The *Dictionary of North Carolina Biography*, the most comprehensive state project of its kind, provides information on some four thousand notable North Carolinians whose accomplishments and occasional misdeeds span more than four centuries. Current plans call for six volumes to be published over a period of several years. Volume 3, H–K, includes 543 entries.

The *Dictionary* contains the first compiled biographical information for many of these individuals. Included are native North Carolinians, no matter in what area they made their contributions, and non-natives whose contributions were made in North Carolina. All persons included are deceased.

Explorers, inventors, engineers, writers, chemists, business leaders, architects, artists, musicians, colonial leaders, military figures, national and state officials, and outstanding teachers and clergymen are among those recognized. And there are the infamous and eccentric—pirates, criminals, a hermit, and the man who weighed more than one thousand pounds. Averaging about eight hundred words, each sketch includes the full name of the subject, dates and places of birth and death (when known), family connections, a career description, and a bibliography. Most of the sketches are based on manuscript and contemporary printed sources that are rare or difficult to find. Some research was conducted in Europe.

William S. Powell has been working on the *Dictionary* since 1971 with the help of several hundred volunteer contributors.

DICTIONARY OF NORTH CAROLINA BIOGRAPHY

EDITED BY WILLIAM S. POWELL

VOLUME 3 H–K

DICTIONARY OF NORTH CAROLINA BIOGRAPHY

EDITED BY WILLIAM S. POWELL

VOLUME 3 H-K

The University of North Carolina Press

Chapel Hill and London

The paper in this book meets the
guidelines for permanence and durability
of the Committee on Production
Guidelines for Book Longevity of the
Council on Library Resources.

Printed in the United States of America

92 91 90 89 88   5 4 3 2 1

Library of Congress Cataloging-in-Publication Data

(Revised for vol. 3)

Dictionary of North Carolina biography.

   Includes bibliographies.
   1. North Carolina—Biography—Dictionaries.
I. Powell, William Stevens, 1919–
CT252.D5   920'.0756   79-10106
ISBN 0-8078-1329-X (v. 1)
ISBN 0-8078-1656-6 (v. 2)
ISBN 0-8078-1806-2 (v. 3)

In Memory of

Jonathan Worth Daniels
26 April 1902–6 November 1981

Sam J. Ervin, Jr.
27 September 1896–23 April 1985

Charles Sylvester Green
23 September 1900–10 January 1980

Mary Lynch Johnson
13 May 1887–17 July 1984

George Myers Stephens
19 July 1904–20 December 1978

Robert Hilliard Woody
11 March 1903–30 December 1985

whose scholarly assistance contributed to the usefulness of the *Dictionary of North Carolina Biography*

Acknowledgments

I am grateful to the North Carolina Society of the Cincinnati for a generous grant to the University of North Carolina Press to assist with the publication costs of this volume; to Claiborne T. Smith, Jr., for his research skills and for his gifts for clerical assistance; to Amanda Upchurch for her work in verifying and arranging many of the bibliographies appended to the sketches; to my wife, Virginia Waldrop Powell, for her careful reading of both manuscripts and proof; to Stevie Champion for her skill as a copyeditor and for her interest in this work beyond the call of duty; to Matthew Hodgson, director, and to Sandra Eisdorfer, managing editor, of The University of North Carolina Press for their continuing interest and help in many ways; and most important of all, to the many authors of the biographies without whose careful and generous work this volume would never have been possible.

Volume three of the *Dictionary of North Carolina Biography*, like the first two, has been produced without grant money of any kind from the federal government. It is the product of the willing scholarly labor of numbers of people who contributed their knowledge and ability. I take great pride in our joint accomplishment and extend my hearty thanks to all who have participated in this important undertaking. We intend to persist until the series is completed.

Dictionary of North Carolina Biography

Hackett, Richard Nathaniel *(4 Dec. 1866–22 Nov. 1923)*, attorney and congressman, was born in Wilkesboro, the son of Dr. Robert Franklin and Caroline Gordon Hackett. His mother was a sister of Brigadier General James B. Gordon. Hackett received his early education in the local schools and was graduated from The University of North Carolina in 1887. He studied law under Colonel George N. Folk in Caldwell County and was admitted to the bar in 1888. He established a practice in Wilkesboro and became a prominent figure in the local Democratic party, serving as chairman of the Wilkes County Democratic Executive Committee from 1890 to 1923. In 1889 he represented North Carolina at the centennial of Washington's inauguration in New York City. He served as mayor of Wilkesboro from 1894 to 1896, when he was an unsuccessful candidate for Congress. In 1906, however, he was elected to the Sixtieth Congress but was defeated for reelection by the Republican candidate, C. H. Cowles, in 1908.

Following his defeat, Hackett became active in the Masonic order and served two terms as Grand Master of the Grand Lodge of North Carolina in 1910 and 1911. It was during his administration that the movement to establish the Masonic and Eastern Star Home crystallized; the cornerstone of the home was laid before his retirement from office.

Hackett married Lois Long, daughter of B. F. Long of Statesville, on 31 Jan. 1907 and they were the parents of Mary Mayo. He died in Statesville and was buried in St. Paul's Episcopal churchyard, Wilkesboro. The Dialectic Society at The University of North Carolina owns an oil portrait of him.

SEE: *Biog. Dir. Am. Cong.* (1961); John L. Cheney, Jr., ed., *North Carolina Government, 1585–1974* (1975); Grand Lodge of Ancient, Free, and Accepted Masons of North Carolina, *Proceedings* (1924); North Carolina Bar Association, *Proceedings* 26 (1924); Oxford, *Orphan's Friend and Masonic Journal*, 9 Dec. 1910, 20 Jan. 1911; C. Beauregard Poland, *Twentieth Century Statesmen, North Carolina's Political Leaders, 1900–1901* (n.d.).

GEORGE T. BLACKBURN II

Hagler (Arataswa or Oroloswa) *(d. 30 Aug. 1763)*, king or head man of the Catawbas (ca. 1749–63), lived and died in the region that was in bitter dispute between the two Carolinas. Upon the murder of The Young Warrior (Yanabe Yalangway) by northern Indians, Hagler was recognized by provincial authorities in Charles Town as king. Governor James Glen of South Carolina and his counterpart in New York attempted to end the ancient feud between the Catawbas and the Six Nations composing the Iroquois Confederacy by arranging a meeting in Albany in 1751. Hagler, accompanied by Lieutenant Governor William Bull, led the Catawba delegation to New York. Although an agreement was reached, the Catawba chief complained in subsequent years of continued harassment of his people by members of the Six Nations.

Although Hagler remained a stalwart ally of the British, he was not above attempting to play upon the rivalries among the southern provinces for the best interests of his nation. As early as 1752 he informed the Charles Town government of the encroachment of whites on Catawba lands. A similar complaint was made to North Carolinians at a meeting in Rowan County in 1754. The frequency of white encroachments increased as settlers fled south after General Edward Braddock's defeat in 1755. Hagler became involved in the controversy between Virginia's Governor Robert Dinwiddie and North Carolina's Governor Arthur Dobbs on one side and Glen on the other. Virginia had requested Catawba braves to accompany Braddock's army and accused South Carolina of preventing the Indians from participating by calling a meeting with them at the time they were supposed to march to Virginia. Also, at about this time Dobbs sent a captain's commission to Jimmy Bullen, a Catawba head man. Some have interpreted this as an attempt by the North Carolina government to establish a rival leader among the Catawbas.

During the early spring of 1756 Virginia commissioned William Byrd III and Peter Randolph to negotiate with Hagler at a site on the Broad River. North Carolina was invited to participate and Captain Hugh Waddell, then commanding the frontier rangers in that province, was appointed commissioner. Hagler agreed to send forty Catawba braves at once to aid the Virginians. This assistance was not forthcoming. The Catawba king later claimed that Glen had instructed him not to go.

In mid-May 1756, a group of Cherokee braves returning from service on the Virginia front terrorized and pillaged the North Carolina backcountry. Hagler and his band, along with some Rowan settlers, captured the offending Indians and delivered them to authorities in Salisbury. On 26–27 May the Catawba king met with Peter Henley, chief justice of North Carolina, at Salisbury. At this meeting he requested gifts, ammunition, and a fort to be built to protect his people while his warriors were away fighting for the British. Dobbs and the North Carolina Assembly reluctantly agreed to this. A site was selected and subsequently purchased for the tribe. Hugh Waddell, who had just constructed Fort Dobbs, was sent with a group of rangers to build the Catawba fort. For some reason relations between the Catawbas and North Carolina cooled, perhaps due to continued white settlement from that colony within Catawba lands. Hagler requested that the North Carolinians cease work on the fort as he wished the stronghold to be built by South Carolinians. In August 1757 Dobbs ordered the work suspended.

From 1756 to 1759 the Catawbas journeyed north to aid the British in their campaigns against the French and their Indian allies. In the fall of 1758 about twenty-five Catawbas took part in General John Forbes's expedition. When these braves returned home, they brought with them the dreaded smallpox which decimated the nation during the winter of 1759–60. It was estimated that between one-half and two-thirds of the tribe died. Hagler withdrew to the Camden area while the disease ran its course. Later the principal settlement of the nation was established at Pine Tree Hill, away from white incursions.

During 1760 Hagler was ill and unable to make trips to Charles Town in May and October. Nevertheless, he participated in the negotiations for the Treaty of Pine Tree Hill (July 1760) with Edmond Atkin, Superintendent of Indian Affairs for the Southern District. By this agreement the Catawba tribe was restricted to a fifteen-square-mile territory. This boundary was not established until after the Augusta Congress of 1763 due to the objections of Arthur Dobbs.

South Carolina finally built the oft-promised Catawba fort in the winter of 1760. The following year Hagler met with Chief Silver Heels of the Iroquois at Charles Town to reaffirm the peace between the two tribes. Also, in the spring of 1761 a number of Catawbas joined Colonel James Grant in his expedition to crush the Cherokee. Although peace was achieved with the Cherokee in December 1761, sporadic fighting continued among the ancient Indian rivals. Two years later, while out hunting, Hagler was ambushed and killed by seven Shawnee braves. One tribal tradition states that his grave was looted by whites, whereas another story contends that his remains were secretly buried. No likeness of Hagler is known to exist. A weather vane in Camden is said to be an effigy of the Catawba king; however, the artisan who made it did not arrive in the area until over a half century after Hagler's death.

SEE: Douglas S. Brown, *The Catawba Indians: The People of the River* (1966); Walter Clark, ed., *State Records of North Carolina*, vol. 22 (1907); William L. McDowell, Jr., ed., *Colonial Records of South Carolina, Series Two*, vols. 2, 3 (1958, 1970); Chapman J. Milling, *Red Carolinians* (1940); William L. Saunders, ed., *Colonial Records of North Carolina*, vols. 5, 6, 8 (1887–90); M. Eugene Sirman, *Colonial South Carolina: A Political History* (1966).

JERRY C. CASHION

Haid, Leo (15 July 1849–24 July 1924), D.D., O.S.B., Roman Catholic abbot, orator, and educator, was born in Latrobe, Pa., the son of nurseryman John Haid and Mary A. Stader Haid. The family name originally was Hite. After preparatory education in the local schools, Haid entered the Benedictine Order's St. Vincent's College near Latrobe in 1862, was graduated from the theological seminary, and was ordained on 21 Dec. 1872. He also received an M.A. degree from Duff's Business College. After his ordination, Father Haid taught at St. Vincent's for thirteen years; in addition, he was secretary of the college and chaplain. In 1885 he was elected abbot of the faltering Maryhelp Abbey, located in Belmont, Gaston County, an area in the Scotch-Irish Presbyterian Catawba Valley described as perhaps the most non-Catholic country in what was "without doubt the most non-Catholic state in America." Under Haid's leadership, for seven years the abbey added new buildings and extensions and over 200 acres of land with accompanying growth in clergy, lay staff, and students. Maryhelp became a mother abbey to the Benedictine schools Haid erected in Florida, Georgia, Virginia, and West Virginia.

On 1 July 1888 Haid was consecrated Bishop of Messene and Vicar Apostolic of North Carolina, and by decree of Pope Pius X was allowed to continue as abbot of Belmont—a double honor accorded no other ecclesiastic in the United States. Besides his service as president of the American Cassinese Congress of the Benedictine Order of the Southern Benedictine Society of North Carolina, he presided over the World Council of Benedictine Abbots in Rome in 1893. On 18 Oct. 1910, the silver jubilee year of Haid's abbacy, Pope Pius designated Belmont Abbey as an "abbatia nullius" or cathedral abbey, of which Haid had been made Abbot Ordinary on 13 June. In recognition of Haid's preeminence in the American Catholic hierarchy, on 15 July 1914 the pope named him assistant to the papal throne and a member of the Roman Patriate or nobility. Although Haid could not participate in political affairs, he was identified by vote with the Democratic party.

After a year of declining health and hospitalization in Charlotte, Bishop Haid died at age seventy-five. Funeral services were held on 30 July 1924 in the abbey cathedral at Belmont, where he was buried in the monastic cemetery.

SEE: Samuel A. Ashe, ed., *Biographical History of North Carolina*, vol. 4 (1906); J. S. Bassett, "A North Carolina Monastery," *Magazine of American History* 29 (1893); Paschal Baumstein, *My Lord of Belmont: A Biography of Leo Haid* (1985); John P. Bradley, *The First 100 Years: Belmont Abbey College, 1876–1976* (1976); *DAB*, vol. 8 (1960); Leo Haid, *Short Sketch of Belmont Abbey* (1910); Raleigh *News and Observer*, 25, 30 July 1924; *Representative Men of the South* (1880); *Who Was Who in America*, vol. 1 (1943).

CATHERINE MYERS BENNINGTON

Hairston, Peter (24 Feb. 1752–1 Dec. 1832), Revolutionary War officer, North Carolina state senator, planter, iron manufacturer, and merchant, was born in Franklin County, Va. His father was Robert Hairston, a landowner and officer, and his mother was Ruth Stovall Hairston.

Peter Hairston, who was named for his grandfather, a Scottish immigrant, was—judging from the voluminous records he left—a man of some education. It is said that he could spell but often he did not. In 1780, he moved with his father's family to that part of Pittsylvania that later became Henry County, Va. In the American Revolution he took part in the 1776 raid against the Cherokees, in the first battle of the Shallowford, and, as a captain, in the Battle of Guilford Court House.

In 1782 Hairston was a deputy under his father, who had been appointed sheriff of Henry County. In April of the same year he married Aylcie Perkins, a daughter of Peter Perkins. Hairston, as early as 1781, began acquiring large tracts of land in Stokes (then Surry) County, N.C. In the spring of 1786 he moved with his wife and only daughter, Ruth Stovall Hairston (1784–1867), to upper Saura Town. There he engaged in many business enterprises including ironworks, a country store in Germanton, the exporting of ginseng and bearskins, and increasingly large tobacco and corn plantings. Hairston also served four terms in the North Carolina state senate (1792–1800) as a Federalist. In 1814, his wife died and his daughter Ruth took over much of his record keeping. Ruth married her cousin Peter Wilson Hairston and their only child, Agnes, married Samuel Hairston.

In 1817, Peter Hairston purchased from Jesse Pearson

the 2,300-acre Cooleemee Plantation in Davie and Davidson counties, thereby adding cotton growing to his enterprises. His landholdings extended over 12,000 acres in Piedmont North Carolina. He died and was buried at Saura Town. His property was willed to his daughter and her descendants, except Cooleemee, which was devised separately to a great-grandson, Peter Wilson Hairston.

SEE: Berry Hill Papers, Peter Wilson Hairston Papers (Southern Historical Collection, University of North Carolina Library, Chapel Hill); Deeds of Davidson, Rowan, Stokes, and Surry counties (North Carolina State Archives, Raleigh); Clement Eaton, *The Growth of Southern Civilization* (1961); Norman Eliason, *Tar Heel Talk* (1956); Elizabeth S. Hairston, *The Hairstons and Penns and Their Relations* (1940); Frances H. Hurt, *An Intimate History of the American Revolution in Pittsylvania County, Virginia* (1976); Legislative Papers and Senate Journals of North Carolina, 1792, 1796, 1799, 1800 (North Carolina State Archives, Raleigh); Tombstone of Peter Hairston, Saura Town, Stokes County; Wills of Peter Hairston and Ruth S. Hairston (Office, Clerk of Superior Court, Danbury).

PETER WILSON HAIRSTON

Hairston, Peter Wilson *(25 Nov. 1819–17 Feb. 1886)*, planter, was born in Pittsylvania County, Va. His father was Samuel Hairston, cited by Clement Eaton as the largest slave owner in the South. Agnes John Peter Wilson, a granddaughter of Peter Hairston, Revolutionary captain and four-term North Carolina state senator, was his mother. He attended the plantation school at his father's Oak Hill, Va., residence and the Bingham School in Hillsborough, N.C.; he was graduated from The University of North Carolina in 1837. It is typical of his later foresight that his graduation oration was addressed to "The Future Prospects of Our Country." Afterward he attended the University of Virginia Law School but found it not to his taste and withdrew before graduation.

In 1832 he received, by devise, from his great-grandfather the Cooleemee Plantation of 2,300 acres in Davie and Davidson counties, N.C., and, though only thirteen years old, took charge of its management. During his college years he continued to travel there and handle management problems. After leaving law school, Hairston began to assume other family responsibilities, including travel to Europe in 1842 in the hope of finding a cure for the illness of his younger brother George. His diary (unpublished) gives a detailed description of his journey and what he saw. He returned at the end of two years and became deeply engrossed in the management of the family estates. In 1849 he married Columbia Lafayette Stuart, a sister of James Ewell Brown ("Jeb") Stuart (the famed Confederate major general who commanded the cavalry of the Army of Northern Virginia).

Hairston increased crop production at Cooleemee, shipping tobacco, hogs, and cotton as far away as Petersburg, Va. The number of slaves on the plantation grew to 300. Between 1853 and 1855 he built the present plantation house, an Anglo-Grecian villa with a double spiral staircase, which stands today as an outstanding example of late Greek Revival architecture. At the time, the building of this house was a mammoth undertaking in Piedmont North Carolina.

As a director of the Yadkin River Navigation Company, Hairston participated in its effort to make that river navigable to the sea. The attempt was only partially successful.

In 1857 Columbia died, and in 1859 Hairston married Fanny M. Caldwell, daughter of Davie Franklin Caldwell, a Superior Court judge and bank director. The couple spent their honeymoon in Europe, returning just before the outbreak of the Civil War. The bridegroom immediately became a volunteer aide on Stuart's staff but soon found that family business required his presence at home. After a short stay, he joined the staff of General Jubal A. Early. Hairston's younger brother had died, his father was senile, and his grandmother was over seventy-five. The responsibility of looking after the combined estates, which involved over 4,000 slaves and thousands of acres during wartime, required many trips home from the front.

At the end of the war, Hairston's policy of kind but firm treatment of his former slaves paid off and they stayed on as hired hands to till the soil of the plantation while he moved to Baltimore, Md., and carried on a business as a grain and fertilizer merchant until his death.

By his first wife Hairston had three children: Samuel, Betty, and Archibald. All of them died before coming of age. By his second marriage he had four children: Agnes W. (1861–1914); Frank Caldwell (1865–1902), sometime North Carolina senator; Ruth Wilson (1868–1947); and Peter Wilson, Jr. (1871–1943).

SEE: Kemp P. Battle, *History of the University of North Carolina*, vol. 1 (1907); Berry Hill Papers, Peter Wilson Hairston Papers (Southern Historical Collection, University of North Carolina Library, Chapel Hill); Cooleemee Plantation Papers (in possession of the author, Mocksville); Deeds of Rowan, Stokes, Davie, and Davidson counties (North Carolina State Archives, Raleigh); Clement Eaton, *The Growth of Southern Civilization* (1961); Elizabeth S. Hairston, *The Hairstons and Penns and Their Relatives* (1940); J. W. Wall, *History of Davie County* (1969); T. T. Waterman, *Early Architecture of North Carolina* (1940); Wills of Peter Hairston and Ruth S. Hairston (Office, Clerk of Superior Court, Danbury).

PETER WILSON HAIRSTON

Hale, Edward Jones *(9 Sept. 1802–2 Jan. 1883)*, editor and publisher, was born in Chatham County, the son and youngest child of Joseph and Dorothy Herndon Hale. An orphan before he was ten, he became the ward of his namesake, Colonel Edward Jones. The young lad was apprenticed to Joseph Gales of the *Raleigh Register*, and he completed his journalistic training in the office of Gales and Seaton's *National Intelligencer* in Washington, D.C. Returning to Fayetteville in January 1825, Hale purchased the *Carolina Observer*, which had changed hands a number of times since its establishment in 1817 by Francis W. Waldo. On his way to amassing a considerable fortune in printing from the successful office of his renamed *Fayetteville Observer*, Hale enlarged his connections with the elite of the state by marrying the prominent socialite, Sarah Jane Walker of the Mallett and Walker families, on 24 May 1828.

Although his archenemy W. W. Holden said Hale exhibited good sense by never running for political office, he was a powerful force in politics. It was said that "the editorial and personal enmity of the two men had considerable influence on the history of the state." By 1850, the *Observer* had the greatest circulation of any newspaper in North Carolina, and Hale had gained a national reputation as a first-rate editor. In 1857 he refused a bid to manage A. S. Barnes and Company, and in 1858 he turned down a munificent offer to be chief editor of the *New York World*. Before the Civil War he brought his sons, Edward Jones, Peter Mallett, and Edward Joseph, into his shop as partners.

During the year he spent with the *Intelligencer*, Hale met John C. Calhoun, Daniel Webster, and, even more importantly, Henry Clay. Hale became the friend as well as the political supporter of "the Great Commoner." In 1834 he joined with George E. Badger, Edward B. Dudley, and Willie P. Mangum to organize the Whig party in North Carolina. He supported the Whigs until 18 Apr. 1861, when he renounced Lincoln's proclamation asking for troops, an action that he believed altered affairs beyond the control of either those with peaceful intentions or those dedicated to the Union. In the presidential election of 1860, Hale joined Badger and William A. Graham to endorse John Bell, and he played a vital role in the election of Zebulon B. Vance, exacerbating the conflict with Holden which reached a climax in 1864.

In 1865, General William T. Sherman ordered the destruction of the *Observer*, one of the preeminent Confederate newspapers. Hale had already moved its files to the home of Colonel Thomas Hill in Chatham County. Finally in the fall of 1866, Hall and his sons moved to New York City where at first they engaged in job printing, but in 1867 they released their first book, R. L. Dabney's *Defence of Virginia and the South*. The Hale firm specialized in printing Southern authors for the Southern market; its leading title was Alexander H. Stephens's *History of the United States*. By 1875 E. J. Hale and Sons, which had its offices on Murray Street and later at 55 Chambers Street, had 124 titles in its catalogue, and by 1883 had released over 500 titles.

Hale was an Episcopalian, and, like many prominent North Carolinians, he was a trustee of The University of North Carolina. He died at age eighty in New York City and was buried in Brooklyn's Greenwood Cemetery. A portrait in oil by James Bogle painted in 1855 was reproduced in Ashe's biographical sketch and in the *Fayetteville Observer*, 17 Sept. 1967.

SEE: Samuel A. Ashe, ed., *Biographical History of North Carolina*, vol. 8 (1917); *Fayetteville Observer*, 17 Sept. 1967; W. W. Holden, *History of Journalism in North Carolina* (1881); *New York Times*, 3 Jan. 1883; J. Tebbel, *History of Book Publishing in the United States*, vol. 1 (1972).

D. A. YANCHISIN

Hale, Edward Joseph *(25 Dec. 1835–15 Feb. 1922),* journalist and statesman, was born in Fayetteville. His father, Edward Jones Hale, was the longtime publisher (1825–65) of one of the South's leading Whig newspapers, the *Fayetteville Observer*. His mother, Sarah Jane Hale, was a descendant of Elder Brewster of the *Mayflower*, and her father, Carlton Walker, had been a major on the staff of General Edmund P. Gaines in the War of 1812. Peter Mallett Hale, Edward Joseph's oldest brother, helped establish the Raleigh *Observer* in 1876.

Edward Joseph Hale received his early education at Donaldson Academy in Fayetteville, and in 1857 he entered the sophomore class at The University of North Carolina. He capped a brilliant academic career by graduating valedictorian of his class in 1860; fifty years later, the university awarded him an LL.D. After graduation Hale joined his father and brother as a partner in the publication of the *Fayetteville Observer*. At the outbreak of the Civil War, he volunteered as a private in

the Fayetteville Independent Light Infantry, which became Company H, First North Carolina Volunteers. He served throughout the war from Bethel to Appomattox, acquiring a reputation for extraordinary valor and rising to the rank of major in James H. Lane's brigade. Having lost his fortune when General William T. Sherman destroyed the press and plant of the *Observer*, after the war Hale moved to New York City and for a time was associated with his father in printing and publishing. Afterwards he became an associate in a large wholesale firm.

In 1872, failing health forced him to retire to Hickory, N.C., where for the next decade he managed several estates entrusted to him. In 1883, he returned to Fayetteville and resumed publication of the *Observer*. The following year, as a member of the platform committee at the North Carolina Democratic state convention, he drafted the party's tariff plank. He also was a delegate to the Democratic National Convention in Chicago. His services to the party were rewarded in 1885, when President Grover Cleveland appointed him consul to Manchester, England.

The former editor's tenure as consul was crowned with success. According to Secretary of State James G. Blaine, his record surpassed that of any official—diplomatic or consular—sent abroad by President Cleveland. Henry White, onetime ambassador to France and Italy and an attaché at the London legation while Hale was at Manchester, recalled that Hale was the first American to be accepted as a social equal by the British nobility. In 1886 he was elected an honorary life member of the famous Cobden Club, a distinction accorded to only a handful of southerners and to only one other North Carolinian, Zebulon Vance. The Fayetteville native also was invited to join the British Association for the Advancement of Science, St. George's Club, the Alorender Club of Manchester, and the Albemarle Club of London. When the newly elected Republican administration of Benjamin Harrison relieved him of his consular duties in 1889, Hale accepted an important position with the Bengal Indigo Manufacturing Company, Limited. He went to India on company business and after his return declined a lucrative offer from the firm to remain in England as its barrister. Prior to his departure for America, Hale was named vice-president of the International Congress on Internal Navigation, and before that prestigious organization he presented his country's case for a Nicaraguan canal.

After spending the year 1891 in New York as commissioner for the Manchester Ship Canal, Hale returned to Fayetteville and once again assumed the editorship of the *Observer*. After Grover Cleveland's reelection to the presidency in 1893, he was offered the Turkish mission and was considered for the post of minister to Russia, but the North Carolinian turned down both positions. During the next two decades, he devoted much of his time and energy to promoting the interests of his city, state, and party.

Hale was the chief advocate of a scheme for the canalization of the upper Cape Fear River, and it was largely through his efforts that the United States Congress approved the project in 1910. In connection with his interest in inland water transportation, he served as director of the National Rivers and Harbors Congress and as president of the Upper Cape Fear Improvement Association. A leader in Fayetteville community affairs, he was chairman of a committee that obtained a new charter for the city in 1893 and president of the Chamber of Commerce in 1909 and 1910. He also headed successful campaigns that resulted in the construction of a municipal waterworks and the paving of the town's streets. Hale attended St. John's Episcopal Church and for a number of years was a vestryman. At the state level he was a trustee of The University of North Carolina (1899–1915) and in 1910 was elected to the board's Executive Committee. A loyal Democrat, Hale attended all the party's national conventions between 1896 and 1912 and for a time he served on the party's state Central Committee. In 1902, the former Confederate officer was an unsuccessful candidate for North Carolina's Sixth District congressional seat, but in 1913 he reentered public service as minister to Costa Rica. Although he returned to the United States in April 1917, he officially held the position of minister until 1921.

Hale was married twice, the first time on 15 Jan. 1861 to Maria Rhett Yeamans, the oldest daughter of Thomas and Eliza Yeamans of Hailbron in Chatham County. She was descended from Sir John Yeamans, a governor of North Carolina's Clarendon County during the Proprietary period. Edward Joseph and Maria Hale were the parents of four children: Edward J., Jr., who succeeded his father as editor of the Fayetteville Observer (1914–19); Frederick Toomer; Louis Bond, who died in 1915; and Thomas H. Maria Hale died in November 1902. In 1905, Hale married Caroline Green Mallett, the daughter of Charles B. Mallett, onetime president of the Cape Fear and Yadkin Valley Railroad. Hale died at his Haymount home in Fayetteville. Funeral services were held at St. John's Episcopal Church, and he was buried in Cross Creek Cemetery.

The Edward Joseph Hale Papers in the Southern Historical Collection at the University of North Carolina Library contain copies of a daguerreotype made when Hale was seventeen and of a photograph made in 1890.

SEE: Samuel A. Ashe, ed., *Biographical History of North Carolina*, vol. 8 (1917 [portrait]); Fayetteville Committee, *A Short Sketch of the Life of Major E. J. Hale* (1910); *Fayetteville Observer*, 15 Feb. 1922; Daniel L. Grant, *Alumni History of the University of North Carolina* (1942); University of North Carolina *Alumni Review* 2 (November 1913).

CHARLES H. MCARVER, JR.

Hale, Peter Mallett (10 Nov. 1829–2 June 1887), newspaper editor and publisher, was born in Fayetteville, the son of Edward Jones Hale, the longtime publisher of the influential Whig newspaper, the *Fayetteville Observer*. His mother was Sarah Jane Walker, daughter of Carlton Walker, who had been a major on the staff of General Edmund P. Gaines in the War of 1812. Peter Hale had one sister, Sarah Caroline, who married George H. Haigh. Hale's younger brother, Edward Joseph, served with distinction as U.S. consul to Manchester, England, and as minister to Costa Rica.

Peter Hale received his early education in the schools of Fayetteville. In June 1846, he entered The University of North Carolina. At his graduation in 1849, he was awarded first distinction along with Thomas Jefferson Robinson and Kemp P. Battle and he delivered the salutatory address. In 1850, he went to Raleigh where he studied law under Judge George E. Badger. Sometime later he returned to Fayetteville to aid his father in the publication of the *Observer*.

At the outbreak of the Civil War, Hale enlisted as a private in the Fayetteville Independent Light Infantry. He served in the Bethel Regiment under General D. H. Hill and fought in the Peninsula campaign. When his enlistment term ended, Hale returned to Fayetteville

and resumed work on the *Observer*. However, when a Union attack on Fort Fisher seemed imminent, he reentered the army briefly. He attained the rank of major before resigning to rejoin his father in the newspaper business.

In 1865, troops under General William T. Sherman destroyed the offices and property of the *Observer*, and in the following year Hale and his father moved to New York City where they established the publishing firm of E. J. Hale and Son. While residing in New York, Peter Hale was offered the presidency of the New York Publishers' Association, but he declined the honor.

The Fayetteville native returned to North Carolina in 1876, and for the next three years he and Colonel William L. Saunders published the Raleigh *Observer*. As editor of the *Observer*, Hale advocated the development of North Carolina's natural resources and supported a strong program of internal improvements. When the newspaper began to experience financial difficulties, Hale resigned but he soon initiated publication of *Hale's Weekly*, which was merged with the Raleigh *News* in 1880. Hale served briefly as editor of the *News*, and between 1880 and 1885 he published the strongly pro-Democratic Raleigh *Register*. In addition to his journalistic accomplishments, Hale was the author of several books including *In the Coal and Iron Counties of North Carolina* (Raleigh, 1883) and *The Woods and Timbers of North Carolina* (Raleigh, 1883). In February 1885 he became state printer, a post he held until 1887.

Hale, who had suffered for more than a year from cancer of the mouth, died in Fayetteville and was buried in Cross Creek Cemetery. He was survived by four daughters and one son. His wife, Mary Badger, whom he had married on 1 Oct. 1855, died in 1884.

SEE: Samuel A. Ashe, ed., *Biographical History of North Carolina*, vol. 8 (1917 [portrait]); Kemp P. Battle, *History of the University of North Carolina*, vol. 1 (1907); *Fayetteville Observer*, 16 June 1887; Raleigh *News and Observer*, 3 June 1887; Raleigh *Signal*, 9 June 1887; Raleigh *State Chronicle*, 9 June 1887; Wilmington *Morning Star*, 4 June 1887.

CHARLES H. MCARVER, JR.

Hall, Allmand (1772–4 Feb. 1831), printer, of Scottish ancestry, was the son of Sarah Hall Burney who had been widowed and married William Burney of New Bern. In 1795, Hall moved to Wilmington where he operated a book and stationery shop on Market Street and is said to have established a circulating library. However, Hall is best known for publishing *Hall's Wilmington Gazette*, which he began on 5 Jan. 1797. He later changed the name of the paper to the *Wilmington Gazette* which, in 1807, had a yearly subscription rate of three dollars and was published each Tuesday. In 1808, Hall sold the *Wilmington Gazette* to William S. Hasell and was no longer involved in printing.

During his days as a Wilmington printer, Hall found himself in the midst of a feud between the Federalists and the Anti-Federalists. Each group wanted a man who shared their beliefs to serve as public printer. In 1798 Hall was elected public printer, displacing Abraham Hodge who had backed the Federalists. Federalist leader Samuel Johnston's statement that Hall's election "mortified" him is evidence that the Federalists opposed Hall. Hall remained neutral, a move that apparently pleased neither the Federalists nor the Anti-Federalists, and he only served one term.

Between 1811 and 1817 Hall moved to Rowan County,

where he was active in the Episcopal church. On 28 Apr. 1821, he represented Christ Church at the third convention of the Episcopal Diocese in Raleigh, when Christ Church was admitted to union with the diocese.

Hall married Ann Howard at Wilmington on 23 Jan. 1800; she died in 1810. They had six children: Sarah (b. 24 May 1801); Thomas (b. 14 Aug. 1802); Ann (b. 23 Dec. 1803), who married William McKoy of Clinton; Isabella (b. 25 July 1805), who married Richard C. Holmes; Caroline (b. 31 Aug. 1807), who married Chambers McConnaughey; and Maria (b. 12 July 1809).

In 1811, Hall married Rebecca Howard, his first wife's sister; she died in 1817 in Rowan County. He then married Mrs. Margaret Cowan Pennington. There were no children of his second and third marriages. Hall died in Rowan County at age fifty-nine and was buried at Thyatira Presbyterian Church.

SEE: Clarence S. Brigham, *History and Bibliography of American Newspapers*, vol. 2 (1947); *Hall's Wilmington Gazette*, 16 Feb. 1797; Elizabeth F. McCoy, *Early New Hanover County Records* (1973); Henry B. McCoy, *The McKoy Family of North Carolina* (1955); Jethro Rumple, *A History of Rowan County, North Carolina* (1881); Mary L. Thornton, "Public Printing in North Carolina," *North Carolina Historical Review* 21 (1944).

H. K. STEPHENS II

Hall, Clement (*May 1706–January 1759*), Anglican missionary and author, was born in Warwickshire, England, probably in or near Coventry where he is known to have had relatives. He was baptized at St. Mary's Church, Warwick, on 29 May 1706 and educated at a public school in Warwick. By 1731, he and his brother Robert were living in Perquimans County, N.C. Their mother either accompanied them or arrived soon afterwards; she died in Edenton on 8 Feb. 1752, at age seventy-three, and was buried in St. Paul's Church. Clement Hall bought a 104-acre plantation on the northeastern side of Perquimans River in 1731 and was appointed a justice of the Perquimans County Court in 1739. He also began regular service as a lay reader for the local Anglican parish. Early in the summer of 1742, he married twenty-year-old Frances Foster, daughter of Francis Foster who had held various positions in the government of the colony since 1689. Just sixteen days later Robert Hall married Ann Leary of Chowan County.

In the summer of 1743 Clement Hall's wish to seek ordination as a missionary in the service of the Church of England was recognized when a number of prominent men in the colony signed a certificate testifying to his "Honour, Diligence and Integrity" and that he was "esteemed a true Churchman, and one of very good Repute, Life & Conversation." He was recommended to church officials in London as a suitable itinerant missionary for service in North Carolina, where there were only two such missionaries to serve over 15,000 white inhabitants. By the end of the year Hall was in London, and through the good opinion of the Bishop of London, the Right Reverend Edmund Gibson, and the Reverend Thomas Spateman, a member of the staff of St. Paul's Cathedral, he was ordained. By mid-August 1744 he sailed for home.

The vestry of Chowan Parish (St. Paul's, Edenton) found a house for Hall, and he and his family soon moved there. He began to hold services in Edenton and on a regular basis made long journeys through the northern portion of the colony. In some years he re-

ported that he traveled over 2,000 miles, sometimes preaching to as many as 600 people at a time when services were held under large trees; on some of his trips he administered the Holy Communion to as many as 300 people on a single tour. Shortly before his death, Hall estimated that he had baptized at least 10,000 people during thirteen years of his ministry. Frequently he noted that he also had instructed Negroes and children to prepare them for baptism, churched women (conducted a service of prayers and thanksgiving for women after childbirth), visited the sick, and distributed tracts supplied by the Society for the Propagation of the Gospel in London.

At his own request, Hall in 1757 was permitted to serve St. Paul's Parish alone. By this time he was often subjected to periods of illness and was building a small house on land he had purchased near Edenton shortly before selling his plantation in Perquimans County. The house he had formerly occupied was burned in 1755, the fire consuming his books, sermons, clothes, "and necessaries to the value of £300 & upwards." This was perhaps equivalent to six years' salary. His death must have been unexpected as bills submitted to his estate included the cost of building materials for the house. Hall and his wife, who survived him, were the parents of seven daughters and two sons: Mary, Sally (or Sarah), Betsy (or Elizabeth), Ann, Deborah, Molly, Nancy, Clement, and Robert. A final accounting of his estate in 1761 revealed that over £407 had been paid out and £413 received, leaving his family a few shillings over £6, about a month's salary.

While riding horseback around the colony, Hall wrote a little 50-page book, *A Collection of Many Christian Experiences*, which he referred to as "a Pocket-Companion . . . to keep my Thoughts employed on good Subjects; which I believe most People find are naturally apt to be vain and wandring when we are alone, notwithstanding our greatest Care." And then, he wrote, "considering that it might also be of some Use to others, who have a Desire to improve their Time upon the like Occasions, or when on a Winter's Night or a rainy Day they have Leisure to peruse it, instead of Drinking, Gaming, or telling of an idle or slandrous Tale; I have ventured to put this my small Mite into the Treasury." The first 21 pages contain "A Miscellaneous Collection of Many Christian Experiences, &c." consisting largely of quotations or paraphrases from Ecclesiastes, Proverbs, Job, Psalms, and the New Testament books of Matthew, Luke, John, Corinthians, and Timothy. Most of the volume, however, is devoted to proverbs, many of which undoubtedly were original with Hall—"Collected and Composed . . . by C. H.," the title page reads. Others of the pithy sayings appear to be derived from Benjamin Franklin; one is from Tertullianus, another from Thomas Fuller, while a careful comparison would perhaps reveal the source of still others. With a separate title page, Hall reproduced the 11-page text of *Serious Advice to Persons Who have been Sick* for which he gave no author, but it actually was written by the Right Reverend Edmund Gibson, Bishop of London, who had ordained Hall. Hall's concluding contributions include a number of prayers, various forms of grace to be said before and after meals, and some prayers for children. Although some of these are clearly derived from the Book of Common Prayer, others may well have been original compositions by Hall.

Hall's *Collection*, printed by James Davis in New Bern in 1753, was the first nonlegal book to be written and published in the colony. Davis had established a printing press in the colony in 1749, but until the appearance of Hall's book only official material had been printed. The only known copy of the book is in the Rare Book Collection, Duke University Library, Durham.

SEE: William S. Powell, ed., *Clement Hall, A Collection of Many Christian Experiences, Sentences, and Several Places of Scripture Improved, A Facsimile of A North Carolina Literary Landmark* (1961); William L. Saunders, ed., *Colonial Records of North Carolina*, vols. 4–5 (1886–87); Society for the Propagation of the Gospel Letterbooks, series B, vol. 11, document nos. 196–198 (microfilm, Division of Archives and History, Raleigh).

WILLIAM S. POWELL

Hall, David McKee (*16 May 1918–29 Jan. 1960*), congressman, was born in Sylva, Jackson County, the son of David McKee and Edith Moore Hall. He attended the public schools in Jackson County until the age of twelve, when he was stricken with osteomyelitis. This affliction three years later resulted in paraplegia. Confined to a wheelchair in 1933, Hall was unable to finish public high school and underwent some two hundred operations over an eight-year period. Despite this, he entered The University of North Carolina as a special student. A remarkably gifted undergraduate, he went on to earn a Certificate of Law in June 1947 and the LL.B. in June 1948. While in law school, he joined Phi Delta Phi legal fraternity and was selected the Vance Inn Phi Delta Phi student of the year for 1946–47. Hall was the first special student to be graduated from The University of North Carolina Law School with the LL.B. degree.

In the summer of 1947, Hall demonstrated paraplegic mobility methods he had developed at the Congress of Physical Medicine in New York; his innovations were featured in *Time* magazine. Admitted to the bar in August of that year, he began a law practice in Sylva in 1948 in the firm of Hall and Thornburg. He served as attorney for the towns of Sylva, Dillsboro, and Webster, and for Jackson County. In 1952, he helped organize and was secretary-treasurer of the Jackson County Savings and Loan Association, and was appointed to the Twentieth Judicial District Committee. He also became president of Jackson County Industries, Inc.

Hall was elected to the North Carolina Senate but served only one term, resigning on 5 Aug. 1955 to become a member of the North Carolina Board of Water Commissioners until 1958. However, he continued to work with Young Democrats clubs and was vice-chairman of the Jackson County Democratic Committee from 1948 to 1954. This political experience enabled him to win a seat in the Eighty-sixth Congress, where he served from 3 January 1959 until his death.

In addition to his personal interests in farming and cattle raising, Hall was active in many civic organizations. He was an Elk, Rotarian, and Methodist trustee, and he worked with the local United Fund and the Carolinas Community Services. On 14 July 1944, he married Sarah McCollum. They had three daughters: Sarah Anne, Edith Allison, and Hannah McKee. Hall was buried in the Webster Memorial Cemetery, Webster.

SEE: *Biog. Dir. Am. Cong.* (1971); *Memorial Services Held in the House of Representatives and the Senate of the United States: Together with Remarks Presented in Eulogy of David McKee Hall, Late Representative of North Carolina* (1960);

Raleigh *News and Observer*, 1 Aug. 1958; *Who Was Who in America* (1963).

PHILLIP W. EVANS

Hall, Edward Dudley (*27 Sept. 1823–11 June 1896*), Confederate officer and public official, was born in Wilmington, the son of Edward Pearsall and Eliza J. Hall. Educated at Donaldson Academy, Fayetteville, as a young man in Wilmington he was an active member of the Thalian Association, a local dramatic group. The 1850 census lists his occupation as manufacturer; at the time, he was involved in turpentine distilling and had interests in a rice mill. Hall represented New Hanover County in the state House of Commons in 1846–47 and was sheriff of the county from 1852 to 1860. He was also the inventor of a machine for gathering, stemming, and shelling peanuts.

In May 1861, even before North Carolina seceded from the Union, Hall organized and served as captain of a company that became Company A, Second Regiment of North Carolina Troops; it afterwards became Company H, Fortieth Regiment. In August 1861 Hall was promoted to major in the Seventh Regiment and saw service in eastern North Carolina, including action at the Battle of New Bern. The following March he was promoted to colonel and transferred to the Forty-sixth Regiment. With this command he saw extensive service, particularly at the Battle of Sharpsburg, at Bristoe Station, and elsewhere in Virginia. He declined a promotion to brigadier general.

Colonel Hall resigned his commission in 1863 upon being elected sheriff of New Hanover County. Within a short time he was elected to the state senate, where he served three terms between 1864 and 1867. In 1868 he was a candidate for lieutenant governor on the Conservative ticket, but his party was defeated. In 1883 he began a four-year term as mayor of Wilmington, after which he was elected chief of police. He also served as special inspector of customs for the Wilmington district for three years and, for four years before his health failed, as major general of the North Carolina Division, United Confederate Veterans.

In 1845 Hall married Susan Hill Lane of Wilmington, who died five years later; they were the parents of a son. Hall afterwards married Sallie Loudon Green, and they became the parents of two sons and three daughters.

SEE: John L. Cheney, Jr., ed., *North Carolina Government, 1585–1979* (1981); Walter Clark, ed., *Histories of the Several Regiments and Battalions from North Carolina in the Great War, 1861–1865*, vols. 1–5 (1901); Clement A. Evans, ed., *Confederate Military History*, vol. 4 (1899); L. L. Polk, *Handbook of North Carolina* (1879); James Sprunt, *Chronicles of the Cape Fear River, 1660–1916* (1916).

WILLIAM S. POWELL

Hall, Enoch (*d. 18 Oct. 1753*), chief justice, was born in England and lived at Newbegin, Northumberland. He was educated at Staple's Inn, one of the Inns of Chancery. On 21 Apr. 1744 he was appointed chief justice of the province of North Carolina by the king's warrant, replacing the deceased William Smith. The letters patent empowered him to hold office "during Our pleasure and his Residence within our said Province" and to convene supreme courts of judicature as necessary. Although it is not known when Hall assumed his post in the colony, his immediate predecessor, the interim chief justice John Montgomery, died in May 1744. Hall was an active chief justice, for there is evidence that he rode the circuits on assizes as well as hearing cases in the formal chambers of his court. His judicial competence was questioned by his adversaries, and in fact he was only called to the bar in England in May 1750, after entering Gray's Inn on 28 Nov. 1749.

As chief justice, Hall served on many commissions and he was closely associated with two efforts at judicial reform. In March 1746 he was named to a commission to revise and print the laws of the province. This obligation required Hall and three others to compile and index the laws then in force, noting statutes that were obsolete, and to print the results. The books of colonial laws were then to be distributed to leading officials of the province. In 1749, Hall sponsored a bill calling for the speedy establishment of more courts of justice and, interestingly, for more equal representation of all subjects in the lower house of the Assembly.

Several cases indicate the political connection of Hall with the faction of Governor Gabriel Johnston. Henry McCulloch alleged that Hall unfairly suppressed evidence in his case against the governor, but Samuel Swann, a member of the Provincial Council, supported Hall. In April 1749 Governor Johnston complained that Hall and Joseph Anderson, judge of the Admiralty Court, had exceeded their authority in the investigation of Macrora Scarborough, another councillor. The charge was that they heard too many witnesses, allowed several changes of venue to obtain more evidence, and heard some testimony in secret. Two weeks later, Hall wrote to Scarborough that he would no longer give summons to his witnesses and that all depositions must be taken at New Bern.

In July 1749, Hall obtained a royal license to return to England for eighteen months to recover his health. The General Assembly had acted in April to see that he was paid a debt of £222 for riding circuits. The county sheriffs had been delinquent in payments to Hall, and it appears from a list of March 1773 that his estate was then owed nearly £1,200 in arrears. It was probably this default that led him to return to England. In 1750 Hall was still active, writing to advise the governor that six counties had withheld their taxes and refused to provide jurors for assize courts. He urged the passage of his bill to increase the number of courts and to provide better regulation of them. Three years later, the Board of Trade noted his long absence from his colonial post and urged him to return. Nevertheless, Hall died in England without resuming his duties in North Carolina. He was replaced by Peter Henley on order of the secretary of state on 20 May 1755.

SEE: John L. Cheney, Jr., ed., *North Carolina Government, 1585–1974* (1975); Walter Clark, ed., *State Records of North Carolina*, vols. 11, 23 (1895, 1904); John Foster, ed., *Register of Admission to Gray's Inn, 1521–1889* (1889); E. Alfred Jones, *American Members of the Inns of Court* (1924); Charles Musgrave, *A General Nomenclature and Obituary*, vol. 3 (1900); William L. Saunders, ed., *Colonial Records of North Carolina*, vols. 4, 5, 9 (1886–1900).

JON G. CRAWFORD

Hall, Frank Gregory (*12 Feb. 1896–19 Feb. 1967*), aerospace scientist, was born in Johnstown, Wis., the son of Frank Dexter and Evelyn Kidder Hall. After receiving his preparatory education in local schools, he entered Milton College, Milton, Wis., and was graduated with the B.A. degree in 1917. He was an aviator in the U.S. Army Air Corps during World War I, then attended the University of Wisconsin at Madison, from which he was awarded an M.A. (1921) and a Ph.D. (1923). From 1923 to 1926 he was a professor of biology and head of the department at Milton College. In 1926, Hall moved to Durham to be assistant professor of biology at Duke University. Instrumental in the expansion of the department, he became its acting chairman in 1930.

Hall held a postdoctoral fellowship at Cambridge University, England (1933–34), where he studied with Sir Joseph Bancroft, a pioneer in the field of high-altitude research. On his return to Duke, Hall joined a group of other scientists who promoted an international high-altitude expedition to South America in 1935. For seven months they lived on the highest peaks of the Andes Mountains.

After his study in England, Hall began to build a scholarly reputation for his research in high-altitude breathing. He used a low-pressure chamber to simulate thin air at incredible heights, testing the limits a man could go without the aid of oxygen equipment and noting the body's responses to high altitudes. On 9 Dec. 1941, two days after the Japanese attack on Pearl Harbor, Hall—now hailed as an aerophysiology expert—was called upon to train bomber and fighter pilots to use oxygen equipment and to set up training chambers that became mandatory in pilot training. As chief of the Physiological Branch of the U.S. Air Force (1942–45), he developed the "G-suit" designed to prevent blackouts in a high-speed dive. He experimented with dummies and scales to determine the ratio of tolerance to gravity. From that effort came the "free fall" to safe levels and later a low-level automatic opening device for parachutes. It further resulted in the substitution of nylon for silk in their construction.

In late 1943, Hall was designated as head of the hydroponics program (the growing of plants in nutrient solutions). Subsequently, he successfully grew fresh vegetables, even in lava mounds, to substitute for the traditional canned "C" rations. Shortly before the Japanese surrender, he was rushed to India as a consultant in the "Hump" operation, a shift within several hours from 200 to 5,500 feet above sea level. Blackouts were occurring, he discovered, because the soldiers were generously donating blood and thereby robbing themselves of needed oxygen. Hall was awarded the Legion of Merit for his "brilliant work in solving the many complex problems of human physiology in relation to flying personnel." He was further cited by General Nathan Twining for his outstanding service during the war.

Afterwards he was an official delegate to the United Nations Educational, Scientific, and Cultural Organization (UNESCO), a unit established in 1946, with headquarters in Paris, France, "for the purpose of promoting international collaboration in education, science and culture." In 1949 he participated in a symposium on high-altitude biology in Lima, Peru.

When he returned to Duke in 1946, Hall was named chairman of the Department of Physiology and Pharmacology in the university's Medical Center, dividing his time between administrative duties, teaching, and his laboratory. During that period, he turned his low-pressure, high-altitude experiences around and experimented with hyperbaric oxygenization, a process available to treat certain diseases. The pressure chamber for that purpose was initially used at Duke in 1962. That year he returned to full-time teaching and research; following his retirement in 1965, he continued his research and publication activities.

Always searching "to determine how man's system acclimates to its surroundings," Hall went around the world many times to find the answer. On one of those trips he conducted a study alone on the Jungfrau in Switzerland, 13,642 feet in the Bernese Alps. His subsequent research provided the scientific basis for modern space administration technologies. He helped develop a face mask and "became internationally known as an authority in aerospace medicine when such research was not only new but equipment for it primitive and often inadequate," making possible early progress in the field. For this leadership he was named a Fellow in Aerospace Medicine during a meeting of the Aerospace Medical Association. The same year Hall participated in two research expeditions. The first, sponsored by the National Science Foundation, took him to the Mojave Desert in southern California, at the south end of the Sierra Nevada, to study the effects on man of the physical environment below sea level. The second was a study on Mount Bancroft (14,000 feet), where he was joined by scientists from the University of Nevada and the University of Illinois.

Although Hall was best known for his altitude impact studies, his whole span of research was highly diversified; among his subjects were unhatched chicks, blood, limestone and caves, perspiration, and turtles. He was the author of more than a hundred articles published in various scientific journals. Hall was proud of an autographed photograph he received from Astronaut Edward H. White, along with a statement from White that his "walk in space" (1965) was made possible in part by Hall's work in solving the problems of human physiology in relation to flying.

Hall was married first to Mary Kidder; they had one daughter, Elizabeth Anne (Mrs. Kent Boutwell). Mrs. Hall died in 1920. He later married Stephanie Daland of Milton, Wis., and they were the parents of one son, Kenneth Hall, who became an anesthesiologist at the Duke University Medical Center. Following Hall's death in Duke Hospital, a memorial service was held in the Duke University Chapel; he was buried in Milton, Wis.

In 1969, during the annual Medical Alumni Week at Duke, the Frank Gregory Hall Laboratory for Environmental Research was dedicated at the Duke University Medical Center. Previously known as the hyperbaric unit, the laboratory has been used by physicians and other scientists with the Environmental Biomedical Research Program to determine how modified environments such as increased pressures of oxygen affect illness in man, and to measure and evaluate the biochemical responses of healthy individuals to unusual environments.

SEE: *Durham Morning Herald* and *Durham Sun*, 21 Feb. 1967; Records of the Office of Information Services and the Alumni Records Office, Duke University, Durham.

C. SYLVESTER GREEN

Hall, James (22 Aug. 1744–25 July 1826), clergyman, was born in Carlisle, Pa., to James and Prudence Roddy Hall. James, Sr., a Scotch-Irish immigrant, arrived in America with his father prior to 1723. In 1751, the Halls migrated to North Carolina, settling among the Bethany Presbyterian congregation near Fourth Creek (later Statesville). James, Jr., received a local education, although he may have attended Crowfield Academy near Centre Church. Influenced by his pious home community and by itinerant preachers, he vowed to consecrate his life to the ministry. His preparation for a clerical career was delayed when his father's health faltered. As the oldest son at home at the time, the third of at least five brothers, James shouldered the burden of principal provider until the younger children matured. Sometime during that period, he was engaged to marry. Subsequently he became convinced that a wife would prevent his fulfilling his vow of total dedication to God's service, so he broke the engagement and never married.

As soon as circumstances permitted, Hall entered the College of New Jersey at Princeton, where he studied theology under John Witherspoon and was graduated in 1774. After declining a mathematics professorship there because of his vow, he returned to North Carolina. In late 1775 or early 1776 the Orange Presbytery licensed him to preach, and in the latter year he received a call to Fourth Creek Presbyterian Church. On 8 Apr. 1778 he was ordained by the Orange Presbytery and installed as pastor of the Fourth Creek, Bethany, and Concord congregations, a parish that encompassed roughly 600 square miles.

During the Revolutionary War Hall subordinated his patriotic impulses to his pastoral obligations. However, when immediate threats to the backcountry reconciled the two responsibilities, he helped organize irregular militia units and participated in expeditions against the British. In 1779, outraged by British depredations in South Carolina, he raised a company from his congregation and was captain during an incursion into the western part of that state. Later, he joined a two-month march into Georgia's Cherokee country and, as chaplain, preached the first gospel sermon in the area. In 1781, he was again drawn away from his ministerial duties when General William Lee Davidson appealed to him to help muster opposition to the advancing Lord Cornwallis. Hall reorganized his company and joined Davidson for the skirmish at Cowans Ford. Of an imposingly tall, muscular physique and a dark, forceful personality, Hall was offered command of the militia force after Davidson was killed but he declined.

After the war Hall intensified his activities within his wide parish and broadened them to affect the National Presbyterian Church. Shortly after hostilities ended, he fostered a two-year revival during which 140 communicants joined his congregation. His fervid efforts severely strained his health. In 1786, he undertook a therapeutic sea voyage to New York, with excellent results. In New York he attended a meeting of the New York–Philadelphia Synod, which then held jurisdiction over North Carolina churches, and he helped organize the General Assembly of the Presbyterian Church. He represented the Orange Presbytery and later the Concord Presbytery a total of sixteen times at general assembly meetings and moderated the 1803 conclave. In 1788, Hall helped form the Synod of the Carolinas. He attended all but one of its annual meetings, until it was superseded by the Synod of North Carolina in 1813, serving as moderator in 1812. He remained active in the North Carolina synod until infirmity precluded his involvement after 1819. During the decade 1810–20 he assisted in the formation of the American Bible Society and the North Carolina Bible Society, serving as first president of the latter.

As early as 1790 Hall relinquished his pastorates at Fourth Creek and Concord to free himself for wide-ranging missionary work. In 1793, he began journeying to the west and southwest, eventually making fourteen extended expeditions as well as numerous shorter trips. On his most notable journey he established the first Protestant mission in the lower Mississippi valley, at

Natchez, in 1800. After his return from Mississippi, he wrote a series of newspaper articles providing the most detailed description of that region by an American to that time. In 1801, he collected the articles as *A Brief History of the Mississippi Territory*. The following year he published another book, *A Narrative of a Most Extraordinary Work of Religion in North Carolina*, reflecting his own role as a fervent leader of the camp meeting revivals sweeping the western part of the state. Differing from those of his colleagues who rejected the revivals' emotionalism as satanic, Hall insisted that the movement was transforming public morals for the better and disseminating truly Christian godliness.

To his religious concern, Hall conjoined an educational concern. As a young pastor, he established a school called Clio's Nursery and an Academy of the Sciences in his Bethany home. He personally provided a classical education and a background in theology for numerous westerners who later attained prominence in North Carolina Presbyterianism, including John Makemie Wilson, Humphrey Hunter, James McIlheny, John Robinson, and Andrew Flinn. There are indications that Hall was the author of an English grammar for his students' use, which was circulated widely in manuscript form and was later published. He worked heartily on behalf of his alma mater and The University of North Carolina, each of which conferred upon him an honorary D.D. He was instrumental in raising the endowment for Princeton Theological Seminary and bequeathed the seminary 250 acres in Tennessee. He also donated some sixty volumes to The University of North Carolina Library.

During the period of his most extensive activity, Hall retained his pastorate at Bethany, and he remained titular pastor there until his death. Throughout his career he had exhibited manic-depressive symptoms which apparently emanated from an inconsistently repressed, ineradicable insecurity about his personal salvation; at one point he refused to preach for a year and a half, until an elder symbolically exorcised a "deaf-and-dumb demon" from him. His depressive tendency dominated his last seven years as his inescapable final judgment drew near. Hall was buried in the Bethany churchyard. At least one of his published sermons survives, *A Sermon preached at the ordination of Mr. Samuel C. Caldwell, as Pastor of Sugar Creek Church* (1792).

SEE: *DAB*, vol. 4 (1960); W. H. Foote, *Sketches of North Carolina, Historical and Biographical* (1846); C. L. Hunter, *Sketches of Western North Carolina* (1877); Jethro Rumple, *The History of Presbyterianism in North Carolina* (1966); W. B. Sprague, *Annals of the American Pulpit*, vol. 3 (1858); R. H. Stone, *A History of Orange Presbytery, 1770–1970* (1970); *Who Was Who in America, 1607–1896* (1963).

TIMOTHY J. WIEST

Hall, James King (*28 Sept. 1875–10 Sept. 1948*), psychiatrist, was born in Iredell County, near Statesville, the son of Dr. Eugenius Alexander and Amanda McCullough Howard Hall. Eugenius Alexander's ancestral line derives from James Hall, born in Ireland (ca. 1705), who married Prudence Roddy in 1730. In 1751, James Hall moved his family from Pennsylvania to land then in Rowan (now Iredell) County. They had ten children, one of whom was Alexander Hall, great-grandfather of James King. Alexander's son, Hugh Roddy Hall, established a classical school later chartered as Ebenezer Academy. The father of James King was born in 1839; though he lost part of his hand in active duty in the

Confederate Army, he completed his medical studies at the University of Maryland in 1868 and practiced medicine in Iredell County.

James King Hall attended Ebenezer Academy and Statesville High School. In 1897, he entered The University of North Carolina where he distinguished himself by membership in Phi Beta Kappa and the debate club, as president of the Athletic Association, and as assistant editor of *The Tar Heel*. In his senior year he completed the first year of medical school, and in 1901 he was graduated magna cum laude. After finishing the second year of medical school at Chapel Hill, he transferred to Jefferson Medical College in Philadelphia, receiving his degree in 1904. He served his internship at the Philadelphia Polyclinic Hospital, where he was influenced by a neurologist, William G. Spiller, and a psychiatrist, Francis X. Dercum, to specialize in the nascent field of psychiatry.

When Hall completed his internship, he was invited to join the staff of the North Carolina State Hospital in Morganton. From 1905 to 1911 he remained there as an assistant physician and performed original research under the direction of Dr. Patrick Murphy. In 1911, Hall and two of his associates at Morganton, Dr. Paul V. Anderson and Dr. E. M. Gayle, purchased the country estate of Major Lewis Ginter in Richmond, Va., where they founded Westbrook Sanatorium, the first private hospital in Virginia to specialize in the treatment of emotional illness.

Hall was president of Westbrook from 1911 until his death. Under his guidance it became, in the judgment of Dr. Karl Menninger, one of the most progressive psychiatric hospitals in the nation. Hall believed that the diagnosis and treatment of emotional diseases were as open to scientific inquiry as diseases of the body, and that emotional illness should incur no more social stigma than physical illness. Becoming a vigorous proponent of preventive psychiatry and mental hygiene, Hall campaigned for humane, medically enlightened treatment of criminals. He took an active interest in the relationship between emotional disorder and crime, and sought to supply detention centers with personnel who could treat the psychiatric problems of inmates.

A prolific writer, Hall made his most important single contribution to medical literature as editor of *One Hundred Years of American Psychiatry*. Published by the American Psychiatric Association in 1944, it was a definitive historical document on the subject. From 1919 to 1944 he was a regular contributor to *Southern Medicine and Surgery*, for which he was also an associate editor. Most of his writings were aimed at both professional and general audiences.

Hall stimulated professional intercommunication, especially through his extremely active participation in regional and national organizations. In 1941–42 he was president of the American Psychiatric Association. Also as president he directed the Tri-State Medical Association, the National Association of Private Psychiatric Hospitals, the Southern Psychiatric Association, and the Richmond Academy of Medicine. He was vice-president of the Medical Society of Virginia and chairman of the (Virginia) Governor's Advisory Board on Mental Hygiene. Other societies in which Hall was active included the American Association on Mental Deficiency, American Association for the Advancement of Science, American College of Physicians, American Medical Association, North Carolina State Medical Society, Southern Medical Society, Central Neuropsychiatric Hospital Association, Neuropsychiatric Society of Virginia, Virginia Academy of Science, North Carolina

Literary and Historical Association, and American Prison Association. The University of North Carolina conferred upon him an honorary LL.D. in 1935.

On 29 Feb. 1912 Hall married Laura Witherspoon Ervin of Morganton, the sister of Senator Samuel Ervin. Their union produced three sons: James King, Jr., Dorman Thompson, and Samuel Ervin. Hall was buried in Morganton.

SEE: *Biographical Directory of Fellows and Members of the American Psychiatric Association* (1949); William deB. MacNider, "James King Hall, 1875–1948," *Southern Medicine and Surgery* 111 (1949); *Men of Mark in Virginia* (1936); *Who Was Who in America*, vol. 2 (1950).

JOHN MACNICHOLAS

Hall, John (*31 May 1767–29 Jan. 1833*), justice of the North Carolina Supreme Court at the time of its organization in 1818, was born in Augusta County, Va. His father, Edward Hall, a native of Ireland, settled in Pennsylvania about 1736 but later made his home in Virginia. In the spring of 1744 Edward married Eleanor Stuart, a daughter of Archibald Stuart, Sr., of the noted family that produced Judge Archibald Stuart, Jr., the Honorable A. H. H. Stuart of President Fillmore's cabinet, and General J. E. B. Stuart of the Confederate Army.

After due preparation John Hall entered William and Mary College. He then studied law at Staunton, Va., under his kinsman, Judge Archibald Stuart, for whom he cherished an ardent gratitude and later named a son. At about age twenty-five Hall, having completed his legal studies, located at Warrenton, N.C., where he remained throughout his life. He was not a talented orator, but his splendid intellect and rich store of legal knowledge soon drew a profitable clientele.

In 1800, Hall took his seat on the Superior Court bench, a position he held until 1818, when he became one of the justices of the newly established North Carolina Supreme Court. Upon the organization of this court on 1 Jan. 1818, John Louis Taylor was appointed chief justice with Leonard Henderson and John Hall as associate justices. The court first sat for the dispatch of business on 1 Jan. 1819. Hall remained on the bench until December 1832, when he resigned because of ill health. In 1829, he·was chosen one of the presidential electors from North Carolina. Although his position on the court prevented his active participation in the political campaigns of the day, he was a pronounced Democrat of the Jeffersonian school. He was also a Mason and Senior Grand Warden from 1802 to 1805.

Hall initially was a Presbyterian, but he eventually joined the Episcopal church and received its sacraments upon his death from cancer of the throat. On 31 January, when news of the death of Judge Hall reached Raleigh, a joint meeting of the bench and bar was held in honor of his memory. At this meeting Chief Justice Leonard Henderson presided, and William H. Haywood, Jr., afterwards a U.S. senator, acted as secretary. Among other resolutions it was resolved that, "in testimony of this respect and affection, we will wear the usual badge of mourning for thirty days."

Hall married Mary Weldon, the daughter of William Weldon and granddaughter of Lieutenant Colonel Samuel Weldon, an officer of North Carolina militia during the American Revolution. By her he left a large number of children, including Dr. Issac Hall, a physician in Warrenton and later of Pittsboro, who married Eliza, the daughter of Peter Evans, and Judge Edward Hall,

who occupied a seat on the Superior Court bench in 1840–41. An oil portrait of John Hall hangs in the Supreme Court, Raleigh, and another is owned by the Masonic Grand Lodge of North Carolina.

SEE: Samuel A. Ashe, ed., *Biographical History of North Carolina*, vol. 5 (1906); University of North Carolina *University Magazine* 9 (April 1860); John H. Wheeler, *Historical Sketches of North Carolina* (1851).

ELIZABETH W. MANNING

Hall, Josephus Wells (*19 Mar. 1805–6 Dec. 1873*), physician, was born near South River in Rowan (now Davie) County, the son of Joseph Hall (1770–1850) and Margaret Linster Hall (1771–1842). His mother was the daughter of Moses Linster of Ireland (1740–1817) and Sarah Wells of Pennsylvania (1747–1818). His father was the son of Dr. Joseph Hall, who built the first gristmill on South River which later became known as the Foard and Lindsay Mill.

Hall was prepared for college by Dr. Jonathan Otis Freeman of the Presbyterian church in Salisbury. Following in the footsteps of his grandfather, he began the study of medicine under Dr. Joseph McDowell at Transylvania College. After earning his degree he practiced in Frankfort, Ky., where he met and married Henrietta Stockton of Indiana in 1836. He then went to Europe for further study, returning in 1839 to Louisville, Ky., his home. He later moved to St. Louis, Mo., where his wife died in 1849. While in St. Louis, Hall was associated with the founding of the Kemper School of Medicine in 1839. However, a disagreement with the head of the school necessitated a move after one year to a rival medical school at St. Louis University. Subsequently the two schools merged to form the present medical school of Washington University. In 1846 Hall was named St. Louis health officer.

For some reason that is not clear, his land in Missouri was confiscated and he returned to Salisbury, N.C., about 1850, a widower with one child and destitute of his former fortune. But he soon improved his prospects by courting the spinster daughter of Thomas L. Cowan, one of Salisbury's wealthiest merchants. He married Mary Cowan in 1853, and they lived with her parents on the south square until they purchased the former Salisbury Academy building on Jackson Street. Written on an inside wall of the house's only closet is the information that they moved into their new home on 19 Oct. 1859. Hall embellished the structure by adding iron grillwork around the porches and entrance gate fashioned by Peter Frercks of Salisbury.

Now that his wife had made him a wealthy man, Hall confined his medical practice to needy cases and spent his time in busy leisure by forming an artillery company and giving frequent lectures on geology and other scientific subjects at the newly formed YMCA in Temperance Hall. At the outbreak of the Civil War, he was commissioned as an army surgeon on 13 Dec. 1861 and assigned responsibility for the Confederate prison hospital in Salisbury. In addition, he worked tirelessly with the Wayside Hospital established by the Ladies Aid Society at the east corner of Lee and Council streets near the depot. When a general hospital consisting of ten buildings was erected along Bringle Ferry Road in the winter and spring of 1864, he was placed in charge. For his services to the Confederate medical corps he had to obtain a pardon after the war from President Andrew Johnson; this was granted on 11 May 1866.

After the war, Hall resumed his building and real estate business that he and his brother, Newberry F. Hall, had begun in 1858 when they erected a three-story brick shop on South Main Street. In the 1860s and early 1870s he built two brick stores on Innes Street and another group of large brick stores on North Main Street.

At age sixty-nine Hall died at his home on Jackson Street. The house was purchased by the Historic Salisbury Foundation in 1972 and designated the Josephus W. Hall House. "In his death," wrote the editor of the *Carolina Watchman*, "Salisbury has lost an excellent and highly valued citizen and one of her best, most cautious, yet judicious and active business characters." He was buried from St. Luke's Episcopal Church where he had been a member of the vestry for many years. His remains were placed in the Old English Cemetery but were later moved to the Chestnut Hill Cemetery. His wife, Mary Cowan Hall, died in 1902 and left all her real property to Hall's daughter, Henrietta, who was the wife of Julius D. McNeely.

SEE: Josephus W. Hall Papers (Manuscript Department, Duke University Library, Durham); McCubbins Papers (Rowan Public Library, Salisbury); Original documents in the Josephus W. Hall House, Salisbury; Jethro Rumple, *History of Rowan County* (1927); Salisbury *Carolina Watchman*, 29 Apr., 15 May 1858, 13 Dec. 1859, 14 Feb., 26 June 1860, 30 Dec. 1861, 20 Aug., 8 Sept. 1866, 31 Oct. 1872, 24 July, 21 Aug., 2 Oct., 11 Dec. 1873, 22 Jan. 1874; *Salisbury Truth-Index*, 7 Nov. 1902; Salisbury *Watchman and Old North State*, 1 May, 10 Sept. 1868.

JAMES S. BRAWLEY

Hall, Thomas Harmison *(June 1773–30 June 1853)*, physician, planter, and congressman, was born in Prince George County, Va., and, after studying medicine, began a practice in Tarboro, N.C. In 1803 he married Mrs. Martha Jones Green Sitgreaves, the daughter of General Allen Jones and the widow, respectively, of James W. Green and John Sitgreaves. Hall was first elected to Congress in 1817 to take the seat previously held by James W. Clark. On Capitol Hill he always stayed at Dowson's No. 2, where he was closely associated with Nathaniel Macon, Weldon Edwards, John Randolph, and other Old Republicans of the Roanoke area. During the presidential campaign of 1824, the Old Republicans supported William H. Crawford; when the House selected Adams over Crawford and Jackson in February 1825, Hall cast his vote for Crawford. Later that year, that vote became the major issue in Hall's campaign for reelection and he was narrowly defeated by Richard Hines. In a rematch two years later, however, the physician regained his seat from Hines.

Hall was unopposed in 1829 and overcame strong opposition from Joseph R. Lloyd in 1831. Two years later Hall bested Richard Sullivan, but in 1835 he was defeated by a Whig, Ebenezer Pettigrew of Tyrrell County. In his eight terms in Congress, Hall consistently held to the convictions of the Old Republicans, advocating strict construction of the Constitution, economy in government, and states' rights. He served on House committees on Indian Affairs, Elections, and Foreign Affairs. During his second tour of duty, he was chairman of the powerful Committee on Expenditures in the Treasury Department. After his second defeat, Hall returned home to be elected by his constituents to a term in the 1836 state senate. He then resumed his medical practice and agricultural pursuits.

Hall's sister, Dorothy, was the wife of the Tory Ralph MacNair. One of their children, Edmond Duncan, prac-

ticed medicine in Edgecombe County, as did his uncle. Hall was buried in the MacNair Cemetery near Tarboro. His tombstone bears the inscription, "Friend of Macon and Randolph."

SEE: *Biog. Dir. Am. Cong.* (1971); P. M. Goldman and J. S. Young, eds., *The United States Congressional Directory* (1973); W. S. Hoffmann, *Andrew Jackson and North Carolina Politics* (1971); Daniel M. McFarland, "Rip Van Winkle: Political Evolution in North Carolina, 1815–1835" (Ph.D. diss., University of Pennsylvania, 1954).

DANIEL M. MCFARLAND.

Hall, William *(11 Feb. 1775–7 Oct. 1856)*, governor of Tennessee and congressman, was born in Surry County, the son of William and Thankful Doak Hall. His father was a major in the Surry County militia during the early period of the Revolutionary War. In 1785, at age ten, he moved with his family to Sumner County (now in Tennessee). Later his father and two brothers were killed by hostile Indians. Hall grew to maturity in Sumner County and continued to live there until his death.

In 1796, he was commissioned a second major in the Sumner County militia. The following year he was elected to represent Sumner County in the Tennessee General Assembly, a position he held until 1805. With the outbreak of the War of 1812, he became a colonel of the First Regiment of Tennessee Volunteer Infantry and served under General Andrew Jackson in the Creek war and against the British. He was promoted to brigadier general in September 1813.

Elected to the Tennessee state senate in 1821, Hall represented Sumner County in the fourteenth, fifteenth, and sixteenth sessions. In the seventeenth assembly he was elected speaker. On the resignation of Governor Samuel Houston in 1829, Hall was inaugurated as governor of the state on 16 April. He served as interim governor until the inauguration of William Carroll on 1 Oct. 1829. In 1831 Hall was elected as a Democrat to the U.S. House of Representatives, where he remained until 3 Mar. 1833.

Hall married Mary B. Alexander, and they had seven children: William H., Richard A., Thankful J., Martha, Mary, Alexander, and John A. He died at his home near Castalian Springs, Sumner County, and was buried in the family graveyard on his estate.

SEE: *Biog. Dir. Am. Cong.* (1961); J. S. Jones, *Biographical Album of Tennessee Governors* (1903 [original photograph, available in the copy of this book in the Genealogical Room of the Chattanooga-Hamilton County Public Library]); R. McBride, ed., *Biographical Directory of the Tennessee General Assembly*, vol. 1 (1975); J. T. Moore, *Tennessee, The Volunteer State*, vol. 2 (1923).

EMMETT R. WHITE

Halling, Solomon *(ca. 1754–24 Dec. 1813)*, physician-surgeon, teacher, and Episcopal clergyman, was a native of Pennsylvania; he was said to have been "bred in medicine." He served as surgeon of the Fourth North Carolina Regiment from 1779 to the end of the Revolutionary War in the commands of General John Ashe and General Benjamin Lincoln. About 1784 he went to New Bern, N.C., to teach in the academy and to practice as a physician and druggist. Halling assisted in the services at Christ Church. He also became an active member of St. John's Masonic Lodge from 11 June 1789, delivering St. John's Day and other addresses, and serving on a lodge committee on the occasion of President Washington's visit to New Bern in 1791; later he was successively elected as Orator, Worshipful Master, and Chaplain of the Lodge.

In the 1790 census, Halling was listed as the head of the household with three females and five slaves. He and his wife Eunice were witnesses to the will of Mary Oliver in 1794. Mrs. Halling died in 1796; their daughter, Francina Greenway, married James Usher in 1807. His second wife, Sarah, died in Georgetown, S.C., on 27 Feb. 1810.

Recommended for Holy Orders by the standing committee of the Episcopal church after the 1790 meeting in Tarboro, Halling was ordained by Bishop James Madison of Virginia in 1792 and became rector of Christ Church, New Bern, succeeding the Reverend Dr. Leonard Cutting. He took part in the continuing efforts to organize a diocese in North Carolina, attending the 1793 and 1794 meetings at Tarboro, at which he served on the committees to draw up a constitution and a form of recommendation of Bishop-elect Charles Pettigrew; he was elected a member of the standing committee and a delegate to the General Convention. In 1796, Halling accepted a call to be rector of St. James's Church, Wilmington, and principal of the Wilmington Academy. From Wilmington he went to Georgetown, S.C., where he was rector of the Parish of Prince George Winyah (1809–13) and participated in the work of the diocesan convention, including the election of South Carolina's second bishop, the Right Reverend Theodore Dehon, who later preached Halling's funeral sermon.

SEE: Gertrude S. Carraway, *Crown of Life* (1940) and *Years of Light* (1944); Joseph B. Cheshire, *Sketches of Church History in North Carolina* (1829) and *The Early Conventions Held at Tawborough, 1790–1793, 1794* (1882); Walter Clark, ed., *State Records of North Carolina*, vols. 15, 18, 22 (1898–1907); Frederick Dalcho, *An Historical Account of the Protestant Episcopal Church in South Carolina* (1820); Gertrude S. Hay and others, comps., *Roster of Soldiers from North Carolina in the American Revolution* (1932); *Heads of Families at the First Census of the United States Taken in the Year 1790* (1908); Archibald Henderson, *Washington's Southern Tour, 1791* (1923); Sarah Lemmon, ed., *The Pettigrew Papers*, vol. 1 (1971); Elizabeth Moore, ed., *Records of Craven County*, vol. 1 (1960); *One Hundredth Anniversary Commemorating the Building of St. James Church, Wilmington, North Carolina* (1939); *Raleigh Register*, 14 May 1807, 15 Mar. 1810; State Convention of the Protestant Episcopal Church in the State of South Carolina, *Minute Book* (1809–13).

LAWRENCE F. BREWSTER

Halton, Robert (d. Mar./Apr. 1749), colonial official, first appears in North Carolina when he took the oaths of a royal councillor in Edenton, 25 Feb. 1731. He seems to have been a soldier in England and may have known Governor George Burrington through the army. When Burrington came to North Carolina from England in 1731, Halton probably accompanied him on the voyage. The governor nominated Halton as one of the earliest members of North Carolina's first royal council, and during the initial year of Burrington's administration he supported the volatile chief executive in all crucial votes. His early loyalty was rewarded when Burrington named Halton as provost marshal of Bath County in March 1731. This office was a profitable one by any measure; when it was abolished by the shift from pre-

cinct to county organization in 1738, Halton was allowed £2,000 in provincial currency as compensation.

By the fall of 1732, Halton probably realized the risk of being too closely identified with the uneven Burrington and did not attend council sessions after October. Two years later the governor suspended him for excessive absences, but Gabriel Johnston restored Halton to his council seat in November 1734. From the earliest days of Johnston's administration Halton was a firm supporter of the governor, and he was rewarded handsomely in return. He became a justice of the peace for New Hanover Precinct in December 1734, apparently having moved there from Edenton during 1732 or 1733. In March 1735 he was made a collector of quitrents and an usher of the Exchequer Court. Two years later he served as a commissioner for running the boundary with South Carolina. During the controversial maneuvers to incorporate Wilmington in 1739, he voted with the pro-Wilmington faction in the council to push through the crucial measure. His loyalty here further endeared him to Governor Johnston, and he became one of Wilmington's original commissioners in 1740 and an assistant justice of the General Court in 1743.

During late 1740 and early 1741 Halton served as a captain of North Carolina troops going to Jamaica and Cartagena. As a man of some military experience, Halton was a colonel in the New Hanover militia. He also participated in the earliest part of the Granville District survey in 1744 and, in September 1746, became an agent for the sale of such lands. Earlier in 1746, Halton journeyed to England (possibly to seek the office of land agent from Earl Granville) and appeared before the Board of Trade to discuss conditions in North Carolina.

Halton remained active until his death. He spent roughly the last sixteen years of his life at his plantation, called Halton's Lodge, on Smith's Creek near Wilmington. However, he returned to Edenton to die, as his will was written there on 22 Mar. 1748/49. In his will Halton named a wife, Mary, who was residing in England, but he left the bulk of his estate to Sarah Groves and his son by her, Robert Halton, Jr.

SEE: Tillie Bond Manuscripts and Governors' Office Papers (North Carolina State Archives, Raleigh); Donald R. Lennon and Ida B. Kellam, *The Wilmington Town Book* (1973); William L. Saunders, ed., *Colonial Records of North Carolina*, vols. 3–5 (1886–87).

WILLIAM S. PRICE, JR.

Ham, George Caverno (8 Dec. 1912–26 Sept. 1977), psychiatrist and teacher, was born in Edgewood, Pa., near Pittsburgh, the son of Thomas C. Ham and his wife, Lola Trickey. A brother, Dr. Thomas Hale Ham, also achieved distinction in medical teaching and research. The family later moved to the Philadelphia area where George was graduated from Radnor High School in Wayne. After completing his undergraduate studies at Dartmouth College, he entered the medical school at the University of Pennsylvania and was awarded an M.D. degree in 1937. Ham was successively intern, resident, and Edward Bok Fellow in medicine at the Hospital of the University of Pennsylvania. After a year as a Commonwealth Fund Fellow in medicine at the University of Virginia, he returned to the University Hospital in Philadelphia as an instructor.

With the advent of World War II, Ham joined the Army Medical Corps. He was assigned to research, first in the study of physiological changes in man associated with rapid changes in velocity, and then in the effects of drugs on the nervous system. As a result of his experience during the war years, Ham found his lifework: the interactions between the human personality and physiological functions. Hence, when he resumed his career after the war, he entered the field of psychiatry. He first became a psychiatric resident at Michael Reese Hospital in Chicago as well as a training candidate at the Chicago Institute for Psychoanalysis, then under the direction of Dr. Franz Alexander. On completion of his residency in 1949, Ham for two years was a research associate in both the Chicago Institute and the Michael Reese Department of Psychiatry. While in Chicago, he made valuable contributions in the field of psychosomatic medicine and published a series of papers that remain as models for workers in the field.

Late in 1951, Ham accepted the appointment of professor and first chairman of the Department of Psychiatry in The University of North Carolina Medical School, which was in the process of expanding its program to four years. Ham had entered his profession at a time of momentous change. Dynamic psychiatry, founded on much of the best in Western humanism, had proved its worth during the late war. Though widely accepted throughout most of the United States, it was little known in the South. Ham, who possessed both high intelligence and an attractive personality, was an ideal choice to implement this new field of learning. A competent administrator and an enthusiastic teacher, he quickly made his department one of the strongest in the new medical school and one of the best in the nation. But Ham did not confine his efforts to the medical school in Chapel Hill. With the collaboration of state legislator John Umstead and Dr. David Young, he helped modernize and improve the state mental hospital system in North Carolina. In 1964, he retired from teaching and entered private practice in Chapel Hill.

Active in many organizations, Ham was honored by his profession on several occasions. In 1976, he received The University of North Carolina School of Medicine's Distinguished Service Award. He was a charter fellow of the American College of Psychoanalysis and a member of numerous state, regional, and national psychiatric councils and advisory bodies. He lectured internationally and his talents were recognized in many areas.

Before leaving Philadelphia, Ham married Sally Watt who predeceased him by only a few months. They were the parents of a son, George C., Jr. ("Jay"), and a daughter, Mrs. Susan Ham Todd.

SEE: *American Men of Science* (1966); *Biographical Directory of the American Psychiatric Association* (1968); *Chapel Hill Newspaper*, 27 Sept. 1977; Arthur Prange and others, "Commemorative Statement to the Faculty Council of UNC, 9 Dec. 1977" (typescript, Office, Secretary of the Faculty, University of North Carolina, Chapel Hill).

CLAIBORNE T. SMITH, JR.

Hambley, Egbert Barry Cornwall (2 May 1862–13 Aug. 1906), mining engineer and industrialist, was born in Penzance, Cornwall, England, the son of James and Ellen Read Hambley. His father was a civil engineer who had explored mining regions throughout the world, including South America and Africa. E. B. C. Hambley, like his father, pursued a career in civil and mining engineering. He studied at Trevath House School in Cornwall and at the Royal School of Mines in Kensington. At the death of his father in 1880, Hambley left school and began working for J. J. Truran, a businessman whose enterprises extended throughout the British Empire.

In January 1881, he was sent to North Carolina and served as assistant to the principal of the Gold Hill Mines in Rowan County. This property had been among the most valuable gold mines in the state before the Civil War but was worked only intermittently after the war. Hambley remained at Gold Hill for three years, then returned to England to join a major engineering firm, John Taylor & Sons. In his capacity as special engineer, Hambley was dispatched to southern India, the Gold Coast and Transvaal in Africa, Mexico, California, Spain, and Norway. During this intensive three-year period, he became acquainted with the latest techniques of mining engineering and also with the design of power facilities.

He returned with this knowledge to North Carolina in 1887 and took up permanent residence (he was never naturalized), serving as a contact for British investment capital in the state. At one time, he was consulting engineer to no less than eight mining companies and managing director for the Sam Christian Hydraulic Company in Montgomery County. Hambley also promoted business and industry in the Salisbury vicinity. He organized the Salisbury Gas and Electric Light Company and served on the board of the Salisbury Cotton Mills, the Davis and Wiley Bank of Salisbury, and the Yadkin Railroad Company.

From 1898 until his death, Hambley's energies were absorbed by an ambitious project to harness the hydroelectric power of the Yadkin River and to develop an industrial complex in Stanly, Rowan, and neighboring counties. In partnership with local businessmen, he formed the North Carolina Power Company and began to search for potential investors. Shortly after 1900, Hambley engaged the interest of George I. Whitney, a financier from Pittsburgh and a member of the banking and brokerage firm of Whitney and Stephenson. Whitney purchased a controlling share of the power company and formed Whitney Company, with Hambley as vice-president and general manager. The Whitney Company served as an umbrella for several subsidiary enterprises, including the Whitney Reduction Works at Gold Hill, the Rowan Granite Company at what became Granite Quarry, the Barringer Gold Mining Company near New London, the Yadkin Land Company, the Yadkin River Electric Power Company, the Yadkin Mines Consolidated Company, and the Virginia Copper and Land Company. Textile mills and electric power outlets were also planned. Rights-of-way for power lines were secured as far away as Knoxville, Tenn.

Within the first few years of the twentieth century, the Whitney Company owned large tracts of land in Stanly and surrounding counties and had stirred the imagination of contemporary observers. Local newspapers saw the company as spearheading a "revolution in manufacturing," turning North Carolina's Piedmont into "the New England of the South." "The master minds at Whitney," exclaimed one journalist, "are engaged in carrying out a giant scheme to grapple with and subdue elemental nature, forcing her with many inventions to lend her untamed energy, wasted for ages, to the direction of human intelligence, that much good may result to the world of men."

The pivotal element in the Whitney-Hambley plan was a hydroelectric power dam at the Narrows of the Yadkin River. The dam, projected at 35 feet in height and 1,100 feet in length, was to generate 27,000 horsepower (the equivalent of about 20,000 kilowatts of electric power) to towns and industries throughout the Piedmont. A five-mile canal was also planned to connect the dam to a power plant on the river just below Palmer Mountain. A spur line was constructed from New London to the dam site. A model manufacturing town called Whitney was designed, and company engineers laid out streets and boulevards. Hundreds of workers, including Sicilian masons, were imported to build the dam out of huge granite blocks quarried in Rowan County.

Despite the prodigious labors of these men and the visionary concepts of Whitney and Hambley, the project stalled after the first few years. Accidents at company mines and at the dam site, as well as outbreaks of typhoid, depleted the labor force. Hambley himself contracted typhoid in the summer of 1906 and died at age forty-four. His death was a shock to the industrial and engineering community of North Carolina. The *Charlotte Observer* called it "a most deplorable event" and editorialized that "few men have done more for [North Carolina] in a material way, and his value to it and the extent of the loss it has sustained in his death are beyond estimate." The Whitney Company outlived Hambley by only one year. The panic of 1907 cut off George Whitney's lines of credit and, although he continued to operate some subsidiary companies for several years, the bold plan to harness the power of the Yadkin was abandoned. A decade later, the Aluminum Company of America implemented Hambley's basic concept with a new dam a few miles downstream to provide power for its reduction works at Badin.

In 1887 Hambley married Lottie Clark Coleman, the great-granddaughter of North Carolina's Governor William Hawkins. They had five children: Littleton Coleman, Gilbert Foster, William Hawkins, James Young, and Charlotte Isabel. The Hambleys first resided at the farm of Mrs. Hambley's father, Dr. Littleton W. Coleman, near Rockwell where Hambley bred valuable herds of Jersey cattle. In 1903, they moved to a large new home on Fulton Street in Salisbury. The house, designed by Charles C. Hook of Charlotte, was constructed not only to accommodate the growing Hambley family but also to entertain potential investors in the projects of the Whitney Company. Hambley had migrated to America as a member of the Church of England and belonged to the Episcopal church throughout his life. He was buried at Chestnut Hill Cemetery, Salisbury.

SEE: Samuel A. Ashe, ed., *Biographical History of North Carolina*, vol. 2 (1907); *Charlotte Observer*, 14 Aug. 1906; Lexington *Dispatch*, 14 Feb. 1906; Salisbury *Evening Post*, 18 Jan. 1956.

BRENT D. GLASS

Hambright, Frederick (*17 May 1727–9 May 1817*), colonial officer and local patriot, was born in Germany, probably the son of Conrad Hambright. Along with several members of the Hambright family, he emigrated to Philadelphia in 1738 on the ship *St. Andrew*. The family settled in Lancaster County, Pa. As a young man, Hambright moved to Virginia where he married Sarah Hardin, daughter of Benjamin Hardin. In the early 1750s they moved to the area that became Tryon County, N.C., with Joseph, John, and Benjamin Hardin, Nathaniel Henderson, James Kuykendall, Robert Leeper, and others. For protection from Indians he set-

tled near the fort at the mouth of the South Fork of the Catawba River.

Hambright was a member of Captain Samuel Cobrin's company during the Spanish Alarm in 1747–48 at Wilmington. As commanding officer of the Tryon County militia, he campaigned against the Cherokee Indians in 1771.

In 1774, the Provincial Congress elected him to serve as a commissioner to help decide where to place the courthouse. He also served on a jury to lay out a road from Tryon Court House to Tuckasege Ford in present Gaston County on the Catawba River. Continuing civil offices in 1775, he was a venireman at the term of the Court of Oyer and Terminer for the Salisbury district and an active member of the Committee of Safety of Tryon County. Although he arrived a day late, he served as a member of the Provincial Congress at Hillsborough. Along with others, he signed the petition opposing Parliamentary taxation and supporting the Provincial and Continental congresses. After receiving permission to leave in September, he was elected by the Provincial Congress to be second major of Tryon County. In the following year, the Congress also elected him justice of the peace. Throughout 1776 he attended safety committee meetings in Wilmington and at Tryon Court House.

As a Revolutionary War officer, Hambright served under General Griffith Rutherford in his campaign into Georgia in 1776. Promoted to lieutenant colonel, he went to the relief of Charles Town in 1779 as a member of Colonel Alexander Lillington's brigade, but retired before the surrender. In the summer of 1780, he served under Colonel Charles McDowell in the Broad River region.

In the fall of 1780, Cornwallis sent Major Patrick Ferguson to stop the colonial militia. When Ferguson claimed on Kings Mountain that "all the Rebels from hell" could not drive him away, Hambright was second in command of a segment of troops under Major William Chronicle. In one of the four columns that converged on the British, Chronicle was shot in the first charge. His undisciplined militia then followed Hambright to participate in the victory. In a thick German accent, he is reported to have said, "Huzza, my brave boys, fight on a few minutes more and the battle will be over." Although wounded in the thigh by a rifle bullet, he remained in the saddle for the entire battle; when Samuel York of York County, S.C., suggested that he leave the field because of his profuse bleeding, he refused. After the battle, he was conveyed to a cabin on Long Creek. The deep wound required a long time to heal and caused him to limp for the rest of his life.

Hambright's first wife died, and he married Mary Dover in 1781. The following year he sold his Long Creek property near Dallas, N.C., and bought land near King's Creek, S.C., where he built a large two-story log cabin which burned in 1927. When he left North Carolina, he resigned the offices of lieutenant colonel and justice of the peace in what was by then Lincoln County. His bravery at Kings Mountain was rewarded by the North Carolina General Assembly in 1786, when he and the other commanders at the battle received an elegant mounted sword. Hambright's is now in the museum at Kings Mountain National Military Park.

For the remainder of his life, Hambright engaged in farming. He also served as a Presbyterian elder. At the time of his death he owned 700 acres of land, four slaves, and three mares. He had twelve children by his first wife and ten by his second. After fighting at Kings Mountain, his son John was named a captain in the

Revolutionary Army and his son Frederick, Jr., became a major. Hambright was buried at Shiloh Presbyterian Church, one mile east of Grover, N.C. In 1931, the Daughters of the Revolution erected a monument to him on Kings Mountain.

SEE: T. D. Bailey, *Commanders at Kings Mountain* (1926); Walter Clark, ed., *State Records of North Carolina*, vols. 15, 17, 19, 22–24 (1898–1905); Clarence W. Griffin, *History of Old Tryon and Rutherford Counties, North Carolina, 1730–1936* (1937); Laban M. Hoffman, *Our Kin* (1968); C. L. Hunter, *Sketches of Western North Carolina* (1877); Bonnie S. Mauney, *The Colonel Frederick Hambright Family* (1964); William L. Saunders, ed., *Colonial Records of North Carolina*, vol. 10 (1890); William L. Sherrill, *Annals of Lincoln County, North Carolina* (1972).

MICHAEL EDGAR GOINS

Hamilton, John *(d. 12 Dec. 1816)*, merchant in late colonial North Carolina and Virginia, commander of the largest provincial corps of North Carolina loyalists, and British diplomat, was born in Scotland, probably near Glasgow. The Clyde ports became the locus of Scotland's spectacular economic growth in the eighteenth century—a movement in which John Hamilton and his kinsmen participated. Sometime between 1755 and 1760 Hamilton arrived in Nansemond County, Va., where in 1760 his three brothers, Archibald, William, and James, were already engaged in commercial ventures. John formed a partnership with Archibald, perhaps William, and their uncle, John Hamilton of Dowan, a Glasgow merchant. The firm, originally called William Hamilton and Company, seemingly prospered; it spread into North Carolina within two years and established a major commercial center at Hamilton Hill on Elk Marsh, six to eight miles west of the town of Halifax.

Due to the nature of their trade and clientele, the Hamiltons extended a great deal of credit, thereby making a major contribution to the development of the Piedmont. Moreover, their firm engaged in extensive land speculation. These two strains merged in the attempt to establish a commercial outpost in Wake County—a project that never succeeded due to the American Revolution. Hamilton and Company's large-scale involvement in the backcountry seems to suggest that east-west sectionalism in colonial North Carolina may have been overemphasized by scholars. The Atlantic network of trade and credit in which the firm operated, however, required that the British Empire, at least in a commercial sense, remain intact. Thus, the coming of the American Revolution doomed Hamilton and Company.

By 1775 the firm found it nearly impossible to collect its debts, despite the respect it apparently earned from many North Carolinians, and was forced to greatly restrict its activities. The inevitable occurred in August 1777, when John and Archibald Hamilton, as well as several of their employees, refused the oath of allegiance required by the new state. Given two months to leave North Carolina, the Hamiltons tried desperately to reduce their losses before sailing from New Bern on a ship purchased for that purpose on 25 Oct. 1777. The brothers would later claim that their departure, a consequence of their loyalism, cost them close to £200,000 in land, personal property, and especially debts.

In New York the Hamiltons separated; John offered his services to the British military, whereas Archibald, burdened by a family, returned to Glasgow. After serving as a messenger between General William Howe and General Sir Henry Clinton, John Hamilton received authorization to raise loyalist troops in conjunction with the new British campaign in the South. His commission specified that the number of men he recruited would determine his rank. When the British attacked Savannah, he took about 30 refugees there; they formed the nucleus of the North Carolina Volunteers (later the Royal North Carolina Regiment). Lieutenant Colonel Hamilton commanded the corps, which mustered a peak membership of about 750 men. North Carolinians—refugees in South Carolina and Georgia, as well as those who joined Cornwallis's march through North Carolina—composed the main part of the unit. Hamilton commanded his troops at the siege of Savannah and the battles of Briar Creek, Kettle Creek, Stono Ferry, Monck's Corner, Hanging Rock, Camden, Guilford Court House, and Yorktown, where he surrendered with 80 of his men. He was wounded three times in the king's service. Cornwallis later wrote that "his conduct as a citizen and soldier appear to me highly meritorious and I think he deserves a mark of the gratitude of his country." In 1782 the Royal North Carolina Regiment absorbed the North Carolina Highlanders, organized by royal governor Josiah Martin before the Battle of Moore's Creek Bridge and reactivated in 1781.

When the British evacuated Charles Town in the autumn of 1782, the 142 men remaining in the Royal North Carolina Regiment, along with the South Carolina Royalists and the King's Carolina Rangers (primarily a Georgia group), were transferred to St. Augustine, Fla., under Hamilton's command. When the loyalists in East Florida learned that their new home had been ceded to Spain, plans for an insurrection to prevent the Spanish from taking possession gained currency. These schemes led to the proposal that the erstwhile merchant lead a mutiny to spark the uprising; his firm refusal and his avowal to oppose any such activities contributed greatly to maintaining the peace in East Florida during this difficult time.

From East Florida the Royal North Carolina Regiment went to Nova Scotia and disbanded there in November 1783. Hamilton probably went with the troops, but by June 1784 he was in London seeking compensation for his losses as a loyalist—an endeavor that would occupy the next six years. Receiving half pay as a lieutenant colonel, Hamilton settled at Portland Place in a London neighborhood frequented by Tory refugees. He apparently married during this period, for by the summer of 1785 he listed a wife and small child among his dependents. Little is known about his personal life except for a suggestive statement by Willie Jones in a letter to Archibald Hamilton, dated 19 May 1786, that he was "exceedingly sorry for his [John Hamilton's] misfortune in loosing his children." In London, despite any personal problems, Hamilton became a spokesman for a group of former southern merchants. The British government gave him and two partners £8,000 as compensation for their American losses. In 1790, however, this entire sum went to their Scottish creditors. In 1806, Hamilton and his partners received further compensation of £5,630 after their case was reopened as a result of the Jay Treaty.

Like many once wealthy southern loyalists, Hamilton looked to the Bahama Islands as a favorable place to rebuild his life, trying in vain to secure appointment as governor there. Finally in 1790 he became British consul in Norfolk, Va.—a post he held until returning to England shortly after the outbreak of the War of 1812. Only two other American loyalists received such consular appointments. The poet Thomas Moore, who visited the consulate in Norfolk during 1803, found Hamilton "a plain and hospitable man, and his wife full of homely, but comfortable and genuine civility." Moreover, Moore felt that the consul "is one among the very few instances of a man, ardently loyal to his King, and yet beloved by the Americans. His home is the very temple of hospitality; and I sincerely pity the heart of that stranger who, warm from the welcome of such a board, could sit down to write such a libel on his host, in the true spirit of a modern philosophist."

Hamilton died in England. Friends and enemies alike remarked on his kindness and integrity. He was described as " 'a short, stout, red-faced man; well bred, and well fed.' "

SEE: Chapman Papers, Lawrence Collection, and Muster Rolls of North Carolina Volunteers and Royal North Carolina Regiment (Public Archives of Canada, Ottawa); Joseph B. Lochey, *East Florida, 1783–1785*, ed. by John W. Caughey (1949); Thomas Moore, *The Poetical Works of Thomas Moore* (1857); Public Record Office, London: A.O. 12/36. 95, 100, 109, 13/54, 107; W.O. 65/65; T. 64/23, 79/44; Raleigh *Minerva*, 14 Mar. 1816; Lorenzo Sabine, *Biographical Sketches of Loyalists of the American Revolution with an Historical Essay*, 2 vols. (1864); Paul Smith, "The American Loyalists: Notes on Their Organization and Numerical Strength," *William and Mary Quarterly* 25 (1968); Treasurer's and Comptroller's Papers (North Carolina State Archives, Raleigh).

CAROLE WATTERSON TROXLER
ARTHUR C. MENIUS

Hamilton, Joseph Grégoire de Roulhac (6 Aug. 1878–10 Nov. 1961),

university professor, was born in Hillsborough, the son of Daniel Heyward and Frances Gray Roulhac Hamilton. After study at home, he prepared for college at the Sewanee Academy in Tennessee and was graduated from the University of the South with the M.A. degree in 1900. He studied at Columbia University (1902–4) with the distinguished historian, William Archibald Dunning, and was awarded the Ph.D. degree in American history in 1906.

Hamilton began his teaching career in 1901 at the Horner Military School in Oxford and was principal of the Wilmington High School (1904–6). With his appointment in 1906 as associate professor of history at The University of North Carolina, Hamilton began his long and productive career on the university faculty which was to last until his retirement in 1948. He became Alumni Professor and head of the History Department in 1908 and was named Kenan Professor of History and Government in 1920.

The university's History Department grew in stature under his leadership and emerged as one of the important centers for graduate work in American history. He resigned as its head in 1930 in order to devote his major attention to the Southern Historical Collection, of which he became founder and director in that year. He continued to teach one or two quarters each year until 1936, but thereafter gave his full attention to the Southern Historical Collection. Hamilton was an imaginative, dynamic, and stimulating teacher, and many of his former students who attained distinction as professional historians, lawyers, journalists, and public officials readily acknowledged his influence. He became widely known as a teacher and scholar, and taught in summer sessions at the University of Michigan (1928), Harvard University (1931), the University of Chicago (1933, 1934, 1936), and the University of Southern California (1939).

During his more than forty-year tenure at Chapel Hill, Hamilton contributed to the enrichment of the university in many ways. His years as secretary of the Historical Society of The University of North Carolina and his articles in the *Carolina Magazine, Alumni Review*, and university *Extension Leaflets* contributed to an awakening of interest in the state's history and encouraged wider public support for the university. Hamilton played an important part in the early development of the university's Institute for Research in Social Science, directed by Howard W. Odum. Thus it was fitting that in 1972 the new building housing the departments of history, political science, and sociology was named for Hamilton, who had been a key figure in the emergence of the modern social sciences at Chapel Hill.

Professor Hamilton participated in the educational programs of the War Department during World War I as director of the War Issues Course, Fourth District, Students Army Training Corps (1918); lecturer, citizenship unit, Army Educational Corps, American Expeditionary Force (1919); and consultant in general education to the war plans division, General Staff (1920–22). Although Hamilton covered the broad field of American history and government in his teaching, in his research and publications he concentrated primarily on North Carolina state history, the American Civil War, Reconstruction, and American biography. He was a prodigious worker, and he wrote rapidly and with ease. He was the author of about one hundred articles, an equal number of biographical sketches, five monographs, and one or more chapters in several cooperative works. His articles appeared in historical journals, scholarly reviews, and literary and popular magazines. His best known books are *Reconstruction in North Carolina* (1914), *Party Politics in North Carolina, 1835–1860* (1916), *North Carolina Since 1860* (1919), and biographies of Robert E. Lee (1917) and Henry Ford (1926). He edited *Truth in History and Other Essays by William A. Dunning* (1937) and fourteen volumes of documentary sources, including the correspondence and papers of Jonathan Worth, Thomas Ruffin, Abraham Lincoln, Thomas Jefferson, Randolph A. Shotwell, and William A. Graham. He was the editor of the *James Sprunt Historical Publications* from 1908 to 1924. Hamilton published many articles on governmental reforms in the state press, the most notable of which was "A Plea for a Constitutional Convention," published serially in the Raleigh *News and Observer* (19 Dec. 1912–19 Jan. 1913) and reprinted in several other newspapers and in pamphlet form.

Although Hamilton's contributions to teaching and scholarship entitled him to rank with the leading historians of his generation, he placed greater value on his establishment and development of the Southern Historical Collection which made The University of North Carolina the leading center for research in southern history. Under Hamilton's direction and as a result of his incomparable talents and skills as a collector, the collection became the largest single depository of nonpublic manuscripts in southern history and culture in existence. His work drew wide praise from other historians. Claude G. Bowers wrote that "no greater contribution to the truth of history has ever been attempted"; Douglas Freeman said that "all historical investigators were in eternal debt" to Hamilton; and Allan Nevins said that all historians would have reason to be grateful to him.

Throughout his career, Hamilton was active in professional associations and read numerous papers before scholarly meetings. He served as a member of several committees of the American Historical Association, including its Executive Council (1929–33). He was elected president of the North Carolina Literary and Historical Association in 1920, of the Southern Historical Association in 1943, and of the Historical Society of North Carolina in 1954.

He was elected to membership in Phi Beta Kappa by the mother chapter at the College of William and Mary, and he was awarded the Columbia University Medal of Honor (1932) and honorary degrees by the University of the South (1942), Washington and Lee University (1942), and The University of North Carolina (1957). In 1949, a group of his former students dedicated a volume of *Essays in Southern History* to him.

Hamilton was a member of the Episcopal church and of the Kappa Alpha fraternity. He was a Democrat with an active interest in public policies, but he was not a "joiner" in the conventional sense. He did, however, enjoy and greatly value his many friends; his warm personality, infectious laugh, sparkling conversation, and seemingly endless fund of stories made him in great demand among his friends and acquaintances.

On 22 Dec. 1908 Hamilton married Mary Cornelia Thompson of Raleigh. She was coauthor with him of *The Life of Robert E. Lee for Boys and Girls* (1917), and was his constant companion and coworker in his thousands of miles of travel to collect manuscripts. Mrs. Hamilton died on 7 June 1959 and Hamilton two years later, both in Chapel Hill. He was buried in the old Chapel Hill Cemetery. There is a portrait in the Southern Historical Collection (University of North Carolina). Two sons survived: Joseph Grégoire de Roulhac Hamilton, Jr., a Washington, D.C. news correspondent, and Dr. Alfred Thompson Hamilton, a physician and surgeon of Raleigh.

SEE: *Chapel Hill Weekly*, 6 June 1947, 13, 16 Nov. 1961; *Durham Morning Herald*, 28 Jan. 1954; Fletcher M. Green, "Joseph Grégoire Hamilton" (typescript, 1962, Office, Secretary of the Faculty, University of North Carolina, Chapel Hill); J. G. de Roulhac Hamilton Papers (Southern Historical Collection, University of North Carolina Library, Chapel Hill); Raleigh *News and Observer*, 12 Aug. 1951, 13, 14 Nov. 1961; *Who Was Who in America*, vol. 6 (1976); Louis R. Wilson, *The University of North Carolina, 1900–1930* (1957).

J. CARLYLE SITTERSON

Hamilton, William Baskerville (7 Mar. 1908–17 July 1972), historian, was born in Jackson, Miss., the oldest son of William B. and Bessie Cavett Hamilton. After attending the public schools in Jackson, he received an A.B. degree from the University of Mississippi in 1928 and an M.A. in 1931. He taught in the public schools of Holly Springs and Jackson, Miss., from 1928 until 1934, when he entered the Graduate School of Duke University. Beginning two years before he received his Ph.D. in 1936, Hamilton taught in the Department of History at Duke until his death.

He began his career as a specialist in the history of the American South, having written a much-used dissertation on the Mississippi Territory under the supervision of Professor William K. Boyd. Hamilton also received solid training in British history from Professor William T. Laprade, and most of his teaching and publishing were in the areas of modern British constitutional and political history and the history of the British Commonwealth. These interests led him to play a prominent part in the establishment of the Center for Commonwealth Studies at Duke University and to

make numerous trips to Canada and England in connection with his scholarly projects. He also made similar trips to New Zealand, Australia, Ghana, and Nigeria.

At Duke University, Hamilton took a special interest in the library and served on the library council for a number of years, including one term as its chairman. He was also the chief builder of the British Historical Manuscripts Collection in the Perkins Library of Duke University. As president of the Duke chapter of the American Association of University Professors in 1949–50, he took the lead in presenting the faculty's proposals for a Faculty Senate and was elected a member of the Committee on Faculty Reorganization, which was created in 1951 and led to the rewriting of the university's bylaws and the establishment of a University Council. After serving as a member of the Council for several terms, Hamilton held the vice-chairmanship (with the president of the university as chairman) in 1960–61. From 1962 to 1964 he served as the first chairman of the Academic Council, which was the successor of the earlier body.

A Fellow of the Royal Historical Society of Great Britain, Hamilton was also a member of a number of professional organizations in addition to Phi Beta Kappa and Omicron Delta Kappa. He was a longtime member of the Southern Historical Association and served as the chairman of its European History Section in 1962–63.

Hamilton became the managing editor of the *South Atlantic Quarterly* in 1956, after he had edited and written an introductory essay for an anthology, *Fifty Years of the South Atlantic Quarterly* (Durham, 1952). His most important book was *Anglo-American Law on the Frontier: Thomas Rodney and His Territorial Cases* (Durham, 1953); he also edited a volume on the British Commonwealth, *The Transfer of Institutions* (Durham, 1964), and was the author of over two dozen scholarly articles and chapters in books.

He married Mary Elizabeth Boyd on 27 May 1938, and they had one child, Elizabeth Cavett, who was born in 1940. Mrs. Hamilton died 5 Mar. 1954.

SEE: *Directory of American Scholars: History* (1969); W. B. Hamilton Papers (Manuscript Department, Duke University Library, Durham); Richard L. Watson, Jr., "William B. Hamilton," *South Atlantic Quarterly* 72 (1973).

ROBERT F. DURDEN

Hamlin, Courtney Walker (27 Oct. 1858–16 Feb. 1950), congressman from Missouri, was born in Henderson (now Transylvania) County, probably in present Cathey's Creek Township, the son of Eliakim Smith and Julia Ann Barton Hamlin. Moving with his parents to nearby Pickens County, S.C., before 1866 and to Missouri in 1869, he grew up on a farm and was educated in local common schools and at Salem (Mo.) Academy. His parents apparently returned to North Carolina, as his father died in Transylvania County in 1910 and his mother three years later.

After reading law, young Hamlin was admitted to the bar on 21 Mar. 1882. He served two years as attorney for the town of Bolivar and for six years was a member of the board of education in Springfield, both in the southwestern part of the state. A Baptist, he also taught a men's Sunday school class. Hamlin served a term in Congress from 1903 to 1905. Although defeated for reelection in 1904, he recaptured his seat in the next election and continued to serve five more terms. On

Capitol Hill he was an advocate of woman suffrage. Returning to Missouri in 1919, he practiced law in Springfield until his retirement in 1935. He then moved to Santa Monica, Calif., to live near his daughters. He died at age ninety-one, believed at that time to be the oldest living former congressman. His remains were returned to Springfield for burial in East Lawn Cemetery.

Hamlin married Annie L. Lamar of Bourbon, Mo., in 1881, and they were the parents of Pearl, Cressie, and Carl.

SEE: *Biog. Dir. Am. Cong.* (1971); *Official Manual of the State of Missouri* (1918); *Springfield News*, 17, 18 Feb. 1950; John H. Wheeler, *Reminiscences and Memoirs of North Carolina* (1884).

PHILLIP W. EVANS

Hammer, Minnie Lee Hancock (14 Dec. 1873–30 Oct. 1959), religious, civic, and cultural leader, and newspaper manager, was the daughter of Dr. J. M. and Jane Page Hancock and the granddaughter of James Page, doorkeeper in the Congress of the Confederate States of America. Her father was a major in the Confederate Army. After graduating from Salem College in 1893, she married, on 21 December, William Cicero Hammer who served as solicitor, U.S. district attorney, and member of the U.S. House of Representatives. Mrs. Hammer assisted her husband in his political activities and took an active part in the management of the *Asheboro Courier*, which they owned and operated for more than forty years. She was a member of the North Carolina Press Association and in 1938 was made an honorary life member. Following her husband's death, on 26 Sept. 1930, Mrs. Hammer was asked by the Democratic party to fill his unexpired term in Congress, but she declined because of her family and business interests.

Mrs. Hammer was for twenty-five years president of the Woman's Missionary Society of the North Carolina Annual Conference of the Methodist Protestant church. When the Foreign and Home Missionary societies were merged into the United Branch of Missions of the Methodist Protestant church, she was made the national president of that group. In 1910, she conceived the idea of creating the Methodist Protestant Children's Home, which was first located in Denton but moved to High Point in 1913. To the hundreds of children who went to live in this home, Mrs. Hammer was affectionately known as "Mother Hammer." In addition, she took an active role in the establishment of High Point College by the North Carolina Annual Conference. She was a charter member of the Asheboro Methodist Protestant Church (now the Central Methodist Church) and for several years before her death was a member of the board of trustees of the Methodist Retirement Home of the Western North Carolina Methodist Conference in Charlotte.

Mrs. Hammer was the first woman to be named a member of the executive committee of the General Conference of the Methodist church after the unification, in 1939, of the three splinter branches.

For fifty-one years, she was president of the Randolph Book Club. She also served as president of her local chapter of the United Daughters of the Confederacy, as a member and president of the Randolph County Historical Society, as first president of the Asheboro Woman's Club, and as chairman of the Seventh District, North Carolina Federation of Woman's Clubs.

Her daughter, Harriette Lee Hammer Walker, a feature writer, editor, and author, died on 26 Sept. 1943. Mrs. Hammer, generally regarded as "Asheboro's First Citizen," was buried in Asheboro City Cemetery.

SEE: *Asheboro Courier*, 2 Nov. 1959; Mrs. Cuthbert W. Bates (Weatherville) and Miss Sarah Esther Ross (Asheboro), letters to the author; J. Elwood Carroll, *History of the North Carolina Annual Conference of the Methodist Protestant Church* (1939); Nolan B. Harmon, ed., *Encyclopedia of World Methodism*, vol. 2 (1974); *High Point Enterprise*, 1 Nov. 1959; *Randolph Guide*, 4 Nov. 1959; Mabel W. Russell, *History of the Methodist Protestant Children's Home, 1910–1935* (1935).

RALPH HARDEE RIVES

Hammer, William Cicero (24 Mar. 1865–26 Sept. 1930), lawyer, editor, and congressman, was born in Randolph County four miles southwest of Asheboro. His parents were William Clark and Hannah Jane Burrows Hammer. The son and grandson of ministers of the Methodist Protestant church, he became a charter member of the First Methodist Protestant Church of Asheboro, as well as a member of the Asheboro Rotary Club and of the Masonic and Junior Orders. He was educated in the public schools of Randolph County before attending Yadkin Institute, Western Maryland College, and The University of North Carolina. Admitted to the bar in 1891, he practiced law as a partner in the firm of Hammer and Wilson in Asheboro.

Before beginning a political career, Hammer taught in the public schools of Randolph and Davidson counties. His first public position was as a member of the Asheboro City Council; he also served as mayor of Asheboro for one term. In the years 1891–95 and 1899–1901 he was superintendent of public instruction in Randolph County. Early in 1902 Governor Charles B. Aycock appointed Hammer as solicitor in the Superior Court of what was then the Fifteenth Judicial District to fill the vacancy left by the death of Wiley Rush. In the fall of that year Hammer was elected to the office. In 1914, President Woodrow Wilson appointed him U.S. attorney for the Western North Carolina District; he served until September 1920, when he received the Democratic nomination to the House of Representatives from the Seventh North Carolina District.

The record of Hammer's congressional career, which spanned the decade 1920–30, was noteworthy in several respects. Among his priorities was legislation to end adult illiteracy and to expand education throughout the nation. His attitude towards education became evident when he supported the Towner-Sterling Educational Bill, one that would not only create a department of education but also help to eliminate illiteracy, promote physical education, and attempt to equalize educational opportunities. Hammer also consistently strove for farm relief. A supporter of the McNary-Haugen Act, he earnestly believed that this bill "would bring about real orderly marketing of farm products, so that the farmers themselves would get the full benefits therefrom." Hammer was the only member of the North Carolina delegation who voted consistently for the McNary-Haugen farm bill. In addition to educational opportunities and farm relief, he favored the building of better roads even when this position was unpopular. To assure getting the best for his own county, he accompanied the surveyors when the roads were being laid out.

In the 1920s, sentiment was divided on the issue of

child labor regulations and restrictions. In a speech before the House, Representative Hammer advocated a child labor law; thus he urged "cooperation with the states for the protection of child life through infancy and in the prohibition of child labor." Nevertheless, no federal child labor law was enacted until 1938.

In Congress, Hammer served on the Judiciary, Patents, Pensions, Expenditures, and Executive committees. His chief work was conducted in the District of Columbia Committee, where he devoted much attention to educational affairs in Washington. Yet he still found the time to familiarize himself with proposals to mitigate the ills of agriculture. In the Judiciary Committee Hammer dealt with impeachment cases and worked out the details of the administrative program for law enforcement as it related to prohibition, including the preparation of a provision for the transfer of enforcement from the Treasury Department to the Department of Justice.

For more than forty years Hammer owned and edited the *Asheboro Courier*, which was widely read in Randolph County. Before he bought the paper in 1891, the *Courier* had been known as the *Randolph Regulator*, which dated back to 1876 and had been operated by M. S. Robins. Prior to entering politics, Hammer had ample time for his newspaper work; even after becoming the Seventh District representative, he maintained close ties with the editors in North Carolina. He served the North Carolina Press Association as president and in other official capacities. But gradually his wife, Minnie Hancock Hammer, took over his business affairs and assumed the management of the newspaper. Mrs. Hammer also helped him in other ways. On 4 July 1930, when the congressman was too ill to fill his speaking engagement at Guilford Battleground, his wife delivered the speech for him. After Hammer's death, she was invited to fill his seat in Congress for the remainder of the term but declined because of home, church, and business obligations. She continued to operate the *Asheboro Courier* until 1938, when the newspaper was sold. Congressman and Mrs. Hammer were the parents of a daughter, Harriette Lee.

SEE: *Asheboro Courier*, 7 Dec. 1922; John L. Cheney, Jr., ed., *North Carolina Government, 1585–1974* (1975); *Greensboro Daily News*, 20 Aug. 1921, 27 Sept. 1930; *Randolph Guide*, 4 Nov. 1959; Sixty-seventh–Sixty-ninth U.S. Congresses, *Congressional Record* (1923–27); Thad Stem, Jr., *The Tar Heel Press* (1973); Harriette H. Walker, *Busy North Carolina Women* (1931); Laura S. Worth, "The History of Education in Randolph County," *North Carolina Education* 12 (September 1945).

KAY M. HAMILTON

Hammon, John (29 Jan. 1760–1868), second-to-the-last Revolutionary War veteran to die, was born in Goochland County, Va. He was the son of James Hammon[d], who died in 1763, and Mary Hargis Hammon, who later married John Holbrook of Goochland County. In 1774, his uncle, William Hammon, moved to Wilkes County, N.C., apparently with the other members of the Holbrook and Hammon families, and became minister of the Roaring River Baptist Church.

In January 1777, John Hammon enlisted in the North Carolina militia under the command of Captain (later Colonel) Benjamin Cleveland of Wilkes County to fight the Tories and also the Indians in the west. He was at Kings Mountain and served to the end of the Revolution with the Wilkes County unit.

Almost immediately after the war ended, Hammon's mother died, and he moved to Kentucky, stopping by Charlottesville, Va., to sell a 319-acre farm. He settled near Bryan's Station (on the outskirts of present-day Lexington) and participated in the action against the Indians there. He also was present at the disaster of Blue Licks in August 1782. Subsequently he marched with Colonel Benjamin Logan on the punitive Miami River Expedition against the Ohio Shawnee towns.

The petition to the Virginia General Assembly of October 1788 for separation from the old Commonwealth was signed by John, James, and Edmund Hammon. John married about this time and settled in that part of Scott County, Ky., which became Owen in 1819. His last military experience was in 1794, as a captain, under "Mad Anthony" Wayne at Fallen Timbers. After the death of his first wife, he married Mildred Ann Morgan, daughter of Major Charles Morgan, also from Wilkes County, N.C. In all, Hammon had twenty-two children.

In 1822 he moved to Cincinnati, barely forty miles north of his Owen County home. There he and his sons contracted to build "steamboat Gothic" superstructures for river steamers. He must have been a citizen of some stature, for he numbered among his acquaintances William Henry Harrison, Vice-President Richard Mentor Johnson, and Congressman Robert Todd Lytle. Hammon never gave up his membership in the Mussel Shoals Baptist Church in Owen County and was said to have commuted regularly by horseback to the old home place on weekends. He was last listed in the Cincinnati directory in 1843 and probably returned to Owen County at that time. He lived with his daughter Lucinda (Mrs. Zachariah Holbrook) until he died at the extreme age of 108, the penultimate Revolutionary soldier to die.

SEE: Deposition of John Hammon (Archives, Veterans Administration, Washington, D.C.); Stratton Owen Hammon, *The Saga of John Hammon, Revolutionary War Hero and Owen County, Kentucky, Pioneer* (1979); Robert Todd Lytle Papers (Cincinnati Historical Society, Cincinnati, Ohio).

LAWRENCE S. THOMPSON

Hampton, John Robinson (1 Apr. 1807–9 Feb. 1880), politician and planter, was the son of George W. and Cornelia Henderson Hampton. Hampton, whose father was sheriff of Mecklenburg County in 1810, was born in Charlotte and raised as a Presbyterian. Little is known about his youth except that he was orphaned at an early age, and, having received only three months of formal education, he learned the printing trade. He left North Carolina to set up a newspaper in Macon, Miss., before moving to Tuscaloosa, Ala., where he married Frances Ann Webb. In 1843, after having two children, Henry and Susan, they moved to Union County, Ark., where Frances soon died. He later married Nancy Gabeen by whom he had two sons, J. E. and George, and two daughters, Charlotte and Fannie.

Hampton's political career began in 1843, when he was appointed to a commission to select a county seat for Union County. Shortly afterwards he moved to Bradley County and settled on a 1,300-acre plantation, Forest Home. A Democrat, he was elected in 1846 to represent Bradley County in the state senate, then reelected to serve in 1848–49 and 1850–51. During the latter term he was elected president of the senate, and because of his position he served as acting governor in

September 1851 during the absence of Governor John Roane. He was returned to the senate by Union County in 1852. In the following year, he and several others incorporated the Cairo and Fulton Railroad.

While serving as senator from Bradley and Union counties in 1856–57, he was again elected president of the senate. From 21 April to 14 September 1857, he became acting governor for the second time when Governor Elias Conway had to leave the state due to illness. In 1856, the county seat of Calhoun County was named for Hampton. Bradley and Dallas counties sent him back to the senate in 1858 and 1862.

In 1861 Hampton was chosen one of Arkansas' six electoral delegates supporting Jefferson Davis's bid for the presidency of the Confederacy. In the fall of 1864 Hampton was a delegate from Bradley and Dallas counties to the Confederate legislature in Washington, Ark., then the state capital while a part of the state was in federal hands. His political career ended with service as senator from the Eighteenth District in the general assemblies of 1877 and 1879. He died in office and was buried in the Bradley County cemetery.

SEE: Margaret Ross, *Arkansas Gazette: The Early Years, 1819–1866* (1969); Josiah H. Shinn, *History of Arkansas* (1900); Robert Sobel and John Raimo, eds., *Biographical Directory of the Governors of the United States*, vol. 1 (1978).

DAVID PFAFF

Hancock, Franklin Wills, Jr. *(1 Nov. 1894–24 Jan. 1969)*, real estate developer, farmer, North Carolina legislator, U.S. congressman, federal official, and county judge, was born in Oxford, the only son and one of four children of Franklin Wills and Lizzie Hobgood Hancock. His father was a descendant of William Hancock, the brother of John Hancock, signer of the Declaration of Independence; he became a registered pharmacist in North Carolina in 1881, was a member of the state pharmacy board for fifty years, and helped organize the School of Pharmacy at The University of North Carolina. On the younger Hancock's maternal side, his great-grandfather, William Royall, was a noted Baptist minister and professor at Wake Forest College. His uncle, Frank P. Hobgood, Jr., was special assistant to the U.S. attorney general in the prosecution of oil land suits.

Hancock was educated in the Oxford public schools until age thirteen, then attended Horner Military Academy for one year before entering The University of North Carolina in 1912. There he pursued regular academic work and studied law, using borrowed funds to pay his way through college. After working as a secretary to his maternal uncle, Frank Hobgood, in Wyoming in 1915, he was admitted to the bar in North Carolina on 28 Aug. 1916 and began to practice law in Oxford. As a well-respected attorney and businessman, Hancock was active in many civic and business organizations, including vice-president of the Granville Real Estate and Trust Company. He became chairman of the Democratic executive committee in Granville County and was a Democratic presidential elector in 1924.

Without opposition Hancock was elected in 1926 to the North Carolina Senate, representing Granville and Person counties. Also without opposition he was elected in 1928 to represent Granville County in the North Carolina House of Representatives. He was author of an education act in the General Assembly, which, although unpopular among teachers and school

superintendents, did reduce school taxes in many counties of the state.

On 7 June 1930, Hancock defeated Andrew Fuller Sams in the Democratic primary to succeed Charles Manly Stedman as U.S. representative for the Fifth Congressional District (Caswell, Forsyth, Person, Rockingham, Stokes, and Surry counties). When incumbent Congressman Stedman died on 23 Sept. 1930, the way was cleared for Hancock's election to complete his unexpired term as well as to fill the new term. Thus, on 1 Dec. 1930, Hancock entered Congress and served through repeated elections until 1938, becoming a prominent member of the House Committee on Banking and Currency.

Ambitious for higher office, he considered challenging Josiah Bailey for the U.S. Senate in 1936, but in October 1937 he announced his candidacy for the Senate seat held by Robert Rice Reynolds. In the primary Hancock sought unsuccessfully to court the more conservative wing of the Democratic party, claiming that his voting record was less supportive of the New Deal than that of Reynolds. He also attacked the flamboyant Reynolds's style, which had made the senator an object of derision by much of the press. Defeated by Reynolds, Hancock was appointed to a six-year term on the Home Loan Bank Board, an appointment that Reynolds had coveted for his supporter George A. Coan, Jr., Works Progress Administrator in North Carolina. Hancock had the backing of building and loan officials over the nation as well as in North Carolina. He served in the new position from 4 Jan. 1939 until 24 Apr. 1942.

The Home Loan Bank Board was an agency that chartered and supervised federal home loan banks and federal savings and loan associations. During World War II, in an executive reorganization, the board became the Federal Home Land Bank Administration in the National Housing Agency. With the abolition of the board, Hancock lost his post and was appointed by President Franklin D. Roosevelt as a special representative to the Reconstruction Finance Corporation and to the Defense Plant Corporation where he served until June 1943. Because these appointments did not require his constant presence in Washington, he was able to return to Oxford where friends persuaded him in 1943 to run, unopposed, for another term in the North Carolina House of Representatives.

While a member of Congress in the 1930s, Hancock supported passage of the Bankhead-Jones Farm Tenant Act, which provided low-interest loans to sharecroppers and tenant farmers. The administration of these rural relief programs was located in the Farm Security Administration (FSA), which in the 1940s came under increasing criticism from conservative congressmen and agricultural interests. Much of the criticism focused on the program's creation of experimental cooperative farms and on FSA administrator C. B. Baldwin. After Baldwin was forced to resign in August 1943, Hancock was named as his replacement. Hancock's earlier ties with congressmen and his more conservative administrative posture made him an appropriate choice for the position. He was called to testify before a special investigating committee headed by North Carolina's Harold D. Cooley. As FSA administrator, he attempted to operate the programs on a more businesslike basis while rapidly liquidating resettlement projects and discontinuing the cooperative farm associations supported by the FSA. For example, in his first letter to divisional directors in November 1943, Hancock urged them to survey their spending of funds "in the same way and with the same degree of interest you would do and manifest if the funds allocated to your region were coming out of your own personal earnings." He sought through these measures to demonstrate an economy of operation to cajole sufficient appropriations from a skeptical Congress.

In general, Congress was pleased with his administration of the program although its appropriations continued to decline. Even Hancock became discouraged, however, and resigned from the position in November 1945. Meanwhile, from 1 Dec. 1944 until August 1945, he also served as president of the Commodity Credit Corporation, another agricultural support program that was being phased out in response to conservative criticism in Congress. For these efforts in Washington, Hancock was named by the *Progressive Farmer* "Man of the Year for North Carolina" in 1945. He had helped tenants become home owners, he had brought greater efficiency to the FSA, and he had handled $4.5 million in farm loans to returning veterans.

Back in North Carolina, Hancock first indicated that he might consider running for governor. But the climate was not right for such a race, and instead he resumed his law practice and became immersed in the development of commercial and residential real estate. In his later years the latter ventures were as far afield as Florida and Virginia. In addition, he was elected to serve as judge of the Granville County Recorder's Court from 1950 to 1954. He continued his civic activities and his abiding devotion to the Baptist church. His philanthropic interests included establishment of the Hancock Health Center, which he donated to Granville County as a memorial to his parents.

In 1917 Hancock married Lucy Osborne Landis of Oxford. They had four sons (Franklin Wills III, who followed his father in the General Assembly from Granville County in 1947; and Charles Hamlin, Robert Denard, and Alexander Hamilton, all of whom remained in the Oxford area) and three daughters (Mrs. Faison Keuster of Charlotte, Mrs. G. T. Moore of Oxford, and Mrs. J. M. Faulkner, Jr., of Raleigh).

Hancock died in Oxford, where he was buried in the Elmwood Cemetery.

SEE: Sidney Baldwin, *Poverty and Politics: The Rise and Decline of the Farm Security Administration* (1968); *Biog. Dir. Am. Cong.* (1972); John L. Cheney, ed., *North Carolina Government, 1585–1974* (1975); *Durham Morning Herald*, 13 Mar. 1945; Farm Security Administration, *Annual Reports*, 1942–43, 1943–44, and Record Group 96 (National Archives, Washington, D.C.); Daniel L. Grant, *Alumni History of the University of North Carolina* (1924); Julian Pleasants, "The Senatorial Career of Robert Rice Reynolds" (Ph.D. diss., University of North Carolina, 1971); William S. Powell, ed., *North Carolina Lives* (1962); *Progressive Farmer* 61 (January 1946); Raleigh *News and Observer*, 5 Oct. 1930, 22 Nov. 1935, 13 Oct. 1937, 23 Dec. 1938, 9 Nov. 1943, 16 Dec. 1944, 4 Jan. 1947, 1 Feb. 1949, 26 May 1953, 11 Feb. 1967, 24 Jan. 1969; U.S. Congress, House Committee on Agriculture, *Activities of the Farm Security Administration* (1944).

THOMAS S. MORGAN

Hancock, Molly McCoy *(28 June 1863–13 Dec. 1951)*, operator of a custom dressmaking shop in Winston from about 1885 to 1945, was one of the few Americans and possibly the only North Carolinian ever to merit the title of "modiste" or "couturiere." Known affectionately as "Madame Hancock" or simply as "Miss Molly,"

she reigned for some sixty years as fashion arbiter and creator of designs for a clientele from a wide area in North Carolina. She was reported to have sent dresses and trousseaux as far away as California and, at least in one instance, to China.

Madame Hancock was the daughter of Josiah Kirksey McCoy, a Confederate soldier, and Elizabeth Ellington McCoy of Reidsville. Mrs. McCoy, who wove her own cloth, owned one of the first sewing machines in her area; it had no foot pedal and while one hand guided the cloth, the other cranked the wheel. Mollie McCoy and her five brothers and sisters attended the Reidsville Academy; afterwards, she entered the Reidsville Female Seminary where her talent for fashioning clothes emerged. She designed her own as well as those of her three younger sisters and even some for her classmates. Later she took courses in fashion design in New York City and opened a shop in Reidsville. On 28 June 1884 she married Thomas Wheeler Hancock, a tobacconist; they had one son, Thomas W., Jr.

After her marriage, "Miss Molly" and her husband lived in Winston where she opened a dressmaking shop. She made everything from christening gowns to shrouds, and her shop eventually occupied the entire second floor above Owen's Drug Store.

Thomas Hancock proudly referred to his wife as "the madame"; from this came the name by which she was to be known by many of her clients and friends. Madame Hancock made regular trips to New York to purchase fabrics and paid large sums of money in order to copy original creations from such Parisian design houses as Poiret and Patou. At the beginning of World War II, she had some forty seamstresses executing her designs. One employee did nothing but iron; another was saleslady for accessories. Madame Hancock trained Allan Chambers to assist her in designing the clothes for which her shop became famous.

In an interview shortly before her death, Madame Hancock observed that modern women worked on their figures and did not leave it up to the dressmaker to hide their defects. "I really thought the bustles were pretty and elegant," she said. "We made the skirts straight and tight in the front and draped them gracefully over the bustle in the back and sometimes it was just tied on. Sometimes the string broke, too!" The ugliest styles, she thought, were those of the period around World War I, when the short, long-waisted, shapeless frocks were topped with potlike hats down over the ears. "And nothing, to my mind, was ever worse than the sight of a bridal gown up to the knees in front with a long train trailing out behind!"

Madame Hancock was a member of the Methodist church and the Order of the Eastern Star. When living in Reidsville she was organist at Main Street Methodist Church. When her eyesight failed, she went to live in the Eastern Star Home in Greensboro. She and her husband, who died in 1915, were buried in Reidsville. She was survived by her son and several grandchildren and great-grandchildren.

A collection called "Gowns by Madame Hancock" was prepared by Pete Ballard, curator of the Reynolda House Costume Collection, for exhibition at Reynolda House in Winston-Salem from December 1975 to December 1976.

SEE: *Greensboro Daily News*, 14 Dec. 1951; Mildred O. Randolph, "Madame Hancock" (manuscript in her possession, Enfield); Reynolda House Museum of American Art, "Gowns by Madame Hancock" (leaflet, 1976);

"Tar Heel Couturiere," *State Magazine* 43 (November 1975); *Winston-Salem Journal*, 14 Dec. 1951.

RALPH HARDEE RIVES

Hanes, Frederick Moir *(18 Sept. 1883–25 Mar. 1946),* physician, educator, and researcher, was born in Salem, the son of John Wesley and Anna Hodgin Hanes. He was graduated from The University of North Carolina in 1903, received the M.A. degree from Harvard the following year, and was awarded the M.D. degree from Johns Hopkins in 1908. His first position was as assistant professor of pathology at Columbia University when he also served as a pathologist at Presbyterian Hospital in New York City. In 1912 he began a year's work with the Rockefeller Institute where he investigated fat metabolism digestion, motility of cancer cells, and techniques of chick and tissue embryo culture. Returning to Winston-Salem, he began the practice of internal medicine.

Shortly before World War I, Hanes was professor of therapeutics at the Medical College of Virginia. With the coming of war he became a lieutenant colonel, serving as an assistant neurologist at Queen's Square Hospital in London and later in France as commanding officer at Base Hospital 65.

After the war, Hanes resumed his practice in Winston-Salem. In 1933 he became head of the Department of Medicine at Duke University, Durham, where he also taught and conducted research in pathology and neurology. The author of numerous articles in medical journals, Hanes was named Florence McAllister Professor of Medicine and a Fellow in the American College of Physicians; he held memberships in the American Association of Physicians and in the Clinical and Climatological Association. In addition to his medical interests, he was a founding member of Phi Beta Kappa Associates and served as president (1928–32) and chairman of the board of directors of the Security Life and Trust Company in Winston-Salem. He was a lover of art, a bibliophile, a horticulturist, and an admirer of Samuel Johnson's works.

A Methodist, Hanes was married to Elizabeth Peck; they had no children. He was buried in Salem Cemetery, Winston-Salem.

SEE: Daniel L. Grant, *Alumni History of the University of North Carolina* (1924); *North Carolina Medical Journal* 7 (1946), 8 (1947); *Southern Medicine and Surgery* 95 (1933), 108 (1946); Winston-Salem *Twin City Sentinel*, 25 Mar. 1946.

CAROLYN F. ROFF

Hanes, James Gordon, Sr. *(12 June 1886–22 July 1972),* manufacturer and civic leader, was born in Salem, one of six sons of John Wesley and Anna Hodgin Hanes, and grandson of the first P. H. Hanes who moved to Salem in 1880 and founded one of the large tobacco factories later absorbed by the R. J. Reynolds Tobacco Company. After attending the local public schools, he entered The University of North Carolina and was graduated in 1909 with the B.A. degree.

Returning to Salem, Hanes immediately joined the staff of the local Shamrock Mills, a manufacturer of men's hosiery owned by his father. He found the company debt-ridden, but within five years—through his skillful management—the firm had become solvent and was renamed the Hanes Hosiery Mills. He was elected

president of the company in 1917 and chairman of the board of directors in 1938, a post he held with pronounced success and expansive growth until his retirement. By then, Hanes was recognized as the "world's largest producer of women's seamless nylon hoisery." He lived to see his son, J. Gordon Hanes, Jr., succeed him in the long line of offices until he too became chairman of the board of the Hanes Corporation.

Known for his business acumen, Hanes was long regarded as one of the most astute men in Winston-Salem, a city of financial giants. He served on the board of directors of many corporations, including the Norfolk and Western Railway Company, the Savoy Plaza Hotel in New York City, the Wachovia Bank and Trust Company, and the Hanes Dye and Finishing Company. Although he held offices in many organizations directly connected with his business, one of his greatest prides, and one to which he gave conspicuous leadership, was as a director of the National Association of Manufacturers.

Hanes had a special interest in local government, and believed every businessman should make community service a part of his life. With that philosophy he was elected to the Board of Aldermen of Winston-Salem and then became mayor for four years (1921–25). In 1928, he was elected to the Board of County Commissioners of Forsyth County, serving until 1950; for more than half of those twenty-two years he was chairman of the board.

As both a businessman and a government official, Hanes was an outspoken and effective advocate of a kind of conservatism that demanded economical operation. When times were good, he encouraged expansion of the city. While he was mayor, Waughtown, West Highlands, and Buena Vista were annexed; and five public schools, three fire stations, and four public buildings were erected. When times were bad, he led the county in reducing its tax rate by 16 percent, reduced the bonded indebtedness of the county by 50 percent, and "foisted off on the city government a number of services that counties ordinarily pay for." One editorial writer claimed that "probably more than anything else, his conservatism in county government established the long-standing division between City and County governments." To avoid a surplus of hospital beds in metropolitan Winston-Salem, Hanes proposed building a new community hospital on Cloverdale Hill and forming an expanding medical center built around the Baptist Hospital and Bowman Gray School of Medicine. This effort was aborted, but two new community hospitals were built on the outer fringes of the city during the 1960s.

One of Hanes's greatest contributions to Winston-Salem was made in the mid-1950s when he "spearheaded an effort to get the city's key leaders behind the [city] school board as it moved toward desegregation policies." From that effort came the excellent Winston-Salem Community Relations Project, in which Hanes was the central figure. Through the project, black and white leaders were brought together to work for harmonious race relations.

Hanes also served on numerous boards of local and state significance. For many years he was a trustee of Greensboro College. A study he headed to test the intelligence of urban children led to the establishment of the Human Betterment League of North Carolina, of which he served as perennial treasurer. For his multiple services to social projects, he received the North Carolina Conference for Social Service award in 1965 as a "leader, benefactor and servant of the people" of the state.

Loyal to his alma mater, Hanes found many ways— tangible and intelligible—to provide assistance. In 1960, he gave The University of North Carolina library a cash gift of $8,000 to finance the publication of a catalogue, *Incunabula in the Hanes Collection*, of the library. In 1961, he established the endowment necessary to fund the James Gordon Hanes Professorship in the Humanities.

The city of Winston-Salem named its community center in appreciation of James Gordon Hanes, who survived to see it as the hub of civic work, utilized by craftsmen, artists, volunteers, businessmen, and social servants. The very nature and use of the building epitomizes his constructive life in Winston-Salem and Forsyth County.

On 12 Nov. 1911 Hanes married Emmie Dewry; they had one son, James Gordon Hanes, Jr. Mrs. Hanes died in 1916. On 1 Apr. 1924, he married Molly Ruffin, who died in 1957. Hanes remained in unusually good health until his death in Colorado Springs, Colo., where he had gone two days before on a business trip. Funeral services were held at the Centenary United Methodist Church, Winston-Salem, with interment in Old Salem Cemetery.

SEE: *Durham Morning Herald*, 6 Apr. 1965; Raleigh *News and Observer*, 22 Sept. 1960, 1 June, 22 July 1972; *Who Was Who in America*, vol. 5 (1973); *Who Was Who in the South and Southwest* (1950); *Winston-Salem Journal*, 22, 24 July 1972.

C. SYLVESTER GREEN

Hanes, John Wesley (3 Feb. 1850–22 Sept. 1903), industrialist and civic leader, was born in Fulton, Davie County. The Hanes family in the United States began with Philip Höhns (the phonetic spelling "Hanes" soon came into use) who arrived from Germany with his son Marcus to settle in York County, Pa., in 1738. In 1748 Marcus, a member of the Reformed church, married Anna Kerber, a Lutheran, and the two soon joined the Moravian congregation in Lancaster. In 1774, they moved with their ten children to 1,060 acres of land in Friedberg near the North Carolina Moravian settlement of Salem. One of the children, Philip, located near Clemmonsville and married Johanna Salome Frey, from which union was born Joseph, who settled in Fulton. The marriage of Joseph Hanes to Catherine Sehner (varied spellings) produced two sons, George and Alexander Martin Hanes. The latter continued in Fulton where he operated a farm and, among other businesses, one of the largest tanneries in that section of the state. Alexander Martin Hanes married Jane March, daughter of Jacob and Margaret Hinkle March. John Wesley Hanes was their sixth son in a family of eleven children.

In 1861, Alexander Martin Hanes died. The Civil War cost the lives of three of John Wesley's brothers—Spencer, Jacob, and George. A fourth brother, Pleasant Henderson Hanes, served as a courier for General Robert E. Lee and surrendered with him at Appomattox. John Wesley remained at home to help manage the family farm, which was now on Hickory Hill near Mocksville. During the war he received most of his secondary education from his mother and from books in the home. For a time after the war, he attended Trinity College (later Duke University).

In 1872, Hanes joined with his brother Pleasant Henderson and a Davie County friend, Thomas Jethro Brown, to organize P. H. Hanes and Company to manufacture tobacco. Pleasant Hanes had returned from the Civil War to establish a wagon trade in tobacco; it was so successful that he became a partner in the tobacco manufacturing firm of Dulin and Booe in Mocksville. His prowess as a salesman and the managerial skills of John Wesley made the entrepreneurial venture promising. When the business burned in 1874, Brown left the organization, to be replaced briefly by a younger brother, Benjamin Franklin Hanes. After the fire the company operated in Greensboro while rebuilding in Winston. With Pleasant often traveling to promote the market and John Wesley remaining at the plant to attend to the manufacturing process, P. H. Hanes and Company became by the 1800s one of the leading flat-plug producers in the country. By the 1890s, the company was increasingly pressed by James B. Duke's American Tobacco Company to consolidate the industry. After resisting for several years, the Hanes brothers sold their business to Duke's American Tobacco trust through Richard Joshua Reynolds who was one of its independent partners.

Though the brothers could have retired on the yield from the sale of their tobacco company, they chose instead to apply their entrepreneurial talents to the rising field of knitwear. Pleasant joined with two sons to establish the P. H. Hanes Knitting Company for the manufacture of men's and boys' underwear. In 1901, John Wesley Hanes opened the Shamrock Hosiery Mill to make infants' and men's socks. Named Hanes Hosiery Mills in 1914, the company grew to be the largest producer of circular knit hosiery in the world. Its management would later pass to his son, James Gordon.

In addition to his manufacturing activities, John Wesley Hanes served as president of the Roanoke and Southern Railroad and was on the board of directors of several banks in the thriving Piedmont area.

Hanes married Anna Hodgin, daughter of Stephen H. and Lucy Moir Hodgin, on 2 Dec. 1879. Their eight children were Alexander Stephen, James Gordon, Frederic Moir, Robert March, John Wesley, Jr., Ralph Philip, Daisy, and Lucy M. He died in Atlantic City, N.J., and was buried in Salem.

SEE: Samuel A. Ashe, ed., *Biographical History of North Carolina*, vol. 2 (1905); *Hanes Hosiery News* (Fall 1972); *The Hanes Story* (company publication, 1965); Hugh T. Lefler, *History of North Carolina*, vol. 4 (1956); *North Carolina Biography*, vols. 4, 5 (1928, 1941); *Winston-Salem Journal-Sentinel*, 24 Apr. 1938, 3 Aug. 1952, 21, 28 Feb. 1965; *Winston-Salem Twin City Sentinel*, 17 June 1959.

JAS. HOWELL SMITH

Hanes, John Wesley, Jr. (24 Apr. 1892–24 Dec. 1987), financier and government official, was born in Winston, the son of Anna Jannette Hodgin and John Wesley Hanes. He was graduated from Woodberry Forest School in Virginia, attended the University of North Carolina (1910–12), and was graduated from Yale in 1915. He became a salesman for the American Tobacco Company and during World War I served in the navy. After the war he joined a Wall Street banking house. In 1932, during the depression, at the request of Governor O. Max Gardner and the Council of State, Hanes was able to secure an extension of the due date for $2½ million when short-term securities fell due and the state was unable to pay. In 1934 Hanes became president of the New York Tobacco Exchange and was a member of the New York Cotton Exchange, the Chicago Board of Trade, and the advisory committee of Stock Exchange

Firms. He was also a senior partner in the Wall Street house of Chas. D. Barney & Co. He became a member of the Securities and Exchange Commission in 1937, and in 1938 he was named assistant secretary of the Treasury. To accept the latter appointment he was obliged to sell his seats on four exchanges and relinquish directorships in over twenty corporations. In his new post he became a close adviser to President Franklin D. Roosevelt on financial matters and was influential in planning economic recovery from the depression. Retiring from the Treasury in 1940, he returned to New York City as a financial adviser to business. Among other actions, he participated in arrangements leading to the sale of the Ecusta Paper Corporation of Brevard (of which he had been president) to Olin Industries. He played a key role in the merger of P. H. Hanes Co. with Hanes Hosiery Mill to become Hanes Corp.

Hanes was an avid sportsman, especially active in polo and interested in horse racing. He served as chairman of a committee to revitalize racing in New York, and he was the first president of the New York Racing Association.

His first wife was Elizabeth Agnes Mitchel, and they were the parents of Agnes Phillips, John Wesley III, and Ormsby Mitchel. Following her death he married Hope Yandell Hanger, and they were the parents of Susan Yandell and David Gordon. Hanes died at the age of 95 after a long illness at his home in Millbrook, N.Y.

SEE: Daniel L. Grant, *Alumni History of the University of North Carolina* (1924); Jo White Linn, *People Named Hanes* (1980); Raleigh *News and Observer*, 27 Dec. 1987.

WILLIAM S. POWELL

Hanes, Lewis (1826–19 Jan. 1882), newspaper editor, was born in Forsyth County but spent most of his life in Davidson County. In addition to his work as a journalist, Hanes was active in politics. He was a Whig member of the House of Commons from Davidson County in 1860 and again for the term 1864–65. An opponent of secession and war, in 1863 he prepared a series of able articles against the war for the *North Carolina Standard,* published by W. W. Holden in Raleigh. These letters, signed "Davidson," attracted wide attention and were a force in the peace movement. Hanes was briefly private secretary to Governor Holden in 1865, but quickly found himself in the wrong camp. Although Holden's staunch ally during the peace movement, Hanes noted the governor's penchant for building his own political machine and resigned. In the fall of 1865 Hanes was elected to Congress; however, he failed to secure the removal of disabilities (imposed on many former Confederates which made them ineligible to vote) and was not seated.

In 1866 Hanes moved to Salisbury, where he began to publish the *Old North State,* an independent organ in opposition to the *Carolina Watchman,* a Conservative newspaper published by John J. Bruner. In 1868 the *Watchman* and the *Old North State* combined, with Hanes taking charge of the editorial department and Bruner of the job shop. Hanes later stated that he established the journal as an independent paper, and it remained such except for a brief period from February to November 1868. During that time, he sided with the Conservatives in an attempt to defeat the constitution of 1868, which was, nevertheless, adopted. For his efforts he was elected a member of the national executive committee of the Democratic party but declined to accept.

In 1871, the Conservatives were able to get a bill through the legislature calling for a convention to amend the constitution of 1868. As most members of the press were Conservative, they naturally supported the proposal. Hanes, however, on constitutional grounds used his influence through the *Old North State* to oppose it and thereby lost his standing with the Conservatives. The convention was outvoted by 95,252 to 85,007.

After this Hanes remained in Salisbury only a short time and put his newspaper up for sale. Bruner purchased it, ceased publication, and immediately reissued the *Carolina Watchman* on 15 Sept. 1871. Hanes was then engaged as a political writer for the *Raleigh Era,* an organ of the Republican party which he, with Marcus Erwin, produced in an able and dignified manner. After six months he withdrew because of an argument with the paper's owners, who wanted him to defend a corrupt and radical judge whom the Democrats were attacking. When he resigned in March 1872, his former partner, John J. Bruner, commented that Hanes was too good for the radicals and that "he is the only man in the state that has rapport with decent people in the Republican party."

Hanes returned to Salisbury to practice law with W. H. Bailey, a former law partner of Nathaniel Boyden who had recently been appointed an associate justice of the North Carolina Supreme Court. While there, Hanes became a member of St. Luke's Episcopal Church and served on its vestry. He did not long remain in Salisbury but left to engage in newspaper work over the state. In 1880, he was elected to the North Carolina Senate from Davidson County and served until his death. He also was made a trustee of The University of North Carolina.

A complex character, Hanes apparently supported both political parties during the unsettled days following the war, but whether on the Democratic or Republican side he was always a conservative. While editing the *Old North State* he was asked in 1871 to testify before a congressional committee inquiring into Ku Klux Klan activity in Rowan County. His testimony absolved Rowan from any involvement in the Klan and convinced the investigators that elections were as peaceful in Rowan as in any northern community.

On 29 May 1848 Hanes married Mary C. Eccles in Davidson County. They were the parents of four children. He died at his home near Clemmonsville at age fifty-six. His former partner in the *Carolina Watchman* said of him: "He was a Christian gentleman who sought to know the truth and adhered to it when he believed he found it."

SEE: James S. Brawley, *The Rowan Story* (1953); *Carolina Watchman,* 29 March 1872; John L. Cheney, Jr., ed., *North Carolina Government, 1585–1979* (1981); Davidson County Marriage Bonds (North Carolina State Archives, Raleigh); J. G. de R. Hamilton, *Reconstruction in North Carolina* (1941); John Nichols, *Directory of the General Assembly of the State of North Carolina* (1860); *Old North State,* 7 Apr., 15 Sept., 1871; *Senate Report* no. 1, Forty-second Congress, 1st Session; Max R. Williams, ed., *The Papers of William A. Graham,* vol. 6 (1976).

JAMES S. BRAWLEY

Hanes, Pleasant Henderson (16 Oct. 1845–9 June 1925), manufacturer and civic leader, was born in Fulton, Davie County. A descendant of a Saxon family which spelled its name in various generations as

Hoenes, Höhns, Haenes, Haines, Haynes, and Hanes, his earliest American ancestor was Philip Höhns, who came from Zweibrucken, Germany, in 1738 to settle at York, Pa. Höhns's son Marcus Hoenes, a member of the Reformed church, married Anna Elizabeth Kerber, a Lutheran, in 1748 and the two joined the Moravian church in 1752. In 1774, the family purchased 1,060 acres in the North Carolina Moravian settlement of Wachovia and migrated to their Piedmont farm at Friedberg, near Salem. Their son Philip married Johanna Salome Frey and settled near Clemmonsville in future Forsyth County. The line of descent was continued through the marriage of their son Joseph who, by his first wife Catherine Sehner (varied spellings), had two sons, George and Alexander Martin Hanes. Alexander settled at Fulton where he operated a large farm, tannery, and mill. He married Jane March, daughter of Jacob and Margaret Hinkle March. Pleasant Henderson Hanes was the sixth of their eleven children.

During the Civil War, Hanes's older brothers Jacob H. and George A. were killed and Spencer J. was critically wounded. Pleasant Henderson served in the first two years of the war as first lieutenant in the Home Guard, but volunteered in 1863 to join the Confederate Cavalry at Richmond, enlisting in Company E, Sixteenth North Carolina Battalion. He soon earned a position as special courier to General Robert E. Lee, with whom he served until the surrender of Appomattox.

The Fulton community schools offered the only formal education Hanes received, but his military experience and help in managing the family farm provided him the skills and motivation to expand his activities. In 1870, he became a tobacco salesman for Dulin and Booe, tobacco manufacturers in Mocksville, and traveled across much of the South. Acknowledging his initiative and shrewdness as a salesman, competing agents dubbed him "Early Bird" Hanes because of his reputation for rising early and making sales to their clients while they were still having breakfast. In 1871, he became a partner in Dulin and Booe which moved to Winston, a growing town that was rapidly becoming a world center of bright leaf tobacco manufacturing.

In 1872, Hanes organized P. H. Hanes and Company to manufacture tobacco. His partners were his younger brother, John Wesley Hanes, and a friend from Davie County, Major Thomas Jethro Brown. The first factory was a two-story frame building measuring forty by sixty feet. In its second year the factory burned, and Brown retired from the firm to be replaced by another brother, Benjamin F. Hanes. A few years later Benjamin withdrew, leaving the company in the hands of Pleasant Henderson and John Wesley Hanes. Together they built a thriving business in the manufacture and marketing of chewing tobacco. By 1900, the business had a capacity of 5 million pounds annually and was reputed to be the third largest manufactory of flat-plug tobacco in the South. Under presssure from James B. Duke's American Tobacco trust, the Hanes brothers sold their company in 1900 to Richard Joshua Reynolds, whose burgeoning tobacco company was at the time an independent participant in the trust.

At ages fifty-five and fifty respectively, the Hanes brothers could have retired on the income from the sale of the company, but instead they entered the textile business. John Wesley opened the Shamrock Hosiery Mills. Pleasant Henderson joined with his sons Pleasant Huber and William Marvin to set up the P. H. Hanes Knitting Company in 1902 to manufacture knitted underwear for men and boys. In addition to directing that company successfully until his death, he was

also vice-president of the Washington Mills of Fries, Va., and of the Security Life and Annuity Company of Greensboro.

Hanes maintained a farm west of Winston-Salem which could serve as a model for Piedmont agriculture. He was one of the first to introduce tractors and the modern methods of scientific agriculture to the area and to demonstrate their value. He invested heavily in his Holstein stock and dairy farm to improve the breeding of stock in the Piedmont.

As a civic leader in the growing community of Winston-Salem, he served several terms on the Board of Aldermen, was a member of the committee that built the city's first waterworks system, helped found the city graded school system, donated fifty acres for the P. H. Hanes Athletic Park to serve the school children, and was chairman of the Board of County Commissioners. At the state level, he was one of the strongest advocates of highway improvement. He was the first president of the North Carolina Good Roads Association, organized in Raleigh in 1902, and was appointed by Governor Charles B. Aycock to represent the state at National Good Roads Congress meetings in Buffalo, Philadelphia, and St. Louis.

A devout Methodist, Hanes was a steward of Centenary Methodist Episcopal Church in Winston-Salem. He was also a trustee of Trinity College (now Duke University), a Mason, a Knight of Pythias, and an officer in the North Carolina division of the United Confederate Veterans. In politics he was a Democrat.

On 29 April 1873 he married Mary Lizora Fortune of Marlin, Tex. Their six children were Katherine Jane, Pleasant Huber, William Marvin, Margaret Lizora, Frank Higgins, and Ruth March Hanes. Hanes was buried in Winston-Salem.

SEE: Samuel A. Ashe, ed., *Biographical History of North Carolina*, vol. 2 (1905 [portrait]); "Hanes Knitting Company Executives 'Chop Wood While Resting,' " *America's Textile Reporter*, 12 Sept. 1957; *The Hanes Story* (company publication, 1965); *Nat. Cyc. Am. Biog.*, vol. 22 (1932); *North Carolina Biography*, vols. 3, 2 (1928, 1941); Winston-Salem *Journal-Sentinel*, 24 Apr. 1938, 3 Aug. 1952, 21, 28 Feb. 1965; Marjorie W. Young, ed., *Textile Leaders of the South* (1963).

JAS. HOWELL SMITH

Hanes, Pleasant Huber, Sr. (5 Mar. 1880–1 Sept. 1967), was born in Salem, the son of Pleasant Henderson and Mary Lizora Fortune Hanes. His mother was a native of Texas; his father was a native North Carolinian, a direct descendant of Philip Höhns, who immigrated from Germany in 1738 and settled in York, Pa. The name, Höhns, was early Anglicized to Hanes. Philip's son, Marcus Hanes, and his wife, Anna Kerber, moved to North Carolina in 1774, when he acquired 1,060 acres in the Moravian settlement of Wachovia. There were ten children in that family, one of whom was Alexander Martin Hanes who married Jane March. One of their eleven children was Pleasant Henderson Hanes.

After preparatory schooling in Salem, Huber Hanes entered Trinity College, Durham, in the fall of 1896. There he was manager of the baseball team and president of the Athletic Association; he was awarded a B.S. degree in 1900. He was also graduated with honors from the Eastman Business School, Poughkeepsie, N.Y., in 1901.

Returning home, Hanes joined his father and other

members of the family in organizing the P. H. Hanes Knitting Company, which became one of the nation's largest manufacturers of knitted underwear. He was secretary and treasurer (1903) and vice-president and treasurer (1917). When his father died in 1925, Huber Hanes succeeded him as president and general manager, posts he filled with great success. On his retirement in 1954, he became honorary chairman of the board of directors. The top administrative positions were then assumed by his son, Pleasant Huber Hanes, Jr.

In addition to his own business interests, Hanes for many years was a director of the Wachovia Bank and Trust Company, the Security Life and Trust Company (later the Integon Corporation), West End Properties, Inc., and the Carolina Board of the Liberty Mutual Insurance Company. On occasion he served as chairman or president of those boards.

A loyal alumnus of Duke University, the successor of Trinity College, Hanes was chairman of its centennial fund-raising committee in 1939 and a longtime trustee. Two business honors of which he was proud were his membership in and onetime presidency of the associated Knit Underwear Manufacturers of America. He also held the position of director and regional vice-president of the National Association of Manufacturers. For two years (1927–29) he was a member of the State Salary and Wage Commission of North Carolina, a gubernatorial appointment. He was also a member of the North Carolina Citizens Association, the North Carolina Folklore Society, the Roanoke Island Historical Association, the Sons of the American Revolution, the Newcomen Society of England, the University Southern Club of New York, and the Merchants Club and the New York Club (both of New York City).

In Winston-Salem, Hanes was a member of the Centenary United Methodist Church, serving several times on its Board of Stewards; a charter member of the Winston-Salem Club of Rotary International; and a member of the Twin City Club, the Forsyth Country Club, Winston Lodge No. 167 of the Ancient Free and Accepted Masons (Knights Templar, Shriner), and the Wachovia Historical Society. He also joined the Sedgefield Country Club near Greensboro.

For nearly seventy years in Winston-Salem, Hanes was active in many civic, cultural, religious, and social service agencies. To all of them he gave liberally of his time, and to them and to many statewide causes he also gave generously of his money. A friend wrote of him, "Few civic or philanthropic movements in Northwestern North Carolina are activated without the enthusiastic support of Mr. Hanes."

On 27 Oct. 1909 he married Evelyn Hazen of Knoxville, Tenn.; they had two children, Rosalie (Mrs. Thomas O. Moors) and P. Huber Hanes, Jr. Hanes was buried in Salem Cemetery, Winston-Salem.

SEE: William S. Powell, ed., *North Carolina Lives* (1962); Raleigh *News and Observer*, 1 Sept. 1967; James R. Toung, *Textile Leaders of the South* (1963); *We, the People of North Carolina* 14 (July 1956); *Who's Who in America* (1954–55); *Who's Who in the South and Southwest* (1956).

C. SYLVESTER GREEN

Hanes, Robert March (*22 Sept. 1890–10 Mar. 1959*), banker, legislator, government official, and business and civic leader, was born in Salem, one of eight children of John Wesley and Anna Hodgin Hanes. After attending the local public schools, he enrolled at Wood-

berry Forest School, Va., in 1907 and was graduated with honors from The University of North Carolina in 1912. He studied at the Harvard University School of Business Administration in 1912–13. In 1945, The University of North Carolina awarded him an honorary LL.D. degree.

Hanes's business career began in 1913, when he was secretary-treasurer of the Crystal Ice Company in his native city. It was interrupted in 1917 for military service in World War I. After training at Fort Oglethorpe, he went to France as a captain in the 113th Field Artillery and saw action at St. Mihiel, the Argonne, and with the First and Second Armies. He was discharged as a major after a distinguished war record.

In 1919, Hanes joined the Wachovia Bank and Trust Company. It was the beginning of a long relationship that identified him with the expansion and growth of the bank to the largest in the Southeast. He became a vice-president in 1920, served as a loan officer in the Winston-Salem office during the next few years, and was then elected administrative vice-president, working closely with Colonel Francis H. Fries, Wachovia's president, in the overall affairs of the system. Following the death of Fries in 1931, Hanes was elected president of the bank. He retired twenty-five years later and became honorary chairman of the board.

A Democrat, he represented Forsyth County in the 1929 and 1931 state House of Representatives and in the 1933 Senate. As a legislator he emerged as a strong leader in the fight for adoption of a sales tax in 1933.

Hanes held top leadership posts within the nation's banking associations. In 1928, he was elected third vice-president of the North Carolina Bankers Association and became its president in 1931. In the difficult days of the Great Depression and thereafter he held a steady hand on banking matters, reflecting qualities that commanded the respect of financial, business, and governmental circles alike. To assist banks during the depression he was instrumental in the development of the National Credit Association, the forerunner of the Reconstruction Finance Corporation. Nationally, he became a leader in the American Bankers Association, held many important committee positions, and in 1939 concluded as the association's president, the first North Carolinian to serve in that office. As a prominent spokesman for banking in the United States, Hanes was acclaimed at home and abroad as an able advocate of the American system as the threat of global conflict was developing. In 1945, he was elected president of the Association of Reserve City Bankers. He was offered the presidency of the Chase National Bank of New York (later the Chase Manhattan Bank) but declined to accept.

The Hanes influence and interests were widespread. In addition to Wachovia, Hanes was a director of numerous major corporations such as the Southern Railway, P. H. Hanes Knitting Company, Hanes Dye & Finishing Company, Colonial Stores, Borden Manufacturing Company, Carolina Power and Light Company, Security Life & Trust, Thomasville Chair, Chatham Manufacturing Company, Ecusta Paper, Piedmont Publishing Company, R. J. Reynolds Tobacco Company, and State Capital Life Insurance.

As a civic leader, Hanes served on the board of the North Carolina State Sanatoriums. In 1946–47 he helped organize the Business Foundation of The University of North Carolina, and served two years as its president. He was also prominent in the establishment of the North Carolina Citizens Association. In 1948, he was appointed to the State Education Commission. He was named to the Board of Conservation and Development in 1952 and served as chairman of the Commerce and Industry Division. At the national level, he was district chairman of the federal Committee for Economic Development, adviser to the finance section of the Navy Department's Office of Procurement and Materiel, and chairman of the finance department committee of the Chamber of Commerce of the United States. He was also active on national committees for the Community Chests of America.

The zenith of his citizen-statesmen career was reached in April 1949, when the U.S. government named him chief of the Belgium-Luxembourg Mission of the Economic Cooperation Administration with headquarters in Brussels. Six months later he was appointed economic adviser to the high commissioner of West Germany and chief of the Economic Cooperation Administration, ending his service in 1951.

Hanes then took a leadership role to organize the state's Research Triangle program in the Raleigh-Durham-Chapel Hill area, serving as chairman of the committee for its development. Failing in health, he attended a special meeting in Raleigh on 10 Jan. 1959, at which Governor Luther H. Hodges announced that Hanes had been elected chairman of the board of the Research Triangle Foundation and that a $1.5 million fund had been assured for the project. Further, Hodges said that $300,000 had been raised for the first building, which was to be named in honor of Hanes.

Hanes was a trustee of The University of North Carolina, the Morehead Foundation, Salem College, and Winston-Salem Teachers College, as well as the head of numerous civic organizations in Winston-Salem. He was a member of the Centenary Methodist Church.

On 3 July 1917, Hanes married Mildred Borden of Goldsboro. They had two children, Sarah Anne and Frank Borden. He died in Winston-Salem at age sixty-eight and was buried in Salem Cemetery. The Wachovia Bank and Trust Company, Winston-Salem, owns a portrait of him.

SEE: John L. Cheney, Jr., ed., *North Carolina Government, 1585–1974* (1975); *Greensboro Daily News*, 11, 12 Mar. 1959; *Tarheel Banker* 37 (April 1959); Gary Trawick and Paul Wyche, *One Hundred Years, One Hundred Men* (1971); John C. Whitaker, *Robert M. Hanes, Citizen, Banker, Statesmen* (1956); *Who's Who in America* (1950–51); *Winston-Salem Journal*, 19 Jan., 11 Mar. 1959.

T. HARRY GATTON

Hanks (Lincoln), Nancy (5 Feb. 1784–5 Oct. 1818), mother of Abraham Lincoln, sixteenth president of the United States, was born in Campbell County in southwestern Virginia. The identity of her father has never come to light and it is assumed that her mother, Lucy Hanks, bore her out of wedlock. Lucy Hanks married Henry Sparrow of Mercer County, Ky., in 1791 and apparently left her young daughter Nancy to live with and help in the household of Richard Berry of Beechland in Washington County, Va. During this period, Nancy Hanks is said also to have lived with Thomas and Elizabeth Sparrow and then with her uncle, Richard ("Dicky") Hanks.

Carl Sandburg in his biography of Lincoln has the infant Nancy Hanks accompany her mother Lucy to Kentucky, but he ignores completely a vast array of North Carolina tradition as well as the lore indicating that she lived in the Berry and Sparrow households. Also included in this lore are accounts of Nancy's traveling

into North Carolina, prior to 1790, with the household of her uncle Dicky Hanks. They settled in what was then Lincoln (now Gaston) County on the banks of the Catawba River, near the present town of Belmont, where a marker stands claiming that Nancy Hanks once lived there.

Dicky Hanks left the Belmont area, but it is said that Nancy stayed and went to work in the household of Abram [Abraham] Enloe in what is now Rutherford County, between Ellenboro and Bostic. The Enloe family later moved farther west to Swain County and, according to western North Carolina tradition, took Nancy with them.

Virginia tradition includes the "Hanks-Hitchcock" story, which says that Joseph Hanks of Virginia married Nancy Shipley and moved to Nelson County, Ky. Their youngest daughter, Nancy, is said to have married Tom Lincoln in 1806. Other traditions have Nancy Hanks growing up in the area near Linville, Va. The truth is difficult to determine because there were a number of Hanks (and Hauks) living in southwestern Virginia at the time, and "Nancy" was a very popular name for a girl.

It is certain that by 1806 Nancy Hanks was living in Kentucky, where on 12 June 1806 she married Thomas Lincoln, a barely literate homesteader with North Carolina connections. They lived first in Elizabethtown, Ky., where she bore a daughter, Sarah, on 10 Feb. 1807. In May 1808 they moved from Elizabethtown to a nearby farm, then to another farm on the South Fork of Nolin Creek near Hodgenville. Here on 12 Feb. 1809 she bore her son, Abraham. The midwife attending referred to Sarah Lincoln as "a little girl there." In the spring of 1811 they moved ten miles to the northeast, to a new farm on Knob Creek. There another son, Thomas, was born in 1812, but he soon died.

Because of difficulty with land titles in Kentucky, Tom Lincoln decided to move his family to the Indiana frontier to settle on public land. In 1816, the Lincolns migrated to Perry (Spencer) County, Ind., and staked a claim on the banks of Pigeon Creek, about one and a half miles from Gentryville. They were joined there in less than a year by Tom and Betsy Sparrow and Dennis Hanks. The Sparrows died in September 1818 of a dehydrating illness called milk sickness, and Nancy Hanks Lincoln died of the same disease on 5 Oct. 1818.

Rumors circulated widely in the last decades of the nineteenth century, and persist even to the present, that Abraham Lincoln was born of an illicit affair between Nancy Hanks and any number of North Carolinians. All these tales seem to be unfounded, especially in the light of Abraham's birth three years after his mother's marriage to Tom Lincoln, and especially if one accepts the argument that his birth was preceded by that of Sarah. Perhaps the tenacity of these derogatory tales, coupled with their diversity (including at least three candidates for paternity and more for look-alike "half brothers"), caused Sandburg to discount completely the North Carolina tradition in connection with Nancy Hanks. Sandburg certainly admits to a cloud surrounding the character of Lucy Hanks. Perhaps Nancy followed in her mother's footsteps and in fact gave Mrs. Abram Enloe reason to send her packing to Kentucky. She may have been pretty, with "light hair, beautiful eyes, a sweet, sensitive mouth"; moreover, she has been described as intellectually vigorous, spiritually inclined, affectionate, and amiable. Less kind descriptions would indicate that she was sallow, sad, and pitiful.

Much of her life was spent, as with many in that period of frontier expansion, in moving again and again to the edge of civilization. As a result, many of the facts of her life are lost or are relegated to oral tradition. It is known, however, that she died in the wilderness at Pigeon Creek and was buried there.

SEE: Paul M. Angle, *The Lincoln Reader* (1947); *Asheville Citizen*, 10 Feb. 1972; *Burke's Presidential Families of the United States of America*, ed. by Hugh Montgomery Massingberd (1975); *Concise Dictionary of American Biography* (1964); *DAB*, vol. 6 (1961); Ruth Hairston Early, *Campbell Chronicles and Family Sketches, Embracing the History of Campbell County, Virginia* (1927); Raleigh *News and Observer*, 10 Feb. 1952, 12, 30 Dec. 1977, 6 Jan., 7 Feb. 1978; Raleigh *Sunday Observer*, 4 Nov. 1923; Carl Sandburg, *Abraham Lincoln, The Prairie Years* (1954); Tim Taylor, *The Book of Presidents* (1972); *Tyler's Quarterly* 8 (1927); John W. Wayland, *The Lincolns in Virginia* (1946); *Winston-Salem Journal*, 12 Sept. 1926.

MEADE B. B. HORNE

Hanmer, Daniel *(fl. 1733–43)*, colonial chief justice and councillor, was described by Governor George Burrington as "bred to the profession of the Law"; he was a nephew of Sir Thomas Hanmer, the leading Tory member of Parliament who was speaker of the House of Commons in 1714–15. Hanmer probably served as chief justice from the death of his predecessor, William Little, in late August or early September 1734, although he was sworn into office on 28 September. Burrington wrote to the duke of Newcastle on 7 Oct. 1734 to inform him that the colonial council had been purged of several members. It was this political dismissal that led to Hanmer's appointment as councillor on 28 Sept. 1734, although neither the governor's instructions nor custom granted an ex officio seat on the council to the chief justice. During his brief tenure as councillor and chief justice, Hanmer administered the oaths of office to legislators and introduced a bill for promoting trade in the province.

Because Hanmer owed his political fortune to Burrington, he was not in the favor of Burrington's replacement, Gabriel Johnston. Hanmer was removed from his posts shortly after the arrival of Johnston late in 1734. Among those who had been purged from the council in September 1734 was the new chief justice, William Smith. Although Hanmer claimed he was "suffering innocent," Smith believed Hanmer was partly responsible for the new chief justice's earlier disgrace. Consequently, Hanmer was imprisoned and his property sequestered. A citizens' petition of 1735 charged Smith with "trampling liberty underfoot," and it appears that Hanmer was the somewhat reluctant champion of the colony against the governor and his agents. Hanmer may have left the colony for England soon after his dismissal from office.

On 15 Oct. 1736, *The Virginia Gazette*, reporting news from Edenton, noted that the brigantine *Inverness* from London had arrived with a cargo of European goods belonging to "Colonel Hanmer, who was sometime ago, Chief Justice of this Province, by the appointment of the late Governor Burrington, but remov'd by the present Governor. He is come in her, with his Wife and Family, and has brought a Cargo of European Goods, with which, 'tis said, he intends to purchase Tobacco, to load her back again, and so to continue that Trade, as long as it will answer."

Hanmer petitioned the Assembly in 1740, claiming that he had earlier been libeled and that the decision against him was unfair and illegal. But the Assembly, with William Smith as its president, conceived this charge to be a libel against the chief justice and censured Hanmer. A last petition to the king in council in 1743 went unheard, and we may accept Hanmer's claim that he was financially ruined by the conflict. His political eclipse was mirrored in the fortunes of his more famous uncle, Sir Thomas Hanmer, who withdrew from political life at about the same time. His death must have occurred soon afterwards as the estate of Eliza or Elizabeth Hamner, presumably his widow, was sold between January 1744 and October 1745.

SEE: Robert J. Cain, ed., *Records of the Executive Council, 1664–1734* (1984); John L. Cheney, Jr., ed., *North Carolina Government, 1585–1974* (1975); William L. Saunders, ed., *Colonial Records of North Carolina*, vols. 3, 4 (1886).

JON G. CRAWFORD

Happoldt, Christopher *(27 Nov. 1823–10 Oct. 1878)*, physician and editor, was born in Charleston, S.C., of German and English ancestry. His father was Christian David Happoldt, a Charleston merchant, and his mother was Sarah Elizabeth Marlen, granddaughter of Edward Marlen, senior customs inspector at the port of Charleston in the early 1800s. As a boy of fifteen, he traveled to Europe with the learned pastor-naturalist Dr. John Bachman, minister of St. John's Lutheran Church in Charleston and collaborator of John James Audubon. On this journey he and Bachman stayed at the Audubon residence in London for several weeks.

Happoldt received his classical education in Charleston and was graduated from the South Carolina Medical College in 1851 at the head of his class. He next spent several years in Europe further pursuing his medical studies at the universities of Paris and Berlin. Following his return to America in 1854, he became the editor of the *Charleston Medical Journal and Review*, one of the most prestigious medical journals in the country. This position brought him in contact with the best physicians in the United States and in Europe, and secured for him a position of authority in his profession.

On 28 Oct. 1856, Happoldt married Emily Amelia Greenlee of Morganton, N.C. The Greenlees were a prominent family of Burke County, descendants of David Washington Greenlee, owner of a large plantation on the Catawba River. After his marriage Happoldt took his bride to live in Charleston, where he continued his career as physician and editor. For a few years all went well. His wife had given him a lovely daughter, Minerva, and his journal and medical practice were both highly successful. In 1858, his career was completely changed when his wife wished to return to her home in Morganton. Happoldt relinquished his editorship of the *Charleston Medical Journal* and moved to Morganton where he began a new medical practice. Even though Morganton was not an important medical center, it was a beautiful town with a distinguished history. Here he found cultivated and intellectual company with such gentlemen as Colonel John Pearson and members of the Ervin family.

In 1861, with the outbreak of the Civil War, Happoldt was commissioned as a surgeon in the Confederate Army. After the war he returned to his practice in Morganton. Life moved slowly and uneventfully for him until September 1873, when a yellow fever epidemic struck the Mississippi Valley. He volunteered his services and was sent to Memphis, where he proved to be one of the most outstanding physicians fighting that dread disease. The epidemic was brief and in a few months he returned to Morganton. When the fever struck again in 1878, he volunteered to battle his old enemy in Vicksburg. This epidemic was much worse and the doctor himself fell a victim to the disease. He died at Vicksburg, struggling to overcome the deadly pestilence that had swept towns and villages out of existence. On his gravestone is the inscription: "At the call of the Howard Association he volunteered for duty in the yellow fever district and was assigned to Vicksburg where he nobly died in helping to keep others alive."

In Morganton Happoldt was survived by his wife and four daughters: Minerva, Lucy Greenlee, Mary Greenlee, and Sarah Elizabeth. His heroic life was later commemorated by Miss Minnie May Curtis of Raleigh in a poem, "The Uncrowned Hero," published in the Morganton *Herald* on 23 Mar. 1893.

SEE: *Charleston Medical Journal and Review* 13 (1858); Ralph S. Greenlee, *Genealogy of the Greenlee Family in America* (1908); Morganton *Herald*, 23 Mar. 1893; C. H. Neuffer, ed., *The Christopher Happoldt Journal* (1960); Joseph F. Waring, *A History of Medicine in South Carolina, 1825–1900* (1967).

CLAUDE H. NEUFFER

Haralson, Herndon (12 Oct. 1757–27 May 1847), soldier, politician, and planter, was born in what is now Person County, one of thirteen children of Paul and Nancy Lea Haralson. His grandfather had immigrated from Holland to Virginia in 1715. In 1750, Paul Haralson left Virginia and settled on Hyco Creek, a small branch of the Dan River running through present Person County. Young Haralson's formal education was limited. At age nineteen, when the land office of North Carolina was opened, he was appointed deputy surveyor for the newly formed Caswell County. He continued in this position until 1780, when he was appointed deputy clerk of court under Archibald DeBow Murphey, Sr. Murphey soon joined the Revolution and left the office to Haralson. When Cornwallis and his army passed near the county office, the young clerk stored the records in a safe place and then applied for and received a commission to raise a volunteer company of militia. In a few days he assembled a company, equipped it, and joined General Nathanael Greene in Hillsborough.

On 21 Feb. 1781, Captain Haralson attacked a surprised band of Tories under the command of Dr. John Pyle. The battle was a great success: the Tories were "cut to pieces," and 180 of their number were killed. On 2 March, Haralson and his men fought in the Battle of Wetzell's Mill, on the Reedy Fork of the Haw River, followed by a skirmish at Alamance Creek. On 15 March, they saw action in the Battle of Guilford Court House. Haralson then marched with General Greene to Eutaw Springs. In this bloody battle, Haralson was promoted to major and given a command of mounted infantry called the "Marshall Corps." After this engagement, he took 500 prisoners to Salisbury, where he was discharged from the army. He returned to Caswell County, a hero.

Haralson again took charge of the clerk's office in Caswell County until 1784, when he accepted an offer to work as a clerk for the Robert Donald Company, importing merchants in Petersburg, Va. He continued in this position for three years before returning to his former post in Caswell County.

On 4 Oct. 1791 Haralson married Mary Murphey (1771–1847), the daughter of Archibald DeBow Murphey, Sr. They had eight sons and three daughters: Archibald, Jonathan, Herndon, Jr., Paul Anderson, Green Lea, Betsy, William Henry, James Madison, Mary, Jane, and John Haywood.

In 1792, the county of Caswell was divided and Haralson took charge of the newly created Person County clerk's office. In 1793, he was elected to the House of Commons. He served four terms in the Assembly up to 1800, after which he declined to run for reelection. That year he was appointed judge of the Superior Court; he also reclaimed his former post of Clerk of Court. Haralson remained in these positions until 1816, when he resigned and moved to Danville, Va. In 1818, he moved to Haywood, N.C., and in 1820, to Tennessee, settling in the wilderness on Forked Deer River. In 1822, as the western district of that state was being organized, he moved to Madison County and from there to Haywood County, Tenn. In 1826 he was made an agent for the Bank of the State of Tennessee. From 1831 until his death, he lived the life of a planter. By that time his possessions and landholdings were fairly extensive. An active Methodist, he was buried in Brownsville, Tenn.

SEE: Lyman C. Draper, *History of the Battle of King's Mountain* (1881); A. R. Foushee, *Reminiscences, A Sketch and Letters Descriptive of Life in Person County in Former Days* (1921); Danny K. Haralson, *Haralson-Harrelson Family History and Lineage* (1974); Herndon Haralson Diary (1837–47) and Personal Papers (Southern Historical Collection, University of North Carolina Library, Chapel Hill); Harrelson Papers (in possession of Douglas Harrelson, Ruffin); Archibald DeBow Murphey Papers (North Carolina State Archives, Raleigh).

RONALD HARRELSON

Harden, John William (22 Aug. 1903–6 Feb. 1985), newspaperman, publicist, and author, was born in Graham, the son of Peter Ray and Nettie Cayce Abbott Harden. Upon graduation from high school he became circulation and advertising manager for the *Burlington Daily Times* as well as news editor for the Graham news department. In 1923 he was classified advertising manager for the Raleigh *News and Observer*, but in the fall entered The University of North Carolina. In Chapel Hill he worked under Bob Madry, head of the university news bureau. Following his graduation in 1927, he joined the *Charlotte News* as a reporter and columnist and in 1937 became news editor of the Salisbury *Evening Post*, where he remained until 1944. Moving to Greensboro, he became executive news editor of the *Daily News* of that city.

In 1944 Harden was named director of public relations in the gubernatorial campaign of R. Gregg Cherry. After Cherry's inauguration, Harden was appointed executive secretary to the governor. While living in Raleigh, he moderated a series of programs on radio station WPTF on "Tales of Tar Heelia." Drawing from his personal file of ghost stories and mysteries, he continued this program for eighteen months during 1946–47. Out of this grew two books, *The Devil's Tramping Ground and Other North Carolina Mysteries* (1949) and *Tar Heel Ghosts* (1954), both published by The University of North Carolina Press.

Resigning his post in the executive office, in 1948 Harden became head of public relations in the reelection campaign of U.S. Senator William B. Umstead. After the election he joined Burlington Mills Corporation as director of public relations and shortly afterwards was made assistant-vice president. Leaving Burlington

Mills in 1958, he undertook pioneer work in the state when he formed his own public relations firm, John Harden Associates, in Greensboro. A year later he was engaged by the North Carolina Department of Conservation and Development to lead a tour of North Carolina business and state representatives through western Europe, and in 1971 he assisted Cannon Mills Company of Kannapolis as director of public relations. Harden received wide recognition for his work in public relations. After selling his company in 1981, he continued in an advisory capacity until his death while working at his desk.

On 13 June 1928 Harden married Josephine Holt; they were the parents of Glenn Abbott and John William. Mrs. Harden died in 1951, and two years later he married Sarah Plexico. They were the parents of twin sons, Holmes Plexico and Mark Michael, and of Jonathan Holder.

Harden was a Democrat and an Episcopalian. He worked with the Greensboro Council of the Boy Scouts of America, the Carolina Regional Theater, and the North Carolina Historic Preservation Society. He also served as chairman of the 1951 campaign of the North Carolina League for Crippled Children and in 1955 was president of the General Alumni Association of The University of North Carolina. Harden was also the author of *Alamance County: Economic and Social* (1928) and *North Carolina Roads and Their Builders* (1966).

SEE: *Chapel Hill Newspaper*, 7 Feb., 10 Feb. 1985; *Greensboro News & Record*, 14 Oct. 1984; Raleigh *News and Observer*, 31 Oct. 1954, 11 June 1958, 9 Sept. 1959, 12 Sept. 1982; Salisbury *Evening Post*, 31 Oct. 1978; *Who's Who in America* (1984).

POLLY A. PIERCE

Harding, Edmund Hoyt (10 July 1890–19 Sept. 1970), salesman, humorist, and promoter of historic restoration, was born in Washington, N.C., the ninth of eleven children of the Reverend Nathaniel Harding and the first produced by his second wife, Marina Brickell Hoyt. His father was for forty-four years rector of St. Peter's Episcopal Church in Washington.

Young Harding received his education in the public schools of Washington and at Trinity School, Chocowinity, from which he was graduated in 1907. His first jobs were those of shoe salesman and later mule salesman in his native town, but he soon began to exhibit signs of the showmanship and infectious humor that would one day bring him national recognition as a speaker and entertainer. From 1924 to 1940 he was a fertilizer and insurance salesman for the Washington firm of William Bragaw and Company.

After 1940, Harding devoted most of his time to speaking engagements, his first speech having been delivered in Newport News, Va., on 6 May 1937. From 1940 until his death, he entertained groups in each of the fifty states, Canada, and Mexico, and gave nearly 5,000 talks. As a speaker and entertainer, Harding combined the qualities of storyteller, clown, and homespun philosopher. His imagination was remarkable, his presentations animated, and his stories seemingly without number. Beginning with Governor R. Gregg Cherry in the late 1940s, he was designated by each governor of the state as "North Carolina's Ambassador of Goodwill."

In 1955, Harding assumed leadership of a nascent movement to preserve and restore historic Bath, North Carolina's oldest town (incorporated in 1706). His production of the pageant, "Queen Anne's Bell," in Octo-

ber of that year gave lasting impetus to this movement. As president of the Beaufort County Historical Society and chairman of the Historic Bath Commission, it was he who made the eventual restoration of Bath a reality.

On 3 June 1914 Harding married Katherine Bragaw of Washington. To this union were born Katherine Blount (14 June 1915) and Rena Hoyt (12 July 1916). Harding's first wife died on 29 Dec. 1954. On 5 July 1969 he married Nina Carolyn Whitley of Aurora, who survived him.

A natural extrovert, Harding was active in numerous clubs and organizations, including the Masons, the Shriners, the Washington Chamber of Commerce, and the Rotary. In 1961, he was president of the North Carolina Society for the Preservation of Antiquities. A lifelong Episcopalian, he served as organist at St. Peter's Church for nearly forty years. He died in Rome, Ga., while returning from a speaking engagement, and was buried in Washington's Oakdale Cemetery.

SEE: Wilson Angley, "The Life and Work of Edmund H. Harding" (Historic Sites Section, North Carolina State Archives, Raleigh); Edmund H. Harding Papers and Memorabilia (Visitors Center, Historic Bath State Historic Site, Bath; also in possession of Mrs. Henry L. Hodges, Washington); John H. Harding, ed. and comp., *Genealogy of the Harding Family in the Eastern Counties of North Carolina* (1908); William S. Powell, ed., *North Carolina Lives* (1962); Raleigh *News and Observer*, 31 Oct. 1954; Washington *Daily News*, 5 May 1966, 21 Sept. 1970.

WILSON ANGLEY

Harding, Henry Patrick (14 Aug. 1874–13 July 1959), teacher and public school administrator, was known most of his life as Harry P. Harding. He was born in Aurora, one of eight children (two of whom died in infancy) of Confederate Army Major Henry H. and Susan Elizabeth Sugg Harding. Harry Harding grew up in Greenville, where his father was a teacher, farmer, and for four years superintendent of schools. He attended Greenville Male Academy and The University of North Carolina. Following a family tradition, he left Chapel Hill between his sophomore and junior years to earn money to help pay for the education of his brothers and sisters but was graduated in 1899. While at the university, he was elected to Phi Beta Kappa and to Sigma Alpha Epsilon social fraternity. He later received the M.A. degree from Columbia University (1931) and an honorary doctorate of pedagogy from Davidson College (1951).

Early in life Harding decided to teach. From Charles D. McIver and Edwin A. Alderman, who toured North Carolina in the 1880s and 1890s campaigning for better schools, he acquired what has been described as "a mystical belief" in public education. While an undergraduate, he planned to teach Latin and Greek in college, but after receiving the B.A. degree he became principal of New Bern High School. In 1901 he left that position to organize the Oxford schools, and from 1902 to 1904 he was superintendent of the New Bern schools. In 1904, the superintendent of the Charlotte schools, Alexander Graham, another of the "evangels of education," persuaded Harding to become principal of one of three graded schools there. In 1912, he was appointed assistant superintendent but continued to teach mathematics. In 1913, he became superintendent.

During Harding's tenure, the Charlotte school system was greatly expanded and improved. In 1912, he supervised the organization of a high school where teachers specialized in one subject instead of teaching a grade. By 1923, Charlotte had the first junior high school in North Carolina; in 1924, it added the twelfth grade. During the years 1912–30, many elective courses were instituted, with the result that more students remained in school longer. Harding was more interested in building character, developing personality, and helping each child to "find himself" than in teaching facts. Many times he was instrumental in persuading Charlotte voters to approve special taxes and bond issues. The money went for new buildings; supplements to teachers' salaries; manual training, business, physical education, and music courses; ungraded classes for retarded children; and health services. Harding was not satisfied until he had replaced old buildings with fireproof ones. In 1925, he convinced the school board to hire a professional consulting firm of architects.

Perhaps his toughest fight for funds came during the "dark days" of 1933 and 1934, after the state legislature annulled the charters that had allowed cities to levy special taxes for schools. Charlotte schools lost almost two-thirds of their budget, most of their special courses, many teachers, the twelfth grade, and a month of the school term. When the Charlotte school district regained the right to levy special taxes, the first attempt to do so failed. After Harding lobbied earnestly among the city's businessmen, voters approved a supplement in 1935.

Harding was quiet, unassuming, gentle, deeply religious, and dedicated to his work. He taught a Bible class at Charlotte's First Methodist Church for twenty years and held offices in the church. When he retired in 1949 at age seventy-four, 5,000 people heard U.S. Senator Frank P. Graham, the son of Harding's predecessor, describe Harding as a "soldier of peace," and one of those who, "without earthly rewards, build the future in the schools of the children of the people."

During his career Harding served as a trustee of The University of North Carolina and as president of the North Carolina Association of City School Superintendents, of the South Piedmont Teachers Association, and of the North Carolina Education Association. He taught for two summers at The University of North Carolina, served on the North Carolina High School Textbook Commission, and was a charter member of the "96 Club," made up of two school superintendents from each state. He was a Rotarian and a member of the Charlotte Chamber of Commerce and the Executives Club. After retirement, he continued to maintain an office and, as superintendent emeritus, to visit schools. He also served on the Charlotte Civil Service Commission.

In 1903, Harding married Lucia Ella Ives of New Bern. The couple had one daughter, Lucia Elizabeth, and a son who died in infancy. Harding's brothers also achieved distinction. William Frederick Harding, a Superior Court judge, lived in Charlotte. Fordyce C. Harding, a lawyer, served in the North Carolina Senate (1915–20). Jarvis B. Harding, a civil engineer, built roads in Mexico. Their sisters, Sudie Harding Latham and Mary Elizabeth Harding, were teachers.

Harry Harding was buried in Elmwood Cemetery, Charlotte. Two portraits of him hang at Harding High School nearby.

SEE: *Charlotte News*, 14 July 1959; *Charlotte Observer*, 9 Feb. 1936, 26 Apr., 30 May 1949, 26 Jan. 1951, 15 Nov. 1953, 14 July 1959; Daniel L. Grant, *Alumni History of the University of North Carolina* (1924); H. P. Harding, "History of the Charlotte City Schools" (typescript, Curriculum Library, Charlotte-Mecklenburg Education Center, Charlotte); H. T. King, *Sketches of Pitt County* (1976); *North Carolina Biography*, vol. 3 (1928, 1941); *Who's Who in the South and Southwest* (1952).

LAURA PAGE FRECH

Hardison, Osborne Bennett (*22 Dec. 1892–16 Mar. 1959*), naval officer, was born in Wadesboro, the second of six children of Harriet Bennett and William Cameron Hardison. Educated in private school through his thirteenth year, he attended Horner Military Academy for one semester before entering The University of North Carolina at age fourteen. He was graduated with an A.B. degree in 1911 and was appointed to the U.S. Naval Academy the following year. Upon his graduation there in 1916 as one of seven honor men in his class, he was commissioned ensign and joined the USS *Texas*, commanded by Captain Victor Blue, also a North Carolinian. Hardison served on this ship throughout World War I and until 1920. From February 1918 until after the armistice, the *Texas*, in the Sixth Battle Squadron, operated in the war zones in association with the British Grand Fleet and was present at the surrender of the German fleet.

Before transferring to naval aviation in 1923, Hardison served several brief assignments including one aboard the USS *Mayflower*, the presidential yacht in Washington, D.C. On completing flight training he began duty with the aircraft squadron at Hampton Roads, Va.; following temporary duty at the Naval Academy he became an instructor in its Department of Engineering Aeronautics, leaving in August 1927 to assume command of aircraft squadrons based on the USS *Lexington*. Afterwards he served for several years in the Bureau of Aeronautics and in the office of the Chief of Naval Operations as aviation officer.

In June 1938, Hardison joined the USS *Ranger* as executive officer; a year later he became aviation officer and subsequently fleet aviator on the staff of the Commander in Chief, U.S. Fleet. After a little more than a year as commander of the Naval Air Station, Anacostia, D.C., in September 1941 he become aide to the Assistant Secretary of the Navy for Air and in that capacity represented the assistant secretary at the commissioning of the Naval Pre-Flight School at The University of North Carolina.

In October 1942, with the rank of captain, he was ordered to command the USS *Enterprise*, one of two aircraft carriers the United States had left in the Pacific. The day after he began this duty, the *Enterprise* participated in the Battle of Santa Cruz Island when the *Enterprise* and the USS *Hornet* inflicted severe damage on a powerful Japanese fleet moving to support land operations at Guadalcanal. For his role in this action Hardison was awarded the Navy Cross. Under his command the *Enterprise* also participated in the Battle of the Soloman Islands (14–15 Nov. 1942), and his ship was awarded a Presidential Citation.

On being detached from command of the *Enterprise* later that month, he was promoted to the rank of rear admiral and assumed command of Fleet Air, South Pacific. For this service he was awarded the Legion of Merit "for exceptionally meritorious conduct. . . . Faced with numerous handicaps and difficulties attendant upon operations in the forward area [he] acted aggressively and with thorough comprehension of the many problems involved, resolutely accomplishing a steady increase of resources necessary to carry the conflict to the enemy. By his able leadership in the planning, procurement, and utilization of materials and personnel for the air branch [he] contributed materially to the prosecution of the war in this area."

In January 1944, Admiral Hardison became Chief of Naval Air Primary Training Command charged with the administration of a naval command distributed throughout the United States. He created a basic aviation training program designed to equip every potential navy aviator with a complete mastery of aircraft in flight. During this period the Pre-Flight School at The University of North Carolina was one unit of Hardison's command, and he visited the campus often on inspection trips. In February 1945, he delivered the university's commencement address.

Reporting in September 1945 as commander, Air Craft Philippines Sea Frontier, he was the U.S. naval representative at the celebration pursuant to Philippine independence. In 1946, he assumed command of Carrier Division Five which supported occupation forces in the Far East. A tour of duty followed in the Office of Naval Operations where he served as Chief of Pan American Affairs, U.S. Navy, and in January 1950 he became Commander of Naval Forces, Mariannas, with additional duty as deputy military governor of the Bonin Volcano Island. In August 1951, he was named Commander of the Air Fleet, Jacksonville, Fla., and later went to Washington, D.C., as Special Assistant to the Deputy Chief of Naval Operations (Air). On 1 Jan. 1954, Hardison was transferred to the retired list and was advanced to the rank of vice-admiral "on the basis of his combat awards."

In 1926, Hardison married Ruth Morgan of Washington, D.C.; they had two sons, Osborne Bennett, Jr., and William Gerry Morgan.

At the time The University of North Carolina celebrated its sesquicentennial, the trustees and faculty voted to confer an honorary degree upon Hardison; however, duty in the Pacific prevented his attending the 1945 commencement to receive this honor. But in 1950, when his son Osborne was graduated, the admiral was awarded the LL.D. degree. The citation read, in part: ". . . carrying on a great tradition, he has ably demonstrated in his long career the contributions made by the sons of this State and this University to the Armed Services of this Nation in peace as well as at war."

Hardison was killed in a street accident in Washington, D.C.; at his expressed wish, he was buried in Arlington National Cemetery.

SEE: Daniel L. Grant, *Alumni History of the University of North Carolina* (1924); Osborne B. Hardison, "This University Is Doing Great Work for the Navy" (commencement address, University of North Carolina, Chapel Hill, 25 Feb. 1945), and "Training a Naval Aviator," *DAR Magazine* 86 (March 1962); William S. Powell, ed., *North Carolina Lives* (1962); Raleigh *News and Observer*, 15 Feb. 1945, 18 Feb. 1959; Records, Bureau of Personnel, Department of the Navy, Washington, D.C., for information regarding Admiral Hardison; Wadesboro *Messenger and Intelligencer*, 20 Feb. 1959; *Who Was Who in America*, vol. 3 (1960); *Who's Who in the South and Southwest* (1954).

HARRIET H. ROBSON

Hargett (or Harget), Frederick (*ca. 1742–January 1810*), Revolutionary War captain, planter, and lawmaker, was probably born in the area that became Pitt County. The second son of Frederick Hargett, he had only one sibling, Peter Hargett, who married Ann Isler and died in Jones County in October 1797. The Hargetts were descendants of the Palatine colony which settled in New Bern in 1710. Hargett probably attended the school in Rocky Run (now Reed Branch) established by John Martin Franck in 1713. While growing up on a plantation, Hargett learned many trades such as joiner and blacksmith. Sometime before 1769, he moved to Craven County. As a planter in Craven and later Jones counties, he owned vast tracts of land and many slaves.

On 28 Nov. 1776, Hargett was commissioned captain in the Eighth Regiment of the North Carolina Continental Line. He had previously served as captain of a Craven County militia company in the expedition to Moore's Creek Bridge. His company also marched to the defense of Wilmington in March 1776.

After the Revolution, Hargett was a prominent planter in Jones County, and rose to the rank of brigadier general of the militia of his division. He served in the General Assembly for fifteen years. Elected to the House of Commons in 1779, he became a member of the House Committee of Claims and served many military petitions for land grants. In 1784, Hargett began his ten-year service in the state senate. There he fought corruption of local officials, officiated on the Council of State, and served many petitions of soldiers of the Continental line. He was a member, and eventually became chairman, of the committees of Claims, Propositions and Grievances, and Privileges and Elections. Hargett attended the state constitutional conventions of 1788 and 1789, at which he was an active Anti-Federalist. He was also one of nine commissioners appointed to select the exact site and lay out the capital city of Raleigh.

Noted for his concern about public education in the state, Hargett was named as one of the original trustees of The University of North Carolina. He headed the trustees' committee in choosing New Hope Chapel (now Chapel Hill) as the site of the university. Hargett was active as a trustee for many years. He also donated land for a public school in Onslow County.

The local activities of the Jones County planter were numerous. During his lifetime, he served as registrar, justice of the peace, chairman of the county court, and town commissioner of Trenton.

Hargett married Penelope Miller, the sister of Daniel Miller, a Continental soldier. She was the great-granddaughter of Jacob and Catherine Miller, Palatine colonists. The Hargetts had five sons and three daughters: Frederick, Jr., William, John, Abner, and Daniel (named for Daniel Miller), Philipine Brook, Susannah Westbrook, and Betsy Bryan.

SEE: Moses Amis, *Historical Raleigh* (1913); John L. Cheney, Jr., ed., *North Carolina Government, 1585–1974* (1975); Walter Clark, ed., *State Records of North Carolina*, vols. 11–13, 17–25 (1895–1906); R. D. W. Connor, *A Documentary History of the University of North Carolina*, vol. 1 (1953); Zoe Hargett Gwynn, *Abstracts of the Records of Jones County, 1779–1868* (1963); Ernest Haywood Collection (Southern Historical Collection, University of North Carolina Library, Chapel Hill); Sybil Hyatt, comp., "Hargett-Thompson, Onslow County, North Carolina" (typescript, North Carolina Collection, University of North Carolina Library, Chapel Hill); Hugh Talmage Lefler and Albert Ray Newsome, *North Carolina: The History of a Southern State* (1973); *New Bern Herald*, 29 Jan. 1810; North Carolina Secretary of State, *North Carolina Troops in the Continental Line* (1884?); Fred A. Olds, *Abstracts of North Carolina Wills, 1760–1800* (1925); William C. Pool, "An Economic Interpretation of the Ratification of the Federal Constitution in North Carolina," *North Carolina Historical Review* 27 (1950); Treasurer and Comptroller's Papers (North Carolina State Archives, Raleigh).

CATHERINE L. ROBINSON

Hargrave, Janie Carlyle *(30 Nov. 1893–23 Oct. 1975)*, missionary, educator, philanthropist, and humanitarian, was born in Lumberton, the daughter of William Watts and Lillian Ottelia Vampill Carlyle. Her maternal grandfather was German-born Dr. Rudolph Ertel Vampill, who began a medical practice in Lumberton in 1881. Frank Ertel Carlyle, a U.S. congressman, was her younger brother. Her dual interest in religion and education manifested itself early in life. She became a Sunday school teacher at age thirteen. At sixteen she was graduated from Lumberton High School, after which she attended the State Normal and Industrial College at Greensboro for two years. Her family belonged to the Christian Missionary Alliance Church, and she was eager to become a missionary. Because her father would not permit her to leave home at age eighteen, she began one of her remarkable careers in the 1912–13 school year.

In her first teaching assignment, she taught sixty-three first graders at the three-teacher, four-month East Lumberton School. When it closed she went to teach at West Lumberton, thus receiving credit for two years of teaching in one year. In the fall of 1913 her father allowed her to attend Nyack Missionary Training College, Nyack, N.Y., from which she was graduated in 1915. Her first appointment was in Puerto Rico, but illness soon forced her to return home. From this time she combined the careers of teaching and missionary work.

Miss Janie, who did not need her teaching salary, spent her total pay on missions, church work, charities, and the Woman's Christian Temperance Union. At times she paid out as much as $300 a month on postage alone, not just for missionaries from her own church but also from other denominations that called on her for help. She could spend hours recounting the miracles that had come her way in answer to requests from missionaries. Before the war in Vietnam, for example, missionaries there wrote for new clothes to outfit Vietnamese girls who were to be sent to college—all in size nine. Miss Janie wondered where she could get so many clothes in such a small size. Two days later, the owner of Ida's dress shop in St. Pauls contributed eighty-one dresses and two skirt-and-sweater outfits, all in size nine.

After returning home from Puerto Rico, Janie Carlyle joined the trek of teachers to summer school and at various times did graduate work at Columbia and Duke universities with a major in general education and a minor in religious education. She also acquired a principal's certificate. During this period she taught at Ellerbe and at various schools in Robeson County. In 1932, she became principal of East Lumberton, which was renamed the Janie Carlyle Hargrave School long before her retirement in 1967.

In the mill village of East Lumberton, Mrs. Hargrave included religious training in her school curriculum, taught Christian principles in human relationships, and instructed students and their parents in good health habits and family life. In her methods of discipline, she was an individualist and a psychologist; in her seventies she was still finding new ways to handle problems in the school. She spent much of her time visiting families in the town, teaching them the Bible and taking care of their needs, and she had much influence among them.

During the 1930s a kindergarten teacher visiting from Maryland inspired Mrs. Hargrave to undertake a new project. In due course she persuaded East Lumberton authorities to renovate an old hotel, pay for the utilities, and allow her to use it rent free as a public kindergarten for all the mill children. Then she traveled to Nyack, N.Y., to find five female students who would teach the children without pay in return for food, lodging, and clothing. Over the next fifteen years, forty-four young women, called "Miss Janie's girls," came to teach at the first kindergarten in Robeson County.

Mrs. Hargrave also sent students from Lumberton to college. Among them were Dr. Kelly Barnes, vice-president of Toccoa Falls Institute and Bible College, Toccoa Falls, Ga., and Dr. William Watson, founder and president of Florida's Trinity Bible College. Some years after Barnes went to Toccoa he requested Miss Janie's permission to send two of his female students to Lumberton to teach at the Daily Vacation Bible School. The young women taught for two weeks in East Lumberton and then for two weeks in North Lumberton. These also were the first schools of their kind in the county. In addition, Mrs. Hargrave conducted the first Negro Vacation Bible School at Sandy Grove Baptist Church.

Among her humanitarian activities, Miss Janie visited jails and helped with services for inmates. For many years she was responsible for arranging to send unwed pregnant girls to an institution where they could be cared for; it often became her duty to inform their parents. She also helped establish a mission among the Indians of Robeson County, did some work with orphanages, and assisted Miss Grace Garthwaite in the Children's Bible Mission. When a graduate of Nyack who was ministering to Americans in Vietcong prisons contacted Miss Janie, she not only gave him advice but also collected money to send him for the purchase of chewing gum, candy, and whatever else he could take into the prisons.

For most of her life Mrs. Hargrave fought against the use of alcohol. She was associated with the Woman's Christian Temperance Union for six decades and was president of the Sixth District for much of that time. In 1971, she financed her own campaign against liquor stores in Lumberton. Many Robesonians say that through her efforts Robeson County was dry until the 1970s and Lumberton was dry at the time of her death. In later years she worked with the Good Shepherd Home for Alcoholic Men at Lake Waccamaw.

After her marriage to George Hargrave in 1930, she became a Presbyterian and served that denomination in several capacities. When she retired from teaching at age seventy-three, she received awards from the Civitan Club, the Lumberton Board of Education, the Robeson County Board of Education, and the children of Hargrave School. In 1962 the Civitans gave her a plaque as the "Outstanding Citizen of Lumberton" of that year. On her eightieth birthday, a dinner in her honor was sponsored by the administration of Toccoa Falls Institute.

Until his retirement George Hargrave owned a dairy. The couple lived on the farm, and Mrs. Hargrave worked with Home Demonstration Clubs. The Hargraves had no children.

SEE: Dr. Kelly Barnes, Toccoa Falls Institute, Toccoa Falls, Ga. (letter to the author); Janie Carlyle Hargrave,

George Hargrave, Ethel Ivey, Hazel Powell, and Charles Thomas Smith (interviews); Lumberton *Post*, 28 Jan. 1973; Lumberton *Robesonian*, scattered issues, 1930–75, but see esp. 24 Oct. 1975.

MAUD THOMAS SMITH

Hargrave, Richard (*5 Dec. 1803–23 June 1879*), clergyman and author, was born in Caswell County, the son of William and Sallie Ellis Hargrave. His father was first an O'Kellyite minister but afterwards became a devout Methodist. After attending a local school, young Hargrave moved with his family in 1818 to Indiana because of their opposition to slavery. They settled in Pike County where no schools were available. In August 1819, Hargrave later recorded, he felt a call to a religious life and in 1823 joined the O'Kelly Christian church, accepting the doctrine of Arianism. Soon, however, he was persuaded to abandon Arianism and join the Methodist church. He was invited to accompany a clergyman in riding the circuit to hold services and they visited many sparsely settled sections of Indiana. Assigned to a circuit in his own right, Hargrave served faithfully for a number of years before being transferred to Illinois.

In 1844 Hargrave was the author of a *Treatise upon the Lord's Supper and Baptism, with a Specific Argument Deduced from the Significance of Baptism*, published in Lafayette, Ind. In 1862 his *Sermons, Expository and Practical* was published in Cincinnati. Throughout most of his life Hargrave composed poems based upon both the Old and the New Testaments. He also wrote seventeen hymns and several miscellaneous poems. They were carefully constructed with good rhyme schemes. After his death his son, the Reverend William P. Hargrave, published *Sacred Poems of Rev. Richard Hargrave, D.D. with a Biography of Himself, and Biographical Sketches of Some of His Coadjutors*, printed in 1890 in Cincinnati; this volume contains an engraving of Hargrave. Indiana Asbury University (now DePauw University) awarded the degree of doctor of divinity to the Reverend Richard Hargrave. Although he retired from the formal ministry in 1871, he continued to preach until his death in Attica, Ind.

In 1829 Hargrave married Nancy Ann Posey. They were the parents of Sarah Frances (who married the Reverend Noah Lathrop), William Posey, Caroline Indiana, Richard Watson, Mary Elizabeth, Martha Ann, John Wesley, and Lucy Ellen.

SEE: Hargrave's autobiography in his *Sacred Poems* (1890); Donald E. Thompson, comp., *Indiana Authors and Their Books, 1917–1966* (1974).

WILLIAM S. POWELL

Harley, George Way (*8 Aug. 1894–7 Nov. 1966*), Methodist missionary, physician, blacksmith, geographer, anthropologist, and researcher, was born in Asheville to George Gamewell (1862–1925) and Lillie [Lily] Way (1871–1959) Harley. His father was a Methodist minister. Young Harley grew up in Brevard, Bessemer City, Norwood, and Concord, where he was graduated from high school as class valedictorian. After receiving the B.A. degree from Trinity College (now Duke University) in 1916, he taught high school science in New Bern for one year. He next headed a carpenter gang at Camp Jackson, S.C.

In June 1918, Harley enlisted in the Medical Corps and was sent to the Chemical Warfare Unit located at the Brady Laboratory of the Yale University Medical School. There his work was noticed by a pathologist who promised him a job and a room while he attended medical school, so just before entering Yale in 1919 he went to McGill University to study pathological museum technique and to take a course in embalming. He received the M.D. degree from Yale in 1923, then interned for one year at Hartford (Conn.) Municipal Hospital. During that time he applied to the Board of Missions of the Methodist Episcopal church for a position at a new station in Ganta, Liberia. He was accepted and studied from September 1924 to February 1925 at the Kennedy School of Missions, a facility of the Hartford Seminary Foundation, after having spent the summer at Grenfell's Harrington Hospital in Labrador. While at the mission school he took an evening course in metal working at a local high school. From May to September 1925 he was at the London School of Tropical Medicine, where he was awarded a diploma. In London, he also took a course in mapmaking at the Royal Geographical Institute and spent a month with a craftsman potter.

In October 1925, Harley left for Ganta, Liberia, where he remained for the next thirty-five years except for furloughs. At Ganta he built a hospital, dispensary, church, school, several residences and shops, and a leper village and two "sick villages," largely from the resources he found there. Although not ordained, he served as pastor of Ganta Church until 1948. He also found time for research. His study of native African medicine was compiled into a thesis for which he was awarded the Ph.D. from the Kennedy School of Missions in 1938; it was published under the title *Native African Medicine* by Harvard University Press in 1941. In addition, he was the author of medical, geographical, and anthropological works that appeared in various journals, as well as several articles on missionary work. Harley's interest in the religious beliefs of the indigenous people led him to collect over 1,000 ceremonial masks of secret African societies and provide documentation regarding their usage and origin. Many are in American museums today and 33, along with 150 other artifacts, comprise the Harley Collection in the Duke University Museum of Art.

Harley served as Research Associate in Anthropology at the Peabody Museum of Archaeology and Ethnology, Harvard University, and was a fellow of the Royal Geographical Society, the Royal Anthropological Institute, and the Royal Society of Tropical Medicine and Hygiene. Because he was a skilled blacksmith he was initiated into the Guild of Blacksmiths in Liberia, "the only white man to gain such native confidence." He was honored by the Liberian government on numerous occasions and in 1946 was made Knight Commander of the Liberian Humane Order of African Redemption, the highest award given by the government except to visiting potentates. In 1955, a hospital at Sanoquelle, Liberia, was named for him. In 1957 he was awarded the doctor of humanities degree by Duke University, and in 1961 *World Outlook* magazine named him "Methodist of the Year."

On 4 Aug. 1923, Harley married Winifred Jewell of Merrimac, Mass. They had three sons: Robert William, Charles Alfred, and Eugene Lincoln, a 1957 graduate of the Duke University Medical School. The Harleys retired in 1960 to Merry Point in Lancaster County, Va. Harley died there and was cremated. The ashes were flown to Liberia where they were buried near the cornerstone of Ganta Church. In memoriam, the Western

North Carolina Conference of the Methodist church donated $100,000 to purchase an airplane and fuel, drugs, and equipment, and to build the George W. Harley Memorial Social Center—all for the Ganta mission.

SEE: Winifred J. Harley, *A Third of a Century with George Way Harley in Liberia* (1973); Edward H. Hume, *Doctors Courageous* (1950); *Monday Afternoon Club Magazine* 12 (January 1950); *New Haven* (Conn.) *Register*, 20 Mar. 1949; *North Carolina Christian Advocate*, 23 June 1960, 24 Nov. 1966; Katherine E. M. Somerville and Gerald W. Hartwig, *Knowing the Unknown* (1978); Charles D. White, ed., *Journal of the 1967 Session of the Western North Carolina Conference of the Methodist Church, Lake Junaluska, N.C.* (1967).

SUZANNE S. LEVY

Harnett, Cornelius (*d. 1742*), colonial official, planter, and innkeeper, formerly a merchant of Dublin, Ireland, settled in Chowan County by 1720. In 1722, when he sold land on Queen Anne's Creek to Chief Justice Christopher Gale, Harnett referred to himself as a planter. He allied himself with the erratic Proprietary Governor George Burrington; and when Sir Richard Everard replaced Burrington in 1725, Harnett sided with his deposed friend. On the night of 7 Dec. 1725, the two men led a riot in Edenton directed against Everard and his supporters. According to the indictment brought against them, the rioters "assaulted" the governor's residence, broke into two other houses, assaulted three men, and caused one man's wife to miscarry due to fear for her husband's safety. On this occasion, Harnett was referred to as "a Ruffianly Fellow."

With criminal charges lodged against them, Burrington and Harnett left Edenton. Harnett settled on the Cape Fear River where he purchased lots in the town of Brunswick. He subsequently opened an inn in the town and operated a ferry across the river at that point.

Upon Burrington's return to power in 1730 as the first royal governor of North Carolina, Harnett was named to the governor's council. Burrington was thereupon accused by the opposition of packing the council with men who would do his bidding, men "of such vile characters and poor understandings, that it is the greatest abuse of power imaginable upon the ministry to recommend such of them." These "characters" included Matthew Rowan, Edmund Porter, and John Baptista Ashe. Much to the governor's chagrin, Harnett soon took issue with several major questions. Along with Ashe, Porter, and William Smith, he reproached the governor for his method of addressing the council and for the wording of his message concerning justices and assistant judges. When Burrington dismissed Porter from the council, Ashe and Nathaniel Rice joined Harnett in strongly opposing the action.

Early in 1732 Burrington complained to the Board of Trade and Plantations that he had appointed Harnett on the advice of others without knowing him personally, and that his presence on the council was a disgrace. Obviously the governor chose to forget the events of 1725, when the two men had been allied against the Everard faction. Privately, Burrington informed Harnett that he "was no longer his friend" and berated him in his own home as a "fool, blockhead, puppy, and Ashe's tool." After receiving repeated abuses from the governor, Harnett resigned from the council in October 1732.

Harnett subsequently served as vestryman for St. Philips Parish at Brunswick, justice of the peace for Bladen (1732) and New Hanover (1736–41) counties, and sheriff of New Hanover County (1739–40). He apparently had large landholdings in Bladen and New Hanover counties where he operated plantations and sawmills. Upon his death, he was survived by his widow, Elizabeth, and a son, Cornelius, Jr., the Revolutionary War statesman.

SEE: Samuel A. Ashe, ed., *Biographical History of North Carolina*, vol. 8 (1905); Walter Clark, ed., *State Records of North Carolina*, vol. 23 (1904); Deeds of New Hanover County (North Carolina State Archives, Raleigh); J. R. B. Hathaway, ed., *North Carolina Historical and Genealogical Register*, vol. 3 (April 1903); William L. Saunders, ed., *Colonial Records of North Carolina*, vols. 2–4 (1886); Alexander M. Walker, *New Hanover County Court Minutes, 1738–1800*, 4 vols. (1958–62).

DONALD R. LENNON

Harnett, Cornelius, Jr. (*20 Apr. 1723–28 Apr. 1781*), Revolutionary War statesman, was born in Chowan County, the son of Cornelius and Elizabeth Harnett. The family moved to Brunswick Town when young Cornelius was only three, and he spent the remainder of his life in the Cape Fear area. Harnett became a leading Wilmington merchant with interests in farming, milling, and mercantile ventures. Along with other business activities, he was a partner in distillery operations which included a still house, wharf, warehouse, and schooner. He became involved in public affairs in 1750, when he was elected to the Wilmington town commission; during the same year, he was appointed by Governor Gabriel Johnston as a justice of the peace for New Hanover County. In 1754, he was elected to represent Wilmington in the General Assembly, a position he held for every legislative session until the end of the colonial period. Harnett's reputation and influence developed rapidly throughout the province. During his career in the legislature, there were few committees of importance on which he did not serve and few debates in which he did not participate.

When the British Parliament in 1765 passed the Stamp Act in an effort to gain revenue from the colonies, Harnett moved to the forefront of the resistance to the act in North Carolina. Along with Hugh Waddell and John Ashe, he was a leader of the citizens' march on Brunswick Town in February 1766, and he served as spokesman for the "inhabitants in arms" in their confrontation with Governor William Tryon. From the Stamp Act resistance was born the Sons of Liberty, and Harnett was chairman for that group in Wilmington. In June 1770, he was elected chairman of a committee to enforce the nonimportation association in an effort to thwart the British Townshend duties.

Throughout the Tryon and Josiah Martin gubernatorial administrations, Harnett was vocal on the major issues facing the province. He advocated government reforms that would curtail abuses complained of by the Regulators in the Piedmont, but at the same time he opposed the riots and excesses of the Regulators. In the Assembly debates over the civil court law, Harnett, along with Robert Howe, William Hooper, Samuel Johnston, and others, led the fight to retain the controversial attachment clause, much to the chagrin of royal Governor Martin.

As resistance to British policy developed during 1773 and 1774, Harnett was in the vanguard of the move in

North Carolina. Massachusetts Revolutionary leader Josiah Quincy, after visiting Wilmington in 1773, commented that Harnett was the "Samuel Adams of North Carolina." He was a vocal supporter of the concept of a continental correspondence committee and was a leading force in setting up the North Carolina Committee of Correspondence in December 1773. When the Wilmington-New Hanover Committee of Safety was organized in November 1774, he was the master spirit and chairman of the committee.

On 19 July 1775, Governor Martin watched helplessly from the British warship *Cruizer* as a group of colonists led by Harnett, John Ashe, and Robert Howe burned Fort Johnston at the mouth of the Cape Fear River. Martin subsequently wrote to Lord Dartmouth requesting proscription of the three revolutionaries because of "their unremitted labours to promote sedition and rebellion here from the beginning of the discontent in America to this time, that they stand foremost among the patrons of revolt and anarchy."

In 1775, a provincial Council of Safety was created to exercise executive and administrative powers over the province. With the flight of Governor Martin from North Carolina during the early summer, the council and provincial congress had become the government of the province. Harnett was elected president of the council, an appointment which in effect made him the chief executive of North Carolina though without the title.

As a member of the provincial congress and as president of the Council of Safety, Harnett was deeply involved in military planning, raising troops, and arming and equipping an army. During 1776 he served on more committees concerned with devising measures for defending the state than any other man. On 4 April, the Fourth Provincial Congress appointed him chairman of a committee to consider the "usurptions and violences attempted and committed by the King and Parliament." The committee report, which was adopted unanimously on 12 April, became known as the Halifax Resolves. The resolution empowered North Carolina delegates to the Continental Congress to "concur with the delegates of the other Colonies in declaring Independency and forming foreign alliances." When, on 5 May, Sir Henry Clinton offered to pardon all North Carolina citizens who would lay down arms and submit to the laws, Cornelius Harnett and Robert Howe were specifically excluded from the pardon.

During the remainder of 1776, Harnett continued to guide the state through his presidency of the Council of Safety. He is generally credited with delivering the first public reading in North Carolina of the Declaration of Independence when he addressed a crowd at Halifax on 1 August. He also had a leading role in writing the North Carolina state constitution, which was drafted in the fall of 1776. When the new government was organized early in 1777, he was elected president of the seven-member council of state established to assist the governor.

Contrary to his own personal wishes, Harnett was elected to the Continental Congress on 1 May 1777; and despite his desire to return home to his plantation, his sense of public duty forced him to remain in the Congress for the full three years permitted by law. Throughout that period his service was capable and statesmanlike. He was committed to the cause of confederation and fully supported the writing and ratification of the Articles of Confederation.

When the British under Major James H. Craig invaded Wilmington early in 1781, Harnett attempted to flee. Crippled by severe gout, he was captured in Onslow County and returned to Wilmington "thrown across a horse like a sack of meal." Imprisoned in an open blockhouse, his health declined rapidly. Although paroled from prison, he died soon afterwards.

A man of liberal mind, Harnett was reputed to be a Deist. His gravestone epitaph would seem to support this conclusion: "Slave to no sect, he took no private road. But looked through nature up to nature's God." Despite these claims, he was a vestryman of St. James Parish in Wilmington and was Deputy Grand Master of North America for the Masonic Order.

Harnett married Mary Holt, the daughter of Martin Holt. They lived at Maynard (later known as Hilton) north of Wilmington and owned a second plantation, Poplar Grove, at present-day Scotts' Hill on Topsail Sound. She died in New York City in April or May 1792. They apparently had no children.

SEE: Samuel A. Ashe, ed., *Biographical History of North Carolina*, vol. 2 (1905); Walter Clark, ed., *State Records of North Carolina*, vols. 11–17, 22–25 (1895–1906); R. D. W. Connor, *Cornelius Harnett: An Essay in North Carolina History* (1909); Deeds and Wills of New Hanover County (North Carolina State Archives, Raleigh); David T. Morgan, "Cornelius Harnett: Revolutionary Leader and Delegate to the Continental Congress," *North Carolina Historical Review* 49 (1972); William L. Saunders, ed., *Colonial Records of North Carolina*, vols. 4–10 (1886–90); Alan D. Watson and others, *Harnett, Hooper & Howe, Revolutionary Leaders of the Lower Cape Fear* (1979).

DONALD R. LENNON

Harper, George Washington Finley (7 July 1834–16 Mar. 1921), merchant, soldier, railroad builder, banker, and entrepreneur, was born at Fairfield Plantation in Wilkes County. One of three children of James and Caroline Finley Harper, he received classical school training near his home and in 1855 enrolled at Davidson College, graduating four years later. After college he entered the general merchandise business with his father, a founder of the town of Lenoir in 1841 when Caldwell County was formed.

The Civil War interrupted young Harper's business career as well as his duties as county register and justice of the peace. In the summer of 1862 he enlisted in the Confederate Army as a private in Company H, Fifty-eighth Regiment of the North Carolina Infantry, but soon was promoted to first lieutenant. Harper fought in skirmishes with Union forces near Cumberland Gap in Tennessee, participated in raids in Kentucky, and became the captain of his company. In the summer of 1863 the Fifty-eighth North Carolina Regiment joined the Army of Tennessee at Chattanooga, and the following September Captain Harper led his troops in the Battle of Chickamauga, where over half of the regiment was killed or wounded. The Union Army pushed the Confederate forces into Georgia for the winter; during its follow-up invasion of the state in spring of 1864, Harper received a leg wound at the Battle of Resaca and was sent home to convalesce.

By the time Harper, now a major, rejoined the Fifty-eighth North Carolina Regiment in the fall of 1864, Atlanta had fallen and his regiment was stationed at Columbia, Tenn. Following his participation in the Battle of Franklin in November, the major was put in charge of captured Union prisoners, transporting 1,700 of them to Corinth, Miss., in December. By February 1865,

Union forces had pushed the Army of Tennessee into North Carolina, and in March Harper fought at the Battle of Bentonville, the last serious Confederate effort to halt the Union advance.

After the war, Harper rejoined his father in business. Not content to devote all of his time to the firm of H. Harper & Son, he became involved in railroad expansion. In 1873, Harper began rail construction from Lenoir to Hickory for the Chester and Lenoir Narrow Gauge Railroad Company. He was elected chairman of the company in 1884, and from 1893 to 1900 served as president and general manager of the reorganized line, Carolina and Northwestern Railway Company (using standard gauge rails).

In addition to retail merchandising and railroad building, Harper found time for other business and community endeavors. He was a commissioner for the town of Lenoir; director of Lenoir's Fire and Hose Company (organized in 1876), of a local building and loan association, and of the Lenoir Furniture Factory (reorganized in 1899 as the Harper Furniture Company); trustee of the North Carolina Hospital for the Insane at Morganton and of Davidson College; organizer of the Lenoir Board of Trade; president of the Green Park Improvement Company, holding a controlling interest in the summer resort at Blowing Rock; and vice-president of the Lenoir Cotton Mill. In 1893 Harper founded the Bank of Lenoir, and, from 1894 until his death, served as its president.

Harper's numerous activities did not prevent his pursuit of political and literary interests. He won election as state representative during the 1880–81 legislative session, as mayor of Lenoir in 1886, and as a delegate to the Democratic Convention of 1888 in St. Louis. In addition to financially supporting the establishment of a local library, he contributed some works of his own: "Sketch of the Fifty-Eighth Regiment North Carolina Troops" (1901), *Emma Lydia Rankin* (1908), and *Reminiscences of Caldwell County, North Carolina, in the Great War, 1861–1865* (1913).

In 1859, Harper married Ella A. Rankin, daughter of the Reverend Jessie and Ann Delight Rankin. They had two children, George Finley Harper and Ellen D. Harper Bernhardt. An active Presbyterian layman, Harper was buried in Belleview Cemetery, Lenoir.

SEE: Nancy Alexander, *Here Will I Dwell: The Story of Caldwell County* (1956); George Washington Finley Harper Papers (Southern Historical Collection, University of North Carolina Library, Chapel Hill); George Washington Finley Harper, comp., *Reminiscences of Caldwell County* (1913); "Major Harper Is Claimed by Death" (unidentified newspaper article, North Carolina Collection, University of North Carolina Library, Chapel Hill).

RICHARD A. SHRADER

Harper, James (*14 May 1799–26 Jan. 1879*), merchant and manufacturer, was the son of John Harper II (1767–1839) and Elizabeth Witherow Harper. Born on Butcher Creek in Cumberland County, Pa., he moved about 1815 with his family to Marsh Creek in Adams County a few miles from Gettysburg. He had one brother, John Witherow Harper III. James was the great-grandson of James Harper of County Antrim, Ireland, whose two (of four) sons migrated to Pennsylvania in 1762 and settled at Octoraro in Cumberland County. One of these sons, John, in 1756 married Jean McGaa who bore him seven children, one of whom was John Harper II, James's father.

James Harper settled in North Carolina for reasons of health and business. Suspecting that Harper had tuberculosis, his physician advised him to travel on horseback and to live in the open. A visit in 1827 with his kinsman Samuel Finley in Augusta County, Va., secured an invitation to call on other Finleys in Wilkesboro, N.C. The North Carolina Finleys had a chain of stores extending from Shoun's Crossroads, Tenn., to Columbia, S.C. At their invitation, Harper agreed to establish a partnership with their kinsman, John Waugh, to open a store in Burke County near Fort Grider or Tucker's Barn.

The partnership with Waugh launched Harper on a lengthy business career. The store prospered from its opening about 1827 near the crossing of the Morganton-Wilkesboro and Statesville-Watauga roads. Nearby Harper and Waugh constructed a large tannery where boots and shoes were manufactured, a smithy, a harness shop, a tailor's business, and a carriage manufactory. Later, with Samuel Patterson, Edmund Jones, and James Clarence Harper, Harper established the first cotton mill in the area. People brought cotton to the mill to have it spun into yarn for use in home looms. About 1841 Harper became sole owner of the Fairfield store, and he founded stores near Collettsville and at James Crossroads. Harper's stores bartered for animal skins, hides, herbs, brandy, apples, cotton, and gold dust. These surplus products, and Harper's yarn, were shipped by wagon to Columbia, Charleston, Fayetteville, and Petersburg and sold. In the early years, Harper obtained his store stock largely from Baltimore and Philadelphia. During the Civil War he used Confederate money to purchase large amounts of cotton and store it. When the war ended, he sold the cotton on a rising market to keep himself solvent.

Harper was public-spirited and used the wealth he acquired to benefit the community. He donated the land on which the town of Lenoir was laid out in 1841 and constructed a turnpike in 1845 from Lenoir to Watauga. He also donated land and money to help found Finley Academy in 1857 and Davenport Female College in 1858. In 1852 Harper organized the First Presbyterian Church in Lenoir. He served as postmaster at Fairfield and later for many years at Lenoir, as well as a justice of the peace.

In 1833 Harper married Caroline Ellen Finley (1808–67), daughter of Samuel and Mary Tate Finley of Augusta County, Va. They were the parents of five children: George Washington, Mary E., Cornelia, Samuel, and John (who died in childhood). George became a major in the Fifty-eighth North Carolina Regiment and wrote its history. Samuel served as a clerk to General Albert Potts Hill. For his family Harper constructed Fairfield, named after his former home near Gettysburg.

People who knew Harper commended his kindness to his slaves, his support of temperance, his abstinence from tobacco, his hospitality and generosity, and his quiet dignity. He was buried in the First Presbyterian Church cemetery, Lenoir.

SEE: Nancy Alexander, *Here Will I Dwell: The Story of Caldwell County* (1956); James C. Harper, Sr., to the author (letter, 2 Oct. 1976); Harper Family Scrapbook (in possession of James C. Harper, Sr., Lenoir); Portrait of James Harper (Photograph File, North Carolina Collection, University of North Carolina Library, Chapel Hill).

JOHN L. BELL, JR.

Harper, James Clarence (*6 Dec. 1819–8 Jan. 1890*), surveyor, manufacturer, and congressman, was born in Cumberland County, Pa., the son of John Witherow Harper III, whose grandfather had emigrated to America from Ireland, and Eliza Love Horner Harper. James Clarence was one of six children; the others were Jane, Elizabeth, Mary Ann, Alexander, and Margaret. In 1831 Harper moved with his family to Darke County, Ohio, where he was educated in the common schools. At the invitation of his uncle, James Harper, young James Clarence Harper moved from Ohio to Caldwell County, N.C., which became his permanent home.

Before the Civil War, Harper's major activities centered on his surveying and business ventures. In 1841, he laid out and surveyed the town of Lenoir. In 1846–47 he surveyed the turnpike from Lenoir to Blowing Rock and helped to found the turnpike company; in 1856, he became the company's president after securing a majority of the stock. On or near his farm on the Yadkin River at Patterson (seven miles from Lenoir), Harper initiated numerous enterprises in the 1850s. He built a tannery, a gristmill, cotton and woolen mills which manufactured sizing and yarn, an oil mill, an icehouse, a saw mill, a paper mill, a blacksmith shop, and a mercantile house. He farmed and logged, and initiated banking by paying drafts written on him for credit balances. By 1855, Harper had a net worth of at least $38,000.

Harper was also committed to public service. In addition to holding several local offices, he entered the state militia as a private in 1861. He was defeated at a muster for colonel in October of that year, and his poor health prevented his active service during the Civil War. In 1865 and 1866 he served in the North Carolina House of Commons. In 1870, after Plato Durham declined to run for Congress on the Conservative ticket, Harper was nominated and won the election. He served in the Forty-second Congress, although poor health and a natural reticence minimized his role. Harper introduced only two bills, both private, and he made only one prepared speech, to oppose the Civil Rights Bill of 1872. For many years he served on the board of directors of the Western North Carolina Hospital at Morganton and assisted in the construction of the buildings. Also Harper was a longtime trustee of the Davenport Female College in Lenoir, was active in the Western North Carolina Conference of the Methodist church, and was one of the founders of the Yadkin Valley High School in 1852.

On 12 Sept. 1843 Harper married Louisa C. McDowell of Caldwell County, the granddaughter of Major Charles Gordon and the great-granddaughter of General William Lenoir. They had three children: Emma (d. 16 Oct. 1922); John Witherow, who was killed at the Battle of Southwest Creek near Kinston in 1865; and an infant son who died in 1873. Emma married Colonel Clinton A. Cilley of the Union Army who commanded the Freedmen's Bureau in the western district of North Carolina. They were the parents of three sons: Lenoir, a banker in Hickory; John, a technician and machinist in Hickory; and Gordon, advertising manager of the John Wanamaker store in Philadelphia. Harper was buried at Harper's Chapel in Patterson.

SEE: Nancy Alexander, *Here Will I Dwell: The Story of Caldwell County* (1956); *Biog. Dir. Am. Cong.* (1961); James C. Harper to the author (letter, 3 Sept. 1976); James C. Harper Diary, 1840–89 (Southern Historical Collection, University of North Carolina Library, Chapel Hill).

JOHN L. BELL, JR.

Harper, Robert Goodloe *(January 1765–14 Jan. 1825)*, Revolutionary soldier, congressman, and senator, was the son of Jesse and Diana Goodloe Harper. Jesse Harper grew up in Caroline County, Va., and was originally a cabinetmaker by trade. In 1755, he purchased 100 acres of land in St. George Parish, Spotsylvania County, took up residence there soon afterwards, and married Diana Goodloe. In 1768, the Harpers sold their farm in Spotsylvania County and the following year moved to Granville County, N.C., with their four-year-old son Robert Goodloe. His mother taught him to read and write, and at age ten he began attending school in the neighborhood. Harper was fifteen when Lord Cornwallis invaded North Carolina, following the defeat of General Horatio Gates at Camden. Against the wishes of his parents, he left school and joined a volunteer cavalry unit which served under General Nathanael Greene until the enemy had left the state. This military experience had a profound impact on young Harper; he always yearned for a military career and made several attempts to get a "proper" commission.

He spent most of 1783 on a surveying tour in Tennessee and Kentucky, accompanied by John Henderson, where he acquired a taste for land speculation and a habit of indebtedness. The latter plagued him for the rest of his life. After six months of idleness following his surveying venture, Harper was persuaded to attend college and in the summer of 1784, at age nineteen, enrolled at Princeton. Governor Richard Dobbs Spaight of North Carolina advanced him a sum of money, and Princeton President John Witherspoon gave him a teaching position, which enabled him to graduate in September 1785. At this point Harper left North Carolina, never to return except for an occasional visit. Both of his parents died in 1788. Alone and penniless he took up residence in Charleston, S.C., in November 1785.

Aided by former friends at Princeton, Harper found employment teaching in a large grammar school in Charleston owned by a Mr. Thompson. Through Benjamin Hawkins of North Carolina, Harper was introduced to several prominent men in Charleston who provided him the opportunity to study law with Edward Rutledge. One year after his arrival, he was admitted to the bar. In 1787, he began to practice in the small community of Cambridge in Abbeville County, located in the extreme southwestern corner of the state in the district known as Ninety-Six. Although constantly employed, his clients could pay only very small fees or neglected to pay at all. In the fall of 1789 he won a seat in the state legislature, but served only two months in the latter part of the 1794 session.

From 1789 to 1794, Harper's major occupation was land speculation, acting as agent for others as well as for himself while residing in Charleston. In the summer of 1794, he returned to Ninety-Six, where he still owned property, and successfully ran for Congress. Because his term would not begin until the fall of 1795, he went back to Charleston and won the congressional seat for Orangeburg District recently vacated by the death of Alexander Gillon. This enabled him to go to Philadelphia in 1794 where he hoped to dispose of numerous tracts of land while serving out the remainder of Gillon's term. Sour land deals and shaky partners resulted in the accumulation of more indebtedness. Nevertheless, on 9 Feb. 1795 he took his seat in Congress as a representative of the district of Ninety-Six and served until 4 Mar. 1801.

There is still some controversy about Harper's changing political views in 1794–95. He has been accused of being strongly pro-French; in fact, he served as vice-president of the Jacobin Club of Charleston at the time of his election to Congress in 1794. Soon after his arrival in Philadelphia, however, he discovered that the great and powerful men were on the other side of the political fence. He supposedly immediately shifted his position: he supported the Jay Treaty in 1795, favored Adams or Pinckney over Jefferson for the presidency in 1796, and displayed strong pro-British sentiments. In any event, Harper became an ardent Federalist; he was the most frequent and loquacious debater in the party, and served as chairman of the powerful Ways and Means Committee in Congress and as leader of the Southern Federalists. In 1797, his *Observations on the Dispute Between the United States and France* attracted much attention at home and abroad. His anti-French attitude grew with his importance, and he became belligerent and less tolerant of those who disagreed with him. He was once accused of being the most insolent man in Congress. In 1798, he was one of the strongest supporters of the Alien and Sedition Laws, urged limitation of citizenship to the native-born, and was eager for war with France.

In the meantime, Harper had been introduced to the wealthy and prestigious Carroll family in Maryland and had developed a friendship with James McHenry, the secretary of war, also from Maryland, who urged him to settle there. Despite his reelection to Congress in 1798 by his South Carolina constituents, in July 1799 Harper opened a law office in Baltimore and two years later married Catherine Carroll, daughter of Charles Carroll of Carrollton, over his vigorous opposition. It was Harper's indebtedness rather than his lukewarm Protestantism that Carroll objected to. Harper established a sound reputation as a lawyer and built up a fine estate, Oakland, on the Falls Road in northern Baltimore, which became a social mecca. Charles Warren, in his *History of the American Bar*, wrote: "The lawyer whose name appears in more cases than any other member of the bar between 1800 and 1825 also came from Maryland—Robert Goodloe Harper—able in mercantile cases, a thorough lawyer and a felicitous and graceful orator."

At the beginning of the War of 1812, he was antiwar and was labeled a "Blue Light Federalist." However, when the British attacked Baltimore in 1814, he commanded troops in the crucial North Point engagement and was given a commission as major general. Harper was elected to the U.S. Senate in March 1815, but did not take his seat until January 1816; he resigned the following December on the ground that business affairs prevented him from serving longer. A Federalist candidate for vice-president in 1816, he received the votes of Delaware electors that year and one electoral vote in 1820. In 1825, Harper decided to reenter politics but died shortly after his announcement that he would run for Congress in the autumn of 1826.

In his last years Harper's greatest interest was the Negro problem. In 1800, he opposed emancipation but favored abolition of the slave trade. Later he became involved in projects calling for the colonization of blacks outside the United States. He was one of the original members of the American Colonization Society, and was influential in the selection of Africa as the place and Liberia and Monrovia as names for the colony and its capital.

Harper died suddenly and was given a military funeral in Baltimore. He was originally interred in the family burial ground on his estate, Oakland, but his remains were later moved to Greenwood Cemetery, Baltimore. He was survived by his wife and two children. A portrait of him is owned by the Maryland Historical Society.

SEE: Annapolis *Maryland Gazette*, 20 Jan. 1825; Baltimore *American and Daily Advertiser*, 15 Jan. 1825; *Biog. Dir. Am. Cong.* (1971); Joseph W. Cox, *Champion of Southern Federalism, Robert Goodloe Harper of South Carolina* (1972); W. A. Crozier, *Spotsylvania County Records, 1721–1800* (1955); Robert Goodloe Harper, autobiography (Harper-Pennington Papers, Maryland Historical Society Archives, Baltimore); U. B. Phillips, "The South Carolina Federalists," *American Historical Review* 14 (1909); C. W. Sommerville, *Robert Goodloe Harper* (1899).

G. MELVIN HERNDON

Harrar, Ellwood Scott, Jr. *(18 Jan. 1905–5 Feb. 1975)*, wood technologist and educator, was born in Pittsburgh, Pa., the son of Ellwood Scott and Lucetta Elsie Sterner Harrar, both former residents of Allentown, Pa. His father, an engineer, was the son of George Washington and Lillian E. Osterstock Harrar, and a grandson of George Harrar who came from England in the early 1800s and settled in Virginia. The family moved to Painesville, Ohio, later to Ashtabula, and then to Youngstown. Young Harrar began his elementary education in Ashtabula and continued in nearby Poland. He was graduated from South High School in Youngstown and in the fall of 1922, at age seventeen, entered Oberlin College. After one and one-half years, he transferred to the New York State College of Forestry at Syracuse University, from which he received the B.S. degree in 1927. At Syracuse (1926–28) he was an assistant in dendrology and wood technology, and completed the requirements for the M.S. degree.

The following fall Harrar went to the College of Forestry of the University of Seattle, Washington, where for three years he was an instructor in forest products and, subsequently, for three years assistant professor. At commencement exercises in June 1936, he was awarded the Ph.D. degree in forestry at the New York State College of Forestry. That summer he became an original faculty member of the new School of Forestry of Duke University. He served first as associate professor of wood science, then as professor and as dean of the School of Forestry from 1957 to 1967. Retiring from the deanship, he continued as a James B. Duke Professor of Wood Science until his full retirement in August 1974 at age sixty-nine.

Harrar was a member of many professional and civic groups. In 1928 he joined the Society of American Foresters, where he became a Senior Member (1935) and a Fellow (1965), and served as a member of the Committee on Tree Nomenclature and as onetime vice-chairman of the Appalachian Section. He was also a member of the International Society of Wood Anatomists, Forest Products Research Society, North Carolina Forestry Council, American Forestry Association, Forest Farmers Association, Society of Wood Science and Technology, and International Society of Tropical Foresters. Syracuse University awarded him the honorary doctor of science degree in 1961.

In addition to his continuous teaching responsibilities, Harrar was a consultant to the Southeastern Procurement Division, Corps of Engineers, U.S. Army; a consultant on veneers and plywood to the U.S. Army Corps of Engineers; a project coordinator for the Civilian Conservation Corps, state of New Jersey; and a consultant for the Crop Division, Biological Laboratories, U.S. Army, Fort Detrick, Md. He was also a member of

President Eisenhower's Bipartisan Committee for Increased Use of Agricultural Products; of the Governor's Advisory Committee for Forestry in North Carolina; and of the Advisory Committee for the Bent Creek Research Center, U.S. Forest Service, Southeastern Forest Experiment Station, Asheville. In 1966, he was cited by the governor for his outstanding contribution to forestry in North Carolina.

On leave from Duke University in 1942–45, Harrar served as chief administrative engineer of the Airplane Division, Curtiss-Wright Corporation, Louisville, Ky. Earlier he was forester of the Society for the Protection of New Hampshire Forests (1928) and research associate of the West Coast Lumbermen's Association, Seattle, Wash. (summers, 1929, 1930).

Through his multiple writings, Harrar made significant contributions to the study of wood science and technology. He was either author or coauthor of the "Douglas Fir Use Book" (1930), "Technology of Papermaking Fibers" (1936), *Textbook of Dendrology* (1936 and subsequent editions), *Guide to Southern Trees* (1946; 2d ed., 1962), seven volumes in *Hough's Encyclopedia of American Woods*, *Forest Dendrology* (1935), more than sixty-five new or revised articles on timber trees of the world in the *Encyclopaedia Britannica*, and later adviser in dendrology and forestry to the *Encyclopedia Americana*. He also wrote numerous articles, research papers, and reviews for technical, professional, and scientific journals in this country and abroad.

Harrar was particularly recognized as an expert on the anatomical, physical, and chemical properties of wood; and on woods of temperate and tropical America, and of Queensland, Australia. While dean of the School of Forestry at Duke University he conceived and put into operation a cooperative program involving Duke and more than sixty liberal arts and sciences colleges in the United States. In this program a student spent three years in preforestry and liberal arts in the cooperating school, then two years in professional forestry study at Duke, receiving a bachelor of forestry degree from his or her original college and a master of forestry degree from Duke.

Further, during his tenure as dean, the faculty of the School of Forestry doubled, and programs of forest business management and of forest production were added to the curriculum. With the financial support of the Ford and Rockefeller foundations, Harrar organized and implemented a five-day Tropical Forestry Symposium at Duke attended by twenty-three internationally known tropical foresters from a dozen countries and three major tropical areas. They met to identify and define, from a world point of view, the chief obstacles to the development of sound policies and practices in tropical forestry.

Among his unique contributions to the field of wood science, Harrar collected over forty years' examples of various woods from the world's forested areas. The collection of more than 5,000 specimens was placed, with Duke University's permission, in the DuPont Winterthur Museum, Winterthur, Del., where it can be used in scientific studies by wood scientists from all parts of the world.

For many years Harrar had a hobby of geology. After his retirement from all duties at Duke, he enrolled in classes in gemology at The University of North Carolina at Chapel Hill. He cut and polished several stones, especially prized by himself and his family.

On 10 Sept. 1927, Harrar married Marion Green of Cleveland, Ohio; they had two daughters, Helen Joanne and Carolyn (Mrs. James Michael Wolfe). Early in life he was a Baptist, but later joined a Presbyterian church with his family. He died in Durham and, by his request, his ashes were scattered over his beloved Duke Forest.

SEE: *American Men and Women of Science: The Physical and Biological Sciences* (1967); *Duke Alumni Register* 61 (April 1975); *Leaders in Education* (1971); *Nat. Cyc. Am. Biog.*, vol. J (1964); Records, Office of Information Services, Duke University, Durham; *Who's Who in America* (1974–75); *Who's Who in American Education: Presidents and Deans of American Colleges and Universities* (1967); *Who's Who in the South and Southwest* (1969–70).

C. SYLVESTER GREEN

Harrell, Costen Jordan (*12 Feb. 1885–30 Nov. 1971*), Methodist bishop, was born in Holly Grove, Gates County, the son of Samuel Isaac and Ira Costen Harrell. He was educated at Trinity College (now Duke University) and the School of Theology, Vanderbilt University. In 1910, he joined the North Carolina Conference of the Methodist Episcopal Church, South, and held pastorates in Raleigh, Durham, and Wilson. Later he served the First Methodist Church, Atlanta; Epworth Methodist Church, Norfolk; Monumental Methodist Church, Richmond; and West End Methodist Church, Nashville. He was ordained a deacon by Bishop Elijah Embree Hoss and an elder by Bishop Richard Green Waterhouse.

Following election to the episcopacy of the Methodist church in 1944 (the Methodist Episcopal Church, the Methodist Episcopal Church, South, and the Methodist Protestant Church united to form the Methodist church on 25 Apr. 1939 in Kansas City), Harrell served as bishop of the Birmingham Area for four years. In 1948, he was assigned to the Charlotte Area and served eight years, presiding over the sessions of the Western North Carolina Annual Conference between 1948 and 1955. (His predecessor in the Charlotte Area was Bishop Clare Purcell; his successor was Bishop Nolan Bailey Harmon.) In 1956, Harrell retired from the episcopacy and during the next thirteen years was a visiting professor at the Chandler School of Theology, Emory University. During that period he resided in Decatur, Ga.

Harrell was the author of *Walking with God* (1928), *Friends of God* (1931), *The Gospel in Homespun* (1946), *The Local Church in Methodism* (1952), *Stewardship and the Tithe* (1953), *The Unfolding Glory* (1958), *Christian Affirmations* (1961), *The Wonders of His Grace* (1966), and other books, as well as a contributor to several religious periodicals. He was the recipient of several honorary doctorates. As a special project, the Western North Carolina Conference of the Methodist Church built the Costen J. Harrell Church in a suburb of Havana, Cuba.

In 1917, Harrell married Amy Patton Walden; they had one son, Julius Walden, who died in his youth. Bishop Harrell was buried in Mount Olivet Cemetery, Nashville, Tenn.

SEE: E. T. Clark, *Methodism in Western North Carolina* (1966); Greensboro *North Carolina Christian Advocate*, 16 Dec. 1971; Costen J. Harrell, *The Wonders of His Grace* (1966); Joseph Mitchell, *Episcopal Elections in the Southeastern Jurisdiction of the United Methodist Church* (1971); John H. Ness, ed., *Methodist History*, vol. 7 (1968); William W. Sweet and Umphrey Lee, *A Short History of Methodism* (1956); *Who's Who in the South and Southwest* (1950).

GRADY L. E. CARROLL

Harrell, John (21 Oct. 1806–8 Dec. 1876), minister, educator, and Methodist missionary to the Indian Territory, was born in Perquimans County. He was probably the son of John Harrell, the only member of this family listed in the 1800 census of the county. Young Harrell was licensed to preach in 1823 and admitted to the Tennessee Conference six years later. When the Missouri Conference of the Methodist church was unable to supply ministers to the Arkansas District in 1831, Bishop Robert P. Roberts journeyed to the Tennessee Conference at Paris, Tenn., and recruited eight men including Harrell. Harrell ministered on the western border of Arkansas, primarily directing his energies to mission work among newly arrived tribes in the Indian Territory but also establishing and serving as pastor of new churches in Arkansas. In 1832, he created the first circuit among the Cherokee Nation. He became Arkansas' first delegate to a General Conference, when he attended sessions at Baltimore in 1836. In the same year he served the Washington County circuit in Arkansas as a pastor and had a part in establishing the First Methodist Church of Fayetteville, Ark. In 1837 the Cherokee and Creek mission work was placed under the Fayetteville District, of which Harrell was presiding elder.

His role as an Arkansas educator apparently began with the appointment as secretary to the Female Academy at Fayetteville in 1837. Later he served on the Board of Visitors for the Far West Seminary of Fayetteville (1844), the first degree-granting institution in Arkansas. His mission work among the newly transplanted tribes in Oklahoma focused on education also. During the fifteen years preceding the Civil War, Harrell had a part in directing the Fort Coffee Academy which served the Northern Choctaws. The Methodist church secured the fort after the army abandoned it to return its forces to Fort Smith. In 1845, one hundred Indian students boarded at the school. A few miles away the church established New Hope Seminary, a boarding school for girls. These schools, founded by two Northern antislavery ministers, were left to Harrell's supervision after the Methodist church divided over the slavery question in 1845. A high school for Creek Indians at Asbury Mission (Eufaula, Okla.) was founded in 1882 and posthumously dedicated to the missionary educator as Harrell Institute.

Before the Civil War Harrell helped found numerous Methodist churches in Arkansas, including those at Fayetteville, Van Buren, and Fort Smith. He was pastor of the Little Rock Methodist Church during 1848–49. He held many positions of trust in the church, including that of delegate to the General Conference of 1845 which created the Methodist Episcopal Church, South, presiding elder of the various districts of the Indian Mission Conference, and superintendent of that conference.

Harrell's influence touched Arkansas history at various points. During the Civil War he served one brief term in the state's General Assembly and was elected speaker of the house. Afterwards he spent three years as chaplain in the Confederate Army. When Isaac Parker of Fort Smith, the famous hanging judge, sentenced dozens of men to the gallows, Harrell often prayed with the victims on the scaffold.

His ministry to the Indian Territory began early in his career, but in 1850 he transferred his official connection to the Indian Mission Conference and spent the next twenty-six years in the saddle ministering to mission churches and schools. He won the respect of the Indian peoples and, according to his obituary in *The Van Buren Press*, "was probably better and more generally known in the Indian Territory than any white man" of that era. He died of pneumonia after a brief illness at Vinita, Indian Territory, and was buried at Old Asbury Mission, Eufaula. In 1832, Harrell married Eliza Williams in Washington County, Ark. She died in the same month as he.

SEE: James A. Anderson, *Centennial History of Arkansas Methodism* (1935); Deane G. Carter, "Some Historical Notes on Far West Seminary," *Arkansas Historical Quarterly* 29 (1970); *DAB*, vol. 4 (1960); Grant Foreman, *The Biography of an Oklahoma Town* (n.d.); Horace Jewell, *History of Methodism in Arkansas* (1892 [portrait]); John B. McFerrin, *History of Methodism in Tennessee* (1873); William Brown Morrison, *Military Posts and Camps in Oklahoma* (1936); *The Van Buren Press*, 19 Dec. 1876; Walter N. Vernon, *Methodism in Arkansas, 1816–1976* (1976).

RICHARD L. NISWONGER

Harrell, William Bernard (17 Dec. 1823–25 Nov. 1906), songwriter, physician, and preacher, wrote the seven quatrains of "Ho! for Carolina!" which at one time rivaled William Gaston's "The Old North State" as a North Carolina anthem. The story goes that in the opening months of the Civil War, a train carrying troops to the Virginia battlefields made a stop at Wilson. A young Georgian stuck his head from the train window and shouted to the crowd gathered there, "Hurrah for old North Carolina! My folks were all from North Carolina, and a grand old state she is. Hurrah! Hurrah!" As Harrell walked home from the railroad platform, the Georgian's words kept recurring to him. He soon wrote down the well-known lines with its chorus beginning, "Ho! for Carolina! that's the land for me; / In her happy borders roam the brave and free," and his wife composed music to fit them. Immediately the song gained popularity and was sung throughout the state. Harrell's many lyrics, hymns, and patriotic verses have never been collected.

Though his paternal line came from Gates County, Harrell was born in Suffolk, Va., the younger of two surviving sons of James and Martha McGuire Harrell. He grew up in North Carolina, but later attended the Norfolk schools and Randolph-Macon Academy in Boydton, Va. In 1849, he was graduated from the School of Medicine of the University of Maryland. He was married in 1851 to Anne Judson Battle, daughter of Amos J. Battle of Edgecombe County, one of the first trustees of Wake Forest College. In 1863–64 he was acting assistant surgeon and served as an inspector of hospitals at the Camp of Instruction in Dublin, Va. On 1 May 1865, at Staunton, Va., he was paroled from his post as medical examiner on the Board of Conscript Surgeons and allowed to return home.

During an 1868 revival in Snow Hill, Harrell entered the ministry of the Baptist church and became the first pastor of the church there. Though he gave up the practice of medicine, he continued to teach in small schools both before and after his call to the pulpit. At various times he held pastorates in Stanly County, Smithfield, Clayton, Selma, Durham, Hillsborough, Graham, Winston, and Monroe. He moved to Dunn about 1888, and in 1893 he had charge of three churches of the Cedar Creek Association.

Harrell and his wife, who died three days before he did, were buried in Greenwood Cemetery, Dunn. The oldest of his four sons and seven daughters was Eugene G. Harrell, an educator. Five children survived their parents: Mabel (Mrs. J. L. Hines); Rosa (Mrs.

Stoller); Albert B. Harrell, a Baptist preacher; William Payton Harrell; and Ida Caroline (Mrs. Hardy Horne), the author of two books of poems.

SEE: *Biblical Recorder*, 19 Dec. 1906; Clipping file, North Carolina Collection (University of North Carolina Library, Chapel Hill); *Greensboro Daily News*, 9 Apr. 1939; *North Carolina Teacher* 10 (March 1893); Raleigh *News and Observer*, 27 Oct. 1946; *State Magazine* 28 (20 Feb. 1960).

RICHARD WALSER

Harrelson, John William (28 June 1885–12 Mar. 1955), educator and soldier, was born in the Double Shoals Community of Cleveland County, the son of John H. and Ellen Williams Harrelson. His father was a tenant farmer. In 1905, young Harrelson entered the North Carolina College of Agriculture and Mechanic Arts (North Carolina State University at Raleigh) to study textiles. His interest soon turned to mechanical engineering, however, and he received his bachelor's degree in that field in 1909, graduating first in a class of sixty-three.

Although he had passed a competitive examination for a regular army commission, Harrelson chose instead to stay at his alma mater as an instructor in the Mathematics Department. By 1921, he had become a full professor. He was granted a leave of absence from State in 1929, when Governor O. Max Gardner appointed him director of the State Department of Conservation and Development. Harrelson returned to North Carolina State in 1933, and after a year as head of the Mathematics Department he was appointed dean of administration (title changed to chancellor in 1945) under the Consolidated University System. He was the first State alumnus to head his alma mater. During his administration, there was tremendous growth in the teaching, research, and extension programs of the university. Twenty-one major buildings were added to the campus, the faculty increased by four times, and the student body tripled in size. When he retired as chancellor in 1953, Harrelson was appointed college archivist, a position he held until his death. He received an honorary doctor of laws degree from Wake Forest College (1941) and an honorary doctor of education degree from North Carolina State (1954).

Harrelson's military career spanned four decades and included two periods of active service. He was a lieutenant in the Coast Artillery, North Carolina National Guard, when the United States entered World War I in April 1917; in July his unit was mustered into service. By the summer of 1918, he had been promoted to major and was serving in the personnel branch of the War Department's General Staff in Washington, D.C. Shortly after receiving his discharge in August 1919, Harrelson was commissioned a lieutenant colonel in the Coast Artillery Reserve. He was promoted to colonel in 1923. In 1927, he was transferred to the Field Artillery Reserve and assigned to the 316th Field Artillery Regiment, 81st Division. In 1934, he was appointed North Carolina's civilian aide to the secretary of war, a post of responsibility in handling enrollment for the Citizens Military Training Corps. During World War II he served as deputy chief of the army's Specialized Training Program, in the Fourth Service Command, with headquarters in Atlanta. At the time of his death, he was a colonel in the U.S. Army Reserve.

In 1935 Harrelson married Elizabeth Connor; they had no children. He was active in the civic, social, and religious life of Raleigh and was a member of a number of honorary, professional, and social fraternities. He died while preparing to take part in ceremonies dedicating North Carolina State's new library, and was buried in Oakwood Cemetery, Raleigh.

On 7 Mar. 1962, North Carolina State dedicated Harrelson Hall to honor the memory of its former chancellor. The unique, round classroom building has joined the Memorial Tower as one of the familiar landmarks on the State campus. By the terms of his will, Harrelson's entire estate was to be given to North Carolina State upon the death of his wife. The will stipulated that "all property, securities, bonds and monies" were to be properly invested and that a portion of the income was to be used by the university for lectures, books, works of art, and appropriate markers for buildings named for individuals. The Harrelson Lectures series was inaugurated on 7 Mar. 1962, with the U.S. ambassador to the United Nations, Adlai E. Stevenson, as speaker.

SEE: "Faculty and Staff News Releases and Clippings, John W. Harrelson" (Office of Information Services, North Carolina State University, Raleigh); John William Harrelson Papers (North Carolina State University Archives, Raleigh); David A. Lockmiller, *History of the North Carolina State College, 1889–1939* (1939); *Who Was Who in America*, vol. 3 (1960).

MAURICE S. TOLER

Harrington, Henry William (*12 May 1747–31 Mar. 1809*), brigadier general in the American Revolution, legislator, and planter, was born in London. He emigrated first to Jamaica, but after a short time moved to South Carolina where he settled on the Pee Dee River across the river from Cheraw and later at Welch Neck. He was interested in education and other improvements and soon became active in church and civic affairs, serving as vestryman and warden of St. David's Parish at Cheraw Hill, as a member of the first grand jury of the county, and later as deputy clerk of court. A prominent Whig, Harrington in August 1775 was commissioned captain of a volunteer company of foot and named chairman of the Committee of Observation for St. David's. His duties involved reporting on the state of the colonial militia, measures of defense, the powers to be granted the Committee of Safety, and the manufacture of saltpeter for the colony. In March 1776, when the Provincial Congress dissolved the king's Privy Council for a Legislative Council, Harrington was elected sheriff for the Cheraw District. In June of that year he marched his company of foot to Haddrell's Point near Charles Town to take part in the campaign against Sir Henry Clinton, but saw no action; however, shortly thereafter he exercised his office of sheriff by receiving prisoners to be confined in the Cheraw District jail.

On 31 July 1776, at age twenty-nine, Captain Harrington married Rosanna, daughter of Rosanna Piper and Major James Auld. Rosanna Piper, the daughter of an Episcopal clergyman, the Reverend Michael Piper, had married, first, Howes Goldsborough, and, second, James Auld, a native of the Eastern Shore of Maryland and a lawyer. James and Rosanna settled in Anson County, N.C. After Harrington's marriage he left South Carolina to take up residence in that county on the east side of the Pee Dee a few miles from the border of the two colonies. In 1779 Richmond County was formed from part of Anson County, and on 25 November of the same year Harrington was commissioned a colonel with command of that county's militia. The following spring he took part in the defense of the coast of South Carolina under the command of General Benjamin Lincoln, but, before the city of Charles Town fell in May 1780, he had returned to North Carolina to sit in the Assembly. Harrington had left Charles Town "with the advice and unanimous consent of the Lieut-Governor and Council, and by General Lincoln's order" to carry a request for the aid of the North Carolina militia, according to a letter he wrote to his wife from Georgetown on 30 Apr. 1780.

In June 1780, he was promoted to brigadier general of the Salisbury District in the absence of General Griffith Rutherford. This was a pro tem appointment, and the Board of War instructed him to use his best judgment until an older and more experienced officer could be named. Harrington's headquarters were in the area of Cross Creek (Fayetteville), and his principal mission was the procurement of provisions as well as the protection of supplies. He was recommended to General Horatio Gates as "a very intelligent gentleman, who is well acquainted with this part of the country and with particular circumstances relating to the enemy and to us." Harrington held this command only five months. The General Assembly named Colonel William Lee Davidson to command the Salisbury District with the rank of brigadier general. Harrington received this news in late September with keen disappointment. He had excellent recommendations but western interests had prevailed in the Assembly. Determined to resign, he resolved, however, to remain with his troops because of news of an enemy advance towards his position. By November 1780 he wrote the Board of War that "the time I waited for is now arrived, and I have the happiness to know that the last of our foe has been obliged to retreat, and that by our own exertions." He was content to relinquish his command, saying, "so this my country is but faithfully served, it is equal to me whether it be by me or by another." He enclosed his commission and stated that he would remain at his post until relieved.

During these final weeks of his service Harrington, from evidence supplied in letters from Francis Marion and General William Smallwood to General Gates, was reluctant to commit his troops until his successor had arrived. Marion said he had asked him "to spare me his horse to endeavor to remove the post at King's Tree . . . but from what I know of the General I do not expect he will part with them," adding that "Harrington has not done any service with the troops he commands." Marion was piqued because Harrington had written to Gates regarding a regiment under his command and he did not believe that Gates had intended that he should serve under Harrington. General Smallwood proposed certain military positions, with Harrington's force drawn up midway between the Pee Dee and the continental encampment for the purpose "of cooperating with us occasionally, suppressing the Tories, or covering such supplies as might be necessarily drawn from the settlements."

Harrington submitted his resignation on 3 Nov. 1780; however, General Gates wished him to remain in the army. He had rendered efficient and honorable service, but he was compelled to decline. He wrote: "I would, with pleasure, continue to serve my country and think myself honored by your orders, but a brigadier's commission, without either District or Brigade, . . . cannot with honor be held. After what the Assembly have done in favor of another, it would appear like begging both commission and brigade; that in justice to myself I

cannot think, even for a single moment, of altering my resolution."

Returning home, he sat in the General Assembly in January 1781. He had suffered great personal hardships during the campaigns. His home near Hailey's Ferry was plunderd by the British and livestock as well as slaves were seized. Mrs. Harrington and her children sought refuge with friends in South Carolina. In July 1780 Harrington had requested a flag of truce for Colonel John Donaldson and Lieutenant Reuben Wilkinson to enter Charles Town and escort his wife and family home. She returned, but the fall of Camden to the enemy forced her to flee again, this time to Maryland. En route her party was attacked by the infamous Tory, Captain John Leggett, and her household goods were stolen or destroyed. Lost in this raid were the general's personal papers and much of his library. But the greater loss was that of a baby daughter, Harriet, who died from the rigors of the journey. Mrs. Harrington returned to her father's home in Anson County while her brothers went in pursuit of Leggett and his band. They could not overtake them and none of her property was found.

After the war Harrington brought suit for the return of a Negro servant taken in the raid at Hailey's Ferry. This servant then belonged to a Captain Campbell, a former British officer who settled on the Pee Dee. He had been sent to Jamaica but Captain Campbell had him returned to Harrington. The general also sued and obtained judgment against Leggett, who had transferred title to his lands to another to avoid confiscation. The land escheated to the state and Harrington was given title. When he learned of the poverty of Leggett's daughters, he gave them title to their land. Thus, on Harrington's death the Raleigh *Register* and the Raleigh *Star* observed that "the nicest sense of honor and strictest principles of justice marked every transaction of his life."

The Harringtons left the vicinity of Hailey's Ferry when peace returned and moved farther down the river. He represented Richmond County in the Assembly and in the senate at Hillsborough in 1783 and at New Bern in 1785. In 1787, he was nominated as a delegate to Congress but was defeated. He was appointed trustee of Salisbury Academy in 1784 and a trustee of The University of North Carolina in 1789, serving in that position until 1795. In 1791, he was one of the commissioners to fix the seat of government. He had contributed his services and part of his personal fortune to the cause of defense and continued to devote his time to his state and to his county, although he preferred the peaceful life of a planter. Harrington has been called Richmond County's leading citizen after the Revolution, when he held various positions such as chairman of the county court, administrator of estates, and bondsman for guardians, administrators, and officials. He owned large tracts of land and was a knowledgeable planter who earned the titles of "The First Farmer in the State" and the "Father of Export Cotton in North Carolina."

Nine children were born to Rosanna and Henry William Harrington, four dying in infancy. The oldest son, named for his father, served in the navy during the War of 1812 and later was prominent in the legislature. Another son, James Auld Harrington, was graduated from The University of North Carolina in 1808 and became a planter in South Carolina.

General Harrington died at home at age sixty-two and was buried in Wolf Pit Township, Richmond County, in the family graveyard overlooking the Pee

Dee River. A marble slab marks his grave and etched upon it are the words: "Here lies one who united in himself the bold achievements of the statesman and patriot with the mild virtues of social life, the kind neighbor, the tender husband and the fond parent."

SEE: Samuel A. Ashe, ed., *Biographical History of North Carolina*, vol. 4 (1906); *Charlotte Observer*, 2 Mar. 1941; Walter Clark, ed., *State Records of North Carolina*, vols. 13–15, 24–25 (1896–1906); Alexander Gregg, *History of the Old Cheraws* (1867); Alice Keith, ed., *John Gray Blount Papers*, vol. 1 (1952).

HENRY A. ROBERTSON, JR.

Harriot (Hariot or Harriott), Thomas (*1560–2 July 1621*), explorer, navigational expert, mathematician, scientist, and astronomer, participated in Sir Walter Raleigh's early expeditions to America. His parentage or ancestry are unknown. Records of his matriculation at Oxford University show him to have been born and reared in Oxford, England, and to be of plebeian stock. He entered St. Mary's Hall (a subsidiary of Oriel College) on 20 Dec. 1577, at age seventeen, and was graduated with a bachelor of arts at the Easter Convocation of 1580. Acquisition of this degree gave Harriot the right to call himself "Master Harriot," a title he carefully used for the rest of his life.

Shortly after leaving the university, Harriot entered the household of Walter Raleigh, where, according to Richard Hakluyt, he not only instructed Raleigh in the mathematics of navigation but also conducted instructional programs for Raleigh's sea captains, that they might "very profitably unite theory with practice" in their explorations. This teaching (resulting in a navigational text called the *Arcticon*, which has not survived) further stimulated young Raleigh to follow in the footsteps of his half brother, Sir Humphrey Gilbert, in attempting to explore and colonize the New World.

On Gilbert's death in 1583, Raleigh purchased a new ship, renamed it the *Bark Ralegh*, and began to prepare for an exploratory visit to America to seek a site for colonization. Helping to plan this expedition was Thomas Harriot working closely with two other young sea captains in Raleigh's household, Philip Amadas and Arthur Barlowe. Raleigh hoped to command the 1584 voyage himself, but he was by this time a courtier rising in the eyes of Queen Elizabeth and she would not permit him to accept the danger of an ocean crossing where Sir Francis Drake and the Spaniards were still fighting. Possibly Harriot may have gone on this voyage. Though he is not listed among the ten names signing the report, there is some evidence that it was at this time that he learned the Algonquin language, perhaps on the return voyage with the two Indians, Manteo and Wanchese. John White is not listed either, though he later indicates that he was a member of this exploratory party. The return of the first voyage was most successful: Manteo and Wanchese made a great impression on the queen and on the court. Their friendliness and the reports of extensive economic potential in the new land appeared so favorable that the queen granted Raleigh a patent for colonizing, knighted him in January 1585, appointed him governor of the new colonies, and permitted him to name his proposed colony "Virginia" (in her honor as Virgin Queen) rather than the Indian name of Wingandacoa it had previously borne.

During the winter of 1584–85, Raleigh and Harriot made extensive preparations for a colonizing effort in Virginia. Seven ships were assembled with nearly six hundred men, half of them sailors and the other half soldiers and colonists who were prepared to spend at least a year in the New World. On 9 Apr. 1585, under the command of Sir Richard Grenville, this flotilla sailed from Plymouth. Because he could not go himself, Raleigh named Harriot as his official representative and charged him with assessing the economic potential of Virginia and reviewing the nature and inclinations of the natives. John White was assigned to help with the making of maps and to bring back drawings and sketches of the new land and its inhabitants. Both men, along with Grenville as general of the expedition, Ralph Lane as high marshall and later governor of the colony, Simon Fernándes as chief pilot of the fleet, and a number of other gentlemen who were to make up the council, sailed on the flagship, *The Tiger*.

During the long sea crossing, Harriot made a number of scientific observations. He tested the traditional and crude dead reckoning against the more accurate celestial navigation, probably using the backstaff he had developed for better observation by his sea captains. He noted the variation of the compass, measuring the magnetic north against the position of the pole star. On 19 April, ten days after leaving Plymouth, he must have observed the eclipse of the sun, though the eclipse was not total where he then was, so it could not be used for an accurate calculation of longitude as he had hoped. As the flotilla proceeded through the islands, Harriot gathered fruits and vegetables, sugar, ginger, tobacco, and pearls to be returned to Raleigh, along with White's drawings of many of the same things, as samples of the richness to be obtained by colonization.

On 26 June, after repeatedly searching navigable waters with extreme difficulty and much loss of vessels, the fleet anchored at Wococon Island, approximately where modern Ocracoke is, and began negotiating with the natives. On 3 July an expedition was sent to Roanoke Island, the site that had been chosen by the 1584 expedition for colonization, to notify the Indian chief Wingina of their arrival. On 11 July Grenville, Lane, Harriot, White, and a few others crossed to the mainland on a voyage of exploration through a number of Indian towns which took them as far as Lake Mattamuskeet, which the natives called Paquype. Within the next month the settlers had been moved to Roanoke, had unloaded their provisions, and were building a fort and houses and beginning to function like a colonial outpost. Harriot and White began in earnest to survey the land resources, and to draw for a permanent record what they could observe of the people and products of the New World.

During the whole of the year they spent at Roanoke Island, Harriot and White kept busy at their recording assignments. In addition to studying the people, they took careful notes on commercially profitable plants and mineral resources that might lead to further investment in colonial ventures. So successful was their publicity that more than two decades later, Harriot was working with Raleigh to prevent the importation of Virginia sassafras roots from glutting the market.

In his contacts with the natives, Harriot did not ignore his scientific bent. He exploited the science and technology of his day in such a way that he should undoubtedly be recognized as the first scientist of the New World—not only in his scientific study of the land and its people, but also in introducing scientific artifacts into Virginia. According to him, the native Americans were most impressed with the scientific instruments they first saw in Harriot's possession. Yet with all his frightening guns, magnets, clocks, and "wildefire works" (a compound used in warfare that was difficult to extinguish once set afire), Harriot earned the confidence and affection of the Indians, including Chief Wingina's, whereas Lane, using force to punish any observed unconformity, attracted only their hatred and distrust.

By the next spring, the new colonists were in dire straits; they badly needed the promised relief supplies, and they counted the days until the arrival of Raleigh's second-year colonists who would bring them. The Indians, too, were uneasy. On 10 June, Lane, suspecting an uprising, struck on the mainland, killing Chief Wingina. Additional search actions scattered his men and left them vulnerable to further attack. On the same day, however, Sir Francis Drake, sailing north from his battles with the Spaniards, anchored at Port Ferdinando. The next day he met with Lane, offering him one of his larger ships for reconnoitering the Chesapeake Bay area to seek a safer and more healthful colonial site. Transfer of the vessel had just begun when, on 13 June, a violent storm grounded some of Drake's vessels and blew others, including the one offered to Lane, out to sea where their only safe action was to set sail for England. The remaining ships were too large for Lane's use; and, because their supplies had been depleted, Lane decided that the colonists still at Roanoke should board Drake's ships and return home. The severe weather made boarding difficult, and, as Lane told the story, Drake "sending immediately his pinnaces vnto our Island for the fetching away of fewe that there were left with our baggage, the weather was so boysterous, and the pinnaces so often on ground, that the most of all wee had, with all our Cardes, Bookes and writings, were by the Sailers cast ouer boord." There can be little doubt that the great portion of Harriot's notes and White's drawings were thus lost in the frantic boarding on that day.

When he returned home, Harriot learned that Raleigh was unable to send relief to Virginia because of the Spanish threat to England; moreover, he was already engaged in a new colonial venture, this time in southern Ireland. Harriot, posing as one of the colonists, joined him there and was given for his use the Abbey of Molanna in the county of Waterford, near Youghal. Here, Harriot gathered his remaining notes and prepared for publication the first English treatise on the New World. This book, published in February 1588 under the title *A briefe and true report of the new found land of Virginia: of the commodities there found and to be raysed, as well marchantable, as other for victuall, building and other necessarie vses for those that are and shalbe the planters there; and of the nature and manners of the naturall inhabitants . . . By Thomas Hariot; seruant to . . . Sir Walter, a member of the Colony, and there imployed in discouering . . .*, exists in only eight copies but remains one of the most important early accounts of the country as it was first seen by the English settlers. It attracted immediate attention and was included by Hakluyt in his *Principall navigations* of 1589. The following year, Theodore de Bry issued elaborate editions in Latin, English, French, and German, adding plates of twenty-one of John White's drawings of the new land and the Indians, for which Harriot wrote headnotes. Though this was the only work Harriot ever published, it was enough to establish Harriot and White as among the foremost authorities on early colonial America.

Harriot was also involved in the preparations for the invasion of the Spanish Armada. Though he was living in Ireland, he frequently visited London, and many of his extant manuscript notes indicate that he was preparing seamen for more scientific approaches to their craft. It is true that superior seamanship (and God's weather) gave England the victory, and Harriot must have felt some satisfaction in his new science of navigation. Among other activities, he collected for Raleigh and government officials a large number of maps and rutters (sets of sailing directions, tide tables, and carefully drawn profiles of ports or entrances to harbors as seen from the sea, usually the first thing seized from a captured ship), particularly those dealing with Virginia; worked with Emery Molyneaux to improve terrestrial globes; and assisted Gerard Mercator in developing more accurate map projections than had been used before this time. But increasingly his interests turned to theoretical and mathematical subjects. Harriot was one of the first of the new scientists to seek a mathematical solution to natural phenomena. His study of the piling of bullets led him to examine the possible atomic structure of matter as one of the earliest of the new atomists. His investigation of the trajectory of bullets and cannonballs led him to consider the laws of motion and falling bodies. In fact, he was performing the same experiments in England that were occupying Galileo in Italy. Both atomic theory and the laws of motion led Harriot to study refraction; he discovered the law of sines many years before Wilebrord Snel (whose name the law bears) and began work on mirrors and lenses that may have resulted in his independent discovey of a telescope some years later.

During this period, Sir Walter Raleigh's fortunes began to decline. His colonization attempts in the New World had yielded only trouble and high costs. The relief vessels for the 1585–86 colony had arrived two weeks too late, and had returned to England leaving only a small contingent at Roanoke Island. The 1587 colonial effort with John White as governor had been extremely difficult to finance, and once landed could not be supplied or rescued. In all, these projects had cost Raleigh at least £40,000 and denied him the possibility of ever visiting Virginia himself. His Irish colonies were disastrous, too. The lands were poor, the settlers unhappy, the natives vicious, and English import duties on Irish products prevented any profit from his plantations. His popularity with Elizabeth, the source of his wealth, had been jeopardized by his courtship of one of the queen's ladies-in-waiting, Elizabeth Throckmorton, whom he married secretly in late 1591 or early 1592, an act that prompted the queen to confine him in the Tower of London and strip him of many of his honors.

In light of Raleigh's predicament, Harriot sought a new patron, and found one in Raleigh's longtime friend, Henry Percy, ninth earl of Northumberland. Percy was a quiet, retiring, serious-minded young man, intensely interested in the new science of which Harriot was an outstanding exponent. Percy himself was known as "The Wizard Earl," and was beginning to gather about him men with similar interests. During much of Raleigh's imprisonment, Harriot was, according to the kitchen accounts of the ninth earl that still exist, dining regularly at the Wizard Earl's table. Though he continued to be one of Raleigh's closest friends and worked with him to find financial support for Raleigh's ventures, Harriot gradually rose in favor with Percy. In 1593, when Percy received the Order of the Garter, he gave Harriot a handsome gift of money. Two years later he granted him a lifetime interest in his landholdings at Brampton in County Durham (now called Barmpton, a rural suburb of Darlington) and established him in a house adjacent to his London residence, Syon House, Isleworth, though Harriot was still using his rooms in Durham House (Raleigh's London residence) when in the city.

By 1597, Harriot was listed as a regular pensioner of the ninth earl at £80 per annum—the same amount received by Percy's younger brothers. In the same year, in a will drawn by Raleigh on 10 July just before he sailed with Robert Devereux, earl of Essex, to intercept the Spanish fleet in the Azores in a dangerous attempt to recoup their fortunes, Raleigh named Harriot as one of the overseers of the will, left him "all my bookes & the furniture in his own Chamber and in my bedchamber in Durham House Togeather with all such blacke suites of apparell as I haue in the same house," and arranged for Harriot to be paid an annual pension of £100 from his royal grants. Though this will was never probated, the sums mentioned indicate the kind of support that Raleigh must have been giving Harriot. From these incomes, Harriot could live like a gentleman, keep his own house and servants, and indulge his every whim in the pursuit of scientific knowledge without the worry of income, fame, or reputation.

Shortly after his accession to the throne, King James had Raleigh accused of treason on trumped-up charges, convicted by a hand-picked jury, and again thrown into the Tower of London at the sovereign's pleasure. Two years later, Henry Percy followed him to the Tower because James suspected a remote connection with the Gunpowder Plot. Harriot, who was questioned about the plot and accused by James of having cast his horoscope, was imprisoned for a time, but then released to pursue his scientific research at Syon House. Nevertheless, he remained the main link between Raleigh and Percy in the Tower and the outside world, visited them often, assisted Raleigh in the writing of his *History of the World*, and instructed young Algernon, Percy's heir, in the elements of mathematics and navigation, both of which would stand him in good stead in later life when, as the tenth earl of Northumberland, he was Admiral of the Fleet.

Between 1606 and 1608 Harriot corresponded with Johannes Kepler; the two men compared notes on their experiments in the refraction of light, explaining, for the first time, the refraction within a sphere and providing a scientific explanation for the dispersion of light in the rainbow. By 1609, Harriot had in his possession a six-power telescope and began a series of observations of the moon. During the next four years he developed at least eight new telescopes, ranging in power from eight to fifty magnifications. With these telescopes (called by Harriot "perspective truncks") he observed the phases of Venus which proved the validity of Copernican over Ptolemaic astronomy, recorded more than thirty drawings of the moon leading to the first telescopic moon map, and determined the time of quadrature so that he could calculate the distance of the moon from the sun. In December 1610, almost simultaneously with Galileo, he discovered sunspots; during the next four years he made and recorded 199 observations. A few months earlier, in October, he first saw the satellites surrounding Jupiter and after two years of observation was able to calculate the distance of the moons from the planet and to compute the periods of their rotation. He also observed, using a cross-staff, the comets of 1607 (Halley's comet) and 1618, observing their orbits and determining that they followed an elliptical orbit.

During these later years, Harriot suffered from cancer of the nose. Theodore Turquet de Mayerne, the king's physician, was called in as a consultant on 28 May 1615. His notebooks still survive to record his impressions of this visit. He saw Harriot as a very melancholy man, about age sixty (actually Harriot was fifty-five, so his illness must have aged him). He noted that Harriot was the man who first brought tobacco out of Virginia and recorded, for the first time, the possible connection between smoking and cancer. His indication that Harriot had had cancer for about two years appears to be borne out by Harriot's own manuscripts, for except for the comet of 1618 his notes are sparse after 1612. Harriot was able, however, to attend the execution of his old friend and patron, Sir Walter Raleigh, at Westminster on 29 Oct. 1618, and his notes of Raleigh's final speech on the scaffold are among his papers.

Harriot died at the home of Thomas Buckner, a mercer who lived on Threadneedle Street near the Royal Exchange. He may have been on his way to visit Henry Percy, who was still in the Tower, or he may have been visiting an old friend, as "Thomas Bookener" had been with Harriot on Roanoke Island in 1585–86. Harriot was buried in the chancel of St. Christopher le Stocks, on the site of the present Bank of England. His grave, and the monument erected there by Percy, were destroyed in the Great Fire of 1666.

In his will, Harriot left his telescopes and scientific instruments to his executors and his mathematical and scientific papers to his patron, Henry Percy. He requested Nathaniel Torporley, a retired clergyman whom he had known for a long time, to edit and publish his papers. But the records of his visit to the New World are not mentioned. A canvas bag of Irish accounts, "the persons whom they concerne are dead many yeares since in the Raigne of Queene Elizabeth," and another bag of "divers wast papers . . . of my Accomptes to Sir Walter Rawley" he asked be burned. Thus died any additional traces beyond his published book of the personal observer of Raleigh and the author of the first English book about "the new found land of Virginia."

SEE: Thomas Harriot, *A briefe and true report* (Clements Library, University of Michigan, Ann Arbor); David B. Quinn, *The Roanoke Voyages, 1584–1590*, 2 vols. (1955); Muriel Rukeyser, *The Traces of Thomas Hariot* (1971); John W. Shirley, ed., *Thomas Harriot: Renaissance Scientist* (1974); Henry Stevens, *Thomas Hariot, the Mathematician, the Philosopher, and the Scholar* (1900).

JOHN W. SHIRLEY

Harris, Bernice (Christiana) Kelly (*8 Oct. 1891–13 Sept. 1973*), writer, was born in eastern Wake County. Both of her parents, William Haywood and Rosa Poole Kelly, came from a long line of sturdy, independent farmers. She had two older sisters and four younger brothers. Her girlhood was centered on the Mt. Moriah Academy, where she was educated, and the Mt. Moriah Baptist Church. Her aunts and uncles and cousins lived nearby, and the families frequently assembled at neighborhood box suppers, hog killings, Saturday night parties, baseball games, Sunday school excursions, and Christmas celebrations. After attending Cary High School for one year as a boarding student, Bernice entered Meredith College and was graduated in 1913. The quotation beside her picture in the annual was from Tennyson's *The Princess*: "A rosebud set with little willful thorns." Following a brief term as principal of a school at Beulaville in Duplin County, she taught for three years at the South Fork Institute, near Maiden in Catawba County, an academy for training rural Baptist preachers. From there she went to Seaboard High School in Northampton County, where she taught English from 1917 to 1927 except for a year in Rich Square (1921–22).

Meanwhile, Miss Kelly had attended summer school at The University of North Carolina, studying playwriting in 1919 and 1920 under Frederick H. ("Proff") Koch. Inspired by his fervor for the folk play, and recalling her childhood excitement in writing poems and stories, she returned to Seaboard determined to spread the "folk gospel," as well as to do some writing of her own. Her marriage in May 1926 to Herbert Kavanaugh Harris, a Seaboard farmer with associated agricultural interests, did not sidetrack her enthusiasm. Into the living room of her new home, where she continued to be called "Miss Kelly," she invited the women of the town for classes in playwriting; these were moderately successful whenever the ladies could be turned aside from swapping recipes and local gossip. She was instrumental in organizing the Northampton Players among the younger people, its purpose to write and produce plays at home before moving the best of them to the state drama festival.

At first, the publication of her own work and that of her group was not a goal, but after 1930 Mrs. Harris took playwriting more seriously. Too, she began sending human-interest stories and feature articles to the Norfolk and Raleigh newspapers. Four of her character sketches appeared in *These Are Our Lives* (1939), a Federal Writers' project. It was Jonathan Daniels who suggested that she try a novel. *Purslane* (1939), some eighteen months in the writing, won the Mayflower Society Cup as the best North Carolina book of the year. Based on the author's happy, nostalgic memories of her youth, the episodic narrative relates the home and community events of "Pate's Siding," twelve miles east of Raleigh. The success accorded *Purslane* prompted the publication of *Folk Plays of Eastern Carolina* (1940), seven one-act plays written during the prior eight years.

After *Purslane*, six more novels were published with fair regularity. *Portulaca* (1941), named for the plant that is a cultivated variety of the wild-growing purslane, transported some of the rural characters of the earlier book into town, where bridge parties supplanted candy-pullings. *Sweet Beulah Land* (1943) was about a freedom-loving wanderer and his unavoidable confrontations with the conservative people in an agricultural community. *Sage Quarter* (1945) was Mrs. Harris's pastoral romance, a novel about twin girls with broad and circumscribing family ties. In *Janey Jeems* (1946), saga of an ambitious, hard-working, religious country family, the author cleverly and only inferentially indicated that it was a black family of whom she was writing. When most reviewers missed the point, the publishers circularized a notice that *Janey Jeems* was the only book ever written about blacks to have the humanity not to mention race. *Hearthstones* (1948) concerned a Confederate soldier who was "read out" of the church for his desertion; then it moved to World War II for a similar incident in the same family. *Wild Cherry Tree Road* (1951) returned to the scene of *Purslane*.

Mrs. Harris's husband died on 13 July 1950, at age sixty-six. Once again she became involved in community dramatics, with informal classes in the writing of plays and their eventual production in the county towns and at the state festival. In 1957, a dramatization of "Yellow Color Suit," her 1944 short story that had been expanded into *Hearthstones*, was televised over a national network. Wake Forest University presented her an honorary Litt.D. in 1959, as did The University of North Carolina at Greensboro in 1960. In 1961, she was

president of the North Carolina Literary and Historical Association, and in 1966 she was the recipient of the North Carolina Award for "notable accomplishments," presented by the governor. She wrote two little Christmas-gift booklets, *The Very Real Truth about Christmas* (1961) and *The Santa on the Mantel* (1964). In these years she served on the board of trustees of the State Library Commission and the North Carolina Arts Council, and was active in the North Carolina Writers Conference and the Roanoke-Chowan Group.

In 1963, Mrs. Harris started teaching a noncredit course in creative writing at nearby Chowan College, and there she met with imaginative people from all walks of life. "People, not books," she often said, "have always been my first interest in life." From her classes at Chowan came two collections in which she seemed to take more pride than in anything she had written herself. *Southern Home Remedies* (1968) prescribed cures and frequently appended a narrative as corroborative evidence. *Strange Things Happen* (1971) collected sixty-eight stories about ghosts, reincarnation, coincidences, and other odd events. For these two books, she received a Brown-Hudson Folklore Award posthumously from the North Carolina Folklore Society.

Mrs. Harris was a Democrat and a Baptist. Her portrait in oil was painted by Marguerite L. Stem. She died in Durham several weeks before her eighty-second birthday, and was buried in the city cemetery at Seaboard.

SEE: *Durham Morning Herald*, 14 Sept. 1973; *Greensboro Daily News*, 4 Aug. 1940; Bernice Kelly Harris, *Southern Savory* (1964); Bernice Kelly Harris Papers (Southern Historical Collection, University of North Carolina Library, Chapel Hill); Bernadette Hoyle, *Tar Heel Writers I Know* (1956); William S. Powell, ed., *North Carolina Lives* (1962); Raleigh *News and Observer*, 9 Sept. 1951; Richard Walser, *Bernice Kelly Harris: Storyteller of Eastern Carolina* (1955).

RICHARD WALSER

Harris, Bravid Washington (6 Jan. 1896–21 Oct. 1965), Episcopal priest and bishop, was born in Warrenton, the son of Bravid Washington and Margaret Burgess Harris. After receiving his preparatory education in Warrenton, he attended St. Augustine's College, Raleigh. Following his graduation in 1917, he joined the U.S. Army, receiving the rank of first lieutenant. While on active duty in France during 1917–19, he was cited for "Meritorious Service" in the Moselle sector.

Upon returning to civilian life Harris enrolled in the Bishop Payne Divinity School, Petersburg, Va., from which he received the B.D. degree in 1922. He was ordained deacon on 18 Dec. 1921 and in August of the following year was advanced to the priesthood by Bishop Henry B. Delany, who placed him in charge of All Saints' Church, Warrenton. Harris remained there until 1924, when he moved to Norfolk to become rector of Grace Church. During the nineteen years he served that parish, Harris took an active part in community affairs. He was president of the Norfolk Community Hospital for ten years, director of the Norfolk Community Fund, and a district chairman of the Boy Scouts of America. From 1937 to 1943 he was the Archdeacon for Negro Work in the Diocese of Southern Virginia. His contributions as archdeacon received churchwide attention when, in 1943, he was appointed Secretary for Negro Work in the Home Missions Department of the National Council.

Harris's accomplishments as an administrator and

priest were recognized when the House of Bishops on 1 Feb. 1945 elected him to be bishop of the Missionary District of Liberia. He was consecrated on 17 April in Christ and St. Luke's Church, Norfolk, by Presiding Bishop St. George Tucker, Bishop Edwin A. Penick of North Carolina, and Bishop William A. Brown of Southern Virginia. At this time Harris was the only active Negro bishop in the Episcopal church. When he arrived in Liberia, he found four schools and one hospital operated by his church. All of them were understaffed and poorly equipped. One of his first actions was to improve the schools and establish new ones. Throughout his episcopate he emphasized the importance of education in any Christian program. He was responsible for the rebuilding and reopening of Cuttington College, Monrovia, which had been closed from 1929 to 1949. This project was jointly supported by the Episcopal church and the Liberian government.

After nineteen years of productive service, Harris retired from his work in Liberia. Upon returning to the United States, he was appointed acting director of the Foundation for Episcopal Colleges and continued in this position until his death. He served for several years as a trustee of the Bishop Payne Divinity School and of St. Paul's School, Lawrenceville, Va. In 1946 the Virginia Theological Seminary awarded him the D.D. degree, and in 1961 St. Augustine's College conferred on him the doctorate of humane letters. He was the author of "A Study of Our Work," published in 1937. On 23 May 1918 he married Flossie Mae Adams. They had no children.

Harris's burial service was held in the Cathedral of St. Peter and St. Paul, Washington, D.C., conducted by Presiding Bishop John Hines and three assisting bishops. On the day of his funeral President Tubman of Liberia ordered all schools, businesses, and offices closed and the flag of the republic flown at half-mast throughout the country. Harris was buried in Arlington National Cemetery.

SEE: *Carolina Churchman* 55 (December 1965); Diocese of North Carolina, *Journals*, 1921–24; General Convention of the Protestant Episcopal Church in the U.S.A., *Journals*, 1946, 1958; New York *Herald Tribune*, 24 Oct. 1965; Raleigh *News and Observer*, 18 Apr. 1945, 13 Oct. 1961; *Who's Who in America* (1954).

LAWRENCE F. LONDON

Harris, Caroline (Carrie) Aiken Jenkins *(27 Mar. 1847–1903[?])*, writer and editor, is believed to have been born at Buena Vista, the Jenkins family plantation on the edge of Williamsboro, a then thriving village in what is now Vance County. Her father, Robert Alexander Jenkins, was the owner of the Jenkins Tobacco Factory, which began by making "plug" and eventually expanded to regular smoking tobacco. Her mother was Elizabeth Tatum Hicks Jenkins, "a fine school teacher and an excellent musician." Elizabeth's great-great-grandfather, William Hicks, came to North Carolina with two brothers from Westbury, Long Island, N.Y., prior to 5 Mar. 1749, when he bought two parcels of land totaling 502 acres at Tabbs Creek from the estate of Earl Granville. The Long Island Hicks were well established, at least in the nineteenth century, when one of them gave a considerable grant to Swarthmore College.

Carrie, the oldest of ten children of Robert's second wife, probably attended the Henderson Female Academy, opened in 1855. A younger sister, Elizabeth, was graduated from the Salem Academy and a brother, Thomas Leoline, attended the U.S. Naval Academy and became a civil engineer in the Philippines.

In 1873, Carrie taught "Music, Drawing, Painting and Waxworks" at the Wilson Collegiate Institute. That year she appeared, one suspects in a leading role, in a play, *Lady of Lyons*, at the Mamona Hall. In the fall she found time to dash back to Henderson, where she had a booth at the county fair. The Henderson *Tribune* of 2 Oct. 1873 noted that "Miss Carrie Jenkins will have an exhibition at the Fair, several paintings, executed by her own artistic hands, besides other articles of beauty."

She married Cicero Willis Harris on 1 July 1874, most likely at St. John's Episcopal Church in Williamsboro, to which the Jenkins family belonged. Members of the Harris family were long residents of the area, and a mutual interest in writing may have been a factor in the marriage. However, Carrie's talents lay in the area of the dramatic, whereas Cicero's were in economics and government, especially in connection with the South. Accounts survive of strong divergent Whig and Democratic party loyalties held in local families. Lucilla R. Harris, a strong Whig supporter of Henry Clay, made a silk vest and presented it to him when he appeared at Raleigh during one of his presidential campaigns. Towards the end of the century, when Carrie and her husband appear to have separated, Cicero published such works as *A Glance at Government* and *The Sectional Struggle*. In any case, in September 1874 the Harrises were living in Wilmington, where Carrie from January to December 1875 was a regular contributor to *Our Living and Our Dead*, a journal of memories of a lost cause, with other items of general interest and some poetry.

Carrie's major literary contribution was *Margaret Rosselyn*, a romantic novel set in her native Williamsboro. It opens with a lament on the state of decay in the vacated old colonial St. John's Church: "Wicked men and women, straying sheep and goats wandered at will up and down the broad, bare aisle," while horse jockeys settled bets in the churchyard. *Our Living and Our Dead* ceased publication in 1876.

Next came *The South Atlantic*, "a monthly magazine of Literature, Art and Science," begun in November 1877 with Carrie as editor. Among the articles included was one by Cicero on "Corrupt Use of Money in Elections" and Carrie's "Omeroh," a biographical account of a Moslem "prince" [Omar Ibn Said] captured by slavers on the Senegal River and eventually owned by Governor John Owen. Converted to Presbyterianism, he spent some time at Fayetteville. His Bible was said to have been given to Davidson College. An 1880 issue, one of the last, ran a half-page advertisement: "WANTED for Prof. T. A. Edison, One Million Ounces of Platinum. I will pay cash for all the platinum in North Carolina. Mrs. Cicero W. Harris, Wilmington."

James Sprunt observed that the Harrises "were conspicuous in Wilmington for their literary attainments." Cicero was both editor of the Wilmington *Star* and the short-lived *Sun* at different times. Of the latter James Sprunt said, "it left a pleasing memory in the community, which held in the highest esteem its editor, Mr. Cicero W. Harris." Of Carrie, Sprunt remarked, "she was a woman of most attractive personality and remarkable energy" who but for the financial depression of the time might have prospered.

In 1881, *The South Atlantic* was being published in Baltimore with C. A. Harris listed as editor. In January 1888 she was living in Washington, D.C., from which she wrote to Colonel Walter Lenoir of Watauga County about the possibility of her building a "stone castle" set in the "shadow of the splendid peaks." This was to be named "Leolyn." The Jenkins were of Welsh extraction, according to family tradition, and Sir Leolyn Jenkins of Jesus College, Oxford, England, was regarded as an ancestor. Carrie was then contributing to the New York papers, receiving $8 a column. *Harpers* had offered her $100 for an article to be called "The Southern Portrait Gallery." She seemed confident of earning her living as a free-lance writer from her contemplated mountain fastness. In 1893, she published *A Romantic Romance* and in 1899, *State Trials of Mary Queen of Scots, Sir Walter Raleigh,* and *Captain William Kidd;* the latter was a condensation of Francis Hargrave's work (London, 1776), written under her pen name, Charles Edward Lloyd.

Carrie Jenkins Harris possibly died in Baltimore, a Celtic romanticist to the last.

SEE: Henderson *Tribune,* 2, 16 Oct., 20 Nov. 1873; Lenoir Family Papers and Matt Whitaker Ransom Papers (Southern Historical Collection, University of North Carolina Library, Chapel Hill); *National Union Catalogue, Pre-1956 Imprints,* vol. 231; James Sprunt, *Chronicles of the Cape Fear River* (1916); John B. Watkins, *Historic Vance County* (1941).

JOHN MACFIE

Harris, Charles Joseph (*11 Sept. 1853–14 Feb. 1944*), businessman, was the son of William Harris, a farmer, and Zilpah Torrey Harris of Putnam, Conn. His paternal ancestor was Thomas Harris, who in 1630 sailed on the *Lyon* in company with Roger Williams from Bristol, England, to Salem, Mass. His brother, William Torrey Harris, was U.S. Commissioner of Education from 1889 to 1906. Harris received his early education in the schools of Putnam. In 1874, he was graduated from Yale where he was a fraternity brother of William Howard Taft, a relative with whom he corresponded until Taft's death. In 1876, Harris received the LL.B. from Washington University in St. Louis, Mo., where his brother was superintendent of schools. He then taught high school in Kansas (1876–77) and in Denver, Colo. (1877–78). After engaging in the hardware business in Denver, he built irrigation ditches in the West, from which he gained much of his wealth.

About 1888, Harris moved to Dillsboro, N.C., and from this base engaged in a variety of business enterprises. His major activity was the mining of kaolin, a clay mineral used in the manufacture of porcelain. At first associated with the Equitable Manufacturing Company which mined kaolin near Dillsboro, Harris in 1890 became secretary-treasurer and a chief stockholder of the new Carolina Clay Company with plants in Dillsboro and Webster. This company shipped large quantities of kaolin to East Liverpool, Ohio, and Trenton, N.J. Eventually he formed and became president of his own company, the Harris Kaolin Company, with operations in Jackson, Swain, Haywood, Mitchell, Yancey, and Avery counties.

With the capital acquired from his kaolin operations, Harris contributed to the economic development of western North Carolina. He was president of the Harris-Woodbury Lumber Company, which owned some 76,000 acres of timberland in what became the Great Smoky Mountains National Park. This land was sold to the Champion Paper and Fibre Company and the Norwood Lumber Company before it became part of the park. In 1903, Harris established the C. J. Harris Tannery in Sylva, the first industry of any size there, and sold it in 1916 to the Armour Leather Company. In 1907, he constructed the dam and power plant on Scotts Creek for the Dillsboro and Sylva Electric Light Com-

pany, of which he was president until 1941. A larger dam and power plant were constructed on the Tuckasegee River at Dillsboro in 1913. His involvement in banking included the presidency of the Jackson County and Spruce Pine banks, the vice-presidency of the American National Bank in Asheville, and a sizable stockholding in Wachovia Bank and Trust Company. Harris was also president of the Blue Ridge Pin Company of Dillsboro, which manufactured locust wood utility pole pins on which glass insulators were placed, and of the Harris Granite Quarries with headquarters in Salisbury. His one venture into publishing was as president of the Asheville Daily Times Company. During this period, his major economic enterprise outside North Carolina was as president of the Appalachicola Lumber Company in Florida.

In addition to business, Harris had a keen interest in politics. He attended every Republican National Convention from 1892 to 1936 and was elected a delegate-at-large in 1908, the year William Howard Taft, his kinsman, was nominated. From 1898 to 1902 he was a member of the U.S. Industrial Commission. In the early 1900s he was president of the North Carolina Republican League, and in 1904 he accepted the nomination of the Republican party for governor of North Carolina. His nomination was a strategem of his party to obtain greater support from business interests; it did not succeed, as Harris was defeated by the Democratic nominee.

Harris was also active in social organizations. He was a member of the Yale Alumni Association of North Carolina, the University and Yale clubs of New York City, the Metropolitan Club of Washington, D.C., and the Asheville and Biltmore Forest country clubs. He was an Episcopalian. His philanthropic activities included gifts to the C. J. Harris Community Hospital in Sylva and the construction of the memorial tower to Elisha Mitchell atop Mount Mitchell. Moreover, except during World War I, he traveled abroad every year from 1910 to 1935.

In June 1881, in Milwaukee, Wis., Harris married Florence Rust, the daughter of David Ward Rust, a lumberman of Saginaw, Mich. Florence bore him two sons, David Rust and Robert Ward. She died in 1918. Harris suffered a broken hip in 1938 and was confined to bed for the rest of his life; he died at his son Robert's home in Biltmore Forest and was buried in Riverside Cemetery, Asheville.

SEE: *Asheville Citizen,* 15, 16 Feb. 1944; *Jackson County Centennial* (1951); *Nat. Cyc. Am. Biog.,* vol. 15 (1916); Joseph F. Steelman, "The Progressive Era in North Carolina, 1884–1917" (Ph.D. diss., University of North Carolina, 1955); Sylva *Jackson County Journal,* 1 June 1906; Sylva *Tuckaseigee Democrat,* 21 May 1890; *Who's Who in America* (1901–2, 1922–23).

JOHN L. BELL, JR.

Harris, Charles Wilson (*1771–15 or 26 Jan. 1804*), educator and lawyer, was born at Mill Grove plantation, about seven miles west of Concord. His paternal grandfather, Charles Harris, emigrated with four brothers and a sister from Ayrshire, Scotland, to Pennsylvania about 1725 and thence to the Poplar Tent district of what was then Anson County sometime between 1745 and 1751. His father, Robert Harris, served under General Joseph Graham in the Revolutionary War and lost his right arm in the skirmish at Clapp's Mill, preliminary to the Battle of Guilford Court House. His uncle,

Dr. Charles Harris, is credited by Kemp P. Battle with having "taught at his home probably the first medical school in the State."

Charles Wilson Harris was the second of three children born to Robert and Mary Wilson Harris. His older sister, Jane Wilson Harris, married Nathaniel Alexander. His younger brother, Robert Wilson Harris, was briefly engaged in commerce at Salisbury and later undertook farming near Sneedsborough in Anson County. His mother died in his youth, and his father married Mary Brevard Davidson, the widow of General William Lee Davidson for whom Davidson College was named. Although no record of Harris's preparatory education survives, it is known that a classical school was conducted in association with the Poplar Tent Presbyterian Church of which his father was for many years the presiding elder. Harris attended the College of New Jersey (Princeton) and was awarded the Mathematical Oration at his graduation in 1792.

For the next two years Harris was a teacher in Mecklenburg County, N.C., and later in Prince Edward County, Va. Although impossible to substantiate, this was probably at Hampden-Sydney College. At some point, he attended William and Mary College in Williamsburg to obtain, as he wrote some years later, a smattering of experimental philosophy, a subject that he felt had been shamefully neglected in his studies at Princeton. On returning to North Carolina, Harris studied medicine for a while with his uncle Dr. Charles Harris, a well-known physician. During his later tenure at Chapel Hill, there being no physician at the university, he kept a stock of medicines, both for the students and the townspeople, which he sold at cost. In March 1795, he joined the faculty of The University of North Carolina as professor of mathematics. The only other member of the academic staff at this time was the presiding professor, David Ker. In the summer of 1796 Ker resigned under pressure of the trustees, and Harris thereafter acted as presiding professor until the time of his own resignation the following December.

Although his tenure on the faculty was brief, Harris played a seminal role in the early direction of the university. On 3 June 1795 he organized the students to form a debating club, which in succeeding months became the Dialectic and Philanthropic Literary Societies. Organized exercises were conducted by these societies each Friday evening and Saturday morning to provide practice in public speaking, English composition, and debate. The exercises were drawn from modern history and literature, subjects not included in the standard classical curriculum prevailing at colleges of the day. The sessions implemented Harris's belief that "true learning consists rather in exercising the reasoning faculties and laying up a store of useful knowledge, than in overloading the memory with words of dead languages," a pedagogical theory he shared with General William R. Davie, the moving spirit among the trustees. His second lasting contribution to the university's early development lay in persuading Joseph Caldwell, a graduate of the class of 1791 at Princeton, to join the faculty in October 1796. Caldwell succeeded Harris as presiding professor in 1797 and continued to guide the university's growth until his death in 1835.

Harris undertook to complete his legal studies in April 1797, reading law under General Davie at Halifax. He was admitted to the bar in the latter part of that year and succeeded to Davie's practice when Davie was elected governor. While in Halifax, Harris maintained his interest in The University of North Carolina, which in 1799 granted him the honorary master of arts degree;

in 1800, he was elected a trustee. In 1802, he was induced by Davie and others to accept an appointment on the bench. However, he was forced to prevent his nomination from being considered by the legislature because of a worsening tubercular disease which had first afflicted him in October 1798. In the spring and summer of 1803, Harris traveled to the Bahamas attempting to recover his health. He arrived in New York in September, and after a brief stay returned to the family home at Mill Grove.

On 14 Apr. 1798 Harris was admitted to the Order of Freemasons at Chapel Hill. Although both his grandfather and father had served as elders of the Poplar Tent Presbyterian Church, Harris himself appears to have held no religious convictions until the period immediately preceding his death. It seems likely that his religious lassitude as well as his membership in the Freemasons were attributable to the influence of his mentor, General Davie. During the weeks before his death, Harris confessed the Christian faith and instructed that no Masonic rites be included in his funeral service. He died at Sneedsborough while visiting his brother Robert and was buried in a private cemetery in Anson County. Although his tombstone records his date of death as 15 Jan. 1804, both the Raleigh *Minerva* and the *Register* in their issues of 15 Feb. 1804 report his death as having occurred on 26 January.

SEE: Kemp P. Battle, *History of the University of North Carolina*, vol. 1 (1907); Battle Family Papers, William R. Davie Papers, Charles Wilson Harris Papers, and Cornelia Phillips Spencer Papers (Southern Historical Collection, University of North Carolina Library, Chapel Hill); Blackwell P. Robinson, *William R. Davie* (1957); H. M. Wagstaff, ed., "The Harris Letters," *James Sprunt Historical Publications* 14 (1916).

GEORGE T. BLACKBURN II

Harris, Diana. *See* **Foster, Diana Harris**.

Harris, Edward (*5 Mar. 1763–29 Mar. 1813*), attorney, judge, and legislator, was born in Iredell County, the son of James and Rebecca Morrison Harris. James Harris, a native of Harrisburg, Pa., moved in 1758 to that part of Rowan County that later became Iredell where he was a justice of the peace. His son Edward was educated under the Reverend James Hall at the noted Clio's Academy, then read law with William Sharpe. After being licensed he practiced law in New Bern where he was living by 1791. Harris married Sarah Roulhac of Orange County but they had no children. His second wife was Sarah H. Kollock, of Elizabeth Town, N.J., whom he married on 5 July 1809.

In the spring of 1802 Harris was appointed to the bench of the United States Court for the Fifth Judicial District to fill the unexpired term of Henry Potter. Only three months later, this temporary court passed out of existence, but Harris had apparently made a mark as a judge. In November 1802 he was sent to the legislature as the borough representative of New Bern, and he served in the same capacity the following year. From 1805 until his death he was a trustee of The University of North Carolina. In 1807 he represented Craven County in the legislature, and in 1811 he was elected by the General Assembly to the Superior Court bench.

Harris had a reputation for honesty and learning which he used to good effect in difficult cases. On one occasion in 1810 he argued unsuccessfully in the case of

Earl Granville, who was attempting to enforce a title obtained in 1744. The appeal to the United States Supreme Court was never prosecuted due to the outbreak of the War of 1812. Harris's judicial career was terminated by his untimely death after less than two years on the bench. He died while holding court in Lumberton and was buried there.

SEE: Kemp P. Battle, *Early History of Raleigh* (1893); John L. Cheney, Jr., ed., *North Carolina Government, 1585–1974* (1975); Walter Clark, ed., *State Records of North Carolina*, vols. 17, 24 (1899, 1905); David M. Furches, undated biographical sketch from Statesville *Landmark* (Clipping files, North Carolina Collection, University of North Carolina Library, Chapel Hill); Marshall De Lancey Haywood, unpublished biographical sketch (Van Noppen Papers, Manuscript Department, Duke University Library, Durham); William S. Powell, *Patrons of the Press* (1962); Raleigh *Register*, 27 July 1809, 2 Apr. 1813.

JON G. CRAWFORD

Harris, George Emrick (*6 Jan. 1827–18 Mar. 1911*), U.S. representative from Mississippi, was born in Orange County, N.C. The family moved during Harris's childhood to Tennessee and eventually to Mississippi; he attended the common schools of both states. After studying law, he was admitted to the bar in 1854 and began to practice in Mississippi. At the beginning of the Civil War he entered the Confederate Army and served as a lieutenant colonel throughout the war. Following the defeat of the Confederacy and the establishment of Reconstruction governments, the Mississippi lawyer was elected a district attorney in 1865 and reelected the following year.

When Mississippi was readmitted to the Union, Harris, a Republican, was elected to both the Forty-first and Forty-second congresses, serving from 23 Feb. 1870 to 3 Mar. 1873. From 1873 to 1877 he was attorney general of Mississippi. Still active in state politics at age fifty, Harris served as lieutenant governor from 1877 to 1879. His longtime involvement in Reconstruction government as a Republican was unusual for a former Confederate officer and probably brought him some of the same social ostracism that haunted General James Longstreet.

Harris eventually moved permanently to Washington, D.C. He was the author of a great many legal books including *A Treatise on the Law of Contracts by Married Women* (1887), *A Treatise on the Law of Damages by Corporations* (1892), *A Treatise on the Law of Identification* (1892), *A Treatise on Sunday Laws* (1893), and *Certiorari at Common Law and under the Statutes* (1893).

A widower, he died of an asthma attack at his home in Washington and was buried in that city's Oak Hill Cemetery, in a grave above Mrs. Harriet S. Harris (1854–9 July 1905), presumably his wife.

SEE: *Biog. Dir. Am. Cong.* (1971); Hugh T. Lefler and Paul Wager, *Orange County, 1752–1952* (1953); *National Union Catalog*, vol. 232 (1972); Records of Oak Hill Cemetery, Washington, D.C.

PHILLIP W. EVANS

Harris, Hunter Lee (*16 Dec. 1866–13 July 1893*), geologist and poet, was born at Sassafras Fork (Stem) in Granville County, son of Adam Clarke and Martha Hunter Harris and the youngest of six. He had two sisters and three brothers. The families of both parents were prominent in the business and social affairs of Granville, Vance, Halifax, and Edgecombe counties. His father was a physician, farmer, and local Methodist preacher. Educated at home and at a neighborhood school, Harris grew fond of reading, especially Dickens. He wrote that he found more pleasure in the company of domestic animals than of boys his own age. In 1885 one of his brothers and he went on a tramping tour of the North Carolina mountains as mineral surveyors.

After several years of keeping books for a merchant, Harris entered The University of North Carolina in January 1886. At Chapel Hill he specialized in chemistry and geology, sang in the Glee Club, was editor of the *University Magazine*, and in his senior year was class poet and president of the YMCA. In 1889 he was named an "honor graduate" with a B.S. degree. Somewhat later he became secretary of the North Carolina Experiment Station in Raleigh, returning to the university in 1891–92 as instructor in geology. The following year he took advanced courses in geology and geography at Harvard on a university scholarship and received a second B.S.; his thesis was entitled "History of the Atlantic Shore Line."

For three years beginning in 1891, Harris was assistant geologist for the North Carolina Geological Survey. At a field camp in Harnett County near Spout Springs on the lower Little River, he was drowned while swimming. He was buried in the family cemetery in Vance County.

During his college days, Harris drafted a "Map of Chapel Hill and Vicinity." His poems appeared in the *University Magazine* and the *Detroit Free Press*. In 1890, he printed *Twilight Songs and Other Youthful Poems* as a Christmas souvenir for his friends. Along with thirteen poems, it contained a photograph portrait as its frontispiece and some of his drawings. In 1903 the university first presented the annual Hunter Lee Harris Memorial, a gold medal awarded for the best short story by a student.

SEE: Biographical sketch of Hunter Lee Harris (in possession of George S. Wills, Westminster, Md.); Harvard University Archives (Cambridge, Mass.) for information regarding Harris; *University* of North Carolina *Magazine* 13 (December 1893), 21 (December 1903).

RICHARD WALSER

Harris, Isaac Foust (*21 Apr. 1879–31 Jan. 1953*), chemist, was born in Chapel Hill, the son of Thomas West Harris, organizer and first head of the medical and pharmacy schools of The University of North Carolina, and Sally M. Foust Harris. He attended the Bingham School in Mebane and The University of North Carolina, earning a B.S. degree in 1900 and an M.S. degree in 1903; his first thesis in biochemistry was entitled "Nucleic Acid of the Wheat Embryo." The work was actually done at the Connecticut Experiment Station, where he had been a Carnegie research student since 1901 and would continue until 1907. Afterwards the city of New York invited him to join its Lederle Antitoxin Laboratories, where he studied the preparation of antitoxins. In 1909, he received wide recognition for the purest and most potent preparation of diphtheria antitoxin made until then; that summer he was called to demonstrate his techniques in the most important laboratories in Europe.

From the Lederle Laboratories Harris moved to the Arlington Research Laboratories in Yonkers, N.Y., in

1912. Three years later, when he was awarded the Ph.D. degree from Yale, he left the Arlington Laboratories to oversee the department of biochemistry at E. R. Squibb & Sons in New York. There he developed and supervised the manufacture of chloramines for the use of army medical units in World War I. He resigned in 1919 to form his own company.

Harris Laboratories, in Tuckahoe, N.Y., was the first, and for ten years the only, commercial producer of vitamins. The U.S. Public Health Service sought Harris's products for use across the country; indeed, his preparation of Vitamin B was the key to ridding his native South of the scourge, pellagra. Research at the company was conducted not only on the preparation of vitamins but also on a broad range of biochemical topics: vegetable proteins, especially ricin from the castor bean and urease from the soybean; thromboplastin; and blood serum immunity. Eventually the laboratories' annual business was measured in hundreds of millions of dollars. In 1942 Harris retired as owner and director of the company, which was purchased by Bristol Laboratories and moved to Syracuse, N.Y.

On 29 July 1915, Harris married Elizabeth Heroy of Stamford, Conn. They had two daughters: Elizabeth (Mrs. John Hahn of Kansas City, Mo.), born 13 Oct. 1916; and Helen (Mrs. Tristam B. Johnson of Princeton, N.J.), born 11 Feb. 1921. In 1932 the Harrises moved to Rockledge, their home in Rye, N.Y., where he died.

SEE: *American Men of Science*, 9th ed. (1949); M. M. Bursey, *Carolina Chemist* (1982); Daniel L. Grant, *Alumni History of the University of North Carolina* (1924); *New York Times*, 2 Feb. 1953; *Westchester County and Its People* (1946); Yonkers, N.Y., *Tuckahoe Record*, 21 July 1947.

MAURICE M. BURSEY

Harris, James Henry *(1832–31 May 1891)*, North Carolina politician, was born in Granville County. Described as "a base born boy of color," he was apprenticed on 3 Aug. 1840 to Charles Allen to learn the carpenter trade; at age nineteen he was described as a dark mulatto. After his apprenticeship, he started his own business in Raleigh. Later he attended school for two years in Oberlin, Ohio, followed in 1862 by travel to Canada, Liberia, and Sierra Leone. In 1863, he was commissioned by Governor Levi Morton of Indiana to help raise the Twenty-eighth Regiment of U.S. Colored Troops. In June 1865, he returned to Raleigh as a teacher for the New England Freedmen's Aid Society.

Harris quickly realized that blacks needed legal and political equality to ensure their freedom. Thus, he entered politics, playing a major role in the state and the nation from 1865 through the 1880s. Elected to the 1865 North Carolina Freedmen's Convention, Harris began his political career by urging moderation, reconciliation with whites, and education for blacks. However, by 1866, as president of the 1866 freedmen's convention, he was pushing forcibly for black rights. He began his national political involvement as a vice-president of the National Equal Rights Convention of 1865 and as deputy president of the 1867 convention.

During congressional reconstruction, Harris emerged as one of the most prominent black politicians in North Carolina. He was a charter member of the state's Republican party, a delegate to the state's 1868 constitutional convention, a state legislator for several terms (house, 1868–69, 1869–70, 1883; senate, 1872–74), a Raleigh city alderman for many years, and a deputy tax collector. In 1869, he served as president of the Na-

tional Convention of Colored Men as well as chairman of the delegation that presented a memorial to President Ulysses S. Grant, urging him to use his influence with Congress to pass supplemental legislation securing equal rights for blacks. In 1877, Harris was vice-president of the National Black Convention. He also attended the 1868, 1872, and 1876 Republican National conventions and was a presidential elector in 1872. In the 1880s he edited and published the *North Carolina Republican*, dedicated to work "in behalf of the Republican party and the advancement of the negro."

As a politician and officeholder, Harris was an eloquent spokesman for a variety of causes. His major interests were education for blacks and an end to legal discrimination. He also pushed for legislation for prison reform, aid to mechanics and laborers, protection for women and debtors, and care for orphans. In addition, he worked for the erection of the Colored Institution for the Deaf, Dumb, and Blind in Raleigh and became one of its first trustees. Throughout his career, Harris believed that blacks and whites had to work together, that their interests were intertwined. This is why he so actively opposed black emigration to Africa. But although often urging moderation, he always insisted that blacks fight to keep their political rights and to gain equality before the law.

Harris also held a life membership in the North Carolina Agricultural Society, was one of the original trustees of St. Ambrose Episcopal Church, and attended the National Labor Conference in Washington, D.C., in 1869.

He married Bettie Miller, who died in 1935; they were the parents of two children, David Henry (d. 1955) and Florence (d. 1889). Harris died in Washington, D.C., and was buried at Mount Hope Cemetery, Raleigh. He was eulogized by both Democratic and Republican newspapers as a gifted politician and a talented orator.

SEE: Elizabeth Balanoff, "Negro Legislators in the North Carolina General Assembly, July, 1868–February, 1872," *North Carolina Historical Review* 49 (1972); Jerome Dowd, *Sketches of Prominent Living North Carolinians* (1888); Frank Emory, Doris Lucas, and others, eds., *Paths toward Freedom* (1976); James H. Harris Papers and St. Ambrose Episcopal Church *Centennial, 1868–1968* (North Carolina State Archives, Raleigh); W. H. Quick, *Negro Stars* (1898); Raleigh *North Carolina Republican*, 30 July, 30 Nov. 1880.

ROBERTA SUE ALEXANDER

Harris, John Cebern Logan *(14 Sept. 1847–17 Mar. 1918)*, attorney, newspaperman, and Republican political leader, was born in Rutherfordton, the son of Cebern Lemuel and Susan Logan Harris. In 1862, at age fifteen, he went to Raleigh where he was employed as a printer's devil in the printing establishment of W. W. Holden, who published the Raleigh *Standard*.

Harris began the study of law under Edward Graham Haywood and completed his instruction under Chief Justice Richmond M. Pearson and Judge Thomas Settle at Wentworth. He was admitted to the bar in 1868 and continued to practice for nearly half a century. In 1874, he was elected solicitor of the former Sixth District and served for several years. During the 1890s he represented the State Board of Agriculture and several other state departments as attorney. Harris won a notable victory in the Patapsco Guano Company case before the United States Supreme Court, which established the right of a state to collect a tax on foreign manufactured fertilizers. He appeared as counsel in many of the leading criminal cases in the district, and during the last ten years of his life he served as chairman of the Wake County Bar Association.

During his brilliant career as an attorney, Harris never lost his love for newspaper work. From 1884 to 1894 he edited and published the Raleigh *Signal*, a weekly Republican paper. For many years he was the North Carolina correspondent for the *New York Times*, the *Chicago Herald*, and other papers.

The son of a staunch "Union man" and a disciple of Governor Holden, Harris was a participant in the birth, and a leader in the organization, of the Republican party in North Carolina. For many years he was secretary of the Republican state committee. In 1892, he was the pioneer advocate of fusion between the Republicans and the Populists. Failing to consummate his plan in the Republican convention, he took the stump for the Republican candidate for president, Benjamin Harrison, and the Populist candidate for governor, Dr. W. P. Exum, who was opposed by Justice David M. Furches, the Republican gubernatorial nominee. In 1894, the plan Harris had fathered was adopted and a fusion legislature elected. He at once began his successful advocacy of his friend Judge Daniel Russell for governor. From 1896 to 1900 he was Governor Russell's most trusted adviser. During this period he was chairman of the State Board of Agriculture and president of the Board of Trustees of the College of Agriculture and Mechanic Arts; for several years he also served as adjutant general of North Carolina. In the latter capacity he acquired the title of "Colonel," which remained with him until his death. Twice he represented his district in Republican National conventions.

On 27 Dec. 1869 Harris married Florence Upchurch, the daughter of W. C. Upchurch of Raleigh, who survived him. He was also survived by eleven children: Mrs. Will X. Coley of Raleigh; Mrs. Charles C. Johnson of Richmond, Va.; Cebern D. Harris of Louisville, Ky.; J. C. L. Harris, Jr., of Kingsport, Tenn.; Mrs. M. W. Crocker of Columbus, Ohio; Charles U. Harris, attorney of Raleigh; William Clinton Harris, longtime judge of the Superior Court of Wake County; Gordon Harris of Schenectady, N.Y.; Winder R. Harris, later U.S. congressman from Norfolk, Va.; Dr. Jack H. Harris, naval surgeon; and Leland S. Harris of Raleigh.

Harris was buried in Oakwood Cemetery, Raleigh.

SEE: North Carolina Bar Association, *Proceedings* 20 (1918); Raleigh *News and Observer*, 18 Mar. 1918.

CHARLES AYCOCK POE

Harris, Reginald Lee (9 Sept. 1890–27 Oct. 1959), lieutenant governor of North Carolina, politician, industrialist, and community leader, was born in Roxboro, one of eight children of William Henry and Rosa Lee Jordan Harris. His father was a merchant and leader in the tobacco and textile community of Roxboro, where the younger Harris resided his entire life.

After attending the Roxboro Central School and the Virginia Military Institute in Lexington, Harris was employed by the Roxboro Cotton Mills and served as president from 1941 to 1956; during the same period he was also president of the Peoples Bank of Roxboro. At his death he was chairman of the board of both organizations. Among his numerous other business affiliations, he served as president of the North Carolina Cotton Manufacturers Association and as a director of the North Carolina Textile Foundation, the Business

Foundation, the Home Economics Foundation, and a variety of other business and charitable enterprises.

As a community leader, Harris was especially active in religious, educational, and health affairs. A lifelong member of Long Memorial Methodist Church in Roxboro, he served as treasurer, Sunday school teacher, Sunday school secretary, trustee, and chairman of the official board. He was also an ardent supporter of Grace Methodist Church, which, on 27 Feb. 1967, named its educational building for Harris in recognition of his service. The Person County Memorial Hospital, which opened in 1950, was built largely through Harris's unstinting efforts. He headed the fund-raising drive and saw the project through to its completion; the hospital annex bears his name.

It was in politics, however, that Harris earned his statewide reputation. First elected to the North Carolina House of Representatives in 1927, he served five consecutive terms, and in 1933 he was chosen speaker of the house. The 1933 legislative session proved to be one of the most controversial in North Carolina history, as the state tried to cope with the paralyzing problems of drastically reduced revenues brought on by the depression. Faced with the possibility of closing public schools, the legislature passed the much-debated 3 percent sales tax—against strong opposition—thereby keeping the schools open. Harris was active in that controversy. In 1940 he attained his political pinnacle, winning the Democratic nomination for lieutenant governor. In the general election, Harris and gubernatorial nominee Joseph Melville Broughton received the largest majority ever given candidates for offices in North Carolina. While lieutenant governor, Harris was prominently mentioned as a future gubernatorial candidate, but he never sought the office. Afterwards, he returned to the legislature for two additional terms (1947, 1949).

During his political career, Harris served on many influential panels. He was a member of the legislature's powerful Advisory Budget Commission, chairman of the State Board of Education (1943–45), director of the North Carolina State College Foundation, and for many years a trustee of the Consolidated University of North Carolina. Long active in Democratic party politics, he was a delegate to national conventions in 1936, 1940, and 1944.

In December 1913, Harris married Katharine Jones Long, the daughter of William H. and Rachel Reade Long of Roxboro. They had six children: Reginald L. Harris, Jr., William H. Harris III, Katharine Long (Mrs. N. B. Schloss), Dr. A. Page Harris, Mary Louise (Mrs. Kedar B. Brown), and Betsy Reade (Mrs. Gordon P. Allen). Harris died in his native Roxboro at age sixty-nine following several years of declining health; he was buried at Burchwood Cemetery, Roxboro. Portraits of him hang in the lobby of the Person County Memorial Hospital and in the entrance of the educational building of Grace Methodist Church.

SEE: *Durham Morning Herald, Greensboro Daily News*, and Raleigh *News and Observer*, 28 Oct. 1959; North Carolina General Assembly, Bills and Resolutions, House, no. 95, 24 Feb. 1961; Roxboro *Courier-Times*, 29 Oct. 1959.

A. M. BURNS III

Harris, Reuben Rivers (1867–11 Jan. 1933), educator, was born in Unionville, Ky. After briefly studying law, he turned to teaching and for fourteen years was principal of the public schools in Decatur, Ala. Having prepared himself for the ministry, he served Episcopal parishes in Florence and Gadsden, Ala., until 1908 when he accepted an invitation to become headmaster of Christ School south of Asheville, N.C. He proceeded to convert the school from one of four impoverished Episcopal mission schools in the Blue Ridge Mountains into what came to be recognized as "one of the most important institutions of learning in the southern mountains." It drew its students from the surrounding areas as well as from low-country South Carolina, New Orleans, La., and Virginia.

The course of study at Christ School offered "a thorough education and training in good citizenship and the knowledge of Christ and His church." Citizenship was taught by allowing the students to operate the school's physical plant, including a farm, and by permitting them to enforce discipline. The chapel was the central focus of the school. High Church services were sung and an Angelus was rung twice a day. Mass was said every morning and evensong came with twilight.

While in New Orleans on a fund-raising trip Headmaster Harris, who had not enjoyed good health in recent years, became ill and died. He was buried outside the wall of a new chapel erected in his memory. Harris was survived by his wife, Emiline Rigard Harris, formerly of Akron, Ohio, and three sons and a daughter. One son, David Page Harris, succeeded him as headmaster of Christ School.

SEE: *Asheville Citizen*, 12, 13 Jan. 1933; Christ School student annual, *Angelus*, 1961; James B. Sill, *Historical Sketches of the Churches of the Diocese of Western North Carolina* (1955).

WILLIAM F. W. MASSENGALE

Harris, Stanley Austin (*31 Oct. 1882–13 Aug. 1978*), Boy Scouts of America executive, son of the Reverend William Jacob and Rachel Martitia Netherly Harris, was born in Trade, Tenn., but his family soon moved to Avery County, N.C. After attending the local schools, he went to what is now Tennessee Wesleyan College in Athens and was graduated in 1903. He taught for a year at Cove Creek Academy in Avery County, became a salesman for a while, and then took a position as secretary of the YMCA in Frankfort, Ky.

Harris began taking a group of boys on hikes, and, after reading about the Boy Scout movement in England, he applied to Lord Baden-Powell for a charter. In 1908, he organized the first Boy Scout troop in the United States. In 1910 Harris became a charter member of the national Boy Scouts of America organization, and in the next year was appointed a Scout commissioner for Kentucky. Seven years later he joined the national staff in New York City; because of his experience in helping councils in his area solve the problems involved in making scouting available to the Negro population, he was given the special assignment of promoting interracial scouting in the southeastern states. The first black Boy Scout troop had been started in Louisville, Ky., and soon there were others. Later Harris became director of the Boy Scouts of America Inter-Racial Service, and expanded his work to include American Indian and Mexican-American boys. The first American Indian troop was started in 1927. In recognition of his accomplishments, Harris was given an honorary doctor of humanities degree by Tuskegee Institute.

Until his retirement in 1947, Harris worked out of the Boy Scout headquarters in New York City; he also maintained a home in Watauga County, first at Sugar

Grove and later in Boone. After retiring to Boone, he helped to raise money for building the town's outdoor theater, was treasurer for the outdoor drama, "Horn in the West," and served for ten years as secretary of the Boone Chamber of Commerce. He was also president of the Rotary Club and board chairman of the local hospital. Harris was a founder and director of Watauga Citizens, Inc., and Watauga Developer, Inc., two community corporations organized to promote existing industry and to attract new industry to the county. He remained active in local Boy Scout work until 1975, when, because of his wife's failing health, he moved to the Friends' Home in Greensboro where he lived until his death. His funeral service was held in the United Methodist Church in Boone, and he was buried in the cemetery there.

He was survived by his wife, Mary Swift Harris; a son, Stanley Austin Harris, Jr., of Boone; and a daughter, Martha Harris Farthing of Greensboro.

SEE: *Charlotte Observer*, 26 July 1975; *Greensboro Daily News*, 31 Aug. 1975; *Winston-Salem Journal*, 14 Aug. 1976.

DOROTHY LONG

Harris, Thomas (*d. October 1677*), clerk of the council and public register, settled in the North Carolina colony, then called Albemarle, in or before 1665. He probably migrated from Virginia, where there were several men named Thomas Harris, but none of them has been identified as the Albemarle settler.

Harris first appears in North Carolina records on 15 Nov. 1665, when he was clerk of the Albemarle Council. He held that position through most of the following decade. By 5 Nov. 1675 he held the office of public register, which was equivalent to secretary for the colony. His tenure probably was ended at some stage of the disorders that afflicted the colony in 1676 and succeeding years. Harris lived near Muddy Creek in Perquimans Precinct, where he held 600 acres by patent and additional land by purchase. In the early 1670s he was operating a public house, or inn. At his death he left a substantial estate in addition to his land.

He was married at least once and had two sons, Thomas and John. His wife, Diana, was listed among his headrights in 1669, when he received two land grants. It appears, however, that Diana was not the mother of Thomas, although it is clear that she was the mother of John. Harris bequeathed his estate to his wife and sons, provided Thomas, who had left home, should return within five years; otherwise, the estate was to go to Diana and John. Thomas appears not to have returned. Although a Thomas Harris was in Albemarle in the 1680s and later, the available evidence indicates that he was not the son named in Harris's will.

By March 1680/81 Harris's widow had remarried. Her second husband was William Foster, a Perquimans neighbor, who administered Harris's estate. After Foster's death, Diana was married to Thomas White and subsequently to Thomas Mercer. In 1687 or 1688 Harris's son John married Elizabeth Waller, widow of Thomas Waller and daughter of George and Ann Durant. Elizabeth died soon after the marriage, and Harris remarried. His second wife, Susanah, gave birth to a daughter, Sarah, on 20 Sept. 1689. John Harris died between May and November 1693. Sarah, his only surviving child, married Nathaniel Nicholson.

SEE: Albemarle Book of Warrants and Surveys, 1681–1706, and Council Minutes, Wills, Inventories, 1677–

1701 (North Carolina State Archives, Raleigh); J. Bryan Grimes, ed., *Abstract of North Carolina Wills* (1910); J. R. B. Hathaway, ed., *North Carolina Historical and Genealogical Register*, 3 vols. (1900–1903); Mattie Erma E. Parker, ed., *North Carolina Higher-Court Records, 1670–1696*, vol. 2 (1968), and *1697–1701*, vol. 3 (1971); Perquimans Births, Marriages, Deaths and Flesh Marks, 1659–1739 (North Carolina State Archives, Raleigh); William S. Price, Jr., ed., *North Carolina Higher-Court Records, 1702–1704*, vol. 4 (1974); William L. Saunders, ed., *Colonial Records of North Carolina*, vol. 1 (1886).

MATTIE ERMA E. PARKER

Harris, Thomas West *(15 Dec. 1839–19 Nov. 1888)*, physician, educator, and first dean of The University of North Carolina Medical School, was born in Chatham County, the son of Thomas Brooks and Nancy Clegg Harris. His father was a planter, stock raiser, and large slave owner. Following his early education, Harris enrolled at The University of North Carolina where he was one of four honor graduates in the class of 1859.

At the outbreak of the Civil War, Harris enlisted as a private in the Confederate Army, serving in the Pittsboro company known as the Chatham Rifles. Subsequently, he was commissioned as captain to organize and command Company E, Sixty-third Regiment, Fifth North Carolina Cavalry, a unit that served with General Robert E. Lee during the Battle of the Wilderness in Virginia. Harris received a serious gunshot wound at the Battle of Dinwiddie Courthouse during Lee's evacuation of Petersburg, and he returned home to recuperate as the war came to an end.

With the collapse of the Confederacy, Harris decided to pursue a medical education in Europe. After his marriage to Sally M. Foust in the autumn of 1865, he moved to Paris, France, where he studied surgery and anatomy under Dr. D. Velpeau at L'hôpital de la Charité. Harris was awarded his certificate from Velpeau in late 1866, returned to America, and received the M.D. degree from New York University in 1868. He then returned to North Carolina, where he practiced medicine in the eastern part of the state and later in Chatham County.

In the autumn of 1877, Harris moved to Chapel Hill and established a large practice in the village and surrounding rural community. Concerned about the shortage of qualified physicians in North Carolina, in 1878 he began teaching private courses in anatomy and materia medica. On 12 Feb. 1879, The University of North Carolina executive committee formally established the School of Medicine and appointed Harris as its first dean and professor of anatomy. The curriculum provided two years' instruction in basic medical and clinical science to prepare students for more advanced studies at major medical institutions outside the state. In addition to lectures by Harris, the first year of study included instruction in chemistry by Professor A. Fletcher Redd and in physiology by Professor Frederick W. Simmons. During the second year, Harris taught materia medica, therapeutics, surgery, and anatomy, which included human dissection and the use of a large collection of models. Lectures were delivered in Old West Hall, and dissections were performed in a small building near the site of present Venable Hall. Harris conducted free clinics each week, allowing students to observe and treat a variety of diseases. Unfortunately, the university was unable to provide a salary for Harris, who was thus forced to devote much of his time to private practice. In recognition of his contributions to

medical education, the institution awarded him an honorary M.A. degree in 1880. By 1885, the conflict between teaching and practice caused Harris to resign his position with the university. The School of Medicine then ceased operation until 1890, when it reopened under the deanship of Dr. Richard H. Whitehead.

Following his resignation, Harris moved to Durham where he continued a general and surgical practice until his death three years later. He was survived by his wife and several children. A portrait, commissioned by Dr. Isaac Harris, hangs in The University of North Carolina Medical School library.

SEE: *Asheville Citizen-Times*, 3 Apr. 1949; Kemp P. Battle, *History of the University of North Carolina*, vol. 2 (1912); *Durham Herald*, 3 Apr. 1949; Daniel L. Grant, *Alumni History of the University of North Carolina* (1924); W. Hadley, D. G. Horton, and N. C. Stroud, *Chatham County, 1771–1971* (1971); Pittsboro *Chatham Record*, 22 Nov. 1888.

MARCUS B. SIMPSON, JR.

Harris, Wade Hampton *(1 Jan. 1858–14 Sept. 1935)*, newspaper editor, was a native of Sandy Ridge, Cabarrus County, the oldest of seven children born to Richard Sadler (4 Jan. 1835–6 July 1911) and Mary Annette Hampton Harris (1837–12 Jan. 1929). His maternal grandfather was Joseph Wade Hampton, proprietor of newspapers in Salisbury and Charlotte in the 1830s and 1840s. His father, a native of Rock Hill, S.C., served for a time as sheriff of Cabarrus County.

Harris was educated in a private school operated near his home by General James H. Lane and B. Frank Rogers. At age fifteen he began to learn the printing trade in the office of the *Concord Sun*, which was owned by his uncle, Charles F. Harris. In January 1875, Harris entered the Virginia Agricultural and Mechanical College (now Virginia Polytechnic Institute and State University) at Blacksburg. There he again came under the influence of General Lane, who was then head of the school's military department. While a student, Harris started a newspaper known as the *Yellow Jacket*; it is said to have been the first college paper published in the South.

Returning to Concord, he joined the staff of the *Concord Sun* as local editor on 1 Feb. 1876. By mid-July of that year, at age eighteen, he had become the *Sun's* general editor and proprietor. In his first issue as editor, Harris declared that "The SUN is strictly Democratic and will leave nothing unsaid that will redound to the interest and welfare of our party." He maintained a lifelong devotion to the Democratic cause.

In October 1878 Harris sold the *Concord Sun* and moved to Wilmington, where he became city editor of the *Wilmington Sun*, a newly founded daily. He remained there until November 1879, when he moved to Greensboro to be local editor of the *Greensboro Patriot*. The following year he returned to Concord, repurchased the *Sun*, and was its editor and proprietor until May 1882, when he again disposed of the journal. He then moved to Charlotte to accept a position as local editor of the *Daily Charlotte Observer* (later the *Daily Journal-Observer*). There, on 27 Feb. 1884, he married Cora Springs (7 Dec. 1860–16 Aug. 1937), daughter of John and Elizabeth Stafford Springs of Charlotte.

On 30 Dec. 1886 Harris became local editor of the *Charlotte Daily Chronicle*. He resigned in November 1888 in order to found the *Charlotte News*, the city's first afternoon daily. He remained editor and publisher of the *News* until March 1895, when he sold the paper to W. Carey Dowd; for a time, however, he continued as local editor. About 1903 the owners of the *Charlotte Observer* began publishing an afternoon daily known as the Charlotte *Evening Chronicle*. Harris soon joined the staff and later became editor in chief. By this time he was already hailed as a "veteran editor."

In 1896, at his own expense, Harris published *Sketches of Charlotte*, a booklet designed to publicize the attractions of the Charlotte area and the city's potential for commercial growth. This publication, reprinted at least eight times, enhanced Harris's reputation as a civic promoter. Between 1896 and 1924 he published several other booklets to make known Charlotte's commercial advantages.

Harris was named editor in chief of the prestigious *Charlotte Observer* on 10 June 1912. His selection was commended by the state's press corps. Several papers attributed Harris's appointment to his well-known loyalty to the Democratic party and particularly to his championship of the presidential candidacy of Woodrow Wilson. As a leading promoter of civic improvements in Charlotte, Harris began shaping the editorial columns of the *Observer* into a vehicle for his generally progressive views on broader state and regional issues. He reportedly exerted considerable influence upon public opinion in the areas of road improvement and the development of a tourist industry in North Carolina.

A recognized leader of the state Democratic party, Harris cooperated with Governor Charles B. Aycock's efforts to establish an educational revival in the state. Widely credited with helping to bring about the reelection of Furnifold M. Simmons to the U.S. Senate in the celebrated Simmons-Kitchin-Clark campaign of 1912, he was also instrumental in the election of Cameron Morrison as governor in 1920. A staunch supporter of Woodrow Wilson, Harris served as an alternate delegate to the Democratic National Convention of 1916. That year he was a member of the North Carolina delegation sent to Shadow Lawn, N.J., to inform Wilson of his renomination for the presidency. Harris also attended the Democratic National conventions of 1920, 1924, and 1928.

In addition to his political activities, the newspaper editor was appointed to serve on various state and national boards and commissions. In 1921 Governor Cameron Morrison named him president and director of the North Carolina Railroad Company, a largely ceremonial post. During this time Harris was also a director of the Woodrow Wilson Foundation. He served in 1934 as a member of the State Advisory Board of the National Recovery Administration.

Harris toured Europe with a group of newspapermen in 1919, 1927, and 1932, and attended U.S. naval maneuvers in the Caribbean in 1924. An extensive world traveler, he nevertheless prided himself on his travels in, and vast knowledge of, the Carolinas. He was regarded as an expert on North Carolina's people, history, resources, institutions, and potential. His years of effort on behalf of a better North Carolina were recognized in 1926 when Davidson College awarded him an honorary doctor of laws degree. And his attempts to promote tourism in his beloved North Carolina mountains were cited when a newly constructed highway bridge in Wilkes County was named for him in August 1931. Spanning the 112-foot Lewis Fork Creek gorge, the structure was then the second highest bridge in the state. Harris was also the author or editor of several books and pamphlets, including *My School Days: Reconstruction Experiences in the South* (1914), *The City of Char-*

lotte and the County of Mecklenburg (1924), *Letters to the Charlotte Observer* (1927), and *The Editor Abroad* (1934). He was a member of Kappa Sigma fraternity and the Charlotte Chamber of Commerce.

In January 1933 Harris, at age seventy-five and in failing health, relinquished a portion of his editorial duties to Julian Miller, a junior associate; he was then by far the state's oldest living newspaper editor. He died two years later and was buried in Elmwood Cemetery, Charlotte. A Presbyterian, he was survived by his wife, his son Richard Pegram Harris of Hendersonville, and his daughter Cora Annette Harris of Charlotte (d. 18 Jan. 1983), a newspaper columnist and horticulturist; another son, James Pinckney Harris, died 10 Mar. 1933. He was known as "Colonel" Harris, but the appellation was honorary.

SEE: LeGette Blythe and Charles Raven Brockmann, *Hornets' Nest: The Story of Charlotte and Mecklenburg County* (1961); *Charlotte Daily Chronicle*, 30, 31 Dec. 1886; *Charlotte Democrat*, 14 Dec. 1888, 22 Mar. 1895; *Charlotte Evening Chronicle*, 11 June 1912; *Charlotte Home and Democrat*, 19 May 1882; *Charlotte Observer*, 17 Nov. 1925, 13, 14 Jan. 1929, 15 Jan. 1933, 14, 15, 16 Sept. 1935, 30 Nov. 1939, 28 Feb. 1950; *Concord Sun*, 1 Feb., 18 July 1876; *Concord Times*, 6 July 1911; *Greensboro Patriot*, 5 Nov. 1879; Wade Hampton Harris Papers (Southern Historical Collection, University of North Carolina Library, Chapel Hill); *North Carolina Biography*, vol. 4 (1928); *Wilmington Sun*, 22 Oct. 1878; *Who Was Who in America*, vol. 1 (1962); *Who's Who in the South* (1927).

ROBERT M. TOPKINS

Harris, Winder Russell (3 Dec. 1888–24 Feb. 1973), newspaperman and congressman, was born in Raleigh, one of eleven children of Raleigh attorney John Cebern Logan and Florence Upchurch Harris. After attending the Raleigh public schools and what is now Belmont Abbey College at Belmont, he began his newspaper career in 1908 as a sports writer for the *Raleigh Times*. He then became successively sports editor, *Charlotte News*; news editor, Spartanburg (S.C.) *Herald*; state news editor, *Charlotte Observer*; managing editor, *Charlotte Chronicle*; telegraph editor, Raleigh *News and Observer*; manager, United Press Bureau, Raleigh; news editor, Richmond *Virginian*; news editor, Newport News *Times-Herald*; city editor, Norfolk *Virginian-Pilot*; and reporter, *Norfolk Ledger-Dispatch*.

From 1918 to 1925 Harris was a correspondent for the Universal Service in Washington, D.C., covering the House, Senate, White House, and many other news beats. He reported on the Republican, Progressive, and Democratic National conventions in 1924. He also covered the presidential campaigns of Governor James H. Cox in 1920 and Senator Robert M. LaFollette in 1924, and traveled as a reporter with Presidents Warren G. Harding and Calvin Coolidge. In 1924 and 1925, he served as assistant secretary of the American delegation to the International Narcotics Congress at the League of Nations Headquarters in Geneva, Switzerland.

Harris returned to Norfolk in 1925 to become managing editor of the *Virginian-Pilot*, a position he held for sixteen years. In 1934 he was honored by the Cosmopolitan Club, which designated him as "Norfolk's First Citizen." Among his many civic activities, he headed the Community Chest and Rotary Club, and he served on the board of directors of the Association of Commerce, Maritime Exchange, Norfolk General Hospital, Boy Scouts, and Red Cross.

On 8 Apr. 1941, he won a special election as a Democrat to fill the vacancy in the Seventy-seventh Congress when Colgate W. Darden resigned to run for governor. Harris was reelected without opposition, but resigned on 15 Sept. 1944 to become vice-president of the Shipbuilders' Council of America and head of its Washington office. Soon afterwards he established residence in Alexandria, Va., where he remained for the rest of his life. On 31 Dec. 1958 he resigned from the Shipbuilders' Council and for the next six years was editor of the *Alexandria Journal*, the *Arlington Journal*, and the *Fairfax County Journal-Standard*. While living in Alexandria, he served from 1953 to 1961 as a member and vice-chairman of the city's Redevelopment and Housing Authority. On the occasion of his eightieth birthday, he was awarded the Medal of Good Citizenship by the Sons of the American Revolution, of which he was a member.

Harris was an Episcopalian. He died of cancer at George Washington University Hospital at age eighty-four and was buried in Oakwood Cemetery, Raleigh. He was survived by his wife, the former Charlotte Meares, and four daughters: Mrs. Anne H. Marshall of Virginia Beach, Va.; Elizabeth Lea Harris; Florence Caroline Harris; and Mrs. Charlotte H. Bill of Alexandria, Va.

SEE: *Biog. Dir. Am. Cong.* (1961); *Washington Post* and *Washington Star & News*, 26 Feb. 1973; *Who Was Who in America*, vol. 5 (1973).

CHARLES AYCOCK POE

Harrison, Richard (*30 Jan. 1768–19 May 1856*), planter and legislator, was born at Leonardstown, St. Mary's County, Md., the son of Kenelm and Mary Harrison. Having inherited a plantation in Edgecombe County, N.C., as provided in the will of his father in 1777, Richard Harrison moved there in 1789. He became a member of the Royal White Hart Lodge in Halifax in 1791 and represented Edgecombe County in the state senate from 1801 to 1807. As a planter he was unusually successful, and in his lifetime he amassed a large landed estate.

Harrison married Martha Smith, the daughter of Arthur and Anne Ruffin Smith of Halifax County and the widow of Marmaduke Bell. They had three children, whom Harrison survived. He and his family were first buried on the plantation; their graves were later moved to Greenwood Cemetery, Tarboro.

In his long and involved will of twenty-four pages, Harrison left his estate to the children of his sisters Mary Dicken Powell and Ann Lewis. His home plantation a few miles west of Tarboro went to his nephew, Dr. Joseph John Willis Powell. In 1857 Dr. Powell began building Coolmore on the Harrison homeplace. Considered a fine example of Victorian architecture, Coolmore took three years to complete. Powell lived in his new home for only a few weeks before he died. At the sale of Bennett Bunn, Richard Harrison had bought the fine house Bunn had erected near the falls of the Tar River at Rocky Mount. Referred to in Harrison's will as "The Brick House," it was left to "nephew Kenelm N. Lewis." Presently known as "The Lewis Place" or "Stonewall," the house has been restored and is maintained by the Nash County Historical Society.

SEE: T. C. Parramore, *Launching the Craft* (1975); Records of the Powell family at Coolmore; Thomas T. Waterman, *The Early Architecture of North Carolina* (1941); John H. Wheeler, *Historical Sketches of North Carolina* (1851); Wills

and deeds of Halifax and Edgecombe counties (North Carolina State Archives, Raleigh); Wills of St. Mary's County (Maryland State Archives, Annapolis).

CLAIBORNE T. SMITH, JR.

Harrison, Thomas Perrin (*11 Oct. 1864–1 Nov. 1949*), college professor, was born in Abbeville, S.C., at the home of his maternal grandfather, Thomas Chiles Perrin. The son of Francis Eugene (1826–78) and Mary Eunice Perrin Harrison (1832–74), he spent his boyhood on his father's plantation at Andersonville, which lay at the confluence of the Tugaloo and Seneca rivers, forming the Savannah. For fifty years this was the most important river port in upper South Carolina; from it tobacco, cotton, and other products were loaded on barges for the 100-mile trip to Hamburg, S.C., and Augusta, Ga. At Andersonville he enjoyed the outdoor life of swimming, fishing, boating, and at night much storytelling. Formal schooling began in a nearby one-room schoolhouse, which he attended with an older brother and sister.

After his parents' death, at age fourteen Harrison moved to Abbeville to live with the Perrins, and for two years attended the Abbeville Academy. In 1882 he entered the South Carolina Military Academy at the Citadel (later known as the Citadel), where in 1886 he was graduated with second honors. This was the first class to enter and, four years later, to graduate after the Civil War. For two years Harrison remained at the Citadel as lieutenant, adjutant, and professor of English. Years later, in 1929, he delivered the commencement address and was awarded the honorary LL.D. degree. Of all the institutions with which he was later associated, he was proudest of the Citadel, a symbol of his lifelong pride in a military bearing.

In 1888 he faced a new and different challenge when he enrolled as a graduate student in Johns Hopkins, Baltimore, with a major in English and minors in German and French. All English majors fell under the direction of Dr. James W. Bright, the eminent pioneer in English philology based on the German school of linguistic research emphasizing historical grammar rather than literature. Harrison so mastered the rigorous program that after two years he was appointed University Scholar and later Fellow in English, the stipend of which enabled him to study in England. In May 1891, he was awarded the Ph.D.; his dissertation was entitled "The Separable Prefixes in Anglo-Saxon." The value of the exacting discipline at Johns Hopkins is undeniable, though, like most of his contemporaries there, he turned with relief to the teaching of literature. Not surprisingly, the optimist Robert Browning became a favorite poet.

The fall of 1891 found Harrison at Clemson College as associate professor, a post he held for four years. On 9 Jan. 1894 he married Adelia Lake Leftwich, in Atlanta, to whom he had become engaged before leaving Baltimore; she was the daughter of the Reverend James Turner Leftwich, pastor of the First Presbyterian Church.

Harrison's move to Davidson College in 1895 marked the beginning of a contented and successful period of teaching in a congenial community. With a balanced curriculum leading to the liberal arts degree and an atmosphere inspired by the Presbyterian church, Davidson has maintained the highest ideal in education since its establishment in 1837. Fortunate in sharing this aim, Harrison remained at the school for thirteen years. At midyear 1908–9, he resigned to accept a professorship at the College of Agriculture and Mechanic Arts (later called the College of Agriculture and Engineering, then State College of Agriculture and Engineering) in Raleigh. Here he adapted his talents towards a utilitarian end. In 1911 he was appointed dean of the college, a position he held until his retirement as Dean Emeritus in 1939. For several years he also taught summer school at The University of North Carolina.

During World War I he did not meet the physical requirements for active military service, but in July 1918 he embarked for France as YMCA secretary. After the armistice he continued as a member of the Army Educational Corps, American Expeditionary Force, until July 1919.

Soon after his return to State College, Harrison was instrumental in establishing the West Raleigh Presbyterian Church; for many years he served as elder. At his suggestion, in 1927 Dr. Ben R. Lacy, a Davidson alumnus, was the first to address the small congregation; later that year Lacy was succeeded by the Reverend Joseph R. Walker as regular minister. Harrison was a member, and occasional speaker, of the National Council of Teachers of English, North Carolina State Teachers Assembly, National History Club, North Carolina Literary and Historical Association, Society for the Promotion of Engineering Education, Folklore Association, and Modern Language Association of America. Scholarly articles by him appeared in *Modern Language Notes* (1920, 1943) and *Shakespeare Association Bulletin* (1945).

Harrison and his family spent every summer in the North Carolina mountains, staying first in boardinghouses and later in the Ravenel home in Biltmore. He and his sons made frequent backpacking trips to the Craggies, Mount Mitchell, and lesser peaks. In 1925 he acquired an old farmhouse on 130 acres at the foot of Whiteside Mountain, near Cashiers. For him, the simple life here was reminiscent of his plantation boyhood. Cashiers became the scene of perennial reunions of his own scattering family as well as of many South Carolina kin.

On his retirement from State College at age seventy-five, Harrison remained mentally and physically active. His daily routine still included early morning calisthenics and jogging through the pines behind his Raleigh home in late afternoon, followed by a cold bath. He made almost a fetish of physical fitness and he never suffered a serious illness. After his wife's death in 1944, he spent his last years at his daughter's home in Asheville. He died during an operation to mend a broken hip. According to his wish, he was buried beside his parents in the family cemetery in Andersonville, S.C. Harrison was survived by four children: James Leftwich, Thomas Perrin, Jr., Florence Leftwich, and Lewis Wardlaw.

SEE: American Genealogical Research Institute, *The Harrison Family* (1972); *Asheville Citizen*, 5 Nov. 1949; Joseph E. Birnie, *The Earles and the Birnies* (1974); *Charlotte Observer*, 2 Nov. 1949; Greenwood, S.C., *Index-Journal*, 3 Nov. 1949; James Harrison Papers (South Caroliniana Library, University of South Carolina, Columbia); Thomas P. Harrison, *Recollections of Andersonville* (1947); Thomas P. Harrison Papers (Southern Historical Collection, University of North Carolina Library, Chapel Hill); Thomas P. Harrison, Jr., *The Harrisons of Andersonville, South Carolina* (1973), and *Supplement* (1975); Wade C. Harrison, "Genealogy of the Perrins" (ca. 1965); Joseph G. Wardlaw, *Genealogy of the Wardlaw Family* (1929); *Who Was Who in America*, vol. 2 (1950).

T. P. HARRISON, JR.

Hart, Julian Deryl (*27 Aug. 1894–1 June 1980*), surgeon and university president, was born in Prattsburg, Ga., the son of John Deryl, a farmer, and Fannie Walter Matthews Hart, a descendant of Sir Anthony Drane, nephew of the second Lord Baltimore. Brought up on a plantation of several hundred acres in Taylor County, Ga., Hart attended public schools in Buena Vista and then matriculated at Emory University, where he distinguished himself in mathematics and oratory, compiling the best record in math over four years of any student at the university. During his senior year, without telling his parents, he determined to become a doctor, although he remained at Emory beyond graduation in 1916 to take an M.A. degree in mathematics in 1917. Admitted to the Johns Hopkins University School of Medicine on the strength of a recommendation from his chemistry professor, for whom he supervised the premedical chemistry laboratory, he made his highest clinical grade in medicine but was most attracted to surgery. After receiving the M.D. degree in 1921, Hart continued at Johns Hopkins as intern in surgery (1921–22), assistant in pathology (1922–23), instructor in surgery (1923–29), assistant resident in surgery and surgical pathology (1923–27), resident surgeon (1927–29), and associate surgeon (1929–30). While a resident he wrote *Surgery of the Hand*, a text in the *Practice of Surgery* series edited by Dean Lewis.

Hart's southern background and long period of preparation at Johns Hopkins were prominent among the considerations that led Dr. Wilburt C. Davison in 1928 to offer him the position of professor of surgery and chairman of the department in the Duke University School of Medicine and Hospital, then under construction. From 1930, when he arrived in Durham to assume these duties, to 1960, when he retired from the medical faculty to become president of Duke University, Hart commented that he was an enthusiast for nothing else.

Because the Duke medical school was in the process of building a national reputation, his career had a clinical rather than a research orientation; its primary products were grateful patients and well-trained students, a number of whom later headed surgery departments. With Dr. Frederick M. Hanes and the cooperation of other members of the clinical faculty, Hart led in the development of the private diagnostic clinics at Duke. His pioneering work on the use of ultraviolet radiation as a means of combating airborne infections in the operating room won national acclaim in the late 1930s and early 1940s. In 1949, he and Dr. James Moody claimed national attention for their work on changing the male-female ratio in litters of rats. Relating their results to human experience, they suggested that it made a difference, in terms of sex determination, how early in the period of fertility an egg was fertilized. For many years after this work was published, Hart served—often informally—as a counselor to childless couples or couples desiring a child of a certain sex. His other publications reflect a broad clinical practice, with important contributions to the surgical treatment of peptic ulcers, spinal fluid drainage, the role of anesthesia in lowering surgical morbidity and mortality, and tidal irrigation of empyema in the chest.

During his surgical career, Hart was a member of the board of governors of the American College of Surgeons and served on its executive committee. He was vice-president (1953) and president (1956–57) of the Southern Surgical Association, vice-president (1956) and president (1957–58) of the Southern Society of Clinical Surgeons, and a member for thirty years and president (1956–57) of the Durham-Orange County Medical Society. In addition, he was a member of Nu

Sigma Nu, Alpha Omega Alpha, Sigma Xi, and Rotary, fraternal organizations; Phi Beta Kappa, the national scholastic society; and many medical organizations, including the International Surgical Society, American Medical Association, American Surgical Association, and Society of University Surgeons.

In April 1960, Hart was asked to assume the duties of president pro tem of Duke University. Subsequently he was appointed president, retroactive to that date. Hart brought to the university, then in a period of administrative turmoil, a concept of leadership defined by the need for teamwork. During his presidency, the relationships among trustees, administrators, and faculty were reorganized to eliminate sources of conflict and friction. Always active in the planning of additions to the physical plant of the hospital and medical school, Hart presided over major expansions of the university plant as well. Under his leadership, faculty salaries were raised substantially and the number of endowed, distinguished professorships doubled. He retired from the presidency in 1963.

Hart married Mary Elizabeth Johnson of Raleigh in 1932. They had six children: Elizabeth Hicks Hart King, Julia Drane Hart Warner, Julian Deryl Hart, Jr., John Martin Hicks Hart, William Johnson Hart, and Margaret Louise Hart Harrison. Hart was a Democrat and a member of Duke University Methodist Church. A portrait of him hangs in the Duke University School of Medicine. His collected works are available in the Medical Center Library, and his personal and professional papers are in the university archives.

SEE: *Annals of Surgery*, 145 (1957); *Duke Alumni Register* 49 (1963); *Durham Morning Herald*, 2 June 1980; J. F. Gifford, *The Evolution of a Medical Center* (1972); Julian D. Hart, *The First Forty Years at Duke in Surgery and the P.D.C.* (1971); William S. Powell, ed., *North Carolina Lives* (1962); Raleigh *News and Observer*, 2 June 1980.

JAMES F. GIFFORD

Hart, Nathaniel (*1734–82*), pioneer, Revolutionary officer, and proprietor in and chief negotiator for the Transylvania Company of Kentucky, was born in Hanover County, Va., the son of Thomas and Susannah Rice Hart. His grandfather, Thomas Hart, a merchant, emigrated from London, England, to Hanover County about 1690 and left an only son, Thomas (1632–1755), father of Nathaniel. His mother was an aunt of Daniel Rice, the renowned Presbyterian minister who, before moving to Kentucky in 1781, is said to have taken part in the establishment of one or more early Presbyterian churches in Orange County (now Caswell County), N.C., among which Hyco (now Red House) is one of the oldest in central North Carolina.

Shortly after Thomas Hart's death, his widow and children moved to Orange County and settled on Country Line Creek, where three of her sons—Thomas, Nathaniel, and David—in the late 1750s and early 1760s obtained land grants in the area that was cut off from Orange in 1777 to form Caswell County. Nathaniel Hart's estate, known as Red House, located at Nat's Fork on Country Line Creek, was of considerable proportions. Referred to as "Captain Hart," he was not only a polished member of society but also an "accomplished and complete gentleman." As one of the proprietors of the Transylvania Company, he was a leading spirit in opening the Kentucky territory and in establishing the town of Boonesborough. At the Battle of Alamance, Hart led a company of infantrymen in Governor Tryon's army; after the battle, he was highly complimented by the governor and his officers for the gallant and spirited behavior of the detachment under his command.

Following the efforts of Daniel Boone and his brother, Squire Boone, to settle Kentucky, Richard Henderson of Granville County in association with Nathaniel Hart, Thomas Hart, John Williams, William Johnson, and John Lutterell, on 27 Aug. 1774 organized the Louisa Company for the purpose of purchasing from the Cherokee Nation a large territory lying on the west side of the mountains on the Mississippi River. In the autumn of 1774, Nathaniel Hart, the chief negotiator, along with Richard Henderson, president of the company, visited the territory and met with the chiefs of the various tribes in the Cherokee country to discuss their interest in buying the land west of the Cumberland Mountains. Nathaniel Hart, Jr., wrote that his father returned to his home with six or eight of the principal men of the Cherokee Nation, who remained with him until the latter part of the year and assisted in the selection of a large supply of goods to be used in exchange for the land.

By 1775 the enterprise had outgrown the Articles of Agreement of the Louisa Company. After a reorganization, a new company, called the Transylvania Company, was formed and Daniel Boone was hired to explore the territory. Soon Nathaniel Hart and Richard Henderson brought vast quantities of goods from Cross Creek (now Fayetteville) to Sycamore on the Watauga River near what is now Elizabethton, Tenn. The Watauga meeting, arranged by Hart, lasted twenty days and was attended by 500 to 1,000 Cherokee Indians along with their chiefs. The Transylvania Company was represented by Hart and his brother Thomas, Henderson, and John Williams. Negotiations broke down and the Indians left, but it is said that Nathaniel Hart overtook them the next day, persuaded them to return, and an agreement was reached. On 17 Mar. 1775, the conveyance or treaty was signed, by which the Transylvania Company acquired all of the territory from the Kentucky to the Cumberland rivers. Title to the land was taken in the name of Richard Henderson, Nathaniel Hart, and the other seven proprietors of the company as tenants in common. This purchase was said to have been the largest private land deal ever undertaken in North America.

Nathaniel Hart and his associates invested much of their time and private fortunes in the venture; they succeeded in obtaining for the colonies peaceful possession of the land from the Indians, thus permitting the opening of the Kentucky territory for colonization. Nevertheless, they received very little for their efforts. Because of a proclamation by the royal governors of Virginia and North Carolina that prohibited treaties or purchases of land from Indians by individuals, the Crown refused to recognize the transaction and declared it null and void. The same proclamation, in substance, was reenacted by the Virginia assembly after the colonies gained independence from Great Britain. As a consequence, the Transylvania Company retained only that small area of the land lying on the Green River in Kentucky and that portion lying on the North Carolina side of the Virginia line, and its plan to establish an original fourteenth colony in America resulted in failure.

In 1760 Hart married Sarah Simpson, daughter of Captain Richard Simpson, a large plantation owner who was one of the earliest settlers in what is now Caswell County. Their daughter, Susanna, in 1783 married General Isaac Shelby, planner of the Battle of Cowpens and hero of the Battle of Kings Mountain, who became the first governor of the state of Kentucky and for whom the towns of Shelby, N.C., Shelbyville, Tenn., and Shelby County, Ky., were named. Nathaniel and Sarah Hart's grandson, Thomas Hart Shelby of Traveler's Rest, Ky., was said to have been the first importer of thoroughbred livestock, including racehorses, into the state of Kentucky.

Hart was appointed a justice of the peace by the royal governor. He served as captain of militia before the outbreak of the Revolution and as captain in the army during the American Revolution. He was killed by Indians near Logan's Station in Lincoln, Ky., where he left his will. In 1783 his widow and their son Nathaniel, Jr., went to Logan's Station to prove the will.

SEE: John R. Alden, *John Stuart and the Southern Colonial Frontier* (1966); Walter Clark, ed., *State Records of North Carolina*, vols. 16, 19, 22, 24 (1899–1905); Lewis Collins, *Historical Sketches of Kentucky* (1850); Dartmouth Papers, 5, 127, 1353 (North Carolina State Archives, Raleigh); Lyman C. Draper Papers (Wisconsin Historical Society, Madison); Genealogical Narrative, "The Hart Family in the United States" (North Carolina State Library, Raleigh); Archibald Henderson, *The Transylvania Company and the Founding of Henderson, Kentucky* (1929); Land grants of Caswell and Orange counties (Office of the Secretary of State, Raleigh); William S. Lester, *The Transylvania Colony* (1935); George N. MacKenzie, *Colonial Families of the United States*, vol. 2 (1966); W. P. Palmer, ed., *Calendar of Virginia State Papers*, vol. 1 (1875); William L. Saunders, ed., *Colonial Records of North Carolina*, vols. 6, 8–10 (1888–90); *Tyler's Quarterly* 31 (1949), 32 (1950); *Virginia Magazine of History and Biography* 7 (1899–1900); Frederick A. Virkus, *The Abridged Compendium of American Genealogy*, vol. 5 (1933).

VANCE E. SWIFT

Hart, Thomas (ca. 1730–23 June 1808), merchant, public official, and militia officer, the son of Thomas and Susannah Rice Hart, was born in Hanover County, Va., on a plantation settled in 1690 by his English-born grandfather, also named Thomas. John, Benjamin, David, and Nathaniel were his brothers, and Ann his only sister. The family moved to Orange County, N.C., in 1755 after their father died. By 1779, Thomas had received a total of 2,282 acres of land in grants and erected his home, Hartford, near Hillsborough. In addition to farming, he built a gristmill on the nearby Eno River and conducted other business enterprises at the location that became known as Hart's Mill. Later he became a partner with Nathaniel Rochester and James Brown in a mercantile establishment in Hillsborough.

After establishing himself financially, Hart married Susannah Gray, the daughter of the wealthy and politically prominent Colonel John Gray. In 1775, the colonel died and left his entire estate to his son-in-law, including the large plantation Grayfields. With capital resources thus increased, Hart shrewdly expanded his business and by his industrious management accumulated a considerable fortune according to the Orange County tax books for 1779. In addition to his financial prosperity, Hart was successful politically. Shortly after settling in North Carolina, he became an intimate of James Watson, James Thackston, Thomas Burke, James Hogg, William Johnston, and Richard Henderson, and an acquaintance of Governor William Tryon and Edmund Fanning. This led to his appointment as a ves-

tryman of St. Matthew's Parish as well as county sheriff for a two-year term and another beginning in 1768. In the latter year he was also made a captain in the Orange County militia and commissary for the troops of Orange and Granville counties.

Throughout his tenure of office, the sheriff was in constant controversy with the increasingly active Regulators. In 1765, the Assembly passed a bill introduced by Edmund Fanning to award Hart £1,000 for his losses as sheriff, and the previous legislature had included Hart in a group exempt from the payment of taxes. These acts infuriated the Regulators, who claimed the sheriff had no losses, but was being rewarded at public expense for using his influence in the election of Fanning to office. Hart also displeased the government by his failure to collect the unpopular poll tax, either because he disapproved of the law or did not understand it. In 1765, the Assembly ordered him to make the collection. Whether or not he did, he settled his financial account in the colony satisfactorily, which won for him a tribute from Orange County residents because he was the only sheriff ever to do so.

When Governor Tryon decided in 1768 to have Herman Husband arraigned in court for his Regulator activities, Sheriff Hart served the warrant and took the accused into custody. In the same year, and again in 1771, Hart was ordered to raise five hundred troops for the defense of the colony. He was unable to enlist the requested manpower but on both occasions accumulated sufficient provisions to sustain the troops Tryon assembled at Hillsborough. The actions of the royal government increasingly incited the wrath of the Regulators, and the sheriff was one of a group of officials they severely whipped in 1770. In view of such treatment, Hart undoubtedly received considerable satisfaction in serving as quartermaster for Tryon when the governor dispersed the Regulators at the Battle of Alamance.

During the relative calm that ensued after the War of the Regulation, Hart was able to concentrate on business enterprises. The role of an entrepreneur appealed to him, and in 1774 he became one of the partners in Richard Henderson's Louisa Company to buy and develop lands in what became Tennessee and Kentucky. Hart journeyed to the Watauga section of Tennessee as one of the company's representatives at a meeting arranged by Daniel Boone with the Cherokee Indians. John Sevier and Isaac Shelby, who attended as spectators, saw the Indians accept several loads of "trading goods" in return for their titular rights to a huge area of western land. After this transaction, the company was reorganized as the Transylvania Company with Richard Henderson, Thomas Hart, Nathaniel Hart, William Johnston, James Hogg, John Luttrell, John Williams, David Hart, and Leonard Henly Bullock as shareholders. Trading with the Indians for western lands strictly violated the Royal Proclamation of 1763, but, as many Americans were engaging in land speculation despite the king's fiat, the Transylvanians ignored it also. The potential profit in the venture was enormous, and the partners lost no time in enlisting settlers to buy or rent land in the territory. Thomas Hart visited the Watauga again in 1775 and his brother, Nathaniel, became a resident agent for the company in the west until he was killed by Indians in 1782.

The outcome of the American Revolution relieved the Transylvania Company of any interference in its affairs from the British government but presented a new dilemma because the states of North Carolina and Virginia claimed Tennessee and Kentucky, respectively, as part of their territory. The partners determined to establish their claim to the western land if possible and years of litigation followed. The final decision rendered that the company's purchase was illegal but a tract was awarded the partners to recompense them for the expenses incurred in the transaction. Hart traded part of his share for land in Kentucky and eventually settled on it.

After the War of the Regulation, Hart continued to fill an important role in political affairs, serving as a juror; member of a commission to build a new jail in Hillsborough; member of the colonial Assembly from Orange County in 1773; and then representative in the First, Second, and Third Provincial congresses. When the Revolution began, he was appointed commissary for the Sixth North Carolina Regiment with the rank of colonel. In addition, he was elected a senator in the North Carolina General Assembly for the 1777 session where he became involved in the work of so many committees that he resigned his military commission in order to attend to them.

Although Hart, with many others, could not condone the violent tactics of the Regulators, he felt no compunction in becoming an ardent patriot in the American Revolution when independence was formally declared. In doing so, he incurred the hatred of the loyal Tories who unleashed their persecutions when Lord Cornwallis approached Hillsborough with the British Army. Concerned for the safety of his wife and several daughters, Hart removed to Hagerstown, Md., accompanied by Nathaniel Rochester, one of his former business partners. Shortly after his departure the Battle of Hart's Mill was fought on his property, which the British occupied.

Hart and Rochester built a mill and a nail and rope factory, both of which prospered. The colonel gradually disposed of his North Carolina property and never returned to the state. He sold his homeplace, Hartford, to Jesse Benton, husband of his niece, Nancy, and father of Thomas Hart Benton. As the purchaser died before paying for the place, Hart became the mortgagee of the property through a friendly lawsuit and allowed the widow and her family to continue to live there. The mortage was never fully redeemed, which apparently caused no ill will as Hart left the Bentons an additional tract of land when he died.

In 1794, Hart moved to Lexington, Ky., where he resided for the remainder of his life. He built up his rope and hemp business into a highly profitable commercial enterprise and engaged in various forms of trade and investment. Due to his affluence, pleasing personality, and shrewd mind, Hart soon became one of the most prominent men in Kentucky. His daughter, Ann (Nancy), married James Brown who had engaged in business with the colonel and Rochester back in Hillsborough, and who later became the U.S. minister to France. Another daughter, Lucretia, born after the Harts left North Carolina, married Henry Clay. A niece married Isaac Shelby, and the other members of the family made marital connections in influential circles.

In Maryland, Hart was a communicant of All Saints' Parish (later renamed St. John's), of the Protestant Episcopal church. In Kentucky, he joined an Episcopal society which eventually became Christ Church in Lexington. He was buried in the Old Episcopal Graveyard in that city. No portrait of Hart has been found.

SEE: Walter Clark, ed., *State Records of North Carolina,* vols. 11, 16, 24 (1895, 1899, 1905); Lyman Copeland Draper Letters (Kentucky Historical Society, Frankfort); William S. Lester, *The Transylvania Colony* (1935); Frank Nash, *Hillsboro: Colonial and Revolutionary* (1953); Records of Orange County (Offices, Register of Deeds and Clerk of Courts, County Courthouse, Hillsborough); William L. Saunders, ed., *Colonial Records of North Carolina,* vols. 7, 8 (1890); Durward T. Stokes, "Thomas Hart in North Carolina," *North Carolina Historical Review* 41 (1964).

DURWARD T. STOKES

Hartley (Hartly, Heartley), Francis (*d. February 1691/92*), secretary and Council member, was appointed secretary by a commission from the Lords Proprietors dated 3 June 1684. Whether Hartley was then living in North Carolina is not known. The earliest date for which there is evidence of his presence in the colony is 5 Feb. 1684/85, when he was defendant in a suit brought in the County Court of Albemarle.

Hartley, who was acting as secretary in February 1690/91, presumably held the office from 1684 until his death. From 1689 to 1691 he sat on the Council and on the courts held by that body, which he appears not to have done in earlier years. He bore the title colonel, which probably indicated his rank in the local militia. The sparse surviving records of the period tell little more about his public career.

Information on Hartley's private life is sparse. He was married in Perquimans Precinct, 2 Aug. 1685, to Susanna Garraway, daughter of John and Frances Garraway. The names of his own parents, given in the marriage record, were William and Elizabeth Hartley. He appears to have patented about 1,100 acres of land in Perquimans Precinct, but he lived, at least in his latter years, on a plantation owned by Governor Seth Sothel.

Hartley must have been a close friend, or perhaps a relative, of Sothel, whose will provided that Hartley was to have "the plantation where he [Hartley] now dwells for the tearme of five years" and two-thirds "of my signory bounding on Flatty Creeke and Pascotank River" during the lifetime of Hartley and his wife. The phrase "my signory" may have been a loose use of the term "seigniory" to designate one of several large tracts for which Sothel obtained patents while he was governor. As defined in the Fundamental Constitutions, however, a seigniory in Carolina was a tract of 12,000 acres attached to a proprietorship. It could not be alienated, in whole or in part, and could be inherited only in its entirety and in conjunction with the proprietorship to which it was attached. The bequest, therefore, raises several questions, including the possibility that there was some blood relationship between Hartley and Sothel, who left no heir-at-law. Whatever the circumstances prompting it, the bequest did not benefit Hartley, whose death occurred before Sothel's.

With the exception of several minor bequests to friends, Hartley left his estate to his wife, Susanna. If he had children, they apparently did not survive him. On 28 Nov. 1694 Susanna married William Duckenfield.

SEE: J. Bryan Grimes, ed., *Abstract of North Carolina Wills* (1910); J. R. B. Hathaway, ed., *North Carolina Historical and Genealogical Register,* 3 vols. (1900–1903); Mattie Erma E. Parker, ed., *North Carolina Higher-Court Records, 1670–1696,* vol. 2 (1968); William L. Saunders, ed., *Colonial Records of North Carolina,* vol. 1 (1886). Manuscript sources, North Carolina State Archives, Raleigh: Albemarle Book of Warrants and Surveys, 1681–1706; Colonial Court Records; Council Minutes, Wills, Inventories, 1677–1701; Perquimans Births, Marriages,

Deaths, and Flesh Marks, 1659–1739; and Perquimans Precinct Court Minutes, 1688–93.

MATTIE ERMA E. PARKER

Harvey, John (d. December 1679), Proprietary governor of Albemarle, was probably born in Warwickshire, England, the son of Thomas and Mary Harvey who received a grant on Harvey's Neck, James City County, Va., in July 1640. John Harvey married Dorothy Took, the daughter of James Took who had settled in Isle of Wight County by 1653. By 1659 the Harveys had moved to the "Southward" to the region that in 1663 became Albemarle County, Carolina, and they are among the earliest known permanent settlers in North Carolina. After the Carolina Proprietary was established, John Harvey secured grants from Sir William Berkeley, governor of Virginia and a Lord Proprietor, to 850 acres in two tracts. Harvey settled on a 600-acre plantation on Currituck Creek (now called Symons Creek) in Pasquotank Precinct and later sold his 250-acre grant in Chowan Precinct. On his plantation he emphasized livestock, eventually acquiring a herd of nearly sixty cattle, "a great stock" of hogs, and forty sheep.

Harvey began his service on the governor's Council during the term of Governor Samuel Stephens (1667–70); he remained on the Council until 1676. The Council, an important institution in the colony's government, advised the governor, comprised the upper house of the General Assembly, and constituted the General Court, the highest court in the colony. Harvey, a highly respected member, was selected by the Council in April 1672 to accompany and assist Governor Peter Carteret on a mission to England to present a list of grievances to the Lords Proprietors. Pressing business matters, however, forced Harvey to abort his journey at New York in July.

Although sympathetic with the anti-Proprietary party, Harvey was not actively involved in the factional strife that culminated in Culpeper's Rebellion. He retained the trust of both parties, and on 5 Feb. 1679 the Lords Proprietors commissioned him president of the Council. The appointment of Harvey as acting governor was acceptable to the rebel council and contributed to the lessening of tension in the colony.

Harvey was survived by his wife, Dorothy, although the Harveys may have had a son, James, who died as a youth. Dorothy Harvey died in December 1682, leaving her estate to her brother, Thomas Took, and his family. A cousin of John Harvey, Thomas Harvey, was deputy governor of the colony from 1694 to 1699.

SEE: Lindley S. Butler, "The Early Settlement of Carolina: Virginia's Southern Frontier," *Virginia Magazine of History and Biography* 79 (1971) and "The Governors of Albemarle County, 1663–1689," *North Carolina Historical Review* 46 (1969); John L. Cheney, Jr., ed., *North Carolina Government, 1585–1974* (1975); J. Bryan Grimes, ed., *Abstract of North Carolina Wills* (1910); J. R. B. Hathaway, ed., *North Carolina Historical and Genealogical Register*, vol. 3 (1903); Nell M. Nugent, comp., *Cavaliers and Pioneers: Abstracts of Land Patents and Grants, 1623–1696* (1934); Mattie Erma E. Parker, ed., *North Carolina Higher-Court Records, 1670–1696*, vol. 2 (1968); William S. Powell, ed., *Yᵉ Countie of Albemarle in Carolina: A Collection of Documents, 1664–1675* (1958); William L. Saunders, ed., *Colonial Records of North Carolina*, vol. 1 (1886).

LINDLEY S. BUTLER

Harvey, John (11 Dec. 1724[?]–3 May 1775), colonial and Revolutionary leader, was born at the family home at Harvey's Neck in Perquimans County, one of twins, the son of colonial justice and Council member Thomas Harvey (1692–1729) and Elizabeth Cole Harvey. He was the grandson of Thomas Harvey (d. 1699) who was deputy governor of the colony during 1694–99, and great-grandson of colonial leader Benjamin Laker. He was also the brother of Miles Harvey (1728–76), a leader in the movement for independence.

Not a great deal is known about Harvey's early life. He was born into considerable wealth for the time, even receiving two of his own personal slaves before his fifth birthday. The will of the second Thomas Harvey called for his sons to attain good educations, but no records are known of how young John Harvey received his schooling. It would not have been unusual for one of his class to have had a personal tutor or to have studied in England.

Whatever his educational background, he must have shown considerable political aptitude, because he was elected one of Perquimans County's five representatives in the Assembly when he was only twenty-one. However his first appearance in the Assembly was brief, for this sixteen-day session was to be the last that Albemarle representatives would attend for the next eight years because of a dispute over how many members the counties were entitled to. During this period he remained active in public affairs. He served as a justice of the county in 1751 and was continually elected to the Assembly, but these elections were all voided by the governor. By the time the representational issue was settled in 1754, Harvey headed the Perquimans delegation. In this first Assembly since the dispute he held many key positions on committees. He was especially instrumental in the committees responsible for appropriations for the French and Indian War, and was occasionally called upon to preside over the Assembly sitting as a Committee of the Whole to consider war appropriations. By 1756 Harvey had emerged as the leader of the northern faction in the Assembly. In that year he was presented by his group as a candidate for speaker of the Assembly. Although his supporters were in the majority, there were not enough of them present on the first day of the session; therefore, Samuel Swann, longtime leader of the southern faction, was once again elected to the speakership by a narrow margin. Over the next ten years the factions patched up most of their differences, so Harvey made no more challenges to the speaker's post but continued to dominate many important committees, such as the one to establish a postal route through the colony in 1765.

In the first session under Governor William Tryon in November 1766, the speakership was open. The sectional differences were well healed now, as exemplified by Harvey's being nominated for the position by Richard Caswell of Dobbs County. His election by the full Assembly was unanimous. Little did they realize at the time that John Harvey was to be the last speaker of the colonial Assembly.

In November 1768 Harvey took the lead in the colony's resistance to Crown policies. He believed that the imposition of the Townshend duties was unconstitutional and injurious to the rights of the colonists, and that the only remedy to such problems was for the colonies to present a united front in opposition. On placing the circular letters from Massachusetts and Virginia before the Assembly, Harvey met with a rather complacent response: a committee was appointed to look into the matter and to reply to the Crown. As head of this committee, he went beyond his instructions in corresponding with other colonies to assure them that North Carolina would be among those to stand by them "in pursuing every constitutional measure for redress of grievances." At this point Harvey took on the role of "Father of the American Revolution in North Carolina," as he was called by R. D. W. Connor.

In the next Assembly, which met in October 1769, Harvey had more cooperation from his comrades. In this session he presented the Assembly with resolutions passed earlier by the Virginia assembly that Parliament had no right to tax the colonies, that petition for redress of grievances was a right of all British subjects, and that they were still loyal to the Crown but only trying to preserve their rights as Englishmen. The Assembly passed these resolutions verbatim, largely at Harvey's instigation. Soon afterwards the governor dissolved the Assembly to prevent the passage of a nonimportation association. On this note Harvey took the bold, unprecedented step of calling an extralegal body, independent of the governor, to act on the matter. Elected moderator, Harvey presided over this convention, which passed the association easily and then adjourned. North Carolina was now in the mainstream of a united colonial front, due primarily to Harvey's power and influence.

When the Assembly met in December 1770, Harvey was absent due to ill health, but he maintained his influence in government through correspondence with such leaders as James Iredell and even Governor William Tryon. In this period Harvey supported Tryon's attempts to quell the Regulator movement.

Harvey was next in the Assembly in January 1773, when recognition of his leadership ability was once again shown by his being nominated for the speakership by the man who had held that position in his absence, Richard Caswell. One of the major events of this session was the final settlement of the quorum controversy, which had hung over the colony for decades. When Governor Josiah Martin introduced the issue, Harvey plainly stated that the members of the Assembly felt that it was not in the best interest of their constituents to act without a majority of the members present. Harvey's word was so respected, even by the governor, that the question was never raised again.

The colony's work on behalf of the American Revolution really began with the session of December 1773. Harvey put before the Assembly a letter from Virginia proposing that each colony establish a committee to communicate with the other colonies the actions of the Crown that were detrimental to colonial interests. The creation of such a committee was approved, and Harvey was named a member of this first North Carolina Committee of Correspondence. Yet he was still held in high favor by Crown officials. In 1773 and 1774 he was voted special bonuses of £100 and £200 respectively; both were approved by the governor and Council "with greatest pleasure . . . as a token of respect . . . for Col. Harvey." This was soon to change, however, for the next item on the Assembly's agenda was the election of delegates to the Continental Congress. Governor Martin was determined to keep this from happening, just as Governor Tryon had prevented delegates from being sent to the Stamp Act Congress nine years earlier. Enraged by Martin's refusal to call the Assembly back into session, Harvey again turned to the option of convening a meeting independent of the governor. He spearheaded the organization of the convention, even having broadsides on the subject printed and distributed under his name. Although Martin issued a proclamation forbidding that it take place, North Carolina's First Provincial Congress met at New Bern on 25 Aug. 1774. Harvey was named moderator. Among other things the Congress elected delegates to the Continental Congress, banned all trade with Britain and the importation of slaves, and passed a "no tea" resolution. On closing, it empowered Harvey to convene another such congress when he saw fit.

When Governor Martin called the next Assembly to meet at New Bern on 4 Apr. 1775, Harvey convened the Second Provincial Congress at the same place on the day before. The Congress reelected its delegates to the Continental Congress and engaged in other revolutionary activities, which were endorsed by the Assembly. Both sessions were short: the Assembly was dissolved on 8 April by a frustrated Governor Martin, and the Congress adjourned later that day.

Harvey had always been somewhat sickly and was seriously ill on a number of occasions, as demonstrated by his missing the Assembly sessions in 1770 and 1771. By the end of the Second Provincial Congress his health must have been declining rapidly, because that body made provision that Samuel Johnston should call the next Congress in the event of Harvey's disability. The exact date of his death is unrecorded, but a letter of 19 May 1775 from New Bern relates that he had recently died at his home in Perquimans County as a direct result of a fall from his horse. From the date and place of this letter, he probably died sometime between 15 April and 12 May 1775. Griffith McRee, in *The Life and Correspondence of James Iredell*, mentions the date of death as 3 June 1775. This could well have been a printing error which was meant to read 3 May 1775; because McRee's work was published in 1857, it is likely that he had access to the inscription on Harvey's tomb. The colonial leader was buried at Belgrade Farm, Perquimans County, in a large granite tomb on the shore of Albemarle Sound. In over two centuries of erosion, the structure has been washed out into the sound, though reportedly it is still intact.

Aside from his other activities Harvey always maintained an interest in his home county of Perquimans, encouraging special legislation on its behalf. He was one of those responsible for the charter of the town of Hertford in 1758.

He married Mary Bonner, probably in early 1745. They had ten children, seven of whom survived to adulthood. Of these Thomas and Miles served in the 1776 Assembly, which adopted the Halifax Resolves.

SEE: Samuel A. Ashe, ed., *Biographical History of North Carolina*, vols. 1, 4 (1905, 1906); *Charlotte Observer*, 21 Oct., 16 Dec. 1906; John L. Cheney, ed., *North Carolina Government, 1585–1974* (1975); R. D. W. Connor, "John Harvey," *North Carolina Booklet* 8 (1908), *Makers of North Carolina History* (1911), and *Revolutionary Leaders in North Carolina* (1916); J. Bryan Grimes, ed., *North Carolina Wills and Inventories* (1912); J. R. B. Hathaway, ed., *North Carolina Historical and Genealogical Register*, 3 vols. (1900–1903); Hugh T. Lefler and Albert R. Newsome, *North Carolina: The History of a Southern State* (1973); Griffith McRee, *The Life and Correspondence of James Iredell*, vol. 1 (1857); New Bern *North Carolina Gazette*, 2 Sept. 1774, 24 Feb., 7 Apr. 1775; Fred A. Olds, ed., *Abstract of North Carolina Wills* (1925); Raleigh *News and Observer*, 18 July 1937, 10 Apr. 1938, 29 Apr. 1945, 13 Jan. 1954, 8 Aug. 1976; Lou Rogers, "John Harvey—Colonial Leader," *We, The People of North Carolina* 6 (June 1948); William L. Saunders, ed., *Colonial Records of North Carolina*, vols. 4–10 (1886–90); *Sketches of Church History in North Carolina*

(1892); *Tar Heel Spotlight*, 9 Aug. 1976; George Troxler, "John Harvey," *North Carolina Bicentennial Newsletter*, special ed., 4 July 1976; John H. Wheeler, *Historical Sketches of North Carolina* (1851).

MARTIN REIDINGER

Harvey, Miles *(17 Dec. 1728–12 Dec. 1776)*, colonial official, was born on Albemarle Sound, Perquimans Precinct, the son of John and Elizabeth Cole Harvey. He began his public service in Perquimans County as an officer and clerk of the Inferior Court. Active in politics, he became a member of the Committee of Safety for Edenton, and in time was elected to the Provincial Congress that met at Hillsborough on 20 Aug. 1775. There he signed the customary test oath professing allegiance to the Crown but denying the right of Parliament to tax the colonies. This Congress named him colonel of the Perquimans militia. The next year he was a delegate to the Provincial Congress at Halifax, on 4 Apr. 1776, which drew up the Halifax Resolves. In addition, Harvey served on committees inquiring into the conduct of insurgents and other persons suspected of aiding the loyalists at the Battle of Moore's Creek Bridge. He was also a member of the committee that drafted instructions and orders for recruiting officers and considered requisitions of the militia.

At the final Congress, which met at Halifax on 20 Nov. 1776, Harvey again represented his county. He served on the Committee of Privileges and Elections, and continued to investigate loyalist activities by drafting instructions for a party of light horse to pursue disloyal persons in North Carolina. According to the journal of the Congress, Harvey was present and active a few days before his death, so it must have been unexpected.

He was survived by children of two wives, the first of whom was Elizabeth Baker, daughter of Colonel William Baker, who represented Nansemond County, Va., in the House of Burgesses, 1742–47. Their children were Mary, Mildred, and Augustus. Harvey's second wife was Elizabeth Jones, and they were the parents of Albridgton, Elizabeth, Agatha, Lucy, Robert, and Miles.

SEE: John B. Boddie, *Southside Virginia Families* (1955); Walter Clark, ed., *State Records of North Carolina*, vol. 22 (1907); J. R. B. Hathaway, ed., *North Carolina Historical and Genealogical Register*, vols. 1, 3 (1900, 1903); James B. McNair, comp., *McNair, McNear, and McNeir Genealogies* (1923); William L. Saunders, ed., *Colonial Records of North Carolina*, vols. 5, 9, 10 (1887, 1890); Marilu Smallwood, *Some Colonial and Revolutionary Families of North Carolina* (1964).

JOHN BURKE O'DONNELL, JR.

Harvey, Thomas *(d. 3 July 1699)*, deputy governor, Council member, and justice of the General Court and of the county court of Albemarle, was the son of John and Mary Harvey of the Heath, in Snitterfield Parish, Warwickshire, England. He was a cousin of John Harvey, who was a Council member in Albemarle in the early 1670s and later president of the Council and acting governor.

Thomas Harvey was in the North Carolina colony, then called Albemarle, by 1670, although he appears to have taken little if any part in public affairs until the 1680s. A trip to London that he and John Harvey made in 1676 may have had political objectives, but its nature is not indicated in surviving records. Although the

Harveys returned to Albemarle in the summer or fall of 1677, neither appears to have taken an active part in the uprising called Culpeper's Rebellion, which occurred late that year.

Insofar as extant records show, Thomas Harvey's first public office was that of justice of the county court of Albemarle, which he held from March 1683 through the following September. By February 1684 Harvey was a member of the Albemarle Council, on which he sat for the rest of the year, in 1687, and in 1690–94. He may have been on the Council in some or all of the intervening years, for which the names of few Council members are known.

In July 1694 Harvey was serving as deputy governor in the absence of Philip Ludwell, who was then acting as governor during intermittent visits to Albemarle from his home in Virginia. Beginning in September 1694, Ludwell appears to have left the government of Albemarle largely to Harvey, who was still serving as deputy governor in 1695, when John Archdale arrived en route to Charles Town to take office as governor of the entire province of Carolina. In accordance with the authority conferred in his commission, Archdale reappointed Harvey as deputy governor. Harvey continued as chief executive of the colony until his death.

As deputy governor, Harvey faced difficult tasks, which on the whole he and his Council handled effectively. Land titles were in disarray because of abuses practiced by Governor Seth Sothel, who had unlawfully seized extensive tracts of land for himself, had granted land already held under earlier patents, and had seized official land records and apparently had destroyed them. Furthermore, the Lords Proprietors had recently agreed to liberalize land policies, which made it advantageous for many colonists to take out new patents in place of those they held. The crucial tasks of validating titles, restoring an orderly record system, and implementing the new policies consumed much time and effort on the part of Harvey and other officials.

Harvey and his Council also had the task of completing a government reorganization directed by the Proprietors in 1691 but scarcely begun when Harvey took office. By the end of his administration the reforms had been implemented, including conversion of the unicameral Assembly to a bicameral body, increased participation in legislative action by the elected members of the Assembly, extension of the suffrage to include all freemen, and reorganization of the court system. For several years Harvey presided over the General Court, which was reestablished under the new system, but in 1698 the deputy governor and Council ceased to sit as justices of the court and instead appointed the justices.

In addition to these and other internal responsibilities, Harvey was confronted by problems arising from efforts by Parliament and administrative officials in London to extend Crown control to the Proprietary colonies; the Lords Proprietors considered this an infringement on rights granted to them in their charter. The Albemarle officials were caught in the middle in the ensuing struggle between the Proprietors and the Crown. These problems were aggravated by efforts of Virginia officials to aid the attempt to extend Crown control over the Carolina colonies, a change that was expected to have great advantage for Virginia. As a result of the movement for charter resumption, Harvey and his government were forced to cope with such matters as new restrictions on trade and the vessels engaged in it, a requirement that governors of Proprietary colonies take oaths and give bonds to enforce certain laws, the establishment in Virginia of a vice-admiralty court with jurisdiction over the North Carolina colony, and other measures encroaching on the power of the Proprietors. From Virginia came complications in relations between the two colonies, including numerous charges of misdoings against North Carolina inhabitants and renewal of the long-standing boundary dispute, along with various controversies stemming from the dispute.

These and other actions by Crown officials in London and America presented Harvey and his Council with the delicate assignment of protecting the interests of the Proprietors without incurring retaliation from London or worsening relations with Virginia. By various means, including evasion and delay, the North Carolina officials avoided compromising the Proprietors' interests. Harvey did not take the newly required oath or give bond. The controversies with Virginia were patiently negotiated, and agents were sent to Jamestown to resolve the boundary dispute. The latter measure, however, was unsuccessful, for Virginia officials refused to deal with the North Carolina agents, apparently preferring to continue the dispute for tactical purposes in promoting charter resumption.

In handling the numerous problems, Harvey made severe personal sacrifices. In a letter to John Archdale, dated 10 July 1698, he discussed his deteriorating health and the great worry and strain under which he labored in performing his responsibilities. He entreated Archdale "to take the burden from off my shoulders," but the burden remained until his death.

Some have thought that Harvey was a Quaker, but available evidence neither supports nor refutes that belief. The supposition is based chiefly on the facts that Harvey was appointed deputy governor by John Archdale, the Quaker Proprietor, and that he never took the oath required of colonial governors. Neither of these facts necessarily has religious significance. Harvey first served as deputy governor under Philip Ludwell, who was not a Quaker, and he was holding the office when Archdale arrived as governor. It is doubtful that religious considerations played a part in his appointment by either Ludwell or Archdale. Likewise, Harvey's failure to take the newly required oath indicates nothing as to his religion, for the Proprietors were resisting that requirement as an invasion of the prerogatives granted them in their charter. By various devices they succeeded for several years in avoiding compliance with the requirement, both on the part of governors of the entire province and the deputy governors of North Carolina, who technically were only the agents of the governor of the province and, in the Proprietors' view, were not subject to the requirement. Whatever his religion, it is unlikely that Harvey would have taken the oath under the circumstances that existed.

Harvey lived in Perquimans Precinct on the peninsula now known as Harvey's Neck. He held 931 acres by patent and additional land acquired by purchase. He was first married, on 13 Apr. 1682, to Johanah Jenkins, widow of John Jenkins, who had been president of the Council and acting governor. Johanah died on 27 Mar. 1688, and Harvey subsequently married Sarah Laker, daughter of Benjamin and Jane Laker. Harvey had no children by his first marriage, but three were born of the second. The oldest child, John, born 19 Sept. 1689, died when he was two. A second son, Thomas, and a daughter, Mary, lived to adulthood. Thomas, Jr., married Elizabeth Cole, daughter of James Cole. He became prominent in public affairs and held several offices, including that of Council member. Mary married Robert West of Chowan Precinct, who also was prominent in public affairs.

Harvey was buried on his plantation in a cemetery that has since crumbled into Albemarle Sound. He left a large estate to his wife and to his son and daughter, who were then age six and four respectively.

In his will Harvey mentioned two brothers, Richard, "late of London," and Robert, then living at the family home in England. He also mentioned two nephews, Thomas and John, sons of his brother Richard. The nephew Thomas is believed to have been the Thomas Harvey of Perquimans who married Margaret Fletcher, daughter of Ralph and Elizabeth Fletcher, in January 1702. That Thomas Harvey appears to have moved to Beaufort Precinct before 1712 and to have died before May 1716. It is possible that the brother Richard, "late of London," and the nephew John also moved to North Carolina. They may have been the Richard Harvey and John Harvey who were living in Hyde Precinct about 1716.

On 17 Jan. 1702 Thomas Harvey's widow, Sarah, married Christopher Gale, who had recently arrived in the colony and soon would become an important public figure.

SEE: J. Bryan Grimes, ed., *Abstract of North Carolina Wills* (1910) and *North Carolina Wills and Inventories* (1912); J. R. B. Hathaway, ed., *North Carolina Historical and Genealogical Register*, vols. 1, 3 (1900, 1903); Mattie Erma E. Parker, ed., *North Carolina Higher-Court Records, 1670–1696* (1968) and *1697–1701* (1971); William L. Saunders, ed., *Colonial Records of North Carolina*, vols. 1– 3 (1886); Ellen G. Winslow, *History of Perquimans County* (1911). Manuscript sources in North Carolina State Archives, Raleigh: Albemarle Book of Warrants and Surveys, 1681–1706; Albemarle County Papers, 1678–1714; Colonial Court Records; Council Minutes, Wills, and Inventories, 1677–1701; Perquimans Birth, Marriages, Deaths, and Flesh Marks, 1659–1739; Perquimans Deeds, Book A; Perquimans Precinct Court Minutes, 1693–98.

MATTIE ERMA E. PARKER

Harvey, Thomas, Jr. *(6 Dec. 1692–20 Oct. 1729)*, member of the Council and of the Assembly, and justice of the General Court, of the Admiralty Court, and of the Perquimans Precinct Court, was the son of Deputy Governor Thomas Harvey and his second wife, Sarah Laker Harvey, and presumably born at his parents' plantation in Perquimans Precinct. The family was descended from the Harveys of the Heath, Snitterfield Parish, Warwickshire, England. His father died when he was six, and a few years later he became the stepson of Christopher Gale, to whom his mother was married on 17 Jan. 1702.

Following in the footsteps of his father and stepfather, Harvey was active in public affairs throughout his adult life. Social position with the Albemarle aristocracy, family connections, and extensive property holdings naturally and rapidly brought Harvey public responsibilities extending to nearly every branch of government in precinct and province. In 1713, the year he came of age and entered into full possession of his father's large plantation on Harvey's Neck, he served as a juror in the General Court, and in October 1714, when he was not yet twenty-two, he was associate justice of the same court, a position that he held intermittently through 1726. He was sitting on the bench when indictments were presented against Edward Moseley and others in 1719 for seizing provincial records and against former governor George Burrington in 1726 for assaulting Governor Sir Richard Everard. The General Assembly made him a vestryman of Perquimans Parish in 1715.

In November 1719 and again in 1720 he was appointed by the Assembly to the commission for examining and settling the public accounts disordered since the Tuscarora War, a fiscal task requiring four years. Appointment to such a commission, usually composed of members of the lower house of the Assembly, indicates that he was a member of that body in 1719 and 1720, for which the journals have not survived. It is certain that Harvey was a member of the lower house in 1722 and 1723, which are among the few years of that period for which Assembly journals are extant. From March 1721 through March 1723 Harvey also was provost marshal, or sheriff, for the county of Albemarle.

By January 1724 Harvey was a member of the Council, on which he sat for the remainder of his life, serving under governors Burrington and Everard. In that capacity, he was ex officio member of the upper house of the Assembly. In order to improve the quality of justice administered in the precinct courts, Harvey and several other Council members were persuaded by the governor to accept appointments as justices of the peace for their precincts. Accordingly, Harvey served as justice of the Perquimans Precinct Court, as well as Council member, from about 1724 until his death. He also served as justice of the Admiralty Court at some period, but the dates are not known.

Throughout his career, Harvey seems to have been active in the militia of the colony. In the early 1720s he bore the title major, and in later years he was called colonel.

Harvey lived in Perquimans Precinct on the family plantation at Harvey's Neck. He also owned several other plantations, a number of slaves, and other valuable property. His wife was Elizabeth Cole, daughter of Samuel Cole or Coles. The couple had four sons: Thomas, John, Benjamin, and Miles.

Harvey died before his thirty-seventh birthday and was buried beside his father in the family graveyard on his home plantation. The cemetery has since been eroded away by Albemarle Sound, but in 1865 Harvey's gravestone, bearing the family arms, was moved to a cemetery farther from the sound, where presumably it still stands. At the time of Harvey's death his sons were small children, ranging in age from ten months to ten years. All lived to adulthood, but the oldest, Thomas, died unmarried before he was thirty. John, Benjamin, and Miles married and had children. John, like his father and grandfather, entered public life. He was a prominent leader in the early stages of the American Revolution, and his death in 1775 was widely regarded as a public loss.

Harvey's widow, Elizabeth, married Edward Salter of Beaufort Precinct. After Salter's death she married one Calldrom (or Caldoun). She died in 1761 and was buried on the Harvey plantation beside her first husband.

SEE: Robert J. Cain, ed., *North Carolina Higher-Court Minutes, 1724–1730* (1981) and *Records of the Executive Council, 1664–1734* (1984); J. Bryan Grimes, ed., *Abstract of North Carolina Wills* (1910) and *North Carolina Wills and Inventories* (1912); J. R. B. Hathaway, *North Carolina Historical and Genealogical Register*, 3 vols. (1900–1903); Perquimans County records (North Carolina State Archives, Raleigh); William S. Price, Jr., ed., *North Carolina Higher-Court Records, 1702–1708* (1974) and *1709–1723* (1977); William L. Saunders, ed., *Colonial Records of North Carolina*, vols. 2, 3 (1886); Ellen Good Winslow, *History of Perquimans County* (1931); Raymond A. Winslow, Jr., "Harvey Cemetery and Exhibit," *Perquimans County Historical Society Yearbook* (1967).

MATTIE ERMA E. PARKER
RAYMOND A. WINSLOW, JR.

Hasell, James (*d. February 1785*), judge, councillor, and acting governor, was a native of Bristol, England, the son of James Hasell, a merchant. He served an apprenticeship in Bristol from 1714 to 1721. After immigrating to Philadelphia, where he remained briefly, Hasell settled in New Hanover County, N.C., around 1735. Samuel Hassell of Philadelphia, perhaps a relative, had lived in Newton (afterwards named Wilmington) at some time between 1733 and 1739.

Hasell married Susannah (or Sarah) Sampson, the widow of John Sampson; his stepdaughter, Ann Sampson, became Edward Moseley's second wife. Thus Hasell was early allied with one of the most prominent political leaders in the colony. He purchased three town lots in Wilmington and became a justice of the peace in 1739. Within seven years he was one of the largest planters in the county, with over 2,000 acres of land. As a prominent Cape Fear social figure, Hasell came to the attention of Governor Gabriel Johnston, who nominated him to the royal Council in 1747. Two years later, on 2 October, he assumed the seat of the deceased Edward Moseley under an emergency appointment, his official mandamus not arriving until 1752. Hasell served on the Council until it was abolished in 1775 and was its most dominant member during its final fifteen years.

Although he had no formal legal training, much of Hasell's career in the colony was tied to the higher courts—those above the county level. He served as chief justice of the General Court (and its later offshoots, both supreme and superior courts) from 1750 to 1755, 1758 to 1759, and 1766 to 1767. In September 1753 he was named chief baron of the Exchequer Court, a largely honorary function that paid a salary of £40 a year. He retained this office until the American Revolution, resigning it temporarily in 1758 and 1766 during his brief service as chief justice. Governor Arthur Dobbs, who criticized his lack of formal training in 1754, saw fit to appoint Hasell chief justice again in 1758 on the death of Peter Henly, while Governor William Tryon praised Hasell as chief justice in 1767.

Despite his distinguished service on the bench, it was as a royal councillor that Hasell performed his major services. His work in the Council was commended by governors Dobbs, Tryon, and Josiah Martin, all of whom frequently sought his counsel, and his loyalty to the Crown was steadfast. Martin even tried to have him made lieutenant governor in 1771. Whereas some councillors vacillated during the Stamp Act agitation in 1765, Hasell openly supported Crown policy. During the critical years just before the Revolution, he remained the only councillor on whom Governor Martin felt he could rely consistently. Hasell was president of the Council from early 1760 to 1775, and as such sometimes acted as chief executive during the governor's absence from the colony, serving, for example, after Tryon departed in 1771 and before Martin arrived. When Martin was in New York on business in January 1775, Hasell prorogued the Assembly because of the revolutionary fervor building there. In April he urged the governor to disrupt the Provincial Congress when every other councillor advised caution.

After July 1775 the Council did not meet again, and Hasell withdrew to his plantation, Hasell's Place, just above present-day Carolina Beach and opposite Cabbage Inlet. His property was not confiscated during his lifetime, but was seized after his death; however, it was restored to his family in 1802. At his death Hasell owned 12,000 acres of land. His will mentions his son, James (1727–69) (by his first wife), and his second wife, Ann Sophia Von Blade Durlace, widow of Baron Von Rosentine, with whom Hasell signed a marriage agreement on 20 Dec. 1755. Hasell left a large and varied library, his books bearing an engraved armorial bookplate. Many of them are now in the North Carolina Collection in Chapel Hill. To his son he left "all the family pictures."

SEE: Bristol Record Office, letter—citing sources—to William S. Powell, 5 June 1980; Ida Brooks Kellam, "James Hasell" (typescript, North Carolina State Library, Raleigh); H. B. McKoy Collection (Southern Historical Collection, University of North Carolina Library, Chapel Hill); Elizabeth Moore, *Rice, Hasell, Hawks and Carruthers Families of North Carolina* (1966); New Hanover County Wills (North Carolina State Archives, Raleigh); William L. Saunders, ed., *Colonial Records of North Carolina*, vols. 5–10 (1887–90); Alfred M. Waddell, *History of New Hanover County* (1909); Stephen B. Weeks, "James Hasell" (Van Noppen Papers, Manuscript Department, Duke University, Durham).

WILLIAM S. PRICE, JR.

Hasell, William Soranzo (*15 Nov. 1780–6 Oct. 1815*), newspaper editor and civic leader, was born in Charles Town, S.C. He was the great-grandson of James Hasell, chief justice and president of the Council in colonial North Carolina. His mother, Susanna Hasell, married Parker Quince, the son of Brunswick merchant Richard Quince. It is said that, because no descendants of James Hasell survived bearing the name, Susanna Hasell Quince asked her son, William Soranzo Quince, to take the Hasell name in order to perpetuate it. This plan was thwarted when William S. Hasell died in his thirties, childless.

Hasell was graduated from Yale in 1799 at age eighteen. He studied law but abandoned its practice to pursue his newspaper and literary interests. This included editing the *Minerva*, an organ of the Federalist party. In 1808 Hasell bought the *Wilmington Gazette* from Allmond Hall, and served as either editor, publisher, or both until his death. Among his other achievements was the establishment of a circulating library and reading room in Wilmington. According to the *Gazette* of 15 Nov. 1808, the reading room contained "all new and interesting pamphlets, and a variety of the best reviews." The subscription rate was ten dollars a year, or one dollar a month for "strangers."

In 1805 Hasell married Elizabeth G. Tart of Charleston, S.C. His early death cut short a life dedicated to the advancement of knowledge and the improvement of Wilmington. He was buried with the Quince family at Rose Hill Plantation, on the Northeast Cape Fear River in what is now Pender County.

SEE: Henry B. McKoy, *The McKoy Family of North Carolina* (1955); James Sprunt, *Chronicles of the Cape Fear River, 1660–1916* (1916); Mary Wescott and Allene Ramage, comps., *A Checklist of United States Newspapers: Part 4, North Carolina* (1936).

H. K. STEPHENS II

Hasell, Cushing Biggs (*14 Oct. 1809–11 Apr. 1880*), businessman, politician, and educational official in Mar-

tin County, became the leading Primitive Baptist minister in the state during the mid-nineteenth century. His father, Joshua Hassell, suffered an unfortunate lot, never professing the religious faith his son considered so crucial in life, and leaving his family penniless on his death in 1824. Cushing's mother, Martha Biggs Hassell, was said to be a pious follower of the Primitive Baptist church. Her "resigned and cheerful" manner aided her ongoing battle with rheumatism, which she endured for thirty years prior to her death in 1860.

Born in Martin County, Hassell spent his childhood alternately with his parents in Williamston and with his grandparents on Albemarle Sound. From an early age he attended school irregularly until he was fifteen; when his father died, however, he went to work to support his mother and the rest of his family (apparently he was the oldest brother). Between various clerking jobs in Williamston, he also worked in Halifax and Plymouth. At age eighteen Hassell resolved to abstain from alcohol, tobacco, gaming, and profanity, and "to be strictly honest, truthful and upright" in all his endeavors. In 1828, during a period of religious excitement in Halifax, he was converted. Two months later Elder Joseph Biggs baptized him in Williamston, and he became a faithful member of the Skewarkey Primitive Baptist Church.

In June 1831, Hassell opened a store with Henry Williams of Williamston, in the partnership of Williams and Hassell. Hassell received only one-third of the profits, but acquired valuable business experience. Upon the dissolution of the enterprise in 1834, he went into business with William Williams, brother of Henry. According to Hassell, their effort floundered for three years owing to Williams's lazy habits, and their partnership dissolved in the wake of the economic panic of 1837. In 1831 and 1832, Hassell also had been instrumental in a survey of Williamston.

In addition to his business ventures, Hassell was chosen a deacon of the Skewarkey Church in 1833. Ordained in 1842, he became a pastor of both the Skewarkey and Spring Creek churches, although he commonly traveled to neighboring churches on two Sundays a month. From 1859 until his death, he served as moderator of the Kehukee Association; founded in Halifax County in 1765, it was the oldest Primitive Baptist association in America.

In May 1832 Hassell married Mary Davis, daughter of Durham and Elizabeth Davis. They were the parents of seven children, two of whom had died by the time of Mary's death in June 1846. Hassell entrusted the care of his remaining five children to her mother Elizabeth; after her death in October of that year, he returned to Williamston with his children. In 1849 he married Martha Maria Jewitt, formerly the wife of Elder Daniel E. Jewitt, founder of the *Christian Doctrinal Advocate and Monitor*; she bore him four more children.

During his lifetime, Hassell served his community and state in a number of capacities. He was president of the Roanoke Steam Navigation Company, and he held various positions related to education: trustee and member of the Board of Examiners for The University of North Carolina, trustee of the Williamston Academy, founder and secretary-treasurer of the Williamston Library Association, and agent of the Chairman of the Board of Superintendents for the common schools of Martin County. A Democrat, he served at different times as clerk, master in equity, and treasurer for Martin County, and as a delegate to the Constitutional State Convention of 1875. In his role as a Primitive Baptist minister, he published a number of works on his denomination, including a history of the Kehukee Association and the churches composing it, a statistical table of all old-school Baptist associations in America, and a history of the Primitive Baptist church "for 4,350 years, from the creation to A.D. 350"—a work completed after his death by his son, Sylvester.

Hassell remained active up to the time of his death in Williamston after an illness of forty-two days. Near the end of his life, he reportedly requested to be buried at Skewarkey, "by the side of my children."

SEE: Samuel A. Ashe, ed., *Biographical History of North Carolina*, vol. 5 (1906); Cushing Biggs Hassell, *History of the Church of God, from the Creation to A.D. 1885* (1886); Cushing Biggs Hassell Papers (Southern Historical Collection, University of North Carolina Library, Chapel Hill); R. H. Pittman, *Biographical History of Primitive or Old School Baptist Ministers of the United States* (1909).

MITCHELL F. DUCEY

Hassell, Sylvester *(28 July 1842–18 Aug. 1928)*, educator, scholar, and Primitive Baptist preacher, was born and reared in Williamston, Martin County. His father, the Elder Cushing Biggs Hassell, was an esteemed minister of the Primitive Baptist faith. His mother, Mary Davis Hassell, died when he was four. After Cushing Hassell married Martha Maria Jewitt three years later, Sylvester grew fond of his stepmother, and she wielded a strong influence on the young boy's moral life. Though a healthy infant, Hassell in his youth exhibited a tendency to be "frail and delicate."

He was educated at the Williamston Academy and then attended The University of North Carolina from July 1858 to August 1861. Afterwards, he returned to Williamston to assist his father in business. While at Chapel Hill, Hassell consistently achieved first distinction in his class; he was also a member—and, in 1861, president—of the Philanthropic Literary Society. In 1867 the university awarded him the honorary A.M. degree.

At the outbreak of the Civil War, the rather unhealthy young man was examined by Confederate recruiting officers seven times, and each time was exempted on account of afflictions of the lungs and throat. In the winter of 1862, however, Hassell served as secretary to Colonel Samuel Watts of the Martin County militia unit stationed at Fort Hill, near Washington, N.C. At the time of the fall of the Roanoke region, the regiment was disbanded and Hassell returned home. During the remaining years of the war he served primarily as tutor to the younger siblings in the Hassell household. His older brother, Theodore, was a lieutenant in the Seventeenth North Carolina Regiment.

When the war ended, Hassell entered his "chosen profession" of teaching, first as an instructor (1865–68) at the Williamston Academy. In 1869 he moved northward to the State Normal College at Wilmington, Del., where he occupied a chair in the ancient languages. In 1871 he also taught at the William Penn Public School in Newcastle, Del. After the death of his first wife, Hassell returned to North Carolina in 1872 to establish the Wilson Collegiate Institute. He managed the school for fourteen years and, during his final six years there (1880–86), claimed half-ownership. In addition to his duties at the institute, the respected educator was principal of the State Normal School between 1882 and 1884.

For six years after the death of Cushing Biggs Hassell in 1880, Sylvester worked diligently to complete his father's magnum opus, *History of the Church of God . . .*, the third major history of the Kehukee Primitive Baptist Association. Upon its publication in 1886, Hassell left

Wilson and returned to his old hometown. There he was principal of the Williamston Academy from 1886 until 1890, when failing health forced him to retire from teaching and gave him the opportunity to visit Primitive Baptist churches in several states.

In August 1863, soon after his twenty-first birthday, Hassell had been converted, receiving "the evidence that his sins were forgiven." On 11 Jan. 1864, he was baptized by his father in the Roanoke River, despite the day being so cold that "the ice in the river was more than an inch thick." He began giving public sermons in 1871 and was ordained in 1874. At various times he was pastor for the Skewarkey, Conetoe, Jamesville, Great Swamp, and Hamilton Primitive Baptist churches. After his father's death, Hassell became moderator of the Kehukee Primitive Baptist Association, a position he held for thirty-five years.

In 1892, Hassell became both county examiner for the public school teachers of Martin County and associate editor of *The Gospel Messenger*, the monthly magazine of the "Primitive Baptist Faith and Order." Six years later he purchased *The Gospel Messenger* and assumed the editorship, remaining closely associated with the magazine until 1922 when its publication was discontinued.

Hassell was married twice, first to Mary Isabella Yarrell, daughter of Julius and Emeline Yarrell of Martin County, in September 1869. She died in 1871, in her twenty-second year, while the couple was living in Delaware. Their only child, Paul, died in 1886 at age fifteen. Hassell's second wife—whom he married in May 1876—was Frances ("Fannie") Louise Woodard, daughter of Calvin and Winifred Woodard of Wilson County. They had at least five children before her death in 1889: Francis Sylvester, who became a lawyer in Wilson; Charles, who became an auditor; Calvin Woodard, who became an attorney for the U.S. Post Office Department and handled cases of mail fraud; Mary, who furnished a home for her father from the time of her marriage to John Hassell in 1914 until she died in 1923; and Frances Winniefred, who died in infancy shortly after her mother's death.

Hassell was recognized not simply for his role in perpetuating the tenets of the Primitive Baptist faith in his many articles in *The Gospel Messenger*. He established an academy in North Carolina and aspired to excellence in his diverse teaching positions. An accomplished linguist, he continually expanded his own mind at a time when "most of his fellow-ministers know only the English language and have had very limited educations."

Late in life, Hassell lived with his niece, Mrs. G. W. Hardison, and her family. Despite the frailty of his health throughout life, he lived to be eighty-six. He was buried in the cemetery at Skewarkey Church, near the graves of his father and other loved ones who had preceded him.

SEE: Samuel A. Ashe, ed., *Biographical History of North Carolina*, vol. 5 (1906); Sylvester Hassell, ed., *The Gospel Messenger* (1878–1922); Sylvester Hassell Papers (Southern Historical Collection, University of North Carolina Library, Chapel Hill); Julius C. Moore, "In Memory of Elder Sylvester Hassell," *Minutes of the One Hundred and Sixty-Third Annual Session of the Kehukee Primitive Baptist Association* (North Carolina Collection, University of North Carolina Library, Chapel Hill); *North Carolina Biography*, vol. 5 (1919).

MITCHELL F. DUCEY

Hathaway, James Robert Bent *(9 Feb. 1841–22 Sept. 1904)*, businessman and historical editor, was born in

Edenton. The Hathaway family, of Welsh origin, migrated in the mid-eighteenth century from Dartmouth, Mass., and settled first in Tyrrell County and later in Chowan County. Although born into a family of at least six children, Hathaway was one of only two children and the only son of Burton Walker and Sarah Ann Bent Hathaway to reach maturity. He received his education from private tutors and at the Edenton Academy. As a young boy he joined the Methodist Episcopal church, in which he was active throughout his life.

His lawyer-planter father died when he was sixteen, and he soon assumed the management of the extensive family holdings in land and slaves. Hathaway suffered heavy financial losses during the Civil War, but in 1866 he established a successful general mercantile business in Edenton. This large and originally prosperous business was destroyed by the panic of 1873. In 1879 he began a general collecting and business agency which evolved into the first private bank in Chowan County. Hathaway's bank, locally known as "The Counting House," served a broad area about Edenton and prospered until the depression of 1893 forced it to close in 1895. During his business career, Hathaway was elected mayor of Edenton on four occasions.

His heavy financial losses and his lack of any steady employment following the collapse of his banking business placed Hathaway in severe financial straits. His situation was relieved somewhat with the recovery through the U.S. government of some French spoliation claims. This last windfall made it possible for the former businessman, now in his late fifties, to undertake a new career.

Hathaway had long been noted in Edenton as "an exceptionally well read person" with a strong interest in North Carolina history and "a flair for mathematics." In 1898 a letter from a woman in Georgia awakened in him an interest in genealogy. It was while in pursuit of his family's history that he became aware of the vast storehouse of early public records to be found in the county courthouses of eastern North Carolina. He determined to make these available to anyone interested in the state's history, and in 1900 he launched a quarterly called *The North Carolina Historical and Genealogical Register*. From 1900 to 1903 Hathaway published ten issues; an almost completed eleventh number was published after his death by his son. Although the *Register* contained a few historical articles and features, at least 90 percent of its pages were devoted to the publication of records from the courthouses of the Albemarle region and from the secretary of state's office in Raleigh.

In his last years Hathaway was permitted to actually live in the Chowan courthouse. His intimate knowledge of the records it contained was especially fortuitous, as Edenton had served as the first capital of North Carolina and many seventeenth- and early eighteenth-century provincial records were still housed in the colonial courthouse building. Most of these he published in the *Register*. The journal eventually obtained subscribers in thirty states, but each issue brought a small financial loss. At Hathaway's death, his books showed a total deficit of $450. It was reliably reported that he "often went without the necessaries of life that he might publish the magazine containing the fruits of his efforts." A number of important primary source items that he published have since disappeared, and they are now known only because of their publication in his quarterly.

Hathaway penned an occasional article for his journal, but he wrote only one other published item. This was an article describing the erection and probable location of the first church in Chowan and the erection of

the present St. Paul's Church in Edenton. The piece was included in a commemorative volume published in 1901 honoring the two hundredth anniversary of St. Paul's Parish.

On 23 July 1861 Hathaway married Margaret Grizzell Reed of Perquimans County, the daughter of James V. and Mary C. Reed and a descendant of the Proprietary governor, William Reed. The couple had two children, Burton Walker (1862–1917) who became a physician, married, and had four children, and Lorena Bent who never married. Hathaway died at the home of his son at Merry Hill in Bertie County and was buried in Beaver Hill Cemetery, Edenton.

SEE: Mrs. L. T. Avery, interview (Southern Pines, 12 Mar. 1978); J. Bryan Grimes, "J. R. B. Hathaway," *Literary and Historical Activities in North Carolina, 1900–1905* (1907); J. R. B. Hathaway, "The Historic Corner Stone of the Church of England in North Carolina," *The Religious and Historic Commemoration of the Two Hundred Years of St. Paul's Parish, Edenton, N.C.* (1901), and ed., *North Carolina Historical and Genealogical Register*, 3 vols. (1900–1903); *Historical and Descriptive Review of the State of North Carolina, Including the Manufacturing and Mercantile Industries . . . and Sketches of Their Leading Men and Business Houses*, 2 vols. (1885); Willis Smith, "James Robert Bent Hathaway—A Gleaner in North Carolina History," *Trinity Archive* 11 (1908); Mrs. Beverly D. Tucker, Jr., "James Robert Bent Hathaway," *Yearbook: Pasquotank Historical Society*, vol. 2 (1956–57).

HERBERT R. PASCHAL, JR.

Haughton, John Hooker (29 Aug. 1810–30 May 1876), lawyer and planter, son of John and Mary Ryan Hooker Haughton, was born in Chowan County. His parents later moved to Tyrrell, his mother's home county. He received his preparatory education in the Edenton schools and entered The University of North Carolina in 1828, graduating in the class of 1832 with a B.A. degree. In 1840 his alma mater awarded him an honorary M.A. degree. He read law under his kinsman, Thomas B. Haughton of Edenton, and on receiving his license practiced law for a few years in Tyrrell County. In 1837 Haughton moved to Pittsboro, Chatham County. The same year his father, a planter, moved to Chatham where he had acquired large landholdings on the Deep River in the southern part of the county.

During the next thirty years, Haughton established a successful law practice in Chatham and surrounding counties. He was a member of the Whig party and a staunch supporter of all its principles. In 1844 the Whigs elected him as one of Chatham's representatives in the House of Commons. Among the measures he successfully sponsored in the session of 1844–45 was the incorporation of Pittsboro, which gave the town a commission form of government. Six years later his party elected him state senator from Chatham. In the legislature of 1850–51 he demonstrated his support of the Whig program of internal improvements by introducing five bills providing for building plank roads and turnpikes, opening coal mines, and improving water transportation to the mines, all of which were passed. In this session Haughton voted for the resolutions endorsing the Compromise of 1850. He was outspoken in his support of the Union while at the same time a firm defender of the institution of slavery. Reelected to the senate for the session of 1854–55, he again sponsored measures for internal improvements. In two bills passed at this session which incorporated the Gulf and Deep River Manufacturing Co. and the Gulf Coal Mining Co., Haughton was named an incorporator and a director. When the Free Suffrage Bill, sponsored by the Democrats, was being considered in 1854, he voted with the Whig minority against it.

Haughton's most important personal venture into the field of internal improvements began when the legislature of 1849 chartered the Cape Fear and Deep River Navigation Company. He was appointed the company's attorney and became one of its largest stockholders. The company was chartered to make possible the navigation of the Cape Fear and Deep rivers by steamboat from Fayetteville to Waddell's Ferry in Randolph County. One of the objects of the improved waterway was to transport coal and iron from the mines in southern Chatham County. In consequence of poor management and the Civil War, the company was never able to complete this ambitious project. Haughton continued as its attorney until the company's dissolution in 1873. He lost a large part of his personal fortune in the once promising enterprise.

In addition to his law practice, Haughton engaged in farming. He owned plantations in Chatham and Jones counties. In 1858 he purchased a home in New Bern, where he lived and practiced law during the winter months. A member of the Episcopal church, he frequently served on the vestry of St. Bartholomew's Parish, Pittsboro, and was one of its delegates to most of the diocesan conventions from 1838 to 1868.

On 11 Dec. 1834 Haughton married Polly Ann Williams, daughter of Dr. Robert and Elizabeth Ellis Williams of Pitt County. She died in 1835 shortly after the birth of their only child, Mary Ann (Mrs. Ross R. Ihrie). On 17 May 1837 he married Eliza Alice Hill (1812–64), daughter of Colonel Thomas and Susanna Mabson Hill of Chatham County. Their children were Thomas Hill, John Ryan, Arthur Lawrence, William Graham, Maria Caroline (Mrs. William L. London), Margaret Lane, Susan Mabson, and Alice Hill (Mrs. Thomas C. James). Four years after the death of his second wife, Haughton married Martha Harvey of New Bern, 13 Aug. 1868. He was buried in the churchyard of St. Bartholomew's, Pittsboro.

SEE: Annual Convention of the Diocese of North Carolina, *Journals*, 1838–68; General Assembly, *Session Laws of North Carolina*, 1844/45, 1850/51, 1854/55; Herbert D. Pegg, *The Whig Party in North Carolina* (1969); Raleigh *Daily Sentinel*, 1 June 1876; Raleigh *Register*, 6 June 1837; Senate and House of Commons, *Journals*, 1844/45, 1850/51, 1854/55; Charles C. Weaver, *Internal Improvements in North Carolina Previous to 1860* (1903); John H. Wheeler, *Reminiscences and Memoirs of North Carolina and Eminent North Carolinians* (1884).

LAWRENCE F. LONDON

Hauser, Charles Roy (*8 Mar. 1900–6 Jan. 1970*), chemist and educator, was born in San Jose, Calif., the son of Charles H. and Elizabeth Rogan Hauser, but moved to Florida at an early age. He attended the University of Florida, where he received a B.S. in chemical engineering in 1923 and an M.S. in 1925. His Ph.D., on organic chloramines, was obtained at the University of Iowa in 1928 under the direction of George H. Coleman. After a year as instructor in organic chemistry at Lehigh University, he joined the faculty of Duke University as an instructor in 1929. There he became a professor in 1946 and James B. Duke Professor in 1961.

For almost ten years after he received his doctoral degree, Hauser's work was neither prolific nor especially notable. He reportedly told a colleague that it took him a long time to learn how to do research. The first of his important discoveries came in 1937 and 1938, in association with W. B. Renfrow, Jr., and David S. Breslow. It concerned his studies on the Claisen condensation and the Perkin synthesis, reactions that produce new carbon-carbon bonds with the aid of basic catalysts. These papers laid the groundwork for understanding the role of acid-base relationships in condensation reactions, and also prefigured a theme of his later research: the improvement of yields and the development of new applications of organic synthesis through understanding of the fundamental mechanism of the chemical reaction. In the second paper of the series in 1938, he enunciated what was to become known as "Hauser's rule": in condensations of esters, the base formed is weaker than the base that initiates the reaction. The prime example of this fundamental reaction was the development of the base-catalyzed rearrangement of benzyl quaternary salts, now called the Sommelet-Hauser rearrangement (despite the relatively minor contribution of Sommelet); Hauser elaborated the theoretical implications of the reaction in collaboration with Simon W. Kantor and Donald N. van Eenam.

His most significant discoveries resulted from his studies of organic polyanions, or organic species with several negative charges, beginning in 1962 in a collaboration with Thomas M. Harris. New carbon-carbon bonds formed by the reaction of these polyanions with suitable alkylating agents are often at different positions in the molecule than the carbon-carbon bonds formed by the reaction of simple singly charged organic anions. Their use makes possible the easy synthesis of compounds that would be quite difficult to prepare by other means.

For his major discoveries on the fundamental mechanisms and synthetic applications of these base-catalyzed condensations, Hauser was elected to the National Academy of Sciences in 1958; he was the first chemist from a university in the Southeast to be so honored. During World War II he had been awarded a certificate of merit for his work on the synthesis of antimalarial compounds. For his principal studies he received the Florida Section Award of the American Chemical Society as "the outstanding chemist of the South" (1957), the Herty Medal (1962), the American Chemical Society Award for Creative Work in Synthetic Organic Chemistry (1962), and the medal of the Synthetic Organic Chemical Manufacturers Association (1967).

Research in organic chemistry was both vocation and avocation to Hauser, and he communicated his enthusiasm to all with whom he worked. His research conferences continued during his final long confinement in the hospital, the last occurring only a few hours before his death. More than seventy chemists earned their doctorates under his direction, and he published more than four hundred research papers in organic chemistry.

In 1929 Hauser married Madge L. Baltimore. Their children were Elizabeth (Mrs. R. L. Grate) of Pacific Grove, Calif.; Frances (Mrs. J. E. Yourison) of Toledo, Ohio; and Dr. Charles F. Hauser of Charleston, W.Va., who, like his father, was an organic chemist.

SEE: *Charlotte Observer*, 11 Apr. 1957; Duke University News Service Files, Charles Roy Hauser, 1931–75 (Duke University Archives, Durham); *Durham Morning Herald*, 18 May 1961; *McGraw-Hill Modern Scientists and Engi-*

neers, vol. 2 (1980); *Milledgeville* (Ga.) *Union-Recorder*, 3 May 1962; *Who's Who in America, 1968–69*.

MAURICE M. BURSEY
CHARLES K. BRADSHER

Hauser, William (*23 Dec. 1812–15 Sept. 1880*), composer, music teacher, editor, physician, and minister, was born near Bethania (then Stokes County). He was a great-grandson of one of the town's earliest settlers, Martin Hauser, an Alsatian carpenter who came to America in 1727 and arrived in North Carolina in 1753, shortly before the first company of Moravians. Martin was a Lutheran but converted after taking shelter in the Moravian stockades during Indian troubles. Many of his descendants remained Moravians, but Hauser's father—Martin Hauser III—turned to Methodism and served that denomination as a local preacher. The Reverend Martin Hauser married Leah Billeter, daughter of a Maryland Quaker, by whom he had eleven children. The youngest was William, who was only two when his father died.

Hauser had little opportunity for education until he reached manhood. Two years after his marriage in 1837 to Eliza M. Renshaw of Rowan County, he moved with his bride to Virginia where he studied Greek and Latin at the newly founded Emory and Henry College. In 1841 they resettled in Georgia, first in Richmond County, where Hauser taught school, then in Burke. Five years later they moved to a farm they named Hesperia, near Wadley, Jefferson County, where they remained for the rest of their lives and were buried. The couple had three children: Carolina Elizabeth (m. Parker White), William Clarke, and Victor McLanndhton.

While residing in Burke County, Ga., Hauser studied medicine under a local physician and began a practice that he continued nearly to the end of his life. Between 1859 and 1861 he contributed seven articles to the *Oglethorpe Medical and Surgical Journal*, serving as assistant editor for sixteen months during this period. He had performed similar duties in 1854 for a humorous medical journal, the *Georgia Blister and Critic*. During the 1859–60 school year, he was professor of physiology and pathology at the Oglethorpe Medical College in Savannah.

Hauser joined the Methodist church in 1827. He is said to have served as a local or supply preacher during much of his life. A Southern patriot, he enlisted in the Confederate Army at age fifty and served for ten months as a chaplain in the Forty-eighth Regiment of Georgia Volunteers, until he was severely wounded in the Battle of Chancellorsville.

The physician-preacher is remembered, however, for his work as a musician. Though trained only in rural singing schools and spending most of his life as a country doctor, he built a sizable library of musical publications—journals, encyclopedias, treatises on musical theory, the scores of operas and oratorios, anthologies of songs, and instruction books for the violin, flute, and banjo. This collection was the basis for a series of thirty-eight essays he wrote for publication in the *Greensborough* (N.C.) *Times* from 1857 to 1859. More importantly, Hauser was a shape-note singing master and composer. His compositions are printed with those of many other rural musicians in two tunebooks he edited, *The Hesperian Harp* (1848) and *The Olive Leaf* (1878). These volumes were well known in the rural South. As early as 1837 Hauser anticipated publishing a song collection under the title *The Southern Harmony*, but the book seems never to have been issued.

Hauser intended his tunebooks to please a wide range of musical tastes and was himself free from the musical prejudices common among Methodists of his day (the Iredell Circuit Quarterly Conference censured him in 1838 for venturing to employ the flute and fiddle at his singing schools). But the music he loved most was the singing of "happy christian white-folks and negroes" who, "filled with the Holy Ghost" during services and at camp meetings, "drop the trammels of form and give forth, from full hearts, the sense of what they sing." Accordingly, he absorbed a large repertory of camp meeting and revival spirituals. For his songbooks, he transcribed many of these tunes, giving them three- and four-part vocal settings, often labeling the tunes as ones learned in his youth from his mother or from other North Carolina singers in the 1820s and 1830s. These melodic transcriptions by Hauser provide the earliest known musical record of North Carolina folk singing.

SEE: Richard M. Boling, "The Life and Work of William Hauser" (M.A. thesis, Tulane University, 1962); William E. Chute, "Rev. Wm. Hauser, M.D.," *Musical Million* 12 (May 1881); Kenneth J. Hauser, Jr., *Alsatian-American Family Hauser* (1977); George P. Jackson, *White Spirituals in the Southern Uplands* (1933); Methodist Episcopal Church South, N.C. Conference, *Iredell Circuit Quarterly Conference Minutes*, 2 June 1838 (Manuscript Department, Duke University Library, Durham); Annie Laura Hauser Schmidt, *Eight Known Generations of the Hauser Family in America from 1726 to 1956* (1956).

DAN PATTERSON

Hawkins, Benjamin (*15 Aug. 1754–6 June 1816*), Revolutionary soldier, U.S. senator, and Indian agent, was born at Pleasant Hill plantation in present Vance County, one of four sons of Philemon and Delia Martin Hawkins. All of the sons served as colonels in the American Revolution. Benjamin Hawkins was educated at the College of New Jersey (now Princeton University). When the Revolution began he joined the staff of General George Washington; his fluency in French earned him an appointment as interpreter between Washington and the French allies. He fought in the Battle of Monmouth and other engagements, and was an original member of the Society of the Cincinnati, formed in 1783 by officers of the Continental Army.

Hawkins served in the North Carolina General Assembly in 1778 and 1784, and acted for the state as commercial agent in Holland, France, and Spain during the Revolution. In 1781–82 and 1786–87, he was a member of the Continental Congress. He was present at Annapolis when Washington resigned his commission as commander-in-chief. In 1785, Hawkins was appointed to a commission to negotiate with the Cherokees and all Indians south of them in the United States.

With Samuel Johnston, Hawkins was elected the first U.S. senator from North Carolina under the Constitution, and he served in the first three congresses from 1789 to 1794. At the close of his senatorial term, Hawkins was appointed by President Washington as Indian agent for the three great Indian tribes and all other Indians south of the Ohio River. He assumed these duties at Fort Hawkins, Ga., in December 1796 and remained in the post until his death twenty years later. His "Sketch of the Creek Country" was published in the *Georgia Historical Society Collections*, volume 3 (1848), and his letters appeared in volume 9 (1916).

In 1789, the General Assembly elected Hawkins to the first board of trustees of The University of North

Carolina; he served diligently until he left the state in 1798. He also was a delegate to the 1789 constitutional convention. Hawkins was a member of the Anglican (later Episcopal) church.

Once established in the Indian territory as agent, he took a common-law wife, Lavinia Downs of Georgia; they had one son, James Madison Hawkins, and four daughters. Four years before his death, when Hawkins thought he was fatally ill, he and Lavinia Downs were married. He died in Georgia and was buried in Crawford County.

SEE: Samuel A. Ashe, ed., *Biographical History of North Carolina*, vol. 5 (1906); A. H. Chappell, *Miscellanies of Georgia* (1874); C. L. Grant, ed., *Letters, Journals and Writings of Benjamin Hawkins*, 2 vols. (1980); C. L. Grant and Gerald H. Davis, "The Wedding of Col. Benjamin Hawkins," *North Carolina Historical Review* 54 (1977).

ARMISTEAD JONES MAUPIN

Hawkins (Hawkings), John (d. 12 Dec. 1717), Council member, Assembly member, and justice of the General Court and of the Pasquotank Precinct Court, emigrated from England to North Carolina before November 1682. He probably came from County Kent, where he was arrested and fined for attending a Quaker meeting in 1670. Settling in Pasquotank Precinct, Hawkins joined the Pasquotank Monthly Meeting of the Society of Friends; he became an elder of the meeting and served on various committees. His devotion and services to his chosen faith are mentioned in a number of Quaker writings.

In following Hawkins's career, one must take care to distinguish between records pertaining to him and those concerning other individuals with the same name, for at least four other colonists were named John Hawkins. One, whose will was proved in 1688, may have been the John Hawkins mentioned in court records as jury foreman in September 1670 and as juror in county court in the early 1680s, although some of those references may pertain to the subject of this sketch. Another John Hawkins, born in February 1671/72 and a resident of Perquimans Precinct, was the son of Francis Godfrey's daughter, Frances, and her husband, Thomas Hawkins, both of whom died during the infancy of their son, who eventually became the ward of his uncle, John Godfrey. A third John Hawkins, born about 1682 and a resident of Chowan Precinct, was the son of James Blount's daughter, Elizabeth, and her first husband, Thomas Hawkins, who died during his son's childhood. The boy was first made the ward of his paternal grandmother, Alice Hawkins Wade, but subsequently was the ward of his stepfather, Michael Lynch. A fourth John Hawkins, who apparently lived in Chowan, probably was an uncle of the younger John Hawkins of Chowan, but his identity is not certain.

The subject of this sketch seems to have been the only John Hawkins who lived in Pasquotank and was a Quaker. No doubt he is the one whose name appears as witness on the wills of several Quakers of that vicinity, including Dorothy Harvey, widow of John Harvey, who made her will in November 1682. He probably was the John Hawkins who, in 1690, was appointed attorney by Elizabeth Banks of London to act with Francis Tomes in prosecuting certain claims against Governor Seth Sothel. Records relating to the estate of Thomas Hunt of Pasquotank indicate that the John Hawkins named as Hunt's administrator in 1696 was the one of present interest.

At an unknown date Hawkins became justice of the Pasquotank Precinct Court, a position he held in July 1694 and in January 1697/98. The exact period of his tenure has not been established because of the sparseness of surviving records of that court. On 6 Nov. 1697 Hawkins was commissioned justice of the General Court. He took his seat the following March and retained it through July 1703.

In the early 1700s Hawkins was elected to the lower house of the Assembly and served at least one session, probably in 1702 or 1703. He was reelected but was barred from taking his seat because of a policy, instituted in 1704, requiring all members to swear to, not merely affirm, the oath of allegiance and other oaths of office. The discontinuance of an earlier policy permitting Quakers to affirm instead of swearing served to disqualify Hawkins and the other burgesses elected from Pasquotank, all of whom were Quakers and prohibited by their religion from swearing. A special election was called to replace the Pasquotank burgesses.

Widespread dissatisfaction with the new policy led to changes favorable to Quakers, and by November 1707 Hawkins held a seat on the Council and was ex officio member of the upper house of the Assembly. He remained in those positions through November 1709, soon after which he appears to have left public life.

In private life Hawkins was a merchant-planter. He owned at least 600 acres of land in Pasquotank and at his death was part owner of a vessel engaged in the coast-wise trade. He also left a substantial estate in possessions of other types, including a number of slaves. He and his wife, Sarah, had two sons, John and Thomas, who were living in 1688, but they apparently died before their parents. There is no mention of children or grandchildren in the will of either parent.

According to Quaker records, Hawkins was "upwards of three score years" at the time of his death. Sarah was also more than sixty when she died on 28 Oct. 1722. In their wills, which complemented each other, John and Sarah left most of their estate to Hawkins's cousin, Thomas Merreday, and to the children of Hawkins's sister, Elizabeth, who had remained in England. They bequeathed the remainder of their estate to various friends.

SEE: F. C. Anscombe, *I Have Called You Friends* (1959); Joseph Besse, *A Collection of the Sufferings of the People Called Quakers*, 2 vols. (1753); "Dictionary of Quaker Biography" (typescript), and John Smith, "The Lives of the Ministers of the Gospel among the People Called Quakers" (Haverford College Library, Haverford, Pa.); J. Bryan Grimes, ed., *Abstract of North Carolina Wills* (1910); J. R. B. Hathaway, ed., *North Carolina Historical and Genealogical Register*, 3 vols. (1900–1903); W. W. Hinshaw, comp., *Encyclopedia of Quaker Genealogy*, vol. 1 (1936); Mattie Erma E. Parker, ed., *North Carolina Higher-Court Records, 1670–1696*, vol. 2 (1968), and *1697–1701* (1971); William S. Price, Jr., ed., *North Carolina Higher-Court Records, 1702–1708*, vol. 4 (1974); William L. Saunders, ed., *Colonial Records of North Carolina*, vol. 1 (1886). Manuscript sources at North Carolina State Archives, Raleigh: Albemarle Book of Warrants and Surveys, 1681–1706; Albemarle County Papers, 1678–1714; Colonial Court Records, Box CCR 192; Wills of Pasquotank County.

MATTIE ERMA E. PARKER

Hawkins, John Davis (15 Apr. 1781–5 Dec. 1858), lawyer, legislator, and planter, was born at Pleasant Hill plantation in Granville (now Vance) County, the fourth of twelve children of Philemon Hawkins III and Lucy Davis. He was a grandson of Colonel Philemon Hawkins, Sr., who was aide-de-camp to Governor William Tryon at the Battle of Alamance in 1771 and held a colonel's commission in the American Revolution. John's brother, William Hawkins, was governor of North Carolina during the War of 1812.

Hawkins was graduated from The University of North Carolina in 1801 and became a lawyer. At an early age he was made a trustee of the university, a position he held for fifty-one years. He was a member of the Episcopal church.

It has been said that Hawkins "possessed rare and extraordinary qualities—a man of great willpower and force of character, intelligent and influential." He represented Franklin County in the House of Commons in 1821–22 and 1834–35, and in the senate for three terms between 1836 and 1841. For many years he also served as a county judge. In private life, Hawkins was a planter of some magnitude and invested a portion of his wealth in the development of early railroads, particularly the Raleigh and Gaston Railroad.

In 1803, he married Jane Boyd, daughter of Alexander and Ann Swepson Boyd of Boydton, Va. They had thirteen children, born between 1805 and 1827. Hawkins was buried in Oakwood Cemetery, Raleigh.

SEE: Samuel A. Ashe, ed., *Biographical History of North Carolina*, vol. 5 (1906); John L. Cheney, Jr., ed., *North Carolina Government, 1585–1974* (1975).

ARMISTEAD JONES MAUPIN

Hawkins, Micajah Thomas (20 May 1790–22 Dec. 1858), legislator, congressman, and planter, the youngest son of John and Sally Macon Hawkins, was born in Warren County. His paternal grandparents, Philemon and Delia Martin Hawkins, who migrated to North Carolina from Gloucester County, Va., about 1737, were among the first settlers in the area that became Bute County, which in 1779 was divided into Warren and Franklin counties. Micajah was the nephew of Congressman Nathaniel Macon and Benjamin Hawkins, a U.S. senator and an Indian agent.

Hawkins attended the Warrenton Academy and The University of North Carolina. During the War of 1812, he was a member of the Seventh Company, Third North Carolina Regiment. He attained the rank of major general in the North Carolina militia. Hawkins became a large-scale planter; according to the 1840 census, he owned 105 slaves, 60 of whom were engaged in agriculture.

At an early age Hawkins entered politics, serving in the North Carolina House of Commons in 1819 and 1820. In 1823 he moved to the state senate, where he remained until 1827. When Robert Porter resigned his seat in the U.S. House of Representatives, Hawkins, a Democrat, was chosen to replace him in the Twenty-second Congress, taking his seat on 6 Jan. 1832. He was elected to the Twenty-third Congress and served for three successive terms thereafter, until 3 Mar. 1841. He declined to run for reelection in 1840.

Returning to North Carolina, Hawkins resumed his agricultural activities, but he was unable to resist the lure of politics. In 1846 he won another seat in the state senate, and in 1854–55 he was a member of the Council of State.

On 20 Sept. 1810, Hawkins married Priscilla M. Moss. Apparently she died childless. His second marriage, to Mariah E. Baker, who was thirty-nine years his

junior, was performed on 13 Feb. 1849. They were the parents of two daughters and a son: Ella Thomas, Martha Hamlin, and John Harrison. Hawkins was buried in the family plot on his plantation in the Sandy Creek district of Warren County near Warrenton.

SEE: *Biog. Dir. Am. Cong.* (1971); family Bible records of Marshall De Lancey Haywood and wills of Warren County (North Carolina State Archives, Raleigh); marriage records of Warren County (Tennessee Archives, Nashville); U.S. Census, 1820–60, North Carolina; Manly Wade Wellman, *The County of Warren, North Carolina, 1856–1917* (1959); John H. Wheeler, *Historical Sketches of North Carolina* (1851); *Who Was Who in America, 1607–1896* (1963).

MILDRED MARTIN CROW

Hawkins, Philemon, II (28 Sept. 1717–10 Sept. 1801), planter, Revolutionary soldier, and public officeholder, was born in Virginia. He was the oldest son of Philemon and Ann Eleanor Howard Hawkins, founders of this branch of the Hawkins family in America. His parents were born in Devonshire, England, and settled in Virginia in 1715. Philemon the emigrant, the great-grandson of Sir John Hawkins, Elizabethan naval commander, was a young man when he died in Gloucester County, Va., in 1725.

In 1735, at age eighteen, Hawkins moved his mother, his brother John, and his sister Ann to Bute County where he soon became the wealthiest man in the county. He was a member of the Anglican church and filled many public positions from 1743 until the end of the Revolutionary War. Hawkins took an active part in the events of 1771–76, serving as aide-de-camp to Governor William Tryon on the expedition against the Regulators in 1771 and later as a member of the two Provincial Congresses that met at Halifax in 1776. The Congress named him a lieutenant colonel of cavalry, but he soon resigned his commission to raise his own battalion. Between 1779 and 1787 he served seven terms in the General Assembly, and in 1782–83 he was a member of the Council of State.

In 1743 Hawkins married Delia Martin, daughter of Colonel Zachariah Martin of Mecklenburg County, Va. They had four sons—John, Joseph, Benjamin, and Philemon—all of whom were colonels in the Continental Army during the Revolution, and two daughters, Delia and Ann. Mrs. Hawkins died in 1794. Both she and her husband were buried at the old homestead in Warren County.

SEE: Samuel A. Ashe, ed., *Biographical History of North Carolina*, vol. 5 (1906); John L. Cheney, Jr., ed., *North Carolina Government, 1585–1979* (1981); John D. Hawkins, *An Oration Commemorative of Col. Philemon Hawkins, Senior, Deceased* (1829); William S. Powell, ed., *The Correspondence of Governor William Tryon*, vol. 2 (1981).

ARMISTEAD JONES MAUPIN

Hawkins, Philemon, III (3 Dec. 1752–28 Jan. 1833), Revolutionary official, landholder, and planter, was born at Pleasant Hill plantation, the seat of the Hawkins family in present Warren County, the son of Philemon and Delia Martin Hawkins. His brothers, John, Joseph, and Benjamin, served as colonels in the Continental Army during the Revolution. The subject of this sketch was the great-grandson of Philemon and Ann Eleanor Howard Hawkins of Devonshire, England, founders of this branch of the family in America in 1715.

Young Philemon was long in public life, serving eleven terms in the General Assembly between 1787 and 1818 and three on the Council of State between 1781 and 1791; in the latter year, he was president of the Council. He held thousands of acres of land and erected his residence, also named Pleasant Hill after his birthplace, near Middleburg in present Vance County. He was a member of the Church of England, afterwards the Episcopal church.

At age nineteen, Hawkins fought alongside his father, who was Governor William Tryon's chief aide, at the Battle of Alamance during the War of the Regulation; however, both father and son later became ardent supporters of the Revolution. In the colonial period he was commander of the county militia, and in May 1776, as a colonel, was named one of the officers to organize recruits in the Halifax and Edenton districts. He resigned ten days later, perhaps because he was a member of the Provincial Congress. Later he was a member of the 1789 convention at Fayetteville, which ratified the federal Constitution.

Hawkins married Lucy Davis of Roanoke on 31 Aug. 1775, and they became the parents of thirteen children, the oldest of whom was Governor William Hawkins. It is said that he left 131 children, grandchildren, and great-grandchildren.

SEE: Samuel A. Ashe, ed., *Biographical History of North Carolina*, vol. 5 (1906); John L. Cheney, Jr., ed., *North Carolina Government, 1585–1979* (1981); Walter Clark, ed., *State Records of North Carolina*, vols. 13, 17, 21 (1896, 1899, 1903); William L. Saunders, ed., *Colonial Records of North Carolina*, vol. 10 (1890).

ARMISTEAD JONES MAUPIN

Hawkins, William (20 Oct. 1777–19 May 1819), lawyer and governor of North Carolina, was born at Pleasant Hill in Granville (now Vance) County, the oldest of seven sons of Philemon III and Lucy Davis Hawkins. He was the grandson of Philemon II and Delia Martin Hawkins, and the great-grandson of the first Philemon and Ann Eleanor Howard Hawkins of Devonshire, England, who emigrated to Virginia in 1715.

Hawkins attended Princeton University and read law under Judge John Williams at Williamsboro, Granville County. After receiving his law license in 1797, he went to Fort Hawkins, Ga., where he was assistant to his uncle, Senator Benjamin Hawkins, who was agent for all the Indian tribes south of the Ohio River. He resided there for two years, then went to Philadelphia to continue the study of law and the French language. Two years later he returned to his father's home at Pleasant Hill and began to practice law.

In 1801 Hawkins was called to public service by Governor James Turner, who appointed him commissioner to settle a claim with the Tuscarora Indians. He won a seat in the legislature in 1805 and became speaker of the house. Elected governor of North Carolina in 1810, he was twice reelected and served as chief executive during the War of 1812.

A member of the Episcopal church, Hawkins married Ann Swepson Boyd in 1803. She was the daughter of Alexander Boyd, a prominent Scottish merchant of Boydton, Mecklenburg County, Va. Her sister, Jane Anderson Boyd, had previously married William's brother, John Davis Hawkins. In 1816 Hawkins's health declined

and he retired to his plantations. He died on a visit to Sparta, Ga., and was buried there.

SEE: Samuel A. Ashe, ed., *Biographical History of North Carolina*, vol. 5 (1906); Beth G. Crabtree, *North Carolina Governors, 1585–1958* (1958); Robert Sobel and John Raimo, *Biographical Directory of the Governors of the United States, 1789–1978*, vol. 3 (1978); John H. Wheeler, *Historical Sketches of North Carolina* (1851).

ARMISTEAD JONES MAUPIN

Hawkins, William Joseph (27 May 1819–28 Oct. 1894), physician and railroad official, was born on his father's plantation in Franklin (now Vance) County. His grandfather was Revolutionary War Colonel Philemon Hawkins II and his father was John Davis Hawkins, one of the largest planters in his district; his mother was Jane A. Boyd of Mecklenburg County, Va. For several years William studied at home under tutors and at the Spring Grove Academy in Franklin County. In 1837 he entered The University of North Carolina, but transferred after two years to William and Mary College, graduating with distinction in 1840. In 1842 he was graduated from the medical department of the University of Pennsylvania and began practicing at Ridgeway, N.C.

Hawkins quickly developed a large medical practice and by 1850 owned twenty-five slaves and real estate valued at $13,000. Soon, however, he became absorbed in the business world. Following his father's interest, he invested in the Raleigh and Gaston Railroad and was appointed to its board of directors. In 1855 he became president of the railroad.

Four years of heavy traffic, accentuated by the inability to maintain rails and rolling stock properly, had reduced the Raleigh and Gaston to a deplorable condition by 1865. To revitalize the line, Hawkins conceived the idea of acquiring and completing the Chatham Railroad and of leasing the North Carolina Railroad and several others to form the Raleigh and Augusta Airline. In October 1869, he offered an annual rental of $240,000 for a twenty-year lease of the North Carolina Railroad. The directors were receptive to the offer, but the Raleigh *Sentinel* contended that the figure was ridiculously low and termed it "Plundering the State." The stockholders became convinced that Hawkins, W. W. Holden, and M. S. Littlefield were plotting to defraud them and in November voted against the lease. The inability to acquire the North Carolina Railroad defeated Hawkins's plan, but the Seaboard Airline grew out of his concept. By 1873 the Seaboard completely controlled the Raleigh and Gaston, and the friends of the North Carolina Railroad accused Hawkins of selling out to the Virginia-based railroad. Soon the Seaboard was selling tickets from Boston to Atlanta. Hawkins remained president of the Raleigh and Gaston until rheumatism forced his retirement in October 1875.

Hawkins was also a large stockholder in and a director of the Raleigh National Bank, and in 1870 he was instrumental in the founding of the Citizens National Bank of Raleigh. He became its president in 1890 and served until his death. From 1881 to 1891 he was a trustee of The University of North Carolina. He died in Philadelphia, where he had gone for medical treatment.

On 4 Jan. 1844 Hawkins married Mary Alethea Clark, daughter of David Clark of Halifax County; they had two sons, Colin M. and Marmaduke J., before her death in September 1850. On 27 Dec. 1855 Hawkins married Mary's sister, Lucy Norfleet Clark; they had two daughters, Louise and Alethea. The second Mrs. Hawkins died on 9 Oct. 1867, and on 12 May 1869 Hawkins married Mary Ann White, daughter of Andrew B. White of Pottsville, Pa.; they had one daughter, Lucy C.

SEE: Samuel A. Ashe, ed., *Biographical History of North Carolina*, vol. 5 (1906); Kemp P. Battle, *History of the University of North Carolina*, 2 vols. (1907–12); Cecil K. Brown, *A State Movement in Railroad Development* (1928); Hawkins Family Papers (Southern Historical Collection, University of North Carolina Library, Chapel Hill); *Membership and Ancestral Register . . . of the North Carolina Society of the Sons of the Revolution* (1898); Raleigh *News and Observer*, 30 Oct. 1894; *Souvenir Presentation Ceremonials of a Silver Service, to Dr. W. J. Hawkins* (by the Raleigh and Gaston Railroad, September 1875).

BUCK YEARNS

Hawks, Cicero Stephens *(26 May 1811–19 Apr. 1868)*, Episcopal bishop, was the youngest son of Francis and Julia Airay Stephens Hawks of New Bern and a grandson of John Hawks and Sarah Rice. The uncle for whom he was named, Marcus Cicero Stephens, also of New Bern, was a banker and Episcopal vestryman. Educated in his hometown by the Reverend Thomas P. Irving, Episcopal priest and schoolteacher, young Hawks also was an amateur actor in some of the "theatrical exercises" directed by Irving. In 1830 he was graduated with an A.B. degree from The University of North Carolina and began to study law in New York City. He was almost ready for admission to the bar when he decided to enter the ministry and was tutored by his brother, the Reverend Francis Lister Hawks. In 1836 he was ordained to the priesthood.

His first parish was at Saugerties, N.Y. In February 1837 he became the first rector of Trinity Church, Buffalo, N.Y., and in October 1843 he accepted a call to Christ Church, St. Louis, Mo. The next year, on 20 October, during a General Convention at Christ Church, Philadelphia, he was consecrated as the first Episcopal bishop of the new Diocese of Missouri.

As a pioneering missionary on the western frontier, Hawks labored tirelessly through a wide area, traveling by horseback, wagon, stagecoach, and steamboat. For ten years he was also rector of the St. Louis church until the diocese was able to assume his support. When that city was scourged by an epidemic of Asiatic cholera in 1849, he remained heroically at his post, ministering to the sick and burying the dead.

Throughout the twenty-five years of his bishopric, Hawks traversed the entire state, conducting services, organizing parishes, and winning friends for himself and his church by his attractive personality, eloquent sermons, and dedicated devotion to his calling. Even during the Civil War he continued his arduous journeys, carrying consolation to grieving homes and trying to bind up the wounds of civil strife. "I hope all my flock go to church now," he wrote, in his earnest efforts to "harmonize all elements in the church."

Having taken the earlier oath of loyalty to the Union, Hawks advised other clergymen to decide according to their own consciences whether or not to take the postwar "Ironclad Oath," though he deplored some of its features. In those stormy times his health began to fail. Weak from his labors, he held an Easter Sunday service in 1868 at St. Louis with the assistance of a visiting minister. A week later he died, and was buried in Bellefontaine Cemetery, St. Louis.

On 19 Feb. 1835 in New Bern, Hawks married Anne Jones, daughter of Dr. Hugh Jones and Anna Maria Guion, and a great-niece of Governor Benjamin Williams.

SEE: Gertrude S. Carraway, *Years of Light* (1944); Hawks and Guion Family Papers (Southern Historical Collection, University of North Carolina Library, Chapel Hill); *Kansas City Star*, 8 Oct. 1940; *Living Church Annual* (1944).

GERTRUDE S. CARRAWAY

Hawks, Francis Lister *(10 June 1798–27 Sept. 1866)*, clergyman, educator, and historian, was born in New Bern, the second son of Francis (10 Dec. 1769–20 Dec. 1831) and Julia Airay Stephens Hawks (1 Dec. 1773–3 Apr. 1813). He was a grandson of John Hawks (1731–31 Oct. 1790), supervising architect of Tryon Palace. While a pupil of the Reverend Thomas P. Irving at the New Bern Academy, young Hawks had roles in home-talent plays in the new Masonic Theater. In 1815 he was graduated with honors from The University of North Carolina. Afterwards he studied law in New Bern under William Gaston and John Stanly and in Litchfield, Conn., at the law school of Tapping Reeve and James Gould. Admitted to the bar, "the young prodigy" in 1820 became a reporter of the North Carolina Supreme Court for six years. In addition to other duties, he compiled four volumes of *North Carolina* [Supreme Court] *Reports*, and he represented New Bern in the 1821 House of Commons. An active Mason, like his father, Hawks was Orator on St. John's Day, 24 June 1822, for St. John's Lodge, Post No. 3, A.F. & A.M. That December he was elected the lodge's Worshipful Master and delivered the sermon on St. John the Evangelist's Day. From 1824 to 1827 he was Deputy Grand Master, presiding at the 1825 Grand Lodge Communications.

Hawks, who had been a devout communicant of St. Matthew's Church in Hillsborough, and who often read sermons at Christ Episcopal Church in the absence of its rector, gave up the practice of law in 1826 to begin training for the ministry. He studied theology with the Reverend William Mercer Green, a college mate and later Bishop of Mississippi, and was ordained deacon at New Bern in 1827. Shortly afterwards he was ordained priest.

After serving as assistant to Dr. Harry Croswell at Trinity Church, New Haven, Conn., and then to the Right Reverend William White at St. James Church, Philadelphia, Hawks was named professor of divinity at Washington College, Hartford, Conn., in 1830. The next year he accepted the rectorate of St. Stephens' Church, New York City. Within a few months he transferred to St. Thomas Church, in Flushing, N.Y., where he remained for twelve years. During that period he had charge of St. John's Church for a time, and was assistant secretary of the 1832 General Convention and secretary of the 1834 New York diocesan convention. In 1835 he was appointed Missionary Bishop of the Southwest, but declined the office because it had no endowment.

Hawks was professor of ecclesiastical history at the General Theological Seminary, 1833–35, and the following year was chosen historiographer of the Episcopal Church of the United States. He traveled through the Holy Land, England, and other countries, gathering material for his religious histories, especially *Contributions to the Ecclesiastical History of the United States*. For several months in 1837 he was editor of the *New York Review*, of which he was a cofounder.

St. Thomas Hall, a classical school for girls, was started by him in 1839 in Flushing, N.Y.; there he was literary master, spiritual almoner, and temporal head. Its financial difficulties contributed primarily to his resignation from St. Thomas Church in 1843 and his removal to Holly Springs, Miss. While in the state Hawks was an original trustee of the University of Mississippi, but he rejected an offer to be Bishop of Mississippi. Moving to New Orleans, La., in 1844, he was for five years rector of Christ Church. Besides rebuilding the church, he helped establish the University of Louisiana and was its first president.

In 1849 Hawks returned to New York to become rector of the Church of the Mediator, soon merged with Calvary Church. In 1853 he was instrumental in founding the *Church Journal*. Elected Bishop of Rhode Island, he declined a bishopric for the third time, preferring to remain a parish pastor and pulpit orator. In 1846 he had volunteered to be professor of history at The University of North Carolina; however, at that time there was no provision for the chair. When offered the post in 1859, he turned it down.

At the outbreak of the Civil War, due to his Southern heritage and sympathy, Hawks resigned the New York rectorate and went to Baltimore, Md., as rector of Christ Church. After the war he once again returned to New York to be associated with the Church of the Annunciation. In 1865 friends assisted him in organizing the Church of the Holy Saviour and the Parish of Iglesia de Santiago, where he conducted services in Spanish.

Stephen F. Miller reported that when a parishioner, remonstrating with Hawks for accepting a call to a more lucrative field, reminded him, "The young ravens would be fed," Hawks replied, "Ah, yes, but unfortunately there is no such promise for the young Hawks!"

Throughout his colorful career, Hawks, "never to be idle," engaged in innumerable pursuits with great ability. As a young lawyer he had proved learned and logical in his convincing arguments. These traits were apparent in his pulpit appearances, drawing theologians from as far away as Europe to hear his scholarly and inspirational sermons "beginning and ending with Christ." Noted for his "graceful elocution, mellifluous composition, and finely-modulated voice," he could recite from memory many hymns and long passages from the Bible and the *Book of Common Prayer*. With his "streams of eloquence unequalled," quick wit, gracious charm, and fund of knowledge on widely diversified topics, Hawks was a popular conversationalist and lecturer.

His prolific writings for children as well as adults on varied religious and secular topics ranged from church histories, a two-volume history of North Carolina, and a book on the English language to works about Egyptian monuments, Peruvian antiquities, and the papers of Commodore Matthew C. Perry and Alexander Hamilton. For some time he was an editor of *Appleton's Cyclopaedia of Biography*.

Hawks was generous in his assistance to numerous literary and historical publications and organizations, particularly the New-York Historical Society, which he helped reorganize and to which he left his family records and historical collections. He was a founder of the American Ethnological Society and its vice-president from 1855 to 1859; he also helped establish the American Geographical and Statistical Society, serving for several years as president.

Scheduled to make the address at the laying of the foundation stone for the coquina shell entrance to Cedar Grove Cemetery in New Bern, he was unable to get there in time for the program. With the $130 in receipts from his talk upon his later arrival, the iron gates under the entrance arches were purchased. The four lines on a marble table above the main arch were taken from a hymn he composed for the event:

> Still hallowed be the spot where lies
> Each dear loved one in earth's embrace,
> Our God their treasured dust doth prize,
> Man should protect their resting place.

Hawks was also the speaker in New Bern, 29 Apr. 1858, at a celebration on completion of the "Old Mullet Line" between that city and Goldsboro by the Atlantic and North Carolina Railroad Company.

A "Memorandum of things to be done, or that should be done in Newbern, by degrees" was drafted by him in 1860. For "Local Improvements" he recommended waterworks, gas lighting, flagging on sidewalks and curb stones, the use of brick for buildings, a "battery" at Union Point, and reestablishment of the New Bern Library Company. Under "For Commercial Prosperity" he suggested lines of screw propellers to New York and Baltimore, a large ocean steamer to run from Beaufort to Liverpool, and railroad connections to several places in East Carolina. "For social and intellectual enjoyment" he proposed good common schools, a polytechnic school, a boarding and day school for males and a similar one for females. (Previously, he had attempted in vain to get a polytechnic school for New Bern.) The memorandum was concluded with this advice: "At present exchange is against us. . . . We buy at the North and do not ship for ourselves. . . . Have our own shipping port, do our own exportation, and begin to form a system of foreign importations for ourselves."

On 11 Nov. 1823 Hawks married Emily Kirby (19 Nov. 1803–12 July 1827), the fifth child of Abner and Anna Plum Kirby of Connecticut. They were the parents of two children. After her death he married Mrs. Olivia Trowbridge Hunt of Danbury, Conn., who survived him. They had six children. Hawks died in New York City; the funeral was held from Calvary Church and his remains were interred at Greenwich, Conn.

SEE: Gertrude S. Carraway, *Crown of Life* (1940) and *Years of Light* (1944); *DAB*, vol. 4 (1960); Stephen F. Miller, *Recollections of New Bern Fifty Years Ago* (1974); John D. Whitford, "Historical Notes" (transcript, Craven County Public Library, New Bern).

GERTRUDE S. CARRAWAY

Hawks, John (*1731–31 Oct. 1790*), architect, contractor and accountant, and the supervising architect (1767–70) of Tryon Palace at New Bern, was born in Lincolnshire, England. Trained under Stiff Leadbeater of Eton, who designed the Harcourt Mansion, Nuneham Courtenay, in Oxfordshire, he became surveyor of St. Paul's Cathedral, London, in 1756. Evidently he had other experience before being selected as "a very able worthy . . . master builder" to accompany Lieutenant Governor William Tryon to North Carolina for the purpose of planning a government house for the colony. Not long after his arrival at Brunswick on 10 Oct. 1764, Hawks moved to New Bern where he was a prominent citizen for the remainder of his life.

His first drawings for the government house and governor's residence were dated 29 Dec. 1766. A contract was signed on 9 Jan. 1767 by "His Excellency, William Tryon, Esquire, Captain General Governor and

Commander-in-Chief in and over the province of North Carolina, of the one part, and John Hawks, of New-bern, architect, of the other part." It provided that Hawks would design and superintend the construction, under the supervision of Tryon, to whom the Assembly—with an initial appropriation of £5,000, later increased to £15,000—had entrusted "sole Direction and Management." The agreement stipulated the payment of an annual salary of £300 proclamation money to Hawks as "a person acquainted with the value of the work, qualified to adapt the proportions, experienced to direct the quality and choice of materials, and of ability to judge the performance of the several craftsmen and tradesmen."

Under modified specifications approved by the Crown, the edifice was designed like a London vicinity house "in the pure English taste," with which Hawks was most familiar. The first bricks were laid on 26 Aug. 1767. With a letter of introduction from Tryon, Hawks went to Philadelphia to secure the services of expert artisans. Although not finished, the "palace" was ready for Tryon, his wife, and young daughter to move in by early June 1770. A gala celebration was held there on 5 December while the Assembly was in session. In his official address to the assemblymen, Tryon commended "the ability of the architect" and praised the structure as a "public ornament." Replying to his message, both houses of the Assembly thanked the governor and complimented the "elegant and noble" building.

Tryon wrote: "Several persons who have passed through here from the other colonies esteem this house the finest capitol building on the continent of North America." The handsome Georgian brick main building was destroyed by fire on the night of 27 Feb. 1798, after the state's capital had been moved to Raleigh. A complete and authentic reconstruction of it and two large brick wings was accomplished between 1952 and 1959 by the Tryon Palace Commission, a state agency, with funds provided by the late Mrs. James Edwin Latham, of Greensboro, a native New Bernian.

To protect New Bern against threats from Regulators, Tryon appointed Hawks and Claude Joseph Sauthier to erect extensive fortifications. Hawks was in charge of making gun carriages. For this and other assignments, he acted as a paymaster and commissioner of finance, disbursing and reporting public funds authorized in March and April 1771 by Tryon.

The first professional architect to remain in America, Hawks did much other architectural and construction work. Tryon's successor, Governor Josiah Martin, referring to Hawks as "a man of unexceptionable character, of known sufficient Qualifications," contracted with him to build a fence around the Palace Square and a smokehouse, pigeon house, and poultry house on the palace grounds. Additions for the Craven County courthouse were also designed and supervised by Hawks. He was commissioned to erect for the district and town of New Bern a jail and a jailer's house, of which he was a trustee, and twice received commissions to superintend jail repairs. He was probably the architect hired to complete the John Wright Stanly house in New Bern and the brick plantation home, Bellair, several miles from the city.

Besides undertaking tasks for Samuel Johnston of Edenton, Hawks drafted plans and dimensions for a "Cupola for Edenton Church Novr. 22nd 1769." Although this cupola is reported not to have been put on the church, it appears similar to the one on the Chowan County courthouse. An oversized "Plan and Elevation of a Prison for the District of Edenton June 1st 1773,"

with measurements for each portion, is not signed but authorities claim it to be "clearly by the same person who did the drawing of the cupola in 1769."

At the Metropolitan Museum of Art in New York is displayed a hand-carved doorway attributed to Hawks. The Southern Historical Collection at The University of North Carolina, Chapel Hill, contains a drawing of "Hillsborough" church, with another sheet of dimensions and specifications in John Hawks's handwriting. Drawings for a church in Granville County, dated 1771, are among the Hawks papers collected by his grandson, the Reverend Francis Lister Hawks, and deposited in the New-York Historical Society Library.

The architect's activities were not confined to his profession. A member of Christ Episcopal Church, he witnessed Tryon's signature and seal on a 1765 commission to "empower Thomas Clifford Howe . . . to induct the Reverend James Reed, Clerk, A.B., into the Rectory" of that church, of which Reed had already been rector for almost twelve years.

Hawks held numerous political offices beginning on 30 Oct. 1766, when he acted as mace bearer for the upper house of the Assembly. The next year he was nominated by Tryon to be "Collector of his Majesty's Customs for the port of Beaufort," the governor expressing confidence that he would serve "with ability, diligence and integrity." From 1770 to 1772 he was clerk of the pleas. "Particularly recommended to my patronage by my friend, Governor Tryon," Governor Martin had Hawks appointed clerk of the Council or upper house, a post he held in 1773 and 1774. Martin referred to him as "a very ingenious and worthy man."

After the American Revolution, Hawks continued to hold public office in North Carolina. He was a justice of the peace, for three years he was on New Bern's board of tax assessors, and for some time from 1781 he was a district auditor. In 1782, he was serving on a commission to handle claims of officers and soldiers of the North Carolina Continental Line; but, because Halifax was considered a more convenient location than New Bern, the three New Bern members were replaced the following year by three residents of Halifax. From 1784 to 1786 the assemblies elected Hawks to the Council of State, of which he was president in 1785. He was long the state's first auditor; his last payment for auditing was recorded in November 1789.

In 1785 he was appointed a trustee for the proposed Dobbs Academy at Kinston. Two years later he was one of the five managers named by the legislature to conduct a lottery to raise money for a Craven County home. During December 1788 he was made judge of the court mercantile and maritime for the New Bern district; however, on 4 Jan. 1789 he submitted his resignation to Governor Samuel Johnston, explaining that he did not feel qualified.

For the last five years or more of his life, Hawks suffered from gout. He died in New Bern. The inventory of his estate was filed 10 Mar. 1791 by his son, Francis, at the Craven County courthouse. He was also survived by another son, Samuel.

In 1768 Hawks married Sarah Rice, the daughter of John Rice, secretary of the Crown, and the granddaughter of Nathaniel Rice, who as Council president served as acting governor from 15 Apr. to 27 Oct. 1734, when royal Governor Gabriel Johnston arrived, and again, after Johnston's death, from 17 July 1752 until his own death on 29 Jan. 1753.

Their son, Francis (1769–1831), was for three decades collector of customs at New Bern. On 7 Mar. 1793 he married Julia Airay Stephens (1 Dec. 1773–3 Apr. 1813).

After her death he married Elizabeth Pugh Guion (10 Sept. 1778–25 Feb. 1816). His grave is between the graves of his two wives in Cedar Grove Cemetery, New Bern.

Francis and his first wife, Julia, were the parents of five sons and five daughters. It is said that he "tuned up" the boys every Monday morning with a whipping. If one of them demurred and pleaded innocence, he would say, "Oh, you will deserve it anyway before the week is half gone." That this chastisement was effective is suggested by the fact that all the sons became successful in their respective pursuits. John Stephens Hawks (21 Mar. 1796–16 Oct. 1865) was a lawyer. The epitaph on his tombstone in St. Peter's Churchyard, Washington, N.C., reads: "An Honest Man." Samuel Cicero Hawks (1 Mar. 1807–16 Feb. 1843) was a businessman and educator. He died at Flushing, N.Y., but was buried in Cedar Grove Cemetery, New Bern; the gravestone inscription reads in part: "The Triumph of a Brother's Love to a Brother's Memory."

The other three sons were Episcopal clergymen. The Reverend Francis Lister Hawks (19 June 1798–27 Sept. 1866) and the Right Reverend Cicero Stephen Hawks (26 May 1811–19 Apr. 1868) are the subjects of sketches in this volume. The Reverend William Nassau Hawks (b. 4 Mar. 1809), was successively rector of St. Peter's Church, Washington, N.C.; teacher at the Moses Griffin School, New Bern, one of the first free trade schools for poor girls; rector of Christ Church, New Bern (1847–53); and rector at Columbus, Ga., where he died.

SEE: Carrie L. Broughton, ed., *Marriage and Death Notices from the Raleigh Register and North Carolina State Gazette, 1799–1825* (1944); Gertrude S. Carraway, *Crown of Life* (1940); Walter Clark, ed., *State Records of North Carolina*, vols. 13, 16–22, 24 (1896–1905); *DAB*, vol. 4 (1960); Alonzo T. Dill, *Governor Tryon and His Palace* (1955); Hawks Family Bible records (in possession of Mrs. Henry Francis DuPont, Winterthur, Del.); Francis Lister Hawks Letterbook, John Hawks Papers, and Mathias Evans Manly Papers (Southern Historical Collection, University of North Carolina Library, Chapel Hill); Stephen F. Miller, *Recollections of New Bern Fifty Years Ago* (1875); William S. Powell, ed., *Correspondence of William Tryon*, 2 vols. (1980–81); Records of Christ Church Parish (Parish House, New Bern); Records of Craven County (North Carolina State Archives, Raleigh); William L. Saunders, ed., *Colonial Records of North Carolina*, vols. 7–9 (1890); Tombstone inscriptions, Cedar Grove Cemetery (New Bern); John D. Whitford, "Historical Notes" (Craven County Public Library, New Bern).

GERTRUDE S. CARRAWAY

Hawley, Joseph Roswell (31 Oct. 1826–18 Mar. 1905), attorney, editor, Union general, congressman, and senator, was born in Stewartsville, Richmond (later Scotland) County, the son of Mary McLeod and the Reverend Francis Hawley. Hawley's mother was born in Fayetteville of Scottish descent and was related to prominent families in the county. His father, whose English ancestors arrived in New England in 1629, was a native of Farmington, Conn.; he came to North Carolina in the 1820s as an itinerant merchant and became a Baptist minister in 1834. Francis held staunch antislavery views, which were to have a significant influence on his son's character and political career. Joseph, who attended school in Cheraw, S.C., recalled only two other Unionist boys during the Nullification crisis, both with Northern fathers. Francis was threatened with assault by mobs and individuals as a result of his abolitionist views and finally left North Carolina with his family in 1837, never to return. Joseph, then age eleven, was never to forget the bitterness and insecurity of those early years.

The Hawleys settled in Connecticut, where Joseph worked summers on the family farm and for two years attended Hartford Grammar School. In 1842, the family moved to Cazenovia, N.Y.; there Joseph prepared for college at the Oneida Conference Seminary. Francis Hawley remained in Cazenovia until his death in 1884, became a Congregationalist, and remained a powerful figure of speech and letters in the abolitionist and related movements. Mary McLeod Hawley was a woman of great dignity, strength, piety, and kindness. Joseph had two sisters, Mary Ann and Diadumena ("Dia"). Both married; Mary, the oldest, who became the wife of a New York farmer, a Pettibone, survived her brother.

In the fall of 1844, young Hawley entered Hamilton College as a sophomore and was graduated with honors in 1847. At school, he excelled as an orator and debater, talents that became hallmarks of his career. Throughout life, Hawley was a man of great physical vigor; his rugged physique and excellent health carried him through many difficulties.

Following graduation, he taught for two winters and in June 1849 began to study law with John Hooker. In May 1850 Hawley was invited to become a partner with Hooker, and Hartford, Conn., became his permanent residence. In 1855, he married Harriet Ward Foote, of a prominent Connecticut family. Because of his strong abolitionist views, Hawley became coeditor of the *Republican*; he was active in the Free Soil party and also toyed briefly with Nativism. In February 1856, in his law office, he founded the Connecticut Republican party, along with Gideon Welles, later President Lincoln's secretary of the navy, and other distinguished political figures. While his law and newspaper career flourished, Hawley also made his name as a political speaker for John Charles Frémont in 1856.

Hawley soon withdrew from the law practice to become editor of the Hartford *Evening Press*. Initiated by Welles, Hawley's new venture became the foundation for an impressive political career, allowing his voice and pen to reach a much larger audience. Charles Dudley Warner, a college chum and lifelong friend, joined the editorial staff in 1860. Together they made the *Press* a persuasive Republican organ throughout New England.

An early supporter of Abraham Lincoln, Hawley attended the 1860 nominating convention and feted the candidate in Hartford. Following the attack on Fort Sumter, he was the first from his state to enlist in the Union Army after Lincoln's call for volunteers. Captain Hawley received special commendation for his service at Manassas. He then returned home to help raise a new regiment, the Seventh Connecticut, and as lieutenant colonel served under Colonel Alfred Howe Terry. Hawley rose rapidly in rank owing to his dynamic leadership, tactical abilities, courage, deep personal concern for his men, but also significant political support.

He served in nineteen engagements with his regiment and other units. On 20 Jan. 1862, Terry was promoted to general and Hawley took command of the Seventh, which eventually came to be known as "Hawley's Regiment." The unit served in various campaigns on and off the coasts of Georgia and South Carolina, including forts Wagner and Pulaski in 1862 and 1863. Following service at New York during the draft riots of 1863, the Seventh under Colonel Hawley saw stiff action at Olustee in Florida, at Bermuda Hundred in Virginia, and in furious battles around Richmond and Petersburg. By the fall of 1864, he was promoted to brevet brigadier general. Early in 1865, Hawley participated, as Terry's chief of staff, in the capture of Wilmington, N.C. He was then detached to establish a supply depot for Sherman's forces and placed in command of eastern North Carolina.

In addition to providing for some 15,000 released Union prisoners, Hawley energetically prepared his native state for Reconstruction. His impetuousness, however, occasionally led to regrettable incidents. Early in the occupation period, he was angered by the rector of St. James Episcopal Church, Wilmington, who refused to offer prayers for President Lincoln and the Union in lieu of earlier ones for Jefferson Davis. Ignoring the rector's strong theological arguments, Hawley ordered the church cleared and turned into a hospital for the liberated Union prisoners. St. James was subsequently returned to church use after Hawley's departure in the summer of 1865.

Despite intermittent episodes of rashness, Hawley contributed significantly to the rapid revival of the region's turpentine industry, farming, and trade. His attempts to turn plantation lands over to the former slaves largely failed, although some freedmen did continue as freeholders. Extensive educational, relief, and hospital assistance by both General and Mrs. Hawley proved more durable. Years later, at Hawley's death, a North Carolina newspaper observed that, in spite of everything, the general "was never the outspoken enemy" of the South and "was never heard to abuse his mother's people" or North Carolinians.

Mustered out as brevet major general in January 1866, Hawley returned to Hartford. Ever restless and ambitious, he ran successfully for the governorship of his home state. After his defeat for reelection, Hawley did not hold another public office until 1872. In the meantime, he pursued a vigorous Radical Republican editorial policy for the Hartford *Courant*, which was combined with the *Press* in 1867. He served as lobbyist for several firms, and spoke frequently on behalf of Radical candidates and causes in all the Northern states. In addition, he strongly encouraged Reconstruction governments and educational programs through a number of friends and admirers in the South.

Although a resident of Hartford's Nook Farm district and a friend of the Charles Warners, Stowes, Beechers, Clemenses, and others, Hawley had little time for extensive socializing. His life was increasingly consumed by the solicitous care of an invalided wife, politics, and journalism.

Hawley was president of the Republican National Convention of 1868 and held important party posts in 1872 and 1876. A potent force among the Radicals, he supported Ulysses S. Grant throughout that general's flawed political career. It was at the 1868 meeting that Hawley enunciated his best known contemporary national slogan, "Every bond shall be as sacred as a soldier's grave." This sentiment expressed lifelong, deeply rooted, hard-money fiscal convictions. Although still a social reformer vis-à-vis the freedmen, he increasingly advocated and shaped conservative Republican monetary policies. He also assumed a rather conservative position with respect to the rising power of labor.

In 1871, the rather disreputable but influential Benjamin F. Butler charged that Hawley had been removed from his command during the Civil War because of incompetence and cowardice. An outraged Hawley responded immediately. Calling Butler a "liar and a Blackguard," he stated that, in his last official contact with

Butler, the general had approved Hawley's promotion to brigadier general. The charges died out much to the discredit of Butler, and Hawley generally was accorded overwhelming public support.

In November 1872, Hawley was appointed to fill a congressional seat vacated by the death of Julius S. Strong. Six years later he won election to the Forty-sixth Congress (1879–81), and in January 1881 he was sent to the senate, where he served until his death, following reelection in 1887, 1893, and 1899. In 1876, Hawley was named president of the Centennial Commission and presided over its programs with considerable administrative ability, vigor, and eloquence. He also was nominated as a unanimous favorite-son candidate for the presidency in 1872, 1876, and 1880. But Connecticut proved to be an inadequate foundation for this ambition, and Hawley had made many enemies over the years due to his occasional uncompromising positions and his honest, though blunt remarks.

While in the U.S. House of Representatives, Hawley served on important committees such as Claims, Military Affairs, Banking and Currency, and Appropriations. In the U.S. Senate, he became an authority on military affairs, the civil service, railroads, coastal defense, and printing. His work on a special naval committee contributed significantly to U.S. naval preparations before the Spanish-American War, especially in improving military steel production and naval gun manufacture. As chairman of the Civil Service Committee, Hawley was characteristically energetic in furthering civil service reform legislation.

Harriet Ward Foote Hawley, the senator's first wife, died on 3 Mar. 1886. The following year Hawley married English-born Elizabeth Horner. They were the parents of two daughters; in addition, Hawley had adopted a niece of his first wife.

Notwithstanding the turbulence and pressures of his public career, Hawley remained an outstanding proponent of social reform and a popular, generous, warmhearted figure. Once when Butler mounted a tirade against the Chinese, Hawley stepped forward and in ringing tones reminded his audience of the American ideal of equality and the nation's historic welcome of foreign immigrants. His image as a social reformer of conviction was paralleled by his reputation for integrity at a time when corruption in government was all too common. On one occasion, Mark Twain introduced him as an honest man in the Senate, and quipped that he was also "mighty lonely there." A number of portraits of Hawley have survived.

SEE: Anonymous Manuscript Collection (Stowe-Day Foundation, Hartford, Conn.) for information regarding Hawley; *Biog. Dir. Am. Cong.* (1961); Biographical Index (North Carolina Collection, University of North Carolina Library, Chapel Hill); Marian Hawley Coudert to J. Nicholson (letter, 20 Mar. 1970); W. M. Evans, *Ballots and Fence Rails: Reconstruction on the Lower Cape Fear* (1967); Caroline D. Flanner, *St. James Church* (1962); Hartford *Courant*, 23, 27 Mar. 1905; Joseph Roswell Hawley Collection (Connecticut Historical Society, Hartford); Joseph Roswell Hawley Collection (Connecticut State Library, Hartford); Joseph Roswell Hawley and Gideon Welles collections (Library of Congress, Washington, D.C.); P. C. Headley, *Public Men of To-day, Hon. Joseph R. Hawley* (1882); John T. Morse, *Diary of Gideon Welles* (1911); *Nat. Cyc. Am. Biog.*, vol. 1 (1892); John Niven, *Connecticut for the Union: The Role of the State in the Civil War* (1965); E. P. Parker, "Memorial Address," *Joint Report of the Commission on Memorials to . . . Joseph*

Roswell Hawley to the General Assembly of Connecticut (1915); Stephen W. Walkley, *History of the Seventh Connecticut Volunteer Infantry, Hawley's Brigade* (1905); *War of the Rebellion: Official Records of the Union and Confederate Armies*, vols. 2, 14, 28, 33, 35, 36, 40, 42, 43, 46, 47, 51, 53 (1890–1900); Wilmington *Herald*, scattered issues, February–July 1865.

JOHN NICOLSON

Hay, James, Jr. *(28 Jan. 1881–7 May 1936)*, journalist and novelist, was born in Harrisonburg, Va., one of two sons of James and Constance Tatum Hay. Besides his brother William, he had two half sisters from the second marriage of his father, who was a lawyer and congressman (1897–1917). Following preparatory school at Clay Hill Academy in Virginia, he attended the University of Virginia, graduating in 1903. On 4 May 1904, he married Lindsay Howell Walker.

After a few months with the *Washington Post*, Hay joined the staff of the *Washington Times* where his political assignments led to his appointment as White House reporter. A founder and charter member of the National Press Club, he was a friend of presidents William Howard Taft and Woodrow Wilson. For seven years Hay was a free-lance writer of stories and magazine articles. When his health broke in 1917, he was taken to Asheville on a stretcher. There he continued to write and became associate editor of the *Asheville Citizen*. His second wife, whom he married on 19 July 1922, was Maud Millicent Larrick, a nurse who he always said saved his life. In 1929 Hay returned to Washington, and in 1931–32 he directed magazine publicity for the George Washington Bicentennial Commission.

Most of Hay's ten books are detective stories, of which three have their settings in Asheville: *The Winning Clue* (1919) is a murder story involving jewel thieves, *The Bellamy Case* (1925) mixes murder and a political campaign, and *The Hidden Woman* (1929) combines murder and newspaper reporting. Several of his other detective stories use Washington as their setting.

He had a daughter, Lindsay, by his first marriage. Hay was a Democrat and an Episcopalian. He was buried in the family cemetery in Madison. Va.

SEE: *Asheville Citizen*, 8, 10 May 1936; *Asheville Times*, 8 May 1936; *Who's Who in America* (1920–21); *Who's Who in the South* (1927).

RICHARD WALSER

Hay, John *(ca. 1757–20 June 1809)*, lawyer and legislator, was born in Belfast, Ireland. In 1779, while still in Ireland, he purchased 2,800 acres of land in Duplin County, formerly the property of royal governor Arthur Dobbs. Hay left Belfast in September 1779, sailing for America with forty other prominent Irishmen. In December, he landed in Virginia and there took an oath of loyalty to the Revolutionary cause. In April 1780, he proceeded to North Carolina to claim his lands, which were not formally granted to him until April 1782.

Educated as a lawyer, Hay presented his license to the New Hanover Court of Pleas and Quarter Sessions in Wilmington in April 1783 and was admitted to the practice of law in the courts of North Carolina. While a lawyer in the Court of Admiralty in 1784, Hay was involved in a confrontation with Judge Samuel Ashe, with the intention of removing Ashe from the Superior Court bench. This action was part of a general rivalry between Federalist lawyers and Anti-Federalist judges

Ashe, John Williams, and Samuel Spencer, which continued through 1787. Charged with insolent behavior toward Judge Spencer in the Court of Admiralty in 1786, Hay was banned from practicing law in that court. As a member of the legislature in 1787, he retaliated by preferring charges of "negligence of their duty and delay of business" against the three judges. The Assembly, however, voted to sustain the judges.

It was said of Hay that he "ranked among the first men in his profession at the bar of North Carolina." He was nominated for the post of councillor of state in 1783 but failed to win that position. In December 1784, as a justice of the peace in Sampson County, Hay presided over the first session of the Sampson County Court of Pleas and Quarter Sessions. In 1786 he moved to Fayetteville, where he practiced law until his death. In 1789 Hay was nominated for U.S. attorney for the Fayetteville district and in 1790 for U.S. district judge, but was not elected to either post.

Hay served as a representative to the North Carolina General Assembly intermittently from 1784 to 1805; in 1784–85 he represented Sampson County, and in 1786, 1790, 1793, 1799, and 1805, Fayetteville and Cumberland County. While in the legislature he was instrumental in drawing up several bills reforming the state court system. In 1786, he was appointed to the committee on finance wherein he investigated the embezzlement of public money by the army commissioners for liquidating army accounts at the end of the war. Hay was reputedly an eloquent orator in the General Assembly.

At the second North Carolina convention to ratify the Constitution, held in Fayetteville in 1789, Hay served as a member from Cumberland County and voted in favor of ratification. He was also appointed to a committee of seven that prepared suggested amendments to the Constitution, eight of which were accepted and sent on to the federal government.

A prominent citizen of Fayetteville, Hay resided at his estate, Hay Mount, which later became a residential section of the town. In 1783 he was appointed a town commissioner, his task being to aid in planning the streets of Fayetteville. One of those streets, Hay Street, bears his name. At the convention in 1789, he introduced a measure that gave Fayetteville representation as a borough town in the General Assembly. In April 1791, he served as chairman of a public meeting called to invite George Washington to the town on his visit to the South. Hay ran as a Federalist candidate for the United States Congress from the Fayetteville district in 1803, but was defeated by the Republican candidate. His affiliation with the Federalist party, which was never popular in North Carolina, often worked against his political career.

In 1783 Hay was appointed a trustee of Innes Academy in Wilmington, and in 1789 he was made one of the original trustees of The University of North Carolina. In the early years of the university he served on committees to establish a curriculum and to choose faculty members. In 1795 he served on the first committee of visitation to report on "the progress of the Students, and the State of the Institution."

In February 1786, Hay married Susannah Rowan, the daughter of Colonel Robert Rowan. Her stepbrother, William Barry Grove, also of Fayetteville, was one of the state's first U.S. congressmen. Hay had one son, David, and a daughter, Susan; she married Judge William Gaston, a distinguished North Carolina jurist who wrote the words for "The Old North State," which since 1927 has been the official state song of North Carolina. Hay died at his residence in Fayetteville at age fifty-two.

SEE: Samuel A. Ashe, ed., *Biographical History of North Carolina*, vol. 6 (1907); Walter Clark, ed., *State Records of North Carolina*, vols. 16–22, 24, 25 (1899–1906); R. D. W. Connor, *Documentary History of the University of North Carolina, 1776–1799* (1953); R. Don Higginbotham, ed., *The Papers of James Iredell*, 2 vols. (1976); Minutes of New Hanover County Court, 1738–1800 (North Carolina State Archives, Raleigh); John A. Oates, *The Story of Fayetteville and the Upper Cape Fear* (1972); *Raleigh Register*, 29 June 1809; Louise Trenholme, *Ratification of the Federal Constitution in North Carolina* (1932); H. M. Wagstaff, ed., *The Papers of John Steele, 1764–1815*, 2 vols. (1924).

LINDA HAWKINS

Hayes, Hubert Harrison (*3 Aug. 1901–30 July 1964*), actor, author, producer, promoter, and folklorist, was born in Asheville, the son of Ernest L. Hayes, a master mechanic, and Elizabeth Ingle Hayes. In 1922–23 he attended Trinity College (now Duke University), Durham, but due to a serious injury he lost his athletic scholarship and had to end his college career. Soon afterwards he was employed by the Augustin Stock Company and toured with the company for three years. Returning to Asheville, Hayes joined the Fire Department but his interest in the theater continued. He wrote a number of plays and became a producer of his own plays and those of others. The first of his plays, written in collaboration with John Tainter Foote, was *Tight Britches*, which portrays life among the mountain people; it was first produced in Asheville in 1933 and appeared on Broadway the following year. Hayes's outdoor drama, *Thunderland*, about the Daniel Boone era, was produced during the summers of 1952 and 1953 in the amphitheater at Skyland. He also wrote numerous radio scripts.

During World War II, Hayes taught meteorology and navigation to soldiers stationed in Asheville. He was a licensed pilot and a member of the Civil Air Patrol.

From 1945 to 1954, Hayes was manager of the Asheville City Auditorium and in that capacity promoted entertainment and talent, bringing to the auditorium top names in show business. In 1948 he founded the Mountain Youth Jamboree, a program to promote and perpetuate folk culture and train children to perform on stage. In cooperation with his wife, Leona Trantham Hayes, whom he married on 9 June 1934, he produced the jamboree annually until his death. Mrs. Hayes continued it through its twenty-sixth anniversary performance in 1973. From the start of the jamboree, Hayes had the support of the Asheville Chamber of Commerce in assembling youths from the Appalachian Mountains each spring to participate in folk dancing, music making, and folk and ballad singing in the Asheville auditorium. Every year he auditioned hundreds of children for the jamboree; during the twenty-six years of its existence, 52,000 children performed. It was in aiding, encouraging, and fostering the development and talent of young people that Hayes made his most lasting contributions.

Hayes was first a Baptist and then an Episcopalian. He died at age sixty-three and was buried in Calvary Episcopal Church cemetery in Fletcher, N.C. In addition to his widow, he was survived by his daughter, Yvonne, and two sisters. As a tribute to his endeavors, Mrs. Hayes gave the Hubert Hayes Memorial Cabin, along with his portrait and bust, to Western Carolina University.

SEE: Alumni Records (Alumni Office, Duke University, Durham); Hubert Harrison Hayes Papers (Manuscript Department, Duke University Library, Durham); Personal papers of Hubert Harrison Hayes (in possession of Leona Trantham Hayes, Asheville); Recordings, Mountain Youth Jamboree (Duke University Library, Durham).

MATTIE U. RUSSELL

Hayes, Johnson Jay (*23 Jan. 1886–22 Sept. 1970*), federal district court judge, was born in his parents' cabin between Cole and Purlear creeks, near Purlear, in Wilkes County. His father was John Lee Hays, son of Joseph Washington ("Wash") Hays, and his mother was Sarah Julia McNeil Hays. Johnson's older brother, Thomas, changed the spelling of their surname by adding an "e." Johnson said the event was "like a scrambled egg; we can't undo it."

After attending the Whitsett Institute in Whitsett, N.C., Hayes entered Wake Forest College in 1907 and was graduated from Wake Forest Law School in 1909: In October of that year he formed a law partnership with John A. Holbrook, but Holbrook died the following April. With John R. Jones, Hayes then established the law firm of Hayes and Jones on 1 June 1910. Four years later Hayes was elected to serve a four-year term as solicitor for the Seventeenth North Carolina Judicial District, beginning 1 Jan. 1915. He was reelected twice, but decided not to seek a fourth term.

In February 1926, the Republican state executive committee elected Hayes to succeed John Parker as national committeeman from North Carolina. Later that year, Hayes waged an unsuccessful campaign against U.S. Senator Lee S. Overman. On 1 Jan. 1927, he moved to Greensboro and joined the law firm of Brooks, Parker, and Smith.

In March 1927, Congress created the Middle District of North Carolina. After Hayes received endorsements from the chief justice, two of the four associate justices, sixteen of the twenty state Superior Court judges, and three-fourths of the lawyers in the district, President Calvin Coolidge appointed him over Frank Linney as Middle District Court judge. He took the oath of office on 6 April and, for the next thirty years, was the only judge of the district. The chief justice also assigned Hayes to hold court in New York City; Richmond, Va.; Columbia, S.C.; and Bluefield, W.Va. Between 1927 and 1957, he heard an average of 750 criminal and 150 civil cases each year.

In 1933, Hayes was the first federal judge to hold that the repeal of the Eighteenth Amendment intentionally rendered the Volstead Act inoperative, leaving the courts powerless to punish crimes committed under it. The attorney general directed the U.S. attorney to appeal directly to the United States Supreme Court. The Supreme Court upheld Hayes's decision and 30,000 defendants awaiting trial were set free.

Hayes helped organize the Wilkes Building and Loan Association (now Wilkes Savings and Loan Association) and the Kiwanis Club in Wilkes County, of which he was an active member until moving to Greensboro in 1927. Always interested in education, he was instrumental in establishing Wilkes Community College and in moving Wake Forest College from Wake County to Winston-Salem. A committed Baptist layman, Hayes served on the state general board and was a trustee of Wake Forest College and of Baptist Hospital in Winston-Salem.

In 1957, while holding court in Greensboro, Hayes

suffered a heart attack, forcing him to retire. Fearing he might grow tired with nothing to do, he wrote *The Land of Wilkes*, a history of Wilkes County for the Wilkes Historical Society. Even during retirement, Judge Hayes often presided in court when it was necessary to clear a backlog of cases. In fact, he presided in Wilkesboro a little more than two weeks before his death.

Hayes and his wife, Willa Virginia Harless Hayes, were the parents of six children: Joseph Hadley, Johnson Jay, Jr., Hayden Burke, Willa Jean (Mrs. J. Thor Wanless), Carol Virginia (Mrs. Marion D. Elliott), and Sarah Rebecca (Mrs. Robert C. Hubbard). The judge died unexpectedly of a heart attack while "salting" his cattle near Bluffs Lodge on the Blue Ridge Parkway. He was buried in Mountlawn Memorial Park, North Wilkesboro.

SEE: Joseph Aicher, "A Biographical and Behavioral Portrait of Judge Johnson Jay Hayes," *North Carolina Central Law Journal* 4 (1972); *Biblical Recorder*, 31 Oct. 1970; Johnson Jay Hayes, *Autobiography of Johnson Jay Hayes* (1968); Crockette W. Hewlett, *United States Judges of North Carolina* (1978); William S. Powell, ed., *North Carolina Lives* (1962).

GREGORY L. HUGHES

Haynes, Raleigh Rutherford (*30 June 1851–6 Feb. 1917*), textile manufacturer, the fourth child and oldest son of Charles H. and Sarah Walker Haynes, was born at Ferry, in Rutherford County. Charles Haynes, a landowner, teacher, and sheriff of the county, died when Raleigh was about eight, leaving his widow with eight children to rear. Young Haynes received instruction from his oldest sister, Letitia, but further education was sacrificed so he could help his mother operate the 200-acre farm left by his father.

At about age twenty, Haynes went to Union County, S.C., with his younger brother, John, to work in the cotton fields. After about two years, he returned to Rutherford County to invest his savings in a general store and a sawmill. In addition to these enterprises, he farmed. By reinvesting his profits, he became one of the largest landowners in western North Carolina.

With the timber and waterpower available on his Main Broad River land, Haynes initiated the first successful textile industry in Rutherford County in 1885, when he began to survey the site for a cotton mill at Henrietta. The building was started in 1887, with Spencer B. Tanner as a business partner. When completed, it was equipped with 5,000 spindles and was said to be the largest textile mill in North Carolina. Tanner, the first president of the Henrietta Mills, and Haynes opened a second mill at Caroleen in 1896. The two plants operated 62,000 spindles and 2,000 looms. In 1897, the Florence Mills unit at Forest City was completed with 12,200 spindles. Between 1916 and 1923, the Haynes Mill at Avondale was finished.

Haynes's last and most enduring project was Cliffside, a mill and town built on the Second Broad River in 1900. Reportedly the largest gingham mill in the South, with 41,000 spindles and 1,500 looms, it employed 900 workers, consumed 7,500 bales of cotton annually, and produced about 70,000 yards of gingham daily. The well-planned town included some 400 houses; a general store, library, park and playground, post office, flour mill, steam laundry, and skating rink; and a movie house built adjacent to the mills for the convenience of the employees. After Haynes's death, his sons, Charles H. and Walter Hayner, and his son-in-

law, Z. O. Jenkins, continued to expand and improve the model town and mills at Cliffside. Charles succeeded his father as president.

Haynes also had an extensive lumber business, a line of general stores, and numerous banking interests. He was president of the Haynes Bank at Henrietta and of the Commercial Bank at Rutherfordton, and a director of the Charlotte National Bank and of the Southern Loan and Savings Bank at Charlotte.

On 29 Jan. 1874, Haynes married Amanda Carpenter, the daughter of Tennessee Carpenter, and they became the parents of five sons and four daughters: Robert E., Charles H., Walter Hayner, Grover C., and Elisha; and Florence (Mrs. Z. O. Jenkins), Eulah (Mrs. J. R. Shull), Sarah (Mrs. Robert Love), and Virginia (Mrs. Baron Pressley Caldwell). After the death of Amanda in 1890, Haynes married Litia Kelley, who lived only a year. He then decided to raise his children himself.

Haynes died at his St. Petersburg, Fla., home and was buried at Cliffside Cemetery, Cliffside, N.C.

SEE: Court Records of Rutherford County (North Carolina State Archives, Raleigh); Clarence W. Griffin, *History of Old Tryon and Rutherford Counties, North Carolina, 1730–1936* (1937); Mrs. Grover C. Haynes, *Raleigh Rutherford Haynes: A History of His Life and Achievements* (1954); *North Carolina Biography*, vol. 5 (1919); *Rutherford Sun*, 26 Aug. 1920; U.S. Census, 1880–1920, Rutherford County.

MILDRED MARTIN CROW

Haywood, Edmund Burke (*15 Jan. 1825–18 Jan. 1894*), physician, Confederate surgeon, and medical administrator, was born in Raleigh, the youngest son of Eliza Eagles Asaph Williams and John Haywood, state treasurer. He was a descendant of North Carolina's early English settlers and Revolutionary patriots. His paternal great-grandfather was John Haywood, who emigrated to North Carolina from Barbados about 1730 as the agent of Earl Granville; his paternal grandparents were Charity Hare and Colonel William Haywood of Dunbar Plantation, Edgecombe County. His maternal grandfather was Captain John Pugh Williams of the North Carolina Continental Line.

Haywood received his early education at the Raleigh Academy and in 1843 entered The University of North Carolina. Although he was an excellent student, ill health forced him to leave the university in 1846 without a degree. After regaining his health, he entered the University of Pennsylvania School of Medicine and was graduated with distinction in 1849. Returning to Raleigh, he went into private practice.

At the outbreak of the Civil War in 1861, Haywood enlisted as a private in the Raleigh Light Infantry and was elected its surgeon. Recognizing Haywood's superior professional qualifications, Governor John W. Ellis soon detached him from his unit and directed him to inspect the military hospitals then established on Morris Island, in preparation for organizing a military hospital in North Carolina. Afterwards, he established the first military hospital in the state and on 16 May 1861 was appointed surgeon of the North Carolina state troops. His first assignment was as administrator of the hospital at the fair grounds and as surgeon of the Raleigh military post and training camp. In July of the same year, he was named president of the Board of Surgeons which examined and approved applications for appointment as surgeon in the North Carolina state troops.

As the war progressed, Haywood became more involved in practical military surgery and he saw heavy fighting in the Peninsular Campaign and in the Seven Days' Battle around Richmond. His compassion for, and attention to, the enemy wounded was widely noted. At the conclusion of his Virginia service in August 1862, he was commissioned a surgeon in the Confederate Army and served for a time as president of the Army Medical Board, which granted medical discharges and convalescent furloughs. In the same year he also became acting medical director of the Department of North Carolina and was placed in charge of the Raleigh military hospitals. His headquarters were at Pettigrew Hospital at New Bern Avenue and Tarboro Road, with subsidiary hospitals at Peace Institute and the state fair grounds.

Near the end of the war, as General William T. Sherman's victorious troops approached Raleigh, Haywood continued to attend the wounded and ill of both Union and Confederate armies. After Appomattox and the collapse of the Confederate government, Haywood, at his own expense, remained at his hospitals until the last patient was released or evacuated. During the war years he became known as a progressive and innovative physician who developed unusual and complex surgical procedures. He was also known and loved as a humanitarian and as a compassionate friend of all ranks and classes.

His military duties over, Haywood, in the tradition of Cincinnatus, refused compensation and returned to private practice in Raleigh. When the state institutions were reorganized in March 1866, he became a member of the board of directors of the North Carolina Insane Asylum; he served for twenty-five years and as president from 1875 to 1879. In the latter year, Governor Daniel Fowle appointed him chairman of the Board of Public Charities. In June 1879, he became vice-president of the North Carolina Medical Society and held the chair of surgery of the North Carolina Board of Medical Examiners. Haywood, who had helped organize the Raleigh Academy of Medicine in 1870, served on the boards of other local and national professional societies until his death. In 1889, he became the first physician to receive the LL.D. degree from The University of North Carolina; in 1868, the university had awarded him the A.M. degree.

Over the years, Haywood became increasingly interested in the plight of prisoners and mental patients of both races. In 1890, he was directly responsible for establishing the Negro mental hospital at Goldsboro and the Western State Hospital at Morganton.

An Episcopalian, Haywood was a member of Christ Church, Raleigh, and a vestryman for twenty-five years. It was said that he never missed a vestry meeting during his tenure. His numerous professional, civic, and church activities were credited with weakening his health and causing the acute pleurisy that finally took his life. He died at Haywood Hall, the house in which he was born.

In November 1850, Haywood married Lucy Ann Williams of Franklin County. They had seven children: Edmund Burke, Jr., Alfred Williams, Hubert (who also became an eminent physician), Elizabeth, Ernest, Edgar, and John.

SEE: Samuel A. Ashe, *History of North Carolina*, vol. 2 (1925); Kemp P. Battle, *Sketches of the History of the University of North Carolina* (1889); Horace H. Cunningham, "Edmund Burke Haywood and Raleigh's Confederate Hospitals," *North Carolina Historical Review* 35 (1958); Ernest Haywood Collection, Edward McCrady L'Engle Papers, and Griffith John McRee Papers (Southern Historical Collection, University of North Carolina Library, Chapel Hill); Hubert B. Haywood, Sr., *Sketch of the Haywood Family in North Carolina* (1956); Fitzhugh Lee Morris, comp., *Lineage Book of Past and Present Members of the North Carolina Society of Sons of the American Revolution* (1951); *North Carolina Medical Journal* 20 (1894), 21 (1895).

MARSHALL DE LANCEY HAYWOOD

Haywood, Egbert (1730–30 Sept. 1801), Revolutionary patriot, was the son of Colonel John Haywood, a surveyor for Earl Granville and treasurer of the northern counties of the province of North Carolina, and Mary Lovett Haywood of New York. In 1773 he was one of eight commissioners appointed to contract with workmen to repair the "public goal" in the town of Halifax, and in 1774 he was one of three commissioners assigned to lay off and mark the line to divide Edgecombe Parish in Halifax County into two parishes.

The North Carolina Provincial Congress in August 1774 appointed Haywood one of eleven members of the Halifax County Committee of Safety. On 9 Sept. 1775, the Congress elected him second major of North Carolina troops for Halifax County, a position he held until 22 Apr. 1776. At the same session, he was appointed one of two men to procure arms and ammunition from the county for the Continental Army. When the Congress reconvened in November 1776, Haywood was elected to the vacancy left by one of its five members from Halifax County who resigned to accept an appointment in the Continental Army. He took his seat on 7 December. On 23 December, he was selected as a justice of the Court of Pleas and Quarter Sessions for Halifax.

Haywood represented Halifax County in the 1777 and 1778 sessions of the Congress as well as in the first 1779 session of the House of Commons, which was the lower house of the legislative branch of the new state government. Among other duties, he served on committees dealing with Indian affairs, privileges, and elections. In 1788, he was a commissioner for purchasing tobacco for the state in Halifax County. In July of that year, he represented his county in the convention at Hillsborough which had assembled to consider ratification of the Constitution. Haywood agreed with Halifax delegate Willie Jones, a leader against ratification on the ground that it would infringe on states' rights. Ratification was rejected by a vote of 184 to 84.

Haywood and his wife Sarah Ware had ten children: Dr. Lewis Green, who married Sarah Ann Cressy; Thomas, who was unmarried; William, who married Abby Jones; Dr. Henry, who married Sarah Ruffin; Mary, who married Captain Robert Bell; Jane, who married Marmaduke Johnson; Sarah, who married her cousin, Adam John Haywood; Margaret, who first married Edward Bignal and afterwards Oliver Fitts; Elizabeth, who married Colonel William Shepard; and Judge John, who served on the Supreme Court of North Carolina and later the Supreme Court of Tennessee. According to the census of 1790, Haywood owned 17 slaves and 1,500 acres of land. He was a Mason and a member of the Royal White Hart Lodge in Halifax.

SEE: W. C. Allen, *A History of Halifax County* (1918); Samuel A. Ashe, ed., *Biographical History of North Carolina*, vols. 3, 6 (1906, 1907); Walter Clark, ed., *State Records of North Carolina*, vols. 12, 18, 21–23 (1885–1904); Charles B. Gault, *Haywood-Bell Genealogy* (1968); Hubert B. Haywood, Sr., *Sketch of the Haywood Family in North*

Carolina (1956); Margaret M. Hofmann, *Genealogical Abstracts of Wills, 1758–1824, Halifax County, North Carolina* (1970); William C. Pool, "An Economic Interpretation of the Ratification of the Federal Constitution in North Carolina (Part 2)," *North Carolina Historical Review* 27 (1950); William L. Saunders, ed., *Colonial Records of North Carolina*, vols. 9, 19 (1890); Frederick G. Speidel, *North Carolina Masons in the American Revolution* (1975).

JOHN D. HAYWOOD

Haywood, Ernest *(1 Feb. 1860–14 Dec. 1946)*, attorney, was born in Raleigh, the son of Edmund Burke and Lucy A. Williams Haywood. He attended Lovejoy's Academy in Raleigh, Horner and Graves Military Academy in Oxford, and The University of North Carolina, from which he was graduated with an A.B. degree in 1880. Haywood then entered the law school conducted in Greensboro by Robert P. Dick and John H. Dillard and was admitted to the bar in 1882.

Practicing in Raleigh, he specialized in commercial, insurance, corporation, and real estate law and was counsel to the defendants in the Hawkins and Sexton will cases. Haywood was one of the founders of the original North Carolina Bar Association in 1885 and one of the subscribers to its charter and bylaws. He was honorary vice-president of the U.S. Chief Justice Roger B. Taney National Memorial Foundation, a sponsor for the Robert E. Lee Memorial Foundation at Stratford Hall, Va., a national trustee of the Sons of the American Revolution, and a member of the Sons of Confederate Veterans. Haywood was deeply interested in local history and was the author of many articles published in Raleigh newspapers. In 1937, he made an all-air trip around the world and had been scheduled to return home from Europe on the *Hindenberg* but changed his plans shortly before his departure. A Democrat and a member of Christ Episcopal Church, he was buried in Oakwood Cemetery, Raleigh.

SEE: Daniel L. Grant, *Alumni History of the University of North Carolina* (1924); *North Carolina Biography*, vol. 3 (1941); C. L. Van Noppen Papers (Manuscript Department, Duke University Library, Durham); *Who's Who in the South* (1927).

WILLIAM S. POWELL

Haywood, Fabius Julius *(26 Oct. 1803–20 May 1880)*, physician and surgeon, was born in Raleigh of English ancestry. His father, John Haywood, born 23 Feb. 1755 at Dunbar Plantation in Edgecombe County, was state treasurer for forty years; his mother, Eliza Eagles Asaph Williams, was the daughter of Colonel John Pugh Williams, a prominent Revolutionary War leader. Eliza was John's second wife; his first wife, Sarah Leigh, died childless. Haywood's paternal ancestor, Colonel John Haywood, born 1685 on St. Michael's Island, Barbados, British West Indies, emigrated to North Carolina in 1729 as surveyor for Earl Granville. It is said that the colonel, who was an engineer, laid off and supervised construction of the fortifications of the colony along the mouth of the Cape Fear River near Old Brunswick Town in Brunswick County.

Fabius Julius Haywood was graduated from The University of North Carolina in 1822, and received a medical degree from the University of Pennsylvania School of Medicine in 1827. He then established a medical practice in Raleigh.

Haywood is credited with being the first surgeon in the state to use a general anesthetic during an operation. The *Raleigh Star* of 9 Feb. 1848 had a vivid account of a procedure Haywood performed on Leroy Moore, a citizen of Wake County, in which was taken "a wen (weighing one pound, four ounces) which grew immediately under his arm. This is not the first time such operations had been successfully performed by Dr. Haywood; though it is the first time, we believe, that chloroform has been used in the state; and the effect was so perfect and happy as if an allwise and merciful providence had prepared it especially for the purpose. Dr. Haywood had previously used Letheon (Martan's trade name for ether) with happy effect in tapping a lady afflicted with dropsy, who twice submitted to the operation without suffering the smallest pain. . . . The anaesthetic properties of chloroform had been described by Sir James Young Simpson of Edinburgh only three months earlier (November 11, 1847)."

During the occupation of Raleigh by the Union Army in 1865–66, Haywood's property, valued at $27,000, was confiscated under the Federal Confiscation Act, and the War Department refused to return it until he had executed an oath of allegiance and received a pardon from President Andrew Johnson granting him amnesty from all acts of wrongdoing against the United States during the recent war.

Haywood was one of the seven original directors of the North Carolina Medical Society, which he helped organize on 17 Apr. 1849. Incorporated on 15 Feb. 1859 as the Medical Society of the State of North Carolina, it, in turn, established the state Board of Medical Examiners.

On 8 Dec. 1831 Haywood married Martha Helen Whitaker, daughter of Cyrus and Mary Rogers Whitaker. Cyrus, a wealthy Wake County landowner, was the son of Thomas and Mary Whitaker of Putnam County, Ga., and the grandson of John Whitaker (1732–84) of Halifax County, N.C. Mary Rogers Whitaker was the daughter of Michael Rogers, onetime Wake County sheriff and a member of the Provincial Congress from Wake County. Dr. Haywood and his wife had a son, Fabius Julius, Jr. (b. 1 Oct. 1840), who entered the Confederate Army soon after enrolling at The University of North Carolina. He was wounded in the leg and captured after successfully passing through enemy lines as courier for his commanding general.

Both Haywood and his wife were interested in the culture of silkworms and planted mulberry trees in their spacious backyard for them to feed on. The top floor of their three-story brick house, which stood on the corner of Fayetteville and Morgan streets opposite the state capitol, was used to store the cocoons from which their slaves spun the silk.

Haywood was a member of Christ Episcopal Church in Raleigh. With his papers in the State Archives is a certificate entitling him to a pew in that church. He died at age seventy-seven and was buried in Oakwood Cemetery, Raleigh. His wife, who died 30 May 1880, was buried beside him.

SEE: Walter Clark, ed., *Histories of the Several Regiments and Battalions from North Carolina in the Great War, 1861–1865* (1901); Fabius Julius Haywood Papers, Marriage bonds of Wake County, and Petitions for Pardon, 1865–68 (North Carolina State Archives, Raleigh); Hubert B. Haywood, Sr., *Sketch of the Haywood Family in North Carolina* (1956); Weymouth T. Jordan, comp., *North Carolina Troops, 1861–1865*, vol. 4 (1973); Dorothy Long, *Medicine in North Carolina* (1972); *North Carolina Medical Society Journal* 33 (1972); Vance E. Swift, "Col. John Whitaker, Judge, Revolutionary War Patriot, Squire of Echo Manor Plantation, Wake County, North Carolina, and Some of His Descendants and Connections" (North Carolina State Library, Raleigh).

VANCE E. SWIFT

Haywood, Hubert Benbury, Sr. (30 Dec. 1883–20 Aug. 1961), physician, who practiced largely in Raleigh, was a member of a distinguished family of medical practitioners. His great-uncle Fabius Julius Haywood, his grandfather Edmund Burke Haywood, his father Hubert Haywood, and his son Hubert Benbury Haywood, Jr., were all eminent physicians in Raleigh. The son of Hubert and Emily Benbury Haywood, he received his early education in the public schools and at the Raleigh Male Academy. He was graduated from The University of North Carolina in 1905 and four years later received the M.D. degree from the University of Pennsylvania Medical School. Haywood continued his studies with postgraduate work at the University of Edinburgh, Scotland, in 1914 and 1923. In 1948 The University of North Carolina awarded him the honorary LL.D. degree. As a student he had been editor of the *Yackety Yack* and the *Carolina Magazine*. He was a member of the Order of the Golden Fleece and, in 1934, president of the General Alumni Association.

Haywood's medical career spanned nearly fifty years. He served as physician for North Carolina State College (1915–20), medical director at St. Mary's College (1924–52) and Peace College (1921–57), and physician and medical director of the North Carolina State School for the Blind (1922–52). He was a member of the board of directors and medical director of the State Capital Life Insurance Company (1938–56). He also taught for a time at the Wake Forest College Medical School.

During World War II, Haywood was commissioned in 1943 as a senior surgeon with the U.S. Public Health Service. For his work as chairman of the Procurement and Assignment Service for Physicians of the State of North Carolina, he received a presidential citation from Harry S Truman.

Haywood was active in a number of professional organizations and served many of them as an officer. They included the American Medical Association, the American College of Physicians (Fellow), the North Carolina Medical Society (president), Subcommittee of the North Carolina Medical Society on the Foundation of a Four-Year Medical School at Chapel Hill (chairman), North Carolina State Board of Health (vice-president), Medical Advisory Board of North Carolina Mental Hospitals (chairman), Wake County Medical Society (president), Raleigh Academy of Medicine (president), and Hospital Care Association of Durham (director). In addition, he was president of the staff at Rex Hospital in Raleigh.

Although he retired from active practice about 1953, Haywood continued his association with the State Capital Life Insurance Company. A lifelong member of Christ Episcopal Church, Raleigh, he served as vestryman and senior warden at different times. In retirement, he worked in his rose garden, enjoyed sketching, and researched his family's history. He was the author of *Sketch of the Haywood Family in North Carolina*, published in 1956.

In October 1915 Haywood married Marguerite Lynn Manor of Harrisonburg, Va., and they became the parents of Hubert Benbury, Jr., and Shirley Benbury, who married Thomas W. Alexander, Jr.

SEE: Clipping file (North Carolina Collection, University of North Carolina Library, Chapel Hill); Daniel L. Grant, *Alumni History of the University of North Carolina* (1924); Hubert B. Haywood, Sr., *Sketch of the Haywood Family in North Carolina* (1956); Jesse A. Helms, *Stateline*, 22 Aug. 1961; *North Carolina Biography* 4 (1919); William S. Powell, ed., *North Carolina Lives* (1962).

LINDA MACKIE GRIGGS

Haywood, John (1685–1758), engineer, legislator, and soldier, was born in Christ Church Parish, Barbados, British West Indies. His family had emigrated to that island from the parish of Bolton, Lancashire County, England, in 1662. Haywood went to New York and then to North Carolina, where, about 1741, he settled in the northern section of present Halifax County.

Haywood was made a justice of the peace in 1746, and from that year until 1752 he was also one of the county's representatives in the Assembly. An active legislator, he served on committees to examine public claims, to revise the laws of the province, to facilitate navigation in provincial waters, and to form a bill to regulate the practice of the courts of justice. He was the author of the bill "of encouragement of James Davis to set up and carry on the business of a Printer." Davis's press, established in 1749, was the first in the colony.

When war with Spain threatened the safety of the colony, Haywood was made commissioner to erect forts along the coast to protect the ports of entry. Because of the inconveniences caused by the Granville District, two provincial treasurers were necessary; Haywood was treasurer for the northern counties. When he relinquished this position, he became commander of the Edgecombe County militia, which then consisted of more than 1,300 officers and men.

Later in life, Haywood and his sons served as assistants to Francis Corbin, chief agent of Earl Granville, owner of that part of the province in which Edgecombe lay. Growing dissatisfaction among those who lived in the Granville District resulted in riots and threats of armed resistance. Corbin and his assistants were accused of charging excessive quitrents and the Haywoods of asking exorbitant fees for their services as land surveyors. At the height of the unrest, Haywood was away from home on business, and upon his return was taken suddenly ill and died. The unruly colonists, suspecting this to be a ruse to enable him to escape their fury, went to his grave, dug up his coffin, and found that the death was indeed a fact. This macabre act brought to an end the history of a useful citizen. An active supporter of the Church of England, Haywood had been a vestryman and churchwarden of his parish.

During his residence in New York, Haywood married Mary Lovatt. They had four sons and three daughters: William married Charity Hare, Sherwood married Hannah Gray, Egbert married Sarah Ware, and John died unmarried; Mary married the Reverend Thomas Burges, Elizabeth married Jesse Hare, and Deborah married John Hardy. All but two left descendants, among whom have been many leaders in the state.

SEE: Samuel A. Ashe, ed., *Biographical History of North Carolina*, vol. 3 (1905); William L. Saunders, ed., *Colonial Records of North Carolina*, vols. 4, 5 (1886, 1887); Joseph K. Turner and John L. Bridgers, Jr., *History of Edgecombe County, North Carolina* (1920).

JAQUELIN DRANE NASH

Haywood, John (23 Feb. 1755–18 Nov. 1827), state treasurer and public official, was born in Edgecombe

County, the son of William and Charity Hare Haywood. He first entered public life upon his election on 27 Jan. 1781 as clerk of the state senate. He served in that capacity until 30 Dec. 1786, when the legislature elected him state treasurer, a position he held for forty years.

With the passage of legislation requiring state officials to reside in Raleigh, the newly established capital, Haywood purchased two lots (190 and 191), bounded by Person, Edenton, Blount, and New Bern streets, where he built a house which is still standing. When the city of Raleigh was chartered by the General Assembly in 1795, Haywood was named one of the seven commissioners responsible for governing it.

As one of the original trustees of The University of North Carolina named by the General Assembly in 1789, he was a member of the building committee that located and was responsible for the construction of the first building on the campus and for laying out the village of Chapel Hill and selling lots there. He served on the board of trustees of the university until his death. He was also instrumental in establishing the Raleigh Academy and became a member of its board of trustees. In 1808, a newly created county was named Haywood in his honor. Following the organization of Christ Episcopal Church in 1821, he served as a vestryman.

Haywood was married twice. His first wife was Sarah Leigh, who died without issue. On 9 Mar. 1798 he married Eliza Eagles Asaph Williams (more commonly known and referred to in his will as Elizabeth), who bore him fourteen children. Haywood was originally buried in a private plot in the northwestern corner of the garden of his home on New Bern Avenue. Subsequently his remains, with those of his wife and seven of their children, were reinterred in Oakwood Cemetery, Raleigh.

After his death, a committee of the 1827–28 legislature examined Haywood's accounts and found that $68,906.80 was missing. All private claims to his property by his heirs, except his widow's dower rights, were surrendered; his land and slaves were sold; and his stock in the Bank of Newbern was transferred to the state. His estate reimbursed the state a total of $47,601.37, but a difference in the Cherokee bonds increased the shortage to $21,735.96. Suit was entered against the estate for this amount, plus interest; however, the jury found that the executor had fully administered all of Haywood's assets except for $7,160.60 in bonds. The court rendered judgment for the state in this amount, with the balance to be recovered from any remaining lands of the deceased treasurer. Despite the shortage in his accounts, Haywood's popularity was high at the time of his death, and many citizens of the state believed that he was not guilty of wrongdoing.

SEE: Samuel A. Ashe, ed., *Biographical History of North Carolina*, vol. 6 (1907); Kemp P. Battle, *History of the University of North Carolina*, 2 vols. (1907–12); William K. Boyd, *History of North Carolina*, vol. 2 (1919); General Assembly, *Session Laws of North Carolina* (1794–95, 1828–29). Manuscript sources in North Carolina State Archives, Raleigh: Records, Court of Pleas and Quarter Sessions of Wake County; Treasurers' and Comptrollers' Papers; Wills of Wake County.

THORNTON W. MITCHELL

Haywood, John (*16 Mar. 1762–22 Dec. 1826*), Revolutionary soldier, lawyer, jurist, and historian, was born in Halifax County where his grandfather had migrated from Virginia. His parents were Egbert and Sarah Ware

Haywood, both of whom were of English heritage. Egbert Haywood was active in the political life of the colony, was an officer in the North Carolina militia during the Revolutionary War, and, after the Revolution, was a member of the state legislature.

John Haywood, too young to enter military service at the beginning of the war, volunteered near the end of the conflict and was assigned as an aide to a North Carolina officer. Although he had received only a limited education, he apparently was admitted to the Halifax bar soon after the Revolution, because in 1785 the General Assembly elected him judge of the Superior Court of Davidson County (Tenn.), a position he declined. In 1791 he was named attorney general, and in 1793 he was appointed to the Superior Court of North Carolina. Haywood established himself as the dominating legal mind on the court and was, as one observer noted, "as completely *the* court as Chief Justice [John] Marshall was of the Supreme Court of the United States." Before resigning from the bench in 1800, he published two volumes of the court's decisions, which are the earliest of the North Carolina law reports. He later published two other works in North Carolina: *A Manual of the Laws of North Carolina* (1808) and *The Duty and Authority of Justices of the Peace* (1810).

Haywood moved to Tennessee—one source indicates as early as 1802 and another as late as 1807—and purchased a farm near Nashville, which he named Tusculum. Recognized immediately for his acute legal mind, he became both a successful practitioner before the Nashville bar and a teacher and counselor of young men who wished to "read law." In 1816 he was elected to the Supreme Court of Errors and Appeals (court of last resort) and served until his death. Haywood edited and reported the opinions of the court and, in association with Robert L. Cobbs, compiled *The Statute Laws of the State of Tennessee* (2 vols., 1831).

Sometimes referred to as "Tennessee's Earliest Historian," Haywood organized in 1820 the Tennessee Antiquarian Society, a forerunner of the Tennessee Historical Society, and became its first president. His interest in history led him to read widely on the subject and to publish several works, the first of which was a book of some 350 pages entitled *The Christian Advocate* (Nashville, 1819). In this philosophical account, he attempts to trace the aboriginal inhabitants of Tennessee and of America to Asia. Much of the material in this volume appeared a few years later in his *The Natural and Aboriginal History of Tennessee* (Nashville, 1823). In the same year he published his best known work, *The Civil and Political History of Tennessee* (Knoxville, 1823). Both trace the development of the Tennessee country to the time of statehood.

Physically, Haywood was massively formed and weighed more than 350 pounds at the time of his death. Judge Nathaniel Baxter, who believed him to have only Felix Grundy as a peer, described him thus: "His arms, his legs, and his neck were all thick and short, his abdomen came down on his lap and nearly covered it to his knees. His head, which rested nearly on his shoulders, was unusually large and peculiarly formed. His under jaw and his lower face looked large and strong, and his head above his ears ran up high and somewhat conical, and viewed horizontally it was rather square and round. His mouth was large, expressive, and rather handsome."

Haywood died at Tusculum and was buried there.

SEE: W. C. Allen, *History of Halifax County* (1918); Joseph B. Cheshire, *Nonulla* (1930); *DAB*, vol. 4 (1960);

John W. Green, *Lives of the Judges of the Supreme Court of Tennessee, 1796–1947* (1947); J. G. de R. Hamilton, ed., *Papers of William A. Graham*, vols. 1, 3 (1957, 1960); L. L. Knight, comp., *Library of Southern Literature*, vol. 15 (1907); John H. Wheeler, *Historical Sketches of North Carolina* (1851); *Who Was Who in America, 1607–1896* (1963).

ROBERT E. CORLEW

Haywood, Marshall De Lancey (6 Mar. 1871–20 Sept. 1933), historian and author, was born in Raleigh, the son of Richard Bennehan and Julia Ogden Hicks Haywood. His father was a distinguished physician and his grandfather, Sherwood Haywood, with his three brothers, was among the first settlers of Raleigh. He was educated at the Raleigh Graded School, Raleigh Male Academy, and Johns Hopkins University. Before assuming duties as marshal and librarian of the North Carolina Supreme Court, a position he held for fifteen years (1918–33), Haywood worked briefly in the office of a cotton broker, as secretary to the North Carolina attorney general, as local editor of the Raleigh *Daily Times*, as assistant state librarian, as librarian of the North Carolina College of Agriculture and Mechanic Arts (now North Carolina State University), and for a year as assistant librarian of the Supreme Court.

An avid interest in history and membership in one of the most prominent families in the state prompted Haywood in 1893 to found the North Carolina Society of the Sons of the American Revolution. As its secretary and in other offices, he led the organization to a position of importance in the state. He was also instrumental in the revival of the North Carolina Society of the Cincinnati, which, although organized in 1783 by the officers of the Continental Army, had been inactive since the Civil War. Haywood, who became an honorary member before his election as a hereditary member, served the society for more than thirty years as assistant secretary (1897–1908) and secretary (1908–33). His interest, however, was not confined to the Revolutionary period, for he was also active in the United Sons of Confederate Veterans.

Haywood was highly regarded in his field, a fact that is borne out by his service as historian of the U.S. War and Navy departments, Historian General of the Sons of the Revolution, historiographer of the Protestant Episcopal Diocese of North Carolina, and historian of the Masonic Grand Lodge. He was a member of the State Literary and Historical Association, the Roanoke Colony Memorial Association, the Church Historical Society in Philadelphia, and the North Carolina Library Association. In addition to numerous articles and monographs, he was the author of *Governor William Tryon and His Administration in the Province of North Carolina, 1765–1771*, *Lives of the Bishops of North Carolina*, *The Beginnings of Freemasonry in North Carolina and Tennessee*, and *Builders of the Old North State*. He also was assistant editor of Samuel Ashe's *Biographical History of North Carolina*.

Martha Hawkins Bailey of Florida became his wife on 16 Oct. 1926, and they were the parents of one child, Marshall De Lancey Haywood, Jr. A lifelong resident of Raleigh and an Episcopalian, Haywood was a member of Christ Church. He was buried in Oakwood Cemetery.

SEE: Samuel A. Ashe, ed., *Biographical History of North Carolina*, vol. 6 (1907); Hubert B. Haywood, Sr., *Sketch of the Haywood Family in North Carolina* (1956); Marshall

De Lancey Haywood, Jr. (Raleigh), personal information; *Who's Who in America* (1926–27).

LUCIUS MCGEHEE CHESHIRE, JR.

Haywood, Richard Bennehan (5 Nov. 1819–2 Jan. 1889), physician and surgeon, was born in Raleigh, the son of Sherwood and Eleanor Hawkins Haywood. He was educated at the Raleigh Academy and in 1841 was graduated from The University of North Carolina. Haywood then entered the Jefferson Medical College in Philadelphia from which he was graduated in 1844.

Returning to Raleigh, he began to practice medicine, although he continued his studies in Europe in 1851. During the Civil War, Haywood was commissioned a surgeon, serving in the surgeon general's office in Raleigh and in the military hospitals in and around Richmond. Following the Battle of Bentonville and the approach of General William T. Sherman's army, he was one of a group of seven or eight persons who surrendered the city of Raleigh to the Union forces.

In 1849, Haywood was one of the founders of the North Carolina Medical Society, which he served as president in 1880–81. He also was president of the Wake County Board of Health and a member of the State Board of Medical Examiners. On 30 June 1868, Governor Jonathan Worth appointed him a director of the North Carolina Railroad on the part of the state; a year later, he was elected a director on the part of the private stockholders and remained in the position until his death. In addition, he served as a member of the board of trustees of the North Carolina Insane Asylum and as physician to the North Carolina Institution for the Deaf and Blind.

On 19 Nov. 1851, Haywood married Julia Ogden Hicks in New York City. They were the parents of ten children, two of whom died in infancy. He was buried in Oakwood Cemetery, Raleigh, with his wife and seven of their children.

SEE: Samuel A. Ashe, ed., *Biographical History of North Carolina*, vol. 6 (1907); Hubert B. Haywood, Sr., *Sketch of the Haywood Family in North Carolina* (1956); *The City of Raleigh: Historical Sketches from Its Foundation* (1887).

THORNTON W. MITCHELL

Haywood, Sherwood (17 Feb. 1762–5 Oct. 1829), banker, was born in Edgecombe County, the son of William and Charity Hare Haywood. He first entered public life as clerk of the state senate, a position to which he was elected on 4 Jan. 1786, following the resignation of his brother, John Haywood, to accept the post of state treasurer. He continued to serve as clerk of the senate until 24 Dec. 1798. Early in 1800, he moved from Edgecombe County to Raleigh, where he purchased four lots from John Haywood which comprised the block bounded by Wilmington, Edenton, Blount, and Jones streets. In 1804, when the Bank of Newbern was chartered by the state, Sherwood Haywood became Raleigh agent of the bank, a position that he held until his death.

Haywood was one of the original trustees of the Raleigh Academy, serving for the rest of his life. He also subscribed to the fund to complete the Main (South) Building at The University of North Carolina. Calvin Jones described him as a "good, polite, clever, worthy man, who never contradicted anyone in his life."

He married Eleanor Hawkins, by whom he had nine children; one son was Richard Bennehan Haywood, who became a physician and surgeon in Raleigh. Haywood and his wife were buried in City Cemetery, Raleigh, in the Colonel William Polk plot.

SEE: Kemp P. Battle, *History of the University of North Carolina*, 2 vols. (1907–12); William K. Boyd, "Currency and Banking in North Carolina," *Historical Papers, Trinity College Historical Society* 10 (1914); Charles L. Coon, *North Carolina Schools and Academies, 1790–1840* (1915); Deeds and wills of Wake County, and Raleigh Academy *Journal*, 1802–11 (North Carolina State Archives, Raleigh); General Assembly, *Session Laws of North Carolina* (1840).

THORNTON W. MITCHELL

Haywood, William *(1730–79)*, merchant and politician, was the oldest of seven children of John Haywood and his wife Mary Lovatt of New York (perhaps born in Beverly, Mass., on 27 Nov. 1695). John Haywood was born near St. Michael in Christ Church Parish on Barbados, British West Indies, in 1685; he arrived in North Carolina about 1730. He served as vestryman and churchwarden of the Anglican parish in Edgecombe County, sheriff, colonel of the county militia, member of the Provincial Assembly, and treasurer for the northern counties. He was also employed by Earl Granville as surveyor for Edgecombe County, an office that embroiled him in political disturbances and caused the exhumation of his body after his death in 1758 to verify his demise.

William Haywood's public career spanned two decades beginning in 1760 when he was named justice of the peace of Edgecombe County, commissioned colonel of the Edgecombe militia, and appointed surveyor of the county by Granville. Haywood proved active in county affairs as magistrate by serving on commissions to build bridges, erect a jail, and examine the sheriff's accounts. During the year of his death he was one of the tax assessors of the county. His devotion to public duty is best exemplified by his constant attendance as justice of the peace at the sessions of the county court. Between 1760 and 1775, he missed only eight quarterly court gatherings.

Haywood was also active in provincial politics. He represented Edgecombe County continuously in the Provincial Assembly from 1760 to 1775, and served on committees of propositions and grievances, public accounts, public claims, and privileges and elections. In 1764 legislation he was designated one of the commissioners to relocate the courthouse of Edgecombe County. In 1774, Haywood introduced legislation for the better observance of the Sabbath and the suppression of vice and immorality in the province.

During the colonial struggle with Great Britain for independence, Haywood demonstrated his allegiance to the American cause. The Third Provincial Congress, which met at Hillsborough in 1775, appointed him to the Committee of Safety for the Halifax District. In 1776, he represented Edgecombe in the Fourth and Fifth Provincial Congresses at Halifax. In the Fifth Congress he was chairman of the committee on privileges and elections and sat on the committee that drafted the state constitution. The same Congress elected Haywood to the Council of State, in which capacity he remained until resigning in 1778. In 1779, he was elected to represent Edgecombe in the lower house of the state legislature.

Haywood belonged to the Anglican church and served as vestryman in St. Mary's Parish. On 2 Mar. 1754 he married Charity Hare, daughter of Moses Hare of Hertford County. They had nine children: Jemima, who married John Whitfield of Lenoir County; John, who was state treasurer for forty years; Ann, who married Robert Williams of Pitt County; Charity, who married Josiah Lawrence of Pitt County; Mary, who married Ethelred Ruffin of Edgecombe County; Sherwood, who was U.S. commissioner of loans; Elizabeth, who married Henry Irwin Toole of Edgecombe County; William, who was clerk of a U.S. district court; and Stephen, who was a state senator of North Carolina. William Haywood died in late 1779 and presumably was buried at his home, Dunbar Plantation, in Edgecombe County.

SEE: Samuel A. Ashe, ed., *Biographical History of North Carolina*, vol. 3 (1905); Walter Clark, ed., *State Records of North Carolina*, vols. 11–25 (1895–1905); Hubert B. Haywood, Sr., *Sketch of the Haywood Family in North Carolina* (1956); Minutes, Edgecombe County Court of Pleas and Quarter Sessions, 1760–79 (North Carolina State Archives, Raleigh); William L. Saunders, ed., *Colonial Records of North Carolina*, vols. 6–10 (1888–89).

ALAN D. WATSON

Haywood, William Henry, Jr. *(23 Oct. 1801–7 Oct. 1852)*, U.S. senator, legislator, and lawyer, was born in Raleigh. His father, William Henry Haywood, Sr., planter and banker, was a prominent public figure in the newly established capital of North Carolina. Young Haywood attended the Raleigh Male Academy and in 1819 was graduated from The University of North Carolina. After studying law, he was admitted to the state bar in 1822. He served in the House of Commons of the North Carolina General Assembly in 1831 and 1834–36; in the latter year, he was speaker of the house.

Haywood was active in keeping Raleigh as the state capital when there were efforts to remove it after a fire destroyed the capitol in 1831. He also pushed an appropriation for the construction of a new state house in Raleigh. As a friend and correspondent of David L. Swain (governor and president of The University of North Carolina), Haywood was interested in the North Carolina Historical Society which Swain had founded. He wrote Swain of his hopes that the society would arouse state pride in its citizens and advised him to seek a set of "State Papers" for the university library.

Elected to the U.S. Senate by the Romulus Saunders and Bedford Brown wing of the Democratic party, Haywood served from March 1843 to July 1846. He was a university classmate and lifelong friend of James K. Polk and supported Polk in the presidential election of 1844, offering advice on campaign procedures and rallying the Democratic party in North Carolina. He was critical of the state's lack of interest and noninvolvement in national politics. Haywood was active in arrangements for President Polk's return to speak at a university commencement in Chapel Hill.

Haywood also corresponded with President Martin Van Buren. He was offered an appointment as chargé d'affaires to Belgium by Van Buren but declined. In letters to Van Buren, he expressed his views on the national bank, the deposit act, and the subtreasury bill. On the matter of public lands, Haywood protested the instruction of senators to vote against reducing or graduating the price of these lands because it was contrary to the interest of the "Old States." In the U.S. Senate, he was a member of the committee on privileges and elections; he also prepared a sketch on the bill for the annexation of Texas. When the low tariff bill, reflecting the views of Robert J. Walker, was introduced in 1845, Haywood opposed it as an unwise measure which he could not support. Rather than vote against his party, he resigned his seat in the Senate, returning to North Carolina and the practice of law. He was regarded by his contemporaries as the "able and astute Haywood," who achieved "a high position at the bar."

Haywood was a member of the Protestant Episcopal church. In February 1826 he married Jane Graham of New Bern, and they had three sons and six daughters: Edward Graham, Duncan Cameron, William Henry, Elizabeth, Annie, Jane, Minerva, Margaret, and Gertrude. Haywood was buried in City Cemetery, Raleigh.

SEE: *Biog. Dir. Am. Cong.* (1928); D. L. Corbitt, *Calendar of Manuscript Collections* (1926); Elizabeth G. McPherson, "Unpublished Letters of North Carolinians to Andrew Jackson," *North Carolina Historical Review* 14 (1938), and "Unpublished Letters of North Carolinians to Polk," *North Carolina Historical Review* 16 (1939); A. R. Newsome, "Twelve North Carolina Counties in 1810–1811," *North Carolina Historical Review* 6 (1929); W. J. Peele, *Lives of Distinguished North Carolinians* (1897); *Raleigh Register*, 1 Feb. 1826; U.S. Census, 1850, Wake County.

BETH CRABTREE

Heartt, Dennis *(6 Nov. 1783–13 May 1870)*, newspaper editor and publisher, was born in North Bradford, Conn. Beyond the fact that he was the son of an English sea captain who settled in Connecticut and married a New England woman, virtually nothing is known of his childhood. At an early age Heartt was apprenticed to Ezra Read and Abel Morse, printers in New Haven. In 1802, having completed his apprenticeship, he moved to Philadelphia where he practiced his trade. He began his publishing career in May 1810 with the establishment of the *Philadelphia Repertory*. This paper, which concerned itself primarily with literary topics, remained in business for two years. In 1812, in Philadelphia, he issued another magazine, *The Bureau; or Repository of Literature, Politics, and Intelligence*. Heartt apparently continued his employment as a printer in Philadelphia until he contracted smallpox, when his physician advised him to move south.

In seeking a better climate, Heartt chose to settle in Hillsborough, N.C., where, in February 1820, he began publication of the *Hillsborough Recorder*. In doing so he filled a void, as there was at that time no newspaper published west of Raleigh. He continued to publish and edit this paper for nearly fifty years. He sold the *Recorder* in 1869 shortly before his death.

As a pioneer newspaper publisher, Heartt saw many newspapers come and go. The *Recorder* meanwhile became a staple in the lives of readers in Orange and adjacent counties. Heartt's paper was a source of news and opinions for and about the political leaders of North Carolina, who were situated in surprising numbers in Hillsborough and its vicinity. It provided practical suggestions for farmers and housewives. Its pages also reflected Heartt's literary interests, as it included efforts of local talent and contributions copied from other journals. Along this same literary bent, in 1845 Heartt published an edition of poems by the slave poet, George Moses Horton.

During his long career Heartt trained numerous apprentices—the most notable of whom was William Woods Holden, who became a well-known newspaperman and governor of the state. In 1837, Heartt gave impetus to improving the press of North Carolina by initiating a movement that led to an editorial convention of thirteen North Carolina editors. This convention, which met in Raleigh, adopted a series of resolutions to improve the standards of newspapers in the state.

In politics Heartt was a Whig, and he championed the party's candidates and programs in his columns, though with a restraint unusual for the papers of the day. He was a charter member and secretary of the Hillsborough Literary Association, which he helped organize in 1842. A Presbyterian, he served as an officer in the Hillsborough church for a number of years.

In 1804, while residing in Philadelphia, Heartt married Elizabeth Shinn, a Quaker. They were the parents of four children: Leo, Edwin, Caroline, and Henrietta. Heartt died in Hillsborough, and his funeral was held in the Presbyterian Church. The location of his burial place is unknown.

SEE: Ruth Blackwelder, *The Age of Orange* (1961[portrait]); William K. Boyd, "Dennis Heartt," *Historical Papers, Historical Society of Trinity College*, ser. 2 (1898); *Hillsborough Recorder*, 18 May 1870, and scattered issues, 1820–69; W. W. Holden, *Address on the History of Journalism in North Carolina* (1881); Hugh Lefler and Paul Wager, *Orange County, 1752–1952* (1953); Herbert D. Pegg, *The Whig Party in North Carolina* (n.d.); Thad Stem, *The Tar Heel Press* (1973); Charles L. Van Noppen Papers (Manuscript Department, Duke University Library, Durham).

H. THOMAS KEARNEY, JR.

Heath, Robert *(20 May 1575–30 Aug. 1649)*, Proprietor of Carolana, and English attorney and judge, was the son of Robert Heath of Brasted, Kent, and his wife, Anne Posyer. He was born at Brasted and attended Tunbridge grammar school and St. John's College, Cambridge. Having read law at Clifford's Inn and the Inner Temple, he was called to the bar in 1603. He was elected to Parliament in 1620, appointed solicitor-general and knighted in 1621, and appointed attorney-general in 1625. As a member of Parliament Heath supported the royal prerogative, and as attorney-general he enforced laws against recusants and ordered the arrest of Jesuits; it was he who conducted many Star-chamber prosecutions of the 1630s and 1640s. In 1631, he became lord chief justice of the common pleas.

King Charles I on 30 Oct. 1629 granted to Heath the land between 31° and 36° north latitude—the territory between Albemarle Sound and the modern Georgia-Florida boundary and extending from the Atlantic to the Pacific oceans. The land was named Carolana and under his charter Heath had broad feudal powers, yet laws for his colony were to be enacted by the freeholders or their representatives. A local nobility might be created and a gold crown was to be kept in Carolana for use by the king when he should visit there. Heath's attempts to attract Huguenot settlers failed, and after a few years he transferred his rights to Henry Frederick Howard, Lord Maltravers. The name assigned to the region survived in a slightly modified form and various provisions of Heath's charter were retained in subsequent charters.

Heath married Margaret Miller by whom he had five sons and a daughter who survived him. Towards the end of the Civil War, he fled to France where he died at

Calais. He was buried in Brasted Church. A portrait of him hangs in St. John's College. Another is in the Inner Temple, London, and in 1866 another version was in the possession of Lord Willoughby de Broke at Kingston.

SEE: *Dictionary of National Biography*, vol. 9 (1950); Mattie Erma E. Parker, ed., *North Carolina Charters and Constitutions, 1578–1698* (1963).

WILLIAM S. POWELL

Heaton, David (*10 Mar. 1823–25 June 1870*), lawyer, bureaucrat, and congressman, was born in Hamilton, Ohio, the son of James and Mary Heaton. He attended Miami University in Oxford, Ohio, in 1841–42, read law, and was admitted to the Ohio bar, practicing in Middletown until 1857. During some of this time he also served as a justice of the peace, and for a brief period after December 1852 he was editorial co-manager of the local newspaper, *The Middletown Emblem*. In 1855 he was elected to the Ohio state senate and served one term before moving to Minneapolis, Minn., in 1857. Characteristically seeking political preferment, Heaton was soon elected to the Minnesota state senate for the first of three terms. He had been postmaster in Middletown from 1849 to 1852, and after settling in Minneapolis he was postmaster there. He was the author of *Summary Statement of the General Interests of Manufacture and Trade Connected with the Upper Mississippi*, published in Minneapolis in 1862.

In 1863, after serving five years, Heaton resigned his senate seat to accept appointment by Salmon P. Chase as special agent of the Treasury Department and U.S. Depository in New Bern, N.C. Later he declined the position of third auditor in the Treasury Department in order to pursue his fortune in the conquered South.

In the fall of 1865 Heaton became president of the New Bern National Bank, but this was merely a prelude to his activities in Reconstruction politics. One of the founders of the North Carolina Republican party, he was author of the platform adopted by that party on 27 Mar. 1867, contributed frequently to the Republican press, and was influential in the councils of the Union League. Heaton was one of the leading Carpetbaggers in the Constitutional Convention of 1868 and was chairman of the committee on the bill of rights. His ambition led him to compete with Joseph C. Abbott and Albion W. Tourgée for prestige and power in that assemblage. To gain a following, Heaton sometimes supported the position taken by native southerners; especially notable was his defense of the death penalty in rape cases.

Once the work of the convention was completed, congressional elections were held. In the Second District Heaton defeated the Conservative candidate, Thomas S. Kenan, and was thus eligible for a seat in the Fortieth Congress. He took the oath of office on 15 July 1868 and was assigned to the Committee on Elections; he also served as chairman of the Committee on Coinage, Weights, and Measures. His most successful legislative venture seems to have been in securing for his constituents a post road from Pollocksville via Palo Alto to Swansboro. Heaton was reelected and served without distinction in the Forty-first Congress until his death in Washington. His last words are said to have been "God bless the colored people!" A few days before his death he was renominated for the Forty-second Congress. He was buried in the National Cemetery, New Bern.

Heaton married Mary Vaness in Hamilton, Ohio, on 29 Nov. 1843 and they became the parents of Harriet, James, and Cornelia.

SEE: *Appletons' Cyclopaedia of American Biography*, vol. 3 (1888); *Biog. Dir. Am. Cong.* (1971); Butler County, Ohio, 1850 Census (typescript, Smith Library of Regional History, Oxford, Ohio); *Congressional Globe*, *passim* (1868–70); William Coyle, *Ohio Authors and Their Books* (1962); George Crout, "Middletown Diary" (typescript, Middletown Public Library, Middletown, Ohio); Early Marriage Records of Butler County (typescript, Middletown Public Library); *General Catalogue of the Graduates and Former Students of Miami University* (1909); J. G. de R. Hamilton, *Reconstruction in North Carolina* (1906); *A History and Biographical Cyclopaedia of Butler County, Ohio* (1882).

MAX WILLIAMS

Heazel, Francis James (*10 Dec. 1891–17 Jan. 1977*), lawyer and civic leader, was born in Page County, Va., the son of James F. and Catherine Morrisey Heazel. After attending Mount St. Mary's College in Emmitsburg, Md., he received the LL.B. degree from Washington and Lee University. Before opening an office in Asheville, N.C., he practiced law in Roanoke, Va., and in Kingsport, Tenn. Long active in civic affairs, he was president of the Asheville Area Chamber of Commerce and held virtually every office in the United Fund; he was also involved in community hospital leadership. He served on the Sinking Fund Commission and the North Carolina National Park, Parkway, and Forest Development Commission.

For the mountain region in the early 1940s he helped to organize the Western North Carolina Associated Communities and was chairman of its project committee. A major accomplishment of this group was to transform the life of the Eastern Band of the Cherokee through the Cherokee Historical Association, a nonprofit corporation chartered by the state, which produced the highly successful outdoor drama, *Unto These Hills*. With the support of Chief Jarrett Blythe of the Cherokees, the enterprise from the first season far exceeded the expectations of its organizers. Heazel's financial experience helped conserve the proceeds for an equally successful venture nearby, led by association chairman Harry E. Buchanan. Oconaluftee Living Village drew an even larger attendance; its earnings paid for a scholarship program for young Cherokees such as Amanda Crowe, who became a renowned wood sculptor.

Perhaps the source of his greatest pride came near the end of Heazel's life—a new home for the Samuel E. Beck Collection of museum pieces, which had been housed in a wooden building. With assistance from principal chief John A. Crowe and tribal council chairman Jonathan Ed Taylor, Heazel drew up a legal instrument to provide control of a substantial museum with a board of tribal council members and trustees of the Cherokee Historical Association. Associate chairman Frank A. Brown took an active part in securing state funds for the museum building. Its design won an award of distinction from the state association of architects.

As a Roman Catholic layman, Heazel was national treasurer of the Knights of Columbus. In recognition of his services, he was appointed to the Papal Order of Knights of St. Gregory by Pope Pius XI.

Heazel and his first wife, Anna Flanagan, had two daughters, Mary Gertrude and Anna Catherine, and a son, Francis J., Jr. After Mrs. Heazel's death, he married Jane Harwell Rutland who survived him.

SEE: *Asheville Citizen*, 18 Jan. 1977; *Greensboro Daily News*, 23 Oct. 1938; *Who's Who in the South and Southwest* (1947).

GEORGE MYERS STEPHENS

Heck, Fannie Exile Scudder *(24 June 1862–25 Aug. 1915)*, mission leader, was born in Buffalo Lithia Springs, Va., the second of ten surviving children of Colonel Jonathan McGee and Mattie Calendine Heck. Colonel Heck was for a time in Confederate service; though taken prisoner, he was released under a parole of honor. He was later elected to the Virginia legislature; however, when fighting around Richmond seemed likely, he took his family first to Raleigh and later to Buffalo Lithia Springs, Va. It was there that his second daughter was born; the name "Exile" came from the fact that she was born during the family's period of exile. Years later she added "Scudder" to her name to honor her great-grandmother, Jane Scudder Chadwick, a devout pioneer Baptist of Morgantown, Va.

The Heck family moved to Warren County, N.C., in September 1862, and after the war settled in Raleigh. Fannie E. S. Heck was educated at Professor F. P. Hobgood's seminary in the capital city and at Hollins Institute in Virginia. An active member of Raleigh's First Baptist Church, she developed an intense interest in missions and dreamed of an organization whereby missionary causes could be fostered by women of the South. In January 1886, when the State Mission Board formed a Woman's Central Committee of Missions, she was named president. For several years the committee functioned as an arm of the Baptist State Convention.

On 11 May 1888, the Woman's Missionary Union (WMU), Auxiliary to the Southern Baptist Convention, was organized in Richmond. Although North Carolina was not one of the ten states to vote for the new organization, its Central Committee favored the movement and sent two representatives, including Miss Heck, to Richmond. Two years later the committee was authorized to affiliate with the Southern WMU, and in 1891 the North Carolina Central Committee made its first report to that organization. Miss Heck continued as president of the North Carolina group. In 1892, at age thirty, she was elected president of the Southern WMU, an office she held for a total of fifteen years—1892–94, 1895–99, and 1906–15. Illness prevented continuous service. She was also president of the North Carolina WMU from the time of its organization until her death. During her tenure in North Carolina, the number of societies grew from 14 to 1,200, with the annual contribution to missions increasing from $1,000 in 1886 to nearly $50,000 by 1915. Branches were established for young women, boys, girls, and small children.

Miss Heck was influential in the organization of the Woman's Missionary Union Training School in Louisville, Ky., an adjunct of the Southern Baptist Theological Seminary. The Heck Memorial Chapel there is a reminder of her contribution. She was a delegate to the first Ecumenical Conference, held in New York in 1900, and she spoke at the Baptist World Alliance in Philadelphia in 1911. Her concern for youth was shown by her participation in the Student Volunteer and Young People's Missionary Education movements; in appreciation of her work with students at Meredith College, the WMU placed the Heck Memorial Fountain on the campus. She was also involved with a plan to send volunteer teachers to the North Carolina mountains during the summer months, a program launched in 1900 and continued for three years.

In Raleigh, Fannie E. S. Heck engaged in personal missionary work among the underprivileged. She was active in the organization of the Associated Charities, serving as the first president. Her interest in social welfare programs led to her role as a representative from North Carolina to the Social Service Conference in Memphis, Tenn., in 1913. She was one of the founders and the first president of the Raleigh Woman's Club.

Miss Heck wrote many leaflets; a book entitled *In Royal Service*, which was a history of the first twenty-five years of the Southern WMU; and the words to "Come, Women, Wide Proclaim," also known as "The Woman's Hymn." For a time she published a monthly paper called *The Missionary Talk*; later she was coeditor of *Our Mission Fields*, a quarterly of the Southern WMU.

Fannie E. S. Heck died after an illness of many months. In addition to legacies to members of her family, she left $100 to the Woman's Missionary Society of Raleigh's First Baptist Church, the interest of which was to be used to pay her annual membership perpetually; $200 to the WMU Training School in Louisville for a new building; and money for several other causes. In two codicils she left small sums to the Raleigh Woman's Club, the YWCA of Raleigh, and other charitable causes. Finally, she left $100 to her brother Charles M. Heck, professor of physics at North Carolina State College, to aid in the employment of a lawyer and a draftsman and to provide other assistance needed to carry through a patent on heat absorption.

The North Carolina WMU, at its annual meeting in 1924, voted to establish an annual offering in her memory, the proceeds to be used for various missionary projects for which other funds were not available. Later renamed the Heck-Jones Offering to honor also Sallie Bailey (Mrs. W. N.) Jones, who succeeded Miss Heck as president in North Carolina, the earnings have been used for buildings, equipment, and projects in mission fields worldwide.

SEE: Foy J. Farmer, *Hitherto: History of North Carolina Woman's Missionary Union* (1952); Edna R. Harris, *Ten Years with Heck Memorial Offering* (1934); Fannie E. S. Heck, *In Royal Service* (1920); Minnie K. James, *Fannie E. S. Heck* (1939); North Carolina Woman's Missionary Union, *Memorial Program* (1928); Raleigh *News and Observer*, 26, 27 Aug. 1915; Will of Fannie E. S. Heck (North Carolina State Archives, Raleigh).

MEMORY F. MITCHELL

Heck, Jonathan McGee *(5 May 1831–10 Feb. 1894)*, businessman and developer, and Baptist layman in the post-Civil War era, was born in Monongalia County, Va., located in that part of the state that became West Virginia, the son of George and Susan McGee Heck. He attended Rector College and studied law in Morgantown, Va. Admitted to the bar, Heck soon established a large practice and served briefly as justice of the peace and commonwealth attorney. As early as 1855 he bought property along the Monongahela River; he continued buying land in the region until 1866 and owned property there as late as 1892. In 1859, Heck and an associate contracted to furnish gas and water to the city of Morgantown for fifty years, but the project was abandoned after one gas well was dug. On 10 Mar. 1859 Heck married Mattie A. Callendine.

As civil war threatened, Heck found that his loyalties

lay with Virginia and the South: "Leaving his young wife and child and the handsome home which he had provided for them, renouncing all his former ambitions and accumulated wealth, he came to Richmond, and once and forever cast his lot with that of the southern states." On 10 May 1861 he was commissioned colonel of the Thirty-first Regiment of Virginia Volunteers, which he was to raise and equip. At the Battle of Rich Mountain against the troops of General George B. Mc-Clellan, Heck was captured and paroled with others; "for some unaccountable reason, [he] was held under parole long after those with him were allowed to return to active service." One account suggests that he was "cheated out of his command at Rich Mountain." As a parolee, he was nevertheless elected to serve in the Virginia General Assembly. As soon as permitted, Heck returned to active service in the Confederate cause—not as a soldier this time, but as a "purchaser of materials for the manufacture of implements of war."

During the war his growing family moved several times, settling briefly at Staunton, Va.; Raleigh, N.C.; and Buffalo Lithia Springs, Va. The family was to locate finally in North Carolina, living first in Warren County and later in Raleigh. On 25 Aug. 1863, Heck (still identified as a citizen of Monongalia County, Va.), bought from William D. Jones of Warren County, N.C., 2,012 acres on Shocco Creek in Warren County for $45,000. As the owner of the "large and then far-famed health resort, Jones's Springs, . . . he with generous-handed liberality threw it open to the many homeless refugees, who were then seeking refuge in North Carolina." Among those who had taken refuge at Shocco were the wife and children of General Robert E. Lee; Lee's daughter, Annie Carter, died there in 1862 and was buried in the Jones family cemetery. When in 1866 Warren County citizens arranged for a monument to be erected there for Annie Carter Lee, Heck wrote to the former general, who responded from Lexington, Va., that "when able to visit the grave of my daughter, for which I have a great desire, I will remember your kind invitations [to] go to your house."

Evidently through his experience as purchaser of materials for the Confederacy and as contractor for making war materials, Heck developed both a familiarity with North Carolina's industrial potential and perhaps much of his substantial personal capital—resources that would stand him in good stead after the war. He traveled far and wide to acquire goods for the war effort, and he was involved in several enterprises, among them a bayonet factory in Raleigh and the firm of Heck, Brodie, Inc., which manufactured bayonets using the rich mineral deposits along the Deep River in Chatham County. In October 1864, Heck, Brodie & Co., "Government contractors," were authorized to "select from the military prisons at Salisbury, N.C., and Danville, Va., sixty prisoners who may volunteer to work in their bayonet factory on Deep River, N.C."

Unlike many of his contemporaries, Heck emerged from the war with energy and investment potential, ready to expand his fortune and that of his adopted state amid the new order—in contrast to many whose fortunes had depended on a slave-based agricultural system. Colonel Heck, as he was consistently known, was, recalled his associate Kemp P. Battle, "the first man in Raleigh to endeavor to break up the business lethargy prevailing after the surrender." He was, another author stated, "one of the men who built the New South, and was extraordinarily successful in promoting the industrial and agricultural development of the State." At thirty-four, six feet tall, with black hair

and beard and eyes, Heck was a strikingly attractive young man, and he combined undeniable southern credentials and connections with useful northern associations and a supply of capital. Whether his capital derived from retained West Virginia holdings, profits made during the war and invested in other than Confederate currency, or other sources is not certain.

Heck's first project after the war was remarkable more for the promptness of organization and spirit of enthusiasm amid prevailing discouragement than for long-term success. He joined with Kemp Battle, William J. Hawkins (president of the Raleigh and Gaston Railroad Company), and Bailey P. Williamson to form Battle, Heck, and Company, whose goal was to "make known in all feasible ways the lands in North Carolina for sale and to induce Northern people to buy and settle among us." Losing no time after the surrender, Heck obtained in June 1865 the necessary warrant of pardon and by 8 July the company's first issue of the *North Carolina Advertiser* was out.

The *Advertiser*, notable in its positive approach to the new day so soon after the surrender, is an interesting document of a very early attempt to promote immigration and investment into the South—a precursor of many such projects in the years that followed. The *Advertiser* analyzed and described in glowing terms the state's wealth of development potential—its temperate climate, wide range of possible crops, rich mineral deposits, sources of waterpower, and forest resources. The North Carolina Land Agency, as the firm's real estate arm was titled, offered for sale a multitude of properties ranging from William S. Pettigrew's 7,000-acre Magnolia Plantation on the Scuppernong River, to 15,000 acres of turpentine land on the Cape Fear River, to the High Shoals mining and manufacturing operation in Lincoln and Gaston counties. Late in 1865 the agency listed for sale a total of 132 separate offerings, including 146,700 acres of agricultural land plus manufacturing, commercial, and residential property. The consistent theme of the publication was the need "under the recent change in the system of labor," to begin anew in "starting North Carolina in a career of prosperity heretofore unknown." The effort met with favorable response from Governor W. W. Holden and from newspapers in North Carolina and beyond, including the *New York Times*. Heck and Battle made a long promotional journey to northern cities and established an office on Broadway in New York, where inquiries were numerous. Yet the project failed by the end of 1865. Recalled Battle later, "Seldom did an enterprise have greater prospects of success, seldom did an enterprise so suddenly and completely collapse." The *Advertiser*, and in later years Kemp Battle, cited the threat of confiscation of southern lands during Reconstruction as the chief reason for the hesitancy of investors and hence the failure of the company.

The partners emerged from the venture still ready for new projects; Battle recalled that, despite the loss of money, they had "had for months . . . active, interesting work in exchange for gloom and despondency and . . . made connections." Two of Heck's next enterprises involved innovative development ideas concerning resources he had become acquainted with during the war years—the Deep River industrial development and the Ridgeway Company.

Geological reports before the war indicated that the coal and iron deposits along the Deep River were among the best in the nation, with potential for a "national foundry." During the war, these resources were vital to the Confederate effort, and Heck had investments in the area. Soon after the war, George Lobdell of the Lobdell Car Wheel Company of Wilmington, Del., sought to use the iron there—reportedly after being impressed with the quality of Confederate steel used in train wheels, which had been made from Deep River ore. He joined Heck in an ambitious development plan for the region, including navigational improvements to allow access to the port at Wilmington, development of the existing furnace at Endor, construction of a big furnace and a dam at Buckhorn, expansion of mining at nearby Egypt and elsewhere, and development of the towns of Lockville and Haywood. Some of these tasks were accomplished, and the firm estimated that a half-million dollars was sunk into the project. Under a series of names—such as the Deep River Manufacturing Company, Cape Fear Iron and Steel Company, and American Iron and Steel Company—Lobdell, Heck, and others created one of the most extensive industrial development enterprises in the state in the early 1870s. Again, however, grand ambitions were thwarted, this time by the discovery that the mineral deposits were smaller than anticipated and the fact that the navigation system on the Deep and Cape Fear rivers was never completed satisfactorily. The operation soon declined.

During the decade after the war, Heck was also involved in an immigration and development plan for Ridgeway, a community on the railroad in Warren County, and home of William J. Hawkins, an associate of Heck, Battle, and Company. The Ridgeway Company was chartered on 22 Aug. 1868, with Heck, Hawkins, Peter R. Davis, and A. F. Johnson as incorporators. Extensive advertising was done in the North and abroad, in hope of creating a bustling city amid the sad fields of Warren County. Orchards were planted, streets laid out, some construction done, and a stone placed to mark the center of the metropolis. Immigrants did come—Germans, Englishmen, and others; in fact, a community of German farmers established there maintains its cultural identity to the present. But Ridgeway never became the thriving city its developers envisioned.

Despite the failure of these schemes, Heck's vision, energy, and willingness to take risks contributed to the renewal of business and industry in the state. Far from being a dreamy idealist, he was an astute and adventurous investor, a successful businessman whose fortunes grew rapidly. Other enterprises, less colorful perhaps, did succeed, making him a wealthy and respected business leader. Among these were several iron or coal operations, including the Moratock Mining and Manufacturing Company near Danbury, the Coal Creek mining operation in Tennessee, and copper enterprises in Virginia. In addition, Heck was a major developer, along with R. S. Pullen, of the new residential section of Raleigh, called Oakwood, which grew as the town recovered from Reconstruction.

Heck's confidence in the new day was expressed in the house he built on North Blount Street, soon to be Raleigh's fashionable avenue. Actually Mrs. Heck's house, the impressive three-story frame dwelling in the modishly ornate Second Empire style, was the first major home to go up in Raleigh after the war; it was built in 1869–70 by contractors Wilson and Waddell, and designed by architect G. S. H. Appleget. The contract for the house survives, along with an almost identical contract for a house for Heck in Ridgeway, but no information has been found to suggest the latter was built; certainly no similar house now stands in Ridgeway.

As his fortunes rose, Heck became a "liberal contrib-utor to many causes for his town and state," with particular interest in Baptist affairs. A member of the First Baptist Church in Raleigh, he had been elected a trustee of Wake Forest College in November 1865, and along with John G. Williams he funded the school's first postwar building—the Heck-Williams Building, constructed in 1878. For some years Heck was president of the board of trustees. He contributed substantially to the Baptist Female College in Raleigh and was a Baptist lay leader, serving as president of the Baptist State Convention. Other civic activity included participation in the reorganization of the state agricultural society, providing "a handsome house and property for a North Carolina Confederate soldiers home," and in 1892 service as chief marshal for Raleigh's centennial celebration.

Colonel and Mrs. Heck had thirteen children, of whom adult sons were George C., John M., and Charles M., and daughters were Mary Lou (Mrs. W. H. Pace), Fannie E. S., Minnie C. (Mrs. B. G. Cowper), Mattie A. (Mrs. J. D. Boushall), Susie, and Pearl. Of interest in North Carolina are Charles, for over thirty years head of the physics department at North Carolina State College, and Fannie, an influential leader in the Woman's Missionary Union of the Southern Baptist Convention. Heck died in Philadelphia, where he had gone for treatment of cancer. He was buried in Oakwood Cemetery, Raleigh.

SEE: Samuel A. Ashe, *Cyclopedia of Eminent and Representative Men of the Carolinas of the Nineteenth Century*, vol. 2 (1892); Kemp P. Battle, *Memories of an Old-Time Tar Heel* (1945); J. M. Heck Collection (North Carolina State Archives, Raleigh); Minnie K. James, *Fannie E. S. Heck* (1939); George W. Paschal, *History of Wake Forest College*, vol. 2 (1935); Rodney A. Pyles to author (letter, 1 Sept. 1971). Unpublished nominations to the National Register of Historic Places in North Carolina State Archives, Raleigh: Catherine Bisher, "Heck-Andrews House" (Wake County); Jerry L. Cross, "Hawkins House" (Warren County); Ruth Little-Stokes, "Moratock Iron Furnace" (Stokes County) and "Endor Iron Furnace" (Lee County).

CATHERINE W. BISHER

Hecklefield, John (d. August[?] 1721), militia officer, justice of the peace, provost marshal, and vestryman, moved to North Carolina from England in 1701. Court records of 1701 and 1702 refer to him as a doctor. His family name was rare. Settling in the Little River area of Perquimans County, he quickly became one of the growing community's leading citizens. Hecklefield married Elizabeth Abington Godfrey, daughter of Thomas Abington and widow of John Godfrey. He apparently was a man of some means before arriving, for provincial courts, the Council, and the Assembly all met at their home between 1701 and 1715. Court had been held at the same place during Godfrey's lifetime, and afterwards when the house was occupied by his widow. It may have been Hecklefield's marriage that drew him into public office almost immediately after his arrival. He was given power of attorney by a local resident in 1701, and later in the year he became captain of the militia. In 1703 he was provost marshal and a few years later was a justice of the peace for Perquimans County.

Like many of his contemporaries, he began acquiring large tracts of land. In 1713 the Assembly named him to prepare a rent roll for his precinct, and in 1715 he became a vestryman for his parish. Hecklefield also was appointed deputy to Lord Proprietor William Craven, but he declined to serve because of ill health.

His wife died before he did, and he was survived by a five-year-old son. His will, dated 30 May and probated 8 Aug. 1721, provided bequests to such prominent friends as Governor Charles Eden, Edmund Gale, and George Durant. His son did not survive long afterwards, and the bulk of the estate was then willed to Hecklefield's sister-in-law, Mrs. Mary Fox, who lived near Essex Bridge, Dublin, Ireland.

SEE: Robert J. Cain, ed., *Records of the Executive Council, 1664–1734* (1984); John L. Cheney, Jr., ed., *North Carolina Government, 1585–1979* (1981); Walter Clark, ed., *State Records of North Carolina*, vol. 23 (1904); J. Bryan Grimes, ed., *Abstract of North Carolina Wills* (1910) and *North Carolina Wills and Inventories* (1912); Mattie Erma E. Parker, ed., *North Carolina Higher-Court Records, 1697–1701* (1971); William S. Price, Jr., ed., *North Carolina Higher-Court Records, 1702–1708* (1974) and *1709–1723* (1977); William L. Saunders, ed., *Colonial Records of North Carolina*, vols. 1, 2 (1886); Ellen G. Winslow, *History of Perquimans County* (1931).

NEIL C. PENNYWITT

Hedrick, Benjamin Sherwood (*13 Feb. 1827–2 Sept. 1886*), educator, chemist, and antislavery leader, was born in western Davidson County near Salisbury, the son of Elizabeth Sherwood and John Leonard Hedrick, a farmer and bricklayer of comfortable means. The family was descended from German immigrants who settled in the Piedmont section of North Carolina in the 1700s. After attending local schools, Hedrick received college preparation at Rankin's (or Lexington) Classical School, an academy directed by the Reverend Jesse Rankin near Lexington. In 1848 he entered The University of North Carolina as a sophomore; he distinguished himself particularly in mathematics, and upon his graduation in 1851 he was awarded "first honor in the senior class." President David L. Swain recommended Hedrick to former governor William A. Graham, secretary of the navy, for a clerkship in the office of the Nautical Almanac in Cambridge, Mass. Graham made the appointment, and while in Cambridge Hedrick also took advanced instruction at Harvard College under such prominent scientists as Eben N. Horsford, Benjamin Pierce, and Louis Agassiz.

Although offered a position at Davidson College as professor of mathematics in 1852, Hedrick declined it, deciding instead to return to his alma mater when the opportunity arose. In January 1854 the university appointed him to the chair of analytical and agricultural chemistry.

In Chapel Hill Hedrick acquired a certain notoriety because of his antislavery views in the antebellum South, although initially he had made no attempt to disseminate his opinions on the issue. But in August 1856 he was asked at the polls whether he would vote for the Republican presidential candidate, John C. Frémont, in the national election. Hedrick replied that he would do so if a Republican ticket was formed in North Carolina. The next month a short article entitled "Frémont in the South" appeared in the *North Carolina Standard* of Raleigh, a leading Democratic newspaper in the state. The article recommended that those with "black Republican opinions" at schools and seminaries in the state be driven out, apparently suggesting that Hedrick be dismissed. Against much advice, he published a defense in the *Standard*, explaining his opposition to slav-

ery and likening his beliefs to those of George Washington and Thomas Jefferson. Subsequently the university faculty passed resolutions denouncing Hedrick's political views, and on 11 October the executive committee of the board of trustees formally approved the faculty's action, which in reality was a dismissal. Meanwhile, the state newspapers were generally unsympathetic to Hedrick's case. On 21 October, while he was attending an educational convention in Salisbury, an unsuccessful attempt was made to tar and feather him. He soon left for the North, where he remained except for visits south in January 1857 and in 1865.

For a time Hedrick lived in New York, where he was employed as a chemist and then as a clerk in the mayor's office. He also did some lecturing and teaching at such institutions as Cooper Union. His services in the mayor's office were terminated after 1 Jan. 1860. In 1861 he went to Washington, D.C., to seek a job with the newly elected Republican government. There he was successively appointed assistant examiner, examiner, and chief examiner in the Chemical Department of the U.S. Patent Office, remaining with that agency until his death.

In 1865 Hedrick attempted to secure a speedy restoration of North Carolina to the Union. He failed to convince state leaders that they should agree to Negro suffrage because it would certainly be demanded by Congress. He also strongly advised a policy of moderation in the development of the Republican party and placing governance of the state in the hands of the ablest men. Evidently he was well acquainted with both President Andrew Johnson and Governor Jonathan Worth. In April 1865 Hedrick petitioned the president for permission to visit North Carolina. Afterwards H. M. Pierce appointed him an agent of the American Union Commission to ascertain the condition of refugees and the poor in the South, paying particular attention to the schools. In 1867 Hedrick was nominated as a delegate to the North Carolina constitutional convention but was defeated in the election. From 1872 to 1876 he was professor of chemistry and toxicology at University of Georgetown.

Hedrick married Mary Ellen Thompson, daughter of William Thompson, on 3 June 1852 in Orange County. They had four daughters and four sons, one of whom, Charles, J., became a patent lawyer in Washington, D.C. Hedrick died there.

SEE: John Spencer Bassett, *Anti-Slavery Leaders of North Carolina* (1898); Kemp P. Battle, *History of the University of North Carolina*, vol. 1 (1907); J. G. de R. Hamilton, *Benjamin Sherwood Hedrick* (1910); Benjamin Sherwood Hedrick Papers (Manuscript Department, Duke University Library, Durham); *Nat. Cyc. Am. Biog.*, vol. 9 (1899); *North Carolina Biography*, vol. 2 (1941).

SHARON E. KNAPP

Hege, Constantine Alexander (*13 Mar. 1843–26 July 1914*), merchant, inventor, and manufacturer, was born near Friedburg Moravian Church in Davidson County, the son of Solomon and Catherine Guinther Hege. Joining the Moravian church at age twelve, he attended the Moravian Boys' School at Salem and the Yadkin Institute in his native county. As a Moravian he was opposed to the war, but nevertheless was obliged to enlist in the summer of 1862; he served for fourteen months in Company H, Forty-eighth Regiment, participating in battles at South Mountain, Va., and Sharpsburg, Md., as well as in several skirmishes. At the Battle of Bristow

Station, Va., on 14 Oct. 1863, he was captured and confined in the Old Capitol prison in Washington. While there he was visited by some North Carolina Moravians working in the capital, and under their guidance young Hege decided to take the oath of allegiance to the United States. After his release, he went to Bethlehem, Pa., where he found employment in the iron works.

In August 1865 Hege returned to North Carolina, but a few months later entered the Bryant & Stratton Commercial College in Philadelphia where, upon completing the course, he was employed by a mercantile firm. In the spring of 1867 he opened a small country store at Friedburg, N.C. A few years later he moved to Salem to start a small foundry. After acquiring a steam engine his business expanded, and in 1877 he obtained a patent for an improved set of works for circular sawmills. He then began manufacturing sawmills and woodworking machinery which he also invented. The sawmills produced at Hege's Salem Iron Works were sold throughout the United States and in several foreign countries. The first sawmill in Alaska was one he gave to the Moravian mission there.

Hege was married in 1870 to Frances Mary Spaugh from an area near Salem, and they were the parents of Walter Julius, Ella Florence, and Rose Estelle. Following the death of his first wife, Hege married Martha Caroline Spaugh in 1895.

SEE: *Cyclopedia of Eminent and Representative Men of the Carolinas* (1892); Memoir of Constantine Alexander Hege (Moravian Archives, Winston-Salem).

WILLIAM S. POWELL

Heitman, John Franklin (*17 Apr. 1840–15 June 1904*), educator, clergyman, editor, and historian, was born in Davidson County near Lexington, the son of Henry and Eve McRary Heitman. In 1861 he entered Trinity College around which most of his career would revolve. His first year at Trinity, then located in Randolph County, was cut short when he joined a stream of other students who entered military duty in the service of the Confederacy. In the spring of 1862 he enrolled as first sergeant in Company H, Forty-eighth Regiment of North Carolina troops; by the end of the war he had advanced to captain. He was wounded at Fredericksburg on 13 Dec. 1863 and was twice hospitalized due to illness. On 6 Apr. 1864 he was captured at Appomattox and detained on Johnson's Island until his release on 18 June 1865. His exploits in the last year of the war are chronicled in a diary now in the Duke University Archives.

Upon his return to Davidson County, Heitman spent a year operating a sawmill business and teaching school before completing his education at Trinity. Receiving the A.M. degree in 1868, he began a career in teaching and as a clergyman in the Methodist Episcopal Church, South. During his service in the North Carolina Conference, he held several distinguished pastorates, including that of Winston Station, later Centenary in Winston-Salem (1873–76) during its formative years. In 1881 he left the parish ministry to enter business in Chapel Hill. Among his pursuits was the establishment of the *North Carolina Education Journal*, which he edited and published monthly from 1881 through 1885 as the "organ of the North Carolina State Teachers Association."

In 1883, when he was appointed professor at Trinity College, Heitman moved the *Education Journal* and his other business interests back to Randolph County. From his arrival at Trinity until the college was relocated

in Durham in 1892, he devoted himself to saving the school from financial collapse. Although his fields of scholarship were German, Greek, metaphysics, and theology, his greatest contributions were in the area of college administration. Upon the resignation of Marquis Lafayette Wood from the presidency of Trinity in December 1884, Heitman was appointed chairman of the faculty and served for three years as virtual president of the institution. Working closely with a three-member committee of management named by the college trustees, Heitman doubled the enrollment, increased church support, collected overdue bills, and entered into a lucrative contract with the U.S. Department of the Interior for the education of Indian students at Trinity.

Except for an embarrassing personal crisis which became a public scandal involving his brother Charles, an attorney in Lexington who fled to Canada to escape debtors, it is likely that Heitman would have succeeded to the presidency of Trinity. Instead, the trustees passed over Heitman in favor of John F. Crowell. Heitman, nevertheless, remained on the faculty until the school moved. When the move occurred, he chose to stay behind as the headmaster of Trinity High School on the old college campus. When the high school was also moved to Durham in 1899, Heitman moved with it, finishing his career as its head. During his last two years in Randolph County, he launched a second monthly paper, the *North Carolina Home Journal*, which was "designed to be a pleasant, as well as useful, visitor to all North Carolina homes." The paper concluded with his move to Durham.

Heitman's contributions to history were made largely in connection with his editorship of the *North Carolina Educational Journal* and the *North Carolina Home Journal*. Both publications contained numerous accounts and biographical sketches relating to North Carolina history written by Heitman. Noting the absence of a readable, reliable, and popular history of the state, in January 1884 he began writing and publishing in monthly installments a new history of North Carolina. Arranging the state's past into eight general periods from 1492 to the present (1884), Heitman began issuing the new history in monthly pieces of approximately 3,000 words. By the time the *Educational Journal* ceased publication at the end of 1885, he had covered the Introductory Period (1492–1663), the Proprietary Period (1663–1729), and a part of the Royal Period (1729–August 1774). The history was continued unbroken in the first issue of the *Home Journal* in 1897 and in all subsequent issues until December 1898 when it, too, ended. By that time Heitman had brought his narrative through August 1774 and the First Provincial Congress at New Bern. Whether he continued his history is unknown; his manuscript has not been located. By the time of the last issue of the *Home Journal*, however, he had written nearly 100,000 words of what appears to be an original and in many cases a carefully researched history of North Carolina.

Heitman married Emma Carr, sister of Durham tobacco manufacturer Julian Shakespeare Carr, with whom he carried on a lively and enlightening correspondence. The Heitmans were the parents of Eva (Mrs. W. Bivens), Polly (Mrs. R. B. Terry), and John, who never married. He and his wife were buried in Trinity Cemetery, Trinity.

SEE: Nora C. Chaffin, *Trinity College, 1839–1892* (1950); John Franklin Crowell, *Personal Recollections of Trinity College, North Carolina, 1887–1894* (1939); John Franklin Heitman Papers (University Archives, Duke University

Library, Durham); *Nat. Cyc. Am. Biog.*, vol. 3 (1893); *North Carolina Educational Journal*, scattered issues, 1881–85; *North Carolina Home Journal*, scattered issues, 1897–98; Tombstone inscriptions, Trinity Cemetery (Trinity).

LARRY E. TISE

Helper, Hardie Hogan (21 Mar. 1822–19 Sept. 1899), abolitionist, Union soldier, journalist, and moderate Republican Reconstruction leader, was born two miles west of Mocksville, the son of Daniel J. and Sarah Brown Helper. He probably attended the Mocksville Academy on Salisbury Street and may have been taught by the Reverend Baxter Clegg and Peter Stuart Ney at the Mocksville Academy on Depot Street. Helper became a member of the Whig party, and in 1850 went to Washington, D.C., to work for the Navy Department. Returning to Salisbury, he was clerk of the Superior Court of Rowan County in 1855.

Helper was a brother of Hinton Rowan Helper, author of the highly controversial abolitionist volume, *The Impending Crisis of the South: How to Meet It*, published in New York in June 1857. Sometime after its publication, H. H. Helper moved to Illinois; extant records imply that he left North Carolina involuntarily because of the hatred generated by his brother's book.

During the Civil War Helper fought with the Union armies in North Carolina and Florida. While assigned to the staff of General A. E. Burnside, he incurred some disability; this may have taken place when he was involved in an attempt to blow up a railroad bridge across the Trent River in eastern North Carolina. In 1888 a Senate committee recommended Helper for a pension for "the disability as though he was at that time actually enlisted in the Federal Army." After about 1880 he was in very poor health. In his writings to Lyman C. Draper, concerning the Boone family and the Squire Boone homesite (Helper's birthplace), he blamed his failing health on his military service.

A staunch Republican, Helper became deeply involved in Reconstruction in North Carolina both as a candidate for political office and as an outspoken newspaper editor. He was a federal tax assessor for the Sixth Congressional District from about 1865 until about 1870 and the postmaster of Salisbury for several months in 1871. An account of his death, written by his son and published in the *Baltimore Sun*, states that President Andrew Johnson once asked him to submit a plan for readmitting the Confederate states to the Union. According to this account, the plan submitted was a very moderate one but did provide for limited Negro suffrage. In 1870 Helper was an unsuccessful candidate for Congress. He advocated complete universal amnesty, limited Negro suffrage, equal distribution of the proceeds from the sale of western land, protective tariffs, industrial development in the South, and several other reform proposals. During the campaign, he strongly emphasized that he was a "Conservative Republican."

In the late 1860s Helper was co-publisher and editor of the Raleigh *Register*, and for a time was its publisher and editor. In 1868, while holding the latter position, he also published a political paper, *The Holden Record*, devoted to scathing attacks on W. W. Holden, Republican leader and governor associated with radical Reconstruction policies and measures in the state. By 1870 Helper had broken completely with the Radical Republicans in Rowan County and North Carolina, denouncing their leaders as "incompetent and worthless . . . for the most part pestiferous ulcers feeding upon the body politic." He blamed the rapid spread of the Ku Klux Klan on the changes forced upon the South by the Radicals. James S. Brawley, in *The Rowan Story*, states that this opposition by a liberal, reform-minded Republican cost Helper his job as postmaster of Salisbury. In 1872, in Salisbury, Helper edited and published for a while the weekly *Tribune*, which strongly supported the Republican presidential candidate Horace Greeley and the liberal reform wing of the Republican party opposing Grant's reelection.

Believing that the Southern Negro should return to Africa, Helper became involved in the work of the American Colonization Society. He maintained that the Negro and the working-class white were "in each other's way" to progress, and that the Negro presence stymied the South's overall development just as slavery had. Helper corresponded at length with the colonization society and in an interview with the editor of the *Davie Times*, 17 Aug. 1883, declared his intention to "raise a colony—one family from each of the ex-slave states . . . not less than seventy-five souls . . . by and through his own efforts and accompany the said colony into the highlands of Liberia in Africa." Nothing further is known about this proposal.

On 16 May 1848 Helper married Elizabeth Long. His second wife was Anna Selena Folk. By these marriages he had two sons, Alexander and Daniel Ott, and one daughter, Mattie. Helper spent his last years on the small farm site that had been his birthplace. He was buried at Center United Methodist Church in Davie County.

SEE: *Baltimore Sun*, 19 Sept. 1899; J. S. Brawley, *The Rowan Story* (1953); Hugh T. Lefler and Albert R. Newsome, *North Carolina: The History of a Southern State* (1973); Martin Collection (Davie County Library, Mocksville); Mocksville *Davie Times*, 17 Aug. 1888; North Carolina Collection (University of North Carolina Library, Chapel Hill), for newspapers, clippings, political addresses, and pension reports concerning Helper.

JAMES W. WALL

Helper, Hinton Rowan (27 Dec. 1829–9 Mar. 1909), abolitionist author and lecturer and consul to Argentina, was born on the Squire Boone homesite two miles west of Mocksville, the son of Daniel J. and Sarah Brown Helper. He was educated at the Mocksville Academy taught by Peter Stuart Ney and the Reverend Baxter Clegg. Graduating in 1848, he was apprenticed to a printer, Michael Brown, of Salisbury.

In 1850 Helper went to the California gold fields but failed as a prospector; according to his own account, he worked one mine claim for three months and made 93¾ cents. The California experience, however, provided material for his first book, *California Land of Gold: Reality vs. Fiction*. Published in 1855, it presented a most unfavorable view of California and its potential, consisting largely of fabricated and garbled statistics intended to serve the purpose of the writer. In this volume Helper praised and advocated the extension of slavery, and scolded "meddling abolitionists."

Helper returned to Salisbury and then moved to New York. In June 1857 he published *The Impending Crisis of the South: How to Meet It*, a work destined to help elect Abraham Lincoln president in 1860 and to rank perhaps next to *Uncle Tom's Cabin* in its impact as an abolitionist document fueling the fires of secession and war. Helper, scorned by proslavery elements in the North, unable to find employment, and harassed and threatened with physical harm, applied to Lincoln for a consular appointment. The request was granted and in November 1861 he was sent to Buenos Aires. While there he married Maria Louisa Rodriquez.

In 1867 Helper settled in Asheville. He was described at this time as a "tall, strongly built man . . . and always alone." Despite the former Southern hatred and threats against his life, he was not molested in any way. He later lived in New York, St. Louis, and Washington, D.C.

Helper wrote five other books, three of which were extremely racist and unleashed intense hatred towards the Negro race. His writings contained rational, progressive, and farsighted viewpoints and ideas as well as irrationalities and illogical ideas which sometimes sounded like the ravings of a maniac. Historians John Spencer Bassett and J. G. de R. Hamilton have portrayed him as a man of keen intellect with a touch of genius which at times bordered on insanity. The Louisville *Courier Journal* once described him as having "an expression of unmistakable resolution written all over his countenance and an air of manifest sincerity in his every utterance."

After about 1890 Helper spent most of his time in Washington, D.C. His wife became blind and returned to South America with their son. Helper's mental instability worsened and he eventually committed suicide. His burial plot was donated, and the burial expenses were paid by the Authors Society of New York. His grave is unmarked.

When he died, the *Courier Journal* wrote: "The world had wrestled with him and thrown him. His mind was shattered and his heart broken. Friendless, penniless, and alone, he took his own life, and died at the age of eighty—this man who had shaken the Republic from center to circumference and who at a critical period had held and filled the center of the stage."

Helper and *The Impending Crisis* indeed "had shaken the Republic from center to circumference." Though he said that the book was intended to help the nonslave-holding whites (three-fourths of the South's population disadvantaged by slavery), it was, in reality, a powerful and dangerous abolitionist work. The 150 pages of statistics from the census of 1850, indiscriminately used to show that the slave states were at a disadvantage in every area of comparison with the free states, had little influence. The real impact of the book came from its scathing denunciation of Southern slave owners, whom the author branded as "robbers, thieves, ruffians, and murderers," and the admonishment to the slave to gain freedom by violence if necessary.

Republican party leaders endorsed the printing of a compendium of the book for distribution in the presidential campaign of 1860. This endorsement led to the "Speakership Flight" in the House of Representatives between 5 Dec. 1859 and 1 Feb. 1860. The debate there about *The Impending Crisis* and the Republican party's endorsement of it gave the book nationwide recognition far out of proportion to its merit. Southern states passed stringent laws against the circulation of abolitionist literature, and persons were punished for possessing the Helper volume.

Hinton Rowan Helper and *The Impending Crisis* shaped history. Historian James Ford Rhodes wrote that the book "proved a potent Republican document especially in the doubtful states of New Jersey, Pennsylvania, Indiana, and Illinois, where it was easier to arouse sympathy for the degraded white than for the oppressed Negro." James Gordon Bennett, editor of the New York *Herald*, reportedly handed a copy to President James Buchanan in the summer of 1857 with the statement: "There is gunpowder enough in that book to blow the Union to the devil." In January 1861 the *Herald* declared that Lincoln's election had been due to "this very work of Mr. Helper, and kindred speeches and documents."

SEE: H. C. Bailey, *Hinton Rowan Helper: Abolitionist-Racist* (1965); *DAB*, vol. 4 (1960); Hugh T. Lefler, "Hinton Rowan Helper, Advocate of a 'White America,'" *Southern Sketches* 1 (1935); Martin Collection (Davie County Library, Mocksville) for information regarding Helper; North Carolina Collection and Southern Historical Collection (University of North Carolina Library, Chapel Hill), Manuscript Department (Duke University Library, Durham), and North Carolina State Archives (Raleigh), for printed and manuscript sources on Helper; James W. Wall, *The History of Davie County* (1969); and "Hinton Rowan Helper and *The Impending Crisis*" (M.A. thesis, University of North Carolina, 1949). The St. Louis (Mo.) Mercantile Library Association has a collection of Helper's books and pamphlets including his personal copy of *The Impending Crisis* with his marginal notes.

JAMES W. WALL

Henderson, Archibald (7 Aug. 1768–21 Oct. 1822), congressman, legislator, and lawyer, was born near Williamsboro in Granville County. His father was Richard Henderson, promoter of the Transylvania colony in Kentucky and a descendant of Thomas Henderson who emigrated from England to Virginia early in the eighteenth century. His mother was Elizabeth Keeling. Young Henderson attended a local academy, studied law under Judge John Williams, and began to practice in Salisbury. Returning to Granville County, he was clerk of the county court from 1795 to 1798. He was elected to Congress in 1798 and served two terms. As a Federalist, he voted for Aaron Burr instead of Thomas Jefferson in the House election of 1801. On 23 Feb. 1801 Henderson published a three-page letter—apparently sent to his constituents—in which he discussed the presidential election, the meaning of freedom of the press, and other timely topics. (A copy of this letter is in the North Carolina Collection, University of North Carolina Library, Chapel Hill.) Because the Republicans controlled the state, he declined to run for a third term; instead, he represented Salisbury in the North Carolina legislature for five terms between 1807 and 1820.

Henderson's chief distinction was his long and extensive practice of law. He was considered by John Marshall to be "unquestionably" one of the ablest lawyers of his time. Henderson also served as president of the Salisbury branch of the State Bank of North Carolina and vice-president of the Raleigh chapter of the American Colonization Society. Following his death the state bar association erected a monument over his grave in Salisbury.

Henderson married Sarah Alexander in 1801, and they were the parents of Roger (died young), Archibald, and Jane Caroline.

SEE: John L. Cheney, Jr., ed., *North Carolina Government, 1585–1979* (1981); Archibald Henderson, *North Carolina: The Old North State and the New*, vol. 5 (1941); Lucy Henderson Horton, *Family History* (1922); Archibald D. Murphey, "Sketch . . . of Archibald Henderson," *Raleigh Star*, 10 Jan. 1823, reprinted in W. H. Hoyt, ed., *The Papers of Archibald D. Murphey*, vol. 2 (1914); *North Carolina Booklet* (July, October 1917); *Raleigh Register*, 1 Nov. 1822.

STANLEY J. FOLMSBEE

Henderson, Archibald (17 July 1877–6 Dec. 1963), mathematician, teacher, literary critic, biographer, and historian, was born at Lombardy, his grandfather's home in Salisbury. He was the son of Elizabeth Brownrigg Cain and John Steele Henderson, Democratic representative to the United States Congress from 1885 to 1895. His ancestors included Richard Henderson, president of the company that sent Daniel Boone to explore the western lands of Tennessee and Kentucky; John Steele, George Washington's comptroller of the Treasury; and Archibald Henderson, a U.S. congressman and state legislator between 1799 and 1820.

Archibald Henderson, third of that name, was a man of astonishingly varied virtuosity and undeniable genius. Towards the end of his career, he himself divided his many interests thus: "Mathematics, and the allied sciences of physics and astronomy, have absorbed . . . my fullest interest through some fifty years of my life. . . . Concurrently with these scientific studies ran another deep and abiding impulse: the passion for a grasp and mastery of some of the leading thought movements of the time, especially in . . . literature, drama, history and philosophy." The pure science of his first love was, of course, without boundary; in the "thought movements" of the second, he was consistently both internationalist and regionalist.

He began his studies at home under the tutelage of his grandmother, who instilled in him a love of reading and, as he said, "an insatiable interest in world affairs." He entered The University of North Carolina in 1894, was graduated first in his class in 1898, and earned a master's degree the following year. For fifty years Henderson was a member of the Department of Mathematics at Chapel Hill: he received a doctorate in 1902, became a full professor in 1908, succeeded his uncle, Dr. William Cain, as department head in 1920, and was appointed Kenan Professor in 1925, serving until his retirement in 1948. In 1915 he had earned a second Ph.D. from the University of Chicago. Under his direction, the mathematics department expanded enormously, increasing its graduate program, adding (to a curriculum largely designed for engineers) extensive opportunities in pure mathematics, and acquiring a departmental library that is among the best in the South.

Henderson was a prolific writer on scientific topics. His *Twenty-seven Lines Upon the Cubic Surface* (1911), completed during a year of study at Cambridge, the Sorbonne, and the University of Berlin, was the first American book included in the prestigious series of Cambridge Tracts in Mathematics and Mathematical Physics. It was also the first volume on the subject and for over thirty years the only one.

About 1920 he became interested in Einstein's theory of relativity and within two years was writing articles about it. The year 1923–24 he spent on sabbatical, studying at Cambridge and the University of Berlin where he came to know Einstein personally. Among his important interpretations of the German physicist's work was "The Triumph of Relativity," the defending portion of a debate published in *Forum* (July 1924); Dr. Einstein himself commented that it left little room for refutation. Related articles included "The Size of the Universe," his presidential address to the North Carolina Academy of Science in 1923; and "Is the Universe Finite?" an address to the American Association for the Advancement of Science in 1925. Henderson collaborated with J. W. Lasley, Jr., and A. W. Hobbs on a textbook, *The Theory of Relativity*, published in 1924.

The breadth and depth of his learning was made available not only to the scientific community but also to students, who found him a skillful and challenging teacher. Because he had the true teacher's wish to make pure science intelligible to the layman, Henderson wrote more than 750 brief articles on scientific subjects which were syndicated in Hearst newspapers.

His second interest, in the cultural and philosophical movements of his time, was most evident in his relationship with George Bernard Shaw. In 1903, inspired by an amateur performance of Shaw's *You Never Can Tell*, he began a study of the Irish dramatist and resolved to bring public attention to a man he felt was an "unappreciated and undiscovered genius." He wrote to Shaw asking for biographical information; Shaw answered, and other letters were exchanged—one of them a manuscript of more than 12,000 words, written by Shaw in January 1905. Henderson was accepted as Shaw's authorized biographer, visited Ayot St. Lawrence in 1907, and for the rest of the older man's life they were in close correspondence. He wrote three complete biographies: *George Bernard Shaw: His Life and Works* (1911), *Bernard Shaw: Playboy and Prophet* (1932), and *George Bernard Shaw: Man of the Century* (1956)— each of which received an award from the North Carolina Literary and Historical Association as well as wide notice internationally. Interspersed with the books were nearly 100 articles and speeches on Shaw's plays, his novels, his socialism, and his public, some of which were translated into other languages for publication in Europe. His studies were often compared with Boswell's study of Dr. Johnson, frequently to Boswell's disadvantage. In 1933, the Carolina Playmakers staged a Shaw-Henderson Festival in Chapel Hill, featuring *You Never Can Tell*, the play that started it all. Acclamations for Henderson's work poured in from university presidents, editors, dramatists, critics, theatrical producers, and writers of several countries including W. B. Yeats, Edwin Markham (who had, fifteen years earlier, written an appreciation of Henderson in the *Sewanee Review*), Arthur Pinero, and his old friend Albert Einstein.

Henderson's interest in theater neither started nor ended with Shaw. He had published articles on Maurice Maeterlinck before he discovered Shaw, and to those he added, over the years, evaluations of Ibsen, Hauptmann, Rostand, Wilde, Strindberg, and many others of many lands. Most noted were two books, *European Dramatists* (1913) and *The Changing Drama* (1914), both recognizing the international theatrical revolt that followed the work of Ibsen.

From its beginning in 1918, the drama department at Chapel Hill found Henderson an ally and a collaborator. In several articles, he demonstrated an optimism about the future of American drama before most people had noticed its past. He wrote about early drama and entertainment in North Carolina, collected American plays, composed a foreword for Frederick Koch's anthology of *Carolina Folk Comedies*, and edited and contributed to the *Carolina Play-Book*.

On the ship that carried Henderson to England for his first meeting with Shaw, a fellow passenger was Mark Twain. The two men formed a friendship, out of which were born several articles by Henderson and a complete biography, *Mark Twain* (1911). Again, a general interest in fiction had preceded the meeting with a great writer, for Henderson had already written about George Meredith. He was also drawn to regional writers, like Frances Christine Fisher Tierman ("Christian Reid") of Salisbury.

Henderson's roots were deep in North Carolina, by choice as well as by birth. Several times he declined offers from magazines and from prestigious universities (including presidencies) because he preferred to stay in Chapel Hill. His family's illustrious past may have originally awakened an interest in history, particularly of his own state and region; in that field, too, he was an eager student and a knowledgeable writer. Some of the subjects were his ancestors: Elizabeth Maxwell Steele, John Steele, Richard Henderson, and the first Archibald. He produced a history of St. Luke's Parish in Salisbury and a book about the Chapel of the Cross in Chapel Hill, his own churches. Fervent devotion to his native state made him a defender of the "Mecklenburg Declaration of Independence," said to have been written before Jefferson's Declaration.

Although a Jeffersonian Democrat, Henderson wrote little of a political nature. But he did advocate in print, at least as early as 1910, extending the franchise to women.

His chief historical works included *The Conquest of the Old Southwest* (1920), concerning westward expansion into Kentucky and Tennessee (in which his forebear was involved); *Washington's Southern Tour* (1923); and *North Carolina: The Old North State and the New* (1941), for which he wrote two volumes of history to be followed by three volumes of biographies composed by various persons. The last work was praised by historians for its attention to cultural development as well as economic and political matters. In 1949 he wrote about The University of North Carolina in *The Campus of the First State University.* At various times over a period of years, he wrote nearly 150 short pieces on state history for North Carolina newspapers.

Even that phenomenal amount of writing together with his teaching and administrative duties did not exhaust the energy of Archibald Henderson. Genial and sociable, he was a frequent and sought-after public speaker and, during much of his life, an enthusiastic sportsman, participating in tennis, baseball, and hiking.

His various projects resulted in enormous collections of research materials, and the generosity of the man and his survivors has enriched several libraries. When the University Library in Chapel Hill was dedicated, he established a collection of American drama, which he subsequently enlarged. In 1937 he donated many of his Shaw materials to Yale University in memory of his grandfather, who had attended that school. On his retirement he gave to The University of North Carolina Library a large collection of Shaw materials—first editions, inscribed copies, manuscripts, and letters. Both that library and the Rowan Public Library in Salisbury have his materials on southern history. Portraits of Henderson hang in the Chapel Hill and Rowan libraries, as well as in the Dialectic Society at Chapel Hill.

Honors rained upon him. Besides his four earned degrees, he held honorary degrees from the University of the South, Tulane, the College of William and Mary, Oglethorpe, Catawba, and his alma mater. On his seventy-fifth birthday, he was elected a Fellow of the Royal Society of Literature, the first American to be so honored.

In 1903 Henderson married Minna Curtis Bynum (Barbara), and they had five children: Mary Curtis, Elizabeth Brownrigg, Barbara Gray, Archibald, and John Steele. After his first wife's death he married, in 1957, Lucile Kelling, then dean of the School of Library Science at The University of North Carolina.

Henderson died at Fordell, his home in Chapel Hill, and was buried in the Chestnut Hill Cemetery, Salisbury.

SEE: *Baltimore Evening Sun*, 3 June 1937; *Charlotte Observer*, 2 Oct. 1932; *Durham Morning Herald*, 3 Oct. 1948; *Greensboro Daily News*, 22 Dec. 1957, 26 Jan. 1964; Archibald Henderson, "Fifty Years at the University," *State Magazine* 12 (24 June 1944); Lucile Kelling Henderson, "Archibald Henderson," *Shaw Review* 7 (1964); Eldon C. Hill, "Shaw's Biographer-in-Chief," *Modern Drama* 2 (1959); S. S. Hood, ed., *Archibald Henderson: The New Crichton* (1949); Salisbury *Evening Post*, 25 Apr., 7 Dec. 1963; Shaw-Henderson Festival, "Archibald Henderson" (monograph, 1933); C. Alphonso Smith, "Archibald Henderson," *Library of Southern Literature*, vol. 17 (1923).

ROSAMOND PUTZEL

Henderson, Barbara Bynum (12 Dec. 1880–25 Mar. 1955), poet, translator, and pioneer leader in the North Carolina woman suffrage movement, was born into a family closely connected with the Episcopal church. Her father, William Shipp Bynum, was an Episcopal clergyman and her mother, Mary Louise Curtis, was the daughter of the Reverend Moses Ashley Curtis, headmaster of the Episcopal School for Boys (predecessor of Saint Mary's College, Raleigh), rector of several churches in the state, and noted botanist and mycologist. Her formative years were spent in Salem (where she was born), Charlotte, and Lincolnton. After graduating with high honors from Saint Mary's College in 1899, she continued her studies at The University of North Carolina where she was elected to Phi Beta Kappa and was graduated in 1902 with the A.B. and M.A. degrees. In college, she wrote numerous poems which were widely copied by college papers and published in anthologies of American college verse.

While attending The University of North Carolina she became engaged to fellow student Archibald Henderson, and in June 1903 they were married. The couple lived in Chapel Hill, where Dr. Henderson was a member of the university faculty, and became the parents of five children: Mary Curtis (b. 8 Nov. 1904), Elizabeth (b. 5 Nov. 1908), Barbara (b. 14 May 1914), Archibald (b. 20 Dec. 1916), and John (b. 3 Mar. 1918).

Mrs. Henderson is best known for her translation from German of Hans Ernst Lissauer's "Hassgesang gegen England" ("Hymn of Hate against England"). The translation was published widely in newspapers and periodicals in this country and abroad, shortly becoming more famous than the original German poem. When it appeared in *The Times* of London, that paper in a long and enthusiastic editorial commented, "She is to be congratulated on a piece of extraordinarily good work in one of the most difficult arts. The lines have a fine natural swing and the language glows with the fire of intense sincerity."

Mrs. Henderson also gained considerable recognition as a poet in her own right. "The March of Women," published in 1915 during the suffrage struggle, became very popular and helped to rally the women of North Carolina in their battle for the ballot. A poem she wrote about Colonel Charles A. Lindbergh was chosen for a commemorative volume, *The Spirit of Saint Louis.* The last of her poems to receive wide publication was "Prayer for All-Souls," which appeared in the *Saturday Review of Literature* in 1944. *Wars and Rumors of War*, a volume of eighteen poems and translations concerning World Wars I and II, was published in 1950. On her death, she left a large number of unpublished poems.

In addition to her literary interests, Mrs. Henderson distinguished herself as a leader of the suffrage movement in North Carolina. In 1913 she organized and was elected president of the Equal Suffrage League of North Carolina, and in 1915 she was unanimously reelected for a second term. Besides organizing and leading the movement, she was responsible for carrying the battle into the General Assembly when a special session was called to consider woman suffrage. She also published several poems and bulletins to help the cause.

Mrs. Henderson died after an illness of several years, survived by her husband, five children, sixteen grandchildren, and four great-grandchildren. She was buried at Calvary Episcopal Church in Fletcher.

SEE: *Chapel Hill Weekly*, 1 Apr. 1955; *Charlotte Observer*, 26 Mar. 1955; Eliza Polk McGehee, "Barbara (Bynum) Henderson" (Manuscript Department, Duke University Library, Durham).

CAROLYN MURRAY HAPPER

Henderson, Isabelle Bowen (23 Mar. 1899–19 May 1969), portraitist and floriculturist, was born in Wilmington, the daughter of Arthur Finn Bowen, who was for many years business manager of North Carolina State College, and Isabelle Woodward Bowen, of an old Wilmington family. After attending the Raleigh public schools, she entered Peace College in 1917 and was graduated in 1919. She taught art at the Centennial School in Raleigh from 1919 to 1921; at College Hill School, Easton, Pa., from 1922 to 1924; and at various times prior to 1930 in summer sessions at North Carolina State and at Wake Forest College. In 1921–23 she continued to study art during the summer at Columbia University and at the School of Fine and Applied Arts (now Parsons School) in New York City. In 1924–25 she was a student at the Pennsylvania Academy of Art in Philadelphia.

She began her career as a professional portraitist in Raleigh in the late 1920s. After her marriage to Professor Edgar H. Henderson in 1932, she moved to Williamstown, Mass., where her husband was a member of the faculty of Williams College. On returning to Raleigh in 1936, she opened a studio and became widely known in the eastern part of the state especially for her crayon portraits of children. In the 1940s she continued painting in Raleigh and in Gainesville, Fla., where her husband had joined the faculty of the University of Florida. In addition to her crayon portraits for many leading North Carolina families, she was commissioned to do oil portraits of such prominent figures as President Frank Porter Graham of The University of North Carolina, President Wallace Carl Riddick of North Carolina State College, Supreme Court Justice Beverly Lake, and Dr. Charles Carroll of the North Carolina Department of Public Instruction.

Mrs. Henderson's garden early became famous both in the area and beyond for its collection of iris and hemerocallis, for the hybridization of which she received the highest award of the National Society of State Garden Clubs in 1951 and recognition from the National Horticulture Society. She was active in the Raleigh Garden Club as well as a popular lecturer in garden clubs throughout the region. She was also an important and forceful member of the North Carolina Art Society and was one of the moving spirits in the establishment and development of the North Carolina Art Museum. Mrs. Henderson was mainly responsible for the museum's excellent collection of Jugtown pottery.

SEE: Ola Maie Foushee, *Art in North Carolina* (1972); Raleigh *News and Observer*, 7 July 1957, 20 May 1969.

LODWICK HARTLEY

Henderson, James Pinckney (31 Mar. 1809–June 1858), soldier, lawyer, diplomat, and first governor of Texas, was born in Lincolnton, the son of Lawson and Elizabeth Carruth Henderson. He received his early education at Lincoln Academy, apparently studied law privately in Chapel Hill, was admitted to the bar in 1829, and practiced in North Carolina. Having demonstrated an interest in the militia, Henderson was named aide-de-camp with the rank of major at age twenty-two; later he served as colonel of a regiment. In 1835 he moved to Canton, Miss., where he developed a popular legal practice, an excellent reputation, and a desire to participate in the Texas revolution. In the spring of 1836 he organized a company of Mississippi volunteers to assist the struggling republic, but the Mexicans surrendered before Henderson reached Texas. He then joined other newly arrived Americans to prevent the return of Santa Anna to Mexico by Texas authorities. The Texas government appointed him a general and sent him to recruit troops in the United States. He is reported to have brought a company of North Carolina men to Texas at his own expense.

When Sam Houston took office as president of Texas in 1836, he named Henderson attorney general. Following the death of Stephen F. Austin a short time later, Houston made him secretary of state. In 1837, the president commissioned Henderson as agent and minister plenipotentiary to England and France to seek recognition for the new republic. Henderson failed to persuade the British to recognize Texas, but they did agree to a trade convention. He was more successful in France, which recognized the new nation in 1839. Henderson returned to Texas in January 1840 with his bride, Frances Cox of Philadelphia, whom he had recently married in London. They settled in San Augustine where he practiced law. The Hendersons had five children, two of whom died young.

In 1844, Houston sent him to Washington, D.C., to assist Isaac Van Zandt, Texas chargé d'affaires, in annexation negotiations. Representatives of the two countries agreed to a treaty, but the U.S. Senate rejected it. Houston then recalled Henderson. The next year, however, by joint resolution, the United States agreed to annex Texas, and the Texans accepted the offer. Henderson served as a member of the convention to draw up a state constitution for Texas, as required for its admission to the Union. In the same year he was elected governor of Texas and took office on 19 Feb. 1846, when the republic formally came to an end.

When war with Mexico broke out in 1846, the state legislature granted the governor a leave of absence to serve in the army as a major general. He participated in the Battle of Monterey and was one of three American commissioners who negotiated the surrender of that city.

After completing his term as governor, Henderson returned to his law practice. In 1857, the legislature elected him to fill the unexpired term of the late Senator Thomas J. Rusk. Henderson died while in Washington, D.C., and was buried in the Congressional Cemetery. His body was reinterred at Austin, Tex., in 1930. Henderson County, Tex., was named in his honor.

SEE: *DAB*, vol. 4 (1960); George P. Garrison, ed., *Diplomatic Correspondence of the Republic of Texas: Annual Report of the American Historical Association*, 3 vols. (1908–11); Elizabeth Y. Morris, "James Pinckney Henderson" (Master's thesis, University of Texas, 1931); Joseph W. Schmitz, *Texan Statecraft: 1836–1845* (1941); F. B. Sexton, "J. Pinckney Henderson," *Quarterly, Texas State Historical*

Association 1 (1897–98); Robert G. Winchester, *James Pinckney Henderson: Texas' First Governor* (1971).

J. TUFFLY ELLIS

Henderson, John Steele (6 Jan. 1846–9 Oct. 1916), member of the General Assembly, U.S. congressman, city planner, lawyer, and a founder of rural free delivery of the mail, was born in Salisbury of English ancestry, the son of Archibald II and Mary Ferrand Henderson, a descendant of General John Steele, comptroller of the U.S. Treasury under Washington, Adams, and Jefferson. He was born in the old John Steele Home, educated at Alexander Wilson's school in Alamance County, and entered The University of North Carolina in January 1862. Five months after the death of his brother at Cold Harbor on 1 June 1864, Henderson left the university at age eighteen and enlisted as a private in Company B, Tenth Regiment, North Carolina troops.

Following the surrender, he and other former students who had left The University of North Carolina before qualifying were granted degrees. Henderson then studied law, first under Nathaniel Boyden, then under Judge Richmond Pearson beginning in January 1866. Five months later he obtained his license, and although not of age, opened a law office in Salisbury. He was soon elected register of deeds, serving until September 1868, and in 1867 he obtained a license to practice in the superior courts. In 1871 he was elected a delegate to a proposed constitutional convention, but the convention question was not approved by a vote of the people. After declining nominations to the General Assembly in 1872 and 1874, he was elected a delegate to the constitutional convention in 1875 and became an active member of that body. He was a member of the 1876–77 General Assembly, which implemented changes made at the constitutional convention. In the next General Assembly (1879) he was returned to the state senate, and in 1880 he was elected a delegate-at-large to the Democratic National Convention. Henderson was one of three men selected to codify the laws of North Carolina; they did the job so well that these law remained unchanged for twenty years. In 1884 he was elected presiding justice of the inferior court of Rowan County, and the following October was nominated for a seat in the United States Congress. Henderson was elected to the Forty-fifth Congress and to four succeeding congresses, serving from 4 Mar. 1885 to 3 Mar. 1895.

In Congress, he was a member of the judiciary committee and chairman of the committee on post offices and post roads. His speeches on tariff reform and the internal revenue system attracted wide attention as campaign documents. In 1890, when the Farmers' Alliance was in the ascendant in the state, he declared that the subtreasury scheme was unconstitutional. His stand on the issue was opposed by most Democratic leaders, but so great was the public confidence in his judgment that he was reelected by a majority of more than 4,000 votes.

Henderson's most important work in Congress came in 1893, when he safeguarded an appropriation bill for the Post Office Department, amended to provide for free rural mail delivery, and an appropriation of $10,000 to carry it out. The first trial routes under the appropriation after it had been gradually increased to $40,000 were at Charleston, Halltown, and Uvilla in West Virginia, the native state of William L. Wilson, then postmaster general. At about the same time a trial route was established out of China Grove near Salisbury,

Henderson's birthplace and residence. His opposition to the free coinage of silver in 1894 was contrary to the view of most of the farmers in his district and probably caused him not to seek reelection the following year. But time has shown his wisdom in opposing such a scheme in that day of frenzied financial panaceas.

Henderson was no less active in the development of his county and state. It was he to whom the Southern Railway turned in acquiring land near Salisbury for its large shops to repair steam engines. On this land stands the town of Spencer, which was begun in 1898. In the development of the Narrows of the Yadkin River, he was associated with Captain E. B. C. Hambley who secured capital for the development of water power in that area. Financial depression during this period aborted the scheme, yet the Aluminum Company of America took it over and later completed the development, including the great dam at Badin. As general counsel, Henderson won a crucial case in defending the rights of his clients against the aggression of other investors.

As probably the largest landowner in Salisbury and surrounding areas, Henderson was one of the city's earliest planners. When the Zion Wesley Institute (now Livingstone College) was established in Salisbury in 1882, Henderson with H. N. Woodson purchased 23 acres adjoining the institute and laid out streets and lots. In July 1891 he bought a large portion of land from Edwin Shaver and developed streets and lots in east Salisbury under the name of the Central Land Company. In 1900 Henderson's real estate company purchased land on the east side of the Southern Railway opposite Spencer and established Southern City. After its incorporation in 1901, the name was changed to East Spencer.

Henderson was generous with his vast holdings. In October 1889 he and his first cousin, Archibald Henderson Boyden, offered the Mill Bridge Alliance 25 acres of land in Salisbury for twenty-five years if it would move its annual fair to Salisbury. Again, in May 1900 Henderson offered a site for a proposed Lutheran college in the city. Both of these offers were declined, however. His son, John S. Henderson, Jr., later gave part of his father's land to the city of Salisbury for a park and donated land on which the Rowan Memorial Hospital is situated.

A member of St. Luke's Episcopal Church, Henderson was for many years senior warden. He wrote a history of the episcopacy in Rowan County which appeared in Dr. Jethro Rumple's *History of Rowan County*, published in 1881. During the 1880s Henderson and the Reverend Francis Murdoch published *The Register*, a quarterly parish paper. Henderson also was instrumental in acquiring a large house and lot in Chestnut Hill for a boys school, which operated successfully from 1891 to 1899.

His interest in education was further demonstrated in 1880, when, as a member of the General Assembly, he adjusted the city tax rate so that the graded school law for Salisbury could pass on the local level. As a result, the law passed in the city by a vote of 311 to 11 and two new graded schools, one for each race, were erected. This action probably explains why he was made chairman of the Rowan County school board, a post he held for many years. The year before his death he expressed the desire, while chairman, "to extend the school terms in the county . . . for the full period of nine calendar months."

After retiring from Congress, Henderson served as a state senator (1900–1902) and as an alderman for the city of Salisbury (1900). He was a trustee of The University of North Carolina from 1877 to 1886 and received an LL.D. from Trinity College (now Duke University) in June 1890. In 1877 he was elected a director of the Western North Carolina Railroad and served until 1880, when the railroad was sold by the state. He cooperated in the completion of that road and favored its sale. He was also a director of the Yadkin Railroad which ran from Salisbury to Norwood, a bank director, and a director in the Yadkin Valley Fair Association.

In October 1874 Henderson married Elizabeth Brownrigg Cain in Asheville; she was the daughter of William Cain of Hillsborough and a sister of Dr. William Cain, electrical engineer and mathematics professor at Chapel Hill. They were the parents of Elizabeth Brownrigg Henderson, who married Captain Lyman Cotton; Archibald Henderson, Kenan Professor of Mathematics at Chapel Hill; John Steele Henderson, Jr., electrical engineer for Westinghouse; and Mary Ferrand Henderson, who spent much of her life working in the Democratic party and promoting women's political rights.

Henderson died at Blythewood, the home he built on the edge of Salisbury in 1878, and was buried in the Chestnut Hill Cemetery.

SEE: Samuel A. Ashe, ed., *Biographical History of North Carolina*, vol. 1 (1905); *Biog. Dir. Am. Cong.* (1928); *Cyclopedia of Eminent and Representative Men of the Carolinas of the Nineteenth Century*, vol. 2 (1892); *Makers of America*, vol. 2 (1916); *National Cyclopedia of American Biography*, vol. 9 (1899); Raleigh *News and Observer*, 10 Oct. 1916, 13 Jan. 1935; Salisbury *Carolina Watchman*, 8 Oct. 1874, 22 Apr. 1880, 19 Oct. 1882, 16 July 1891; *Salisbury Post*, 17 July 1907, 31 Jan. 1954; *Salisbury Herald*, 10 Oct. 1889, 10 May 1900; *Sketches of Prominent Living North Carolinians* (1888).

JAMES SHOBER BRAWLEY

Henderson, Leonard (*6 Oct. 1772–13 Aug. 1833*), lawyer, teacher, and chief justice of the North Carolina Supreme Court, was born in the Nutbush community near Williamsboro, Granville County, the third son of six children of Richard and Elizabeth Keeling Henderson. His grandfather was Samuel Henderson, first sheriff of the county, and his wife, Elizabeth Williams, who had moved there from Hanover, Va., in 1740. At their home, Jonesboro, the Richard Hendersons raised two daughters (Fannie, who married Judge Spruce Macay; and Elizabeth, who became Mrs. William Lee Alexander) and four sons (Richard, who moved to Virginia and became a judge; Archibald, who moved to Salisbury and there married the sister of Governor Nathaniel Alexander; Leonard; and John Lawson, who often represented the borough of Salisbury in the General Assembly, and was comptroller of the state and clerk of the Supreme Court in Raleigh).

Leonard's education was confined to instruction by local teachers and the Reverend Henry Pattillo, the prescribed courses at Springer College, and one or two sessions at a school in Salisbury. Afterwards he studied law at Williamsboro under Judge John Williams, of Montpelier, who had married Henderson's maternal grandmother and with whom he lived after the death of his parents. He was admitted to the bar and for a time was clerk of the district court in Hillsborough. A Freemason, in 1797 he was senior warden of Hiram Lodge No. 24. In 1802 he was elected to the Council of State, and in 1807 he was appointed a commissioner of the town of Williamsboro.

In 1808, two years after the district system of courts was abolished, Henderson was elected by the General Assembly to fill a vacancy on the Superior Court bench caused by the death of Judge Spruce Macay. The election of Henderson, a thoroughgoing Federalist and an ardent supporter of Alexander Hamilton and John Marshall, was a high tribute to his character and eminent qualifications, as the legislature was solidly Republican. About this time Henderson opened a law school at Williamsboro and soon earned a reputation for thoroughness and accuracy. Although he did not formulate the case method of instruction, his pupils were well versed in concrete cases selected by Henderson from numerous volumes. Among the many young men who studied with him were Richmond M. Pearson, William Horn Battle, Robert Ballard Gilliam, Robert H. Burton, and Hutchins G. Burton. The school at Henderson's home, Jonesboro, was the forerunner of Richmond Hill and The University of North Carolina law schools.

After eight years as a Superior Court judge and with a growing family, Henderson resigned in 1816 to resume his law practice in Williamsboro and teach in his law school. In 1817 he was elected a trustee of The University of North Carolina, serving until his resignation in 1828. Late in 1818 the court system was again changed and the Supreme Court of North Carolina was established. Judges Henderson and John Hall, with John Louis Taylor as chief justice, comprised the first court. In 1829, after the death of Taylor, Henderson became chief justice, a position he held until his own death.

Henderson County and the cities of Henderson and Hendersonville were all named in the judge's honor. He was described as a large man, over six feet tall and weighing 212 pounds, with dark hair, gray eyes, a large, symmetrical head, and a long chin. He was buried at Montpelier, his childhood home, and survived by his wife, Frances Farrar, whom he had married on 3 Nov. 1795; she was the niece of Judge John Williams, who had guided his legal studies at Williamsboro. They had four sons and two daughters: Archibald Erskine, William Farrar, John Leonard, and Richard (who died three years before his father), Fannie (who married Dr. William V. Taylor and moved to Memphis, Tenn.), and Lucy (who married Dr. Richard Sneed and moved to Henderson, Ky.).

A portrait of Chief Justice Henderson was presented to the North Carolina Supreme Court on 20 Apr. 1909.

SEE: John L. Cheney, Jr., ed., *North Carolina Government, 1585–1979* (1981); *DAB*, vol. 4 (1960); T. B. Kingsbury, "Chief Justice Leonard Henderson," *Wake Forest Historical Society Papers* (1899); Samuel T. Peace, "Zeb's Black Baby," *Vance County, North Carolina* (1955); Nannie May Tilley, "Studies in the History of Colonial Granville County" (M.A. thesis, Duke University, 1931); C. L. Van Noppen Papers (Manuscript Department, Duke University Library, Durham); John B. Watkins, *Historic Vance County* (1941); John H. Wheeler, *Historical Sketches of North Carolina* (1851).

LUCY B. ROYSTER

Henderson, Mary Ferrand (*13 Oct. 1887–4 July 1965*), Democratic party official and promoter of women's political rights, was born in Salisbury, the daughter of John Steele Henderson, a North Carolina legislator and congressman, and Elizabeth Cain Henderson. One of seven children, she was the sister of Archibald Henderson, mathematician and professor, and Elizabeth Henderson Cotton, Democratic party activist and woman suffragist.

Mary Henderson spent her childhood in Salisbury where she received her early education. She was graduated from St. Mary's School, Raleigh, in 1903, attended the Stuart School in Washington, D.C., and studied law at The University of North Carolina in 1915–16 and 1933–34.

Working ardently for woman suffrage, she became the first legislative chairman of the Equal Suffrage League of North Carolina. In 1920 she served as vice-chairman of the Democratic party in Rowan County. Appointed first vice-chairman of the North Carolina Democratic party executive committee in 1922, Miss Henderson was the first woman to serve in that position. In 1924 she was elected to the office and served until her voluntary resignation in 1930.

When the number of North Carolina delegates-at-large was increased in 1924 from four to eight, she figured prominently in the successful drive to establish a four-man–four-woman delegation, and she was elected as one of the four women. Between 1928 and 1930, Miss Henderson led the voter registration drive for Democratic women. During the 1930s she continued to be an active campaigner for her party. In 1934, she was an unsuccessful candidate for the position of national committeewoman from North Carolina to the Democratic party.

Miss Henderson was the first woman to serve on the Alumni Council of The University of North Carolina. Throughout her life she advocated the adoption of the Australian ballot, longer school terms for rural communities, and more widely based welfare legislation. She also held offices in the Daughters of the American Revolution, United Daughters of the Confederacy, YWCA, and the Woman's Club. She died in Chapel Hill where she had resided since 1933.

SEE: Lyman Cotton Papers, Archibald Henderson Papers (Southern Historical Collection, University of North Carolina Library, Chapel Hill); *North Carolina Biography*, vol. 5 (1941); Raleigh *News and Observer*, 22 July 1934, 5 July 1965.

CAROLYN HOWARD CARTER

Henderson, Philo P. *(February 1823–21 July 1852)*, poet, was born in Central Mecklenburg County, the son of James P. and Harriet Wallace Henderson. The Henderson family was a proud one of Scottish descent. Philo had two brothers and two sisters: Matthew, who died young; Thomas Cairns, salutatorian of the 1856 class at Davidson College; Martha (Mrs. E. L. Burney); and Lilly (Mrs. J. C. Caldwell). A well-to-do farmer and later a merchant, the father early recognized Philo's potential and sent the boy to the Latin academy at Sugar Creek Church after elementary schooling near the farm.

In 1839 Henderson was enrolled at Davidson College, where his intellectual qualities were somewhat offset by an arrogant impetuosity. On one occasion, at a meeting of the Philanthropic Society, he was "fined 6¼ cts. for leaning against the wall." Later, after a minor altercation in the dining hall, he drew a knife on the steward and the next day threatened the man with a pistol. For this offense—to the distress of the students among whom he was "entertaining, popular and magnetic"—he was expelled. He then entered The University of North Carolina as a sophomore. At Chapel Hill "he was rather wild," wrote a contemporary of his, "but never guilty of anything dishonorable." His record was with-

out distinction, his marks were only average, and his irregular attendance at required assemblies was reprehensible. In his senior year he was absent from chapel 12 times, from prayers 46, and from lectures 57. Even so, he was graduated with a B.A. in 1843 and went to Mocksville to study law with Judge Richmond Pearson.

After visiting his Henderson relatives in Missouri in 1844, he was granted a license to practice his profession and settled in Charlotte. At that time he was a handsome fellow, "his eye bright and beaming with poetic fire," his "luxurious curls" dropping "to his shoulders in rich profusion." His name, Philo, was indeed prophetic. The young ladies were attracted to him, and he to them. Often he fell in love, and always he wrote poems to commemorate his rapturous encounters. First there was Mary, and when they parted, he succumbed to a debilitating period of drink. At least thirty-nine of his uncollected poems have been cited in manuscript and in print. While five are addressed to a damsel named Rotha, the love of his life was Ada (Miss M. Addie McCleary of Mecklenburg County), about whom he wrote his most frequently reprinted poem, "The Flower of Catawba." Like the heroines in the works of Edgar Allan Poe, whose influence on Henderson is obvious, his young ladies seemed to be fragile maidens soon to die. Other typical verses of Henderson are "The Anthem of Heaven" and "On Receiving a Present from a Lady." Though not credited on the masthead, he served as unofficial assistant to editor J. Lawrence Badger of the weekly *Hornets' Nest* in Charlotte, where many of his poems first appeared.

It is said that "false friends betrayed Ada, and made her break, *at the same time that it broke her heart*," her plighted troth with Philo. And then *his* heart-strings snapped like the strings of a madman's taut-strung harp." He returned to his parents' home to recover, then, on a visit to Charlotte, became ill and died. "The Isle of Long Ago" and "Swannanoa," two esteemed poems of the day, have frequently been attributed to Henderson, but his authorship is not only unauthenticated but also unlikely. He was buried in the second cemetery at Sugar Creek Church, Charlotte.

SEE: J. B. Alexander, *The History of Mecklenburg County* (1902); Charlotte *North Carolina Whig*, 28 July, 4 Aug. 1852; Mary Bayard Clarke, ed., *Wood-Notes* (1854); John N. McCue, comp., *Henderson Chronicles* (1915); F. B. McDowell, "Davidson's Early History," *Charlotte Daily Observer*, 8 Feb. 1903; *North Carolina Booklet* (1926); *North Carolina University Magazine*, December 1856, March, August 1857; Philanthropic Society Minutes (Davidson College); Philo Henderson Manuscript and University Records (Southern Historical Collection, University of North Carolina Library, Chapel Hill); U.S. Census of 1850.

RICHARD WALSER

Henderson, Pleasant *(9 Jan. 1756–November 1840)*, pioneer, soldier, and merchant, was born in Granville County, possibly the youngest son of Samuel and Elizabeth Williams Henderson. In his late teens he became associated with his elder brother Richard, who had formed the Transylvania Company, in the opening of Kentucky to settlement. In 1775 he joined Daniel Boone and his party in cutting the Wilderness Road; he was described as a "fellow pioneer with Boone at Booneborough," the fort-settlement on the Kentucky River. Here on 23 May 1775 the first elected government of Transylvania met under the leadership of Richard Henderson. Nevertheless, the proposed fourteenth American colony failed to gain recognition by the Second Continental Congress chiefly because of the opposition of the Virginia delegation.

Pleasant Henderson returned to his parents' home in Granville and early in 1776 volunteered for duty in a county militia unit, which was sent to Cross Creek to meet the Highland Tory units gathered in support of the Crown. Henderson's unit arrived after the Battle of Moore's Creek Bridge and participated only in the rounding up of Tory supporters in the area. After several months' service, the unit was released. In late 1778 Henderson again volunteered for a militia company being formed at Charlotte to aid the states of South Carolina and Georgia, threatened by a new British invasion. He served as a lieutenant until April or May 1779 but was not involved in any major battle. During this campaign he briefly met his older brother William, who was a resident of South Carolina. Later in the war William became a general.

In 1779, North Carolina and Virginia agreed to extend the dividing line between their respective states and Richard Henderson was chosen a North Carolina commissioner. In November and December of that year, when the line was extended to the Tennessee River, Judge Henderson and his brothers Pleasant, Nathaniel, and Samuel were parties to the survey. The Henderson brothers continued on to Boonesborough and during the first half of 1780 were involved in efforts to form a government for Kentucky, bringing together the various Cumberland settlements and the remainder of the Transylvania Company. The result was the famous Cumberland Compact, prepared chiefly by Richard Henderson.

In 1781, following the Battle of Cowpens and the invasion of North Carolina by Cornwallis, Pleasant Henderson was called into service for the last time. Appointed major under the command of Colonel Malmedy, a Frenchman, he and his regiment joined General Nathanael Greene's army at Troublesome Iron Works two days after the Battle of Guilford Court House. They were later involved in a skirmish at Ramsey's Mill.

As clerk of the Council of State from 1782 to 1784, Henderson served as the private secretary of Governor Alexander Martin. The governor's sister, Anne Jane Martin, had married Henderson's brother, Thomas, in 1778 and from that time the two families were very close. In 1783 Pleasant was assigned a grant of 640 acres, which came to be known as Mt. Pleasant, adjoining Alexander Martin's Danbury estate.

When Judge Richard Henderson died in 1785, Pleasant acted as the executor of his estate. In January of the following year he married, in Surry (now Stokes) County, Sarah Martin, the daughter of Colonel James and Ruth Rogers Martin and a niece of Governor Alexander Martin. It appears that the couple resided primarily in Granville County until at least 1790, when they were listed in the census as living in Henderson District of that county. Soon afterwards they took up residence at Mt. Pleasant in Rockingham County.

In 1797 Henderson moved from Mt. Pleasant to Chapel Hill, where on 9 December he was chosen steward of The University of North Carolina. He built a large home on Franklin Street for his growing family and student boarders. In 1802 he gave up the job of steward and, though elected a trustee of the university, declined the office. At this time he opened a store called Henderson and Searcy. In 1807 he was elected clerk of the House of Commons, succeeding John Hunt who had held the office since 1778. Henderson served

until 1830, continuing his residence in Chapel Hill. In 1816 he sold his Mt. Pleasant home to his nephew, Alexander Henderson of New Bern.

On 21 May 1830 the Hendersons left Chapel Hill and on 7 July arrived in Carroll County, Tenn., where they established a new home. They were the parents of seven children: James Martin, William, Tippoo Saib, Mark Mitchell, Eliza Jane (Mrs. Hamilton C. Jones), Pleasant, and Alexander Martin. Henderson died in Tennessee.

SEE: John L. Cheney, Jr., ed., *North Carolina Government, 1585–1974* (1975); *Early Families of the North Carolina Counties of Rockingham and Stokes with Revolutionary Service* (1977); Archibald Henderson, *The Campus of the First State University* (1949) and "Richard Henderson: The Authorship of the Cumberland Compact and the Founding of Nashville," *North Carolina Booklet*, vol. 21, July-October 1921, January-April 1922; Pension Application: 12 Sept. 1832—Pleasant Henderson S1912 (National Archives, Washington, D.C.); Worth S. Ray, ed., *Colonial Granville and Its People* (1973 reprint); Rockingham County Deeds; U.S. Census of 1790; John H. Wheeler, *Reminiscences and Memoirs of North Carolina and Eminent North Carolinians* (1966 reprint).

CHARLES D. RODENBOUGH

Henderson, Richard (*20 Apr. 1735–30 Jan. 1785*), land speculator, judge, and politician, was born in Hanover County, Va., the son of Samuel and Elizabeth Williams Henderson. Before Richard was ten the family moved south to Granville County, N.C. Under his mother's watchful eye, he was educated by a private tutor and directed his energies towards a career in law. Samuel Henderson was the Granville sheriff, and young Richard found his first employment at his father's side as a deputy. With that experience Richard next arranged to read law under his mother's cousin, John Williams, a young and gifted attorney. Henderson was soon admitted to the bar and joined Williams in his practice. Their association would become a lifelong friendship; it was enhanced further in 1763, when Henderson married Williams's stepdaughter, Elizabeth Keeling, the daughter of an English peer, Lord Keeling.

Henderson's career took a major step forward in March 1768, when royal governor William Tryon appointed him associate justice on the colony's Superior Court. Tryon, in writing to the British colonial secretary, the Earl of Shelburne, described Henderson as a "gentleman of candor and ability . . . for whom [the inhabitants] entertain an esteem." Henderson's tenure in office occurred during a turbulent period for the Piedmont. As the Regulators reached their zenith in 1770–71, Henderson felt the full fury of their wrath. In September 1770, while court was in session at Hillsborough, Regulators stormed into the town and besieged the courthouse. Henderson managed to escape out a back door, but several other colonial officials, including John Williams, were less fortunate. In November, the Regulators burned Henderson's home near Williamsboro. In the trial following the Battle of Alamance in 1771, he was one of the presiding justices who convicted twelve Regulators, of whom six were executed. When his term ended in 1773, Henderson retired from the bench in order to pursue his real ambition.

From a young age the West had always held a fascination for him. Perhaps as early as the mid-1760s Henderson had begun to formulate a plan of exploration, and while riding the circuit through western North

Carolina he had met a young man who shared his enthusiasm. By 1769 Henderson felt the time had come to equip an expedition to explore the lands beyond the Appalachians and to locate areas suitable for settlement. The little band set out on a two-year mission led by Henderson's friend, Daniel Boone.

Despite Boone's glowing reports, Henderson was in no position to capitalize until the demands of the bench had been lifted from his shoulders. Once that had been accomplished, he lost little time and in 1774 formed the Louisa Company. Consisting of six prominent citizens, including John Williams, the association determined to purchase from the Indians a sizable tract of land and then as Lords Proprietors to direct its settlement. The following year the company was enlarged and renamed the Transylvania Company. In March 1775 the proprietors signed a treaty with the Cherokee at Sycamore Shoals on the Watauga River, thereby gaining title to an immense tract of land consisting of present-day Kentucky and a large section of Tennessee. Boone was again commissioned to travel west and begin a settlement, which was soon called Boonesborough.

The company was beset with troubles from the beginning. The governors of North Carolina and Virginia both issued proclamations denouncing Henderson and the company and invalidating any agreement with the Indians. As the proprietors tried to organize the settlers and establish a government in Kentucky, James Hogg, a member of the company, traveled north to Philadelphia to present to the Continental Congress a memorial from the Transylvanians seeking admission as the fourteenth colony. The Congress, appeasing the states' claims to western lands and respecting imperial jurisdiction over the West, wanted no part of the Transylvania colony. Without federal recognition, the colony's fate was sealed. The Transylvania Company lingered for several years but effective control of the land had been lost. Eventually North Carolina and Virginia each granted the company 200,000 acres as compensation for its expense and services in the undertaking. Henderson, though, was far from finished with land speculation. In 1779–80 he spearheaded another group of settlers into the Cumberland Valley in Tennessee and founded French Lick (present-day Nashville).

Henderson was equally as busy on the eastern side of the mountains. With the coming of the Revolution he became an ardent supporter of the American cause and maintained an active role throughout the war. In 1778 he was nominated as a delegate to the Continental Congress but stepped aside when John Williams was also being considered. During the same year he declined an appointment to the Council of State. Also in 1778 he returned to the bench as judge but resigned a short time later. For the next two years, Henderson served on the boundary commission to determine the line between Virginia and North Carolina. That finished in 1780, he was a member of the state's Board of War until the hostilities ended in 1781. A militia colonel himself, he assisted in recruitment and the procurement of supplies.

With peace restored, Granville County elected Henderson to the state legislature in 1781, and he served on the Council of State from 1782 to 1783. His life was cut short by death at age forty-nine. He was buried on his farm where his house still stands near Williamsboro on Nutbush Creek. Henderson was an Anglican and a vestryman in the Parish of Granville. His children were educated by Henry Patillo, an eminent Presbyterian clergyman. Henderson, who was always interested in education, played a key role in the establishment of

Granville Hall, an academy begun in 1779. The Hendersons had six children: Fanny (b. 1764), Richard (b. 1766), Archibald (b. 1768), Elizabeth (b. 1770), Leonard (b. 1778), and John (b. 1780).

SEE: Walter Clark, ed., *State Records of North Carolina*, vols. 12–23 (1895–1904); Lyman C. Draper Collection (State Historical Society of Wisconsin, Madison), which contains the richest source material for the period of westward migration in general and Richard Henderson in particular, especially Draper's life of Boone and the Kentucky, Virginia, and North Carolina Papers; Archibald Henderson, *The Conquest of the Old Southwest* (1920), "The Creative Forces in Westward Expansion: Henderson and Boone," *American Historical Review* 28 (1914), "Richard Henderson and the Occupation of Kentucky," *Mississippi Valley Historical Review* 1 (1914), and *Star of Empire* (1919); William S. Lester, *The Transylvania Colony* (1935); George W. Ranck, *Boonesborough* (1901)—No. 16 of the Filson Club Publications contains a copy of Henderson's journal of his trip to Kentucky in 1775; William L. Saunders, ed., *Colonial Records of North Carolina*, vols. 7–10 (1890).

MARK F. MILLER

Henderson, Samuel (*6 Feb. 1746–1816*), pioneer and western agent, was born in the Nutbush area of Granville (now Vance) County, the fourth son of Samuel and Elizabeth Williams Henderson. His father was commissioned sheriff of Granville County on 6 Mar. 1754. A brother, Judge Richard Henderson, was a principal of the Transylvania Company, which engaged in the purchase and settlement of lands in the area of present-day Tennessee and Kentucky. Nothing is recorded of Samuel's education. Extant letters disclose a well-developed vocabulary but rudimentary skill in written expression. In September 1768 he served with the Granville regiment of militia dispatched to maintain peace at Hillsborough during the Regulator incidents there. These centered around the operation of the colonial court conducted by his brother Richard and other officials appointed by the government at New Bern.

Samuel accompanied Richard to Kentucky in 1775 and was present when the Treaty of Watauga or Sycamore Shoals was concluded during 14–17 March. Under this treaty, the Transylvania Company, consisting of speculators chiefly from Orange and Granville counties, acquired claim to lands in the Tennessee and Kentucky areas by purchase from the Cherokee nation. Samuel was among the original party of settlers of the lands obtained under the treaty, and he served as a representative for the settlement of Boonesborough in the legislative assembly convened by the settlers on 23 May 1775.

In July 1776 Frances and Elizabeth Callaway (daughters of Colonel Richard Callaway) and Jemima Boone (daughter of Daniel Boone) were abducted by Indians. Samuel Henderson was one of the party that rescued the women. The incident, one of the most celebrated in the early history of Kentucky, has been cited as the source of the abduction in James Fenimore Cooper's *Last of the Mohicans*. Henderson married Elizabeth Callaway at Boonesborough on 7 Aug. 1776, the first wedding recorded to have taken place in the Kentucky settlement.

Henderson returned to North Carolina about 1777 and settled in Guilford County where he became prominent, especially in the local militia. Despite this relocation, he continued to participate in the western settlement. On 3 July 1779, the Council of State commissioned him commissary to the detachment of militia accompanying the boundary commission for extension of the North Carolina-Virginia boundary westward; the council authorized an initial draft of £10,000. This effort continued into the next year and was largely conducted for North Carolina by his brother Richard.

On 13 May 1780 Samuel participated as a signatory in the adoption of the Cumberland Compact at French Lick (now Nashville, Tenn.). This document was the original instrument of government for the settlement area. In October of that year, he served as a captain of the Guilford County militia in the suppression of an insurrection in Surry County. And, in the following spring, he fought at the Battle of Guilford Court House, 15 Mar. 1781.

By 1782, Henderson had lost possession of the property he had obtained in the western lands under the Transylvania Company, and most of his coadventurers had been killed or dispersed. For the next twenty-five years, his activities were concentrated in North Carolina. On 3 June 1784 he was appointed a tax collector for Guilford, and during the next several years he participated in various capacities in the formation of Rockingham County. He served on the commissions that drew the boundaries and erected the courthouse and prison.

In 1784, Henderson was dispatched by Governor Alexander Martin to convey official communications to the disaffected western settlers who had formed the state of Franklin under the leadership of General John Sevier. Martin's letter of appointment instructed Henderson to ascertain whether the secession of this area from the state was intended to be permanent or temporary, and whether it was supported by a majority or by only a few leaders. Henderson executed this commission in the spring of 1785 and conveyed official responses of the legislature of Franklin and of General Sevier declining to stop the secession and stating the westerners' grievances. In 1807 Henderson moved to Tennessee, where he died at McMinnville in Warren County.

SEE: *The Career of Colonel Samuel Henderson* (1938); Walter Clark, ed., *State Records of North Carolina*, 16 vols. (1886–1907); *The Conquest of the Old Southwest* (1920); *The East Tennessee Historical Society's Publications*, nos. 26, 33 (1954, 1961); Archibald Henderson, *North Carolina: The Old North State and the New* (1941); Alice Barnwell Keith, ed., *John Gray Blount Papers* (1952); William L. Saunders, ed., *Colonial Records of North Carolina*, 10 vols. (1886–90).

GEORGE T. BLACKBURN II

Henderson, Thomas (*19 Mar. 1752–15 Nov. 1821*), merchant and legislator, was born in Granville County, the son of Samuel and Elizabeth Williams Henderson. In the early 1770s he operated a store at Guilford Court House with Thomas Searcy under the name Henderson and Searcy. Searcy's brothers, Reuben, Bartlet, and Richard, participated with Henderson's brother, Richard, in the formation of the Transylvania Company.

Thomas Henderson was elected a delegate from Guilford County to the Third Provincial Congress, which convened at Hillsborough during 20 Aug.–10 Sept. 1775. Another delegate from Guilford was Alexander Martin whose sister, Anne Jane Martin, became Henderson's wife in March 1778. For the rest of their lives the brothers-in-law remained close associates. As the Revolutionary War was ending, the fighting drew near Guilford Court House. Henderson was called into

the militia as a private and acted as a guide to General Nathanael Greene in the maneuvering of the armies on either side of the Dan River.

Soon afterwards Alexander Martin became governor for the first of seven terms. He and Henderson acquired 350 acres of land at Guilford Courthouse confiscated from the Tory, Edmund Fanning. On this land, adjacent to the courthouse, they laid out a town called Martinsville (Martinville, according to the original deed) where the governor built his home. Martin, who never married, provided a home for his mother, and apparently the Hendersons also came to live with him.

Henderson became clerk of court for Guilford County, which was now politically controlled by Martin. In 1786, when Rockingham County was formed from Guilford, Henderson resigned as clerk of Guilford to take the same office in the new county. He then moved his family to Governor Martin's home, Danbury, on Jacobs Creek of the Dan River. Although Henderson acquired several tracts in Rockingham, he seems to have made his residence at Danbury for the remainder of his life. For this reason, according to local tradition, prior to the establishment of a central courthouse, much of the public business of Rockingham County was conducted by Clerk Henderson at Danbury (the governor's home—not to be confused with the county seat of Stokes County, established much later).

In 1789 Henderson served a single term as clerk of the Council of State, succeeded the next year by his wife's nephew, Thomas Rogers. In 1795 he was for one term a member of the Council of State. Between 1792 and 1795 Henderson served two terms as a representative of Rockingham County in the House of Commons, and in 1796 he served one term in the state Senate.

On 2 Nov. 1807 Alexander Martin died at Danbury and by his will left that home to Henderson and his wife on the condition that they continue to provide a home for Martin's mother. But Jane Martin died just four days after her son, relieving the Hendersons of this responsibility.

Henderson remained politically active in league with such local leaders as Colonel James Hunter, Theophilus Lacy, and Alexander Sneed. He died in Rockingham County.

Thomas and Jane Henderson had seven children: Samuel; Alexander, who became the owner of the Danbury estate during his father's lifetime; Mary (Polly), who married John Lacy; Thomas, editor of the Raleigh *Star*; Jane; Nathaniel, who married Susan Searcy; and Frances (Fanny).

SEE: Ethel Stephens Arnett, *Greensboro, North Carolina: The County Seat of Guilford* (1955); *Charlotte Observer*, 31 Oct. 1926; John L. Cheney, Jr., ed., *North Carolina Government, 1585–1974* (1975); *Early Families of the North Carolina County of Rockingham and Stokes with Revolutionary Service* (1977); Worth S. Ray, *Colonial Granville County and Its People* (1973 reprint); Rockingham County Deeds (North Carolina State Archives, Raleigh).

CHARLES D. RODENBOUGH

Henderson, Thomas, Jr. (*25 Mar. 1787–22 June 1835*), Raleigh editor, was born in Rockingham County. His father was Thomas Henderson, Sr. (1752–1821), a county clerk in Guilford and Rockingham counties; and his mother was Jane Martin Henderson, a sister of Governor Alexander Martin. After receiving a common school education, he entered the printing profession. From early October 1806 until early March 1807, he printed the *North-Carolina Journal* for the heirs of Abraham Hodge at Halifax.

Shortly afterwards Henderson moved to Raleigh, where he formed a partnership with Dr. Calvin Jones to publish the Raleigh *Star*. Announcing their intentions with a notice in the rival Raleigh *Register*, the prospective editors said they "would attempt to pursue a firm yet liberal line of conduct, often giving facts, more seldom opinions, and those ever so candid and dispassionate; solicitous always to stifle the baneful spirit of faction, and looking with a single eye to the happiness and honour of United America." The first issue of the *Star* appeared on 3 Nov. 1808. After a year or so, Jones apparently withdrew as co-editor while remaining a financial partner. The issue of 20 Apr. 1809 stated that it was published by Thomas Henderson, Jr., "for self & company," whereas the issue of 3 Jan. 1812 said it was published by "Thomas Henderson, Jr." A 13 Feb. 1815 notice in the *Star* announced the dissolution of the partnership effective 1 Jan. 1815, when the paper became the sole property of Henderson. On 5 Jan. 1816 he changed the title to *The Star and North Carolina State Gazette*. The paper was published each Thursday at "the upper end of Fayetteville Street near Casso's Corner."

From the beginning, the *Star* was a unique newspaper. The editors announced they would print intelligence, congressional, and legislative news in summary only but would not print rumors or "stud horse advertisements." One of their guiding principles was the advancement of agricultural interests in the area and the state. Henderson, in fact, was a proponent of the establishment of an agricultural society in Wake County as well as in North Carolina. Although he was a Federalist, the *Star* remained fairly neutral politically and devoted most of its attention to agriculture, literature, and culture. For a few years, the pages were numbered consecutively and the editors published a detailed index for each volume. It was later described as the forerunner of the general-interest family newspaper.

Concerned about the lack of communication between the eastern and western parts of the state, Henderson attempted to use the *Star* as a vehicle for exchange between those areas. On 30 Mar. 1810 he sent a circular letter to citizens in several counties, asking them to provide detailed information about their county's history, geography, and social conditions, presented within about twenty subject areas. In explaining the project to his readers on 26 July 1810, he requested that "men of information" supply a "description of such county as each may be particularly acquainted with." He repeated the notice on 26 Apr. and 3 May 1811, publishing "A Statistical Account of Edisto Island" from David Ramsay's *The History of South Carolina* as an example of the kind of report he wanted from his contributors. On 1 May 1812, the editors told their readers they were still interested in the project and again requested their assistance. Sketches of twelve counties were written and presumably received by the editors in 1810 and 1811, but apparently none were published in the *Star*. A. R. Newsome said the editors may have wanted to wait until they received reports of all sixty-two counties or may not have had room to publish them because of the mounting pressure to provide political and military news surrounding the War of 1812. The reports were preserved, however, and were later published in other sources, including the *North Carolina Historical Review*.

Henderson was also an active citizen of Raleigh. He was a city commissioner, a member of the Town Watch, a director of the leading bank, and a state printer. While he published the *Star*, he also ran the Star Store

on the lower floor of his building on the west side of Fayetteville Street, just opposite the Stone Fountain. The store sold all kinds of merchandise, including books like the *Star Almanac* and several others he had printed. In Raleigh, as he had done in Halifax, he promoted the cause of drama—organizing and participating in amateur productions, athletic contests, and open-air entertainment. As a major in the state militia, Henderson commanded the Wake Dragoons when the unit accompanied Governor William Hawkins on an inspection of coastal defenses after reports of a British invasion in the summer of 1813. Henderson eventually attained the rank of colonel, for he was universally referred to as "Colonel Henderson."

His participation in community affairs involved Henderson in a near-fatal accident which influenced the life of a later president of the United States. Sometime in the spring of 1811 (Archibald Henderson's account says 1810, but that conflicts with most other reports), while attending a picnic at Hunter's Mill Pond on Walnut Creek, Henderson and two companions were in a canoe that capsized in about 10 feet of water. One of the men could not swim and grabbed Henderson's coat, pulling them both to the bottom of the river. Jacob Johnson, a somewhat poor but respected member of the community, who was on the bank, immediately jumped in, dived to the bottom, and pulled the men to safety. Henderson was believed dead, but was revived by his partner, Dr. Jones, who fortunately happened to be on the bank, too. Henderson suffered ill effects of the experience for nearly a year, but Jacob Johnson was less fortunate. He never recovered his good health and died from exhaustion while tolling bells in January 1812. His son Andrew (born 29 Dec. 1808 in Raleigh) was left fatherless and penniless; because there were no public schools, he could not afford any education. He became a tailor's apprentice in Raleigh before moving west to Tennessee and back east to Washington, D.C., as vice-president and then president upon the assassination of Abraham Lincoln. Henderson remained ever grateful to Jacob Johnson, and honored him with a glowing obituary on 12 Jan. 1812.

The conclusion of the nation's difficulties with the Chickasaw Indians on 19 Oct. 1818 marked a turning point in Henderson's life. The University of North Carolina had received gifts of land in the Chickasaw country from Benjamin Smith and Major Charles Gerrard. In addition, the state legislature had given the university—by way of escheats—all lands in western Tennessee allotted to Revolutionary War veterans but not claimed by their heirs. The state of Tennessee, of course, was not very happy; moreover, concerned about the influx of people from North Carolina, Tennessee appealed to the North Carolina General Assembly to stop the emigration. In the summer of 1821, Colonel Thomas Henderson accompanied a delegation from The University of North Carolina to Murfreesborough, then the capital of Tennessee, to present the university claims for the lands. On 5 Aug. 1821 Colonel William Polk, a university trustee, hired Henderson to oversee the processing of the claims. For his assistance, which he completed in two months, Henderson received one-half of all the land legitimately claimed by the university. The university received 147,853 acres and, even though Henderson had to share some of his portion with his agents in Tennessee, he still received enough to make him a wealthy man.

He returned to Raleigh, but the lure of his western land was too strong to resist. In the *Star* of 3 Jan. 1823, he informed his patrons that he had sold the newspaper to John Bell and A. J. Lawrence and that he was moving to Tennessee. In his farewell editorial, he wrote, "If I have not promoted the public good in a ratio commensurate with the humble spheres in which I have acted—if I have failed to render due 'service to the state,' it has not been for the want of a willing hand and a devoted heart." A week later, his major rival in Raleigh, the *Register*, said Henderson "will take with him the good will of his fellow citizens. . . . We believe no personal feeling ever mingled with Editorial duties on either side—and we too wish our worthy fellow-citizen the prosperity and happiness which enterprize and industry always merit." On 27 Mar. 1823, many of Raleigh's citizens gave a farewell dinner in Henderson's honor at Wynne's Bell Tavern.

Henderson, his wife and her parents, and his twin brother Alexander left Raleigh later in the spring of 1823, arriving on 23 May at Mount Pinson in Madison County, Tenn., the estate Henderson had inherited from his father a year earlier. Their home became a center of hospitality and the Hendersons were often entertained at the governor's mansion. The former editor also counted Colonel (then Congressman) David Crockett among his friends. In his own foray into politics, Henderson was defeated in an 1834 bid to be a delegate to the state constitutional convention. In June 1825, he gave notice of the establishment of Mount Pinson Academy, and remained one of its patrons and supporters. When General Andrew Jackson visited Jackson, Tenn., on 18 Sept. 1825, Henderson helped organize a public dinner in Jackson's honor.

Early in 1835 Henderson traveled to a site near Gainesville, Ala., where his brother Alexander had acquired a plantation, with a "view to settling." He became ill on the way and was treated for dropsy by Dr. Robert Hunter Dalton (who had married one of Henderson's nieces) at the physician's home near Livingston, Ala. After remaining there for some time, he went on to his brother's plantation where he died.

On 29 May 1811 Henderson married Anne McKinney Fenner at The Oaks in Franklin County; the ceremony was performed by President Joseph Caldwell of The University of North Carolina. His wife was the daughter of Dr. Richard Fenner, who had been a lieutenant in the Continental Army, and Anne Geddy Fenner. The Hendersons had eight children. Born in Raleigh were Calvin (21 Apr. 1813), who died in Louisiana in 1843; Richard (5 May 1815), who was graduated from West Point in 1835 and was killed at Dade's Massacre, Fla., on 28 December of that year; William (28 July 1817); Thomas (5 June 1819), who died in 1877; and Corinna (9 Sept. 1821), who died 19 June 1850. Born at Mount Pinson were Samuel (6 Aug. 1823), who died in 1897; Alexander (5 June 1826); and Nathaniel (23 Feb. 1828).

SEE: C. S. Brigham, *History and Bibliography of American Newspapers, 1690–1820*, vol. 2 (1947); M. D. Haywood, *Builders of the Old North State* (1968); Archibald Henderson Papers (Southern Historical Collection, University of North Carolina Library, Chapel Hill); G. G. Johnson, *Ante-Bellum North Carolina* (1937); A. R. Newsome, "Twelve North Carolina Counties in 1810–1811," *North Carolina Historical Review*, vol. 5 (October 1928); E. I. Williams, *Historic Madison* (1946).

THOMAS A. BOWERS

Henderson, William B. *(fl. 1892–98),* Negro state senator, farmer, and resident of Middleburg, was elected to the North Carolina General Assembly in 1892 as a Republican representative from the Eleventh District (Vance and Warren counties). Almost immediately, on 24 Jan. 1893, Henderson's seat was challenged by his recent opponent, John P. Leach of Warren County. Leach claimed that he was the "legitimate" candidate. Henderson and several other Republicans found themselves displaced by legislative action. He appealed to Congressman Thomas Settle, pointing out that his election had been certified by the Democratic Canvass Board and that he had defeated Leach by 653 votes.

The appeal was unsuccessful. The era was one of great emotion, rivalry, and charges by the Democrats of collusion between the Populists and the Negro Republicans. Henderson ran again, was elected, and served in the North Carolina Senate in 1897 and 1898. He was not active and seldom spoke, although on occasion he proposed measures pertaining to fences and livestock as well as the desirability of a register of deeds and a dispensary for Vance County. He served on committees dealing with penal institutions, public roads, the insane asylum, and claims. In 1898 Governor D. L. Russell named Henderson to be chief fertilizer inspector, replacing James Young.

SEE: John L. Cheney, Jr., ed., *North Carolina Government, 1585–1974* (1975); Helen G. Edmonds, *The Negro and Fusion Politics in North Carolina* (1951); *Senate Journal* (1897); Thomas Settle Papers (Southern Historical Collection, University of North Carolina Library, Chapel Hill).

JOHN MACFIE

Hendren, William Mayhew *(13 Oct. 1871–19 July 1939),* lawyer, was born in New Bern, the son of the Reverend Linville L. Hendren, Methodist Episcopal Church, South, and Mary Elizabeth Mayhew Hendren. Through his maternal line he was a direct descendant of Thomas Mayhew, governor and patentee of Martha's Vineyard, Nantucket, and Elizabeth Isles, Mass., who began a settlement at Edgartown, Martha's Vineyard, in 1642.

Young Hendren received his elementary and preparatory education in various public schools in North Carolina and at the Hill School in Statesville. He attended The University of North Carolina as an undergraduate from 1890 to 1892, then returned to study law from 1893 to 1895. Admitted to the North Carolina bar in 1894, he joined the Winston (now Winston-Salem) firm of Glenn and Manly in 1896, which then became Glenn, Manly and Hendren. For more than forty years he was a partner in this and the successor firms of Manly and Hendren (1905) and Manly, Hendren and Womble (1911). He was senior partner of the latter from 1929 until the time of his death. The firm engaged in general civil practice, specializing in corporation, insurance, and banking law. It was counsel for the R. J. Reynolds Tobacco Company, Wachovia Bank and Trust Company, P. H. Hanes Knitting Company, Chatham Manufacturing Company, Security Life and Trust Company, Pascal Mirror Company, Haverty Furniture Company of Winston-Salem, and Rawls Dickson Candy Company.

Hendren's firm also served as assistant division counsel for the Southern Railway Company and as local counsel for the Western Union Telegraph Company, American Express Company, Duke Power Company, Standard Oil Company of New Jersey, Montgomery Ward Company, New York Life Insurance Company, Penn Mutual Life Insurance Company, Prudential Insurance Company of America, Metropolitan Life Insurance Company, Equitable Life Assurance Society of the United States, and a number of other life, fire, and liability insurance companies.

Hendren was a member of the board of directors of the Wachovia Bank and Trust Company and of the Security Life and Trust Company. He raised money for good causes in Winston-Salem, notably for the fund to build Baptist Hospital. A Democrat, he represented Forsyth County in the North Carolina Senate in 1931–32. He was a member of the Forsyth County Bar Association, the North Carolina Bar Association (president, 1925–26), the American Bar Association (general council, 1932–35), Delta Kappa Epsilon, Rotary International, Knights of Pythias, Forsyth Country Club, Twin City Club (president, 1919), and Cosmos Club. A member of the Centenary Methodist Church, he served on the Board of Stewards and for many years taught the Men's Bible Class.

On 28 Mar. 1899, in Winston-Salem, Hendren married Annie J. Rawley, daughter of Taylor Lindsay Rawley of that city. They had two daughters: Mary Elizabeth (Mrs. Charles W. Long) and Carrie Shelton (Mrs. Alfred Z. Smith, Jr.). Hendren died in Winston-Salem and was buried in Salem Cemetery.

In 1966 his daughters made a gift honoring their father to The University of North Carolina Law School to furnish a seminar room.

SEE: *Martindale-Hubbell Law Directory*, vol. 1 (1938); J. C. Schwarz, ed., *Who's Who in Law*, vol. 1 (1937). Information on Hendren is in the possession of Office of Records and Registration, University of North Carolina, Chapel Hill; Mrs. A. Z. Smith, Jr., 630 Carolina Circle, Winston-Salem; Womble, Carlyle, Sandridge and Rice, Winston-Salem.

ELIZABETH R. CANNON

Hendrick, John Kerr *(10 Oct. 1847–20 June 1921)*, congressman and lawyer, was born in Caswell County, the son of William H. and Susan Bennett Hendrick, both natives of Virginia. In 1856 the family moved to Logan County, Ky., where young Hendrick continued his education in local schools and at Bethel College, Russellville, Ky. While teaching school, he studied law under his uncle, Judge Caswell Bennett, and was licensed in 1875. Practicing first at Smithland, he moved to Paducah in 1898.

Hendrick was a delegate to the Democratic National Convention at St. Louis in 1888. A state senator for four years, he was elected to Congress in 1894, serving from 4 Mar. 1895 to 3 Mar. 1897. In 1877 Hendrick married Lula Grayot, and they became the parents of Alfred A., W. R., Harry B., and Nellie. He was buried in Maplelawn Cemetery, Paducah.

SEE: *Biog. Dir. Am. Cong.* (1961); William E. Connelley and E. M. Coulter, *History of Kentucky*, vol. 5 (1922); U.S. Census, 1850, Caswell County.

WILLIAM S. POWELL

Henkel, David *(4 May 1795–15 June 1831)*, theologian, Lutheran minister, and founder of the Tennessee Synod, was the son of the Reverend Paul and Elizabeth Negeley Henkel. Apparently his family had tutored him because he exhibited early intellectual prowess, showing a good understanding of both the English and German languages; before his career ended, he also learned Greek and Hebrew. Henkel began his ministry

in South Carolina on 4 Oct. 1812 at age seventeen. During the next year, the Lutheran Synod of North Carolina approved him as a catechist to serve several rural churches in Lincoln County (including present Gaston, Lincoln, Catawba, and part of Cleveland counties), which became his lifetime home and parish. In October 1815 he became a ministerial candidate.

In the years that followed, the fiery Henkel formulated questionable doctrines and often went against the grain of North Carolina Lutheranism. After a visit to his father, who lived in New Market, Va., Henkel expected to be ordained, but in October 1816 the North Carolina Synod denied his request. As a result, Henkel's Lincoln County churches caused some "bitterness" in the synod. In 1817, after he had visited his brother, the Reverend Philip Henkel, in Tennessee, the synod again failed to ordain him. On 20 Oct. 1818 Gottlieb Shober, the Moravian-turned-Lutheran who was a leader in the synod, tongue-lashed Henkel for objectionable doctrines and "bad rumors."

As the year 1819 approached, conflict seemed imminent. Early correspondence before the synod indicated that Henkel and his allies and Shober and his allies anticipated a showdown. Although the synod's constitution provided for its annual meeting to be held on Trinity Sunday, Shober decided to meet earlier to allow the synod to select delegates to a General Synod meeting in Pennsylvania. On 26 Apr. 1819, the North Carolina Synod convened at Buffalo Creek in Cabarrus County. Henkel was present, but his father, brother Philip, and associate, Joseph E. Bell, stayed away "in defiance." After the absent ministers were verbally attacked, the synod held an inquiry into charges against David Henkel. Certain Presbyterians and other denominational members were among Henkel's accusers. Andrew Hoyle, a Presbyterian minister, charged that Henkel had tried to defame his reputation. Others accused him of lying, of teaching doctrines foreign to Lutheranism, and of excommunicating a certain person illegally. The latter accusation was shown to be well founded, and the charges concerning Hoyle were proved by the convention. During his "trial," Henkel had no counsel and could not cross-examine witnesses. At its conclusion, the synod revoked his candidacy status and put him on probation as a catechist for six months. Henkel, who denied all the charges, "promised to do better." Nevertheless, Shober and the synod later accused him of perpetrating the division that followed this meeting.

On 6 June 1819 Henkel and his associates attended the regularly scheduled synod meeting at Buffalo Church; they considered the April meeting to be unconstitutional. The next day Philip Henkel ordained his brother David and Joseph E. Bell as Lutheran ministers with all powers and responsibilities of the office. The service was held under an oak tree because the church doors were locked. The dispute had approached the breaking point.

Although some of the complaints against Henkel were reasonable and his firebrand sermons could have been considered objectionable by other denominations, other charges relating to doctrine were made by persons ignorant of his profound theology. Yet, his disagreement with the Reverend Mr. Hoyle appeared to be personal, not theological. Shober, in addition, desired the repudiation of Henkel and his vigorous teachings. In a letter of 6 Nov. 1819, Shober thanked Hoyle for his assistance in disposing of Henkel.

Henkel's parishes responded by writing petitions vindicating their spiritual leader. The 1819 synod minutes indicate that he far exceeded his fellow ministers in the performance of his duties. In one year he had baptized 377 children (about three times as many as his associates), 49 adults, and 38 slaves (only one other minister had baptized any slaves), and he had confirmed 135 young people. Bell urged Henkel not to break with the synod, and apparently he agreed to attempt a reconciliation at the next synod meeting.

The causes of the controversy were threefold. First and primarily, Henkel, Shober, and others had personality conflicts. Second, Henkel and his allies opposed the General Synod, whereas Shober and Carl Storch, synod president, favored sending delegates. Finally, the two groups had doctrinal differences.

On 29 May 1820, the seventeenth annual North Carolina Synod Convention was held at Emmanuel Church in Lincolnton. Henkel, his father, his brother Philip, and Joseph Bell all attended. During the morning session, synod leaders debated the status of David Henkel. Shober and Storch considered Henkel's ordination to be illegal, whereas Henkel contended that the synod had departed from proper Lutheran practice, failing to adhere to the Augsburg Confession and the synod constitution. After lengthy and violent argument, the synod adjourned until the afternoon. Because the Henkels had been repudiated, they did not attend the afternoon session. However, Henkel sent two members of his churches with instructions. They argued that, because the synod had ratified Bell's "oak tree" ordination, it should also recognize Henkel's. They also presented a letter by Henkel indicating that he would rejoin the synod if it promised to abide by its constitution. But the synod refused to compromise.

With the schism complete, the Henkel faction met during 17–19 July 1820 to organize the Tennessee Synod. Although unable to attend this first meeting, David Henkel became the leader and spokesman of the new synod. On 22 Oct. 1821, he attended the second convention of the Tennessee Synod and was elected secretary. At this time, he had baptized 444 infants, 56 adults, and 69 slaves, and confirmed 156 persons.

Meanwhile, charges and countercharges between the two synods persisted. On 26 Apr. 1822, Henkel wrote a conciliatory letter to the North Carolina Lutheran Synod in which he suggested that the opposing groups meet to determine who was at fault in the controversy, and to restore peace and unity for the good of the Christian church. The North Carolina leaders, at their own convention, replied "that D. Henkel is no minister of the Lutheran Church." This response ended any hopes for reconciliation, and the two synods went their separate ways.

Henkel continued to lead the Tennessee Synod for the rest of his short life. During his ministry he delivered 3,200 sermons, baptized 2,997 infants and 243 adults, and confirmed 1,105 persons. He also made two missionary journeys into Kentucky and Indiana, and he was the author of numerous pamphlets and essays. His most outstanding writings included "The Essence of the Christian Religion, and Reflections on Futurity" (1817), "The Carolinian Herald of Liberty, Religious and Political" (1821), "Objections to the Constitution of the General Synod" (1821), "The Heavenly Flood of Regeneration, or Treatise on Holy Baptism" (1822), "An Answer to Joseph Moore" (1825), "The Tennessee Synod Constitution" (1828), "A Translation from the German of Luther's Smaller Catechism, with Preliminary Observations by the Translator" (1829), "An Essay on Regeneration" (1830), and "A Treatise on the Person and Incarnation of Jesus Christ, in which some of the principal

Arguments of the Unitarians are examined" (1831). In addition, Henkel wrote a number of essays concerning the synodical break, such as "Plain Truth, Vindicated," "Reasons shewn why this debate with the North Carolina Synod was proposed," and "Reasons" why the 1819 North Carolina Convention was unconstitutional.

On 17 May 1814 Henkel married Catharine Hoyle, daughter of the Honorable Peter, state legislator and political leader, and Elizabeth Carpenter Hoyle. They were the parents of Susan (m. Philip Benick), Elizabeth (m. Henry Ingold), the Reverend Polycarp C. (m. Rebecca Fox), the Reverend Socrates (m. Elenora Henkel), Cicero (m. Elenora Little), Flora (m. Laban Fox), and Elenora (m. Peter Little).

After an illness of about a year, Henkel died at his home in Lincoln County at age thirty-six. He was buried at St. Johns Lutheran Cemetery, now in Catawba County. A likeness of him is among the Charles L. Coon Papers at Duke University.

SEE: G. D. Bernheim, *History of the German Settlements and of the Lutheran Church in North and South Carolina* (1872); Curtis Bynum, *Marriage Bonds of Tryon and Lincoln Counties, North Carolina* (1929); Diary of the Reverend David Henkel, 1812–30 (in possession of Elon C. Henkel, New Market, Va.); *Evangelical Review*, vol. 8 (1856–57); L. A. Fox, "Origin and Early History of the Tennessee Synod," *Lutheran Quarterly*, vol. 19 (1889); Henkel Family Papers, Charles Lee Coon Papers (Manuscript Department, Duke University Library, Durham); David Hinkle Papers (Southern Historical Collection, University of North Carolina Library, Chapel Hill); Laban Miles Hoffman, *Our Kin* (1915); L. L. Lohr, "David Henkel: Sketch of His Life and Labor" (Lutheran Archives, Salisbury); Lutheran Archives (North Carolina Synod House, Salisbury); *Minutes of the Evangelical Lutheran Synod of North Carolina, 1803–1826* (1894).

ROBERT C. CARPENTER

Henkel, Paul (15 Dec. 1754–20 Nov. 1825), Lutheran pastor, missionary, and organizer on the American frontier, was born on Dutchman's Creek in present Davie County, the oldest son of Jacob and Mary Barbara Dieter Henkel, who had just moved to the North Carolina frontier on the eve of the French and Indian War. When the Cherokees overran that section in 1760, Jacob Henkel, like so many of his neighbors in the Forks of the Yadkin, went back to Virginia, settling in what is now Pendleton County, W.Va., on the headwaters of the South Fork of the Potomac River.

It was there that Paul Henkel was reared and that he married Elizabeth Negeley on 20 Nov. 1776. He was trained for the cooper's trade but preached his first sermon in 1781. Encouraged by the Reverend John Andrew Krug of Frederick, Md., he studied Latin, Greek, and theology with the Reverend Christian Streit at Winchester, Va. He was licensed to preach in 1783 and ordained in Philadelphia on 6 June 1792 by the Ministerium of Pennsylvania. It is not surprising that Henkel should turn to the ministry. His father's grandfather, the Reverend Anthony Jacob Henckel, after twenty-five years of service in Germany, had been one of the first Lutheran ministers to emigrate to America, settling in Pennsylvania with his family about 1718.

In 1790 Paul Henkel moved to New Market on the North Fork of the Shenandoah River in Virginia, which from then until his death was—with three exceptions—his base of operations. In 1800 he arrived in North

Carolina for a five-year stay, and twice he went to Point Pleasant at the confluence of the Great Kanawha and Ohio rivers in present-day West Virginia. But he called New Market home.

Before settling at New Market, Henkel was in North Carolina. The church on Dutchman's Creek in Davie County, in the same section where he was born, lists him as pastor from 1785 to 1789. His diary, begun in 1790, makes numerous references to his ministry in North Carolina during those years, but they are vague and do not indicate how far his work extended. In 1800 he was called from New Market by several churches in Rowan and Stokes (now Davie, Davidson, and Forsyth) counties, N.C. Besides his old church at Dutchman's Creek, those listing him as their pastor are Bethany, Pilgrim, and St. Luke's in Davidson County and Nazareth and Shiloh in Forsyth. He was given a home south of the Moravian town of Salem in a community the Moravians referred to as "Opossum Town, where Pastor Henkel lived."

His five years there coincided with the Great Revival that began in Piedmont North Carolina in 1801, and he wrote copiously about it in his diary. Whereas some of the other Lutheran pastors were inclined to go along with the revivalists, Henkel spoke out against their emotional excesses. He even went so far as to debate the matter with the Reverend James Hall, the eminent Presbyterian divine, at the big camp meeting at Shepherds Cross Roads in the southern part of Iredell County in 1802. Later, however, he admitted that the revivals had brought the North Carolina churches closer together when acting in an official capacity.

In March 1803, Henkel met at Pine Church near Salisbury with three other Lutheran pastors and fourteen lay delegates to organize the North Carolina Synod of the Lutheran church. The other pastors were J. C. Arends, dean of North Carolina Lutherans, Carl A. Storch, and Robert Johnstone Miller, but there is evidence that Henkel was the moving force. In his relationship with the other pastors he increasingly assumed a supervisory role, preaching for Arends west of the Catawba so often that several churches there listed him as one of their pastors. Moreover, he brought his son Philip to Guilford and was supervising his work there, and arranged for his brother John to go to Cabarrus County as pastor. (John Henkel died before he could reach his new field.) Even after leaving North Carolina, Paul Henkel considered himself a member of the North Carolina Synod and either met with it or reported to it until the organization of the Tennessee Synod in 1820. During those years, he was often back in the state, visiting his sons, attending the synod, or taking orders for books or delivering them. His impact on the Lutheran church in North Carolina cannot be limited to the five years he spent near Salem.

In the years following his departure from his pastorate near Salem, Henkel was appointed annually as a missionary to the frontier by the Ministerium of Pennsylvania, especially to the Ohio region; later, the ministerium permitted Henkel to go where he chose. As he covered the frontier from South Carolina to Ohio, preaching in German and English, he tried to persuade the Germans to retain their language and religious background, and insisted on loyalty to an unaltered Augsburg Confession. Where he could locate them, he organized Germans into congregations and attempted to find pastors for them.

In many ways, Paul Henkel was to the Lutheran church of the frontier what Francis Asbury was to the Methodist church. There was, however, one major difference. Asbury passed up marriage rather than be encumbered with a wife on his journeys. Henkel frequently took his wife Elizabeth with him, riding in a chaise or wagon instead of on horseback. Often his entering a new field of work depended on her decision, as when they came to North Carolina in 1800. Asbury left no descendants to carry on his work. Henkel founded a dynasty, with five of his six sons ordained Lutheran ministers. It is far more appropriate to speak of the Henkels than just Paul Henkel.

At New Market the Henkels founded the first Lutheran publishing house in America. Paul Henkel had felt one was needed in order to furnish congregations with copies of the Augsburg Confession. Solomon, his oldest son, a pharmacist and doctor who had settled in New Market, bought a printing press in 1806, and Ambrose, his third son, learned the printing trade and ran the Henkel Press. As long as he lived, Paul Henkel contributed to it, editing the Augsburg Confession, catechisms, and hymn books in English and German, and translating the German hymns into English. His diary also mentions an "ABC Book" on which he was working.

Ambrose Henkel, who was ordained a Lutheran minister by the Tennessee Synod, gradually took over his father's work around New Market. Sons Andrew and Charles became Lutheran ministers in Ohio. Two other sons, Philip and David, carried on the Henkel ministry in North Carolina. Philip, who went to Guilford County when his father arrived in the state in 1800, moved to Lincoln County about the time Paul Henkel returned to New Market, and most of his work was in that area.

In 1813 Philip was joined by his eighteen-year-old brother, David. The North Carolina Synod licensed David to preach, but with some hesitancy because of his youth. Strong-willed and brilliant, David Henkel found himself in conflict with others in the synod, especially Gottlieb Shober, a Moravian minister who was supplying a Lutheran charge. The disagreement came to a head in 1820, when a meeting of the synod was called two weeks early to choose a delegate to a proposed General Synod. The Henkels and one other minister met at the appointed time and decided to withdraw from the North Carolina Synod and form the Tennessee Synod. Paul Henkel was absent when the split occurred but was present at the organization of the new synod in Tennessee later that summer. It was the third time he had participated in the creation of a Lutheran synod on the frontier; in 1818 he had helped establish the Joint Synod of Ohio.

From the beginning, the Tennessee Synod was based not on geography but rather on doctrinal differences, with the Henkels insisting on an "unaltered" Augsburg Confession and bitterly opposing the General Synod. Its organization brought about a split in North Carolina Lutheranism that was not healed for a century. During that period the Tennessee Synod was strong in North Carolina, comprising almost as many congregations as the North Carolina Synod and all the congregations west of Statesville. The Henkel Press at New Market gave it unusual strength in upholding its conservative stance. The final merger of the North Carolina Synod and the Tennessee Synod into the United Lutheran Synod in North Carolina took place in 1921.

Paul Henkel did not live many years after the Tennessee Synod was organized. In 1823 he suffered a stroke which slowed him down; two years later he was stricken a second time and died within ten days. He was buried first at Davidsburg Church, but following his wife's death in 1843 they were both reinterred in the cemetery of Emmanuel Church, New Market.

SEE: *DAB*, vol. 4 (1932); William J. Finck, trans., *A Chronological Life of Paul Henkel from Journals, Letters, Minutes of the Synods, etc.* (1935–37); Homer M. Keever, "A Lutheran Preacher's Account of the 1801–10 Revival in North Carolina," *Methodist History* (October 1968).

HOMER M. KEEVER

Henley, Peter *(1724–25 Apr. 1758)*, chief justice of North Carolina, was the son of John Henley of Wotton Abbas, Dorset, a member of Parliament. The family had been granted Wotton Abbas early in the reign of Queen Anne. Peter obviously was related to Sir Robert Henley, Earl of Northington and lord chancellor, who was also from Wotton Abbas. Phocion Henley (1728–64), musical composer, may have been his brother. Peter Henley was educated at Corpus Christi College, Oxford, admitted to Middle Temple on 26 Apr. 1744, and called to the bar on 28 June 1748. Letters patent from George II, dated 15 Nov. 1755, named him chief justice of North Carolina in place of Enoch Hall, deceased.

Hall, as early as January 1753, had been asked by the Board of Trade to explain his absence of almost four years from the colony and to inform the board of his plans to return and resume his duties. These queries were prompted by the representation of Thomas Child, attorney general of North Carolina, who was then in England. When Arthur Dobbs arrived at New Bern in October 1754 to take office as governor, he found James Hasell serving as chief justice. Hasell was not trained in the law and, although Dobbs said "he seems a good-natured man and bears a good character here in private life," was not considered suited for the position. Dobbs, therefore, requested that a "worthy good lawyer" be appointed. Upon the death of Hall, Henley received the royal warrant and qualified in the colony as chief justice on 5 Dec. 1755, when he took the oaths required by the Assembly.

Henley's principal accomplishment during his brief tenure in the office was to meet with King Hagler of the Catawba Indian Nation to reassure him and his people that the government of North Carolina intended to honor the provisions of the treaty negotiated in February 1756 between the North Carolina and Virginia governments and the Cherokee and Catawba nations. This conference, held in May 1756 at the home of Peter Aaran in Salisbury, resulted from a dispute between the Cherokees and the Catawbas. Hagler spoke of the perfidy of the Cherokees, who planned to enter an alliance with the French; however, he promised that his own people would remain loyal to the English and defend them "or go down into the grave with them."

One concern of the Catawbas was the disposition of a white woman they had taken from the Cherokees who had seized her as they came from Virginia after an abortive engagement with the Shawnees. At her persuasion they had stolen horses, saddles, and other goods. When Hagler expressed the hope that she would not be put to death, Chief Justice Henley assured him that the woman, an indentured servant, would be returned to her master. With solemnity Hagler said: "I am glad of it. I am always sorry to lose a woman. The loss of one woman may be the loss of many lives because one woman may be the mother of many children." The report of the conference noted that his audience was

amused, and, observing this, the king added that he "spoke nothing but the truth."

In the same serious tone Henley addressed Hagler, his warriors, and young men. He reiterated the determination of his government to preserve peace and harmony, to suggest the enactment of laws against the sale of strong liquor to the Indians, to propose to the governor an allocation of public money as a gift for certain obligations, to supply them with ammunition, and to build a fort for their protection. As a token of his sincerity Henley presented the king with powder and lead, adding a promise to honor a prior commitment that a house be built for him.

Henley's public reputation and performance of his official duties impressed Governor Dobbs, who recommended on 27 Dec. 1757 that he be appointed a member of the Council if his health was restored, but Henley died the following spring. He was interred in St. Paul's Church, Edenton.

Before leaving England, Henley had been on the point of marrying Agnes Tucker of Corytown, Devon, towards which she advanced £400 "out of her own private fortune." However, as Henley wrote, "the Marriage was postponed to be compleated at a future Day," and he gave her his bond for the amount advanced. In his will, made a few months before his death, he provided that the amount, with interest, be paid to her. The will also left property to a son, John, but there is no mention of a wife or the mother of the son. When specifying the name of an executor of his will, Henley made provisions for the education of his son and the protection of his property for the benefit of the child. Henley held over 1,500 acres of land in Anson, New Hanover, and Orange counties as well as three lots in Edenton. Among his extensive and valuable estate, he listed furniture, china, silver, livestock, a chariot, five slaves, a print of Governor Dobbs, five busts of members of the royal family (purchased by Thomas Baker at the sale), books, and personal apparel.

In an address of the Assembly to the Council on 2 Jan. 1760 on the occasion of complaints that the incumbent chief justice had extorted legal fees from his clerks, the character of Peter Henley was cited. He was described as a man who impartially administered his office, dividing the fees fairly with his clerks, and as a just executor of the laws and of justice. His death, the address continued, was lamented by everyone who wished to see the government strengthened.

SEE: *Acts of the Privy Council, Colonial Series*, vol. 4 (1911); Abel Boyer, *Political State of Great Britain*, vol. 43 (1732); John L. Cheney, Jr., ed., *North Carolina Government, 1585–1979* (1981); Chowan County Estate Records (North Carolina State Archives, Raleigh); John Foster, *Alumni Oxonienses*, vol. 2 (1891); J. Bryan Grimes, *North Carolina Wills and Inventories* (1912); John Hutchins, *The History and Antiquities of the County of Dorset*, vol. 2 (1863); *Register of Admissions to the Honourable Society of the Middle Temple*, vol. 1 (1949); William L. Saunders, ed., *Colonial Records of North Carolina*, vols. 5–6 (1887–88); Stephen B. Weeks, "Peter Henley" (C. L. Van Noppen Papers, Manuscript Department, Duke University Library, Durham).

HENRY A. ROBERTSON, JR.

Henry, Jacob *(ca. 1775–October 1847)*, legislator, was the son of Joel and Amelia Henry. His birthplace is not known, but by the time of the 1790 census Jacob, then under age sixteen, and his parents were living in Carteret County. The family owned eight slaves.

Despite the fact that the North Carolina constitution of 1776 forbade the holding of public office by those who denied the "truth of the Protestant religion" or the "divine authority" of the New Testament, Henry, a Jew, was elected to the North Carolina House of Commons in 1808 and reelected in 1809. On 5 December, soon after the beginning of his second term, Hugh C. Mills, a member from Rockingham County, cited the constitution in declaring that Henry was not qualified as he "denies the divine authority of the New Testament, and refused to take the oath prescribed by law for his qualification." The house resolved itself into a committee of the whole with Thomas Love, of Haywood County, presiding; no proof was presented to support the charges and the resolution was rejected. Henry continued to hold his seat. At the time of the 1810 census Henry was living in the town of Beaufort, Carteret County, but by 1820 he had moved to Charleston, S.C.

In 1801 he married Esther Whitehurst, and they were the parents of at least seven children: Denah, Joel, Philip Jacob, Samuel, Judah (Judith), Cordelia, and Sarah. Esther died in Charleston in July 1823; Henry's mother died there in June 1825. Henry also died in Charleston and probably was buried alongside his wife and mother in the local Hebrew cemetery.

SEE: *Charleston Courier*, 14 Oct. 1847; *Journal of the House of Commons of the State of North Carolina* (1809); A. R. Newsome, "A Miscellany from the Thomas Henderson Letter Book, 1810–1811," *North Carolina Historical Review* 6 (October 1929); Ira Rosenwaike, "Further Light on Jacob Henry," in Leonard Dinnerstein and Mary Dale Palsson, eds., *Jews in the South* (1973).

ALICE R. COTTEN

Henry, Louis Debonair (*1788–13 June 1846*), state legislator, was a native of New Jersey, the son of Michael D. Henry (A.B., Rutgers, 1783); his mother was the daughter of Edward and Elizabeth Batchelor Graham of New Bern. After graduating from Princeton College in 1809, he studied law in New Bern under his uncle, Edward Graham (1764–1833), who had been a law pupil of John Jay, first chief justice of the United States Supreme Court.

One of Henry's best friends at New Bern was a Princeton classmate, Thomas Turner Stanly (1789–1813), the youngest son of John Wright Stanly, who was studying law with his oldest brother, John Stanly, a state legislator and former congressman. Edward Graham had been John Stanly's second in the 1802 political duel at New Bern when former Governor Richard Dobbs Spaight, Sr., was fatally wounded.

At a party in the home of William Gaston, Thomas Stanly wanted to attract the attention of Lucy Hawkins, a visitor from Warren County, who was with Henry on the other side of the tea table. Picking up a small piece of cake, Stanly flipped it across the table and it fell into a cup of tea. Some of the liquid splashed on Henry's vest. The lady exclaimed, "Do you stand that?" Henry took her question seriously and challenged Stanly to a duel.

The pistol duel took place Sunday afternoon, 14 Feb. 1813, a few miles south of Suffolk, Va. Stanly's second was his eighteen-year-old first cousin, George E. Badger, who became a Superior Court judge, secretary of the navy, and U.S. senator. On the first fire Stanly was

killed instantly by a shot in his right side. Henry lost a finger on his left hand in the duel. He fled to New York but, without threat of prosecution, returned to North Carolina and practiced law at Fayetteville. It is reported that for the rest of his life he never would sleep alone in an unlighted room, perhaps in fear that Stanly's ghost would come to haunt him or that a Stanly relative or friend might seek revenge.

During December 1814, in Warren County, Henry married Lucy Hawkins. She was the youngest daughter of Colonel Philemon Hawkins, Jr., Revolutionary patriot, and the sister of Mrs. William Polk and of William Hawkins, who the previous month had completed his third term as governor of North Carolina.

In 1821 and 1822 Henry represented Cumberland County in the state House of Commons, and from 1830 to 1832 he was the legislator from the borough town of Fayetteville, serving in the 1832 session as speaker of the house. The 1834 and 1835 assemblies elected him as a councillor of state. He declined an offer to be minister of Belgium, but in 1837 accepted President Martin Van Buren's commission to settle claims arising from a treaty with Spain.

On 10 Jan. 1842, the Democratic state convention nominated Henry as its candidate for governor. His campaign was hampered by illness, and he was defeated by the Whig incumbent, John Motley Morehead. Two years later at Baltimore he was a delegate to the Democratic National Convention, which nominated James K. Polk, a native Tar Heel, for president. His last official act was to preside over the Democratic state convention at Raleigh in January 1846. Death came suddenly five months later at his home in Raleigh, where he had moved some years before from Fayetteville.

Henry's wife had died on 17 Feb. 1819, at Raleigh, without issue. On 27 Dec. 1821, at Fayetteville, he married Margaret Haywood, the only child of Adam John Haywood, by whom he had seven children: Louis D., Virginia (m. Colonel Duncan McRae of Wilmington), Caroline (m. Colonel John H. Manly of Raleigh), Augusta (m. Captain Robert P. Waring of Charlotte), Margaret (m. Colonel Edward Graham Haywood), Mary (m. General Matthew P. Taylor), and Malvina (m. Douglas Ball of Norfolk, Va.). She died on 3 Apr. 1874 at Raleigh.

SEE: Samuel A. Ashe, *History of North Carolina*, vol. 2 (1925), and ed., *Biographical History of North Carolina*, vol. 2 (1905); Carrie L. Broughton, comp., *Marriage and Death Notices from Raleigh Register and North Carolina State Gazette, 1799–1825* (1944), and *1867–1887* (1951); Gertrude S. Carraway, *The Stanly (Stanley) Family* (1969); R. D. W. Connor, ed., *North Carolina Manual* (1913); Marshall De Lancey Haywood, *Builders of the Old North State* (1968); Princeton University alumni files; John D. Witford, manuscript, *Historical Notes* (1900). A genealogical chart compiled by Governor H. T. Clark is in the possession of Mrs. Pembroke Nash, Tarboro.

GERTRUDE S. CARRAWAY

Henry, Matthew George (*25 Oct. 1910–19 Mar. 1974*), bishop of the Protestant Episcopal church, was born in Chapel Hill, the son of Dr. George Kenneth Grant and Mary Elizabeth Harding Henry. His father was professor of Latin and later assistant registrar at The University of North Carolina. His mother came from a family long active in the Episcopal church in the state: her father, the Reverend Nathaniel Harding, was rector of St. Peter's Church, Washington, for forty-seven years; her grandfather, the Reverend N. C. Hughes, D.D., lived at Chocowinity.

Henry attended the public schools in Chapel Hill and entered The University of North Carolina in 1927, receiving the A.B. degree in chemistry in 1931. A member of Phi Beta Kappa, he held a teaching fellowship at the university while doing graduate work for a year. He subsequently enrolled at the Virginia Theological Seminary, Alexandria, where he was graduated with the bachelor of divinity degree in 1935. After his elevation to the episcopate, he was awarded honorary doctor of divinity degrees from the University of the South (1948) and the Virginia Theological Seminary (1949).

On Trinity Sunday, 16 June 1935, Henry was ordained to the diaconate in the Chapel of the Cross, Chapel Hill, by the Right Reverend Edwin A. Penick, Bishop of North Carolina. He was advanced to the priesthood by Bishop Penick in the Church of the Messiah, Mayodan, on 23 May 1936.

Following his ordination to the diaconate, Henry went to St. Philip's Church, Durham, for a short time. In November and December of the same year he was stationed at St. Paul's, Winston-Salem. Afterwards, Henry became deacon and later priest-in-charge at Christ Church, Walnut Cove; Messiah, Mayodan; St. Philip's, Germantown; and Emmanuel, Stoneville. In 1936 he moved to Tarboro to become rector of Calvary Church. He remained there until 1943, when he took charge of Christ Church, Charlotte. He arrived in Charlotte to find a fledgling mission; he left the church in a flourishing condition, and it afterwards became the largest Episcopal congregation in North Carolina.

In 1948 Henry was elected the third bishop of the Diocese of Western North Carolina, and on 29 September was consecrated at Trinity Church, Asheville. Thus began a remarkable episcopate of twenty-seven years, ending only with the bishop's death.

During his long association with the Episcopal church, Bishop Henry served in various capacities. He was a trustee of the University of the South, of the board of managers for Thompson Orphanage in Charlotte, of St. Mary's Junior College and of St. Augustine's College, both in Raleigh; president of the board of Patterson School near Lenoir; and on the board of managers of the Kanuga Conference Center in Henderson County. From 1965 to 1967 he was president of the North Carolina Council of Churches. He also served as president of the Fourth Province of the Episcopal church and in 1955 received the Worldwide Rural Worker's Fellowship Award for his work in rural church areas. Before his election to the episcopate, he had worked in Charlotte with the Mental Hygiene Board, Traveler's Aid, Medical Aid, Medical Social Service, and Community Chest. As bishop he was instrumental in forming the Asheville Human Relations Council and was appointed to the Governor's Special Committee for Religious Concern for Traffic Safety.

On 30 June 1937, Henry married Cornelia Catharine Sprinkle of Lexington. They were the parents of four children: Anna Catharine (m. Peter Wortham Howes), the Reverend Kenneth Grant, Matthew George, Jr., and Elizabeth Harding.

Bishop Henry died of a heart attack just a few months before his sixty-fifth birthday, when he had planned to retire. He was buried in Calvary Churchyard, Fletcher.

SEE: *Asheville Citizen*, 20 Mar. 1975; *Asheville Citizen-Times*, 29 Sept. 1968; *Chapel Hill Weekly*, 2 Oct. 1968; *Durham Morning Herald*, 20 Mar. 1975; Raleigh *News and Observer*, 26 Sept. 1948.

JAMES ELLIOTT MOORE

Hentz, Caroline Lee Whiting (1 June 1800–11 Feb. 1856), novelist, was born in Lancaster, Mass. Her father, John Whiting, who served as a colonel in the Revolutionary War, was descended from Samuel Whiting who came to the colonies in 1636 and became the first minister in Lynn, Mass.; her mother was Orpah Danforth Whiting. Little is known about her childhood except that she supposedly wrote fiction, drama, and poetry as an adolescent.

On 30 Sept. 1824 she married Nicholas Marcellus Hentz, an emigré who had fled his native France with his family in 1816. The following year she, her husband, and their first child, Marcellus, began their residence in Chapel Hill. She devoted herself to the care of the five children who were born in the first decade of their marriage: Marcellus died before his second birthday, but Charles, Julia, Thaddeus, and Caroline survived their parents. Her husband accepted an appointment as professor of modern language and belle lettres at The University of North Carolina, taught French, and spent his spare time in entomological studies. She found the years in North Carolina satisfying and nostalgically recalled the "kindness, warm feeling, hospitality, and union of Chapel Hill."

In the fall of 1830 Nicholas Hentz, who was described by his son Charles as "a rolling stone; never abiding long in one place," moved the family to Covington, Ky., where he found employment as the head of a female academy. From that point on, Caroline Hentz divided her energies between teaching in various female academies and writing short stories and novels. Beginning with the academy in Covington, she and her husband supervised and taught in girls' schools in Cincinnati, Ohio; Florence, Tuscaloosa, and Tuskegee, Ala.; and Columbus, Ga. Her ambivalent reaction to the teaching profession was reflected in her relatively negative attitude towards her duties along with a recognition that her efforts were necessary in the support of the family: "School again—Alternate coaxing and scolding, counsel and reproof—frowns and smiles—oh! what a life it is—oh woe is me—this weary world! I am often tempted to say—Yet man is doomed to earn his subsistence by the sweat of the brow and the fire of his brain and why not woman also?"

Simultaneously, she was constantly writing fiction and issued dozens of short stories and twelve novels before the end of an extremely successful career during which she gained a popular and national audience. Her first novel, *Lovell's Folly*, appeared in 1833; her last, *Ernest Linwood*, was published in 1856. Mrs. Hentz's literary endeavors were motivated partially by the need to supplement the family's income, and her correspondence with publishers indicates that she sought to profit from the increasing demand for sentimental-domestic fiction, a genre that addressed itself to women and their concerns.

Aside from the financial motivation, she sought in her fiction to fulfill a dual purpose. The first was rooted in a transplanted but undeviating loyalty to the antebellum South. Setting nearly half of her fiction in the South, she attempted to defend that section's commitment to slavery. She claimed that the institution of slavery was misunderstood by Northerners and in fact benefited Southerners, both white and black. Convinced that the misunderstanding stemmed at least in part from the antislavery writings emanating from the North, she responded directly to Harriet Beecher Stowe's *Uncle Tom's Cabin* by defending slavery in *The Planter's Northern Bride*. She noted in a letter to her publisher that Stowe's characterization was completely inaccurate: "Slavery, as she [Stowe] describes it, is an entirely new institution to us." In her preface to the novel, she described relations between whites and blacks in positive terms, writing that "we have been touched and gratified by the exhibition of affectionate kindness and care on the one side, and loyal and devoted attachment on the other."

Her second and more important literary purpose expressed concerns regarding women and their status in society that went beyond sectional boundaries. Along with other women writers of the nineteenth century who focused on women and the home in their fiction, she sought to promote and legitimate the role of women in society. Arguing that women were different from—and morally superior to—their male counterparts, she emphasized that women were the primary inculcators of a virtue and morality necessary for the maintenance of the social fabric and that women performed this function most effectively by remaining in the home and providing models for their husbands and children. Women, she felt, should provide a peaceful haven for their husbands and serve as their spiritual guides. They should also mold their children's character and prepare them for the tasks assigned by society. In short, woman in her fiction was seen as the controlling force in the family, and the family in turn was portrayed as the institution upon which society depended for its continuance and survival.

During the 1840s, Mrs. Hentz's familial responsibilities increased in proportion to the decline of her husband's health. She maintained their last girls' school in Columbus by herself but soon decided that her pen was the surest path to security. She had already produced some short stories and two novels during the years in which she had combined teaching and writing, and the reaction to them determined her decision to concentrate on writing alone to support herself and her family. As she commented, "I am compelled to turn my brains to gold and sell them to the highest bidder." Increasing her production to a startling degree, she achieved her aim, writing eight novels and five collections of short stories all of which were published in the first half of the 1850s.

While visiting her son Charles during the winter of 1855–56 she contracted pneumonia in Marianna, Fla., died, and was buried there. Her husband died nine months later and was buried beside her. Both had joined the Presbyterian church in 1835.

SEE: *Alabama Review*, vol. 4 (October 1951); Rhoda C. Ellison, articles in *American Literature*, vol. 22 (November 1950); Hentz Family Papers (Southern Historical Collection, University of North Carolina Library, Chapel Hill); Historical Society of Pennsylvania; Mary Kelley, "The Unconscious Rebel: Studies in Feminine Fiction, 1820–1880" (Ph.D. dissertation, University of Iowa, 1974); Overbury Collection, Barnard College Library; Manuscripts Collection, Boston Public Library; Manuscripts Collection, Huntington Library; Helen White Papashvily, *All the Happy Endings* (1956).

MARY KELLEY

Hentz, Nicholas Marcellus (25 July 1797–4 Nov. 1856), teacher and America's first arachnologist, was born in Versailles, France, the youngest child of Nicholas and Marie-Anne Thérèse Daubrée Hentz. He was the brother of Jean Nicholas Richard, Françoise Constance Eleonore, and Jean François Victor. In 1810 the youth began to study miniature painting in Paris, and three years later took up medicine and became a hospital assistant. In 1816, after the downfall of Napoleon, political circumstances in France forced his father to escape to America. The elder Hentz and his wife, with their oldest and youngest sons, settled in Wilkes-Barre, Pa.

As a teacher of French and painting, young Hentz resided in Boston and Philadelphia, and then on Sullivan's Island, S.C., where he was a tutor on a plantation. There he intensified his entomological studies with a special interest in spiders. At Harvard he attended lectures in medicine, but abandoned his studies to join the faculty of a boys' school in Northampton, Mass. On 30 Sept. 1824 he married Caroline Lee Whiting of Lancaster, Mass., and in 1827 assumed the "chair of modern languages" at The University of North Carolina. For the next four years he pursued his study of spiders and published a number of articles in scientific journals.

In Chapel Hill, life was not always pleasant. During his second year the trustees ruled that each professor "be in his room on the campus from 9–12, 2–5 each day," and Elisha Mitchell, his noted associate on the faculty, wrote that, although he thought Hentz was "one of the most accomplished Entomologists, perhaps the most accomplished in America," he feared the Frenchman might leave the university, for his field trips required him to "ramble in the woods two or three evenings [afternoons] in the week." In 1829, when the university awarded him an honorary M.A. degree, Hentz revealed to a correspondent that he had then collected about "two-thirds of the American spiders, and that in the South the spiders of a given species are much larger than in the North." In spite of his recognized scholarship, the narrow Presbyterian community at the university frowned upon Hentz's having been reared a Roman Catholic, and suspected him of French revolutionary liberalism. Even the students felt that somehow the study of French was contrary to religious tenets. Though normally genial, the small, slightly built professor was subject to a severe nervous disorder, and then he would become suspicious and jealous. His fits of "ejaculatory prayer," regardless of where he was, disturbed the sedate villagers. Hentz decided to try to improve his locale and his finances.

On 6 June 1831, Mrs. Winifred M. Gales, a close friend of the Hentz family, wrote Jared Sparks that the Hentzes "left Raleigh this day on their way to Kentucky where he has an engagement of 2,000$ a year. For their sakes I rejoice for they were not agreeably suited at Chapel Hill," where the inhabitants persecuted unbelievers "after the most approved manner of dealing with Heretics? There is a great revival amongst the students at Chapel Hill, and Gossip Report says that the Preachers (Missionaries) inculcate the idea that it is adverse to piety and devotion to study profane subjects." After Hentz's departure, French was dropped from the curriculum.

For the next eighteen years Hentz and his wife conducted female academies in Covington, Ky.; Cincinnati, Ohio; Florence, Tuscaloosa, and Tuskegee, Ala.; and Columbus, Ga. In Florence, Hentz joined the Presbyterian church. In 1849 his health began to deteriorate and, after moving to the home of a son in Marianna, Fla., he died there and was buried in the Episcopal Cemetery. From 1850 on, Mrs. Hentz contributed to the family finances by the sale of her widely read fiction.

After Hentz's death, his collection of insects found their way to the Boston Museum. His first scientific publication in 1820 concerned alligators. In addition to three French textbooks issued between 1822 and 1839, he brought out a novel in 1825, *Tadeuskund, the Last King of the Lenape, an Historical Tale*, about an Indian massacre of 1778 in the Wilkes-Barre region. His masterwork, *The Spiders of the United States*, with "two new plates from his skillful pencil," was finally published in 1875.

Nicholas and Caroline Hentz were the parents of five children: Marcellus Fabius (1825–27), Charles Arnould (1827–94), Julia Louisa (Mrs. John W. Keyes, 1828–77), Thaddeus William Harris (1830–78), and Caroline Theresa (Mrs. James Orson Branch, b. 1833).

SEE: Kemp P. Battle, *History of the University of North Carolina*, vol. 1 (1907); Collier Cobb, sketch in *Elisha Mitchell Scientific Journal*, vol. 47 (January 1932 [portrait]); Gales Papers (North Carolina State Archives, Raleigh); Samuel Wood Geiser, sketch in *Field and Laboratory*, vol. 24 (October 1956); Hentz Papers (Southern Historical Collection, University of North Carolina Library, Chapel Hill); *Occasional Papers of the Boston Society of Natural History*, vol. 2 (1875); Helen Waite Papashvily, sketch of Mrs. Hentz, *Notable American Women*, vol. 2 (1971); Laura Coachman Varty, Digest of *Le Conventionnel Hentz, Député de la Moselle* by Jules Florange (1911).

RICHARD WALSER

Hepburn, Andrew Dousa (14 Nov. 1830–14 Feb. 1921), professor and president of Davidson College, was born in Williamsport, Pa., the son of Samuel, an attorney and Democratic state judge, and Rebecca Williamson Hepburn. Andrew grew up in Carlisle, Pa., and attended Jefferson College in Canonsburg, leaving briefly in 1850 to teach at a small school in La Porte, Ind. In 1851 he entered the University of Virginia to pursue two years of advanced study in Latin, Greek, German, natural science, and moral philosophy without taking a degree. After a year of "general reading," or independent study, during 1853 and 1854, he enrolled in the Princeton Theological Seminary and was graduated in 1857. Until his ordination in the southern Presbyterian church (Lexington Presbytery) on 22 Oct. 1858, he was "stated supply" at a church in Harrisonburg, Va.; he then became pastor of a church in New Providence, Va.

At its meeting in December 1859, the board of trustees of The University of North Carolina elected Hepburn professor of metaphysics, logic, and rhetoric; he assumed his chair in the autumn of 1860. Siding with the Confederacy during the Civil War, he remained in Chapel Hill until the 1864–65 academic year, when he took leave to serve as temporary supply pastor for the First Presbyterian Church in Wilmington. While there, in February 1865, he led a delegation of civilian dignitaries who formally surrendered the city to Union forces; his address on this occasion, considered excessively conciliatory by some, caused a brief controversy from which he nonetheless emerged unscathed. During the summer of 1865 he traveled in Germany and studied at the University of Berlin.

In 1867, unable to support his family on his truncated postwar salary, Hepburn resigned his professorship; yet he remained close to the university for the rest of his life. At the commencement of 1867, he delivered the eulogy for the Reverend Dr. James Phillips, the senior professor, who had died in April. Later that year, the board of trustees officially consulted him about reforms to the curriculum. In 1881 he was awarded the honorary LL.D. degree, and in 1883 he delivered the baccalaureate sermon. Before leaving the state, Hepburn represented the Orange Presbytery at a conference in Philadelphia in November 1867, aimed at reconciling the northern and southern branches of the Presbyterian church; however, he declined to vote for any merger plan, in accordance with his instructions as a delegate.

In 1868, Hepburn joined the faculty of Miami University of Oxford, Ohio, as professor of English literature; in 1871, he became president of the university. When Miami temporarily closed in 1873, he returned to North Carolina as a professor at Davidson College, first in the chair of Latin and French (1874–75), then in his preferred chair of mental philosophy and English literature (1875–85).

Davidson's board of trustees elected Hepburn president of the college in 1877. While in office, he succeeded in having abolished the master of arts degree, at that time awarded automatically to select alumni regardless of academic effort in imitation of archaic English academic custom. His comprehensive proposals for curriculum reform included increased course offerings in English, French, and German; elective, rather than mandatory, programs in Latin and Greek; and a four-year program in Bible studies. Each of these was eventually adopted by the college. Impressed with the systems of self-regulation through an honor code, which he had observed at Virginia and North Carolina, he attempted to set up a similar system at Davidson in place of faculty proctoring. In this case, however, he was frustrated by tradition-minded professors and trustees. The Davidson honor system, tentatively enacted in 1880, was rescinded by the trustees after an unfortunate hazing episode at the commencement of 1881 (it was reenacted years later). Other initiatives proceeded slowly, if at all.

These frustrations, plus a desire to return to active teaching, led Hepburn to resign the presidency at Davidson in 1885 and to accept reappointment as professor of English literature at Miami of Ohio, which had reopened the same year. He held the latter position until his retirement in 1908.

Hepburn died in Oxford, Ohio. In addition to his honorary degree from The University of North Carolina, he received an M.A. degree from Jefferson College (1860) and a doctor of divinity degree from Hampden-Sydney (1876). Hepburn Hall, on the campus of Miami of Ohio, was named in his honor.

On 10 July 1857, Hepburn married Henriette McGuffey, a daughter of William Holmes McGuffey, author of the celebrated *Eclectic Reader* series and Hepburn's instructor in moral philosophy at the University of Virginia. One son, Charles McGuffey Hepburn, was valedictorian of the Davidson class of 1878; he later studied law at the University of Virginia (1878–80), practiced in Ohio, served as dean of the University of Indiana Law School, and wrote a widely used hornbook on torts.

Hepburn was the author of a *Manual of English Rhetoric* (1875), as well as several reviews and critical articles. Yet he was most highly regarded by his contemporaries for his abilities as a classroom teacher. In the words of Kemp P. Battle, "Dr. Hepburn's career . . . was distinguished for excellent scholarship, inspiring teaching and preaching, a style in writing which was a model of pure English, and for the lofty virtues of a gentleman and a Christian."

SEE: Archives (Davidson College Library); Kemp P. Battle, *History of the University of North Carolina*, vols. 1, 2 (1905–12); Hepburn Letters (Southern Historical Collection, University of North Carolina Library, Chapel Hill); Andrew D. Hepburn Papers (Archives, Miami University, Oxford, Ohio); Philip N. Moore, *Remarks at the Unveiling of the Hepburn Memorial Tablet . . .* (1923); Cornelia Rebekah Shaw, *Davidson College* (1923); Robert Hamlin Stone, *History of the Orange Presbytery* (1970).

BENNETT L. STEELMAN

Hepburn, James (*ca. 1752–May 1798*), Loyalist merchant, attorney, politician, and planter, was born in Scotland. The year and circumstances of his migration to America are unknown, but prior to 1772 he was a clerk for the firm of Alston, Young, and Co., merchants trading extensively in Virginia and North Carolina. In 1771 he entered into partnership with Joseph Montfort, treasurer of the northern district of North Carolina, and Robert Nelson, merchant, as Hepburn, Nelson, and Co., for trading on the Cape Fear River. In 1771 or 1772 Hepburn went to London and purchased goods for the company, but the venture was unsuccessful and in 1774 the firm was dissolved. Hepburn had by then achieved sufficient local prominence to be appointed, in April 1774, justice of the peace for Cumberland County. Also in that year he was licensed as an attorney and qualified in the courts of Cumberland, New Hanover, and Halifax counties.

Hepburn's Loyalist sympathies were in evidence as early as July 1775, when Governor Josiah Martin considered him reliable enough to furnish wagons to transport the records of Lord Granville's land office to safety. In the same month the Wilmington Committee of Safety denounced him in the strongest terms as a traitor to American liberties. The following month he petitioned the committee to be restored to favor, and was ordered to sign the association not to engage in trade with England. Within a few weeks he took his seat as a delegate from Campbellton to the Third Provincial Congress convening at Hillsborough on 20 August. He signed the test and was appointed to several committees, including one charged with securing the support of Scottish immigrants.

His adherence to the patriot cause was of short duration. In February 1776, he took part in the Moore's Creek Bridge campaign as secretary to Donald MacDonald. Before the battle he was sent under a flag of truce to demand Richard Caswell's surrender, and reported back to MacDonald that the patriot position could be attacked. After the battle he was imprisoned successively at Halifax, Charlotte, Salisbury, and again at Halifax.

In September 1778 Hepburn appeared in New York City, where he was licensed to practice law, and remained there until at least November 1779. By June 1780, shortly after the capture of Charleston by the British, he had established himself in that city as a public notary and attorney. When Governor Thomas Burke of North Carolina was imprisoned on James Island near Charleston in November and December 1781, Hepburn was among several prominent Loyalists from North Carolina who attempted unsuccessfully to obtain for him a parole within American lines.

When the British evacuated Charleston in December 1782, Hepburn was among the large number of Loyalists who went to St. Augustine. He was befriended by the governor of East Florida, Patrick Tonyn, and received appointments as proctor of the court of vice-admiralty, attorney general, and member of the council of the province.

In July 1784, Hepburn migrated to the Bahama Islands, the British colony eventually to receive many southern Loyalists. A sizable number had gone there already, and had begun an insistent demand for land, provisions, and offices that alarmed the governor, John Maxwell. Within a few days of his arrival Hepburn had assumed the presidency of the dissidents, who styled themselves the Board of American Loyalists. The governor had no military force at his disposal, and during the following months the Loyalists, led by Hepburn and Robert Johnston of South Carolina, refused to recognize Maxwell as governor and attempted to gain their demands through rioting, the disruption of law courts, and petitions to the king and various officials in England. Maxwell retaliated by refusing Hepburn and Johnston licenses to practice law, dissolving the troublesome assembly, and issuing a precept prohibiting the election of Hepburn to that body. When the new assembly met in February 1785, Hepburn was returned as member for Cat Island, and the governor promptly prorogued the assembly. Maxwell was recalled to England, and the new governor, John Powell, soon was embroiled in the same difficulties. Powell complained to authorities in England that Hepburn, "the most vociferous," and Johnston, "the most able and dangerous," were inflaming the Loyalists.

The new assembly, however, proved more tractable to the government. Hepburn and several other dissident members failed to prevent the return of members supporting the governor, and in September 1785 the assembly expelled Hepburn and four of his supporters. After this incident he ceased active opposition to the government, withdrew to his substantial estate on Cat Island, consisting of some 1,300 acres and 65 slaves, and proceeded to become a prominent cultivator of cotton. In 1796 he again was elected to the assembly, but this time his service was uncontroversial. At his death he left a widow, Mary, and three children, James, John, and Eliza.

SEE: Audit Office Papers and Treasury Papers (Public Record Office, London, England); Bahamas, *Journal of the General Assembly, 1779–1786* (1912); Burke Letter Books and Cumberland County Court Minutes (North Carolina State Archives, Raleigh); Nassau, Bahamas, *The Bahama Gazette* (1789–98); Hugh F. Rankin, *The North Carolina Continentals* (1971); *The Royal South-Carolina Gazette*, 20 June 1781; William Saunders and Walter Clark, eds., *Colonial and State Records of North Carolina*, 26 vols. (1886–1905); Kenneth Scott, comp., *Rivington's New York Newspaper: Excerpts from a Loyalist Press, 1773–1783* (1973); Will Books (Bahama Archives).

ROBERT J. CAIN

Herbst, Johannes (*23 July 1735–15 Jan. 1812*), Moravian composer, was born at Kempten, Allgäu, Germany, to Lutheran parents. He was educated at Hernhut, Germany, where he served an apprenticeship in clockmaking. From 1762 to 1766, Herbst worked in the Moravian children's schools in England. He then returned to Germany, was ordained deacon in 1774, and served the Moravians in Gnadenfrey for six years. Subsequently, he was called to Lancaster, Pa., and emigrated to the United States with his wife, Rosine Louise Clemens. Their three children—Sophie Louise, Johann

Ludwig, and Samuel Heinrich (who died young in 1786)—were left behind in Germany to be educated in Moravian schools.

In 1791 Herbst moved to Lititz, Pa., where, for almost twenty years, he served first as assistant pastor, then pastor. Among his many responsibilities he led the worship services, directed music, played the organ when necessary, and kept "the official Diaries, Minutes, and Financial Accounts of the Congregation." Herbst composed anthems for special days in the Moravian religious calendar and copied music that was used in the Moravian schools. A major accomplishment at Lititz was his music collection. In the catalogue of music he compiled in 1795, and afterwards updated regularly, he arranged pieces alphabetically according to the first words of the text, not according to the composer. Apparently this was a standard procedure for early catalogues of music in Pennsylvania Moravian settlements.

Herbst is considered the most prolific composer among musicians who served the Moravian church in America. The present catalogue of Moravian compositions, derived from that compiled by Herbst in 1795, lists more than one hundred compositions by him. About fifty of them were probabliy written in America. According to one source, "A few of his European compositions are expressive and even audacious, but most of them are rather dull and uninteresting." When Herbst arrived in this country, his style of composition underwent a change. He "attempted larger forms, wrote more florid and independent parts for the strings, and added wind instruments to his orchestra." In the Moravian settlements, Herbst's anthems were popular, apparently because of their plain, obvious style.

In 1811 Herbst was called to Salem, N.C. Two days prior to leaving Lititz, he was made Bishop of the Moravian Church. However, he served as pastor of the Salem congregation only a few months before his final illness. Despite ill health, he remained interested in church music and continued to contribute manuscripts of performing parts to the congregation's library. His death in Salem was noted both within and outside the Moravian community. Afterwards the Elders' Conference took the unusual action of instructing one of its members to contact a Raleigh printer and ask that "the home-going of our departed Brother, Johannes Herbst, shall be announced in a suitable manner in the public papers."

SEE: Hans T. David, *Musical Life in the Pennsylvania Settlements of the Unitas Fratrum* (1959); Hans T. David and Albert G. Rau, *A Catalogue of Music by American Moravians, 1742–1842* (1938); Marilyn Gombosi, *Catalog of the Johannes Herbst Collection* (1970).

GEORGE BOWLING

Heron, Benjamin (*21 Dec. 1722–22 June 1770*), mariner and colonial official, was born in Lymington, Hampshire, England. He served in the British Navy and took part in the Cartagena Expedition before settling in North Carolina. His brother Charles was an apothecary and a surgeon at Corhampton, Hampshire, England.

Captain Heron became master of a ship sailing between England and the colonies. He was in Wilmington by 1755, when he was authorized by the town commissioners to purchase a fire engine in London and transport it to Wilmington for the protection of that city. By 1761, Heron had been appointed clerk of the pleas of the province, deputy surveyor, and deputy auditor of the king's revenue. Subsequently he became clerk of the Crown (1762), secretary of the province, naval officer for North Carolina (1762), a commissioner of pilotage for the Cape Fear River (1764), and a member of the governor's Council (1764–69). In the Council, he frequently served on the committee to settle public claims. During the Regulator rebellion in the backcountry of North Carolina, he was appointed lieutenant general of the governor's forces (1768) although he left the colony before actual hostilities began.

Heron is best remembered for building one of the first drawbridges in America, across the Northeast River above Wilmington. Authorized by the General Assembly in 1766, the bridge was to have "one wide arch of thirty feet for rafts and pettiauguas to pass through and six feet high above high water mark, and be made to draw up occasionally for the navigation of vessels of larger burthern." The drawbridge was described by a traveler in 1775 as a "noble" structure which "opens at the middle to both sides and rises by pullies, so as to suffer ships to pass under it."

Along with other interests, Heron owned several plantations, including Marle Bluff, Mulberry, Mount Blake, and Four Mile House. In 1769 he embarked for England on a one-year journey to recover his health. Instead, he died at Islington, a borough of London, and was buried in St. George's Chapel, Windsor.

Heron's first wife was Mary Howe, daughter of Job Howe and sister of Revolutionary War general Robert Howe. After her death, he married Alice Marsden, daughter of Rufus and Alice Marsden. His children included Mary (m. Thomas Hooper), Elizabeth (m. John McKenzie), and Frances (m. Samuel Swann).

SEE: Arthur Adams, *Living Descendants of Royal Blood* (1949); Donald R. Lennon and Ida Brooks Kellam, eds., *The Wilmington Town Book* (1973); New Hanover County Deed Books, New Hanover County Will Books; William L. Saunders, ed., *Colonial Records of North Carolina*, vols. 5, 6 (1887, 1888).

DONALD R. LENNON

Herring, Harriet Laura (*27 July 1892–18 Dec. 1976*), social science researcher and student of socio-industrial relations in the South, was born in Kinston, the seventh and last child of William Isler Herring and his second wife, Laura E. Loftin. Members of the Herring family were among the founders of Johnston and Lenoir counties. A member of the class of 1913 at Meredith College, Harriet spent a year as a high school teacher in Scotland Neck (1914–15), then two years on the staff of Chowan College (1915–17). She went on to receive a master's degree in history from Radcliffe in 1918 and a special certificate in industrial relations from Bryn Mawr College the following year.

Beginning what was to be a lifelong commitment to the industrial community and the welfare of its workers, Miss Herring in 1918 took a position as employment manager with the Roxford Knitting Company in Philadelphia. Returning to North Carolina, she became a community worker for the Pomona Mills in Greensboro and in 1922 personnel director for the Carolina Cotton and Woolen Mills, a division of Marshall Field and Company, in Spray. There, with the support of Luther H. Hodges, then personnel manager for Marshall Field in the Leaksville-Spray area, she instituted the first comprehensive employee welfare system for cotton mill workers in the South.

In 1925, she accepted the invitation of director Howard W. Odum to join the staff of the Institute for Research in Social Science (IRSS) at The University of North Carolina. Her appointment as a research associate charged with examining reports of social ills connected with the industrialization of the South was sought by Odum in the belief that, having been "born here of the same folk," she would be an investigator acceptable to mill owners and others in positions of power and influence. The institute's projected study of the wide-ranging effects of paternalism in the textile industry was, however, rejected by the North Carolina Cotton Manufacturers Association and attacked by David Clark, editor of the *Southern Textile Bulletin*. As a result, Miss Herring's initial research focused on the company's role in shaping life in the mill village. Published as *Welfare Work in Mill Villages: The Story of Extra-Mill Activities in North Carolina* (1929), this was but the first of many investigations of the textile industry in particular and the industrialization of the region in general she would conduct as the institute's specialist in industrial research. During her forty-year association with the IRSS, she wrote numerous articles and reports on these subjects and two more books, *Southern Industry and Regional Development* (1940) and *Passing of the Mill Village: Revolution in a Southern Institution* (1949).

She also contributed to the institute's research in other areas. During the 1930s, with Odum and T. J. Woofter, Jr., she directed a group of related projects on "A State in Depression." She was coauthor of *Part-Time Farming in the Southeast* (1937), a research monograph prepared for the Works Progress Administration, and one in a series of IRSS studies on the plight of the southern farmer. With George L. Simpson she wrote *North Carolina Associated Communities: A Case Study of Voluntary Subregional Organization* (1953), one of a number of community surveys prepared during the directorship of Gordon W. Blackwell. Throughout this period Miss Herring also served on the faculty of the Department of Sociology, teaching a course on the industrial community.

Her continuing investigation of social welfare questions and her commitment to the industrialization of the state and the region influenced her activities outside the institute and the university. She participated in the work of the North Carolina Conference for Social Service, serving as secretary from 1928 to 1931. She was frequently a consultant to the state government of North Carolina. On leave from the IRSS, she served as state superintendent of reemployment during the 1930s, and later she produced a section-by-section study entitled *Industrial Development in North Carolina*, issued by the State Planning Board in 1945. Governor William B. Umstead appointed her to the Commission on Reorganization of State Government (1953–57). With other members of the institute staff, she provided the leadership for the state Commission on Revenue Structure's Conference on Economic and Social Factors in the Development of North Carolina (1955–56). In addition, Miss Herring was active in politics at all levels; in 1960 she was a delegate to the Democratic National Convention.

After retiring from the university in 1965, she continued to live in Chapel Hill for several years as professor emeritus of sociology. She then returned to the Kinston area. At the time of her death at age eighty-four, she was working on a social history of industrial communities through the ages.

SEE: *Chapel Hill Weekly*, 13 Apr. 1945; Harriet Laura Herring Papers (Southern Historical Collection, University of North Carolina Library, Chapel Hill); Guy Benton Johnson and Guion Griffis Johnson, *Research in Service to Society: The First Fifty Years of the Institute for Research in Social Science at the University of North Carolina* (1980); Talmage C. Johnson and Charles R. Holloman, *The Story of Kinston and Lenoir County* (1954); Minutes of the Faculty Council, University of North Carolina, 18 Feb. 1977 (University of North Carolina Library, Chapel Hill); Raleigh *News and Observer*, 12 Aug. 1933; *Who's Who of American Women: A Biographical Dictionary of Notable Living American Women*, vol. 2 (1961–62).

KATHERINE F. MARTIN

Herring, Herbert James (*11 Dec. 1899–23 Sept. 1966*), educator and university administrator, was born in rural Pender County, the son of Julian Fletcher and Minnie Alice Johnson Herring. After graduating with honors from high school, he entered Trinity College (now Duke University) in the fall of 1918 and was graduated with a B.A. degree in 1922. He taught English in R. J. Reynolds High School, Winston-Salem (1922–24), then returned to Durham in mid-1924 to become assistant dean of Duke University, thereby forming an affiliation that continued through his professional career. In 1928–29 he was granted a leave of absence for graduate study at Columbia University, receiving an M.A. degree in 1929. Later, he was awarded an honorary LL.D. degree from Juniata College, Huntingdon, Pa. (1948).

At Duke University, Herring taught speech (1925–43) and was promoted to dean of men (1935). In 1942 he became dean of Trinity College, the university's undergraduate college for men, and held the position until mid-1956. In 1946 he was given the dual appointment of dean and vice-president in the Division of Student Life, serving until his retirement on 31 Dec. 1964. On that occasion Duke president Douglas M. Knight said of him: "Few men in American education are privileged to serve their University so long and so well as he has done—for these 40 years of devoted and single-minded service to Duke. Dr. Herring's primary interest and his primary responsibility were the same—a constant concern for the welfare of students during their undergraduate days." Herring was appointed vice-president emeritus in 1965. During the final year of his life, he served as general consultant to the administration of Louisburg College, Louisburg.

Herring was a member of the Newcomen Society, Tau Kappa Alpha, Sigma Upsilon, Phi Eta Sigma, Omicron Delta Kappa (leadership), Phi Beta Kappa (scholarship), and Sigma Chi (grand praeter, 1937–45). Organizations with which he was affiliated included the Rotary Club of Durham (president, 1947–48), Executives Club (president, 1949), Durham County Chapter of the American Red Cross (first vice-president, 1955–57), Durham United Fund (campaign chairman, 1958; president, 1959); North Carolina Association of Collegiate Registrars (president, 1939), Academic Deans of Southern States (chairman, 1946–47), North Carolina College Conference (executive committee, 1950; president, 1956–57), Committee on International Exchange of Persons (1950–54), Louisburg College Board of Trustees, American Council on Education Advisory Committee for the State Department's Leadership and Specialists Program (1957–60), and Educational Advisory Committee to the Committee on Education, U.S. House of Representatives, Seventy-eighth Congress (1944).

He was the recipient of many honors for his outstanding work in both civic and educational circles. He was selected in 1957 by the Durham Merchants Association as one of five "Fathers of the Year"; served as an official North Carolina delegate to the Southern Regional Conference on Education beyond the High School; was cited for outstanding leadership of the United Fund campaign in 1959; and was presented the Tau Kappa Alpha Distinguished Alumni Award for 1959, one of eight selected in the United States.

A dedicated layman, Herring was a member of Trinity Methodist Church, Durham, where he long taught the Julian S. Carr Bible Class, for which he was given a special citation in 1951. He saw military service as a member of the Student Army Training Corps at Trinity College in September-December 1918.

On 31 Dec. 1929, he married Virginia Cozart, of Stem, daughter of Wiley S. and Virginia Bacon Cozart. They had two children: Virginia Frank (Mrs. B. A. Lenski) and Herbert James, Jr. Herring died in Durham and was buried in Maplewood Cemetery.

SEE: *Durham Morning Herald*, 31 Dec. 1946, 24 Sept. 1966; *Durham Sun*, 31 Dec. 1946; Info Sheet (Office of Information Services, Duke University, Durham); *Who Was Who in America*, vol. 5; *Who's Who in American Education*, vol. 16 (1954); *Who's Who in the South and Southwest* (1947).

C. SYLVESTER GREEN

Herrington, William D. *(b. 1841)*, Confederate soldier and author, was born in Pitt County, probably the son of Moses Herrington and the brother of Lewis W., James L., and Mary A., all of whom were orphaned in 1858. The family name sometimes appears as Harrington, but apparently in error. William in 1858 became the ward of Churchill Perkins of Pactolus, the wealthiest man in the county, a planter, merchant, and longtime member of the General Assembly. Perkins was one of the founders of Jordan Plain Academy, which young Herrington may have attended; he was listed as a student and a member of Perkins's household in the 1860 census. The Pitt County Guardian Returns for 1858 indicate that Perkins held $595.95 for Herrington. On 5 May 1862 Herrington spent $115 for a horse, followed soon afterwards by other amounts for a pair of gaiters, a pair of fine blankets, several kinds of cloth probably for a uniform (as an additional sum was paid "to Mrs. May for work"), socks, and a shirt collar.

On 14 May 1862, in Raleigh, Herrington enlisted in the Third North Carolina Cavalry (also known as the Forty-first Regiment) and served in Company I until 15 Dec. 1864, when he transferred to the First Battalion, Sharp Shooters; either then or shortly afterwards he was promoted to corporal. It was reported that he sought this transfer "for the purpose of gathering material necessary to the completion of a Tale of the war, the plot of which was laid in the Shenandoah Valley." Herrington contributed "popular romances" to the Raleigh weekly, *The Mercury*.

In 1864, while still a member of the Third Cavalry, Herrington was the author of a "novelette," *The Captain's Bride: A Tale of the War*, published in Raleigh by Wm. B. Smith & Co. It was dedicated to Perkins "as an humble tribute of Gratitude to his Kindness and Benevolence, by his ever grateful ward the Author." The first printing of 5,000 copies was quickly sold out, and a second edition was published in February 1865, although a copy of only the first edition has survived. An advertisement reported that "This charming Story has been pronounced by both the press and the public as one of the most delightful contributions that has been made to Polite Southern Literature." It was followed by *The Deserter's Daughter* from the same publisher, copy-

righted in 1864 but with the imprint date 1865 and actually published in early February. Both tales had previously been published in *The Mercury*. No separate printing of a third novel, *The Refugee's Niece*, is known to have survived, but it appears in *The Mercury* of 7 May 1864. A fourth story, "Viola; or, The Victim: A True Story of War and Love," was published in *The Mercury* of 22 and 29 Oct. 1864. These brief stories are well written, thoroughly loyal in sentiment to the Confederate cause, and tell of overcoming great odds. The settings are clearly eastern North Carolina, and undoubtedly reflect the author's military experience there.

While on duty in Virginia, Herrington was reported missing at Hatcher's Run on 6 Feb. 1865. Federal records describe him as a "Rebel deserter. Has taken the Oath of Allegiance." He actually signed an Oath of Amnesty at City Point, Va., 9 Feb. 1865, where he was described as "complexion-light; hair-light; eyes-blue; height-5 ft. 7 in." A Register of Refugees and Rebel Deserters, Provost Marshal General, Washington, D.C., states that he was received on 14 Feb. 1865, after which transportation was furnished to Madison, Wis.

No further trace has been found of Herrington. There is nothing in Madison to suggest that he ever lived there, nor can any record of him be found by the state historical agencies in the other states that existed at that time. A Raleigh newspaper, in reporting Herrington missing, observed that "he is possessed of indomitable energy. We hope he may soon be exchanged." When state indexes to the 1870 census become available, it may be possible to determine where he located and whether he continued to write.

Perkins, whose home still stands at Pactolus, made his last report as Herrington's guardian on 1 Jan. 1864. He died on 8 Nov. 1867 and his will, proved in February 1868, makes no mention of Herrington.

SEE: Confederate Roster Project files (North Carolina State Archives, Raleigh); Wm. D. Herrington, *The Captain's Bride* (copy in Duke University Library, Durham) and *The Deserter's Daughter* (copy in the North Carolina Collection, University of North Carolina Library, Chapel Hill); Pitt County census returns, 1850, 1860 (microfilm, North Carolina Collection, Chapel Hill); Pitt County Wills and Guardian Returns (North Carolina State Archives, Raleigh); Raleigh *The Mercury*, 7 May, 4, 11 June, 30 July, 6 Aug., 22, 29 Oct. 1864; Raleigh *Southern Field and Fireside*, 24 Sept. 1864, 28 Jan., 25 Feb., 11 Mar. 1865; Salem *People's Press*, 29 Sept. 1864, 23 Feb. 1865.

WILLIAM S. POWELL

Herritage, William *(ca. 1707–69)*, lawyer and planter, served for thirty years as clerk of the General Assembly of North Carolina. His early life remains shrouded in mystery and his parentage unknown. Herritage arrived in North Carolina from Essex County, Va., in the early 1730s. By 1736, he had settled in Craven County and had begun to acquire large tracts of land. Evidently well educated and knowledgeable in the law, he quickly won the respect of colonial leaders.

Herritage became a resident of New Bern and by 1740 had married Susannah Moore, daughter of Adam Moore (Mohr) who had been one of the original Palatine settlers of the town. Herritage took part in various civic activities, and he served on the commission responsible for building Christ Church. In 1741 he provided the Craven County Court with the first census of New Bern, which listed twenty-one families.

As a member of the colonial aristocracy, Herritage

was a major planter in his area and held extensive land on the Neuse and Trent rivers. In the 1750s, he established residence a few miles from New Bern at a plantation known as Springfield. During his life, he took part in land transactions involving fifteen town lots in New Bern and over 7,000 acres in Craven and Dobbs (now Lenoir) counties. At his death, his heirs inherited three plantations, seven lots, and two stores in New Bern, an additional 2,200 acres, and sixty-five slaves. The inventory of his estate revealed a personal library of over two hundred books. Almost half of his literary holdings were law books, but his reading interests ranged from the *Book of Common Prayer* to the works of Aristotle and Locke.

As a notable lawyer, Herritage appeared frequently before the Craven County Court of Pleas and Quarter Sessions, representing clients in cases involving land titles, the settlement of estates, and the licensing of businesses. In 1739, he was appointed the first King's Attorney for Craven County.

Herritage played an influential part in the political life of the colony as clerk of the lower house of the Assembly. He was chosen unanimously for the office in 1739 and continued in the position until his death, serving under six different speakers of the house and three royal governors. During his unusually lengthy term, he became involved in controversy and was called upon to give evidence in charges against the chief justice and in arguments over representation in the Assembly. Paid by the house, responsible to it rather than to the governor, and involved in the passage and recording of the colony's laws, Herritage held a legislative office second in importance only to that of the speaker.

One law of personal interest to Herritage was that of 1762 which provided for the establishment of Kingston on land he owned on the Neuse River, thus earning him the title of founder of present-day Kinston. He had acquired the land, known as Atkins Bank, in 1744 for £399. From his 640-acre plot, he provided 100 acres for town lots and 50 for a town common. The bill was introduced in the Assembly by his son-in-law, Richard Caswell, and members of the Herritage and Caswell families became prominent in the early development of the town and in efforts to further trade along the Neuse.

Herritage was married three times, first to Susannah Moore, then to Susannah Franck (daughter of John Martin Franck), and in 1761 to Sarah Lovick (widow of Thomas Lovick of Carteret County). He had seven children who survived to adulthood: Sarah, Heneage, Susannah, Anna, John, William Martin, and Elizabeth. John saw action in the Revolutionary War and service in the lower house; Sarah married Richard Caswell, who became governor of the new state in 1776.

Herritage died in the spring of 1769 and was probably interred at Springfield plantation. He left no known portrait or likeness, but he did leave a reputation as a prosperous, respected colonial leader. In 1914, historian R. D. W. Connor described Herritage's accomplishments: "The records of his time reveal him to us as a planter who cultivated his broad acres with great skill and success; as an attorney who managed large affairs for his clients with distinguished ability and fidelity; as a citizen whose services were always at the command of the community; as a public official who for thirty years bore a large and significant part in directing the legislation of the Colony."

SEE: Blanche Humphrey Abee, *Colonists of Carolina* (1938); Robert Digges Wimberly Connor, "Tower Hill," *North Carolina Booklet* (1914); Craven County Deeds, Inventories, and Wills (North Carolina State Archives, Raleigh); Craven County Land Grants (North Carolina Land Grant Office, Raleigh); Alonzo Thomas Dill, Jr., "Eighteenth Century New Bern: A History of the Town and Craven County," *North Carolina Historical Review* 22, 23 (1945, 1946); Talmage C. Johnson and Charles R. Holloman, *The Story of Kinston and Lenoir County* (1954); Minutes of the Craven County Court of Pleas and Quarter Sessions (North Carolina State Archives, Raleigh); William L. Saunders, ed., *Colonial Records of North Carolina*, vols. 4–8 (1886–90).

GEORGE-ANNE WILLARD

Herty, Charles Holmes (4 Dec. 1867–27 July 1938), chemist, the son of Bernard and Louisa Turno Herty, was born in Milledgeville, Ga. He attended Middle Georgia Military and Agricultural College for four years before enrolling in the University of Georgia, where he received the Ph.B. degree in 1886. Four years later he was awarded a Ph.D. by Johns Hopkins University. During 1899 and 1900 he studied under Otto N. Witt at the University of Berlin and Alfred Werner at the University of Zurich.

Herty's varied career was characterized by service to his state and to the South. He was an assistant to the state chemist of North Carolina in 1888, and served in the same capacity at the Georgia Agricultural Experiment Station in Athens in 1890–91. From 1891 to 1902 he taught at the University of Georgia and from 1905 to 1916 at The University of North Carolina, where he was Smith Professor of General and Industrial Chemistry, dean of the School of Applied Science (1908–11), and a member of the athletics committee. At both schools he stressed the importance of applied chemistry as a solution to the South's economic problems.

While working for the U.S. Forestry Bureau from 1902 to 1904, Herty designed a cup-and-gutter method for collecting rosin from pine trees. His new technique replaced the old practice of collecting rosin from boxes cut into the base of the trees, thereby saving the turpentine industry millions of dollars. With grants from the Chemical Foundation, the state of Georgia, and the city of Savannah, Herty in 1931 began research in Savannah concerned with the production of rayon and paper from the cellulose and pulp of the southern pine tree. He successfully demonstrated that newsprint could be made from pine pulp, previously thought to be too resinous. This discovery stimulated the paper industry throughout the southern coastal region.

Herty attained a position of national prominence in his field, serving as president of the American Chemical Society for two terms (1915–16) and of the Synthetic Organic Chemical Manufacturers Association (1921–26), as well as editor of *The Journal of Industrial and Engineering Chemistry* (1917–21). From 1926 to 1928 he was adviser to the Chemical Foundation, and in 1928 he opened a consulting office in New York City. In addition to several separate publications, Herty wrote numerous articles for such periodicals as the *Journal of the Elisha Mitchell Scientific Society*, *American Chemical Journal*, *Journal of the American Chemical Society*, *Journal of Industrial and Engineering Chemistry*, and *Science*. His honors included an LL.D. degree awarded by The University of North Carolina (1933); degrees from the University of Florida, the University of Georgia, Duke University, Colgate University, the University of Pittsburgh, and Oglethorpe University; and the medal of the American Institute of Chemists (1932). On 17 Dec.

1946 a bronze memorial to Herty was unveiled at the Georgia capitol in Atlanta.

On 23 Dec. 1895, Herty married Sophie Schaller of Athens, Ga. They had three children: Charles Holmes, a metallurgist; Frank Bernard, a businessman; and Sophie Dorothea, a plant physiologist. An Episcopalian, Herty created while in Chapel Hill a retirement plan for clergy of the local parish; a system based on it was adopted by the entire denomination in 1917. He died in Savannah, and his cremated remains were buried in the old city cemetery in Milledgeville.

SEE: *Atlanta Constitution*, 18 Dec. 1946; Frank K. Cameron, "Charles Holmes Herty, 1867–1938," *Journal of the American Chemical Society* 61 (1939); *DAB*, vol. 9 (1958); *Milledgeville* (Ga.) *Times*, 29 July 1938; Raleigh *News and Observer*, 9 May 1932; J. Maryon Saunders to Jaques Cattell, 23 June 1943 (Herty clipping file, North Carolina Collection, University of North Carolina Library, Chapel Hill); *University of North Carolina Catalogue* (1905–17).

MAURY YORK

Herty, Charles Holmes, Jr. *(6 Oct. 1896–17 Jan. 1953)*, metallurgist and chemical engineer, was born in Athens, Ga., the son of Sophie Schaller and Charles H. Herty, then a faculty member at the University of Georgia. The family moved to Chapel Hill, N.C., in 1904, when his father became head of the Department of Chemistry at The University of North Carolina. He attended the Asheville School and The University of North Carolina, where he studied chemistry and received a B.S. degree in chemical engineering in 1918.

In the summer of 1918 Herty joined the army as a private in the Chemical Warfare Service and headed the chemical plant at Saltville, Va.; he was discharged in 1919 as a sergeant in the Ordnance Department. At the Massachusetts Institute of Technology he earned the M.S. degree in 1921 and the D.Sc. degree in 1924, conducting research that was to be the foundation of his life's work in steelmaking metallurgy at the Buffalo Station of the institute's School of Chemical Engineering Practice, at the Lackawanna Plant of the Bethlehem Steel Company. He continued at the Buffalo Station as a research associate until 1926, when he was appointed head of ferrous metallurgy research at the U.S. Department of Mines in Pittsburgh. In 1931 Herty became director of the Metallurgical Advisory Board, also in Pittsburgh, established in 1926 by a consortium of thirty interested steel companies to carry out research on the physical chemistry of steelmaking at the Carnegie Institute of Technology and the Pittsburgh Station of the U.S. Bureau of Mines.

Prior to his pioneering investigations, few of the chemical reactions involved in the production of steel had been clearly established, and practical open-hearth operators based production on rules of thumb without a theoretical basis. Herty's principal theoretical contributions foresaw the end to this empirical era: he developed the first dependable method for chemical determination of the oxygen content of the steel bath, demonstrated the mechanism of formation of nonmetallic inclusions when deoxidizers are added to steel, showed how to minimize the content of nonmetallic oxide inclusions, devised the first scientifically based system to control iron oxide in slag, determined quantitatively the effects of oxygen and deoxidation methods on the physical properties of finished steel, evaluated deoxidation constants for several important deoxidizing agents in steel, and made many important studies of the fluidity and viscosity of steel slags. Matching his gift of insight into theory was his rare ability to understand and talk with the practical steel operator. It was this combination of scientific and practical talents that translated his theoretical discoveries into practice in steel plants; both executives and operators came to realize that the previously mysterious factors governing steel production actually had a sound scientific basis and could be controlled.

In 1934, when the goals of the Metallurgical Advisory Board had been met, Herty joined the staff of the Bethlehem Steel Company as a research engineer. Named assistant to the vice-president of the steel division in 1942, he continued his work on improving the open-hearth practice and in controlling slag reactions with molten steel. During World War II he served on advisory committees to the War Production Board, especially on the recovery of manganese, a metal required for many kinds of steel; much of the manganese used by the United States had to be imported.

In recognition of his work, Herty received the Robert W. Hunt Medal and Prize of the American Institute of Mining and Metallurgical Engineers (1928), the Francis J. Clamer Medal of the Philadelphia Technical Society (1935), the Albert Sauveur Achievement Award of the American Society for Metals (1943), the Bradley Stoughton Award of the Lehigh Chapter of the American Society for Metals (1946), and the Sc.D. from Lehigh University (1950). In 1946 he was president of the American Society for Metals, and in 1947 he was elected to the National Academy of Sciences, the first metallurgist so honored.

On 13 Nov. 1929, Herty married Kathleen Malloy of San Francisco, and they became the parents of four children: Dorothea, Charles H., III, Kathleen, and Timothy. He died in Bethlehem, Pa., where he was buried in Nisky Hill Cemetery.

SEE: *Bethlehem* (Pa.) *Globe-Times*, 19 Jan. 1953; *Biographical Memoirs of the National Academy of Sciences* 31 (1958); *Who Was Who in America*, vol. 3 (1960).

MAURICE M. BURSEY

Hewes, Joseph *(23 Jan. 1730–10 Nov. 1779)*, merchant, colonial leader, delegate to the Continental Congress, and signer of the Declaration of Independence, was raised at Mayberry Hill, the family's 400-acre plantation near Kingston, West Jersey. He was the oldest son of Aaron (1700–53) and Providence Worth Hewes.

Young Hewes inherited many traditions that would serve him well throughout life. The more important of these were a love of the land, a belief in the duty of public service, and a firm indoctrination in the "Puritan Ethic" of diligence, hard work, and thrift as the prerequisites for success. The influence of these values can be seen in his decision to renounce his intention to enter the College of New Jersey (later Princeton). Following his classical education at the Kingston Friends' Grammar School in 1749 and attracted by Philadelphia's opportunities for a mercantile career, Hewes apprenticed himself to Joseph Ogden, a relative and successful merchant-importer in that city. From August 1749 to September 1754, Hewes learned the trading business from dock laborer to cargo master. In the latter year he turned down a partnership offered by Ogden and, aided by funds from his father's estate, established his own retail concern. Discouraged by the lack of progress, he soon began to search for a more opportune site to relocate his business. His choice was Edenton, N.C.

Hewes arrived in Edenton in early 1755. In the spring, he entered into partnership with George Blair and Charles Worth Blount, both prominent merchants. The firm of Blount, Hewes and Company prospered, and by 1757 Hewes found time for political and civic affairs. That year he was appointed a justice of the peace for Chowan County and inspector for the Port of Roanoke. He also became an early leader in the movement to establish an academy in Edenton, a member of the building committees for the county courthouse and jail, and an official of St. Paul's Parish.

By 1760 Hewes had gained a position among the elite of Edenton society. No doubt his status was enhanced by his engagement late in that year to Isabella Johnston, the younger sister of Edenton lawyer and political leader Samuel Johnston. Although Isabella's death within the year brought this relationship to a tragic end, Johnston continued to consider Hewes as a member of his family. In 1760, Johnston, who had served as Edenton's representative in the Assembly since 1754, convinced Hewes to stand for the borough seat. Thus began the merchant's career in politics that would run with few interruptions until his death about twenty years later.

Hewes's business ability was early recognized by his fellow representatives, and he was repeatedly appointed to appropriation and finance committees. In filling these and other committee posts, he became intimately involved in the often bitter legislative-executive contests over the power to originate appropriation bills, to audit accounts of public expenditures, to issue paper currency, to collect and appropriate quitrent revenue, to determine the Assembly quorum, to appoint and instruct the provincial treasurers and agents, and to structure the colony's judicial system. Although his service to the colony was exhaustive, Hewes did not neglect the interests of his constituents. From 1760 to 1774 he sponsored local bills to finance construction of a courthouse, church, and academy; to reorganize the town's court and tax system; to improve navigational aids in the Albemarle Sound and Edenton Bay; and to regulate the inspection of exports through the Port of Roanoke.

As the movements towards increased intercolonial cooperation and colonial independence from Britain gathered momentum during the early 1770s, Hewes assumed a place among the Whig leadership of the colony. On 4 Dec. 1773, the North Carolina Assembly in response to a Virginia resolution created a "Committee of Correspondence." The committee consisted of Hewes, Speaker of the House John Harvey, Jr., Robert Howe, Cornelius Harnett, William Hooper, Richard Caswell, Edward Vail, John Ashe, and Samuel Johnston. These men would become the "revolutionary high command" of the colony. In the spring of 1774, the committee approved a Massachusetts circular proposing that an intercolonial congress be convened in Philadelphia to formalize opposition to "British tyranny." Forced to meet in extralegal session due to Governor Josiah Martin's refusal to convene a regular meeting, members of the Assembly met in New Bern on 25 August, approved Hewes's report of the Committee of Correspondence, and on 27 August selected Hewes, Caswell, and Hooper as the colony's delegates to the Continental Congress.

Hewes and Hooper arrived in Philadelphia on 14 September. Soon after taking his seat Hewes became acutely aware of the lack of unity among the delegates. On one extreme were the advocates of an uncompro-

mising defense—by force if necessary—of American rights, led by the representatives of Massachusetts, Virginia, and South Carolina. The opposition, led by the representatives of Pennsylvania and New York, argued for reconciliation with the Crown and were willing to recognize a wide latitude of Parliamentary authority over colonial affairs. The majority of the delegates, including those of North Carolina, found themselves somewhere between the two extremes. These moderate Whigs favored reconciliation with Britain, but they also stressed the need for guarantees against further infringements on American liberty. In succeeding weeks the moderates were able to control the tone of the debates and the actions of the Congress. After it adjourned on 26 Oct. 1774, Hewes remained in Philadelphia to renew old friendships and visit relatives. He also traveled to New York on business.

In late November, he returned to Edenton suffering from an "intermittent fever and ague." In all probability Hewes had malaria, a disease common in Edenton due to the mosquito-infested swamps surrounding the town. His health also had deteriorated under the effects of the cold weather and heavy work load in Philadelphia. However, his activities in North Carolina from November 1774 to April 1775 allowed little time for rest and recuperation. His mercantile firm, which had been reorganized with Robert Smith as "Hewes and Smith," was valued at £20,000 in 1774; in addition, Hewes owned a shipyard on the bay south of Edenton. While attending to business affairs, he also served on Edenton's Committee of Safety, which was responsible for enforcing the Continental Association in the Port of Roanoke.

By early 1775, the work of the moderate Whigs throughout the colonies for peaceful reconciliation with Britain had suffered massive setbacks. The failure of the Crown to consider the Declaration of Rights and Grievances, Parliament's rejection of the conciliatory proposals of Lords North and Chatham, the declaration that a "state of rebellion" existed in Massachusetts, and the ordering of 10,000 additional troops to Boston provided evidence that George III had chosen force to answer colonial complaints. This somber realization was pressed home in late April when news of the battles of Lexington and Concord reached Hewes and the other delegates as they prepared to return to Philadelphia.

When the Continental Congress reconvened, Hewes began to urge North Carolina to strengthen its defenses. To counter Governor Martin's efforts among the colony's Loyalists, Hewes enlisted the aid of Presbyterian ministers in Philadelphia. First, a pamphlet was written for distribution to Highland Scot immigrants explaining the work of the Continental Congress. In November 1775, two of the ministers traveled south—with instructions drafted by Hewes—to further stem the tide of Loyalism in North Carolina.

Because of failing health and in order to attend the colony's Third Provincial Congress, Hewes left Philadelphia six days before the 1 August adjournment of the Continental Congress. His stay in North Carolina, though brief, was marked by participation in the organization of a provincial government for the colony and in the authorization to raise the colony's quota of Continental troops. On 22 October he rejoined his fellow delegates in Philadelphia. Among his committee assignments during this session, his service on the Naval Board proved to be the most exhaustive and most significant. From November 1775 to February 1776, he served as the board's secretary, keeping its business records and conducting much of its voluminous correspondence. Possibly one of Hewes's most noteworthy achievements on the board was to secure John Paul Jones's first commission in the Continental Navy.

In 1776, King George III not only rejected the Olive Branch Petition, but also proclaimed the colonies to be in a state of rebellion. This was closely followed by the Congress's authorization for independent governments in each colony. In January 1776 Thomas Paine's incendiary *Common Sense* appeared, and, against Hewes's urgings, was sent to North Carolina for distribution. The following month, Governor Martin's efforts among the Loyalists reached fruition only to be thwarted by patriots at the Battle of Moore's Creek Bridge. The final blow to moderate hopes came in March with news of the Crown's Prohibitory Act closing colonial ports and placing the colonies under military rule. Hewes stated that "nothing is left now but to fight it out." All hope of reconciliation had vanished and separation from England was now formally debated in the Continental Congress. Hewes's pleas for instructions from North Carolina on the issue of independence were answered on 12 April by the Fourth Provincial Congress meeting at Halifax. The colony's delegates were told "to concur with the delegates of the other colonies in declaring Independency." On 7 June Virginia's Richard Henry Lee introduced the long-awaited resolution, which was approved in final form on 4 July 1776.

Some historians have stated that Joseph Hewes was openly indecisive on the issue of declaring independence from Britain. The basis for this assertion lies in John Adams's letter to William Plummer dated 28 Mar. 1813. But records of the Continental Congress, specifically those covering the period from March to July 1776, provide no support for Adams's recollection. Rather, these records, coupled with the writings of other delegates, show Adams to be in error. It has been argued that Adams in his letter to Plummer was recalling the actions of South Carolina's Edward Rutledge rather than those of Hewes. Whatever the nature of Adams's confusion may have been, Hewes's attitude from March to July 1776 is clear from his correspondence—he supported independence. This decision was made reluctantly, but once made, there was no infirmity of will or allegiance. In March 1776, Hewes became a revolutionary—albeit a reluctant one—but a revolutionary just the same.

Early in August 1776, Hewes left Philadelphia for a much-needed "recess from Publick Employment." For almost a year he had been at work in that city and, from March through July, he had carried the entire work load of the North Carolina delegation alone. His health, already poor, by August had deteriorated to a dangerous degree. He complained of continual headaches, high fevers, and fading vision.

His hoped-for rest had to be postponed, for shortly after returning to Edenton he was elected the borough's representative to the Fifth Provincial Congress. The main concern of this Congress, which met in Halifax during November-December 1776, was the drafting of a state constitution. This proved to be a most divisive process. The "Conservatives," led by Samuel Johnston, James Iredell, and Hewes, supported a political system based on a strong executive and property qualifications for suffrage and officeholding. In vehement opposition were the "Radicals," led by Willie Jones and Thomas Person, who argued for the establishment of a "direct democracy." The constitution, as adopted on 14 December, improved the political position of the lower classes, but far from satisfied either faction. The debates over the document did produce one unfortunate result—an embittered and continuing division in the ranks of North Carolina Whigs.

Following the adjournment of the Provincial Congress, Hewes was able to rest in Edenton for a few months. Late in March 1777, his health had improved to the extent that he was planning to return to Philadelphia and the Continental Congress. That the state's General Assembly would fail to appoint him was never considered. However, when the Assembly convened on 7 April, the previous Conservative-Radical factionalism reappeared in all its bitterness, and the major point of contention became the reappointment of Joseph Hewes as delegate to the Continental Congress. Led by John Penn, the Radicals accused Hewes of plural officeholding, a violation under the new state constitution, and of reaping personal profit from his position as delegate. After many days of emotional debate, Hewes was bypassed and Penn was appointed as delegate. Although this defeat was a harsh one for Hewes, a more significant result may have been the withdrawal of many Conservatives, notably William Hooper, from politics.

Feeling that his reputation had been unjustly smeared, Hewes retired from public life, refusing in both 1777 and 1778 to stand for Edenton's seat in the General Assembly. For two years he devoted his attention to regaining his health and supervising his extensive business affairs. Early in 1779, however, he acceded to popular demand and returned to the General Assembly. Soon after taking his seat, he allowed his name to be placed in nomination as a delegate to the Continental Congress. This time his election was not contested.

Soon after his arrival in Philadelphia, Hewes was appointed to the Treasury and Marine committees, two of the Congress's most important and busiest standing committees. Within a month, he received two additional assignments. By the middle of August 1779, Hewes wrote that he again suffered from severe headaches and by late September he was so ill that he could not walk to Carpenter's Hall. On 29 October, sensing that he could no longer fulfill his duties as delegate, Hewes submitted his resignation. Unable to travel, he remained in Philadelphia hoping that complete rest would restore his strength. However, his health was beyond repair and he died about two weeks later at age forty-nine.

When news of Hewes's passing reached the Continental Congress, the delegates voted to attend the funeral as a body and proclaimed a one-month period of mourning. At 3:00 P.M. on 11 November, a most distinguished gathering met at Hewes's rooming house and escorted the body to Christ's Church for burial. The *Pennsylvania Packet*, in its 16 November obituary, paid a deserved tribute to Joseph Hewes and to the devotion to duty which his life exemplified: "His mind was constantly employed in the business of his exalted station until his health, much impaired by intense application, sunk beneath it."

The only known likeness of Hewes is a 1¾-inch by 1⅝-inch miniature painted on ivory by Charles Willson Peale in 1776. The oval portrait was framed as a lady's broach and was a gift from Hewes to Helen Blair, the niece of Isabella Johnston. The miniature is now owned by the U.S. Naval Academy Museum in Annapolis, Md.

SEE: Michael G. Martin, Jr., "Joseph Hewes: 'Reluctant Revolutionary'?" (Master's thesis, University of North Carolina, 1969).

MICHAEL G. MARTIN, JR.

Hiatt, Houston Boyd *(16 Sept. 1886–28 Aug. 1941),* physician, surgeon, and radiologist, was born in Greensboro, the son of John Rufus and Ella Leora Otwell Hiatt. He attended Mrs. Bettie Wright's School in Sampson County, Fayetteville Military Academy, Horner's Military Academy, and The University of North Carolina. Hiatt was graduated from the University of Maryland School of Medicine, interned at Johns Hopkins Hospital, and pursued postgraduate work at Johns Hopkins and in St. Louis, Mo., under Dr. George Dock. He entered private practice first in Clinton with Dr. Algernon Lee, then went to Asheboro. Beginning in 1913 he practiced in High Point until ill health forced his retirement.

In 1916 Hiatt was a lieutenant with the First North Carolina Field Hospital, North Carolina National Guard, on the Mexican border. During World War I he served as medical examiner for the local draft board. One of the first radiologists in the state, Hiatt was a Fellow of the American Medical Association and a member of the North Carolina Medical Society and the Guilford County Medical Society (president, 1931). He was the local surgeon for the Southern Railway, a visiting consultant in internal medicine and X-ray to the State Hospital at Morganton, and a staff member of the Guilford General Hospital in High Point and of Sternberger's Hospital in Greensboro.

Among his civic activities, Hiatt served as first chairman of the Parks and Juvenile Commission, an organizer and official of the Boy Scouts of America, president of the Rotary Club, and member of the board of directors of the Salvation Army and of the Board of Associated Charities. An Episcopalian, he was a vestryman of his church.

On 8 July 1907 Hiatt married Kathleen Cromwell Sadtler, daughter of George Washington and Delia Cromwell Banks Sadtler. They had three children: John Rufus, who died in infancy; Houston Boyd, Jr., who died in 1929; and Leora Cromwell, who married Edward Merritt McEachern. Hiatt died in Tarpon Springs, Fla., and was buried in High Point.

SEE: High Point *Enterprise,* 16 Nov. 1922, 29 Aug. 1941; Fayetteville Military Academy Commencement Program, 27 May 1898; Family Bible and Papers.

L. H. MCEACHERN

Hickerson, Thomas Felix *(30 Apr. 1882–8 Aug. 1968),* Kenan Professor of Applied Mathematics at The University of North Carolina and world-famed authority on highway engineering, was born on the Roundabout farm near Ronda in Wilkes County, the fourth son of Dr. James and Anne Eliza Hickerson. His parents lived at the family home in the Happy Valley area of the Yadkin River. Hickerson studied this region and its people, publishing the results in two books, *Happy Valley* (1940) and *Echoes of Happy Valley* (1962). In 1964 he wrote a booklet, *The Faulkner Feuds,* in which he vindicated Richard J. Thurmond of Happy Valley who in 1889 shot and killed Colonel W. C. Faulkner, the great-grandfather of novelist William Faulkner.

Hickerson received his schooling in Ronda and at the Bingham Military School in Asheville. At The University of North Carolina, he won the Holt Medal for his mathematical abilities in his senior year, graduating with a Ph.B. degree in 1904. He taught for a year at the Bingham School and in 1905 returned to Chapel Hill for graduate work in mathematics and engineering; he also was an instructor in mathematics. After receiving the

A.M. degree in 1907, he studied civil engineering at the Massachusetts Institute of Technology, earning a B.S. degree in 1909. Later he attended a graduate course in highway engineering at Columbia University (winter, 1911–12) and a teachers' seminar on applied mechanics at Cornell University (summer, 1927).

In 1909 Hickerson joined the faculty of The University of North Carolina as associate professor of civil engineering; in 1920 he was promoted to full professor in the School of Engineering. When the School of Engineering was dissolved in 1936, he chose to remain in Chapel Hill as a member of the mathematics department rather than move to Raleigh. In 1938 his title was established as professor of applied mathematics, and in 1945 he received a Kenan professorhip. He retired in 1952.

Hickerson's books on bridge and road building, including *Route Surveys and Design, Highway Curves and Earthwork,* and *Highway Surveying and Planning,* served a generation of civil engineers (a complete list of his publications is in the *North Carolina Engineer,* July 1965). Two accounts reflect this: a highway engineer working on the Burma Road in World War II found his *Route Surveys and Design* extremely helpful; and in 1967, when an engineer in Africa needed help on a problem of road intersections and tangents, Hickerson sent him the fifth revised edition of his book with up-to-date and precise information—in Hickerson's own handwriting—on how to do it. He developed and contributed to the profession ideas, tables, and methods relating to such things as spiral curves and their super elevation, the laying out of circular and spiraled curves by deflections from the point of intersection of the tangents, the bearing strengths of columns, analysis of stresses in bridge and building frames, and the solution of spherical triangles applicable to celestial observations in the determination of azimuth, latitude, and time.

Many road systems, including the North Carolina system, were developed with his assistance. Hickerson was a member of the first Highway Commission from 1915 to 1919 and served frequently as consultant on such projects as the Blue Ridge Parkway from Linville Falls to Bull Gap near Asheville. He also was president and a life member of the North Carolina Academy of Science, a Fellow of the American Society of Civil Engineers and president of the North Carolina Section, a charter member of the North Carolina Society of Engineers and of Tau Beta Pi, a longtime member of the former Society for the Promotion of Engineering Education, a life member of the American Mathematical Association, and active in the Elisha Mitchell Scientific Society and the Society of Sigma Xi.

For fifty-one years Hickerson was a member of the Order of Gimghoul and a trustee for twenty-eight years. He participated in the concept, planning, and establishment of the Order's real estate development; later, with A. H. Patterson, he supervised the erection of the Waldensian Castle. Hickerson planted the boxwood bushes that circle Dromgoole Rock and in later years supervised the maintenance of the castle and grounds.

Hickerson, a bachelor, was known for his hospitality and old-world courtesy. He delighted in entertaining his students and friends at his home on Battle Lane and in sharing his flowers. Some years before his death he established a scholarship fund for his students. A member of the Episcopal church, Hickerson was buried in the family plot at Ronda. A drawing of him by Adrian Lamb is published in Howell's *The Kenan Professorships.*

SEE: *American Men of Science*, 9th ed. (1955); *Chapel Hill Weekly*, 29 Dec. 1968; Faculty Tribute by L. A. Cotton and others, 11 Aug. 1968 (Archives, University of North Carolina, Chapel Hill); A. C. Howell, *The Kenan Professorships* (1956); *North Carolina Engineer* (July 1965).

MARTHA B. CALDWELL

Hickman, Franklin Simpson *(14 Sept. 1886–11 Nov. 1965)*, minister, author, and educator, was born in Fort Wayne, Ind., the son of John Wesley and Emma Tessier Hickman. His early education was sporadic and was not completed until he had worked for eight years (1903–11) for the Pennsylvania Railroad. When he felt called to the ministry in 1911, he finished his high school studies and enrolled in De Pauw University, Greencastle, Ind., in 1913, the same year he was ordained a Methodist minister. In 1917 he was graduated at age thirty-one with a B.A. degree and then spent three years in graduate study at Boston University, earning the bachelor of sacred theology degree (equivalent to a current bachelor of divinity) in 1920.

After his ordination Hickman served in various local church assignments, but focused his objectives on teaching. To that end, he accepted a position as instructor in the Chicago Training School for City, Home and Foreign Missions from 1920 to 1924. Simultaneously, he was enrolled in Northwestern University, Evanston, Ill., from which he received an M.A. degree in 1922 and a Ph.D. degree in 1924, with a major in the psychology of religion. De Pauw University awarded him the honorary doctor of divinity degree in June 1950.

For the session 1924–25, Hickman was associate professor of religion at Hamline University, St. Paul, Minn. Continuing his preaching ministry, he was pastor of the First Methodist Episcopal Church of Minneapolis and director of the Wesley Foundation (student work) in St. Paul from 1925 to 1927. In the summer of 1925, he taught at Emory University, Atlanta, Ga., and the following year the Abingdon Press published his authoritative *Introduction to the Psychology of Religion*.

His addresses before many church gatherings and his scholarship attracted the attention of the administration of Duke University, Durham, which in 1927 appointed him professor of the psychology of religion in the newly formed School of Religion (now Duke Divinity School), an affiliation that continued until his retirement in 1953. For a number of years Hickman also taught homiletics and continuously served on major academic committees of the faculty. He taught at Hampton Institute, Hampton, Va., in the summer of 1928 and spent the spring semester of 1937 on sabbatical teaching at Soochow (China) University. In the summer of 1941 he was guest teacher at Iliff School of Theology.

Hickman's fame as a preacher found expression at Duke through his ministry as preacher to the university (1927–45) and as dean of the chapel (1939–48). He held the added title of professor of preaching in 1939–41. During those years he was in great demand as a speaker on campuses, before church conferences, and in the pulpits of many denominations.

In addition to teaching and preaching, Hickman was an avid reader and researcher, and he wrote extensively. Following his 1926 text on the psychology of religion, he published *Can Religion Be Taught, Evangelical Religion Faces the Question?* (1929), which was an outgrowth of an address he delivered before the Methodist Sunday School Council in Nashville, Tenn., on 28 Dec. 1928. He was a contributor to *Education and Religion*,

edited by Homer Henkel Sherman (1929). *Christian Vocation—A Study in Religious Experience* (1930) was the script of the Belk Lectures (second series) delivered at Wesleyan College, Macon, Ga., in April 1930. He was also the author of *The Possible Self—A Study in Religious Education as Adaptation* (1933), *A Child in the Midst of Democracy* (1934), and *Signs of Promise* (1943). His last volume was *Religion Tomorrow*, comprising the Norton Lectures delivered at the Southern Baptist Theological Seminary, Louisville, Ky., in 1940 and the Mendenhall Lectures delivered at De Pauw University in 1942. In 1947 he wrote "Wings for the Spirit—The Spiritual Message of First Corinthians" for the *Upper Room Bible Series*.

Through the years Hickman was contributing editor of *The Christian Advocate* and frequently wrote articles for many church publications. He contributed several meditations for *Holidays and Holy Days* (1946), edited by H. E. Spence. His most extensive writing project was a daily devotional article, "Just a Minute," begun in 1944 and published continuously for more than twenty years on the editorial page of the *Durham Morning Herald* and the Augusta, Ga., *Herald*, a feature read daily by more than 150,000 people.

He was a member of the North Indiana Conference of the Methodist Episcopal church, a frequent delegate to the Federal Council of Churches and the major conferences of the Methodist church (he was once nominated to the office of bishop), and the founder (1931) and longtime director of the Phillips Brooks Club, an interdenominational gathering of clergymen at Duke University. His fraternities included Phi Beta Kappa (scholarship), Delta Sigma Rho, Phi Delta Kappa, Omicron Delta Kappa (leadership), and Theta Phi (theology). Travel was a lifetime hobby, and he visited many parts of Britain, the Near East, Europe, and Alaska.

On 28 June 1913 Hickman married Veva Beatrice Castell of Angola, Ind.; they had one child, Anna Jeannette, who died in infancy. Upon his retirement from Duke, the Hickmans established residence in Angola, Ind., and spent four months of each year in Deland, Fla. He died and was buried in Angola.

SEE: *Durham Morning Herald*, 12 Nov. 1965; Info Sheet, Office of Information Services, Duke University; *Who's Who in American Education*, vol. 20 (1962); *Who's Who in the Clergy*, vol. 1 (1935–36).

C. SYLVESTER GREEN

Hicks, Ellen Thompson *(9 Sept. 1866–21 Oct. 1951)*, nurse and Episcopal missionary, was born in Oxford, the daughter of Edward Hubbell and Harriet Virginia Britton Hicks. Her father, a lawyer and a graduate of The University of North Carolina, had given up his practice to manage the family estate after the death of his mother.

Ellen received her first formal education at a private school and then attended Oxford Female Academy for two years. When she was twenty-one, her father died after a long illness. The experience of caring for him inspired her to become a professional nurse. Shortly after her husband's death, Harriet Hicks learned of a training program for nurses at Philadelphia General Hospital. Ellen applied and was accepted. Because of opposition from family and friends, however, she did not enroll. Nursing had not yet been established as an acceptable occupation for women. Many years later, Ellen recalled that relatives and acquaintances feared either that the training would be too strenuous for her, or that, because of her career, she would disgrace the family name.

Yet Ellen did not abandon her ambition. The following year she earned money by chaperoning a statewide tour of the Oxford Orphanage's singing class. She then reapplied to the nursing program at the Philadelphia hospital and again was accepted. She enrolled in September 1899 and was graduated a year later. During the next few years she gained a variety of medical experience, working at St. Timothy's Hospital, Roxborough, Pa.; the Home of the Merciful Saviour for Crippled Children, Philadelphia; and Dr. Howard Kelly's private sanitorium in Baltimore, Md. She returned to Philadelphia to become superintendent of the Bryn Mawr Hospital, a post she held until 1903.

After her resignation she traveled in Europe for several months. Upon returning to the United States, she decided to enter the mission field and applied through the Protestant Episcopal church for an assignment in China. Before the arrangements could be made, she met Charles Henry Brent, Bishop of the Philippines, who persuaded her to go to Manila. She sailed in 1904. Failing health forced her return home a year later, but in 1905 she went back to the Philippines where she remained for twelve years. At St. Luke's Hospital in Manila, she was instrumental in establishing a nurses' training program for young Filipino women.

Miss Hicks left the Philippines in 1917, intending to go to Europe to nurse soldiers wounded in World War I. Instead, the church mission board sent her to St. Luke's Hospital in Ponce, Puerto Rico. Although originally planning to stay only three months, she lived in Puerto Rico for twenty years. There she assisted in rebuilding the hospital after an earthquake in 1918 and a hurricane in 1928, and taught in the hospital's nursing school. She retired in 1938 and moved with her sister, Harriet Britton Hicks, to Sarasota, Fla., where she died at age eighty-five.

During Ellen Hicks's lifetime, a nurses' dormitory at St. Luke's Hospital in Ponce was named after her. In 1974 St. Stephen's Episcopal Church, her home church in Oxford, established a nursing scholarship in her name in the Diocese of the Northern Philippines.

SEE: Charles H. Brewer, Jr., *A History of St. Stephen's Episcopal Church, Oxford, North Carolina, 1823–1980* (1980); Hicks family notes supplied by E. C. Hicks, Jr., Wilmington; "A Tribute," *Southern Churchman*, vol. 104, 6 Aug. 1938; Mrs. J. A. Yarborough, "Interesting Carolina People," *Charlotte Observer*, 6 Dec. 1942.

ANASTATIA SIMS

Hicks, Thurston Titus (14 Oct. 1857–28 July 1927), attorney, was born at White Oak Villa in Granville County, the oldest son of Benjamin Willis and Isabella Jane Crews Hicks. The Hicks lands were obtained by deed from Earl Granville to William Hicks on 5 Mar. 1749 and descended undiminished, undivided, and unencumbered to Thurston's father. Thurston was the second of seven children, and his childhood was characteristic of that period of privation and struggle following the Civil War. During the winter months of 1866–75 he attended Pleasant Hill Academy, a local private school operated by Mrs. Asenath F. Cheatham. In 1875 he obtained instruction in Latin by private tutoring under Professor Fred A. Fetter at Oxford.

From 1876 to 1879, Hicks attended Yadkin College, a Methodist-Protestant church college founded in 1856 in Davidson County. This college, presided over by the Reverend Shadrock Simpson, offered the standard curriculum of classics, mathematics, and basic sciences with additional offerings of modern languages and Shakespeare. Its activities included two competitive literary societies, the Ciceronian and the Clark, for student discussion and debate. Hicks distinguished himself as a medalist debater. He was graduated with an A.B. degree in the class of 1879.

In the following year, Hicks served as principal of Shiloh Academy in Davidson County while preparing for the bar. He received his license on 5 Jan. 1881 and, after an unsuccessful year in Oxford, established a permanent practice in Henderson, the seat of newly formed Vance County. Over the years he was involved in a number of cases resulting in legal precedents. Hicks was one of several attorneys for the defense in *Gattis v. Kilgo*, perhaps the most controversial legal battle in the state's history. This case evolved from criticisms brought by North Carolina Chief Justice Walter Clark, a trustee of Trinity College, that its president, John C. Kilgo, had allied the school's fortunes with the Duke tobacco trust, perverting it from its purpose as a Methodist denominational college. Kilgo responded at a formal hearing of the Trinity trustees. Unwilling to attack Clark directly, he charged that T. J. Gattis, an elderly Methodist minister, was the source of the accusation. Kilgo further charged that Gattis had perjured himself by stating that Kilgo had a reputation as a "wire-puller" but gave conflicting statements at other times. Kilgo's remarks were published by Benjamin N. Duke and others, and Gattis brought suit for libel and slander. The suit was heard four times in the state Supreme Court without Clark's participation and was ultimately resolved in the defendant's favor upon the court's finding that the statements were made under privileged circumstances of response to adverse criticism. The suit was brought in Granville County, and Hicks participated in the defense on its second, third, and fourth hearings. At one point, his brother Archibald, whom he had trained for the bar, appeared as a counsel for the plaintiff.

Hicks was originally a Democrat and so served as mayor of Henderson (1889–91). However, he changed his registration to the Republican party because he objected to the electoral amendment of 1900, modeled on the Louisiana "grandfather clause," insisting on qualifying by literacy (to vote, one had to be able to read and write any section of the Constitution) despite considerable pride of lineage. In 1910, five years after settlement of *Gattis v. Kilgo*, Hicks received the Republican nomination for state chief justice against the incumbent, Walter Clark, but was defeated in the general election.

On 6 Dec. 1883 Hicks married Mary Horner, daughter of the Reverend Thomas J. and Isabella Norwood Horner. He was survived by two sons and a daughter.

SEE: Samuel A. Ashe, ed., *Biographical History of North Carolina*, vol. 8 (1905); Thurston Titus Hicks, *Sketches of William Hicks, etc.* (1926); Olin Bain Michael, *Yadkin College, 1856–1924: A Historic Sketch* (1939); *North Carolina Reports* 133 (1899), 403 (1901), 199 (1902), 106 (1905); Samuel Thomas Peace, *Zeb's Black Baby* (1955).

GEORGE T. BLACKBURN II

Hicks, William Jackson (18 Feb. 1827–14 Jan. 1911), farmer, machinist, carpenter, industrialist, and architect, was born in Spottsylvania County, Va., the son of Martin (1789–1848[?]) and Nancy Pendleton Hicks (d.

1830), daughter of Robert Pendleton of Spottsylvania County. His great-grandfather, Peter Hicks, was born in England in 1720 but settled in Spottsylvania early in adulthood and became a farmer and sheriff of the county. His grandfather, also Peter Hicks, fought in the Revolutionary War and was sheriff of the county for a number of years.

Hicks entered school at age thirteen but left, due to the long illness of his father, to manage the family farm. After his father's death, he continued to operate the farm for a short time. In the winter months he studied to further his education.

Always fond of mechanical work, Hicks soon was engaged in quarrying stone and stone cutting. During this time he also became interested in the business of a millwright and in carpentry, fields in which he developed a high degree of skill. In 1852 he was hired by Smith, Colby, & Company of New York to install a mining plant for the McGulloch Gold Mine in Guilford County; he then installed a plant for Garden Hill Gold and Copper Mills in the same county. After completing his work near Greensboro, he was employed by James F. Jordan & Company of Raleigh to assist in the installation of papermaking machinery for the Manteo Manufacturing Company on the Neuse River.

Hicks next turned his attention to house building until the Civil War. When the war began he was employed by Waterhouse & Bowes for the construction of the first powder mill in North Carolina, located on Smith's Creek five miles from Raleigh. After these mills blew up, he was employed by the same company to erect a second set of mills on Crabtree Creek, three miles from Raleigh. These mills continued to operate until the end of the war, when they were destroyed by Federal troops.

After the war Hicks entered the resin business and then returned to carpentry. In 1869 the state appointed him assistant architect and superintendent of construction of the new penitentiary near Raleigh, and in 1877 he was named architect and warden, a position he held for twenty-five years. Other buildings built by Hicks were the governor's mansion and the old Supreme Court and State Library buildings. After the penitentiary was completed, he eventually resigned his post there and entered into partnership with a Mr. Ellington of Raleigh. In 1898 he moved to Oxford to become superintendent of the Oxford Orphanage Asylum. However, he continued his ties with Raleigh, helping to establish the Raleigh Savings Bank of which he was a director for some years. He also was a member of the Agricultural Society and president of the North Carolina Building and Supply Company at Oxford.

Although never a member of the armed services, Hicks was affectionately known for most of his life as "Colonel Hicks." He was a staunch Democrat and an officer of the Masons. On 4 Mar. 1858 he married Julia Louise Harrison (13 Nov. 1887–8 Apr. 1912), daughter of John R. Harrison of Raleigh; they had eight children. After his death, his wife returned to the Hicks home in Raleigh, located at 304 West Edenton Street, at the intersection of Dawson Street, where she remained until her death.

SEE: Samuel A. Ashe, ed., *Biographical History of North Carolina*, vol. 2 (1905); *Raleigh City Directories*; Stephen B. Weeks, "The History and Biography of North Carolina" (Scrapbook, North Carolina Collection, University of North Carolina Library, Chapel Hill).

JOHN LEONARD RIGSBEE

Highsmith, Jacob Franklin (Frank) *(1 Sept. 1868– 22 June 1939),* surgeon, was born at Hives (now Roseboro), the son of John James and Mary Ann Fowler Highsmith. His father, a well-to-do farmer, supported the Confederacy and fought with the Sixty-first North Carolina Regiment throughout the Civil War; his mother was a descendant of the Parkers, Revolutionary patriots. Young Highsmith attended private schools near his home, Old Salem Academy in Sampson County, and Glenwood Academy in Johnston County. He was graduated from Wake Forest College in 1887 and from Jefferson Medical College, Philadelphia, in 1889, shortly before his twenty-first birthday. In the latter year he began a practice in Fayetteville, but his pursuit of learning was lifelong. He regularly visited the Mayo Clinic in Rochester, Minn., as well as other prestigious hospitals in the United States, and observed hospitals abroad in 1906, 1914, and 1928.

In 1896 Highsmith opened a brick office in the business section of Green Street. The building, which had rooms on the second floor to accommodate patients overnight, quickly assumed the name of Highsmith Hospital. In 1899, Highsmith and Dr. J. H. Marsh, who also had an office on Green Street, joined to establish a three-story hospital—known as the Marsh-Highsmith Hospital—in the same location, extending the building to Market Square. Two years later Highsmith bought out Marsh, enlarged the hospital, and improved the equipment. This hospital was said to be one of the most modern in the South in the early part of the twentieth century. It had operating, anesthetic, sterilizing, and X-ray rooms; a surgeons' washroom and nurses' dressing room; lavatories with porcelain tubs and basins; a kitchen, pantry, and laundry; an elevator, electric lights (and gas lights for emergencies), call bells, telephones, screened windows; a private ambulance service; and rules for patients and visitors similar to hospital rules in force seventy-five years later. There were set rates for ward rooms, private rooms, and special nurses.

Highsmith Hospital was one of the first in the state to establish a training school for nurses; to provide hospital beds; to keep charts, records, and case histories; and to use ultraviolet-ray machines. It also was among the first to have a physiotherapy department and a high-voltage deep X-ray machine. In 1926 the hospital became so crowded, and that part of the town so noisy, that Highsmith erected a larger and even more modern hospital in a quieter location. Then, as from the beginning, the hospital had an outstanding staff. Dr. W. T. Rainey, a leading diagnostician in North Carolina who had begun his career with Highsmith in 1913, remained with the hospital until his death. Highsmith Hospital was one of the first in North Carolina to use insulin in the treatment of diabetes, and Rainey was one of the state's first physicians to acquire the state license then required to administer insulin.

As a boy, Highsmith began to practice surgery on his father's farm to assist animals in distress; his first operation was on a sheep. As a physician, his first operation on a human was for a hernia. In the early days, he sometimes operated on the patients' kitchen tables. While still a young surgeon, he performed so many successful operations, including the removal of large tumors, that he soon became known as "the miracle man."

Highsmith was chief surgeon in his hospital until succeeded by his oldest son, Dacosta. His two other sons, Frank, Jr., and W. C., who became specialists, also joined the staff. In 1949, after Dacosta's death, the hospital was bought and run by a board of directors.

In addition to his work at the hospital, Highsmith was surgeon for both the Atlantic Coast Line and the Norfolk and Southern railroads, was a consultant and visiting surgeon in many hospitals in North Carolina and elsewhere, and contributed articles to medical journals. Over the years he was active at various times in the Cumberland County Medical Society (president, 1903), North Carolina Medical Society (first councilor, 1902; president, 1909), the Jefferson Medical College Alumni (president, 1908), American College of Surgeons (life member from 1913), and the Tri-State (North Carolina, South Carolina, and Virginia) Medical Society (president, 1938). He organized the North Carolina Hospital Association and became its first president. Highsmith also was a delegate to the American Medical Society in 1907 and 1908, chairman of the Medical Advisory Board of the United States, and a member of the Mississippi Valley Medical Association.

A man of remarkable energy, he was deacon of the First Baptist Church; a member of the Sons of the Revolution and of the Fayetteville Chamber of Commerce; and a Mason, a Shriner, an Elk, and a Knight of Pythias. He was president of the local Rotary, which he helped organized, and of the National Bank.

On 14 Nov. 1889 Highsmith married Mary Lou White of Sampson County, who survived him. They had eight children: Dr. James Dacosta, Mrs. Mamie Wells, Mrs. Annie Campbell, Juanita (Nita), Mrs. Louise Hardee, Frank (Dr. J. F., Jr.), Bill (Dr. W. C.), and Mrs. Rachel Caldwell. Highsmith died of a heart attack on the farm where he was born. He was buried in Cross Creek Cemetery, Fayetteville.

At his death, Highsmith owned a home on Green Street, a large mountain cottage at Ridgecrest, and the 18,000-acre farm in Sampson County. After his parents' death, he had made the farm into a private recreation center with fishing, hunting, and bathing; it was open to all employees of the Highsmith Hospital.

SEE: Samuel A. Ashe, ed., *Biographical History of North Carolina*, vol. 2 (1905); Cumberland County Courthouse, *Deeds; Fayetteville Observer*, 1 Feb., 1 July 1896, 2 Jan., 5 Sept. 1899, 18 Oct. 1937, 22 June, 15 Nov. 1939, 12 Apr. 1954, 10 Feb. 1963, 17 Sept. 1967; Charles H. Hamlin, *Ninety Bits* (1946); Annette P. Highsmith, *Highsmiths in America* (1971) and *Highsmith Hospital* (n.d.); Highsmith Hospital (portrait); Miss Nita Highsmith, 608 Forest Rd., Fayetteville, N.C. 28305 (photographs); Junior Service League, *Spirit of Cumberland* (1970); John Oates, *Story of Fayetteville* (indexed ed., 1972); Raleigh *News and Observer*, 5 May 1940; Lou Rogers, *We the People* (April 1951 [portrait]); Warner Wells, *Medicine in North Carolina*, vol. 1, and *Surgical Practice in North Carolina: A Historical Commentary* (1954); *Who's Who in America*, vol. 18; Mary Lewis Wyche, *The History of Nursing in North Carolina* (1938).

LOU ROGERS WEHLITZ

Highsmith, John Henry (5 Oct. 1877–8 May 1953), public educator, was born in McDaniel Township, Sampson County, the son of Lewis Whitfield and Margaret Tatum Highsmith. He grew up in Durham where he was graduated from public high school in 1896 with a scholarship to Trinity College (now Duke University), receiving the B.A. degree in 1900 and the M.A. degree in 1902. From 1901 to 1904, he served as principal of North Durham School. After attending Teachers College, Columbia University, from 1904 to 1906 as a graduate scholar, he was professor of Bible and philoso-

phy at Meredith College (then known as the Baptist University for Women), Raleigh. In 1907, he became professor of education at Wake Forest College where he taught for ten years.

Highsmith began his career with the state public school system in 1917, when he was appointed by Governor Thomas W. Bickett to the State Board of Examiners and Institute Conductors. In 1920 he was named state inspector of high schools, a position later entitled state high school supervisor, and in 1932 he became director of the Division of Instructional Service of the State Department of Public Instruction where he served until his death. He continued to teach throughout his life, primarily in the summer school sessions at the University of Louisiana, North Carolina State University, The University of North Carolina at Greensboro, and Duke University. He was awarded a doctor of letters and law degree by Catawba College in 1925 and a doctor of education degree by Wake Forest College in 1934.

Highsmith was known for his unwavering commitment to quality high school education for all children in North Carolina. He was a staunch advocate of the consolidated high school that offered a comprehensive curriculum, of the accreditation of secondary schools to promote and assure high standards in high school facilities and teaching, and of higher standards of instruction through better teacher training by the colleges and teacher certification. His plan for reorganizing the state's high schools in 1925–26 was heartily endorsed by the North Carolina College Conference. As a representative of the General Education Board, Highsmith served as director of the reorganization of the high schools in Oklahoma in 1928 and in Mississippi in 1929. In the latter year he was president of the National Association of State High School Supervisors.

Through the Southern Association of Colleges and Secondary Schools he served the cause of better education in the South, principally by work on various committees. He was chairman of the Committee on Libraries for several years when the group did much to raise the standards for libraries in high schools and colleges in southern states. He was also chairman of the Committee on Negro Schools, responsible for the accreditation of Negro high schools and colleges throughout the South. He served as chairman of the Committee on Secondary Education and as vice-president of the Southern Association of Colleges and Secondary Schools in 1946. Among the significant programs he developed to raise the standards of instruction in North Carolina high schools was the professional supervisor staff within his division.

Highsmith wrote extensively for professional journals and participated in educational organizations at all levels. In 1939 he was president of the North Carolina Education Association, which elected him posthumously to its Hall of Fame. The citation, read on 16 Mar. 1960, stated: "It must be said . . . that public education was the passion of his life."

A Baptist, he was active in the work of his church throughout his life, serving as president of the Board of Education of the Baptist State Convention from 1932 to 1938 and as a long-term deacon and superintendent of the Sunday school of the First Baptist Church in Raleigh. He was a member of Phi Beta Kappa, a Rotarian, a Mason, and a Democrat.

In 1907 Highsmith married Lula V. Johnson, who died in 1919; they had one son, John Henry, Jr., and one daughter, Lula Belle (Mrs. Orus N. Rich). In 1921 he married Kate M. Herring, and they had two daughters, Katherine Herring (Mrs. Kern Holoman) and Louise Westbrook (Mrs. Louis R. Wilkerson). Highsmith was buried at Montlawn Cemetery in Raleigh, where he had made his home for thirty-three years.

SEE: *Charlotte Observer*, 11 May 1953; *Greensboro Daily News*, 10 May 1953; Annette Paris Highsmith, *Highsmiths in America* (1971); *North Carolina Education* (May 1960); Raleigh *News and Observer*, 21 Oct. 1938, 9 May, 10 May 1953; *Who Was Who in America*, vol. 3 (1960); *Who's Who in America*, vol. 20 (1938–39).

KATHERINE HIGHSMITH HOLOMAN

Hill, Charles Applewhite *(1784–17 July 1831)*, state senator, schoolmaster, minister, textbook writer, and author of the state's first Literary Fund law for the financing of public schools, was born in Franklin County. His father was William Hill (1750–ca. 1786), a landowner of substantial means, who was named a militia lieutenant for Bute County Company No. 6 in 1776. William was one of the witnesses to the deeding of the 100-acre tract on which the town of Louisburg, seat of Franklin, was established in 1779. After his death, his brother Henry qualified as guardian for William's four sons—William Bennett, Samuel Sugan, James Jones, and Charles Applewhite. In 1788 Thomas Brickell disputed the legality of Henry Hill's holding the post of guardian on the ground that he, as public register, thus held two offices. Green Hill, the clerk of court, upheld this position, removing his brother and appointing as new guardian William Brickell, brother of the objector. Several years after Henry Hill appealed through the courts, the decision was overturned and his nephews were restored to him.

Charles Applewhite Hill, like his cousins, Confederate Major General Matt W. Ransom and Congressman, House Speaker, and U.S. Senator Nathaniel Macon, was a descendant of Edward and Abigail Sugan Jones, pioneer eighteenth-century settlers on Shocco Creek in present Warren County. Another cousin of Hill was U.S. Senator Augustus Hill Garland, of Arkansas, who was attorney general of the United States under President Grover Cleveland. His uncle, Henry Hill, was elected to fourteen one-year terms in the state senate (1780–95); his uncle, Green Hill, Jr., served one term in the state house (1779); his first cousin, Jordan Hill, served three house terms (1787–88, 1790) and five terms in the senate (1799–1805); and his brother, James Jones Hill, served in the house (1805, 1808–9) and in the senate (1812–13, 1817–18). Charles himself served four terms in the senate (1823–26). In total, the Hills of Franklin County served thirty-three terms in the state legislature between 1779 and 1826.

When Hill entered The University of North Carolina in 1802, his residence was listed in university records as Franklinton. That year he was a member of the Philanthropic Society. In 1804, he was one of twenty students who left the university to protest the "Monitorial law, imposing an oath on all by turns to act the part of spies on each other's conduct." This anti-honor code group is said to have enrolled en masse at the Franklin Academy in Louisburg under the tutelage of the aggressive Yale graduate Matthew Dickinson when he opened the school in January 1805. Dickinson was later accused of trying to rival the university.

During 1807 and 1808 Hill served as a trustee of Franklin Academy. After 1808, he moved to Georgia and taught school for several years. He was in Washington County, N.C., in 1812 and returned to

Louisburg in 1815. At that time he decided to finish his studies at Chapel Hill; he was graduated in 1816 with an A.B. degree at age thirty-two. In 1818 his textbook, *An Improved American Grammar of the English Language for the Use of Schools*, was published by the Gales printing firm in Raleigh. Two years later he was granted the M.A. degree by The University of North Carolina in recognition of his teaching career.

For four years (1816–20), Hill conducted the Warrenton Male Academy. Afterwards he taught a private school in Warrenton for one year and then moved back to Franklin County. From 1822 to 1828, he was principal of Midway Academy, which he founded in Franklin County, about halfway between Louisburg and Warrenton, near the present Ingleside community. The school burned in 1824, but was soon rebuilt and reopened. In newspaper advertisements for his school, Hill announced that if advice and admonition were unheeded he would use the rod, with parental prudence, to administer corporal punishment to his charges. And he further gave notice that his plan of education was designed to be preparatory for entrance to The University of North Carolina.

Hill was elected to the North Carolina Senate for four consecutive terms in 1823–26, when he was known as a champion of public education and a foe of lotteries. In 1824 he was chairman of the senate committee on education, and on 6 December of that year he introduced a bill to create a public school, or literary, fund by using the proceeds from state-owned bank stock and taxes from "gates, natural and artificial curiosities, peddlers, negro traders, and Billiard tables." On the third reading the Senate passed the bill 38 to 16, but it failed in the House of Commons, which earlier had postponed indefinitely a similar bill by one of its own members. Hill tried again, and on 22 Dec. 1825 he introduced legislation which, with slight amendment, passed both houses of the legislature and became the Literary Fund law, titled "An Act to Create a Fund for the Establishment of Common Schools." It was to be backed by income from various stocks, taxes, and vacant state lands. The money thereby generated was inadequate to institute any significant program on a statewide scale, and efforts to increase the fund's income failed for ten consecutive years. Nevertheless, the legislature's initial action eventually led to establishment of the state's public school system. "It has so often been asserted by North Carolina writers that [Bartlett] Yancey was the author of the Literary Fund Law of 1825, that I hesitate to utter a dissenting opinion. But the credit for the authorship of that law belongs to Charles A. Hill of Franklin," wrote Charles L. Coon in his 1915 history of North Carolina schools. In 1826, Hill was a leader of the opposition to lotteries and was a factor in creating enough sentiment to do away with what he considered gambling devices that ostensibly were for the aid of schools and churches.

In 1827 Hill announced that he was going to devote full time to school work, and in 1828, in addition to his duties at Midway, he became principal of Louisburg Academy. He retained both connections until his death, and for many years he was also a Methodist preacher.

In 1806 Hill married Rebecca Wesley Long, daughter of Colonel Gabriel and Sarah Anne Richmond Long, and granddaughter of Colonel Nicholas Long of Halifax. They had nine children: William George, Mary Ann, Daniel Shine, Kemp Plummer, Nicholas Long, Richard Henry, Martha Caroline, Sarah Richmond, and Charles J.

A copy of Hill's grammar is in the North Carolina

Collection of The University North Carolina Library, Chapel Hill.

SEE: Charles L. Coon, *North Carolina Schools and Academies, 1790–1840* (1915) and *Public Education in North Carolina: A Documentary History, 1790–1840*, vol. 1 (1908); E. H. Davis, *Historical Sketches of Franklin County* (1948); Thomas Neal Ivey, *Green Hill*, ed. by J. Edward Allen (n.d.); *University of North Carolina Alumni Directory* (1954); Stephen B. Weeks, ed., *Register of Members of the Philanthropic Society, University of North Carolina* (1887).

E. T. MALONE, JR.

Hill, Daniel Harvey *(12 July 1821–24 Sept. 1889)*, soldier and educator, was born in York District, S.C., the son of Solomon and Nancy Cabeen Hill and the grandson of William Hill, noted ironmaster and Revolutionary War soldier. After his father's death in 1825, his mother raised the boy, the youngest of eleven children, in genteel poverty. Nancy Hill, a devout Presbyterian, managed, however, to convey to young Daniel her own deep religious convictions. These he retained through life. During the Civil War few, if any officers, went into combat with a firmer faith than did Daniel Harvey Hill.

Desiring a military career, he entered West Point in 1838. He was graduated four years later number twenty-eight in a class of fifty-six that teemed with future Civil War generals. The young officer served with distinction in the Mexican War, gaining two brevet promotions as well as a gold sword from the state of South Carolina given in appreciation of his services. Following his resignation from the army in February 1849, Hill became a professor of mathematics at Washington College (now Washington and Lee University), Lexington, Va.

On 2 Nov. 1852 he married Isabella Morrison, daughter of the first president of Davidson College and sister of Thomas J. Jackson's second wife. At the time Jackson, the future "Stonewall" of the South, was teaching at the Virginia Military Institute, also in Lexington. Two years later Hill joined the faculty at Davidson College in North Carolina. In 1859 he resigned his chair of mathematics at this small liberal arts college to become superintendent of the North Carolina Military Institute at Charlotte.

When the Civil War began, Hill, at the request of Governor John W. Ellis, organized North Carolina's first camp of instruction at Raleigh. As a colonel he led the First North Carolina at Big Bethel, Va., the first important engagement of the war. In September 1861 he was promoted to brigadier general and the following March to major general.

Hill's division distinguished itself in the Peninsular campaign of 1862, as it did later at Second Manassas, South Mountain, and Sharpsburg. In early 1863 Hill assumed command in eastern North Carolina, where he conducted operations against New Bern and Washington. Recalled to defend Richmond during the Gettysburg campaign, he was promoted to lieutenant general (from North Carolina) on 11 July 1863. He was then ordered to the Army of Tennessee. In the Confederate victory at Chickamauga he commanded a corps. But his recommendation to President Jefferson Davis that Braxton Bragg be removed from command on the ground of incompetence prompted the president to relieve Hill instead. Furthermore, Davis refused to send Hill's commission to the Senate for approval. Thus he served as a lieutenant general for only a short period (19 July–15 Oct. 1863) while Congress was not in session. Except for a short stay in Petersburg in 1864, Hill saw little further service until the closing stages of the war. At Bentonville, N.C., in March 1865, he commanded, as a major general, a division in Joseph E. Johnston's small force.

There was no greater waste of general-officer material during the war than Daniel Harvey Hill, one of the best combat soldiers and most literate men to serve in the Confederate Army. Unfortunately, he suffered from an incontrollable impulse to criticize his associates. The result was a war record marked by brilliant episodes, but an overall Confederate career that was both disappointing and unhappy.

After the war Hill settled in Charlotte where he established in 1866 a periodical, *The Land We Love*, and in 1869 a weekly paper, *The Southern Home*. During these years he became aware of the necessity for a new and broader approach to education in the South. He wanted emphasis placed on technical training. "Is not a practical acquaintance with the ax, the plane, the saw, the anvil, the loom, the plow, and the mattock," he wrote, "vastly more useful to an impoverished people than familiarity with the laws of nations and the science of government?"

From 1877 to 1884 Hill served as president of Arkansas Industrial University (the future University of Arkansas) and then, after a year's rest, headed until 1889 the Middle Georgia Military and Agricultural College at Milledgeville (later Georgia Military College). He died in Charlotte and was buried in the cemetery at Davidson College.

Hill was the author of a textbook, *Elements of Algebra*; several religious tracts; and numerous articles relating to the Civil War, notably those in *Battles and Leaders of the Civil War*. He also contributed to his own publications.

Daniel Harvey Hill, Jr., one of nine children, followed in his father's footsteps and became an educator. From 1908 to 1916 he was president of North Carolina College of Agriculture and Mechanic Arts (now North Carolina State University) at Raleigh.

SEE: A. C. Avery, *Memorial Address on the Life and Character of Lieutenant General D. H. Hill* (1893); L. H. Bridges, *Lee's Maverick General* (1961); Walter Clark, ed., *Histories of the Several Regiments and Battalions from North Carolina in the Great War, 1861–1865*, vols. 1–5 (1901); C. A. Evans, ed., *Confederate Military History*, vol. 4 (1899); *The War of the Rebellion: A Compilation of the Official Records of the Union and Confederate Armies* (1880–1901).

JOHN G. BARRETT

Hill, Daniel Harvey, Jr. *(15 Jan. 1859–31 July 1924)*, college president, teacher, writer, and historian, was born at Davidson College, the son of Isabella Morrison and Daniel Harvey Hill. His father was an outstanding lieutenant general of the Confederate Army, president of Arkansas Industrial University and of the Georgia Military and Agricultural College, and a mathematics teacher at Davidson College. His great-grandfather was Colonel William Hill of the Revolutionary War. His maternal great-grandfather, General Joseph Graham, also served in the Revolutionary War; and his maternal grandfather, the Reverend R. H. Morrison, was president of Davidson College.

Young Hill received a bachelor of arts degree from Davidson College after preparatory work at the North Carolina Military Institute in Charlotte and at Horner and Graves Military Academy in Hillsborough. Also from Davidson he received a master of arts degree in 1885 and a doctor of literature degree in 1905. The University of North Carolina awarded him a doctor of laws degree in 1910.

After graduating from Davidson in 1880, Hill accepted a professorship of English at the Georgia Military and Agricultural College in Milledgeville, Ga., which he held for nine years. In 1889 he was elected professor of English in the original faculty of the newly established North Carolina College of Agriculture and Mechanic Arts (now North Carolina State University) in Raleigh. The young professor made many contributions to the academic life of the new college. Under President Alexander Q. Holladay he served as professor of English and bookkeeping, secretary of the faculty, and bursar. He took charge of the library in its formative years and served as its first librarian on a part-time basis for ten years. In 1905, as his reputation as an educator grew, he was elected vice-president of the college by the board of trustees. Three years later he became the school's third president, upon the retirement of Dr. George T. Wilson.

Hill served as president from 1908 until 1916, a time of significant growth for the college. By the purchase of two adjacent tracts of land, the size of the campus was enlarged and several major new buildings were added, including the Nineteen-eleven Dormitory, the Engineering Building (renamed Winston Hall), the Dining Hall (renamed Leazar Hall), the YMCA Building (renamed King Religious Center), and South Dormitory (renamed Syme Hall). There were also dramatic increases in both student enrollment and faculty. The student body nearly doubled, increasing from 446 to 723. At the time Hill became president, the college had a staff of nine. At the time of his resignation, the faculty consisted of 20 full professors, 6 associate professors, 8 assistant professors, and 28 instructors. The Agricultural Extension Service, which has become an important channel for communicating research findings to the state's agricultural community, began on 1 July 1909.

During his tenure at the college, Hill did considerable historical research and writing. He was the author of the volume on North Carolina in the twelve-volume *Confederate Military History*, edited by Clement Anselm Evans and published in 1899. His *Young People's History of North Carolina* first appeared in 1907. With Charles William Burkett and Frank Lincoln Stevens, he wrote *Agriculture for Beginners*, a widely used textbook, and edited *The Hill Readers*, a series of five volumes published in 1906.

After serving the college for twenty-nine years, Hill resigned as president to accept an offer by the North Carolina Historical Commission to write a history of North Carolina troops in the Civil War. The project was conceived and promoted by J. Bryan Grimes, secretary of state of North Carolina and chairman of the North Carolina Historical Commission; it was funded by the Ricks Foundation, created in 1916 by Robert Henry Ricks of Rocky Mount. Hill planned to write four volumes, but illness and death intervened and he completed only the first two. The two-volume work, entitled *Bethel to Sharpsburg: North Carolina in the War Between the States*, was published in 1926 by Edwards and Broughton of Raleigh, two years after Hill's death. His research was exhaustive and meticulous. For his writing he collected between five and six thousand volumes relating to the Civil War, an exceptionally fine working library on the subject which was later turned over to the North Carolina Historical Commission.

Hill became a member of the North Carolina Histori-

cal Commission in 1904 and served as its secretary from 1921 until his death. He was chairman of the North Carolina Council of Defense during World War I, and at various times served as president of the North Carolina Folklore Society, the North Carolina Teachers Assembly, and the North Carolina Literary and Historical Association.

On 22 July 1885 he married Pauline White, of Milledgeville, Ga., daughter of Dr. Samuel G. White, a surgeon in the U.S. Navy. They had five children: Pauline, Daniel Harvey, Samuel White, Elizabeth (Mrs. Max Abernethy), and Randolph Isabel. Hill died in Blowing Rock, where he had gone with relatives in the hope that the mountain air would help restore his health.

In 1926 the new library at North Carolina State College was appropriately named the D. H. Hill Library. The original library building has been renamed Brooks Hall, but the present library building, which was built in 1954 and expanded in 1971, retains the name of the college's first librarian and third president.

SEE: Daniel Harvey Hill, *Bethel to Sharpsburg*, vol. 1 (1926); David A. Lockmiller, *History of the North Carolina State College of Agriculture and Engineering of the University of North Carolina, 1889–1939* (1939); Alice E. Reagan, *North Carolina State University: A Narrative History* (1987).

I. T. LITTLETON

Hill, Frederick Jones (*15 Mar. 1792–27 Mar. 1861*), physician, planter, and legislator, was born at his father's plantation, Fairfields, in New Hanover County. He was the son of Elizabeth Jones and John Hill, an officer in the Continental Army. His grandparents were William and Margaret Moore Hill, and Frederick and Jane Swann Jones. For one year (1805–6) Hill attended The University of North Carolina, where he was a member of the Dialectic Literary Society. In 1811–12 he studied medicine at the College of Physicians and Surgeons, New York City. Hill practiced medicine in Wilmington but later gave it up for agriculture. Nevertheless, his reputation in the state as a physician continued. In April 1849 he was elected chairman of the State Medical Convention, which met at Raleigh to form a medical society. Following the organization of the Medical Society of the State of North Carolina, Dr. Edmund Strudwick of Hillsborough nominated Hill to be its first president. Hill asked that his name be withdrawn as he had not been in active practice for many years. The society then unanimously elected him an honorary member.

On 2 Apr. 1812 Hill married Ann Ivy Watters, of Chatham County, the daughter of William and Mary Watters. The ceremony was performed at Forceput, a relative's plantation in New Hanover County. The couple had no children. In 1825 Hill purchased from his mother-in-law a property near Pittsboro he named Kentucky, which became the Hills' summer home. A year later he bought Orton Plantation, located on the Cape Fear River in Brunswick County, from the estate of the late Governor Benjamin Smith. Orton was built about 1725 by Roger Moore, a collateral ancestor of Hill's. The principal crops of the 4,975-acre plantation were rice and cotton. About 1840 Hill made considerable improvements to his home by adding a second floor and attic as well as four Doric columns to the facade of the house. In 1854 he sold Orton to Thomas C. Miller, who had married his wife's niece, Annie W. Davis. Hill then returned to Wilmington where he had retained his earlier home.

A staunch Whig, Hill first served in an elective office as a representative from Brunswick County to the North Carolina Constitutional Convention of 1835, but he did not play a significant role as delegate. On the major reforms of the old constitution he voted for biennial sessions of the General Assembly, popular election of the governor, and religious toleration by substituting the word "Christian" for "Protestant" in the state constitution. He voted against the amendment to abolish borough representation in the legislature.

In 1835, Hill represented Brunswick County for one term in the North Carolina Senate. During this session he was elected a trustee of The University of North Carolina, serving until 1860. He represented his county in the House of Commons in 1836, 1838, and 1840, and in every session was appointed a member of the Committee on Internal Improvements. He supported the measures of the Whig party to build roads, canals, and railroads. His most valuable contribution, however, was in the field of education. In a speech delivered in the House of Commons on 10 Dec. 1838, Hill advocated using a part of the funds derived from the sale of state land to support public schools. He said that it had always been one of his most cherished desires "to furnish the means of a plain education to every citizen within our limits." Moreover, he continued, the word "education" meant "something more than the mere imparting of instruction; it is the engrafting of knowledge upon a good stock, the application of all those means calculated to develop the physical, moral, and intellectual faculties of man." In conclusion, Hill declared that "In a government founded upon the popular will, Education is necessary for all classes, and for each individual in the community—and it is the duty of such Government to take care that this great end be secured." Three weeks after making this speech, Hill introduced in the House "A Bill for the establishment of Common Schools." A similar bill had been introduced in the Senate a few days earlier by William W. Cherry of Bertie County. After several amendments had been made to the Hill and Cherry bills, the two houses agreed on a measure, which was passed on 7 Jan. 1839, to begin North Carolina's common school system. At the next session of the General Assembly, Hill introduced another bill to provide for the better regulation of the common schools; it was passed with amendments on 9 Jan. 1841.

In 1840 Hill was a delegate to the Whig National Convention, held in Harrisburg, Pa., where he voted for William Henry Harrison and John Tyler as his party's candidates for president and vice-president. He was a strong supporter of the Whig party's attempt to reestablish the Bank of the United States, which Tyler later opposed. When Hill ran for reelection to the House of Commons in 1842, he was defeated. He wrote a friend that "Mr. Tyler has thrown the weight of his name (or rather that which hangs around the office he accidentally fills) into the canvass to my prejudice." This defeat marked the end of his political career.

A member of the Episcopal church, Hill represented St. James Parish, Wilmington, ten times in the diocesan conventions and St. Bartholomew's, Pittsboro, twice. In 1831 he and his uncle, Dr. Nathaniel M. Hill, gave the land in Pittsboro on which St. Bartholomew's Church was built; they also guaranteed the cost of its construction. When Hill died, he left the Diocese of North Carolina his residence in Wilmington, 20 acres of land, and $10,000 "for the benefit of the poor orphans of the state

of North Carolina"; he also bequeathed $4,000 to St. Bartholomew's Church, Pittsboro. The bequests were not to take effect until the death of his wife. Hill was buried in the family lot in Oakdale Cemetery, Wilmington.

SEE: J. G. de R. Hamilton, ed., *The Papers of William A. Graham*, vol. 2 (1959); Hill Family Bible (in the possession of Mrs. Douglas Marshall, Charlotte); Frederick J. Hill Papers (Southern Historical Collection, University of North Carolina Library, Chapel Hill); Frederick J. Hill, *Remarks . . . Delivered in the House of Commons of North Carolina*, 10 Dec. 1838 (1838); *Journal of the Proceedings . . . of the Protestant Episcopal Church in the State of North Carolina*, 1821–51; North Carolina Constitutional Convention of 1835, *Proceedings* and Debates (1836); North Carolina, *Journal of the Senate and House of Commons*, 1835–41; *Proceedings of the State Medical Convention, Held in Raleigh, April 1849* (1849); *Raleigh Register*, 17 Apr. 1812, 6 Apr. 1861; Royal G. Shannonhouse, ed., *History of St. Bartholomew's Parish, Pittsboro, N.C.* (1933); J. Lawrence Sprunt, *The Story of Orton Plantation* (1966).

LAWRENCE F. LONDON

Hill, Green, Jr. (3 Nov. 1741–11 Sept. 1826), pioneer Methodist minister, Revolutionary patriot, planter, and public servant, was born in Granville (later Bute) County, the son of Grace Bennett and Green Hill. His father, a member of the established church, was appointed to the vestry of the Parish of St. George in 1758; little else is known of him except that he was a farmer and landowner of substantial means. His maternal grandfather, William Bennett, resident of Northampton County, was captain of the Roanoke Company of 101 Men, Northampton Regiment, colonial militia, in 1748. U.S. Senator Augustus Hill Garland, of Arkansas, who was attorney general in the cabinet of President Grover Cleveland, was a descendant of Hill's brother, William.

No accounts are known to exist of Hill's childhood, and there is no record of the extent and manner of his formal education. He was a member, along with his brothers William and Henry, of Blandford-Bute Masonic Lodge. Hill was a delegate from Bute County to the colonial Assembly at New Bern on 25 Aug. 1774, to the Assembly at New Bern on 3 Apr. 1775, and to the Second Provincial Congress in Hillsborough beginning 21 Aug. 1775. At the Halifax Congress of 4 Apr. 1776, where he represented Bute, he was named second major of the Bute militia regiment. On 11 Jan. 1777 he was appointed a justice of the court (equivalent to the modern magistrate) for Bute County. In the same year Hill represented his county in the first session of the state legislature at New Bern. When Bute was split in 1779 to form Franklin and Warren counties, he and his brother William were two of the four witnesses to the deed recording the purchase of the 100 acres of land for the new county seat, Louisburg. He also served as a land processioner (a kind of surveyor) for the Franklin County Court of Pleas and Quarter Sessions.

In 1781 Hill enlisted as chaplain of the Tenth Regiment, Sharp's Company, and saw service that year as far west as Salisbury, when American armies were retreating. In 1783 he was elected treasurer for the District of Halifax; he was also elected one of the councillors of state, a position he held until 1786. In December 1785 he became clerk of the Court of Pleas and Quarter Sessions for Franklin County and was named to a four-man committee to see that a bridge was built across the Tar River at Louisburg. In 1786 he built and began to operate a gristmill at Massie's Falls on the Tar River. A legislative committee, assigned in 1789 to report on an alleged shortage of funds under his management, found instead that Hill, as Halifax district treasurer, was due a reimbursement of 233 pounds, 13 shillings, and sixpence, which the Assembly paid him.

Sometime in the early 1770s, Hill became interested in the Protestant religious movement known as Methodism. Bishop Francis Asbury preached to "about 400 souls" at Hill's home on 9 July 1780. Clergy present at the Ellis' Preaching-House conference in Virginia voted on 30 Apr. 1784 to meet three times in 1785, "the first at Green Hill's (North Carolina) Friday 29th and Saturday 30th of April." This gathering, the first conference of the Methodist church ever held in North Carolina, actually took place on 20 Apr. 1785. It was also the first Annual Conference of the new Methodist Episcopal church since its formal organization in December 1784, thus, the first conference of the organized Methodist church ever held in the United States. Although at the time Hill was merely a local preacher, at this session at his home Methodist historian Jesse Lee was "admitted into full connexion" of the ministry. Lee, prior to then, had worked for a number of years as an overseer on the Halifax plantation of Colonel Gabriel Long. Hill was the brother-in-law of the English scholar, preacher, and physician, Dr. John King, who had come to America to establish Wesleyan societies. King had preached the first Methodist sermon in Baltimore before moving southward in 1780 to Louisburg. Hill is said to have been the first native son of North Carolina to become a Methodist preacher.

Other conferences were held at Hill's home near Louisburg in January 1790, December 1791, and December 1794. Methodist Bishop Francis Asbury described in his journal, dated 19 Jan. 1792, his visit to the home of Green Hill, whom he ordained as a deacon on 21 January.

In 1796 Hill crossed the Alleghenies, moving westward and preaching along the way. He was not, however, one of many North Carolinians who were granted land in Tennessee, then still part of North Carolina, on account of distinguished service in the Revolutionary War. He moved his family to Tennessee in 1799 and settled about 12 miles south of Nashville, where he built a home, called Liberty Hill, which was in some ways a duplicate of the house he had left behind in Franklin County. There, in 1808, met the Western Conference of the Methodist church, which included the states of Tennessee, Kentucky, Alabama, Mississippi, Louisiana, Ohio, Indiana, Illinois, and all territory west of the Mississippi River. Hill was ordained an elder on 4 Oct. 1813 by Bishop William McKendree.

Hill was married twice, first on 13 Oct. 1763 to Nancy Thomas. Their children were Jordan, who became a state legislator and sheriff of Franklin County; Hannah, who married Thomas Stokes of Chatham County; Nancy, who married Thomas Knibb Wynn of North Carolina; Martha, who married Jesse Brown of North Carolina; and Richard, who died in infancy. Nancy Thomas Hill died on 16 Jan. 1772, and on 3 June 1773 Hill married Mary Seawell, daughter of Benjamin Seawell of old Bute County. The children of this second marriage were Green Hill III (trustee of Franklin Academy when it was chartered by the legislature in 1802 and trustee board clerk when it opened in 1805), who married Mary Long, daughter of Colonel Gabriel and Sarah Richmond Long; Lucy, who married the Reverend Joshua Cannon; John; Thomas; Sally Hicks, who never married; Mary Seawell, who married Adam de

Graffenreid of Tennessee; William; and Joshua C., who married Lemiza Lanier of Beaufort County.

Hill died and was buried at Liberty Hill, his home in Tennessee. His old home in Louisburg, where the Methodist conferences were held, still stands and is occupied by descendants of his brother, William. The poet and novelist Edwin Wiley Fuller was buried there in a family cemetery. The country club and the city cemetery in Louisburg both are named for Hill. The library of Vanderbilt University has some of his books.

SEE: James R. Cox, *Pioneers and Perfecters of Our Faith* (1975); E. H. Davis, *Historical Sketches of Franklin County* (1948); W. L. Grissom, *History of Methodism in North Carolina, From 1772 to the Present Time* (1905); Thomas Neal Ivey, *Green Hill*, ed. by J. Edward Allen (n.d.); *Minutes of the Methodist Conferences, Annually Held in America, From 1773 to 1813, Inclusive* (1813); M. H. Moore, *Pioneers of Methodism in North Carolina and Virginia* (1884).

E. T. MALONE, JR.

Hill, Henry Harrington (*20 Sept. 1894–17 May 1987*), educator, was born in Statesville, the son of James Henry and Anne Harrington Hill. The elder Hill was the leading educator in Iredell County for over fifty years. He served briefly as county superintendent of schools, a position he originally refused, then for almost twenty years was chairman of the county board of education. But James Henry Hill is perhaps best remembered for his association with Statesville Male Academy, the school he headed from 1898 to 1905; at various times he also taught at Statesville's Simonton College.

Henry Hill received his education under his father's supervision until the age of fifteen, when he entered Davidson College; after spending three years there, he transferred to the University of Virginia. At Virginia he was elected to Phi Beta Kappa, and earned both the bachelor's and master's degrees. His Ph.D. from Teachers College, Columbia University, was awarded in 1930. Hill began his teaching career in Walnut Ridge, Ark., in 1916, and from 1922 to 1927 was the town's superintendent of schools. From 1927 his rise in the profession was rapid. In sequence he became principal of North Little Rock High School; supervisor of high schools for the state of Arkansas; professor of school administration at the University of Kentucky; superintendent of the Lexington, Ky., schools; assistant superintendent of schools for the city of St. Louis;, and, in 1941, dean of the University of Kentucky's School of Education. He occupied the deanship for one year before moving to Pittsburgh, Pa., to become superintendent of schools.

In 1945 Hill was elected president of George Peabody College for Teachers in Tennessee and served with distinction until his retirement in 1961. His presidency was marked by a period of substantial growth in enrollment, an increase in the number of faculty members, and additions to the physical plant. Hill was a competent administrator who worked well with faculty and staff. As one writer observed, "He was a talented, intelligent man who could have chosen [any one of] many professions," but instead "chose to be a teacher." He possessed a clear vision of Peabody's mission, and though educated in private schools was a tireless and outspoken supporter of public schools. As an individual Hill was dignified in appearance and in every respect the cultured gentleman; also, his gentle sense of humor tended to place individuals and groups at ease.

Widely recognized as a leader in education, Hill received honorary degrees from a number of institutions, among them Columbia University, the University of Pittsburgh, the University of Kentucky, Harvard University, and Davidson College. He was an active member of the American Association of School Administrators, a trustee of the Educational Testing Service, and president of the Southern Association of Colleges and Schools. When Felix Robb, who succeeded him as president of Peabody, resigned to accept an executive position with the Southern Association, Hill was persuaded to return as interim president, a position he held from July 1966 to August 1967.

Hill gave freely of his time and talents. He was president of the Lexington Community Chest, a director of the Pittsburgh chapter of the American Red Cross, and president (1954) of Nashville's United Givers Fund. He served as a trustee and vice-president of the American Automobile Foundation for Traffic Safety, and was a member of Nashville's Downtown Rotary Club.

In 1922 Hill married Elizabeth Eloise Wilkes of Durant, Miss.; she died in 1979. Funeral services for Dr. Hill were held in Nashville's Westminster Presbyterian Church, where he had served as an elder; interment was in Mount Olivet Cemetery. Hill was survived by his daughter, Adrienne (Mrs. Kirkland W. Todd), four grandchildren, and four great-grandchildren.

It is interesting to note that two other Peabody presidents in this century were native North Carolinians—Bruce Ryburn Payne of Morganton (1911–37) and Sidney Clarence Garrison of Lincolnton (1937–45).

SEE: Alfred L. Crabb, *Peabody and Alfred Crabb*, ed. by John E. Windrow (1977); Homer Keever, *Iredell—Piedmont County* (1976); *Nashville Banner*, 18 May 1987; *Nashville Tennessean*, 7 Nov. 1985, 8 Jan. 1986, 20 May 1987; *Who Was Who in America*, vols. 1, 2 (1897–1942, 1942–50); *Who's Who in America* (1968–69).

J. ISAAC COPELAND

Hill, James (*fl.* 1676–81), Council member, was appointed to that position by a commission issued by the Lords Proprietors on 21 Nov. 1676. He probably assumed office the following summer, when his commission reached the northern Carolina colony, then called Albemarle.

Hill may have lived previously in Virginia, where a James Hill was granted 350 acres in Northumberland County in 1661. Whether he came to Albemarle before his appointment to the Council is not known.

A few months after Hill took office, the Albemarle colonists revolted against the acting governor, Thomas Miller, in the uprising called Culpeper's Rebellion. Like all but one of the other Council members, Hill supported Miller, but he does not seem to have been a chief target of the insurgents. Although Miller and certain Council members were thrown into prison and charged with heinous crimes, Hill was only confined to his home by a guard, from which he escaped to Virginia. Upon his return to Albemarle, after order was restored, he was arrested but apparently was soon released. In August 1679 he again was sitting on the Council, then presided over by John Harvey. The same month or soon after, Hill and several others helped Thomas Miller escape from prison, where he had been confined by order of a court held by the Council, of which Hill was a member. In 1680 Hill resigned his seat on the Council to protest certain actions of Robert Holden, then secretary and customs collector as well as a Council member.

Hill, a Quaker, was a member of the Perquimans Monthly Meeting and presumably lived in Perquimans Precinct. Records indicate, but do not clearly show, that his wife was Hannah Hill, who seems to have been married previously to Henry Phelps. If so, Hill had three stepchildren: John, Jonathan, and Hannah Phelps. Whether he had children of his own is uncertain.

Hill's name has not been found in records of later date than 10 Sept. 1681, when the Perquimans Monthly Meeting appointed him to a committee to settle differences between two of its members. He probably died soon after that date.

SEE: William Wade Hinshaw, comp., *Encyclopedia of American Quaker Genealogy*, vol. 1 (1936); Minutes and Records of Perquimans Monthly Meeting, 1680–1762 (Quaker Collection, Guilford College Library, Greensboro); Nell Marion Nugent, comp., *Abstracts of Virginia Land Patents and Grants, 1623–1800* (1934); William L. Saunders, ed., *Colonial Records of North Carolina*, vol. 1 (1886–90). Manuscript sources in North Carolina State Archives, Raleigh: Albemarle Book of Warrants and Surveys, 1681–1706; Council Minutes, Wills, Inventories, 1677–1701; Entry Book of Lords Proprietors of Carolina (microfilm).

MATTIE ERMA E. PARKER

Hill, John (*9 Apr. 1797–24 May 1861*), planter, county official, legislator, and congressman, was born near Germanton, the son of John and Mary Elizabeth Hill. After attending country schools, he entered The University of North Carolina as a member of the class of 1820 but failed to graduate. He returned home to Stokes County, where for the rest of his life he combined his public and private careers. From 1819 to 1823 he represented Stokes in the North Carolina House of Commons, and served in the North Carolina Senate in 1823, 1825–26, 1830–31, and 1848–49. At various intervals over a thirty-year period he held the post of clerk of court.

During the political controversies of the 1830s, Hill, an admirer of Andrew Jackson, emerged as one of the leaders of the Democratic party in North Carolina. In 1836 he ran as an elector on the Van Buren ticket, and the following year challenged Augustine H. Shepperd, a former Jacksonian then in the Whig ranks, for the Fifth District seat in Congress, narrowly losing by 117 votes. In an 1839 rematch Hill, running on a platform of opposition to rechartering the United States Bank and support for the Independent Treasury plan, defeated Shepperd by 47 votes.

Hill's service in the Twenty-sixth Congress was generally undistinguished. He made few speeches and confined his activities primarily to defending the policies of President Martin Van Buren, particularly the Independent Treasury idea which was finally enacted into law in 1840. Hill declined to stand for reelection in 1841. Back in Stokes County, he devoted himself to his planting interests but still remained active in state and local politics.

After representing Stokes in the 1848–49 session of the Senate, Hill became chief clerk of that body in 1850 and served for several years. In 1861, he was elected to represent Stokes in the secession convention that took North Carolina out of the Union. While attending the convention in Raleigh, Hill had a stroke and died. He was buried in the Old Hill Burying Ground near Germanton.

SEE: *Biog. Dir. Am. Cong.* (1971); *Congressional Globe,* 26th Congress; Greensboro *Patriot*; Raleigh *North Carolina Standard*; John H. Wheeler, ed., *Historical Sketches of North Carolina from 1584 to 1851* (1851).

RALPH J. CHRISTIAN

Hill, John Sprunt (17 Mar. 1869–29 July 1961), philanthropist and banker, was born near Faison, the son of William Edward and Frances Diana Faison Hill. Among prominent relatives were his grandfather General William Lanier Hill and his great-uncle Governor Edward Bishop Dudley. At age twelve he completed the course at Faison High School and, being too young for college, he worked as a clerk until entering The University of North Carolina in 1885 as a freshman. In Chapel Hill he was active in extracurricular activities, especially in the Dialectic Society of which he was president. He shared highest honors in his class and was graduated with a Ph.B. degree in 1889. Returning to Duplin County, Hill taught in local schools until 1891, when he returned to the university to study law. The following year he entered the Columbia University Law School, from which he was graduated in 1894.

After a brief association with the New York City firm of Peckham and Tyler, Hill established his own law firm, Hill, Sturcke, and Andrews. While attorney for a finishing school in New York, he met Annie Louise Watts, of Durham, the only daughter of George Washington Watts. They were married on 29 Nov. 1899, and became the parents of George Watts, Laura Valinda, and Frances Faison.

At the outbreak of the Spanish-American War, Hill enlisted in New York Troop A as a private and served in the Puerto Rican campaign. In 1900 he unsuccessfully sought a seat in Congress on the Democratic ticket in a traditionally Republican section; afterwards he worked as a legal counsel for Tammany Hall. Owing to his father-in-law's illness, Hill left New York in 1903 to settle in Durham, taking over Watts's management of the American Tobacco Company. In the same year he also established the Home Savings Bank and the Durham Bank and Trust Company.

At this time Hill turned his attention to local improvements, with particular emphasis on The University of North Carolina as well as Durham civic life. In Chapel Hill he outlined his concerns at the commencement of 1901 in a speech entitled "Needs of the University"; he was elected to the board of trustees in 1905. The university was a substantial beneficiary of Hill's interest in North Carolina history: in 1891 he established a Hill Prize, in 1905 he donated a scholarship, and in 1906 he endowed the North Carolina Collection. In later years he obtained a permanent home for the collection through his efforts to build a new library at the university in the late 1920s, capping these achievements with the founding of the Friends of the Library organization.

For the benefit of the university and its alumni, Hill also built the Carolina Inn in 1924. When the university library was moved to its new quarters, the old Carnegie Library was converted into Hill Music Hall at the urging of Hill and his wife. In addition, Hill was chairman of the university trustee committee on university buildings during the growth period of 1923–31. Later he patronized the University Press. In recognition of his continuing service to the university, he was awarded an honorary doctor of laws degree in 1933.

In Durham, Hill coupled business interests with civic improvements. Besides his banking activities, he was a director of Erwin Mills (1916–46) and of Home Security Life Insurance. He served on the Durham Board of Aldermen (1908–10) and on the board of the Durham Public Library. From 1933 to 1938 he represented Durham in the state senate. Whether in an official or private capacity, Hill worked to improve the city of Durham, donating playgrounds, the Durham Athletic Park, the Hillandale golf course, and numerous parks and other gifts, including contributions to Watts Hospital and founding funds to the Research Triangle Institute.

Hill made lasting contributions to the state. In many speeches, including a report on the "Needs of North Carolina Farmers with Regard to Credits, Marketing and Cooperation," he championed the formation of rural credit associations, culminating in the passage of the Credit Union Act of 1915 by the state legislature. Shortly afterwards he established a rural credit association at Lowe's Grove in Durham County. In 1920 he entered the program for better roads with a speech before the Good Roads Association and then served on the State Highway Commission (1920–31). In a speech before the North Carolina Forestry Association in 1920, Hill urged the state to build up forestry stocks for greater profits while providing for the conservation of natural resources. Hill was also a strong advocate of prohibition. A devout Presbyterian and supporter of a pious religious life, he pushed for the State Alcoholic Beverage Control system as a rational approach to the problem and control of liquor.

Hill's interests extended beyond North Carolina. In 1913 he was a delegate to the International Congress of Foresters, held in Paris, from which stemmed his concern for forestry and natural resources in general. In countless speeches Hill pressed for improvements in these areas not only in North Carolina but in the South and the United States as well. He was a fellow of the American Geographical Society and held memberships in the American Institute of Genealogy and the American, North Carolina, and Virginia Historical societies. For many years, he served as a trustee of the Union Theological Seminary in Richmond, Va.

The philanthropist was active until his death at age ninety-two from the complications of pneumonia. He was buried in the Hill family plot in Maplewood Cemetery, Durham. The citation on his honorary degree stated of Hill: "A builder without vainglory, a fighter with abandon but without guile, a dreamer whose youthful dreams go daily into the making of a better University and a more beautiful state."

SEE: Samuel A. Ashe, ed., *Biographical History of North Carolina*, vol. 8 (1917); William D. Carmichael, *John Sprunt Hill '89: Nullum Quod Tetigit Non Ornavit* (1953); Dialectic Society Minutes, 1885–89 (Southern Historical Collection, University of North Carolina Library, Chapel Hill); *Durham Morning Herald*, 30, 31 July 1961; *Durham Sun*, 1 Aug. 1961; Daniel L. Grant, *Alumni History of the University of North Carolina* (1924); Archibald Henderson, *John Sprunt Hill: A Biographical Sketch* (1937); John Sprunt Hill Papers (Southern Historical Collection, University of North Carolina Library, Chapel Hill); Gary B. Trawick and Paul E. Wyche, *100 Years, 100 Men: 1871–1971* (1971).

ROGER N. KIRKMAN

Hill, Joseph Alston (1800–35), orator and lawyer, was the younger son of William Henry Hill (1767–1808) and his wife Eliza Ashe, the daughter of General John Ashe (1720–81) and Rebecca Moore Ashe, who was the daughter of Colonel Maurice Moore and the sister of General James Moore and Judge Maurice Moore. Hill was born at Hilton, his father's residence on the Cape

Fear near Wilmington. He was named for Governor Joseph Alston, his first cousin, the son of his aunt Mary Ashe and William Alston of Waccamaw, S.C.

William Henry Hill, Joseph's father, represented the Wilmington district in Congress from 1799 to 1803. He was the son of William Hill, the ancestor of the distinguished family of that name on the Cape Fear. William Hill, the father, was a native of Boston and a graduate of Harvard in 1756. He had come to North Carolina because of his health and settled at Brunswick, where he taught school and married Margaret Moore, daughter of Nathaniel Moore. His oldest son, John, was an original member of the Society of the Cincinnati, having taken part in the Battle of Eutau Springs as a lieutenant in the Fourth Regiment, North Carolina Continental Line. His other son, William Henry Hill, was appointed by President George Washington as U.S. district attorney. He served in the Sixth and Seventh Congresses when party feeling ran deep and bitter, because, for the first time, the election of president in 1801 was thrown into the House of Representatives. William Henry Hill voted with Henderson, Grove, and Dickson for Aaron Burr against Alston, Stone, Stanford, Mason, and Spaight for Thomas Jefferson. (Hill's nephew was Governor Joseph Alston of South Carolina who married Theodosia Burr, the only daughter of Aaron Burr.) A Federalist, Hill was appointed judge of the United States District Court for the District of North Carolina by President John Adams at the close of his term, but the designation was withdrawn by President Jefferson. Hill returned to Hilton, his home near Wilmington, where he died at age forty-two.

Joseph Alston Hill was nine when his father died, and his mother immediately directed his education. He was graduated from Yale College and trained for the bar at the celebrated Litchfield Law School. He came to the bar with a mind probably better disciplined than any man who had preceded him in North Carolina. He seems to have inherited rare oratorical powers from his grandfather, General John Ashe, one of the most influential political leaders of the colony who was a member of the Committee of Correspondence (1773) and, earlier, speaker of the North Carolina Assembly (1762–63); he died in Continental service on 4 Oct. 1781. (Ashe was the son of John Baptista Ashe, prominent in the colonial annals of North Carolina, and his wife Elizabeth Swann, daughter of Speaker Samuel Swann and Elizabeth Lillington Swann.)

In the Internal Improvement Convention at Raleigh in 1833, when he debated the ablest men of the state, Hill carried—over great opposition—all the resolutions he submitted. According to tradition, so remarkable was his ability in these debates that his claim to leadership was generally, if not universally, conceded. At the time Judge William Gaston pronounced Hill the most brilliant man of his age in North Carolina.

Hill had served in the North Carolina legislature in 1826, 1827, and 1830. He died a young man, but one who had developed extraordinary talents.

SEE: Samuel A. Ashe, ed., *Biographical History of North Carolina*, vol. 4 (1906); Walter Clark, ed., *State Records of North Carolina*, vol. 20 (1902); *The Compendium of American Genealogy*, vols. 3, 4; Marshall De Lancey Haywood, *Governor Tryon of North Carolina* (1903); Francis B. Heitman, *Historical Register of Officers in the Continental Army* (1893); A. M. Hooper and Griffith McRee, *A Memoir of General John Ashe in the Revolution* (1854); Alice Keith, ed., *The John Gray Blount Papers* (North Carolina State Archives, Raleigh); Hugh F. Rankin, *North Carolina*

Continentals (1971); William L. Saunders, ed., *Colonial Records of North Carolina*, vol. 9 (1890); John H. Wheeler, ed., *Historical Sketches of North Carolina from 1584 to 1851* (1851) and ed., *Reminiscences and Memoirs of North Carolina and Eminent North Carolinians* (1884).

WILLIAM A. BLOUNT STEWART

Hill, Robert Andrews (25 Mar. 1811–2 July 1900), jurist, was born in Iredell County, the son of David and Rhoda Andrews Hill. In 1816 his family moved to Tennessee, settling in Williamson County where he managed to acquire a good education. He taught school in 1832 and 1833, and was elected constable the next year. From 1836 to 1844 he served as justice of the peace, studying law in his spare time. After beginning a practice in Waynesboro, he was elected by the legislature in 1847 for two terms as district attorney general. Moving to Mississippi in 1855, he practiced law in Jacinto, Tishomingo County. He was elected probate judge in 1858 and served until the end of the Civil War. During the hostilities he maintained a neutral position because of his opposition to secession.

Afterwards, when Mississippi's duly elected national representatives were not seated, Judge Hill spent many months in Washington, D.C., arranging for pardons and the reimbursement to citizens for property seized by the army, as well as pleading successfully for the suspension of the direct land tax. Recognizing his farsightedness, the people of his county elected Hill by an overwhelming majority as delegate to the constitutional convention of 1865, and Provisional Governor Sharkey appointed him chancellor of the district. In 1866 President Andrew Johnson appointed Hill federal district judge, a position he held for twenty-five years.

During the two-year period of military occupation and the subsequent years of readjustment and recovery, Hill's leadership and advice were sought and followed by southerners and northerners alike. For example, the 1866 national legislation giving civil rights and privileges to Negroes was at variance with Mississippi's newly enacted freedmen's laws; the state laws were repealed to avert conflict. The Reconstruction Act of 1867 declaring all state jurisdictions to be without authority over acts of the military was interpreted by Hill to be constitutional, but he held that the constitutional rights of citizens remained in effect and that the military courts should be used only in certain offenses. The act of 1870, prompted by Ku Klux Klan activity, allowed the suspension of the writ of habeas corpus and the institution of military law. Hill believed that the matter could be better dealt with in the civil court and so ruled in the first case tried under the act in 1871. He maintained jurisdiction over the defendants, allowed them to agree to a guilty verdict from the jury, and fined and released all but four of the twenty-eight defendants on bond, subject to their own recognizance to keep the peace for two years.

Hill's judicial responsibilities during this period and for much of his professional life in Mississippi were made difficult because of the lack of a superior or adviser for the most part. Because the new national and state laws had not been passed on by a Superior Court, Hill of necessity had the responsibility of construing them. His loyalty to the Union was never questioned nor were his interpretations challenged. His legal reasoning was sound and had been from his early years as justice of the peace in Tennessee where, with many litigated cases, only one of his decisions was appealed and that was upheld by a higher court. In 1868, at the time of the Mississippi constitutional convention, Hill—although not a delegate—prepared the article establishing the judicial system of the state, including the Supreme Court, setting up the appointive method of choosing judges and chancellors and establishing separate common law and equity courts. In a letter to the judicial committee of the 1900 state constitutional convention just completed, Hill spoke with pride of his earlier work which the convention had sustained more than thirty years later.

At age eighty, he retired to his home in Oxford with his wife of fifty-eight years, the former Mary Lucky Andrews. He was interested to the last in many things but especially the judiciary; his church, the Cumberland Presbyterian Church; and higher education. Hill had served as a longtime trustee and law lecturer at the University of Mississippi. He died at age eighty-nine and was buried in St. Peters Cemetery, Oxford.

SEE: J. F. H. Claiborne, *Mississippi as a Province, Territory, and State* (1880); *DAB*, vol. 9 (1932); James Wilford Garner, *Reconstruction in Mississippi* (1964); N. E. Gillis, *Abstract of Goodspeed's MISSISSIPPI* (1962); Goodspeed, *Biographical and Historical Memoirs of Mississippi*, vol. 1, part 2 (1891); *Nat. Cyc. Am. Biog.*, vol. 2 (1892); M. B. P., "Robert Andrews Hill" (4-page biography in subject file at the Mississippi State Department of Archives and History); Franklin L. Riley, ed., *Mississippi Historical Society Publications*, vol. 5 (1902); Dunbar Rowland, *Mississippi*, vol. 1 (1907); James W. Silver, "North Carolinians in Mississippi History," *North Carolina Historical Review* 22 (1945); *Vicksburg Herald* (Vicksburg, Miss.), 3 July 1900; *Weekly Clarion-Ledger* (Jackson, Miss.), 5 July 1900; *Who Was Who in America: Historical Volume, 1607–1896* (1963).

CLARA HAMLETT ROBERTSON FLANNAGAN

Hill, Theophilus (*1741–20 Dec. 1790*), interstate merchant and planter, was a son of the wealthy Abraham and Judith Hinton[?] Hill of Chowan County. By the end of 1761 he had established himself near Contentnea Creek in what is now Wilson County. In 1763 he sold his patrimony of 990 acres, including the Punch Bowl, and invested most of the proceeds in Hill & Company, buying and selling merchantable commodities between Peacock's Bridge and New Bern. The firm was involved in a lawsuit in the Edgecombe County Court of July 1764. Hill was replaced as a road overseer in 1765 and was living in New Bern by 22 Nov. 1768, when he sold all his land in Edgecombe and Dobbs (soon to become Wayne) counties.

Within a year or two he decided to try the mercantile and planting potentialities of the South Carolina upcountry, establishing himself on the South Fork of the Edisto River (in present Saluda County) about 40 miles north of Augusta. By 1786 Hill had left his capable oldest son, Lodowick, in charge of the Edgefield District plantation and had transferred his principal operations to the vicinity of San Diego Plains some 20 miles north of St. Augustine, Fla. By the time of his death, his wife and younger children had become communicants of the Roman Catholic church, despite her unusual Baptist background. Undocumented tradition states that he lost a large plantation near Santo Domingo, Haiti, during the bloody insurrection of 1790–91.

On 3 Sept. 1762 Hill was bonded to marry Theresa Thomas (1744–ca. 1825), daughter of the Reverend John Thomas, Sr., and his wife Christenater Roberts of Tosneot Baptist Church in Edgecombe (now Wilson) County. On 4 Feb. 1792 she married as her second husband Don Manuel Marchal.

Hill and his wife had at least seven children: Lodowick (1763–22 July 1822), who in 1785 married Susannah ("Susan") Grigsby of Edgefield County, S.C., after serving as sergeant in Captain Isaac Ross's Troop, Second Regiment, South Carolina State Dragoons; Sarah (María del Carmen), who married Francisco Xavier Sánchez, 28 Dec. 1787; Christiana, who married José Sánchez de Ortegosa, 15 Sept. 1794; María Antonia, who married Bernardino Sánchez de Ortegosa, 4 Feb. 1799; Elizabeth (Isabel), who married Joseph Burnell from Lynn, Norfolk, England, 7 Feb. 1797; and Anna María (6 June 1787–23 June 1849), who married Samuel Williams of St. Augustine, 12 Aug. 1805, and General José Mariano Hernándes, 25 Feb. 1814.

SEE: St. Augustine Cathedral Records, Canova Transcripts; Lodowick Johnson Hill, *The Hills of Wilkes County, Georgia* (1972).

HUGH BUCKNER JOHNSTON

Hill, Theophilus Hunter (*31 Oct. 1836–29 June 1901*), poet and librarian, was born near Raleigh at Spring Hill plantation in the home of his maternal grandfather, Theophilus Hunter, Jr. His great-grandfather was the Reverend William Hill, a chaplain in the American Revolution; his grandfather, also William Hill, was North Carolina's secretary of state for more than forty years; and his father, Dr. William G. Hill, was an eminent physician. His maternal great-grandfather was Theophilus Hunter, pioneer Wake County settler. Hill's mother, Adelaide, was the daughter of Theophilus Hunter, Jr. Young Hill received his early training from an aunt, Eliza Hill, who later conducted a private school in Raleigh. He then attended the Raleigh Male Academy while it was under the direction of J. M. Lovejoy. In 1852 he entered The University of North Carolina but because of family financial reverses was obliged to complete his studies at home.

In 1853 Hill became editor of a Raleigh newspaper, *The Spirit of the Age*. At the time he was encouraged by Judge Daniel Fowle, who later became governor, to take up the study of law. Having read law under Fowle, Hill was licensed in 1858, but because he did not care for the law he never opened a practice, preferring instead a literary life. In Raleigh in 1861 his first volume of poems, *Hesper and Other Poems*, became the first book published under the copyright laws of the Confederate States. His second volume, *Poems*, was published in New York in 1869, and his final volume, *Passion Flower*, was published in Raleigh in 1883. Other poems appeared in newspapers and periodicals.

From 1871 to 1873 Hill served as state librarian until he became editor of *The Century*, published in South Carolina although he remained in Raleigh. He also represented several book concerns and insurance companies. Hill was a lifelong Democrat and kept fully informed on political issues, but he never ran for public office.

His first wife, whom he married on 22 Jan. 1861, was Laura Phillips of Northampton County; she died in 1878. Their children were Theophilus Hunter, Frank E., and Rosa. In September 1879 he married Mattie Yancey of Warren County, and they had one child, Tempe. She painted a portrait of her father for the State Library.

Hill died of a fever in Raleigh at age sixty-four. He was buried in Oakwood Cemetery.

SEE: Edward A. Oldham, "Theophilus Hunter Hill," *North Carolina Poetry Review*, vol. 3 (September–December 1935); R. D. W. Connor, ed., *North Carolina Day, Dec. 23, 1910* (1910); *Raleigh City Directories*, 1886, 1887; John H. Wheeler, ed., *Reminiscences and Memoirs of North Carolina and Eminent North Carolinians* (1884).

ELIZABETH E. NORRIS

Hill, Thomas Norfleet (*12 Mar. 1838–24 July 1904*), jurist, was born at Kenmore, Halifax County, the son of Lavinia Dorothy Barnes and Whitmel John Hill, the grandson of Colonel Whitmel Hill who was prominent in the American Revolution. His mother had been a noted belle in her day, and the refusal of her cousin Jesse Bynum to introduce her to Robert Potter at a ball in Halifax was the cause of a long, celebrated, and bitter feud.

Hill was educated at the Vine Hill Academy in Scotland Neck and later at the Warrenton Male Academy. After graduating from The University of North Carolina with a B.A. degree in 1857, he studied law with Judge Richmond Pearson for two years. In 1860 Hill settled in Scotland Neck to practice. With the advent of the Civil War, he served for a year as a private in the Scotland Neck Mounted Riflemen (later Company G of the Third North Carolina Cavalry). In May 1862 he was elected solicitor for Halifax County and resigned from military service; he held that office until 1866. In 1877, with the creation of the inferior court system, he was elected chairman of the Halifax County inferior court board of justices and so remained until the system was abolished. After that, he practiced law in the town of Halifax.

Hill was considered learned in the law and was often called upon to serve as referee. Though urged by his friends to run for public office, he was by nature reserved and not a good politician. He ran unsuccessfully for the position of associate justice of the North Carolina Supreme Court in 1878 and again in 1888. In 1902 he challenged Judge Walter Clark as chief justice of the North Carolina Supreme Court. In that unsuccessful bid, Hill ran as an Independent with Republican support. He died two years later and was buried in Trinity Cemetery, Scotland Neck.

In 1861 Hill married Eliza Hall, the daughter of Dr. Isaac Hall of Pittsboro and his wife Eliza Evans. Louisa Hall, her only sibling, married John Manning, professor of law at The University of North Carolina. Thomas and Eliza Hill were the parents of four sons and six daughters. Hill's second wife was Mary Amis Long, the daughter of Colonel Nicholas Long; they had no children.

In later life, several of Hill's unmarried and widowed daughters resided together in the town of Weldon where they become local celebrities; one of them, Rebecca, lived to be over one hundred. His son, Stuart Hall Hill (1876–1948), attended The University of North Carolina from 1893 to 1896 and later settled in New York City. For a short time he was private secretary to Theodore Roosevelt. Stuart married Madeline Blossom but they had no children. On his death, he was buried in Scotland Neck. As a hobby, Stuart Hill prepared a series of manuscript volumes relating to the genealogy of many eastern North Carolina families. Copies of these attractively written studies, rich in the local history of the region, were deposited in the North Carolina Col-

lection of The University of North Carolina Library, the Department of Archives and History in Raleigh, the New York Public Library, and other institutions.

SEE: W. C. Allen, *History of Halifax County* (1918); Joseph B. Cheshire, *Nonnulla* (1930); Stuart H. Hill, "The Hill Family" (North Carolina Collection, University of North Carolina Library, Chapel Hill); William S. Powell, ed., *Dictionary of North Carolina Biography*, vol. 1 (1979); C. T. Smith and Stuart Smith, *Trinity Parish* (1955).

CLAIBORNE T. SMITH, JR.

Hill, Whitmel (*12 Feb. 1743–12 Sept. 1797*), Revolutionary officer and government official, delegate to the Continental Congress, state senator, and member of the Council of State, was born into a wealthy family in Bertie County. Little is known of his early life or when he moved to what is now Martin County. He was graduated from the University of Pennsylvania in 1760. Hill married Winifred Blount, great-granddaughter of James Blount of Chowan County, and they had four children, two of whom died in infancy. Their son was Thomas Blount, their daughter, Elizabeth. The extent of Hill's landholdings is not known though his estate, Palmyra, at Hill's Ferry, was undoubtedly large. In the census of 1790, his 140 slaves was the largest number held by anyone in Martin County.

At the beginning of the American Revolution, Hill, already a justice of the peace, was elected lieutenant colonel of the Martin County militia. He was second in command to William Williams, for whom Williamston was named. Hill remained lieutenant colonel from September 1775 to April 1778, when Williams's "infirmities" forced his resignation and placed Hill as colonel of the regiment. Previously he had held several important positions in the Revolutionary government. In August 1775, Hill was elected to the Assembly which met at Hillsborough and established the provisional government in the "absence" of the last royal governor of North Carolina, Josiah Martin—the man, ironically, for whom Hill's county was named. In April 1776, Hill was a delegate at Halifax where the provisional government changed its name to the Council of Safety and declared its independence from England. When the next Congress assembled in Halifax in November 1778 and established the state constitution and the bill of rights, Hill was once again a member. Previously, Hill had represented Martin County in North Carolina's first General Assembly in 1777. At the following session of the General Assembly in New Bern in April 1778, Hill, now a senator, was elected speaker of the Senate.

In July 1777, Hill had uncovered a Tory plot "to assassinate all the leading men" of the Revolution in North Carolina on "some certain night." As a result of this information Governor Richard Caswell was able to circumvent the plans of the "traitors," most of whom were arrested. Shortly before Hill's discovery of the Tory conspiracy, his name had been placed in nomination as a delegate to the Continental Congress, a position won by Cornelius Harnett. Nevertheless, he was named a delegate to the Congress meeting in Philadelphia shortly after he was chosen speaker of the Senate. Hill served in the Congress from 1778 to 1781.

In a letter to Dr. Thomas Burke, his roommate in Philadelphia, fellow delegate to the Continental Congress, and future governor of North Carolina, Hill wrote that he had made the 350-mile journey to Philadelphia in only seven and one-half days, "a ride scarcely performed before in so short a time." With apparent pride, Hill later wrote that he had covered 65 miles in one day! In another letter from Philadelphia, Hill expressed his irritation with South Carolina's refusal to accept the paper money of North Carolina troops serving in the Palmetto State or adequately to provide for the Tar Heels. "Our distrest militia," he wrote, "have been obliged to rescue that Country from the Dominion of Britain" and had been met with constant affronts. He hoped that the North Carolina troops would therefore "claim to themselves some compensation for their services, which compensation they will seize and bring home to their ruined families."

In October 1779, Hill and Burke received special recognition from the North Carolina General Assembly for "their able, faithful and diligent and public spirited services" in Philadelphia. Hill was then appointed to the prestigious Council of State. In 1783 he was elected senator from Martin County, and in 1787 and 1788 he was reappointed to the Council of State. In the latter part of 1788 Hill was reelected to the Senate, and in 1789 he was appointed to the state commission on Indian affairs and public revenue and to the committee on propositions and grievances. These were the last public offices he would hold.

Meanwhile, Hill had spent considerable effort attempting to develop Martin County. In 1785 he successfully petitioned the state to incorporate a town on the Roanoke River on property he donated "to promote the trade and navigation of the said river." No trace now exists of this town, Blountsville, though it was probably located to the east of Williamston. Hill also encouraged the building of a canal to open the Albemarle Sound to the Atlantic Ocean near Roanoke Island. Nothing else is known of his life except that he died on his plantation.

SEE: Fairfax Braxton, "Patriots of North Carolina," *National Republic*, April 1930; Walter Clark, ed., *State Records of North Carolina*, vols. 12, 19 (1895, 1901); Marshall De Lancey Haywood, comp., *Membership and Ancestral Register, North Carolina Society of Sons of the Revolution* (1898); William C. Poole, "An Economic Interpretation of the Ratification of the Federal Constitution in North Carolina," *North Carolina Historical Review* 27 (April, July, October 1950); David Lowry Swain, "Life and Letters of Whitmill Hill," *University of North Carolina Magazine*, vol. 10 (March 1861); John H. Wheeler, ed., *Historical Sketches of North Carolina, 1584–1851*, vol. 1 (1851).

JAMES R. YOUNG

Hill, William (15 Apr. 1737–23 Aug. 1783), colonial official and merchant, was born in Boston, Mass., the son of John and Elizabeth Maxwell Hill and the grandson of Henry Hill who arrived in Boston in the latter part of the seventeenth century from Isle of Thanet, County Kent, England. Henry died in Boston in 1726, leaving his family large holdings of property including distilleries near Essex Street.

William Hill and his brother, John (1732–58), attended Harvard College, graduating in the class of 1756. In their freshman year they boarded in the home of President Holyoke. They were described as "quiet and orderly undergraduates." Shortly after his graduation William went to Brunswick, N.C., a port town on the Cape Fear River, to become the local schoolmaster. On 29 Sept. 1757 he married Margaret Moore, of Brunswick, daughter of Nathaniel and Elizabeth Webb Moore and granddaughter of Governor James Moore of South Carolina. The ceremony was performed at Orton Plan-

tation by the Reverend John McDowell, an Anglican missionary in the Cape Fear section. They had nine children but only four reached maturity: John (1761–1832), William Henry (1767–1808), Nathaniel Moore (1769–1842), and Thomas (1770–1818).

Not long after settling in Brunswick, Hill gave up teaching to enter the mercantile business with Parker Quince as his partner. His business was successful, and he seems to have been respected and liked in the Lower Cape Fear section where he was commonly referred to as "the elegant gentleman from Boston." In 1764 Governor Arthur Dobbs appointed Hill collector of duties "on rum, wine and other distilled liquors" for the port of Brunswick. He held this position until the end of the colonial period, and at the same time continued his mercantile business, exporting and importing goods to and from England.

Although the approaching break with the British government seriously affected his business, Hill was sympathetic towards the grievances of his fellow colonists. On a visit to North Carolina in March 1773, Josiah Quincy, Jr., of Massachusetts, wrote: "Lodged last night in Brunswick, N.C., at the house of William Hill, Esq., a most sensible, polite gentleman, and though a crown officer, a man replete with sentiments of general liberty, and warmly attached to the cause of American freedom." On 25 July 1774, Hill wrote the English firm of Kelly and Co. that the tea he had repeatedly ordered had not arrived but that he did not complain because "the flame into which this whole Continent is thrown by the operation of the Boston Port Bill will presently show itself in an universal stop to all intercourse between Great Britain and the Colonies. My little connection in trade must cease with the rest." Three months later Hill wrote Kelly that he had received a shipment of tea that he was returning in the same vessel, remarking that even if he was disposed to accept it "the people here would not suffer it to be landed. Poison would now be more acceptable." He pointed out that the British were greatly mistaken in their belief in "a disunion among the American Provinces, and I can venture to assure you that North Carolina will not be behind any of her sister Colonies in virtue." In the same letter he refused to accept the agency "for supplying his Majesty's ships," and declined further trade until "the present difficulties are happily over, which, as a warm friend of Great Britain and her Colonies, I sincerely wish may be speedily accomplished."

In November 1775, there being no longer any commerce out of the port of Brunswick, Hill gave up his position as naval officer and shortly afterwards moved to Wilmington. In 1780 he was elected to the House of Commons from New Hanover, but was declared ineligible to take his seat because he already held a county office, commissioner of forfeitures. Remarking on his election Hill said that the "Choice was made without my Privity or Consent, and I knew not that any Person had set me up as a Candidate till near the close of the Poll." Following this reversal, he was placed in charge of administering the law relative to encouraging the importation of arms and munitions into the port of Brunswick. When commerce on the Cape Fear was resumed, he was appointed one of the commissioners to regulate pilotage on that river.

A member of the Anglican church, Hill served as a vestryman and lay reader of St. Philip's Parish, Brunswick, where he was buried. Referring to Hill's death in a letter to a friend, Archibald Maclaine Hooper said, "Mr. Hill died . . . of obstinate quackery," not calling in a physician until "about four days before his death."

SEE: Walter Clark, ed., *State Records of North Carolina*, vols. 14–15 (1896–98); "Extracts from the Letter-Book of William Hill, of Cape Fear, N.C.," *New England Historical and Genealogical Register* 13 (October 1859); Don Higginbotham, ed., *The Papers of James Iredell*, vol. 2 (1976); Archibald Maclaine Hooper, "William Hill, of Cape Fear, N.C.," *North Carolina University Magazine* 2 (1853); William L. Saunders, ed., *Colonial Records of North Carolina*, vols. 6, 7, 9 (1888–90); Clifford K. Shipton, ed., *Biographical Sketches of Those Who Attended Harvard College in the Classes of 1756–1760*, vol. 14 (1965); Alfred Moore Waddell, *A History of New Hanover County* (1909).

LAWRENCE F. LONDON

Hill, William (23 Sept. 1773–29 Oct. 1857), public official, son of William and Eliza Halbert Hill, was born in Surry (now Stokes) County. His father, a Baptist minister, attended the Provincial Congress at Hillsborough in August 1775 and later served as a chaplain in the American forces that fought at Guilford Court House in the Revolutionary War.

Though Hill pursued a variety of occupations, most of his career was devoted to public service. He taught school for a brief time beginning at the age of sixteen. In July 1795 he obtained a position as clerk in the Raleigh law office of James Glasgow, secretary of state. In 1803 Hill moved to Haywood, Chatham County, and worked as a merchant. Returning to Raleigh the next year, he entered business, and during the 1804–5 session of the General Assembly he was appointed magistrate for Wake County. In February 1806 he was elected registrar of Wake County. The following year he became clerk of court and held that office until 1811, when the General Assembly appointed him secretary of state to succeed the late William White. Hill was reelected (annually until 1835 and biennially thereafter) with regularity until his death forty-six years later. By that time he was known as "Old Sec." Hill also served as state librarian from 1812 until 1842, except for the period between 1827 and 1831.

Hill married twice. His first wife was Sarah Geddy, whom he married in January 1803; they were the parents of Cynthia, Eliza, Louisa, and William Geddy, who became a physician. A year or so after the death of his first wife he married Frances G. Blount on 14 Feb. 1833. He died in Raleigh, and following a funeral at the local Methodist Episcopal church he was buried in the Raleigh City Cemetery.

SEE: Kemp P. Battle, *Early History of Raleigh* (1893); Raleigh *Weekly North Carolina Standard*, 4 Nov. 1857; Wake County Wills (North Carolina State Archives, Raleigh); John H. Wheeler, ed., *Reminiscences and Memoirs of North Carolina and Eminent North Carolinians* (1884); Maury York, "A History of the North Carolina State Library, 1812–1888" (research paper, Research Branch, Division of Archives and History, Raleigh).

MAURY YORK

Hill, William Geddy (11 Sept. 1806–4 May 1877), physician, was born in Raleigh, the son of William Hill, North Carolina's secretary of state for more than forty years, and Sarah Geddy Hill, a native of Halifax County. He was the grandson of William Hill, Revolutionary patriot and in August 1775 a representative of Surry County in the Provincial Congress at Hillsborough. Hill received his education at the Raleigh Male

Academy, whose principal was the Reverend William McPheeters; The University of North Carolina; the office of Dr. Joseph W. Hawkins, eminent physician of Warren County; the office of Dr. Rufus Haywood in Raleigh; and the University of Pennsylvania, from which he was graduated in medicine and surgery in 1827.

Hill entered the medical profession in Pittsboro, but in deference to his wife he settled in Raleigh where he was a successful practitioner until his death. In 1849 he was an organizer of the Medical Society of North Carolina, successor to an earlier group founded in 1799, and in 1872 served as president. In 1870, at the organization of the Raleigh Academy of Medicine, Hill was elected its first president and regularly attended its meetings. In addition to his private practice, he was physician to the state penitentiary. During the Civil War, in the administration building of Peace Institute (now College), Hill ministered to the sick and wounded soldiers of the Confederate and Union armies.

For many years Hill was active in the Masonic order. In February 1830 he was initiated, passed, and raised in Hiram Lodge No. 40, Raleigh; then, briefly, he belonged to Columbus Lodge No. 40, Pittsboro. On returning to Raleigh, he renewed—in 1842—his membership in Hiram Lodge, where he was Junior Warden (1844–45) and Worshipful Master (1846–47, 1856). During 1849–50 he was Senior Grand Warden of the Grand Lodge of North Carolina, and on 3 Dec. 1861 he received the highest honor of Ancient Craft Masonry when elected Grand Master of the Grand Lodge, serving for one year. He was also Grand Representative near the Grand Lodge of North Carolina of both the Grand Lodge of Vermont and the Grand Lodge of Mississippi. In 1864 a company of Masons dimitted from Hiram Lodge in Raleigh and organized a lodge which was named in Hill's honor; the first meeting was held on 18 May, and the charter was dated 7 December. A portrait of Hill is on display at the Masonic Temple (former residence of Josephus Daniels) on Glenwood Avenue in Raleigh.

Hill married first, Adelaide Hill, a daughter of Theophilus Hunter Hill of Wake County and later Rachel Jones of the well-established Wake County family. Hill's son, Theophilus Hunter (1836–1901), was a Wake County poet. William G. Hill became a Methodist and "was an exemplary member for twenty years." He was interred in the Raleigh City Cemetery on New Bern Avenue and East Street near the grave site of his father.

SEE: *Guide to North Carolina Historical Highway Markers* (1961); Marshall D. Haywood, *Builders of the Old North State* (1968); Richard B. Haywood, *Memoirs of Dr. William G. Hill, Late President of the Raleigh Academy of Medicine* (1877); G. G. Johnson, *Ante-Bellum North Carolina* (1937); H. G. Jones, *For History's Sake* (1966); Raleigh Sesquicentennial Commission, *Raleigh: Capital of North Carolina* (1942); Henry Jerome Stockard, Sketch of Theophilus Hunter Hill (Charles Van Noppen Collection, Duke University Library, Durham); Elizabeth C. Waugh and Ralph Mills, *North Carolina's Capital, Raleigh* (1967).

GRADY L. E. CARROLL

Hill, William Henry (1 May 1767–9 Dec. 1808), lawyer, legislator, congressman, and planter, the son of William and Margaret Moore Hill, was born at Brunswick town in Brunswick County. He attended schools in Boston, his father's birthplace, and studied law there under a Mr. Barrett.

In 1790 President Washington appointed Hill district

attorney for North Carolina, a position he held for the next eight years. In 1794 he was elected to the state senate from New Hanover County. In politics he was a Federalist and a strong supporter of the administrations of Washington and Adams. His district elected him to the U.S. House of Representatives in 1798 and again in 1800. During his four years in Congress, Hill was an outspoken advocate of all Federalist measures. He believed in a strong central government. When in 1802 the Republicans introduced a bill to repeal the Judiciary Act, passed in President Adams's administration, Hill made a long speech opposing its repeal. His action was in opposition to the wishes of the majority of the North Carolina legislature, which had instructed the state's representatives in Congress to vote for repeal of the act. Hill denied the right of the legislature to instruct the state's representatives how to vote. When he ran for reelection in 1802, he was defeated by a Republican primarily on this issue. In 1801, when the presidential contest between Thomas Jefferson and Aaron Burr was thrown into the House of Representatives, Hill and his Federalist colleagues from North Carolina voted for Burr. This was another reason for his defeat in 1802. Just before leaving office President Adams appointed Hill a federal judge for the District of North Carolina, one of the so-called "midnight judges." Jefferson, however, refused to honor the appointment.

After his failure to be reelected to Congress, Hill withdrew from politics, devoting his efforts to his law practice and to agriculture. He owned a plantation near Wilmington called Hilton and another, Belmont, in Chatham County. He acquired the latter in 1796 as a summer home.

Hill took an active interest in the founding of The University of North Carolina. He was elected a member of the first board of trustees in 1791 and served until his death. In 1792 the board appointed him to the commission of eight trustees to select the site for the university. He was one of those who in 1793 donated funds to the university and who later gave books to its library.

Hill first married Elizabeth Nash Moore, widow of James Moore and daughter of Governor Abner Nash; and second, Alice Starkey, daughter of John Starkey of Onslow County. He had no children by either marriage. His third wife was Elizabeth Ashe, daughter of John and Rebecca Moore Ashe. They became the parents of William H., Jr., Joseph Alston, Anna (m. Charles Wright), Mary (m. Dr. James F. McRee), and Julie (m. Dr. Ezekiel Hall). Hill died at his home, Hilton, and was buried in the family cemetery on the plantation.

SEE: *Annals of the Congress of the United States* (Sixth and Seventh Congresses, 4 Mar. 1799–3 Mar. 1803); Samuel A. Ashe, ed., *Biographical History of North Carolina*, vol. 4 (1906); Kemp P. Battle, *History of the University of North Carolina*, vol. 1 (1907); *Biog. Dir. Am. Cong.* (1961); Raleigh *Star*, 22 Dec. 1808; Henry McG. Wagstaff, "Federalism in North Carolina," in *James Sprunt Historical Publications*, vol. 9 (1910).

LAWRENCE F. LONDON

Hilliard, Henry Washington (*4 Aug. 1808–17 Dec. 1892*), lawyer, congressman, diplomat, and author, was born in Fayetteville but shortly after his birth moved with his parents to South Carolina. After graduation in 1826 from South Carolina College (now the University of South Carolina), he studied law in the office of William C. Preston in Columbia. He later moved to Athens, Ga., where he continued his legal studies under a

Judge Clayton and was admitted to the bar in 1829. From 1831 to 1834 he held the first chair of literature at the University of Alabama but resigned to enter the more lucrative practice of law in Montgomery.

From 1837 to 1839, Hilliard served in the Alabama General Assembly as a member of the Whig party. In the legislature he opposed a resolution supporting the Sub-Treasury and the general ticket plan, which called for a statewide election of congressmen from all districts and was designed to ensure Democratic control of all congressional seats. A delegate to the Whig National Convention in Harrisburg, Pa., in 1839, Hilliard was one of the early supporters of John Tyler for vice-president. Although he favored Henry Clay rather than William Henry Harrison for the presidency, he loyally supported the ticket in the election of 1840. In 1841 he sought election to the U.S. House of Representatives as a Whig, but, even though he won a majority in his own district, he was defeated in the statewide contest required under the general ticket system. In May 1842, after having refused other offers of diplomatic posts, Hilliard was appointed chargé d'affaires to Belgium, a post he held with distinction until June 1844.

In 1845 Hilliard was the first Whig elected to Congress from the Montgomery District and the only Whig congressman elected from Alabama that year. He was reelected in 1847 (without opposition) and in 1849 but declined to run for reelection in 1851. In his maiden speech, for which he was complimented by John Quincy Adams, he supported an aggressive policy in Oregon even at the risk of war with Great Britain. He advocated adequate financing of military forces during the Mexican War. When the Wilmot Proviso was under consideration, he conceded that Congress could legislate for the territories of the United States but insisted that it "must regard the rights of the States" and not "legislate for the benefit of one section at the expense of another."

Although he had reservations about some features of the Compromise of 1850, Hilliard accepted it as a means of reducing sectional differences. When Southern rights associations were formed and threatened secession, he actively supported the cause of compromise, attending a "Union" convention in 1851 at which he was largely responsible for its taking the position that a state had no constitutional right to secede.

Also in 1851 he spoke extensively on behalf of the Whig candidate for the seat Hilliard had held in the House of Representatives, debating William Lowndes Yancey. Throughout his political career, he was the opponent of Yancey and was regarded as the only man in Alabama who could debate him on equal terms. Hilliard was disturbed when adoption of the Kansas-Nebraska Bill brought about repeal of the Missouri Compromise because he feared that its adoption would lead to reawakened prejudice outside the South.

When the national Whig party drifted towards abolitionism, Hilliard joined a number of other former Whig leaders in shifting his support to the American or Know-Nothing party. A presidential elector of the American party in 1856, he made an extensive speaking tour on behalf of Millard Fillmore's candidacy. Soon after the inauguration of James Buchanan, however, he transferred his allegiance to the Democratic party on the ground that conservative forces in the United States should not be divided. At a commercial convention held in Montgomery in 1858, he opposed adoption of any measure that might lead to the reopening of the slave trade.

When the Constitutional Union party nominated

John Bell and Edward Everett in 1860, Hilliard left the Democratic party and joined the Union party, which he considered to be the successor to the Whig party of the past, and spoke widely on behalf of the candidates. After the election of Abraham Lincoln, Hilliard opposed secession unless aggressive steps were taken by the national government. In a Montgomery speech that was heard with respect but with little sympathy, he advocated that the rights of Southerners should be asserted within the Union and that all possible remedies should be exhausted before the Union was abandoned.

Hilliard took no part in the measures that resulted in the secession of Alabama nor in the early proceedings of the Confederate government. When Lincoln issued the call for troops to coerce the Southern states, however, he joined the Southern cause. In 1861 he was appointed by President Jefferson Davis as agent of the Confederate government to persuade the state of Tennessee to secede and join the Confederacy. Successful in this assignment, he returned to Alabama and organized "Hilliard's legion," which became part of Bragg's army and was commanded by Hilliard with the rank of brigadier general. In 1862 he resigned from the army and returned to Montgomery, where he resumed the practice of law.

In 1865 he moved to Augusta, Ga., and later to Atlanta. He supported Horace Greeley for president in 1872 and was an unsuccessful candidate for Congress in 1876. In 1877, after considering Hilliard for other diplomatic posts, President Rutherford B. Hayes appointed him minister to Brazil, where many Southerners had settled after the war in self-imposed exile. During the period of his service in Brazil, the emancipation of more than a million slaves was pending. When he was called upon for information about the results of emancipation in the United States, he wrote a letter that helped ensure the success of the movement and made a highly publicized banquet speech. Although questions were raised about the propriety of his action, he became a hero among the supporters of emancipation. In 1881, he returned to Atlanta and lived there until his death.

An author of considerable ability, Hilliard prepared the introduction and notes for a translation of Alesandro Verri's *Roman Nights* (1850); published *Speeches and Addresses* (1855), a collection of his speeches; and wrote a novel, *De Vane: A Story of Plebeians and Patricians* (1865), and his reminiscences (his best work), *Politics and Pen Pictures at Home and Abroad* (1892).

Although Hilliard was criticized for vacillation during his political career, from his own point of view he was consistent. As a supporter of the Constitution and the Union, he worked for the party that offered him the greatest opportunity to preserve them. An outstanding orator, his debates with Yancey attracted large audiences and nationwide attention. In his early years, he became a Methodist minister and never entirely severed his connection with that profession.

Hilliard was married first to a Miss Bedell and second to a Miss Mays Glascock. After his death in Atlanta, he was buried in Oakwood Cemetery, Montgomery, Ala. His portrait appears as the frontispiece of his *Politics and Pen Pictures*.

SEE: *Atlanta Constitution*, 18 Dec. 1892; *Biog. Dir. Am. Cong.* (1928); Toccoa Crozart, "Henry W. Hilliard, 1808–1892," in *Trans. Ala. Hist. Soc.*, vol. 4 (1904); Lewy Dorman, *Party Politics in Alabama from 1850 through 1860* (1935); J. W. DuBose, *The Life and Times of William Lowndes Yancey* (1892); "Hon. Henry Washington Hilliard," *American Whig Review* (1849); B. F. Riley, *Makers and Romance of Alabama History* (n.d.).

JOHN M. MARTIN

Hilliard, Louis (*24 Dec. 1837–20 Aug. 1894*), Confederate officer, legislator, and judge, was the son of William Henry and Sallie Dortch Hilliard of "The Meadows" in Nash County. His grandfather, Robert Carter Hilliard (1771–1828), was the brother of Isaac Hilliard; he attended The University of North Carolina in 1799 and represented Nash County in the House of Commons in 1813–15 and in the Senate in 1817.

Hilliard was graduated from The University of North Carolina with a B.A. degree in 1858. His senior graduating thesis, "William Walker—the Great Fillibuster," is in the North Carolina Collection of the university library in Chapel Hill. During the Civil War he was a captain in the Confederate Army, serving as assistant commissary of subsistence with the Second Regiment from July 1861 until July 1863; he was then transferred to the Quartermaster Department. After the war Hilliard practiced law and was a member of the General Assembly from Pitt County in 1866. He was elected a Superior Court judge in 1874, but his appointment was questioned and the matter went to the state Supreme Court where his election and commission were declared void. From 1875 to 1877 he served as a trustee of The University of North Carolina. About 1880 he moved to Norfolk, Va., where he entered the cotton commission business.

Hilliard married first Claudia Gorham, by whom he had four children: Churchill, Emma, David, and Lillie. His second wife was Nellie Cherry, daughter of William and Mary Gorham Cherry. They had six children but only two, Landon and Elinor, married and left descendants. Elinor married Richard Blackburn Tucker, son of the Right Reverend Beverly Tucker, Bishop of Southern Virginia.

SEE: Alumni Records (University of North Carolina, Chapel Hill); Kemp P. Battle, *History of the University of North Carolina*, 2 vols. (1907, 1912); John L. Cheney, Jr., ed., *North Carolina Government, 1585–1979* (1981); Louis H. Manarin, ed., *North Carolina Troops, 1861–1865*, vol. 3 (1971).

CLAIBORNE T. SMITH, JR.

Hilliard, "Nancy" Ann Segur (*17 Oct. 1798–8 Nov. 1873*), hotel keeper, was a native of Granville County, the daughter of William and Lucy Walker Hilliard. The family moved to Chapel Hill in 1817. During the 1830s and 1840s, Nancy was the proprietor of a boardinghouse or inn previously run by Orange County sheriff Thomas D. Watts and his wife Lucy. Located near the site of present Graham Memorial, it was known for a time as the Hilliard Hotel and then the Eagle. For years it was considered *the* hotel in town.

The Eagle catered mainly to student boarders who paid from eight to ten dollars a month for meals described as "too good for college boys." Generous to a fault, Miss Hilliard too often extended credit to students pleading lack of money. It was said that she had energy and pluck, enjoyed extraordinary popularity and success, and was a candid and kind counselor. She was an institution in her own time.

Adult patrons arrived by coach and consisted of traveling men, general visitors, and relatives of students. President James K. Polk, a graduate of The University of North Carolina, arrived on 31 May 1847, at the invitation of university president David L. Swain, to attend commencement. He and his entourage were housed in a wing of the Eagle especially built for the occasion.

Reportedly, in 1852 Miss Hilliard sold the Eagle and built a house of her own, a neat white structure nicknamed the "Crystal Palace," where she kept a few boarders. It stood on the lot now occupied by the Planetarium gardens. Still later, it is said, she was manager of the "North Carolina Railroad eating-house at Company Shops, now Burlington."

Miss Hilliard's fortunes declined sharply with the advent of the Civil War and the closing of the university. In December 1869, the Crystal Palace was sold at auction for an unpaid debt of $750.23, the buyer paying $150.00. There followed a brief and disastrous attempt at hotel keeping in Raleigh. She returned to Chapel Hill and was given a free room at "the old Hotel." Odd sums sent by former students kept her going for a while. Yet she died virtually destitute and was buried in a grave next to her mother, close by the Philanthropic lot. Thirteen years later, "certain alumni" erected a stone enscribed: "in grateful remembrance of her unfailing kindness and hospitality."

SEE: *Abstracts of the Wills and Estates of Granville County, N.C., 1746–1808*, Kemp P. Battle, *History of the University of North Carolina* (1907–12); Deed Records, Hillsborough; Archibald Henderson, *The Campus of the First State University* (1949 [photograph]); Louis R. Wilson, *Selected Papers of Cornelia Phillips Spencer* (1953).

JOHN MACFIE

Hilton, Ernest Auburn (20 Sept. 1879–28 Sept. 1948), master potter, was born in Catawba County near Hickory, the son of John Wesley Helton (or Hilton), a farmer and manufacturer of jugs. The family lived in the first section of the state to be known as "Jugtown," a region some eight miles square in Catawba and Lincoln counties. Ernest began making pottery under the direction of his father when he was eight, and within four years he was throwing one-quart jars and jugs on the potter's wheel. After working for a time with relatives in Catawba and Iredell counties, in 1934 he established his own pottery four miles west of Marion in McDowell County. He turned the basic pieces himself while his wife, Clara Maude Cobb, and their daughters, Tommie, Lera, Ernestine, and Mozell, applied the glazes and decorations.

The Hilton pottery became noted for its dogwood patterns, featuring raised white dogwood blossoms on a dark beige background. Hilton also produced blue-edge pottery (cobalt blue on beige) resembling the wares of colonial days. He created painted nature scenes as well as numerous designs of vases, flower pots, pitchers, and sets of dishes. The pottery was fired in a groundhog kiln and coated with ground-up Coca Cola bottles, his favorite glaze. He used local clay, of course, but also some from Enka, Morganton, Seagrove, Spruce Pine, and Statesville. Hilton experimented with different clays, mixing "long" clay from the east with "short" clay from the west to give more life and color to his pieces. His work has been the subject of a number of exhibitions at the Metropolitan Museum of Art in New York City and the North Carolina Museum of History in Raleigh.

SEE: *Asheville Citizen*, 30 Sept. 1948, 23 June 1952; Leon E. Danielson, "The Hilton Potteries of Catawba Valley,

North Carolina," *Journal of Studies Ceramic Circle of Charlotte* 4 (1980); Exhibition notes, North Carolina Museum of History, 1986.

ROBERT O. CONWAY

Hilton, William (1617–75), leader of expeditions to the Cape Fear River region of North Carolina in 1662 and 1663, was born in Northwich, Cheshire, England. He arrived in New Plymouth with his mother in 1623 to join his father, William, who had crossed on the *Fortune* in 1621 and eventually settled at the Piscataqua.

Hilton evidently went to sea at a fairly early age and led a busy life, as there are references to his having been to Surinam, London, and Barbados in addition to Carolina. In 1662, he was chosen as captain of the ship *Adventure* on a voyage to explore the area then known as Florida, which included the eastern coast apparently as far north as the Carolinas. The expedition sailed from Charlestown, Mass., on 14 Aug. 1662, and was composed of New Englanders seeking a more desirable place to live. The *Adventure* reached the Cape Fear area on 3 September but was blown off course, probably by a hurricane, before she could enter the mouth of the river. Hilton finally guided the ship up the river mouth on 3 October and set about exploring the waterway and the land on either side. The main river was called the Charles River (later the Cape Fear River) and its numerous branches and tributaries were named after some of the explorers on board, particularly Samuel Goldsmith, Lieutenant Enoch Greenleaf, John Greene, James Bate, Edward Winslowe, and Hilton himself. The group scouted the river area for several weeks, sailing as far as the present Northeast Cape Fear River—a distance of some 35 miles from the mouth of the Cape Fear River. The earliest known map of the Cape Fear area was prepared by Nicholas Shapely from information written down in chronicle form in November 1662 when the expedition returned to New England.

The chronicle of this first voyage was not known to have existed for some time; it was published in the April 1970 issue of the *New England Historical and Genealogical Register* in an article by Louise Hall. The chronicle, which was most likely written by John Greene, praises the beautiful land, abundant land and water wildlife, bountiful forests, and wild fruits, especially grapes, that the explorers found. The glowing description of the area led to an attempt at settlement by another group of New Englanders, in which Hilton played no role; the effort failed, and the New Englanders returned home.

Hilton's seafaring life took him to Barbados, where in 1663 he was named commander and commissioner with Captain Anthony Long and Peter Fabian of a voyage to what is now the coast of North Carolina and South Carolina. The expedition, which "was set forth by several Gentlemen and Merchants of the Island of Barbadoes," left from Spikes Bay, Barbados, aboard the *Adventure* on 10 Aug. 1663. Land was sighted on 26 August near Port Royal, S.C., and the ship anchored farther north in St. Helena Sound. The explorers were visited numerous times by Indians, from whom they learned of a party of shipwrecked Englishmen held by the Indians. The expedition was able to rescue them and set sail on 28 September. Hilton's enthusiastic description of the area later led to a number of attempts at settlement in South Carolina.

While sailing northward up the coast, Hilton was once again blown off course almost to "Cape Hatterasse," according to his chronicle. The ship finally anchored in the Cape Fear River on 12 Oct. 1663 but was unable to proceed—because of unfavorable winds—until 24 October. The *Adventure* continued slowly up the river for two days, then anchored. Twelve men rowed farther in a long boat, returning on 2 November. In the succeeding days the various tributaries and some of the shoreline were explored and described in Hilton's chronicle. Most of the land was found to be very desirable; it offered "as good tracts of land, dry, well wooded, pleasant and delightful as we have seen any where in the world," wrote Hilton, and contained an abundance of good timber and wildlife. As a final testimony to the Cape Fear and in an attempt to refute the complaints of the New Englanders, which he found in the form of "Writing left on a post" in the area and described as "scandalous," Hilton noted in his chronicle "that we have seen facing on both sides of the River, and Branches of Cape-Fair aforesaid, as good Land, and as well Timbered, as any we have seen in any other part of the world, sufficient to accomodate thousands of our English Nation, lying commodiously by the said River." The party set sail for Barbados on 4 December and arrived on 6 Jan. 1664.

When the expedition returned, Sir Thomas Modyford and Peter Colleton—two of the organizers of a group of two hundred Barbadians (known as the Barbadian Adventurers)—made numerous proposals for settlement of the area by their group, but were refused by the Lords Proprietors, holders of the newly granted Carolina charter. Hilton, Long, and Fabian were granted 1,000 acres of land for their efforts but none claimed the grant within the specified time period.

Little is known of Hilton after his "A Relation of a Discovery," describing the Barbadian expedition, was published in 1664. The primary record of a man's life during this time was his will, but Hilton's will disappeared after his death. His name survives in several ways, particularly in South Carolina where Hilton Head and Hilton Head Island were named for him.

SEE: Charles M. Andrews, *The Colonial Period of American History*, vol. 3 (1937); Louise Hall, "New Englanders at Sea: Cape Fear before the Royal Charter of 24 March 1662–63," *New England Historical and Genealogical Register* 124 (April 1970); A. S. Salley, ed., *Narratives of Early Carolina* (1911).

CHRIS FURR

Hines, Lovit (*23 Jan. 1852–1 Sept. 1921*), merchant, the son of James Madison and Nancy Thompson Hines, was born in Wayne County but the next year the family moved to Lenoir Institute, Lenoir County. During the 1870–71 session, he attended Wake Forest College where he studied Latin, English, and mathematics. Returning to Lenoir County, Hines worked as a farmer and in his father's sawmill. After operating his own lumber business for several years, he formed a partnership with his brother, Wait T., at Dover in 1889. In 1893 the Hines brothers purchased the Greenville Land and Development Company, and, with P. H. Pelletier and S. C. Hamilton, created the Greenville Lumber Company. The firm burned in 1896.

The following year Lovit and Wait Hines went back to Lenoir County and organized the Hines Brothers Lumber Company at Kinston. Their $6,000 investment, consisting of lumber and machinery from the Dover mill, was matched by Henry C. Riley of Charles S. Riley and

Company, Philadelphia. This manufactory produced railroad crossties, bridge timber, tobacco sticks, moldings, bed slats, and fence posts, as well as lumber for tobacco hogsheads and boxes. The company owned 24 miles of narrow-gauge railway from Kinston into the surrounding forest, and operated a train on standard-gauge track from Kinston to Snow Hill in Greene County. The firm also operated heavy equipment in connection with its logging activities. By 1919, Hines Brothers Lumber Company employed 300 men and produced 65,000 feet of lumber a day.

Hines married Mollie Jane Murphy on 23 Dec. 1879; they had eleven children, seven of whom survived. Mollie Hines died on 31 Dec. 1907. He then married Polly Jones on 1 Sept. 1908; this union produced five children. Hines was buried at the Maplewood Cemetery, Kinston.

SEE: Samuel A. Ashe, ed., *Biographical History of North Carolina*, vol. 8 (1917); *Catalogue of Wake Forest College, Thirty-Sixth Session, 1870–'71* (1871); Talmage C. Johnson and Charles R. Holloman, *The Story of Kinston and Lenoir County* (1954); *North Carolina Biography*, vol. 6 (1919); William S. Powell, *Annals of Progress: The Story of Lenoir County and Kinston, North Carolina* (1963).

MAURY YORK

Hines, Peter Evans (*28 July 1828–14 Aug. 1908*), physician, was born in Warren County, the son of Congressman Richard Hines and his second wife, Ann Edmunds Spruill. He was named for his mother's older half brother, Peter Evans of Old Sparta, Edgecombe County. Hines was prepared for college at Lovejoy's Academy in Raleigh and in 1849 was graduated from The University of North Carolina, where he received an M.A. degree in 1852. In July 1849, he began to study medicine under Dr. C. E. Johnson of Raleigh. He was graduated with high honors from the medical school of the University of Pennsylvania in 1853. The following year he was an intern at St. Joseph's Hospital in Philadelphia.

During 1854–55 Hines continued the study of medicine in the great hospitals of Paris. He then established a practice in Raleigh. When the Civil War broke out, Governor John W. Ellis appointed him surgeon of the First Regiment of North Carolina Volunteers, the famous Bethel Regiment. In 1862 he was named medical director of all the hospitals in the Petersburg, Va., division. Later that year he was made medical director of the general hospitals of North Carolina, a post he held until the war ended.

After the war Hines was president of the Wake County Medical Society, of the Raleigh Academy of Medicine (1876–95), and of the North Carolina Board of Medical Examiners (1878–84). From 1894 until his death he was superintendent of health of Wake County, and for many years he was city physician of Raleigh.

A devout Episcopalian, Hines served in 1890 as a vestryman of Christ Church, Raleigh, and as a member of the Standing Committee of the Diocese of North Carolina. He filled both of these positions at the time of his death. In 1882 he married Frances Iredell Johnson of Raleigh, but they had no children. Hines was buried in the family plot in the Old City Cemetery, Raleigh. His widow gave his medical library of 500 volumes to the library of The University of North Carolina.

SEE: Kemp P. Battle, *History of the University of North Carolina* (1924); Daniel L. Grant, *Alumni History of the University of North Carolina, 1795–1924* (1924).

CLAIBORNE T. SMITH, JR.

Hines, Richard (25 June 1792–20 Nov. 1851), attorney and congressman, was born in the Old Sparta section of Edgecombe County, the son of Jesse Hines and his wife Celia, daughter of Colonel Jonas Johnston. His grandfather Richard Hines, a native of Sussex County, Va., had moved to North Carolina and settled on Town Creek, Edgecombe County, in 1770. Jesse Hines died intestate in 1793, and his widow married Elias Carr.

Hines seems to have been educated locally. He was admitted to the bar in 1816 and for several years practiced in Washington, Beaufort County. He returned to Edgecombe and represented the county in the House of Commons in 1824. He was elected as a Democrat to the Nineteenth Congress but lost his bid for reelection in 1826. Hines became a strong Whig and continued to be interested in politics, though he never again held office. He later moved to Raleigh and was involved in the reception given Henry Clay there in 1844.

The historian John H. Wheeler described Hines as a "gentleman of great personal worth and liberal feelings." The Hines residence in Edgecombe County, the Hermitage, is no longer standing. Areta Ellis of New Bern, who visited the estate in 1838, wrote her family from "The Hermitage near Sparta" on 2 May: "Just as the sun was setting we drove up the avenue of a quarter of a mile leading to Mr. Hines' house. I can give you no idea of the place, unless I possessed some of the descriptive powers of those who have written of the style of English scenery. It was far superior to anything in our little town. Caroline and Mr. Hines are extremely kind and attentive, and Miss Hines one of the most accomplished and interesting young ladies I have ever met."

Hines married first a cousin, Susan Wilkins. She died in 1819, leaving a daughter Susan who never married. His second wife was another cousin, Ann Edmunds Spruill, who died in 1830. They had a daughter, Rowena, who never married, and five sons: Peter Evans, Benjamin S., Jesse Davidson, Elias Carr, and Richard, Jr. Peter, who became a prominent physician in Raleigh, married Frances Iredell Johnson but had no children. Benjamin, who attended The University of North Carolina in 1842, never married. Jesse married Elizabeth Poole and left issue. Elias, who received A.B. (1847) and M.A. (1850) degrees from the university, was for many years solicitor of the Edenton District; he died in the Civil War, leaving a widow, Margaret, daughter of Thomas F. Norfleet of Bertie, and two sons. Richard, Jr., who received an A.B. degree from the university in 1850 and in 1852 was appointed tutor in ancient languages, became an Episcopal minister and in 1867 was given a D.D. by his alma mater; he married Helen Huske and later moved to Memphis, Tenn.

The third wife of Richard, Sr., was Caroline Snead, of New Bern, who left one son to reach maturity, John S.; he received an A.B. degree from the university in 1856 and settled in St. Louis, Mo. Congressman Richard Hines was buried in the Old City Cemetery, Raleigh.

SEE: *Biog. Dir. Am. Cong.*; John B. Boddie, "The Hines Family," in *Southside Virginia Families*, vol. 1; Daniel L. Grant, *Alumni History of the University of North Carolina,*

1795–1924 (1924); John H. Wheeler, ed., *Historical Sketches of North Carolina from 1584 to 1851* (1851).

CLAIBORNE T. SMITH, JR.

Hinsdale, John Wetmore (4 Feb. 1843–15 Sept. 1921), Confederate officer, attorney, and president of the North Carolina Bar Association, was born in Buffalo, N.Y., the son of Dr. Samuel J. and Elizabeth Wetmore Hinsdale; he moved to Raleigh with his parents when only a few months old. On his father's side he was descended from Comfort Sage and Jabez Hamlin, both colonels in the Continental Army. Through his mother he was descended from Richard Cogdell, New Bern patriot, and from Governor William Bradford and Elder William Brewster of Massachusetts.

Hinsdale was educated at Donaldson Academy in Fayetteville and Starrs Military Academy in Yonkers, N.Y.; in 1858 he entered The University of North Carolina. In 1861, at the outbreak of the Civil War, he was commissioned a second lieutenant in the Eighth North Carolina Regiment. He served with distinction as aide de camp to Brigadier General T. H. Holmes; as adjutant general with Brigadier General J. Johnston Pettigrew, General W. D. Pender, and General T. H. Holmes; and as inspector general with General Sterling Price. Afterwards he was elected colonel of the Third Regiment Junior Reserves (Seventy-second North Carolina), a post he held until the end of the war.

After being paroled at Bush Hill, N.C., on 2 May 1865, Hinsdale attended the Columbia University Law School and in 1866 was admitted to practice in New York and North Carolina. He was associated first with John Devereaux in the firm of Hinsdale & Devereaux, practicing in Fayetteville and Carthage; the firm later expanded to include Raleigh. About 1875 Hinsdale moved to Raleigh but for several years continued to maintain offices in Fayetteville and Carthage.

Hinsdale's practice in both state and federal courts, including the United States Supreme Court, was concerned primarily with railroad, insurance, corporation, and commercial law. In a sketch of Hinsdale, published in the *24th Annual Report of the North Carolina Bar Association* (1922), Judge Robert W. Winston said: "It may be doubted if the state has had a more painstaking laborious lawyer than John W. Hinsdale. His pleadings, drawn with great care and caution, were comprehensive to a degree; his cases were prepared with meticulous attention to details . . . his briefs were the apple of his eye, collecting, digesting, assimilating decided cases from every imaginable jurisdiction, often becoming full-grown textbooks."

His professional activities were varied. In addition to providing an annotated edition of Winston's *North Carolina Reports* in 1878, over a period of years Hinsdale contributed digests of North Carolina laws, forms, and a court calendar to legal directories including *Martindale's Legal Directory* and *Sharp and Alleman's Lawyers and Bankers Directory*. His interest in improving court procedures resulted in his authorship of the Equity Reference Act and the Non Suit Act, both of which were adopted by the North Carolina legislature. Until the law on non suits was revised in 1970, attorneys regularly made the motion for non suit by stating, "I would like to make the usual motion under the Hinsdale Act." He was elected president of the North Carolina Bar Association in July 1909.

On 23 Sept. 1869 Hinsdale married Ellen Devereaux,

the daughter of Major John Devereaux. They had six children: John W., Jr., S. J., Mrs. John Englehard, Mrs. J. M. Winfree, Mrs. H. V. Joslin, and Nellie. Hinsdale was a Democrat, an Episcopalian, and a member of Christ Church, Raleigh.

SEE: Samuel A. Ashe, ed., *Biographical History of North Carolina*, vol. 1 (1905); *Cyclopedia of Eminent and Representative Men of the Carolinas of the Nineteenth Century*, vol. 2 (1892); North Carolina Bar Association *Report*, vols. 11, 24 (1909, 1922); Raleigh *News and Observer*, 16 Sept. 1921; *Who Was Who in America*, vol. 1 (1943).

MARY W. OLIVER

Hinton, Charles Lewis *(18 Jan. 1793–23 Nov. 1861)*, major of militia, planter, legislator, and state treasurer, was born at The Oaks plantation, Wake County, about ten miles east of Raleigh. His father was David Hinton, the youngest son of Colonel John and Grizelle Kimbrough Hinton. His mother was Jane Lewis, the daughter of Howell and Isabella Willis Lewis of Granville County.

Hinton was a member of the House of Commons and a senator from Wake County. He also served as a member of the commissions for rebuilding the state capitol and for building a state hospital. He was a commissioner for the sale of Indian lands and for eleven years served as treasurer of North Carolina. He was a trustee of The University of North Carolina for twenty-eight years.

Although his fine mind and great leadership ability impelled him towards public service, Hinton was a planter at heart—a true country gentleman. A deeply religious man, he was an active member of Hepzibah Baptist Church in Wake County until he helped organize and changed his membership to Oak Grove Methodist Church. At his death he was a member of Christ Episcopal Church in Raleigh.

Hinton married Ann Perry, the daughter of Joshua and Mary Boddie Perry of Franklin County. They had three sons and three daughters, but only David and Anne Perry reached maturity. Hinton died at Midway Plantation, Wake County, and was buried at his childhood home, The Oaks. A portrait of him by Garl Brown hangs at Midway Plantation.

SEE: Charles Lewis Hinton file (Secretary of State's Office, Raleigh); Legislative Records (North Carolina State Archives, Raleigh).

CHARLES HINTON SILVER

Hinton, James *(ca. 1750–12 June 1794)*, planter, legislator, Revolutionary soldier, and county official, was born in Johnston (now Wake) County, the second son of Colonel John and Grizelle Kimbrough Hinton. Little is known of his early life, but he could have been a private in his father's militia regiment in Johnston County. He is listed as a captain in that regiment (by that time in Wake County) at the general muster on 6 Oct. 1773 when his father was colonel, his father-in-law Theophilus Hunter lieutenant-colonel, and his brother John major. Hinton was still a captain when he served with the regiment in the Moore's Creek expedition in 1776; he was paid for his services and the use of his horse for twenty-seven days. By June 1780 he was colonel of the regiment, a commission his brother, Major John Hinton, had declined in 1777.

Management of his 7,000-acre plantation and the 36

slaves listed in the 1790 census, as well as his activities with the militia, by no means occupied all of Hinton's time. For more than ten years he represented Wake County in the General Assembly; he was first elected to the state Senate in 1780 and then to the House of Commons for the next seven sessions (1781–88). After attending the state constitutional convention at Hillsborough in 1788 as a delegate from Wake County, he was returned to the Senate in 1793, defeating his brother-in-law, Joel Lane, who had served for the six preceding sessions. Hinton's election may have indicated the dissatisfaction of a majority of the voters with the selection of Lane's land as the site of the permanent state capital in preference to the Hinton land, which had been considered.

During all of this time, Hinton served as register for Wake County, a position he held from June 1777 until his death, when he was succeeded by his nephew Willis Hinton. He was also justice of the peace for Wake County from December 1782 presumably until his death.

By his marriage in 1773 to Delilah Hunter, Hinton had four sons and two daughters—all of whom are named in the will of their grandfather, Theophilus Hunter, who outlived his son-in-law. Their son Theophilus died young, but the other five children—including sons Henry, Ransom, and James, Jr.—married and had descendants.

Hinton was buried in an unmarked grave in the burying ground at Silent Retreat, his home in Wake County. This plot is enclosed by a wall of hewn granite blocks and is located quite near his house, which still stands about two miles from Shotwell near Bethlehem Church on Poole Road, about one mile southeast of The Oaks, his brother David's plantation home.

SEE: Bible Records of Colonel William Hinton, Pension Claim of Johnathon Smith (North Carolina State Archives, Raleigh); Walter Clark, ed., *State Records of North Carolina*, vol. 14 (1896); Court Minutes, Estate Papers, and Marriage Bonds of Wake County (North Carolina State Archives, Raleigh); William L. Saunders, ed., *Colonial Records of North Carolina*, vol. 9 (1890); Treasurer and Comptroller Journal A, Treasurer and Comptroller Military Papers (North Carolina State Archives, Raleigh).

MARY HINTON DUKE KERR

Hinton, John *(ca. 1718–11 May 1784)*, colonial and Revolutionary pioneer, planter, patriot, legislator, and soldier, was born in Chowan Precinct (now Gates County). He was the son of "Col." John Hinton, an emigrant from England to Virginia who had come to North Carolina in 1700 by way of Nansemond County, Va. His mother, Mary Hardy Hinton, arrived in North Carolina from Virginia in 1695 with her parents, John and Charity O'Dwyer Hardy.

Hinton was among the early trailblazers who opened up the wilderness of present Wake County. He was not yet eighteen when his father wrote his will in 1730. Nine years later he was granted land in the part of Craven County that would be cut off into Johnston and then Wake County by means of a grant said to be the earliest known document identifying land now included in Wake County. The "Entry" (for less than the 640 acres this well-to-do young man could have asked for) indicated his intention of establishing a home surrounded by open grazing forest with the advantage of a "burnt marsh," a landmark left by Indian hunters. Here he built a log house on the south side of the Neuse

River about six miles east of the present city of Raleigh. The dwelling was entered by a ladder to the upper portion, as protection from marauding Indians and wild beasts. Later Hinton built a house facing the river from the opposite side, called The Square Brick House because of the unusual shape of the brick used in the foundation and chimneys. One of the bricks has been preserved in the Mordecai House in Raleigh, which was built by Henry Lane, one of Hinton's grandsons whose wife was Hinton's granddaughter. Over the years Hinton took up several thousand acres of land by Granville grants and additional acreage by purchase, becoming one of the largest planters in this section. His land followed the course of the Neuse River, and in some places the property ran four miles to the east and west of the river.

A justice of the peace for Johnston County in 1759, Hinton was named with other justices to find a suitable location for the Johnston courthouse. The site selected, Hinton's Quarter, was on the property of his brother William. Hinton also represented Johnston County in the Second, Third, Fourth, and Fifth Provincial Assemblies of Governor Arthur Dobbs in 1760–62.

For over twenty years, Hinton served as an officer in the colonial and then state militia. Listed as captain of foot in the Johnston County militia in 1754, he held the ranks of major by 1761 and colonel by 1769; he served as colonel for eight years or longer. In 1768, just after the onset of the Regulator disturbances, Hinton—then a major in the Johnston County militia—was one of the "General and Field officers" of the army at the council of war called by Governor William Tryon at Hillsborough Camp on 22–23 September. Convinced that the Regulator dissension could not be settled peaceably, Tryon raised an army in the spring of 1771 and began an expedition against the insurgents on the western frontier on 20 April. Hinton, by now colonel of the militia in the newly formed Wake County, participated in this expedition, but Governor Tryon's journal refutes the claim of Hinton's former biographers that he and his Wake County detachment were present at the Battle of Alamance on 16 May. The detachment had been ordered to remain in Wake County to collect fines from the men who had appeared at the general muster on 6 May without arms, as well as to prevent the disaffected from joining the Regulators. It was not until 20 May, four days after the two-hour conflict, that Hinton and his men joined the army, having successfully carried out their assignments. They remained with the army until discharged at Captain Theophilus Hunter's Quarter in Wake County on 21 June, after Hinton had presided at the trial of prisoners held at Hillsborough Camp three days earlier.

When his land came under Wake County jurisdiction in 1771, Hinton served as one of the seven commissioners appointed to select a site for the Wake County courthouse. As a representative from Wake County, he attended the Second Provincial Congress at New Bern on 3 Apr. 1775 and the Third Provincial Congress at Hillsborough, beginning 20 Aug. 1775, where he subscribed to the oath of allegiance to the Association just adopted by the Continental and Provincial Congresses. At the latter Congress he was appointed a member of the Committee of Safety for the Hillsborough District and the same day designated colonel of the Wake County minutemen, thus being transferred from the colonial to the state militia. A delegate from Wake County to the Fourth Provincial Congress at Halifax, Hinton participated in the adoption of the Halifax Resolves and was named (5 Apr. 1776) a member of the Safety Com-

mittee "to enquire into and make report to this Congress of ammunition now remaining in the Province," a fitting appointment for a veteran who had commanded his regiment in the Moore's Creek expedition only a month before.

Because he was already a colonel in the Johnston County militia, it appears that Hinton, with his regiment, had simply been transferred to Wake County in 1771. The muster rolls show Hinton as colonel of the Wake militia, his son-in-law Theophilus Hunter as major in 1772 and lieutenant colonel in 1773, his son-in-law Joel Lane as lieutenant colonel in 1772, his son John, Jr., as captain in 1772 and major in 1773, and his son James as captain in 1773. When the British yoke could no longer be borne, he was as loyal to the cause of freedom as he had been to the king as a British subject and officer of the royal governor's militia forces. After a campaign of about a month's duration, the Battle of Moore's Creek Bridge was fought on 27 Feb. 1776. The state comptroller's accounts show that Colonel Hinton was paid for his services for thirty days as well as for furnishing a cart, four horses, and two servants for twenty-seven days in this campaign. One of the servants was "Uncle Brisco" who, after Hinton's death, lived at The Oaks, the plantation of his youngest son David, where Brisco drove the first carriage brought into Wake County, hitched a horse to the last gig brought within its boundaries, and told many a tale about having gone off to war with his master.

In 1776, Hinton also spent five days organizing the Wake County militia regiment and collecting provisions for an intended expedition to Cape Fear. Apparently, although alerted for the expedition, Hinton and his regiment did not participate in it.

About 1745, Hinton married Grizelle Kimbrough, the daughter of Buckley and Elizabeth English[?] Kimbrough who had arrived in Edgecombe County in 1735/36 from New Kent County, Va. They had four sons and five daughters, all of whom married and had descendants. Hinton and his wife lived to see their second son, James, serve as colonel of the Wake County militia in 1780, after that commission had been declined by their oldest son, Major John Hinton, in 1777.

Hinton's unmarked grave is at the site of his river plantation home, The Square Brick House, which burned two years after his death. It appears that his wife, who survived him by fourteen years and was buried beside him, lived with their son Kimbrough at his home, The Red House, after her home burned. Following her death, Kimbrough Hinton went to Tennessee where he died.

SEE: Census of 1790; Walter Clark, ed., *State Records of North Carolina*, vols. 12, 13, 19, 22, 23 (1895, 1896, 1901, 1907, 1904); Benson J. Lossing, *Pictorial Field Book of the Revolution*, vol. 2 (1860); William L. Saunders, ed., *Colonial Records of North Carolina*, vols. 6, 7–10 (1888, 1890). Manuscript sources in North Carolina State Archives, Raleigh: Map Collection; Court Martial Minutes, Court Minutes, and Militia Returns of Johnston County; Deeds of Edgecombe County; Charles M. Heck Collection; Precinct Court Records of Chowan County.

MARY HINTON DUKE KERR

Hinton, John (14 Mar. 1748–19 Oct. 1818), colonial and Revolutionary soldier, legislator, councilor of state, justice, and sheriff of Wake County, was born in that part of Johnston County that became Wake in 1771. He was the oldest son of Colonel John Hinton, a soldier, patriot, public servant, and planter of Johnston (now Wake) County; his mother was Grizelle Kimbrough, daughter of Buckley Kimbrough of Virginia and Edgecombe County, N.C., and his wife (a Miss English[?]). His paternal grandparents were the immigrant "Col." John Hinton of Chowan County and his wife, Mary Hardy. Hinton was of English-Scottish ancestry: the Hintons entered England from Normandy with William the Conqueror and the Kimbroughs, according to genealogists, were Scottish-English.

Although raised as the oldest son of a wealthy and prominent family, Hinton followed the pattern of his ancestors in self-reliance, initiative, industry, and dedication to personal achievement as well as to the progress of his community and state. His education is undocumented but there is ample evidence that his training far exceeded the mere rudiments of literacy. Devoted to and closely associated with his famous father, young Hinton was, nevertheless, a man of great presence and influence and a leader in his own right. He built his home, Clay-Hill-on-the-Neuse, in what was then Johnston County and on 27 June 1765, at age seventeen, married sixteen-year-old Pheribee Smith, daughter of John Smith, Jr., and his wife, Elizabeth Whitfield, of Smithfield, named in Smith's honor.

During the Battle of Alamance on 16 May 1771, Hinton, a captain, was with his regiment in Wake County, his commanding officer and father, Colonel John Hinton, having remained there on direct orders from the governor to "support the proper officers in forthwith collecting the fines due from the militia men agreeable to the Militia Law, for appearing at the general muster of the 6th Inst., without arms." Four days later, on 20 May, he was with Colonel Hinton's Wake County regiment when it joined Governor Tryon's army at Sandy Creek. By 6 Oct, 1773, he had been promoted to major in his father's regiment. When North Carolina joined the other colonies in the American Revolution, Major Hinton gave his full support to the cause of independence and fought with the Wake militia regiment in Governor Richard Caswell's army at the Battle of Moore's Creek Bridge on 27 Feb. 1776. He continued to serve with great personal courage throughout the war. Soon after April 1777 he was promoted to colonel to succeed his father, but declined to serve in that rank.

Returning to Wake County, Hinton served as a member of the House of Commons in 1779, councilor of state from 3 Dec. 1799 to 1801, justice from 1780 to February 1818, and sheriff for some time prior to 1788, when he settled his account by sheriff's return (turned over revenue collected to state treasurer) to September 1789.

Hinton had vast landholdings in Wake County, some inherited and some acquired through land grants and his own business acumen. When he came into his inheritance in 1784, Hinton was not only one of the wealthiest men in the county but one of the most influential as well.

Major John and Pheribee Hinton had seven known children: John, William, Willis, Samuel, Mary (Polly), Grizelle, and Elizabeth (Betsy). The few references to marriages of daughters Nancy and Sarah are undocumented and are not supported by the dates involved; there was no mention of the so-named daughters in Hinton's will. Samuel, who was graduated from The University of North Carolina in 1798, died in January 1802; he was unmarried. Willis died unmarried in 1806. John married Sarah (Sally) Bryan; William married Candace Rosser; Mary married her cousin, Henry Lane; and Grizelle married Judge Henry Seawell. All had

families. Elizabeth died unmarried at Clay-Hill-on-the-Neuse in 1865.

Pheribee Hinton died in 1810, eight years before her husband; her death was reported in the *Raleigh Register* of 27 Dec. 1810. Hinton's death was reported in the *Raleigh Register* of 23 Oct. 1818: "Died at his seat on Neuse River in this vicinity, Major John Hinton, an old and universally respected citizen, and one of the best and most extensive Farmers in the County. He has left a numerous family connection, and many friends to bewail his loss." Both husband and wife were buried in the family cemetery at Clay-Hill-on-the-Neuse in graves marked simply "J. H." and "P. H."

By his will of 25 Aug. 1818, Hinton devised his pew in the Presbyterian Church in Raleigh to his two surviving daughters, Grizelle and Elizabeth. He left in trust to his son William one acre of land at Maloby's Crossroads, including the site of a meeting house, for "the use of all Christian clergymen to preach on & for the benefit of the community to be used solely as a place of Divine worship." An old, small brick church stands at this site, east of Raleigh, and is used by a black congregation of the Baptist denomination.

For his valiant military service during the Revolutionary War and for his many public services, Hinton was honored by a commemorative marker near the site of his home, Clay-Hill-on-the-Neuse, about five miles east of Raleigh. The marker was presented by the Bloomsbury Chapter of the Daughters of the American Revolution. The home fell many years ago, but the family cemetery remains, enclosed by the original stone wall. Pictures of the house are extant. There are no known likenesses of Major Hinton.

SEE: John L. Cheney, Jr., ed., *North Carolina Government, 1585–1974* (1975); Walter Clark, ed., *State Records of North Carolina*, vol. 13 (1896); Court Minutes of Wake County, DAR Records, Governor's Letters, Legislative Papers, Marriage Records of Wake County, Minute Book D from Inferior Court of Pleas and Quarter Sessions in Wake County (North Carolina State Archives, Raleigh).

EUDORA COLEMAN HODGES

Hinton, Mary Hilliard (7 June 1869–6 Jan. 1961), author, artist, genealogist, and historian, was born at Midway Plantation, Wake County, eight miles east of Raleigh. Her father was Major David Hinton, alumnus of The University of North Carolina and a leading citizen; he was the son of Charles Lewis Hinton, also a graduate of the university and longtime state treasurer. Her mother was Mary Boddie Carr, of Edgecombe County, a member of two distinguished families and a sister of Governor Elias Carr.

Mary Hilliard Hinton was educated at St. Mary's Episcopal School and Peace Institute (now College), Raleigh. Later she studied and practiced portraiture under Mrs. Ruth Huntington Moore of the Peace Institute faculty. Miss Hinton was a heraldic artist of great ability, holding for several years the office of heraldic artist for the North Carolina Society of the Daughters of the Revolution. For many years she served as editor of the society's *North Carolina Booklet*.

Membership in numerous patriotic and allied organizations reflected the wide variety of Miss Hinton's talents and interests. She was a member of the Daughters of the Confederacy, Association for the Preservation of Virginia Antiquities, North Carolina Literary and Historical Association, Daughters of the Revolution (registrar and state regent for many years), National Council of the Colonial Dames, Order of the Crown of America, Audubon Society, Colonial Dames of America, National Geographic Society, Daughters of the Barons of Runnemede (charter member no. 5), and Raleigh Woman's Club (chairman of the art department).

Miss Hinton was an active member of Christ Episcopal Church, Raleigh; a leading worker in the Anti-Suffrage League; and a world traveler. She died at her ancestral home, Midway Plantation, and was buried in the Hinton graveyard at The Oaks plantation near Raleigh.

SEE: Samuel A. Ashe, ed., *Biographical History of North Carolina*, vol. 3 (1906); Margaret Collier, *Biography of Representative Women of the South, 1861–1929*, vol. 2 (1923); Family records in the author's possession; *Woman's Who's Who of America* (1914–15).

CHARLES HINTON SILVER

Hobbs, Allan Wilson (12 July. 1885–19 Oct. 1960), educator, was born in Greensboro, the son of Dr. Lewis Lyndon Hobbs, president of Guilford College, and Mary Mendenhall Hobbs. His brother Lewis Lyndon, Jr., became a surgeon in Philadelphia, and his brother Richard J. M. was appointed dean of the School of Commerce at The University of North Carolina.

Hobbs was educated in Pennsylvania at Westtown Friends School (1901–2) and Haverford School (1902–4). In 1907 he was graduated at the head of his class from Guilford College and the following year studied at Haverford College. A brilliant athlete, he played professional baseball with Montreal and the New York Yankees. Hobbs taught for one year at Saxapahaw School, N.C. (1908–9) before returning to Guilford as instructor (1909–11) and as assistant professor of mathematics and dean of students (1913–15). On completion of his doctorate at Johns Hopkins University in 1917, Hobbs became instructor in mathematics at The University of North Carolina where he was appointed full professor in 1925. He served as dean of the College of Liberal Arts from July 1930 until his retirement in 1955.

Continuing his interest in sports, Hobbs represented the university in the North Carolina Intercollegiate Athletic Conference, the Atlantic Coast Conference, and the Southern Conference of which he was president in 1942–43. He was chairman (1928), vice-president (1929), and a member of the executive committee (1930) of the Southeastern Section of the Mathematical Association. A Quaker, Hobbs was a co-founder of the Chapel Hill Friends Meeting. He was coauthor, with Archibald Henderson and John W. Lasley, of *The Theory of Relativity* and author of a number of pamphlets and articles.

On 4 Sept. 1924 Hobbs married Nell Blair of Montevallo, Ala.; they had one son by adoption, William Galen. Hobbs died in Fort Lauderdale, Fla., and was buried in the family plot in New Garden Friends Meeting. On Saturday, 6 Nov. 1971, he was honored posthumously by membership in the Guilford College Athletic Hall of Fame.

SEE: Chapel Hill *News Leader*, 21 May 1956; *Durham Morning Herald*, 24 Oct. 1960; Grimsley Taylor Hobbs (personal contact); *Greensboro Daily News*, 6 July 1930, 24 Oct. 1960; Raleigh *News and Observer*, 21 July 1946, 30 May 1956, 23 Oct. 1960; Southern Pines *The Pilot*, 10 Nov. 1971; *Who Was Who in America*, vol. 4 (1968).

HENRY HOOD

Hobbs, Lewis Lyndon (17 May 1849–13 May 1932), educator, religious leader, and college president, was born one mile west of Guilford College, the youngest of nine children of Lewis and Phoebe Cook Hobbs. His father taught in the "little brick schoolhouse" at New Garden (later Guilford College), and was a man of above-average education and spiritual refinement. Lewis Lyndon inherited his father's love of learning and, after her husband's death, Phoebe Hobbs nurtured it in the tradition of the Society of Friends.

Young Hobbs attended New Garden Boarding School as a day student and was graduated in 1876 from Haverford College, where he later (1882) received a master of arts degree. He returned to New Garden as a teacher of Greek, Latin, and mathematics, and in 1878 was chosen principal of the Quaker school, a post he held until 1885. When New Garden's charter was changed to that of a four-year college in 1888, he was elected its first president; he served in that post until his resignation in 1915. In 1908 he was awarded an honorary doctor of laws degree by both Haverford College and The University of North Carolina.

Under Hobbs's guidance, Guilford College grew in enrollment, faculty, endowment, buildings, and equipment, and was recognized throughout the state for academic thoroughness. During this period of quantitative growth, however, Hobbs never lost sight of the worth of each student and was always concerned that the students develop all their capabilities. His effective service as president was paralleled by his participation in the affairs of the Society of Friends. At age twenty-seven he was chosen clerk of the New Garden Monthly Meeting and assistant clerk of the North Carolina Yearly Meeting of Friends; he served as clerk of the Yearly Meeting for forty-eight years. In addition, he was a member of various committees of the Meeting, and held the office of trustee for fifty-two years. It was said that as presiding clerk he listened with patience, discernment, and a clear interpretation of the matters at hand; as a result, business sessions ran easily, with a sense of unity and peace.

Hobbs worked tirelessly for the improvement of public schools. He spent much time in personal persuasion and made many addresses in their behalf. Partially because of his efforts, the first tax levied in North Carolina for a rural graded school was in Guilford County, and went for the elementary school at New Garden, among others. He also served as a member of the Guilford County Board of Education and for four years as a member of the first state board of examiners for public school teachers.

In 1880 Hobbs married Mary Mendenhall, also a teacher in New Garden Boarding School. Together they worked for better educational opportunities for all youth. The couple had five children: Walter, Lewis Lyndon, Jr., Allan Wilson, Richard J. M., and Gertrude.

SEE: *Greensboro Daily News*, 13, 14 May 1932; Mary Mendenhall Hobbs, "Lewis Lyndon Hobbs," *Guilford Collegian* 11 (November 1898); New Garden Monthly Meeting of Friends, "Memorial for Dr. Lewis Lyndon Hobbs" (read at a memorial service, 18 May 1932).

TREVA W. MATHIS

Hobbs, Mary Mendenhall (30 Aug. 1852–20 July 1930), educator, writer, and speaker, was born at Florence, near Jamestown, to Nereus and Oriana Wilson Mendenhall. She was tutored by her father, an outstanding teacher, attended village schools and New

Garden Boarding School, and was graduated from Miss Howland's School on Lake Cayuga, Union Springs, N.Y. After graduation she taught at Howland for a year, then returned home to teach Latin and history for two years at New Garden Boarding School. The principal was young Lewis Lyndon Hobbs, whom Mary had known since childhood. They were married in 1880. Their strong Quaker background, their beliefs in good educational opportunities for male and female alike, and their own excellent education formed the basis for a long, happy, and very compatible union. They were the parents of five children: Walter, Lewis Lyndon, Jr., Allan Wilson, Richard J. M., and Gertrude.

As early as her student days at Howland, Mary's interest in the education of young ladies was apparent. When asked to write an essay on what she would do if given $10,000 to spend as she wished, she said that she would establish a school for girls. Later, while serving as assistant clerk of the 1889 North Carolina Yearly Meeting, she was moved to ask the women's meeting for subscriptions to help educate Quaker girls. They responded with contributions of $103. Heartened by this success, she summoned her courage to appear before the men's meeting to ask for money. It was "an unlooked for, inexplicable thing to do." Nevertheless, they, too, responded generously and, as a result, the Girls Aid Committee of the Yearly Meeting was formed. Mrs. Hobbs intended that the girls live in cottages and save expenses by supplying much of their food and doing all the cooking, cleaning, and so forth. The plan was so successful that soon a dormitory was built. It was called New Garden Hall, but in later years was renamed Mary Hobbs Hall.

Mary Hobbs's interest in education was not limited to Quaker girls. She envisioned better opportunities for all girls and worked hard for the cause. She was asked to speak often—on many topics—and did, but always requested additional time to give her views on the unpopular subject of education for girls. She wrote petitions to the legislature for various women's organizations, but gave them to Charles Duncan McIver to present when she learned that he also was interested in the education of women. She appeared before the education committee of the General Assembly to plead for an appropriation for the founding of a "normal and industrial school for white girls," and it was her earnestness that helped persuade the legislature to establish the school now known as The University of North Carolina at Greensboro. In recognition of her work for higher education, The University of North Carolina awarded her the honorary doctor of literature degree in 1921.

While continuing to write and speak for women's education, she also used her expressive voice and pen in many other causes—among them temperance, woman suffrage, home missions, capital punishment, Indian affairs, orphanages, and the League of Nations. She remained active in the affairs of the Yearly Meeting, serving on a long list of committees and organizations. With all her activities, she never neglected her family and home life. Arcadia, the family home near the Guilford College campus, was the center of warm, friendly hospitality to students, faculty, and community. Mrs. Hobbs mothered neighborhood boys and girls as well as her own, and arranged for many of them to attend New Garden Boarding School by paying their expenses from her own funds.

SEE: Frances Renfrow Doak, *Mary Mendenhall Hobbs* (lecture delivered at Guilford College on Founders Day,

1955); Mary Mendenhall Hobbs, "History of New Garden as Written by Mrs. Mary Hobbs," *Guilfordian* (1920); Carol Inglis, "Mary Mendenhall Hobbs" (paper written at Guilford College, 1976); "Mary Mendenhall Hobbs," *Greensboro Daily News*, 21 July 1930; New Garden Monthly Meeting, "Memorial for Dr. Mary Mendenhall Hobbs" (read in a memorial service, 17 July 1932); Lynda S. Swofford, "A Long Ago Vision . . . A Force Today," *Greensboro Daily News*, 14 May 1972.

TREVA W. MATHIS

Hobbs, Richard Junius Mendenhall (6 July 1888–17 Sept. 1967), lawyer, educator, and administrator, was born at Guilford College, the third son of Lewis Lyndon Hobbs, president of the college, and Mary Mendenhall Hobbs, members of a prominent Quaker family. He was named after Richard Junius Mendenhall, a promoter, with James J. Hill, of the Great Northern Railway and a founder of Minneapolis.

Hobbs attended Westtown Friends School, Pa., and in 1909 was graduated from Guilford College where he won the Orator's Prize and was, like his brother Allan Wilson, a baseball star. In 1911 he received an M.A. degree from Haverford College, where he was elected to Phi Beta Kappa. At Columbia University Law School, Hobbs studied under Harlan Stone and was elected to Delta Sigma Rho, the honorary legal fraternity; he earned the LL.B. degree in 1914. From 1915 to 1929 he practiced law in Greensboro and Gastonia. Moving to Chapel Hill, Hobbs was professor of business law at The University of North Carolina from 1929 to 1967 and dean of the Business School from 1954 to 1956. He was coauthor of *Britton and Brauer's Cases and Materials on Business Law*.

During World War II, Hobbs was a member of the panel of arbitrators of three organizations: the American War Labor Board, the North Carolina Department of Labor, and the Mediation and Conciliation Services. In Chapel Hill, he was active on the school board and served as alderman of the town for seventeen years, occasionally as mayor pro tem. He was a member of Orange County Board of Commissioners for ten years and of the North Carolina Bar Association. Hobbs was one of the principal founders of the Chapel Hill Friends Meeting.

He married Gretchen Taylor and had three sons: Richard, Grimsley, and Lewis Lyndon III. After the death of his first wife in 1956, he married Katherine Smith.

SEE: Dudley DeWitt Carroll and others, "UNC Faculty Pays Tribute to R. J. M. Hobbs," *Chapel Hill Weekly*, 24 Jan. 1968; Grimsley Taylor Hobbs (personal contact); "R. J. M. Hobbs: A Tribute from Dr. Frank," *Chapel Hill Weekly*, 20 Sept. 1967.

HENRY HOOD

Hobbs, Samuel Huntington, Jr. (4 Feb. 1895–16 Nov. 1969), rural sociologist, was born on a family farm near Clinton, the first son and second child of seven children of Samuel Huntington and Mary Broddy Hobbs. His father, a leading Sampson County farmer, was active in the North Carolina Cotton Growers Association and the National Farmers Union, and served from 1929 to 1931 as the county's Democratic representative in the state senate. On the farm where he grew up and helped his father with the chores, Hobbs received practical lessons in rural social economics. Hobbs's father also played an important role in his son's formal education. For two years, Hobbs attended classes in a school his father had established on the family farm. Later, he was a student at the newly formed public schools, which offered instruction only through the tenth grade. In 1913, after a year at Elon College, Hobbs entered The University of North Carolina where he received a B.A. degree in 1916.

Although Hobbs had majored in geology, E. C. Branson, head of the Department of Rural Social Economics, offered him a job as instructor. Hobbs accepted the position and completed his master's thesis, "Gaston County: Economic and Social," the following year. Except for two years in the navy during World War I and a year at the University of Wisconsin to complete his doctoral degree (1928), Hobbs never left The University of North Carolina, where he taught for fifty-two years.

Not long after Hobbs joined the department, Branson began referring to him as "my right hand man." Branson also likened their relationship to that of a father and son. Hobbs later named one of his sons after Branson. Hobbs was Branson's choice to succeed him as head of the department, a position Hobbs held from 1933 to 1939, when the department was merged with the Department of Sociology. His teaching, writing, editing, and public service activities all reflected the influence of his mentor and friend.

The work of Branson and Hobbs was a significant part of the university's effort to aid the people of North Carolina by improving economic and social conditions in the state. This idea of service to the state led to the university's designation, "the Wisconsin of the South." While completing his graduate studies at the University of Wisconsin, Hobbs had an opportunity to see how the university that pioneered in service to the state worked. Under his direction, the Department of Rural Social Economics at Chapel Hill continued to develop a library of information about the state and region, to conduct state and regional studies, and to answer calls for information from citizens and state institutions.

Many of the courses Hobbs taught—on such topics as the rural community, cooperation in agriculture, and North Carolina land economics—had few precedents. He developed them on his own, before there were any relevant textbooks. The development of these courses and Hobbs's research and writing activities were closely related. Material gathered by him, or under his direction, became the basis for courses, articles, and books.

Through the pages of The University of North Carolina *Newsletter*, Hobbs and his contributors made the entire state their classroom. They provided information about social and economic developments and needs to newspaper editors, officeholders, and concerned citizens throughout the state. In addition to editing the *Newsletter* from 1922 to 1956, Hobbs wrote scores of articles for the paper. The *Newsletter* was widely appreciated as an influential promoter of public welfare in North Carolina.

Hobbs also encouraged and guided the work of the North Carolina Club and the various county clubs organized by faculty members and students. The North Carolina Club each year focused on a specific problem confronting the state and published its findings in the *North Carolina Yearbook*. County clubs worked in a similar manner. Hobbs helped facilitate the work of the clubs and often edited their publications. In addition to shedding new light on specific concerns, he aimed to develop informed and concerned citizens who would be prepared to address the needs of their counties and state.

State officials drew not only on the information Hobbs had accumulated, but also on Hobbs himself. A walking library of facts about North Carolina and the South, he served on countless committees and planning boards such as the North Carolina Farm Tenancy Commission, North Carolina Rural Electrification Authority, North Carolina Rural Telephone Authority, Medical Care Commission, and Chapel Hill Planning Authority. He helped shape state legislation creating the Department of Conservation and Development, and the Local Government Commission. In 1936–37, he served as national supervisor of field work in rural research for the Works Projects Administration, and wrote or edited several studies for that New Deal program. Numerous professional organizations requested his services as a writer, editor, consultant, and organizer. His colleagues in various fields related to his work elected him president of the Southern Association of Rural Economists and Sociologists, of the North Carolina Conference for Social Service, and of the Historical Society of North Carolina.

Notwithstanding his demanding schedule, Hobbs found time to write numerous articles and books. His most noteworthy studies were *Gaston County: Economic and Social* (1920), *North Carolina: Economic and Social* (1930), and *North Carolina: An Economic and Social Profile* (1958), a revised and expanded edition of his 1930 study. In addition to a voluminous compilation of facts on the natural resources of North Carolina, agricultural and industrial production, size of farms, public services, personal income, level of education, and related matters, each of these studies displayed scrupulous accuracy and a determination to face facts, even when they were not flattering to the state. Hobbs's work was based on an underlying assumption that if North Carolinians were presented with the relevant information they would take the appropriate action to develop the state's natural and human resources. Nevertheless, despite his appeal to a common interest, there were issues of justice and equality involving conflicting interests that were not inevitably solved by economic development. Hobbs did not address these issues, nor did he offer theories to explain the causes and consequences of modernization. And perhaps because he grew up in a poor county, in a poor state, he expressed few reservations about the noneconomic costs of growth and development. Yet within the limits of his approach, he helped develop methods and institutions to obtain and interpret the mass of data necessary to make policy decisions in a modern state.

Hobbs's interest in agriculture was never simply in the abstract; it involved farms and farmers, childhood memories, and a love of the soil. In 1936 he acquired a farm in Orange County where he grew crops, raised livestock, and experimented with ways to increase productivity.

In 1922 Hobbs married Mary Virginia Thomas of Baltimore. They were the parents of three sons: Samuel Huntington III, William T., and Robert Branson. Not long after his retirement from teaching, Hobbs died in The University of North Carolina's Memorial Hospital and was buried in the old Chapel Hill Cemetery.

SEE: *Asheville Citizen*, 18 May, 6 June, 17 Oct. 1956; Eugene Cunningham Branson Papers (Southern Historical Collection, University of North Carolina Library, Chapel Hill); *Chapel Hill Weekly*, 19 Nov. 1965; Richard N. Current, "Tarheels and Badgers," *Journal of Southern History*, vol. 4 (1970); *Daily Tar Heel*, 15 Dec. 1935; *Durham Morning Herald*, 21 July 1957; Faculty Records, vol.

1:23 (Archives, University of North Carolina, Chapel Hill); Daniel L. Grant, *Alumni History of the University of North Carolina, 1795–1924* (1924); Samuel Huntington Hobbs, Jr., Papers (Southern Historical Collection, University of North Carolina Library, Chapel Hill); *North Carolina Manual* (1929); William S. Powell, ed., *North Carolina Lives* (1962); Raleigh *News and Observer*, 6 July 1930, 24 May 1953, 21 Sept. 1965, 17, 21 Nov. 1969.

JERROLD M. HIRSCH

Hobgood, Franklin P (*22 Feb. 1847–16 Feb. 1924*), teacher and college administrator, was born near Oxford, the eighth of twelve children of James Benton and Elizabeth House Hobgood. His father was a prominent agriculturist and leading citizen of Granville County. His paternal grandfather, Thomas Fowler Hobgood, is said to have emigrated from Wales in about 1770.

Young Hobgood prepared for college at the Horner Academy, Oxford, to which he rode daily on horseback from his home about six miles away. Following six months of service with Company B, Seventieth Regiment, North Carolina Junior Reserves Brigade, he entered Wake Forest College in January 1866, graduating as class valedictorian with a B.A. degree in 1868. He subsequently received M.A. (1871) and LL.D. (1918) degrees from his alma mater. After teaching for a few months at St. John's College, Oxford, Hobgood became principal of the Reidsville Classical and Mathematical School, Reidsville, in 1869. Thus began his long and distinguished career in education that would span the next fifty-five years.

In January 1871 Hobgood left the Reidsville school to join his father-in-law, William Royall, as co-principal of the Raleigh Female Seminary. When Royall moved to Louisburg in the summer of 1871, Hobgood became sole principal of the Raleigh seminary, continuing in that capacity until 1880. On 1 September of that year, Hobgood—joined by many faculty members whom he had attracted to the Raleigh school—opened a school at Oxford, occupying the premises formerly used by Mrs. M. A. Stradley in the operation of an academy for young women. Here he reestablished the Oxford Female Seminary (Oxford College after 1910), resuming an educational enterprise that had been inaugurated under the auspices of the Baptist denomination in that region in 1851. Except for a two-year period (1890–92) when ill-health forced his temporary retirement, he continued as president of the Oxford school until his death.

Hobgood's educational philosophy was expressed in an article entitled "The Education of a Girl—What It Is," which appeared in the *Biblical Recorder* of 19 June 1901. Developing his thought around the symmetry desired between the attainment of "power" (the capacity to accomplish a given end) and "poise" (a sense of proportion and good judgment), Hobgood argued that any difference between the education accorded men and women should be one of degree, rather than kind. He admitted that women might profitably concentrate more on the "spiritual" disciplines and men on the "material" ones, though he recognized that more concern in the curriculum for the spiritual, or aesthetic, could benefit the male populace as well. After discussing the role of the sciences, mathematics, languages, history, and aesthetics in the education of women, Hobgood summarized: "the design of colleges for girls should be to surround their pupils with such influences as to train their minds, cultivate taste, refine and polish manners, develop and strengthen the spiritual sense,

and fit them to occupy with ease and grace every department of social and domestic life."

A Mason (Grand Master, 1915), a Democrat, and a Baptist, Hobgood was active in the educational, civic, and religious affairs of his community and state throughout his adult years. In addition to his responsibilities as a college administrator, he served on the boards of trustees of Wake Forest College (1879–1924), The University of North Carolina (1907–24), and the Baptist Orphanage at Thomasville (1897–1924). He was chairman of the Granville County Board of Education for six years and served one term as president of the Teachers' Assembly of North Carolina. Elected to four one-year terms as a vice-president of the Baptist State Convention of North Carolina (1887, 1905, 1906, 1910), he served on numerous boards and committees of the Convention for over a half century and was respected for his leadership and counsel among the churches of the Flat River Baptist Association.

On 6 Oct. 1868 Hobgood married Mary Ann Royall, daughter of the Reverend William Royall, in Wake Forest. They had six children: Franklin P., Royall, James Edward, Lizzie (m. Franklin Wills Hancock, Sr.), Mamie (m. Beverly Sampson Royster, Sr.), and Carrie.

Hobgood was interred in the family burial plot in Elmwood Cemetery, Oxford. Portraits are in the possession of various descendants, including Mrs. James H. Bost, of Charlotte, a great-granddaughter.

SEE: Samuel A. Ashe, ed., *Biographical History of North Carolina*, vol. 4 (1906); *Biblical Recorder*, 19 June 1901, 8 Mar. 1916 (photograph); George Washington Paschal, *History of Wake Forest College*, vol. 2 (1943); Annual *Proceedings of the Baptist State Convention* (1874ff).

R. HARGUS TAYLOR

Hodge, Abraham (*1755–3 Aug. 1805*), state printer and Federalist activist, was born in the colony of New York in 1755. He had at least one sibling, a sister Elizabeth, who married John Boylan; they were the parents of William Boylan. Hodge may have been related to the New York printer Robert Hodge (1746–August 1813).

During the American Revolution, Hodge worked for Samuel Loudon, a patriot printer of New York who published the *New York Packet and American Advertiser* (later *Loudon's New York Packet*) and became the state printer of New York. Hodge also conducted George Washington's traveling press while the army was stationed at Valley Forge. Throughout the Revolution, he was noted for his dedication to spreading Republican principles and cheering his countrymen.

About 1784 or 1785, Hodge established a printing office in Halifax County, N.C. It is often said that he moved to North Carolina at the request of prominent citizens of the state. Hodge was elected state printer by the General Assembly in 1785. At various times during his career, he owned presses in Edenton, Halifax, Fayetteville, and New Bern.

With a partner, Andrew Blanchard, Hodge printed the *State Gazette of North Carolina* in New Bern from 17 Nov. 1785 to March 1788. In January 1786, he formed a brief partnership with the printer Silas W. Arnett to publish the *Laws of the State of North Carolina*. When the General Assembly met in Fayetteville in 1786–87, Hodge and Blanchard moved there to print the *State Gazette*. In 1788, Blanchard was replaced by Henry Wills, and the *State Gazette* moved to Edenton. Although the names "Hodge & Wills" continued to appear in the paper until 1795, the firm dissolved in 1793, when Hodge left for

Halifax to publish the *North Carolina Journal*, a newspaper he had established in the summer of 1792. For many years the *North Carolina Journal* had the largest circulation of any newspaper in the state. It reflected Hodge's Federalist leanings and was often criticized for these unpopular views of government. Hodge continued to edit this paper until his death.

In the spring of 1796, the firm of Hodge & Boylan founded the *North Carolina Minerva and Fayetteville Gazette*. William Boylan, the son of Hodge's sister, had come to the state from Pluchamine, N.J., as a youth. In 1798, a law requiring the state printer to live in the capital city was passed; accordingly, Hodge & Boylan moved its presses to Raleigh in 1799 and renamed the newspaper the *North Carolina Minerva and Raleigh Advertiser*.

Hodge's outspoken Federalist views brought him a violent confrontation with Thomas Blount in the summer of 1798. Hodge had published several anonymous handbills and newspaper accounts degrading the character of Blount, a Republican candidate for Congress. When Hodge refused to name the author of the articles, Blount attacked him, hitting Hodge several times with his cane.

Hodge and his partners served as state printers from 1785 to 1800 uninterrupted, except in 1798 when Allmond Hall held the office. In 1800, Joseph Gales, backed by Blount and other staunch Republicans, won the office. Hodge continued to publish the *Minerva* until he retired in 1803.

Abraham Hodge died in Halifax. He probably never married, as William Boylan was his sole heir and executor of his will. Besides his fifteen-year-service as state printer, Hodge was involved in five firms and he established three newspapers. He printed religious publications and his own *North Carolina Almanac* (1794). In addition, he was one of the first men in the state to contribute to the library of The University of North Carolina.

SEE: W. C. Allen, *History of Halifax County* (1918); Clarence S. Brigham, *History and Bibliography of American Newspapers, 1690–1820*, vol. 2 (1947); R. D. W. Connor, *A Documentary History of the University of North Carolina* (1953); D. H. Gilpatrick, *Jeffersonian Democracy in North Carolina, 1789–1816* (1967); William Woods Holden, *Address on the History of Journalism in North Carolina* (1881); Douglas C. McMurtrie, *A History of Printing in the United States*, vol. 1 (1936), and *Pioneer Printing in North Carolina* (1932); George Washington Paschal, *A History of Printing in North Carolina* (1946); Isaiah Thomas, *The History of Printing in America* (1970); Mary Lindsay Thornton, "Public Printing in North Carolina, 1749–1815," *North Carolina Historical Review* 21 (1944), and "Public Printing in North Carolina, 1749–1815" (M.A. thesis, University of North Carolina, 1943); A. J. Wall, "Samuel Loudon," *New-York Historical Society Quarterly Bulletin* 6 (1922–23); Stephen B. Weeks, *The Press of North Carolina in the Eighteenth Century* (1891).

CATHERINE L. ROBINSON

Hodge (Hodges), William *(1747/50–1819/20)*, clergyman, was born in the Hawfields section of Orange (later Alamance) County. Evidence is almost conclusive that he was the son of John and Agness Hodge, whose family also included sons John, Robert, George, and Samuel. Hodge joined the Hawfields Presbyterian Church during the pastorate of John DeBow and planned to enter the Christian ministry, but the un-

timely death of DeBow discouraged him and he resigned himself to farming.

Hodge married Charity White, daughter of Stephanus and Ann Ross White; increased his real estate holdings; and was a successful planter until he neared the age of fifty. At that time, inspired by the evangelistic zeal of James McGready, his interest in religion revived and he studied under McGready and David Caldwell to prepare himself for the ministry. When the Presbytery of Orange met on 4 Oct. 1792, Hodge had just been ordained and shortly afterwards became pastor of the Hawfields and Cross Roads Presbyterian churches. Thus, he was the first son of Hawfields to become a minister and he was influential in the decision of Robert Tate to become the second.

Active in the affairs of the Presbytery, Hodge was elected treasurer of the organization of 6 Mar. 1797. He was also an effective preacher. A sermon he delivered in 1791 at Alamance Presbyterian Church on the subject "God Is Love" was primarily responsible for the conversion of Barton Warren Stone, who later founded the denomination known today as the Disciples of Christ. However, Hodge's emphasis on evangelism offended some of the staid members of his congregations and a number withdrew from his churches. As a result, Hodge resigned his pastorate on 4 Apr. 1799 and the following year was dismissed from his Presbytery so he could go to the West.

In 1800, he became pastor of the Shiloh Presbyterian Church in Sumner, Tenn., and was associated with McGready, Stone, and others in the Great Revival which began that year in the Southwest. During the Revival, the practice soon became widespread for members of the congregations to exhibit strange physical exertions, which the sympathetic called "The Exercises" and scoffers called the "jerks." Unlike the fiery McGready, Hodge preached in a calm but convincing manner, and became known as "a Son of Consolation," though his influence was equal to that of his more dynamic associates.

Revivalism, of which Hodge had always approved, sparked the rapid formation of congregations of converts but there were no ministers to serve as pastors for the new organizations. To meet this crucial need, Hodge, McGready, and their colleagues in the Cumberland Presbytery proceeded to license young exhorters who did not have the educational qualifications demanded by the Presbyterian church in general. This led to a rebuke from the Presbyterian Synod of Kentucky, which met on 21 Oct. 1806 and suspended the Shiloh minister and John Rankin from the ministry for insubordination. McGready and others soon received similar sentences. Hodge eventually made peace with his church and on 6 Dec. 1809 was restored to good standing as a minister. The same action followed one year later in McGready's case, but the others involved refused to yield to the denominational authority and organized the Cumberland Presbyterian Church.

The dissension that existed among the clergy had repercussions among the church members, and Hodge encountered increasing difficulties with his congregation at Shiloh. In 1818, he resigned the pastorate and moved to Logan County, Ky., where he died a year or two later. His burial place is unknown.

SEE: William Henry Foote, *Sketches of North Carolina, Historical and Biographical* (1846); *Minutes of Orange Presbytery* (Office of Orange Presbytery, Burlington, N.C.); James Smith, *History of the Presbyterian Church from Its Origin to the Present Time, including a History of the Cum-*

berland Presbyterian Church (1835); Herbert Snipes Turner, *Church in the Old Fields* (1962).

DURWARD T. STOKES

Hodges, Luther Hartwell *(9 Mar. 1898–6 Oct. 1974)*, businessman, lieutenant governor, governor, secretary of commerce, and civic leader, was born at Cascade, Pittsylvania County, Va., the son of John James and Lovicia Gammon Hodges. They moved to North Carolina soon after his birth.

Luther Hodges, who attained success in business, who altered the direction of a state, who influenced presidents, and who traveled the world preaching "service above self," began his life as the next to youngest of nine children of a tenant farmer. At age twelve he went to work as an office boy in a textile mill in Spray. Later he worked his way through The University of North Carolina, where he was president of the Student Council and of his senior class. Upon graduation in 1919, Hodges accepted a job as secretary to the general manager of the Marshall Field and Company mills in the Leaksville-Spray (now Eden) area. He rose rapidly in the company—as personnel manager, production manager, general manager for all Marshall Field mills, and vice-president. Throughout his business career, he was involved in various civic affairs, including the YMCA and Rotary Club, and in politics by working in the election campaigns of others.

In North Carolina during this period, Hodges served as a member of the State Board of Education and the State Highway and Public Works Commission. In 1944, while living in New York, he volunteered for service with the federal government and was made price administrator of the textile division of the Office of Price Administration. He later served briefly as a consultant to the secretary of agriculture, and as textile consultant for the U.S. Army in Germany.

After his retirement from Marshall Field in 1950, Hodges became chief of the industry division of the Economic Cooperation Administration in West Germany. In 1951 he was a consultant for the State Department on the International Management Conference, a top-level technical assistance program for European business corporations. Throughout his career to this point, Hodges had practiced a theory of his that businessmen should be involved in government.

Upon returning to North Carolina, Hodges in 1952 became a candidate for the Democratic nomination for lieutenant governor. Although virtually unknown in many areas of the state, he conducted a vigorous grass-roots campaign against more established politicians and led the field in the primary. No runoff was called and Hodges was elected lieutenant governor in the fall. He was sworn in during the inauguration ceremonies of Governor William B. Umstead in January 1953.

Hodges became governor when Umstead died in November 1954. In the six years that followed, Governor Hodges literally charted a new course for North Carolina. He utilized his experience in business to develop new approaches to the problems of the state, particularly that relating to needs for jobs. His industrialization program was the hallmark for the South. He led trade missions at home and abroad, created a system of community colleges to provide needed training and education, supported the state's first minimum wage law, and conceived the Research Triangle Park, which he called "the heart and the hope of North Carolina's industrial future."

He sought to bring business management to govern-ment, creating a Department of Administration to coordinate fiscal and planning operations. In education Hodges was able to increase appropriations, initiate a grass-roots campaign to gain public support for schools, and set a moderate course for school desegregation, and he sponsored a board of higher education to coordinate the state's college and university system. He was instrumental in court improvement and in prison rehabilitation programs, including work release.

His leadership ability was recognized throughout the state, the South, and the nation. In 1956, when he ran for his own four-year term, Hodges carried every county. He served as chairman of the Southern Governors' Conference and of the Southern Regional Education Board. At the end of his term, Governor Hodges was selected by then President-elect John F. Kennedy to be his secretary of commerce.

In his four years as commerce secretary under presidents Kennedy and Lyndon B. Johnson, Hodges breathed new life into the Department of Commerce and into American business. He reorganized the department, created an Area Development Administration to help depressed areas, and was instrumental in the passage and implementation of the Trade Expansion Act. He worked for greater international trade and tourism. And he was the nation's chief spokesman for free enterprise and business ethics in the period.

After his term as secretary of commerce, Hodges returned to Chapel Hill but not to retire. He went to work for the North Carolina Research Triangle Foundation at a salary of one dollar a year paid quarterly and continued to work for the sound economic development of the state. He lectured in the School of Business Administration at the university in Chapel Hill. In 1967, he became president of Rotary International and for the next year traveled around the nation and the world for Rotary.

While governor, Luther Hodges asked that no buildings or bridges or monuments be named for him. His memory needs no such reminders. Hodges was in a sense a spirit of ethics, hard work, dedication, and success. He touched many things in his life, and all he left better than he found them. His monument is the record of service he gave to the state and to the nation.

In 1922 Hodges married Martha Blakeney of Union County, and they became the parents of two daughters, Betsy and Nancy, and a son, Luther, Jr. Mrs. Hodges died in 1969 after a fire in their Chapel Hill home. The following year Hodges married Mrs. Louise Finlayson, who survived him. He was buried in Eden.

SEE: Beth G. Crabtree, *North Carolina Governors, 1585–1958, Brief Sketches* (1958); Luther H. Hodges, *Businessman in the Statehouse* (1962); *North Carolina Manual* (1953–59); James W. Patton, ed., *Messages, Addresses, and Public Papers of Luther H. Hodges*, 3 vols. (1960, 1962, 1963); Raleigh *News and Observer*, 7 Oct. 1974; Gary E. Trawick and Paul B. Wyche, *100 Years, 100 Men, 1871–1971* (1971); *Who's Who in the South and Southwest* (1954, 1959).

CHARLES DUNN

Hodgson, John *(ca. 1705–47)*, Edenton lawyer, attorney general, assemblyman, speaker of the house, provincial treasurer, judge of the admiralty court, and commissary of North Carolina troops in the War of Jenkins' Ear, served the town of Edenton for many years as commissioner and treasurer. In 1734 he was appointed attorney general by Governor George Burrington to replace John Montgomery, who had been suspended. Hodgson qualified for the position before the Council on 29 Sept. 1734 and served until 1741, when Governor Gabriel Johnston appointed Joseph Anderson in his place. His removal from office may have been caused by Johnston's "silencing" or disbarring the lawyers who did not agree with him. According to Governor Arthur Dobbs, who referred to Johnston's silencing of Hodgson and Samuel Swann, this was the case. Hodgson was speaker of the house and later Swann became speaker. As speaker, Hodgson was a member of the committee to revise the North Carolina laws, but it was Swann who carried through the revision of the laws after Hodgson's death.

Hodgson first served in the Assembly in 1735 (it was Governor Johnston's first Assembly) as a representative of Bertie County. He was then elected to represent Chowan County in 1738–39 and became speaker of the house in 1739–40. Chowan returned him to the Assembly in 1742–44 and in 1746. In 1740 Hodgson was appointed provincial treasurer for the northern district, a position he held until his death. Shortly afterwards he became involved in the controversy caused by Governor Johnston's attempt to favor the southern members of the Assembly at the expense of the northern ones. When the Assembly at New Bern was prorogued to Wilmington on 12 June 1741, Hodgson and Benjamin Hill refused to go. Other members from the northern counties agreed not to go to Wilmington or to pay taxes. Johnston was fishing in troubled waters. He favored the Wilmington area, it is believed, because he hoped to limit the number of northern members attending the Assembly in order to get some of his bills passed. Some northern members did attend and blocked the governor's moves. In 1746, however, two laws were passed providing for a southern capital and for two delegates from each of the northern counties instead of the usual five. For thirteen sessions (1741–51), the same Assembly met in the south and few members from the northern counties attended. In 1752, two years after Johnston's death, the Privy Council disallowed the 1746 laws.

Hodgson's first wife was Elizabeth Pagett (5 Nov. 1716–1744[?]), the daughter of Samuel Pagett, a physican-planter, and Elizabeth Blount Pagett, daughter of James Blount. They were the parents of three children: Isabella, John, and Robert. Isabella married a Deloach in Halifax or Northampton County and had two children, William John Hodgson Deloach (d. August 1788) and Sarah Blount.

With three children under the age of ten, Hodgson probably did not wait longer than the usual six months or so after his wife's death before marrying his teenage sister-in-law, Penelope Pagett, in 1744 (see her biography in volume 1, pp. 95–96). By this second marriage, he had two more sons: Samuel and Thomas Craven. Penelope qualified as Hodgson's administratrix, with her uncles John and James Blount as sureties. Her uncle Charles Blount panicked when, in checking her accounts, he discovered that she had little cash on hand to pay her husband's debts. Moreover, the court threatened to take both the children and their property away from her, believing that she—a twenty-one-year-old widow with five children ranging from ages five to twelve—was not rearing and educating them satisfactorily. Subsequently, Peter Payne was appointed guardian of John Hodgson and Charles Blount of Robert Hodgson. In October 1751 the guardianship of Isabella, John, and Robert was restored to Penelope.

Just before his marriage to Penelope Hodgson, James

Craven in April 1752 petitioned for division of John Hodgson's estate and that of his son Samuel (Penelope's first child). In April 1756 Joseph Eelbeck was appointed guardian of Isabella Hodgson (he had married her aunt, Sarah Pagett) and Charles Eliot as guardian of her brother Robert. By the following year Isabella had married, and Thomas Barker, the current husband of Penelope, was appointed guardian of John and Robert Hodgson. But three months later, in July, Robert was allowed to choose for himself, and he selected Penelope's uncle, Charles Blount.

There are no known pictures of John Hodgson. However, John Wollaston, the English painter who toured New York City, Annapolis, Virginia, and Philadelphia, did portraits of Penelope Hodgson Barker (the heroine of the Edenton Tea Party), Betsy Barker, Thomas Hodgson, and presumably Thomas Barker in Williamsburg, Va. The Barkers were visiting his daughter Betsy, who was attending school in Williamsburg.

SEE: John L. Cheney, Jr., ed., *North Carolina Government, 1585–1974* (1975); Walter Clark, ed., *State Records of North Carolina*, vol. 23 (1904); J. R. B. Hathaway, ed., *North Carolina Historical and Genealogical Register*, vol. 5 (October 1900); Blackwell P. Robinson, *The Five Royal Governors of North Carolina, 1729–1775* (1963); William L. Saunders, ed., *Colonial Records of North Carolina*, vols. 2, 3, 4 (1886), vol. 6 (1888), vol. 7 (1890); Nicholas B. Wainwright, comp., *Paintings and Miniatures at the Historical Society of Pennsylvania* (1974).

VERNON O. STUMPF

Hodgson, John, II (*ca. 1740–16 Nov. 1774*), Chowan plantation owner and Edenton merchant, was the son of John Hodgson, attorney general, assemblyman, and provincial treasurer, and Elizabeth Pagett Hodgson. Upon the death of his mother, young John, his sister Isabella, and his brother Robert were placed under the care of their teenage aunt, Penelope Pagett (later Barker), who married their father in 1744. When Robert Hodgson died about 1760, his brother John was old enough to be appointed administrator of his estate. With Robert's death, John and his half brother Thomas Craven were the only Hodgsons left in Edenton. Isabella had married a Deloach in Halifax or Northampton County.

In June 1769, when Thomas Craven Hodgson was licensed as an attorney, John Hodgson II was a planter-merchant in Edenton. The two half brothers must have been very fond of each other, for Thomas's will, written three days before his death on 19 Feb. 1772, left everything but two slaves to John, his executor. The will was witnessed by Jasper Charlton and Thomas Blount.

Hodgson was a sick man when he made his own will on 6 May 1774, with bequests to his sister Isabella's son, William John Hodgson Deloach (a minor under the care of Joseph Harrison Eelbeck, who had been a guardian of the boy's mother), and to his Eelbeck first cousins: Joseph Harrison, John Daniel, and William Eelbeck. The slaves left to Hodgson by his half brother Thomas Craven were given to the Eelbeck cousins. Hodgson also left bequests to his friends Samuel Johnston, Andrew Little (son of John Little), and Margaret Blair (daughter of George Blair); Samuel Johnston and Andrew Little were to be the executors. The residue of his estate was to be sold and invested, with the interest going to his aunt, Penelope Barker, for her lifetime; afterwards, the principal was to go to the Eelbeck cousins.

Six weeks before his death, Hodgson gave bond for his appearance at court in December to satisfy the parish that he was the father of Elizabeth and Sarah, born of Joanna Kippen, who had so sworn. He also promised to support and maintain them according to the orders of the court. Hodgson died before December and there is no further record of his daughters by Joanna Kippen.

SEE: Walter Clark, ed., *State Records of North Carolina*, vol. 22 (1907); J. R. B. Hathaway, *North Carolina Historical and Genealogical Register*, vol. 5 (October 1900); Miss Elizabeth V. Moore, Edenton (letter to the author, 17 Sept. 1980); Wills of Chowan County (North Carolina State Archives, Raleigh).

VERNON O. STUMPF

Hoerr, Lucile Marie. *See* **Charles, Lucile Marie Hoerr**.

Hoey, Clyde Roark (11 Dec. 1877–12 May 1954), printer, newspaper publisher, state legislator, attorney general, governor, congressman, and U.S. senator, was born in Shelby, the fifth child of Mary Charlotte and Samuel Alberta Hoey, a Confederate captain. At age twelve, when his father's health failed, he left school to earn a living. From the time of his first job as a printer's devil at the Shelby *Aurora*, beginning 1 Oct. 1890, Hoey expressed a maturity beyond his years. After a brief period in Shelby, he became a printer at the *Charlotte Observer*. While in Charlotte he heard that the Shelby *Review* was in financial straits. He hurried home and purchased the newspaper on 1 Aug. 1894 with promises to pay off the creditors; at sixteen he became publisher of the paper under the name of the *Cleveland Star*.

When he was only twenty, the Democrats of his native Cleveland County nominated Hoey for the General Assembly. He was elected after a hotly contested campaign and served in 1899; two years later he was reelected. In 1903 he was a state senator from the Thirty-third District, and from 1903 to 1909 he served as chairman of the Cleveland County Democratic Executive Committee.

Meanwhile, Hoey read law in Shelby, then continued his legal studies at The University of North Carolina from June to September 1899. The same year he was admitted to the state bar. A growing law practice forced him to give up his work at the *Star*, though he retained ownership of the paper until 1908.

In 1913 Hoey was appointed assistant U.S. attorney for the Western District and served until 1919, when Congressman Edwin Yates Webb, also of Shelby, resigned to accept appointment as a federal judge. Hoey won the nomination for his seat in a special primary on 24 November, defeating Republican John Motley Morehead; he served in Congress from 16 Dec. 1919 to 3 Mar. 1921. Declining to seek reelection, he returned to Shelby and resumed the practice of law. Although identified with his brother-in-law, Governor O. Max Gardner, as a part of the Democratic party leadership centered in Shelby, Hoey did not assume a major role in the primary campaigns of the time, but took to the stump for the party ticket as a "silver-tongued" orator.

On 15 May 1935, as the state was emerging from the depths of the depression, Hoey—as expected—announced for governor. Raised in the primary campaign was the sales tax imposed by the General Assembly of 1933 which angered the people and caused turmoil within the Democratic party. Dr. Ralph W. McDonald, a young Salem College professor and legislator from Forsyth County, entered the race and made the sales tax a major issue in the contest with Hoey and former speaker A. H. Graham of Orange County, the leading Democratic candidates. In the first primary, Hoey led McDonald by 4,468 votes; in the second primary, many of the Graham voters switched to Hoey, who was nominated by a margin of nearly 52,000 votes. After an easy victory in the fall, Hoey was inaugurated governor on 7 Jan. 1937 for a four-year term that ended on 9 Jan. 1941.

During the Hoey administration the state began furnishing free textbooks for elementary school children, a pay increase for teachers was approved, the highway system was expanded, the first advertising and publicity program for tourism and industry was established, graduate courses were offered in Negro colleges, a modern parole system was developed, child labor laws were passed by the General Assembly, and the State Bureau of Investigation was established. Although Hoey was a "dry," he accepted the legislature's verdict against a statewide referendum on the liquor question and the Alcoholic Beverage Board of Control was created. Early in 1937, when the nation was faced with widespread sit-down strikes, he warned in a radio broadcast on 27 March that "sit-down strikes are unlawful, and will not be tolerated in North Carolina."

A popular governor, Hoey made a total of 976 speeches, visited all parts of the state, and twice daily walked down Raleigh's Fayetteville Street for a Coca Cola break at a drugstore. He did not seek to build a political machine and refused to become involved in the selection of his successor. When his gubernatorial term ended he continued to serve his party as Democratic national committeeman from 1941 to 1944.

Entering the race for the U.S. Senate in 1944, Hoey defeated former governor and former senator Cameron Morrison in the primary and easily won in the general election. He took his seat in the Senate on 3 Jan. 1945. His long white hair, frock coat, striped pants, wing collar, floral tie with a diamond stickpin, high-top shoes, and cordial and courtly manner soon set him apart as a senator who possessed the essence of that office. Some of his colleagues called him "The Duke." He was unopposed in the 1950 primary and was overwhelmingly reelected in the general election.

Senator Hoey was an effective member of the Finance and Agriculture committees. He received acclaim for his work as chairman of the Permanent Investigating Subcommittee, leading the investigations of the "five percenter" scandals with a calm hand and refusing to succumb to the appeal of publicity. His unshakable poise, rapierlike wit, repartee with a subtle sting, and polished diplomacy became Hoey hallmarks in Congress.

A Methodist layman, he taught Sunday school at Central Methodist Church in Shelby and, while governor, instructed the Men's Class at Edenton Street Methodist Church in Raleigh. He was a Mason and a member of the Odd Fellows, Woodmen of the World, Knights of Pythias, Junior Order, and Omicron Delta Kappa and Sigma Chi fraternities. He was given honorary LL.D. degrees by Davidson College (1937), The University of North Carolina (1938), and Duke University (1938).

Hoey married Bessie Gardner of Shelby on 22 Mar. 1900; she died on 13 Feb. 1942. They had three children: Clyde R., Jr., Charles A., and Isabel Y. (m. Dan M. Paul).

On 12 May 1954, Hoey went to his office and did a radio broadcast tape recording but he appeared to be tired and weak. Afterwards he attended a Senate Finance Committee meeting, had lunch, and returned to his office for his usual brief rest. His administrative assistant, Jack Spain, became concerned when he did not resume his normal schedule. Investigating, he found Hoey slumped in a chair at his desk, dead from a stroke at age seventy-six. Many of his colleagues and other prominent governmental officials attended the funeral in Shelby. He was buried in the town's Sunset Cemetery.

Senator Hoey, the last of the "Shelby Dynasty," was proud of his record of political leadership that spanned most of his life.

SEE: *Addresses and Papers of Governor Clyde R. Hoey, 1937–1941* (1944); *Biog. Dir. Am. Cong., 1774–1961* (1961); *Charlotte Observer*, 13 May 1954; John L. Cheney, Jr., ed., *North Carolina Government, 1585–1974* (1975); *Congressional Directory* (1953); *Memorial Services in the Senate and House of Representatives, Clyde Roark Hoey, A Late Senator from North Carolina* (1954); Joseph L. Morrison, *Governor O. Max Gardner* (1971); *North Carolina Manual* (1949); *Shelby Daily Star*, 13 May 1954; *Who's Who in America*, (1950–51).

                                                                    T. HARRY GATTON

Hofmann, Julius Valentine *(20 Feb. 1882–17 Aug. 1965)*, teacher, administrator, forester, and conservationist, was born in Janesville, Minn., the youngest surviving child of Valentine and Rosalia Frodl Hofmann. His parents emigrated to America from Austria (now Czechoslovakia), purchased land, and operated a farm. Hofmann grew up in a farming community, was graduated from Janesville High School, and spent two years as a book salesman. He later attended the University of Minnesota where he received a diploma from the School of Agriculture (1909) and a B.S. (1911), an M.S. (1912), and a Ph.D. (1914) in forestry. His was the first Ph.D. awarded in forestry in the United States. In 1915 he married Ella Kenety, the daughter of William and Anna Powers Kenety of Fulda, Minn. They had two children, Eileen Rose and Julian George.

Hofmann began his professional life in 1903 teaching school. During his college career he was a teaching fellow in botany. After graduation he joined the U.S. Forest Service and became technical forester of the Priest River Experiment Station in Idaho and then director of the Wind River Experiment Station in Carson, Wash., where he remained until 1924. At Wind River he developed techniques for and initiated studies in fire control and the natural establishment of forests following fire. He also developed the first tests related to forest genetics in the West.

Afterwards he moved into college administration and teaching. As assistant director of the Pennsylvania State Forest School, Hofmann taught classes in forest management and initiated studies to determine the extent of heart rot in forests of sprout origin. In 1929 he was named head of the Department of Forestry at North Carolina State College; in 1932 the department was upgraded to become the Division of Forestry. Hofmann initiated a program of land use by purchasing tracts of land on a self-liquidating basis and building a sound forestry program. The present School of Forestry has the use of over 80,000 acres of land purchased under this concept.

Hofmann was known throughout the forestry profession for bringing modern forestry to the South. After bitter political fighting in Pennsylvania, he established the new forestry department at North Carolina State College, where forty-six students followed him and seventeen fully trained foresters were graduated the first year.

He was the author of a U.S. Forest Service bulletin, *Relative Humidity and Forest Fires* (1923) and U.S. Department of Agriculture Bulletin no. 1200, *The Natural Regeneration of Douglas Fir in the Pacific Northwest* (1924); contributed to such periodicals as *Ecology, Journal of Forestry, Timberman, West Coast Lumberman, American Forest, Journal of Agricultural Research,* and *We the People*; and wrote numerous newspaper articles. His Ph.D. dissertation was entitled "The Importance of Seed Characteristics in the Natural Reproduction of Coniferous Forests" (1918).

Hofmann was a fellow of the American Academy of Science and a member of the Ecological Society of America, Botanical Society, Geographical Society, Society of American Foresters (chairman, Appalachian Section, 1934), North Carolina Forestry Association, and Alpha Zeta, Xi Sigma Pi, Sigma Xi, and Alpha Gamma Rho fraternities. In 1959 he was honored by the Society of American Foresters for outstanding contributions to the forestry profession, and in 1960 he was the recipient of the University of Minnesota's Outstanding Achievement Award reserved for former students who attained high eminence and distinction. In 1964 he received the annual award of both the national fraternity of Alpha Gamma Rho and the Southern Forest Institute, representing southern forestry industries.

Active in community affairs, Hofmann was chairman of the committee that acquired and organized the National Park Recreation Area at Crabtree Creek (now Umstead Park), which was turned over to the state of North Carolina. He was a member of the Rotary Club from 1924 until his death. His lifelong desire to help boys led to his participation in the Boy Scouts; he served as president of the Occoneechee Boy Scout Council for four years and received the Silver Beaver Award in 1942.

Hofmann traveled extensively in the United States, central and western Canada, central and western Europe, Mexico, and all countries of South America except Paraguay. He also took a trip around the world. He enjoyed life and kept young growing and developing plants, playing golf, and taking care of his farm and woodland holdings.

SEE: Recollections of the author; *Who's Who in the South and Southwest* (1947).

                                                                    JULIAN G. HOFMANN

Hogg, Gavin *(8 Aug. 1788–28 Oct. 1835)*, lawyer, was born in the town of Wick, Caithness, Scotland. He came to the United States with his parents, James and Mary Finlayson Hogg, in about 1797. After arriving in Wilmington, the family moved to Hillsborough and later settled in Chapel Hill. Hogg attended The University of North Carolina, where he was a member of the Dialectic Society; he was graduated in 1807, then spent a year as a tutor at the university. While teaching in the Atkinson family in Dinwiddie County, Va., he read law.

After receiving his license, Hogg went to Windsor in Bertie County to practice law. It was reported by his contemporaries that, when he arrived in town, he drove up to a tavern in a single-stick gig after a long and fatiguing day's drive. He told the landlord that he had no money or local acquaintances, but showed him his license and said he intended to practice law. In asking for room and board, he noted that he would be unable to pay if he did not find work. The landlord, impressed by his candor, welcomed him cordially and gave him a place to stay while he became established. In this way he began his lifework.

As a Federalist, Hogg strongly opposed the War of 1812 and expressed his views with vigor. According to Pulaski Cowper, "public sentiment was fiercely arrayed against him, and so excited and defiant had it become, that his life was threatened, and he defied, singly and alone, a mob in the streets of Windsor, and stationed on his front porch with gun in hand, threatened death to the first who should invade his domain." But despite his opposition to the war, the patriotic Hogg raised a company of soldiers in Bertie County and, as their captain, participated in the Battle of Craney Island near Norfolk, Va. After his return from the war, he enjoyed great popularity among the very people who had wanted to lynch him and his legal services were eagerly sought. On one docket, he was attorney for 400 out of 423 cases.

Later in life Hogg became a Jacksonian Democrat. Sometime after the war, he moved to Raleigh and bought a number of lots in the vicinity of the capitol. The Archives and History/State Library building is located on property where the Hogg home stood for over a hundred years; the Supreme Court building is on a lot formerly owned jointly by Hogg and his close friend, George Mordecai.

On 22 May 1822, Hogg married Mary Ann Bayard Johnson of Stratford, Conn. She was the great-granddaughter of Samuel Johnson, first president of Kings College (afterwards Columbia University), and the granddaughter of William Samuel Johnson, second president of the same college and a signer of the United States Constitution for Connecticut. Hogg and his wife had several children who died in infancy and one son, Thomas Devereux Hogg, a longtime resident of Raleigh. Upon her death, Hogg married Sarah Leigh Haywood, the widow of James Gray Blount, but their marriage was of short duration due to his death at age forty-seven. The second Mrs. Hogg raised her orphaned stepson with enduring love.

Though originally a Presbyterian through his parents, Hogg became a member of the Episcopal church. He was a devoted friend of Bishop John Stark Ravenscroft, who spent the last months of his life at the Hogg residence where he died on 5 Mar. 1830. Hogg, with a small group of influential friends, was appointed in 1826 to make plans for erecting the first (wooden) structure for Christ Church, Raleigh. He was a delegate to the diocesan convention for four years (1825–28), and to the General Convention for two years (1829, 1832).

Pulaski Cowper, in praising Hogg as a fine criminal lawyer with a large and lucrative practice, wrote: "He was bold, aggressive and determined. He would in strict conscience, prosecute or defend to the full limit, confining himself strictly and solely to the evidence detailed; no inducement could alter or swerve his convictions. In his speeches to the jury he would frequently ask the court to stop him if he transcended the limits not warranted by the evidence presented. He was a fine advocate, and argued his points of law and evidence clearly, forcibly and intrepidly. He was one of the most positive and determined men the East ever had. He never gave a threat or took one. Courteous, respectful, and affable, yet dignified, deferential, though of easy approach."

Hogg was appointed by the General Assembly to prepare a codification of the statute law, but ill health forced him to resign the commission. As his health declined further, he relinquished his law practice in 1834. He died in New York while seeking medical advice. Due to the fame and stature of the man, Grace Episcopal Church in New York designated its famous sexton, Sexton Brown, to accompany the body back to North Carolina. Hogg was buried in the old Raleigh City Cemetery. Later his remains and those of his two wives and infant children were moved to Oakwood Cemetery. A portrait of Hogg hangs in the library at Hayes, near Edenton, the home of his good friend, James Cathcart Johnson.

SEE: Pulaski Cowper, "Reminiscences and Anecdotes of the North Carolina Bar," *University Magazine* (April 1895); Archibald Henderson, "Mystery of Relation of Hoggs Still Remains Unsolved in North Carolina," undated newspaper clipping (North Carolina Collection, University of North Carolina Library, Chapel Hill); Hogg Family Bible (in possession of Elizabeth Dortch); Raleigh *News and Observer*, 22 June 1941; *Raleigh Register*, 23 Sept. 1834, 13 Jan., 10 Nov. 1835.

ELIZABETH DORTCH DIX KEYES

Hogg, James (1729–9 Nov. 1804), planter, merchant, and university official, was born in East Lothian, Scotland, one of six children of Gavin and Helen Stevenson Hogg. Nothing is known of his early life, education, or career. In 1764 he married McDowal Alves, the daughter of Alexander and Elizabeth Ingles Alves, and five years later moved to Borlum, near Thurso, in the parish of Reay, Caithnesshire. Hogg rented a farm, and the family prospered and became respected members of the community. That success would be short-lived. Conditions in mid-eighteenth-century Scotland were extremely troubled; the dislocation—economic, political, and social—was complete. With the decline of the linen industry and the development of sheep raising, huge numbers of people were thrown out of work and forced to roam the countryside or squat on the land of others.

Hogg complained bitterly that the country was being overrun by vandals and gangs, and that the land was no longer safe for his wife and children. Matters came to a head in 1771 when he discovered a shipwreck near his farm. The beleaguered captain was putting up an ineffective defense against the onslaught of looters when Hogg came to his assistance. The attackers were run off but Hogg paid dearly for his gallantry. Shortly afterwards, a band of ruffians descended upon his house, attempted to murder him, and burned his home to the ground.

Hogg had had enough. In 1772 his brother Robert visited the family in Scotland from Wilmington, N.C., where he had lived since 1756. With his brother's help, James made ready for the voyage. He contracted a vessel and organized 280 emigrants to undertake the passage to America. After several delays, the group arrived in Wilmington in 1774. His brother had purchased a 1,160-acre farm for him near Hillsborough along the Eno River, but Hogg elected to settle first in Cross Creek where he became a partner in the mercantile company operated by Robert Hogg and Samuel Campbell of Wilmington.

After a year, Hogg moved to Hillsborough to open the company's office and take up residence at Old House on his land east of town. Also in 1775 Hogg became a member of the Transylvania Company, a large-scale land speculating venture conceived by Judge Richard Henderson. As the proprietors struggled in Kentucky to establish title and organize settlement, Hogg was commissioned as emissary to the Continental Congress in Philadelphia to present the company's memorial to be admitted as the fourteenth colony. But that august body felt any decision on its part to be unwarranted. Appeasing the states' claims to western lands and respecting the Crown's authority to determine policy in the West, the Congress simply elected not to consider the Transylvania petition.

Active in the American Revolution, Hogg served on the Hillsborough Committee of Safety during the war and in 1777 sat on the town's board of commissioners. The state later sent him to Connecticut on public business. In the British campaign through North Carolina in 1781, he was captured in his newly built house, Poplar Hill, but was soon released.

Hogg had long been interested in education. When Hillsborough founded its first academy, Science Hall, in 1779, he was a chief benefactor and trustee. Ten years later, The University of North Carolina formed its first board of trustees and named Hogg a member. For the next thirteen years Hogg played a critical role in the formation and development of the university. He presented to the board a gift of 20,000 acres in western Tennessee from General Benjamin Smith to enhance the school's endowment. In November 1792 he was one of the commissioners charged with the selection of a suitable site for the school. When Chapel Hill was chosen, Hogg organized the donation of 1,390 acres from the residents of the area. He remained active in university affairs until he was felled by a stroke in 1802.

Hogg outlived his wife by four years. They were buried in the Old Town Cemetery, Hillsborough, in the same plot with lifetime friend and signer of the Declaration of Independence, William Hooper. Before he died Hogg petitioned the legislature to change his childrens' name from Hogg to his wife's maiden name, Alves. Apparently the years of ridicule had proven too much and the assembly happily assented. The couple had six children: Walter, Gavin, Elizabeth, Anne, Helen, and Robina.

SEE: Bernard Bailyn, *Voyagers to the West* (1986); Kemp P. Battle, *Letters of Nathaniel Macon, John Steele, and William Barry Grove* (1902); Joseph Blount Cheshire, comp., "Memoranda relating to James Hogg of Hillsborough, 1774–1805" (microfilm of a typescript, North Carolina Collection, University of North Carolina Library, Chapel Hill); Archibald Henderson, "The Transylvania Company: A Study in Personality: Part I, James Hogg," *Filson Club Historical Quarterly* 21 (1947); James Hogg Papers (Southern Historical Collection, University of North Carolina Library, Chapel Hill); *Raleigh Register*, 19 Nov. 1804.

MARK F. MILLER

Hogg, John (*fl. 1756–79*), merchant and Loyalist, the son of Gavin and Helen Stevenson Hogg, emigrated to North Carolina from Scotland sometime after 1756. His brother, Robert, who arrived in Wilmington in 1756, established the successful mercantile house of Hogg and Campbell, with branches in Cross Creek, Hillsborough, Wilmington, and elsewhere. John, with a third brother James, became a member of the firm.

John Hogg was a loyal subject of the Crown, and one of the last official acts of Governor Josiah Martin was to commission him a magistrate for Orange County on

14 Apr. 1775. Two years later, in April 1777, while awaiting passage to England, Governor Martin wrote from New York to Lord George Germain citing Hogg, among others, as risking life and reputation to supply the Loyalists of North Carolina with provisions when they took up arms.

Hogg sought refuge in New York, but by 1778 he was anxious to return home and wrote to Colonel Thomas Clark, a fellow North Carolinian who was encamped with the colonial army at White Plains, to request a meeting; he also asked for time to study the new Constitution and laws before taking the oath of allegiance. On 6 Sept. 1778, Clark informed James Hogg of Hillsborough that because of gout John had been unable to travel to White Plains; however, Clark promised to help him procure a safe conduct home because, he said, "I have always had a great friendship for your brother and never considered him as an enemy to this country."

Among Council papers before the General Assembly in January 1779 was the petition of John Hogg to take the oath of allegiance.

SEE: Walter Clark, ed., *State Records of North Carolina*, vols. 11, 13 (1895, 1897); Harry Roy Merrens, *Colonial North Carolina in the Eighteenth Century: A Study in Historical Geography* (1964); Lorenzo Sabine, *The American Loyalists* (1847); William L. Saunders, ed., *Colonial Records of North Carolina*, vol. 9 (1890).

HENRY A. ROBERTSON, JR.

Hogg, John (*5 Feb. 1765–28 Oct. 1826*), legislator, arrived in Wilmington from Anstruther, Fife, Scotland, about 1797. He, it is assumed, was a cousin of Robert, John, and James Hogg of the mercantile house of Hogg and Campbell—with branches in Wilmington, Cross Creek, Hillsborough, and elsewhere—and a member of that firm. Hogg was elected to the legislature from Hillsborough in 1794 and 1796. In 1809 he contributed $25 to the building fund for the Main or South Building at The University of North Carolina. He died in Fayetteville.

SEE: Alice Keith, ed., *John Gray Blount Papers*, vols. 2, 3 (1952, 1959); Raleigh *News and Observer*, 22 June 1941.

HENRY A. ROBERTSON, JR.

Hogg, Robert (*d. 1780*), merchant, a native of East Lothian in northern Scotland and the son of Gavin and Helen Stevenson Hogg, emigrated to North Carolina about 1756 according to one source, but the New Hanover County Court Minutes record the transference of a deed to a Robert Hogg in 1739. James and John Hogg were his brothers. Because James, apparently a younger brother, was forty-six years old in 1774, Robert must have been born before 1728.

Hogg settled in Wilmington where he formed a business partnership with Samuel Campbell, and together they established "one of the most important mercantile firms on the Cape Fear." Hogg and Campbell operated branches in Cross Creek, Hillsborough, Swansboro, New River, and Bladen County, in addition to the store maintained in Wilmington, and carried on a widespread trade with merchants in Great Britain, the West Indies, and the other continental colonies. The firm exported a wide variety of products, including naval stores, deerskins, and flour (the latter from Cross Creek), and sold various manufactured goods, sugar, coffee, tea, rum, and sometimes slaves to their local customers. Their annual profits approximated £1,200 sterling; when the company was dissolved in 1778, it had assets of £18,330 sterling. Because an established merchant was expected to earn more than £500 sterling per annum in the Revolutionary Era, the firm was obviously prospering. The Scottish lady, Janet Schaw, called Hogg a merchant "of eminence" and trusted his judgment.

On the eve of the American Revolution, Hogg was one of the leading gentlemen of Wilmington. He took part in civic activities, was elected a town commissioner in 1770 and 1772, and later served on the Committee of Safety from November 1774 to June 1775. As perhaps indicative of his social status, he defaulted on road work. On another occasion he was accused of "dealing & trafficking with negroes." Although Hogg was at first a member of the Committee of Safety, he evidently became disenchanted with the Revolutionary cause and sailed for England in 1775. Governor Josiah Martin wrote that Hogg was "a merchant of first consideration in the colony, where he has resided many years, and who is compelled by popular clamour and resentment to abandon his important concerns here, because he will not renounce his principles, which he has maintained with a manly firmness and steadiness, which do honour to his heart and understanding." Hogg stayed in England from the fall of 1775 to the summer of 1778, when he returned because a confiscation act had been passed declaring that all property of persons living outside the province after October 1778 would be confiscated by the state. Upon his arrival, he and another merchant, John Burgwin, were "on their parol" at Burgwin's plantation. In January 1778, the motion carried 16 to 10 in the legislative committee to admit Hogg as a citizen of the state. The minority legislators seemingly did not believe in Hogg's sincere friendship for the new government. In contrast, the majority accepted as proof of his loyalty his "instructions to his Factors and Agents" before he had left in 1775 "to appropriate one-half of his property, if they found the same necessary, in the Defense of the American Cause." Hogg's position on independence, then, is somewhat ambiguous.

Apparently Robert Hogg never married. On a visit to Scotland in 1772, he urged his brother James to emigrate, and in 1774 James Hogg arrived with all his family. James worked for his brother by managing first the Cross Creek store and later the outlet at Hillsborough. Robert Hogg died before 7 July 1780, when he was supposed to have sat on a grand jury. He left his estate to James, whose loyalty both to the Revolutionary cause and to his brother was unquestionable.

SEE: Evangeline Walker Andrews, ed., in collaboration with Charles McLean Andrews, *Journal of a Lady of Quality; Being the Narrative from Scotland to the West Indies, North Carolina, and Portugal, in the Years 1774 to 1776* (1939); Walter Clark, ed., *State Records of North Carolina*, vol. 13 (1901); Charles C. Crittenden, *The Commerce of North Carolina, 1763–1789* (1936); Robert Hogg Account Books (Southern Historical Collection, University of North Carolina Library, Chapel Hill); Donald R. Lennon and Ida Brooks Kellam, eds., *The Wilmington Town Book, 1743–1778* (1973); Harry Roy Merrens, *Colonial North Carolina in the Eighteenth Century: A Study in Historical Geography* (1964).

ALICE E. MATHEWS

Hogg, Samuel E. [Edwards?] *(18 Apr. 1783–28 May 1842)*, physician, legislator, and congressman, was born in Halifax, the son of Thomas and Rebecca Edwards Hogg. He attended public schools in Caswell County and later taught school briefly. In 1804, while in his early twenties, Hogg studied medicine in Gallatin, Sumner County, Tenn., but soon afterwards moved to Lebanon County, Tenn.

On 21 Nov. 1812 Hogg became a surgeon for the First Regiment of Tennessee Volunteers, a position he held until 22 Apr. 1813. His medical talents were appreciated by Major General Andrew Jackson, who placed his fellow Carolinian-turned-Tennessean on his staff as hospital surgeon for the expedition against the Creek Indians from 22 Feb. to 25 May 1814. Nearly six months after Jackson's victory at Horseshoe Bend, Hogg again took to the field as hospital surgeon on the staff of Major General William Carroll from 13 Nov. 1814 to 13 May 1815.

After a brief postwar respite, Hogg served in the Tennessee House of Representatives before holding a seat in the Fifteenth Congress from 4 Mar. 1817 to 3 Mar. 1819. He then resumed his private medical practice successively in Lebanon, Tenn. (1819–28), Nashville (1828–36), Natchez, Miss. (1836–38), and again in Nashville (1838–40). In 1840, he was president of the State Medical Society of Tennessee. Hogg died in Rutherford County, Tenn., and was buried in the Nashville City Cemetery.

SEE: *Biog. Dir. Am. Cong.* (1971); Robert M. McBride and Dan M. Robinson, *Biographical Directory of the Tennessee General Assembly* (1975).

PHILLIP W. EVANS

Hogg, Thomas Devereux *(1 Oct. 1823–30 Sept. 1904)*, businessman and philanthropist, was born in Raleigh. His father, Gavin Hogg (1788–1835), a native of Wick, Caithness, Scotland, settled in Raleigh after having lived in Bertie County. His mother was the former Mary Ann Bayard Johnson (1802–30) of Stratford, Conn., a descendant of Samuel Johnson, first president of Kings College, and of his son William Samuel Johnson, first president of the school after it became Columbia University.

Hogg obtained his early education at the Episcopal School for Boys (later St. Mary's School and Junior College), Raleigh, and at Isaac Webb's preparatory school in Middletown, Conn., where Rutherford B. Hayes was a classmate. After graduation in 1844 from the College of New Jersey (later Princeton University), he obtained the M.D. degree from the Jefferson Medical College of Philadelphia, although he did not remain active in the practice of medicine.

A resident of Raleigh thereafter, except for a short time in New Orleans, Hogg was, according to his obituary, "an active participant in every movement which tended to the upbuilding of his state." A major stockholder in the Raleigh and Gaston Railroad, completed in 1840, he was instrumental in securing financial aid for that company as well as for the Wilmington and Weldon Railroad at crucial periods in their development. In the 1850s he promoted the proposed Greenville and Raleigh and other plank roads. Appointed by Governor David Reid in 1853 to the board of commissioners for the State Hospital for the Insane (later renamed Dorothea Dix Hospital), Hogg was a member of the three-man executive committee during construction of the institution's first buildings.

As an incorporator, director, and stockholder of the Raleigh Gaslight Company, chartered in 1859, he spearheaded the company's successful effort to furnish Raleigh with gas. The same year a group of citizens, who according to the Raleigh *Standard* preferred "the brightness of gaslight to the dripping dimness of the olden style," presented him a silver pitcher inscribed "as a mark of their appreciation of his public spirit and enterprise." Earlier he had also been a Raleigh city commissioner, representing the Eastern Ward in 1852 and serving as a member of a special "Fire and Water Committee," which, after the widely destructive fire of December 1851, reorganized and augmented Raleigh's fire department and improved the water supply.

In January 1860 Hogg was elected first president of the Oak City Savings Bank, chartered by the General Assembly of 1858–59. In April 1861, his fellow commissioners elected him president of the board of the Chatham Railroad (later the Raleigh and Augusta). Among other antebellum interests was his partnership with Robert W. Haywood in the Raleigh Planing Mills, which began operating near Raleigh in the summer of 1853. In the federal census of 1860, Hogg was listed as owning 22,000 acres of land in Wake County.

Hogg opposed separation from the Union until North Carolina seceded; he was then commissioned a major and served from September 1861 throughout the Civil War as chief commissary of the Subsistence Department of North Carolina. In his brief postwar report on its operations, he wrote that before the end of the war his department was "feeding about half of Lee's army," a statement with which editor-historian Walter Clark and others concurred.

His business interests after the war included grape culture in a vineyard near Raleigh owned jointly with Henry Mahler, and a partnership in a Baltimore distillery with James L. Bryan, his late wife's uncle. The state of North Carolina appointed him inspector of the North Carolina Railroad in 1871, following lease of the line to the Richmond and Danville Railroad Company.

When Mayor Joseph Separk died in office in 1875, the Raleigh board of aldermen elected Hogg to succeed him. He declined, reported the Raleigh *Sentinel*, "on the ground that his private engagements would not admit of his giving that attention which the office would require." He served the following year, however, as a member of the board, representing the First (Northeast) Ward. For some years thereafter he advocated, albeit unsuccessfully, the building of a steel roadway for vehicles in Raleigh's streets, which remained unpaved until after 1886. Towards the end of his life, he served as a delegate—appointed by Governor Thomas Holt—to the Nicaraguan Canal Convention of 2 June 1892 in St. Louis, Mo.

On 13 Dec. 1848, Hogg married Janet Bryan (9 Feb. 1831–22 Feb. 1855), of Plymouth, the daughter of John Stevens and Lucy Davis Haywood Bryan and granddaughter of Sherwood Haywood of Raleigh. In 1850 they built the residence that until 1962 occupied the entire square on which the Archives and History/State Library building was constructed in 1969. Mrs. Hogg died shortly after the birth of their third daughter Lucy, who later married Isaac Foote Dortch and was the mother of eight children. The oldest daughter, Sally, did not marry; the second, Janet, married Colin Hawkins but had no children.

An Episcopalian, Hogg was a lifelong member of Christ Church, Raleigh, where he served as senior warden and treasurer for a number of years. Politically, he was a Whig. He was the author of two short treatises on mining interests and municipal improvements; copies of both are in the North Carolina Collection, University of North Carolina Library, Chapel Hill.

An accident claimed the life of Hogg in Raleigh; he was buried in Oakwood Cemetery from Christ Church. Portrait miniatures, a daguerreotype, and photographs of Hogg are in the possession of his granddaughter, Miss Elizabeth Dortch of Raleigh, who also owns the 1859 silver pitcher described above.

SEE: Moses N. Amis, *Historical Raleigh* (1913); Levi Branson, *Branson's North Carolina Business Directory, 1877–1878*; Christ Church (Raleigh), *Centennial Ceremonies . . . 1821* (1922); *Christ Church: 150 Years at the Heart of the City* (1971); Walter Clark, comp., *History of the Raleigh and Augusta Air-Line Railroad Co.* (1877); Miss Elizabeth Dortch, Raleigh (interviews, 1972, 1975); Hogg Family Bible and other family papers (in the possession of Miss Elizabeth Dortch, Raleigh); Gavin Hogg Papers (Manuscript Department, Duke University Library, Durham); Thomas Devereux Hogg Papers (Southern Historical Collection, University of North Carolina Library, Chapel Hill); Thomas D. Hogg Papers and Marriage Bonds of Wake County (North Carolina State Archives, Raleigh); *North Carolina Laws (Private), 1858–1859*, c. 74, c. 108, c. 109, *1860–1861*, c. 129; Raleigh *Daily Sentinel*, 4 Sept. 1875; Raleigh *Morning Post*, 2 Oct. 1904; Raleigh *News and Observer*, 1 Oct. 1904, 1 Aug. 1954; Raleigh *North Carolina Standard*, 14 Dec. 1859, 18 Jan. 1860; *Raleigh Register* (weekly), 21 Jan. 1852; *Raleigh Register* (semiweekly), 16 Dec. 1848, 4 Jan., 30 Apr. 1851, 28 Jan., 11 Feb., 18 Feb., 8 Mar. 1852, 9 Mar., 8 Oct. 1853, 24 Feb., 17 Nov. 1855, 15 Mar. 1856, 19 Mar. 1859, 18 Jan. 1860; *Raleigh Times*, 1 Oct. 1904, 11 July 1957.

ELIZABETH REID MURRAY

Hogun, James (d. 4 Jan. 1781), politician and Revolutionary soldier, a native of Ireland, settled in Halifax County around 1751. He married Ruth Norfleet of a prominent North Carolina family. One son, Lemuel, survived him.

There are no records of his life during the next twenty-three years after his arrival, but the fact that in 1774 he became a member of the Halifax County Committee of Safety suggests that he had become a person of some prominence. Hogun represented Halifax County in the Provincial Congresses of 20 Aug. 1774, 4 Apr. 1776, and November 1776, where he demonstrated an interest in military affairs. On 22 Apr. 1776, he was appointed first major of the Halifax militia by the Provincial Congress. In the November 1776 Congress he served on a committee appointed to study the reorganization of the militia.

Possibly because of his demonstrated interest in military affairs Hogun was appointed colonel of the Seventh North Carolina Continental Regiment on 26 Nov. 1776. He joined George Washington in July 1777 and participated in the battles of Brandywine and Germantown; it was said that in the latter conflict he conducted himself with "distinguished intrepidity."

In 1778, when the Continental Congress authorized four new regiments for North Carolina, Hogun was ordered home to aid in raising and recruiting the men. Assigned command of the first regiment to be raised, in August 1778 he marched his command into Washington's camp at White Plains, N.Y. In November, perhaps because they were poorly armed, his men were ordered to West Point to work on the fortifications.

Major General Benedict Arnold, commandant of Philadelphia, requested Washington to send him a regiment or two of Continentals to guard the stores and perform the housekeeping chores in that city. Possibly because Hogun's command was made up of men whose enlistments were short, it was selected for this task. His regiment left the Hudson around the middle of December and arrived in Philadelphia sometime before 19 Jan. 1779.

On 9 Jan. 1779, the Continental Congress voted on two brigadier generals for the North Carolina Line. The state delegates, as directed by the North Carolina legislature, voted for Thomas Clark and Jethro Sumner, but the Congress selected Sumner and Hogun. Hogun, it was said, was chosen over Clark because he was senior in rank and had behaved well in the Battle of Germantown. But Thomas Burke, a delegate from North Carolina, had worked behind the scenes to frustrate Clark's appointment.

On 19 Mar. 1779, Hogun succeeded Benedict Arnold as commandant of Philadelphia. He served in that post until 22 November, when he was ordered to march the North Carolina brigade to the relief of Charles Town, S.C. He became a prisoner of war when Major General Benjamin Lincoln surrendered to the British on 12 May 1780, and was sent to prison camp on Haddrel's Point. The British offered to parole Hogun to some other community, but he declined, declaring that he wished to share the hardships of confinement with the men of his brigade. He feared that in his absence enemy recruiting officers might succeed in enlisting North Carolina prisoners of war for service in the West Indies. Hogun attempted to maintain a military atmosphere among his men, but his health began to fail during the winter of 1780. He died on Haddrel's Point.

James Hogun, who was relatively obscure in the years prior to the outbreak of the Revolution, rose rapidly in military affairs once the shooting war began, perhaps because of his role in North Carolina Whig politics. He was more of a competent and reliable officer than a spectacular soldier. He did his job in a quiet fashion, but he did it well.

SEE: Walter Clark, ed., *State Records of North Carolina*, vols. 11–15 (1895–98); Hugh F. Rankin, *The North Carolina Continentals* (1971); William L. Saunders, ed., *Colonial Records of North Carolina*, vols. 9, 10 (1890).

HUGH F. RANKIN

Hoke, John Franklin (*30 May 1820–27 Oct. 1888*), lawyer, legislator, and Confederate officer, was born in Lincolnton of German parentage. His father was Colonel John Hoke, who arrived with his family in Lincolnton from Pennsylvania at the end of the eighteenth century. A merchant in Lincolnton, together with James Bivens and Michael Schenck he built the first southern cotton factory. He married Barbara Quickle in January 1808 and raised a distinguished family, including John Franklin Hoke, the subject of this sketch, and Michael Hoke, also a prominent lawyer, Democratic nominee for governor of North Carolina in 1844, and father of Robert F. Hoke, a major general in the Confederate Army.

John F. Hoke was graduated from Pleasant Retreat Academy in Lincoln County and in 1841 from The University of North Carolina. He studied law with former governor David L. Swain and Judge Richmond M. Pearson, later chief justice of the North Carolina Supreme Court. After receiving his license in 1843, Hoke began

practicing law in Lincolnton, a career he pursued for the remainder of his life.

He began his military career in March 1847, when he was commissioned a first lieutenant and assigned to Company G in the Twelfth Regiment of U.S. Infantry. Promoted to captain in June, he saw action in Mexico during the Mexican War. After his company was mustered out in June 1848, he returned to North Carolina to resume his law practice. He soon became active in politics, serving in the 1850, 1852, and 1854 sessions of the North Carolina Senate as a states' rights Democrat. As a member of the House of Commons in 1860, Hoke argued for the right of secession in a resolution in which he declared that "the people of North Carolina has the right to withdraw from the Union whenever a majority of them . . . assembled should decide that withdrawal is necessary for one of two reasons, viz., to protect their property or person from unconstitutional and oppressive legislation by the general government, or when the general government fails to fulfill its constitutional obligations."

During the same year, Hoke was appointed adjutant general of North Carolina and in that capacity, in May and June 1861, organized and sent to Virginia fourteen regiments. On 10 July, he was commissioned a colonel in the Twenty-third Regiment of North Carolina Infantry (also known as the Thirteenth Regiment of North Carolina Volunteers). Because of transportation problems, his regiment arrived too late to fight at the first Battle of Manassas, but Hoke saw action in the Peninsula campaign. In 1862 his regiment was reorganized and he failed to be appointed as a colonel. Therefore, he, along with the other officers who were not selected, left to seek new positions. Not finding a suitable appointment, he returned to Lincolnton and was elected to the state senate in 1863. In the fall of 1864 he was commissioned a colonel of the Fourth Regiment of North Carolina Reserves, a senior reserve unit composed of men between the ages of forty-five and fifty assigned to guard prisoners, protect bridges, and arrest deserters. Serving in this capacity until the end of the war, Hoke came into contact with Union troops only once when a brief skirmish took place as the Union Army tried to gain the release of some prisoners.

After the war, Hoke was elected a representative to the House of Commons from Lincoln County in 1865 as a Conservative. Although he remained an active Democrat for the rest of his life, he sought no other political office. Instead, he became a prominent lawyer in Lincoln and the surrounding counties. The *Shelby New Era* called him "one of the most distinguished members of the bar of Western North Carolina." He also engaged in business pursuits—he owned a gold mine and sawmills, and was active in railroad promotion—and he served as a trustee of The University of North Carolina from 1874 to 1879. An active Episcopalian although his parents had belonged to the German Reformed church, Hoke was a vestryman in his parish for many years.

On 30 Oct. 1850 he married Catherine Alexander, the daughter of William Julius Alexander of Charlotte and granddaughter of Joseph Wilson. She died on 23 Dec. 1857 and Hoke never remarried. They had three children: William A., also a Democratic legislator and lawyer who served as a judge on North Carolina's Superior Court and as chief justice of the North Carolina Supreme Court; Sallie Hoke Badger; and Nancy Hoke Childs.

Hoke died suddenly while viewing a political parade from the front porch of his home in Lincolnton. He was buried in the churchyard of St. Luke's Episcopal Church in his hometown. A portrait of Hoke is in the second volume of Walter Clark's *Histories of the Several Regiments and Battalions from North Carolina in The Great War 1861–'65.*

SEE: J. H. Boykin, *North Carolina in 1861* (1961); Walter Clark, ed., *Histories of the Several Regiments and Battalions from North Carolina in The Great War 1861–'65*, vols. 2, 3 (1901); J. Dowd, *Sketches of Prominent Living North Carolinians* (1888); William A. Hoke Papers (Southern Historical Collection, University of North Carolina Library, Chapel Hill); Miscellaneous Papers (North Carolina Collection, University of North Carolina Library, Chapel Hill); J. Nichols, *Directory for the General Assembly* (1860); A. Nixon, "History of Lincoln County," *North Carolina Booklet* (January 1910); W. L. Sherrill, *Annals of Lincoln County, North Carolina* (1937); Van Noppen Papers (Manuscript Department, Duke University Library, Durham); John H. Wheeler, *Reminiscences and Memoirs of North Carolina and Eminent North Carolinians* (1884).

ROBERTA SUE ALEXANDER

Hoke, Michael *(2 May 1810–9 Sept. 1844),* lawyer, politician, and public figure, was the second of eight children born to John and Barbara Quickle Hoke in Lincoln County. The Hoke ancestors had come from the Alsace district of France in the early eighteenth century and settled in the Lincoln County area. By the time of Michael's birth, the family was already well known across the state; his father then was associated with Michael Schenck in the manufacture of cotton textiles in the South.

Hoke was first educated in the schools of his native county. In 1827 he was enrolled at Captain Alden Partridge's school at Middletown. Among Hoke's contemporaries who attended the school were Thomas and Paul Cameron, Thomas Bragg, and George Little. Hoke left the institution in 1829 and began his legal studies with Judge St. George Tucker of Virginia. He later received instruction from Judge Robert H. Burton, of Lincoln County, whose daughter he would eventually marry.

In time, Hoke became a brilliant lawyer and a conspicuous figure in public life. He represented Lincoln County in the House of Commons in the 1834, 1835, 1836, 1838, and 1840 sessions, serving on the committees on education, privileges and elections, and rules of order, as well as other special committees. From 1838 until his death, he was a trustee of The University of North Carolina.

In 1844 the Democrats nominated Hoke for governor of North Carolina against the highly celebrated Whig candidate, William A. Graham. The two men were intimate friends, born in the same county, and at the height of their careers. Both were highly respected across the state, regardless of political lines. During the campaign the Whigs called their opponents "Locofocos," but did not feel they could apply this title to Hoke, whom they considered to be unlike most leaders of the Democratic party. Although the Democrats were defeated in the election, Hoke's campaign dealt the first serious blow to Whig supremacy in North Carolina.

After the election Hoke resumed his legal practice. A few weeks later, he was taken ill at a court session in Mecklenburg County and died in Charlotte at age thirty-four. The cause of death was attributed to a fever (probably malaria) contracted during the summer while he was campaigning in the eastern counties. His death was mourned by the entire state, and his remains were interred at Lincolnton.

Hoke was survived by his wife, Frances Burton Hoke, and six children including Mary Brent, who married Hildreth H. Smith, onetime professor at The University of North Carolina; Robert Frederick, the noted Confederate general; and George, a physician.

SEE: Daniel L. Grant, *Alumni History of the University of North Carolina, 1795–1924* (1924); J. G. de R. Hamilton, ed., *The Papers of William Alexander Graham*, vol. 4 (1961); John H. Wheeler, *Reminiscences and Memoirs of North Carolina and Eminent North Carolinians* (1884); *Who Was Who in America*, vol. 1 (1943).

CLAUDE H. SNOW, JR.

Hoke, Michael *(28 Sept. 1874–24 Sept. 1944),* pioneer orthopedic surgeon, was born in Lincolnton, the second surviving son of Major General Robert Frederick Hoke, of the Confederate Army, and Lydia Ann Van Wyck Hoke. He was named for his paternal grandfather, who died in 1841 after a strenuous campaign for the governorship of North Carolina. His maternal uncle, Robert Van Wyck, was the first mayor of metropolitan New York City. During his infancy the family moved to Raleigh, where he received his early education. At age fifteen, Hoke entered The University of North Carolina. At Chapel Hill he was an outstanding student, athlete, and captain of the football team; he was graduated in 1893 with a B.S. degree in electrical engineering and entered medical school the next fall. Hoke received an M.D. degree from the University of Virginia in 1895. His internship and residency were at the Johns Hopkins Hospital, where Sir William Osler was chief of medicine and William S. Halsted was chief of surgery.

Influenced by his father, Hoke began the practice of general surgery in Atlanta in 1897. After three years he left to spend a year in Boston under Dr. Joel E. Goldthwait, the first orthopedic surgeon in America. Hoke returned to Atlanta to specialize in orthopedic surgery, being the first to practice this specialty in Georgia as well as one of the few pioneers in orthopedics in the nation.

On 20 Apr. 1904 he married Laurie H. Harrison of Atlanta. They had two daughters: Mrs. Charles McGee of Atlanta and Mrs. Edward Jastrum of Rehoboth, Mass.

Hoke's chief interest was in the crippled child, and for years he gave his services without pay. Operations were performed at the Wesley Memorial Hospital, which later became the Emory University Hospital. The cost of the children's hospitalization was defrayed by a group of women who sold pencils on their behalf. The long convalescence and treatment required special quarters, so two cottages were rented in Decatur. A clinic was then opened for the local poor. From this beginning the Scottish Rite Hospital for Crippled Children was established and rapidly expanded; its permanent quarters were occupied in 1919. Thereafter the Shriners took over the project, and their work led to a chain of hospitals for crippled children throughout America. Hoke was among the first to serve on the advisory board for these hospitals.

The flail foot that often resulted from poliomyelitis had been treated for years by sacrificing the heel bone. Because of his mechanical training and innovative mind, Hoke was able to devise an operation that stabilized the foot by causing complete union of the three major bones of the foot. This and other tested operations were given the name "the Hoke operations" by his peers.

As Hoke's reputation grew, many orthopedists traveled to Atlanta to observe his work on limbs incapacitated by disease or from birth. He was credited with an improved treatment for curvature of the spine, well-leg traction for fracture of the thigh, and numerous procedures for deformity.

In 1932, the year he was awarded an honorary LL.B. by The University of North Carolina, Hoke was persuaded by Franklin D. Roosevelt to become surgeon-in-chief at the Warm Springs Foundation. Moving to Warm Springs, Hoke and his wife occupied the Little White House except when the president was visiting. By 1935 he considered his work there finished and returned to private practice in Atlanta. The same year ill health forced him to retire, although he maintained his interest in the Alfred E. Dupont Hospital for Crippled Children, in Wilmington, Del., where he had received an appointment years before.

Upon retirement, Hoke and his wife moved to a restored antebellum home in Beaufort, S.C., where he remained until his death. He was buried in the Hoke family plot in Raleigh.

SEE: *Atlanta Journal*, 28 Sept. 1944; Hoke family records (in possession of the family); J. H. Kite, *Clinical Orthopedics* 14 (1959); A. R. Shans, Jr., *AOA News* (September 1974); W. L. Sherrill, *Annals of Lincoln County, North Carolina* (1937).

ALEXANDER WEBB, JR.

Hoke, Robert Frederick (27 May 1837–3 July 1912), Confederate officer and industrialist, was born in Lincolnton, the son of Michael and Frances Burton Hoke. His father, a lawyer, was the Democratic candidate for governor in 1844. Young Hoke attended school in Lincolnton and was graduated from the Kentucky Military Institute in 1854. Afterwards he returned home to help his widowed mother manage the various family business interests, including a cotton mill and iron works.

Hoke entered the Confederate Army as a second lieutenant of the First North Carolina Volunteers. At Big Bethel, on 10 June 1861, D. H. Hill commended him for his "coolness, judgement and efficiency." By September Hoke had attained the rank of major. He was subsequently transferred to the Twenty-third North Carolina and promoted to lieutenant colonel. Following the Battle of New Bern on 14 Mar. 1862, Hoke assumed temporary command of the Thirty-third Regiment, its colonel, C. M. Avery, having been captured at New Bern. Hoke led the regiment at Hanover Court House, the Seven Days before Richmond, Second Manassas, and Sharpsburg. When Avery returned to the Thirty-third, Hoke became commander of the Twenty-first North Carolina, Trimble's Brigade, Jubal Early's division. At Fredericksburg in December 1862, Hoke earned the praise of both Early and "Stonewall" Jackson for his part in repulsing the Union attack on the Confederate right. Shortly after this battle he was promoted to brigadier general and given command of Trimble's Brigade. During the Chancellorsville campaign, Hoke, serving with Early at Fredericksburg, was severely wounded. At the time of Gettysburg he was still recovering, but in the fall of 1863 he was sent to the central counties of his native state to quell outlawry and armed deserters.

Early 1864 found him in the eastern part of North Carolina serving under General George E. Pickett. Fol-

lowing an unsuccessful attack on New Bern, Pickett was recalled to Virginia and Hoke assumed command of the forces in eastern North Carolina. For his capture of Plymouth and its 3,000-man Union garrison, in which he was aided by the ram *Albemarle*, Hoke was elevated to major general. The date of his commission and that of the battle, 20 Apr. 1864, were the same. General Robert E. Lee wrote President Jefferson Davis that he was pleased to learn of Hoke's promotion, "though sorry to lose him, unless he can be sent to me with a division."

After Plymouth Hoke returned to Virginia and assisted General Pierre G. T. Beauregard at Drewry's Bluff and General Lee at Cold Harbor. From the Petersburg trenches in December 1864, Hoke's men were ordered to North Carolina to help with the defense of Fort Fisher and Wilmington. The fort capitulated on 15 Jan. 1865 and the city on 22 February. Hoke's division next faced the Union Army on 8 March at Southwest Creek near Kinston, and on 19–21 March at Bentonville west of Goldsboro. Hoke remained with Joseph E. Johnston, his superior at Bentonville, until the surrender of the Confederate forces to General William T. Sherman at Bennett's Farm House near Durham. In his farewell address to his men, Hoke reminded them that they were "paroled prisoners not slaves." He urged them to cherish "the Love of Liberty," to transmit it to their children, and to "teach them the proudest day in all your proud career was that on which you enlisted as Southern soldiers."

After the war Hoke was engaged in various business enterprises. Among his principal interests were gold and iron mining, insurance, and railroads. For many years he served as a director of the North Carolina Railroad Company. He was an Episcopalian and a Democrat.

On 7 Jan. 1869 he married Lydia Van Wyck, by whom he had six children. Hoke died at age seventy-five and was buried in Raleigh. Hoke County is named for him.

SEE: Samuel A. Ashe, ed., *Biographical History of North Carolina*, vol. 1 (1905); Walter Clark, ed., *Histories of the Several Regiments and Battalions from North Carolina in the Great War, 1861–1865* (1901); C. A. Evans, ed., *Confederate Military History* (1899); *The War of the Rebellion: A Compilation of the Official Records of the Union and Confederate Armies* (1880–1901).

JOHN G. BARRETT

Hoke, William Alexander (25 Oct. 1851–13 Sept. 1925), lawyer, legislator, and North Carolina chief justice, was born in Lincolnton of German and Scotch-Irish ancestry, the only son among the three children of John Franklin and Catherine Wilson Alexander Hoke. Alexander County was named for his maternal grandfather, William Julius Alexander. His father, a veteran of the Mexican War, was appointed adjutant general of North Carolina by Governor John W. Ellis in 1861 and later, as colonel, commanded the Thirteenth and, subsequently, Twenty-third North Carolina regiments of the Confederate Army.

Educated at the Lincolnton Male Academy, young Hoke grew to manhood during the years of the Civil War and Reconstruction. Having studied law under Chief Justice Richmond M. Pearson at Richmond Hill, he was admitted to the bar on 25 Oct. 1872. After practicing for eight years in Shelby, he returned to Lincolnton and formed a law partnership with his father, which continued until the latter's death in 1888. In 1889 he represented Lincoln County in the state legislature.

Elected to the bench in 1890, Judge Hoke served in the Superior Court until 1904, when he was elected an associate justice of the North Carolina Supreme Court. Reelected in 1912 and 1920, he was appointed chief justice on 2 June 1924, succeeding the late Walter Clark. He was elected to the same post in November, but resigned on 16 Mar. 1925 because of ill health, assuming the status of an emergency judge until his death. His remains were taken from Raleigh to Lincolnton and buried in the graveyard of St. Luke's Episcopal Church. He had been a lifelong member of the Episcopal church.

Familiarly known as "Alex," Hoke, a staunch Democrat, was "in his day the most beloved North Carolinian," according to Archibald Henderson. Walter P. Stacy, his friend and colleague on the high court, described Hoke as a "superb lawyer," "splendid judge," and "noble spirit," standing "second to none in their [the people's] esteem and affection." Stacy further remarked: "His striking appearance and military bearing at once arrested attention and commanded respect. He was one of North Carolina's truly great men; great in mind and heart; great in character and achievement; great in breadth and quality of his sympathies."

The judicial opinions of Justice Hoke appear in fifty-three volumes of the Supreme Court Reports (#137–#189, inclusive) and deal with a wide range of subjects. In particular, several Supreme Court decisions prepared by Hoke show his mastery of the law of real property. In *Hicks v. Manufacturing Co.* (138 N.C.), one of the outstanding cases to come before the court during his tenure, Hoke wrote the decision that settled questions of assumption of risk and contributory negligence as affected by the negligence of a master or employer. He also wrote significant decisions concerning other matters of civil law, such as contracts, wills, conveyances, notes, and various suits in equity. His opinions in criminal cases reflected the right of every citizen to a fair and impartial trial.

Hoke apparently regarded the high point of his life to have been his role as chairman of the commission to provide a suitable statue of his friend, Governor and later Senator Zebulon Baird Vance, for the Hall of Fame in the capitol in Washington, D.C., where he delivered the address of presentation on 22 June 1916. Hoke was awarded the honorary doctor of laws degree by The University of North Carolina in 1909 and by Davidson College. From 4 July 1902 until his death he belonged to the Society of the Cincinnati, as a direct descendant of Lieutenant William Lee Alexander (Fourth North Carolina Continental Infantry), for whom, together with his maternal grandfather, Colonel William Julius Alexander, he presumably was named.

On 16 Dec. 1897 Hoke married Mary McBee of Lincolnton, who predeceased him. Their only child, Mary, survived both parents and later married Edward Slaughter of Charlottesville, Va.

SEE: Archibald Henderson, *North Carolina: The Old North State and the New*, vol. 2 (1941); A. Nixon, "History of Lincoln County," *North Carolina Booklet*, vol. 2 (January 1910); W. L. Sherrill, *Annals of Lincoln County, North Carolina* (1937); Walter P. Stacy, *William Alexander Hoke* (1926).

WALSER H. ALLEN, JR.

Holden, Joseph William (30 Sept. 1844–21 Jan. 1875), poet, newspaperman, and state political leader, was born in Raleigh, the son of William Woods and Ann Augusta Young Holden. He attended the Lovejoy School in Raleigh and later the military academy in

Charlotte conducted by Daniel H. Hill. With the outbreak of the Civil War, he enlisted as a private in the state troops before his seventeenth birthday and was stationed on Roanoke Island. Holden distinguished himself for gallantry in service but was captured by the Union forces and confined as a prisoner of war for a year. After his parole, he returned to his home in Raleigh.

In 1862–63 Holden attended The University of North Carolina, but a strong desire to return to military service caused him to give up his formal education; however, he was persuaded by his father to work for the *North Carolina Standard*, having previously gained newspaper experience working during summer vacations. He continued in this capacity, as well as participating in his father's political campaigns, until 1868.

In 1868 Holden won a seat in the General Assembly as a Republican from Wake County, and, through the influence of his father, who was then governor, was elected speaker of the house. He presided over the chamber with grace and, given his youth, displayed a surprising knowledge of parliamentary law. In March 1870 he resigned the speakership to assume editorial control of the *Standard*, then under the financial control of N. Page & Co., after an unsuccessful bid for the U.S. Congress.

After Governor Holden's impeachment and removal from office in 1871, Joseph left the state and attempted to make a new career for himself, first in Washington, D.C., and then in Leavenworth, Kans., where he worked for the *Times*, a newspaper edited by the brother of Susan B. Anthony. He was immediately promoted to the post of managing editor, but ill health forced him to leave the paper after a tenure of only eighteen months.

Returning to Raleigh, Holden was elected mayor in 1874. Through his temperate and judicious actions in office, he reestablished and maintained the affection of his fellow citizens—having had the reputation of a warm, friendly, but hot-tempered personality. He died before completing his term. In the last months of his life, he wrote occasional newspaper stories and even began a novel.

It was through his pen, and especially his poetry, that Holden was most remembered. He began writing verse as a young boy, often publishing it in the *North Carolina Standard*. Among his best poems are "Love's Melancholy," "Hymn," "A Home Above," and "Hatteras." The latter (original manuscript now owned by Salem College) was written when he first saw the whitecaps of Cape Hatteras while on board ship as a prisoner of war. Described by Walter Hines Page as the "best in sentiment and tone written in the South," "Hatteras" was included in Henry Wadsworth Longfellow's collection of writings published under the title *Poems of Places*. Had his life and times been different, the young poet might have achieved national recognition. Certainly he was greatly respected and admired by another of North Carolina's famous writers, John H. Bonner.

Holden, who never married, died in his father's house and was buried in Oakwood Cemetery, Raleigh. He was known for his lovable spirit, discriminating mind, fertile and poetic imagination, cultivated taste, and courteous and generous manners.

SEE: Samuel A. Ashe, ed., *Biographical History of North Carolina*, vol. 6 (1907); Daniel L. Grant, *Alumni History of the University of North Carolina, 1795–1924* (1924); J. G. de R. Hamilton, *Reconstruction in North Carolina* (1914); Horace W. Raper, "William W. Holden: A Political Biography" (Ph.D. diss., University of North Carolina, 1951); "Studies in North Carolina Poems," *North Carolina Education* (September 1911).

HORACE W. RAPER

Holden (Holding), Robert *(fl. 1671–1709)*, Council member, secretary, customs collector, receiver general, and escheator, was identified in January 1678/79 as a "Merchant Lately belonging to Virginia and now bound for the County of Albemarle in the Province of Carolina." Holden was then in London, where he would soon receive commissions for several offices in Albemarle.

Although his known association with the northern Carolina colony began in 1679, he may have lived in Albemarle briefly about 1671. In a letter dated 5 Sept. 1671, the Lords Proprietors directed Albemarle officials to grant Holden a certain tract of land that he wanted unless another had prior right. They also directed the officials to permit Holden to explore Indian territory and trade with the Indians for the purpose of discovering a land route between Albemarle and the South Carolina colony on Ashley River. Holden, who was then in London, was given the letter and other papers to bring to Albemarle. Presumably he delivered the documents after 11 Dec. 1671, when he was in Virginia en route to Albemarle. It is not known whether he then lived in the Carolina colony, as his request for a particular plot of land suggests, or whether he remained there after delivering the papers from London. If so, his stay was temporary, for he was living in Virginia in 1676 and apparently had done so for some time.

In the Virginia disturbance of 1676 known as Bacon's Rebellion, Holden was one of "the most eminent Rebels." Subsequently he was called to testify before a commission sent by the Crown to investigate the governor's handling of the uprising. The Virginia Assembly, in granting a general pardon to participants in the rebellion, in February 1676/77, excepted Holden and other "great offenders" from the pardon. By an act "inflicting pains and penalties" on those excluded from pardon, the assembly fined Holden 5,000 pounds of tobacco and ordered his imprisonment until he gave security for payment of the fine and for his future good behavior. No doubt his leaving Virginia was prompted by his situation after the rebellion. Within two years after the order for his arrest, he was in London arranging for his appointment to offices in Albemarle.

The Albemarle positions that Holden obtained were lucrative and carried substantial pay. His governmental posts included that of customs collector, conferred by Crown officials, and the offices of Council member, secretary, receiver general, and escheator, conferred by the Proprietors. In addition, the Proprietors commissioned him to receive on their behalf all wrecks, ambergris, and other "ejections of the sea" to which they were entitled by their charter. All of those posts provided remuneration, either in the form of fees or as a percentage of the funds handled. Moreover, the Proprietors themselves now commissioned Holden to explore Indian territory and to command all military forces involved in the venture. That authorization afforded him opportunity to engage in the extremely profitable trade with the piedmont and mountain Indians.

In early June 1679 Holden arrived in Boston, where he remained about two weeks before proceeding to Albemarle. From Boston he sent to customs officials in London an account of fraudulent practices of New England traders in Albemarle tobacco and other common violations of English trade laws. Although he professed to have obtained such information for the benefit of the Crown, later events would show that knowledge of the mechanics of fraud in the colonial trade could be useful in promoting his own interests.

Holden reached Albemarle in mid-June, bringing commissions and instructions for John Harvey, whom the Proprietors had appointed acting governor, and for other Council members, as well as his own commissions. By November the new government had been organized and, as his commissions provided, Holden was taking a prominent role in it. His power was further strengthened at the end of the year by Harvey's death and the appointment by the Council of an acting governor to fill the vacancy. Holden now had the prestige of being the only important official who had been directly appointed by the Proprietors. Moreover, the recently chosen acting governor, the aged John Jenkins, owed his position in part to Holden.

Despite the opportunities for legitimate financial gain afforded by his various offices, Holden lost little time in putting to use the information he had obtained on fraudulent practices in the colonial trade. Soon after his arrival he challenged the authority of his fellow customs official, Timothy Biggs, who held a commission as surveyor of customs from Crown officials. Claiming that he, as collector of customs, had sole authority to enforce trade laws, Holden undertook to prevent Biggs from performing his assigned duties. Those duties included the inspection of vessels entering Albemarle, in order to discover and seize any articles imported unlawfully, and, when the vessel was ready to depart, the issuance of clearance papers certifying compliance with customs and other laws. Holden in effect nullified Biggs's authority by ordering shipmasters not to permit Biggs or his assistants to board their vessels and by having the assistants arrested and held in prison without bail when they attempted to perform their duties despite his orders. Meanwhile, Holden appears to have used the power of inspecting and clearing vessels, properly belonging to Biggs, as a weapon held over the heads of shipmasters. By some such means he forced shipmasters to take on board rotten and trashy tobacco for shipment as customs collections, at financial loss to themselves, and to turn a blind eye on other questionable actions, such as placing Holden's mark on tobacco collected as customs duties and having it shipped and sold for his own benefit.

Biggs protested Holden's obstructionist activities, both to Albemarle officials and to the London customs office, but without avail. Holden's ascendancy over the Albemarle government was such that in March 1680 the Council, sitting as the General Court, suspended Biggs's commission and authorized Holden to officiate in his stead. London officials ignored the protests until July 1681, when they replaced Holden as customs collector.

By the summer of 1681, however, the Albemarle colonists had delivered themselves from Holden's domination. At some date in the winter or spring Holden was arrested and placed in the custody of the marshal, probably on order of the Council or the Assembly. The particular charges are not known, but there is evidence of many that could have been the basis for his arrest. According to an extant collection of twenty depositions by prominent colonists, Holden had committed numerous crimes. Among his alleged offenses were the arbitrary valuation of tobacco, in which customs duties usually were paid, so that the duties amounted to two pounds of tobacco for each pound shipped; forcing, by threats and other means, the lading of rotten and trashy tobacco despite the fact that shipmasters could not collect freight charges on its delivery and the crews involved could not collect wages; mismarking tobacco collected as customs and having it shipped on his own account; public expression of contempt for the acting governor and other officials; illegal alteration of the text of an act of the Assembly left in his custody; appropriation of ammunition placed in his custody for the public defense; the issuance of illegal orders for the arrest of colonists, holding them in prison without bail, and subjecting them to abuse; and intimidating a grand jury and securing indictments by threats, without presenting any evidence against the accused except his own word.

It is not known whether Holden was brought to trial. The existing depositions appear on their face to have been testimony presented in such a trial, and the text of some indicates that they were so presented. In others, however, internal evidence suggests that the depositions may have been assembled as evidence to be sent to London to justify whatever action the colony had taken. It is likely that a formal trial was not needed to persuade Holden to leave Albemarle, which he did, either voluntarily or under sentence of banishment. The date of his departure, like the circumstances, is uncertain. He is not named as a Council member in extant documents after March 1680/81.

Little is known about Holden after he left Albemarle, although he appears to have taken to seafaring as master of a small trading vessel. Despite his record in Albemarle, he continued to have influence with the Carolina Proprietors, or at least some of them. In 1707 he sought appointment as governor of the Bahama Islands, which were owned by six of the eight Proprietors of Carolina. He stated that he sought that appointment in order to benefit from the commission earlier given him to handle wrecks, ambergris, and other "ejections of the sea" for the Proprietors. On 20 May 1707 the Proprietors of the Bahamas requested the Board of Trade and Plantations to approve the appointment of Holden as governor. During the board's consideration of the request, indirect inquiries concerning Holden were made of John Archdale, whose Proprietorship in Carolina did not include an interest in the Bahamas. The board was informed that Archdale had said that he knew Holden well in Albemarle and that he "related a very slender carrector" of Holden and indicated that Holden was "no wayes quallified for the meanest Post in the Government." Although at one stage the board appears to have been inclined to approve the appointment, its final action is not known. Whatever the fate of the appointment, Holden appears not to have officiated as governor of the Bahamas.

Holden's contacts with the Proprietors continued at least until 1709. In July of that year he attended a meeting of the Proprietary Board and was given certain papers "to Peruse." The nature of his business on that occasion is not given in extant records. No later reference to Holden has been found except a statement in records of the Council of Trade and Plantations, dated 25 July 1720, reporting that he did not go as governor to the Bahamas. Whether he was then alive was not indicated.

Available sources shed no light on Holden's marital status or other personal affairs.

SEE: J. R. B. Hathaway, ed., *North Carolina Historical and Genealogical Register*, 3 vols. (1900–1903); William Waller Hening, ed., *Statutes at Large; being a Collection of . . .*

Laws of Virginia . . . (1823); Mattie Erma E. Parker, ed., *North Carolina Higher Court Records, 1670–1696* (1968); William S. Powell, ed., *Yᵉ Countie of Albemarle in Carolina* (1958); W. Noel Sainsbury, ed., *Calendar of State Papers, Colonial Series, America and West Indies*, vols. for 1677–81, 1706–8, 1720–21; William L. Saunders, ed., *Colonial Records of North Carolina*, vol. 1 (1886); *Virginia Magazine of History and Biography*, vol. 6 (October 1898). Manuscript sources in North Carolina State Archives, Raleigh: Albemarle Book of Warrants and Surveys, 1680–1706; Council Minutes, Wills, Inventories, 1677–1701, particularly a letter of John Nixon, attorney, to Holden, 18 Jan. 1678/9; Papers on Holden in collections of photocopies of documents in the Public Record Office, London, catalogued by North Carolina Archives as "English Records" and "British Records."

MATTIE ERMA E. PARKER

Holden, William Woods *(24 Nov. 1818–2 Nov. 1892),* printer, editor, politician, governor, and the most controversial state figure during Reconstruction, was born near Hillsborough, the son of Thomas Holden and Priscilla Woods, who were never married; he was reared after his sixth birthday by his stepmother, Sally Nichols Holden. His grandfather, who was English, first settled in Massachusetts but later moved to Orange County, N.C., to engage in farming. At age ten, Holden was apprenticed as a printer's devil to Dennis Heartt, editor of the *Hillsborough Recorder*, who was responsible for his early education and political views. Striking out on his own at age sixteen, he first worked as a printer for the *Milton Chronicle*, then for a Danville, Va., paper (in which his own compositions were first published), and later, in 1836, for the Raleigh *Star* which was edited by Thomas Lemay.

Despite the lack of formal education, Holden studied law at night under Henry Watkins Miller of Raleigh and received his license to practice on 1 Jan. 1841. Although he could have played a major role in city politics and civic affairs, the legal profession did not offer the fascination of newspaper work. Thus, when the *North Carolina Standard*, the official organ of the Democratic party in North Carolina, was made available in 1842, Holden purchased control. Through it he became the state's most militant champion of minorities, reform, and state ideals. He served as publisher and editor of the *Standard* until elected governor in 1868.

As editor, Holden had a brilliant record, and his editorial influence was unsurpassed in the state. By building upon such issues as equal suffrage, internal improvements for all sections, universal education, and improved labor conditions in an industrial economy, he became the tactical leader of the Democratic party. By the 1850s he had made it the dominant and most popular party in the state. (Later, he was mainly responsible for similar success by the Conservative [1862] and Republican [1868] parties.) Throughout life his major goal was reform, especially to alleviate human wants and human misery, and, if the state leaders were unwilling to work for it, he was ready to lead the political fight himself.

In 1844, when elected to the House of Commons, Holden immediately sponsored legislation calling for the creation of a deaf and dumb institution in Raleigh. Later he served as state printer; a member of the Literary Board and the board of trustees of The University of North Carolina; and commissioner of the deaf and dumb institution and of the insane asylum. In 1858 the Democratic state convention in Charlotte rejected his bid for the governorship because of his humble origins and vigorous support for the "common folk," as well as the fear by members of the state's aristocracy (especially those from the east) that they could not control him. In the same year, he failed to win election to the U.S. Senate. No doubt these rejections caused him ultimately to break away from the Democratic party and to completely change the direction of the state during the Civil War and Reconstruction eras.

While Democratic spokesman for North Carolina, Holden played an active role in national issues and in the party. Throughout the 1840s and 1850s he advocated Southern rights to expand slavery and at times championed the right of secession, but by 1860 he had shifted his position to support the Union. Thus, at both the Charleston and Baltimore Democratic National conventions, he worked diligently to keep the state from bolting the party and leaving the Union, prophesying that should secession occur a long and devastating war would result. In early 1861 he led the forces that defeated the proposed state secession convention, but when the fighting began he joined with leaders from the other political factions at the second convention in voting for secession.

During the Civil War, Holden waged a continuous battle for individual liberty, helped to secure the nomination and election of Zebulon B. Vance for governor in 1862, and by 1864 was the avowed leader of the state's "peace movement." Recognizing the futility of the war, he declared that it was far better to make an honorable peace while still possible rather than being forced to accept unconditional surrender. Moreover, he thought the time had come to overthrow the agrarian aristocratic rule and, based on the rising tide of industrialism, to create a progressive state for the welfare of the masses rather than continue the existing order for the privileged few. For such views Holden was denounced as a traitor. In September 1863, the *Standard* office was attacked by Georgia troops and his personal papers and type were destroyed. Nevertheless, he continued to publish the *Standard* until suspension of the writ of habeas corpus took away the freedom of the press. As a matter of principle, Holden opposed and was defeated by Governor Vance in 1864 on the peace issue. (He had accepted the nomination only after he could not persuade any other prominent politician to enter the race.)

In May 1865 President Andrew Johnson summoned state Union leaders to Washington, D.C., to discuss North Carolina's reentry into the Union, and from that meeting came the decision to appoint Holden provisional governor of the state, in which capacity he served from 29 May to 28 Dec. 1865. In this office he exerted leadership in the reorganization of state, county, and local governments, making more than 3,000 nonpartisan appointments in an effort to unify the state; supervised the taking of amnesty oaths; revised the state constitution to meet national demands and restore federal authority; and worked towards the state's economic recovery. Despite these efforts, he was again denied the governorship in late 1865, when he was defeated by Jonathan Worth. As compensation, he was offered a seat in the U.S. Senate, but declined in order to resume the editorship of the *Standard*. Later, President Johnson offered him the post of minister to San Salvador, which he chose not to pursue in view of potential confirmation difficulties.

During this period Holden continued to help restore North Carolina to the Union. In 1866, sensing the waning strength of the president to control the Northern Radicals and realizing that it would be disastrous for

the state to resist congressional rule, he began to work with the new political forces. He was instrumental in organizing the Republican party in the state, and in the winter of 1866–67 he spent much time in Washington working with the radical leaders. In 1868 Holden headed the Republican ticket in the state elections and was elected governor by a vote of 92,325 to 73,594, defeating Thomas Samuel Ashe. He carried with him six of the seven congressmen, all executive and judicial officials except one judge and one solicitor, and both houses of the state legislature. When Governor Worth refused to recognize the Republican victory or to vacate his post before his term expired, Holden assumed the governorship through the direct interdiction of General Edward Canby and the Reconstruction laws.

Holden faced enormous challenges during his administration: reorganization of local and state governments, reestablishment of public schools open to all children, penal reform and the construction of a state penitentiary, development of a deteriorating economy by encouraging northern migration of labor and capital, expansion of railroads and other internal improvements, and obtaining equal justice for all persons. The last issue caused the greatest concern, as many North Carolinians were unwilling to extend full civil rights and suffrage to the Negro. Thus, as elsewhere in the South, the Ku Klux Klan was organized to restore whites to local and state offices. Holden attempted to maintain law and order by suppressing the Klan, although the state was unable to convict known offenders; by encouraging prominent men to take active roles in preventing depredations; and by securing from President Ulysses S. Grant and federal authorities the military aid to maintain peace.

In March 1870, when civil authority weakened in Caswell and Alamance counties, Holden declared them to be in a state of insurrection as authorized by the Shoffner Militia Act. Troops were organized, first under the command of William J. Clarke but soon transferred to George W. Kirk, who had made a reputation for himself as a terrorist during his Union raids in the western part of the state. Holden originally had appointed W. W. Robbins of Marshall, who declined in order to keep a federal job and in turn recommended Kirk. The troops made many arrests in the two counties, ignoring the writ of habeas corpus and causing much fear and alienation. Later, Holden ordered the arrest of Josiah Turner, Jr., editor of the Raleigh *Sentinel* and "King of the Ku Klux" for his avowed opposition to Republican rule.

Holden hoped to have the Klan prisoners tried by state military commissions, an action initially endorsed by Chief Justice Richmond M. Pearson. However, on 6 Aug. 1870 Judge George W. Brooks, U.S. district judge at Salisbury, issued a writ of habeas corpus that they should be tried in a federal court for possible violation of their constitutional rights. Thus began a series of legal maneuvers culminating in the dismissal of the state troops and any effort to control the Klan, as well as the demise of Governor Holden.

On 9 Dec. 1870 Frederick W. Strudwick of Orange County, a former Klan leader, introduced in the state house of representatives a resolution calling for Holden's impeachment for high crimes and misdemeanors. The resolution was adopted on 14 December. Five days later, the house approved eight articles of impeachment against Holden: the first two alleged that he had illegally declared Alamance and Caswell counties in insurrection; the third and fourth concerned the "unlawful" arrest of Josiah Turner, Jr., and others without benefit of trial; the fifth and sixth accused the governor of disobeying the writ of habeas corpus; and the last two charged him with the unlawful recruitment of troops and their illegal payment from the state treasury.

When the state senate was notified of the charges on 20 December, Holden immediately turned over the duties of his office to Tod R. Caldwell. His trial began on 23 Jan. 1871. On 9 February the house voted a ninth indictment, charging Holden with conspiring with George W. Swepson to defraud the state in connection with railroad bonds. This article was never presented to the senate, nor mentioned in the press, for fear of implicating Conservative leaders who were active in the Holden trial. No legitimate claim could ever be made that Holden was personally dishonest or that he had used his office for personal gain. The defense based its arguments on the fact that the violent activities of the Klan required stringent enforcement regulation, that the governor was authorized under state law to use such force, and that any maltreatment of prisoners was done contrary to orders. After a highly partisan trial, the senate—on 22 March—rendered a guilty verdict on the last six charges (the minor ones insofar as constitutional rights were concerned), and ordered that Holden be removed from his post and denied the right to hold office again in the state.

The verdict came as no surprise to Holden, who was in Washington at the time. He expected assistance from his Republican friends, and two possibilities were extended: diplomatic service or the editorship of a newspaper that the Republican National Committee proposed to establish in the nation's capital. Holden declined a ministerial post in Peru or the Argentine Confederation, and the proposed newspaper never materialized. Forced to find employment on his own, in September 1871 he assumed the political editorship of the Washington *Daily Chronicle*. Despite his success in greatly expanding the paper's circulation, Holden soon longed to return to his native state. The opportunity was offered and accepted in February 1872, when he was appointed to the postmastership in Raleigh, a position he retained until 1883.

Although many efforts were made to remove his political disabilities, Holden refused to participate, insisting that such movement must come voluntarily from the people of the state and without political friction. Until 1889 he participated in local affairs, acting as unofficial head of the state Republican party (until he could no longer support the national policies of high tariffs, pro-business, and nonsupport for the South), writing for the Raleigh and Charlotte newspapers, composing poetry, taking part in church functions, and lecturing. His address, "History of Journalism in North Carolina," delivered before the press association on 21 June 1881 in Winston, came to be considered one of the masterpieces of the state's journalistic history.

Retirement emphasized Holden's outstanding personal traits—kindness, charity, warm hospitality, fearlessness, close family ties, and constant interest in the welfare of the common folk. He also enjoyed his two-story frame colonial residence that he had built in 1852 on the corner of Hargett and McDowell streets. He had chosen to live at home during his two terms as governor rather than occupying the executive mansion. It was considered one of the finest homes in Raleigh, had one of the first bathtubs in the city, and was noted for its sunken garden. He spent much time there among the blooming flowers, boxwoods, and a weeping elm which was the only one of its kind in Raleigh. After suffering a stroke in 1889, Holden lived quietly until his death. He was buried in the Holden family plot in Oakwood Cemetery, Raleigh.

Holden was married twice. His first wife was Ann Augusta Young (19 Feb. 1819–20 June 1852), whom he married in 1841; she was the daughter of John Wynne Young, a native of Baltimore, Md., and Nancy Peace, and the niece of William Peace, founder of Peace Institute. After her death he married, in 1854, Louisa Virginia Harrison, the daughter of Robert Harrison, a prosperous Raleigh citizen. His children included Laura (Mrs. W. P. Olds), Joseph William (1844–75), Ida Augusta (Mrs. Calvin J. Cowles), Henrietta (Mrs. Fritz Mahler), Mary Eldridge (Mrs. Claude A. Sherwood), Beulah (Mrs. Walter R. Henry), Charles C., and Lula (Mrs. F. T. Ward).

SEE: Samuel A. Ashe, ed., *Biographical History of North Carolina*, vol. 3 (1906); *DAB* (1932); Edgar E. Folk, "W. W. Holden and the Election of 1858," *North Carolina Historical Review* 21 (October 1944), and "W. W. Holden and the North Carolina Standard, 1843–1848," *North Carolina Historical Review* 19 (January 1942); J. G. de R. Hamilton, *Reconstruction in North Carolina* (1914); William W. Holden, *Memoirs*, ed. by W. K. Boyd (1911); Horace W. Raper, "William W. Holden and the Peace Movement in North Carolina, *North Carolina Historical Review* 31 (October 1954), "William W. Holden: A Political Biography" (Ph.D. diss., University of North Carolina, 1951), and *William Woods Holden, North Carolina's Political Enigma* (1985); John H. Wheeler, *Reminiscences and Memoirs of North Carolina and Eminent North Carolinians* (1884); A. A. Wilkerson, "Caswell County and the Kirk-Holden War," *Durham Sun*, 14 July 1946.

HORACE W. RAPER

Holderness, George Allen (*15 June 1867–23 Dec. 1947*), businessman, farmer, banker, and state senator, was born in Caswell County near Milton, the son of Sarah Foreman and William H. Holderness. In his youth he was a traveling salesman, operating out of both Baltimore and Philadelphia, and covering especially the towns along the Tar River where he became a popular drummer. He lived in Snow Hill for a few years before moving in 1893 to Tarboro, where he spent most of his life.

In the fall of 1894, Holderness and several others raised $2,500 to establish the Tarboro Telephone Company. In October 1895, an exchange with a capacity of 50 lines was opened in an upstairs office in the 400 block of Main Street; it had 30 subscribers. From this modest start, exchanges were established in other towns, and in 1900 the Carolina Telephone and Telegraph Company was incorporated. Holderness was elected secretary-treasurer and general manager, and in 1926, president. He served as chairman of the board from 1938 to 1944. During the half century of his leadership, the company became a ten-million-dollar corporation with 96 exchanges virtually covering eastern North Carolina. Under his son, Haywood Dail, who was with the company for thirty-eight years, Carolina Telephone and Telegraph would earn hundreds of millions of dollars.

Holderness served on the directorate of countless business concerns in North Carolina and adjoining states. He was one of the organizers of Jefferson Standard Life Insurance Company, of which his son Howard was president. For a few years Holderness lived in Richmond, Va., where he became president of the Virginia-Carolina Chemical Company. A prominent banker, he participated in the founding and became president of the First National and the Farmers Banking and Trust Co., both in Tarboro, and he served on the board of directors of the First and Merchants Bank of Richmond.

Applying his business acumen to farming, Holderness for many years progressively and successfully operated over 2,000 acres in Edgecombe County. His Panola and Cotton Valley farms served as examples for others in the use of silage and tile drainage. He pioneered locally in extensive dairying and raising beef cattle in addition to the normal crops of his day.

An active Democrat, Holderness was elected to the state senate in 1916 and 1918. During his tenure he served as chairman of the powerful appropriations committee.

On 29 Nov. 1899 he married Harriet Howard of Tarboro. In addition to their sons Howard and Dail, they were the parents of George Allen, rear admiral in the U.S. Navy; William Henry, Greensboro attorney; Thomas Thurston, Greensboro financier; Anna Stamps (Mrs. William Munford Transom) of Greensboro; and Harriet (Mrs. Lee Ferguson Davis) of Richmond. In addition to achieving success in their chosen fields, as well as in the area of public service, each of their five sons and two daughters—and their spouses—were active in church and civic affairs.

Harriet Howard Holderness was a lifelong member and supporter of Howard Memorial Presbyterian Church in Tarboro. Both she and her husband were buried in Greenwood Cemetery. There is a portrait of George Holderness in the headquarters of the Carolina Telephone and Telegraph Co. in Tarboro.

SEE: Henry C. Bridgers, *The Story of Banking in Tarboro* (1969); *Carolina Telephone and Telegraph Company—History—Officers—Directors—Statistics* (1972); Greenville *Kings Weekly*, Tarboro *The Southerner*, Washington *Weekly Progress*, various dates; Marvin E. Holderness, Sr., *History and Genealogy of the Holderness Family* (1958); *North Carolina Biography*, vol. 4 (1919).

H. C. BRIDGERS, JR.

Holderness, William Henry (1 July 1904–20 July 1965), attorney and philanthropist, was born in Tarboro, the son of George Allen and Harriet Howard Holderness. His father, a businessman, served two terms in the state senate (1917–20) where he was chairman of the appropriations committee; in 1896, with M. H. Powell, he organized North Carolina's first telephone company, which later merged with three other firms to become the Carolina Telephone and Telegraph Company. His brother, Howard (b. 2 Nov. 1902), was for many years president and chairman of the board of the Jefferson Standard Life Insurance Company. Another brother, Haywood Dail (b. 30 July 1909), served as president (1957–73) and chairman of the board (1973–74) of Carolina Telephone and Telegraph.

"Willie" Holderness, as he was familiarly known, attended Tarboro High School and Augusta Military Academy in Fort Defiance, Va., and was graduated from The University of North Carolina in 1924. While at Chapel Hill, he became a member of Phi Beta Kappa and Delta Kappa Epsilon fraternities. After his graduation from the Harvard Law School in 1927, he entered practice in Greensboro in association with A. L. Brooks. For many years he was a partner in the firm of Brooks, McLendon, Brim, and Holderness (later McLendon,

Brim, Holderness, and Brooks). He also served as a director of Carolina Telephone and Telegraph.

A Democrat, Holderness was appointed to the Guilford County Alcoholic Beverage Control Board in 1955 and served as chairman from 1959 until his death. As an active member of the North Carolina Association of Alcoholic Beverage Control Boards, he played a major role in determining the state's liquor policies. Much of his private life was devoted to promoting charities, particularly the United Fund (he was twice president of Greensboro's Fund drive), the state Children's Home Society, and the Boy Scouts of America.

A bridge player of professional caliber, Holderness regularly participated in state and national tournaments. In addition, he was a longtime president of the Greensboro Country Club.

He was married twice: first to Martha Jane Broadhurst of Greensboro and later to Brent Blackmer Woodson of Salisbury. He was survived by his six children: two daughters, Jane Howard (Mrs. Robert H. Carrington) of Oyster Bay, N.Y., and Brent Blackmer; and four sons, William Henry, Jr., Charles Woodson, Hays Ragland, and Thomas Pearson.

Holderness died in Wilmington of pneumonia induced by serious injuries in a boating accident, and was buried with Presbyterian services in Forest Lawn Cemetery, Greensboro. His will provided a generous bequest to The University of North Carolina Law School, which was used to endow the Holderness Moot Court Competition, named in his honor.

SEE: *Chapel Hill Weekly*, 6 July 1966; *Greensboro Daily News*, 21 July 1965; Hugh T. Lefler, *History of North Carolina*, vol. 3 (1956); Raleigh *News and Observer*, 21 July 1965.

BENNETT L. STEELMAN

Holding, Robert Powell (31 Dec. 1896–26 Aug. 1957), banker, was born in Wake Forest, one of seven children of Minta Royall and Thomas Elford Holding. He attended the local public schools, then entered Wake Forest College in the fall of 1912. After receiving a B.A. degree in 1916, he immediately enrolled in the Wake Forest Law School from which he was graduated in 1917. Holding passed the North Carolina Supreme Court examination for a license six months before he was of age to practice law. He took a position as bookkeeper-teller in the Bank of Morehead City and in less than a year was assistant cashier.

In January 1918, Holding joined the First National Bank of Smithfield as assistant cashier and bookkeeper-teller. The bank was an outgrowth of the Bank of Smithfield, begun in 1898 with a paid-in capital of $10,000. In 1916 First National purchased the Smithfield Savings Bank and in 1919, when Holding was appointed cashier, its total resources amounted to $500,000. In 1921 the bank merged with Citizens National Bank and became the First and Citizens National Bank. Holding, who by age thirty had established himself as a hardworking, farseeing, and aggressive leader, was elected president of this growing firm in 1926. Adopting a state charter in 1929, the bank changed its name for the last time to First-Citizens Bank & Trust Company. During the ensuing depression years a great many banks failed, but not First-Citizens. From 1929 to 1934 First-Citizens, under Holding's leadership, opened banks in fifteen towns throughout eastern North Carolina.

In 1932 Holding was made president of the Regional Agricultural Credit Corporation, established that year by the federal government to serve the two Carolinas, Georgia, and Florida. With all the millions of dollars loaned by the corporation, 99.9 percent of the principal and interest was collected. During the depression, he also was a financial adviser to President Franklin D. Roosevelt. In 1934 the board of First-Citizens elected Holding president and chairman, positions he held until his death. By 1938, when a wrecked national economy had spawned a rash of defunct banks across the country, First-Citizens had paid its eightieth consecutive semiannual dividend.

Under Holding's direction, the First-Citizens Bank & Trust Company continued to grow and prosper, adding four more offices in the 1940s and additional branches in communities already served. By the end of 1949, the bank's total resources amounted to more than $132 million. It was the first bank in the state to establish an installment loan or time payment department. At the time of Holding's death, the bank was operating in 32 communities through 45 separate offices with resources totaling more than $200 million.

Notwithstanding his countless hours at the bank, Holding found time for public service. In 1939, he was appointed to the newly created State Banking Commission by Governor Clyde R. Hoey, and served until his death. As president of the North Carolina Bankers Association during 1942–43, Holding began an illustrious career of service to numerous professional organizations, including a period on the executive committee of the American Bankers Association. He was one of the original members of the North Carolina Securities Advisory Commission and became widely recognized in the national bond market as a securities expert. Holding personally handled the investment portfolio of First-Citizens.

He also was president of Seashore Transportation Company and a director of State Capital Life Insurance Company, Carolina Telephone and Telegraph Company, and Textron, Inc. He served on the board of trustees of Wake Forest College, which in 1957 awarded him the honorary doctor of laws degree, and of Campbell College. In addition to his work in the Baptist church and the Kiwanis Club, Holding was a generous yet unassuming philanthropist, making countless contributions to individuals and educational institutions.

On 11 Jan. 1922 he married Maggie Brown of Bethel. They had three sons: Robert Powell, Jr., Lewis Royall, and Frank Brown.

SEE: "Biographical Material, Robert Powell Holding" (Clipping file, North Carolina Collection, University of North Carolina Library, Chapel Hill); *North Carolina Biography*, vol. 3 (1956); Raleigh *News and Observer*, 27 Aug. 1957, 19 Jan. 1960; *Who's Who in the South and Southwest* (1950, 1952); *Who Was Who in America*, vol. 3 (1960).

ALEX G. MACFADYEN, JR.

Holladay, Alexander Quarles *(8 May 1839–13 Mar. 1909)*, educator, was born in Spottsylvania County, Va., the son of Alexander Richmond and Patsy Quarles Poindexter Holladay. He grew up in an area where his ancestors had lived for five generations. His father was for several years a member of the Virginia General Assembly and served two terms in the U.S. House of Representatives (1849–53). His great-grandfather, Lewis

Holladay, was commissioned a lieutenant of militia in 1775 and participated in a number of campaigns during the Revolutionary War.

Young Holladay received his preparatory education in the schools of Richmond and in 1857 entered the University of Virginia, where he studied languages, philosophy, and law. In 1859 he went abroad to travel and pursue special studies at the University of Berlin. With the outbreak of the Civil War in the spring of 1861, Holladay returned to Virginia where he volunteered as a private in the state militia. One month later, on 25 May 1861, he was commissioned a second lieutenant in the Nineteenth Virginia Infantry. He participated in many early battles of the war before he was stricken with typhoid fever. Although his recovery was slow, Holladay eventually returned to active service. At one time during the war he served on the staff of General Braxton Bragg. He was paroled at Greensboro in April 1865.

After the war, Holladay studied law under his father in Richmond; in 1870, they formed the law firm of Holladay and Holladay. The same year he was elected to the Virginia senate, serving two terms (1871–75). After his father's death in 1877, Holladay gave up the practice of law and entered the field of education. He taught in the Richmond schools until 1881, when he was elected principal of Stonewall Jackson Institute at Abingdon, Va. In 1884, Holladay was appointed head of the Department of English Literature at Florida Agricultural College, Lake City (forerunner of the University of Florida). He was named president of the college in 1885 and served in that capacity until 1888. He remained in Lake City one more year as professor of English.

In the summer of 1889, Holladay applied for the professorship of English in the new North Carolina College of Agriculture and Mechanic Arts (now North Carolina State University). On 30 Aug. 1889, the board of trustees unanimously elected him president. When the college opened on 3 October, the main building had just been completed. It housed all college activities during the academic year 1889–90. The workshop, kitchen, dining hall, storeroom, and gymnasium were in the basement; offices, classrooms, and the library were on the first floor; and the second and third floors served as dormitories. The building was later named Holladay Hall in honor of its first president.

During Holladay's ten-year tenure as president, eleven buildings were constructed, including five dormitories, engineering and agricultural buildings, and an infirmary. When he resigned in June 1899, the college had already abandoned many of the manual labor and trade school features of its early years and was developing into a professional institution for the training of agricultural leaders and civil, mechanical, chemical, and electrical engineers. Under Holladay's leadership, the college had justified the faith of its advocates by proving its worth to the state.

On 17 Apr. 1861, six days before enlisting in the Virginia state militia, Holladay married Virginia Randolph Bolling, the daughter of Thomas Bolling of Bolling Island in the upper James River. They had five children: William Waller, Alexander Randolph, Charles Bolling, Mary Stewart (Mrs. Peyton Harrison Hogue), and Julia Cabell (Mrs. James M. Pickell). Charles Bolling Holladay was a member of the first graduating class (1893) of the North Carolina College of Agriculture and Mechanic Arts.

Holladay received an honorary doctor of laws degree

from Davidson College in 1895. After his departure from Raleigh in 1899, he spent some time in Delaware and New York. He then purchased a farm in Nelson County, Va., where he resided until failing health compelled him to live with a daughter in Raleigh. He died there and was buried in Oakwood Cemetery.

SEE: Alexander Quarles Holladay Papers (Archives, North Carolina State University, Raleigh); David A. Lockmiller, *History of the North Carolina State College, 1889–1939*; Office of Information Services, "Faculty and Staff News Releases and Clippings, Alexander Q. Holladay" (Archives, North Carolina State University, Raleigh); *The Twentieth Century Biographical Dictionary of Notable Americans*, vol. 5 (1904); *Who Was Who in America*, vol. 3 (1951–60).

MAURICE S. TOLER

Holland, Annie Wealthy *(1871–6 Jan. 1934)*, educator, was born in Isle of Wight County, Va., on a plot of land contiguous to the Wealthy plantation, where her grandmother had been a slave. She was the daughter of John Daughtry and Margaret Hill, a surname she received at her baptism a year before her marriage. Mrs. Holland was named after Annie Wealthy, mistress of the Wealthy plantation.

At age sixteen, Annie completed her studies at the Isle of Wight county school. Afterwards her grandfather, Friday Daughtry, sent her to Hampton Institute, but his health failed and she never earned a diploma. She worked in New York City for a year as a nurse and later as a dressmaker, then returned home and earned a certificate to teach the second grade. In 1888 she married Willis B. Holland, an 1884 graduate of Hampton Institute who also became a teacher.

The records of Mrs. Holland's early career are sparse. In 1897, after teaching for nine years, she became assistant to her husband, then a school principal. In 1899, by choice, she left to teach in a rural school ten miles from her home, but returned to succeed her husband as principal in 1905. Around 1911 Mrs. Holland became a teaching supervisor in North Carolina for the Jeanes Fund, a private trust founded to promote rural Negro education. She served first in Gates County, N.C., then in Chesapeake and Reynoldson counties, Va.

In 1915 Mrs. Holland became the Jeanes Fund's state demonstration agent for North Carolina, which effectively made her the state supervisor of Negro elementary schools. This position was funded by the Jeanes Fund and the North Carolina Colored Teachers Association until it was incorporated into the state educational organization in 1921. Mrs. Holland's post was not administrative, but rather involved constant travel to all North Carolina counties to conduct meetings, organize fund drives, and teach demonstration classes in every subject from reading to nutrition and sewing. Her itinerary for the month of April 1917, documented in a letter from State Supervisor N. C. Newbold, required her to visit 21 counties in 35 days, with 10 of those days in the vicinity of her home in Franklin, Va. Newbold further advised her to omit a stop if she found her schedule so tight that she had to travel at night.

Mrs. Holland is best known as the founder of the first Negro parent-teacher association in North Carolina, which held its first meeting at Shaw University on 14 Apr. 1928. Her husband, Willis, died in Franklin, Va., in 1925. She died nine years later, during a speaking engagement, and was buried in Franklin. In 1938, on the tenth anniversary of the founding of the North Carolina Congress of Colored Parents and Teachers, the exercises of the annual meeting included the planting of a tree at Shaw University in Mrs. Holland's memory.

SEE: N. C. Newbold, ed., *Five North Carolina Negro Educators* (1939 [photograph]); Records of the Jeanes Fund and of the State Division of Negro Education (North Carolina State Archives, Raleigh).

SARAH R. SHABER

Holland, James *(1754–19 May 1823)*, Revolutionary officer, legislator, and congressman, was born in either Pennsylvania or present-day Anson County, N.C., to which his parents moved about the time of his birth. He was the son of Mary Harrison and William Holland, an English immigrant. Although apprenticed to a carpenter at age fifteen, Holland acquired an adequate education, read law, and developed a successful business as a contractor. At twenty-three he became sheriff of Tryon County, N.C., and served until July 1778.

During the Revolutionary War, he held a commission as second lieutenant in Colonel Francis Locke's regiment of North Carolina militia, seeing action at Ramsour's Mill, Cowpens, and Guilford Court House. In 1782 he became superintending commissioner of specific supplies in the District of Morgan. Promoted to the rank of first major of the Morganton District militia in 1787, he used the title "major" until his death.

Following the creation of Rutherford County in 1779, Holland was named county commissioner and trustee, and he constructed the county courthouse on his property at Gilberttown. He entered the state senate in 1783 and returned in 1797. Between his two terms in the senate, he served in the house in 1786 and 1789. In the General Assembly he won attention for his ability in finance and for his judgment and impartiality on numerous committees of inquiry.

As a delegate to the second constitutional convention in 1789, Holland favored ratification of the federal constitution. The same year he was appointed to the North Carolina Council of State as well as becoming one of the original members of the board of trustees of The University of North Carolina, a post he held until 1795.

In 1794, Holland announced his candidacy for Congress and handily defeated his opponent, Colonel Joseph McDowell. His first term (March 1795–March 1797) was marked by his energetic, determined opposition to the Jay Treaty and his open hostility to enlargement of the U.S. Navy. Declining to stand for election to the Fifth Congress, Holland instead expanded his law practice into Buncombe County and reentered the North Carolina Senate. He ran for election to Congress again in 1798, but in the Federalist sweep lost to Joseph Dickson. In 1800, however, he won an easy victory and would continue to win with comfortable margins until he declined to seek reelection in 1810.

An orthodox Jeffersonian Republican, Holland followed the party line with few deviations. He led the Republican resistance to the military establishment until the shocking events of 1807 (the Aaron Burr conspiracy occurred, the British stopped American ships, and Congress passed a nonimportation act) and the contagiousness of Henry Clay's leadership led to a reversal of sentiment. Even in 1810, Holland advocated a large militia force, preferring that as a natural American institution to a standing army.

He stoutly defended the embargo that halted U.S. trade with foreign nations, displaying a sectional bias against New England commerce. Always a partisan for agriculture and free land, he also advocated on numerous occasions a balanced economy through the encouragement of domestic manufacturing. He early promoted the direct election of the president and vice-president, and proposed that violation of the nonimportation of slaves agreement be considered a capital offense. A defender of General James Wilkinson, he maintained an embarrassed quiet during the Aaron Burr and Salmon P. Chase impeachment discussions.

In 1811, Holland followed his sons who had preceded him to a new home on the Duck River in middle Tennessee. There he became a large, wealthy landowner and participated in local affairs, serving as justice of the peace from 1812 to 1818. "Big Jim" Holland stood for election to Congress once more in 1822, but he lacked the popularity in Tennessee he had enjoyed in North Carolina and was defeated. He died and was buried at his home in Maury County, Tenn.

In January 1780 Holland married Sarah Gilbert, the daughter of a conspicuous Rutherford County citizen, William Gilbert. Children surviving him were Cynthia (Mrs. Tyree Rodes and later Mrs. Peter R. Booker of Pulaski, Tenn.), Sophia Salina (Mrs. Harden Perkins of Tuscaloosa, Ala.), and James, Jr. (married Winifred Sanford, daughter of Tennessee Congressman James Turner Sanford), who lived in Maury County.

SEE: *Annals of Congress*; Walter Clark, ed., *State Records of North Carolina*, vols. 18, 19, 20 (1900, 1901, 1902); S. S. L. P. Cochrane, "Memorabilia of Her Family" (Tennessee Archives); C. W. Griffin, *Old Tryon and Rutherford Counties* (1977); Haywood Papers (Southern Historical Collection, University of North Carolina Library, Chapel Hill); Nashville *American*, 11 Oct. 1896; H. H. Newton, *Rutherford County, North Carolina, Abstracts of Minutes*; Pulaski *Citizen*, 2 Dec. 1897; Tennessee Land Grants (Tennessee Archives); Wills of Rutherford County (North Carolina State Archives, Raleigh).

N. C. HUGHES, JR.

Holloman, George Vernon (*17 Sept. 1902–19 Mar. 1946*), inventor and Army Air Corps officer, who from 1931 to 1945 pioneered in aeronautical engineering research and development, was born in Rich Square, the son of George Lycurgus and Hulda Eggleston Holloman. He attended local schools and was graduated from high school just as the first radio receiving set arrived in Rich Square. Fascinated by the new device, Holloman promptly enrolled in a course at Southern Radio College in Norfolk, Va. He then was employed by and sent to Europe and Asia as a representative of the American Marconi Company (later Radio Corporation of America). He gradually accumulated funds that enabled him to earn an electrical engineering degree with honors at North Carolina State College. As an ROTC student, he was commissioned a second lieutenant in the infantry and spent two years at Fort Benning, Ga., as regimental communications officer and adjutant of the Special Weapons Battalion of regimental headquarters.

In 1927 Holloman was transferred to the Army Air Corps, sent to Brooks Field, San Antonio, Tex., for flight training, and was graduated with wings in June 1928. His first assignment as an Air Corps pilot was at Post Field, Fort Sill, Okla., where he and four other young officers were charged with reactivating the old Eighty-eighth Observation Squadron. The Eighty-eighth

had had a brilliant World War I record but had been demobilized in 1922. Holloman served as engineering officer of the squadron until it joined a Composite Air Force Group under Major Lewis H. Brereton.

From February to May 1934, Holloman was detailed to the U.S. Air Mail responsibilities of the Army Air Corps and flew the night mail circuit between Pittsburgh and Newark. Later, as control officer of the western end of the Eastern Air Mail zone, he was stationed at Chicago on temporary detached service from a permanent post of duty with the Army Air Corps Materiel Division at Wright Field. He spent the summer of 1934 at the Air Corps Technical School at Chanute Field, Ill., for advanced study in communications. For the remainder of the year and much of 1935, he attended the Air Corps Engineering School at Wright Field to take advanced training in aeronautical engineering.

Upon completion of the advanced communications program at Chanute Field, Holloman was made assistant director of the Instrument and Navigation Laboratories at Wright Field. Eventually eleven in number, the laboratories conducted research and development of various types of aircraft instrument navigation equipment such as automatic pilots, instrument landing systems, and automatic flight and landing equipment to serve by night as well as by day or in foul or fair weather. By August 1937, the completely automatic landing of an airplane was accomplished for the first time, with George Holloman and R. K. Stout as passenger-observers. A series of such automatic landings that month demonstrated the reliability of the invention. A growing stream of exciting, imaginative engineering achievements came from the laboratories, adding strength and flexibility as well as range and reliability to aircraft operations, and helping to lay the foundations for the powerful American air fleets of World War II and postwar air transport development.

In April 1941, war conditions in the world and apprehensions of U.S. involvement led to the formation at Wright Field of a new group of laboratories known collectively as the Special Weapons Unit. Colonel Holloman was placed in charge of the unit and served in that post until World War II approached its end in Europe in the spring of 1945. (Having been commissioned second lieutenant in June 1925, Holloman was promoted to first lieutenant in July 1931, to captain in August 1935, to major in November 1940, to lieutenant colonel in December 1941, and to colonel in April 1942.) In March 1945 he transferred from the Wright Field Laboratories to take a then secret assignment in the Pacific Theater of war.

On 19 Mar. 1946 a B-17 bomber, piloted by Major General James E. Parker, commanding general of the Twentieth U.S. Air Force, crashed into a mountain on the island of Formosa while on a flight from Shanghai, China, to Manila in the Philippine Islands. The general and nine other Army Air Force personnel aboard the plane were killed. Colonel Holloman was among them. Holloman Air Force Base, New Mexico, was named for him.

Holloman was married in 1932 at Kenilworth, Ill., to Dorothy Darling, a niece of John Motley Morehead of North Carolina and Rye, N.Y. Their only child, George V., Jr., was born in Chicago in 1934.

SEE: George A. Holloman, *The Hollyman Family* (1952)); Holloman family record collection (Charles R. Holloman, Raleigh); *New York Times*, 22 Mar. 1946; North Carolina State College, *Alumni Magazine*, May 1942; Raleigh *News and Observer*, 22 July 1938, 10 May

1942, 15 Mar. 1944, 1 Apr. 1945; *Saturday Evening Post*, 25 Mar. 1944.

CHARLES R. HOLLOMAN

Holman, Clarence Hugh (*24 Feb. 1914–13 Oct. 1981*), educator and writer, was born in Cross Anchor, S.C., the son of David Marion and Jessie Pearl Davis Holman. He received his early schooling in Gaffney and Clinton, S.C., before entering Presbyterian College, from which he was graduated magna cum laude with a B.S. degree in chemistry in 1936. From 1936 to 1939 he was director of public relations for the college, and from 1939 to 1941 director of its radio programs, receiving meanwhile an A.B. degree in English cum laude in 1939. In 1939, he studied radio programming at New York University. From 1939 to 1942 he was on the faculty of Presbyterian College, and in 1945 became its academic dean after serving as state publicity director for the Council for National Defense (1942–44) and as academic coordinator and instructor in physics for the U.S. Army Air Force (1943–45). As an avocation during these busy years, he—admittedly "a life-long and devoted reader of detective stories"—published a series of popular mystery novels: *Death like Thunder* (1942), *Trout in the Milk* (1946), *Up This Crooked Way* (1946), *Another Man's Poison* (1947), and, as "Clarence Hunt," *Small Town Corpse* (1951).

But Holman was at heart an educator. In 1946, he entered The University of North Carolina as a graduate student and instructor in English, receiving his doctorate in 1949 with a dissertation on "William Gilmore Simms's Theory and Practice of Historical Fiction"; the same year he was elected to Phi Beta Kappa. From this time, his rise in the university was rapid. Within a decade he was appointed assistant professor (1949), associate professor (1951), professor (1956), and Kenan Professor (1959). In 1954 he served as an assistant dean and from 1955 to 1957 as acting dean of the College of Arts and Sciences. From 1957 to 1962 he was chairman of the Department of English, also serving as a member (1957–73) and chairman (1961–73) of the Board of Governors of the University Press and as chairman (1959–62) of the Division of Humanities. From 1963 to 1966 he was dean of the graduate school, from 1966 to 1968 provost, and from 1972 to 1978 a special assistant to the chancellor, organizing and compiling a self-study survey of the university at Chapel Hill.

Holman was the recipient of a Simon Guggenheim Fellowship (1967), the Thomas Jefferson Award (1975), an award for excellence in writing from Winthrop College (1976), and the Oliver Max Gardner Award (1977). He was awarded a Litt.D. by Presbyterian College in 1963, and a L.H.D. for "dedicated classroom teaching" by Clemson University in 1968. In 1975 he became a member of the board of trustees of the Triangle Universities Center for Advanced Study, and in 1976 was named chairman of its executive committee. In the latter year he also became a member of the board of trustees, a member of the executive committee, and vice-president of the National Humanities Center in the Research Triangle Park, and in 1980 he was elected a fellow of the American Academy of Arts and Sciences. Holman was a deacon of the First Presbyterian Church in Clinton and an elder of the Trinity Avenue Presbyterian Church in Durham.

Known beyond his university for capacities as an administrator, Holman was chairman of the American Literature Section of the South Atlantic Modern Language Association (1953–54); chairman of the bibliographical committee (1957–61), member of the executive committee (1964–65), program chairman (1966, 1979), and chairman (1970) of the American Literature Section, and a member of the executive committee of the Twentieth-Century American Literature Group (1978–81) of the Modern Language Association of America; president of the Southeastern American Studies Association (1958–59); consultant in English to the U.S. Air Force Academy (1962); and president of the Virginia-North Carolina College English Association (1962–63). In 1957–60, he was on the editorial board of *College English*; in 1967, an advisory editor of the *Encyclopedia Americana*; in 1968, a founding editor (with Louis D. Rubin, Jr.) of the *Southern Literary Journal*; and, from 1970, a member of the editorial boards of *Essays on Literature* and *Resources for American Literary Study*, and an adviser on American literature for the *Encyclopedia of World Literature*.

Holman's principal concern and greatest skill was teaching. In the classroom he was rigorous and demanding, but also sympathetic, a friendly leader, and an experienced guide. Students who flocked to his lectures remember him as blunt, firm, and intense, but at the same time witty, lighthearted, and pleasingly informal. To them, he was a storehouse of knowledge and a fount of wisdom, both commodities freely shared. As one of his colleagues put it, "he will be best remembered for an exceptional presence, a sense of justice and proportion matched only by his wisdom, . . . a man of grace for whom knowledge seemed to come so easily that he parted with it gladly." On resigning from his administrative duties, Holman remarked, "I am returning to the work I have always considered my primary responsibility, teaching and research." He knew that these two went hand in hand, that what best fed teaching was a lively mind, constantly renewing itself through study.

As an inquiring scholar, Holman had as his major interest prose fiction, particularly fiction of the South, a subject on which he earned an international reputation for authoritative critical judgments. The author, coauthor, or editor of twenty-six books and some seventy professional articles, he is perhaps most remembered for *A Handbook to Literature*, with W. F. Thrall and Addison Hibbard (2nd ed., rev. and enl., 1960; 3rd ed., 1972; 4th ed., 1980); *Thomas Wolfe* (1960), which has been translated into six languages; *The Thomas Wolfe Reader* (1962); *Three Modes of Southern Fiction* (1966); *The Letters of Thomas Wolfe*, with Sue Fields Ross (1968); *Southern Fiction: Renaissance and Beyond*, with Louis D. Rubin, Jr., and Walter Sullivan (1969); *Southern Writing, 1585–1920*, with Richard Beale Davis and Louis D. Rubin, Jr. (1970); *Thomas Wolfe and the Glass of Time*, with Richard S. Kennedy and Richard Walser (1971); *The Roots of Southern Writing* (1972); *The Loneliness at the Core: Studies in Thomas Wolfe* (1975), winner of the Mayflower Society Award; *Southern Literary Study: Promise and Possibilities*, with Louis D. Rubin, Jr. (1975); *The Immoderate Past: The Southern Writer and History* (1977); and *Windows on the World: Essays on American Social Fiction* (1979).

In his last published essay, "American Literature: The State of the Art" (1980), Holman defined the kind of literary scholarship to which he had dedicated his life: "It sees and prizes the utility of accurate fact and data. It operates on the simple—perhaps naive—doctrine that all literary work is about something other than itself or the making of itself. Although its adherents embrace from time to time a variety of often conflicting critical stances, the tradition itself is critically eclectic. It seems to have a relatively simple—although by no means simplistic—view of reality and history, and it tends to subject literature to the customary American pragmatic tests."

On 1 Sept. 1938, Holman married Verna Virginia McCleod of Ocala, Fla. They were the parents of two children: Margaret McCleod Stroud (b. 1949) and David Marion (b. 1951). Holman was buried in the Chapel Hill Memorial Cemetery.

SEE: *American Literature* (November 1980, March 1982); *Chapel Hill Newspaper*, 14 Oct. 1981; *Chapel Hill Weekly*, 28 Apr., 29 May, 5 Oct. 1966; Durham *Herald*, 16 June 1965; Raleigh *News and Observer*, 26 May, 2 Oct. 1966, 15 Oct. 1981.

LEWIS LEARY

Holmes, Gabriel (*1769–26 Sept. 1829*), lawyer, governor, and congressman, was a native of Duplin (now Sampson) County. He attended Zion Parnassus Academy in Rowan County and for a time was a student at Harvard. Afterwards he studied law with John Louis Taylor in Raleigh, was admitted to the bar in 1790, and began to practice in Clinton. Holmes represented Sampson County in the House of Commons in 1793, 1794, and 1795, and served in the North Carolina Senate in 1797, 1801, 1812, and 1813. He was a trustee of The University of North Carolina from 1801 to 1804 and again from 1817 until his death. The General Assembly honored him eight times between 1810 and 1820 by appointments as a councilor of state.

In the General Assembly of 1820, Holmes was nominated as a candidate for governor but was defeated by Jesse Franklin. The following year, however, Franklin declined a second term and Holmes was elected over Hutchins G. Burton of Halifax, James Mebane of Orange, and Joseph H. Bryan of Bertie counties. He served as governor of North Carolina from 7 Dec. 1821 to 7 Dec. 1824. As chief executive, Holmes was committed to expanding the functions of state government and tried to persuade the Assembly to spend more on transportation facilities and education. He advocated the teaching of agricultural courses at the university, and during his administration the Board of Agriculture was established and money was appropriated for the promotion of agriculture and industry.

In the political caldron of the 1820–24 period, Holmes wavered between support of John Quincy Adams or John C. Calhoun. After Congressman Charles Hooks of the Wilmington District voted for William H. Crawford in the House vote of February 1825, Holmes successfully contested his seat and was sent to Washington. On Capitol Hill he was a messmate of U.S. Senator John Branch at Mrs. Dunn's establishment. Both of the former North Carolina governors were identified as friends of Vice-President Calhoun. While in Congress, Holmes served on the Select Committee on the Militia and for a time was chairman of the Committee on the Post Office. He was easily reelected in 1827 and narrowly defeated Edward B. Dudley in 1829. A few weeks after the 1829 election he died suddenly at his home near Clinton, and in a special election future governor Dudley was selected to replace him in Congress.

Holmes married Mary Hunter, the daughter of Theophilus Hunter, Revolutionary hero of Wake County. One of their sons, Theophilus Hunter Holmes, was a classmate of Robert E. Lee and a year behind Jefferson Davis at West Point; he became a lieutenant general in the Confederate Army. A state historical highway marker four miles north of Clinton indicates the former home of Governor Holmes.

SEE: Samuel A. Ashe, ed., *Biographical History of North Carolina*, vol. 3 (1906); *Biog. Dir. Am. Cong.* (1971); R. D. W. Connor, ed., *A Manual of North Carolina* (1913); B. G. Crabtree, *North Carolina Governors* (1958); P. M. Goldman and J. S. Young, *The United States Congressional Directory* (1973); A. R. Newsome, *Presidential Election of 1824 in North Carolina* (1939).

DANIEL M. MCFARLAND

Holmes, Joseph Austin (*23 Nov. 1859–13 July 1915*), geologist, mining engineer, and conservationist, was born in Laurens, S.C., of English and Scotch-Irish ancestry, a descendant of William Holmes (1592–1678) of Marshfield, Plymouth, Mass. His parents were Nancy Catherine Nickels and Zelotes Lee Holmes, a Presbyterian minister and teacher with a strong scientific interest. His uncle, Joseph E. Holmes, represented the American machinery exhibitors at the London Crystal Palace Exposition.

After receiving his early education at Laurens Academy and the Holmes Academy, Holmes worked his way through Cornell University, graduating in 1881 with a B.S. degree in agriculture. Appointed professor of geology and natural history at The University of North Carolina in 1881, he headed that department until 1891 and lectured there until 1903.

Exceptional knowledge of North Carolina's economy and resources earned Holmes an appointment as state geologist to head the new Geological Survey, created to study the state's resources and encourage economic development. He brought to this task the qualities that typified his life: ability, dedication, and energy. Sometimes working from 9:00 A.M. until 2:00 A.M., Holmes used the survey to greatly benefit the state's economy and to make North Carolina the premier state in southern conservation. Under his direction a systematic study of the state's resources began; the resulting knowledge and publicity of mineral, timber, fish, wildlife, and water resources led to important economic investment and development. Holmes aimed to conserve as well as develop, and much of the survey's work stimulated long-range planning and less wasteful practices. He initiated studies of reforestation and turpentining methods to better utilize and protect timber resources. Additional studies sought a similar goal for North Carolina's other resources. Though handicapped by limited funds, his efforts demonstrated the value of study and planning in resource protection and use. Among the first to urge that a federal forest reserve be established in the South Appalachians, Holmes supported the movement for establishing eastern forest reserves and facilitated passage of the Weeks Act by accumulating evidence of deforestation's adverse impact on the mountain slopes.

While residing in North Carolina Holmes became well known for his efforts to improve state roads, organizing and leading the North Carolina Good Roads Association. His advocacy of increased state funding and the use of county convicts on road work resulted in a large increase in the construction of macadam roads. He assisted similar efforts in other states and was adviser to the U.S. Department of Agriculture for southern roads.

In 1903 Holmes was appointed director of the department of mines and metallurgy at the St. Louis World's Fair. His success in this enterprise led to decorations by several foreign governments and his appointment to a congressionally authorized committee investigating the more efficient use of American fuels and structural materials. In 1905, he was placed in charge of the fuel investigations and resigned as North Carolina state geologist. Soon appointed chief of the technological branch of the U.S. Geological Survey, Holmes achieved its reorganization as the U.S. Bureau of Mines in 1910. President William Howard Taft appointed Holmes director of the new bureau although he was identified with those who opposed Secretary of the Interior Richard A. Ballinger.

At the federal level, Holmes concentrated on reducing waste in the use of mineral resources and on lowering the appalling accident rate in U.S. mines. Studies by him or under his direction resulted in great savings in the mining and metals industries, including improvements in radium extraction and coking coal. He is best known for his efforts to reduce mining accidents and to improve rescue and emergency procedures, adopting and making famous the slogan "Safety First" for the Bureau of Mines. He disproved the established theory that coal dust would not explode unless in the presence of gas, thus revealing the true hazard of coal dust to mine safety. He sponsored a national mine safety meeting in 1911 with beneficial results—the increased availability of trained rescue and first-aid personnel, and of modern safety and rescue devices such as oxygen breathing apparatus. He also traveled abroad on several occasions to study mining techniques and invited foreign experts to the United States to suggest improvements.

Well-liked and respected by his colleagues, Holmes was noted for unselfishness. He sometimes used his own money to complete projects in North Carolina and once reduced his salary to increase an assistant's. North Carolina State Geologist Joseph Hyde Pratt described him as "a splendid representative of the Southern Christian gentleman."

On 20 Oct. 1887, Holmes married Jane Isabella Sprunt of Wilmington, N.C. They had four children: Jean Dalziel, Joseph Austin, Jr., James Sprunt, and Margaret Catherine. A Presbyterian and a Democrat, Holmes was not politically active except in lobbying for state funding and for the creation of the Bureau of Mines. The author of seventy-five articles, he directed work described in many more publications by state and federal agencies.

Holmes belonged to the Geological Society of America (charter member); American Association for the Advancement of Science; American Institute of Mining Engineers; American Society for Testing Materials; American Society of Mechanical Engineers; Academy of Science, Washington, D.C., St. Louis, Raleigh; American Forestry Association; Sigma Xi and Tau Beta Pi fraternities; Elisha Mitchell Scientific Society, Chapel Hill (a founder); Cosmos Club, Washington, D.C.; St. Louis Club; and Engineer's Club, New York. He served on the National Conservation Commission, International Mining Commission, and Mining Legislation Commission of Illinois. Holmes was decorated by the governments of Germany, Belgium, Italy, and Japan, and received honorary doctorates from the University of Pittsburgh in science and The University of North Carolina in law.

Holmes died in Denver, Colo., of tuberculosis and was buried in Rock Creek Cemetery, Washington, D.C. His death was hastened by overwork, by site inspections of mine disasters, and by an arduous trip to investigate Alaska coal fields in 1913. After his death, the Joseph A. Holmes Chair of Safety and Efficiency Engineering was created at the Colorado School of Mines and the Joseph A. Holmes Safety Administration was formed by the Bureau of Mines.

SEE: W. W. Ashe, "Joseph Austin Holmes—An Appreciation," *American Forestry* (March 1916 [portrait]); Bureau of Mines Records (North Carolina State Archives, Raleigh); Cornell University alumni file; *Denver Post*, 13, 17 July 1915; *Evening Star* (Washington, D.C.), 13, 17 July 1915; Holmes biographical file (U.S. Bureau of Mines); Holmes's manuscripts (Southern Historical Collection, University of North Carolina Library, Chapel Hill); Information provided by Joseph Austin Holmes, Jr. (Lake Wales, Fla.–Black Mountain, N.C.); *New York Times*, 14 July 1915; Oliver H. Orr, Jr., *Charles Brantley Aycock* (1961); Gifford Pinchot, *Breaking New Ground* (1947); Joseph Hyde Pratt, "Memorial of Joseph Austin Holmes," *Bulletin of the Geological Society of America* (March 1916); John R. Ross, "Conservation and Economy: The North Carolina Geological Survey, 1891–1920," *Forest History* (January 1973).

FRANK BEDINGFIELD VINSON

Holmes, Moses L. (*6 Apr. 1817–7 Jan. 1889*), gold miner and merchant, was born on Big River near Flat Swamp in Rowan (now Davidson) County, the son of Jesse and Nancy Owen Holmes. His father owned a large farm and gristmill in the Flat Swamp vicinity. As a young man, Holmes worked for a country merchant, James Ellis, and learned the fundamentals of business. He apparently received no formal education either in business or mining, but as one biographer noted: "[Holmes] graduated at a higher school—the school of practical business. There are some men who, with the best college education, are without common sense, and who seem to learn nothing of men or business. There are others who, without any college education, seem to have a quick comprehension of men, and who, by habit of observing closely and storing up what they learn, acquire a large amount of useful knowledge. One of the latter is Mr. Holmes."

By 1846 Holmes and his younger brother Reuben had settled in Rowan County at Gold Hill, one of North Carolina's fastest growing mining communities. The Holmes brothers borrowed $500 from local merchants and established a small dry goods operation. Moses also became principal lessee in the Phillip Earnhardt mine, and both brothers began making small investments in other mining companies in the Gold Hill district and at the McColloch Mine in Guilford County. As merchants they played a significant role not only in the commercial life of the community but also as investors in the machinery and equipment needed for deep mining operations. So absorbed was Holmes in his work that one miner confided that "he is urging on his business with much energy and thinking much more of Gold Mines, Stores, and the price of cotton than Love, Marriage, or domestic happiness." By 1850 the Holmes brothers owned a small store and operated one of the district's more profitable mining companies. When the leases of other companies expired in the early 1850s, Moses developed a plan to consolidate the most valuable properties at Gold Hill under a single owner. In 1853 he obtained a bond for the Old Field, Heilig, and Barnhardt mines and sold the entire property to a New York firm, Sackett and Belcher, for $315,000. The Gold Hill Mining Company was organized in the fall of 1853, with Holmes serving as local agent along with his brother and Ephraim and Valentine Mauney.

During this period Gold Hill achieved recognition as "the prince of mines" in the eastern states. Fully one-third of the gold bullion deposited at the U.S. Mint in Charlotte came from the Gold Hill district. Up to 150 miners and laborers, including Cornishmen and slaves, worked in the shafts that descended 750 feet into the earth and at the ore mills that mechanically separated gold from quartz rock. The success of the operation depended heavily on the leadership of the local management. "The history of the Gold Hill gold mine," wrote state geologist Ebenezer Emmons, "would show the importance of perseverance under discouraging prospects—sufficiently so, it is believed, to have induced many operators to have abandoned the mine at any early day. But owing to the . . . efforts of [the] Messrs. Holmes and the Messrs. Mauney, and the late Captain Peters, it has proved one of the rich mines of the State."

For his efforts, Holmes was rewarded handsomely. By 1860 he was a major stockholder in the Gold Hill Mining Company, operated as a partner in at least four commercial enterprises, and owned valuable personal property including a carriage, a gold watch, and sixteen slaves. The mining business declined in the late 1850s and ended completely with the outbreak of the Civil War. Nevertheless, Holmes was able to maintain his prominent position by operating a woolen mill in Montgomery County and by furnishing bluestone and copperas to the Confederate government. He also speculated in the cotton market, buying 700 bales in 1863 at $0.15 to $1.50 per pound in Confederate money. This he later sold for $0.63 per pound in Union greenbacks and enjoyed a considerable profit.

After the war, Holmes moved to Salisbury where he quickly became a business leader, operating a dry goods store, a boot and shoe business, a tannery, and a tobacco factory. He also served as a member of the North Carolina legislature (1865–67), a director of the North Carolina Railroad, a county commissioner, and mayor of Salisbury (1881–83). Holmes played a central role in organizing the Salisbury Cotton Mills, as well as maintaining his interest in the mines at Gold Hill. In 1874 he and his brother Reuben regained ownership of the principal mining properties. They sold this property to a London-based company for $125,000 in 1881 and served as consultants to several companies working at Gold Hill throughout the 1880s. Work continued intermittently in the Gold Hill district until 1915, although not as profitably as in the antebellum period.

Holmes married Elizabeth A. Richards in 1853. They lived in Salisbury with their daughter Bessie (later Mrs. F. B. Arendell of Raleigh), who was born in 1870, and attended the Methodist church. Holmes died suddenly and was "deeply mourned" by the Salisbury community as a "charitable, eminently practical businessman." He was buried in Salisbury's Chestnut Hill Cemetery.

SEE: Jerome Dowd, *Sketches of Prominent Living North Carolinians* (1888); Ebeneezer Emmons, *Geology of North Carolina* (1856); Salisbury *Carolina Watchman*, 10 Jan. 1889.

BRENT D. GLASS

Holmes, Theophilus Hunter (13 Nov. 1804–21 June 1880), Confederate general, was born near Clinton in Sampson County, the son of Gabriel and Mary Hunter Holmes. His father was governor of the state from 1821 to 1824. In 1825 young Holmes entered West Point, from which he was graduated in 1829 in the same class as Robert E. Lee and one year behind Jefferson Davis. He served in the Seminole War and became a captain in 1838. In 1841 he married Laura Wetmore, of North Carolina, the niece of George E. Badger who was President William Henry Harrison's secretary of the navy;

they became the parents of four sons and two daughters. During the Mexican War Holmes "gallantly led" a storming party at the siege of Monterrey and won promotion to the brevet rank of major. Following that conflict he served mainly in the West. In 1855 he became a regular major, and in 1859 he took command of the army recruiting service with headquarters on Governor's Island, N.Y., where his wife died shortly afterwards.

In April 1861, rather than take part in the Fort Sumter relief expedition, Holmes resigned his commission and returned to North Carolina to assist in organizing the state troops. His friends and fellow officers at Governor's Island urged him to reconsider his decision and offered to obtain a leave of absence for him so he could spend the period of the war in Europe; however, without hesitation he declined. In June President Davis, a close friend, appointed Holmes a brigadier general in the Confederate Army and assigned him to the Aquia Creek area of Virginia. The following month his brigade joined the Confederate forces near Manassas Junction but, through no fault of his, he did not arrive on the field in time to participate in the Battle of First Manassas on 21 July 1861.

Promoted to major general in October 1861, Holmes commanded the Fredericksburg District until March 1862, when Davis assigned him to command the Department of North Carolina where "he did creditably in reorganizing the defenses of the State, though he may not have been aggressive" in combating Union coastal attacks. Summoned by Lee to aid in the defense of Richmond, his division on 30 June 1862 advanced against the Union forces at Malvern Hill but was forced to retreat by overpowering artillery fire. Receiving no orders to do so, he did not join in Lee's futile assault on Malvern Hill the next day.

In July 1862 Davis appointed him commander of the Trans-Mississippi Department with headquarters at Little Rock, Ark., and in October promoted him to lieutenant general, a rank he initially declined. During November and December the War Department repeatedly ordered him to transfer troops across the Mississippi River to Vicksburg, then threatened by Grant's army advancing southward through Mississippi, but he refused on the grounds that this would lead to the Federal occupation of Arkansas. Although Grant's offensive failed, Holmes's noncompliance with orders, plus the defeat of Confederate forces at Prairie Grove, Ark., on 7 Dec. 1862 and at Arkansas Post on 11 Jan. 1863, prompted Davis to place General Edmund Kirby Smith in charge of the Trans-Mississippi and to reduce Holmes's command to the District of Arkansas in February 1863.

In June 1863 Kirby Smith, on urging from the War Department, authorized Holmes to attempt the capture of Helena, Ark., in the desperate hope of relieving pressure on Vicksburg, now besieged by Grant. Early on the morning of 4 July Holmes's 8,000 troops made a poorly coordinated assault on the strongly fortified Union garrison at Helena, and after some initial success were driven back with the loss of over 1,600 men. Not only was the attack ill-conceived, but also it was ill-managed by Holmes who, on realizing he had failed, vainly sought death on the battlefield. On 23 July, giving illness as the reason, he temporarily relinquished his command to Major General Sterling Price, who on 10 September evacuated Little Rock and retreated to southern Arkansas, where later that month Holmes resumed command.

On 29 Jan. 1864, Kirby Smith asked Davis to replace

Holmes with a "younger and more energetic officer." Learning of this, Holmes angrily resigned his post on 28 February and returned to North Carolina where he commanded the state reserve troops until the end of the war. He spent his last years on a small farm near Fayetteville and was buried in the cemetery at MacPherson Presbyterian Church in a soldier's coffin, as he had wished.

SEE: *Appleton's Cyclopaedia of American Biography*, vol. 3 (1887); Samuel A. Ashe, ed., *Cyclopedia of Eminent and Representative Men of the Carolinas of the Nineteenth Century*, vol. 2 (1892); *Battles and Leaders of the Civil War*, vols. 1–3 (1887); J. H. Brown, ed., *Cyclopaedia of American Biographies*, vol. 4 (1901); Albert Castel, *General Sterling Price and the Civil War in the West* (1968); Walter Clark, ed., *Histories of the Several Regiments and Battalions from North Carolina in the Great War, 1861–1865*, vols. 1–5 (1901); *DAB*, vol. 9 (1943); *Fayetteville Observer*, 12 Sept. 1895; D. S. Freeman, *Lee's Lieutenants*, vol. 1 (1942); Raleigh *Observer*, 22 June 1880; Van Noppen Papers (Manuscript Department, Duke University Library, Durham); *War of the Rebellion: A Compilation of the Official Records of the Union and Confederate Armies*, ser. 1, vols. 13, 17, 34 (1885, 1886–70, 1891); John H. Wheeler, *Reminiscences and Memoirs of North Carolina and Eminent North Carolinians* (1884).

ALBERT CASTEL

Holmes, Urban Tigner, Jr. *(13 July 1900–12 May 1972)*, medievalist, Romance philologist, author, and editor, was born in Washington, D.C., the son of Urban Tigner Holmes (1869–1940), a career naval officer who was graduated from the U.S. Naval Academy at Annapolis, and Florence Fielding Lawson Holmes (1871–1951) of Philadelphia. His grandfather, David Thomas Holmes (1832–1905), had been a Methodist circuit rider in Georgia before moving with all of his family to Arkansas in 1867. But when young Tigner's parents became Episcopalians, their son was baptized in the Episcopal church, which would remain his spiritual home throughout life.

Holmes received his early schooling in the nation's capital and in the Danville School for boys in Danville, Va., where, at age eleven, his reading of Irving's *Alhambra* inspired his purchase of a Spanish grammar and aroused his lifelong passion for languages. In 1916 he was enrolled in the U.S. Naval Academy, but resigned the following year because of ear trouble. Entering the University of Pennsylvania in the fall of 1917, he turned to the study of medieval France under the influence of the Bayeux Tapestry and Professor J. P. W. Crawford. In the fall of 1920, with an A.B. degree and honors from Pennsylvania, he entered Harvard on a tuition scholarship and studied Romance languages under J. D. M. Ford and Charles H. Grandgent. That summer, while teaching at the University of Western Ontario in London, Canada, he met Margaret Allen Gemmell (1900–1973), whom he married on 22 June 1922.

Harvard awarded Holmes a master's degree in 1921 and a Ph.D. in 1923, the latter after his return from advanced study on a Sheldon Travelling Fellowship in Europe, where his teachers included Mario Roques, Joseph Bédier, Antoine Meillet, and, for a short time, Edmond Faral and Vendryes. After serving as assistant professor of French from 1923 to 1925 at the University of Missouri, Holmes was appointed associate professor of Romance philology at The University of North Carolina and set about making his department one of the

most outstanding in the country in the field. At age twenty-seven he was appointed full professor. Holmes was a visiting professor at the University of Chicago in the spring of 1929 and at the University of Southern California in the summer of 1939. In the latter year he was on the council of the Modern Language Association of America, and in 1941 he was elected president of the South Atlantic Modern Language Association. In 1941 and 1942 he was director of the Linguistic Institute of the Linguistic Society of America.

During World War II Holmes served in Washington, D.C., as a liaison officer between the Office of Strategic Services and the Department of State. In 1945, after his return to the university, he was named Kenan Professor of Romance Philology and was made a Fellow of the Mediaeval Academy of America. In 1948 and 1956 he was lecturer in the Mediaeval Institute at Notre Dame University. Other honors included a Litt.D. from Washington and Lee University (1948) and Western Michigan University (1965) and an LL.D. from Tulane University (1971). In addition, he was named Chevalier de la Légion d'Honneur (1950); visiting professor at Louisiana State University (1950); distinguished visiting professor at Michigan State University (autumn 1950); Fulbright Lecturer for two terms at the University of Melbourne, Australia (1960); member of the Royal Archaeological Institute (1961); Fellow of the Royal Numismatic Society (1961), of the American Numismatic Society (1962), and of the Royal Society of Antiquaries, FSA, London (1967); clerk (1964–67), second vice-president (1967–69), and president of the Fellows (1969–72) of the Mediaeval Academy of America; Senior Fellow of the Southeastern Mediaeval and Renaissance Institute (1966); and lecturer for the North Carolina Association of Eastern Colleges (1969) and at Notre Dame University (1970).

In 1965 at a banquet honoring his sixty-fifth birthday, Holmes was presented a festschrift volume with contributions by fifteen of his former students. As a fitting tribute to an outstanding career of teaching and scholarship, he was invited to accept an appointment for the spring semester of 1973 at the Institute for Advanced Study at Princeton, N.J. But he was not to enjoy this final honor. In the spring of 1972, while at Memphis State University to deliver a series of lectures, he died suddenly of a heart attack.

Among the most notable of Holmes's numerous books are *The Life and Works of Du Bartas*, with John Coriden Lyons and Robert White Linker (3 vols., 1935–40); *A History of Old French Literature from the Origins to 1300* (1937); *A History of the French Language*, with his friend, Alexander H. Schutz (1940); *Daily Living in the Twelfth Century* (1952), his favorite work; *Chrétien de Troyes and the Grail*, with Sister M. Amelia Klenke (1959); and *Chrétien de Troyes* (1970). He also edited the first volume of *A Critical Bibliography of French Literature: The Mediaeval Period* (1946), as well as *Mediaeval Studies in Memory of E. B. Ham* (1967). In addition, Holmes published scores of reviews in scholarly journals, particularly in *Speculum*, one of the major publications in his field, where his influence was widely felt over the years. His range and versatility are also evident in well over a hundred articles and notes that appeared during his long career on such varied subjects as the chronology of Old French writings, the identity of medieval authors, etymologies, onomastics, literary sources, foreign influences on French vocabulary and syntax, medieval and Renaissance gem lore, the position of the North Star in the thirteenth century, interpretation of the earliest story of the Grail, the beast epic, coins in Old French literature, Waldensian dialects in North

Carolina, the identity of a bird in Chaucer, the bombardier beetle in a poem by Villon, the medieval minstrel, and the medieval concept of the monster. Holmes was for many years an associate editor of *Studies in Philology*. He was the major influence in founding the *University of North Carolina Studies in the Romance Lanugages and Literatures* (1940) and *Romance Notes* (1960), and was editor of both of these internationally known publications until his retirement in 1971.

In nearly half a century as a graduate professor in the university at Chapel Hill, Holmes directed over 150 dissertations and theses, and sent a steady stream of teachers and scholars in Romance philology to important positions in many prominent colleges and universities in the United States and Canada.

Holmes devoted his life to his family, his university, his church, and his community. He was active in dramatic performances, sang in the church choir, and read "The Christmas Story" for the Planetarium in his magnificent bass voice. Both he and his wife were influential members of the Episcopal church, where Holmes served as vestryman and delegate to diocesan conventions. They were among the first members of the American Church Union in North Carolina and were the first couple to receive the Keble Award when the Union's Annual Council met at Raleigh in 1968. The respect and admiration of his churchmen is reflected in a long article that appeared after his death in *The American Church News* on All Saints' Day 1972.

Holmes was buried near the top of the hillside in the new Chapel Hill Cemetery; the following year his wife was buried beside him. He was survived by two daughters, Mary Cleland (Mrs. L. L. Bernard) of South Bend, Ind., and Florence Anne (Mrs. Hampton Hubbard) of Clinton, N.C.; a son, the Very Reverend Urban Tigner Holmes III, dean of the School of Theology of the University of the South at Sewanee, Tenn.; a sister, Mrs. John T. Knight of Metairie, La.; a brother, Edward Lawson Holmes of Kirkwood, Mo.; seventeen grandchildren; and three great-granddaughters.

The annual Urban Tigner Holmes, Jr., Graduate Award in Mediaeval Studies and Romance Theology was established at The University of North Carolina by his former students and his colleagues as a continuing memorial. There is a fine oil portrait of Holmes (the gift of his three children) by Ray E. Goodbred of Charleston, S.C., in Toy Lounge of Dey Hall on the Chapel Hill campus.

SEE: *Directory of American Scholars III: Foreign Languages—Modern and Classical, Linguistics and Philology* (1964); J. Bryan Griswold, obituary in *The American Church News*, vol. 37 (1972); John Mahoney and John Esten Keller, eds., *Mediaeval Studies in Honor of Urban Tigner Holmes, Jr.* (1965); Memorial Statement (Office of the Secretary of the Faculty, University of North Carolina, Chapel Hill); *Who's Who in America* (1972).

ALFRED GARVIN ENGSTROM

Holmes, Urban Tigner, III (*12 June 1930–6 Aug. 1981*), Episcopal priest, teacher, and dean, was born in Chapel Hill, the son of Urban Tigner, Jr., and Margaret Allen Gemmell Holmes. He received undergraduate and graduate degrees from The University of North Carolina, and theological degrees from the Philadelphia Divinity School and the University of the South. Ordained in 1954, he served Episcopal churches in Pennsylvania and North Carolina and was chaplain at Catawba College, Salisbury, and at Louisiana State

University, where he also taught Greek. After teaching at the Episcopal seminary at the University of the South, Holmes became dean in 1973. He was the author or coauthor of sixteen books and numerous articles, many dealing with spirituality and man's concept of God.

Holmes married Jane Wiley Neighbours, and they were the parents of four children: Jane Teresa, David Thomas, Janet Reid, and Allen Tigner. He was buried in Chapel Hill.

SEE: William S. Powell, ed., *North Carolina Lives* (1962); Raleigh *News and Observer*, 7 Aug. 1981.

WILLIAM S. POWELL

Holt, Donnell Shaw (*7 Mar. 1908–20 Mar. 1982*), president and chairman of the board of Cannon Mills, was born in a mill house 100 feet from the gate of Trevora Mills in Graham, the son of Glenna and Seymour Holt, who eventually became superintendent of the mill. His grandfather, Isaac Holt, started as a day laborer, working his way up to head of the carding section of Trevora Mills. Don Holt was graduated from Graham High School in 1925 and The University of North Carolina in December 1929. At Chapel Hill he majored in chemistry, hoping to attend medical school; joined the Delta Tau Delta fraternity and was inducted into the Order of the Davians; and, at 6 feet 2½ inches and 200 pounds, played end for the football team. He was named All-State in 1927 and 1928, and All-Southern in 1929. Though accepted by The University of North Carolina Medical School for the 1930 fall quarter, the depression frustrated his ambitions.

Having spent his summers working in textile mills since age fourteen, Holt found a job with Esther Hosiery Mill that paid $125 a month. After six months he obtained a position in the accounting and business section at Trevora. He took business courses at night for several years and swiftly rose in the organization, becoming vice-president of the mill in March 1937.

With America's entry into World War II, Holt joined the navy and was commissioned as a lieutenant in June 1942. For eighteen months he served in the New Hebrides as ground control officer for an aircraft scouting unit. While helping to pull an American flyer from his plane that had crashed in the ocean, Holt received a permanent injury to his back. He spent the last eighteen months of his three-year tour in Long Beach, Calif., as executive officer for a navy aircraft carrier service unit. Before his discharge in 1945 he was promoted to the rank of lieutenant commander.

After the war Holt returned to Trevora. Shortly after it was acquired by the Cannon Mills as a subsidiary in 1949, he was hired by Cannon and began a meteoric rise in that company. In 1950, he represented the Cotton Manufacturers Institute during an American textile mission to Japan to convince the Japanese to raise textile prices. The following year Charles A. Cannon promoted him to vice-president. Holt subsequently orchestrated the establishment of the decorative fabric and bedsheet division and in 1959 was elected executive vice-president. In 1960 he was named president of Cannon Mills of New York, the sales organization for the company. When Charles Cannon stepped aside in 1962 to fill the newly created position of chairman of the board, Holt—Cannon's personal choice—succeeded him as president and chief executive officer. Under Cannon's watchful eye, he introduced a more modern management style and brought younger men up in the organization. On the death of "Mr. Charlie" Cannon in 1971, Holt was reelected president and named chairman of the board, the first non-Cannon to head the company. He took over an organization recently under fire by the Justice Department for alleged discriminatory practices in company-owned housing and by "Nader's Raiders" for alleged corporate dominance of Kannapolis civic affairs. Holt quickly implemented a public relations campaign to counter negative perceptions of Cannon Mills. He also struggled with a slumping economy and a nearly successful attempt to unionize the company before retiring at the end of 1974. He remained on the board of directors until 1980, when he stepped down because of ill health. Two years later he died of kidney disease.

Holt was long active in civic and church affairs, receiving numerous awards. Before World War II he was appointed secretary to the board in charge of overseeing the bond issue for, and development of, the Alamance County Hospital. He also helped establish the Alamance Country Club. During his career he served on the board of directors of Wiscasset Mills, Wachovia Bank and Trust, North Carolina Cotton Manufacturers Association, National Bank of Alamance, and Alamance County Tubercular Sanatorium. In 1975 he was chairmain of the United Way campaign for Cabarrus County. Elon College and Livingstone College both awarded him a doctor of laws degree. He was inducted as an honorary member of the Phi Psi textile fraternity of North Carolina State University and named its "Man of the Year in Textiles" in 1973.

On 12 July 1932 Holt married Margaret McConnell, who was superintendent of the music curriculum for the Graham schools. They had no children. He was survived by his wife and his younger brother, Sidney.

SEE: Alumni Files (University of North Carolina, Chapel Hill); Linda Bailey, "Holt Steps Down as Cannon Head," Salisbury Post, 10 Dec. 1974; "Chairman of Cannon Mills Announces His Retirement," Raleigh News and Observer, 10 Dec. 1974; "Donnell Holt, Cannon Executive," Charlotte News, 22 Mar. 1982; "Ex-Cannon Mills Chief Don S. Holt Dies at 74," Raleigh News and Observer, 22 Mar. 1982; Everette L. Gilliam, "Don Holt Led Cannon in Period of Change," Concord Tribune, 10 Dec. 1974; "Holt Named President of Cannon Mills Sales," Burlington Times-News, 16 Feb. 1960; "Holt Retires as Cannon Chairman," Kannapolis Independent, 9 Dec. 1974; "Jordan Named Alamance Hospital Board Chairman," Greensboro Daily News, 31 Oct. 1941; Phillip Moeller, "Cannon Mills' New Top Man Accentuates the Positive," Charlotte Observer, 6 June 1971; Conrad Paysour, "Don S. Holt—He's a Down-to-Earth-Man: Cannon Mills Has Fine Year under Graham Native's Leadership," Greensboro Daily News, 2 Apr. 1972; James Ross, "His Early Dream Escaped but Now He's a President," Greensboro Daily News, 2 Apr. 1962; Harold S. Taylor, "Succeeding 'Mr. Charlie,'" New York Times, 8 Aug. 1971; "What's Behind the New Look at Cannon," Textile World (1971, reprint).

JOHN GIBSON

Holt, Edwin Michael (14 Feb. 1807–14 May 1884), industrial pioneer and planter, was one of six children born to Rachel Rainey and Michael Holt III in Orange (now Alamance) County. His father's ancestors had emigrated from Germany to England before settling in Spotsylvania County, Va., and later in North Carolina. Michael Holt III was an influential state representative

and senator who operated a stagecoach stop at his home on the Hillsborough-to-Salisbury route. In addition to his plantation, he managed a store, gristmill, woodworking shop, sawmill, distillery, and blacksmith shop. Experience with his father's business ventures encouraged Edwin's industriousness and versatility. Despite little formal education he was a good businessman, and he learned to accept responsibility while supervising wagons that took produce from his father's plantation to market in Fayetteville, Hillsborough, and elsewhere.

At age twenty-one, Holt married Emily Farish who bore him ten children: Alfred Augustus (1828–56), Thomas Michael (1831–96), James Henry (1833–97), Alexander (1935–92), Fannie H. Williamson (1837–1918), William Edwin (1839–1917), Lynn Banks (1842–1920), Mary Elizabeth H. Williamson (1844–1935), Emma H. White (1847–1904), and Lawrence Shackleford (1851–1937).

A Greensboro cotton mill stimulated Holt's interest in building a mill on Alamance Creek where his father operated a gristmill. Although the elder Holt at first refused to be a partner in the venture, William A. Carrigan, husband of young Holt's aunt, Nancy, agreed to participate. When Michael Holt learned that Judge Thomas Ruffin approved of the project and had even offered to provide capital, he offered his son both capital and waterpower. Holt and Carrigan refused the capital but agreed to buy waterpower from Holt's father. Securing timber and rocks from their farms and making their own bricks, they used slave labor and hired carpenters when necessary. The mill was built and a few houses were erected for the workers. Under the name Holt and Carrigan Cotton Mill, operation began in 1837 with 528 spindles processing yarn. Holt managed the factory while Carrigan operated the store. Despite difficulties encountered when rising water flooded the mill, the firm continued to use waterpower until after 1870. Holt and Carrigan also operated a second store in Hillsborough, and factory and farm products were shipped by wagon to Hillsborough, Fayetteville, and Salisbury as well as to Petersburg and Clarksville, Va. The 1842 inheritance from Michael Holt's estate increased the capital of the Holt-Carrigan firm, which subsequently built an addition to the factory, more workers' houses, and a yarn house. By 1849, twelve looms produced cloth selling for six and seven cents per yard.

After the death of his wife in 1841, William Carrigan decided to sell his partnership to Holt and move to Arkansas in 1851. As a result, Thomas M. Holt returned from business school in Philadelphia to help his father in the mill. It was he who later explained how the famous Alamance plaids, the first goods to be woven of colored yarn south of the Potomac River, came to be produced. By 1854 the mill could hardly keep up with the demand for goods, and was selling quantities of yarn, sheeting, and osnaburgs. By 1860, the Alamance Cotton Mill, as it was known then, had sixty female and eight male employees, and a tax value of $57,000.

Though Holt opposed secession when the Civil War began, he and his sons contributed greatly to the war effort. William, Alexander, and Banks Holt served in the Confederate Army, but William was recalled in 1861 to manage the mill at Alamance for his father, while Thomas took over the Granite Mills on the Haw River. Both Edwin Holt and his brother William, who was a physician in Lexington, believed that the need for cotton would eventually bring European aid for the South, and Edwin considered it strange that England and France did not recognize the Confederacy. During the war the Holt mills produced goods both for the army and for personal use, despite the difficulty in securing materials needed for operation. By 1870 the value of production of the Alamance mills was $73,625, including the manufacture of yarns, sheeting, plaids, ticking, and frilling. After the war, Holt turned over the management of the Alamance Cotton Mill to his sons and the firm name was changed to Erwin M. Holt's Sons. In 1871 fire destroyed the mill, valued at $60,000 but insured for only $25,000. Despite the loss, a new factory was erected and production was resumed. Of the seven mills in Alamance County by 1870, five were cotton mills owned by the Holts; another was later purchased from John Newlin and Son, and operated by Holt, White & Williamson. The latter two partners were sons-in-law of Holt.

Rivaling the interest of Edwin Holt in the textile industry was the life and work on his plantation, Locust Grove. He built the manor house, not far from Alamance Creek, in 1849. In back of the house was the family cemetery where Edwin and Emily Holt and some other members of the family later were buried. Holt experimented with new farm methods, fertilizers, and crop rotation. By 1860, he owned 1,200 acres of improved land and 400 acres of unimproved land in Alamance County. At that time he also owned fifty-one slaves, though twenty-four of them were age ten or less and one was mentally retarded. The Holt plantation produced 1,900 bushels of wheat, 2,800 of corn, and 1,200 of oats, plus fruits, vegetables, dairy products, beef, and pork. The Holts salted down some 14,000–15,000 pounds of pork annually. In 1860 the gristmill produced 5,000 bushels of meal and 666 barrels of flour. In earlier years much corn was used to make whiskey, which was sold for as little as 37½ cents per gallon. Holt was owner of at least one distillery, sawmill, brickyard, and shoe shop and part owner and director of a bank and a railroad.

Like his father, Edwin Holt was concerned with public affairs. A Whig, he went by wagon to Raleigh in April 1844 to hear Henry Clay speak and he attended a number of local Whig meetings. Though not a politician, he did speak out for the election of Thomas Ruffin in 1861. Holt frequently attended Orange County court and participated in activities directed by it. He was one of the commissioners for the building of a new courthouse and he served on the finance committee. When Alamance County was established in 1849, he served on the building committee for the courthouse in Graham, the new county seat. He was also one of the commissioners chosen for the construction of a jail in Alamance County. Both Edwin Holt and his son Thomas served as stockholders and directors of the North Carolina Railroad built between Goldsboro and Charlotte. When surveying began in 1850, Edwin went out with surveying parties.

Holt was particularly interested in education, and he sent his children to schools held at St. Paul's Lutheran Church, Albright's school near their home, Miss Louisa Mason's school, Caldwell Institute, Mr. and Mrs. Burwell's Female Academy, The University of North Carolina, and a business school in Philadelphia. In 1844 he recorded attending a school district meeting. Schools were also held at the factory in Alamance, such as the geography school that began in April 1847. Further, Holt attended school examinations given in Graham Institute.

The most frequently mentioned single item in his diary was the church. A member of St. Paul's Lutheran Church located near his plantation, Holt also attended other churches in the area as well as preaching at services held in the factory. He and his family attended camp meetings such as the one held in October 1854 at Hawfields where three of his children professed religion. One of these was Thomas M. Holt, who united with the Graham Presbyterian Church in June 1856. Eventually Edwin, Emily, and seven of their ten children joined this church, where stained glass windows honored Edwin and Emily Holt and their son Alfred.

In many ways Holt represented the original industrial pioneer. His foresight, ability, and industriousness aided in planting the roots of the textile industry in the soil of his native North Carolina. At his death most of the mills in Alamance County belonged to members of his family. By his life and work Edwin ensured the growth of manufacturing through the work of his children and grandchildren.

With one exception, Holt's children were successful in business and were active in public affairs. When William died in 1917, his estate was valued at approximately $3 million, and his heirs paid the highest inheritance tax that had been paid in North Carolina to that time. Thomas was not only a businessman but he also served in both houses of the state legislature and as lieutenant governor and governor of North Carolina.

SEE: Samuel A. Ashe, ed., *Biographical History of North Carolina*, vol. 7 (1908); John Warren Carrigan Papers (Manuscript Department, Duke University Library, Durham); Isabel Stebbins Giulvezan, "The Paternal Ancestry of Ivan Lee Holt III" (1926, University of North Carolina Library); *Hillsborough Recorder*, 5 May 1842, 19 Sept. 1848, 14 Feb. 1849; Eugene Holt, *Edwin Michael Holt and His Descendants, 1807–1948* (1949); W. P. Huddle, *The History of the Hebron Lutheran Church, Madison County, Virginia, from 1717–1907* (1908); Minutes of Session Book 1, Graham Presbyterian Church, Graham; North Carolina Land Grant Book 14 (North Carolina Department of Archives and History, Raleigh); "Occasional Diary of Edwin Michael Holt 1844–1854" (typescript, Southern Historical Collection, University of North Carolina Library, Chapel Hill); Raleigh *News and Observer*, 16 May, 3 Oct. 1884, 16 Jan. 1917; Thomas Ruffin Papers (Southern Historical Collection, University of North Carolina Library, Chapel Hill); Sally Walker Stockard, *History of Alamance* (1900); U.S. Census Records, 1850; J. W. White Papers (Manuscript Department, Duke University Library, Durham); *Wilmington Daily Journal*, various issues.

RACHEL Y. HOLT

Holt, Jacob W. *(30 Mar. 1811–21 Sept. 1880)*, contractor, architect, and builder, the oldest son of David and Elizabeth ("Betsy") McGehee Holt, was born in Prince Edward County, Va. When he was still quite young his mother died and he and his brother, Thomas J., and two sisters were placed in the care of an uncle, John McGehee. Their father, an impoverished and itinerant carpenter, also died a few years later. The young brothers apparently were apprenticed to a carpenter, most likely William A. Howard of Prince Edward County who often worked in association with brickmason Dabney Cosby, later of North Carolina. Jacob's connection with Howard is not documented but arises from stylistic similiarities in the work of the two men and from the fact that Holt later named a son William Howard Kenneth Holt. In February 1838 Holt married Aurelia Ann Phillips, and by about 1840 they were the parents of a daughter, Mary C.

Evidently by 1844 Holt and presumably his family moved to Warrenton, N.C., where, according to local tradition, he was involved in the construction of the grand residence of William Eaton, completed in 1843; no documentation of this exists, and the house is not much like his known later work. Holt was one of several craftsmen who moved to Warrenton in the early and middle 1840s from Prince Edward County. These included Thomas Holt (probably Jacob's brother), brickmasons Edward T. Rice and Francis Woodson, cabinetmaker Samuel N. Mills, and others. Most were Baptists, and in 1847 Holt, Woodson, Rice, and L. A. Womack bought as trustees of the "intended Warrenton Baptist Church" a lot in Warrenton. Here was soon built a small frame temple-form Greek Revival church— probably Holt's work.

Although Holt lived and worked in Warrenton throughout most of the town's 1840s–1860s boom period, busily employing a work force of sixty including slaves and assistants, there is no documentation for any of his buildings before 1853. Local historian Elizabeth Montgomery (who was a little girl in antebellum days in Warrenton) recorded that "Under the superintendence of these three contractors [Jacob and Thomas Holt and E. T. Rice] most of the handsome residences in the county, as well as those in town, before the War Between the States, were built." More than twenty Greek Revival-style houses stand in Warrenton and there are others in the countryside. Most of these have strong similiarities to Holt's later, documented work and are probably the products of his workshop.

The 1850 census lists Holt as a thirty-eight-year-old carpenter with a wife and three young children. Also in his household were eighteen young men, many from Virginia, presumably workmen, assistants, and apprentices. Holt also owned forty-two slaves, mostly young men. By 1860, at age forty-nine, he had six children. The census listed him as a "master mechanic," with fourteen young men—all carpenters—in the household.

In 1853 construction began on a major project for Warren County—the new courthouse. County court records document regular payments from the "Courthouse Fund" to Holt and to his associates, brickmasons Woodson and Rice, throughout the 1853–57 construction work. The two-story brick temple-form courthouse, for fifty years the centerpiece of Warrenton, bears similiarities to Holt's probably earlier work in the Greek Revival style, but it features the bracketed cornice of the coming Italianate style, in which he was so prolific.

Beginning in 1856 Holt began work on a number of buildings for which documentation survives. All had the basic, boxy Greek Revival form, but were enriched by brackets along cornices, curvilinear and circular motifs on doors and porches, arched elements at windows and in mantels, and other repetitive, distinctive features. Among those well documented by family papers are Vine Hill in Franklin County, built in 1856 for Archibald D. Williams; Sylva Sonora in Warren County, now gone, built for the Boyd family; and Eureka, a grand, towered house built in 1857–58 for the Baskervill family in Mecklenburg County, Va. The contract for Eureka states that the source for the design was W. Ranlett's *The Architect*, a widely used architectural pattern book.

Not documented, but stylistically similar, are half a dozen dwellings in Warrenton plus the Presbyterian Church, and perhaps twenty structures in the county. In addition, and quite different from his other work, is Holt's own house in Warrenton. He did not own the land but leased it from at least 1856 to 1859, and on it

were located his dwelling and workshop. The design Holt obviously took from Andrew Jackson Downing's *Cottage Residences*, a popular pattern book that promulgated the picturesque bracketed and Gothic mode supplanting the classical Greek Revival. The house has a central tower flanked by projecting gabled wings, an inset porch, and ornate eaves—as does Downing's Fig. 72, "A Cottage in the Italian or Tuscan Style." It appears that Holt used Downing's publication for details in many of his houses, but only in his own dwelling did he stray from the traditional boxy house into the more modish villa form.

Holt also worked in Mecklenburg and Charlotte counties in southern Virginia, and in Vance, Granville, Halifax, Nash, Northampton, Franklin, and Wake counties in North Carolina. In both Raleigh and Chapel Hill, too, houses of Holt's mode once existed.

Shortly before the Civil War, Holt expanded his field of operation beyond building for a planter clientele and undertook construction of three of the substantial educational buildings going up in those prosperous years. He took the carpentry contract for the massive St. John's College at Oxford, which was built during the late 1850s, with John Berry, Hillsborough brickmason, undertaking the brickwork. In 1860 Holt gained commissions for both carpentry and brickwork in constructing Peace Institute in Raleigh and the new main building at Trinity College in Randolph County. A newspaper article from the *High Point Reporter*, quoted in the *North Carolina Standard* of 31 Oct. 1860, described him as "one of the first architects in the state," who had "put up many fine residences and public buildings in the eastern part of the state."

In these large projects Holt worked as a contractor building from an architect's designs—in contrast to his accustomed role of accomplishing both design and construction. First William Percival, a talented and itinerant English architect, and then Holt's brother Thomas, who had worked in Jacob's carpentry shop in Warrenton until moving to Raleigh in the late 1850s, served as architect for Peace Institute. Trinity president Braxton Craven was credited with the design of the ambitious new building, fronted by columns. The Civil War prevented completion of the Peace building; it was patched up in makeshift fashion to serve as a hospital, later housed the Freedman's Bureau, and finally was reclaimed for its original purpose as a Presbyterian school for young women. The Trinity project was never begun.

After the war, Holt's work continued many of the motifs of his antebellum buildings, with some accommodation to the increased verticality, roofline complexity, and ornateness of developing late nineteenth-century styles. In 1868 he remodeled the Central Hotel in Warrenton: a newspaper article of 14 February noted that "our friend Jacob Holt Esq., so well known in North Carolina and Virginia, is busily employed in repairing the establishment."

Soon after the war, Holt moved to Virginia and continued to build. In 1873 he constructed the Boydton Methodist Church; a contemporary newspaper commended "Mr. Jacob Holt, a workman of more architectural taste and more faithful to comply with his contracts could not be found." Other buildings in Chase City and Boydton are highly suggestive of his hand. Family tradition at Shadow Lawn in Chase City strongly claims his authorship. His last known work, however, was back in North Carolina, in Murfreesboro. A Norfolk paper of 21 Apr. 1875 reported: "New house of D. A. Barnes about finished. Built by Jacob W. Holt

of Chase City, Mecklenburg Co., Va." An early photograph shows a boxy frame house with ornate, vigorous
woodwork.

Holt died in Keysville, Va. He and his wife, who died
in 1898, were buried at Chase City, Va.

Although not trend-setting or sophisticated, Jacob
Holt's work is important as a consistent and highly per-
sonalized oeuvre within the mainstream of mid-nineteenth-century American vernacular architecture. Particularly significant are three aspects of his work: he
was prolific, constructing dozens of buildings in a
many-county area, perhaps as many as eighty; many of
his buildings are documented and either surviving or
pictured; and at least two mid-nineteenth-century pattern books are known to have been his sources. His
handsome Greek Revival buildings and distinctive,
more ornate Italianate ones are an important element in
the mid-nineteenth-century architectural fabric of North
Carolina.

SEE: Information from Edgar Thorne, Panthea Twitty,
and Mary Hinton Kerr (Warren County); Journal of A.
D. Williams (North Carolina State Archives, Raleigh);
Lizzie W. Montgomery, *Sketches of Old Warrenton* (1924);
Records of Prince Edward County, Va. (Courthouse,
Farmville, Va.); Records of Warren County, N.C. (North
Carolina State Archives, Raleigh).

CATHERINE W. BISHIR

Holt, James Henry *(22 Apr. 1833–13 Feb. 1897)*, textile
manufacturer, was born at Locust Grove, the home of
his parents near the village of Alamance, in Alamance
County. He was the son of Edwin Michael and Emily
Farish Holt. After receiving his elementary education at
home and in private schools, he attended the Caldwell
Institute, near Hillsborough, and studied under the
Reverend Dr. Alexander Wilson. In 1852, at age nineteen, Holt joined his brother, Alfred, in the operation of
a general store at Graham, the seat of Alamance
County, where he was also placed in charge of deposits
in a private bank owned by his father.

On 15 Jan. 1856, Holt married Laura Cameron
Moore, of Caswell County, a sister of Louisa Moore
who married his brother, Thomas. The couple had
twelve children: Ida Cameron, Glenn, Walter Lawrence,
Edwin C., Samuel M., James Henry, Jr., Robert L., William I., Ernest A., Mary Lou, Laura A., and Daisy A.

Interested in banking, Holt became the cashier of a
bank in Thomasville in 1862. Two years later he left that
post to enlist as a private in Company K, Tenth Regiment of North Carolina Artillery. He was stationed at
Fort Fisher from April until December 1964, when he
was commissioned as a captain and sent to Fayetteville
to serve as commandant of a military school. Shortly
afterwards, the war ended; Holt received his parole and
went back to Alamance County.

On returning home, Holt was made a member of the
family firm of Erwin M. Holt's Sons. He also joined his
father and his brothers in the founding of the Commercial National Bank in Charlotte and for many years
served on its board of directors. From the residence he
built in Graham, Holt commuted to the Alamance and
Carolina cotton mills, which he helped manage. In 1879
he and his brother William built the Glencoe Mills, located two miles upstream from Carolina. When William
moved to Charlotte to become a banker, James became
the sole manager of this enterprise. To be nearer his office, he moved to Burlington and resided for the rest of

his life in a house he built on Park Avenue. The site is
now a part of the property of the Macedonia Lutheran
Church.

In 1890, Holt helped his sons, James, Jr. and Robert
to build the Windsor Cotton Mills in Burlington. Two
years later he assisted his sons Samuel and William in
constructing the Lakeside Mills, also in Burlington. The
aging industrialist then aided his son Walter in establishing textiles plants in Fayetteville and Wilmington.
Changes in management were later made in two of the
mills. James, Jr., went to Lakeside when Samuel, accompanied by his brother Ernest, moved to Texas to become a cattle rancher. Robert eventually became the
manager of Carolina and almost the sole owner of
Glencoe. After his death, ownership of Glencoe passed
to his sister, Daisy, whose husband, Walter G. Green,
Sr., managed the operation for a number of years.
When Green died, changes were made in the plant and
it was no longer used as a cotton factory.

Holt was a member of the Graham Presbyterian
Church until a congregation of that denomination was
organized in Burlington. He then became one of the
principal contributors to the construction of that town's
First Presbyterian Church, where he served as an officer until his death. Holt died at his home and was buried in Pine Hill Cemetery, Burlington.

SEE: *The Alamance Gleaner* (Graham), 18 Feb. 1897; *The
Alamance News* (Graham), 25 Mar. 1976; *Burlington Daily
Times-News*, 14 Dec. 1976; Eugene Holt, *Edwin Michael
Holt and His Descendants, 1807–1948* (1949); Julian
Hughes, *Development of the Textile Industry in Alamance
County* (1965); John W. Moore, ed., *Roster of North Caro-
lina Troops in the War Between the States*, 4 vols. (1882);
The North Carolina Presbyterian, 18 June 1896.

DURWARD T. STOKES

Holt, John Allen *(18 Dec. 1852–15 June 1915)*, educator, lay leader in the Methodist Protestant church, and
state senator, was born near Hillsdale, Guilford County,
the son of John Foust and Louisa J. Williams Holt. For
forty-one years he was a teacher and for thirty-nine
years he was principal and senior proprietor of Oak
Ridge Institute, a nondenominational preparatory
school that had close ties to the North Carolina Annual
Conference of the Methodist Protestant church.

Holt attended Oak Ridge Institute, Williams College
in Massachusetts, Ohio Wesleyan University, and the
Ohio Business College from which he was graduated in
1875. The same year he began his association as a
teacher with Oak Ridge Institute, where in 1879 he was
joined by his brother, Martin Hicks Holt (d. 1914). In
1884, the Holt brothers purchased the institution and
operated it until their deaths. John Allen headed the institute's commercial department.

Also interested in the mercantile business and in
banking, Holt was a director of the City National Bank
of Greensboro and of the North State Fire Insurance
Company. In addition, he served for more than twenty
years as a member and/or chairman of the Guilford
County Board of Education. He was a member of the
board of trustees of The University of North Carolina, a
member of the Order of United American Mechanics, a
Mason, and active in the North Carolina Teachers Assembly which was organized in 1884. In 1898, he was
elected president of the Association of Academies of
North Carolina.

In 1907–8 Holt was a member of the state senate,

where he served as chairman of the committee on education and a member of the committees on railroad and finance. Considered to be a debater of rare force, he championed the reduction of railroad passenger and freight rates, better educational facilities for the masses, and the control of trusts. The Raleigh *News and Observer* once observed: "[Holt] has killed the old idea that the teacher is not practical." A frequent delegate to the North Carolina Annual Conference of the Methodist Protestant church, he was a delegate to the General Conference of that denomination in 1884, 1900, 1904, and 1908. As a result of their strong religious convictions, the Holt brothers made a standing offer of free tuition at Oak Ridge Institute to ministerial students of their denomination and to the sons of Methodist Protestant ministers in the North Carolina Conference.

On 29 Dec. 1881, Holt married Sallie Josephine Knight (13 Sept. 1853–23 Apr. 1946), the daughter of Pinkney Knight. They were the parents of two sons and a daughter. One son, Earle, taught for some years at Oak Ridge Institute. Holt was buried in Oak Ridge.

SEE: Samuel A. Ashe, ed., *Biographical History of North Carolina*, vol. 7 (1908); *Biennial Report of the Superintendent of Public Instruction of North Carolina, 1887–1888* (1889), *1896–'97 and 1897–'98* (1898); J. Elwood Carroll, *History of the North Carolina Annual Conference of the Methodist Protestant Church* (1939); Nolan B. Harmon, ed., *Encyclopedia of World Methodism*, vol. 2 (1974); Information from Colonel Zack L. Whitaker (Oak Ridge Institute); *Journal of the North Carolina Annual Conference of the Methodist Protestant Church* (1910, 1915); *Prominent People of North Carolina* (1906).

RALPH HARDEE RIVES

Holt, Lawrence Shackleford *(17 May 1851–15 Jan. 1937)*, textile manufacturer and capitalist, was born in Alamance County at Locust Grove, the home of his parents near the village of Alamance. He was the youngest of ten children of Edwin Michael and Emily Farish Holt. Holt received his elementary education at the Reverend Dr. Alexander Wilson's school at Melville, in the southern part of Alamance County, after which he attended Horner Military Academy at Oxford. He then enrolled at Davidson College as a member of the class of 1871, but did not remain to graduate because he was impatient to enter the business world.

To satisfy his son's ambition, the elder Holt placed him in charge of a wholesale grocery business that he owned in Charlotte. After proving himself in this capacity, the young manager persuaded his father and brothers, Thomas, James, William, and Banks, to join him in founding the Commercial National Bank of Charlotte, which soon became—and remained—a highly successful financial institution.

In 1872 Holt married Margaret Locke Erwin of Burke County. They became the parents of seven children: Erwin Allen, Eugene, Emily Farish, Margaret Erwin, Florence E., Lawrence Shackleford, Jr., and Bertha Harper.

The year after his marriage, Holt returned to Alamance County and built a home near Locust Grove. He became a partner in the family firm of Edwin M. Holt's Sons, operator of the cotton mill at Alamance and the Carolina Cotton Mills which it had built on the Haw River. For the next several years, in cooperation with one or more of his brothers and William A. Erwin, a brother-in-law, Holt helped found the Bellemont Cotton Mills and the E. M. Holt Plaid Mills. He also became one of the owners of a half interest in the

Altamahaw Cotton Mills; the other half was owned by J. Q. Gant, his brother-in-law by marriage to Corinna Erwin. The new firm of Holt, Gant, and Holt operated six miles northeast of Mill Point (now Elon College).

In 1884, Holt attempted to buy the bankrupt Lafayette Mills, at Company Shops, but was outbid by R. J. Reynolds. The tobacco magnate soon changed his plans and sold the factory to Holt for $17,000. In this transaction, the industrialist fulfilled his greatest ambition—to become the sole owner of a textile mill. By concentrating all his resources on this venture, he was able to replace the knitting machines used in the defunct plant with 2,160 spindles and 124 looms. In 1885, the Aurora Cotton Mills began production; thereafter its output increased regularly as various additions were made to the plant.

In order to be near his principal business, Holt moved from his country home to Blythewood, an ornate house he built at Company Shops about the time the town's name was changed to Burlington. Like his father, he firmly believed in a family-owned-and-operated business, and in 1896 he included his sons in the mill's management by forming the firm of Lawrence S. Holt and Sons. Subsequent expansion followed, and the enterprise eventually included the Gem Cotton Mills in Gibsonville and the Sevier Cotton Mills in Kings Mountain. All of the firms were profitable. Moreover, Holt was credited with being the "first manufacturer in the South" to voluntarily shorten the working day from twelve to eleven hours without reducing pay.

While born into a Presbyterian family, Holt married an Episcopalian and became a communicant of that church. In 1879 he played a leading role in the construction of St. Athanasius Protestant Episcopal Church at Company Shops, which still stands. In 1911 he built and endowed the impressive Episcopal Church of the Holy Comforter in Burlington in memory of his daughter, Emily Farish, who died in 1885 at age five.

Grieved by the death of his wife in 1918, Holt closed Blythewood; it remained unoccupied for two decades. Leaving his mill operation in the hands of his sons, the industrialist retired to Washington, D.C.

When new materials were introduced into the textile industry, Eugene Holt advised replacing cotton yarn with rayon, but his father would not agree to the change. Shortly after this difference of opinion, Aurora Cotton Mills ceased operation. The plant was first rented, then sold to other textile corporations. Eugene moved to Richmond, Va., where he pursued his interest in rayon. Lawrence, Jr., became a real estate promoter in Asheville, and Erwin lived a retired life in Burlington. All of the manufacturer's family left Alamance County.

Near the end of his life, Holt moved to western North Carolina in the interest of his health, and he died in a Statesville hospital. His remains were taken to Burlington and interred in the family plot in the cemetery adjacent to St. Athanasius Church. He had been a Republican in politics, a charitable conservative, and a man of keen financial judgment.

SEE: *The Alamance Gleaner* (Graham), 16 Sept. 1886; *Burlington Daily Times-News*, 15 June 1937, 9 May 1949; Eugene Holt, *Edwin Michael Holt and His Descendants, 1807–1948* (1949); Julian Hughes, *Development of the Textile Industry in Alamance County* (1965); Cornelia Rebekah Shaw, *Davidson College* (1923).

DURWARD T. STOKES

Holt, Lynn Banks *(28 June 1842–23 Oct. 1920)*, textile manufacturer, was born near Graham in Alamance County, the son of Edwin Michael and Emily Farish Holt. He was a descendant of Michael Holt, who settled in present Alamance County about 1740. In 1837 his father founded the Alamance Cotton Mill near Graham, one of the oldest mills in the South and the first southern mill to make colored cotton goods.

L. Banks Holt was educated in local schools and at Hillsborough Military Academy. When the Civil War began, he left the academy to enlist as a private in the Orange Guards. For gallantry displayed in the capture of Fort Macon by his company, he was promoted to second lieutenant and assigned to Company I, Eighth North Carolina Regiment, Confederate Army. Later he became a first lieutenant. Holt participated in many important battles in northern Virginia and was wounded during one of the engagements before Petersburg. In the assault on Fort Harrison on 29 Sept. 1864, he was severely wounded and taken prisoner; he was confined first at Point Lookout and then at Fort Delaware until June 1865.

After the war, Holt joined his father at the Alamance Cotton Mill, which the elder Holt later turned over to his sons. L. Banks eventually purchased the interests of his brothers. In 1879 he and one brother, Lawrence S., built near Graham the Bellemont Mill, of which he became sole owner in 1887, and in 1883 founded at Burlington the E. M. Holt Plaid Mills, named for their father. Later he purchased his brother's interest in the plaid mills as well. Meanwhile, he also acquired the Oneida Mill at Graham and the Carolina Mills, both manufacturing colored cotton goods. In 1909 Holt consolidated the Alamance, Bellemont, Oneida, and Carolina mills and incorporated the business as the L. Banks Holt Manufacturing Company. He remained president of both the E. M. Holt Plaid Mills and the L. Banks Holt Manufacturing Company until his death. In addition to these properties, he owned a one-third interest in the Altamahaw Cotton Mills near Burlington and stock in many other mills. He was also a director of the Merchants and Farmers Bank and the Commercial National Bank, both of Charlotte, and of the North Carolina Railroad.

For many years Holt was an elder of the Presbyterian church in Graham. He was active in educational, charitable, and religious movements, to which he contributed generously. In politics he was a Democrat; although keenly interested in local matters, he declined to hold public office. His hobby was agriculture, and on his Alamance and Oak Grove farms near Graham he raised purebred livestock, including Jersey and Holstein cattle, Shetland ponies, and standardbred pacers.

Holt married Mary Catherine Mebane of Caswell County. They had eight daughters: Mary Virginia, Elizabeth Mebane, Frances Yancey, Caroline Banks, Cora Alice, Emily Louise, Martha Lynn, and one who died in infancy.

SEE: *Cyclopedia of Eminent and Representative Men of the Carolinas*, vol. 2 (1892); Robert O. Holt, *The Holts of Alamance County, North Carolina* (1920); Julian Hughes, *Development of the Textile Industry in Alamance County* (1965).

LARRY W. FUQUA

Holt, Martin Hicks *(9 Jan. 1855–26 Nov. 1914)*, educator, lay leader in the North Carolina Annual Conference of the Methodist Protestant church, and legislator, was the son of John Foust and Louisa J. Williams Holt and a great-nephew of the antebellum North Carolina educator and statesman, Archibald D. Murphey. The family on his paternal side pioneered in cotton manufacturing in the North Carolina piedmont.

After attending Oak Ridge Institute in Guilford County and Kernersville High School, Holt received a bachelor's degree from The University of North Carolina and a master of arts degree from Western Maryland College. For a time he also studied law. He began his teaching career at Kernersville in 1872; later he taught at the Tabernacle High School and was a salesman for a wholesale grocery business. In January 1879, Holt joined his brother, John Allen, at Oak Ridge Institute, which they purchased in 1884. The brothers were associated as teachers and joint proprietors of the institute for about thirty-five years. Martin Hicks was junior principal and head of the academic department. As a result of their strong religious convictions, they made a standing offer of free tuition to Methodist Protestant ministerial students and to the sons of Methodist Protestant ministers in the North Carolina Conference.

In 1893 Holt was a member of the North Carolina General Assembly, where he served as chairman of the committee on education and as a member of several other committees including finance and corporations. He was responsible for raising the tax rate for public education and was instrumental in increasing the appropriations for the educational and charitable institutions of the state. Holt became an initial director of the North Carolina Deaf and Dumb School at Morganton and served continuously for many years. From 1893 to 1897, he was a member of the board of trustees of The University of North Carolina. He also was a delegate to the General Conference of the Methodist Protestant church in 1888 and 1912.

Holt was considered to be "a speaker and a debater of more than ordinary ability . . . of poetical temperament, and . . . [one who delighted] in [the] study of the classics." In 1878, he married Mary A. Lambeth of Guilford County; they became the parents of two sons and a daughter. One son, John Harvey, taught for some years at Oak Ridge Institute. Holt was buried in Oak Ridge.

SEE: Samuel A. Ashe, ed., *Biographical History of North Carolina*, vol. 7 (1908); *Biennial Report of the Superintendent of Public Instruction of North Carolina, 1887–1888* (1889), *1896–'97 and 1897–'98* (1898); J. Elwood Carroll, *History of the North Carolina Annual Conference of the Methodist Protestant Church* (1939); Nolan B. Harmon, ed., *Encyclopedia of World Methodism*, vol. 2 (1974); Information from Colonel Zack L. Whitaker (Oak Ridge Institute); *Journal of the North Carolina Annual Conference of the Methodist Protestant Church* (1910, 1915); *Prominent People of North Carolina* (1906).

RALPH HARDEE RIVES

Holt, Michael, Jr. *(6 May 1723–20 June 1799)*, blacksmith and farmer who became a Patriot during the American Revolution, was born in Virginia, the son of Michael Holt, Sr., and his wife Elizabeth, whose maiden name is unknown. Other children born to this couple included William, Peter, and John. About 1740, the family moved to North Carolina and settled on land in present Alamance County.

When grown, the younger Michael obtained his own land by a grant of 150 acres on Little Alamance Creek from Earl Granville's agents. By the practice of his trade and shrewd management, he added to this acreage throughout his life. Holt was appointed one of the justices of Orange County (from which Alamance was later formed) and was a captain in the provincial militia. In 1768, when the Regulators became troublesome to royal governor William Tryon, Holt was ordered to muster out his company and join the militia to maintain order. On his arrival in Orange County to head this force, Tryon set up his headquarters on Holt's farm. When no fighting occurred, Tryon concluded that the agitation had permanently subsided and returned to New Bern. His assumption was incorrect, however, as the following year the Regulators became violent. Holt was one of several local officials "severely whiped" during the rioting in Hillsborough. The governor returned to Orange and Captain Holt again led his company to join the militia in ending the insurrection. After subsequent attempts to negotiate a settlement failed, the War of the Regulation ended with the Battle of Alamance, fought 16 May 1771, ironically on Holt's own farmland. After the confict the sick and wounded were sent to the Holt home for medical attention and nursing. The outcome of the war was retribution for the captain in view of the indignities he had suffered at the hands of the rioters, and he continued to be a loyal subject of the Crown.

When the American Revolution began, Holt was among the militia officers authorized by Tryon's successor, Governor Josiah Martin, to raise companies of fifty men "to resist and oppose" the Patriots. He dutifully recruited his company and led it to join the Scottish Highlander Tories and other Loyalists rallying under General Donald McDonald at Cross Creek (now Fayetteville). En route to the rendezvous, "when he was fully acquainted with the intention of the Tories," he changed his mind and returned home, "inducing a Number of Others to follow his example without a junction with the Scotch Army." Holt then became a Patriot and remained one. Nevertheless, he was arrested as a Tory and sent to prison in Philadelphia. From his confinement there, he explained his change of attitude in a petition addressed to the North Carolina Council of Safety. This was supplemented by a similar petition from the Orange County Committee of Safety. As a result, the Council decided "Michael Holt would not in any wise injure the Caus of liberty in this State," and, upon its recommendation, the Continental Congress pardoned the prisoner.

Holt then returned to his farm and lived peaceably for the rest of his life. Shortly after the Revolution, an English author touring the United States was entertained at the Holt home "with great hospitality." The visitor described his host as a magistrate possessed of a "considerable property" and "the son of Dutch or German parents, for he himself was born in America." Holt was a sensible man of sound judgment, "but without the least improvement from education, or the embellishment of any kind of polish, even in his exterior." The farmer has also been described as five feet ten inches tall and weighing approximately 225 pounds, with a complexion so dark he was known locally as "Black Michael."

He married Margaret O'Neill, and they were the parents of Joseph, Margaret, and Elizabeth. After his first wife's death, Holt married Jean Lockhart in 1767, and their children were Sarah, Joshua, Isaac, Mary, Catherine, Michael III, and William. The blacksmith was buried in a private cemetery on his farm, which also contains the graves of several members of his family, including that of his son-in-law, John Harden, husband

of Sarah Holt, who was a captain in the American Revolution. This burial ground, still intact, is located on the west side of the Hanford Brick Yard Road, a few miles southeast of Burlington. On Holt's tombstone is the epitaph often quoted but seldom actually seen:

> Remember, man as you pass by,
> As you are now, so once was I;
> As I am now so must you be,
> Prepare for death and follow me.

Holt's children inherited his considerable estate and used it with such success that a substantial part of the patrimony remained in the possession of his descendants for three generations.

SEE: Hugh T. Lefler and Paul Wager, eds., *Orange County, 1752–1952* (1953); William S. Powell, James K. Huhta, and Thomas J. Farnham, eds., *The Regulators in North Carolina* (1971); William L. Saunders, ed., *Colonial Records of North Carolina*, 10 vols. (1886–90); John Ferdinand Dalziel Smyth, *A Tour of the United States of America . . .*, 2 vols. (1784); Walter Whitaker, *Centennial History of Alamance County, 1849–1949* (1949); Wills of Orange County (North Carolina State Archives, Raleigh).

DURWARD T. STOKES

Holt, Michael, III *(11 July 1778–20 Apr. 1842)*, farmer, magistrate, and legislator, was born in Orange County, the son of Michael, Jr., and his second wife, Jean Lockhart Holt. He was reared on his father's farm and from him inherited several hundred acres of land along Big Alamance Creek and its tributaries in present Alamance County.

During his youth, Holt received only elementary schooling, but from his parents learned the rudiments of husbandry. Building on this foundation, he became one of the most successful farmers in the Piedmont section of the state. In addition to attaining financial affluence, the agriculturalist cultivated his mind with "diligent reading, reflection, and conversation" and thereby "possessed the respect and good opinion of his fellow citizens." This was demonstrated in his many years of service as a magistrate and by his election in 1804 as a representative of Orange County in the North Carolina House of Commons. He was elected to the state senate in 1819 and reelected for the 1821–22 term.

A member and "worthy communicant" of the Lutheran church, Holt married Rachel Rainey, daughter of the Reverend Benjamin Rainey, a minister in the Christian church founded by James O'Kelly. The couple became the parents of six children: Nancy Mitcham (Mrs. William A. Carrigan), Jane Lockhart (Mrs. John Holt), Edwin Michael, William Rainey, Alfred Augustus, and Polly (Mary), who never married. Holt lived in a farmhouse near the present village of Alamance, where his son Edwin eventually built one of the early cotton mills in the state. Edwin also made some changes in the house and named the place Locust Grove. Later alterations have been publicized in Alex Haley's *Roots*. The house is preserved today as the Alamance County Historical Museum.

Holt trained his sons to be master farmers and, though Edwin and William chose other vocations for their lifework, the family cultivated the ancestral acres profitably for two generations, even surviving the economic loss of slave labor. Holt did not share Edwin's enthusiasm for manufacturing, as he failed to envision the potential of the cotton mill at Alamance. He remained skeptical of his son's plans and did not live to see their ultimate success.

When he died, Holt's numerous slaves and tracts of land were divided by his will equally among his children with meticulous precision. He also bequeathed the sum of $200 to enclose "the graves in the garden" with brick or stone. The executors carried out his instructions, and Holt was buried with numerous members of his family at Locust Grove in a walled cemetery, maintained by his descendants.

SEE: John L. Cheney, Jr., ed., *North Carolina Government, 1585–1974* (1975); *Hillsborough Recorder*, 16 Aug. 1820, 5 May 1842; Hugh T. Lefler and Paul Wager, *Orange County, 1752–1952* (1952); Wills of Orange County (North Carolina State Archives, Raleigh).

DURWARD T. STOKES

Holt, Thomas Michael (*15 July 1831–11 Apr. 1896*), textile manufacturer, legislator, and governor, was born at Locust Grove in Alamance (formerly Orange) County, near the site where the Regulators fought in 1771. He was the second son of ten children born to Edwin Michael and Emily Farish Holt. His father was a pioneer in the North Carolina textile industry, as well as a prominent planter and landowner; his mother was the daughter of a prosperous Chatham County farmer.

Holt received his early education at home under a private teacher. He then entered Caldwell Institute, in Hillsborough, where he studied under the Reverend Dr. Alexander Wilson before enrolling in the sophomore class at The University of North Carolina in June 1849. Holt left the university in 1850 to gain practical experience in Philadelphia. He became an accomplished salesman and expert bookkeeper but, at his father's request, returned to Alamance County the following year to assist in the operation of the factory on the Alamance Creek. When Edwin Holt had bought the interests of his partner, William A. Carrigan, the factory name was changed from the Holt and Carrigan Cotton Mill to Edwin M. Holt's and Sons. Thomas worked industriously at the factory, and it was he who began the dyeing of yarn prior to making cloth from it. This made it possible to produce "Alamance plaids."

When the Civil War began, Holt continued to work at the factory; however, in 1861 he took over the Granite Mills on the Haw River and his brother William was called home from the Confederate Army to manage the Alamance factory. Later with his brother-in-law and partner, Adolphus Moore, Holt built a new factory at the lower end of the old Granite Mills on the Haw. By May 1874 some forty houses, a church, and a school had been built for the 175 employees and their families.

Although concerned with the textile industry throughout his life, Holt had a variety of other interests. He served as a magistrate and in 1872 was elected county commissioner, a position he held for four years. Before the Civil War, Holt had been a Whig, but in 1876 he was elected a state senator on the Democratic ticket. In 1882 he was sent to the North Carolina House of Representatives where he served three successive terms and was chosen speaker of the house in 1884. Elected lieutenant governor in 1888, he became governor of North Carolina upon the death of Daniel G. Fowle in 1891. Holt served until 1893 but declined to run for a full term because of his health.

As part of his public service Holt helped to secure the establishment of the state Department of Agriculture, the North Carolina College of Agriculture and Mechanic Arts at Raleigh, and two other state schools at Greensboro. He also served on the board of trustees of The University of North Carolina and of Davidson College. Holt encouraged the expansion of common schools in the state and urged that appropriations to The University of North Carolina be increased. He sought additional aid for the state hospitals at Morganton, Raleigh, and Greensboro, and for the children's home at Oxford. At the county level, Holt assisted in establishing a new system of government, returning governance to the people through the popular election of county officers. (Previously, that practice had been abolished and elections had been turned over to justices of the peace appointed by the legislature.)

Along with his father, Holt became a stockholder, president, and director of the North Carolina Railroad Company, which built a road between Goldsboro and Charlotte. He was also instrumental in the construction of other railroads in the state. When northern businessmen had a lien on the state-owned stock in the North Carolina Railroad, Holt and other North Carolinians went north and succeeded in compromising the debt and saving the stock. Some estimated that they saved the state as much as $5 or $6 million. As president of the North Carolina State Fair for several years, Holt was active in putting the fair on a financially secure basis. He was also a member of the Patrons of Husbandry, or the Grange, serving as president for thirteen years.

During the Kirk-Holden War, both Holt and his brother-in-law, Adolphus Moore, were arrested on Governor William Holden's orders. Holt saw the whole disturbance as a political move to win election by the Radical Republicans. However, he maintained that the Democrats carried the state by 211,000 votes and would have a two-thirds majority in both houses. Radical Republicans first attempted to try those arrested for murder by a military commission, but could not get anyone to sit on the cases. When they turned the remaining prisoners over to the civil courts, over a hundred were quickly released, including Thomas Holt. He long remembered the indignation of the people and the impeachment and removal of Governor Holden from office.

On 17 Oct. 1855 Holt married Louisa Matilda Moore of Caswell County, and they were the parents of six children: Alice Linwood, Charles Thomas, Cora May, Louisa Moore, Ella Moore, and Thomas M., Jr. Holt became a member of the Graham Presbyterian Church on 2 June 1856 and served as a ruling elder from 1859 until his death. In 1895 he was awarded an honorary LL.D. by The University of North Carolina.

Holt died at his home on the Haw River, near the mill he operated. The funeral was held at the Graham Presbyterian Church, and burial was in Linwood Cemetery, Graham.

SEE: Samuel A. Ashe, ed., *Biographical History of North Carolina*, vol. 3 (1908); John W. Carrigan Papers (Manuscript Department, Duke University Library, Durham); E. M. Holt Diary, J. W. White Papers, Henderson Papers (Southern Historical Collection, University of North Carolina Library, Chapel Hill); Eugene Holt, *Edwin Michael Holt and His Descendants, 1807–1948* (1949); Julian Hughes, *Development of the Textile Industry in Alamance County* (1965); Minute Book 2, Graham Presbyterian Church; Raleigh *News and Observer*, 11, 13 Apr. 1896, 14 Mar. 1898.

RACHEL Y. HOLT

Holt, Walter Lawrence *(1 June 1859–1 Oct. 1913)*, leader in the textile industry, was the son of James Henry and Laura Cameron Holt. His father was a well known manufacturer, his mother was the daughter of a prominent Caswell County farmer, and his grandfather, Edwin M. Holt, pioneered in the manufacturing of textiles such as the Alamanace plaids in Alamance County. After preparatory training, young Holt took courses at Horner Military Academy in Oxford before entering Davidson College. Leaving Davidson in his junior year, he completed his formal education at Eastman's Business College in Poughkeepsie, N.Y.

Holt began work as bookkeeper and shipping clerk at the Carolina Cotton Mills, which belonged to his father and uncle. Later he kept books and was a supervisor at another of the Holt mills at Glencoe on the Haw River in Alamance County. In partnership with his brother, Ernest, Holt built and became president of the Elmira Mills. In 1893 he opened the Lakeside Mills in partnership with Ernest and another brother, Samuel. Two years later he and his family moved to Fayetteville, where they built Holt-Morgan Mills in the suburbs. Holt was president and his cousin, Lawrence A. Williamson, was secretary-treasurer. Walter Holt also served as president and treasurer of the Fayetteville Lakeview Mills. In 1900, when the Tolar-Hart-Holt Mills began operation, he became a director of that firm.

Holt not only was concerned with building new mills but he also tried to provide for the needs of his employees. He was responsible for the construction of neatly laid out villages in the surrounding areas. The houses were supplied with water, and space was made available for gardening. Schools and churches were established, as well as recreation and amusement facilities.

Like most of his family, Holt was a Democrat, but he was less interested in politics than some members of the family.

On 12 Feb. 1890 Holt married Mary De Rosset, and they had four children: Elisabeth Nash, Walter L., Jr., William De Rosset, and Mary De Rosset. While still president of the Holt-Morgan and Holt-Williams mills in Fayetteville, and a director of several mills in the Alamance section of the state, Holt died in Westbrook Hospital in Richmond, Va. The funeral was held in St. John's Episcopal Church, Fayetteville, where he was buried.

SEE: Samuel A. Ashe, ed., *Biographical History of North Carolina*, vol. 3 (1908); Julian Hughes, *Development of the Textile Industry in Alamance County* (1965); Raleigh *News and Observer*, 2 Oct. 1913.

RACHEL Y. HOLT

Holt, William Edwin *(1 Nov. 1839–26 May 1917)*, textile manufacturer and civic and religious leader, was born at Locust Grove in Alamance County, near the site where the Regulators fought in 1771. He was one of ten children born to Edwin Michael Holt, a pioneer in the North Carolina textile industry as well as a prominent planter and landowner, and his wife Emily Farish, the daughter of a prosperous Chatham County farmer. Young Holt's education began at home under a tutor, and at thirteen he attended a school in Germantown. He later studied under the Reverend Dr. Alexander Wilson and in 1855 entered The University of North Carolina. After two years he left the university and returned to be general manager of his father's factory in Alamance County. Edwin Michael Holt had bought the

interests of his partner, William A. Carrigan, and needed William's assistance.

When the Civil War began, Holt joined the Sixth North Carolina Regiment of the Confederate Army. However, Governor John W. Ellis ordered him to return to the factory to help supply cotton goods for the army. Holt remained there throughout the conflict. After the war, in 1866, when his father decided to retire from the textile industry, William Holt became one of the partners in the business. Later, with his brother James, he organized the Carolina Cotton Mills which began operation in 1869; meanwhile, William retained his interest in the Alamance factory. On 24 Apr. 1871, the mill at Alamance burned. With an estimated value of $60,000 the building was insured for only $25,000, but the factory was quickly rebuilt.

In 1880 William and James Holt built the Glencoe Mills. Later William moved to Lexington, where he erected the Wennonah Mills. His ever-expanding textile enterprises included the Anchor Mills, Huntersville; Florence Mills, Forest City; Asheville Mills, Asheville; Spray Mills, Spray; Mineola Mills, Gibsonville; and Francis Mills, Biscoe. Holt tried to treat his employees fairly and received considerable praise for raising their wages 25 percent in 1887 before other owners were willing to do so.

Holt's financial interests were widespread. Particularly concerned with banking in North Carolina, he was a stockholder and president of the Commercial National Bank in Charlotte. He also owned stock in the First National Bank and the Merchants and Farmers National Bank, both in Charlotte, and in the Bank of Lexington. Holt owned stock in the Southern Stock Mutual Fire Insurance Company and the Underwriters Fire Insurance Company of Greensboro, as well as in the North Carolina Railroad, of which he was a director. His real estate holdings included farms in Alamance and Davidson counties and numerous hotel properties in the state. These business affairs left him less time for politics than some other members of his family. He was a Democrat.

Holt married Amelia Lloyd, the daughter of Dr. William Rainey and Louisa Allen Hogan Holt of Lexington. They had seven children: William Edwin, Jr., Ethel, Lois, Maud, Emily, and twins Lora and Lura, who died in infancy.

Holt's funeral was held in Grace Episcopal Church, Lexington, of which he was a member. He was buried in Lexington City Cemetery. Among his bequests, he left his church $4,000. The estimated value of his estate was over $3 million; the estate paid an inheritance tax of $126,000, which was the largest paid to that time in North Carolina. It was believed that, at the time of his death, Holt held more state bonds than any other person in North Carolina.

SEE: Samuel A. Ashe, ed., *Biographical History of North Carolina*, vol. 2 (1908); John W. Carrigan Papers (Manuscript Department, Duke University Library, Durham); E. M. Holt Diary, J. W. White Papers, Henderson M. Fowler Papers (Southern Historical Collection, University of North Carolina Library, Chapel Hill); Eugene Holt, *Edwin Michael Holt and His Descendants, 1807–1948* (1949); Julian Hughes, *Development of the Textile Industry in North Carolina* (1965); Raleigh *News and Observer*, 27 May 1917.

RACHEL Y. HOLT

Holt, William Rainey (*30 Oct. 1798–3 Oct. 1868*), physician, public servant, and planter, was born in Alamance County, the oldest son of Michael and Rachel Rainey Holt, and the grandson of Captain Michael and Jean Lockhart Holt. He had two brothers (Alfred Augustus and Edwin Michael) and three sisters (Jane Lockhart, Polly, and Nancy). His mother was the daughter of the Reverend Benjamin and Nancy Rainey, the former a prominent minister of the Christian church. His father was a prosperous planter who served in the North Carolina House of Commons in 1804 and in the state senate in 1819 and 1821–22, during which terms he advocated internal improvements in the state.

Holt was graduated from The University of North Carolina in 1817 and obtained a medical degree from the Jefferson Medical College in Philadelphia. Always desirous of keeping abreast with the newest scientific and medical discoveries, he attended clinics yearly in Philadelphia even after he was firmly established in his profession. Holt opened a practice in Lexington, where he soon became known not only as a good physician but also as a community builder. Skilled and dedicated, he sought to improve sanitary conditions and to combat many superstitions prevalent in that day.

When Holt moved to Lexington, Davidson County had not yet been created. After the formation act was passed by the legislature in 1822, he became one of the foremost leaders in its implementation. In 1823 he was commissioned a justice of the county Court of Pleas and Quarter Sessions; when a dispute arose over the location of the county seat, Holt was sent by the court to The University of North Carolina to enlist the support of his good friend, President Joseph Caldwell. After Lexington was named the county seat by a new act of the legislature, Holt purchased lots at the county auction and was appointed to various committees concerned with building a courthouse, a poor house, and even a gallows.

The young physician was one of the first members of St. Peters Episcopal Church in the 1820s and served as a vestryman for many years. He was a trustee of the Lexington Academy in 1825 and of the Lexington Female Academy in 1858. During a term in the state senate in 1838–39, he strongly supported passage of the Education Act and was chairman of the committee on internal improvements. At home he worked for a tax for common schools in the county; in 1843, after the tax was finally voted, he became a member of the first Davidson County Board of Superintendents of Common Schools. He also supported the establishment of the first cotton mill in Lexington and pioneering efforts in the cotton industry elsewhere by his brother, Edwin Michael Holt, and others. When the Railroad Act was passed in 1849, he played an important role in the location and building of a railroad through the county; two stations—Holtsburg and Linwood, the name of his farm—were named in his honor.

Soon after settling in Lexington, Holt began buying farmland in the Jersey Settlement near the Yadkin River. Deeply interested in agriculture, he spent much of his time at his farm, trying out new methods about which he had read or heard. He read the latest agricultural publications and maintained a close friendship with scientific agriculturists like the editor Edmund Ruffin, Professor Ebenezer Emmons, and Judge Thomas Ruffin, whom he succeeded as president of the state Agricultural Society. Holt effectively used such advanced practices as deep plowing, proper drainage, and turning under clover and peas to enrich the soil; commercial fertilizers; and the latest farm machinery. The yields per acre at Linwood were considered phenomenal. Not only his neighbors but also agriculturists from all over the state, and even from Richmond and Baltimore, went there to learn of his experiences.

Although cotton was the chief cash crop, no doubt sold to his brother's cotton mills, the plantation was almost self-sufficient with a variety of other products. Newspapermen who rode on the train through this productive farmland became poetic in their descriptions of the green fields and the herds of improved sheep and cattle. Holt purchased outside the state a purebred Short Horn bull and brought him to Linwood, with the registration papers completed a short time afterwards. This was the first registered animal of any breed of cattle in North Carolina. "When his sons and daughters went to college, each week a large wagon of supplies consisting of beef, mutton, pork, vegetables as well as water-ground flour and meal, was sent from the plantation, which was a great help to the schools as well as helping pay for the education of the boys and girls." His slaves were well fed, clothed, and housed. The smartest and most skilled were appointed as overseers.

Because of his agricultural achievements, his public service, and his medical knowledge and skill, Holt was well known across the state. When newspapermen wrote about Lexington, they often closed with the statement, "Dr. Holt lives here." Distinguished judges and attorneys attending court in Lexington would be entertained in Holt's home, considered by all as an ideal residence.

In 1822 Holt built a house on South Main Street where he took his bride, Mary Gizeal Allen, a descendant of William Allen, who had married Mary Parke, of the Parke-Custis family of Virginia. They had five children: Elizabeth Allen, who married Dr. Dillon Lindsay; Elvira Jane, who married Joseph Erwin; Louise, who died young; Mary Gizeal, who married Colonel Ellis, a brother of Governor John Willis Ellis; and John Allen.

In 1834, two years after the death of his first wife, Holt married her cousin, Louisa Allen Hogan, daughter of Colonel William and Elizabeth Allen Hogan. William Hogan was a son of Colonel John Hogan, a Revolutionary War officer whose wife Mary was a daughter of General Thomas Lloyd. Holt bought land adjoining his first house, which he removed, and built The Homestead, an imposing residence of distinctive architectural features (which still stands). Here were born their nine children: Louisa, Julia, Franklin, James, William Michael, and Eugene Randolph, all of whom died unmarried (William Michael, an officer in the Confederate Army, died in Richmond in 1862, and Eugene Randolph died a prisoner of war on Johnson's Island in 1865); Claudia E., who married D. C. Pearson; Frances, who married Charles A. Hunt of Lexington; and Amelia, who married William Edwin Holt, son of Edwin Michael Holt.

Holt was a Democrat and a Secessionist. Firmly believing in the Confederate cause, he was deeply disturbed by the South's defeat. Soon after the war ended, former Governor John Motley Morehead died at Rock Bridge Alum Springs, Va., where Holt had accompanied him in the vain hope of curing his illness.

Although he grieved over the outcome of the war and the loss of his friend and his children, Holt worked resolutely to supervise his plantation under new conditions. His exposure to all kinds of weather caused more suffering from rheumatism and wore down his physical resistance. He was buried in the Lexington City Cemetery.

SEE: Samuel A. Ashe, ed., *Biographical History of North Carolina*, vol. 7 (1908); Minutes of Davidson County Court of Pleas and Quarter Sessions (North Carolina State Archives, Raleigh); M. Jewell Sink and Mary G. Matthews, *Pathfinders, Past and Present: A History of Davidson County, North Carolina* (1972).

M. JEWELL SINK

Holton, Alfred Eugene (29 Oct. 1852–4 Dec. 1928), lawyer and Republican political leader, was one of eight children of Quinton and Harriet Holland Holton. He was born near Jamestown, Guilford County, into a most unusual family that shaped his life. His father was a farmer and a Methodist Protestant minister. The Methodist Protestants had left the Methodist Episcopal Church, South, to protest acceptance of slavery as church doctrine. During the Civil War, the elder Holton apparently served as the state moderator for the Methodist Protestants but was prevented from preaching himself because of his criticism of slavery. Thus, A. Eugene grew up in Iredell and Yadkin counties a confirmed Methodist, but he was also a member of a family that rejected many of the dominant ideas found in North Carolina at the time.

The family also directed young Holton into his career. His early legal training came from his grandfather, Jesse Holton, and his father. According to family tradition, Quinton Holton trained aspiring lawyers and several hundred young men read under his direction. The Holton children were reputed to have walked around with copies of Blackstone under their arms. Four of them became lawyers: A. Eugene, Samuel, John Q., and their sister Tabitha—the first woman licensed to practice law in North Carolina.

After some formal education in the Iredell and Yadkin public schools and a brief experiment as a schoolteacher in Iredell County, Holton began the career his family had chosen for him. He studied the law further with Judge Albion W. Tourgée of Greensboro and received his license to practice in 1874. The fact that Tourgée was a staunch Republican indicates that Holton had followed his father's lead in opposing the dominant political forces of his time. For most of the next two decades he was a law partner of Mann Reece in Yadkin County. In 1880 and 1882, he was elected as a Republican to represent that county in the North Carolina House of Representatives.

In December 1891 Holton married Mary Elizabeth Petty of Guilford County. They continued a family tradition by having a large number of children. There were twelve in all and they all survived to maturity, including George R., Frank P., Mary, John W., Harriet H., Elizabeth P., Theodore R., A. Eugene, Jr., Eleanor, David M., Walter, and Rebecca.

With the appearance of the Populist party in North Carolina politics in 1892, Holton again became active in the Republican party, this time as a leader among Republicans who tried to bring about fusion between their party and the Populists. In the summer of 1894, he was elected chairman of the Republican state committee. He was startled to find that in "some counties we had no organization" and worked diligently to correct the situation. The fusion victory in the fall elections gave Holton great prominence, and he became a candidate for the U.S. Senate. He ran as a traditional Republican against Jeter C. Pritchard, who had endorsed free silver

and had worked closely with Populist leader Marion Butler. At the Republican legislative caucus in January 1895, Pritchard defeated Holton by a vote of 30 to 18 and was subsequently elected to the Senate.

Although disappointed by this reversal, Holton continued to work hard as state chairman. He aligned himself with Congressman Thomas Settle III in an effort to block Pritchard's domination of the party organization. He supported the gold standard and Speaker of the House Thomas B. Reed for president in 1896, when Pritchard worked for free silver and William McKinley. Holton readily accepted McKinley's nomination when the national convention rejected free silver. He then helped to maneuver the Republicans into a complex legislative fusion arrangement in 1896 that allowed the Populists and Republicans to retain control of the state legislature and brought about the election of Republican Daniel L. Russell as governor of North Carolina. In 1896 he also moved to Waughtown near Salem and formed a law partnership with Major J. E. Alexander that lasted until 1902.

As a reward for his services—and probably because Senator Pritchard wanted to remove a dangerous rival from active politics—Holton was appointed U.S. district attorney for the Western District of North Carolina by President McKinley in 1897. He held this position continuously for seventeen years until he was replaced in the spring of 1914 by a Democrat nominated by President Woodrow Wilson. Holton had an excellent record in office and won universal respect for his impartiality by sentencing Republican officeholders to long prison terms for abusing their public trusts. Theodore Roosevelt once remarked "that no man in the United States had a better record as District Attorney than Gene Holton of North Carolina."

After leaving office, Holton remained active in Winston-Salem. He formed a law firm with his son George that would last until his death. He was also the founder and president of the Forsyth Roller Mills, which was started to help local grain farmers. At the same time, he was named to the boards of directors of several banks and businesses. In May 1928, he suffered a severe stroke and lost consciousness. He never recovered and was buried at the Springfield Friend's Church in Guilford County. Holton was an excellent example of a white North Carolinian who became an active Republican. His family background inclined him towards unorthodox politics and a legal career. He never deviated from that pattern and performed his work with dedication and a high degree of skill.

SEE: Helen G. Edmonds, *The Negro and Fusion Politics in North Carolina: 1894–1901* (1951); S. E. Hall, "Alfred Eugene Holton," *Proceedings of the Thirty-first Annual Session of the North Carolina Bar Association* (1929); Gordon B. McKinney, *Southern Mountain Republicans, 1865–1900: Politics and the Appalachian Community* (1978); Thomas Settle Papers (Southern Historical Collection, University of North Carolina Library, Chapel Hill); *Winston-Salem Journal*, 5 Dec. 1928 (photograph).

GORDON B. MCKINNEY

Holton, Holland (13 May 1888–20 Aug. 1947), educator, the son of Samuel Melanchthon and Aura Barrett Chaffin Holton, was born at Dobson, but his family moved to Durham in 1894. He completed his secondary education in Durham High School in 1903 and in the fall of that year entered Trinity College (now Duke University), where he was graduated with the B.A. degree in 1907. Holton began his career as principal of East Durham High School (1907–9). From there he went on to become head of the department of history at Durham High School (1909–10), principal of West Durham High School (1911–14, 1915–19), instructor in public speaking at Trinity College (1912–19), and assistant superintendent (1915–19) and superintendent (1919–21) of the Durham County schools. Meanwhile, he attended the Trinity College School of Law (1910–11, 1914–15) and the University of Chicago Law School (summers, 1915–17). He received the doctor of jurisprudence degree in 1927 after spending the 1926–27 session at Chicago.

In 1921, Holton joined the faculty of Trinity College as professor of education and the legal phases of educational administration, and as head of the Department of Education. He had been named director of the Trinity College Summer School in 1920 and held that post until his death. While at Duke University, Holton devoted much personal and professional time to his contacts with public schoolteachers, providing them with off-schedule classes, seminars, and conferences.

Recognized as a national authority on secondary education, Holton served as secretary of the North Carolina Commission on High School Textbooks (1919–23), a member of the commission on secondary schools of the Southern Association of Secondary Schools and Colleges (1927–47) and editor of the Southern Association *Quarterly* (1937–47); and a member of the North Carolina College Conference (president, 1937–38), North Carolina Education Association, and National Education Association. He was also a member (and secretary) of the Durham County Board of Health (1922–26), of the North Carolina Constitutional Committee against the Repeal of the Eighteenth Amendment to the Federal Constitution (elected 1933), and of the Selective Service System (1940–47).

A Republican, Holton served for two years on the state executive committee. He was a member of Duke Memorial Methodist Church and active in its lay program, particularly the Sunday school. In addition, he was a Mason (3rd degree), a Knight of Pythias, and a member of the Kiwanis Club of Durham (president, one term). Among his fraternal affiliations were Phi Beta Kappa (scholarship), Tau Kappa Alpha, Kappa Delta Pi (education), and Phi Delta Kappa.

On 24 Dec. 1911, he married Lela Daisy Young, the daughter of George Polk and Arthelia Belvin Young. They had three sons: Winfred Quinton, who died in his youth; Samuel Melanchthon; and Holland Young. Holton died and was buried in Durham.

SEE: *North Carolina Biography*, vol. 3 (1929); *Who Was Who in America*, vol. 2 (1950).

C. SYLVESTER GREEN

Holton, Tabitha Anne *(1854–14 June 1886)*, first woman licensed to practice law in North Carolina, was born in Guilford County, the daughter of the Reverend Quinton (5 Feb. 1818–5 May 1890) and Harriet Jacobina Holland Holton (12 Dec. 1823–25 Mar. 1871). Her father was a Methodist Protestant minister.

Little is known about Tabitha Anne Holton's early life, though the Raleigh *Observer* reported that she was well educated, spoke three or four languages fluently, had studied law by reading books lent to her by members of the Greensboro bar, and had occasionally been examined by those lawyers as she had had "no regular preceptor." Otto Olsen, biographer of Albion W. Tour-

gée, mentions in passing that she mastered law while tutoring her brothers.

On 7 Jan. 1878, she and her brother Samuel Melanchthon Holton arrived in Raleigh from Jamestown and reported the next day to take the bar examination given by the North Carolina Supreme Court. A question immediately arose as to the power of the court to admit women to practice law, and the candidate was advised to appear with counsel that afternoon so that the matter could be considered and determined. However, because of the funeral of Chief Justice Richmond M. Pearson, the hearing was postponed until the morning of 9 January. At that time, Albion W. Tourgée appeared as counsel in her behalf; and his long argument (which was reported at length in the Raleigh *Observer* of 10 January) was convincing, despite resistance led by William H. Battle. The court, after a ten-minute recess to consider the question, permitted the applicant to be tested. She was escorted from the National Hotel by her brother, who had taken the bar examination at the regularly scheduled time the preceding day. Though the questioning was done in private, it was reported that Tabitha Anne Holton passed without missing a single question. Her license was dated 8 January, the day on which the men had taken the examination.

According to a newspaper report, the female lawyer planned to move with her newly licensed brother to Kansas where a number of women were practicing law, but nothing has been found to indicate that she did so. She was sworn in as an attorney in the court at Greensboro, and it is thought that she practiced in Yadkinville in partnership with Samuel M. Holton and perhaps with two other brothers, Alfred Eugene and John Quinton Holton. She did research and office work, leaving courtroom appearances to the men.

Tabitha Anne Holton was described as "a sprightly brunette, of medium size, an intellectual cast of countenance, though not strikingly handsome." She dressed "very neatly and in good taste, but not gorgeously." Basically timid, she told reporters she "suffered the horrors of a hundred deaths" while awaiting the court's decision and was tempted to abandon her goal but persevered as she recalled the days of hard study. The Raleigh *Observer* commented, "We certainly admire this noble little woman's pluck, if we can't say so much for her judgment." The *Greensboro Patriot*, in its 16 Jan. 1878 issue, carried a long article entitled "A Female Lawyer," which could easily have been written by a 1975 advocate of the Equal Rights Amendment.

Suffering from tuberculosis, North Carolina's first woman lawyer died intestate in Yadkinville and was buried in the cemetery of Springfield Friends Church, now within the city limits of High Point. Though Springfield was a Quaker church, Jamestown citizens were buried there during a long period when the town had no cemetery of its own.

SEE: Mrs. Alice Holton Edison, personal contact (Winston-Salem); Greensboro *New State*, 10 Jan. 1878; *Greensboro North State*, 24 June 1886; *Greensboro Patriot*, 16 Jan. 1878; Otto H. Olsen, *Carpetbagger's Crusade: The Life of Albion Winegar Tourgée* (1965); Raleigh *News*, 10 Jan. 1878; Raleigh *Observer*, 8, 9, 10 Jan. 1878; Tombstones, Springfield Friends Church (High Point).

MEMORY F. MITCHELL

Hood, George Ezekiel *(25 Jan. 1875–8 Mar. 1960)*, lawyer, legislator, mayor, and congressman, was born in Goldsboro, the son of Edward Bass and Edith Finlayson Bridgers Hood. The Hood family had lived in the area since the eighteenth century. His mother was a member of a prominent eastern North Carolina family which was descended from Colonel Joseph Bridger of White Marsh in Isle of Wight County, Va. Bridger, a Burgess and a member of Sir William Berkeley's Council, played a leading Loyalist role in Bacon's Rebellion.

Hood's formal education began in 1880 when he entered the city schools of Goldsboro. After completing the seventh grade at William Street School, he dropped out and took a job as a messenger with Western Union; a few years later he became manager. He then worked for the Southern Railway Company in Goldsboro and Raleigh. Bright and enterprising, Hood returned to Goldsboro to study law, and was privately tutored by attorneys Isaac F. Dortch and Dail Hardy. In 1896, at age twenty-one, he was admitted to the bar of the North Carolina Supreme Court. He pursued the profession in Raleigh for a year before opening a practice in Goldsboro in 1897. An interest in politics led to his appointment as secretary of the Wayne County Democratic Executive Committee from 1896 to 1900.

Meanwhile, Hood enlisted in the National Guard in 1896 and was promoted to captain of Company B, First Regiment, on 19 July 1901, then to lieutenant colonel and assistant chief of ordnance on 20 Nov. 1905. He was transferred to the inspector general's department as assistant inspector general on 21 Jan. 1907 and retired as a colonel on 25 May 1909.

In the elections of 1898 Hood ran for county treasurer and a seat in the North Carolina House of Representatives on the Democratic ticket. He won both offices, serving as treasurer until 1901, when he was succeeded by James William Croom Thompson. In the house, Hood was appointed to the education committee that set in motion Governor Charles Brantley Aycock's educational reform program to upgrade public schools statewide. Later he was a member of the executive committee of the North Carolina Agriculture Department (1904–10).

Returning to Goldsboro in 1901, he was elected mayor and served with distinction until 1907. In that capacity Hood guided Goldsboro through its first real expansion, voting bonds to build the present city hall, pave streets, and take over public utilities.

In 1909 Hood sought a seat in Congress but lost the nomination by ten votes in a hectic, heated convention held in the Messenger Opera House in Goldsboro. In 1912 he was a presidential elector on the Democratic ticket of Woodrow Wilson and Thomas Riley Marshall. In the 1913 convention he was nominated by acclamation and in the general election led his party to victory over Republican B. H. Crumpler of Clinton; he was reelected to a second term in 1915.

During his four years in Congress, Hood actively supported President Wilson and was much interested in his military policy. He was on the congressional committee to receive the statue of Zebulon Baird Vance, former governor and U.S. senator from North Carolina, when it was placed in the capitol. Declining to seek a third term in 1918 for health reasons, Hood retired to Goldsboro where he again entered the civic and professional life of the county.

Always a student of history, Hood was a member (1903–8) of the State Literary and Historical Association and a charter member of the Wayne Historical Society. For many years he gave the annual address at ceremonies on Confederate Memorial Day, 10 May, in Goldsboro. In 1905 he published a philosophical work, *The Origin of Man.*

A lifelong member of St. Paul's Methodist Church, Hood served on the board of stewards and was frequently a delegate to the district and annual conferences. He was a Knight of Pythias and a Chancellor Commander and delegate to the Grand Lodge of North Carolina. Active in the Wayne County bar, he held every official position of that organization during his lifetime; at the time of his death, he was dean. From 1903 to 1956 he was also a member of the North Carolina Bar Association

On 23 Sept. 1903 Hood married Julia Annie Flowers, the daughter of Dr. Samuel Bryce Flowers and his second wife, Nancy Lofton Kornegay, a widow, of Mount Olive. They had three children: Nannie Bridgers, George Ezekiel, Jr., and Elizabeth. Hood was buried in Willow Dale Cemetery, Goldsboro.

SEE: *Biog. Dir. Am. Cong.* (1774–1949); John Bennett Boddie, *Seventeenth Century Isle of Wight County, Virginia* (1938); *Goldsboro News-Argus*, 25 Jan. 1960; Private papers of George Ezekiel Hood (in possession of George E. Hood, Jr., Goldsboro).

JOHN BAXTON FLOWERS III

Hood, Gurney Pope (*26 Nov. 1884–20 Nov. 1962*), banker, legislator, commissioner of banks, and church and fraternal leader, was born in Grantham Township, Wayne County, the son of Solomon Pope and Betsey Rhodes Hood. His ancestors were among the early settlers of his native region. He attended a one-teacher public school for nine years and a graded school in Goldsboro for one year, then read law for two and a half years under Nathan O'Berry. Although licensed in 1908, he never practiced law.

As a young man Hood was a Western Union messenger in Goldsboro, learned telegraphy, studied at night in business school, and became a telegraph operator, billing clerk, and bookkeeper for the Bank of Wayne. Deciding to make a career in banking, he served as an officer from 1913 to 1923 in banks in Whitakers, Morehead City, Tarboro, and Elizabeth City. In 1923, with his brother, he organized and was president of the Hood System of Industrial Banks.

In his first public office, Hood was alderman of Goldsboro from 1911 to 1913. Shortly after moving to Morehead City he became mayor, serving from 1917 to 1919. Returning to his industrial banking business in Goldsboro, he was elected in 1929 and reelected in 1931 to the North Carolina House of Representatives from Wayne County. In the General Assembly Hood was a member of the finance committee of both sessions, chairman of the subcommittee that wrote the Local Government Act, and a member of the subcommittee that drafted the Revenue Bill of 1931. As a member of the banking committee, he was active in banking legislation and supported the controversial Seawell Bill to remove the banking department from the Corporation Commission and make it a separate department, and to create the office of banking commissioner, one of Governor O. Max Gardner's legislative goals. Named commissioner of banks, Hood took office on 27 May 1931, the date the General Assembly adjourned, and served until 14 Apr. 1951, when he was succeeded by William W. Jones. His tenure encompassed the harsh days of the Great Depression and witnessed the failure of many financial institutions. Hood supported bank education, strengthened bank supervision, and was a leader in the restoration of the banking system after the Banking Holiday of 1933. In 1938 he was elected president of the

National Association of Supervisors of State Banks. While banking commissioner, he was chairman of a committee of state employees other than teachers that drafted the State Retirement Act.

After leaving office, Hood organized and was president of the Hood System Industrial Bank in Raleigh until 1956. That year he was an unsuccessful candidate for the Democratic nomination for lieutenant governor.

A longtime leader in the Methodist church, Hood was honored for his service by the North Carolina Methodist Conference in 1961. He was vice-president of the North Carolina Council of Churches and a member of the board of directors of the National Conference of Christians and Jews. Among other associations, he was state councillor and national councillor of the Junior Order of United American Mechanics, and a member of the Masonic order, Odd Fellows, and Woodmen of the World. Hood was also a trustee of Louisburg College and of Shaw University.

On 16 June 1915 he married Marion Lee Stevens of Goldsboro. They had three children: Robin Pope, Samuel Stevens, and Lee Rawlings. At age seventy-seven Hood died of a stroke in Raleigh and was buried in Willow Dale Cemetery, Goldsboro.

SEE: John L. Cheney, Jr., ed., *North Carolina Government, 1585–1974* (1975); Gurney Pope Hood Papers (in possession of Robin Pope Hood, Marion); Robin Pope Hood, personal contact (Marion); *North Carolina Manual, 1949*; Raleigh *News and Observer*, 21 Nov. 1962; *Tarheel Banker*, May 1931, May 1951, December 1962.

T. HARRY GATTON

Hood, James Walker (*30 May 1831–30 Oct. 1918*), clergyman, educator, and bishop, the son of Levi and Harriet Walker Hood, was born on the farm of Ephraim Jackson in Chester County, Pa., nine miles from Wilmington, Del. His mother, a woman of "extraordinary intelligence," was much interested in all matters affecting blacks, including a separate church for her race. His father was a Methodist minister. While living in Wilmington, Hood's parents became involved in a controversy over a church building constructed by blacks but taken over by white Methodists; henceforth they supported the African Methodist Episcopal Zion church, established as the Methodist church for blacks.

Hood's childhood was a time of hard work, danger, and meager education. Levi Hood opposed binding any of his twelve children to an apprenticeship because he thought it similar to slavery. He did arrange verbal contracts whereby his children would work for food, clothing, and six weeks of school a year until they were sixteen. After young Hood had served a short term under a contract with Ephraim Jackson, the arrangement was ended, and he found work where he could in Philadelphia and New York. He was once kidnapped, apparently to be sold into slavery, but escaped. Although he attended school for only a few months in Pennsylvania and Delaware, his native ability enabled him to pursue general and theological studies without a teacher except for a tutor in Greek.

A religious inclination eventually led Hood into the ministry. At age eleven he experienced conversion, but questioned his beliefs until he was eighteen. At age twenty-one he mentioned to a minister his call to preach, thinking mistakenly that the clergyman would make arrangements for him. In 1856 Hood finally appeared before the New York Conference of the A.M.E. Zion church and secured a license to preach. The next

year he moved to New Haven, Conn., and filled a pulpit there. In 1859 the New England Conference received him on trial and appointed him a missionary without pay to Nova Scotia. Lacking the funds to go, he worked in a New York hotel for thirteen months to become self-supporting. After being ordained deacon at Boston in September 1860, he departed for Nova Scotia. Hood landed at Halifax and walked the forty-five miles to Englewood, a mile from Bridgeton where he found a black community. Although its members were Hardshell Baptists and hostile to Methodism, Hood had gathered a congregation of eleven persons before his departure in 1863. In the interim he was ordained an elder in 1862 at Hartford. After serving in Bridgeport, Conn., for six months in late 1863, he was sent as a missionary to North Carolina where he remained for the rest of his life.

In North Carolina Hood found his major area of service. In early 1864, against the opposition of white Northern Methodists, he persuaded the black Southern Methodist congregations in New Bern and Beaufort to affiliate with the A.M.E. Zion church. When the Northern Methodists contested his conversion of these congregations to Zion, Hood was forced to appeal to the secretary of war for a ruling that permitted the blacks to align with whichever church they desired. In late 1864 he helped to found the North Carolina Conference, and over the years he aided in the establishment of numerous churches within its bounds. Hood was a pastor for three years in New Bern, two years in Fayetteville, and over three years in Charlotte. After becoming a bishop in 1872, he resided in Fayetteville until his death.

Hood became active in North Carolina politics on behalf of his people. In the fall of 1865 he presided over the first statewide political convention of blacks, which met to demand civil and political rights. In 1868 he participated in the state constitutional convention and contributed greatly to placing strong homestead and public school provisions in the constitution. From 1868 to 1871 Hood served as assistant state superintendent of public instruction, with the major duty of founding and supervising schools for blacks. Although hampered by white hostility and the lack of black teachers, he increased attendance to 49,000 students in 1871. Hood remained active in the Republican party, serving as a delegate to the national convention in 1872 and as temporary chairman of the state convention in 1876. He also served briefly as a magistrate and a deputy collector of customs and from 1868 to 1871, without pay, as assistant superintendent of the Freedman's Bureau in North Carolina.

Hood's duties as bishop took him to most states and to Europe. As an itinerant bishop, he had—by 1914—presided over several conferences annually for these total periods: New York, 27 years; New England, 24 years; Allegheny-Ohio, 6 years; Alabama, 4 years; Kentucky and New Jersey, 4 years each; California, 3 years; Philadelphia and Baltimore, 3 years; and Tennessee, 1 year. Yet most of his time he spent in the Virginia, North Carolina, South Carolina, and Georgia conferences which he had helped to found before becoming a bishop.

One of Hood's contributions as bishop was to help establish and guide Zion Wesley Institute (later Livingstone College) in Salisbury, N.C. He presided over its board of trustees for over thirty years, educated six of his children there, and donated a good portion of his annual salary to keep it open. In 1881 Hood attended an ecumenical conference in London to help secure finances for the institute. He appointed a committee of Englishmen to direct the fund-raising, had the name of the college changed to Livingstone in honor of David Livingstone who had recently died, and provided the means for the president of Livingstone to travel in England to assist in fund-raising.

Hood's family life, although disrupted by long absences from home, centered around three marriages. In 1853 he married Hannah L. Ralph of Lancaster, Pa., who died in 1855. In 1858 he married Sophia J. Nugent of Washington, D.C., who before her death bore him seven children, four of whom survived. On 6 June 1877, he married a twenty-seven-year-old widow from Wilmington, N.C., Keziah P. McCoy, who bore him two children. Keziah Hood was a freeborn seamstress and an Episcopalian, educated in Episcopal sabbath schools and at St. Frances Academy in Baltimore.

Hood was a large man of courage, conviction, and persistence. Two of his special interests were temperance and the rights of blacks in public transportation. From 1848 to 1863 conductors of the Pennsylvania Railroad tried on numerous occasions to remove him from first-class cars, but they never succeeded. In 1857 he was put off of streetcars in New York City five times in one night, but he was not deterred. In North Carolina Hood was so insistent in demanding first-class steamer accommodations that he was never bothered after the first contest. He avoided public transportation in the Deep South because asserting his rights absorbed so much energy. Regarding his second interest, Hood participated in every temperance campaign in North Carolina.

It is remarkable that Hood, who had little formal education, should have published five books: *The Negro in the Christian Pulpit* (1884); *One Hundred Years of the African Methodist Episcopal Zion Church* (1895); *The Plan of the Apocalypse* (1900); *Sermons by . . .* (1908); and *Sketch of the Early History of the African Methodist Episcopal Zion Church* (1914).

SEE: American Missionary Association Archives (Dillard University, New Orleans); Benjamin Brawley, *Negro Builders and Heroes* (1937); James Walker Hood, *One Hundred Years* (1895), *Plan of the Apocalypse* (1900), and *Sketch of the Early History* (1914); Frenise A. Logan, *The Negro in North Carolina, 1876–1894* (1964); North Carolina Superintendent of Public Instruction, *Reports* (1869–71); William J. Simmons, *Men of Mark* (1887); U.S. Census, 1880.

JOHN L. BELL, JR.

Hooks, Charles (*20 Feb. 1768–18 Oct. 1843*), planter, legislator, and congressman, was born in Bertie County. At age two, he moved with his parents to Duplin County where the family settled on a plantation near Kenansville. His sister Mary ("Polly") married Ezekiel Slocumb and they were the parents of Jesse, a member of Congress.

In adulthood, Hooks became a planter like his father. He served in the North Carolina House of Commons from 1801 to 1805, and in the senate in 1810 and 1811. A Democrat, Hooks was elected to the Fourteenth U.S. Congress to fill the vacancy created by the resignation of William R. King. He served from 2 Dec. 1816 to 3 Mar. 1817, and was reelected for full terms in the Sixteenth, Seventeenth, and Eighteenth Congresses (4 Mar. 1819–3 Mar. 1825).

After leaving public service, Hooks moved from North Carolina to Alabama in 1826 and settled near Montgomery. There he resumed the agricultural life of his earlier years until his death. Hooks was interred

in the Molton family cemetery on Laurel Hill near Montgomery.

SEE: *Biog. Dir. Am. Cong.* (1971).

PHILLIP W. EVANS

Hooper, Archibald Maclaine (*7 Dec. 1775–25 Sept. 1853*), editor and writer, was born in Wilmington, the son of George and Katherine Maclaine Hooper. His father was a merchant and the Loyalist brother of William Hooper, one of North Carolina's signers of the Declaration of Independence. His mother was the only daughter of Archibald Maclaine.

Hooper is noteworthy chiefly for his early contributions to the writing of North Carolina history and as a literary stimulus to his sons, John De B. and Johnson J. According to his friend Griffith J. McRee, Hooper—through guilelessness, impracticality, generosity, overindulgence to his slaves, and "a fondness for polite letters"—failed as a lawyer in his youth and lost the valuable plantation inherited from his father in middle age. He also apparently had little success as solicitor and cashier of the Wilmington branch of the State Bank of North Carolina, offices that he held briefly.

From 1826 to 1832 Hooper edited the Wilmington *Cape Fear Recorder*, which he filled with literate commentary and with some of the earliest biographical accounts of many of the Revolutionary figures of North Carolina. His best-known sketch is that of William Hooper, signer of the Declaration of Independence, written in 1822 and often reprinted, most notably in John H. Wheeler's *Historical Sketches of North Carolina*. His memoir of General John Ashe, completed by McRee, appeared as a pamphlet at Wilmington in 1854, and his sketch of General Robert Howe was published in the second volume of the *U.N.C. Magazine* (June 1853). At least eight other sketches remain buried in contemporary newspapers.

The *Cape Fear Recorder* burned shortly after it was offered for sale in 1832. Thereafter, Hooper held a position in the U.S. Customs Office at Wilmington for several years, one of numerous Federalists who united with "Jacksonian Democracy." On being removed from office, he published, under the pseudonym "Caius Victor," *A Defence of Andrew Jackson Against the Calumnies of the Whig Press in Relation to the Removal of the Wilmington Collector* (Wilmington, ca. 1845). This 83-page pamphlet is interesting today for its biographies of the successive port collectors of Wilmington.

In 1806 Hooper married Charlotte De Berniere, the daughter of a British Army officer. They had six children. His last years were spent at the home of his oldest son, George, in Russell County, Ala., where he died. Hooper was a member of St. James Episcopal Church, Wilmington.

SEE: Archibald Maclaine Hooper manuscripts (Southern Historical Collection, University of North Carolina Library, Chapel Hill); Information from Mrs. Ida Kellam and Mrs. E. M. McEachern, Wilmington; Griffith J. McRee, "The Late Archibald Maclaine Hooper," *U.N.C. Magazine*, vol. 4 (March 1855); Raleigh *Register*, 12 Oct. 1853.

CLYDE WILSON

Hooper, George (*ca. 1744–19 June 1821*), Wilmington merchant, clerk of court, commissioner of navigation, alleged Loyalist, and later first president of the Bank of Cape Fear, was a native of Boston, Mass. He was a younger son of Mary Dennie and the Reverend William Hooper, who became rector of Trinity Episcopal Church in 1747. George received his preparatory education at the Boston Latin School but unlike his brother, William, the Signer, who studied law, he went into service in a merchant house. After William was admitted to the bar in Boston in 1764, he and his two younger brothers, George and Thomas, went to Wilmington, N.C., where they were welcomed by the planters, merchants, and lawyers of the lower Cape Fear River. The Hooper brothers were said to be handsome, with charm, grace of manner, and cultivated minds but tempered by an aristocratic reserve. In the firm of George and Thomas Hooper, they both prospered in handling British and American goods.

In 1775 George Hooper was a member of the committee to value houses in Wilmington. On 16 Jan. 1778 Governor Richard Caswell appointed him clerk of court, and later in the year he was named one of the commissioners for navigation on the Cape Fear River. On 8 June 1780, Hooper resigned his position as clerk of court after he and some of his fellow merchants were suspected of being Tories. However, it is doubtful whether the George Hooper listed as a prisoner of the Patriots after the Battle of Camden in August 1780 was George Hooper the Wilmington merchant.

Hooper and his brother Thomas then went to Charleston, S.C., where a branch of their company was located. From Charleston, George carried on an extensive correspondence with his influential father-in-law, Archibald Maclaine, Wilmington lawyer and Patriot leader in the General Assembly. Maclaine attempted to restore the citizenship and property of George and Thomas; he was ably supported in his efforts by William Hooper. Eventually, the North Carolina General Assembly allowed George to return as a citizen where he again prospered and later became the first president of the Bank of Cape Fear, chartered in 1804.

Hooper married Katherine Maclaine, the daughter of Archibald and Elizabeth Rowan Maclaine, who inherited several plantations and Wilmington town lots. They had at least two children who grew to adulthood: Archibald Maclaine, lawyer and editor of the *Cape Fear Recorder*, and Mary Hooper Fleming. George and Katherine Hooper were members of St. James Episcopal Church in Wilmington, where Hooper died.

SEE: William K. Boyd, *History of North Carolina*, vol. 2 (1919); Walter Clark, ed., *State Records of North Carolina*, vols. 13, 14 (1896), 15 (1898), 16, 17 (1899); B. A. Konkle, *John Motley Morehead and the Development of North Carolina, 1796–1866* (1971); L. H. McEachern and Isabel M. Williams, eds., *Wilmington-New Hanover Safety Committee Minutes, 1774–1776* (1974); Raleigh *Register*, June 1821; Lorenzo Sabine, *Biographical Sketches of Loyalists of the American Revolution*, vol. 1 (1864).

VERNON O. STUMPF

Hooper, John De Berniere (6 Sept. 1811–23 Jan. 1886), educator, was born at Smithville (now Southport), the second son of Archibald Maclaine and Charlotte De Berniere Hooper. He was called by his middle name of De Berniere or, by family and friends, simply "De B." Hooper's paternal ancestors were prominent citizens of North Carolina, and his mother's father, John De Berniere, was a British Army officer of Huguenot ancestry who brought his large family to North Carolina to be near his wife's brother, Edward Jones.

Hooper grew up in Wilmington with well-educated parents, who managed to send their children to good schools despite the father's financial misfortunes. Through the interest and support of a cousin who was a prosperous widow, he entered The University of North Carolina as a freshman in the middle of the academic year 1827–28. Hooper quickly rose to the top of his class and maintained the position throughout his student years, graduating in 1831 as the only member of his class to achieve the highest grades in every field of study. In addition to excelling in the usual classical course, he was fortunate in studying French with Nicholas Marcellus Hentz, the only native Frenchman to succeed as a professor of French at the university during the antebellum years. Languages were always his special interest, and his contemporaries testified to his proficiency in the French language and literature.

After graduation Hooper remained at Chapel Hill as a tutor in languages, hoping to find time to study theology in preparation for the ministry. At the end of 1833 he left the university to become assistant to Joseph Green Cogswell, headmaster of the new Episcopal School for Boys in Raleigh. His relationship with Cogswell was friendly, but he was dissatisfied with the school's discipline and with his heavy work load, which left no time for private study. But the need to contribute to the support of his parents kept him at his post, and he eventually gave up hope of entering the ministry.

When Cogswell left the school in 1836, Hooper refused to replace him permanently but agreed to be acting head of the institution for a few months until a new headmaster arrived. In July 1836 he was appointed professor of modern languages at The University of North Carolina, and in 1838 he was promoted to professor of Latin. In 1843, he again assumed responsibility for instruction in French in addition to the advanced work in Latin.

On 20 Dec. 1837, Hooper married Mary Elizabeth Hooper, who was doubly related to him as the daughter of Professor William Hooper, his father's cousin, and of Frances Jones Hooper, his mother's cousin. In 1848 he and his wife left Chapel Hill to join her father in farming and conducting a school for boys near Littleton in Warren County. The venture was only moderately successful, and the older Hooper left for other work in 1852. De Berniere remained until 1860, when he joined his brother-in-law, Thomas C. Hooper, in conducting the Fayetteville Female Institute. In 1866 he once more became associated with his father-in-law at the Wilson Female Institute. When The University of North Carolina was reopened in 1875, he was appointed professor of Greek and French. As the enrollment increased, he and the professor of Latin and German asked to be relieved of their responsibility for modern languages; their request was finally met in 1885, when the university had additional resources. The change came too late to benefit Hooper, who became ill in the summer of 1885 and was given a leave of absence by the trustees. In October he tendered his resignation, effective at the end of the year, and he died at his home in Chapel Hill the following January.

Hooper's students and colleagues testified to his fine qualities as a teacher and his superior scholarship, but he was content to serve in North Carolina, refusing to consider a position at the University of Mississippi at the urging of his former classmate, Jacob Thompson. His teaching responsibilities were always demanding and, in accord with the custom of his day, he was not expected to be a productive, publishing scholar in the modern sense. He therefore attained no wide national reputation and left no list of publications to impress later generations. His contemporaries recognized his worth, and the trustees of The University of North Carolina placed a tablet in his honor in Memorial Hall at their own expense, in contrast to their usual practice of using such tablets as a fund-raising device for which relatives were expected to pay.

Friends praised Hooper's taste and critical ability, his wit and humor, his modesty, kindliness, and high standards of personal conduct. He was an active member of the Protestant Episcopal church. His funeral was held at Christ Church in Raleigh, where he was buried in the Oakwood Cemetery. He was survived by his wife, who lived until 23 June 1894, and by four children: Helen (m. James Wills), Fanny (m. Spier Whitaker), Henry De Berniere (m. Jessie Wright), and Julia (m. Ralph H. Graves).

Hooper's personal appearance was described as "delicate and elegant." There is an engraving of him in Ashe's *Biographical History*.

SEE: Samuel A. Ashe, ed., *Biographical History of North Carolina*, vol. 7 (1907); John De Berniere Hooper Papers (Southern Historical Collection, University of North Carolina Library, Chapel Hill); *University Magazine*, vol. 18 (1886); University of North Carolina Archives (University Library, Chapel Hill).

CAROLYN A. WALLACE

Hooper, Johnson Jones *(9 June 1815–7 June 1862)*, lawyer, newspaper editor, and short story writer, was born in Wilmington, the sixth and youngest child of Archibald Maclaine and Charlotte De Berniere Hooper. His forebears from both families were educated, cultivated citizens. William Hooper, his great-grandfather, was a graduate of Edinburgh University who left Scotland to settle in the colonies; he became pastor of Boston's West Congregational Church and, later, rector of Trinity Church. Another William Hooper, a signer of the Declaration of Independence, was his great-uncle. On his mother's side, he was descended from the Huguenot hero, Jean Antoine De Berniere.

Archibald Hooper, honorable and brilliant as he was, failed at every undertaking—planting, law, banking, and journalism—a fact that probably accounts for Johnson's failure to follow his brothers to college. George, the oldest son, attended West Point but withdrew to read law; Maclaine died in childhood; and John, the third son, became a professor of classics at The University of North Carolina. Johnson attended public school in Wilmington, read widely and voraciously, and was taught by his father. As a young lad he became a printer's devil in the office of the *Cape Fear Recorder*, edited by the elder Hooper. At age fifteen he published in the *Recorder* his first known work, a humorous poem entitled "Anthony Milan's Launch," about a British consul who fell into Wilmington harbor during a launching ceremony.

In 1835 Hooper followed his brother, George, to Lafayette, Ala., where he began to read law in the brother's office. The *Dictionary of American Biography* suggests that young Hooper left home because of a family disagreement, but other sources offer the more likely reason that his father's finances were depleted. Whatever the cause, the parents themselves later moved to Alabama and were warmly received by their sons. In 1838 Johnson was admitted to the bar and became active in Whig politics, and in 1842 he entered into a brief partnership with his brother. In 1843 Hooper became editor of Lafayette's first newspaper,

the *East Alabamian*, and began writing Whig editorials; he also began to write the short stories that would make him famous.

From Hooper's experience as a census taker in 1840 came the story, "Taking the Census in Alabama," which appeared in the *East Alabamian* in the summer of 1843. William T. Porter, editor of the highly popular New York magazine, *Spirit of the Times*, happened to read the story, thought it first-rate, and reprinted it in his weekly. Numerous small newspapers scattered over the country printed and reprinted it, resulting in almost overnight fame for Hooper on a national scale. This also marked the beginning of a close friendship with Porter that lasted until the editor's death in 1858.

By the fall of 1843 Porter had printed another of Hooper's stories, "A Three Days Hunt in Alabama"—one that had been published in the *East Alabamian* under the title, "Our Hunt Last Week." Then, for slightly more than a year, no stories appeared; during this period Hooper was busy practicing law, editing his newspaper, and dabbling in politics, but his creative mind was active. In December 1844 he introduced "the remarkable Captain Simon Suggs of the Tallapoosa Volunteers, a shrewd, brazen, farcical backwoodsman whose whole ethical system was snugly summed up in his favorite frontier aphorism, 'It is good to be shifty in a new country.'"

The stories featuring the ready-witted captain, published first in the *East Alabamian*, found immediate favor. When copies reached Porter's desk he was overjoyed; within a few weeks, he reprinted three of the adventures (or misadventures) of Simon Suggs in the *Spirit*. In fact, Porter was so impressed that he delayed the printing of *Big Bear of Arkansas*, a volume of humorous short stories that he was editing, long enough to include one of Hooper's yarns. With the appearance of Porter's anthology, the publishers Cary and Hart almost immediately signed Hooper to a contract that led to the publication in the fall of 1845 of *Some Adventures of Simon Suggs, Late Captain of the Tallapoosa Volunteers*. The first printing of 3,000 copies was soon followed by 5,000 additional copies; by 1851 and 1852 the ninth and tenth editions had appeared and in 1856, the eleventh. The thirteenth edition, with an introduction by Manly Wade Wellman, was published by The University of North Carolina Press in 1969.

Within a few years Hooper had acquired a reputation, national and international, as a master of humor and satire. He, along with Augustus Baldwin Longstreet, whose *Georgia Scenes* had appeared in 1835, provided for the South a special kind of storytelling. With genuine talent they developed the art of putting into written form the tales they had heard—tales that were anecdotal and realistic, and told with directness and gusto. None surpassed Hooper and Baldwin Longstreet, but they were joined by Thomas Bangs Thorpe, William Tappan Thompson, Joseph Glover Baldwin, and George W. Harris in creating what Edgar Allan Poe referred to as a "species of writing." With perhaps two exceptions, each of these men was at one time or another associated with a newspaper, but none could be called a professional; their backgrounds varied widely and writing occupied a secondary role, yet the influence of these men has been considerable. Novelists and short story writers from the late nineteenth century to the present are indebted to them. Mark Twain was definitely influenced by Hooper, and, as Wellman suggests in his excellent introduction, William Faulkner's Snopses are near cousins of Simon Suggs.

In December 1842 Hooper married Mary Mildred

Brantley, the daughter of Green D. Brantley, a well-to-do merchant and planter of Lafayette; three children were born to the couple—William De Berniere, Annie Brantley who died in early childhood, and Adolphus. The marriage was a happy one, and Hooper became a fast friend and political supporter of his father-in-law, who, like himself, was a member of the Whig party.

With the collapse of the Whigs and the approach of war, Hooper supported the Know-Nothing or American party, and then turned to the Democratic party where he took a firm stand for Southern rights. In his new political affiliation he was an admirer of William Lowndes Yancey, and, like Yancey, an advocate of immediate secession. In 1861 Hooper was living in Montgomery, where he was owner and editor of the Montgomery *Mail*; when the Provisional Congress of the Confederate States of America was convened in that city, he was elected its permanent secretary by acclamation. He soon sold his interest in the *Mail*, and in May 1861, with his wife and younger son, moved to Richmond, Va., with the new government. In 1862, as a result of governmental reorganization, Hooper lost his position as secretary of the Congress, but through the influence of Howell Cobb was appointed editor of the proceedings of the Provisional Congress and the constitution of the Confederate States of America.

As Richmond began to feel the effects of war, Mrs. Hooper and Adolphus returned to Montgomery, and Hooper, who had been an Episcopalian but never an ardent churchman, joined the Roman Catholic church. The war, overwork, and illness soon took their toll. He died, probably of tuberculosis, and was buried in Richmond's Shockhoe Hill Cemetery. For almost a century his grave went unmarked, and then, late in 1950, eleven men, "all ardent admirers of one of America's greatest humorists," contributed the funds to erect a suitable monument. A portrait of Hooper hangs in the Alabama Department of Archives and History in Montgomery.

SEE: W. Stanley Hoole, *Alias Simon Suggs* (1952); Louis D. Rubin, Jr., *A Bibliographical Guide to the Study of Southern Literature* (1969); Edgar E. Thompson, "The Literary Career of Johnson Jones Hooper: A Bibliographical Study of Primary and Secondary Material" (M.A. thesis, Mississippi State University, 1971): John D. Wade, "Johnson Jones Hooper," *DAB*, vol. 5 (1932); Manly Wade Wellman, "Introduction," *Adventures of Captain Simon Suggs, Late of the Tallapoosa Volunteers* (1969).

J. ISAAC COPELAND

Hooper, Thomas (ca. 1746–ca. 1821), Wilmington and Charleston merchant, and alleged Loyalist, was born in Boston, Mass., the son of Mary Dennie and the Reverend William Hooper, who became rector of Trinity Episcopal Church in 1747. He was the younger brother of William, a signer of the Declaration of Independence, and George. Thomas received his preparatory education at the Boston Latin School but unlike his older brother William, who studied law, he went into service in a mercantile house with his brother George. After William was admitted to the bar in Boston in 1764, Thomas and his two brothers went to Wilmington, N.C., where they were welcomed by the planters, merchants, and lawyers of the town. The Hooper brothers were said to be handsome, with charm, grace of manner, and cultivated minds but tempered with aristocratic reserve. Thomas and George established a mer-

cantile partnership in the lower Cape Fear and later Thomas opened a branch of their firm in Charleston, where he rapidly accumulated a great fortune.

During the American Revolution, Thomas became suspect as a British merchant and some of his goods were seized by Patriot committees. On 21 Jan. 1779 he petitioned the House of Commons of the General Assembly to be admitted as a citizen of the state but he was rejected. In 1780 Hooper was one of several signers of an address to General Sir Henry Clinton in Charleston, but his large mercantile business still prospered. His wife became ill and went to England in 1782; Hooper followed and they soon traveled to France, returning to Wilmington in July 1785.

In July 1786, Governor William Moultrie of South Carolina wrote to Governor Richard Caswell of North Carolina asking that he intervene with the commissioner of confiscated property to restore Hooper's property to him. Moultrie advised Caswell that Hooper had become a citizen of South Carolina on 10 Oct. 1783. Caswell submitted the letter to the General Assembly and implied that the state should honor another state's request. By the winter of 1786–87, with the ratification of the Definitive Treaty between the former colonies and Britain, Thomas and his brother George were free from threat of banishment and their property was restored to them.

Thomas Hooper married Mary Heron, the daughter of the Honorable Benjamin and Mary Howe Heron. Benjamin was deputy surveyor and auditor of His Majesty's revenue, clerk of the Crown, naval officer, and member of the North Carolina royal governor's Council in 1763; he died in England in 1770. Mary's brother, Edward Heron, remained loyal to the state of North Carolina, although in 1782 he asked for permission to visit his sister when she was ill and on her way to England. It is not clear whether Hooper had any children who survived to adulthood. While he lived in Wilmington or visited there, he attended St. James Episcopal Church. He died in Charleston, S.C.

SEE: Walter Clark, ed., *State Records of North Carolina*, vols. 13, (1896), 15 (1898), 16, 17 (1899), 18 (1900); *DAB*, vol. 9; D. R. Lennon and I. B. Kellam, eds., *The Wilmington Town Book, 1743–1778* (1973); L. H. McEachern and Isabel M. Williams, eds., *Wilmington-New Hanover Safety Committee Minutes, 1774–1776* (1974).

VERNON O. STUMPF

Hooper, William (17 June 1742–14 Oct. 1790), one of North Carolina's three signers of the Declaration of Independence, foremost Patriot leader, writer, orator, attorney, and legislator, was the oldest of five children of the Scots divine, the Reverend William Hooper (1704–14 Apr. 1767), second rector of Trinity Episcopal Church, Boston, Mass., and Mary Dennie Hooper (b. ca. 1720), daughter of Boston merchant John Dennie. He was the grandson of Robert and Mary Jaffray Hooper of the Parish of Ednam, near Kelso, Scotland. It should be noted that William Hooper's blackened sandstone slab in Hillsborough, N.C.'s Old Town Cemetery carries the New Style or Gregorian calendar birthdate, 28 June 1742, eleven days later than the Old Style or Julian calendar date, 17 June 1742, used in the published accounts of Hooper. The slab is thought to have been placed between 1812 and 1818 by the Signer's only daughter and surviving child, Elizabeth (Mrs. Henry Hyrn Watters), who evidently preferred the New Style date.

An unusually delicate, nervous child, William was at first painstakingly taught at home by his father, himself a classicist and orator of some note, educated at the University of Edinburgh. At age eight, the boy was sent to the Boston Public Latin School where he worked so hard under headmaster John Lovell, a celebrated disciplinarian and staunch Loyalist, that at fifteen he entered the sophomore class of Harvard College on 7 Oct. 1757. He was graduated A.B. in 1760 with marked distinction in oratory, surpassing, it is said, even his father in that field.

Although the Reverend Mr. Hooper had hoped that his oldest son and namesake would enter the ministry, William's own inclination led him to law; and in 1761 his father allowed him to study under the brilliant James Otis, famed for his knowledge of common, civil, and admiralty law. Various Hooper biographers have stated that Otis's fiery stands for colonial rights indoctrinated the young Hooper.

In 1763 Harvard College conferred an M.A. on Hooper, and in 1764 he settled temporarily in Wilmington, N.C., to begin the practice of law. Hooper, who was handsome, well-bred and well-educated, with courtly manners and a pleasing personality, was warmly accepted by the planters and lawyers of the lower Cape Fear. By June 1766 he was unanimously elected recorder of the borough.

From the beginning, however, Hooper's health had been precarious in the low-lying Wilmington area. He was seriously considering leaving New Hanover County when his father died without warning one Sunday, "falling down suddenly in his garden." William's education was to be his chief inheritance, although his father's will also left to him "all my Books and Manuscripts," a legacy that he treasured. He apparently made a firm decision to continue his legal career so well begun in North Carolina and, on 16 Aug. 1767, married at King's Chapel in Boston Anne Clark, of New Hanover, the daughter of Barbara Murray and Thomas Clark, Sr., late high sheriff of New Hanover County. Anne was the sister of Thomas Clark, Jr., who became a colonel and brigadier general in the Continental Army. It was the fortunate affluence of the Clark family that enabled the William Hoopers to survive the difficult years of the American Revolution.

Hooper's legal work took him in every direction of the province; he traveled on horseback 150 miles and more to backcountry courts in all seasons and weather. In 1769 he was appointed deputy attorney general of the Salisbury District and inevitably ran afoul of the Regulators, incurring their lasting enmity. A 1768 incident in Anson County was followed by another at the Hillsborough riots of September 1770, when Hooper reportedly was dragged through the streets by the Regulators.

His formal entry into political life came on 25 Jan. 1773, when he sat for the first time in the Provincial Assembly as representative for the Scots settlement of Campbellton (later Fayetteville). The Assembly, meeting at New Bern, lasted only forty-two days, but Hooper became acquainted with such recognized provincial leaders as Samuel Johnston, Allen Jones, and John Harvey. In the same year, Hooper made the first purchase of land for his future home on Masonboro Sound eight miles below Wilmington—108 acres of Caleb Grainger's old Masonborough Plantation. In 1774 he bought 30 adjoining acres on which he built his house, Finian. The Hoopers offered lavish hospitality at Finian to guests from far and wide, and the sound provided pleasant surroundings for their three young children: William (b.

1768), Elizabeth ("Betsy") (b. 1770), and Thomas (b. ca. 1772).

In 1773 a new courts bill agitated the province, and Hooper threw all of his energy and talent into a campaign to defeat it, arguing that the bill meant further encroachment by the Crown on colonial rights. His influential "Hampden" essays, now lost, were written about this time to explain to the citizenry at large the critical issues involved and why the bill should be defeated. The upshot of the conflict was that most provincial courts were closed and that Hooper was disbarred from practicing law for a year.

In December 1773 he was returned to the Provincial Assembly as representative for New Hanover County together with John Ashe, leader of the Whig party. On 8 December the Assembly took the important step of appointing a standing Committee of Correspondence and Inquiry and selected nine of the most significant leaders in the province to serve on it. Hooper's was the fourth name listed, and it was on this committee of communication that he made signal contributions throughout the Revolutionary years. His prophetic observation in a letter of 26 Apr. 1774 to his friend James Iredell is often quoted as a landmark of colonial foresight at this early period. He wrote, "They [the colonies] are striding fast to independence, and ere long will build an empire upon the ruins of Great Britain; will adopt its Constitution, purged of its impurities, and from an experience of its defects, will guard against those evils which have wasted its vigor."

In June 1774 the port of Boston was closed, and Hooper took the lead in mustering aid and support for his native city. At a notable general meeting of lower Cape Fear citizens in Wilmington on 21 July, he was elected chairman and presided over the selection of a committee to issue the historic call for the First Provincial Congress. A significant resolve approved by the New Bern meeting stated, "We consider the cause of the Town of Boston as the common cause of British America, and as suffering in defense of the Rights of the Colonies in general." Two shiploads of provisions and £2,000 in currency were sent for the relief of the Massachusetts port town. Already the thirty-two-year-old Hooper's diverse talents for persuasive oratory and fluent writing plus his ardent, personal commitment to the colonial cause and his trained knowledge of civil and admiralty law had combined to make him a most useful and effective leader in any assembly in which he sat.

When the First Provincial Congress—the first such convention ever to meet without royal assent—duly convened in New Bern on 25–28 Aug. 1774, Hooper was named the first of three delegates to represent North Carolina at the First Continental Congress which met on 20 September at Carpenters' Hall, Philadelphia. The other two envoys were Richard Caswell and Joseph Hewes. Although Hooper was one of the youngest of the fifty delegates in Philadelphia, he was immediately named to a committee "to state the rights of the colonies" and to another to report on legal statutes affecting trade and commerce in the colonies. "[Richard Henry] Lee, Patrick Henry, and Hooper are the orators of the Congress," wrote John Adams. Back in Wilmington, Hooper was named to the Wilmington Committee of Safety, formed on 23 Nov. 1774. He could not, however, be present until 30 December.

There now began the steady, physically exhausting cross-country travel by horseback between Philadelphia and North Carolina that Hooper continued until the spring of 1777. Nearly all of his work in both places followed the same routine: long days of committee sessions and staggering amounts of correspondence, reports, and addresses to be written at night. At Philadelphia there was the added burden of purchasing supplies at warehouses and wharves and dispatching them to Committees of Safety and militia at home. Moreover, yellow fever in Philadelphia and malaria in Wilmington were constant hazards.

Before the close of 1776, Hooper had attended three Continental Congresses, four Provincial Congresses (he did not attend the fifth in Halifax in November 1776 because of the pressure of work in Philadelphia), and four Provincial Assemblies besides meetings of the Wilmington Committee of Safety. Almost invariably he was made chairman or member of any committee with important resolutions or addresses to compose, and some of the most significant statements of the Revolution crystallizing public opinion came either wholly or partially from his pen.

At the lengthy Third Provincial Congress (20 Aug.–10 Sept. 1775), which met for safety's sake far inland at Hillsborough, Hooper was made chairman of a committee to prepare a Test Oath for the 184 delegates. Since the Battle of Lexington on 19 April, tension and alarm had been rampant. Hooper was appointed to a committee to prepare an explanatory address to the people of North Carolina and named chairman of another to prepare an address to the "inhabitants of the British Empire." Hooper alone composed the important British Empire address declaring the views of the Congress on the existing state of affairs. Besides other assignments, he was also one of a committee of 45 delegates to devise a temporary government for the province.

About 1 Feb. 1776 Hooper quietly absented himself from the Continental Congress in Philadelphia to go to his widowed mother's aid in Cambridge, Mass. According to Joseph Hewes, Mrs. Hooper had only "lately got out of Boston," and her Patriot son was greatly alarmed for her safety. Still absent from Philadelphia a month later, Hooper may have seized this opportunity to escort his mother to Milton, N.C., where she is said to have spent her later years. Her death date is unknown.

The Fourth Provincial Congress convened at Halifax on 4 Apr. 1776, and Hooper and John Penn (who had replaced Caswell) appeared on 15 April, three days after the passage of the Halifax Resolves. Hooper was immediately made chairman of a committee to supply the province with ammunition and "warlike stores," and he and Penn were added to a committee to produce a civil constitution and to another on secrecy, war, and intelligence. Both men were placed on committees to consider business necessary to be brought before the Congress and to form a temporary government, as well as on a committee of inquiry. Hooper, Hewes, and Penn were all reappointed delegates to the Third Continental Congress which convened on 10 May 1776.

In Philadelphia Hooper served on Hewes's marine committee; with Benjamin Franklin on the highly important committee of secret intelligence which had broad powers to hire secret agents abroad, make agreements, and even to conceal information from the Congress itself; and on Thomas Jefferson's committee to compose a Declaration of Independence. Although Hooper was absent when independence was actually voted and declared on 4 July 1776, he, like most of the other delegates, affixed his name to the amended Declaration on 2 August.

For the rest of the year Hooper was concerned with committees for the regulation of the post office, the treasury, secret correspondence, admiralty courts, laws of capture, and the like. On 22 December he was appointed chairman of a committee with Hewes and Thomas Burke to devise a Great Seal for the new state of North Carolina.

Early in 1777, Hooper and numerous other delegates were stricken with yellow fever. On 4 February he secured permission to return to Wilmington to attend the General Assembly on 8 April, and on 29 April he formally resigned his seat in the U.S. Congress. "The situation of my own private affairs . . . did not leave me a moment in suspense whether I should decline the honour intended me," he wrote to Robert Morris. He was succeeded by Cornelius Harnett and never again appeared on the national scene.

Hooper resumed his residence at Finian and his law practice in the newly opened courts, again riding the circuits with his friend Iredell as he had done before the Revolution. He attended the General Assembly of 1777, 1778, 1779, 1780, and 1781 as member for the borough of Wilmington, serving on numerous committees. When it appeared that Finian would not be safe from British men-of-war in Masonboro Sound (a house owned by Hooper three miles below Wilmington was burned and Finian was shelled), Hooper moved his family into the town. He himself, at times seriously ill with malaria and his right arm badly swollen, became a fugitive from the British, going from friend's house to friend's house in the Windsor-Edenton area.

On 29 Jan. 1781 Major James H. Craig's men took Wilmington, although the town was not evacuated until November. Then, an ailing Mrs. Hooper and two of her children were forced to flee by wagon to Hillsborough where her brother, General Clark, found shelter for them. Finally, on 10 Apr. 1782, the reunited Hoopers purchased General Francis Nash's former home on West Tryon Street (still standing and in 1972 named a National Historic Landmark). Hooper's preserved *Memorandum Book, 1780–1783* provides valuable records of this period.

With his permanent removal to the backcountry, Hooper was now entirely out of the mainstream of current events, both state and national. His election to the 1782 General Assembly as member for Wilmington was declared invalid, and in 1783 he suffered the first political loss of his career at the hands of Hillsborough tavern keeper Thomas Farmer, who defeated him for a seat in the General Assembly. One absorbing new interest developed, however. Some years before, in 1778, Hooper had been named first on a committee of nine prominent men to begin an academy, "Science Hall," in the vicinity of Hillsborough. The school had made a brave start on Colonel Thomas Hart's Hartford Plantation, but it had been swept aside by Revolutionary activity. Now, Hooper pushed a new academy bill through the 1784 Assembly, to which he was elected, and almost single-handedly began a second venture, a new "Hillsborough Academy," which prospered for a few years. Unfortunately, the November 1786 Assembly at Fayetteville, the last that he attended, tabled a bill to raise funds for the school and thereby ensured its demise.

Hooper's law practice was still a considerable one owing to steady litigation concerning Loyalists' estates, confiscated lands, treason, and all the legal backwash of the Revolution. Like Iredell and other conservative men, Hooper lamented unreasonable severity and vengefulness against Loyalists and absentees and urged moderation in their treatment. In consequence, he found himself at painful odds with some of his old friends and acquaintances. On 22 Sept. 1786 he was appointed to a federal court to settle a Massachusetts–New York territorial dispute, but the matter was resolved locally and the court never met.

A bitter blow fell when Hooper was not elected a delegate to the 1788 Constitutional Convention, which met in Hillsborough's old St. Matthew's Church (then renovated as the new academy), literally within sight and sound of his own house. He never recovered from this second important rejection. The Iredell correspondence indicates that from 1787 onward there had been a perceptible decline in Hooper's health and that, like his fellow townsman, Thomas Burke, he had chosen to drown his increasing disillusionment in rum. He died at age forty-eight, the evening before his daughter Elizabeth's marriage to Colonel Henry Hyrn Watters of the Cape Fear.

Hooper was buried in a corner of his garden, and the brick-walled plot was later incorporated into the adjoining Old Town Cemetery. On 25 Apr. 1894, the grave was opened at dawn before various family representatives, and a very few discernible relics—part of a button and a nail or two—were placed in an envelope and removed, together with the covering sandstone slab, to the Guilford Courthouse National Military Park, Greensboro. There an imposing 19-foot-high monument, surmounted by a statue of Hooper in colonial dress and in orator's pose, honors the patriotic services of William Hooper and his friend and colleague, John Penn. The sandstone slab, with six additional words deeply incised, "Signer of the Declaration of Independence," was later returned to the original Hillsborough grave site.

Hooper's portrait was painted in 1873 by the prominent Philadelphia artist, James Reid Lambdin (1807–89), who was commissioned by the Committee on the Restoration of Independence Hall. Lambdin's portrait copied the head of William Hooper in John Trumbull's (1756–1843) study for his famous painting, *The Signing of the Declaration of Independence*. It remains uncertain, however, whether Trumbull actually painted Hooper from life. In February 1790 Trumbull traveled to Charleston, S.C., to collect likenesses of the Signers, but it seems unlikely that Hooper's swiftly deteriorating condition at that date would have permitted even short sittings for a sketch.

SEE: Edwin Anderson Alderman, *Address on the Life of William Hooper, "The Prophet of American Independence"* (Guilford Battle Ground, 4 July 1894); Samuel A. Ashe, ed., *Biographical History of North Carolina*, vol. 7 (1908 [portrait]); Walter Clark, ed., *State Records of North Carolina*, vols. 11–24 (1895–1905); John De Berniere Papers (Southern Historical Collection, University of North Carolina Library, Chapel Hill); Crockette W. Hewlett, *Between the Creeks: A History of Masonboro Sound, 1735–1970* (1971); Archibald Maclaine Hooper, "Life of William Hooper, Signer of the Declaration of Independence . . . Written in 1822 . . . by Callisthenes," *Hillsborough Recorder*, 13, 20, 27 Nov., 4 Dec. 1822; William Hooper Papers (Southern Historical Collection, University of North Carolina Library, Chapel Hill); Griffith J. McRee, ed., *The Life and Correspondence of James Iredell*, 2 vols. (1857); William L. Saunders, ed., *Colonial Records of North Carolina*, vols. 7–10 (1886–90); "Unpublished Letters of William Hooper," *Historical Magazine* (August 1868); Fanny De Berniere Whitaker, "The Hooper Family," *North Carolina Booklet*, vol. 5 (July 1905); William Hooper Memorandum Book, 1780–83 (microfilm in the North Carolina Division of Archives and History, Raleigh, from the original in the New-York Historical Society Library); Will of Anne Hooper (Orange County Courthouse, Hillsborough); Will of William Hooper (North Carolina Division of Archives and History, Raleigh).

MARY CLAIRE ENGSTROM

Hooper, William (*31 Aug. 1792–19 Aug. 1876*), educator and clergyman, was born in Hillsborough, the oldest son of William and Helen Hogg Hooper. His father, a merchant, was the son of the William Hooper (1742–90) who was one of North Carolina's signers of the Declaration of Independence. His mother was the daughter of James Hogg, resident of Orange County, who was one of the commissioners appointed to select a site for The University of North Carolina. The first William Hooper—great-grandfather of the subject of this sketch—had emigrated to Massachusetts from Scotland about 1737; in Boston, he served as pastor of a Congregational church and, subsequently, as the second rector of Trinity Episcopal Church (1747–67).

After the death of her husband in 1804, Helen Hooper moved to Chapel Hill in order to provide the best educational opportunities for her three sons. Here William entered the preparatory school of The University of North Carolina in the winter of 1804 and was tutored by President Joseph Caldwell and Matthew Troy. The university awarded him the B.A. degree in 1809 and the M.A. degree in 1812. During the academic year 1812–13 Hooper studied theology at the Princeton Theological Seminary. He received additional degrees from Princeton University (M.A., 1817) and The University of North Carolina (LL.D., 1833; D.D., 1857).

Hooper entered the teaching profession as a tutor at The University of North Carolina in 1810. The greater portion of his next sixty-five years was spent as teacher and/or administrator at the preparatory, college, and university levels. His positions at Chapel Hill included principal tutor, 1810–17; professor of ancient languages, 1818–22 and 1828–37; and professor of rhetoric and logic, 1825–28.

Leaving his teaching post at the university in 1837, Hooper was named senior professor (president) at the newly formed Furman Theological Institute, Winnsboro, S.C. He remained at the institute during its first year of operation (1838–39) before becoming professor of Roman literature at South Carolina College where he taught from 1840 to 1846 and served for a time as acting president of the college.

In October 1845 the trustees of Wake Forest College elected Hooper to succeed Samuel Wait as president of the college. He accepted the offer—although he did not assume his duties until January 1847—on the condition that the friends of Wake Forest would make a concerted effort to eliminate its $20,000 debt. Hooper relinquished the presidency at the end of the fall term, December 1848. Thereafter, he served as teacher and/or educational administrator at the following institutions: Hooper's Family School, Warren County, 1849–51; Sedgwick Female Seminary, Raleigh, 1851–52; Chowan Female Institute (now Chowan College), president, 1854–62; Fayetteville Female Seminary, 1862–63, 1865–67; Mt. Vernon Female Seminary, Chatham County, associate principal, 1863–64; and Wilson Collegiate Seminary, associate principal, 1867–75. He retired to Chapel Hill in the latter year, spending the rest of his life with his daughter and his son-in-law, Professor John De Berniere Hooper, a member of the university faculty.

A deeply pious man as well as an erudite scholar, Hooper combined his career in education with a religious calling. Confirmed in the Episcopal church in 1818, he became a lay reader in 1819 and a deacon in 1820. Two years later he was ordained to the priesthood and assumed the pastoral charge of St. Johns Church, Fayetteville, on 24 Apr. 1822. He remained in this position until 1824, when doubts concerning the church's teaching on baptism, confirmation, and Holy Orders led to his resignation.

In 1831, Hooper was baptized into the fellowship of Mt. Carmel Baptist Church, Orange County. Thereafter, he was welcomed into the councils of the Baptist denomination, even though his views on such controversial questions as "intercommunion" and "pulpit affiliation" were far more liberal than those of the vast majority of his fellow Baptist ministers. Hooper's pastoral charges included Wake Forest Baptist Church (1847–48), New Bern Baptist Church (1852–54), Buckhorn Baptist Church in Hertford County (1855 ff.), and Wilson Baptist Church (1868). He also served as co-pastor, with William Hill Jordan, of the Warrenton Baptist Church (1849–50).

A concern for the provision of adequate educational opportunities, especially in the preparatory schools, had been expressed by Hooper during his tenure at The University of North Carolina. Invited to deliver a lecture before the North Carolina Institute of Education, meeting at Chapel Hill on 20 June 1832, he developed the theme, "Imperfections of Our Primary Schools, and the Best Method of Correcting Them." He noted three "imperfections" in particular: indolent and indulgent youth, who were not prepared for the rigors required to attain a sound education; the desire of parents and other patrons for an education that could be acquired both inexpensively and rapidly; and the scarcity of able teachers and tutors. Among the improvements he suggested for schools attempting to prepare men for the university were greater attention to the rudiments of English grammar and penmanship, concentration on "classical" studies, a more lively and spirited manner of instruction, and greater use of the oral lecture to supplement the texts required. Finally, he urged the establishment of a seminary for the education of schoolmasters.

Once he had cast his lot with the Baptists, Hooper was numbered among those advocates of higher education—for both men and women—within the newly formed Baptist State Convention of North Carolina. He was the author of the report to the convention in 1832 recommending the "establishment of a Baptist literary institution in this State"—a report that led to the founding of Wake Forest Institute in 1834.

Hooper's views on the education of women—to which he had made passing reference in the 1832 lecture—appeared in an article in the Biblical Recorder of 22 Apr. 1848 entitled "Importance of Female Education." Here, he contended that women ought to be educated because of the various "offices" and "relations" they occupied in society as daughters, sisters, wives, and mothers. But beyond the familial advantages accruing to the educated, he noted that new fields of philanthropy had been opened to educated women—visiting and instructing the poor, distributing religious tracts, composing juvenile books, teaching in "charity" schools, and cooperating in missionary and other religious societies. Then, in a sentence that might have been penned a century and a half later, Hooper added: "But education has lifted and expanded woman's views to take in the wide compass of her duty—to see that she is the 'daughter of God,' that she can[,] like him[,] diffuse happiness around her; *that she can be man's equal*

if not his superior in the removal of crime and wretchedness in the world" [italics added].

Although he published no books, Hooper was a gifted and prolific writer. Many of his letters, articles, and essays appeared in the pages of the *Biblical Recorder*, the Baptist weekly published in Raleigh. He was also a popular and eloquent speaker—especially before the literary societies of various educational institutions—and at least twelve of his addresses (or sermons) were published frequently in pamphlet form. *Fifty Years Since: An Address Before the Alumni of The University of North Carolina*, delivered on 7 June 1859, was used extensively by Kemp Plummer Battle in writing his history of the university. *The Force of Habit*, originally delivered as a sermon before Chapel Hill students in 1833, is said to have been read often by President Swain to succeeding generations of graduating classes. Hooper's concern for the cultivation of the human spirit, together with the mind, was expressed in *The Discipline of the Heart, to be Connected with the Culture of the Mind: A Discourse on Education, Delivered to the Students of the College, at Chapel Hill, North Carolina, August 22, 1830.*

In December 1814 Hooper married Frances Pollock Jones, the daughter of Edward Jones, solicitor general of North Carolina. They had seven children: William Wilberforce, Edward Jones, Joseph Caldwell, Thomas Clark, DuPonceau, Mary Elizabeth (m. John De Berniere Hooper), and Elizabeth Watters.

Hooper was buried in Chapel Hill beside the remains of his mother and his stepfather, President Joseph Caldwell, whom his mother married in 1809. Portraits of him are in the possession of The University of North Carolina at Chapel Hill, Wake Forest University, and Chowan College.

SEE: Samuel A. Ashe, ed., *Biographical History of North Carolina*, vol. 7 (1908); Kemp P. Battle, *History of the University of North Carolina*, vol. 1 (1907); Charles L. Coon, "Imperfections of Our Primary Schools," *North Carolina Schools and Academies, 1790–1840* (1915); John De Berniere Hooper Papers (Southern Historical Collection, University of North Carolina Library, Chapel Hill); George Washington Paschal, *History of Wake Forest College*, vol. 1 (1935 [portrait]); Thomas Jerome Taylor, *A History of the Tar River Baptist Association, 1830–1921* (n.d.).

R. HARGUS TAYLOR

Hoover, David (*14 Apr. 1781–12 Sept. 1866*), pioneer settler of Indiana, public official, and author, was born on the Uwharrie River in Randolph County, the son of Andrew Hoover, a well-to-do farmer of German descent who owned no slaves. David had virtually no opportunity to receive a formal education but read widely and cultivated a number of talents. In the early fall of 1802, when he was twenty-one, the family possessions were sold and the Hoovers and some neighbors set out for the Northwest Territory. After five weeks they reached a site some 12 miles north of modern Dayton, Ohio, purchased 200 acres as a base, and began to search for a permanent home. David scouted out the country for a considerable distance and in 1806 found a site that offered springwater, timber, and building stone in what is now Wayne County, Ind. After returning to Ohio, he was accompanied back to this site by his father and others, mostly North Carolinians, and they determined to locate there. In 1816 David Hoover platted and named the settlement that developed into the city of Richmond, Ind.

In 1807, soon after arriving in Indiana, Hoover married Catherine Yount, and they became the parents of seven children. Although he was a Democrat in strong Whig country, he served six terms in the state senate between 1832 and 1844. Hoover described himself as a Jeffersonian Democrat and often quoted Jefferson. Earlier he was elected a justice of the peace (1810) and an associate judge (1815). For fourteen years he was also clerk of the Wayne Circuit Court and in time, as a highly respected elder citizen and pioneer settler, he organized an association of early inhabitants which met regularly.

Hoover often made public addresses and was the author of *Some Recollections of My Boyhood Days*, undated but published in Indianapolis, and of *Memoirs of David Hoover*, published in Richmond, Ind., in 1857. Although not a formal member of the Society of Friends, he regarded himself as a Quaker.

SEE: *A Biographical Directory of the Indiana General Assembly* (1980); R. E. Banta, comp., *Indiana Authors and Their Books, 1816–1916* (1949); David Hoover, *Memoirs* (1857).

WILLIAM S. POWELL

Hopkins, Nathan Thomas (27 Oct. 1852–11 Feb. 1927), clergyman and Kentucky legislator and congressman, was born in Ashe County. He attended the common schools, was ordained a Baptist minister in 1876, and engaged in the ministry for half a century. As a youth Hopkins moved to Kentucky, where he became a merchant, timberman, and farmer in the vicinity of Yeager, Pike County. He served as the tax assessor for Floyd County from 1878 to 1890 and as a member of the Kentucky State House of Representatives in 1893–94 and again in 1923–24. As a Republican, he successfully contested the election of Joseph M. Kendall to the Fifty-fourth Congress and served from 18 Feb. to 3 Mar. 1897. In 1900 he was an unsuccessful candidate for election to the Fifty-seventh Congress.

In May 1871 Hopkins married Nancy Johnson (b. 1850) in Pike County, Ky. They had four children: William J. (b. July 1884), Thomas C. (b. January 1887), Rosey B. (b. December 1890), and Benjamin H. (b. May 1894). Hopkins died in Pikesville, Ky., and was buried in Potter Cemetery, Yeager, Ky.

SEE: *Biog. Dir. Am. Cong.* (1971); Leonard Roberts and others, eds., Pike County, *Kentucky Historical Papers #3, 1822–1977.*

JAMES R. MORRILL

Horn, Alexander Grice (11 May 1817–22 Apr. 1886), "one of the greatest news editors of his day" and secretary of the first Secession Convention at Montgomery, Ala., was a native of Wilson (then Edgecombe) County. His parents, Jeremiah and Elizabeth Grice Horn, moved in 1834 to the vicinity of Sumterville, Ala. Horn entered school at Greensboro, Ala., and secured a thorough preparation in the law, which he practiced for a short time at Livingston. It became apparent that his temperament was not suited to that profession but rather to "the editorial pen which he was born to wield" and to "the profession which by his genius and ability he has adorned."

In the autumn of 1836, Horn invested $1,800 in the establishment of the *Macon Transcript* in Noxubee County, Miss., and not long afterwards renamed it the *Mississippi Star*. As a result of "an impecunious and fast

partner" and of "the great crash of '37," the newspaper and its premises were sold at auction by the sheriff in 1838. Sometime before 1850 and until April 1852 Horn held the office of clerk in Clarke County. About 1856 he moved to Mobile, Ala., and founded the *Mobile Mercury*, which appeared with considerable success as late as 4 Aug. 1861, and the weekly *Gulf City Home Journal*, which first appeared on 27 Oct. 1862.

On 7 Jan. 1861 Horn was present as a member and temporary secretary of the Alabama State Secession Convention assembled in Montgomery. On 15 January he was elected by acclamation to serve as permanent secretary. On 8 February the delegates from six seceded states adopted for one year a "Constitution for the Provisional Government of the Confederate States of America," and shortly before adjourning on 21 March passed a resolution of appreciation for the "faithful" services of Horn and three other officials.

After the convention, Horn resumed his journalistic career and outspoken support of the Southern cause. With the occupation of Mobile by the Union Army in the latter part of 1864, he returned to Clarke County, Miss., and established the *Quitman Intelligencer* and the *Chickasawhay Advertiser*. In 1866, "when it was but a small town," he settled in Meridian, Miss., and began to publish the *Mississippi Messenger*, which was renamed the *Meridian Mercury* in 1867. The newspaper flourished under his leadership. In 1873 the *Meridian Mercury* was issued triweekly and also weekly on Fridays by the firm of Horn & Kerlee, Publishers. On 31 Mar. 1884 it was merged with the *Tri-Weekly Observer* as a weekly under the name of the *Meridian Mercury and Observer*. By 24 Dec. 1885 it had passed from Horn's control and subsequently was renamed the *Meridian Daily News*.

The *Mercury* office was on Commerce Street. Horn's sons, Jerry and Alex, worked with him and shared the family residence on Lauderdale Street. Their newspaper advertised "a large circulation in this and surrounding States." On 5 Apr. 1872, Colonel Horn (as he was popularly known) was approved by the Mississippi state legislature for the office of commissioner of deeds for Lauderdale County. The following year he appeared in an advertisement as a partner in the real estate firm of Horn & Kerlee. However, it was his "connection with the Mississippi press," dating "farther back than any other man connected with it," for which he was best known.

About 1883 Horn became partially paralyzed as the result of a brain tumor and was forced to use crutches; nevertheless, he continued to supervise his business affairs until the last three or four months of his life. He died of a cerebral hemorrhage and was buried beside his son Alex in the McLemore Cemetery. Both he and his wife had been communicants of the Episcopal Church of Meridian.

"Col. Horn was an able and vigorous writer," wrote R. H. Henry in *Editors I Have Known*, "and his trenchant pen was never silent when the interest of his country or party was at stake. He was a strict party man, and never flickered one jot or tittle during the dark days following the war, when so many Southern men were ready to go over to the enemy for the loaves and fishes offered them by the radical regime then in power. Horn stood steadfast, firm as the rocks of the mountains, immutable as the law of Moses."

About 1847 Horn married Rebecca S. Jackson (1827–ca. 1852), a native of Choctaw County, Ala., by whom he had a daughter, Ella, who married John McCloud of Wilcox County. On 26 Feb. 1854, at Quitman, he married his second wife Lizzie Blakeney, of Camden, who survived him and by whom he had four children: Jeremiah; Alexander Grice, Jr. (ca. 1858–ca. 1881); Ida, who died as a girl in Mobile; and Minnie, who died unmarried before 1886.

SEE: R. H. Henry, *Editors I Have Known* (1922).

HUGH BUCKNER JOHNSTON

Horne, Ashley *(27 Mar. 1841–22 Oct. 1913)*, businessman and farmer, was born at the family estate near Clayton, one of the nine children of Benajah and Elizabeth Tarboro Horne. His father was of Scottish descent and served the area as magistrate while prospering in farming and business enterprises.

Young Horne had only about two years of schooling, mostly under William B. Jones, a noted educator of the area. Early on, however, he showed a predilection for trading. Unknown to his father, he would with no money buy cattle in Clayton on his father's credit, drive them to Raleigh to sell, and, on returning to Clayton to settle his accounts, usually realize at least a small profit.

In 1861, he enlisted in the Confederate Army as a private and was assigned to the Fiftieth North Carolina Regiment. Later he was assigned to the Fifty-third Regiment, the same group in which his brother Sam was a lieutenant, and served mostly with General Robert E. Lee and the Army of Northern Virginia. He participated in the evacuation of Richmond and the charge at Hare's Hill. As an orderly sergeant, he led nine men to carry the news of the surrender to Johnston's army at Greensboro and Sherman's army at Durham.

The first of his six brothers to return home after the war, Horne found some of Sherman's troops still occupying the plantation. When they left a month later, they took all the stock, produce, and fencing. Using two horses he had stolen by sneaking into Sherman's camp in Raleigh one night, Horne began to replant and rebuild. Around this time, he started accumulating small amounts of capital by trading in wood and tobacco. Dividing his time between farming and business, he became one of the state's most prosperous citizens by the turn of the century. As a farmer, he was president of the North Carolina Agricultural Society and published "cotton letters" with growing advice to other planters. His business prowess earned him the presidencies of many concerns, among them the Clayton Banking Company in 1899, the Clayton Cotton Mill in 1900, and the Capudine Chemical Company in 1904. He was vice-president and director of the Caraleigh Phosphate and Fertilizer Mills and a director of many industries including the Raleigh Standard Oil Mill, Raleigh Commercial and Farmer's Bank, Caraleigh Cotton Mill Company, and Wilson Farmer's Oil Mill. He was one of the first in the state to advocate the formation of insurance companies in North Carolina to keep insurance money within the state and served as director of the Eastern Life Insurance Company and the Goldsboro and Seven Springs Securities Company.

A lifelong Democrat, Horne served one term in the state senate (1884–85) and was a member of the finance committee that established what would become North Carolina State College. He also protested the use of free prison labor in state railroad construction. He was unsuccessful in his one bid for statewide office when he ran for the Democratic gubernatorial nomination in 1908. While in the senate, Horne worked to secure funding for a monument to the North Carolina Women of the Confederacy. Failing to win legislative approval,

he donated $10,000 of his own money and commissioned the sculpture that stands in Raleigh.

Horne was married twice, first in 1871 to Cornelia Frances Lee by whom he had three children and later to Rena Hasseltine Beckwith by whom he had one child. Horne Memorial Methodist Church, Clayton, which he helped establish, was named to honor his service to the church.

SEE: Samuel A. Ashe, ed., *Biographical History of North Carolina*, vol. 1 (1905); *Assembly Sketch Book, Session 1885*; *North Carolina Biography*, vol. 6 (1919).

WILLIAM R. PITTMAN

Horne, Herman Harrell *(22 Nov. 1874–16 Aug. 1946)*, educator, was born at Clayton, the son of Hardee and Ida Caroline Harrell Horne. In 1895 he was graduated with A.B. and A.M. degrees from The University of North Carolina, where he was a member of the Philanthropic Society and of Alpha Theta Phi (later Phi Beta Kappa). Continuing his studies at Harvard, he received the degrees of S.M. in 1897 and Ph.D. in 1899. In 1934 Horne was awarded the honorary LL.D. degree by The University of North Carolina in recognition of his outstanding work in education.

In 1899 Horne became an instructor at Dartmouth College, where he was later promoted to assistant professor and then to professor of philosophy. In 1909 he left Dartmouth to become professor of the history of education and philosophy at New York University. Horne remained on the faculty for thirty-three years, retiring as chairman of the departments of the history of education and the philosophy of education in 1942. During his long career he was often a lecturer at summer conferences for religious education at Blue Ridge, Ga.; Eagles Mere, Pa.; Lake Geneva, Wis.; Silver Bay, N.J.; and Lake Couchiching, Canada. He also taught summer courses at The University of North Carolina, University of California, Dartmouth College, and New York University.

A prolific scholar, Horne wrote numerous articles on philosophy and education in addition to the following books: *The Philosophy of Education* (1904), *Psychological Principles of Education* (1906), *Idealism in Education* (1910), *Free Will and Human Responsibility* (1912), *Leadership of Bible Study Groups* (1912), *Story-telling, Questioning and Studying* (1916), *The Teacher as Artist* (1917), *Jesus Our Standard* (1918), *Modern Principles as Jesus Saw Them* (1918), and *Jesus the Master Teacher* (1920). He also edited *Simple Southern Songs* (1917) and *Songs of Sentiment* (1917).

On 20 Aug. 1901 Horne married Alice Elizabeth Worthington, the daughter of Denison and Julia Munroe Wheeler Worthington. They were the parents of four children: Julia Carolyn, Elizabeth Worthington, William Henry, and Ida Battle. Horne died of a heart attack at his home in Leonia, N.J., and was buried at Clayton, N.C.

SEE: Daniel L. Grant, *Alumni History of the University of North Carolina, 1795–1924* (1924); Raleigh *News and Observer*, 17 Aug. 1946; Albert Gallatin Wheeler, Jr., comp., *The Wheeler Family in America* (1914).

JAMES ELLIOTT MOORE

Horne, Joshua Lawrence ("Josh") *(21 Dec. 1887–15 Mar. 1974)*, newspaperman and civic leader, was born in Nash County, the son of Joshua Lawrence and Lula Parker Horne. Educated first in local schools, he attended Trinity Park School, Durham, from 1903 to 1905 and was graduated from Trinity College (later Duke University) in 1909. Horne began his lifework as city editor of the Rocky Mount *Daily Record* in 1910. The following year he founded his own newspaper, the *Morning Telegram*, whose name was changed in 1912 to the *Evening Telegram*. In 1950 a Sunday edition was published. Influential for many years in northeastern North Carolina, the newspapers were sold to the Thomson chain in 1970.

During his sixty years in the newspaper business, Horne not only won recognition from his profession but also gave liberally of his time and talents to his city and state. As a newspaperman, he served as president of the North Carolina Press Association in 1930 and was director of the Associated Press from 1937 to 1950. He also founded two radio stations in Rocky Mount, WCEC and WFMA. A pioneer in many fields, Horne was a member of the first state rural electrification authority, of the Rocky Mount Air Port Commission (beginning in 1934), and later of the Rocky Mount–Wilson Airport Authority. In the latter capacity, he was instrumental in obtaining better air service for his area of the state.

While Horne was serving on the state Board of Conservation and Development in 1935, a new highway marker program was begun jointly by that board, the North Carolina Historical Commission, and the State Highway Commission. He was a member of a special committee formed at the time to approve markers and their inscriptions. Through this association, Horne developed an intense interest in the heritage of his native state. In 1954 Governor William B. Umstead appointed him to the executive board of the North Carolina Department of Archives and History; Horne served as chairman from 1965 to 1972 and remained on the board until his death. During his chairmanship, the agency's staff doubled and its budget tripled, providing increased services to preserve the history of North Carolina, and new facilities were opened at several state historic sites. Horne had a particular interest in historic Halifax, not far from his home in Rocky Mount.

A devout Methodist, Horne was long a member of the official board of the First United Methodist Church, Rocky Mount. For many years he was a trustee of Duke University and High Point College, and he participated in the establishment of North Carolina Wesleyan College in Rocky Mount.

In 1912 Horne married Mary A. Thorp, the daughter of Judge William Lewis and Mildred Brown Holmes Thorp. They were the parents of a daughter, Mary Louise, who married Mel. J. Warner of Rocky Mount. Horne's second wife was Mildred Nicholson of Orlando, Fla.

On his retirement, a bust of Horne was placed in the foyer of the *Telegram* building by the newspapers he had founded. The inscription read in part: "For fifty years he strove daily to hold up a mirror, not only for the news of his community, but for the conscience of its citizens. His has been a life of unselfish effort and dedication to the best for his church, his profession, his town, state, and nation." He was buried in Pineview Cemetery, Rocky Mount.

SEE: Rocky Mount *Evening Telegram*, 16 Mar. 1974; Fitzhugh Lee Morris, comp., *Lineage Book of the North Carolina Society of the Sons of the American Revolution*

(1951); William S. Powell, *North Carolina Lives* (1962); *Who's Who in America*, vol. 33 (1964).

CLAIBORNE T. SMITH, JR.

Horner, James Hunter (3 Apr. 1822–13 June 1892), educator, was born near Flat River at Red Mountain, Orange County (now Rougemont, Durham County), the son of Colonel William Horner, a native of Pennsylvania who moved to North Carolina in the early nineteenth century. Following his graduation from The University of North Carolina in 1844, he taught for a few years in Florida and in eastern North Carolina. He then founded and became principal of the Horner School at Oxford (which later moved to Hillsborough for a brief period) where he taught from 1851 until his death, with the exception of about a year during the Civil War and a brief illness in 1874 and 1875. Military features were introduced in 1880 and it became Horner Military School.

The customary M.A. degree was bestowed upon Horner by The University of North Carolina, as it was upon most graduates of the time who entered one of the professions. In 1891 he also was honored with an LL.D. degree.

Horner was regarded as a superior teacher, and countless young men who became leaders in the state were graduates of his school. On 5 June 1861, at age thirty-nine, he was elected captain of Company E ("Granville Targetteers"), Twenty-third Regiment, which arrived in Virginia just after the first Battle of Manassas. For most of the summer and winter the regiment encamped near Fairfax Station, but for brief periods was elsewhere in Virginia. On or about 16 Apr. 1862, he was defeated for reelection as captain and returned home to resume teaching. (On 10 May Abner D. Place, aged twenty-three, also of Granville County, was elected captain of the company.)

Preferring to teach in his own school, Horner declined several opportunities to join the faculty of The University of North Carolina. Nevertheless, he lectured at the Normal School there in the summer of 1879, the first summer school in the nation. He also was a trustee of the university from 1885 to 1892. An active member of the Episcopal church, he served for many years as a vestryman and senior warden of St. Stephen's Church, Oxford. The tower of the handsome stone church, erected in 1904, is a memorial to him.

On 18 Sept. 1850 Horner married Sophronia Moore, the granddaughter of General Stephen Moore. They were the parents of seven daughters and three sons.

SEE: Samuel A. Ashe, ed., *Biographical History of North Carolina*, vol. 8 (1917); Kemp P. Battle, *History of the University of North Carolina*, 2 vols. (1907–12); Daniel L. Grant, *Alumni History of the University of North Carolina, 1795–1924* (1924); Weymouth T. Jordan, Jr., ed., *North Carolina Troops, 1861–1865: A Roster*, vol. 7 (1979); *North Carolina Biography*, vol. 5 (1919); Oxford *Public Ledger*, 17 June 1892; Stephen B. Weeks Scrapbook, vol. 8 (North Carolina Collection, University of North Carolina Library, Chapel Hill); University of North Carolina Alumni Office files (Chapel Hill).

WILLIAM S. POWELL

Horner, Jerome Channing (23 July 1853–1 Sept. 1951), educator, was born in Oxford, the son of James Hunter and Sophronia Moore Horner. He attended his father's school, Horner School, and Davidson College from which he received both a bachelor's (1875) and a master's degree. Upon graduation he became principal of the Albemarle Academy, Edenton, where he taught for two years. He then began teaching in the Horner School, which for a brief time was located in Hillsborough, but in 1876 the school reopened in Oxford.

In 1879 Horner's brother, Junius, taught for him while he served as an assistant at the Cape Fear Military Academy to learn something about managing a military school. When he returned to Oxford in 1880, the Horner School became Horner Military School. On 2 Jan. 1914 fire destroyed the barracks, and at the end of the term it was decided to reestablish the school in Charlotte. There it continued to provide excellent training for young men until it closed in 1920.

Horner, an Episcopalian who served his parish as senior warden, treasurer, and lay reader, was married on 22 Nov. 1885 to Kate M. Williams of Wilmington, and they were the parents of two children. Following her death he married Eloise Kent of Wisconsin, and they had four children.

SEE: Samuel A. Ashe, ed., *Biographical History of North Carolina*, vol. 8 (1917); *North Carolina Biography*, vol. 5 (1919); Oxford *Public Ledger*, 17 June 1892; Raleigh *News and Observer*, 2 Sept. 1951.

WILLIAM S. POWELL

Horner, Junius Moore (*7 July 1859–4 Apr. 1933*), Episcopal bishop, was born in Oxford, the son of James Hunter and Sophronia Moore Horner. After attending the Horner School, Oxford, and the University of Virginia, he received the A.B. degree from Johns Hopkins University in 1885 and the B.D. degree from General Theological Seminary, New York, in 1890. Soon after graduating from seminary he was ordained deacon and a year later was advanced to the priesthood. He was associated with his brother, Jerome C., and his father at the Horner School and served a number of missionary stations in the region, particularly in Leaksville and Reidsville.

In October 1898 Horner was elected bishop of the Missionary District of Asheville by the General Convention meeting in Washington, D.C.; he was consecrated in Asheville on 28 December. In 1899 the University of the South granted him the doctor of divinity degree. When the missionary district was reorganized in 1922, he became bishop of the Diocese of Western North Carolina. Although Horner had limited experience in parish leadership, he had the training and ability necessary to succeed. He set about expanding the work of the church and soon established preaching stations, missions, parishes, and, dear to his heart, schools to offer industrial training not otherwise available to the young people of the mountains of North Carolina. With that special education, of course, they also received religious and moral training.

On 14 Dec. 1892 Horner married Eva Harker of Augusta, Ga., and they became the parents of Eva, Katherine, and Junius.

SEE: Samuel A. Ashe, ed., *Biographical History of North Carolina*, vol. 8 (1917); Diocese of Western North Carolina, *Journal of the Twelfth Annual Convention* (1934); *North Carolina Biography*, vol. 6 (1919); *Who Was Who in America* (1943).

WILLIAM S. POWELL

Horton, George Moses (*ca. 1797–ca. 1883*), poet, was born in Northampton County, the property of William Horton who also owned his mother, his five older half sisters, and his younger brother and three sisters. As a child, he moved with his master to Chatham County, taught himself to read, and began composing in his head a series of stanzas based on the rhythms in Wesley hymns. In 1814 he was given to William's son James, at whose death in 1843 he passed to James's son Hall.

By the time he was twenty, George Moses Horton had begun visiting the campus of The University of North Carolina eight miles away. There he sold students acrostics on the names of their sweethearts at twenty-five, fifty, and seventy-five cents. For several decades he "bought his time" from his masters through the sale of his poems and through wages collected as a campus laborer. Caroline Lee Hentz, novelist and professor's wife, encouraged him; his first printed poem, "Liberty and Slavery," appeared in Mrs. Hentz's hometown Massachusetts newspaper, the *Lancaster Gazette*, on 8 Apr. 1829. Soon plans were made to purchase his freedom and transport him to Liberia. To raise funds, Horton's *The Hope of Liberty*, the first book published in the South by a black man, came later that year from the press of Raleigh's liberal journalist Joseph Gales, but profits were inconsiderable and the plans were dropped. From time to time, Horton won the admiration and support of such men as Governor John Owen, presidents Joseph Caldwell and David L. Swain of The University of North Carolina, and newspapermen William Lloyd Garrison and Horace Greeley.

In 1845 Dennis Heartt of the *Hillsborough Recorder* brought out *The Poetical Works of George M. Horton, The Colored Bard of North-Carolina, To Which Is Prefixed The Life of the Author, Written by Himself*. Seldom was Horton without a manuscript for which he was gathering subscriptions from admiring students and friends. In April 1865 he attached himself to Captain Will H. S. Banks, and thereafter followed Banks's Michigan cavalry unit to Lexington and Concord. Banks sponsored Horton's third book, *Naked Genius*, published several months later from the press of William B. Smith in Raleigh.

Horton's last years were spent in Philadelphia writing Sunday school stories and working for old North Carolina friends who lived in the city. Details of his death are unrecorded. Through Horton's unhappy marriage to a slave of Franklin Snipes, he was the father of a son Free and a daughter Rhody, both of whom bore their mother's name. Horton's poems are traditional in vocabulary and style. His academic imitations and the love poems he wrote for student sale are less appealing than the rural pieces and those on slavery. His poetic protests of his status are the first ever written by a slave in America.

SEE: W. Edward Farrison, "George Moses Horton: Poet for Freedom," *CLA Journal* (March 1971); Richard Walser, *The Black Poet* (1966).

RICHARD WALSER

Horton, Wilkins Perryman (*1 Sept. 1889–1 Feb. 1950*), state senator, lieutenant governor, Democratic party official, and Superior Court judge, was born in Kansas City, Kans., the son of Thomas B. and Mary E. Wilkins Horton, who moved to Pittsboro, N.C., when Horton was three years old. His father, born in Virginia, was a livestock dealer and farmer who saw Confederate service during the Civil War. Young Horton grew up in Pittsboro, received his early education in the Chatham County public school system, and attended Draughn's Business College in Raleigh and, from 1912 to 1914, The University of North Carolina where he received a law degree. He worked hard, financed his own education, and in 1915 began a law practice in Pittsboro with H. R. Haynes.

Horton began his political career in 1918 with his first term as state senator from the Thirteenth District. While a senator, he also was Chatham County attorney and for one term was president of the North Carolina Railroad. In 1935 Horton left the senate to run for lieutenant governor and was elected. He served under Governor Clyde R. Hoey until 1939, when he decided to run for governor; at the end of his term as lieutenant governor, the North Carolina Senate commended him for his just leadership and organizational prowess. Finishing second to J. Melvin Broughton by about 40,000 votes, Horton declined a runoff when the third- and fourth-place candidates in a field of seven threw their support to Broughton, citing as his reasons party harmony and the war in Europe. His platform in the race showed him to be a supporter of fair taxes, economical government, better public schools, higher teachers' salaries, resource development, improved libraries, and wildlife conservation. Horton also favored state compensation for children injured in school bus accidents, social security, and better pensions for Confederate veterans. He founded the state commission for the blind. Although the issue was not mentioned in his platform, Horton advocated the prohibition of alcoholic beverages.

After losing the election, he practiced law in Pittsboro with Daniel L. Bell, his former campaign manager, and Harry P. Horton, his adopted son. Tragedy struck in 1943 when Horton's wife, the former Casandra C. Mendenhall of High Point, died. Nevertheless, he reentered public life in 1944 when he was elected Democratic national committeeman. Horton resigned that post in 1947 to become chairman of the North Carolina Democratic Executive Committee, where he served ably until the following year when he relinquished the position to Capus Waynick, the campaign manager of Governor W. Kerr Scott. There had been speculation that Governor R. Gregg Cherry would appoint Horton U.S. senator, but he received the chairman's job instead.

In the spring of 1949, Governor Scott appointed Horton Superior Court judge, a position for which he was reportedly well qualified. He assumed the bench in July but only served until December, becoming ill during a session of the court; he was taken to the Pittsboro Hospital and later to the Duke Hospital. Horton died at home after an extended illness and was buried in the Pittsboro Methodist Church cemetery.

A Mason and a Shriner, Horton was Grand Master of the Grand Lodge of North Carolina and past master of the Columbus Lodge of Pittsboro. At the time of his death, he was chairman of the Chatham County Democratic Executive Committee, chairman of the Chatham County Infantile Paralysis Foundation, and vice-president of the North Carolina Infantile Paralysis Society. He was survived by his adopted son Harry and by his brothers W. B. and D. W. Horton.

SEE: *Charlotte Observer*, 22 Dec. 1940; *Durham Morning Herald*, 2 Feb. 1950; *Greensboro Daily News*, 12 Feb. 1940; Wade C. Hadley and others, *Chatham County, 1771–1971* (1976); Wilkins Perryman Horton (Alumni Office file,

University of North Carolina, Chapel Hill); Platform of Lt. Governor Wilkins P. Horton (North Carolina Collection, University of North Carolina Library, Chapel Hill); Raleigh *News and Observer*, 6 June 1935, 10 May 1947, 3 Feb. 1950.

ROBERT WALKER FULLER III

Hoskins, Charles W. *(January 1818–21 Sept. 1846),* army officer, was born in Edenton. The records of the U.S. Military Academy at West Point indicate that he and his father attested that he was eighteen at the time of his appointment to West Point in 1832, but in two documents his son, John D. C. Hoskins, states that his father was born in 1818. His family was prominent in Edenton, and was connected with the patriot Richard Hoskins whose wife participated in the Edenton Tea Party. His father, James Hoskins, was the son of Thomas and Mary Roberts Hoskins. His mother's name is nowhere listed in any official army documents, but she is mentioned in Ashe's *Biographical History of North Carolina* as having been a Miss Alexander. In Hathaway's *North Carolina . . . Register*, Charles Hoskins is referred to as the son of Mary Norcom who married James Hoskins on 22 Oct. 1775. This date is clearly erroneous and is corrected in another volume containing marriage bonds to 22 Oct. 1795. A Chowan County tombstone shows that a Mary Hoskins, wife of James, was buried at the Strawberry Hill Cemetery, born 17 Mar. 1771. Unfortunately the date of death is partially obliterated.

Charles Hoskins lived as a boy at Pembroke plantation near Edenton and was educated at Edenton Academy. In April 1832 he was appointed to the U.S. Military Academy by North Carolina congressman William Biddle Shepherd. He entered West Point on 1 July 1832 and was graduated fortieth in a class of forty-nine, receiving his commission as a brevet second lieutenant in the Fourth Infantry on 1 July 1836. He was promoted to second lieutenant on 13 Sept. 1836 and served under generals Scott and Wool in the Cherokee Nation as a quartermaster, helping to prepare for the removal of the Indians to the West, from 1836 to 1839. During this time he was promoted to first lieutenant, on 30 Dec. 1838. He also served at Fort Gibson, Ark., from 1839 to 1841, in the Florida War from 1841 to 1842, in the transferral of the Cherokees to the West in 1842, and at Fort Scott, Kans., from 1844 to 1845. While stationed at Jefferson Barracks, Mo., he met and became friends with Lieutenant Ulysses S. Grant. He also met Jennie Deane, who was born in Charleston, S.C., the daughter of Major John Deane of New Rochelle, N.Y. They were married in March 1845 and had one son, John Deane Charles, born on 17 Jan. 1846 in Potosi, Mo.

Hoskins served as regimental adjutant from 10 Sept. 1845 to 21 Sept. 1846. He was active in the military occupation of Texas during 1845–46 and in the War with Mexico, fighting in the Battle of Palo Alto, 8 May 1846; the Battle of Resaca-de-la-Palma, 9 May 1846; and the Battle of Monterrey, 21 Sept. 1846, during which action he was shot and killed.

Ulysses Grant recalled that during this battle to capture Fort Teneria he was the only man in the Fourth Infantry upon a horse. He met Lieutenant Hoskins, "who was not in robust health, found himself very much fatigued . . . and expressed a wish that he could be mounted also." Grant gave him the horse, but discovered a short time later that Hoskins had been shot by the enemy. Grant was then appointed adjutant in his place. Grant's regard for his friend was demonstrated some years later. When Hoskins's only son John Deane Charles applied for admission to West Point in 1864, General Grant asked that President Lincoln appoint the young man to the military academy; his request was honored.

Charles Hoskins was eulogized in the *National Intelligencer* of Washington, D.C., in a tribute that was reprinted in the Raleigh *Register* on 3 Nov. 1846, stating: "Lieutenant Hoskins possessed a quick and lively intellect; he cherished a nice and high sense of honor, and was remarkable for the generosity and chivalry of his character." A resolution in his honor was entered in the Laws of North Carolina for 1846–47. His death at an early age was lamented because of his capability as an army officer and also because of his charm, wit, and "passion for humor." His body was transported from Monterrey to Jefferson Barracks, Mo., where he was buried in the National Cemetery.

SEE: Samuel A. Ashe, ed., *Biographical History of North Carolina*, vol. 2 (1925); *Association of Graduates in the United States Military Academy* (11 June 1937, U.S. Military Academy Archives); Cadet Application Papers, roll 82 (U.S. Military Academy Archives); George W. Cullum, *Biographical Register of Officers and Graduates of the United States Military Academy*, vol. 2; Elizabeth City *Economist*, 18 July, 22 Sept. 1902; George McIver, "North Carolinians at West Point before the Civil War," *North Carolina Historical Review* (August 1930); National Archives and Records Service Microcopy Publ. 688 (U.S. Military Academy Archives); *North Carolina Cemetery Records*, Gen. Rec. Com. by NSDAR of North Carolina (1959, North Carolina State Archives, Raleigh); *North Carolina Laws, 1846–47*; *North Carolina Register*, vol. 1:252 (1823), vol. 3, no. 1 (January 1903); Raleigh *Register*, 3 Nov. 1846; John H. Wheeler, *Historical Sketches of North Carolina*, vol. 2 (1851).

MEADE B. B. HORNE

Hotelling, Addyson Harold (*29 Sept. 1895–26 Dec. 1973*), mathematical statistician and economist, was born in Fulda, Minn., the son of Clair and Lucy Rawson Hotelling. (In later life he dropped his first name.) He moved to Seattle, Wash., with his family in 1905, and attended the University of Washington by earning his own way. During World War I he joined the army, serving at Camp Lewis, Wash. After the war he returned to the university and was graduated in 1919 with a major in journalism.

Hotelling worked briefly for the Puyallup, Wash., *Herald*, and in 1920 married Floy Tracy. His mathematical talent was observed by Eric Temple Bell, whose encouragement induced him to return once more to the University of Washington for an M.A. degree in mathematics (1921) and to go to Princeton for a Ph.D. degree (1924). Hotelling was then appointed a junior research associate at the Food Research Institute of Stanford University, where he remained until 1931 except for a six-month stay in Rothamstead, England, to study with Ronald Fisher, whose work was fundamental to modern statistical theory. While at Stanford, Hotelling conducted his early research in statistical analysis and in 1931 published "The Generalization of Student's Ratio" (*Annals of Mathematical Statistics* 2), introducing a statistic known as "Hotelling's Generalized T^2."

The importance of econometrics, the application of statistical techniques to economics, was receiving increasing recognition and in 1931, largely at the instance of Wesley Mitchell, the Department of Economics at Columbia University appointed Hotelling professor of economics. Hotelling held the post for fifteen years, during which his principal economic work appeared. He was influential in the development of many statisticians and economists, including Nobel laureates Kenneth Arrow and Milton Friedman.

His wife died in 1932, and on 14 June 1934 he married Susanna Porter Edmondson. In 1939 they left New York for an extended visit to India, where Hotelling lectured at Calcutta. After their return in 1940, he engaged in statistical research with certain military applications and was head of Columbia's Statistical Research Group, whose work was devoted to the war effort.

In 1946 Hotelling left Columbia to accept an appointment at The University of North Carolina, which was establishing an Institute of Mathematical Statistics. As head of the institute, he brought to Chapel Hill a number of distinguished statisticians and built one of the nation's leading university departments in the subject; he also taught courses in mathematical economics. In 1965 Hotelling was a visiting professor at the University of Buenos Aires, Argentina. After his retirement in 1966, he remained active in his profession and continued to travel widely for some years. He died in his sleep and was buried in Chapel Hill near the university. He was survived by his wife and seven children.

Hotelling is remembered among economists for his work on the early stages of econometrics. His best known works are "The General Welfare in Relation to Problems of Taxation and of Railway and Utility Rates" (*Econometrica* 6 [1938]), "Stability in Competition" (*Economic Journal* 39 [1929]), and "Economics of Exhaustible Resources" (*Journal of Political Economics* 39 [1931]). The first of these deals with the question of what price to charge where the marginal cost is very low but the total investment may be great, as in bridge tolls and railway rates. The second is a theoretical discussion of how two competitors may divide a market, and the third anticipates some of the conservationist controversies of the 1970s.

His best known statistical work was the introduction of Hotelling's Generalized T^2, and his work in canonical correlations and principal components. These studies have had substantial influence in the development of mathematical statistics.

In 1930 Hotelling participated in a meeting in Cleveland, Ohio, that founded the Econometric Society, of which he was president in 1937. He was one of the first Distinguished Fellows of the American Economic Association (elected in 1965) and received honorary degrees from the University of Chicago (1955) and the University of Rochester (1963). He became a member of the National Academy of Sciences in 1970, was given the North Carolina Award in 1972, and was elected to the Italian Accademia Nationale de Lincei in 1973.

SEE: "In Memoriam—Harold Hotelling," *American Economic Review* 64 (December 1974); Howard Levene, "Harold Hotelling, 1895–1973," *American Statistician* 28 (May 1974); Ingram Olkin and others, eds., *Contributions to Probability and Statistics: Essays in Honor of Harold Hotelling* (1960); R. W. Pfouts, ed., *Contributions to Economics and Econometrics: Essays in Honor of Harold Hotelling* (1960); Walter L. Smith, "Harold Hotelling," *Annals of Statistics*; "Three Papers in Honor of Harold Hotelling at 65," *American Statistician* 14 (June 1960).

HAROLD HOTELLING, JR.

House, Abby (*ca. 1796–30 Apr. 1881*), Confederate "angel of mercy," was the daughter of Green and Ann House of Granville and Franklin counties. It is unclear where Abby was born, but she spent most of her adult life near Franklinton. Although her given name probably was Abigail, she came to be known as "Aunt Abby," and is most remembered for her aid to Confederate soldiers during the Civil War.

When the war began, she pledged to her eight nephews that she would do what was necessary to help them if they became sick or wounded. In fulfilling her promise she made frequent trips to Virginia on foot and by train. Although she rarely had enough money for train fare, her rough features, shrewd eyes, black mourning clothes, feisty personality, and ever-present cane convinced conductors of the expedience of allowing her to travel at no cost. She often neglected her personal safety to nurse or obtain furloughs for her nephews and other soldiers. Aunt Abby labored under fire during the bombardment of Petersburg and was present during or after other battles. Well endowed with self-confidence, she never hesitated to make demands of Robert E. Lee, Jefferson Davis, or Zebulon Baird Vance. By the end of the war all three men knew her personally. Because of her persistence in trying to obtain a furlough for one of her nephews, Marcellus, Vance once referred to Aunt Abby as the "ubiquitous, indefatigable and inevitable Mrs. House." When unable to travel, she gathered food and clothing for soldiers from her neighbors near Franklinton.

Aunt Abby's conspicuousness did not end with the Civil War. She admired Zebulon Vance as much as she loathed William Woods Holden. According to tradition, she was present during the Democratic convention held in Raleigh's Tucker Hall in 1876. Because Clay County was not represented, Paul Cameron moved that Aunt Abby be allowed to cast a vote during the balloting for the gubernatorial nominee. Her vote for Vance was perhaps the first instance of woman suffrage in the state. The following year she attended Vance's inauguration. Cartoonist Willis Holt Furgurson included Aunt Abby in "The Burial of Radicalism in North Carolina, Nov. 7, 1876," a cartoon representing Vance's victory over Judge Thomas Settle in the gubernatorial contest. In it she watches Vance tear asunder the state's shackles and exclaims, "ZEB your setting CAROLINA frae makes me feel like a gal again."

Aunt Abby mellowed in her final years. About 1876, the Reverend William Capers Norman of Raleigh converted her to Christianity and she joined the Methodist church. In March of that year she sat on the stage of the Metropolitan Hall in Raleigh with three bishops of the Methodist church during the celebration of the centennial of Methodism in North Carolina. During the conference she pledged $5,000 towards the construction of a proposed "Methodist Metropolitan Church" for Raleigh. She spent her last years in a cottage built near the old fairgrounds in Raleigh with funds provided by Confederate veterans. Governor Vance was among her regular visitors. She died at about age eighty-five and was buried in what is now an abandoned family cemetery north of Franklinton.

SEE: Mary Bayard Clarke, "Aunt Abby the Irrepressible," *The Land We Love* 3 (1867); W. H. Furgurson, "The Burial of Radicalism in North Carolina, Nov. 7, 1876" (North Carolina Collection, University of North Carolina Library, Chapel Hill); North Carolina Census (1810, 1850, 1880); T. H. Pearce, "Aunt Abby for the Confederacy," *The State* 40 (1972), and "Aunt Abby Finally Got Her Marker," *The State* 41 (1974); Raleigh *Daily News*, 26

Mar. 1876; Raleigh *Observer*, 28 Dec. 1876; Glen Tucker, *Zeb Vance, Champion of Personal Freedom* (1965); R. H. Whitaker, *Whitaker's Reminiscences, Incidents and Anecdotes* (1905).

MAURY YORK

House, Robert Burton (*19 Mar. 1892–17 Aug. 1987*), university administrator, was born in Thelma, Halifax County, the son of Joseph and Susan Drake House. Receiving his early education locally, he was graduated with honors in 1916 from The University of North Carolina where he was a member of Phi Beta Kappa. The following year he received the master of arts degree from Harvard. During World War I he served with the American Expeditionary Forces as a lieutenant of infantry (1917–18).

After teaching in the Greensboro high school in 1919, House became an archivist on the staff of the North Carolina Historical Commission (1919–24), where, as Collector of World War Records, he was responsible for the acquisition of more than 100,000 official and personal documents of the late war. From 1924 to 1926 he was the executive secretary of the North Carolina Historical Commission and managing editor of the *North Carolina Historical Review*, which was established in 1924. During that period he was also executive secretary of the State Literary and Historical Association.

In 1926 House became executive secretary of The University of North Carolina, serving until 1934 when he was appointed dean of administration at the Chapel Hill branch of the newly created three-campus Consolidated University of North Carolina. In 1945, he became chancellor at Chapel Hill. After retiring from that post in 1957, he taught in the English department until 1962. Under the watchful eye of House, the university survived the depression and World War II. During his administration it began or rebuilt fourteen departments or schools, including art, dentistry, journalism, medicine, music, naval science, nursing, public health, sociology, and social work.

House was a popular speaker who demonstrated a keen sense of humor and often delighted audiences with his harmonica as a means of breaking the ice at formal meetings. Active in cultural affairs in the state, he was a leader in organizing the Citizens Library Movement and instrumental in the creation of the North Carolina State Art Society. He was the author of numerous articles and of several books including *Miss Sue and the Sheriff*, about his childhood in Halifax County, and *The Light That Shines*, about his student days in Chapel Hill. He also was the editor of *The Public Letters and Papers of Governor Thomas W. Bickett* and of the *North Carolina Manual*, published in 1921, 1923, and 1925. House received honorary degrees from Catawba College, Bowdoin College, and The University of North Carolina. A Democrat and a Methodist, he taught a men's Bible class for forty-six years.

In 1918 House married Hattie Drake Palmer, and they became the parents of a son and a daughter, Robert Burton and Carolyn Twitty. His wife and both children predeceased him. He died at his home in Chapel Hill and was buried in the local cemetery.

SEE: *Chapel Hill Newspaper*, 18 Aug. 1987; Ola Maie Foushee, *Art in North Carolina* (1972); *North Carolina Historical Review* 1–4 (1924–27), 24 (1947), 37 (1960); Raleigh *News and Observer*, 18 Aug. 1987; *Who's Who in America* (1952).

WILLIAM S. POWELL

Houston, Christopher *(18 Feb. 1744–27 May 1837)*, farmer, soldier, and town planner, was born in Lancaster County, Pa., the fourth son of Robert Houston, a successful Scottish immigrant wheat farmer, and his wife Martha Worke of Philadelphia. Reared in Lancaster County, he was educated by private tutors and in schools in Philadelphia. In 1765 he joined the great wave of settlers migrating from Pennsylvania to the Carolinas and late in the year arrived at Fort Dobbs in Rowan County. Houston settled along the Catawba River and with his brother-in-law and his brother, James, established the first mill in the area at Hunting Creek.

Houston played an active role in the Revolutionary War, both as a civilian and as a soldier. As a civilian, he was responsible for procuring goods for the community from Virginia. As a soldier, he served from 1776 to 1782 in the North Carolina Rangers along with his brother James. Both fought in the Battle of Ramsour's Mill, near present-day Lincolnton, in which James was killed. Houston participated in the Battle of Kings Mountain and was one of a band of patriots assembled by General Nathanael Greene to fight in the Battle of Guilford Court House.

After the war Houston went back to Hunting Creek, where he founded a neighborhood school in his home and served as a town planner. The 1788 Act to Divide the County of Rowan into Rowan and Iredell counties stated that "George Davidson, Christopher Houston, Joseph Sharpe, Jeremiah Nielson, and John Nisbett are directed to agree and contract with workmen for the erecting and building of a courthouse, prison, and stocks for the use of the county of Iredell, at the place that they agree on." During the American Revolution John Oliphant of Rowan County had conveyed a land site of fifty acres to Fergus Sloan, also of Rowan County. Sloan deeded the fifty acres to the newly appointed town commission, and the new county seat, named Statesville, was established in 1789. Shortly after helping to establish Statesville, Houston recognized the need for a town on Hunting Creek, so he founded Houstonville, the second postal station in Iredell County. He served as the first postmaster of the new town.

In 1812 Houston and his wife, with their son James and twenty-seven slaves, moved to Maury County, Tenn. He helped James clear his land and in return James deeded some of the property to his father. Houston spent the rest of his life farming and working in James's marble and slate factory near Columbia, Tenn. He died in Maury County ten days after suffering a "stroke of palsy."

A staunch Presbyterian, Houston was well known for instructing his family and slaves in religious matters. He was considered a good master to his slaves, whom he freed in his will, stipulating that they were to be sent to Liberia. Whiggish in politics, he opposed the presidency of Andrew Jackson, favored the United States Bank, and spoke out against secession in the South Carolina Nullification Crisis of 1832.

Houston was married twice, first to Sarah Mitchell in 1767. She died in 1821, and he married Elizabeth Simpson in 1826. He had seven children: Martha, John, Lillias, James, Placebo, Samuel, and Sarah.

SEE: Gertrude Dixon Enfield, Unpublished biography of Christopher Houston (Southern Historical Collection, University of North Carolina Library, Chapel Hill); F. B. Heitman, *Historical Register of Officers of the Continental Army During the War of the Revolution* (1893); Mary Dalton Kennedy Papers (Southern Historical Collection, University of North Carolina Library, Chapel Hill); North Carolina Historical Commission, *Roster of Soldiers from North Carolina in the American Revolution* (1932).

M. ELAINE DOERSCHUK

Houston, David Franklin ("Frank") *(17 Feb. 1886–2 Sept. 1940)*, educator, author, U.S. cabinet official, and business executive, was born in Monroe, Union County, the youngest child of William Henry and Cornelia Anne Stevens Houston. His father farmed in North Carolina, then moved to Darlington, S.C., in 1872, where he became a horse and mule dealer, and for a time the operator of a general store where young Houston was employed. Although his father barely made the family a living, Frank early demonstrated his energy, ability, and ambition by graduating from the College of South Carolina in 1887. After a year of graduate study and three years as superintendent of public schools in Spartanburg, S.C., he studied political science and economics at Harvard under President Charles W. Eliot, receiving the M.A. degree in 1892.

With that background and the strong support of his famous mentor, Houston rose rapidly in the academic world. While teaching political science at the University of Texas, he married Helen Beall, of Austin, in 1885; published the scholarly *A Critical Study of Nullification in South Carolina* (1896); and served as dean of the faculty for three years. In Austin he also acquired as friends a number of powerful people, including Colonel Edward M. House, who later was chiefly responsible for Houston's appointment as a federal administrator.

In 1902 Houston began a distinguished career in college administration when he was chosen president of Texas A&M College. Three years later he returned to Austin as president of the University of Texas, and in 1908 he became chancellor at Washington University in St. Louis. Within a few years he had gained a national reputation for effective administrative leadership.

Colonel House brought Chancellor Houston to the attention of Woodrow Wilson, who named him secretary of agriculture in 1913. An economic conservative, Houston at first opposed increased federal intervention to aid agriculture such as supporting cotton prices or providing agricultural credits. But he later acquiesced in such measures and even supported federal aid to agricultural education, the building of hard-surfaced roads, and federal licensing of agricultural warehouses. Houston proved to be a model administrator, reorganizing the administrative structure of his department and staying out of matters that did not concern him. His most important legacy as agricultural secretary, however, was to change the department's emphasis from trying to improve production, to improving marketing, prices, and distribution. He led the effort to establish a cooperative Extension Service, an Office of Markets, and an Office of Information, while recruiting many of the country's best-known agricultural economists to work for the Department of Agriculture. Although he apparently did not often attempt to influence policy in other areas, his memoirs, *Eight Years with Wilson's Cabinet, 1913 to 1920* (2 vols., 1926), remain a good source for intimate discussions of Wilson's administration.

From February 1920 to March 1921, Houston served as secretary of the Treasury. As an ex officio member, he was also elected chairman of the Federal Reserve Board. His integrity and economic conservatism led him to adopt stringent policies to halt the inflationary economic boom under way. Although his monetary policies probably had little to do with the depression and the collapse of farm prices that followed in 1920, Houston received much of the blame.

A man who never sought publicity, Houston spent the last two decades of his life in relative obscurity. He shunned a political career, even though mentioned as a possible Democratic candidate for the presidency in 1924. However, he remained extremely active in business and education. From 1921 to 1927 he was associated with AT&T as president of Bell Telephone Securities Company and as financial vice-president of American Telephone & Telegraph Company, and from 1927 to 1940 he was president of Mutual Life Insurance Company of New York. He also served as a member of the Board of Overseers of Harvard and as a trustee of Columbia University.

Houston and his wife had five children: Duval Beall, David Franklin, Elizabeth, Helen Beall, and Lawrence Reid. He was buried in Cold Spring Harbor (N.Y.) Memorial Cemetery.

SEE: *DAB*, vol. 22; David F. Houston Papers (Harvard University Library, Cambridge, Mass.); *New York Times*, 3 Sept. 1940; John W. Payne, Jr., "David F. Houston: A Biography" (Ph.D. diss., University of Texas, 1953); *Who's Who in America* (1913–40).

E. DALE ODOM

Houston, William, Sr. (*d. ca. 1795*), was a physician, apothecary, and local political leader of Duplin County. His early life is obscure until he arrived in North Carolina about 1735 from County Antrim, Northern Ireland. Houston was the nephew of Henry McCulloch, a wealthy London merchant who financed many colonizing expeditions to the Cape Fear region, and served as his uncle's partner, trustee, and agent. In 1742 he built a home, Soracte, on the Northeast River, eight miles from Kenansville.

In 1749, when Duplin County was formed, Houston was an integral part of its development. He was a vestryman of St. Gabriel Parish (Anglican); a justice of the peace, serving frequently from the 1750s onward; Duplin's first representative to the colonial Assembly, from 1749 to 1762; and one of the three men in charge of building the county's courthouse, prison, and stocks. In the Assembly he developed a reputation for industry in the service of his county.

In 1765, after Parliament passed the Stamp Act, Houston was appointed stamp distributor for North Carolina. As he never solicited the office, it is conjectured that he was selected because of his kinship and close relationship with Henry McCulloch. This appointment became the focal point of public demonstrations on 19 and 31 Oct. 1765 in Wilmington, and on 31 October in New Bern and Fayetteville. Houston was hanged in effigy, presumably more in protest against the Stamp Act than against him personally. Unaware of the appointment or the reaction to it, Houston traveled from Soracte to Wilmington on Saturday, 16 November, where he was confronted by a crowd of three or four hundred people led by Colonel John Ashe. Under the circumstances, Houston declared that "he should be very sorry to execute any Office disagreeable to the People of the Province." The crowd was not satisfied until it had escorted him to the courthouse where he put his resignation in writing.

In 1766 Houston became clerk for the Committee of Public Claims at New Bern, and in 1768 and 1771 he was reappointed justice of the peace for Duplin. During the Revolutionary War, he served as chairman of the Court Martial Committee in Duplin, charged with hunting down Tories and deserters to the colonial cause. In 1784, Governor Alexander Martin once again appointed him justice of the peace for Duplin. He served as chairman of the county court from 1784 to 21 Oct. 1793, when he was last mentioned in the court minutes.

A wealthy man, Houston owned several large tracts of land and a number of slaves. In 1786, he donated land for a county seat to be built at Soracte, but Kenansville was later chosen instead. Houston married Ann Jones, the daughter of Squire Griffith Jones of Bladen County. They had five children: William, Jr., Edward, Griffith, Henry, and a daughter who married Captain William Hubbard.

SEE: J. O. Carr, "William Houston, The Stamp Agent—Another Viewpoint," in James Sprunt, ed., *The Chronicles of the Cape Fear River (1660–1916)* (1916); Walter Clark, ed., *State Records of North Carolina*, vols. 11 (1895), 17 (1899), 22 (1907), 25 (1906); Cleburne Huston, *Bold Legacy: The Story of the Houston, Huston, Houstoun Ancestors (1150–1800)* (1968); Kenansville *Duplin Times*, 30 Jan. 1941, 16 Sept. 1949; Faison Wells McGowen and Pearl Canady McGowen, *Flashes of Duplin's History and Government* (1971); William L. Saunders, ed., *Colonial Records of North Carolina*, vol. 7 (1890).

W. MICHAEL GOLNICK, JR.

Houston, William Churchill (*[?]1746–12 Aug. 1788*), teacher, Revolutionary leader, and attorney, was born in the Poplar Tent neighborhood of present Cabarrus County, the son of Margaret and Archibald Houston. He studied at the Poplar Tent Academy under Joseph Alexander, then—with a letter of recommendation from Alexander—rode off to the College of New Jersey where he taught in the grammar school associated with the college to pay for his studies. Houston continued to teach until 1768, when he was graduated with the A.B. degree from Princeton. The same year he became master of the grammar school and served as senior tutor. Continuing his education, he subsequently received the M.A. degree. On 25 Sept. 1771, Houston was elected the first professor of mathematics and natural philosophy at Princeton, where he remained until the Revolutionary War.

On 28 Feb. 1776 Houston volunteered his services to the colonials. He became captain of the foot militia of Somerset County and saw action in the Princeton area. In August he resigned his commission to return to the college. Soon afterwards, when all activities were disbanded at Princeton, Houston reenlisted and served until 6 Mar. 1777.

Meanwhile, in 1775 and 1776 Houston was elected deputy secretary of the Continental Congress. He was a member of the New Jersey Provincial Congress in 1776 and of the New Jersey General Assembly from 1777 to 1779. In 1778 he served as a member of the New Jersey Council of Safety, as well as resuming his professorship at Princeton.

In 1779 Houston was elected to the Continental Congress where he took a particular interest in supply and finance. He managed to find time to study law and in 1781 was admitted to the New Jersey bar. In the latter year he was appointed clerk of the New Jersey Supreme Court, an office he held until his death. Also in 1781 he was elected by Congress as the first comptroller of the Treasury, but declined to serve. From 1782 to 1785 Houston was receiver of the Continental taxes. In 1782, he also served on the commission to adjust the deficiencies in pay caused by depreciated currrency for New Jersey's troops, and on the commission that attempted to settle the Wyoming land dispute between Connecticut and Pennsylvania.

Resigning from Princeton in 1783, Houston proceeded to build up a sizable law practice in the Trenton area. In 1784 and 1785 he was elected to the Continental Congress, where he interested himself in John Fitch and Fitch's steamboat. A year later he was a member of the Annapolis Convention of 1786. One of six New Jersey delegates to the Constitutional Convention in Philadelphia, he took an active part in its deliberations. Although he signed the report of the commissioners to the New Jersey legislature, he did not sign the draft of the Constitution—whether by intention or by accident is not known.

Suffering from tuberculosis, Houston began to travel towards his native North Carolina in the hope of regaining his health. He died suddenly in an inn near Philadelphia and was buried in the yard of that city's Second Presbyterian Church.

Houston married Jean Smith, daughter of Caleb Smith and granddaughter of Jonathan Dickinson, the first president of the College of New Jersey. He was the father of two sons and two daughters. In person, Houston was tall, slender, and dignified.

SEE: *Biog. Dir. Am. Cong.* (1774–61); Walter Clark, ed., *State Records of North Carolina*, vols. 22 (1907), 23 (1904), 25 (1906); *DAB*, vol. 9; *Durham Herald-Sun*, 8 June 1941; *General Catalogue of Princeton University, 1746–1906* (1908); *Greensboro Daily News*, 8 June 1941; William Nelson, *New Jersey Biographical and Genealogical Notes* (1916); *Princeton Alumni Weekly*, 7 June 1929; William L. Saunders, ed., *Colonial Records of North Carolina*, vols. 4 (1886), 5, 6 (1887).

JOE O'NEAL LONG

Howard, Caleb D. *(fl. 1788–94)*, printer and journalist, published in Wilmington *The Wilmington Centinel and General Advertiser* with his partner, Daniel Bowen; their first issue apparently appeared on 5 Mar. 1788. The partnership was dissolved sometime in 1788 or 1789, and Howard moved to Fayetteville. There, he became the partner of John Sibley, and they published *The Fayetteville Gazette* beginning on 24 Aug. 1789. Although Howard was known as a strong anti-Federalist, the *Gazette* printed essays and arguments both for and against the proposed federal Constitution. Early in 1790, the name of the newspaper was changed to *The North Carolina Chronicle; or Fayetteville Gazette*, and according to the imprint was printed by John Sibley and Co. The 13 Sept. 1790 issue said it was printed by George Roulstone for John Sibley and Co., and the 11 October issue noted that it was printed by Howard and Roulstone for John Sibley and Co.

The firm of Sibley and Howard submitted a proposal to print the journal of the 1789 constitutional convention at Fayetteville, but the journal was printed by Hodge and Wills, the official state printers. On 23 Nov. 1789, Sibley and Howard were paid six pounds for printing 300 copies of amendments to the U.S. Constitution.

The *Chronicle* ceased publication in March 1791, and the publishers lamented that their subscribers were tardy in paying their bills. The 25 June 1794 issue of *The North Carolina Journal*, published by Hodge and Wills at Halifax, listed Caleb D. Howard as their agent in Fay-

etteville and told subscribers there that they could pay him. This is the last known reference to Howard.

SEE: C. C. Brigham, *History and Bibliography of American Newspapers, 1690–1820*, vol. 2; C. C. Crittenden, *North Carolina Newspapers before 1790*; D. C. McMurtrie, *A History of Printing in the United States*; S. B. Weeks, *The Press of North Carolina in the 18th Century*.

THOMAS A. BOWERS

Howard, George, Jr. *(22 Sept. 1829–24 Feb. 1905)*, lawyer and judge, was born in Tarboro, the son of George and Alice Thurston Clark Howard. His father, a native of Howard County, Md., moved to Halifax in 1824 and founded, edited, and published the *Free Press*, a weekly newspaper. Two years later he went to Tarboro, Edgecombe County, continuing the *Free Press* until 1836, when it was called the *Tarboro Press*. In 1852 the name was changed to the *Tarboro Southerner*, and today it is called the *Daily Southerner*, enjoying the distinction of being among the oldest newspapers in the state.

Young Howard was educated at the Tarborough Male Academy and in 1849 entered The University of North Carolina, where for two years he studied law under Judge William H. Battle and Samuel F. Phillips. After the first term of the Supreme Court of 1850 granted him a license, he began a practice in Edgecombe County. A year later he received his Superior Court license and was immediately elected to serve as county solicitor in the Court of Pleas and Quarter Sessions of Greene County. At this time the town of Wilson in Edgecombe County had begun to grow in population and importance. In 1854, Howard decided to move there and practice law. In November of that year he went to Raleigh at the opening of the legislature to urge the passage of a bill that would establish Wilson County. The bill was passed and ratified, and on 15 Feb. 1855 that section of Edgecombe County became known as Wilson County. Howard promoted the growth of the town of Wilson, his home for ten years. After the Civil War he returned to Tarboro, where he lived and practiced law until his death.

In 1858 Governor John W. Ellis offered Howard the seat in the Supreme Court vacated by Judge Matthias E. Manly and the General of Assembly of 1859 elected him to the office for life. "His fine presence, quickness of apprehension and legal abilities gave him large success upon the bench" and "he maintained . . . his reputation as a lawyer and as a presiding and administrative judicial officer, he was not excelled by any."

When the state convention of May 1861 was called, Howard and William S. Battle were elected delegates by the people of Edgecombe. Howard believed that as "by the exercise of the sovereignty of the people of the State in Convention assembled, the State had entered into the Union, when in like manner they chose to exercise their sovereign right again, they could withdraw from the Union and in doing so they could not be guilty of treason to either the State or Federal Government." He voted against an ordinance justifying secession because of the course urged by President Lincoln. In the organization of the convention, Howard was made chairman of the Committee on Military Affairs and served for the duration of the convention, which remained in session until May 1862.

On 2 Oct. 1865 he was elected to the convention that met in Raleigh to debate the legal and political effects of the Ordinance of Secession. Howard was one of nine men who were willing to vote to repeal the ordinance, but refused to vote that it was null and void, despite threats of political and perhaps personal destruction. (One of the other nine men was Colonel Dennis D. Ferebee of Camden County. In 1901 Ferebee's granddaughter, Mary, married Howard's youngest son, Stamps.)

Howard did not hold public office after 1866, although he served on a commission appointed by Governor Alfred M. Scales to recommend reforms in the state revenue system. He was for many years a director of the Wilmington and Weldon (later the Atlantic Coast Line) Railroad Company, and from 1885 to 1893 a member of the board of trustees of The University of North Carolina. In his hometown of Tarboro he served as a town commissioner, president of the Pamlico Banking and Insurance Company, and director of the Tarboro Cotton Mills and Fountain Mills. He continued to participate in every phase of the town's social, political, and economic life, and was an elder of the First Presbyterian Church.

On 3 Dec. 1861 Howard married Anna Ragland Stamps, the daughter of Dr. William Lipscombe and Elizabeth Jiggetts Stamps of Caswell County. They had six children: Elizabeth (m. Dr. Julian Meredith Baker), George III (m. Elizabeth Rawls), Harriet (m. George Allen Holderness), Alice (m. Job Cobb), William Stamps (m. Mary MacPherson Ferebee), and Mary Romaine (m. William Thomas Clark).

Howard died at his home in Tarboro, where he was buried beside his wife who died on 11 June 1901. His professional attainments were "splendidly summarized" by Judge Henry Groves Connor at the presentation of his portrait to the North Carolina Supreme Court on 13 Feb. 1917. Another portrait hangs in the Edgecombe County Courthouse, Tarboro.

SEE: Annual Reports of the President and Directors of the Wilmington and Weldon Railroad Company; Samuel A. Ashe, ed., *Biographical History of North Carolina*, vol. 4 (1905); Charters of the Wilmington and Weldon Railroad Company; J. G. de R. Hamilton, *Reconstruction in North Carolina* (1971); "I'm Thinking," *Rocky Mount Evening Telegram*, 31 Mar. 1956; *Journal of the Convention of the State of North Carolina* (1861, 1865 sessions); Personal letters and papers of Judge George Howard, Jr., and of W. Stamps Howard (in possession of the author).

MARY FEREBEE HOWARD

Howard, Henry Frederick (15 Aug. 1608–17 Apr. 1652), third Earl of Arundel and Surrey, Earl Marshal of England, and proprietor of Carolana, was the second but oldest surviving son of Thomas, second Earl of Arundel, and his wife, Lady Althea Talbot, daughter and ultimately sole heiress of Gilbert, seventh Earl of Shrewsbury. His great-grandfather was Thomas Howard, fourth Duke of Norfolk, who conspired against Queen Elizabeth with Mary, Queen of Scots, and was beheaded in 1572 for his part in the Ridolfi Plot. With the fourth duke's attainder, the ducal title and properties were lost to the Howard family for three generations. However, the fourth duke's son, Philip (1557–95), inherited—in right of his mother—the title of Earl of Arundel. This title eventually reached Henry Frederick through his father, Thomas (1585–1646), the second Earl of Arundel.

Throughout much of his life, Howard had only the courtesy title of Lord Maltravers. He was first elected a Member of Parliament in 1628 and continued to serve in Commons until he was summoned to the House of Lords on 21 Mar. 1640 as Baron Mowbray and Maltravers, by which title he was known until the death of his father.

Howard's first notoriety resulted from his youthful marriage in 1626 to Lady Elizabeth Stuart, daughter of Esmé, Duke of Lennox, and ward of King Charles. This marriage infuriated the king who had arranged for Lady Stuart's marriage to Lord Lorne, oldest son of the Earl of Argyle. For a period, Howard's father was confined in the Tower of London and the couple was placed in the custody of the Archbishop of Canterbury. After intervention by the House of Lords, the king relented and all were released.

As son and principal heir of the premier earl of England, Howard enjoyed numerous appointments and honors. From 1633 to 1639 he served as joint lord-lieutenant of Northumberland and Westmoreland. In 1633 he was appointed a commissioner to exercise ecclesiastical jurisdiction in England and Wales, in 1634 he was made a privy councillor of Ireland, and in 1636 he was named joint lord-lieutenant of Sussex and Surrey. In the latter year he was also designated vice-admiral of Norfolk, Cambridgeshire, and Isle of Ely.

These were but a few of the honors bestowed upon Howard in a period in which he was becoming increasingly involved in English colonial and overseas affairs. His interest in these matters probably originated with his father, the second earl, who had been one of the supporters of Sir Walter Raleigh's Guiana voyage of 1617, a member of the Virginia Company and the Council for New England, one of the leading adventurers in a plan to establish a plantation on the Amazon River under Captain Roger North, and in 1634 a member of the Laud Commission.

While still in his twenties, Howard became involved in overseas activities that soon rivaled those of his father. In 1632, he was received in the Council for New England as a councillor and patentee and along with others received grants of territory from that body. Unfortunately these deeds of feoffment were not confirmed by the Crown and were without legal validity. As late as 1638, however, Howard requested of the council "a degree more in latitude and longitude to be added to his portion of lands."

Howard joined with others in a plan to establish a West India Company in 1637. The plan called for an attack on Spain through its West Indian possessions. Some fit port in the West Indies was to be seized as a base of operations against the Spanish islands and as a haven for retreat. The investors in the West India Company planned to divide all spoils from these activities among themselves. In 1638 Howard was given a license for twenty-one years to stamp farthing tokens for distribution in all of the English colonies except Maryland. A colony was to be furnished as many of these farthings as were needed in exchange for commodities vendible in England. Many would have agreed with one seventeenth-century observer that this "Son & heir to the Ld Arundale . . . had a wonderful Inclination & a great Sagacity in promoting the plantation of Northern America and some of the Islands thereunto Adjacent."

Howard's interest in colonial promotion and settlement led him to use his influence sometime before 1637 to obtain a letter from King Charles to the governor and Council of Virginia ordering them to set out a county in the southern part of that colony for him. This letter miscarried in some manner, and on 11 Apr. 1637 another royal letter was sent by Charles to his Virginia government once more instructing that colony's officials to assign Howard "such a competent tract of land in the Southern part of that country as may bear the name of a county and be called the county of Norfolk." The county was to be awarded on conditions that would serve the good of the colony, and Howard was to be granted powers and privileges within the county that befitted "a person of his quality." A yearly rent of twenty shillings was to be reserved for the Crown.

Acting on these instructions from the king, Governor John Harvey and the Virginia Council issued a patent to Howard for the County of Norfolk on 22 Jan. 1637/38. The county was to extend southward from the branches of the Nansemond (now Suffolk) to 35° north latitude or about as far south as the mouth of the Neuse River. It was to extend east and west 1° in longitude on either side of the Nansemond River. The Virginia authorities had rather cleverly drawn Howard's county so that much of it lay within the area of the proprietary province of Carolana, which had been granted Sir Robert Heath in 1629 by King Charles and which extended from 36° to 31° along the coast. The Virginia patent required Howard to people the county within seven years and gave him certain severely circumscribed powers and privileges within the county.

In the end this patent proved of little interest or importance to Howard, for one month before the Virginia government reluctantly issued him a patent to the County of Norfolk, he was able to purchase the princely domain of Carolana from its proprietor, Sir Robert Heath. On 2 Dec. 1637, with the king's entire approbation, Heath, for an unknown sum, conveyed his title to Carolana to Howard. The yet unsettled Carolana extended from 36° to 31° north latitude and from the Atlantic westward to the South Seas. The charter assigned to the proprietor full title to this vast area and the power necessary to govern any settlement that might be made there.

Howard moved rapidly to establish a settlement and government in Carolana. On 2 Aug. 1638 he commissioned Captain Henry Hawley, then deputy governor of Barbados, to settle the southern part of the province, awarding him the title of lieutenant general of Carolana and 10,000 acres of land in that province. At the same time he apparently commissioned a Captain Henry Hartwell to settle the northern part of the province. Whatever his precise arrangements with Howard, Captain Hawley did not personally attempt to lead a colony into Carolana. Instead he appointed his brother, Captain William Hawley, to be deputy governor of Carolana and sent him to Virginia to organize an expedition to establish a colony to the south in Carolana. In April 1640, the Virginia Council under spur of a letter from the Crown granted leave for Carolana to be colonized by an expedition of "one hundred persons from Virginia, 'freemen being single, and disengaged to debt.' "

There is no evidence that Hawley ever led an expedition into Carolana or that Howard or any of his agents ever actually got a colony into that province. Although many decades later there were those who maintained that he had "at great expense planted several parts of the said country," there is no evidence to support such contentions. Certainly no lasting settlement was ever made. Still Howard did not lose interest in the project. In the summer of 1638, when it appeared that the Virginia charter would be restored, he joined with Lord Baltimore in insisting that any new charter contain a clause securing their provinces "from any prejudice or

inconvenience that might accrue to them." In all probability the mounting constitutional crisis in England distracted Howard and left him with little time to develop Carolana. As the difficulties increased in England, Howard took a strong and unyielding stand at the side of the king. He was one of the earlier signers of the "Protestation" in May 1641 by which he bound himself to "maintain and defend" the Protestant faith, and he took an active part in all military operations. After the capture of Banbury, he received the honorary degree of master of arts at Oxford in November 1642. Subsequently, he became joint commissioner for the defense of the county, city, and university. The illness of his father at Padua, Italy, took him from the country for months, and his father's death on 4 Oct. 1646 brought him the title of Earl of Arundel and Earl Marshal of England. When he returned home, he found that his property had been seized, but by vote of Parliament he was permitted to redeem his estates for a payment of £6,000.

In 1649, as the Civil War came to an end, notices began to appear in the London newspapers announcing that an expedition was preparing to sail shortly for Carolana and that a governor had been named. In the following year, a pamphlet was published extolling the virtues of Carolana and announcing that settlers were preparing to go out to that province. Meanwhile a map was published to show prospective colonists the precise location of Carolana. Howard's role in developing these plans for a colony is uncertain, but it seems unlikely that they could have been developed without his full knowledge and consent. Whatever may have been his part in this enterprise, it did not succeed. No colony sailed from England for Carolana.

His last years were devoted to efforts to break his father's will. This led to a bitter and prolonged fight with his mother, who opposed him. This role of the ingrate son has colored much of the subsequent writing about him. He died at age forty-four, two years before the death of his mother.

Howard's marriage to Lady Elizabeth Stuart produced nine sons and three daughters. His oldest son and heir, Thomas (1627–77), began to show signs of insanity while living with his grandfather in Italy in the 1640s. His "hopeless insanity" gradually worsened and "though he lingered many years, he was no more than a cipher." Thomas's brother, Henry, managed his affairs and in 1660 was able to secure the restoration of the title and honors of the dukedom of Norfolk to the Howard family after nearly ninety years. On the death of Thomas, Henry became the second son of Henry Frederick to succeed to the dukedom of Norfolk.

SEE: Clarence Walworth Alvord and Lee Bidgood, *The First Exploration of the Trans-Alleghany Region by the Virginians, 1650–1674* (1912); Charles McLean Andrews, *The Colonial Period of American History*, vol. 3 (1937); Gerald Brenan and Edward Phillips Statham, *The House of Howard*, vol. 2 (1907); British Museum Manuscripts (North Carolina State Archives, Raleigh); Daniel Coxe, *A Description of the English Province of Carolana . . .* (1722); Gordon Goodwin, "Henry Frederick Howard," *DNB*, vol. 10 (1908); William Waller Hening, comp., *The Statutes At Large; Being a Collection of all the Laws of Virginia, From the First Session of the Legislature, in the Year 1619*, vol. 1 (1823); Mary Hervey, *The Life of Thomas Howard, Earl of Arundel* (1921); Hugh T. Lefler, ed., "A Description of 'Carolana' by a 'Well-Willer,' 1649," *North Carolina Historical Review* 32 (1955); Henry R. McIlwaine,

Minutes of the Council and General Court of Colonial Virginia, 1622–1632, 1670–1676 (1924); Edward Daffield Neill, *Virginia Carolorum: The Colony Under the Rule of Charles the First and Second, A.D. 1625–A.D. 1685* (1886); Herbert R. Paschal, Jr., "Proprietary North Carolina: A Study in Colonial Government" (Ph.D. diss., University of North Carolina, Chapel Hill, 1961); William S. Powell, "Carolana and the Incomparable Roanoke: Explorations and Attempted Settlements, 1620–1663," *North Carolina Historical Review* 51 (1974); "Propriety of North Carolina als Florida" (North Carolina Collection, University of North Carolina Library, Chapel Hill); William Noel Sainsbury, *Calendar of State Papers, Colonial Series (America and West Indies)*, vol. 1 (1860); William L. Saunders, ed., *Colonial Records of North Carolina*, vol. 1 (1886); Peter Townsend, ed., *Burke's Genealogical and Heraldic History of the Peerage Baronetage and Knightage* (1963); *Virginia Magazine of History and Biography*, vols. 4 (1897), 8 (1900), 10 (1902), 11 (1903), 12 (1905), 13, 14 (1906).

HERBERT R. PASCHAL, JR.

Howard, Martin (*ca. 1725–November 1781*), Loyalist and chief justice of North Carolina, was born either in England or in New England (authorities disagree) but grew up in Rhode Island where his father, Martin, Sr., was admitted as a freeman of Newport in May 1726. Young Howard read law in Newport under James Honyman, Jr., who later became attorney general of Rhode Island. One of his biographers wrote that he studied at an Inn of Court, but Howard is not listed in Jones's *American Members of the Inns of Court*. On 29 Dec. 1749 he married his first wife, Ann Brenton Conklin of South Kingstown, R.I. They had three children—a son and two daughters. Although a regular attendant at Newport's Anglican Trinity Church, Howard had been born and bred an Anabaptist and was not baptized as an Anglican until the summer of 1770 in North Carolina. During 1752–55 he served as librarian of the famed Redwood Library. The Rhode Island legislature chose him as a delegate to the Albany Congress in June 1754 to negotiate with the Six Nations (composing the Iroquois Confederacy) in the coming hostilities with France. In 1756 Howard was elected to the Rhode Island Assembly and four years later served on the committee to revise the laws of the colony.

During the turbulent years after the close of the French and Indian War in 1763, Howard was a member of the conservative Newport Club, which included such figures as Peter Harrison and Dr. Thomas Moffat. These men abhorred the disorder of Rhode Island politics, and in April 1764 Howard joined with Moffat in a newspaper campaign to have the colony's charter revoked and royal government imposed. As a part of this effort, Howard corresponded with Benjamin Franklin, who was trying to accomplish the same end in Pennsylvania. In February 1765 Howard wrote a pamphlet called *A Letter from a Gentleman at Halifax to his Friend in Rhode Island*. In it he responded to a pamphlet by Governor Stephen Hopkins of the previous November that had attacked the Newport Club. The thrust of Howard's essay, however, was support of Parliament's authority to tax the colonies. Although Howard had not been named as author on the pamphlet's title page, there was no question among his friends or enemies as to who had written it. Undoubtedly when he was attacked as a Stamp Act agent in the summer of 1765, much of the hatred vented against Howard resulted from his identification as the "Gentleman at Halifax."

When leaders of the Stamp Act riots, which occurred

in Newport on 27–28 Aug. 1765, began formulating their plans, they reserved a special enmity for Howard because of his pamphlet allegations that Newport merchants were little better than smugglers. On the morning of 27 August a gallows was erected near Colony House in Newport with effigies of the three stamp agents hanging there. Crowds gathered and by 5:00 P.M. free drinks were provided. After sunset the three figures were cut down and burned. That evening Howard was walking through town with John Robinson, the customs officer, when Robinson was attacked by a small crowd. Howard helped rescue his friend and then upbraided the ruffians for their behavior. The next evening a mob with painted faces and broad axes broke into Howard's house, demolished his furniture, and drank the contents of his wine cellar. Later that night they returned and smashed his doors, floors, and windows, and even cut down the trees in his front yard. By 29 August Howard was so concerned for his own safety and that of his family that he boarded the British ship *Cygnet* and two days later sailed for England, arriving there in October. Seven years later while in North Carolina, he submitted a claim for £524 13s. sterling to the Rhode Island legislature for his losses in the riots. The assembly lowered the award to £111 18s. but never paid it. In a swipe at Howard as a defender of the Crown, the legislature agreed to pay his award when England fully recompensed Rhode Island for its role in the French and Indian War. After he demonstrated the extent of his losses and protested his loyalty to friends in England, the Crown offered Howard the chief justiceship of North Carolina. He accepted, and his commission was issued on 29 July 1766.

By January 1767, Howard was in North Carolina and on the twenty-third of the month qualified as chief justice before the governor and Council. At some time during the year he went to Boston to sit for his portrait by John Singleton Copley. While there he married his second wife, Abigail Greenleaf, daughter of the sheriff of Suffolk County, Mass.

Having escaped from a volatile situation in Rhode Island only a short time before, Howard soon found himself in the midst of the Regulator upheaval in North Carolina. He presided over all higher court trials of Regulators in the fall of 1768 and generally was considered to have been fair by backcountry residents. In fact, when the Regulators planned to disrupt the Salisbury court session of March 1771, they specifically excluded the chief justice from their hatred but not his colleagues. That spring he presided at the trials of the rebel leaders of the Battle of Alamance, six of whom were executed.

A man of considerable intellect as well as courage, Howard condemned the institution of slavery from the Superior Court bench late in 1771. In his charge to a grand jury that had failed to convict a white man for murdering a slave, he said: "Slavery is an adventitious, not a natural state. The souls and bodies of negroes are of the same quality with ours—they are our own fellow creatures, tho' in humbler circumstances, and are capable of the same happiness and misery with us." The entire text of Howard's remarks was published in both the *Cape Fear Mercury* (Wilmington) and the *Newport Mercury* (Newport, R.I.). His remarks were a powerful intellectual indictment of the slave system and may have contributed to passage of an act in 1773 by the General Assembly providing punishments and fines for the killing of black bondsmen.

In January 1770 Governor William Tryon nominated Howard to a seat on the royal Council, and on 19 No-

vember he was sworn in. Faithful in his attendance at
Council sessions, Howard usually sided with the governor—especially during the crucial months prior to the
American Revolution. When the Superior Court system
was suspended in late 1772, he served as chief justice of
the prerogative courts established by Governor Josiah
Martin but his income from fees was diminished. His
salary of £70 per year had not been paid since 1770, but
he had averaged at least £800 a year in fees and other
perquisites. Lorenzo Sabine writes that in the summer
of 1777 Howard said: "I shall have no argument with
the Sons of Liberty of Newport; it was they who made
me Chief Justice of North Carolina, with a thousand
pounds sterling a year." Because of his association with
the hated prerogative courts, Howard had become the
most despised official in the colony (next to the governor) by the summer of 1775. Yet when full-scale fighting
broke out, he was able to withdraw quietly to his plantation, Richmond, on the Neuse River in Craven
County. There he lived a remote existence, as his letter
thanking James Iredell for a personal kindness in May
1777 indicates: "An instance of civility to an obscure
man in the woods, is as flattering as a compliment to a
worn-out beauty. . . . I have lately been so little accustomed even to the common courtesies of life that a sentiment of kindness comes upon me by surprise."

By midsummer 1777, it became necessary for Howard
to leave North Carolina when he refused to take an
oath of loyalty to the state. He moved his family to
New York, and less than a year later went on to England and settled in Middlesex County. Howard was
awarded a pension of £250 per year for his loyalty to
the British government. In November (one account says
the fourth; another, the twenty-fourth) 1781 he died.
After the war, his wife and daughter settled in
Massachusetts.

SEE: Samuel A. Ashe, ed., *Biographical History of North
Carolina*, vol. 3 (1906); Bernard Bailyn, ed., *Pamphlets of
the American Revolution, 1750–1776*, vol. 1; John R. Bartlett, ed., *Records of the Colony of Rhode Island and Providence Plantations in New England*, vols. 4–6; Henry Herbert Edes, *Martin Howard, Chief-Justice of North Carolina
and His Portrait by Copley* (1903); Don Higginbotham and
William S. Price, Jr., eds., "Was It Murder for a White
Man to Kill a Slave? Chief Justice Martin Howard Con-
demns the Peculiar Institution in North Carolina," *William and Mary Quarterly* 36 (October 1979); Loyalist
Claims Commission Transcripts (North Carolina Division of Archives and History, Raleigh); G. J. McRee,
ed., *Life and Correspondence of James Iredell*, vol. 1 (1857–
58); Edmund S. Morgan and Helen M. Morgan, *The
Stamp Act Crisis* and *Prologue to Revolution: Sources and
Documents on the Stamp Act Crisis, 1764–1766*; Lorenzo
Sabine, *Biographical Sketches of Loyalists in the American
Revolution* (1864; reprint ed., 1966); William L.
Saunders, ed., *Colonial Records of North Carolina*, vols. 8–
10 (1890).

                                    WILLIAM S. PRICE, JR.

Howard, William Travis (12 Jan. 1821–31 July 1907),
physician and teacher, was born in Cumberland
County, Va., the son of William Alleyne and Elizabeth
Travis Howard. He was graduated from Hampden-Sydney College, studied medicine under John Peter Met-
tauer in Prince Edward County, and received a degree
from Jefferson Medical College in 1844. He served a
residency at the Baltimore City Almshouse, and about
1845 settled in Warrenton, N.C., where he practiced
medicine and surgery until 1866. He was the author of

a series of highly regarded articles published in the
North Carolina Medical Journal in 1859 and 1860 that disproved the contemporary theory concerning malarial
pneumonia. He was also a pioneer in certain gyneco-
logical techniques and developed a number of instruments used in that area of medical practice.

Like a number of other North Carolinians, Howard
moved to Baltimore at the end of the Civil War. There,
in addition to his private practice, he taught physiology
at the University of Maryland. Within a year he was selected to fill the new chair of diseases of women and
children, the first such in any American medical school.
He continued his practice, research, and publication,
and despite his modesty gained a wide reputation in
his field.

Howard was married three times: to Mrs. Lucy M.
Davis Fitts, of Warren County; to Anastasia Waddill, of
Northampton County, whom he had known as a young
man; and to Rebecca N. Williams, of Baltimore, who
survived him. He was buried in Richmond, Va.

SEE: *DAB*, supp. vol. 1 (1944); Lizzie Wilson Montgomery, *Sketches of Old Warrenton* (1924); *Transactions of the
Medical Society of North Carolina* (1908).

                                    WILLIAM S. POWELL

Howe, George (3 Oct. 1876–22 June 1936), teacher and
administrator, was born in Wilmington, the son of
George and Annie Josephine Wilson Howe. His father
was a distinguished clergyman, and his uncle was the
late president Woodrow Wilson, with whom Howe
lived during his boyhood. From Lawrenceville School
in New Jersey, Howe enrolled at Princeton University
and in 1897 received the A.B. degree, with membership
in Phi Beta Kappa and the Zeta Psi social fraternity. After studying at Oxford University in England, he was
sent by Woodrow Wilson to the University of Halle,
Germany, where he received the A.M. and Ph.D. degrees in 1903. In the latter year he was elected by the
trustees to the faculty of The University of North Carolina as a professor of the Latin language and literature.
Except for a leave of absence in 1912–13 to study at the
American Classical School in Rome, Howe remained at
the university for thirty-three years under the administrations of presidents Venable, Edward K. Graham, and
Harry W. Chase.

In September 1919, Howe, then head of the Classics
Department, was appointed dean of the College of Liberal Arts, a post he held until 1922. As dean, Howe
separated the instructional and disciplinary functions of
that office, devoting himself to the improvement of undergraduate studies and assigning the direction of extracurricular affairs (including discipline) to Frank Porter Graham in the new position of dean of student
affairs. Also valuable to his office were Howe's experience with undergraduate tutorials at Princeton, his administrative expertise as faculty committeeman and
head of a major academic department, and his personal
standards for scholarship.

His participation in programs for university development included service on numerous committees.
Among these boards were E. K. Graham's Committee
on Grounds and Buildings, appointed on 6 Sept. 1913;
the Curriculum Committee, which met in July 1918 to
define the university's role in World War I by designing
a program of American ideals implemented by the Student Army Training Corps; Chase's committee to set cri-
teria for Kenan professorships (1919); and the Administrative Council of the Consolidated University (1933).

During World War I Howe, a Democrat, was a member of the North Carolina State Council of Defense (1917–18).

Howe earned his reputation as one of the most prominent classical scholars in the South through authorship of several well-known Latin texts (including *The Spirit of the Classics*) and through activity in professional societies such as the American Philological Association, the Classical Association of the Middle West and South (first president of the southern section), the American Association of University Professors, and the North Carolina Literary and Historical Association. He was an associate editor of *Studies in Philology* and *Classical Journal*. A bibliography of his work was compiled by Albert Irving Suskin in 1936. Howe was also a member of the board of directors of the Bank of Chapel Hill. He left the university in May 1936 because of declining health.

On 27 Oct. 1903 Howe married Margaret S. Flinn, of South Carolina, the daughter of the Reverend William Flinn, a Presbyterian chaplain and dean of the University of South Carolina. In 1934 Howe traveled to Arkansas and sued for divorce in Little Rock. He then married Mrs. Ethel Eason, with whom he lived in Richmond, Va., until his death. When Howe's first wife contested his will, the Virginia Supreme Court in 1942 declared his second marriage void. The library of George Howe, including rare classical volumes given to him by President Wilson, was presented to the library of The University of North Carolina as a memorial to Howe by Margaret Flinn Howe in 1945.

SEE: Kemp P. Battle, *History of the University of North Carolina* (1912); *Chapel Hill Weekly*, 26 June 1936; Princeton Register; Raleigh *News and Observer*, 22 Jan. 1942; *Register of the Officers and Faculty of the University of North Carolina, 1795–1945*; Albert Irving Suskin, *Dr. George Howe, a Bibliography* (1936); *Who Was Who in America*, vol. 1 (1943); Louis Round Wilson, *The University of North Carolina, 1900–1930* (1957); *Yackety-Yack* (1904–35).

CATHERINE MEYERS BENNINGTON

Howe, Robert (1732–14 Dec. 1786), planter, soldier, and politician, was born in New Hanover (later Brunswick) County, the son of Job Howe (Howes), who moved to North Carolina from Charleston, S.C., and settled on the Cape Fear River where he prospered as a planter. Sarah, Job's wife, was a descendant of Sir John Yeamans; Job's mother, Mary Moore, was the daughter of South Carolina governor James Moore.

Young Howe, according to tradition, was educated in England. In 1754 he married Sarah Grange, daughter of Thomas Grange, but they separated in 1772. The number of both his legitimate and illegitimate children is open to debate. In her will Sarah Howe mentioned a son, Robert, and daughters Mrs. Ann Goodet Daniel and Mary Moore; another source adds a second daughter, and still another includes Robert and six daughters. Howe's reputation as a womanizer was widely commented upon.

Howe received a considerable fortune from his grandmother and from his rice plantation on Middle Sound opposite Barren Inlet. He also owned a plantation in Bladen County where he became captain of a militia about 1755. He was appointed a justice of the peace for Bladen County in 1756, and received a similar appointment in 1764 when Brunswick County was created. From 1760 to 1762 Howe represented Bladen in the Assembly. In 1764 he was elected a member from Brunswick and thereafter was reelected six times. As a captain of militia in 1766–67, he was in command of Fort Johnston, a post he also held from 1769 to 1773. He served with Virginia troops in the French and Indian War, and in Governor William Tryon's expedition against the Regulators he was a colonel of artillery.

With the onset of the revolutionary crisis, Howe became a member of the Committee of Safety for Wilmington and Brunswick County. He also served on the committee that supervised the collection of corn, flour, and pork in August 1774, intended as a gesture of support for Boston. After the news of Lexington and Concord reached North Carolina in May 1775, he assumed command of the drilling of the militia. On 15 July, Howe's command of nearly five hundred militia marched out of Brunswick against Fort Johnston. Early in the morning of 19 July, after Governor Martin had fled, the militia set fire to the fort and the surrounding buildings.

When North Carolina created two regiments for the newly authorized Continental Line, Howe was appointed colonel of the Second North Carolina Regiment on 1 Sept. 1775. Late in the year he marched into Virginia and, although too late to participate in the Battle of Great Bridge, assumed command of the North Carolina and Virginia troops that captured Norfolk. He had been given the post because of his seniority over Colonel William Woodford, of Virginia, who praised Howe as a "brave, prudent & spirited commander." For his services he received the thanks of the Virginia Convention on 22 Dec. 1775 and of the Provincial Congress of North Carolina on 27 Apr. 1776.

In March 1776, along with James Moore, Howe was promoted to brigadier general by the Continental Congress and ordered to South Carolina. While he was away his plantation was destroyed by the British. When Henry Clinton was in the Cape Fear area, he issued a proclamation offering pardon to all those who would take an oath of allegiance with the exception of Cornelius Harnett and Robert Howe. In Charleston, Howe acted as something of a super-adjutant to Major General Charles Lee, and was put in command of the South Carolina militia at the first siege of Charleston in June 1776. Although an expedition against St. Augustine was contrary to Howe's better judgment, he marched from Charleston on 8 Aug. 1778 with the regulars. When Lee was recalled to the northward, Howe was left in command of the troops in Georgia. But the effort to capture St. Augustine ended in failure as a result of British reinforcements, transportation breakdowns, an outbreak of malaria, and lack of cooperation by Governor John Houstoun of Georgia.

After the death of Brigadier General James Moore on 15 Apr. 1777, Howe was appointed to succeed him as commanding general of the Southern Department. He was promoted to major general on 20 October. When Savannah was threatened by British forces under Lieutenant Colonel Archibald Campbell, Howe assumed the defense of that town. Because of the lack of cooperation by Governor John Houstoun, Howe was outflanked and defeated by Campbell on 29 Dec. 1778. Already in disfavor with South Carolina and Georgia politicians, Howe was forced to bear the greater part of the blame for the loss of Savannah, although he was subsequently acquitted by a court martial "with the Highest Honor."

Notwithstanding the loss of Savannah, his recall as commanding general of the Southern Department was more political than usually suspected. As early as 20 Aug. 1777, the South Carolina Assembly had passed a resolution questioning Howe's right to command in that state. An acrimonious dispute with Christopher Gadsden eventually led to a duel on 30 Aug. 1778, with Howe and Gadsden each missing at a distance of eight paces. However, Joseph Hewes attributed Howe's recall to a "little ridiculous matter he has been concerned with in South Carolina, with regard to a female."

The Continental Congress removed Howe as commander of the Southern Department on 25 Sept. 1778. Ordered to the north, he rejoined George Washington's army on 19 May 1779 but was incapacitated for over a month by injuries resulting from a fall. On 18 June, he was sent across the Hudson River to cooperate with General Israel Putnam in the attempt to take Fort Lafayette on Verplanck's Point. Howe could not carry out his orders to concentrate artillery fire on the fort, as there were few field pieces along and, for some reason, those that were there lacked ammunition. Moreover, had these articles been available, there were no entrenching tools, no provisions, and no wagons to transport them. After an engineer had examined the fort and declared that an attempt to take the place by storm would be "ineligible," Howe advised Washington to call off the siege, which was done.

Howe was relatively uninvolved in later military plans, although he was commandant of Fort West Point prior to the Arnold conspiracy and was active in the upper Hudson for the rest of the war. He served as a member of the court martial board that convicted Major John André of spying. And in 1781, when the malignancy of mutiny spread from the Pennsylvania Line to the New Jersey Line, Washington sent Howe with five hundred men to quell the rebellion of the latter group. Marching swiftly through a two-foot snow in the early morning chill of 27 January, Howe surrounded the mutineers' camp with men and artillery. Two of the three leaders convicted by a speedy court martial were executed and the mutiny collapsed.

In 1783 Howe was again in charge of the troops that dispersed the discontented soldiers who had driven the Continental Congress from Philadelphia. In the same year he returned to his North Carolina plantation, Kendall (above Orton), to resume his career as a planter, yet he was in Philadelphia frequently between 1784 and 1785. In 1786 he was elected a delegate to the North Carolina House of Commons. On his way to a meeting of the house, he became ill and died in Bladen County.

As North Carolina's only major general, Howe spent too much time in Continental service to have made significant contributions to the state units. Judging by his performance at the Continental level, one is led to suspect that he leaned too heavily towards the spectacular. Yet, Howe might have been one of the better known general officers of the American Revolution had his timing been better; his opportunities came at times when he did not have the proper field strength to gain favorable recognition.

SEE: Walter Clark, ed., *State Records of North Carolina*, vols. 11–23 (1895–1904); Curtis C. Davis, *Revolution's Godchild* (1976); Hugh F. Rankin, *The North Carolina Continentals* (1971); William L. Saunders, ed., *Colonial Records of North Carolina*, vols. 6–10 (1888–90); Janet Schaw, *Journal of a Lady of Quality* (1939); Alan D. Watson, Dennis R. Lawson, and Donald R. Lennon, *Harnett, Hooper & Howe* (1979).

HUGH F. RANKIN

Howell, Edward Vernon (30 Mar. 1872–14 Feb. 1931), pharmacist, university professor, banker, and founder

and dean of The University of North Carolina School of Pharmacy, was, according to John Grover Beard, his successor, "the most distinct personality Chapel Hill has ever known." Born in Raleigh, he was the son of Virginia Carolina Royster and the Reverend James King Howell, a Baptist minister of Welsh ancestry.

After graduation from the Selma Academy, young Howell entered Wake Forest College where he received the A.B. degree in 1892. At Wake Forest he was a football fullback for three years and captain of the team in 1890. He was also captain of the lacrosse team and winner of the "best-all-around athlete" medal. In his senior year, along with his sister, Emily Royster (later Mrs. P. B. Kyser of Rocky Mount, the first woman pharmacist in North Carolina), he passed the Board of Pharmacy examination for a license to practice in the state. For three months in the summer after graduation Howell got his first pharmaceutical experience at W. H. King Drug Co. in Raleigh. In the fall he entered the Philadelphia College of Pharmacy, from which he was graduated in 1894 with the graduate in pharmacy degree. A keen and enthusiastic researcher, Howell was offered a graduate scholarship in chemistry at Johns Hopkins University; however, because of financial reasons, he returned to North Carolina instead and went into partnership with his sister and brother-in-law, who operated a store, Kyser Drug Co., in Rocky Mount.

Meanwhile, at Chapel Hill, the newly installed university president, Edwin A. Alderman, was looking for someone to revive the defunct School of Pharmacy that had existed for short periods around 1885 and 1889. The position would pay a salary of twenty-five dollars a month, plus small commissions on the tuition fees of any students the new teacher could interest in his courses. Although this was not, perhaps, a brilliant prospect, Howell was an avid scholar and a man of vision. He accepted Alderman's offer, and in the fall of 1897 began the School of Pharmacy with one professor (himself) and seventeen students. For the next thirty years he watched it grow into a nationally recognized professional school with a maximum registration of 148; from a single room in New West, it spread by degrees until, in 1925, it occupied the entire old chemistry building, remodeled under his guidance and renamed Howell Hall in his honor. In 1897 Howell also registered as a graduate student and for two years pursued his studies in chemistry simultaneously with his teaching duties.

Dean W. W. Pierson described Howell as "the most versatile man . . . I have ever known," and the record confirms his opinion. In 1897 and 1898 (during the time when professors and graduate students could participate in college athletics), Howell was drafted to play on the Carolina football team. The rivalry between The University of North Carolina and the University of Virginia was already well established, and Virginia had won most of the previous matches. But in 1898 Howell turned the tide, becoming one of Carolina's immortals by running 55 yards through the whole Virginia team for the touchdown that ended the game with a score of 6 to 2 for Carolina. He also was a member of the Monogram Club and of the Faculty Athletic Committee.

From 1892 onward, Howell held continuous membership in the North Carolina Pharmaceutical Association and he attended every annual meeting except the one in 1900, when he was studying in Europe. Among his many positions in the association, he was a member of executive, legislative, and papers-and-queries committees, and a delegate (fourteen times) to the American Pharmaceutical Association (APA). A member of the

APA from 1900 onward, he served variously as chairman of the Historical Section and of the Scientific Section, and a member of the Committee on Drug Reform. The year before his death he was named to the prestigious committee to revise the U.S. pharmacopoeia.

Howell early turned his attention to finance and was active in real estate and in the management of The People's Bank of Chapel Hill, of which he was president. When economic depression threatened the bank's security, he saw to it—at great personal sacrifice—that depositors were paid in full.

He had numerous hobbies, the most important of which, perhaps, was the collection of antiques—from furniture to old books and papers. Interested in folklore, he was a member of the American Folklore Society and a charter member of the North Carolina Folklore Society. His collected papers contain items relating to the breeding of English setters and to his registered bitch, Flora Belle. An enthusiastic deep-sea fisherman, he owned a boat and an entire island off the North Carolina coast where he had a cottage; there, friends would go for fishing and duck hunting in season. Howell loved to entertain, and was a genial and fascinating host; Foy Baker, his chef and houseman, was famous for his barbecues and turtle stews. For many years they gave a party at Halloween for two to three dozen neighborhood children with ice cream, candy, and a gift for each child.

Among the dean's outstanding qualities were his teaching skills. Students testified to his wit, kindness, vast knowledge, and ability in his lectures to make even a mass of scientific detail interesting. He invented numerous mnemonic devices (some humorous, some anecdotal) for their benefit. At the banquet celebrating the twenty-fifth anniversary of the founding of the School of Pharmacy, the classes of 1920, 1921, and 1922 gave him a gold watch to show their appreciation of his work.

Equally talented as a scholar, Howell devoted hours to private research projects. He was the author of fifty or more scientific articles, most presented at meetings of the North Carolina Pharmaceutical Association and the American Pharmaceutical Association. In addition, he was interested in historical research, especially that relating to his state or university. Howell was an indefatigable collector of historical documents, the bulk of which were given to the manuscript collection of The University of North Carolina after his death. There are papers relating to the Boylan and Benton families, to Daniel Boone, to Judge John Williams, and, most notably, to Henry Harrisse, on which Howell was working at the time of his death.

Howell was a Democrat, a Baptist, and a member of Sigma Alpha Epsilon (social) and Kappa Psi (pharmacy) fraternities, the Junior Order of Gimghouls, the Elisha Mitchell Scientific Society of The University of North Carolina, the North Carolina Literary and Historical Association, and the American Historical Association. In 1923–24 he served as vice-president of the Conference of American Pharmacy Faculties.

One Friday late in January 1931, Howell, after previously informing his class that he intended to visit friends in Raleigh, chalked a hurried note on the blackboard: "Goodbye, I'm gone." He never returned. During the weekend he developed pneumonia, and his niece, Mrs. Carlton Noell (Virginia Kyser), went to his home to direct his nursing care. He died two weeks later. Funeral services were held in Chapel Hill with interment in Raleigh. An oil portrait by William Wirtz

hangs in The University of North Carolina School of Pharmacy.

SEE: John G. Beard, "Edward Vernon Howell," *Carolina Journal of Pharmacy* 13 (October 1931); Clippings File (North Carolina Collection, University of North Carolina Library, Chapel Hill); "Dean Vernon Howell Saw Fondest Dream Realized," Raleigh *News and Observer*, 22 Feb. 1931; Louis Graves, "Dean Edward Vernon Howell," *Carolina Journal of Pharmacy* 7 (March 1931 [portrait]); Edward Vernon Howell Papers (Southern Historical Collection, University of North Carolina Library, Chapel Hill); "Vernon Howell Taken by Death," Raleigh *News and Observer*, 15 Feb. 1931; *Who Was Who in America*, vol. 2 (1943–50).

ERMA WILLIAMS GLOVER

Howell, Rednap (d. 1787), "poet of the Regulators," moved to North Carolina from New Jersey, probably in the early 1760s. He settled first in present Chatham County, then moved about 1768 to what is now Randolph County. Howell is supposed to have been a teacher and certainly was well educated for his time. He wrote several "Regulator poems" satirizing the men and events associated with the Regulator uprising in North Carolina from 1768 to 1771. He may also have written some of the "Regulator Advertisements" that he signed, as well as a pro-Regulator pamphlet entitled "A Fan for Fanning and a Touchstone for Tryon."

Howell first appeared on the Regulator scene in May 1768 as one of the signers of a petition to Governor William Tryon, stating the grievances of the western North Carolina farmers against the appointed county officials. Howell and James Hunter carried the petition to Tryon, who refused to hear their grievances and demanded that the Regulators pay their taxes and obey the laws of the province.

In the summer of 1768 Tryon led a military expedition through the Regulator counties, but met with no formal resistance. This expedition, coupled with a promise to hold new elections in 1769, quieted the opposition for some time. The elections were held and several pro-Regulators were sent to the provincial legislature. However, when that body was dissolved after only four days in session, the Regulators once again took action. In September 1770, they prevented court from being held in Hillsborough, the seat of Orange County. Howell was later indicted in connection with this incident, although he probably did not take part in the more riotous actions of the mob.

In January 1771 Howell learned that Herman Husband, another Regulator leader, had been imprisoned in New Bern and began raising a force to release him. Because Husband was released by the court, the expedition did not take place. Subsequently, Tryon raised another force of eastern militia and again set out to punish the Regulators. At the Battle of Alamance on 16 May 1771, his militia easily defeated the badly organized Regulators. Howell was present at the beginning of the battle, but is thought to have left the field without taking part in the fighting. Nevertheless, he was outlawed by Governor Tryon and a reward was offered for his capture, dead or alive.

After Alamance, Howell fled to Maryland and later returned to New Jersey, where he died. As far as is known, he never married.

SEE: John Spencer Bassett, "The Regulators of North Carolina, 1765–1771," American Historical Association *Annual Report* (1894); William L. Saunders, ed., *Colonial Records of North Carolina*, vol. 8 (1890).

ELMER D. JOHNSON

Howell, Robert Boyté Crawford (10 Mar. 1801–5 Apr. 1868), Baptist minister and leader, was born in Wayne County. Although of Episcopal heritage, he joined the Baptists at age twenty. He attended Columbian College in Washington, D.C., but left for home after the 1825–26 session to study the law. Persuaded to become a missionary instead, Howell was ordained in January 1827. At the same time he became pastor of the Cumberland Street Baptist Church of Norfolk, Va. In April 1829 he married Mary Ann Morton Toy; of their ten children, eight grew to maturity.

In 1834 Howell visited Nashville, Tenn., where he accepted appointment by the American Baptist Home Mission Society as a missionary and pastor of the First Baptist Church. His work, which began on 1 Jan. 1835, coincided with the controversy between Baptists and the followers of Alexander Campbell. Most of the members of the church he was to serve, as well as the former pastor, had gone over to Campbellism, claiming the church building as well. Howell led the successful effort to erect a new building. Within a short time, Howell had become the recognized leader of Baptists in Tennessee. He began a newspaper, *The Baptist*, which he edited for thirteen years; promoted Sunday schools and missionary societies; and organized societies for education and ministerial improvement, as well as for Bible publication and distribution. In addition, he was instrumental in establishing a school called Union University (not the present one) and in the formation of the Baptist General Association (Convention) of Tennessee and Alabama in 1842.

In 1850 Howell moved to Richmond, Va., to become pastor of the Second Baptist Church. After remaining there seven years, he returned to his Nashville pastorate. During his absence, Landmarkism had emerged. This extreme right-wing party, which would have a devastating impact on Baptists in the Southwest, was led by James Robinson Graves, a member of Howell's church, and Nashville was its hub. Howell perceived the danger of the new movement, not only to the local congregation, but also to all institutions of the Southern Baptist Convention. He openly opposed Graves and fought his teachings all the way to a historic session of the Southern Baptist Convention at Richmond, where the convention voted to reject Landmarkism.

Howell was much respected by Baptists throughout the South, serving two four-year terms as the second president of the Southern Baptist Convention. He was reelected at the Richmond convention in 1859, but immediately resigned. His confrontation with Graves broke the power of Landmarkism, but its effects were evident for a hundred years.

When the Union Army captured Nashville in February 1862, Howell's church was seized for military purposes and he and three or four other ministers were imprisoned. Howell was confined for only two months, but his health was impaired. He died several years later in Nashville and was buried in that city's Mount Olivet Cemetery.

Howell was the author of *Terms of Communion at the Lord's Table* (1846), *The Deaconship* (1846), *The Evils of Infant Baptism* (1851), *The Covenants* (1856), *The Early Baptists of Virginia* (1856), *A Memorial of the First Baptist Church, Nashville, Tenn., from 1820 to 1863*, and eighty bound volumes of sermons in manuscript.

SEE: P. E. Burroughs, *The Spiritual Conquest of the Second Frontier* (1942); *Encyclopedia of Southern Baptists* (1958); R. B. C. Howell, *A Memorial of the First Baptist Church, Nashville, Tennessee, from 1820 to 1863*.

LOULIE LATIMER OWENS

Hubbard, Fordyce Mitchell (13 Jan. 1809–1 Sept. 1888), Episcopal clergyman and educator, was born in Cummington, Mass., the son of Roswell and Sarah Mitchell Hubbard. In 1829 he was graduated from Williams College, in Massachusetts, where he remained for several years as a tutor. He studied law and for a time was associated with the Round Hill School in Northampton. Later he taught Latin at a classical school in Boston and in 1836 published an edition of *Poems of Catullus* for the use of the school. While residing in Boston he married Martha Henshaw Bates, the daughter of a U.S. senator from Massachusetts.

In November 1842, having been ordained an Episcopal priest, Hubbard became rector of Christ Church in New Bern, N.C. He remained there until 1847, when he was appointed principal of Trinity School near Raleigh. A year later he was elected to the chair of Latin Languages and Literature at The University of North Carolina, a position he held through 1868. While in Chapel Hill, he served as rector of the Chapel of the Cross in 1852 and again in 1868.

In 1848 his life of William R. Davie was published as a volume in Jared Sparks's *Library of American Biography*. Hubbard also revised the *North Carolina Reader* by Calvin H. Wiley; his editions of Reader No. I appeared in 1855 and 1856 and of No. II in 1856, 1857, 1858, 1859, and 1873. In addition, Hubbard contributed to the *University of North Carolina Magazine*, the *North Carolina Journal of Education*, the *Southern Literary Messenger*, and the *North American Review*. In 1860 he received an honorary D.D. degree from Columbia College in New York and Trinity College in Connecticut.

Hubbard left The University of North Carolina in 1869 to become principal of St. John's School in Manlius, N.Y., and to serve as rector of Christ Church there. He retired to Raleigh in 1881, but remained active in the Episcopal Diocese of North Carolina until his death. His wife and his only child, a daughter, both predeceased him in 1870.

SEE: Fordyce Hubbard Argo, "An Ante-Bellum Professor" (1946; a typescript in the North Carolina Collection, University of North Carolina Library, Chapel Hill); *Journal of the Convention of the Diocese of North Carolina* (1842–88); *North Carolina University Magazine*, vol. 9 (October 1859); Raleigh *News and Observer*, 4 Sept. 1888.

BONNIE L. WILSON

Hubbard, Jeremiah (13 Feb. 1777–23 Nov. 1849), educator and Quaker leader, was born in Mecklenburg County, Va., the son of Joseph and Ann Crews Hubbard. He was the grandson of Hardiman Crews and his Indian wife, whose name has not been found. On several occasions tradition has depicted her as a Cherokee, but according to one reference she was a "daughter of the 'Dochees' "—"Dochee" (or related spellings) is said to be the name of an ancient or mythical Indian tribe of the Virginia backcountry. She could have been from one of the small tribes of the Sioux family that inhabited the south central section of Virginia. In adulthood Jeremiah exhibited several characteristics that prompted his classification as Indian, and he and his four brothers were often referred to as "the big Cherokee boys." Hubbard "was tall, erect and straight as an arrow, being six feet two or three inches in height"; "he had a dark swarthy complexion, keen black eyes, high cheek bones, hair straight and black as coal, a large mouth and firm lips." With these features, he must have made an impressive picture as he presided over the large annual gathering of North Carolina Quakers in their spacious meeting house at New Garden. And he must have inspired the respect and awe of his pupils as he directed their intellectual training in the schoolrooms in Orange and Guilford counties and in Indiana.

Soon after the Revolutionary War, Joseph Hubbard moved his family to Person County. It seems likely that he settled on the upper waters of Richland Creek, just south of the present town of Roxboro. Little is known of Jeremiah or his family during his childhood. Late in life he paid high tribute to his half-breed Indian mother for the care, discipline, and guidance she gave him. No reference has been found to his ever having attended school, although at the height of his career he was referred to as one of the most eminent teachers and most learned persons among the North Carolina Quakers.

In 1802 Hubbard married Margaret Butler in Dinwiddie County, Va. Between the time of their marriage and 1810 they moved from Person County to Hillsborough in Orange County, and in 1815 they moved to the Deep River community near Jamestown. On 15 May 1820, Margaret Hubbard died, leaving Jeremiah with eight children ranging from four to seventeen years. On 9 Oct. 1821, he married Martha Charles of Charles City County, Va.

Hubbard is remembered primarily as a leader in education, despite the fact that he had little if any formal training. He is known to have taught in two schools in Guilford County, and it is assumed that he taught while living in Person and Orange counties. While residing in the Deep River community, he became generally recognized as an outstanding leader of the Quakers in North Carolina. As presiding clerk of the North Carolina Yearly Meeting of Friends for sixteen years, he vigorously campaigned for the establishment of a Quaker-supported boarding school to train teachers, other Quaker leaders, and members of the general public. In this effort he was joined by Nathan Hunt, who became known as the principal founder of the New Garden Boarding School (later Guilford College). Although the work of these two leaders was made more difficult by the economic depression of 1837, the response to their strong and extended appeal was sufficient to enable the Society of Friends to acquire a suitable tract of land, erect an adequate building, and launch the school upon its long history.

In February 1837, only a few months before the opening of the long-awaited New Garden Boarding School, Hubbard and his family succumbed to "Western fever" and migrated to Indiana. Jeremiah was well equipped for leadership in the rapidly developing society of that section of the country. There he continued his dual roles as outstanding teacher and minister of the Society of Friends. He was an excellent speaker, well informed, and energetic.

It is not known whether Hubbard ever sought political office, but he did take a firm stand on the burning issues of his time. He opposed slavery and joined the

Manumission Society to work for gradual emancipation. In view of his Indian blood, he would have been expected to support efforts to protect the lives and rights of the exploited Indians. When Chief Ross and a few others from the Cherokee Nation went to Washington, D.C., to appeal to President Andrew Jackson, they stopped at New Garden to ask Hubbard to go with them. They were aware of his Indian ancestry and knew that he was a friend of the president. One Sunday morning after worship, the Cherokees conferred with some of the prominent Quakers present in front of the New Garden Meeting House. As a result of this conference, Hubbard agreed to accompany them to Washington. There followed an unparalleled scene—the presiding clerk of the North Carolina Yearly Meeting of Friends riding out with a band of Indians, with whom he was united in blood, personal appearance, and sympathy, to seek assistance from the president of the United States. It is said that they obtained Jackson's support for a treaty that would prevent the sale of alcoholic beverages to the Cherokees.

Hubbard died in Richmond, Ind.

SEE: Deeds of Orange County (Register of Deeds, Hillsborough); Willard Heiss, ed., *Encyclopedia of Quaker Genealogy*, vol. 7 (1962); William Wade Hinshaw, *Encyclopedia of Quaker Genealogy*, vols. 1 (1969), 6 (1947); "Memorial of Whitewater Monthly Meeting of Friends to Jeremiah Hubbard," *Friends Review* 7 (12 Dec. 1853); Minutes of Whitewater Monthly Meeting of Friends (Indiana), Abstracts of the Records of the Society of Friends in Indiana, Part One (1962, Indiana Historical Society, Indianapolis). Manuscript sources in Quaker Collection, Library of Guilford College: Charles F. Coffin, "Personal Recollections of Jeremiah Hubbard"; "Genealogy of the Hubbard Family with a Brief History of the Connection with the Cherokee Indians"; Minutes of Deep River Monthly Meeting of Friends; Minutes of Spring Monthly Meeting of Friends.

ALGIE I. NEWLIN

Hubbs, Orlando (14 Feb. 1840–5 Dec. 1930), sheriff of Craven County and congressman, was born on a farm in Commack, N.Y., the son of Platt Ralph and Deborah Reeve Hubbs. His family had lived on Long Island for four generations, and he was the great-grandson of a Revolutionary War veteran. Hubbs attended local public schools and Commack Academy. At age sixteen he left school to learn the trade of carriage and wagon building; later he worked as a ship carpenter in Brooklyn.

In 1865, Hubbs moved with his wife to New Bern. According to family tradition, he came to North Carolina at the request of his brother Ethelbert, a Union veteran who had just settled in the state. Active in a mercantile business, Hubbs became involved in local politics, winning election to the first of five terms as sheriff of Craven County in 1870. No doubt his political base in Craven was strengthened by the activities of his brother, who was for a time editor of the *New Bern Daily Times* and held the important patronage post of New Bern postmaster from 1874 to 1882. By 1880 Orlando was chairman of the Republican executive committee for the second congressional district and a member of the party's state executive committee.

Hubbs was nominated for Congress in 1880 at a Republican convention marred by disorder and factionalism. Some Republicans refused to accept the result of the convention, and for several months there was considerable strife in the party as former Congressman

Curtis H. Brogden campaigned as an anti-Hubbs candidate. The open division among Republicans ended after a Democratic candidate, William H. Kitchin, entered the race. Brogden withdrew, and Hubbs was easily elected in a district that was normally Republican. One of four "carpetbaggers" in the Forty-seventh Congress, Hubbs worked quietly to advance local interests and win patronage for political friends.

He sought reelection in 1882 but was frustrated by disarray within his party. The district convention broke up in confusion, with Hubbs and black attorney James E. O'Hara each claiming to be the true nominee. After weeks of bitter feuding with O'Hara, Hubbs dropped out of the race shortly before election day, noting that a continuing schism would only hurt the Republican party in other races. Later Hubbs unsuccessfully sought appointment as a U.S. marshal. In the 1884 election he held the purely honorary position of presidential elector for the losing Blaine-Logan ticket.

In 1886 and 1888, Hubbs ran for register of deeds in Craven County on a coalition ticket supported by one wing of the local Republican party and by Craven's perennially weak Democratic party. Each time he lost. After serious business reverses, he returned to his native New York in 1890 where he engaged in farming. Beginning in 1903, he served six consecutive terms in the New York Assembly and won a state senate seat in 1908.

Hubbs was married twice, first to Amelia H. Wheeler, and then, upon her death, to her sister Bertha C. Wheeler. Only one of his three children lived to maturity. Hubbs was a teetotaler and an active member of the Methodist church. He died at age ninety and was buried in his hometown of Commack, N.Y.

SEE: E. D. Anderson, "Race and Politics in North Carolina, 1872–1901: The 'Black Second' Congressional District" (Ph.D. diss., University of Chicago, 1978); *Biog. Dir. Am. Cong.* (1961); P. C. Headley, *Public Men of To-Day* (1882); William S. Pelletreau, *A History of Long Island*, vol. 3 (1903); Patricia H. Stewart, "Orlando Hubbs and the Corruption Charges of 1908" (paper, Molloy College, 1974); *Who's Who in New York City and State* (1911).

ERIC D. ANDERSON

Hudson, Arthur Palmer (14 May 1892–26 Apr. 1978), folklorist and teacher, was born in the Hesterville community of Attala County, Miss., the son of William Arthur and Lou Garnett Palmer Hudson. Despite the handicap of growing up on a farm in difficult times, Hudson qualified for study at the University of Mississippi where he received the B.S. degree in 1913. For the next seven years he served in secondary schools in the state, first as principal of the Gulfport High School from 1913 to 1918, then for one year as a teacher of English at the Gulf Coast Military Academy and for another year as superintendent of schools in Oxford.

In 1920 Hudson returned to the University of Mississippi for an M.A. degree and began to teach in its English department. While continuing his studies (he was awarded a second M.A. degree by the University of Chicago in 1925 and a Ph.D. with the Smith Prize for Graduate Research by The University of North Carolina in 1930), he rose to the rank of professor and head-elect of the department. In 1930 he accepted an appointment as associate professor of English at The University of North Carolina, where he taught for the rest of his academic career. Hudson was promoted to professor in

1935, received a Kenan professorship in 1951, and retired as Kenan Professor Emeritus in 1963. He taught principally the literature of the English Romantic period and folklore, his chief interest. From 1950 to 1963 he was executive secretary of the university's Curriculum in Folklore.

Hudson's enthusiasm for folklore had first been aroused at the University of Mississippi by E. C. Perrow. Later he studied under Louise Pound and Archer Taylor at the University of Chicago; his doctoral dissertation at The University of North Carolina was on Mississippi folk songs. His major publications included *Specimens of Mississippi Folklore* (1928); *Folksongs of Mississippi and Their Background* (1936); *Humor of the Old Deep South*, with George Herzog (1936); *Folk Tunes from Mississippi*, with H. M. Belden (1937); two volumes of *The Frank C. Brown Collection of North Carolina Folklore*, with John T. Flanagan (1952); and *Folklore in American Literature* (1958). He also published several monographs and many articles on folklore. From 1954 to 1964 Hudson edited *North Carolina Folklore*, the journal of the North Carolina Folklore Society, which he served as secretary-treasurer from 1943 to 1964. His manuscripts and sound recordings, donated to The University of North Carolina at the time of his retirement, form the nucleus of its Southern Folklore Collection.

In 1916 Hudson married Grace Noah of Kosciusko, Miss., and the couple had three children: William Palmer, Margaret Louise, and Ellen Noah. Both daughters survived him.

SEE: A. C. Howell, *The Kenan Professorships* (1956); Arthur Palmer Hudson, "Account of the Giver," Arthur Palmer Hudson Papers (Southern Historical Collection, University of North Carolina Library, Chapel Hill); Arthur Palmer Hudson, "An Attala Boyhood," *Journal of Mississippi History* 4 (1942); Daniel Patterson, "Folklore Studies in Honor of Arthur Palmer Hudson, *North Carolina Folklore* 13 (1965 [portrait]).

DANIEL W. PATTERSON

Huffman, Robert Obediah (15 May 1890–2 Feb. 1978), industrialist and businessman, was born in Morganton, the son of Samuel and Martha Ann Hildebrand Huffman. His father, a Morganton businessman, was one of five founders and the first president of the Drexel Furniture Company of Drexel. Young Huffman attended the Morganton city schools and The University of North Carolina, where he received the A.B. degree in 1913 and an honorary LL.D. degree in 1954.

Although Huffman held positions in many different businesses and industries, he was most active in hosiery and furniture manufacturing. He was treasurer (1927–44) and president (1944–58) of the Morganton Full Fashioned Hosiery Company; president (1935–56) and chairman of the board (1956–59) of Drexel Knitting Mills; and president (1935–58) of Huffman Full Fashioned Mills, Morganton. In 1935, when the death of his brother, Frank O. Huffman, left the office vacant, he became president of the Drexel Furniture Company; that year the company had sales of $1,336,119. To illustrate the impact of his career on the community, in 1968 at the time of Huffman's retirement as chairman of the board of Drexel Enterprises, which included the Drexel Furniture Company, the corporation had reached annual sales of $78,400,000 and employed 6,300 persons. Drexel Enterprises, a holding company, had been organized in December 1961, with Huffman as president and chairman of the board. Earlier, in 1957, Drexel Furniture had acquired Morganton Furniture Company and Heritage Furniture Company of High Point through stock exchanges. These two companies became known as the Heritage-Morganton division of Drexel Enterprises. In 1962, through a merger, the Southern Desk Company of Hickory also became a division of Drexel Enterprises.

In the fields of banking and insurance, Huffman served one or more terms as director of the First National Bank, Morganton; Charlotte Branch, Wachovia Bank and Trust Company; Jefferson Standard Life Insurance Company, Greensboro; North Carolina Board, Liberty Mutual Insurance Company, Charlotte; and Federal Reserve Bank, Richmond, Va. Additional positions included president of the Burke Farmers Cooperative Dairy (1940–61) and of the Business Foundation at The University of North Carolina (1950–51). For many years he was a director of Grace Hospital in Morganton.

Among his professional associations he was president of the Southern Hosiery Manufacturers' Association (1933–34), vice-president of the National Association of Hosiery Manufacturers (1939); and a director of the American Thread Company, the National Association of Manufacturers, and the Southern Furniture Manufacturers' Association.

During World War II and the postwar period, Huffman served the U.S. government in various positions. He was chief of the men's hosiery unit, textile division, War Production Board (1943); a consultant on hosiery, chief of the hosiery and underwear section, and price executive of the manufactured articles branch, Office of Price Administration (1944); and assistant director of the consumer soft goods division, Office of Price Stabilization (1951).

Huffman was long active in the civic and religious life of his community, including sometime mayor of Morganton and chairman of the Morganton School Board. He was a member of the board of trustees of Mars Hill College and of the Development Council and Board of Visitors of Wake Forest University; on both campuses a building was named for him. He also served on the board of trustees of South Mountain Institute, a child-caring institution at Nebo. For fifteen years he was chairman of the Board of Deacons of the First Baptist Church, Morganton, where for thirty years he taught a men's Bible class.

In 1956 the Rotary Club, with Senator Sam J. Ervin, Jr., as speaker, presented to Huffman the Morganton Man of the Year Award. During a dinner held in Charlotte in 1963, the Newcomen Society in North America honored Huffman and Drexel Enterprises for the leadership they had given the southern furniture industry in the previous quarter century. Huffman was said to have taught the South how to style and market furniture. He explained at the dinner that the most significant element in the philosophy behind Drexel's success was "that every person who works for the company is important . . . that employees may vary in ability and responsibility, but Drexel considers each an individual, himself, and important in the operation."

Huffman was a member of Phi Beta Kappa, Beta Gamma Sigma, and the Golden Fleece. He was a 32nd degree Mason. Other memberships included Kiwanis, New York Athletic Club, Merchants and Manufacturers Club (Chicago), Biltmore Forest Country Club (Asheville), Mimosa Hills Golf Club (Morganton), and Linville Golf Club (Linville). In addition to golf, his hobbies were raising Guernsey cattle and fishing. He was a Baptist and a Republican.

On 4 Nov. 1915, Huffman married Pearl Trogdon of Winston-Salem. They had three daughters, all of whom survived their father: Pearl Trogdon (Mrs. Roy O. Scholz of Baltimore, Md.), Anne Lancaster (Mrs. Jeter C. Pritchard of Morganton), and Martha Roberta (Mrs. Robert Scott Langley of Kinston). Huffman was buried in Forest Hill Cemetery, Morganton.

SEE: *Asheville Times*, 23 July 1963; *Burke County News and Morganton Herald*, 29 Mar. 1956; Drexel Enterprises, Inc., News Release, 7 Mar. 1968; *Home Furnishings Daily*, 13 Nov. 1963; Morganton *News Herald*, 2 Feb. 1978; William S. Powell, ed., *North Carolina Lives* (1962); *Reflections: A History of Drexel Enterprises, Inc., 1903–1963*, with a foreword by R. O. Huffman (n.d.); *Who's Who in America* (1952–53, 1966–67).

HENRY S. STROUPE

Hufham, James Dunn (*26 May 1834–27 Mar. 1921*), Baptist clergyman, editor, and historian, was born near Faison, Duplin County, the second of nine children of the Reverend George Washington and Frances Dunn Hufham. His great-grandfather, Solomon Hufham, an Englishman, settled near the juncture of the Duplin-Bladen-New Hanover county line before 1751. His maternal ancestors went to Virginia soon after the founding of Jamestown, moving later to Maryland. The family arrived in Duplin County in the late eighteenth century.

Hufham studied at Green Academy, near Faison, and was prepared for college by Dr. James Sprunt of Kenansville. He was graduated from Wake Forest College with the B.A. (1856) and M.A. (1860) degrees; in 1878 the college awarded him the D.D. degree.

After graduation, Hufham returned to Duplin County where he taught for a year at Warsaw High School (1858), served as pastor of the Bear Marsh Baptist Church (1857–61), and engaged in itinerant pastoral and missionary work within the bounds of the sprawling Eastern Baptist Association, whose churches were located from Wayne to Carteret to New Hanover counties. He also served for brief periods as pastor, or pastoral supply, for the Baptist congregations at Chinquapin, Clinton, and Kenansville.

In April 1861, Hufham retired temporarily from the pastoral ministry to become editor and sole proprietor of the *Biblical Recorder*, the weekly Baptist journal published in Raleigh. He continued as editor until 1867, and later served as associate editor from 1874 to 1877. Returning to the pastorate in 1868, he subsequently served Baptist churches in Sawyers Creek, Camden County (1868–70); Second Church (now Tabernacle), Raleigh (1874–78); Scotland Neck (1878–91); Tarboro (1891–94); First Church, Shelby (1894–96); and First Church, Henderson (1896–1903). While in Scotland Neck and Tarboro, he was also engaged in pastoral and missionary work throughout Halifax, Edgecombe, Martin, Pitt, Washington, and Beaufort counties. In 1903, he was forced to retire from regular pastoral services due to an injury sustained from a fall.

The *Biblical Recorder* of 24 Apr. 1861—the first edition to appear after Hufham's purchase of the journal—stated his editorial policy succinctly: "I claim for myself perfect liberty to say what I believe and to act as I think best.—I have already received much excellent advice, and I have no doubt but that it will be freely given in the future; but brethren must not complain if even after they express their opinions, I think for *myself*, praise what appears to be commendable, and condemn what is blameworthy." That same liberty was extended to his correspondents. Hufham became widely read and favorably known during this trying period in the state's history. His editorials during the Civil War displayed an ardent patriotism and a profound sympathy for the Confederate cause. Near the end of the war his press was wrecked by Union soldiers, said to have been incensed by the tone of an editorial that he had prepared for publication.

The affairs of the Baptists in North Carolina had no more loyal supporter and advocate than James Dunn Hufham. Apart from championing the work of the denomination and the churches through the pages of the *Biblical Recorder* and in his own ministry, he served the Baptist State Convention as recording secretary (1862–67, 1875–78) and as corresponding secretary (1871–74). He was financial agent for Wake Forest College (1877–78) and a longtime member of its board of trustees (1866–1921). In addition, Hufham was a member of the Convention's Board of Missions—predecessor of the current General Board—from 1874 to 1909. Much credit is due him for encouraging North Carolina Baptists to support the Thomasville Orphanage (now Mills Home of the North Carolina Baptist Children's Home, Inc.) and in the establishment of the Baptist Female University (now Meredith College) in Raleigh.

Hufham's interest in the history of his denomination, in general, and of North Carolina Baptists, in particular, was first evidenced in a lengthy "report" he submitted in 1860 as a member of the History Committee of the Eastern Baptist Association. In 1885 he was instrumental in the organization of the North Carolina Baptist Historical Society, serving as vice-president and historian. He expanded upon his earlier interest in a series of eleven lengthy articles on "The Baptists in North Carolina" that appeared in *North Carolina Baptist Historical Papers* from April 1897 to July 1899. This quarterly—published under the auspices of the North Carolina Baptist Historical Society—was edited by Hufham. The only book he wrote was his *Memoir of John Lamb Prichard, Late Pastor of First Baptist Church, Wilmington, NC*, published in 1867.

On 23 July 1863 Hufham married Mary Anna Faison of Sampson County. They had six children: George, James Dunn, Annie Hinton (m. James R. Singleton), James Needham, Thomas McDowell, and Mary Faison. Hufham was interred beside the remains of his wife and firstborn son in the cemetery adjacent to Trinity Church, Scotland Neck.

SEE: Annual *Proceedings of the Baptist State Convention of North Carolina* (1862); Samuel A. Ashe, ed., *Biographical History of North Carolina*, vol. 3 (1905); *Biblical Recorder*, 2 Jan. 1935 (portrait); George Washington Paschal, *History of Wake Forest College*, vol. 2 (1943); Thomas Jerome Taylor, *A History of the Tar River Baptist Association, 1830–1921* (n.d.).

R. HARGUS TAYLOR

Huggins, James Dwyre, Sr. (24 Aug. 1874–19 Apr. 1932), teacher and educational administrator, was born near Camden, S.C., the son of Theodore Norwood and Martha Joy Huggins. While growing up on a farm, he injured one of his legs in his middle teens and for nearly a year was bedridden. For four years thereafter Huggins was an invalid, but when able to get about on crutches he returned to school until he obtained a teaching position near Lynchburg, S.C. Later, for a year, he attended Welch Neck High School (now Coker College) at Hartsville, S.C., before entering Catawba College, then located at Newton, N.C. When his old injury began to trouble him again, he went home for treatment and stayed to teach for one session near Clyde, S.C. Afterwards, he returned to Catawba where he received the bachelor's degree in 1903. From 1903 to 1905 he was principal of the Bethany, S.C., High School. Two years later he accepted a post in Boiling Springs, N.C., where he remained for the next quarter century.

At a meeting on 10 July 1905 held in the First Baptist Church of Shelby, the board of trustees appointed by the Kings Mountain Baptist Association to select the site for a new denominational high school chose Boiling Springs. Not long after the ground-breaking ceremony early in the spring of 1907, Professor Huggins—as he came to be called—was hired as field agent until the school opened. However, at a meeting of the Boiling Springs High School board of trustees on 25 July 1907, he was elected principal and was authorized to select a faculty. Although the school building was not ready, classes began in October with 135 students, 4 teachers, and the principal. In the early summer of 1909, the board of trustees made Huggins and F. A. Brown, who taught mathematics and science, joint principals for a two-year term. By then enrollment had increased to 219. Yet, the board did not feel it could assume financial responsibility for the teaching staff. The principals agreed to do so, and to employ the teachers with the board's approval. This arrangement was short-lived, for in the summer of 1910 the two men resigned and the board appointed the Reverend J. M. Hamrick principal for the 1910–11 school year. Huggins consented to serve as assistant principal.

In the summer of 1914 Huggins again was elected principal of Boiling Springs High School. One year later, after becoming critically ill from a resurgence of his youthful injury, he was hospitalized and his right leg was amputated above the knee. That summer he could not do his usual public relations work and student recruitment, but by the fall he was back at his desk. Under Huggins's guidance, the institution remained strong during World War I. By the 1920s, however, it was obvious that the school could not compete with the tax-supported state high school system, then rapidly spreading into all areas of North Carolina. On 2 May 1928 Boiling Springs High School closed its doors after twenty-one years of operation; in the fall, it opened as a junior college.

On 3 Sept. 1928, Boiling Springs Junior College (now Gardener-Webb College) began its first session, with the Reverend James Blaine Davis as president and Huggins as dean. But in June 1929 Huggins resigned. A year before, he had understood from Dr. James E. Hillman of the North Carolina Department of Public Instruction that it would be acceptable if only three of the five department heads held M.A. degrees provided the other two were working toward graduate degrees. A year later, however, President Davis was informed by the State Department that Huggins should not head a department without an advanced degree. Six weeks before, Davis had sent Huggins a letter, dated 26 Apr. 1929, stating that the trustees had elected him dean and head of the mathematics department at a yearly salary of $2,200. On 13 June Huggins wrote the board, requesting that he be released from the position. As he explained in another letter, he felt that in order to remain at the college, he would have to continue graduate study—even at the sacrifice of his health.

On 5 May 1930 Huggins was again elected dean, as well as principal of the high school division of the college. He died two years later. After his death, the trustees declared that to Huggins, "more than to any other man or group of men" who had been attached to the institution, Boiling Springs High School and Junior College was indebted for its "material, intellectual, and spiritual achievement." *The Kalarathea*, the college newspaper, observed that "it is impossible for anyone to understand or even imagine all that must be meant when we say 'Professor Huggins and Boiling Springs High School and College.' When we speak of this school, we invariably think of it as a group or institution with Professor Huggins as father."

Huggins married Bessie Atkins on 27 Dec. 1906, and they had three children: James Dwyre, Jr., Evelyn Louise Prince, and Rachel Barron Hedrick. When Huggins died, there was talk of burying him on the campus in front of the building that bore his name. But wisdom prevailed over sentiment, and he was interred in the Boiling Springs Cemetery.

SEE: Francis B. Dedmond, *Lengthened Shadows: A History of Gardner-Webb College, 1907–1957, passim* (1957).

FRANCIS B. DEDMOND

Huggins, Maloy Alton (5 Oct. 1890–11 Apr. 1971), educator and religious administrator, was born in Marion County, S.C., the son of A. R. F. and Alice Lundy Huggins. He attended the common schools of his home county and, from 1905 to 1908, Stinceon Institute in Orrum, N.C. Through a loan from R. C. Lawrence, Huggins was able to enter Wake Forest College in the fall of 1908; he received the B.A. degree in 1912. He was awarded M.A. degrees by Wake Forest in 1916 and by The University of North Carolina in 1929. During the summers of 1916, 1922, and 1923, he studied at Columbia University. From Wake Forest he also received the honorary doctor of laws degree in 1949.

On 13 July 1918 Huggins married Katherine Elizabeth (Katiebet) Morris, the daughter of Mr. and Mrs. E. W. Morris; they had two daughters, Minnie Morris and Katherine Elizabeth (Mrs. Paul V. Beam). Shortly after his marriage he left for France to serve in the 324th Machine Gun Company, 81st Division, for the remainder of World War I. He was one of twelve men chosen from his division to attend the Sorbonne in Paris for five months.

Before his military service, Huggins had been the principal of the Washington, N.C., High School (1912–13); a teacher of Latin and Greek at Union University, Jackson, Tenn. (1913–15); superintendent of schools at Clayton (1915–17); and a teacher in the Durham High School (1917–18). After returning from France, he was the superintendent of schools in Scotland Neck from 1919 to 1924. In the latter year, Huggins was named secretary of Christian Education for the Baptist State Convention of North Carolina, a position he held until 1929 when he became professor of education at Meredith College, Raleigh. In the fall of 1932, he was elected executive secretary-treasurer of the Convention—the first layman to hold this post since 1885.

Huggins was called to serve North Carolina Baptists at the peak of the depression. Disastrous fires at Wake Forest College and the lack of chapel facilities there were just a few of his burdens. The Convention had also assumed a large debt against Meredith College. Huggins carried his appeal from the mountains to the sea on behalf of Baptist educational institutions in the state. He proved to be an excellent financier, as well as a great harmonizer—he had a gift for bringing order out of chaos and did not permit divergent views to divide the members of his denomination. In 1932, mission gifts had dwindled to $199,330; total receipts, including those from the Cooperative Program, amounted to only $480,484. Upon his retirement in the fall of 1958, receipts from the Cooperative Program and mission gifts from the churches totaled $5,912,101, the number of churches had increased from 2,374 to 3,307, and membership had risen 101 percent—from 433,036 to 831,272. There were notable gains in Sunday school enrollment, Training Union and Womans Missionary Union memberships, and Baptist activities as a whole throughout the state.

Other significant accomplishments during Huggins's tenure included the addition of a new wing to the Baptist Hospital and the establishment of the North Carolina Baptist Homes for the Aging. The Baptist State Convention founded Fruitland Baptist Institute and created summer assemblies at Fruitland and Caswell. It also accepted the offer from the Z. Smith Reynolds Foundation to move Wake Forest College to Winston-Salem. Although these achievements might have occurred under other leadership, Huggins's interest and projection of new programs during his twenty-seven-year tenure were instrumental in their success. "Mr. Baptist," as he was known, served longer than any of the twenty-four men who had preceded him since the founding of the Baptist State Convention in 1830.

Huggins was the author of several books and pamphlets—among them, *North Carolina for Christ; Baptists Working Together; Fellowship in World Service; Our Worship and Witness; Baptists Encircling the World through Their Churches; High School Libraries;* and *Baptists Working towards a World Program.* His most important work, *A History of North Carolina Baptists, 1727–1932,* was written during his retirement and published in 1967.

In politics, Huggins was an independent Democrat. He was a deacon and worshipped at the First Baptist Church, Raleigh. He was also a member of the Raleigh History Club. He died on Easter Sunday at Wake Memorial Hospital, Raleigh. The funeral service was conducted by the Reverends John M. Lewis, John E. Lawrence, and W. Perry Crouch at the First Baptist Church, Raleigh; he was buried in the city's Montlawn Memorial Park.

SEE: Baptist State Convention of North Carolina, *Annual* (1971 [photograph]); Maloy Alton Huggins Papers (North Carolina Baptist Historical Collection, Wake Forest University, Winston-Salem); R. C. Lawrence, "Maloy A. Huggins, General Secretary," *Biblical Recorder,* 16 Dec. 1942; William S. Powell, ed., *North Carolina Lives* (1962); John S. Raymond, comp., *Among Southern Baptists,* vol. 1 (1936–37).

JOHN R. WOODARD

Hughes, (Harvey) Hatcher (12 Feb. 1881–18 Oct. 1945), playwright and teacher, was born in Polkville, Cleveland County, the tenth of eleven children of Andrew Jackson and Martha Polk Gold Hughes. He was the brother of Cicero (1865–1939), Cora (Mrs. Robert H. Hardin) (1868–1930), Mollie (Mrs. Greeley Neal) (1868–1951), Sallie (Mrs. Simpson Love) (1870–1940), Dan (1871–1900), John (1873–1937), Charlie (1875–1946), Gordon (1877–1950), George (1878–1906), and Fannie (Mrs. Ed Atkins) (1884–1966).

Hughes attended local schools and during vacations visited his mountain kinfolk, unconsciously absorbing their highland dialect. After high school in Grover, he worked off and on to earn money for college expenses, including writing for the newspapers. In 1901 he entered The University of North Carolina, then took a job in Yorkville, S.C., for two years between his sophomore and junior years. By the time Hughes received the A.B. degree in 1907, he had become prominent in the university literary clubs, was a major contributor to the campus publications, was editor of the annual, and had been elected to Golden Fleece, the student leadership society. While a senior he was an instructor in English, continuing in the post until he was awarded the M.A. degree in 1909. His interest in theater was stimulated by courses in modern drama under Professor James F. Royster. He went to Columbia University to pursue a doctorate, but abandoned his plans upon being appointed lecturer in English at Columbia, where he instituted a course in practical playwriting and organized the Morningside Players. During World War I, Hughes was a captain in the army—much of the time as a member of the American Expeditionary Force in France.

Back at Columbia, his classes were enthusiastically attended by New York theater people as well as students. Often he was called to Broadway as a "play doctor." Hughes was active in theater affairs, at one time serving as chairman of the National Council on Freedom from Censorship. His first play, *A Marriage Made in Heaven*, was written about 1918 but not produced until ten years later. *Wake Up, Jonathan* (1921), a collaboration with Elmer Rice, became a successful vehicle for the famous actress Minnie Maddern Fiske. Hughes was awarded the Pulitzer Prize in 1924 for *Hell-Bent fer Heaven* when the Pulitzer Committee at Columbia reversed the jury's selection of George Kelly's *The Show-Off*. The prize play was based on fresh observations he had made during a visit to the North Carolina mountains in 1921. The melodramatic account of a fanatic mountain preacher, it came at a time when the new realism was permeating the American theater. *Ruint* (1925), his second "folk play," is a comedy in which the North Carolina mountain people take revenge on a northern visitor believed to have "ruint" a local girl. Everything is straightened out when it is revealed that he had only kissed her. These two plays were more successful than three satiric comedies that followed: *Honeymooning on High: A Silly Play for Silly People* (Boston, 1927); *It's a Grand Life* (1930), a collaboration with Alan Williams; and *The Lord Blesses the Bishop* (1934).

In 1930 Hughes married the American actress Janet Cool Ranney, and they had a daughter, Mrs. Ann Ranney Moss, of Missoula, Mont., born in 1935. Hughes loved animals and the country life; on his farm at West Cornwall, Conn., he said he had rather be a farmer than a college professor. He died at his home in New York after becoming ill while attending the rehearsal of a play at Columbia.

SEE: Ruby Hughes Baker, personal contact, 1974 (Kings Mountain); Grace Leake, *Holland's* magazine, February 1937; New York *Herald*, 20 Oct. 1945; *North Carolina Authors* (1952); *Who Was Who in America* (1950); *Yackety-Yack* (1907).

RICHARD WALSER

Hughes, Mary Elizabeth (*8 Nov. 1841–28 Apr. 1888*), pioneer woman physician, was born in Ebensburg, Pa., the second daughter of Ezekiel and Harriet Russell Hughes. Her father was a native of Wales, an engineer, and an active member of the Presbyterian church. Details of her childhood and early education appear unknown, but she attended the Cleveland Homeopathic College in Cleveland, Ohio, and her diploma conferred the degree of doctor of medicine on 15 Feb. 1871. Relatives report that she did postgraduate work and completed an internship in New York City before moving to Tryon, N.C., to establish a practice about 1872. There she specialized in the illnesses and diseases of women and children as well as engaging in general practice. In 1879 she was also listed among the graduates of the Chicago Homeopathic Medical College.

Shortly before her death, apparently from tuberculosis, Dr. Hughes went to the Hughes home in Iowa City, Iowa, where her parents had moved in 1867; her father had died in 1882 but her mother still lived there. She died in Iowa City at age forty-six and was buried in the city's Oakland Cemetery following a funeral that was private at her own request.

SEE: *History of the Cleveland Homeopathic College from 1860 to 1880* (n.d.); Hughes family papers (in possession of Miss Helen Hughes, Iowa City, Iowa); Information from Mr. Dale M. Bentz (Librarian, University of Iowa); Martin Kaufman, *Homeopathy in America* (1971); William Harvey King, *History of Homeopathy*, vols. 2, 3 (1905); Records of Oakland Cemetery (Iowa City, Iowa).

WILLIAM S. POWELL

Hughes, Nicholas Collin (*24 Mar. 1822–20 May 1893*), Episcopal clergyman and teacher, was born near Gulph in Lower Merion Township, Montgomery County, Pa., the son of John and Hannah Bartholomew Hughes. Descended from early Swedish and Welsh settlers in Pennsylvania, he was named for the Reverend Nicholas Collin, the last clergyman sent to America by the kings of Sweden to serve the churches founded in New Sweden during the seventeenth century. Young Hughes entered the University of Pennsylvania in the sophomore class of 1836 and was graduated in 1839. After graduation from the General Theological Seminary in the class of 1844, Hughes was ordained a deacon in St. Thomas Church, New York City, by Bishop Benjamin T. Onderdonk on 30 June 1844.

Almost immediately after his ordination, Hughes moved to North Carolina where his brother, Dr. Isaac Wayne Hughes, had settled in New Bern to practice medicine. On his arrival in the state, he was assigned as missionary in Lenoir, Wayne, and Pitt counties. On 17 Oct. 1848, he was ordained a priest by Bishop Levi S. Ives in Christ Church, Raleigh. In 1850 Hughes founded Trinity School at Chocowinity, Beaufort County; the school was associated with Old Trinity Parish, established by the Reverend Nathaniel Blount in 1775. Hughes was connected with this school at intervals until the end of his life, and it proved to be his most important contribution to his adopted state. Although Trinity School was never large, it exerted a great influence in eastern North Carolina. Its religious instruction was of such a high order that over the years twenty of its students entered the ministry.

In January 1857, Hughes became rector of St. Bartholomew's Church, Pittsboro, and priest-in-charge of St. Mark's, Gulf. Occasional services were held at Egypt on Deep River. Resigning the rectorship in Pittsboro in December 1859, he was for the next five years in charge of St. James' in Hendersonville and Calvary Church in Henderson County. At the close of the Civil War Hughes returned to Beaufort County. From 1865 to 1869 he attempted unsuccessfully to revive Trinity School, serving at the same time as priest-in-charge of St. Paul's

Mission in Greenville. From 1869 until the summer of 1873 he was rector of St. Peter's Church, Washington; the present church building was erected during his tenure. At the diocesan convention in 1873, Hughes was appointed to conduct a canvass to raise funds for a permanent Episcopal endowment fund. His efforts were markedly successful. For the next year he was master of the grammar school at the University of the South at Sewanee, Tenn. Returning to North Carolina early in 1875, Hughes was for several months in charge of missions in Winston, Reidsville, and Durham. Later that year he returned to eastern North Carolina where, until his retirement in 1883, he was rector of St. Paul's Church, Greenville, and missionary in the counties of Pitt, Beaufort, and Craven. In 1878, with the help of his son, Nicholas Collin, Jr., Hughes reopened Trinity School, which operated successfully until 1908.

In recognition of his services as priest and teacher, The University of North Carolina awarded Hughes a doctorate of divinity in 1884. He was the author of a book, *Genesis or Geology*, published in Chocowinity in 1887, and of a popular sermon he delivered in 1878, entitled *Is Christ Divided?* which later appeared in pamphlet form.

In 1848 Hughes married Adeline Edmunds Williams, the daughter of Dr. Robert Williams of Pitt County and his third wife, Elizabeth Ellis. They had five children: Nicholas Collin, Jr., Isaac Wayne, John, Mary (Mrs. Nathaniel Harding), and Hannah (Mrs. Charles C. Calvert). Of their sons, Nicholas and Isaac became Episcopal clergymen. Hughes was buried in Trinity Parish churchyard, Chocowinity.

SEE: Marshall De Lancey Haywood, *Lives of the Bishops of North Carolina* (1910); Anna M. Holstein, *Swedish Holsteins in America* (1892); *Journals of the Diocese of North Carolina, 1845–83*; Royal G. Shannonhouse, ed., *History of St. Bartholomew's Parish, Pittsboro, N.C.* (1933); *University of Pennsylvania Matriculates of the College, 1749–1893* (1894).

LAWRENCE F. LONDON

Hughes, Samuel Wellwood (*4 Mar. 1815–2 Oct. 1884*), Presbyterian educator and churchman, was born near Cedar Grove, Orange County, the third of fourteen children of pioneer teacher Joseph Dunn Hughes (15 Feb. 1785–20 May 1844) of Rowan County and the grandson of Timothy Hughes of Rowan. Joseph D. Hughes married at least twice, and his first wife may have been Mary W[ellwood] (1788–25 Sept. 1829). His will mentions a wife, Sarah, and her four children.

According to family tradition, in the early 1800s the Reverend Samuel Paisley (later pastor of Old Eno Presbyterian Church) heard of Joseph D. Hughes's success as a teacher in Rowan County and invited him to establish a school in the Old Eno community of northern Orange County. A deed to Joseph Dunn Hughes "of Orange County," dated 25 Mar. 1810, for 136 acres of land on the east bank of the Eno River, indicates that he was already a resident of Orange in 1810. Hughes, who became known as "the Father of Schools in Northern Orange," began in his own modest Eno River farmhouse what is said to have been the first organized school in the area. His pupils were his own children and those of neighboring farmers. His avowed purpose was simply "to rescue them from ignorance."

Samuel Wellwood Hughes, born on the Eno farm, attended his father's school and absorbed the plain Presbyterian lessons of discipline, diligence, and honesty

that were to become the underlying principles of his own school. Later he attended the Bingham School on "Academy Square" in northern Hillsborough and for a short time taught there. A Bingham School advertisement in the Raleigh *Register* of 27 June 1839 lists S. W. Hughes as a member of the English Department with A. H. Ray; the other two teachers were W. J. and J. A. Bingham. Afterwards, Hughes worked his way through Hampden-Sydney College, Farmville, Va. Family tradition says that on one occasion he walked home from Farmville, a distance of 160 miles.

On his death at age fifty-nine, Joseph Dunn Hughes named Samuel as one of his executors. Six months later, in December 1844, the son married Elizabeth Jesse Hughes (11 Mar. 1816–24 Oct. 1859), of Prince Edward County, Va., sister of Judge Robert W. Hughes of the U.S. Court of Virginia; they had seven children. In January 1845, at age thirty, Samuel W. Hughes opened his own school, first called the "Cedar Grove Academy" and later simply "Hughes' Academy," which apparently moved several times. It is known to have operated in the 1860s in a small log house above the intersection at Ira Ellis's (later Nelson P. Hall's) Mill on the Eno below Fairfield Presbyterian Church and, still later, farther up the Eno at the old Joseph Dunn Hughes farmstead. There, a new two-frame school was built, together with various outbuildings to house students. The surviving frame structure is now owned by the Hillsborough Historical Society.

Like his father before him and his revered Bingham mentors, Hughes appears to have been a master teacher in the old austere Scots Presbyterian mold. His academy, advertised in flyers as a "Classical and Mathematical School," was modeled directly on the Bingham School in Hillsborough and was to some degree an extension of it. Although full programs in Greek and Latin were offered (tuition, $25), students might take only the English courses (tuition, $15). The Hughes Academy also accepted neighboring girls as had Joseph Dunn Hughes's little school; one of its most distinguished graduates was Annie Lavalette Hughes, daughter of Samuel, later the co-principal with Miss Emma Scales of the Reidsville Female Seminary. The Hughes Academy, incorporated in 1851, apparently never employed more than one assistant at a time. Three of these were the Reverend A[rchibald] Currie (1852), S. M. Wells (1855–56), and H. A. Rogers (1858). Enrollment usually ranged between thirty-five and forty students per session, although it is said to have reached one hundred just before the Civil War ("the number of his pupils often exceeded his wishes," according to the S. W. Hughes Family Papers).

No catalogue of the Hughes Academy was ever issued, and no records or roll books have survived. Some forty-eight former students are known, however, including Needham Bryant Cobb, D. I. Craig, James Lauchlin Currie, Thomas Murphy Jordan, A. L. Phillips, Robert W. Scott, Spier Whitaker, George Tayloe Winston, and Patrick Henry Winston. The academy seems to have been particularly successful in offering solid preparatory training to future physicians, ministers, educators, and leaders in government and law. Its graduates were accepted at The University of North Carolina without examination.

On 12 Mar. 1850 Hughes was appointed to Orange County's first examining board for teachers, together with Cadwallader Jones, Dr. Alexander Wilson, the Reverend J. B. Donnelly, and the Reverend L. K. Willie. In February 1852, Hughes was appointed to an eight-man Board of Superintendents of the Common Schools.

Like his father, he served Old Eno Presbyterian Church as a ruling elder and as stated clerk of the session.

On 11 July 1862 Hughes married as his second wife Margaret J. Murray (29 Feb. 1836–29 Jan. 1924), the daughter of Eli Murray of Alamance County. By this marriage he had six children. Early in the 1880s two strokes curtailed his teaching activities, but even in his final weeks students stood around his bed to recite their lessons in the old Joseph Dunn Hughes farmhouse. A third stroke proved fatal. Hughes was buried in the Old Eno Cemetery, where some twenty members of the large Hughes family had preceded him. Twenty-two later Hughes burials were recorded at New Eno Cemetery, Cedar Grove.

After Hughes's death, his academy was moved to Cedar Grove, where it reopened as the "Cedar Grove Academy" under the principalship of Benjamin C. Patton. Annie Lavalette Hughes returned from Reidsville to take charge of it in 1901, and it continued until after 1914.

A daguerrotype, tintype, and early photograph of Hughes show him to have been an imposing, massive man with black hair and blue eyes. A large picture now hangs in the Orange County Historical Museum.

SEE: T. C. Ellis and Mrs. A. A. Ellis with Annie H. Hughes, *History of Eno Presbyterian Church, 1755–1955* (n.d.); Mary Claire Engstrom, comp., Cemetery Records of Old Eno and New Eno Cemeteries (Hillsborough); *Hillsborough Recorder*, December 1855; *An Historical Program to Commemorate the Hughes Academy* (7 May 1967); "History to Be Recalled May 7 at Old Hughes' Academy," *News of Orange County*, 20 Apr. 1967; Robert B. House, "The Rich and Rewarding History of Hughes' Academy," *Chapel Hill Weekly*, 31 May 1967; S. W. Hughes Family Papers (collection of 14 sheets by Samuel W. Hughes, Hillsborough); Orange County *Deed Books*, 22, 25, 51, and Orange County *Will Book* F-193 (Orange County Courthouse, Hillsborough); "Picture [of Samuel Wellwood Hughes] Presented," *News of Orange County*, 10 May 1973; Raleigh *Register*, 29 June, 23 Nov. 1839.

MARY CLAIRE ENGSTROM

Humber, Robert Lee (*30 May 1898–10 Nov. 1970*), lawyer, legislator, business executive, cultural leader, and founder of the Movement for World Federation, was born in Greenville, the son of Lena Clyde Davis and Robert Lee Humber, Sr. His father owned and operated a machine and repair shop adjacent to the family's residence. Humber attended the Greenville Graded School until 1913, then transferred to the Winterville High School where he studied Greek, Latin, and other college preparatory subjects and from which he was graduated in May 1914. He entered Wake Forest College in the fall of that year and was graduated cum laude in May 1918, having already completed most of the requirements for the M.A. and LL.B. by working during the summers; he received those degrees in June 1919 and May 1921, respectively.

Enrolling at Harvard in the Army Reserve Military Training Camp on 1 July 1918, Humber was one of forty men who were sent to Camp Plattsburg, N.Y., where he completed his training and was commissioned a second lieutenant in the Field Artillery. With the armistice of 11 Nov. 1918, he resigned his commission and returned to private life.

In January 1919 Humber entered Harvard University to pursue a doctorate in the Department of Government, History, and Economics. The following September he served as a volunteer policeman during the Boston police strike and at the end of the month was appointed a faculty tutor in his department. On 3 Nov. 1919 he was awarded the Rhodes Scholarship from North Carolina and was scheduled to enter Oxford University in January 1920. Obtaining a deferment from Oxford until the fall, he shifted his degree program at Harvard to the M.A. and tutored for the balance of the academic year. In the summer of 1920 he was admitted to the North Carolina bar. His M.A. from Harvard was awarded in 1926 after he had met a language requirement through further study in Europe.

Humber spent three years at New College, Oxford, interspersing his studies with periods of extensive travel. He voyaged around the world during the second half of 1921 and visited selected areas of Europe for intervals of more intensive study. While in Paris in the summer of 1922, he met his future wife, Lucie Berthier, then executive secretary of the American University Union, a nonprofit information bureau and center for social contact among American students in Paris. Upon completing his work at Oxford in 1923, when he was awarded the B.Litt. degree, Humber moved to Paris where he continued independent studies and tutored American students in English, American history, literature, and government. Between 1926 and 1928, as an American Field Service Fellow at the University of Paris, he completed his work for a doctor of letters degree except for the publication requirement of the dissertation. Because he would not permit his volume on John C. Calhoun's political thought to be printed, even though a publisher had offered to do so, the degree was never conferred.

In October 1929 Humber married Lucie Berthier and lived in Paris, where he worked for an American oil company as legal representative and head of its European operations. In 1940, the Nazi invasion of France forced the Humbers to flee with their three children, Marcel B., John L., and Eileen Genivieve. During a visit to his boyhood home in Greenville, their infant daughter had died of an illness in the south of France.

Returning to North Carolina on the eve of World War II, Humber retired from business and for the next decade devoted all his time, energy, and resources to what he considered the greatest single challenge confronting mankind—world peace. Stirred by his travels and exposure to other cultures, he was convinced that man's only hope for a permanent and lasting peace lay in the establishment of a world order implemented by a world federal government. In his pamphlet, *The Declaration of the Federation of the World*, he set forth his idea that order among men could be maintained only under law, law restraining the individual rather than the confrontation of nations through military action after the failure of diplomacy.

Humber launched his Movement for World Federation on 27 Dec. 1940 at Davis Island in Core Sound, an old ancestral home. After he had lobbied across the state, the General Assembly passed his resolution, becoming the first legislative body in history to endorse the principles of a world federal government. Humber immediately began a campaign among the other state legislatures, working in nearly all of them himself over the next ten years. Sixteen states adopted his resolution and a number of others accepted his ideas in some modified form. A co-founder of the United World Federalists at Asheville in 1947, he served as vice-president during the next four years and remained on the North Carolina branch's executive council until his death. In

1960 he was elected president of the state organization and served for six years.

Humber never lost his deep commitment to the principles embodied in the idea of world federation, and his widespread public speaking across the nation created numerous opportunities to further his cause. He represented the Southern Council on International Relations at the United Nations Organizational Conference in San Francisco in 1945, and he participated in the White House Conference for International Cooperation in 1965. Humber was the recipient of the World Government News Medal for the most outstanding service by an individual to world federation (1948), the American War Dads Prize for the greatest single contribution towards world peace (1948), and the American Freedom Association's Peace Award (1967). At the time of his death he was writing a book to show how a world federal government could operate successfully, emphasizing his belief that this was man's only hope of survival as a civilization.

In his studies at home and abroad, Humber developed an intense appreciation for the lasting cultural values left by previous generations to assist those that followed in their search for truth, beauty, and meaning in life. As early as 1943, when he joined the board of directors of the State Art Society (of which he remained a member until 1955), he considered the possibility of establishing an art museum in North Carolina and began exploring the means by which a collection of great art could be acquired. He convinced the 1947 General Assembly that an unrevealed donor was ready to give the state one million dollars in cash if the state would match it, having already obtained a verbal commitment from Samuel H. Kress and the Kress Foundation in New York. After the bill was passed, Kress became ill and his brother, Rhush H. Kress, assumed leadership of the foundation. There being no written commitment, yet significant evidence that an agreement had been reached, Rhush Kress offered to donate at least one million dollars in art instead of cash. In 1951 the General Assembly accepted his alternate proposal.

As chairman of the State Art Commission from 1951 to 1961, Humber guided the selection of the old masters that formed the original museum collection, negotiating substantial discounts from the New York art dealers who became keenly interested in participating in the creation of a great public museum in the South. The North Carolina Museum of Art opened its doors in April 1956, and a collection of art valued at around two and one-half million dollars was received from the Kress Foundation in November 1960. In 1955 Humber was elected president of the State Art Society and served until 1961, when he became chairman of the North Carolina Museum of Art Board of Trustees, established by the General Assembly the same year; Humber served as chairman until his death. In recognition of his contributions in the field of art he was awarded the Thomas Gilcrease Institute of American History and Art (Tulsa, Okla.) Certificate of Merit (1955), the North Carolina State Art Society Certificate of Merit and Achievement (1956), and the Salmagundi Art Achievement Medal of the Salmagundi Art Club, New York (1966).

Humber also entered the political arena as a Democrat. After an unsuccessful bid for Congress in 1946, he was elected to the state senate from Pitt County in 1958 and served three consecutive terms through 1964. As chairman of the Senate Higher Education Committee, he led the fight for the establishment of the State Community College and Technical Institute system of education. At the same time he proposed and led the efforts to create Pitt Technical Institute in 1963–64, serving as chairman of the board of trustees until his death. In addition, he worked hard for the adoption of a constitutional amendment that would have ensured representation in the General Assembly based on population and geography (as at the federal level) had the amendment passed. He wrote the bill establishing the North Carolina Awards, the state's highest honor to its citizens, or former citizens, for significant achievements in science, literature, the fine arts, and public service. For his own contributions—the promotion of world peace, leadership in creating the North Carolina Museum of Art, influence on the state's culture, and service in the state senate—he was presented the North Carolina Award for Public Service in 1968.

Humber's leadership in the field of education antedated his interest in Pitt Technical Institute. He served as a member of the board of trustees of Meredith College in 1947–50 and of Wake Forest College in 1951–54 and in 1959–60, when he was chairman of the board. In recognition of his service, Wake Forest awarded him the honorary LL.D. in 1949. From The University of North Carolina he received the LL.D. in 1958 and from Duke University, the D.H.L. in 1967. Between 1967 and 1970 he served as vice-president and then president of the North Carolina Community Education Institutions, which he represented at the National School Boards Association. He also was a member of the North Carolina Rhodes Scholarship Selection Committee from 1946 to 1960 and again in 1963.

Born and raised as a Southern Baptist, Humber was active in the denomination wherever he lived. At his home church, the Memorial Baptist Church of Greenville, he served as a Sunday school teacher, deacon, and chairman of the Board of Deacons and Trustees. While abroad during the 1920s and 1930s, he attended the American Church in Paris, of which he was treasurer (1932–35) and chairman of the Prudential Committee (1935–41). In the latter capacity he was instrumental in raising an endowment fund to perpetuate the financial security of the nondenominational Protestant Church owned by the American Foreign Christian Union of New York City, on whose board of directors he served between 1941 and 1970. After his return from Europe, he immersed himself in the affairs of the Baptist denomination, being particularly concerned about the financial health and academic standards of its institutions of higher education. In 1947 he was elected vice-president of the North Carolina State Baptist Convention.

Through his service on numerous state and local councils, boards, and commissions, Humber participated in many facets of North Carolina's corporate life. Affiliations in the public sector included Advisory Committee on Highway Safety (1950); Pitt County Development Commission (1957–70); North Carolina Commission on Interstate Cooperation (1959–61); Youth Fitness Commission (1961); Coastal Plain Planning and Development Commission (board of directors, 1962–65, 1969–70, and president, 1962–64); North Carolina State Capitol Planning Commission (1962–65); Tar River Basin Development Association (president, 1965–70); Governor's Study Committee for Vocational Rehabilitation (1967–69); North Carolina Council on Prevention of Crime and Delinquency (1968–69); Pitt County Good Neighbor Council (1969–70); Greenville Citizens Awareness Committee (co-chairman, 1970). In addition, he was active in the North Carolina Literary and Historical Association (first life member, 1938–70, and president, 1950–51); North Carolina Symphony Society (executive committee, 1949–70, and board of trustees, 1955–70);

Roanoke Island Historical Association (board of directors, 1955–61, and president, 1955–59); Tryon Palace Commisson (1956–70); North Carolina Conservatory of Music committee (1962–63); Heritage Square Commission (1962–67); Edenton Historical Commission (charter member and chairman, 1962–70); Advisory Committee on Topographic Mapping of North Carolina (1963); Rachel Maxwell Moore Foundation of Art (board of directors, 1963–70); North Carolina Arts Council (chairman, 1964–67); Pitt County Historical Association (president, 1964–68); and North Carolina Society for the Preservation of Antiquities (charter and life member).

He was also a member of Phi Beta Kappa, Omicron Delta Kappa, Epsilon Pi Tau, Phi Delta Phi, Sigma Phi Epsilon, Sigma Pi Alpha, International Platform Association, American Academy of Political and Social Science, American Judicature Society, American Society of International Law, American Legion, Rotary International, Watauga Club (Raleigh), Harvard Club, Salmagundi Art Club, Century Association (New York City), and American Club (Paris, France).

Humber died suddenly in Greenville while attending a film on Tolstoy's *War and Peace*, leaving an unfinished manuscript on his desk. He was buried at Cherry Hill Cemetery, Greenville.

SEE: O. K. Armstrong, "Grassroots Crusader," *Reader's Digest*, May 1946; George W. Blount, *Peace Through World Government* (1974); Ola Maie Foushee, *Art in North Carolina: Episodes and Developments, 1585–1970* (1972); C. Sylvester Green, *Vignettes: Robert Lee Humber* (1976); Robert Lee Humber, "The Crisis of Our Time," *The Danforth Lectures No. 1*, East Carolina College (1959–60), and *The Declaration of the Federation of the World* (1941); David R. Milsten, *Thomas Gilcrease* (1969); *North Carolina Session Laws* for 1941, 1947, 1951; Papers of Robert Lee Humber (in possession of the family, Greenville); William S. Powell, *North Carolina Lives* (1962); "Tar Heel of the Week," Raleigh *News and Observer*, 5 Feb. 1950; Ted N. Williams, ed., *Annual of the Baptist State Convention of North Carolina* (1971); *Who Was Who in America*, vol. 5.

JOHN L. HUMBER

Hume, Thomas *(21 Oct. 1836–15 July 1912)*, educator and clergyman, was born in Portsmouth, Va., the oldest of eight children of the Reverend Thomas and Mary Ann Gregory Hume. His paternal grandfather—a Church of Scotland clergyman, also named Thomas—emigrated from Edinburgh in 1806, settling eventually in Smithfield, Isle of Wight County, Va. His father was a prominent Baptist clergyman in Virginia.

Hume was prepared for college at the Virginia Collegiate Institute, Portsmouth. Entering Richmond College at age fifteen, he was graduated with the B.A. degree in 1855 and awarded the M.A. a few years later. In 1855–58 he attended the University of Virginia, where he earned several of the "school diplomas" being conferred at that time. Later he was the recipient of honorary degrees from Richmond College (D.D., 1881), Wake Forest College (LL.D., 1892), and The University of North Carolina (LL.D., 1910).

Chesapeake Female College in Hampton, Va., was the scene of Hume's earliest labors as a teacher. There he taught English and French from 1859 until 1861, when he enlisted in the Third Regiment, Virginia Infantry. Though not yet ordained to the Gospel ministry, he served his regiment as chaplain; subsequently, he was transferred to the position of post chaplain at Petersburg where he remained until the surrender of the Confederate Army at Appomattox. On 5 June 1865, at

the close of the annual session of the Baptist General Association of Virginia, he was ordained a minister.

The remainder of Hume's career was devoted to education and the church. As an educator, he was principal of the Petersburg Classical Institute (1865–67) and principal and professor of English at Norfolk College (1880–85) before joining the faculty of The University of North Carolina, where he spent the last twenty-five years of his life. At Chapel Hill, he served as professor of English language and literature (1885–1902), professor of English literature (1902–7), and professor emeritus of English literature (1907–12).

Hume's pastoral services had begun during his days in Petersburg, when he ministered to rural churches in Sussex and Chesterfield counties. Later, he served as pastor of the First Baptist Church, Danville (1870–73); Cumberland Street Baptist Church, Norfolk (1874–78); and Berkley Avenue Baptist Church, Portsmouth (1880–81). As a preacher, one biographer noted of him: "He was indeed a fine preacher; language simple and chaste, thought strong and penetrating, illustrated richly from the broad fields of his reading; voice clear and incisive, face aglow with the passion of the hour, made him a speaker good to listen to and easy to learn from."

However, Hume did his finest work as a teacher of English and English literature at The University of North Carolina. Edward Kidder Graham—a colleague and later president of the university—wrote of him on the occasion of his retirement from active teaching: "Dr. Hume wrought at his task of teaching the masterpieces of literature with the zeal of a prophet. Literature . . . was to him not a chance profession; it was a religious faith. . . . He placed but one limit on the number of courses he taught, and that was the number of hours in the day. Day and night he gave himself to active instruction."

Apart from his work in the classroom, Hume organized the university's Shakespeare Club; participated in the work of the YMCA, on campus and throughout the Southeast; and was a frequent lecturer on Shakespeare, Tennyson, and the literary study of the Bible before school groups, clubs, and summer assemblies in various parts of North Carolina and Virginia. In addition to numerous shorter articles and addresses that appeared in the religious press, he was the author of *Helps to the Study of Hamlet in Questions and Answers* (1880) and "Shakespeare's Moral Teaching," published in the *Shakespeare Journal* for 1886. A presidential address prepared for the North Carolina Baptist Historical Society in 1893, entitled "John Milton's Religious Opinions and Connections," appeared as "John Milton and the Baptists" in the *North Carolina Baptist Historical Papers* (April 1897).

On 31 Oct. 1878 Hume married Anne Louise Whitescarver of Waynesboro, Va. They had four children: Thomas, Anne Wilmer (m. William Reynolds Vance), Mary Gregory (m. James Edward Mills), and Helen. Hume was buried in Waynesboro, Va.

SEE: Samuel A. Ashe, ed., *Biographical History of North Carolina*, vol. 4 (1906); Kemp P. Battle, *History of the University of North Carolina*, vol. 2 (1912); *North Carolina Baptist Historical Papers*, vol. 1 (April 1897 [portrait]); George Braxton Taylor, *Virginia Baptist Ministers* (5th ser., 1915); *Who's Who in America* (1908–9).

R. HARGUS TAYLOR

Hunt, John *(ca. 1644–1710)*, Council member and justice, was in the North Carolina colony by 1664. He lived for about a year in the home of George Catchmaid in Perquimans Precinct, but later settled in Pasquotank Precinct.

Hunt was a Quaker and by June 1677 belonged to the Pasquotank Monthly Meeting. In September 1679 he joined other Quakers in a petition to the Lords Proprietors protesting the disturbances known as Culpeper's Rebellion and the conditions following. Although he took no active part in those disturbances, Hunt appears to have sympathized with the faction supporting Thomas Miller, the acting governor.

By 3 May 1684 Hunt had become a member of the Council, a position that he also held in 1687 and 1689. He may have been on the Council in the intervening years, for which the names of Council members are not known.

From April 1685 through December 1687, Hunt was a justice of the County Court of Albemarle. In 1694, 1697, and probably the intervening years, he was a justice of the Pasquotank Precinct Court, of which few records have survived. In November 1697 he was commissioned justice of the General Court, on which he took his seat the following March. He does not appear to have held public office after October 1698, when his term on the General Court expired.

In private life Hunt was a mariner and a merchant-planter. He bore the title "captain," reflecting his rank as mariner. As early as 1680 he was part owner of a vessel engaged in trade with New England. His landholdings, which lay in Pasquotank, comprised at least 1,300 acres. The plantation on which he lived was on Little River. On occasion he appeared in court as attorney, usually representing nonresident clients.

Hunt was married twice, first before June 1677 to Frances Manners, who was the widow of Peregreen Manners and the mother of a daughter, Jane Manners, who married Caleb Bundy. His second wife, Elizabeth, was the widow of one Hatch and the mother of a son, Anthony Hatch. Elizabeth seems to have been related, perhaps as sister, to James Tooke. Apparently Hunt had only one child of his own, a daughter named Elizabeth, who married one Evans.

Hunt died between 7 Apr. 1710, when he made his will, and 26 August, when the will was probated. He bequeathed his estate to his wife and his three grandchildren: Elizabeth Evans, John Hunt Evans, and Bartholomew Evans.

SEE: Albemarle Book of Warrants and Surveys, 1681–1706, Colonial Court Records (Box CCR 192), Folders on House of Burgesses and Appointments and Commissions, Council Minutes, Wills, Inventories, 1677–1701, Wills of John Hunt and Arthur Workman (North Carolina State Archives, Raleigh); J. Bryan Grimes, ed., *Abstract of North Carolina Wills* (1910); J. R. B. Hathaway, ed., *North Carolina Historical and Genealogical Register*, 3 vols. (1900–1903); William Wade Hinshaw, comp., *Encyclopedia of American Quaker Genealogy*, vol. 1 (1936–50); Mattie Erma E. Parker, ed., *North Carolina Higher-Court Records, 1670–1696* and *1697–1701* (1968, 1971); William S. Price, Jr., ed., *North Carolina Higher-Court Records, 1702–1708* (1974); William L. Saunders, ed., *Colonial Records of North Carolina*, vol. 1 (1886).

MATTIE ERMA E. PARKER

Hunt, Memucan (23 Aug. 1729–1808), planter, state senator, and first treasurer of North Carolina, was born in Virginia, the third son of Ralph and Dinah Anderson Hunt. The ancestors of Ralph Hunt had emigrated from

England to Virginia in the seventeenth century. Little is known of Memucan's education and early life. According to tradition, his home from about 1760 was the plantation of Burnside (so named in 1824), where a two-story weatherboarded house was built with interior carved woodwork characteristic of the Classic Revival. It is located near Williamsboro in Vance (then Granville) County.

Hunt's service in the colonial government began at age forty-one. In 1770 he was chosen as sergeant at arms of the North Carolina Assembly, and in 1773 he was elected a representative to the Assembly from Granville and Bute counties. At the March 1774 meeting of the Assembly in New Bern, Governor Josiah Martin and the Council received three bills sent up by Hunt and a Mr. Moore. Of greater significance was Hunt's effort, on behalf of sundry inhabitants of Granville County, to secure passage of a law restraining Negroes from trading with white people. The Assembly ordered the matter to be tabled.

Approving the rising spirit of colonial rebellion, Hunt and the other freeholders of Granville County resolved in August 1774 to support the people of Wilmington's call for a Provincial Congress. When the Congress convened at New Bern on the twenty-fifth of that month, Hunt, along with Thomas Person, sat for Granville County. At the Second, Third, Fourth, and Fifth Provincial Congresses, Hunt was one of the five delegates from Granville County.

When North Carolina was established as an independent state in 1777, financial problems were paramount. The fiscal responsibilities of Memucan Hunt began with his appointment as the Hillsborough district treasurer, one of six in the state. By 1779 he was also a member of the Committee of Accounts and held office as a senator in the General Assembly. Probably as a result of his leadership, the legislature authorized the issuance of £500,000 in currency, on the faith and credit of the state, to defray military and other expenses. Hunt was one of the three commissioners named to oversee the printing. The next year he filled the same role upon the issuance of an additional £1,240,000.

In November 1784, meeting at New Bern, the General Assembly abolished the several offices of district treasurer and established that of state treasurer, electing Hunt to the post. He took office on 1 Jan. 1785 at a salary of £500 per annum. Due to his having honored—in good faith—some fraudulent claims for payment of compensation for military service, Hunt was involved in both litigation and hearings by the General Assembly in 1786. At the end of that year, though not charged with malfeasance, he was not reelected. Retiring from governmental service, he became a wealthy planter and resided at his home with his family. From 1784 to 1792 he served as a justice of the peace for Granville County.

From Hunt's will, recorded on 23 Feb. 1808, there emerges the picture of a man of considerable substance. This is confirmed by the inventory of Hunt's personal property filed in Granville County Court House in February 1809 after his death. He had owned twenty-two slaves, two horses, four mares, one mare colt, fourteen head of cattle, thirty-three hogs, sows, and shoats, a large quantity of household furniture and utensils, a cotton gin, and various other machines and tools for farming. Including 920 acres left to his wife—for the duration of her life as his widow—Hunt's real property apparently totaled 15,875 acres. Among his holdings were half of a 3,000-acre tract on "Dutch River" and half of a 1,000-acre tract in Tennessee. He had evidently sold 250 acres of land in Wilkes County to Thomas

Walsh in 1804. Bonds (debts) due and payable to Hunt's estate included five totaling $384.50, four totaling over £72, one for 8 barrels of corn, and at least one more.

Hunt married Mary ("Polly") Wade, a relative of General Wade Hampton, who survived him; she died in 1825. Among their ten children were Colonel William and Dr. Thomas. Members of the Hunt family are presumed to have been parishioners of St. John's Episcopal Church, Williamsboro, where stands the only colonial church building in the Diocese of North Carolina. Charles Wilson Peale, the famous American artist, did portraits in oil on wood of Hunt and his wife. Photographs of the paintings are extant.

SEE: Samuel A. Ashe, ed., *History of North Carolina*, vol. 2 (1925); Walter Clark, ed., *State Records of North Carolina* (1895–1914); E. H. Hummel, comp., *Hicks' History of Granville County*, vol. 1 (1965); Papers relating to the estate of Memucan Hunt and Granville County records (North Carolina Division of Archives and History, Raleigh); B. P. Robinson, ed., *The North Carolina Guide* (1955); William L. Saunders, ed., *Colonial Records of North Carolina* (1886–98).

WALSER H. ALLEN, JR.

Hunt, Nathan (10 Oct. 1758–8 Aug. 1853), Quaker leader, itinerant minister, and principal founder of the New Garden Boarding School (now Guilford College), was born in the New Garden community (now within the limits of Greensboro), the son of Sarah Mills and William Hunt, a Friends minister. Nathan Hunt characterized his heritage "as a very ancient British family with some Scotch and some Welsh blood in it." His paternal grandfather and great-grandfather located on Rancocas Creek in New Jersey soon after 1670. His father, as a young man, arrived with the pioneer settlers in the New Garden Community and soon married Sarah Mills, the daughter of John and Sarah Beals Mills. The Mills and the Beals families were also among the community's early settlers. All of these relatives of Nathan Hunt had followed the emigrant road from the Philadelphia area across Maryland to the Valley of Virginia, up the valley to suitable passes across the Blue Ridges, and then along trails and emerging frontier roads to New Garden.

When Nathan was fourteen, his father and Nathan's cousin, John Woolman, died of smallpox while on a religious visit at Newcastle-on-Tyne, England. Afterwards, neighbors contributed a sum of money for the purchase of equipment and tools to enable Nathan to learn the blacksmith trade. This act of charity may indicate that his mother found it difficult to support her eight children. Nathan, who had little opportunity for a formal education, said he never attended school more than six months in his life. Fortunately, he lived within three miles of the home of Dr. David Caldwell, then generally considered the area's outstanding intellectual and teacher. Caldwell gave the youth access to his library and encouraged him to follow a continuous discipline in his study.

Around the time of the Battle of Guilford Court House in 1781, the Hunt farm was victimized by foragers from both the American and British armies. All of the horses, one cow, and other resources were seized, leaving the family almost destitute. After the battles on New Garden Road and at Guilford Court House, a large number of the most seriously wounded from both armies were left at New Garden Meeting House and scattered among homes in the community. When some of the wounded contracted smallpox, young Nathan Hunt volunteered to help care for the victims who were being treated at the Meeting House. His family objected to his running such a risk in view of the death of his father and cousin from the disease; moreover, his neighbor, Richard Williams—a young married man with two children—had just contracted smallpox from a wounded British officer. Nevertheless, Nathan felt that it was his duty to try to save the lives of the afflicted soldiers. He did catch the virus, but had a mild case.

Hunt fought the institution of slavery as boldly as he had confronted smallpox. At the time, public bitterness against abolitionists was strong in Guilford County and some were attacked by mobs. Despite the risks, he spoke out forcefully against slavery, even in the presence of a slaveholding governor of North Carolina.

For nearly two hundred years itinerant Quaker ministers, both men and women, fanned out continuously to Quaker meetings in the British Isles and in the Western Hemisphere. Their ministry furnished the lifeblood of the Society of Friends and kept the meetings alive. Nathan Hunt was one of the ablest. Recorded as a minister at age thirty-five, he visited nearly all the meetings in the United States, Great Britain, and Canada. While in Glasgow, Scotland, he preached to an audience of more than four thousand people—among them the Russian ambassador and his wife and attendants. He also carried his Christian message to Indian tribes in the United States and Canada. His travels often kept him away from his family for several months at a time.

Hunt exercised vigorous leadership within the Society of Friends of North Carolina. When the state's Quakers were threatened with a schism, he was quick to evaluate the dispute and use his influence to mend the breach. Living at a time when the yearly meeting (the governing body) directed members to remain aloof from politics, Hunt surprised some when he left a session of the annual assembly of Friends to ride twenty miles to cast his ballot in a general election. He said that he considered voting a debt that he owed his country and he could not neglect it.

Hunt's name heads the list of founders of New Garden Boarding School, which opened in the spring of 1837. Thereafter his role in the school was akin to that of a patron saint. Through frequent visits and talks to the students, he exercised as much influence as any teacher. Members of his family were also deeply involved in the school's establishment and operation. His son, Thomas T. (and wife, Nancy D. Hunt), and daughters, Asenath Hunt Clark (and husband, Dougan Clark) and Abigail Hunt Stanley (and husband, Joshua Stanley), were members of the committees that planned, promoted, and established the school, and all of them were teachers or administrators after it opened.

On 12 Nov. 1777, at age nineteen, Hunt married Mary Ruckman, the daughter of Joseph Ruckman of Guilford County. She died eleven years later, one week after the birth of their sixth child. On 6 Apr. 1791 he married Prudence Thornbrugh, the daughter of Thomas and Abigail Thornbrugh; by her, Hunt had four more children.

Soon after Hunt's second marriage, the family moved to the Pine Woods community, a few miles west of the Springfield community to which they later moved. Prudence Hunt died in 1822, and it is believed that Nathan and the family of his son, Thomas, shared the same home. In 1848 they returned to the old family homestead on New Garden Road. Four years later Thomas Hunt and his family moved to Indiana, and Nathan went to live with his daughter and son-in-law, Abigail and Joshua Stanley, in the Centre community in southern Guilford County.

Hunt died near the Centre Friends Meeting and was buried in the Friends Cemetery at Springfield Friends Meeting House. In recognition of his role in the history of Guilford College, his picture now hangs in the foyer of New Garden Hall, the school's administration building; Nathan Hunt Road runs south from the main campus; and his broadbrimmed hat is prominently displayed in the Quaker Collection of the library.

SEE: *Brief Memoir of Nathan Hunt* (1854); Mary Mendenhall Hobbs, "Nathan Hunt and His Times," *Bulletin of Friends Historical Society of Philadelphia* (November 1907); Nathan Hunt Memorial by Springfield Friends Meeting, Minutes and Records of New Garden Meeting of Friends, Minutes and Records of Springfield Monthly Meeting of Friends, Minutes of North Carolina Yearly Meeting of Friends (Quaker Collection, Guilford College Library).

ALGIE I. NEWLIN

Hunt, William *(1733–9 Sept. 1772),* minister and religious traveler, was born at Rancocas, N.J., the son of William and Mary Woolman Hunt. After the death of his parents when he was very young he was reared by an aunt in Maryland. As a lad he was accepted by the Friends Meeting that he attended regularly in the company of this aunt.

Hunt moved to North Carolina when he was about eighteen, presenting his certificate to the Cane Creek Monthly Meeting of Friends in present Alamance County. In 1733 he married Sarah Mills at the Cane Creek Meetinghouse and settled near New Garden (Guilford College). When a monthly meeting was established at New Garden in 1754, he and his brother Eleazar were among the charter members. The same year he was recommended to become a minister.

It was the custom of Friends ministers to make religious visits to other meetings, whether in their immediate vicinity or in other parts of the colonies or in foreign countries. Often such visits would keep the clergymen away from home and family for years. On 18 Oct. 1770 Hunt, accompanied by his nephew Thomas Thornbrugh, left New Garden to travel through eastern North Carolina, Virginia, Maryland, Pennsylvania, New York, Rhode Island, and Nantucket, Mass. On 4 May 1771, Hunt and Thornbrugh boarded the ship *Mary and Elizabeth* out of Philadelphia for London. They were at sea only twenty-three days, a very short journey for sailing vessels.

In England the two were received at most of the meetings and were housed in the homes of many illustrious Quakers. Leaving England they went to Scotland, Ireland, Holland, and back to England. Hunt was called an eminent minister and was received as a "worthy zealous Friend with a good gift." He became ill with smallpox in August 1772 and died the following month; he was buried in the Friends Burial Ground at Newcastle-on-Tyne.

William Hunt's reputation in North Carolina is somewhat overshadowed by that of his son, Nathan, also a minister and a traveler in religious service, but best known as one of the founders of New Garden Boarding School (later Guilford College).

SEE: Henry J. Cadbury, *Journal of William Hunt's Visit to Europe, 1771–1772, Together with William Hunt—A Memoir* (1968); William Hunt and Nathan Hunt, *Memoirs of William and Nathan Hunt, Taken Chiefly from Their Journals and Letters* (1858).

TREVA W. MATHIS

Hunter, Aaron Burtis *(26 Apr. 1854–12 July 1933),* Episcopal clergyman, educator, book collector, and philanthropist, was born in Philadelphia, Pa., the son of John C. and Sarah A. Clark Hunter. After graduation from public school in Philadelphia, he attended Amherst College, receiving the B.A. degree in 1876. He was elected to membership in the Amherst Club, Delta Upsilon social fraternity, and Phi Beta Kappa. Hunter was graduated from Union Theological Seminary in 1879 and spent the next year studying at the University of Berlin, Germany. Amherst and the University of the South awarded him doctor of divinity degrees in 1916.

Upon ordination as an Episcopal priest in 1882, Hunter was appointed successively assistant to the rector of St. Luke's in Germantown, Ohio; rector of St. Mary's Church in Hillsboro, Ohio (1882–84); and chaplain of Wolfe Hall in Denver, Colo. (1885–87).

On 9 Jan. 1888 Hunter married Sarah Lothrop Taylor of Brooklyn, N.Y. One month later, on 6 February, he accepted an appointment to teach theology at St. Augustine's Normal School and Collegiate Institute in Raleigh—one of the first institutions established in the South to promote higher intellectual development for the Negro. Hunter believed in stimulating the individual's ability for self-help, and that "religion is for the training of . . . body, intellect, heart, and will, not just the expression of . . . emotion." In 1891 he succeeded Robert Bean Sutton as principal, and in the late 1890s his administration spurred a period of energetic activity directed towards enhancement of the Industrial Trade School program. Mrs. Hunter founded and served as head of St. Agnes Hospital and Training School for Nurses, which adjoined the St. Augustine campus.

Many rare books and prints (including incunabula) collected by the Hunters on trips to Europe, particularly Italy, were sold to support the library at St. Augustine's. A large collection of these books is now part of the Rare Books Collection at The University of North Carolina Library.

In 1916 Hunter resigned as principal of St. Augustine's, having worked to change its status from that of a strictly diocesan school to an institution of general higher education, although still supported by the national Episcopal church. In October 1920, he became priest-in-charge of St. James's American Episcopal Church in Florence, Italy, and remained there for more than six years. In 1928, when St. Augustine's achieved the status of college, Hunter was elected honorary president.

He died at age seventy-nine in Manchester, Vt., where he was interred temporarily. On 14 Sept. 1933, his remains were taken to Raleigh for services at St. Augustine's and Christ Church, and he was buried in Oakwood Cemetery, Raleigh. According to his will, Hunter's estate was placed in trust for the care of his widow, and, after her death, for the support of St. Augustine's College and St. Agnes Hospital.

SEE: *Carolina Churchman*, February 1923; Joan Davis Eaton, "A History and Evaluation of the Hanes Collection in the Louis Round Wilson Library, University of North Carolina" (M.S.L.S. thesis, University of North Carolina, Chapel Hill, 1957); Cecil D. Halliburton, *A History of St. Augustine's College, 1867–1937* (1937); Robert Williams Patton, *An Inspiring Record in Negro Education*

(1940); Raleigh *News and Observer*, 13 July, 14, 15 Sept. 1933; St. Augustine's College, *Gifts and Bequests* (1968) and *St. Augustine's Second Century* (1968).

CATHERINE MYERS BENNINGTON

Hunter, Charles Norfleet (*9 Jan. ca. 1852–4 Sept. 1931*), educator, was born in Raleigh at the home of his father, Osborne Hunter, a Negro artisan. His mother, Mary Hunter, though a slave owned by William Dallas Haywood of Raleigh, lived with her husband until her death in 1855. At that time young Hunter, his older brother, and his two sisters were taken to Haywood's property and cared for by their aunt.

At the close of the Civil War, Hunter enrolled in a freedmen's school in Raleigh. He later stated that he had completed one year of course work at Shaw University and the University of South Carolina. For the most part, however, his formal education was limited to occasional summer sessions at Hampton Institute in Virginia and teachers' institutes in North Carolina.

By 1869 Hunter was employed at the Raleigh branch of the Freedmen's Savings and Trust Company. He was assistant cashier when the company failed in 1874. In December of the following year he began teaching at Shoe Heel (Maxton) in Robeson County. In 1878 he became principal of the Garfield School in Raleigh, but resigned three years later to accept a clerkship in the Raleigh post office. After the election of a Democratic president in 1884, Hunter found employment as a traveling agent for A. S. Barnes & Co. of New York. But he soon returned to teaching, first at the Negro grade school in Durham and then as principal, successively, of the Negro school in Goldsboro and the Oberlin and Garfield schools in Raleigh.

Hunter lost his position at the latter school in 1900, apparently because of a drinking problem. He moved to Trenton, N.J., where he was a partner in a real estate and employment agency. In 1902 he returned to Raleigh as principal of the Oberlin School. Transferring to the Chavis School in 1906, he worked also for the North Carolina Mutual and Provident Association as traveling agent and superintendent of the Raleigh office. In 1909 he was appointed principal of the Negro school at Method, which under his leadership became the Berry O'Kelly Training and Industrial School.

Moving to Portsmouth, Va., in June 1918, Hunter obtained employment in the Norfolk Navy Yard. He returned to Raleigh in 1921, but his age and lack of formal education made it increasingly difficult for him to secure and retain teaching positions. Between 1922 and 1931 he was principal of Negro schools in Garner, Haywood, Pittsboro, Wilson's Mills, Manchester, Lumber Bridge, and Palmyra.

Throughout his career, Hunter was involved in numerous activities and organizations intended to promote progress for Negroes and friendly relations with whites. He and his brother, Osborne Hunter, Jr., were among the founders of the North Carolina Industrial Association, which sponsored the first Negro state fair in North Carolina in November 1879. Hunter was active in reforming and reviving the Negro state fair after its suspension in 1926 and was elected secretary and manager of the fair in 1930. As secretary of the North Carolina state organization of the Negro Development and Exposition Company, he was also involved in preparing exhibits for the Jamestown Exposition in 1907.

Hunter wrote numerous articles and letters for newspapers, many of them concerning race relations and the history and progress of Negroes. He also edited a number of newspapers and periodicals. During the 1880s he was an editor of *The Journal of Industry*, weekly paper of the North Carolina Industrial Association, and of *The Progressive Educator*, official organ of the North Carolina State Teachers' Association. In 1891 he became associate editor of the Raleigh *Gazette*; in 1902 he began publishing the *Oberlin School Record*; and in 1910 he edited *Our Advance*, a short-lived monthly. From March 1917 until his departure for Portsmouth, and again in 1921, he edited the Raleigh *Independent*.

For many years Hunter was secretary of the Negro Republican State Executive Committee. He was severely critical of the lily-white Republican organization and actively opposed the appointments of Frank A. Linney and I. M. Meekins to federal judicial posts in the state in the early 1920s. At various times Hunter was also secretary of the Grand Lodge of North Carolina of the Independent Order of Good Templars, recording secretary and book agent for the North Carolina State Teachers' Educational Association, corresponding secretary of the state Negro Business League, and a member of the vestry of St. Ambrose Episcopal Church, Raleigh.

In November 1876 Hunter married Eliza Hawkins (d. 1923), a native of Warrenton who had moved to Raleigh after the Civil War. Of their five children, two survived to adulthood: Emma Hunter Satterwhite and Lena M. Hunter. Charles N. Hunter died and was buried in Raleigh.

SEE: Charles N. Hunter Papers (Manuscript Department, Duke University Library, Durham); John H. Haley, *Charles N. Hunter and Race Relations in North Carolina* (1987); Charles N. Hunter, *Negro Life in North Carolina with My Recollections* (1928 [photograph]); Raleigh *News and Observer*, 5 Sept. 1931.

ROBERT L. BYRD

Hunter, Cyrus Lee (*13 Dec. 1807–15 Dec. 1881*), physician, scientist, and historian, was born in Lincoln (now Gaston) County, one of ten children of the Reverend Humphrey and Jane Ross Hunter. His father, of French Huguenot-Scots ancestry, was born near Londonderry, Northern Ireland, and came to America at an early age; educated in both medicine and theology, he became a Presbyterian minister after a lengthy service in the American Revolution. Jane Hunter was the daughter of Dr. George Ross of Laurens District, S.C.

In 1834 Cyrus Lee Hunter married Sophia Forney, the youngest daughter of General Peter Forney, and settled in the Machphelah area of Lincoln County. There he established a medical practice that extended into the adjacent counties. In addition, Hunter owned a prosperous gristmill, the gift of his father-in-law, situated on a creek near his home. After the Civil War the mill was modernized and operated by his son-in-law, John H. Sharp, until 1885, when it was rendered inoperable by the opening of the channel of the creek. Hunter's ability as a businessman was recognized by his neighbors, many of whom brought him their money to invest, a service he performed with honesty and efficiency. It is said that no one ever lost a penny by him.

Hunter's library was considered to be one of the largest and best in his area of the state, and he was widely recognized as a scholar. He had a strong interest in botany and collected over two hundred specimens of North Carolina woods. Placed on exhibit at the exposition in Venice, Italy, in 1875, this collection was lost and never recovered. Hunter is credited with the development of the Catawba variety of grape and with the discovery of two rare varieties of wild plants. He was also an avid student of entomology, herpetology, and mineralogy. His interest in minerals was stimulated by the fact that he lived within the placer gold mining area of North Carolina. The wedding rings of his daughter and daughter-in-law were made of gold mined on his own estate. Hunter's extensive mineral collection was exhibited at the Centennial Exposition, Philadelphia, in 1876.

Hunter corresponded with a number of scientists, including John James Audubon and Louis Agassiz. Unfortunately, these interesting letters, along with his other papers and his library, were destroyed in the fire that razed his home shortly after his death. Hunter reported some of the results of his scientific investigations in various articles he wrote for such periodicals as the *North Carolina University Magazine* and the *South-Atlantic.*

After the Civil War his scholarly interests turned to history. In 1875 he was one of the incorporators of the Historical Society of North Carolina, and in 1877 he published his *Sketches of Western North Carolina.* Several of these sketches were original, but others, including that of his father, were condensed from John H. Wheeler's *Historical Sketches of North Carolina.* Wheeler also provided Hunter with information from the records of the Pension Bureau, Washington, D.C., relating to the military service of several Revolutionary War soldiers. At the time of his death Hunter had almost completed a similar series of sketches for eastern North Carolina, which would probably have been edited and published had his manuscript not been consumed in the fire that destroyed his white frame mansion, Vine Hill.

Hunter and his wife Sophia had five children. Two daughters died young. Their two sons, Henry Stanhope and Captain George William Hunter, served in the Confederate Army, and the latter was mortally wounded at Chancellorsville. Their youngest daughter, Sophia, married John H. Sharp of Norfolk, Va. Sophia Forney Hunter died about 1845. On 20 May 1851, Hunter married Catharine F. Lyman of Massachusetts. They had one son, Lee, who married Pickett Myers. Myers Hunter, Lee's son, like his grandfather, was a physician and practiced in Charlotte. Cyrus Lee Hunter died suddenly on his way home from attending church services at Castania and was buried in Machphelah Cemetery, Iron Station (Lincoln County).

SEE: Kemp P. Battle, *History of the University of North Carolina,* vol. 2 (1912); *North Carolina University Magazine* 9 (1859–60), 10 (1860–61); Pre-1914 Graves Index (North Carolina State Archives, Raleigh); *South-Atlantic* 3 (1878); *Transactions of the Medical Society of North Carolina* (1930); John H. Wheeler, ed., *Historical Sketches of North Carolina from 1584 to 1851* (1851) and *Reminiscences and Memoirs of North Carolina and Eminent North Carolinians* (1884).

W. CONARD GASS

Hunter, Ezekiel (*d. 1773*), Baptist minister and legislator, served in the Onslow County Regiment of militia during the French and Indian War in 1754 and represented Onslow County in the North Carolina House of Commons in 1773. Although nothing of his parentage is presently known, he was not the son of Nicholas Hunter as George Paschal supposed.

Hunter appears to have been ordained about 1758, when he became pastor of the New River congregation. He is reported to have organized and pastored Baptist congregations in Onslow, Jones, Duplin, Brunswick, Bladen, Carteret, and New Hanover counties. His missionary zeal is credited with the early growth of the Baptist denomination in southeastern North Carolina. Hunter was identified with the Separate Baptists.

His will was made on 10 Nov. 1773, and he apparently died shortly afterwards. Hunter was survived by his wife, Rachel, and four minor children: Lena, Mary, Asa, and Ezekiel, Jr.

SEE: Burkitt and Read, *History of the Kehukee Baptist Association*; Hassell, *History of the Church of God*; George Washington Paschal, *History of North Carolina Baptists,* vol. 1 (1930).

TUCKER REED LITTLETON

Hunter, Hiram Tyram (*26 Mar. 1883–9 Oct. 1947*), educator and college president, was born at Mars Hill, the son of James Hardy and Martha Carolina Bradley Hunter. After attending elementary and secondary schools in Mars Hill, he was graduated from Mars Hill College high school division in 1908. In 1912 he received the B.A. degree from Wake Forest College.

Hunter served as president of Southside Institute, Chase City, Va. (1912–14); headed the Department of English at Woman's College (now Westhampton College of the University of Richmond), Richmond, Va. (1914–16); and did graduate study at Teachers College, Columbia University, New York City (1916–17), where he earned the M.A. degree in 1917. From 1917 to 1919 he was associate professor of education and head of the department of education at Southern Methodist University, Dallas, Tex. The following year he was professor of education at Baylor University, Waco, Tex. In the early summer of 1920 he went to Wake Forest College to direct its summer school and serve as professor of education.

After receiving the master of education degree from Harvard University in June 1922, he spent the summer as assistant dean of Harvard's Graduate School of Education and in the fall returned to Wake Forest for one year. In 1923 Hunter became president of Western Carolina Teachers College (now Western Carolina University), Cullowhee, serving until his death twenty-four years later.

An aggressive advocate of improved training for public school teachers, Hunter designed a program emphasizing the liberal arts as the basis of professional education. He was a member of the National Education Association, the American Association of School Administrators, and the North Carolina Education Association. While at Harvard, he was initiated into Phi Delta Kappa. In 1942 Wake Forest College awarded him the honorary degree of doctor of education.

Hunter was an active Baptist layman and a member of the Cullowhee Church. He was a charter member of the Rotary Club of Sylva, onetime president, and governor of District 190 of Rotary International (1941–42). He died at his home in Cullowhee at age sixty-four and was buried in the Cullowhee Cemetery.

SEE: R. D. W. Connor, *North Carolina Biography* (1919); John R. Logan, *Sketches, Historical and Biographical, of the Broad River and King's Mountain Baptist Association,* 1800–1882; John S. Ramond, *Among Southern Baptists* (1936); *Who Was Who in America,* vol. 2 (1950).

C. SYLVESTER GREEN

Hunter, Isaac (*ca. 1745–19 Mar. 1823*), planter, was probably the son of Theophilus Hunter, although the place of his birth and the name of his mother have not been recorded. He was first known to be in present Wake County when he acted as a chain bearer for the survey of 584 acres of land north of Crabtree Creek for which Theophilus Hunter had made application to Earl Granville. The land was granted to Theophilus on 21 July 1761, and he deeded the property to Isaac for £12 convention money on 3 Mar. 1762. Seven years later, on 28 Feb. 1769, Isaac Hunter was authorized by the Johnston County Court to open a tavern at his dwelling house.

Hunter acquired large tracts of land in the vicinity of and north of Crabtree Creek, including a mill site from John Giles Thomas which was later sold to Durrell Rogers, Hunter's son-in-law. Another mill site near where Crabtree Creek empties into the Neuse River was sold to Joseph Gales, who converted it into a paper mill.

Hunter's tavern was located on the Cross Creek to Petersburg stage road, and evidently was a well known and popular stopping place. In 1788, when the Hillsborough Convention was held to consider the ratification of the United States Constitution, it was also to fix the unalterable seat of government of the state. After it was determined that the convention would not select a particular point but would leave the choice to the General Assembly, provided that it be within ten miles of the place named, seven locations were nominated, including that of Isaac Hunter in Wake County, proposed by James Iredell. On the second ballot, Hunter's tavern was named as the place within ten miles of which the permanent capital of the state was to be located.

The commission chosen by the General Assembly to select the actual site of the capital met at Hunter's house on 22 Mar. 1792. He apparently hoped to sell a site to the state for the permanent capital, but the commission almost immediately adjourned to the house of Colonel Joel Lane, although its members viewed Hunter's land with other sites the next day. The state, however, bought 1,000 acres from Lane. Hunter eventually sold the tavern property to William Camp, the first husband of his daughter, Elizabeth.

Although Hunter had had extensive landholdings in Wake County, he began to dispose of them, apparently to meet his debts and expenses. In 1800, for example, he traded 627 acres to James House of Franklin County for a stud horse named Rufus. By 1822, his property was reduced to 650 acres and two slaves.

Family tradition indicates that Hunter was married twice, but this fact cannot be documented. By his first wife, Rebecca Hart, Hunter had seven children: Jacob, David, Alexander, Michael, Pherebee, Delilah, and Rebecca. By his second, Charlotte Thomas, he fathered Anderson, Norfleet, Elizabeth, Louise, Charlotte, and Frances. He was survived only by his sons Norfleet and Michael and by his daughter, Elizabeth Rogers.

At the time of his death, Hunter had a reputation for intemperance, which apparently contributed to his death. He was heavily in debt when he died, and by 1825 his remaining property was sold to settle his accounts.

SEE: Willis Briggs Papers, Granville Land Grants, Johnston County Deeds, Minutes of the Johnston County Court of Pleas and Quarter Sessions, Report of Commission Establishing Capital in Secretary of State Papers, Wake County Deeds (North Carolina State Archives, Raleigh); Walter Clark, ed., *State Records of North Carolina*, vols. 19, 21 (1901, 1903); Recollections of Joseph and Winifred Gales, David L. Swain Papers (Southern Historical Collection, University of North Carolina Library, Chapel Hill).

THORNTON W. MITCHELL

Hunter, James (*ca. 1735–ca. 1783*), leader of the Regulator movement, was born of Scotch-Irish ancestry probably in Pennsylvania. Tradition has him the son of James, Sr., but his mother was the former "widow Ann Hunter" who in 1755 purchased land of her son-in-law, Gilbert Strayhorn, in Orange County. Strayhorn family records pertaining to New Hope Presbyterian Church, Orange County, note that James Hunter moved to the county as a young man, possibly some years before his mother bought her land there. On 11 May 1757 he was granted 200 acres of land in what was then western Orange County, and in January 1779 he and James Low acquired 640 additional acres adjacent to or near the first grant.

Court minutes of the county indicate that Hunter was active in local affairs and seemed to be better educated than the average person. He early assumed a position of leadership in the Regulator movement through which many people in the backcountry sought to gain more influence in local government. Hunter is credited with having helped to draft some of the Regulator "Advertisements" and petitions. Such petitions to Governor William Tryon seem to have had no effect, and the Regulators believed that their chief opponent was Edmund Fanning, register of deeds and superior court judge in Orange County and holder of other offices. He was a close friend of Governor Tryon.

At each step of the Regulator movement, Hunter took an active part. His signature appears on most of the petitions, and he was entrusted to deliver several of them. In March 1768, after peaceful measures had failed, the Regulators warned officials that future taxes would be collected at the risk of the sheriff's life. The warning was ignored, and a farmer's mare, with saddle and bridle, was seized for unpaid taxes. In response, a party of Regulators proceeded to Hillsborough, the county seat, and "rescued" the mare; they also fired some shots into Colonel Fanning's house. Further incidents occurred after Regulator leaders Herman Husband and William Butler were arrested and charged with inciting the people to riot.

Petitions to the governor failed to bring relief. Although Regulators were elected to the Assembly, they were unable to secure passage of desired legislation—in part, because members of the Assembly were beginning to support early steps that led to the American Revolution. As a result the governor dissolved the legislature. The courts, it seemed, also failed the Regulators when the judges found Fanning guilty of charges of corruption but failed to punish him. When the Regulators broke up one session of court and threatened to repeat such action, the governor called out the militia to restore order in Orange County and elsewhere in the backcountry.

Matters came to a head in the spring of 1771, when Tryon led the militia of some 1,400 men to a site west of Hillsborough where a large number of Regulators were encamped. The Regulators requested a conference with the governor, but he refused as long as they were armed. He would, however, confer with a delegation if the remainder laid down their weapons, and he gave them one hour to reply. At the end of the hour, the governor sent a messenger to seek their answer and to tell them that if they did not respond he would order his force to fire. About this time a few of the Regulator leaders, including the Quaker Herman Husband, left the scene. James Hunter was asked to assume leadership, but he refused with the traditional response that "they were all free men and every one must command himself." Hunter, nevertheless, somehow came to be called "the general of the Regulation."

At the Battle of Alamance, which followed, the absence of a military leader made the outcome of the engagement predictable in favor of Tryon's militia. Twenty Regulators were killed, many were wounded, and twelve were captured, six of whom were later hanged. Tryon's casualties were nine killed and some sixty wounded.

Even though Hunter did not regard himself as a military leader, he was a natural leader among his friends and neighbors. After the Battle of Alamance, Governor Tryon issued a proclamation outlawing him and the other Regulator leaders. Almost a year later, after Tryon had become governor of New York and Josiah Martin had become governor of North Carolina, Hunter was permitted to return to his home and family. Petitions for his pardon, submitted to the governor by his friends and neighbors, show the esteem in which he was held.

The Regulator effort cost Hunter dearly. His plantation was laid waste by Tryon after the battle. As a condition of pardon, he was obliged to take an oath of allegiance to the Crown. Then as events proceeded swiftly into the conflict between America and Great Britain, a new test came. Because he could not in good conscience repudiate his solemn oath, he found himself classified as a Tory. In February 1776, Governor Martin issued a call to the Regulators and Scottish Highlanders to "raise the King's Standard" at Cross Creek on the Cape Fear to repel the "Rebels." Those Regulators called out from the newly formed Guilford County, in which his property now lay, included James Hunter and his brother-in-law, Robert Fields, and Robert's brothers, William and Jeremiah. They all participated in the Battle of Moores Creek, a Patriot victory. The Fields brothers were captured, as was James Low, the man who entered for the land grant with Hunter and who is believed to have been his brother-in-law. Although not apprehended at the scene of the battle, Hunter was subsequently arrested. A few months later he was paroled after taking the oath of allegiance to the new government.

Afterwards it became necessary for Hunter to mortgage his property. It also appears that his health was broken, and he died sometime between October 1779 and February 1783 when his widow Mary was given administration of his estate.

Although no record survives of the marriage of the Regulator, James Hunter, to Mary Walker, the will of Samuel Walker, dated 1773 and probated in 1783, names his sons-in-law, James Hunter and Robert Fields, as his executors. Genealogical research suggests that Hunter's five children were Martha (m. Aaron Hill), Samuel (m. Lydia Deviney), Marion (m. Alexander Strain), Mary (m. William Strayhorn), and James, Jr. (m. Margaret Phipps). James, Jr., and Samuel later moved to Clinton County, Ill., whereas their descendants moved to Texas and the Far West.

SEE: James W. Albright, *History of Greensboro* (1904); Vearl G. Alger, "The Case for James Hunter of Stinking Quarter and Sandy Creek: Regulator Leader, 1765–1771," *North Carolina Genealogical Society Journal* 3 (1977); E. W. Caruthers, *A Sketch of the Life and Character of the Rev. David Caldwell* (1842); D. I. Craig, *Historical Sketch of New Hope Church in Orange County, N.C.* (1891); Granville Land Grants, Records of Guilford, Orange, and Randolph Counties (North Carolina State Archives, Raleigh); Walter M. Hunter, *The Hunters of Bedford County, Virginia* (1972); Hugh T. Lefler and Paul W. Wager, eds., *History of Orange County, 1752–1952* (1953); William S. Powell, James K. Huhta, and Thomas J. Farnham, eds., *The Regulators of North Carolina: A Documentary History, 1759–1776* (1971); William L. Saunders, ed., *Colonial Records of North Carolina*, vols. 7–10 (1890); Sallie W. Stockard, *History of Guilford County* (1902).

VEARL G. ALGER

Hunter, James (8 Apr. 1740–30 Jan. 1821), soldier and legislator, was born six miles above Easton, Pa., in the forks of the Delaware River, the son of Alexander and Elizabeth Hunter. His father was a native of County Antrim, Ireland. In about 1754, James moved with his family to Bedford County, Va., where in 1762 he married Mary McFarland (1743–1821) who was also of Scotch-Irish descent. Moving to North Carolina at the same time as the Hunters were the McFarlands and the Martins. One of James's cousins was Alexander Martin, later governor of North Carolina.

Hunter acquired extensive land on Wreck Island Creek near his father, and all deeds until 1772 list him as living in Bedford County, Va.; in that year, he acquired land on Beaver Island Creek in what became Rockingham County, N.C. In 1778 he was elected to represent Guilford County in the General Assembly and he continued to serve until 1782. In January 1781, as the armies of generals Nathanael Greene and Charles Cornwallis maneuvered prior to the Battle of Guilford Court House, Colonel James Martin was ordered to call out the Guilford militia. James Hunter was a major in the county militia, and he participated in the battle with this unit which was commanded by his cousin, James Martin. Tradition relates that Hunter was selected to carry the official news of the battle to General George Washington. He remained on active duty for the rest of the year and took part in the occupation of Wilmington after the British evacuation.

In 1782 Hunter was selected by the legislature to be auditor for the Salisbury District. He also served Guilford County as treasurer, sheriff, and presiding justice. In 1785, when the county was divided, he became justice of the peace for the new county of Rockingham. Two years later he was commissioned lieutenant colonel of the county militia. Between 1790 and 1792 he was justice of the Salisbury District and in the latter year became chairman of the Rockingham County court.

Hunter was a Presbyterian and a Federalist, although not politically active after about 1792. About two miles south of his residence on Beaver Island Creek he erected a large meeting house for the use of any ministers whose theology did not conflict with his Presbyterian concepts. At his death he was buried on the hill above his house where his wife was also buried at her death less than a month later. Their ten children were Mary McFarland (m. William Deering), twins John and James, Alexander, Rachel (m. Nicholas Dalton), Samuel, Elizabeth, Robert, Pleasant, and Nancy.

SEE: John L. Cheney, Jr., ed., *North Carolina Government, 1585–1974* (1975); Robert Hunter Dalton, "A Brief History of the Dalton Family and the Hunters," a manuscript prepared in Neosho, Mo., 1878; *Early Families of the North Carolina Counties of Rockingham and Stokes, with Revolutionary Service* (1977); Walter M. Hunter, *The Hunt-*

ers of Bedford County, Virginia (1972); Rockingham County Deeds (North Carolina State Archives, Raleigh).

ELMER D. JOHNSON
CHARLES D. RODENBOUGH

Hunter, James (16 May 1767–5 Dec. 1831), pioneer Methodist minister and leader in the establishment of the Methodist Protestant church in North Carolina in the 1820s, was born in Virginia. As a young man, he moved to Halifax County, where he was received into the Methodist Episcopal church in 1792. On 14 Dec. 1797 he married Martha Elizabeth Crowell, and in 1810 he was "located" as a Methodist minister. Hunter early became identified with the movement in his area for more liberal principles in church government, and he actively supported *The Wesleyan Repository*, a reform periodical published in Baltimore.

Hunter was present at the first meeting of the Roanoke Union Society on 6 Nov. 1824, which met at Sampson's Meeting House in Halifax County. At the second session of the society, held later that month, he was elected secretary pro tem. In April 1828 he was summoned to trial for his membership in the Roanoke Union Society and for patronizing *The Mutual Rights*, a periodical that strongly advocated structural changes in the government of the Methodist Episcopal church. On 19–20 Dec. 1828, Hunter attended the organizational meeting of the North Carolina Annual Conference of the Methodist Protestant church at Whitaker's Chapel near Enfield. He and the Reverend Henry Bradford were assigned to serve the historic old Roanoke Circuit in 1829.

During some forty years as a Methodist minister, Hunter served as a traveling preacher, presiding elder, and member of the General Conference.

SEE: Nathan Bangs, *History of the Methodist Episcopal Church*, vol. 3 (1840); John Paris, *History of the Methodist Protestant Church* (1849).

RALPH HARDEE RIVES

Hunter, Theophilus (before 1727–98), colonial officer, Revolutionary leader, justice, early Wake County planter, and member of the North Carolina Assembly, was born in Nansemond County, Va., but settled in present Wake County, N.C., before 1752. His father, Isaac Hunter, was the son of Nicholas and the grandson of William Hunter of Nansemond County. His mother, Sarah Hill Hunter, was the daughter of Abraham and Sarah Pugh Hill. Nicholas Hunter moved to northeastern North Carolina and settled in Northampton County.

Between 1752 and 1761 Theophilus Hunter obtained over 2,000 acres in grants in the Granville district of what was then Johnston County, and by 1771 he had extensive holdings south of Crabtree Creek including Rocky Branch and Walnut Creek. His residence, Hunter's Lodge, was about four miles south of the present city of Raleigh on the Fayetteville stagecoach road and was one of the earliest homes in the area.

By 1759 Hunter was a justice of the peace in Johnston County and in that year was on the committee to lay out ground for a courthouse at Hinton's Quarter, near present Clayton, where in 1760 he and the other justices held court. In 1761 he was on a commission to run the boundary line between Orange and Johnston counties.

Wake County was created by the legislature on 27 Dec. 1770 to be effective 12 Mar. 1771. By this act, Hunter was named one of the commissioners to lay off land on which to erect a courthouse, jail, and stocks, as well as one of the commissioners to contract with workmen to erect the buildings. He was also on the commission to run the line between Wake, Johnston, Cumberland, and Orange counties as specified by the act to create Wake County.

When Governor William Tryon marched against the Regulators in the spring of 1771, he made his headquarters during 5–8 May at Hunter's Lodge, and when the colonial militia marched back after the Battle of Alamance, the Wake County regiment was disbanded at Hunter's Lodge.

On 4 June 1771, when the first Court of Pleas and Quarter Sessions for the new county was held, Hunter was the presiding judge. He continued as a justice of this court throughout the colonial period and was elected to the same position by the Halifax Provincial Congress on 23 Dec. 1776. A major in the Wake County regiment of colonial militia, Hunter was made a lieutenant colonel by the Provincial Congress on 22 Apr. 1776. On the nineteenth he had been made a member of a committee to secure arms and ammunition for the Continental Army.

Hunter was a delegate from Wake County to the Provincial Congress at Hillsborough in 1775, and in 1783 he represented the county in the North Carolina House of Commons. In 1778, he became surveyor for Wake County and served on a committee to contract with workmen to build a new courthouse in Hillsborough. After the creation of Raleigh as the state capital was authorized by an ordinance in 1789, a tract of Hunter's land was offered as a possible site. When his land was not chosen, Hunter purchased four lots in the new capital. In 1793 he and James Bloodworth deeded the property to Wake County on which the present courthouse is located. He also donated a lot on the corner of Dawson and Morgan streets for a Masonic lodge.

The U.S. census of 1790 indicates that Hunter was the second largest slaveholder in the county. Sometime between 1771 and 1798 Hunter's Lodge burned, and Theophilus and his family moved to Spring Hill plantation. Here his land stretched from Walnut Creek in Raleigh almost to the site of Cary, and his home was situated on one of the most beautiful knolls in the county. The original part of Spring Hill built by Hunter has been demolished, but the larger part added by Theophilus, Jr., still stands on the grounds of Dorothea Dix Hospital. In 1940 the Caswell-Nash Chapter of the Daughters of the American Revolution erected a monument to Hunter near the house.

The name of Hunter's first wife is not known, but she was the mother of Delilah and Isaac. His second wife, Jane Smith Williams (widow of Joel Williams of Johnston County), was the mother of Edith, Irene, Mary (Polly), Theophilus, Jr., Osborn, and Henry. Hunter's sons and daughters married into other prominent Wake County families. Theophilus Hunter Hill, who published volumes of poetry in 1861, 1869, and 1883, was a descendant.

Hunter's will was registered in Wake County on 15 July 1798.

SEE: M. N. Amis, *Historical Raleigh* (1913); Samuel A. Ashe, ed., *Biographical History of North Carolina*, vol. 4 (1905); Walter Clark, ed., *State Records of North Carolina*, vols. 19, 23, 24 (1901, 1904, 1905); Johnston County Court Minutes (North Carolina State Archives, Raleigh); *Literary and Historical Activities in North Carolina*, vol. 1 (1907); William L. Saunders, ed., *Colonial Records of North Carolina*, vols. 8–10 (1890); E. C. Waugh, *North Carolina's Capital, Raleigh* (1967).

MARY HINTON DUKE KERR
MARY BATES SHERWOOD

Hunter, Thomas (*ca. 1735–84*), Revolutionary patriot, was the son of Isaac Hunter of Northampton County. He first appears in the North Carolina records in 1761, when he purchased a tract of land in Northampton County called "the rich square." This was the site and origin of the present town of that name. About 1764 he married Priscilla Smith, the daughter of Drew Smith. In 1766 he sold his holdings in Northampton and began buying land in the Scotland Neck section of Halifax County. In 1770 he moved farther to what was then Edgecombe County and bought land on the north bank of Stoney Creek. This property was four miles west of the present city of Rocky Mount and is still known as Hunter's Hill.

From the first, Hunter was active in the Revolutionary movement. He represented Edgecombe in the First Provincial Congress held at New Bern on 21 Aug. 1775, and when the brigade of militia for Edgecombe was reorganized on 22 May 1776 he was appointed second major. In 1777, when Nash County was formed from western Edgecombe, Hunter was placed in charge of the militia of the new county with the rank of colonel. The following year he respresented Nash in the North Carolina House of Commons.

Little is known about Hunter's military service. The major duties of militia officers were to draft men and supplies for the Continental Army and to defend the home ground when under attack. In the state records are several letters from Colonel Hunter regarding military supplies, and in the Nashville Courthouse are records of several courts-martial at which he presided. No doubt he saw action in the spring of 1781, when Lord Cornwallis marched north from Wilmington on his way to Virginia and passed through Nash County. The militia tried unsuccessfully to impede the British advance in skirmishes at Swift and Fishing creeks. The arrival of the British gave impetus to a Tory uprising in the county. Colonel Seawell wrote: "Not a man of any distinction or scarcely any men of property has lain in his house since the British passed through Nash County."

Hunter did not long survive the war. He resigned as justice of the county court in 1784, and died intestate the same year. The inventory of his estate was dated 5 May 1787, with Micajah Thomas as administrator. According to the Nash County Registry, Hunter left sons Thomas, Cordial Norfleet, and Drew, and daughters Elizabeth and Polly, who married Loderick F. Ellin.

SEE: John B. Boddie, *Historical Southern Families*, vol. 7 (1963); Walter Clark, ed., *State Records of North Carolina*, vols. 22, 23, 24 (1907, 1904, 1905); Deeds and Wills of Northampton, Halifax, and Nash counties.

CLAIBORNE T. SMITH, JR.

Huntington, Roswell (*15 Mar. 1763–8 Sept. 1836*), Revolutionary silversmith in Hillsborough and founder of three generations of silversmiths, was born in Norwich, Conn., the son of Ebenezer, Jr. (1740–63), and Sarah Edgerton Huntington, and a descendant of Simon and Margaret Baret Huntington (fl. 1633). Before Roswell was a year old his father died in the West Indies, apparently late in 1763, at age twenty-three. Ebenezer's will was probated in Norwich in January 1764. On 15 June 1765, his widow married Joseph Gale.

On 5 Apr. 1769 the court in Norwich appointed Captain Daniel Throop, of Lebanon, Conn., a relative by marriage, as guardian of six-year-old Roswell, requiring a bond of £500. Before Roswell's majority, two later guardians were successively appointed, William Huntington of Lebanon in 1774 and Andrew Huntington, also of Lebanon, in 1777. Although there are discrepancies in the recorded dates of Roswell's brief military service, both he and his guardian William Huntington apparently enlisted in the Third Connecticut Regiment in early May 1775, and both were discharged on 16 Dec. 1775. The youthful Roswell is said to have participated in the defense of New London.

He was early apprenticed to Norwich silversmith Joseph Carpenter, and in 1784 at age twenty-one (when he had evidently inherited his legacy) advertised himself as a goldsmith and jeweler in Norwich opposite the store of his relative, General Jedediah Huntington. No signed specimens of his early Connecticut work appear to have been preserved.

The precise reasons for Huntington's relocation in the village of Hillsborough are unknown, but there is said to have been a distinct migratory strain or propensity discernible on his paternal side. It is also possible that there was some connection between the movements of Roswell and the Joseph Gale family.

On 3 Mar. 1785, the Orange County Court of Common Pleas and Quarter Sessions bound over to Roswell Huntington as an apprentice thirteen-year-old Francis Nash "to learn the art and Mistery of a silver and goldsmith." On 6 October, Huntington advertised in the North Carolina *Gazette* for a "Journeyman Goldsmith and Jeweller who is a good Workman. . . . [He] will meet with good encouragement and constant employ." At the 25 Aug. 1786 sale of confiscated property in Hillsborough, he purchased corner Lot 21 on West King Street, formerly the property of Edmund Fanning, for £501 which he almost certainly did not pay in cash. Although he kept the lot only fifteen months, Huntington appears to have acquired or rented farmland in the old Quaker community on the Eno River near Maddock's and Low's Mills, to have held another Hillsborough lot (91) briefly, and to have acquired at least a dozen slaves. It has not been determined, however, where his first silversmith's shop was located in Hillsborough.

In 1789 Huntington was paid £5 as one of the nine members of the Orange Company of Horse selected to guard the North Carolina Treasury's money being transferred from the temporary State Treasury (the old Blue House) in Hillsborough to Fayette or Fayetteville. The same year he married (date of bond, 12 October) Mary (May) Palmer, daughter of carpenter and planter Martin Palmer and Priscilla Bivens (or Bivins) Palmer, said to have been the daughter of one Captain Bivens, an itinerant sea captain. Roswell and his wife had seven children: Sarah, William, Martin Palmer, Priscilla, Nancy, Elizabeth, and John, and the three sons were all trained as silversmiths in their father's shop. Although there are various links between the Huntington family and the Eno Meeting of Friends, there appears to be no proof that either the Huntingtons or the Palmers were Quakers.

In 1792, at age twenty-nine, Huntington was commissioned to engrave a bronze plate or plaque to be placed in the cornerstone of Old East, the first building to be constructed on the new University of North Carolina campus and now a National Historic Landmark. A

Latin inscription was engraved in flowing letters on one side of the plate with its English translation on the other, and the whole was signed "R. Huntington, Sculp." The cornerstone was set with due Masonic ceremony on 12 Oct. 1793. This is one of the few identified pieces of Huntington's work, and it is in bronze, not gold or silver. It seems, in fact, likely that he may also have done considerable work as a brazier, for in 1820 he advertised in the *Hillsborough Recorder* for some weeks for "Clean old brass." The historic Huntington plate was removed from the Old East cornerstone during Reconstruction and turned up years later in a pile of scrap metal in a Clarksville, Tenn., foundry, the owner of which formally restored it to the university on 12 Oct. 1916.

Recently, two graceful teaspoons (part of a set of six), bearing the mark "R. H.," have come to light. These carry the initials "J. H." on the front and were apparently made about 1805 for John Holden, Sr. (1764–1842), a well-to-do planter of the St. Mary's Chapel community near Hillsborough. According to Holden family tradition, the spoons were made from John Holden's silver buckles worn on his knee breeches and shoes. A teaspoon in an Oxford collection, bearing the mark "Huntington," may also be Roswell's work. Signed Roswell Huntington silver appears to be extremely rare.

There are few mentions of Huntington in Hillsborough after 1820. It seems certain that his wife, May Palmer Huntington, died between 1831 and 1833, and it is likely that she was buried near her parents in a grave marked only by rough stones in the rock-walled Quaker Cemetery northeast of Hillsborough. In December 1833, the seventy-year-old Huntington, accompanied by four of his children—William, Sarah (a widow), Elizabeth, and Priscilla—migrated to Marion, Perry County, Ala., as part of the considerable movement southward of Hillsborough residents in the 1830s. His youngest son, John, also migrated to the South in 1837 and settled finally at Pontotec, Miss.

Roswell Huntington lived only three years in his new home. He died suddenly, as his obituary in the Milton (N.C.) *Spectator* of 27 Sept. 1836 stated, "of rheumatism of the chest . . . he was greatly esteemed . . . for his amiable disposition and willingness to perform acts of kindness." He was buried in the Marion Cemetery where his tombstone inscription, composed by his grandson, describes him as "a soldier of the Revolution . . . upright and honest in all the relations of life." It is possible that two unidentified oil portraits belonging to the Huntington family are likenesses of Roswell and his wife.

The Huntington-trained group of silversmiths may be said to have included nine craftsmen: Roswell and his three sons, William, Martin Palmer, and John; William's son, William Henry; and the Huntingtons' Hillsborough apprentice, Lemuel Lynch, and Lynch's three sons, Thomas M., Lemuel George, and Seaborn, Jr., the latter known as an "intermittent" silversmith.

SEE: Walter Clark, ed., *State Records of North Carolina*, vols. 21, 22 (1903, 1907); George Barton Cutten, *Silversmiths of North Carolina, 1696–1850* (1948); *Hillsborough Recorder*, 15 Oct. 1820, 8 Jan. 1833; William Johnston Hogan, "Three Generations of Huntington Silversmiths, 1763–1885" (MS, Keysville, Va.); E. B. Huntington, *A Genealogical Memoir of the Huntington Family in This Country* . . . (1863), rev. as *The Huntington Family in America, A Genealogical Memoir of the Known Descendants of Simon Huntington from 1633 to 1915* (1915); Milton

Spectator, 27 Sept. 1836; North Carolina *Gazette*, 6 Oct. 1785; Orange County *Deed Books* 3, 8, 30, 32, 54, Orange County *Marriage Bonds*, Orange County *Will Book* A (Orange County Courthouse, Hillsborough); "The Presentation of the Plate," University of North Carolina *Alumni Review*, vol. 5 (November 1916); Tombstone inscriptions, Marion, Ala., Cemetery.

MARY CLAIRE ENGSTROM

Huntington, William (*8 Sept. 1792–27 Oct. 1874*), Hillsborough silversmith and engraver, Presbyterian churchman, and businessman, was born in Hillsborough, the oldest of three sons of silversmith Roswell Huntington, a native of Connecticut, and his wife Mary (May) Palmer; all three sons were trained as silversmiths in their father's Hillsborough shop. Nothing further is known of William's early education, but the quality of his surviving letters, poems, and inscriptions suggests careful schooling possibly received in the Hillsborough Academy.

By December 1815, at age twenty-three, William had set up his own silversmith's shop in Hillsborough "next door above David Yarbrough & Co.'s store" and advertised that he was ready to execute work "in the most faithful and fashionable manner and upon the shortest notice." On 27 May 1819, he formally joined the new Hillsborough Presbyterian Church of which the Reverend John Knox Witherspoon was the youthful first pastor, and there began one of the great and enduring spiritual experiences of his life. He served until 1833 as stated clerk, ruling elder, and church treasurer, and scores of numbered vouchers survive in his exquisitely neat copperplate handwriting.

On 9 Dec. 1819 Huntington married Frances Robeson Howze (28 Dec. 1802–9 July 1877), of Franklin County, the daughter of John and Patsy Yarbrough Howze, and began a long married life of remarkable felicity.

In the 1820s William and his two brothers, Martin Palmer and John, formed various short-lived partnerships to operate jeweler's and silversmith's shops in the neighboring towns of Milton, Oxford, Salisbury, and Charlotte. Beginning in 1819, William appears to have been a silent partner in the Milton firm of Martin Palmer Huntington & Co.; in 1824 he joined his younger brother John in a similar venture in Oxford. John then briefly joined Robert Wynne in Salisbury in 1827, and in 1828–32 was the partner of the Virginia-born silversmith, Thomas Trotter, in Charlotte. In 1834 he returned to Hillsborough to work with the Huntingtons' apprentice, Lemuel Lynch.

Survived signed pieces of William Huntington silver from the Hillsborough period, bearing the mark "W. H.," indicate that he had a fair amount of custom in his native town and its environs. Extant teaspoons, tablespoons, large serving spoons, cream ladles, and punch ladles—either in private collections or museums—are all graceful, strong pieces with initials and sometimes dates flowingly inscribed, as on Nancy Cabe Latta's second set of wedding silver on the occasion of her 6 Nov. 1820 marriage to Major Robert Donnell. Miss Mary W. ("Polly") Burke, William's lifelong friend, is known to have given small (5½-inch) "W. H." spoons as annual merit prizes at her day school on East Queen Street in Hillsborough; and the Strudwicks, Moores, Waddells, Webbs, Hollemans, and other old Orange County families all ordered Huntington silver for special family occasions. Possibly the outstanding surviving "W. H." piece from the Hillsborough period is a magnificent cream ladle with a unique twisted handle (ca. 1830) now in a private collection.

During these years Huntington also undertook a variety of other business ventures. He early formed a brief partnership with local merchant John Van Hook, Jr., he advertised that he would engrave tombstones "in a handsome manner" (but none bearing his stonecutter's mark has as yet been found in Orange County), he opened a blacksmith's shop in Hillsborough opposite his silversmith's shop, he invested in farmlands northwest of Hillsborough and in town lots (land speculation, in fact, appears to have been in his blood), and he even embarked on a business partnership in Pittsboro, Chatham County, at the same time he was operating a Hillsborough general store in which he sold "Family Flour" and sundry patent medicines. From 1829 to 1833 he reopened the silversmith's shop, which had been closed briefly, in his own home just east of the new Masonic Hall on West King Street. He also served as town commissioner of Hillsborough for twelve years (1821–33) and as a manager of the Orange County Sunday School Union for over a decade.

In December 1833, Huntington and his family and three of his four sisters accompanied their aging father to a new home in Marion, Perry County, Ala., where William set up shop on the same lot where his stone dwelling house stood. His second son, William Henry (the only one of the Huntingtons' seven sons to survive the parents), worked with him as apprentice and partner. Preserved Alabama pieces carry either the mark "W. H." or "W. H. & Son."

Many of these later works are special gift pieces with handsomely engraved presentation inscriptions, such as "Grand Parents to Fannie" on six tablespoons made for William Henry's daughter, Fannie Huntington. Extant silver of the Alabama period includes a dozen tablespoons, a baby cup, and a sugar shell. Notable later gift pieces were two massive gold finger rings, apparently William's last work, both made to send back to his native Orange County. On one, designed in 1869 for Mrs. Cornelia Phillips Spencer of Chapel Hill, were engraved these words inside the heavy plain gold band: "In memory of the University of N.C. as it was. Caldwell, Phillips, Mitchell, Hooper, Swain. A tribute to Mrs. Cornelia P. Spencer." The ring is now thought to have been buried with Mrs. Spencer. The other similar ring, sent to William A. Graham of Hillsborough in March 1874, had the names "Clay, Calhoun, and Daniel Webster" engraved on the inside band. The *Hillsborough Recorder* of 25 Mar. 1874 noted, "The remarkable feature is that Mr. Huntington made the ring and executed the engraving at the age of eighty-one years."

A gentle man of sentiment and sensibility with a marked poetic strain, William Huntington invariably celebrated the passing years, birthdays, his golden wedding anniversary, and so forth with original poems and inscriptions beautifully copied and sent on stiff cards to friends and relatives. For thirty-five years he served as ruling elder and stated clerk in the Marion Presbyterian Church, and his fugitive poetry reflects his lifelong devotion to "the doctrines, order, and fellowship" of his church. He was buried in the Marion Cemetery. A picture of Huntington and his wife exists, as does an old set of silversmith's tools, found in a family desk, which may have been used by several Huntington silversmiths.

SEE: Hope Summerell Chamberlain, *Old Days in Chapel Hill* (1926); George Barton Cutten, *Silversmiths of North Carolina, 1696–1850* (1948), rev. by Mary Reynolds Pea-cock (1973); *Hillsborough Recorder*, 14 June 1820, 19 Sept. 1821, 27 May 1822, 29 Jan. 1823, 16 Dec. 1824, 28 May, 30 July, 10 Sept. 1828, 19 Aug. 1829, 8 Jan. 1833, 25 Mar., 18 Nov. 1874; William Johnston Hogan, "Three Generations of Huntington Silversmiths, 1763–1885" (MS, Keysville, Va.); Letters of William Huntington, Heartt-Wilson Papers, James Webb Papers (Southern Historical Collection, University of North Carolina Library, Chapel Hill); Marion (Ala.) *Standard*, 29 Sept. 1874; Raleigh *Register*, 27 Sept. 1816; Raleigh *Star*, 15 Dec. 1815; *Sessions Books* of the Hillsborough Presbyterian Church (1818–33, Hillsborough); James Webb Papers (North Carolina Division of Archives and History, Raleigh).

MARY CLAIRE ENGSTROM

Husband (or Husbands), Herman (or Hermon, Harman) (3 Oct. 1724–ca. June 1795), legislator, county official, planter, surveyor, miner, pamphleteer, and social radical, was born in Cecil County, Md., the son of William and Mary Husband, wealthy slave-owning planters and the parents of eleven or twelve children. His early education consisted of tutoring at or near the farm of his maternal Dutch grandfather, Herman Kinkey. Husband also read extensively throughout life. His probated inventory notes around eight hundred pamphlets and eighteen "Bound Books" in his estate.

Although his parents belonged to the Anglican church, Husband joined a New Side Presbyterian congregation after hearing evangelist George Whitefield in 1740. After quarreling with the congregation's elders, he joined the Society of Friends at East Nottingham. Husband wrote about his religious odyssey in a pamphlet entitled *Some Remarks on Religion* in 1750. By that year his first wife, whose last name may have been Cox, had died leaving three children. Also in 1750 he received lands in Cecil and Baltimore counties from his parents and traveled to Barbados. In 1751 he spent time in Bladen County, N.C. Back in Maryland, Husband served from 1752 to 1754 on numerous committees appointed by the Friends at East Nottingham to enforce discipline, and in 1753 as overseer of the Deer Creek Preparative Meeting in Baltimore County.

In the fall of 1754, Husband traveled through the backcountry of North Carolina as agent for a land company composed of farmers and artisans from Pennsylvania and Maryland. In the Granville District he looked over lands and met with settlers in Orange and Rowan counties. Acting on rumors of fraud, he went to Earl Granville's land office in Edenton and examined the records. He also petitioned Governor Arthur Dobbs and the Assembly, arguing against appropriations and legal sanctions for the Society for the Propagation of the Gospel. In 1755 Husband went back to Maryland but returned to North Carolina when he discovered that no member of the land company wanted to journey southward. He purchased two lots in Corbinton (later Hillsborough) on which he built a temporary residence. From 1755 to 1762 he acquired more than 10,000 acres in Orange and Rowan counties and moved to land along Sandy Creek.

Husband raised wheat, surveyed and sold land, and set up a public gristmill, but in 1759 he resettled in Maryland and managed the Fountain Copper Works in Frederick County. In 1762 he returned to Sandy Creek and married Mary Pugh, a member of the Cane Creek Monthly Meeting. She probably died before 1765. Husband participated in county government as an overseer of Sandy Creek in 1764 and on a road jury in 1765. In

January 1764, the Monthly Meeting disowned him as a result of a dispute over the society's discipline. The following year he married Amy ("Emey") Allen, nineteen years younger, who was also disowned for marrying out of unity.

Influenced by the Stamp Act protest, Husband and other Sandy Creek farmers formed an association in 1766 to seek a solution to civil corruption, but the organization collapsed due to official intimidation. He did not join the new reformers, the Regulators, in 1768, although he served as their spokesman and pamphleteer. In May 1768 Colonel Edmund Fanning and others seized Husband and William Butler and jailed them at Hillsborough as suspected organizers of the renewed "insurgency." After a crowd assembled near the town, Fanning released the prisoners. Husband also appeared in the Hillsborough Riots of September 1770, but his role remains unclear. He served as assemblyman for Orange County in 1769 and 1770 but was expelled during the latter session and imprisoned in New Bern for allegedly libeling Maurice Moore, Jr., for threatening the Assembly, and for initiating the revolt. He remained incarcerated until February 1771 before being acquitted by a grand jury. Husband wrote two defenses of himself and the Regulators, *An Impartial Relation of the First Rise and Cause of the Recent Differences in Publick Affairs* and *A Continuation of the Impartial Relation*, both in 1770.

Prior to the Battle of Alamance on 16 May 1771, Husband attempted to arrange a truce but left after negotiations collapsed. He then fled, a proscribed traitor, through Maryland into western Pennsylvania under the name "Toscape Death." Although his properties in North Carolina were confiscated, he began another estate in Bedford County, Pa., where his family settled in 1772. All Regulators and outlawed leaders except Husband were pardoned by Governor Josiah Martin in 1775.

Husband supported the American Revolution and the Pennsylvania Constitution of 1776. In September of that year the state convention appointed him to the Bedford County Board of Commissioners and Assessors, and in 1777–78 he represented his county in the legislature, publishing a paper money scheme and urging Quakers to support the state constitution. He also informed the state war board of the location of lead deposits that were mined for ammunition production.

In 1779 Husband believed he saw the New Jerusalem rising west of the Alleghenies. Until his death he mapped out the heavenly city according to the Book of Ezekiel and his own observations gathered on trips through the mountains. He also wrote about the coming of this western New Jerusalem, which he thought fulfilled God's plan to provide small farmers and artisans with land and political democracy. He composed pamphlets proposing alternatives to the federal Constitution and Secretary Alexander Hamilton's financial policies, offering a plan for peace with the Indians, and praising the French Revolution as the final stage before a republican millenium. Many of these ideas were also inserted in articles Husband wrote under the name "Allegheny Philosopher" for Andrew Ellicott's *Maryland and Virginia Almanack* from 1781 to 1792. In addition, Husband prepared designs for internal transportation improvements. His civil services included surveying Brunerstown (later Somerset), Pa., and serving as Bedford county commissioner (1786) and as state representative (1790).

From 1793 to 1795 Husband apparently participated as a moderate in the Whiskey Rebellion, a western Pennsylvania revolt against Secretary Hamilton's excise on whiskey. As a Bedford County delegate, he attended the meeting at Parkinson's Ferry in 1794 and served on a resolutions committee with Albert Gallatin, H. H. Brackenridge, and David Bradford. He was also appointed to committees that negotiated with state and federal commissioners. In 1795 federal troops arrested Husband and sent him with other rebels to stand trial in Philadelphia. He was acquitted and pardoned by President George Washington due to the intercession of Dr. Benjamin Rush, Dr. David Caldwell, and North Carolina senators Alexander Martin and Timothy Bloodworth. Husband died in a tavern outside Philadelphia, allegedly from an illness contracted in prison. His burial place is unknown. He was survived by his wife Amy and eight children.

SEE: William K. Boyd, ed., *Some Eighteenth Century Tracts Concerning North Carolina* (1927); *DAB*, vol. 10 (1946); A. Roger Ekirch, " 'A New Government of Liberty': Herman Husband's Vision of Backcountry North Carolina, 1755," *William and Mary Quarterly* 34 (October 1977); Andrew Ellicott, "Ellicott's *Maryland and Virginia Almanack* (1781–1792)," in Charles Evans, ed., *American Bibliography* (1903–4); Archibald Henderson, ed., "Hermon Husband's Continuation of the Impartial Relation," *North Carolina Historical Review* 18 (1941); Mary Elinor Lazenby Papers, 1933–55 (Darlington Memorial Library, University of Pittsburgh); Mark H. Jones, "Herman Husband: Millenarian, Carolina Regulator, and Whiskey Rebel" (Ph.D. diss., Northern Illinois University); James P. Whittenburg, " 'The Common Farmer (Number 2)': Herman Husband's Plan for Peace between the United States and the Indians, 1792," *William and Mary Quarterly* 34 (October 1977).

MARK H. JONES

Huse, Howard Russel (*20 July 1890–31 Mar. 1977*), college professor and scholar, was born in Omaha, Nebr., the son of Jesse Benjamin and Mary Wearne Huse. The family later moved to Chicago where he attended the local public schools. After a year's study at the University of Chicago, he went to Europe in 1909 and spent a year at the University of Dijon. Here young Huse developed an early admiration for French culture, to which he devoted much of his life. France became for him, as he wrote, "a second country and a second home."

Returning to Chicago in 1910, Huse resumed his studies at the university. In 1911 he was an interpreter for the stage manager of Sarah Bernhardt, the great French actress, during her American tour that year. When Huse received the Ph.D. degree from Chicago in 1913, the world was still open and free; the adventurous, willing to endure hardship, could roam at will without the restriction of passports and permits. Taking advantage of this opportunity, he circled the globe for a year before settling down. He shipped on freighters as a common seaman, taught school in the Philippines, sold hardware in Australia, and worked on the docks in London. These experiences later provided a special dimension to his perception of the world's great literature.

Huse began his academic career as assistant instructor at the University of Chicago (1914–16), then joined the faculty of Newcombe College, Tulane University, as assistant professor (1916–18). During World War I he entered the army as a private in the infantry, rising to the rank of second lieutenant. For a year after the war he was assistant U.S. trade commissioner in Athens and Constantinople.

In 1920 Huse accepted the position of assistant professor of romance languages at The University of North Carolina. After obtaining a second Ph.D. from his alma mater in 1930, he was promoted in 1931 to professor of French and Italian at Chapel Hill. For many years he served as the first acting chairman of the Curriculum of Comparative Literature and was for a time chairman of the Humanities Division in the university's College of Arts and Sciences. On his retirement in 1963, he was emeritus professor of French and Italian until his death.

As a teacher Huse was adept in correlating his knowledge of many other disciplines with the instruction of language and literature. In his classes, he instilled concepts relating to the basis of human existence along with the subject matter at hand. His favorite themes were a hearty skepticism for idealism and metaphysics, a respect for the fragile nature of civilization, and the importance of taste in the arts. In teaching French lyric poetry and French literature of the eighteenth century, he focused on the study of Dante's *Divine Comedy*. His learning and enthusiasm enabled several generations of students to share the wonder of that triumph of the human spirit.

Huse was the author of *Essentials of Written and Spoken French* (1928), a grammar; *Psychology of Foreign Language Study* (1931); *The Illiteracy of the Literate* (1933), a brilliantly written text presenting wise counsel about language; and *Reading and Speaking Foreign Languages* (1945). His final book, published in 1954, offered a new prose translation of the *Divine Comedy*. The translation was widely used in colleges and universities throughout the United States and Canada. At the time of his death, Huse was working on a prose translation of the *Fables of La Fontaine*. In addition to these volumes, he edited *Contes et Recits*, a collection of French literature, and wrote many articles on various subjects and authors, particularly Anatole France and Jean Jacques Rousseau.

In 1920 Huse married Charlotte Vulliemoz, a native of France. They were the parents of two children, Henri and Mary Louise. In 1946 he married Mary Kathleen Martin but had no children by his second wife. He died at age eighty-seven at Duke Hospital, Durham.

SEE: *Chapel Hill Weekly*, 3 Apr. 1977; Alfred G. Engstrom, Address at the Memorial Service for Dr. Huse, University of North Carolina, 4 Apr. 1977; Claiborne T. Smith, Jr., personal recollections; *Who's Who in America* (1964–65).

CLAIBORNE T. SMITH, JR.

Huske, John (d. May[?] 1792), early state and local official, and merchant, may have been related to British Major General John Huske (1692[?]–1761), some of whose family settled in New England. The younger John Huske, a native of Hull, Yorkshire, came to North Carolina alone, apparently arriving in the late 1770s as a merchant. He had been in Europe and the West Indies, could read French, wrote a fine hand, and could keep financial records. He was first mentioned as being in the state in 1781 when he was at Sampson Hall, Duplin County, with a great many other refugees from Wilmington who had left or been driven out by the British when they took the town on 1 February. His business and possessions were lost at that time. Huske and Thomas Maclaine, brother of Archibald Maclaine, were reported to have been the only two inhabitants of Wil-

mington who "refused to sign a petition to be admitted to a dependence upon Great Britain."

William Hooper, writing to Governor Thomas Burke on 17 July 1781, referred to Huske as "the young gentleman whom I mentioned to you as very well qualified to fill the department of a Secretary." Huske, who lived in Hooper's home for a time, was described to the governor as "a gentleman of the most refined honor and unspoiled integrity." As he was seeking "some genteel employment that may support him and keep his mind employed," he was recommended as ideal to serve as the governor's private secretary or as secretary to the Council because James Glasgow, the present secretary, lived too far away to attend the frequent Council meetings. Even if the two offices were combined, Hooper said, "I know no one who would discharge the trust with more reputation."

Bearing newspapers and other sources of information for the governor, Huske went to Hillsborough and there on 2 August was made the secretary. He performed such official duties as signing the commissions of the state's delegates to the Continental Congress on 13 Aug. 1781. He and other members of the executive staff were with Governor Burke on the morning of 13 September when Tories under the command of David Fanning raided Hillsborough. Following an armed encounter, Fanning took them prisoner and set off for Wilmington to turn them over to Major Craig. From there they were sent to Charleston, S.C., and closely confined for a time; in December some, including Huske, were paroled and permitted to return home. Burke, however, was held until he escaped on 16 Jan. 1782. In time Huske applied to the Assembly for his salary and reimbursement of his expenses while a captive of the British. He received £150.

Huske was in Edenton on occasion and was on friendly terms with the people there, particularly James Iredell, perhaps largely through William Hooper. In 1783 he was a member of a commission to regulate pilots on the Cape Fear River and was among the men who chose the site for a lighthouse on Smith Island. He also served on a committee named in 1784 to build a jail in Wilmington, on a committee to seek bequests and donations to build a Presbyterian church in the town, and as a trustee of Innes Academy. In 1787, as Captain Huske, he commanded the Wilmington artillery company. He was one of the justices of New Hanover County between 1784 and 1790 when he resigned, and he was clerk of court in 1785. His health was not good and in 1790, in seeking a place near the sea to improve it, he visited Fort Johnston and suggested that plans be made to lay out an adjacent town. About the time of Huske's death, the present town of Southport began to develop there.

Exactly what Huske did during the final years of the Revolution is not clear, but apparently as an attorney-in-fact he represented some Loyalists in their claims for land in 1783. In the spring of that year, at a heated election in Wilmington, it was reported that many people were afraid to go to the polls. Huske and two other men took up positions to see that no one eligible to vote was hindered from doing so. In another instance, however, he wanted charges against certain officials investigated before they could take an oath under the Act of Pardon and Oblivion (intended to restore former Loyalists to citizenship) and hold office. On another occasion, he demonstrated civic concern when he sought an embargo on the shipment of provisions from Wilmington when they were badly needed after a flood. In 1791 he appeared as the agent of several people, and in that capacity he was engaged by the executors of Robert Hogg.

In the spring of 1784 Hillsborough was excited about the pending marriage of Elizabeth ("Betsy") Hogg and John Huske. William Hooper wrote James Iredell that "the young gentleman is well known to, and beloved by us [Mrs. Hooper] both." On another occasion it was noted that "he and Betsy were destined for each other." In March it was reported that the wedding would be "soon"; in April it was expected to take place in two or three days. The following January Mrs. Huske was delivered of a "chopping" girl, as Archibald Maclaine described her to James Iredell. She was named Ann Alves—the latter being the surname given the younger members of the Hogg family when their father had it legally changed to their mother's maiden name. On 26 Aug. 1786 a son, John, was born, but Mrs. Huske died the same day. "There is reason to fear," Iredell wrote his wife, "owing to a mistake of her case." Hillsborough, of course, was greatly saddened by this event, and Huske "is a walking ghost," William Hooper informed James Iredell, even after a lapse of two years.

Huske was elected to represent New Hanover County in the Hillsborough Convention of 1788 called to determine whether North Carolina would approve the new federal Constitution. Known to be opposed to the document, he appeared to take his seat, but his name does not otherwise appear in the minutes nor is his vote recorded. Illness may have accounted for his subsequent absence. Nevertheless, his point of view prevailed overwhelmingly, and the state declined to accept the document. In 1789 he again represented his county, and at the convention in Fayetteville he was still adamantly opposed to the Constitution. This time, however, it was accepted by a majority of the delegates, whereupon Huske walked out of the convention at the head of the minority delegates.

Huske's stand clearly was unpopular. A number of men who formerly had praised him now turned against him. Archibald Maclaine's reaction was typical. In a letter to James Iredell, he wrote: "Our friend Huske is the loudest man in Wilmington against the new constitution. Whether ambition, or avarice, or a compound of both, actuates him, I leave you to judge."

At the time of the 1790 census, Huske was living in New Hanover County and owned seven slaves. Three males over sixteen, including himself, composed his household plus one "other free person." His two children, who probably were living with relatives in 1790, in time had large families and left numerous descendants in the state. Huske died in Wilmington and was buried in the churchyard at St. James Episcopal Church although he was a Presbyterian.

SEE: Joseph Blount Cheshire, "Memoranda relating to James Hogg" (1903 typescript, North Carolina Collection, University of North Carolina Library, Chapel Hill); Walter Clark, ed., *State Records of North Carolina*, vols. 13, 15–19, 21, 22, 24 (1896, 1898–1901, 1903, 1907, 1905); Don Higginbotham, ed., *The Papers of James Iredell*, vol. 2 (1976); London *Gentlemen's Magazine*, July 1760, January 1761, November 1773; Griffith J. McRee, *Life and Correspondence of James Iredell*, 2 vols. (1857–58); John Potts, "The Location of Smithville," *James Sprunt Historical Monograph No. 4* (1903); John S. Watterson III, "The Ordeal of Governor Burke," *North Carolina Historical Review* 48 (April 1971).

WILLIAM S. POWELL

Hyams, Charles Walter *(1863–8 Nov. 1941)*, botanist and mineralogist, was born in Statesville, the son of Mordecai E. and Caroline Hyams. The catalogues of the North Carolina College of Agriculture and Mechanic Arts for 1898 and 1899 report that he was educated at Trinity College and the University of Tennessee, but recent inquiries suggest that there are no records to support this. As a youth Hyams joined his father on long trips through the Appalachian Mountains in search of botanical specimens, and he was instrumental in the rediscovery of *Shortia galacifolia*.

In the school years 1897–98 and 1898–99 Hyams was instructor in botany at the North Carolina College of Agriculture and Mechanic Arts, and from 1899 until 1901 he was instructor in botany and entomology. During the first two years he was also botanist at the North Carolina Agricultural Experiment Station, and botanist and entomologist during the last two. Minutes of the trustees further indicate that he was elected "Assistant to the Professor of Horticulture and Arborculture and Botany." In these positions Hyams was the author of several reports. *Publications No. 150* of the Agricultural Experiment Station (13 June 1898) pertains to 833 varieties of medicinal plants collected and used in North Carolina; the Station's *Eleventh Biennial Report* (1898) contains information on botanical investigations made by him, as do the annual reports dated 30 June 1900 and 30 June 1901. *Publications No. 164* (19 May 1899) deals with 2,685 species of flora in the state, and *Bulletin No. 177* (December 1900) is entitled "Edible Mushrooms of North Carolina." The executive committee of the board of trustees of the college dismissed Hyams on 9 Apr. 1901, but there is no indication of the reason for this action.

Remaining in Raleigh, Hyams was employed for a time as a storekeeper with the Internal Revenue Service and his wife as a teacher. Their names last appear in the city directory of 1903, and it was around this time that he returned to Statesville. In 1907 he was tried, convicted, and sent to prison for two years for stealing a great many books from local lawyers and selling them to an unsuspecting collector in Raleigh. In 1910 he was living with his family on West End Avenue, and the census of that year listed his occupation as mineralogist and his job as "mines." Apparently soon afterwards he became a recluse, living alone in a very small house adjacent to the Wallace Brothers Herbarium where his father had once been employed. Despite this and his unkempt appearance, Hyams's scientfic knowledge and his ability as a conversationalist made him welcome among lawyers, teachers, and clergymen in the town. He frequently contributed pieces of scientific and literary interest, particularly poems, to the local newspapers and in 1923 published in pamphlet form a tribute to Edgar M. Hallyburton, the first American soldier captured in World War I.

Hyams's wife was the former Maggie Barrett, and her father, Robert G. Barrett (b. 1830), lived with them in Statesville. At his death, Hyams was survived by three children: Margaret, of Winston-Salem; Mrs. D. B. Kanoy, of Charlotte; and Mrs. George Petrella, of Washington, D.C. He also left a brother, F. D. Hyams, of Charlotte. His funeral was conducted by the pastor of the local Associate Reformed Presbyterian Church and included the reading of an impressive poem, "When I Die," written by Hyams for the purpose and left with the clergyman ten years previously.

SEE: Archives, North Carolina State University, Raleigh; Homer M. Keever, *Iredell, Piedmont County* (1976);

Personal information from Mrs. Edna Emerson (Salisbury), Mrs. W. B. Knox (Statesville), and Mrs. Mildred J. Miller (Stony Point); Raleigh city directories, 1901–6; Raleigh *News and Observer*, 9 Nov. 1941; Statesville *Landmark*, 6 Dec. 1907; *Statesville Record*, 10 Nov. 1941.

WILLIAM S. POWELL

Hyams, Mordecai E. (*28 Sept. 1819–16 May 1891*), botanist and herbalist, was born in Charleston, S.C., a descendant of Solomon Hyams who came to America from Prussia in 1744. Although an obituary notice reports that Hyams "graduated at the University at Columbia," alumni records at the University of South Carolina do not contain his name. In 1861 he was living in Magnolia, Fla., when he was detailed to Charlotte, N.C., to buy medicinal roots, barks, and herbs to be used to produce medicine for Confederate soldiers. Enlisting in the Confederate Army, he was in charge of the medical supply department in Charlotte for about a year, after which he moved to Statesville, a center of the herb trade.

In 1868 Hyams moved to Wilkesboro and formed a partnership with Calvin J. Cowles for the purchase and sale of crude drugs. Because of inadequate transportation facilities there, he returned to Statesville in 1869 and joined the firm of Phifer and Turrentine in the crude drug business. In 1871 the company was sold to Wallace Brothers, and Hyams became botanist and manager. From here large quantities of crude drugs were shipped abroad as well as to new drug manufacturers in the United States. During the next fifteen years the Wallace Brothers Herbarium enlarged the number of varieties in which it dealt from 75 to 300, and by 1890 it was processing over 2,300 varieties. One particularly popular product was ginseng root for which a large market existed in China.

Hyams often went on long expeditions through the southern mountains, sometimes accompanied by his son, Charles, identifying and arranging to buy herbs, bark, and roots. It often was necessary for him to train local gatherers. He added 166 new varieties of plants to the identified flora of North Carolina. In 1898 the North Carolina Agricultural Experiment Station published a list of medicinal plants that Hyams's son compiled. The elder Hyams also was the author of "The Crude Drug Industry in the South," prepared for the U.S. Census Bureau, and he arranged exhibitions of botanical specimens sent by Wallace Brothers to the Philadelphia Exposition of 1876 and the Paris Exposition of 1878.

He was an honorary member of the Elisha Mitchell Scientific Society at The University of North Carolina and was a delegate in 1882 to the National Forestry Congress and to the American Forestry Association meeting in Cincinnati. Hyams was asked by the North Carolina Department of Agriculture to prepare a new edition of Moses Ashley Curtis's book on trees, shrubs, and woody vines for which some of his additions appeared in the *Journal of the Elisha Mitchell Scientific Society* in 1885. Failing health prevented his finishing this work, however.

In 1878 Hyams and his son rediscovered the rare *Shortia galacifolia* growing in McDowell County along the Catawba River. It had first been reported by the French botanist, André Michaux, on his visit to the high mountains in 1794, but the exact location was unknown. Hyams was highly commended by Asa Gray and other well-known botanists for his skill in recognizing and identifying this plant.

In the late 1880s he left the Wallace Brothers' employ-

ment because of ill health but worked for a time at another local herbarium. His funeral was held in the local Presbyterian church and he was buried in Oakwood Cemetery, Statesville.

In 1849 in Middlesburg, Clay County, Fla., Hyams married Caroline Ferdinand Sheifler Smith, a native of Wertenburg, Germany. They were the parents of Fred D., Jefferson H., Charles W., George McQueen, and Kate.

SEE: Thos. E. Anderson, "When Statesville Was Nation's 'Yarb' Center," *Southern Medicine and Surgery* 96 (November 1934); Gary R. Freeze, "The Wallaces of Statesville, North Carolina, and Their Root-Herb Trade, 1859–1896," a paper delivered at the Conference on the Jewish Experience in the South, University of North Carolina at Asheville, 10 Apr. 1986; Statesville *Landmark*, 21 May 1891; Personal information from James L. Dalton (Old Fort), Mrs. Edna Emerson (Salisbury), and Mrs. Mildred Miller (Stony Point).

WILLIAM S. POWELL

Hyde, Edward (*1667–8 Sept. 1712*), first to hold the office of governor of North Carolina, was probably born at the family estate of Norbury Manor in Cheshire County, England. He inherited the family manors of Norbury and Hyde and other estates through his father, Robert (d. April 1670). His mother was Phillis or Felice (d. February 1668), the daughter of Ralph Sneyd of Keel and Bradwell in Staffordshire, who brought as her dowry a small amount of property in Shelmenthorpe, Yorkshire.

Hyde's family connections were of great importance to him, for through them he was able to claim kinship with two of England's monarchs, Queen Mary II and Queen Anne. The mother of Mary and Anne was Anne Hyde, first wife of James II and daughter of the famous Edward Hyde, first Earl of Clarendon. Queen Mary, Queen Anne, and Edward Hyde of Norbury and Hyde were descendants of a common ancestor, Robert Hyde (d. 1528) of Norbury and Hyde of Cheshire County. Edward was descended directly from Robert's oldest son, Hamnet, whereas the two queens were descended through the cadet line established by Robert's third son, Lawrence (d. 1590) of West Hatch, Wiltshire County. Lawrence's grandson, Edward Hyde, first Earl of Clarendon, became the famous statesman of the reign of Charles II and subsequently the grandfather of the English monarchs, Mary and Anne.

The scion of the Hydes of Hyde and Norbury, Edward Hyde, the subject of this sketch, was the head of a landed family which had held the manor of Hyde since the days of the Norman Conquest. Norbury Manor had been acquired by marriage during the reign of Henry III. Edward Hyde's mother died a year after his birth and his father died when he was three. He had two sisters, Anne and Penelope, both of whom lived to maturity and subsequently married. The young orphans were raised at Denton by their grandmother, Anne Brooke Hyde, until her death in 1687.

Hyde entered Oxford University at age sixteen, enrolling in Christ Church College on 23 Nov. 1683. He did not take a degree. Little is known of his early career except that he labored under serious financial problems. His grandfather, also named Edward, had supported the Parliamentary cause against the king in the Civil War and at the restoration of Charles II was fined £3,000. This sum was borrowed from a lawyer named Shippon, and by the time Hyde reached his majority, he was being pressed for repayment by his family's creditors. His financial difficulties apparently increased with the passing years. Finally around 1690 or 1691, he was forced to sell Norbury Manor, which the Hydes had held for 450 years, along with his Shelmenthorpe property for £8,000 to the Leigh family of Lyme. Although this amount seems ample for him to have met his financial obligations, other financial concerns seem to have pressed in upon him. By 1708, as Hyde himself admitted, he had been reduced "by divers unhappy accidents and great misfortunes . . . to a very deplorable condition" and was facing "utter ruine."

Battered by financial reverses, Hyde was able to secure some help through the patronage and support of his distant cousin, Lawrence Hyde, first Earl of Rochester, the uncle of Queen Mary and Queen Anne and the second son of the great Edward Hyde, first Earl of Clarendon. Rochester's position as the undoubted head of the Church of England party made him one of the most powerful Tory leaders of his day. Edward Hyde owed him a great deal and on one occasion referred to him as his best friend. It was without question Rochester who, in July 1702, secured for him Queen Anne's appointment to the post of provost marshal of Jamaica with leave to remain in England and appoint a deputy. This position did not prove very lucrative, for in June 1704 Hyde memorialized the Board of Trade to assist him in recovering the fees due him from his deputies in the island colony.

It was probably also Rochester who secured the queen's interest in Hyde's petition in 1708 for a governor's post in Carolina and led her to intervene with the Lords Proprietors on his behalf. Although Colonel Edward Tynte had just been named governor of all of Carolina, the post of deputy governor of northern Carolina was available or could be made available. The deputy governor was normally chosen by the governor for all of Carolina, but early in 1709 the Proprietors issued orders to Colonel Tynte to commission Edward Hyde deputy governor of northern Carolina.

Hyde again petitioned Queen Anne for help. This time he sought a grant of £146 "which with some further helps from your May'ts Charitable bounty" would enable him to transport his wife and family to Carolina. On 4 Apr. 1709 a royal warrant for £146.13.4 was issued in Hyde's favor to be paid from "the arrears of the yearly rent of 20 marks reserved and made payable to us by the Proprietors of our Province of Carolina upon their charter." Hyde next sought and received authorization from Queen Anne for passage for himself and his party on board a naval vessel to Virginia. Meanwhile, the queen "signified her pleasure that Mr. Hyde with his family and servants" be permitted to live and eat aboard the *Rameleis* "until such time as the Convoy sayles to Virginia, in which he is to take his passage to his government of Carolina." The Hyde party numbered fifteen and consisted of his wife, children, and a number of servants. The voyage to Virginia was aboard HMS *Kinsale*. Its captain had orders to feed his passengers in the same manner as the ship's company and to provide them with the best accommodations the ship could afford. On 13 Aug. 1710 the *Kinsale* dropped anchor in the James River, and on 19 August Hyde went ashore as the ship's cannon roared a salute. At Williamsburg he was well received by Governor Alexander Spotswood and other prominent citizens of the Virginia colony.

However, nothing but disappointment awaited Hyde ashore. He soon learned that Colonel Tynte, governor of all Carolina, had died at Charleston and that no one else in America had the authority to issue him his commission as deputy governor of northern Carolina. Without the commission he had no legal claim to the post. Under normal circumstances, Hyde's position would have been a difficult one, but recent political developments in North Carolina made his situation almost impossible. In 1701 a Vestry Act had been passed in North Carolina establishing the Anglican church as the official, tax-supported church of the colony. Strong opposition to the act developed at once among the colony's numerous Quakers. Allied with a large anti-Proprietary faction in the colony, they resisted efforts of pro-Anglican deputy governors to establish the church effectively in the province. In 1708, the two factions rallied behind rival claimants to the deputy governorship and armed conflict was avoided only when one of the claimants, the pro-Anglican William Glover, and a few of his chief adherents fled to Virginia. Thomas Cary, supported by the Quakers and other anti-Proprietary elements, was left in control of the government while his exiled enemies in Virginia denounced what they called the Cary usurpation. The result was great confusion and uncertainty within the North Carolina government and among the colony's residents over the next two years.

The arrival of Hyde in Virginia without a perfected commission now added greater confusion in North Carolina. There was indisputable evidence that the Lords Proprietors intended for Hyde to become deputy governor, but he lacked the necessary documents to establish a legal claim to the office. His arrival in Virginia was the signal for renewed political activity among the North Carolinians. Hyde had already been informed of most of his colony's problems, and the exiled Gloverites soon flocked about him to give their side of the controversy.

Governor Cary quickly made it clear that he would be unwilling to surrender his deputy governorship to Hyde and began to arm his followers. Cary found strong support among the nonconformists who, according to one observer, "did not want to have such a great Tory [Hyde] for governor."

Faced with a determined Cary and lacking the legal right to his post, Hyde remained in Virginia until he could hear further from the Proprietors in London. Individuals and delegations from North Carolina conferred with him at Norfolk and Williamsburg. William Byrd, who dined with him and Mrs. Hyde at the home of Governor Spotswood, characterized Hyde as "a jolly, good natured man but no valiant politician."

Cary found himself under increasing pressure to give way to Hyde and to permit him to assume the government. Those who favored Hyde's acceptance built their case upon his kinship to and his approval by the queen, the statements by eyewitnesses actually present at the Proprietary board at the time of his election to the deputy governorship, and the notice that Governor Tynte had given the North Carolina Council before his death that a new deputy governor was coming out. Cary's support began to fade in the face of this overwhelming evidence and increasingly intense pressure from many sides to accept Hyde despite his lack of proper credentials. Finally "after Long debates" Cary and his followers entered into a written agreement with the Hyde camp to accept Hyde as president of the Council but not as deputy governor until new orders came from the Lords Proprietors. This agreement was ultimately signed by all of the Proprietors' deputies in North Carolina including Thomas Cary.

Hyde now moved into the colony and settled with his family in "a rather fine dwelling" at the William Duckenfield plantation on Salmon Creek not far from Balgra, the residence of Colonel Thomas Pollock, one of his chief supporters. Duckenfield may well have played a major role in inducing Hyde to come to North Carolina. In all probability they were friends of long standing; certainly they were contemporaries, near neighbors in Cheshire, and related by marriage.

Hyde assumed responsibility for the government on 22 Jan. 1711. From the beginning his position was precarious. Much of his support came from those with deep and unswerving hatred for Cary. These individuals sought revenge for past injustices and were unwilling to follow a course of reconciliation and moderation which the situation demanded. The prisoner of his friends' smoldering anger and resentment, Hyde lacked the necessary moral strength or political ability to check the vindictiveness of his followers.

Hyde's Council reorganized the courts, which had been dormant since 1708, and called for the meeting of an Assembly in March. The activities of this Assembly soon brought Hyde and his followers into conflict with the Caryites, for the Assembly enacted laws voiding acts of the courts in North Carolina since 1708 and calling into question the legality of many of the actions of Cary and his government. Its passage of a new and more comprehensive Vestry Act showed clearly that the religious issue was far from dead in the colony.

The Caryites bitterly denounced this legislation, which they realized was designed to punish them. Within a short time Cary and John Porter, Sr., were arrested and impeached on charges of high crimes and misdemeanors, but they quickly escaped from the custody of the provost marshal, denounced Hyde, and proclaimed Cary as the true chief executive of the colony. Soon Cary had a large body of armed followers in Bath County where he fortified a plantation on Bath Creek with breastworks and cannon.

The armed uprising that followed is known as Cary's Rebellion. The events of this rebellion show clearly that Hyde's hold on the government was tenuous, and that the harshness and extreme nature of the laws adopted in the March Assembly had cost him a great deal of support.

Hyde marched overland from the Albemarle to Bath with a force of armed men to recapture Cary, but retreated when he found Cary's position too strong to attack. Heartened, the Caryites armed two vessels and sailed to attack Hyde and his followers in the Albemarle. The assault was beaten back by Hyde and his small force, and Cary's vessels with their cannon were captured. Hyde meanwhile sought support from the Governor of Virgina, Alexander Spotswood, who offered to mediate the dispute. When Cary refused to accept Spotswood's mediation, the Virginia governor dispatched a force of Marines from the guard ships off Chesapeake Bay to North Carolina to aid Hyde in suppressing the Cary forces. On 17 July 1711, HMS *Enterprize* anchored off Currituck Inlet and sent three boats with fifty-five men under the ship's lieutenant to the assistance of President Hyde. By the twenty-ninth the men of the *Enterprize* had returned to their ship. Their appearance in the colony had led to the immediate collapse of Cary's support, for none of his followers had any desire to commit treason by firing on the queen's standard. Cary and four of his chief lieutenants fled into Virginia where they were picked up by the authorities and jailed. Shortly afterwards Spotswood sent them as close prisoners to England where after a year of hearings they were released for lack of proper evidence.

For the first time Hyde was now in full control of the

North Carolina government although he still lacked a commission. In July 1711 Mrs. Hyde returned to England, probably with the intention of obtaining a proper commission for her husband. Long before this, in December 1710, the Proprietors had voted to make Edward Hyde an independent governor of North Carolina although they did not seek Crown approval of his appointment until the following June. On 24 Jan. 1712 the Proprietors signed Hyde's commission, and Catherine Hyde sailed almost immediately with it for America. On 9 May 1712, Hyde presented his commission to the Council and was sworn in as governor of North Carolina.

Long before this event took place, Hyde and his sorely beset colony had experienced the terror and tragedy of Indian warfare. Whether incited by some of Cary's followers as some claimed or simply determined to settle old scores, a portion of the powerful Tuscarora and several smaller tribes decided to attack and destroy the settlements in Bath County, as the settlements on the Pamlico and Neuse were called. Even as the Indians plotted during the summer of 1711, the beleaguered colony suffered drought and an epidemic of yellow fever. Finally, at dawn on 22 September, the Indians struck without warning throughout Bath County. For three days the region reeled beneath the shock of massacre and widespread destruction until the Indians at last turned back towards their villages.

Word of the terrible disaster soon reached Hyde in Albemarle County, which had been spared from the attack. Hyde found himself in an awkward situation. The hatred and ill feeling engendered by Cary's Rebellion remained to hamper efforts to secure full cooperation from the North Carolinians. The Quakers, who comprised an important segment of the Albemarle population, refused to take up arms or to permit anyone to use the arms they possessed. Nevertheless, Hyde moved to put the colony on a war footing. Thomas Pollock was named major general and plans for a retaliatory campaign were made. Messengers were dispatched to Virginia and South Carolina begging for help. Little assistance came from Virginia, but South Carolina proceeded to collect a force of 33 whites and 495 Indians under Captain John Barnwell to go to the aid of its sister colony.

This help was desperately needed, for Pollock's effort in mid-October to lead a force of about 200 men against the Indians failed due to the cowardice of a majority of his troops. Hyde found that massacre and Indian warfare had failed to erase dissensions within the colony. Governor Spotswood reported of the North Carolinians that the "Spirit of disobedience to which they have long been accustomed, still prevails so much he can hardly persuade them to unite for their common safety." In November, an Assembly, called to make plans for the conduct of the war, instead sought to restore several opponents of the Hyde government to office and had to be dissolved by President Hyde.

Fortunately for the strife-torn colony, Barnwell arrived on the Neuse late in January 1712 and immediately attacked the Tuscarora towns. Cutting a wide and destructive swath through the Tuscarora country, he reached Bath only to find that no one had been informed of his coming because the messenger from Charleston had been captured and taken prisoner by a French privateersman.

The Hyde government now bestirred itself to provide support for Barnwell. A new Assembly was hastily convened. It thanked Barnwell for his help, ordered 500 bushels of corn to be collected and sent to his force on the Pamlico, voted to raise 200 men for four months' service, and arranged to erect magazines on the Pamlico and Neuse. The Assembly ordered Barnwell to grant no peace or terms to any Indian towns involved in the massacre.

Only sixty-six men, most of whom had no ammunition, had joined Barnwell by the time he moved out to attack the Tuscarora. Eventually, however, an additional seventy North Carolina troops joined him as the campaign progressed. At first only a limited amount of grain was raised, but in time sufficient supplies were assembled to maintain the expedition in the field. Angered by the scarcity of supplies, Barnwell wrote the governor of South Carolina not to blame Hyde, for, he observed contemptuously, "the people regard him no more than a broom staff, they pay much more deference to my cutlass." Barnwell attacked Hancock's Fort and after a siege forced the Indians to sue for terms which were granted. His decision to sign a treaty of peace with the Indians countermanded his instructions from the North Carolina government, which reacted angrily to his action. Failing to receive from North Carolina the plaudits and rewards he felt he had earned, Barnwell took matters into his own hands. He lured a number of the former hostiles to a conference, took them prisoner, and shipped them off to South Carolina to be sold as slaves. The Indians in the Bath County area retaliated immediately, and soon the war was being waged as fiercely as ever.

Hyde now faced the task of leading a colony whose resources were almost exhausted. An Assembly, called to meet in July, enacted a stringent conscription law which proved difficult to enforce. In an effort to unify the colony, Governor Hyde on 31 July 1712 issued a proclamation pardoning all those who had taken part in Cary's Rebellion except for Cary himself and four of his chief lieutenants. Hyde also announced his intention to take personal command of the military activities against the Indians. He determined to gather the militia of Albemarle County and march at the head of these forces into Bath County. The governor declared that he planned to establish his headquarters at Bath Town and Neuse "that I may be nearer at hand to give such necessary orders, as shall be necessary for the better prosecution of War and I shall always be ready to do the country, the best service even to the hazarding of my life for them, so I hope I shall have . . . the necessary quantity of my militia forces as shall enable [me] to end the war with honor or make such a peace as shall not reflect upon the British Glory." Plans for the campaign were prepared, and Hyde began to gather recruits for the expedition.

These things were not to be, however. Dreaded yellow fever, epidemic in North Carolina in the summer of 1711, had struck the colony again in 1712, and on 1 September Hyde contracted the disease. About noon eight days later he died at his plantation at the head of Albemarle Sound. The governor's Council was in session at Hyde's estate when he became ill, and Graffenried later recalled that "we all became sick at the Governor's with the great heat and without doubt because we ate so many peaches and apples, so that eventually, in a few days the Governor died, which caused me much business, since he was a very good friend of mine." Three days later the Council elected Thomas Pollock to head the government until the Lords Proprietors' wishes could be known. Hyde was most likely buried on the plantation he had rented in Chowan (now Bertie) County.

In 1692 Hyde married Catherine Rigby, the daughter of Alexander Rigby, of Leighton in Lancashire, by whom he had four children: Anne (b. 1693), the oldest; Penelope (b. 1697), who lived to the age of sixty-nine; Derby Lawrence (b. 1700), who died at age eleven in North Carolina; and Edward, who died a bachelor in Spain.

Mrs. Hyde was named administrator of the governor's estate and remained in the colony until March 1713, when she apparently returned to Hyde Hall in England. In the following year, her daughter Anne married George Clarke, of Swanswick near Bath in Somerset, a nephew of William Blathwayt. The couple at once moved to New York, where Clarke had settled earlier and where he eventually became lieutenant governor and served as acting governor from 1736 to 1743. Here they were joined by Catherine Hyde, who remained in New York until her death in 1738; she was interred in the same vault as Lady Cornbury in Trinity Church. Because Anne Clarke alone of the Hyde children had issue, the manor of Hyde passed ultimately to the Clarke family which thereafter assumed the hyphenated name of Hyde-Clarke.

SEE: British P.R.O. C05/9, 1264, 1292, and 1363, ADM 1/2574, ADM 2/41, 44, and 148, ADM 51/302 and 312 in British Archives (North Carolina State Archives, Raleigh); R. D. W. Connor, "Edward Hyde," *DAB*, vol. 5 (1932); Joseph Foster, ed., *Alumni Oxonienses*, vol. 2 (1891); J. R. B. Hathaway, ed., *North Carolina Historical and Genealogical Register*, 3 vols. (1900–1903); Cecil Headlam, ed., *Calendar of State Papers*, Colonial Series (*America and West Indies*), vols. of 1702–3 (1913) and 1704–5 (1916); "Journal of John Barnwell," *Virginia Magazine of History and Biography*, vol. 6 (1898); *Journal of the Commissioners for Trade and Plantations*, vol. for 1704–9 (1920); Ruth Lawrence, ed., *Colonial Families of America*, 21 vols. (1928–42); Henry McIlwaine, ed., *The Executive Journals of the Council of Colonial Virginia*, vol. 3 (1928); George Ormerod, *The History of the County Palatine and City of Cheshire*, vol. 3 (1882); William P. Palmer, ed., *Calendar of Virginia State Papers and Other Manuscripts*, vol. 1 (1875); Herbert R. Paschal, Jr., "Proprietary North Carolina: A Study in Colonial Government" (Ph.D. diss., University of North Carolina, Chapel Hill, 1961) and "The Tuscarora Indians in North Carolina" (M.A. thesis, University of North Carolina, Chapel Hill, 1953); William S. Price, Jr., ed., *North Carolina Higher-Court Records, 1709–1723* (1974); William L. Saunders, ed., *Colonial Records of North Carolina*, vols. 1, 2 (1886); Rebecca Swindell and Norman H. Turner, *Edward Hyde: Governor of North Carolina, 1710–1711* (1977); Norman H. Turner, personal contact (Cheshire, England); Vincent H. Todd, ed., *Christoph Von Graffenried's Account of the Founding of New Bern* (1920); Louis B. Wright and Marion Tinling, *The Secret Diary of William Byrd of Westover, 1709–1712* (1941).

HERBERT R. PASCHAL, JR.

Hyman, John Adams (23 July 1840–14 Sept. 1891), black politician, state senator, and congressman, was born a slave near Warrenton, Warren County. Sold and sent to Alabama, he returned to Warren County in 1865 a free man. With the rise of Negro participation in North Carolina politics, Hyman became a delegate to the second Freedman's Convention held in Raleigh during 1866. The following year, he was a delegate to the first Republican state convention and attended the Republican state executive committee meeting. With North Carolina a part of Military District Number Two, under E. R. S. Canby, he also was chosen a "Register" for Warren County to assist in the registration of voters in 1867. In 1868, he became a delegate to the North Carolina Constitutional Convention.

Also in 1868 Hyman, together with three other Negroes, was elected to the North Carolina Senate. Representing the Twentieth Senatorial District (Warren County) from 1868 to 1874, he supported civil rights for Negroes during both his terms. However, his efforts were clouded by his involvement in frauds and payoffs of significant proportions: irregular activities as a member of a committee to locate a site for a penitentiary, accepting money from lobbyists during the Milton S. Littlefield-George W. Swepson railroad bond scandal, and demanding money from a congressional candidate in return for his support. Aside from these episodes, Hyman's participation in legislative matters was minimal.

Hyman was a strong political campaigner. With Warren County a part of the gerrymandered Second Congressional District, also known as the "Black Second," he decided to run for Congress. Although defeated in 1872, he was elected in 1874, thus becoming the first black to represent North Carolina in the U.S. House of Representatives and the only Republican to represent North Carolina in the Forty-fourth Congress (1875–77). Hyman supported all legislation to secure and protect the rights and privileges of Negroes, and he strongly supported suffrage rights. His votes on issues arising from the Civil War and Reconstruction reflected his Republican sentiments. For example, he opposed the appointment of former Confederate officials to federal posts, as well as the removal of disabilities imposed on southern leaders by the Fourteenth Amendment. His stand on the main issues confronting the Congress also demonstrated his party affiliation. He supported Rutherford B. Hayes over Samuel J. Tilden in the disputed presidential election of 1877, which was decided by Congress; he favored a third term for Ulysses S. Grant, whom he avidly supported; and he opposed the resumption of specie payments.

After serving one term in the House, Hyman failed to obtain his party's nomination in 1876. This was due in part to his limited participation in Congress, an unwillingness of white Republicans to support him, a factional split among the Negroes in the Black Second, and the old accusations of fraud and corruption that still haunted him from his days in the state senate.

In private life, Hyman worked as a farmer and ran a combination liquor-grocery store in Warrenton. In 1872 he began to mortgage his real estate, and by 1878 he had disposed of all his land. Undoubtedly, campaign expenses contributed to his financial reverses, but his extravagances in the nation's capital were his undoing. He was constantly in debt. Writing to Judge Thomas Settle in March 1877, Hyman said that he was in "desperate need." An appointment by President Hayes to the post of collector of internal revenues at New Bern was withdrawn when town residents rallied on behalf of the collector already in office. In 1879, Hyman was accused of using funds from the treasury of the Negro Methodist Church in Warrenton. Shortly afterwards, he left Warrenton for Washington, D.C., to become an assistant mail clerk. He remained an employee of the Post Office Department until 1889, when he obtained a minor position in the Agriculture Department.

Hyman spent his last years in Washington, D.C., where he died of a stroke. He was survived by his widow, two sons, and two daughters.

SEE: *Biog. Dir. Am. Cong.* (1961); *Congressional Record*, 44th Congress, 1875–77; North Carolina *Senate Journal*, 1868–72 (1865); Benjamin Perley Poore, comp., *The Political Register and Congressional Directory: A Statistical Record of the Federal Official, Legislative, Executive, and Judicial, of the United States of America* (1887); Raleigh *Daily Sentinel*, 1867–76; Raleigh *Daily Standard*, 1867–68; *Record of Deeds*, books 32–47 (Warren County Courthouse, Warrenton); *Report of the Commission to Investigate Charges of Fraud and Corruption Under Act of General Assembly*, Session 1871–72 (1872); Warrenton *Gazette*, 1872–84; Warrenton *Indicator*, 1867; *Washington Post*, 1891.

JOSEPH E. ELMORE

Inborden, Thomas Sewell (6 Jan. 1865–10 Mar. 1951), black educator, was born near Upperville, about sixteen miles from Winchester, Va., the son of freeborn parents. His maternal grandmother was descended from a distinguished white family from the "upper neck" of Virginia.

In 1882, after attending a local public school, Inborden left home, on foot, to go to Cleveland, Ohio, where he worked as a bellboy and waiter in the Forest City Hotel for sixteen months. He saved sufficient funds to enter preparatory school at Oberlin College, where he remained for four years. In 1887 he went to Fisk University and four years later was graduated with the B.A. degree. He then joined the American Missionary Association, whose purpose was to provide for the education and the "Americanization" of all minorities of whatever race or nationality. Affiliated with the association for over half a century, he was first assigned as pastor of a church in Beaufort, N.C., and remained there for three months. In the fall of 1891 he went to Helena, Ark., to organize a high school, and two years later he was sent to Albany, Ga., to establish the Albany Normal School.

Transferred to Bricks, N.C., located in Edgecombe County between Enfield and Whitakers, Inborden was the organizer and first principal of the Joseph Keasbey Brick Agricultural, Industrial and Normal School, where he began work on 1 Aug. 1895. The land for the school had been donated to the American Missionary Association by Mrs. Julia Elma Brewster Brick of Brooklyn, N.Y., to establish a self-help school for poor black children. During the first year, the institution enrolled 54 students of whom 13 were boarders. Both boys and girls were admitted up to the fourth grade, although most of them were first and second graders. The 50-acre campus was situated on a tract of 1,129 acres. Eventually, it comprised three large dormitories in addition to a chapel, recitation hall, administration building, and shop where boys were taught blacksmithing, woodwork, mechanical drawing, the use of small machinery, and cabinetmaking. Over the years enrollment increased, reaching as high as 460 students, 260 of whom were boarders. The school produced a variety of farm products, and Inborden developed an extensive mail-order business in honey. Many black teachers—especially in the field of home economics—also served in nearby counties; others went on to graduate work in other institutions and became teachers, dentists, and physicians.

During this period, attendance at the annual farm meetings for Negroes grew from 5 to approximately 2,000. Inborden inspired many blacks to seek the ownership of land, and about 1920 he was instrumental in the founding of the Tri-County Federal Farm Loan Association, which was run by blacks.

Inborden also organized the first YMCA Conference for Negroes in the South. He served as president of the North Carolina Colored Teachers Association for two years, of the North Carolina Fair Association for two years, and of the North Carolina Negro Farmers Congress for eight years. In addition, he was chairman of the Jury of Awards for the Negro Building at the Jamestown Exposition in 1907, a member of the Negro Sociological Congress, and president of the Eagle Life Insurance Company of Raleigh. He held several honorary appointments by North Carolina governors.

In 1909 and 1926, Inborden traveled extensively in the United States on behalf of the American Missionary Association. In 1922 he was granted a sabbatical from the Brick School—with all expenses paid—to travel more than 12,000 miles in the American West.

Inborden married Sarah Jane Evans, the daughter of freeborn blacks who had migrated to Ohio from North Carolina about 1854. She was a graduate of Oberlin College and a teacher for thirty-six years. Before her death on 12 May 1928, the Inbordens had seven children, three of whom grew to adulthood.

John Whitfield McGwigan, a local historian from Enfield, recalls that Inborden was a "courtly figure, a man of slight to medium stature, of light complexion; and I seem to recall that he had a wispy goatee. For years he was an official U.S. Weather Bureau observer. . . . He was considered an authority on the subjects of horticulture and bee keeping. . . . He did much to foster friendship and brotherly love among the races and was universally admired throughout the community." As a result of Inborden's distinguished leadership, the Brick School became Brick Junior College in 1926. The Inborden Elementary School, Enfield, honors his memory. Inborden was buried in Westwood Cemetery, Oberlin, Ohio.

SEE: T. S. Inborden, *History of Brick School* (ca. 1934) and two unpublished autobiographies, 3 Jan. 1931 and ca. 1938 (in possession of Dorothy Inborden Miller, Washington, D.C.; typed copies in possession of R. H. Rives, Greenville); J. E. O'Hara, *Enfield Progress* (8 July 1887); T. H. Phillips, personal recollections (Enfield).

RALPH HARDEE RIVES

Inge, Samuel Williams (*22 Feb. 1817–10 June 1868*), lawyer and congressman, was born in Warren County, the son of Major Francis and Rebecca Coke Williams Inge. He moved to Alabama as a youth, was educated in the schools of Greene and Tuscaloosa counties, and attended the University of Alabama. After studying law with William M. Murphy and W. G. Vandergraff, he began to practice in Eutaw in 1839.

Moving to Livingston where other members of his family lived, Inge was a member of the legislature in 1844. Two years later he was elected to Congress as a Democrat, serving from 4 Mar. 1847 to 3 Mar. 1851. Inge engaged in a bloodless duel in Bladensburg, Md., near Washington, D.C., with North Carolina Representative Edward Stanly, a notorious hothead. On 1 Apr. 1853 President Franklin Pierce appointed Inge U.S. attorney for the northern district of California. He later surveyed the state of Sonora, Mexico, but returned to San Francisco to form a partnership with A. P. Crittenden and resided there for the rest of his life.

Inge married a Miss Hill in Greene County, Ala., and they were the parents of Samuel W., Jr. (m. Imogene Fanny Inge) and Juliette (m. Dr. Inge). He was buried in Mount Calvary Cemetery, San Francisco.

SEE: *Biog. Dir. Am. Cong.* (1961); Thomas M. Owen, *Dictionary of Alabama Biography*, vol. 3 (1921).

ROY PARKER, JR.

Inge, William Marshall (*1802–46*), lawyer and congressman, was born in Granville County, the son of Richard, Sr., and Sally Johnson Inge. He attended The University of North Carolina from 1819 to 1821 but was not graduated. His family moved to Tennessee where he studied law, was admitted to the bar, and practiced in Fayetteville, Lincoln County. He also served as a judge of the Superior Court.

Inge represented Lincoln County in the Tennessee House of Representatives for two terms (1828–33) and, as a Democrat, was elected to Congress, serving from 4 Mar. 1833 to 3 Mar. 1835. Moving to Livingston, Ala., he practiced law and served in the Alabama House of Representatives in 1840, 1844, and 1845. Several of his brothers and sisters had previously settled in Alabama.

He married Susan Marr of Fayetteville, Tenn., and they were the parents of six children: Sally, Mary Turner, Eliza Jane, John, Susan, and William, Jr. Inge was buried in the Livingston cemetery.

SEE: *Biog. Dir. Am. Cong.* (1971); William Garrett, *Reminiscences of Public Men in Alabama* (1872); Robert M. McBride and Dan M. Robison, *Biographical Directory of the Tennessee General Assembly*, vol. 1 (1975); Thomas M. Owen, *Dictionary of Alabama Biography*, vol. 3 (1921).

ROY PARKER, JR.

Innes, James (*ca. 1700–5 Sept. 1759*), colonial officer and official, seems to have been born at Canisby in Caithness in the extreme northern part of Scotland. The parish records there for the time of his probable birth are incomplete. His arrival in North Carolina in 1733, about the same time as Governor Gabriel Johnston, and his appointment by the governor shortly thereafter as a justice for New Hanover Precinct suggest a prior acquaintance in Scotland. In May 1735, Johnston appointed him assistant baron of the Exchequer Court and unsuccessfully recommended him for the Council.

In 1740 Innes was given a position of command in the expedition against the Spanish Caribbean stronghold of Cartagena, a phase of the war between England and Spain that had begun in 1739. It having been decided in London that colonial troops might be better suited for a tropical campaign, a regiment of foot was raised in the North American colonies for service in the West Indies by Alexander Spotswood, a former governor of Virginia. At his death in the spring of 1740, while the expedition was being readied, the command was assumed by Sir William Gooch, his successor as governor of that colony. His regiment, four companies of which were raised in North Carolina, was known variously as Gooch's Americans, Gooch's Marines, or the American regiment.

On 7 June 1740, Innes was appointed captain with a provincial commission in the British Army and assigned command of the Cape Fear company of a hundred men. The names of the captains of the other three companies raised in the Albemarle section of the province—Pratt, Coletrain, and Holton—have been lost in obscurity. These companies met the Cape Fear group at Wilmington, and on 15 Nov. 1740 the North Carolina contingent sailed directly for Jamaica to rendezvous with the British regulars and the other colonial troops. They did not return for two years. According to a contemporary South Carolina newspaper, Innes carried letters of marque, enabling the transport to act as a privateer should it encounter any Spanish ships on the way.

Most of the British colonies in North America were represented in the Cartagena campaign. Among the more prominent colonials who served in the American regiment was Lawrence Washington, the older brother of George Washington. The expedition, poorly planned and executed, ended in disaster. Although the British captured the forts at Boca Chico, the entrance to the harbor of Cartagena, the inner fortifications of the city successfully withstood a three-month siege and the British and colonial troops were decimated by fever. Moreover, the British regulars were strongly prejudiced against the native American regiment. The colonials were quartered on transports and British men-of-war. The field officers of Gooch's regiment, in a memorial to Major General Thomas Wentworth, commander in chief, dated 7 Feb. 1742 at Kingston, Jamaica, complained of the treatment their men were subjected to on the ships. It is significant that the first name on this document was that of James Innes. He was among the twenty-five survivors of the Cape Fear company who arrived in North Carolina in January 1743.

On returning to civilian life, Innes prospered as a planter and he was appointed colonel of militia of New Hanover County. On 5 July 1750 he became a member of the Council following the death of Eleazer Allen and served until his own death nine years later. Innes had been on the Council a little over a month when a Spanish ship was wrecked off Ocracoke on 18 August. Governor Gabriel Johnston immediately sent him to investigate as one well acquainted with the Spanish language and method of trading, no doubt because of his service in the West Indies. From 1751 to 1754, Innes was associated with Francis Corbin as Proprietary agent for Lord Granville in the sale of his land.

Early in 1754, trouble broke out with the French in the Ohio country on the Virginia frontier. North Carolina promptly authorized the use of £12,000 and 750 men to assist in the defense of its sister colony and placed Innes in command of the force. According to historian William L. Saunders, these were the first troops raised by any British colony in America to fight outside its own borders on behalf of a common cause and in a common defense.

Governor Robert Dinwiddie of Virginia, who had an astute perception of the threat posed by the French, spearheaded the Ohio expedition. In a letter of 23 Mar. 1754 to Mathew Rowan—who as president of the Council, was governing North Carolina pending the arrival of Governor Arthur Dobbs—Dinwiddie commended the appointment of Innes, observing that he was a man "whose capacity, judgement, and cool conduct I have great regard for." At some point in their respective careers, he and Innes, a fellow Scot, had become close friends. Dinwiddie, before becoming governor of Virginia in 1751, had been surveyor general of customs for the southern part of British America and may have had contact with Innes in that capacity. Governor Dinwiddie had considered appointing Innes commander in chief of the expedition from the start. Instead, however, the post was given to Joshua Fry, mapmaker, frontiersman, and a Virginia commissioner to continue the dividing line between that colony and North Carolina in 1751. Shortly afterwards, on 15 May 1754, Fry died in camp at Wills Creek, Md., while marching to the Ohio. By a commission dated 4 June, Dinwiddie named Innes to replace him. Young George Washington, who was second in command to Colonel Fry and might have ex-

pected to succeed him, wrote to Dinwiddie on hearing of Colonel Innes's appointment: "I rejoyce that I am likely to be happy under the command of an experienced officer and man of sense. It is what I have ardently wished for." Washington may have known of Innes from his brother Lawrence as the two men had been comrades in arms at Cartagena.

While awaiting the arrival of the new commander, Washington continued the advance to the Ohio and built an entrenched camp called Fort Necessity in the Great Meadows near present Uniontown in southwestern Pennsylvania. Here in late May he surprised a French patrol and killed the leader. The French later retaliated in force and Washington surrendered Fort Necessity on 3 July 1754, withdrawing to Wills Creek. These two skirmishes marked the beginning of what became known as the French and Indian War, which at its end left England mistress of the North American continent.

North Carolina's participation in the Ohio expedition turned out to be unpleasant. In the latter part of June Innes and his troops began to assemble in Winchester, Va., too late to prevent Washington's defeat at Fort Necessity several hundred miles away. In his will, which he made in Winchester on 5 July 1754, Innes stated that the expedition was ready to go into action against the French and their Indian allies who had most unjustly established themselves on land belonging to the English king. But the campaign was plagued with difficulties from the start. The script issued by the province of North Carolina was not accepted outside its borders. No provision had been made for the supply and payment of the North Carolina troops as had been expected, so the men had to be disbanded and sent home. Innes's appointment as commander in chief was not popular among the Virginians or the officers from the other colonies.

Governor Dinwiddie, on the other hand, gave Innes his unqualified support. An obscure Scot settler in the area, writing home to his sister about the troubles on the frontier, reported with pride that a Scotsman was commanding the expedition. Dinwiddie kept a tight control of affairs from Williamsburg. Believing that the force was not strong enough to go into action, he directed Innes to proceed to Wills Creek, Md., a strategic location, and expand the fort George Washington had built there after his defeat at Fort Necessity. Innes renamed the post Fort Cumberland. It was the nucleus of the present city of Cumberland, the second largest in the state of Maryland. Innes remained at the fort with four hundred men, only a few of whom were from North Carolina. Early in October, Governor Horatio Sharpe of Maryland produced a commission from the king appointing him commander of the Ohio expedition. Relieved of the post that he had held for only five months, Innes wished to resign but was persuaded to remain with the title of campmaster general (by a commission dated 24 Oct. 1754), to continue organizing the troops, and to complete the fort. Governor Sharpe, however, did nothing.

In 1755 General Edward Braddock arrived from England with a large force of British regulars to march on the Ohio. On 24 June he appointed Innes governor of Fort Cumberland and left him in command when the forces moved on to Fort Duquesne on the present site of Pittsburgh. With the subsequent death of Braddock and the rout of his troops, his successor, Colonel Dunbar, retreated, stopping at Fort Cumberland long enough to leave in the care of Innes three or four hundred sick and wounded men. Innes was joined at the fort by Edward Brice Dobbs, the son of North Carolina's Governor Arthur Dobbs, who commanded a second detachment of North Carolina troops authorized by the Assembly in October 1754 for service in the Ohio campaign. This regiment missed action with Braddock near Fort Duquesne because at the time it was on a scouting expedition. After the battle, the flight of the British regulars disorganized the provincial troops and many under Dobbs's command deserted.

Innes remained at Fort Cumberland until the early fall, when he returned to North Carolina on a leave of absence. On 10 Oct. 1755, Robert Dinwiddie advised Arthur Dobbs that trouble had broken out around the fort and asked that Innes return. The colonel accordingly went back to Fort Cumberland and remained there until the summer of 1756. The situation by then had quieted down enough to permit his retirement from service. His fellow councillor and friend, James Murray, summed up the Ohio campaign by saying that Innes would have done better to stay at home to gather lightwood.

The few remaining years of Innes's life were uneventful, and he lived quietly at Point Pleasant, his plantation on the northeast branch of the Cape Fear River not far from Wilmington, where he died and was buried. The dwelling house, described in 1775 as a handsome residence built on the British plan, burned in 1783. In his will, drawn up at Winchester in 1754, Innes stipulated that, after the death of his wife, his land, library, and considerable personal property was to be used for a free school for the youth of North Carolina. This legacy, the first private bequest for educational purposes in the history of the state, was not implemented until 1783, when the state legislature established the Innes Academy in Wilmington. Innes also provided in his will for the purchase of a bell for the parish church of Canisby in Caithness and left a bequest of £100 to be invested for the use of the poor of the same parish.

Innes had no children by his wife Jean, whose surname is unknown. It is likely that she, too, was a native of Caithness. In 1761 she married Francis Corbin, with whom her first husband had been associated as agent for Lord Granville. She made her will in 1775, leaving her property to the children of John Rutherford and his wife Frances, the widow of Governor Gabriel Johnston. Mrs. Innes died during the North Carolina visit of Janet Schaw, who left a graphic account in her journal of the lady's last days and funeral; she was buried between her two husbands at the foot of the lawn at Point Pleasant.

James Innes was one of the most important residents of North Carolina in his time. He has been described as an honorable man and an honest and efficient public servant. State historians, beginning with John Hill Wheeler, have tended to assume from a reference in Robert Dinwiddie's correspondence in 1754 to Innes as a former officer in His Majesty's Army, that Innes had had service prior to his arrival in North Carolina in 1733. Recent research in the archives of the War Office in London has not proved this to be the case. No doubt Dinwiddie was referring to Innes's provincial commission as captain in the Cartagena campaign.

SEE: Andrews, ed., *Journal of a Lady of Quality* (1934); Samuel A. Ashe, ed., *Biographical History of North Carolina*, vol. 2 (1905); Mark M. Boatner, *Landmarks of the American Revolution* (1973); Robert A. Brock, ed., *Official Papers of Robert Dinwiddie* (1883); Walter Clark, ed., *State Records of North Carolina*, vols. 11, 23–24 (1895, 1905); Colonial Office Papers (Public Record Office, London);

Concise Dictionary of American Biography (1977); R. D. W. Connor, *History of North Carolina, Colonial and Revolutionary Periods* (1919); Donald Jackson, ed., *Diaries of George Washington*, vol. 1 (1976); Lawrence Lee, *The Lower Cape Fear in Colonial Days* (1965); J. P. MacLean, *An Historical Account of the Settlement of the Scotch Highlanders in America* (1900); William L. Saunders, ed., *Colonial Records of North Carolina*, vols. 4–6 (1886–90); *Virginia Magazine of History and Biography*, vol. 20; Alfred Waddell, *A Colonial Officer and His Times* (1973).

CLAIBORNE T. SMITH, JR.

Iredell, James, Sr. *(5 Oct. 1751–20 Oct. 1799)*, state judge, state attorney general, and United States Supreme Court justice, was born at Lewes, Sussex, England, the oldest of five sons of Margaret McCulloh and Francis Iredell, a Bristol merchant. His father, never a man of substantial means, suffered a stroke in the mid-1760s and was never able to work again. Consequently, young Iredell dropped out of school and in 1768, through his influential McCulloh relatives, was appointed comptroller of customs at Port Roanoke in the town of Edenton, N.C. His yearly salary of £30 was to be paid directly to his parents, while he himself lived on port fees estimated to be worth £100 per annum. Because Henry Eustace McCulloh, the collector of Port Roanoke, was in England most of the time, Iredell had full responsibility for collecting customs as well as looking after McCulloh's numerous properties and other interests. Finally, in 1774, McCulloh negotiated the transfer of the collectorship to Iredell, who maintained the post until he closed his books in June 1776.

During the American Revolution, Iredell sided with America rather than Britain for several reasons. He had become a respected citizen of Edenton, an Albemarle community noted for the talents and accomplishments of its residents, many of whom were connected by a complex web of intermarriages. Intelligent and well versed, Iredell put down deep roots when he studied law under Samuel Johnston—the nephew of a former royal governor and the town's most prestigious individual—and then married his mentor's sister, Hannah Johnston, in 1773. By that date he was practicing law in addition to handling his customs duties, and he became deputy king's attorney for Hertford, Perquimans, and Tyrrell counties. More importantly, in terms of his reputation colony wide, Iredell emerged as the most thoughtful and influential political essayist in Revolutionary North Carolina.

But if Iredell threw in his lot with the Patriots, believing that Parliament had passed numerous acts harmful to the colonists and in violation of their constitutional rights, he rejected until almost the last moment the idea of American independence. Between 1773 and 1776 he attempted, in a series of four essays, to answer a two-part question: How could the empire at once be held together and British-American rights and liberties be revived and guaranteed in the future? Slowly and reluctantly, Iredell concluded that there was no hope of Parliament's ever putting limits to its own authority. He therefore tried, through a scholarly use of British history, to demonstrate that the legislature of the parent country and the legislatures of the colonies were entirely independent of one another but united in a common monarch. This concept, advanced almost simultaneously by three or four writers in different parts of America, would one day gain acceptance with the creation of the British Commonwealth of Nations.

The colonists' final break with England in 1776—

which cost him a considerable fortune when he was disinherited by a wealthy bachelor uncle in the West Indies—found Iredell taking a more active role in public affairs. He not only continued to employ his pen for the Patriots, but he also accepted in 1777 a post as one of the judges of the Superior Court (Supreme Court) system. Resigning the following year, he returned to public life in 1779 as attorney general of North Carolina and served for the two critical years when the state faced repeated threats of British invasion. As attorney general he was responsible for taking legal action against the Loyalists and others who hampered the Revolutionary War effort.

Although Iredell returned to private life and his own law practice near the end of 1781, he continued to maintain an active interest in political matters. A careful reading of his extensive papers suggests that, contrary to long-held historical opinion, no clear-cut party or factional divisions along radical-conservative lines existed in the state during the Revolution and the postwar years. Even so, Iredell in some respects was conservative politically. He preferred the leadership of men of training and talent from respectable families, most of them from his own eastern part of the state; and he was at times critical of "Western men" and the so-called "back-country interest." He was especially concerned in 1783 and thereafter about the legislature's unwillingness to comply with all the provisions of the treaty of peace, just as he wished to see all the states strengthen the authority of the Continental Congress under the Articles of Confederation. He was equally opposed to arbitrary legislative authority by the North Carolina General Assembly, just as he had opposed Parliamentary supremacy in earlier days.

Indeed, there was a remarkable consistency to Iredell's political thinking throughout his life. Both before and after the Revolution he sought to discover methods to confine legislative bodies within their constitutional boundaries. In doing so, he became a pioneering advocate of the doctrine of judicial review; and in 1787, as an attorney for the plaintiff in *Bayard v. Singleton*, he helped convince the state Superior Court to void an act of the legislature. As he had advocated a division of sovereignty under the old British Empire, so now he advocated a similar arrangement in America between the states and the central government. Accordingly, he favored beefing up the power of Congress so that the confederation could function more effectively in matters of national interest. When such amending endeavors failed, he ardently backed the adoption of the federal Constitution of 1787. He and his brother-in-law, Samuel Johnston, played crucial roles in the adoption of that document, which North Carolina had initially rejected in the first ratifying convention. As Iredell wrote, there would now "be two governments to which we shall owe obedience. To the government of the Union in certain defined cases—to our own state government in every other case."

For the first time, Iredell's name was known outside his state, and it led to greater things. For as Hugh Williamson explained from New York, "The North Carolina debates are considerably read in this State especially by Congress members; some of whom, who formerly had little knowledge of the citizens of North Carolina, have lately been *very minute in their inquiries concerning Mr. Iredell*." On 10 Feb. 1790, President George Washington appointed Iredell an associate justice of the United States Supreme Court. The president explained his choice thusly: "I determined, after contemplating every character which presented itself to my view, to name Mr. Iredell of North Carolina; because, in addition to the reputation he sustains for abilities, legal knowledge, and respectability of character, he is of a State of some importance in the Union that has given no character to a federal office."

Iredell's nine years on the highest bench were a formative if unspectacular period in the history of the Supreme Court. It was a time when the justices, besides the two annual terms of the Court, were—according to the Judiciary Act of 1789—required to do circuit duty twice yearly in the lesser federal courts. Iredell, who had ridden the circuits as a rural lawyer and state legal officer, may have been better prepared for this assignment in the saddle than most of his colleagues; he also was the only jurist in the beginning years of the Supreme Court to bring his family to Philadelphia, the nation's capital in the 1790s. Even so, the responsibilities were arduous as the circuits stretched from Portsmouth, N.H., to Savannah, Ga. It was Iredell who took the initiative in working out a fair distribution of these assignments among the judges.

As a justice, Iredell demonstrated, in Julius Goebel's words, "a tough and independent outlook." (Clearly he and James Wilson of Pennsylvania possessed the finest legal minds on the high court during this period.) He "usually had his own characteristic approach" in seeking a solution to cases before the tribunal. He seems to have assumed that the English common law, a part of the colonial legal heritage, would continue as a kind of unwritten underpinning of the federal system of law. An unwavering nationalist so far as federal power over foreign policy and interstate commerce was concerned, as in fact he had been since the Revolutionary War, Iredell was a Federalist politically in the 1790s. Nevertheless, he displayed in such Supreme Court cases as *Chisholm v. Georgia* and *Ware v. Mylton* what Goebel describes as "his continuing interest in maintaining watch and ward over the rights of the states." Yet, on another occasion, in response to a congressional statute calling upon circuit court judges to serve as pension commissioners, Iredell informed Washington that the act was unconstitutional, for it conferred on the Court responsibility neither explicitly nor implicitly found in the national charter of 1787. Whatever else, Iredell saw the judiciary as an active force in the new republic, an equal with the other branches of the federal government.

A man of versatile interests, Iredell read widely and wrote both letters and judicial opinions in smooth, vivid prose. While away from North Carolina, he and his wife Hannah maintained their home in Edenton, where they were members of St. Paul's Episcopal Church. They were the parents of three children who lived to adulthood. Iredell died in Edenton and was buried nearby in the Johnston family cemetery at Hayes Plantation.

SEE: J. Goebel, Jr., *History of the Supreme Court: Antecedents and Beginnings to 1801* (1971); Don Higginbotham, "James Iredell's Efforts to Preserve the First British Empire," *North Carolina Historical Review* (1972), and ed., *The Papers of James Iredell*, 2 vols. (1975); "James Iredell," in L. Friedman and F. Israel, eds., *The Justices of the U.S. Supreme Court, 1789–1969*, vol. 1 (1969); G. J. McRee, ed., *Life and Correspondence of James Iredell*, 2 vols. (1857–58); John Charles Waldrup, "James Iredell and the Practice of Law in Revolutionary Era North Carolina" (Ph.D. diss., University of North Carolina, 1985).

DON HIGGINBOTHAM

Iredell, James, Jr. *(2 Nov. 1788–13 Apr. 1853)*, U.S. senator, North Carolina governor, general of state militia, and Superior Court judge, was born in Edenton. His father was James Iredell, Sr., well-known jurist and member of the first Supreme Court of the United States; his mother was Hannah Johnston, of Edenton, the daughter of Samuel Johnston, Sr., of Onslow County and the niece of royal Governor Gabriel Johnston. James, Jr., attended Edenton Academy, was graduated from Princeton University in 1806, studied law, and was admitted to the North Carolina bar in 1809. He was captain of a company of North Carolina volunteers who were active in the defense of Norfolk in the War of 1812. The following year he served as solicitor of the First Circuit Court.

In 1815 Iredell was appointed a brigadier general of North Carolina militia. He was elected from Edenton as a member of the North Carolina General Assembly in 1813 and served again in 1816–28; from 1817 to 1827 he was speaker of the house. Iredell was elected governor of North Carolina in 1827 and served for a few months before his election to the U.S. Senate to complete the unexpired term of Nathaniel Macon, upon the latter's resignation.

Perhaps much of Iredell's claim to fame was as the son of his illustrious father, who was active in colonial and early state government prior to his appointment to the United States Supreme Court by President George Washington. His uncle and mentor, Samuel Johnston, was equally active in the early history of the colony and state, particularly in the organization of the Revolutionary government and the Continental Congress and later as governor and member of the U.S. Senate. Johnston sponsored his nephew's education at Princeton. The younger Iredell's term as governor was too brief for any outstanding accomplishments. In addressing the General Assembly after his election, he proposed continuation of the program of former governors in emphasizing internal improvements and the development of educational facilities. Joseph Caldwell's *Numbers of Carlton* envisioned a program of railroad expansion to open the western section of the state, providing transportation for the products of that region to a North Carolina port and foreign markets. Iredell suggested the construction of a trial road from Campbellton to Fayetteville.

Iredell did not seek reelection to the U.S. Senate after completing Macon's term. Instead, he returned to North Carolina and moved to Raleigh to practice law. In 1836–37 he was a commissioner to revise the state laws, and from 1840 to 1852 he was a reporter for the North Carolina Supreme Court. He prepared a *Digest of All the Reported Cases Determined in the Courts of North Carolina, from the Year 1778 to the Year 1845*, published in three volumes in Raleigh between 1839 and 1846.

Iredell's wife was the daughter of Samuel Treadwell, collector of the Port of Edenton. They were the parents of seven children: Frances, Penelope, Annie, Jane, James, Helen, and Samuel. Iredell died in Edenton and was buried in the Johnston family cemetery at Hayes Plantation in Edenton.

SEE: *Biog. Dir. Am. Cong.* (1928); Raleigh *Register*, 20 Apr. 1853; John H. Wheeler, ed., *Historical Sketches of North Carolina from 1584 to 1851* (1851).

BETH CRABTREE

Irving, Thomas Pitts *(d. February 1818)*, Episcopal clergyman and teacher, was born in Somerset County on the Eastern Shore of Maryland. He was graduated with high honors from the College of New Jersey (now Princeton University) in 1789. In 1793 he went to New Bern, N.C., to head the New Bern Academy, which he served very effectively until 1813 when he left for Hagerstown, Md., to head a new academy there. In New Bern Irving earned a good reputation not only as a classical and mathematics teacher, but also as an active participant in local events. Among his earliest pupils was William Gaston, later a renowned judge. When he was fifteen Gaston delivered an oration on "the blessings of American independence" on the occasion of the quarterly visitation of the trustees of the academy.

Irving was a musician, both performing and composing musical works, and he directed his pupils in dramatic presentations, some of which he wrote himself, for the pleasure of the community. When funds were being collected for a new Masonic lodge, Irving directed his students in an evening of entertainment for which admission was charged and applied towards the new building. He was chaplain of the lodge in 1798 and Worshipful Master in 1808–10.

He was the owner of a sloop, *The Farmer's Daughter*, valued at a thousand dollars, which sank in the Neuse River in 1809. While the vessel was being used by Moses Jarvis, her cargo shifted in a storm, resulting in considerable damage and loss of property. Irving's stepson, Captain Thomas Fuet, played a role in raising her, but a lawsuit followed in connection with the loss.

In 1795, soon after Irving's tenure at the New Bern Academy began, the building burned and the school was transferred to a room in the Tryon Palace building. About this time Irving undertook to prepare for the Episcopal priesthood; he was ordained in Philadelphia by Bishop William White in 1796. In New Bern he took on additional duties as rector of Christ Church, a position he held until his departure for Maryland. Irving was a subscriber to John Marshall's five-volume *Life of George Washington*, published between 1804 and 1807.

Irving was in Hagerstown, Md., by the end of October 1813 when he obtained certificates for two slaves, Sue and Tom, who accompanied him there from New Bern. He later purchased another slave, David Davis, a blacksmith. Whether Irving had a wife in New Bern does not appear, but Thomas Fuet was identified as his stepson. In Maryland, in 1816, he married Bridget Philburn, who survived him.

SEE: Charles L. Coon, *North Carolina Schools and Academies, 1790–1840* (1915); Alonzo T. Dill, *Governor Tryon and His Palace* (1955); *General Catalogue of Princeton University, 1746–1906* (1908); Elizabeth Moore, *Records of Craven County, North Carolina*, vol. 1 (1960); Raleigh *Register*, 6 Feb. 1818; *Sketches of Church History in North Carolina* (1892); William B. Sprague, *Annals of the American Pulpit*, vol. 5 (1859); David C. Trimble, *History of St. John's Church, Hagerstown, Maryland* (1981).

WILLIAM S. POWELL

Irwin, Henry *(ca. 1725–4 Oct. 1777)*, colonial official and Revolutionary War commander, was born of Scottish descent, probably in Virginia. He purchased land in Tarboro, N.C., in 1760 and was chosen a delegate to the Assembly in the initial election held there after royal Governor Josiah Martin granted Tarboro a charter as a borough town. Irwin was later appointed to the Edgecombe committee formed in 1774 to discharge duties imposed by North Carolina's First Provincial Congress, at which that county had no representatives. The following year he was a member of the Edgecombe delegation to the Provincial Congress at Halifax, and on 9 Sept. 1775 he was appointed lieutenant colonel of the Halifax District.

Irwin returned to Halifax for the Congress that convened on 4 Apr. 1776. This body, which began drafting a state constitution, also instructed its representatives to the Continental Congress to support independence from Great Britain according to the Halifax Resolves and accepted authority from Philadelphia to raise more soldiers for North Carolina's Continental Line. Despite warnings that delegates had "lost all idea of expense, in the zeal of preparing for defense," four additional regiments were created and Irwin became lieutenant colonel of the new Fifth Regiment. As had been predicted, problems arose when attempts were made to put the recently established military units in the field. Irwin, who had received orders to take charge of public provisions and to sell and receive supplies for war, also faced accounting disorders, insurgents, and severe health problems.

In a letter of 19 May 1777 to Governor Richard Caswell, Irwin reported that he had been sick and unable to go to Halifax or move northward with his assembled regiment, but had recovered sufficiently to do so. He also stated that, during this illness, treason was discovered in the eastern counties. Irwin and twenty-five Continentals reacted by disarming some thirty Tories and Loyalists who had "made an attempt" on Tarboro, and Irwin forced them to take an oath of allegiance to forestall their further mutiny. Evidence of difficulty with the expanded forces and his continued poor health reappeared in another letter to Caswell later that summer. On 15 August, Irwin wrote the governor that he was doubtful of success in the further recruitment of men to strengthen the Fifth Regiment. He mentioned a recent bout with smallpox, but stated his continuing desire to be granted permission to rejoin the Continentals.

Irwin eventually resumed command as his troops fought in Pennsylvania. At the Battle of Germantown, he was killed in heavy fighting that also claimed the life of Brigadier General Francis Nash. A monument to Irwin and several other North Carolina soldiers now marks their common grave on the battlefield, although his death was not immediately known. He was at first thought unharmed but captured by the British, as letters to Caswell from John Penn, Cornelius Harnet, Captain Cosmo de Medici, and Colonel Abraham Shephard reveal. This mistaken idea was apparently due to poor communication within General George Washington's army after the battle and because Irwin's recent ailments were presumed to have made him "lame."

He left several children in North Carolina. His daughter, Mary, married Lovatt Burgess, son of Anglican priest Thomas Burgess; another daughter, Elizabeth, married Governor Montfort Stokes. A son, John Alexander, married Sarah Sessums, daughter of Judge Solomon Sessums of Edgecombe County; among their children was Thomas Burgess Irwin, the first husband of Leah Caroline Arrington of Nash County.

SEE: J. B. Boddie, *Southside Virginia Families* (1955); Walter Clark, ed., *State Records of North Carolina*, vol. 16 (1899); Curtis C. Davis, *Revolution's Godchild* (1976); F. B. Heitman, *Historical Register of Officers of the Continental Army* (1967); William L. Saunders, ed., *Colonial Records of North Carolina*, vol. 2 (1886); J. K. Turner and J. L. Bridgers, *History of Edgecombe County* (1920).

JOHN BURKE O'DONNELL, JR.

Irwin, Jared (1750–1 Mar. 1818), Revolutionary War officer and governor of Georgia, was born in that part of Anson County that later became Mecklenburg County, the son of Thomas and Rebecca Lawson Irwin. About 1757 his family moved to Burke County, Ga., where he spent his childhood on the Indian frontier. During the American Revolution he and his father and three brothers saw active service, with Jared attaining the rank of colonel and fighting in South Carolina as well as near Augusta. For their service, these men in 1784 received land grants in Washington County, Ga., where they also built a fort. Jared settled there in about 1787.

Irwin held a number of local offices including inferior court justice, justice of the peace, and road commissioner; after moving to Washington, he served with commissioners in negotiating treaties with the Indians. As early as 1783, he participated in the first of a number of conventions and legislatures in the formation and inauguration of the state government. He also served in the convention that ratified the federal Constitution. He was a member of the state legislature from 1790 to 1811, except during the years when he was governor of Georgia (1796–98 and 1806–8). During his first term as governor, he took satisfaction in signing a bill to rescind the Yazoo land act by which a previous legislature, through bribery, had sold thirty-five million acres of western land to four land companies for 1.5 cents an acre.

Although the records are not clear, it appears that Irwin was married twice. His first wife's maiden name was Steward; his second wife's given name was Isabella, whom he probably married after 1772. His children were Rebecca, Mary Elizabeth, Nancy, Thomas, John, Jared, Jr., Jane, Isabella, and Ann. In addition, he adopted a nephew, Jared, Jr., the son of his brother Alexander. Two of his sons, Jared, Jr., and Thomas, were among the earliest graduates of the University of Georgia after it opened in 1801. Irwin died at his home, Union Hill, where he was buried near Ohoopee Baptist Church.

SEE: *Appleton's Cyclopaedia of American Biography*, vol. 3 (1887); Kenneth Coleman and Charles S. Gurr, eds., *Dictionary of Georgia Biography*, vol. 1 (1983); Wheeler Preston, *American Biographies* (1940); Robert Sobel and John Raimo, eds., *Biographical Dictionary of the Governors of the United States*, vol. 1 (1978).

WILLIAM S. POWELL

Ives, Levi Silliman (1797–14 Oct. 1867), second Bishop of the Protestant Episcopal Church in the Diocese of North Carolina, was born in Connecticut, the son of Levi and Fanny Silliman Ives. Though reared as a Presbyterian, he converted to the Episcopal church in his early twenties, was graduated from the General Theological Seminary in New York, and was ordained deacon in 1822 and priest in 1823. Until his election as bishop in 1832, Ives served various churches in Batavia, N.Y.; Philadelphia and Lancaster, Pa.; and New York City.

Ives had entered the ministry under the auspices of Bishop John Henry Hobart of New York, marrying his daughter Rebecca in 1825. No children of the marriage survived childhood.

Ives was early and consistently identified with the High Church wing of the Episcopal church, of which Bishop Hobart was the acknowledged leader and power broker. This movement was distinguished not so much for any tendencies towards "Romanism," but for accenting differences between it and Protestantism—its emphasis on the centrality of the sacraments, indispensability of the episcopate descending from the Apostles, rejection of theological liberalism and rationalism, rejection of emotionalism and revivalism, wariness of any cooperation with Protestants, and insistence on strict obedience to distinctive Episcopalian traditions and to Prayer Book directives. All of these emphases confined the High Churchmen to a narrow circle of ecclesiastics who, rejoicing in the church's historical catholic past, feared Roman Catholicism as theologically and morally corrupt and Protestantism as hopelessly parochial and volunteeristic.

In 1832 the Diocese of North Carolina was one of the High Church dioceses of the time, and for many years Ives's views and those of the diocese coincided. Lay delegates to the church's General Convention invariably voted with him on issues with High Churchmanship overtones. Ives's episcopate was largely successful for many years because he was able to increase the number of parishes and clergy. In his early years, the diocese at Ives's urging founded a diocesan classical school in Raleigh in hopes that the faculty could be composed of ministerial students who themselves would constitute a small diocesan seminary, but the school closed in 1839 due to inadequate funding and an overly optimistic building project.

Ives's views on slavery were unexceptional. He urged Episcopalians to make provision for the church's ministry to slaves without speaking against slavery as such.

In the 1840s the Tractarian movement in England (also called the Oxford movement and the Puseyite movement) shifted the emphasis of High Churchmanship away from its previously militant rejection of Roman Catholicism. Some writers seriously maintained that proper High Churchmanship required the reintroduction in Anglicanism of practices, rituals, and theological ideas which they felt had too thoughtlessly and hastily been discarded during the English Reformation. Ives, along with other American bishops, was an early supporter of the English writers who, he felt, deserved a considerate reading. Vociferous opposition from American Low Churchmen, however, caused the movement in some quarters to be branded as theologically dangerous; it seemed to them to blur important distinctions between Anglicanism and Roman Catholicism. In response, many High Churchmen were forced to make their public approbation of Tractarian proposals more circumspect and guarded.

In 1847, two factors caused Ives to be party to the founding of the first monastic community in Anglicanism since the Reformation: the financial impossibility of his paying salaries to clergy for a western North Carolina mission station at Valle Crucis, and the application to him of several recent seminary graduates of thoroughgoing Tractarian persuasions who wished to institutionalize themselves as a monastic order. The evidence suggests that Ives consented to the founding of the order more than he actually instigated it, though it is clear that he personally felt that Anglicanism should be broad enough to tolerate a reformed monasticism. Unfortunately for Ives, various ritualist indiscretions on the part of the monastics became public knowledge just at the time when Low Church outcry against the Tractarian movement peaked, and Ives reluctantly dissolved the order with assurances to the diocese that nothing non-Episcopal had ever been intended. At the same time, he had been preaching a series of sermons to the effect that private auricular confession was at least permissible in Anglicanism and perhaps even desirable—a practice that Low Churchmen of the time especially abhorred as puerile and subject to moral abuse. When Ives announced to several diocesan conventions that he was a "true Episcopalian," therefore, he meant that the practices he had espoused were, in his judgment, compatible with the Episcopal church. Low Churchmen, on the other hand, tended to hear his remarks as retractions and recantations when they were not intended as such.

A pamphlet warfare was carried on throughout 1849–51 between Ives and various High Churchmen and Low Churchmen alike, with Ives maintaining that as bishop he was not canonically subject to being judged theologically by a diocesan convention, and his detractors writing that even a bishop was not immune to proper correction from a lowly layman. By 1851, Ives seems to have become convinced that the Tractarian practices that he wished reintroduced were uncanonical and illegal in the Episcopal church, however desirable they might be abstractly considered, and he made a deliberate effort to dissociate himself from them. He later wrote, however, that in that time of silence he was plagued by the feeling that he had betrayed some essential catholicisms and by the fear that a church that so rigidly denied catholic truths could hardly be catholic itself.

In August 1852 Ives and his wife left North Carolina for an extended trip to Europe, with the very private intention of examining the Roman church in Rome itself. In December, while in Rome, Ives became a Roman Catholic and submitted his resignation as bishop to the Episcopal church.

His letter of resignation did not arrive in the United States until February 1853, dating his conversion in December, but for the previous two months Roman Catholic newspapers had been printing unsubstantiated accounts of an abjuration in New York in October 1852. When the Catholic papers failed to print corrections or clarifications, Protestants tended to conclude that Ives was either dishonest (he had offered to return, prorated, his salary as of 22 December) or mentally deranged (mental derangement had been suggested by various Low Churchmen as early as 1849 to explain as charitably as possible Ives's solitary deviations from Episcopal traditions).

Surviving evidence indicates periods of instability in Ives, and the tensions of living in a self-imposed silence to quiet his Roman leanings were agonizing, but mental derangement was a convenient rationale for Episcopalians to explain and accept Ives's resignation. Since then he has been characterized in most Episcopal church historiography as a highly unstable, morbid personality given to excess and overstatement. But in a time of rabid, irrational anti-Catholicism, Ives's espousal of a more inclusive and flexible historical catholicism within Anglicanism received a suspicious and horrified hearing.

Ives returned to the United States in 1854 and was a leading layman in the organization and support of various Roman Catholic charitable institutions. He died at age seventy and was buried in Westchester County, N.Y.

SEE: Marshall De Lancey Haywood, *Lives of the Bishops of North Carolina* (1910); Levi Silliman Ives, *The Trials of a Mind* (1854); Nancy K. Rorie, "Historical Studies of Western North Carolina" (Ph.D. diss., Duke University, 1977).

MICHAEL T. MALONE

Ivey, George Franks (24 June 1870–1 Oct. 1952), textile and furniture manufacturer, author, and churchman, was born at Morganton of English and German ancestry, the eighth child of George Washington and Selina Neal Ivey. His father, a beloved and prominent minister in the Methodist Episcopal Church, South, was reared in Stanly County and served pastorates in South Carolina and west central North Carolina for fifty-two years. Endowed with a good mind, resolute character, and Christian conviction, he had great human understanding and was welcome in any company; he also was industrious and frugal, traits necessary in a man who had to raise ten children on a minister's salary during Reconstruction. Selina Ivey, reared in McDowell County, was a woman of practical judgment who managed her family well.

Young Ivey was educated in the local schools and at Trinity College (later Duke University), from which he was graduated in 1890. Desiring to learn mechanical skills, he went in the fall to Taunton, Mass., where he was employed by Mason Machine Works. Later he worked for Kilburn and Lincoln in Fall River, Mass.

In 1893 Ivey returned to North Carolina and accepted employment at Henrietta Mills at $1.00 a day. After several months he left Henrietta to become superintendent of the cotton mill at Granite Falls at $2.50 per day; there, he upgraded the mill by getting more modern machinery installed. From Granite Falls he went to Bessemer City to superintend the Southern Cotton Mills. Next, he was put in charge of the mill at Forest City.

On the recommendation of S. B. Tanner, Ivey secured a position as instructor in textiles at the North Carolina College of Agriculture and Mechanic Arts in Raleigh. During his first year of teaching, an innocent infraction of postal regulations—of which he was exonerated—led the school's president to ask for his resignation, which was given in March. At the time, Ivey regarded the incident as a great misfortune. Nevertheless, as a result of it he returned to manufacturing where his abilities were successfully employed for the rest of his life.

The next fall he secured the post of superintendent of the Holt Williamson Mill at Fayetteville. He stayed there a year before becoming superintendent of the E. L. Shuford Manufacturing Co. in Hickory and later of the Bessemer City Cotton Mills.

For some time Ivey had wanted to have a mill of his own. In 1903, in collaboration with A. A. Shuford, he built the Ivey Cotton Mill in Hickory and became its manager. This mill produced high quality products, including sateen. For ten years all went well. The mill was enlarged more than once, and as the business expanded additional stock had to be issued. But Shuford's death in 1912 and the sale of the additional stock enabled others to gain control of the mill, and in 1913 Ivey was replaced as manager.

In 1908 Ivey had invented a wooden lug strap that was used in cotton mills. Soon he and a friend began to manufacture the lug straps and other mill supplies. The business prospered. When his associate decided to sell his equity in the firm, Ivey and another partner assumed ownership. Noting that a large portion of the desks in North Carolina schools were made outside of the state, Ivey and his new partner began to manufacture school desks under the firm name of Southern Desk Company. After severing his connection with the Ivey Cotton Mill he became personally involved in the Southern Desk Company. In 1920 he became the sole owner. The company grew to become a major national producer of high quality desks, chairs, church furniture, and other items.

At one time Ivey held stock in his brother's mercantile business in Charlotte. In partnership with J. B. Ivey and E. C. Ivey he went into the manufacture of juvenile furniture, a venture that proved unprofitable even though the company diversified its products. He also became a partner in a dining room furniture manufacturing company that fell victim to the depression and other contingencies in the early thirties.

In addition to manufacturing, Ivey was associated with various other businesses and community enterprises. He became a director in the company that built Hotel Hickory in 1924, and for about twenty-five years he was president of the Howard-Hickory Co., a nursery business. He also had an interest in a feldspar mine in the Spruce Pine area. When he built a new home and could not dispose of his old one advantageously, he made it into apartments and got into the rental housing business.

Ivey helped many young people obtain a college education. He was a trustee of Brevard College until his death, and for twenty-five years he was a trustee and the secretary and treasurer of Rutherford College. In the latter position, he was deeply involved in the difficulties of financing a small church-related institution. Also, seeing the need to help those in retirement, he played a leading role in establishing the Methodist Home for the Aged in Charlotte.

Ivey was the author of *Loom Fixing and Weaving*, written because he was unable to find such a manual while employed at Henrietta Mills. The book went through four editions and for twenty years was used as a text by the Georgia Institute of Technology and for half that long by the Agricultural and Mechanical College of Texas. In 1926 he wrote a book on *The Physical Properties of Lumber*. Another book, *Carding and Spinning*, was published for mill management. His autobiography and other writings appeared in 1945 under the title, *Humor and Humanity*.

Ivey's interest in trees prompted him to give an arboretum to Carolina Park in Hickory. It contains over 250 species of trees. In addition, he accumulated one of the most complete collections of Confederate money to be found anywhere.

Long active in the Methodist church, Ivey became superintendent of the Sunday school of the First Methodist Church soon after his arrival in Hickory in 1903 and held the post for thirty years. As a result of his work and popularity in the Western North Carolina Conference, he was elected a delegate to the 1944 Southeastern Jurisdictional Conference that met in Atlanta.

On 14 June 1899 Ivey married Edith Blanche Sherrill of Sherrill's Ford. They had six children: Elbert, who worked with his father in Hickory and died in 1942; Dorothy (m. Dr. Ralph C. Flowers) of Hickory; Leon S., who worked with his father in Hickory and succeeded him when he died; Christine, who died in infancy; Edith (m. J. E. Pugh) of Hickory; and Lucille (m. H. L. Barrett, Jr.) of Charlotte. Ivey died suddenly of a heart attack and was buried in Oakwood Cemetery, Hickory.

SEE: *Charlotte Observer*, 6 Jan. 1946, 2 Oct. 1952; George Franks Ivey, *Humor and Humanity* (1945 [portrait]).

GARLAND R. STAFFORD

Ivey, Joseph Benjamin (8 June 1864–4 Apr. 1958), merchant and churchman, the fifth child of George Washington and Selina Neal Ivey, was born in Shelby of English and German ancestry. He was the brother of George Franks Ivey. His father, reared in Stanly

County, was a beloved and prominent minister in the Methodist Episcopal Church, South, who served pastorates in South Carolina and in west central North Carolina from 1851 until his death in 1902. His mother was raised in McDowell County.

At age seven Ivey began his formal education at the public school in Morganton but, due to the form of discipline administered by the teacher, was soon transferred to a private school. In Lenoir he was a pupil in the preparatory department of Davenport Female College. In 1876 he entered Finley High School, a private institution. Two of his fellow students were the sons of Governor Zebulon Vance. When the family moved to Denver, he attended Denver Seminary under the tutorage of Professor D. Matt Thompson. Ivey later said that Thompson and his wife influenced the shaping of his life more than any others except his parents. After leaving Denver Seminary in 1860, he did not pursue further education because of poor eyesight. Although this condition was blamed on measles contracted in Lenoir, myopia was actually responsible.

In his last year at Denver, Ivey published a pen-printed school paper, "The Denver Seminary Gazette." As the years passed, writing became an avocation and he contributed numerous pieces—polemics, human interest stories, accounts of his travels (of which there were many), and so forth—to local newspapers and other publications. In 1941 he published *My Memoirs*.

In 1880 his father was appointed to another pastorate and the family left Denver. It was decided that young Ivey, having served as a carpenter's helper, would learn the carpenter's trade. He was apprenticed to a carpenter and cabinetmaker in Lenoir, but left after six months. A friend of the family recommended him to Captain L. J. Hoyle, of Belwood in Cleveland County, who offered him a job in his country store. At first Ivey took little interest in the work and was, according to his own estimate, an indifferent clerk. But after a year or so he changed his mind and decided he would become a merchant. This was the turning point in his career.

At that time merchants had no set price for their merchandise; they sold goods for what they could get. Ivey persuaded Hoyle to establish the one-price system— one price to everyone. Those who wanted to buy "on time" paid a small additional charge for the service. This innovation proved to be popular.

After four years at Belwood, Ivey obtained employment in a store in Newton where he remained about eight months. Seeking better wages, he then went to work for a store in Hickory. One day one of the owners told him that his services were no longer needed, observing that in his opinion Ivey could never become a merchant! When Captain Hoyle heard he was out of work, he offered him a half partnership in his store and a salary if he would return. Ivey went back to Belwood in July 1885 and again introduced new methods of merchandising. That fall he had a one-day sale. To draw the crowds, he employed a brass band and there was a hot-air balloon ascension. Merchandise was displayed on tables outdoors. The sale was a big success. Another time he had an auction. The store also took on new lines, including an agency for buggies.

Ivey stayed at Belwood until the spring of 1893, when he accepted the offer of S. B. Tanner to take charge of the dry goods department of the Henrietta Mills store in Rutherford County. After a few years as a successful manager he concluded that his future lay in having his own mercantile business in a city. In February 1900 Ivey opened a store at 231 North Tryon Street in Charlotte. At the end of the year he bought a business at 13 West Trade Street and moved his store there, and in the fall of 1914 he moved again to 13–15 North Tryon Street. Still another move was made in 1924 to the present location on the southwestern corner of North Tryon and Fifth streets. (The storehouse and land are owned by the company.) By 1940–41, when the building was enlarged as far as Church Street, J. B. Ivey & Company had become the leading store in Charlotte for quality merchandise.

In 1937 a branch store was opened in Asheville, and later a branch appeared in Greenville, S.C. More stores followed in other locations. Ivey was fortunate in those who worked with him. In 1904 David Owens became his lifelong associate. In 1929 W. T. Buice joined the firm as merchandise manager, a post he held until his death in 1951.

Ivey was an active member of the Methodist church throughout life. While at Denver Seminary, at age fourteen, he taught the next Sunday's Sunday school lesson to the primary children on Friday afternoon. In Hickory the seventeen-year-old was active in the Sunday school of which his brother, Will, was superintendent. At age eighteen he became a lifelong tither. At twenty-one he was superintendent of the Kadesh Sunday school at Belwood. In Henrietta he led the movement to secure a full-time pastor. Ivey continued to teach Sunday school classes for many years and was the Sunday school superintendent in several other churches. For a number of years he was president of the North Carolina Sunday School Association. Ivey was a delegate from the Western North Carolina Conference to the General Conferences of 1926, 1934, 1938, 1940, and 1944, and to the United Conference in 1939. A variety of religious and cultural programs received his financial support.

Ivey believed that business should not be conducted on Sunday. Following the lead of John Wanamaker, he did not advertise his merchandise on Sunday and had the shades drawn on the show windows on Saturday night. His personal habits were exemplary. He did not use tobacco and early in life made a pledge to abstain from the use of alcoholic beverages. He loved flowers and cultivated them in variety and quantity at his home in Charlotte and his summer home at Lake Junaluska.

On 2 Feb. 1893 Ivey married Emma Gantt of Cleveland County. They had four children: George Melvin, Emma Virginia (Mrs. C. R. Walker), Ella Marie (Mrs. O. M. Litaker), and Katherine Neal (Mrs. Ervin Jackson). Emma Ivey died on 13 Mar. 1917. On 8 Oct. 1919 he married Mrs. Daisy Smith of Clio, S.C. Ivey died just two months short of his ninety-fourth birthday. He was buried in the family plot in Elmwood Cemetery, Charlotte.

SEE: *Charlotte Observer*, 27 Sept. 1936; J. B. Ivey, *My Memoirs* (1941); Raleigh *News and Observer*, 5 Apr. 1953.

GARLAND R. STAFFORD

Ivey, Thaddeus (*27 June 1855–6 Apr. 1933*), farmer, schoolteacher, and civil servant, was born at Ashpole, Robeson County, the son of the Reverend Stinson Ivey, Baptist minister and educator, and his wife Mary Ann King. The younger Ivey became a farmer and in the 1880s was principal of Ashpole Institute. He was the first person to apply for membership in the Farmers' Alliance, a farm protest organization that began in Texas and spread to North Carolina in 1887. In April of that year, Ivey became the first member of Ashpole Alliance No. 1, the first subordinate alliance chartered in North Carolina. When the North Carolina Farmers'

State Alliance was organized in October 1887, he was elected vice-president and a member of the three-man executive committee. He was reelected to both positions in 1888 and served until August 1889. He declined reelection to the executive committee but remained active in the organization.

In 1891 Ivey moved to Cary to become bookkeeper and cashier for the North Carolina Farmers' State Alliance Business Agency, and on 1 Jan. 1895 he was appointed state business agent, succeeding William H. Worth on his election as state treasurer. Ivey served in the position until August 1897. During his tenure the Farmers' Alliance shoe factory was established at Hillsborough.

A member of the Prohibition party, Ivey ran for the state senate in 1894 on his party's ticket but withdrew in favor of his Republican-Populist opponent, Henry W. Norris. Ivey supported the People's party until its demise, then became a Republican. Although he never won an elective office, he served for many years under Republican administrations as chief deputy in the U.S. marshal's office in Raleigh.

Ivey died of angina pectoris and was survived by his wife and eight children: sons D. R., A. H., George E., and Thaddeus; and daughters Esther M., Mrs. Knud Nisson, Mrs. C. J. Sistare, and Eva Alberta. After funeral services at the Cary Baptist Church, he was buried in the local cemetery.

SEE: Levi Branson, ed., *North Carolina Business Directory*, vol. 7 (1890); Elias Carr Papers (Manuscript Collection, East Carolina University, Greenville); North Carolina State Alliance Minute Book, 4 Oct. 1887, in Farmers' State Alliance Papers and Leonidas Polk Denmark Papers (North Carolina Division of Archives and History, Raleigh); *Proceedings of the Third Annual Session of the North Carolina Farmers' State Alliance, Held in the Town of Fayetteville, North Carolina, August 13, 14, and 15, 1889*; Raleigh *News and Observer*, 6 Apr. 1933; Raleigh *Progressive Farmer*, 26 Mar. 1889 (photograph), 6 Dec. 1892, 25 Dec. 1894, 5 Jan., 17 Aug. 1897.

LALA CARR STEELMAN

Ivey, Thomas Neal (22 May 1860–15 May 1923), Methodist minister, editor, and educator, was born in Marion, S.C., the third child of the Reverend George Washington and Selina Neal Ivey. George Washington Ivey was a circuit rider of the Methodist Episcopal church for fifty-two years, most of the time along the Catawba River in Piedmont North Carolina. By choice he rode the circuit, preferring rural charges to the better city appointments, but few ministers of his time were better known or more respected than "Uncle Ivey." His five sons all excelled in their widely different fields. William, the oldest, was a physician in Lenoir; Eugene, the youngest, was an early electrician in the same town; Joseph Benjamin was the founder of Ivey's department store; George Franks was a Hickory manufacturer, best known as the founder of the Southern Desk Company.

Thomas Neal, the second son, grew up in Methodist parsonages and spent his more formative years in Lenoir, a place he never forgot. He was educated at Finley High School, an academy in that town, where Captain W. C. Fawcette was principal. In 1879 he was graduated from Trinity College (later Duke University), then situated in the corner of Randolph County next to High Point. Trinity awarded him the M.A. degree in 1882 and the doctor of divinity degree in 1897; in 1920 he was made an alumnus member of Phi Beta Kappa.

The eight years following his graduation were spent in school teaching and administration—at River Bend in Lincoln County, at Shelby as assistant principal, at Brevard, and at Oak Institute in Mooresville as principal. At Oak Institute, a Methodist academy, Ivey acquired a reputation as a strict disciplinarian and "a good school man." Also during this period he married Lenora Dowd on 7 Aug. 1883.

In December 1886, while in Mooresville, Ivey joined the North Carolina Conference of the Methodist Church, South, and was appointed to the position he already held at Oak Institute. The next year he was sent to Lenoir as pastor of the church there, for the first time separated from the large Lenoir Circuit. Then followed four years in the Roxboro Circuit and four years at Wilson, one of the stronger appointments in the conference. While he was at Roxboro, the Western North Carolina Conference was organized in 1890. However, Ivey remained in the North Carolina Conference, which covered the eastern part of the state.

At the conference of 1896, he was appointed co-editor of the *North Carolina Christian Advocate*, along with Leonidas W. Crawford from the Western North Carolina Conference. Late in 1893 that periodical had been organized at Greensboro by merging the *Raleigh Christian Advocate* and the *Western Christian Advocate*, published in Asheville. Although the merged paper was owned by a stock company rather than the conferences, both conferences gave it their support and appointed an editor. Just the summer before, Crawford had bought a controlling interest in the stock company and was already at work as editor.

Such an organization had its weakness. The North Carolina Conference was acutely conscious that the stock company relieved it not only of financial responsibility but also of control over editorial policy. The "double-barrelled" editorial arrangement did not work. At the time the state was being rocked by the Kilgo-Clark controversy over the support of higher education and the attendant Gattis-Kilgo lawsuit. Each of the editors had his own editorial pages and used them to full advantage, with Ivey supporting John Carlisle Kilgo, the president of Trinity College, and Crawford numbered among his opponents. Instead of unifying the two conferences, the paper became divisive. At the end of two years, the North Carolina Conference bought half the stock and subscription lists, and reestablished the *Raleigh Christian Advocate*, with Ivey as editor.

It was as editor of the *Raleigh Christian Advocate*, from 23 Feb. 1899 to 1910, that Ivey did his best work, raising the paper's circulation from 2,500 to 7,500. Besides his general editorial excellence, two facets of his work stand out. In 1902 he published the first *North Carolina Methodist Handbook and Almanac*, which he changed in 1906 to the *Southern Methodist Handbook*. It appeared every year—except one during World War I—until his death in 1923, long after he had left the *Raleigh Advocate*. The other significant contribution was his publication of the Bildad Akers letters. In early 1903 letters began finding their way into the *Advocate* from one Bildad Akers, letters with spelling and grammar far below Ivey's standard but with a homespun philosophy that was Ivey at his best. The best of these were published in 1908 in a volume entitled *Bildad Akers—His Book*. In 1910 the General Conference elected him editor of the *Christian Advocate*, the general organ of the church published in Nashville, Tenn. Reelected three times, he held the position until his death.

Beginning in 1898, Ivey was a delegate to every General Conference of the Methodist Episcopal Church,

South, as long as he lived. In 1911 he was a delegate to the Ecumenical Methodist Conference, and at one time he was vice-president of the Federal Council of Churches. He also served on the first commission for the unification of Methodism as a strong advocate of union.

About 1920 Ivey's health began to fail and his doctor prescribed golf. He died three years later, ironically, on a golf course in Nashville. He was buried in Raleigh, the city that had been more home to Ivey and his family than any other.

SEE: Joseph Benjamin Ivey, *My Memoirs* (1941); Marion Timothy Plyler, *Thomas Neal Ivey, Golden Hearted Gentleman* (1925); Plyler and Alva Washington, *Men of the Burning Heart* (1918).

HOMER M. KEEVER

Ivie, Allan Denny (3 May 1873–16 May 1927), state senator and attorney, was born in Patrick County, Va., the son of William Sterling and Sarah J. Elizabeth Scales Ivie. His maternal great-great-grandfather, John Scales, lived and died in Rockingham County, married Lydia McClarg, a native of France, and had six sons and two daughters. Peter Scales, John's son, married Annie Walker whose mother, Susan Warren, was related to Colonel James Warren and General Joseph Warren who made history at Bunker Hill in the American Revolution. Joseph Warren and Paul Revere led the spy group consisting of the unemployed workers of Boston; James Warren was a confidant of John Adams. Dr. James Warren Scales, son of Peter Scales, married Mary Lodoskie Mebane; their only child was Sarah J. Elizabeth Scales, the mother of Allan Denny Ivie. Allan Ivie's paternal ancestors had commercial interests. His great-grandfather lived in Dinwiddie County, Va. His grandfather, John W. Ivie, moved from Dinwiddie to Patrick County, Va.

The origins of the Ivie family, also spelled in English records as Ivey and Ivye, are found in Wiltshire and Oxfordshire, England. The Ivie coat of arms is described as "Gules a lion rampant or; Crest: a demi lion rampant or, supporting a staff raguly vert."

Ivie attended public schools until 1896 when he enrolled at Oak Ridge Institute, a preparatory school for boys in North Carolina; he was graduated in 1898. In the fall of 1899 he entered The University of North Carolina, but left soon afterwards because of illness. Returning in the fall of 1900, he received a degree from both the literary department and the law school in 1902.

At Chapel Hill, Ivie won Orators' and Debators' medals. In 1902, a speech he delivered at the annual college commencement attracted statewide interest and was printed in many of the leading daily newspapers, receiving favorable editorial comment. He was a member of the Dialectic Society, one of the two literary societies on campus at the time. During his second year, Ivie was elected president of the YMCA, an office normally held by third- and fourth-year students. He was also president of his law class in 1902.

Upon graduation, Ivie obtained a license to practice law and settled in Leaksville, where his family had lived since 1892. Over the years he was connected with the law firms of Johnston, Johnston, and Ivie; Johnston and Ivie; Johnston, Ivie, and Dalton; Ivie and Trotter; and Ivie, Trotter, and Johnston. At his death, he was a senior member of the latter firm. Ivie was known for his deep concern for the welfare of his clients. He pursued all cases, large or small, with great vigor and was recog-

nized as one of the leading attorneys of Rockingham County and North Carolina throughout his twenty-five years of practice.

On 11 Oct. 1905 Ivie married Annie Elizabeth McKinney of Reidsville. They had five sons: Allan Denny, Jr., George Harris, Joseph McKinney, William Scales, and James Warren.

Although not active politically, Ivie was very much involved in matters of civic and community interest dealing with the welfare of the people. He always supported the Democratic party. Feeling the duties of citizenship, he accepted the nomination for state senator from the Twentieth District and in 1910 defeated the incumbent by a large majority. In the senate he was primarily interested in legislation that would aid the masses. During the campaign he had promised to work for a bill to shorten the working hours of laborers in manufacturing mills. Through strong advocacy and an excellent speech ending arguments against his proposal (which received compliments from the opposition), Ivie's bill passed with a tremendous majority. The new law came to be known as the "ten hour law."

In 1912 Ivie was reelected from the Nineteenth District by a larger majority than in 1910. During his second term he was chairman of the Committee on Constitutional Amendments. This committee of twenty members was instructed to revise the state constitution and propose amendments.

Ivie was a staunch advocate of temperance and he campaigned for prohibition. In 1913, he was one of twenty-five selected to represent North Carolina in presenting to Congress a petition and request for a constitutional amendment requiring nationwide prohibition. The same year Ivie became vice-president and a director of the Imperial Trust and Savings Co.

An active member of the Methodist Episcopal Church, South, Ivie was president of the first Leaksville Methodist Church County Sunday School Association and a lay reader of the Mt. Airy District Methodist Church. In his community he belonged to the local Rotary Club, Knights of Pythias, and Junior Order of American Mechanics. He had large farming and stock-raising interests. And he was the first president of the Rockingham Alumni Association for The University of North Carolina, remaining involved in university alumni activities throughout life.

Ivie had been ill for two months with a relapse of influenza when he died; death was attributed to an embolism of the brain. On 21 June 1927, the Superior Court in session at Wentworth adjourned from 11:00 A.M. until 2:00 P.M. in Ivie's honor. In the interim, a memorial service was held in the courthouse by the legal fraternity of Rockingham County. Ivie was survived by his wife and children.

SEE: Alumni Records (University of North Carolina, Chapel Hill); Ian R. Christie and Benjamin W. Laboree, *Empire of Independence, 1760–1776* (1976); R. D. W. Connor, ed., *Pocket Manual of North Carolina for 1911* (1911) and *for 1913* (1913); Don Higginbotham, *The War of American Independence: Military Attitudes, Policies, and Practice, 1763–1789* (1971); H. M. London, ed., *Proceedings of the Thirtieth Annual Session of the North Carolina Bar Association* (1928); *North Carolina Biography*, vol. 5 (1941); Leonard Wilson, ed., *Makers of America: Biographies of Leading Men of Thought and Action*, vol. 2 (1916).

ELAINE M. WHITFORD

Jack, James (1731–18 Dec. 1822), Revolutionary War officer, best known for his ride from Charlotte to the Second Continental Congress in Philadelphia to deliver a copy of the Mecklenburg Resolves, was the oldest son and one of nine children of Patrick and Lillis McAdoo Jack. His parents lived along the Conococheague River southwest of Chambersburg, Pa. His grandfather may have been the Reverend William Jack of Laggan Presbytery in Northern Ireland who was removed from his benefice by Charles II for nonconformity to the Church of England.

The French and Indian War caused Patrick Jack to leave Pennsylvania and move to North Carolina. By 1760 the family was living to the west of Salisbury in Thyatira, one of the first Presbyterian communities to be established west of the Yadkin River. On 20 Nov. 1766 James Jack married Margaret Houston and in 1772 moved to Charlotte, where the previous year his father had bought lots on the south side of West Trade Street. There Jack and his elderly parents built a house in which they operated a tavern. In the years that followed Jack became prosperous enough to speculate in Charlotte real estate and was appointed a tax collector and an overseer of the poor in the county of Mecklenburg.

Meanwhile, hostility was growing to the acts of Parliament. When news arrived of the outbreak of fighting at Lexington and Concord in Massachusetts, the Mecklenburg Resolves of May 1775 were drawn up declaring British laws and authority to be null and void. Whether a "Declaration of Independence" was also issued has long been disputed. Jack and his father were active supporters of the patriot cause, and it seems likely that many of the Committee of Safety meetings were held at their tavern. Jack recalled that "for some time previous to, and at the time of those resolutions [of May 1775] were agreed to, I . . . was priviledged to a number of meetings of some of the . . . leading characters of that county on the subject before the final adoption of the resolutions." James Jack was dispatched to carry the Resolves to Congress. He set out on his ride in June and upon arriving in Salisbury had the document read publicly in the district court then in session. On reaching Philadelphia he found that the North Carolina delegates, still hoping for a reconciliation with England, considered the action premature. Apparently, they never informed the other delegates of the Mecklenburg action. Moravian records tell of Jack's return through Salem on 7 July. The forty-three-year-old patriot, averaging around 30 miles of hard riding each day, completed his 1,100-mile trip in about thirty-eight days.

Jack stated that he served "in the Revolutionary War from the commencement to the close." A captain in the Mecklenburg militia, he is said to have been so popular that his company urged him not to accept promotions. When Lord Cornwallis occupied Charlotte in September 1780, British troops dragged Jack's ailing father from his bed and he died not long afterwards; the home was burned to the ground. Though the tavern was rebuilt (a new license was granted in October 1781), the expense of this and the failure to receive reimbursement of his wartime expenditures of £7,646 left Jack financially impoverished. His claim, audited by Colonel Matthew Locke, was paid to a friend who died before delivering the money to Jack.

At the end of the war, Jack moved across the mountains into present Tennessee. In 1784 he was one of the signers of a petition to the North Carolina Assembly urging that the area be created into a separate state. This was not done until 1796, however, and by then

Jack had moved to Wilkes County, Ga., where he engaged in farming. About 1814 he and his wife moved to neighboring Elbert County to spend their last years in the home of their son, William Houston. They had three other sons—Patrick, who became a colonel in the U.S. Army and served in the Mexican War; Archibald; and James, Jr.—and one daughter, Cynthia, who married A. S. Cosby and settled in Mississippi. An obituary in the Raleigh *Register* of 17 Jan. 1823 gave Jack's age as eighty-four, but he, himself, had written on 7 Dec. 1819 that he was then eighty-eight which agrees with other accounts stating that he was ninety-one at his death.

SEE: Samuel A. Ashe, ed., *Biographical History of North Carolina*, vol. 4 (1906); Walter Clark, ed., *State Records of North Carolina*, vols. 15, 22 (1898, 1907); *The Declaration of Independence by the Citizens of Mecklenburg County . . . and the Proceedings of the Cumberland Association* (1831); Adelaide L. Fries, ed., *Records of the Moravians in North Carolina*, vol. 2 (1925); George R. Gilmore, *Sketches of Some of the First Settlers of Upper Georgia* (1885); Cyrus L. Hunter, *Sketches of Western North Carolina* (1877); Mecklenburg County Court Minutes, Books 1, 2 (North Carolina State Archives, Raleigh); Mecklenburg County Wills, Book D (Mecklenburg County Courthouse, Charlotte); Salisbury *Western Carolinian*, 28 Jan. 1823.

NORRIS W. PREYER

Jackson, Andrew (15 Mar. 1767–8 June 1845), seventh president of the United States and the last to be born in the colonial period, was the son of Andrew and Elizabeth Hutchinson Jackson. The elder Jacksons and their two sons, Hugh and Robert, moved to North Carolina from Carrickfergus, Northern Ireland, in 1765 and settled in the Waxhaw region of Mecklenburg (now Union) County. Named for a band of Indians, this area was considered to be "a rich oasis in a region of pine barrens," and it extended across the unmarked boundary between the two Carolinas. The elder Jackson died in February or March 1767, and Mrs. Jackson took his body to the Waxhaw Presbyterian Church, about twelve miles away in South Carolina, for burial. Returning home, she gave birth to a son and named him Andrew. Whether she actually arrived at home or stopped at the home of relatives is not known, and the precise birthplace of Jackson is in dispute.

Andrew Jackson briefly attended an old field school and although very young took part in the American Revolution. He never officially enlisted but served as a courier for General William R. Davie, and the two became close friends. Davie, in fact, is said to have been something of a hero to young Jackson. Andrew and one of his brothers were captured by the British and imprisoned for a time. Both of the two older Jackson brothers lost their lives in the Revolution, and Mrs. Jackson fell victim to a fever contracted while nursing the wounded in Charleston.

Orphaned at fourteen, Jackson worked in a saddler's shop and taught school. He then studied law at Salisbury under Spruce Macay in 1784–85, and was admitted to the bar in Rowan County on 6 Nov. 1787. For a time he practiced there as well as in Guilford County. When Jackson was appointed solicitor of the western district of North Carolina, comprising what is now the state of Tennessee, he and a friend, John McNairy, moved across the mountains to Jonesboro. Jackson soon moved to Nashville and there lodged with the widow of John Donelson, the founder of the town. He married the widow's daughter, Rachel, when they believed her divorce from a jealous husband was final. Much to their embarrassment they learned later that the divorce was not final, and they were married a second time. They had no children of their own, but adopted her nephew who took the name Andrew Jackson Donelson.

An avid land speculator, Jackson acquired many acres including his homesite, The Hermitage, near Nashville, where he lived as a cotton planter. His political career began when he was a member of the convention that framed Tennessee's first constitution in 1796, and he was elected as the state's first representative in Congress. He resigned at the time of the so-called Blount Conspiracy and was elected to the Senate. He also served as a Superior Court judge.

Politically weakened by his association with Aaron Burr and his killing of Charles Dickinson in a duel, Jackson lived as a country gentleman until the War of 1812. Attaining the rank of major general, he acquired fame by defeating the Indians at Horseshoe Bend and the British at New Orleans. He was severely criticized, however, for the "Seminole Affair" of 1818, in which he invaded Spanish Florida and executed two British subjects. Nevertheless, he was appointed governor of Florida after its purchase, but he soon returned to Tennessee where his friends were organizing a campaign to make him president. After serving briefly in the Senate, Jackson resigned and concentrated on his presidential hopes. He was triumphantly elected in 1828 and reelected in 1832. His tenure was noteworthy for the great increase in the power of the president. He was also instrumental in the election of Martin Van Buren as his successor. Jackson spent his last days at The Hermitage and was buried in the garden there.

SEE: John S. Bassett, *The Life of Andrew Jackson* (1911); *Biog. Dir. Am. Cong.* (1961); *DAB*, vol. 9 (1932); Max F. Harris, *The Andrew Jackson Birthplace Problem* (1963); Marquis James, *The Life of Andrew Jackson* (1938); James Partin, *Life of Andrew Jackson*, 3 vols. (1860); William B. Sumner, *Andrew Jackson* (1899).

STANLEY J. FOLMSBEE

Jackson, Herbert Worth (15 Feb. 1865–30 Dec. 1936), banker and civic leader, was born in Asheboro, the son of Elvira Evelina Worth and Samuel Spencer Jackson, a lawyer. Among his forebears were Judge John Alston, who came to North Carolina in 1694 with Governor John Archdale, and Judge Samuel Spencer, a member of the First Provincial Congress held in New Bern in 1774 and of later congresses held at Hillsborough and Halifax. His maternal grandfather, Jonathan Worth, was governor of North Carolina during Reconstruction. His mother served as president of the North Carolina Division of the Daughters of the American Revolution and as co-editor of *The North Carolina Booklet*, a quarterly historical publication. His father died when he was ten, and his mother remarried twice and was widowed three times by 1886.

Jackson received his elementary education under a private tutor in Asheboro before entering Bingham Military School at Mebane in 1877. Six years later he enrolled in The University of North Carolina, where he became first baseman and captain of the varsity baseball team and excelled as a kicker in the not yet widespread game of football; he also held membership in Alpha Tau Omega. He was awarded the bachelor of philosophy degree in 1886. The following year his financial career began with an appointment as clerk in the treasury de-

partment of the state of North Carolina. Three years later he became treasurer of the Wetmore Shoe and Leather Company. In 1891 Jackson was named assistant cashier of the Commercial and Farmers Bank (later Commercial National Bank) of Raleigh. In 1906 he was promoted to cashier, and while in this position was elected president of the North Carolina Bankers Association for the term 1908–9.

In 1909 Jackson was appointed president of the Virginia Trust Company of Richmond, Va. Founded in 1892, this was the first trust company in Virginia and one of the first in the South. When he became president the business was small, with capital stock of $500,000, deposits of $120,000, and trust assets of $600,000. Jackson's imaginative advertisements offering financial advice seem to have contributed to the success of the company, which at the time of his death had increased its capital stock to $1 million, its resources to $8 million, and its trust assets to an aggregate of $50 million.

Over the years Jackson was a member of the Richmond Clearing House Association (president, 1935–36), Virginia Bankers Association, and American Bankers Association. He served on the board of directors of the Raleigh Standard Gas Company, Jefferson Standard Life Insurance Company, Atlantic Fire Insurance Company, Virginia Electric and Power Company, Johnson Publishing Company, Tredegar Iron Works, and Aberdeen and Rockfish Railroad of which he was chairman of the board. He also served as secretary and treasurer of the News and Observer Publishing Company, owned by his cousin-in-law, Josephus Daniels.

Active in church work, he was an elder and, for over seventeen years, superintendent of the Sunday school of the First Presbyterian Church of Raleigh. In Richmond, he became an elder and taught the Men's Bible Class in the Second Presbyterian Church. For a number of years he was treasurer of the Richmond Presbyterian League.

Early in life Jackson demonstrated an interest in history. In Raleigh he served as treasurer of the North Carolina Society of the Sons of the Revolution and in Richmond as president of the parallel organization in Virginia. He also held membership in the Virginia Society of Colonial Wars, of which he became deputy governor and later governor. Through his influence, the General Society of Colonial Wars donated a gate, a gatehouse, and tablets to Stratford, the home of the distinguished family of Robert E. Lee. He was instrumental in having some silver pieces bearing the Lee coat of arms obtained and returned to the home. In addition, Jackson was a member of the Society of the Cincinnati and of the Confederate Memorial Literary Society, and served on the board of directors of the Stone Mountain Confederate Monumental Association and of the Richmond Battlefield Parks Corporation.

While living in Raleigh, he was elected to the board of trustees of The University of North Carolina. He also served on the boards of Peace College in Raleigh, Union Theological Seminary, and Hampden-Sydney College.

Throughout his life Jackson participated in many community projects. In Raleigh, he helped organize the YMCA and served as an alderman, a member of the public school committee, and a member of the Municipal Building Commission. After moving to Richmond, he conceived the idea of the Richmond Foundation, founded by him and others in 1919 as a public trust fund. This trust, derived from gifts from civic-minded citizens, was to be used for charitable, educational, and benevolent purposes for the people of Richmond and the state of Virginia.

During World War I, he served as chairman of the Richmond Victory Loan Campaign in which Richmonders made more than $15 million available for the war effort. He also volunteered his services as a member of the board of directors of the Sheltering Arms Hospital, the Richmond Home for Ladies, and the Retreat of the Sick Hospital. From 1928 to 1936 he was president of the Richmond Police Benevolent Association, a charitable organization.

On 22 Oct. 1890, in Tarboro, N.C., Jackson married Annie Hyman Philips, the daughter of Frederick Philips who was a judge of the North Carolina Superior Court. They had three children: Evelyn Hyman, Herbert Worth, Jr., and Samuel Spencer.

At age seventy-one Jackson died from a heart attack at his home in Richmond; he was buried in Oakwood Cemetery, Raleigh. More than twenty newspapers featured articles about his passing. His will specified funds for five Richmond charities. In 1938 the president of The University of North Carolina announced that his widow had endowed the Herbert Worth Jackson Scholarship as a memorial to him. Portraits of Jackson hang in the boardroom of the Virginia Trust Company and in the homes of Herbert Worth Jackson III and Samuel Spencer Jackson.

SEE: Samuel A. Ashe, ed., *Biographical History of North Carolina*, vol. 8 (1917); Daniel L. Grant, *Alumni History of the University of North Carolina, 1795–1924* (1924); Hampden-Sydney Alumni Association, *Record* (January 1937); Norfolk *Virginian-Pilot*, 31 Dec. 1936; Richmond *News Leader*, 29 Sept. 1909.

B. W. C. ROBERTS

Jackson, Mary Anna Morrison (31 July 1831–24 Mar. 1915), wife of "Stonewall" Jackson and author, was the daughter of the Reverend Robert Hall Morrison and his wife Mary Graham, a daughter of General Joseph Graham of "Vesuvius Furnace" in Lincoln County. At the time of Anna's birth, her father was pastor of Sugaw Creek Presbyterian Church in Mecklenburg County; she was born in the manse (since destroyed) three miles from the center of Charlotte. Shortly afterwards her father became the first president of Davidson College, and, according to Anna's sister, "most of her happy childhood" was spent at Davidson, where the original Presidents' House is still in use, though much enlarged. Anna was educated at Salem Academy (1847–49); in 1914, as the most famous of its alumnae, she was awarded a diploma by Salem College. When her uncle, William A. Graham, was secretary of the navy in the administration of President Millard Fillmore, Anna visited him in the nation's capital. Through her sister Isabella, who was married to Major D. H. Hill of the faculty of Washington College (later Washington and Lee University) in Lexington, Va., she met her future husband, Major Thomas Jonathan Jackson of the faculty of the Virginia Military Institute, also in Lexington.

On 16 July 1857 Anna and Tom Jackson were married at Cottage Home, in Lincoln County, the Catawba River plantation of her father after his retirement from Davidson. She was Jackson's second wife; his first wife had died childless. A few days after their marriage, the couple set on for a northern tour which included Richmond, Baltimore, New York, Saratoga, and Niagara Falls.

The Jacksons were deeply religious and devoted to one another. Their happy home life in Lexington was marred only by the death of their first child, Mary Graham, who lived only a few weeks. When the call to arms was issued for the Confederacy, the cadets at Virginia Military Institute offered their services and Major Jackson was chosen to lead them. Anna Jackson returned to Charlotte to live with relatives. In the home of her sister, Mrs. James Irwin, her daughter Julia was born on 23 Nov. 1862, her only child to survive infancy. Anna remained in Charlotte, although making several trips to see General Jackson, until she received the news of his tragic wounding by his own men. She was at his bedside when he died on 10 May 1863.

It is said that at first Anna did not approve of the nickname "Stonewall," as she did not think it appropriate to Jackson's personality and sensitive nature; however, she later accepted it as a badge of honor. In 1911, she objected strenuously to what she considered a caricature of her husband in Mary Johnston's novel, *The Long Roll*.

From the time of her husband's death until about 1873, Anna lived with her father at Cottage Home. She then moved to Charlotte to provide better educational advantages for her daughter Julia; she remained in that city for the rest of her life, living on West Trade Street at two different residences (now both destroyed). Her interests centered chiefly around the First Presbyterian Church, where her pew is now marked; the Stonewall Jackson Chapter of the United Daughters of the Confederacy; and the Mecklenburg Chapter of the Daughters of the American Revolution. When she attended a meeting of the latter organization in Washington, D.C., she was asked by President and Mrs. McKinley to receive with them.

Anna Jackson wrote several books. The first, *Life and Letters of General Thomas J. Jackson*, was published by Harper and Brothers in 1892. It was republished, with additions, in 1895 as *Memoirs of Stonewall Jackson by His Widow* (Louisville, Ky.). In 1910, the Stone and Barringer Company of Charlotte published her *Julia Jackson Christian, Daughter of Stonewall Jackson*. Julia Jackson had married William Edmund Christian on 2 June 1885, borne him a daughter and a son, and died on 30 Aug. 1889 at age twenty-seven. In 1882 Mrs. Jackson had begun a family history, entitled "Memory's Mirror," giving considerable detail about the families of her husband, her father, her grandfather (General Joseph Graham), and her great-grandfather (Major John Davidson of Rural Hill), but this memoir was never completed or published.

Jackson's widow was much honored in North Carolina and throughout the former Confederate states. After the death of Mrs. Jefferson Davis in 1906, Mrs. Jackson was recognized nationwide as "The First Lady of the South." The "tiny, brown-eyed lady" was the idol of Confederate veterans, many of whom came from all over the South to pay their respects to her and to her husband's memory. She literally lived her legend in her own day. Anna Jackson died in Charlotte at age eighty-three. She was accorded military honors at her funeral, and her body was taken to Lexington for burial beside her world-renowned husband.

SEE: Laura Morrison Brown, *Historical Sketch of the Morrison Family* (1919); Letters of Mrs. Jackson (Stonewall Jackson Memorial, Inc., Lexington, Va.); *Memoir of Mrs. Stonewall Jackson* (1915); Julia Christian Preston, *Stonewall's Widow* (1961) and "A Patchwork Quilt of Memories" (mimeographed, 1971).

CHALMERS G. DAVIDSON

Jackson, Walter Clinton *(28 June 1879–12 Aug. 1959)*, teacher and college administrator, was born in Hayston, Ga., the son of Albert Leroy and Jane Granade Jackson. His father was a farmer who had served in the Confederate Army; his mother was a former schoolteacher. Young Jackson received the bachelor of science degree from Mercer University in 1900 and was awarded the doctor of laws degree in 1926. After teaching in several Georgia schools, he was invited by E. D. Broadhurst to be principal of the Lindsay Street School in Greensboro in 1902. The same year he married Mattie Redford, who had also gone to Greensboro to teach. They had three children: Walter C., Jr., Virginia Elizabeth, and Lillian Murchison (Mrs. C. O. Hunt).

In 1903 Jackson transferred to Greensboro High School as an English teacher and in 1905 became principal.

In 1909, Jackson began his long association with the institution that later became The University of North Carolina at Greensboro. He was head of the Department of History until 1915, when he also became dean. From 1921 to 1932 he was vice-president and department head. In the latter year he went to The University of North Carolina at Chapel Hill as dean of the School of Public Administration, a position he held for two years. In 1934, upon the retirement of Julius Foust, Jackson returned to Greensboro to head what was then the Woman's College of The University of North Carolina. He retired in 1950.

Active in civic affairs, Jackson was awarded citations by the National Conference of Christians and Jews and by the Greensboro Chamber of Commerce. He was president of the North Carolina Conference for Social Service (1925–26) and of the Southern Commission on Interracial Cooperation (1928–32); vice-president of the North Carolina Council of Churches; and a Rotarian. For many years he was a member of the board of trustees of Bennett College and at times was the chairman. In 1949 Bennett awarded him the doctor of humane letters degree for being "a pioneer in the field of better race relations."

Jackson also served a variety of educational organizations. He was president of the North Carolina Literary and Historical Association (1924–25) and a member of the editorial board of the *North Carolina Historical Review*. He was also president of the North Carolina Education Association (1937–38) and of the North Carolina College Conference (1938); vice-president of the Southern Political Science Association (1933–34), and a member of Phi Beta Kappa. He was the author of *A Boy's Life of Booker T. Washington*; *Poetry by American Negroes*, with N. I. White; and *The Story of North Carolina*, with A. M. Arnett.

A junior high school in Greensboro, where Jackson died, is named in his honor, as is the main library at The University of North Carolina at Greensboro.

SEE: Archives, University of North Carolina at Greensboro (Greensboro); *Greensboro Daily News*, 13 Aug. 1959.

ELISABETH ANN BOWLES

Jacobs, Harriet *(11 Feb. 1815–7 Mar. 1897)*, writer and reformer, was born a slave in Edenton. Her grandmother, "Yellow" Molly Horniblow, who was freed in 1828, subsequently bought a house in Edenton and earned her living as a baker. It is probable that her father was the slave Daniel, a skilled carpenter and "old and faithful servant" of Dr. Andrew Knox of Pasquotank County. Her mother was the slave Delilah, property of the tavernkeeper John Horniblow. She had one brother, John S. Jacobs, who was younger than herself. Jacobs had no formal education, but was taught to read and write by Margaret Horniblow, her first mistress.

Publication of Jacobs's pseudonymous slave narrative, *Incidents in the Life of a Slave Girl, Written by Herself* (ed. by L. Maria Child, 1861), established the fugitive slave Harriet Jacobs as an Afro-American activist and writer. Her book was republished in England the following year as *The Deeper Wrong: Or, Incidents in the Life of a Slave Girl, Written by Herself* (ed. by L. Maria Child, 1862). Probably the only slave narrative to focus on sexual oppression as well as the oppression of race and condition, *Incidents* is unique among nineteenth-century American autobiographies. It is a first-person account of a woman's struggle against her oppression in slavery as a sexual object and as a mother. Its avowed purpose was to enlist American women in the struggle against slavery and racism, and it was only after great difficulty that Jacobs published it with the aid of her editor, the abolitionist woman of letters Lydia Maria Child.

Jacobs composed her autobiography between 1853 and 1858. She wrote pseudonymously, calling herself "Linda Brent" and using fictitious names for everyone else. In *Incidents*, she writes that she was orphaned when a child and at the death of her beloved mistress was sent to a licentious master, "Dr. Flint" (Dr. James Norcom). He subjected her to unrelenting sexual harassment. In her teens she bore two children to "Mr. Sands" (probably Samuel Tredwell Sawyer), another white man. When her jealous master threatened her with concubinage, she ran away. With the help of sympathetic black and white neighbors, she was sheltered by her family and for years remained hidden in the home of her grandmother "Aunt Martha," a freed slave. During this period the father of her children, who had bought them from her master, allowed them to live with her grandmother. Although later he took their little girl to a free state, he failed to keep his promise to emancipate the children.

About 1842, Harriet Jacobs finally escaped to the North, contacted her daughter "Ellen" (Louisa Matilda Jacobs), was joined by her son "Benjamin" (Joseph Jacobs), and found work in New York City as a nursemaid for "Mrs. Bruce" (Mrs. N. P. Willis). In 1849 she moved with her brother "William" to Rochester, N.Y., where both became members of an active group of reformers. Jacobs made a confidante of feminist-abolitionist Quaker Amy Post, who urged her to write the story of her life to aid the antislavery cause.

When—after she had corresponded with Harriet Beecher Stowe and William C. Nell—her book finally appeared in the early months of 1861, Jacobs traveled to various northern cities, attempting to swell sentiment for emancipation by publicizing and circulating *Incidents*. During the Civil War, she moved to Washington, D.C., to nurse black troops. Then, with her daughter, she followed the Union armies south.

Well known among reformers as "Linda" because of her book, Jacobs embarked upon a career as a relief worker, making herself a link between the philanthropists of the North and the freedpeople of the South. In 1863 she was at Alexandria, Va., employed by the Quakers of Philadelphia to work among the "Colored Refugees"; in 1865 she was at Savannah, Ga., sent on a similar mission by New York Quakers; in 1868 she was in England soliciting funds for a home for the orphans and the aged among the Savannah freedpeople. The letters Jacobs composed throughout these years and published in the reformers' newspapers comprise an extraordinary series of first-person reports on relief work among the freedpeople.

Little is known of her later years in Cambridge, Mass., and in Washington, D.C., where she died. Jacobs was eulogized as "a woman of strong individuality and marked character" by another prominent former slave, the Reverend Francis Grimke. She was buried at Mt. Auburn Cemetery, Cambridge, Mass.

SEE: Harriet A. Jacobs, *Incidents in the Life of a Slave Girl, Written by Herself*, ed. by L. Maria Child . . . ed. and with an introduction by Jean Fagan Yellin (1987); Dorothy Sterling, ed., *We Are Your Sisters: Black Women in the Nineteenth Century* (1984); J. F. Yellin, "*Written by Herself*: Harriet Jacobs' Slave Narrative," *American Literature* 53 (1981).

JEAN FAGAN YELLIN

Jacobson, John Christian (*8 Apr. 1795–24 Nov. 1870*), educator and Moravian bishop, was born in Burkhall, Denmark. His parents, both missionaries in the Diaspora service of the Moravian church in Denmark, moved to Skjerne, Denmark, soon after his birth. In 1801, at age six, Jacobson was placed in the church boarding school at Christiansfeld. He was transferred to the Niesky Institute in 1809; there he studied classical languages and theology. In 1816, having completed his studies in theology, he was called by the church to America and appointed teacher at Nazareth Hall, a boys' boarding school in Nazareth, Pa. Four years later he was made professor at the theological seminary in Bethlehem, Pa. In October 1826 Jacobson married Lisetta Schnall of Bethlehem; her parents were also missionaries of the church.

In December 1826, having accepted a call to the pastorate of Bethania, the Jacobsons arrived in North Carolina. Jacobson remained in Bethania until 1834, when he was called to nearby Salem as inspector of the girls' boarding school and assistant pastor. His improvements and skillful administration of the academy were noted by the church when in 1844 he was called back to Nazareth Hall as principal. Here he continued to demonstrate his abilities as an educator.

The dividing line between his earlier and later careers was marked by his election as a delegate to the General Synod in Herrnhut, Saxony, in 1848. He was subsequently called to Bethlehem in 1849 to serve as a member of the Provincial Elders Conference of the northern province. Jacobson presided over the synod for eighteen years. During this time several important changes were made within the Moravian church, including the adoption of constitutional policies granting the church in America greater independence. On 15 Sept. 1854 Jacobson was ordained bishop. While serving as bishop and president of the Provincial Synod, he continued to demonstrate his concern for education. He was instrumental in establishing the theological seminary at Nazareth, where he gave occasional lectures on the history of the church. *The Moravian Church Miscellany* for 1852–53 records Bishop Jacobson's recollections of his journey through the northern provinces, in which he comments on the progress of the church.

In 1867 Jacobson retired after serving the church nearly fifty-one years. He died at age seventy-five, survived by his wife and four of his children.

SEE: John Clewell, *History of Wachovia in North Carolina* (1902); Adelaide Fries, ed., *Records of the Moravians in North Carolina*, vol. 8 (1922); *The Moravian* (1 Dec. 1870); W. N. Schwarze, "History of the Moravian College and Theological Seminary," *Transactions of the Moravian Historical Society*, vol. 8 (1909).

CHARLOTTE BENNETT

Jacocks, William Picard (*9 Dec. 1877–17 Feb. 1965*), international public health physician and administrator, was born in Windsor. (His middle name, Picard, is accented on the last syllable.) His ancestors had lived in northeastern North Carolina as early as 1688. His mother was the former Emily Baker Nicholls. His father, Jonathan Joseph Jacocks, a Confederate veteran and staunch Episcopalian, was a merchant specializing in hardware and harnesses. Both mother and father died in August 1892, leaving eight children between the ages of three and twenty. William lived with his oldest brother, Charles, continuing his schooling at Windsor and at Trinity School, Chocowinity, in Beaufort County. He entered The University of North Carolina in 1898, but being short of funds withdrew after a year to teach for the next two winters at Chocowinity. He was graduated from the university with the class of 1904, a Phi Beta Kappa student and distinguished athlete, especially in football and track. Jacocks received a master's degree in 1905 after a year of graduate work in history, French, and pedagogy, serving at the same time as a graduate assistant teacher in French. For the next two years he taught at the Bingham School in Asheville and then returned to Chapel Hill to pursue the two-year medical curriculum. In 1911 he earned a doctoral degree in medicine from the University of Pennsylvania and the following year was an intern at Alleghany General Hospital in Pittsburgh.

In 1912 Jacocks joined the North Carolina State Board of Health to participate in a campaign—sponsored by the Rockefeller Foundation—to eradicate hookworm, working first in the field and later as state campaign director in Raleigh. His association with the Rockefeller Foundation lasted for thirty years. He left North Carolina in 1915 to continue the battle against hookworm in the British West Indies, first in St. Vincent and later in Trinidad where he served as acting director for the region. In 1917 he went to Ceylon, as director, to establish local health units, working out of Colombo. In 1927 he was also made director for India to operate the same type of programs in rural centers. Moving his base over to southern India about 1934 and to Delhi a few years later, he continued his work with hookworm and also with such problems as malaria, cholera, plague, smallpox, maternal and infant care, and sanitation.

His long service in Ceylon and India with the Rockefeller International Health Division was punctuated by scheduled periods of service in the United States, where he did related work and study. In 1918–19, commissioned as a captain, he completed Medical Officers Training at Fort Oglethorpe, Ga., and army bacteriology laboratory courses at Louisville, Ky., and New Haven, Conn. After being mustered out in January 1919, he had six months of study leave in New York and Baltimore before returning to Ceylon. While again in New York and Baltimore, Jacocks completed a doctorate at the Johns Hopkins School of Hygiene and Public Health in 1925. In 1931 he worked in the vicinity of Elizabeth City, N.C., and he made an observation tour for the International Health Division in Eastern Europe in 1936. During his years with the division, he was the author of numerous professional papers, mainly on hookworm and on the rural delivery of public health services. In 1927 he was elected a member of the (British) Royal Society of Tropical Medicine and Hygiene.

In Delhi as regional director of India and Ceylon, Jacocks arrived at retirement age in 1942. His longtime colleague, Dr. John A. Ferrell, wrote of him at that time: "His relationships with governmental authorities, with the people served, with his assistants, and with officers of the Division and the Foundation have been effective and harmonious and were always conducted on a high plane calculated to inspire confidence and co-operation. The projects he formulated were outstanding. . . . He has brought to large populations improved health and higher standards of living."

In vigorous health Jacocks came home to a nation at war, and from among the many opportunities open to him, he chose to pitch in at once with the North Carolina State Board of Health. For three years he was coordinator of school-health services, and for three more years he served as director of the division of nutrition in Raleigh.

In 1948 he "retired" again, settling soon afterwards in Chapel Hill where he lived at the Carolina Inn. The University of North Carolina awarded him the honorary degree of doctor of laws in 1954. Physically fit and mentally alert through the years in Chapel Hill, he was an ardent and regular spectator at athletic events and daily practice sessions of the university teams, each sport in its season. Jacocks was also a familiar figure at the university library, where he pursued his methodical research and purposeful reading. He concentrated especially on the history of his native Bertie County and a compilation of the Jacocks family genealogy, both interests of his father and his brother Charles before him. He was an active member of the Bertie County Historical Association and the North Carolina Society of County and Local Historians.

Off and on for years, Jacocks had been a collector of books, fine prints, paintings, eastern rugs, and objects of art in ivory, brass, jade, and tortoise shell. Two unusual collections that he accumulated were statuettes of Ganehsa, the Hindu god of wisdom and prudence, in as many different materials as possible; and pressed or clear glass celery vases. The latter hobby had its genesis after he returned from India and while he was working for the State Board of Health. Jacocks had set out one day to find something suitable to hold the cut flowers offered by flower sellers in downtown Raleigh, found a celery vase in a nearby store, subsequently found some more for friends, and ended up owning more than 300 matched pairs and about 150 different singles.

His temperament combined an appetite for hours of quiet work and study, with a balancing capacity for enjoyment of group activities, in which he was always a welcome and adaptable companion. The young athlete became the trim and agile octogenarian with a brisk gait. His voice was well modulated, his manners gracious and gentle; his face tended to light up easily and frequently with enjoyment and humor. Modest and considerate, he was an unassuming yet friendly person. Respect and sympathy for others were basic to his nature.

Jacocks never married. He died in Windsor and was buried at St. Thomas Episcopal Church cemetery there. Either during his lifetime or by bequest, he gave most of his books and other fine collections to his alma mater at Chapel Hill and to the Bertie County Historical Society and Public Library at Windsor.

SEE: Articles by Demont Roseman, Jake Wade, Jane Hall, and others (Clippings file, North Carolina Collection, University of North Carolina Library, Chapel Hill); William Picard Jacocks Papers (Southern Historical Collection, University of North Carolina Library, Chapel Hill).

ANNA BROOKE ALLAN

James, Hinton (20 Sept. 1776–22 Aug. 1847), first student of The University of North Carolina, engineer, and legislator, was born in that part of New Hanover County that became Pender County in 1875, the oldest of five children of John and Alice James. The family lived on a portion of the land set apart in 1725 by the Lords Proprietors for Welsh settlers, subsequently known as the Welsh Tract.

On 12 Feb. 1795 James became the first student of The University of North Carolina, which had opened its doors on 15 January. He was the only student for two weeks. James had an outstanding record at Chapel Hill. At the time, original essays were printed in a record book and those of James frequently appeared, including "The Motions of the Earth," "The Slave Trade," "The Pleasures of College Life," and "The Commerce of Britain." He was a member of the first literary club, the debating society, and the Concord or Philanthropic Society. On 4 July 1798, he was awarded the bachelor of arts degree in engineering as one of seven students in the university's first graduating class.

James became an assistant to Hamilton Fulton, an engineer from Scotland hired by the state to make improvements on the rivers of North Carolina to aid navigation. James was put in charge of channel improvements on the Cape Fear River, the first such project undertaken there. In 1807 he was elected to the state legislature and served three terms. He also served as mayor of the town of Wilmington. At the time of his death, he was clerk and treasurer of the city of Wilmington and a magistrate for New Hanover County.

James was buried in the cemetery of Hopewell Presbyterian Church, near Burgaw, in the community where he was born. He was married three times and two of his wives, Mary Ann Watson and Sarah Moorehead, were buried beside him. The name and burial place of his third wife is unknown. A historical marker was erected by the North Carolina Department of Archives near his grave, and a dormitory at The University of North Carolina was named in his honor.

SEE: Kemp P. Battle, *History of the University of North Carolina* (1907–12); A. J. Howell, *The Book of Wilmington* (1930); Louis T. Moore, "Burial Place of Hinton James," *Charlotte Observer*, 23 May 1926.

GARY E. TRAWICK

James, Hinton (24 Apr. 1884–3 Nov. 1948), businessman and congressman, was born in Richmond (now Scotland) County, the son of Alexander Long and Mary Patterson James. He was the great-grandson of Hinton James, the first student at The University of North Carolina. In 1896, when the university observed its centennial, eleven-year-old Hinton attended; fifty years later, at the one hundred and fiftieth anniversary, he delivered an address.

After attending Davidson College, James farmed and engaged in buying and selling produce, particularly watermelons and cantaloupes; he was also a cotton merchant and had banking interests. As a widely known sportsman he hunted, raised prizewinning dogs, and served as state commissioner of game and inland fisheries (1941–45). James was elected as a Democrat to complete the unexpired term of Congressman William C. Hammer from 4 Nov. 1930 to 3 Mar. 1931; he was not a candidate for another term.

He married Anita Bryant of Laurinburg, and they were the parents of five children: Mary Wall, Anita Bryant, Eliza Patterson, Alice Long, and Hinton, Jr. James was buried in Laurinburg.

SEE: *Biog. Dir. Am. Cong.* (1961); *North Carolina Manual* (1931); Raleigh *News and Observer*, 17 June 1945, 4 Nov. 1948.

ANITA BRYANT JAMES

James, Horace (*6 May 1818–9 June 1875*), minister, Union Army chaplain, and Freedmen's Bureau officer, was born in Medford, Mass., the son of Galen C. James of Medford and his wife Mary R. Turner of Scituate, Mass. He was graduated from Yale University in 1840 and was ordained a Congregational minister; he did further study of theology at Andover. In 1843 he married Helen Leavitt in Medford, and they moved to Wrentham, Mass., where he became pastor of the Wrentham Original Congregational Church. Their son and only child, Horace Melville James, was born on 28 Mar. 1846.

In February 1853 James became the pastor of Old South Congregational Church in Worcester, where he served until after the outbreak of the Civil War. Like many New Englanders before the war, he regarded slavery as immoral and was adamant that it should not spread to the U.S. territories acquired during the Mexican War. In 1854 he spoke against the Kansas-Nebraska Bill at a mass meeting in Worcester. Two years later he publically condemned the beating of abolitionist Senator Charles Sumner by proslavery Congressman Preston S. Brooks of South Carolina. He also delivered antislavery sermons from the pulpit.

Despite his attack on the "peculiar institution" James was not an abolitionist, defined by historian James M. McPherson as one of "those Americans who before the Civil War had agitated for immediate, unconditional, and universal abolition of slavery in the United States." Rather, he felt that slavery should be abolished gradually and with compensation to slave owners. When the Civil War began, James, like Abraham Lincoln, considered the goal of the federal war effort to be the restoration of the Union without the immediate abolition of slavery in the South.

In October 1861 James joined the Twenty-fifth Massachusetts Infantry Regiment as a Union Army chaplain. He accompanied the regiment to Fortress Monroe, Va., where Major Benjamin F. Butler placed him in charge of supervising the care and employment of the many "contrabands" or escaped slaves who fled to Union lines. In February 1862 James's regiment participated in the expedition led by Major General Ambrose Burnside that captured Roanoke Island, N.C. Burnside appointed him officer-in-charge of the contrabands who sought federal protection on the island.

When the Twenty-fifth Massachusetts was part of the force that captured New Bern in March, James went to the town. Working under the federal-appointed superintendent of the poor, Vincent Colyer, he assisted black and white refugees who arrived in New Bern and other points held by the Union Army in coastal North Caro-

lina. Colyer was a former Northern YMCA official. James also established evening schools for blacks in New Bern, gave them religious instruction, and solicited food and clothing from Northern philanthropic organizations on his own initiative. By this time, and as a result of his experience with escaped slaves in Virginia, James changed his mind about the gradual, compensated abolition of slavery. He now believed that the eradication of slavery should be part of the Union's war aims, although he still did not consider blacks to be the biological and intellectual equals of whites.

When Vincent Colyer left North Carolina in November 1862, Major General John G. Foster, Burnside's successor, appointed army chaplain James Means to Colyer's post as superintendent of the poor. Means, however, soon died of yellow fever, and in January 1863 Foster named James to the office, which was now called the superintendent of Negro affairs. James had greater responsibility and a more lasting impact on the former slaves who came under his supervision than either of his predecessors. At the time of his appointment, the U.S. government was beginning to allocate more of its resources to the relief of blacks and destitute whites in the South. (This effort eventually led to the creation of the Bureau of Refugees, Freedmen, and Abandoned Lands in March 1865.)

As superintendent of Negro affairs, James was responsible for taking censuses of black refugees in eastern North Carolina and for finding them employment. He also issued rations, medicine, and clothing to destitute freedmen within federal lines, who had been officially liberated by the Emancipation Proclamation issued in January 1863, and he had to supervise the contracts of former slaves with whites. Assisted by New England philanthropic institutions, he established many schools for blacks in Union-held North Carolina. He also gave aid to white refugees.

To furnish the many freedmen with places to live as well as to provide consolidated points from which to implement his programs for assisting them in their transition from slavery to freedom, James created a number of refugee camps on land that had been abandoned by its owners or seized by the U.S. Army. At the camps he hoped to feed and shelter black families until they could become self-sufficient through the programs he planned to establish. These included basic education, vocational education, and the formation of small industries to utilize black labor.

In early 1863 James established the first camp at Roanoke Island, which served as a model for future black colonies. He set up smaller camps at other places in coastal North Carolina including Beaufort, Washington, and Plymouth. At New Bern, he created three camps but in 1864 combined these into the one located inside the federal fortifications and therefore protected from Confederate attack. This camp was just across the Trent River, south of New Bern. Army officers called it the Trent River Camp or the Trent River Settlement, but in 1865 it also came to be called James City in honor of its founder. During Reconstruction the federal government broke up the freedmen camps and restored the land to the original owners. The residents of James City, however, obtained leases from the owners of their tracts and managed to keep their community intact. (Many of the descendants of the original settlers still live in the vicinity of the original camp in a black community known as James City.)

In 1864, James was discharged as chaplain of the Twenty-fifth Massachusetts Infantry and immediately commissioned a captain and assistant quartermaster of

U.S. Volunteers, keeping his position as superintendent of Negro affairs. In March Congress established the Bureau of Refugees, Freedmen, and Abandoned Lands to which passed the responsibility for providing aid to destitute blacks and whites throughout the South. Secretary of War Edwin M. Stanton selected Major General Oliver Otis Howard as commissioner of this federal agency known as the Freedmen's Bureau. With the creation of the bureau James became the assistant commissioner for North Carolina, an office he held for only a short time. He soon asked to be relieved of his duties because of a concern for his family's health (and possibly his own), a strong desire to return to the pulpit full time, and a belief that it would not be long before the federal government abolished the Freedmen's Bureau.

To take James's place General Howard appointed Brevet Brigadier General Eliphalet Whittlesey, a member of Howard's staff. Whittlesey arrived from Washington and established a headquarters in Raleigh in July 1865; he then divided the state into districts to be served by the bureau. At his insistence, James agreed to remain for a short time as subassistant commissioner for the eastern district and to lend his experience in dealing with the freedmen. Whittlesey also appointed him financial agent for the bureau in North Carolina.

James remained as head of the eastern district until December 1865, when Howard finally accepted his resignation. After leaving the Freedmen's Bureau he entered into a plantation and labor scheme in Pitt County. In the enterprise he was the partner of Whittlesey and Winthrop Tappan, a neighbor of Whittlesey in the state of Maine. The plan conceived by Whittlesey and Tappan and presented to James called for the two men from Maine to rent two plantations in Pitt County from the owner, William Grimes. The plantations, named Avon and Yankee Hall, were located about twelve miles from Washington on opposite sides of the Tar River. James received money for expenses and had complete charge of the farms, including hiring and supervising freedmen as laborers and purchasing supplies. On each of the sites he established schools and churches for the freedmen. In overseeing the laborers employed on the plantations, James acted as a civilian agent for the Freedmen's Bureau; he received no salary, but if the project produced a profit he was to share in it equally with his partners.

In the summer of 1866, a black laborer was killed on one of the plantations. In September a military court tried James as an accomplice in the shooting and for allegedly exploiting the freedmen in the profit-making venture. The court also tried Whittlesey for using his position as head of the Freedmen's Bureau in the state to exploit freedmen labor and for not reporting the Pitt County shooting to headquarters in Washington. Both men were acquitted. Whittlesey soon left the state and rejoined Howard's staff in Washington, D.C.

James continued to run the plantations until a crop failure in 1867 led to the venture's termination, after which the land was returned to the owner. James returned to Massachusetts in the same year and took charge of a parish in Lowell, serving also as associate editor of the *Congregationalist*, a church publication. He then traveled abroad. While visiting Palestine, he contracted a severe cold that resulted in consumption and ultimately his death in Worcester, Mass. He was survived by his wife and son.

SEE: American Missionary Association Papers: North Carolina Letters (Dillard University, New Orleans); Thomas W. Baldwin, comp., *Vital Records of Wrentham,* *Massachusetts, to the Year 1850* (1910); Vincent Colyer, *Report of the Services Rendered by the Freed People to the United States Army in North Carolina in the Spring of 1862, After the Battle of New Bern* (1864); Horace James, *Annual Report of the Superintendent of Negro Affairs in North Carolina, 1864: History and Management of the Freedmen in This Department up to June 1st, 1865* (n.d.); *Massachusetts Soldiers, Sailors, and Marines in the Civil War* (1932); William McFeeley, *Yankee Stepfather: General O. O. Howard and the Freedmen* (1968); New York *Freedmen's Advocate* (March, April 1864); *New York Times,* 29 July 1866; *An Oration Delivered in New Bern, North Carolina, Before the Twenty-Fifth Regiment, Massachusetts Volunteers, July 4, 1862* (1862); *Our Duties to the Slave: A Sermon Preached Before the Original Congregational Church and Society in Wrentham, Massachusetts, on Thanksgiving Day, November 28, 1846* (1847); Samuel H. Putnam, *The Story of Company A, Twenty-Fifth Regiment [of] Massachusetts Volunteers in the War of the Rebellion* (1886); Records of the Bureau of Refugees, Freedmen, and Abandoned Lands for North Carolina, Record Group 105 (National Archives, Washington, D.C.); Franklin P. Rice, *The Worcester Book: A Diary of Noteworthy Events in Worcester, Massachusetts, from 1657 to 1883* (1884); Charles Emery Stevens, *Worcester Churches, 1719–1889* (1890); *Trial of Rev. Horace James, Before a Special Military Commission, Convened by Direction of Andrew Johnson, President of the United States in September, 1866* (n.d.); *The War of the Rebellion: A Compilation of the Official Records of the Union and Confederate Armies* (1880–1901); Bell I. Wiley, *Southern Negroes, 1861–1865* (1953); Henry Ernest Woods, ed., *Vital Records of Medford, Massachusetts, to the Year, 1850* (1907); Worcester *Evening Gazette,* 10 June 1875.

JOE A. MOBLEY

Jarrell, Benjamin Franklin (14 May 1880–9 Dec. 1946), musician, was raised in Surry County on the southern slope of the Blue Ridge, the son of Rufus A. and Susan Turney Jarrell. According to his father, the Scotch-Irish family had settled in present Rockingham County in the eighteenth century. Rufus, the son of the colorful horsetrader Fountain Jarrell and his wife Fannie, was born in Surry County in 1848. He fought in the Civil War and became a good tale teller, recounting stories of being hit by minié balls and of being close enough to have heard the shot that killed President Abraham Lincoln. After the war, Rufus became a farmer and was licensed by the government to make apple brandy; he was an expert with traditional recipes and practices. His sons acquired whiskey-making skills and worked with him until Prohibition outlawed their time-honored and quality-controlled family occupation. By the beginning of the twentieth century, the Jarrell home was a social center for the self-sufficient community at Round Peak; it was well known for good stories and music.

Ben and his older brother Charlie apparently acquired their musical talent from their mother's side of the family. When she married Rufus in 1873, she was the widow Susan Turney and had two children, Dave and Mary, who were musical influences on the Jarrell children and grandchildren. Susan, a midwife, died in about 1906, after going out to deliver a baby in an ice storm.

When they were boys, Ben and his brother learned to play both banjo and fiddle from neighbors. Charlie brought an early version of "John Henry" into the area from Alleghany County. Ben learned "The Drunken Hiccups" from a Civil War veteran, "Old Man Houston" Galyean. They frequently played for community dances and sometimes performed at the one-room schoolhouse, especially for the school breaking at the end of the year. They would walk at the head of a line of marching children with their father or another Civil War veteran. These men were innovative musicians; Ben and neighbors Tony and Charlie Lowe even changed and elaborated on some of the tunes. Some popular urban songs made their way into the mountain region by way of recordings or visiting singers. As early as 1910, Ben owned one of the first cylinder phonographs in Round Peak.

Ben Jarrell was one of the finest southern musicians documented for his time. In 1927, he traveled to Richmond, Ind., with patent medicine seller Da Costa Woltz and banjo player Frank Jenkins to record for Gennett records. The eighteen performances completed at the session preserved significant and vital music from the time and region. Ben's incisive vocal and driving fiddle propelled the band and characterized the traditional style of the area. Even the band's recording of the song "Merry Girl" was cast into a traditional framework reflecting local taste.

Jarrell married Susan Letisha Amburn and had eleven children, many of whom became good musicians in their own right. Because Ben did not care for farming, he also played music, traveled to the Northwest, and ran a store in Round Peak until his father died about 1921. Then he moved the family to Mount Airy, where he opened another store and built a new house. Jarrell became a prominent retired farmer and merchant. In 1940, when he ran for Democratic representative of Surry County, his younger children campaigned for him in the schools as a family band. A member of the Round Peak Masonic Lodge, Ben was buried at Ivy Green Baptist Church beside his wife.

SEE: Cecelia Conway, Fieldtapes and interviews with Ben's son, Tommy Jarrell, 1974–85; Tommy Jarrell, 33⅓ rpm phonodiscs and notes, 1972 (County Records, P.O. Box 191, Floyd, Va. 24091). County Records: County 524, Richard Nevins, ed., *Da Costa Woltz's Southern Broadcasters, 1927* featuring Ben Jarrell and Frank Jenkins.

CECELIA CONWAY

Jarrell, Randall (6 May 1914–14 Oct. 1965), poet, critic, and teacher, was born in Nashville, Tenn., the son of Owen and Anna Campbell Jarrell. Owing to his parents' divorce, much of his childhood through 1927 was spent in central and southern California. Returning to Nashville in 1928, he attended high school and was graduated from Vanderbilt University with a B.S. degree in psychology in 1935. During the next two years he pursued graduate work at Vanderbilt, where he fell under the spell of the famed Fugitive and Agrarian poets. With the growth of his own poetic skills, he won the Poetry Prize from *The Southern Review* in 1936.

Jarrell taught at Kenyon College in Gambier, Ohio, from 1937 to 1939, beginning a long career in the classroom and forming lasting friendships with John Crowe Ransom and the young poet Robert Lowell. In 1938 he received an M.A. degree in English from Vanderbilt; his thesis was on the poet A. E. Housman. After leaving Kenyon, Jarrell taught at the University of Texas until 1942, when he published his first collection of poems, *Blood for a Stranger*. In 1940 he married Mackie Langham, who also taught in the English Department

at the University of Texas, but they were divorced in 1951.

World War II claimed Jarrell's time from 1942 to 1946. He aspired to be a pilot but ultimately served in the Air Force as a Celestial Navigation tower operator, principally in Arizona. Even these years were productive for his poetry; in fact, his second volume of verses, *Little Friend, Little Friend* (1945), grew directly from his war experiences and feelings about the war. Its best-known poem is the last, "The Death of the Ball-Turret Gunner."

Immediately after the war Jarrell received a Guggenheim Fellowship, the culmination of growing critical acclaim which included the Jeanette Sewall Davis Prize from *Poetry* magazine and the John Peale Bishop Memorial Literary Prize from *The Sewanee Review*. Combining his triple role as creator, critic, and teacher, Jarrell taught at Sarah Lawrence College in 1946–47 while continuing his writing and serving as literary editor of *The Nation*.

In 1947 Jarrell began a long and important association with North Carolina, becoming associate, then full professor of English at the Woman's College of The University of North Carolina (now The University of North Carolina at Greensboro). Though he took leaves of absence to teach at the Salzburg Seminar in American Civilization, Princeton, the University of Indiana, and the University of Illinois, and to accept an appointment as Consultant in Poetry at the Library of Congress (1956–58), he remained centered in Greensboro where his affection for the college and its students grew over the years. In 1961 he chose to receive the National Book Award at The University of North Carolina at Chapel Hill, and in 1962 he was presented the O. Max Gardner Award, one of the state's highest honors.

In addition to his classroom activities, Jarrell's interest in the arts spurred the founding of a literary magazine, *Analects*, at Greensboro to which he contributed a number of his own works. In 1948, his first full year of residence in North Carolina, Jarrell published his third volume of poetry, *Losses*, with the fourth, *The Seven-League Crutches*, appearing in 1951. Of *Losses*, *Poetry* magazine stated: "The book contains war poems quite as good as any written in this century."

On 8 Nov. 1952, Jarrell married Mary Eloise von Schrader, who later wrote a memoir of their marriage and assisted in his posthumous publications.

As an outgrowth of his years as literary critic for *The Nation* and *The Partisan Review*, Jarrell's first book of literary criticism, *Poetry and the Age*, appeared in 1953. During the next decade he was a judge of such literary contests as the National Book Awards, was poetry critic for *The Yale Review* (1955–57), and was a member of the editorial board of *The American Scholar*. From 1949 until his death Jarrell was involved in selecting, editing, introducing, and sometimes translating works as diverse as Anton Chekhov's *The Three Sisters*, fairy tales of the Brothers Grimm, two collections of Rudyard Kipling's stories, Christina Stead's *The Man Who Loved Children*, and *Selected Poems* by William Carlos Williams.

In 1954 the poet Jarrell's versatile talents took another turn with the publication of his only novel, the satiric *Pictures from an Institution, a Comedy*, based on years of academic observations. The next year there appeared *Selected Poems*, published by Knopf, followed by *The Woman at the Washington Zoo: Poems and Translations* in 1960. Another prose effort, *A Sad Heart at the Supermarket: Essays and Fables*, was published in 1962. A second volume of *Selected Poems*, this published by Atheneum, came out in 1964.

Perhaps it was his interest in fairy tales as a "metaphor for life" as well as his belief in the universal relevance of poetry that inspired Jarrell to write three sensitive children's books, *The Bat-Poet* (1964) and *The Animal Family* (1965), both illustrated by Maurice Sendak, and *The Gingerbread Rabbit* (1964). For *The Bat-Poet* he won the American Association of University Women Children's Book Award.

In 1965, the year of his death, there appeared the last new collection of poems, *The Lost World*, for which he received the Roanoke-Chowan Poetry Award. His widow, Mary Jarrell, describes his final year: "Signs of Randall's nervous breakdown had begun, but they fooled us into explaining them in other terms. Before the worst of it happened, he was granted a few magic weeks of Lisztian virtuosity." During the last months of his life Jarrell was teaching at The University of North Carolina, Chapel Hill. One night, as he walked along a dark road in the town, he was struck by a car and killed. Jarrell was buried in New Garden Friends Cemetery, Greensboro.

His posthumous works include *The Third Book of Criticism*, published in 1969, and *The Complete Poems*, published in the United States in the same year and in England in 1971. *The Achievement of Randall Jarrell: A Comprehensive Selection of His Poems* with a critical introduction by Frederick J. Hoffman appeared as part of the Modern Poets series in 1970, and *Jerome, the Biography of a Poem*, based on Jarrell's original contribution to *Analects* in 1960, was published in 1971. Unfinished at his death were anthologies, translations, individual poems, and another children's book.

SEE: Charles Marshall Adams, *Randall Jarrell: A Bibliography* (1958); Suzanne Ferguson, *The Poetry of Randall Jarrell* (1971); Mary Jarrell, "The Group of Two: A Memoir of a Marriage," *Harper's Magazine*, April 1967; Robert Lowell and others, eds., *Randall Jarrell, 1914–1965* (1967); Karl Jay Shapiro, *Randall Jarrell: Lecture with a Bibliography of Jarrell Materials in the Collections of the Library of Congress* (1967); *Who's Who in America* (1964–65).

MARY FARNHAM

Jarrell, Thomas Jefferson *(1 Mar. 1901–28 Jan. 1985)*, musician, born and raised near Round Peak in Surry County, was the oldest child of Benjamin Franklin and Susan Letisha Amburn Jarrell. He was an exceptional instrumentalist, singer, and tale teller. His music and life story provide the means for reaching beyond the written record to an understanding of the complex roots of southern culture. The National Endowment for the Arts awarded Jarrell one of the first National Heritage Fellowships at the Smithsonian Festival of American Folklife on 4 July 1982; his life stands as a tribute to his heritage, artistry, and cultural contribution.

Tommy Jarrell learned most of his tunes before the influence of commercial recordings and radio. He preserved two generations of the old instrumental styles and repertories that thrived in the region before 1925. In addition to being a remarkable musician, Tommy was a singular vocalist with a powerful style; his repertory included many unusual fiddle and banjo songs, ballads, and Primitive Baptist hymns. An exceptional storyteller, he related family reminiscences and regional lore with a fine wit and was an inspired performer and transmitter of regional styles and repertory. To his last days he continued to add imaginative and subtle variations to his stories and tunes.

Tommy first learned to play banjo when he was eight years old from "Boggy" Cockerham, a man hired to help on the farm. When he was thirteen, he took up the fiddle; he learned from watching his father, his Uncle Charlie, and other neighbors. By the time he was sixteen, Tommy played for dances at Round Peak. In his last years he played sometimes in the same house and for the same people who had been courting when he played as a boy.

Several of his fiddle tunes were acquired from men who were Civil War veterans. He learned "Sail Away Ladies" from "Old Man Pet" McKinny when they met on the road. The old man borrowed his fiddle and played the tune for him twice. Another time, Tommy went up to visit Zack Payne near Lambsburg to learn "Billy in the Low Ground." Instead, he came home having learned "Flatwoods" and "Devil in the Strawstack." He also added to the mountain tradition already influenced by Afro-American banjo music in the nineteenth century. He learned "Bo Weaval" from a black woman singing at a traveling tent show and later "Rylan Spenser" from Jim Raleigh, a Mount Airy stoneworker and guitar player.

Educated in a one-room schoolhouse, Tommy was always interested in words, sounds, spellings, and new ideas. He liked television because he felt that it presented accurate pronunciations of words that he had read but not heard spoken. He told wry anecdotes about spelling crow "krow," and in 1978 he named his dog "Boliver" after a Spanish revolutionary. Tommy had an ear for a good story and could mock the voices of the old folks, as well as the style of several local musicians.

When he was seventeen Tommy helped his grandfather farm, but they lacked $2.47 to cover the fertilizer bill. Later he worked at the sawmill. During those years, he could have gone back across the hill and made moonshine that would have sold for $20 a gallon.

Tommy married Nina Lowe, the daughter of Charlie Barnett and Ardena Leftwich Lowe, and lived with them in Lambsburg. Two years later Nina's parents died, and the couple moved to Mount Airy, where Tommy's folks lived. They had three children: Ardena, a good flat-foot dancer, who worked in a clothing factory; Clarence Wayne, a dancer and caller, who became a storekeeper; and Benjamin Franklin ("B. F."), a bluegrass fiddler, who became a disc jockey in Dobson.

When his children were young, Tommy worked with the highway department and ran a motor grader for thirty years. Over these hard years, he played music only on holidays with "Adam's Charlie" Lowe, an excellent banjo player who knew all of the old tunes and had incredible time. Tommy would say, "Music is like a wheel. It goes around steady—not steady by jerks but steady. That's what my Daddy used to say. It goes around like a wheel, like the wheel of a tape recorder, and never misses a beat." Tommy kept the music going steady.

After his retirement, Tommy had enough time for music again. His playing inspired local elderly musicians from his own region (Fred Cockerham, Kyle Creed, and Sydna Myers) and those slightly younger who had learned from him as boys (Earnest East, Benton Flippen, Paul Sutphin). He traveled to nearby fiddlers' conventions where his brothers Fred Rufus and Early Columbus judged the music. His sisters Julie Lyons and Ottola "Togie" McGee were both good dancers and singers in their own right. They often held get-togethers for Tommy's family, including sisters Ida

Elizabeth Gentry and singer Edith Sylvia Hicks, children, neighbors, visiting musicians, and folklorists. Tommy enjoyed his musical life increasingly in his old age and took his growing national reputation in stride. The time had come when Tommy was the one who remembered the old and the new tunes of his father's generation.

Inquisitive friendliness, humor, and generosity characterized Tommy Jarrell. He performed concerts and festivals across the United States and Canada. Apprentices from many states frequently visited his North Carolina home to learn from him; at the time of his death, they gathered in Mount Airy from as far away as the West Coast and France to honor him. In addition to passing his music on in person, Tommy recorded homemade tapes for visitors, made albums for County Records, and appeared in videotapes and films. The film about his life and music, *Sprout Wings and Fly*, won awards, was translated into Spanish, and was played at international festivals in Scotland, Spain, and South America. The summer before he died, Tommy made another album of previously unrecorded material, *Rainbow Sign*:

> I'll tune up my fiddle, I'll rosin my bow;
> I'll make myself welcome wherever I go.

SEE: Cecelia Conway, Fieldtapes and interviews with Tommy Jarrell and family, 1974–87 (selected tapes are in The University of North Carolina Folk Music Archive, Chapel Hill, and the Library of Congress Archive of Folklife, Washington, D.C.), "Thomas Jefferson Jarrell," *North Carolina Folklore Journal* 30 (1982), and "Tommy Jarrell, Round Peak Fiddler," hour-long radio show, WUNC Radio and University of North Carolina Curriculum in Folklore, Chapel Hill, 1977; Cecelia Conway, Les Blank, Alice Gerrard, and Maureen Gosling, *Tommy Jarrell: Sprout Wings and Fly*, half-hour color film (Flower Films, El Cerrito, Calif., 1983); David Gates, "Pickin' on Tommy's Porch," *Newsweek*, 17 Sept. 1984 (photograph); Tommy Jarrell, 33⅓ rpm phonodiscs and notes, 1972 (County Records, P.O. Box 191, Floyd, Va. 24091); *New York Times*, 29 Jan. 1985. County Records: County 713, *Down to the Cider Mill* with Cockerham, Jenkins; County 717, Charles Faurot, ed., *More Clawhammer Banjo Songs and Tunes from the Mountains* (1969); County 723, Richard Nevins, ed., *Back Home in the Blue Ridge* with Cockerham, Jenkins (1969); County 741, *Stay All Night*; County 748, Charles Faurot, ed., *Tommy Jarrell's Banjo Album: Come and Go with Me* (1974); County 756, Barry Poss, ed., *Sail Away Ladies* (1976); County 757, Blanton Owens, ed., *Clawhammer Banjo*, vol. 3 (1978); County 791, Alice Gerrard, Andy Cahan, Verlen Clifton, eds., *Rainbow Sign* (1986); Heritage 010, Lisa Ornstein, ed., *Music from Round Peak* (1976). Mountain Records (Rt. 3, Box 299, Galax, Va. 24333): Mountain 302, JUNE APPLE, Zane Bennett, ed., *Kyle Creed and Tommy Jarrell* (1972); Mountain 310, Kyle Creed, ed., *Joke on the Puppy* with Chester McMillian and Steve Roberts (1976).

CECELIA CONWAY

Jarvis, Thomas (d. 1694), landowner, member of the Grand Council, and deputy governor of the Albemarle, was one of the earliest settlers in the Carolinas. His birthplace, birthdate, and parents are unknown although he was of English descent. Among his descendants were Samuel Jarvis, leader of the Albemarle militia during the Revolutionary War, and Thomas Jordan Jarvis, a governor of North Carolina.

Nothing is known of Jarvis's education, religion, or early life. He probably arrived in the Albemarle region (which included the precincts of Perquimans, Pasquotank, Currituck, and Chowan) from Virginia, as did the other settlers of the time. He was in the Albemarle as early as 1663, when Governor William Berkeley of Virginia announced on orders from England that settlers on the Roanoke Sound should make claims to their land through the procedures set down in the Virginia law. Among the patents for land issued by Governor Berkeley was one for a tract owned by Captain John Jenkins. The tract was described as being bound on the west by the great swamp that divided that land from the land of Thomas Jarvis. This description places Jarvis's land in what is now known as Harveys Neck in Perquimans County.

In 1672 Jarvis was a member of the governor's Grand Council. He was one of the nine signers of the Council's instructions to be presented to the Lords Proprietors in England by Governor Peter Carteret of the Albemarle region. During Carteret's absence, disputes about taxes and control of the area eventually led to what is known as Culpeper's Rebellion in 1677 during which Thomas Miller, a representative of the Proprietors, and most of his officials were overthrown. Thomas Eastchurch, appointed governor by the Proprietors, was prevented from entering the region by armed forces. Thomas Jarvis was a member of the "rebel" parliament of eighteen men created by Zachariah Gillam, a shipmaster and another one of Miller's opponents. Jarvis may have then returned to Virginia for a short time, for a man by that name served in the Virginia House of Burgesses in 1682.

When Philip Ludwell was appointed governor in 1689, the area of Albemarle included sixty to seventy scattered families. Jarvis acted as Ludwell's deputy from November 1690 to November 1691. On 6 July 1690 one John Gibbs, who had protested Ludwell's appointment, had entered the precinct courts in Albemarle, seized two magistrates, and taken them to Virginia. Afterwards Jarvis and his Council wrote letters to Francis Nicholson, then lieutenant governor of Virginia, and to Governor Ludwell, who was absent from Albemarle at the time, asking for help.

Ludwell's appointment in 1689 differed from that of his predecessors in that he was appointed governor not only of the county of Albemarle but also of the part of the Carolina province north and east of Cape Fear. In November 1691, the Lords Proprietors made Ludwell governor of the entire province of Carolina with the power to appoint a deputy in North Carolina. Jarvis again served as Ludwell's deputy governor until September 1694. Records show that he was paid no salary.

It is probable that Jarvis died early in September 1694. On 24 September Thomas Harvey was acting as the deputy governor. Foster Jarvis, Thomas Jarvis's son, appeared before the General Court on the twenty-third and asked that the estate of the deceased Thomas Jarvis be divided between himself and Charles Neal in behalf of Neal's wife Dorkas, the daughter of Jarvis, and their daughter Dorcas Neal. No mention was made of Thomas Jarvis's wife, and no portrait of him exists.

SEE: Thurman Chatham Collection, Colonial Court Records 148, Civil and Criminal Papers of Early Colonial Courts 1681–1719, Colonial Court Records 101, Minutes Dockets—General Court 1693–95, Colonial Court Records 189, Minutes—General Court 1682–1716, Colonial Court Records 188, Notes and Receipts 1676–1790, Perquimans Precinct Court Minutes 1688–93 (North

Carolina State Archives, Raleigh); Beth G. Crabtree, *North Carolina Governors, 1585–1958* (1958); Bryan Grimes, *Abstracts of North Carolina Wills* (1910); Mattie Erma E. Parker, ed., *North Carolina Higher-Court Records, 1670–1696* (1968); William S. Powell, ed., *Yᵉ Countie of Albemarle in Carolina: A Collection of Documents, 1664–1675* (1958); Hugh F. Rankin, *Upheaval in Albemarle* (1962); William L. Saunders, ed., *Colonial Records of North Carolina*, vol. 1 (1890); Charles L. Van Noppen Papers (Manuscript Department, Duke University Library, Durham).

JUNE DUNN PARKER

Jarvis, Thomas Jordan *(18 Jan. 1836–17 June 1915)*, teacher, lawyer, lieutenant governor, governor, ambassador to Brazil, and U.S. senator, was born in Jarvisburg, Currituck County, the son of Elizabeth Daley and Bannister Hardy Jarvis, a Methodist minister and farmer. He was the brother of George, Ann, Margaret, and Elizabeth. Of English descent, the Jarvis family appears several times in the history of North Carolina. Thomas Jarvis (d. 1694) was deputy governor of the county of Albemarle under Governor Philip Ludwell, and General Samuel Jarvis led the Albemarle militia during the Revolutionary War.

The family of Thomas Jordan Jarvis had the necessities of life but few of the luxuries. Jarvis spent most of his youth working on his father's three-hundred-acre farm and sporadically attended nearby common schools. At age nineteen he decided to attend Randolph-Macon College, which at the time was located at Boydton, Va. Because his parents had little money, he paid his way through college by teaching in his hometown during the summer; he also was assisted by John Sanderson. He was graduated with honors in 1860 and received the master of arts degree in 1861.

In the spring of 1861 Jarvis opened a school in Pasquotank County. When North Carolina entered the Civil War, he enlisted in the Seventeenth North Carolina Regiment and on 16 May 1861 was commissioned first lieutenant of Company B, Eighth North Carolina Regiment. On 22 Apr. 1863 he was made captain. Although he had a good military record, he was wounded in the right arm during the Battle of Drewery's Bluff in May 1864 and never rejoined his regiment. His arm was permanently disabled. When the war ended, he was on sick leave in Norfolk. In May 1865, he was paroled and returned to Jarvisburg.

In order to comply with President Johnson's requirement for the restoration of the North Carolina government, Governor William W. Holden on 8 Aug. 1865 called an election for 21 September to select delegates to a constitutional convention. Elected a delegate from Currituck County, Jarvis opposed the writing of the new constitution which was later rejected by the electorate.

Late in 1865, he formed a business partnership with William H. Happer of Tyrrell County. The two men bought a stock of goods from Norfolk on credit and opened a small general store in the Gum Neck community. But business was poor and in 1867 Jarvis bought out Happer's share of the store. In his spare moments he began to read law. After obtaining a license in June 1867, he gave up his store and moved to Columbia.

In the spring of 1868, North Carolina adopted a new constitution and Jarvis won a seat in the state house of representatives in an uncontested Tyrrell County election. In the fall, the Democratic party nominated him as an elector on the Seymour-Blair ticket and Jarvis made

the first of many statewide canvasses. North Carolina, however, voted for Ulysses S. Grant for president.

In the legislature, Jarvis opposed the passage of a bill for special tax bonds for railroad construction, changes in suffrage, and the organization of special militia to police certain counties. He later helped to establish the Bragg-Phillips Investigating Committee, which studied the corruption regarding the special tax bonds that had passed. In 1870, the Republican-Conservative effort was defeated in both houses and Jarvis was elected speaker of the house. He exercised a controlling role in the impeachment of Governor Holden, reduced the cost of state government, and investigated other railway frauds. In 1872 he was the Democratic elector-at-large on the Horace Greeley ticket.

About this time Jarvis moved to Greenville, where he formed a law partnership with David M. Carter and spent the next three years reestablishing himself. He also became chairman of the county Democratic central committee and helped the party win in county elections.

In 1875, the legislature again called for a convention to revise the state constitution. Jarvis won one of the county's two seats at the convention, where his presence was felt both on and off the floor. Although he was unable to repudiate the entire constitution, thirty significant amendments were made. One important change empowered the legislature to appoint justices of the peace and the county commissioners.

In 1876, Zebulon B. Vance was elected governor and Thomas J. Jarvis lieutenant governor, thereby ensuring Democratic control of the executive as well as the legislative branch of the state government. Jarvis had served two years when Vance won a seat in the U.S. Senate, leaving the governorship to Jarvis. Jarvis took office on 5 Feb. 1879.

As governor, he fought against governmental extravagance and corruption and worked for the reduction of taxes, the state debt, and government control. He sold various state-owned railroads, which were costly to the state, to private businesses. While attempting to reduce government spending, he was instrumental in the state's decision to provide mental health facilities at Morganton and Goldsboro. He also worked for the establishment of normal schools for teachers in North Carolina (in 1879 the state authorized additional normal schools at Davidson, Trinity, and Wake Forest colleges) and helped to organize the State Board of Health at the state and county levels.

Jarvis won reelection to a full term as governor in 1880. During this term, he actively supported establishing a system of county superintendents of education elected by boards of education, grades of teacher certification, standards of examinations for public school teachers, and lists of recommended textbooks. Funds for the mental institutions continued to increase, and the laws of North Carolina were for the first time codified and state insurance laws fully defined. The legislature also gave Jarvis permission to build a governor's mansion. State property in Raleigh was sold and convict labor and convict-made materials were used to build the mansion, which was begun in April 1883. Jarvis never lived in the new governor's residence.

Governor Jarvis won much acclaim for the state during the Boston Exposition of September 1883. North Carolina had the largest exhibit of resources, and Jarvis's "New South" speech focused even more attention on the state's progress in agriculture and industry. The exhibit was so popular that it was also shown in Chicago and New Orleans.

At the end of his gubernatorial term, Jarvis was offered the post of U.S. minister to Brazil, although he had hoped for a place in President Cleveland's cabinet. Soon after starting his duties in July 1885, he became anxious to reenter North Carolina political life; in particular, he wanted the Democratic nomination for governor in 1888. However, Jarvis could not return to North Carolina until after the election, and Daniel G. Fowle became governor.

After President Cleveland died, Jarvis resigned his ambassadorial post and returned to Greenville. He reopened his law office in partnership with Alexander L. Blow; when Blow became clerk of the North Carolina Superior Court in 1912, Jarvis formed a partnership with Frank Wooten. In 1889, Jarvis handled one of his most sensational cases as a member of a team of lawyers who successfully defended Eugene Grissom, superintendent of the North Carolina Insane Asylum, against charges of immorality, corruption, mismanagement, and cruelty.

In 1889, the board of trustees offered him the first presidency of North Carolina State College but he declined. In 1892 he became the permanent chairman of the State Democratic Convention, and in April 1894, when Senator Zebulon B. Vance died in office, Governor Elias Carr appointed him to fill the vacancy. On Capitol Hill, Jarvis busied himself with fiscal matters and tariff reduction; he also advocated a graduated income tax. He did not seek election to the two remaining years of Vance's terms but tried unsuccessfully to win a full term in the other U.S. senatorial seat.

Jarvis then turned his energies towards unifying the Democratic party nationally under a silver standard platform. He attended the Chicago National Democratic Convention in 1896 as a delegate-at-large, with hopes of being elected national committeeman, a position captured by Josephus Daniels.

Because the Democratic party wanted new people to run for public office, Jarvis concentrated on his law practice. In 1901, he and four other lawyers won acquittals for State Supreme Court justices David M. Furches and Robert M. Douglas after impeachment charges had been brought against them by the state house of representatives. Jarvis also assisted in dismissing the charges for contempt of court brought against Josephus Daniels by Judge Thomas Richard Purnell because of several strong editorials published by Daniels about the judge's actions concerning the Atlantic and North Carolina Railroad. In 1904, President John C. Kilgo offered Jarvis the deanship of the new Trinity College law department but Jarvis declined because he felt that he was too old.

The Methodist church and public education were two of his strong interests. In 1891 he represented the North Carolina Methodist Conference in the Ecumenical Conference in Washington, D.C. He was also superintendent of the Sunday school and chairman of the Building Committee of the Methodist church in Greenville which was later named the Jarvis Memorial Methodist Church. In the field of education, Jarvis helped to establish a graded school system in Greenville and was chairman of the board of trustees for the system. He was a trustee of Trinity College and in 1907, with his friend, William Ragsdale, wrote the bill proposed before the legislature that would establish a teachers' training school in Greenville. Later Jarvis served as chairman of the Building Committee of East Carolina College. He was a member of the Odd Fellows and the Knights of Pythias.

In 1874 he married Mary Woodson, the daughter of Judge John Woodson of Goochland County, Va. They had no children. Jarvis was buried in the Cherry Hill Cemetery, Greenville. Jarvis Hall at East Carolina University and Jarvis Street in Greenville were also named in his honor. Portraits of him hang in the Pitt County Courthouse, Jarvis Hall, and the State Archives-Library Building in Raleigh.

SEE: Samuel A. Ashe, ed., *Biographical History of North Carolina*, vol. 1 (1905 [portrait]); *Biog. Dir. Am. Cong.* (1950); Wyatt Brown, personal interview, January 1979; Walter Clark, ed., *Histories of the Several Regiments and Battalions from North Carolina in the Great War, 1861–1865*, vol. 5 (1901); Beth G. Crabtree, *North Carolina Governors, 1585–1958* (1958 [portrait]); *DAB*, vol. 5 (1932); Jerome Dowd, *Sketches of Prominent Living North Carolinians* (1888); *Eighth Census of the United States* 9, Agricultural Schedule 705 (1860) (North Carolina State Archives, Raleigh); Mattie Gaylord, personal interview, January 1979; Greenville *Daily Reflector*, 27 May 1899–9 Dec. 1912; *Thomas J. Jarvis Memorial Issue, East Carolina Training School Quarterly* (July–September 1915 [portrait]); Thomas J. Jarvis Papers (Manuscript Collection, Duke University Library, Durham); Joye E. Jordan, *Thomas Jordan Jarvis* (1945 [portrait]); *Journal of the House of Representatives of the General Assembly of North Carolina* (1868–69, 1869–70, 1870–71) (North Carolina State Archives, Raleigh); Miscellaneous Records of the Jarvis Memorial Methodist Church (in possession of Wyatt Brown, Greenville); Pitt County Deeds, 1891 (Pitt County Courthouse); Raleigh *News and Observer*, 13 Apr. 1881, 8 Sept. 1896; Wilmington *Morning Star*, 4 July 1875–4 Aug. 1880; Frank M. Wooten, Jr., personal interview, January 1979; Wilfred Buck Yearns, ed., *The Papers of Thomas Jordan Jarvis, 1869–1882*, vol. 1 (1969 [portrait]). Unpublished sources in North Carolina State Archives, Raleigh: Governor's Papers, Thomas Jordan Jarvis, 1879–85; Thomas Jordan Jarvis Letter Book, 1879–83; Record of Deeds, Currituck County, Book 43; Record of Deeds, Tyrrell County, 1860–73.

JUNE DUNN PARKER

Jay, Allen (1831–1910), Quaker minister, was born in Miami County, Ohio, the son of Isaac Jay and Rhoda Cooper Jay. His grandparents were from North Carolina. Jay's early schooling was limited to a few months each year, with visiting Friends exerting a vital influence in his life. On 20 Oct. 1854 he married Martha Sleeper. Greenfield (Ohio) Monthly Meeting recorded him as a minister on 21 June 1864. "In the love of the gospel" he visited meetings and families extensively throughout Ohio, Tennessee, and North Carolina, as well as attending the Baltimore and North Carolina Yearly Meetings.

The Baltimore Association of Friends was founded in 1865 to assist and advise the Friends of the southern states. Its specific purposes were to give immediate relief to distressed Quakers in North Carolina through gifts of food and shelter; to repair and rebuild homes and meetinghouses; to restore schools in Quaker communities, and supply teachers and equipment; to set up teacher training institutes; and to conduct agricultural demonstrations, especially on operating a family farm successfully. Allen Jay was called by Francis T. King of the Baltimore Association in the summer of 1868, and he traveled widely in its behalf with good results. The farm of Nathan Hunt at Springfield (Guilford County, N.C.) was bought and made into a model farm where demonstrations and annual institutes attracted farmers and distinguished guests, including the governor. The

Baltimore Association was responsible for the establishment of 44 schools with an enrollment of over 3,000 students taught by 65 well-trained teachers. Fifty-eight meetinghouses were restored and farmers saw, believed, and began to practice a new type of life.

As a result of these activities, the Society of Friends came into a new and more vigorous spiritual life in North Carolina. It is said that had it not been for the Baltimore Association and the efforts of Allen Jay, no Friends Meeting might have survived. Allen Jay High School and the Allen Jay Home in Guilford County are memorials to Allen Jay.

SEE: Seth and Mary Edith Hinshaw, *Carolina Quakers* (1972); Allen Jay, *Autobiography* (1910); North Carolina Yearly Meeting, *Minutes*, 1868–78.

B. RUSSELL BRANSON

Jeffress, Edwin Bedford, Sr. *(20 May 1887–23 May 1961)*, journalist, was born in Canton, the son of Charles James and Maria Love Osborne Jeffress. He obtained his elementary and secondary education in the public schools of Haywood County, for a short period in Salisbury, and then at the Asheville High School where he was graduated in 1903. That fall he entered The University of North Carolina and distinguished himself as a student, earning a Phi Beta Kappa key for scholarship and an Omicron Delta Kappa key for leadership. During the last two years he was an assistant instructor in geology. In 1907 he received the bachelor of arts degree, with a major in general science.

The summer after graduation Jeffress edited the *Canton Observer*, and, although he had planned to make a career of teaching science, the first "printer's ink on his hands" later determined his profession. From 1907 to 1909 he taught at the Bingham Military School in Asheville, but spent his vacations working as a reporter for the *Asheville Gazette News*, beginning a long association with that brilliant journalist of the turn of the century, W. A. Hildebrand. In the summer of 1909, he resigned his teaching post to become a full-time staff member of Hildebrand's paper. Two years later the Asheville publisher acquired the *Greensboro Daily News*. Jeffress is believed to have been the first newspaperman to become a staff correspondent in the state capital, where he wrote special dispatches for both the Asheville and Greensboro papers.

In late 1911, Jeffress purchased (apparently from Hildebrand) a half interest in the *Greensboro Daily News* and assumed the role of business manager. Soon afterwards he became secretary-treasurer of the Greensboro News Company. When Hildebrand sold his part ownership of the Greensboro paper to his employees (many of whom had followed him from Asheville to Greensboro) in 1918, Jeffress became president, succeeding his longtime friend and mentor.

The growth in circulation and influence of the *Greensboro Daily News*, and later its afternoon counterpart, the *Greensboro Record*, was largely attributed to Jeffress, who for the next sixteen years was a dynamo of energy and accomplishment. In 1934, he became seriously ill; subsequent brain surgery resulted in a general incapacitation until his death in 1961. Although he experienced some difficulty in getting around, he remained alert, a ready conversationalist, and a perennial student, having returned to Chapel Hill where he lived out his days at the Carolina Inn among the academic and cultural offerings of his beloved University of North Carolina.

During the twenty-three years he was active, Jeffress demonstrated a deep interest in everything that concerned the growth and development of Greensboro. From the first he was an energetic member of the Chamber of Commerce, serving as president for two terms (1921–22). His leadership in that group and related activities won for him the Civitan Club's Outstanding Citizen Award. He was the logical choice for election to the city council, and, as mayor of Greensboro from 1925 to 1929, he did much to enhance that city. Notable among his achievements was his part in the establishment of the Greensboro-High Point Airport. He was also founder and president of the Greensboro Community Chest.

Elected to the North Carolina General Assembly, Jeffress proved to be an effective legislator in the 1931 session—particularly in his fine service through the Commission to Study the Prison Situation in North Carolina. The same year the governor appointed him to the State Highway Commission, of which he was chairman for two years. In the reorganization of 1933, which produced the North Carolina State Highway and Public Works Commission, including the State Prison System, he was named chairman for a four-year term; however, his tenure was cut short by his illness less than a year after he assumed the expanded office. Capus Waynick, writing about North Carolina roads and road builders, paid high tribute to the constructive and innovative leadership Jeffress provided in the few years of service he gave the state in the interest of improved highways.

Through his active years, he was a member of the American Newspaper Publishers Association, the Southern Newspaper Publishers Association, the North Carolina Press Association, and the National Press Club in Washington, D.C. One of his auxiliary business ventures was the North State Engraving Company, of which he was president and a longtime director. He was also a director of the King Cotton Hotel Company. For a number of years he was a director of the Alumni Association of The University of North Carolina. Other memberships included Kiwanis International, the Merchants and Manufacturers Club, the Greensboro Country Club, and various fraternal organizations: Ancient, Free, and Accepted Masons (Knight Templar, 32nd degree Mason, and the Shrine), Knights of Pythias, and Benevolent and Protective Order of Elks.

Jeffress's life in Chapel Hill for most of his last twenty-seven years was a saga of individualism. Susan Quinn wrote in *The Daily Tar Heel*, "E. B. Jeffress is back, complete with cane, a battered gray felt hat that got a smudge on its crown when it blew across the street in Salt Lake City, Utah, and an opinion on almost any subject anyone wishes to discuss." He was an inveterate traveler by bus, once making an 8,500-mile trip across the continent, averaging 300 miles a day, and returning with an alert observation of the highways, the people, and the places he had seen.

In 1955 Jeffress was honored by his hometown with a testimonial dinner for his multiple contributions to the city and the state. The Greensboro Chamber of Commerce staged the affair, attended by a large contingent of dignitaries headed by Governor Luther H. Hodges. A month after his death, the Tompkins Knob on the Blue Ridge Parkway was renamed E. B. Jeffress Memorial Park in honor of the man who as much as any other contributed to that great highway for North Carolina.

Jeffress married Louise Bond Adams on 17 July 1913, and they had five children: Rebecca (Mrs. Winfield S. Barney, Jr.), twins Edward Bedford, Jr., and Charles (Carl) Osborne, Mary Louise (Mrs. A. Bradford McLean), and Sarah Clark Tate (Mrs. Bruce O. Jolly). He died at Chapel Hill three days after his seventy-fourth birthday. A funeral service was held at the Holy Trinity Church (Episcopal), and he was buried in Forest Lawn Cemetery, Greensboro.

SEE: *Asheville Citizen*, 23 May 1955; Chapel Hill *News Leader*, 13 Sept. 1956; *Greensboro Daily News*, 24 May, 6 June 1961; *North Carolina Biography*, vols. 3, 5 (1956, 1941); Capus Waynick, *North Carolina Roads and Their Builders* (1952); *The Daily Tar Heel*, 12 Oct. 1954; *Who's Who in the South* (1927); *Who's Who in the South and Southwest* (1929).

C. SYLVESTER GREEN

Jeffreys, George Washington (*ca. 1793–15 June 1848*), clergyman, agriculturalist, and author, of Person County, entered The University of North Carolina in 1813 and remained there for one academic year. In 1817 he married Pherebe Smith Hinton, the daughter of Major John and Pherebe Smith Hinton of Wake County. They had four daughters: Mary Mildred, Ann Eliza, Candace, and Cornelia. Mrs. Jeffreys died in 1827, and in 1829 he married Helen Jones, the daughter of Nathaniel "White Plains" and Rachel Perry Jones of Wake County. There were no children from his second marriage.

From Person County Jeffreys was elected to the Council of State in 1824, 1825, 1826, 1827, 1829, 1830, 1831, 1832, and 1834. He was a minister of the Methodist Episcopal church from about 1832 until his death. In 1842 he became a trustee of The University of North Carolina and served until his death.

As corresponding secretary of the Agricultural Society of North Carolina, Jeffreys sought to promote experimentation in agricultural methods in the state. He collected letters on innovative techniques in Virginia and Pennsylvania, and printed the letters in the *American Farmer*, a leading agricultural journal published in Baltimore. This was the first such periodical in the United States and was widely read in North Carolina. In the late 1820s Jeffreys became one of the first systematic writers on the breeding of fine horses in America.

Among his correspondents were Josiah Quincy of Massachusetts; William Painter and Judge Richard Peters of Pennsylvania; and John Slaughter, Robert Russell, Thomas Marshall, Thomas Jefferson, William Meriwether, John Taylor of Caroline, William Noland, and Thomas Melville, Jr., of Virginia. These men discussed the advantages of various new agricultural processes, such as deep ploughing, liming and manuring of fields, crop rotation, and horizontal ploughing, as well as the merits of raising hogs and planting corn. Of each man, Jeffreys inquired about ways to improve exhausted land and the effects of better agricultural methods on his farm. He received from Thomas Jefferson, John Taylor of Caroline, and Judge Richard Peters suggestions of books essential to a good agricultural library.

Jeffreys also advocated that the state of North Carolina encourage and sponsor agricultural experimentation. Writing under the pseudonym " 'Agricola,' A North-Carolina Farmer," he was the author of *A Series of Essays on Agriculture & Rural Affairs in Forty-Seven Numbers* (1819), printed in Raleigh by Joseph Gales.

Early in the summer of 1848, Jeffreys visited Patrick Mineral Springs in Patrick County, Va., to improve his health. There his conditioned worsened, so he moved to Patrick Court House where he could receive better medical attention. He died soon afterwards, however,

and was buried in the family burying ground, probably located in Person County.

SEE: *American Farmer*, 1820–21; Samuel A. Ashe, *History of North Carolina*, vol. 2 (1925); Kemp P. Battle, *History of the University of North Carolina* (1907); *Biblical Recorder*, 1 July 1848; John L. Cheney, Jr., ed., *North Carolina Government, 1585–1974* (1975); Elizabeth W. Dixon, *William Gaston Chapter, DAR, Gaston, North Carolina: Williamson, Bethel, and Allied Families* (1956); Daniel L. Grant, *Alumni History of the University of North Carolina, 1795–1924* (1924); Colonel William Hinton family Bible records (North Carolina State Archives, Raleigh); *National Historical Magazine*, February 1938; Raleigh *Register*, 28 June 1848; University of North Carolina, *Alumni Directory* (1954).

JOHN D. NEVILLE

Jenings (or Jennings), William (*d. 1687*), Council member, leader in Culpeper's Rebellion, and member of the "Rebel Assembly," is thought to have been the William Jenings to whom Virginia authorities granted 350 acres of land in Surry County, Va., in 1657 and 550 acres on New Begun Creek, in the Albemarle area, in 1663. He had moved to the northern Carolina colony, then called Albemarle, by 27 Apr. 1672, when he was a member of the Council. He also was on the Council as of 25 May 1673. The exact length of his tenure cannot be determined because of the sparseness of surviving records of the period.

Jenings took part in the uprising called Culpeper's Rebellion, which occurred in December 1677. He and his son-in-law, William Seares, were leaders of a group of armed men who seized and imprisoned the acting governor, Thomas Miller, and two Council members at the beginning of the uprising. Subsequently, Miller was held prisoner at Jenings's house. Jenings was elected to the Assembly chosen by the colonists after the overthrow of Miller's government.

He lived in Pasquotank Precinct at "the upper end of Pasquotank River," probably on the land granted him by the Virginia governor and Council in 1663. He and his wife, Martha, had at least three children: John, Ann, and another daughter, apparently named Margaret, who married Ralph Garnet. Ann was married first to William Seares, who died about 1679, and later to Paul Lathum. John probably was the John Jenings who in 1684 was a justice of the County Court of Albemarle and subsequently justice of the Pasquotank Precinct Court. A William Jenings who was active in the colony in the 1690s and early 1700s seems to have been John's son.

Jenings died between 24 Jan. 1686/87, when he made his will, and April Court, 1687, when the will was proved. His legatees were his son, John, whom he named executor; his daughter, Ann Lathum; his son-in-law, Ralph Garnet; a granddaughter, Mary Garnet; and a godson, William Barcocke. Presumably, his wife and the daughter who married Garnet died before the will was made.

SEE: Albemarle Book of Warrants and Surveys, 1681–1706, Council Minutes, Wills, Inventories, 1677–1701, Wills of William Jennings and William Seares (North Carolina State Archives, Raleigh); John Bennett Boddie, *Seventeenth Century Isle of Wight County, Virginia* (1938); J. Bryan Grimes, ed., *Abstract of North Carolina Wills* (1910); J. R. B. Hathaway, ed., *North Carolina Historical and Genealogical Register*, 3 vols. (1900–1903); Nell M.

Nugent, comp., *Cavaliers and Pioneers: Abstracts of Virginia Land Patents and Grants, 1623–1666* (1934); Mattie Erma E. Parker, ed., *North Carolina Higher-Court Records, 1670–1696* (1968) and *1697–1701* (1971); William S. Powell, ed., *Yͤ Countie of Albemarle in Carolina: A Collection of Documents, 1664–1675* (1958); Hugh F. Rankin, *Upheaval in Albemarle . . .* (1962); William L. Saunders, ed., *Colonial Records of North Carolina*, vol. 1 (1886).

MATTIE ERMA E. PARKER

Jenkins, David Aaron (5 Apr. 1822–10 Sept. 1886), state treasurer of North Carolina and member of the General Assembly, was born in Lincoln (now Gaston) County of Welsh parentage. He was the son of Aaron and Mary Jenkins. His mother was the daughter of Joseph Jenkins, who is reported to have been a fifer in a company of American Revolutionary soldiers, and the granddaughter of Lieutenant Colonel Frederick Hambright, who commanded an American regiment at the Battle of Kings Mountain.

Although his formal education was limited to the old field schools, Jenkins, according to one source, started teaching at age fourteen. Subsequently, he chopped and sold wood to the Fullenwider furnace, receiving in return manufactured goods that he sold for profit. He also did farm work and split rails. His first real financial opportunity came when he was entrusted with the collection of accounts for three major principals, one of whom, Jesse Holland, later became his father-in-law. Jenkins was elected, first, to the office of constable and, later, to the office of magistrate, serving in the latter capacity for many years. When the Civil War was imminent, he was unquestionably loyal to the South, but he foresaw the inexpediency of secession and was opposed to it. During the conflict he was, as a magistrate, exempt from active field duty. After the war, he became identified with the Republican party, holding the view that the interests of the people could best be served by their taking an active part in politics and seeking, by their influence, to temper and restrain the excesses of those in power.

In 1866, supported by both Democrats and Republicans, Jenkins was elected to the General Assembly and served two years. In 1868, he was the Republican nominee for state treasurer and won the election. On assuming office, he employed as his adviser Kemp P. Battle, who had been the Democratic incumbent and his opponent, reflecting his astuteness and recognition of capability. He also retained Donald Bain, another Democrat, as chief clerk. He was reelected in 1872, serving two four-year terms.

Jenkins's record as state treasurer, in a stormy period of reputed spoils in government, was notable for his personal integrity. However, historian J. G. de Roulhac Hamilton advances this opinion: "D. A. Jenkins seems to have been personally honest so far as the funds in his hands were concerned, but like all in his administration, he was perfectly aware of the wholesale stealing that was going on." A further statement by the same author hints at nepotism: "Jenkins had his son in office." Nonetheless, his personal honesty was widely acclaimed among his contemporaries and earned him the sobriquet, "Honest Dave Jenkins." In 1880 friends urged him to seek the Republican nomination for governor but he declined to do so, and in 1881 he supported the Prohibition party.

Jenkins was a member of the Baptist church. On 20 May 1841, he married Lodema Holland (b. 22 Apr. 1820), the daughter of Jesse and Martha Jane Hanks

Holland. They had ten children: Mary A., Elmina B., Aaron D., William W., Martha J., James C., Benjamin, David H., John F., and Laban L. Jenkins died at age sixty-four and was buried beside his wife in the family burial ground near their home in eastern Gastonia. Portraits of him and of his wife are in the possession of his great-grandsons, James Copeland Craig of Charlotte and Dr. Samuel Austell Wilkins, Jr., of Atlanta; the two portraits are combined and reproduced in Hoffman's *Our Kin.*

SEE: *Cyclopedia of Eminent and Representative Men of the Carolinas of the Nineteenth Century*, vol. 2 (1892); J. G. de R. Hamilton, *Reconstruction in North Carolina: Studies in History, Economics and Public Law*, vol. 58 (1914); Laban Miles Hoffman, *Our Kin* (1915).

ROBERT L. CHERRY

Jenkins, James Lineberry (16 July 1883–21 Mar. 1973), clergyman, educator, and college president, was born in Stanly County, the son of Lewis and Elizabeth Jenkins. He was graduated from Wake Forest College in 1910 and was principal of Southport High School from 1910 to 1912. After attending Southern Baptist Theological Seminary in Louisville, Ky., in 1913, he served as pastor of the Parkton Baptist Church in Robeson County for seven years. During the period 1920–23 he was an evangelist under the Baptist State Mission Board, and from 1924 to 1927 he was pastor of a church in Umatilla, Fla. Returning to North Carolina, he became pastor of Boiling Springs Baptist Church where he served until his retirement in 1952. During some of this time he also served other nearby churches.

In the depression years of 1932–35, Jenkins was the unpaid president of Boiling Springs Junior College (now Gardner-Webb College). He also was head of the college's Bible department for several years, and both before and after his retirement he taught homiletics to hundreds of ministers at Fruitland Bible Institute near Hendersonville. In 1951 he was president of the North Carolina Baptist Pastors' Conference.

In 1918 Jenkins married Kate McArn Watson, a 1912 honor graduate of Meredith College and niece of the poet John Charles McNeill. They were the parents of four children: James L. (Jay), Jr., Catherine Watson, Ella McNeill, and Elizabeth Lewis. Jenkins was buried beside his wife, who died in 1946, in Spring Hill cemetery near Wagram, Scotland County.

SEE: Francis B. Dedmond, *Lengthened Shadows: A History of Gardner-Webb College, 1907–1956* (1957); *Heritage of Cleveland County* (1982); Jay Jenkins, personal contact; M. A. Jolley, *Our Dream of Tomorrow, 1847–1962: A History of Boiling Springs Baptist Church* (1962); John S. Raymond, *Among Southern Baptists* (1936); *Shelby Daily Star*, 22 Mar. 1973.

FRANCIS B. DEDMOND

Jenkins, John (d. 17 Dec. 1681), Proprietary governor of Albemarle County, was born in England and may have been the John Jenkins who was graduated from Clare College, Cambridge, in 1642. On 14 May 1653, he patented 1,000 acres in Westmoreland County, Va. By September of that year he was licensed by the Council of State in England as the master of a vessel bound for Bermuda. Jenkins appears to have resided on Egg Neck in Northampton County, Va., on a 400-acre grant he received in March 1655, but by 1662 he was in Albemarle

County, Carolina. On 5 Sept. 1663 Sir William Berkeley, governor of Virginia and a Lord Proprietor of Carolina, granted Jenkins 700 acres south of the Perquimans River on Harveys Neck, a tract that he had already settled. In addition to his plantation, he was recorded in 1680 as owning one ship, a bark.

The long public career of John Jenkins in Albemarle County began when he became a member of the Council of Governor Samuel Stephens, sometime between 1667 and 1670. On 20 Jan. 1670, Jenkins was commissioned a deputy for the Earl of Craven, a position that also entitled him to a seat on the Council. The Council advised the governor on executive decisions and comprised the upper house of the General Assembly and the General Court, the highest court in the colony. With the exception of several months when he was forcibly removed from office, Jenkins was on the Council from the term of Governor Stephens until 1681.

By April 1672, Jenkins was appointed deputy governor by Governor Peter Carteret, who was dispatched to England by the Council to present a list of grievances to the Lords Proprietors. Jenkins had been appointed lieutenant colonel of the colony's militia in 1670, and after becoming the deputy governor he was called Colonel Jenkins. During his tenure as commander of the militia, the colony fought and won its first Indian war—the Chowanoc War of 1675–77.

During this period a factional struggle for control of the colony surfaced. The anti-Proprietary party, composed of many of the earliest or precharter settlers, was led by John Jenkins; the Proprietary party was led by Thomas Eastchurch, who became speaker of the Assembly. Unrest was encouraged by the weak direction given the colony by the Proprietors, uncertain Proprietary land policy, geographic isolation, and the Navigation Acts passed by Parliament which unfavorably regulated the intercolonial trade. In the fall of 1675 Jenkins was arrested and deposed by Eastchurch, but by March 1676 he had been released and returned to power.

Continuing as acting governor until July 1677, Jenkins relinquished his office to Thomas Miller who had been authorized by Eastchurch, recently commissioned governor by the Proprietors, to serve as acting governor. Excesses in the persecution of his opponents led to Miller's ouster in Culpeper's Rebellion in December 1677, and a rebel council governed the colony for eighteen months until the summer of 1679. Although not a leader of the rebellion, Jenkins was an important member of the rebel council. The rebel council was superseded when the Proprietors appointed John Harvey president of the Council and acting governor in February 1679, but the widely respected Harvey died in December of that year. Upon election by the Council, Jenkins filled the vacancy, serving for two years until his death.

Jenkins was survived by his wife Joanna, who married Thomas Harvey, later governor of the colony, on 13 Apr. 1682. Joanna Harvey died on 27 Mar. 1688. The Joanna Jenkins who married Robert Beasley on 9 Sept. 1689 may have been the daughter of John Jenkins.

There are few glimpses of the personality of John Jenkins in the sparse records of the period. His political enemies characterized him as "the most active and uncontrollable" of their opponents. Yet George Fox, the founder of the Society of Friends, said in November 1672 that he was received "lovingly" by the governor and his wife and that the governor "courteously" guided him the next day through the forest. For nearly seven years Jenkins, deputy governor and president of the Council, served as chief executive of Albemarle

County—longer than anyone else in the Proprietary period, and he was a key figure on the rebel council during its eighteen-month ascendancy. Except for the six months in 1675–76, the periods in which Jenkins was at the helm were characterized by stability. His effectiveness as governor stands in sharp contrast to the unrest and political chaos that typified much of the history of Albemarle County.

SEE: Lindley S. Butler, "The Governors of Albemarle County, 1663–1689," *North Carolina Historical Review* 46 (July 1969); John L. Cheney, Jr., ed., *North Carolina Government, 1585–1974: A Narrative and Statistical History* (1975); J. R. B. Hathaway, ed., *North Carolina Historical and Genealogical Register*, vol. 3 (April, July 1903); Rufus M. Jones, ed., *The Journal of George Fox* (1963); Lawrence Lee, *Indian Wars in North Carolina, 1663–1763* (1963); Nell M. Nugent, comp., *Cavaliers and Pioneers: Abstracts of Virginia Land Patents and Grants, 1623–1666* (1934); Mattie Erma E. Parker, *North Carolina Higher-Court Records, 1670–1696* (1968); William S. Powell, ed., *Yᵉ Countie of Albemarle in Carolina: A Collection of Documents, 1664–1675* (1958); William L. Saunders, ed., *Colonial Records of North Carolina*, vol. 1 (1886).

LINDLEY S. BUTLER

Jennett, Norman Ethre (*10 Mar. 1877–17 Jan. 1970*), artist, illustrator, cartoonist, and author, was born in the Grantham community of Wayne County, the son of Elijah Stanton and Clarissa King Jennett. The boy was only a year old when his father died, and for several years he lived with his mother and grandmother at Grantham and attended Bethany Friends Meeting. Later his mother married William Rufus King, and young Jennett moved with them to Sampson County.

His education was limited to a few years in the common schools, but the youngster exhibited a particular talent for drawing. He whittled likenesses of people on blocks of wood, and at age fifteen he took one of his wood sketches to Marion Butler, then editor of the Clinton *Caucasian*. Butler inked the block and ran it with Jack Bennett's poem, "Summer's Comin'." The sketch of the jaunty black man attracted considerable notice, and Butler paid Jennett a dollar a week to work around the office and occasionally carve out other wood blocks. Soon, however, the competing newspaper, the *Sampson Democrat*, hired him away from the *Caucasian*. Some of his cartoons began to take on a political tone; and Butler, by then the leader of the newly organized Populist party in North Carolina, became his favorite subject for caricature. One cartoon showed Butler selling out to the Republicans; another pictured him as a giraffe reaching for a "senatorial plum."

Jennett's satirical characterization of the Populist leader attracted the attention of Governor Elias Carr who recommended the young man to Josephus Daniels, editor of the partisan Raleigh *News and Observer*. Daniels, the unofficial press agent for the Democrats in their political campaigns against the Populists and Republicans, hired Jennett as an office boy, and caricatures began to appear in the *News and Observer* in August 1895.

Having formerly worked with wood blocks, Jennett now perfected a technique of drawing a picture with a pencil, cutting it on a chalk plate, then making the cut from molten metal. Crude though it was, it introduced a new weapon into the political campaigns of the 1890s. Jennett's cartoons against the Fusionists became a popular feature in the *News and Observer* and won him the attention of many leading Democrats. His colleagues called him the "Sampson Huckleberry."

With loans from Julian S. Carr of Durham, Jennett in 1897 was able to accept a scholarship from the National Academy of Design in New York. The following year he attended the William M. Chase School of Art. Meanwhile, he sold many of his drawings to such publications as *Life*, *Southern Tobacco Journal*, and *American Druggist and Pharmaceutical Record*, and to such New York newspapers as the *World*, *Herald*, and *Journal*.

In the bitter off-year election of 1898, Jennett was persuaded to return to Raleigh for several months to draw cartoons for the Democrats. Daniels wrote, "I do not know how we could have gotten along in the campaigns of 1896 and 1898 without Jennett's cartoons," and in the fall grateful Democrats raised sixty-three dollars for a gift in appreciation for his "services in assisting in redeeming the state."

Jennett continued to draw for various national publications, and for several months in 1899 he worked for the *St. Louis Star*. He returned to New York, however, and for two years was an artist for the *Brooklyn Eagle*. In 1900 he painted six scenes that were exhibited at the Paris Exposition by the Mutual Life Insurance Company. The same year he spent several weeks in Raleigh drawing cartoons during the campaign for passage of the suffrage amendment.

From 1901 to 1917 Jennett was artist for the New York *Herald*, simultaneously working on the *Evening Telegram* in which one of his popular features was the colored comic strip, "The Monkey Shines of Marseleen." In 1906 McLoughlin Brothers published a selection of the strips in a book, *The Monkey Shines of Marseleen*, and three years later Cupples and Leon published an entirely new edition under the same title. Among Jennett's other activities during the period of his association with the *Herald* were the creation of the Pathe Freres' rooster, and of a comic strip called "The Arrow-Plane Girlies" for *McCall's* in 1912.

Jennett was art editor of both *Aerial Age* and *Flying* from 1917 to 1922, and from 1923 to 1939 he was assistant art director of the McFadden Publications. In 1948, he sold his Cedar Grove, N.J., home and moved to California. In his retirement he devoted himself to oils and watercolors, some of which were exhibited in New York, New Jersey, and California.

On 9 July 1901 Jennett married Helen Mary MacGinness, a native of Ireland. Their children, Norman Ethre, Jr., and Charlotte Clara, both lived in California. Helen Jennett died in 1967; she and her husband were buried in the Santa Barbara Cemetery.

SEE: *Book Notes* (October 1899), for Jennett's first few years in New York; Josephus Daniels, *Editor in Politics*, for a discussion of Jennett (with several factual errors); Raleigh *News and Observer*, especially for 1896, 1898, and 1900, for Jennett's cartoons. Unpublished sources in University of North Carolina Library, Chapel Hill: Papers of Norman Ethre Jennett (including scrapbooks of clippings and drawings), Southern Historical Collection; photographs of Jennett, North Carolina Collection.

H. G. JONES

Jenoure, Joseph (or James) (*d. October 1732*), colonial official, first occurs in the records of North Carolina in the 1720s. A resident of Edenton, he appeared before Governor Richard Everard and the Council on 28 May 1728 to deny a charge that he had spoken scandalously of one of Everard's daughters. By July, Jenoure had got-

ten into deeper trouble with the governor. At the General Court that month he and eleven other men were charged with rioting at Everard's house. The mob had been armed with swords and clubs, and at least two men were injured, one of whom was the governor's servant. The case was continued through several sessions until the charges were dismissed on Everard's order in April 1729. The exact causes of the conflict between Jenoure and the governor are unknown, but they probably involved the notorious blank patent controversy under Everard.

It may have been Jenoure's animosity to Everard that persuaded George Burrington to nominate him to North Carolina's first royal Council in August 1730. At the same time he was named surveyor general, one of the most remunerative offices of the colony, but it is unlikely that such a perquisite was Burrington's to bestow. Clearly, Jenoure had powerful friends in England.

Jenoure's animosity to Everard's allies continued, for, with John Lovick and Edmund Gale, he disrupted Edmund Porter's vice-admiralty court in January 1731. Such actions endeared him to the volatile Burrington, and he was sworn as a councillor on the new governor's first day in office, 25 Feb. 1731. He was a frequent attendant at Council sessions and a firm supporter of Burrington. Jenoure nominated his friend John Lovick to a vacancy on the Council in the summer of 1731, and Lovick eventually became the governor's most trusted ally. Jenoure also supported Burrington's move to oust Edmund Porter from the upper house in January 1732.

When he died, Jenoure named a wife, Anne, and a son in his will. Shortly after his death, his house burned and most of his papers as surveyor general were destroyed. The confusion surrounding Jenoure's first name stems from the fact that he is referred to as Joseph by all records originating in North Carolina and as James by all those originating in England.

SEE: J. Bryan Grimes, *North Carolina Wills and Inventories* (1912); William L. Saunders, ed., *Colonial Records of North Carolina*, vols. 2, 3 (1886).

WILLIAM S. PRICE, JR.

Jerkins, Alonzo Thomas (*2 June 1807–7 Apr. 1895*), legislator, banker, merchant, and shipper, was born in New Bern, the son of Thomas Jerkins (11 Apr. 1783–21 Dec. 1855) and his wife Grizzell Sears, a sister of Captain George Sears. A native of Beaufort County, the father was a sea captain operating between New Bern and the West Indies. In 1804 he settled at New Bern and in less than a year was married there; the marriage bond was dated 8 Jan. 1805. While he was away on a lengthy voyage, his wife died on 13 Aug. 1824. Ceasing his sailing trips, he remained in town and turned his attention to other interests. Four fine homes built by him still stand in New Bern.

After his mother's death, young Jerkins left The University of North Carolina where he had been a student in 1823–24. Had she lived longer, he probably would have remained to graduate. For some time he taught school at his home in New Bern, later assisted by his first wife, Sarah McIlwean (28 July 1809–13 Sept. 1874), for whom a marriage bond was issued on 28 June 1831. His second wife, Susan Carr (14 Mar. 1836–19 Feb. 1911), survived him.

Becoming a prosperous businessman, Jerkins was long recognized as one of the community's outstanding citizens, landowners, and religious leaders. In April

1845 he was a trustee of the First Baptist Church when title to its Middle Street lot was obtained for the erection of its present brick edifice, now listed in the National Register of Historic Places. A holder of various church offices, he placed in the church a memorial tablet to his first wife.

In 1850 Jerkins represented Craven County in the North Carolina House of Representatives. In 1854, he was among the original subscribers for the Union Bank at New Bern and one of the first directors of the Atlantic and North Carolina Railroad Company. An incorporator of the Bank of Commerce in 1859, he became its president.

Jerkins was instrumental in helping develop water transportation facilities. Besides having an interest in the Trent River Transportation Company, which ran a regular line of freight and passenger boats from the river's mouth up to Trenton, he held stock in the Neuse River Navigation Company, which among other projects owned and operated the steamer *Johnston* between New Bern and Smithfield. Frequently he shipped upstate by water merchandise from his local stores. According to a bill of 3 Apr. 1855, for goods sent by him to Ashley G. Powell of Smithfield, his charges were 3½ yards of plaid muslin, $1.05; 47⅞ yards of curtain calico, $6.43; 8 yards of Kentucky jeans, $2.00; 7½ yards of apron checks, $1.35; 3 coconut dippers, $1.05; 467 pounds of sugar in two barrels, $35.03; 1 set of cups and saucers, $0.60; 12 white granite plates, $1.40; and 20 gallons of molasses, $6.00.

During April 1846 Jerkins joined St. John's Lodge No. 3, Ancient Free and Accepted Masons, to which his father also belonged. His rise to official positions was rapid, becoming Junior Warden in June, Senior Warden the following year, and Worshipful Master in 1848–50. In December 1850, he was named the Twenty-fourth Grand Master of the Grand Lodge of North Carolina and was twice reelected. Until 1853 he served as High Priest of the reactivated Eureka Chapter No. 7, Royal Arch Masons, and in 1857 he again became the Worshipful Master of St. John's Lodge for another one-year term.

After the Civil War, he did not hold Masonic offices but remained active in the fraternity. He was also an organizing member, a temporary chairman, and a permanent director of the North Carolina Mutual Life Insurance Company, of which records are extant from 19 Sept. 1867 to 21 Sept. 1870.

After a busy career in diversified fields, Jerkins died in New Bern when he was almost eighty-eight. His will, probated on 29 Aug. 1895, named his widow as executrix. The grave in Cedar Grove Cemetery, New Bern, is on a plot with the graves of his two wives. A portrait of him hangs in Lowthrop Hall on the second floor of New Bern's Masonic temple; another portrait is at the Grand Lodge headquarters in Raleigh.

Jerkins had two sisters: Julia E., who married Francis N. McIlwean in July 1826—the marriage bond is dated 27 July; and Nancy Sears (10 Oct. 1810–8 Sept. 1881), who was the wife of Alexander Mitchell (19 Jan. 1807–27 Aug. 1876)—their marriage bond was issued on 18 Oct. 1833.

SEE: Gertrude S. Carraway, *Years of Light*, vols. 1, 2 (1944, 1974); Craven County Deeds, Wills, and Marriage Bonds (North Carolina State Archives, Raleigh); Tombstones, Cedar Grove Cemetery (New Bern).

GERTRUDE S. CARRAWAY

Jerman, Cornelia Petty *(1 Dec. 1874–4 Feb. 1946)*, leader of the North Carolina woman suffrage movement and Democratic party official, was born near Carthage, the daughter of William Cary and Emma Virginia Thagard Petty. She was graduated from Oxford College in Oxford, N.C., in 1892 and studied at the New England Conservatory of Music in Boston, Mass. In 1898 she married Thomas Palmer Jerman of Raleigh. Moving to Raleigh, she immediately became active in the city's social life. She was a charter member of the Woman's Club of Raleigh, serving as president from 1909 to 1911 and as chairman of the building committee during the construction of the first and second club houses. She subsequently became president of the North Carolina Federation of Women's Clubs and a trustee of the General Federation of Women's Clubs.

Mrs. Jerman was in the forefront of the woman suffrage movement in North Carolina. She helped organize the Raleigh Equal Suffrage League and in 1919 was elected president of the North Carolina Equal Suffrage League. At a special 1920 session of the General Assembly, which considered and rejected ratification of the Nineteenth Amendment, Mrs. Jerman fought futilely for women's right to vote. In 1921, she led a movement to organize the State Legislative Council to sponsor constructive legislation in the fields of health, education, labor, and corrective institutions; from 1922 to 1933, she served as president of the council. She also led an effort to organize the Raleigh League of Women Voters and served as its president. When the Democratic state convention met in 1922, she served as vice-president of the convention and became the first woman in North Carolina to address a Democratic state convention as a delegate.

In 1920, 1924, and 1928 Mrs. Jerman was a delegate to the Democratic National Convention. As the gubernatorial campaign began in 1928, there was speculation that Mrs. Jerman planned to run for governor; however, she declined to enter the campaign. She was appointed to the Democratic National Committee in the same year, and she actively campaigned for Al Smith in 1928 and Franklin D. Roosevelt in 1932.

In 1934, the Roosevelt administration selected Mrs. Jerman for the post of assistant collector of Internal Revenue for North Carolina. This appointment required her resignation from the Democratic National Committee and her relocation to Greensboro. She remained in the federal post until 1939, when she resigned and returned to Raleigh.

In June 1943 Mrs. Jerman was awarded an honorary doctor of laws degree by the Woman's College in Greensboro. She also served as a director of the Atlantic and North Carolina Railroad and the Wake County Savings Bank, and was a member of the Fortnightly Review Club, the St. Cecilia Music Club, and the Women's National Democratic Club of Washington, D.C.

On her death in Raleigh, the *News and Observer* called her the "State's First Woman." She was survived by a son, Thomas Palmer, Jr., and a foster daughter, Cary (Mrs. John P. Cooper).

SEE: Cornelia Petty Jerman Papers (Manuscript Collection, East Carolina University, Greenville); *Who's Who in America* (1940–41).

DONALD R. LENNON

Jernigan, Thomas Roberts *(24 Feb. 1847–1 Nov. 1920)*, state senator, consul, editor, and author, was born at Barfields on the Chowan River in Hertford County. His father was Lemuel Jernigan, a prosperous planter and for many years a presiding justice in the Court of Common Pleas and Quarter Sessions. His mother, Mary Harrell, was the first cousin of W. N. H. Smith, chief justice of the North Carolina Supreme Court. Jernigan received his early education at Union Male Academy in Harrellsville. In September 1864, at age sixteen, he enlisted in the Fifteenth Battalion, North Carolina Cavalry. He was captured at Colerain on 22 Jan. 1865 and imprisoned at Fort Monroe, Va., until his release on 14/15 Feb. 1865. After the war, he was graduated from the University of Virginia Law School and returned to his native county to practice law with his brother, John H. Jernigan, also a University of Virginia graduate.

Jernigan began his quest for public office in 1870, when he was nominated for the state house of representatives by the county Democratic party. Though the county contained the usual Republican majority, he was declared legally elected. But further examination of the election results showed Jernigan trailing slightly in the popular vote. When the count of the popular vote was made official, he immediately relinquished his certificate of election although many protested the recount. Some of his political friends questioned his action, but all admired his sense of justice and fair play.

In 1874 Jernigan was nominated for the state senate, again against Hertford County's Republican majority. This time he won the election, representing the First District from 1874 to 1876. Jernigan developed an enviable reputation in the senate, and thereafter his name was often placed in nomination for public office. In 1880, while serving as a presidential elector, he made a moving speech to second the nomination of Winfield S. Hancock. Jernigan's canvass was favorably received by the press, which complimented his diction and easy manner of delivery. But, like his brother John, he became deaf at an early age, cutting short his career in elective office.

Grover Cleveland's election to the presidency in 1884 opened another political avenue to Jernigan. He was appointed consul to Kobe, Japan, and served for four years. In 1889 he returned home and moved to Raleigh, where he edited the *North Carolina Intelligencer*, a paper dedicated in Jernigan's choice of a motto as "Impartial, not neutral; and devoted to the best interests of North Carolina, inseparable from Democratic principles." In 1892, he purchased the *State Chronicle* from Josephus Daniels. The paper failed to show a profit, and within a year he leased it to the *News and Observer*, which for a time called itself the *News and Observer-Chronicle*.

At the beginning of President Cleveland's second administration in 1893, Jernigan was named consul general to Shanghai, China. He was "most popular not only among the foreign community, but among the Chinese." At the end of his term in 1897, he chose to remain in Shanghai, where he practiced law and was an attorney for the Standard Oil Company of China. For several years, he served as chairman of the International Settlement of Shanghai, a position that had been rotated yearly until the time of his appointment. In 1906 he was elected a member of the North China Branch of the Royal Asiatic Society. He also wrote several books and articles about economic and political life in China, including *China's Business Methods and Policy* and *China in Law and Commerce*.

In 1885 Jernigan married Frances Sharp, the daughter of Colonel Starkey Sharp of Hertford County. They had four children: Paul, Frances, Roberts H., and Starkey. Jernigan was buried, according to his wish, on the mount overlooking Nanking, China.

SEE: *The Ahoskie Era of Hertford County* (1939); Samuel A. Ashe, ed., *Cyclopedia of Eminent and Representative Men of the Carolinas of the Nineteenth Century* (1892); John L. Cheney, Jr., ed., *North Carolina Government, 1585–1974* (1975); "Passing of Another 'Old China Hand,'" *The Far East Review*, December 1920; *Who's Who in the Far East* (1907–8); Benjamin B. Winborne, *The Colonial and State Political History of Hertford County* (1906).

THOMAS R. J. NEWBERN

Jessup, Ann Matthews (*10 Oct. 1738–26 Sept. 1822*), Quaker minister, missionary, and horticulturist, was born in Pennsylvania, the daughter of Walter and Mary Matthews. She married first, John Floyd, and second, Thomas Jessup, Jr., of Orange County, N.C., in 1766. During the thirteen years of her marriage with Jessup, she raised his eleven children by two previous wives, her own daughter, Elizabeth Floyd, and three of their four children, one having died in infancy.

Ann Jessup was recorded a Friends minister on 28 Sept. 1765, and for many years was a "beloved friend" in the New Garden Monthly Meeting. After her husband's death in 1783, she returned to Pennsylvania with her three children and soon became an active minister. Jessup's daughter, Sara, had married a British soldier who died on the return trip to England; she soon married a member of the Scots Guards. While visiting Sara in Glasgow, Scotland, and traveling in England over a two-year period, Ann gathered seeds and roots of vegetables, flowers, alfalfa, and cuttings of many kinds of fruit trees. She returned to New Garden in 1792, bringing with her much that she had collected, and in the spring of 1793 she engaged Abijah Pinson to work with her in grafting cuttings. Pinson established a nursery at Westfield, Surry County, from which many Quaker families bought plants and trees to carry with them as they migrated west.

In 1817 Mrs. Jessup moved to Highland County, Ohio, where she joined the Fairfield Monthly Meeting and lived with Thomas's daughter, Hannah Jessup Willis, until her death five years later. She was buried at Fall Creek Monthly Meeting Cemetery in Highland County.

SEE: William Wade Hinshaw, *Encyclopedia of American Quaker Genealogy*, vols. 1, 5 (1936); Katherine Hoskins, "Guilford Woman Was Pioneer Orchardist," *Greensboro Daily News*, 21 Feb. 1960; Edna Harvey Joseph and others, "Descendants of Hunt, Woolman, Borton, Beals, Mills, Hussey, Jessup, Small, Chipman, Shields" (Typescript, Guilford College Library, Greensboro).

TREVA W. MATHIS

Jocher, Katharine (*22 Sept. 1888–2 Aug. 1983*), social worker and university professor, was born in Philadelphia, Pa., the daughter of John Conrad and Lillie Caroline Reichle Jocher. Her undergraduate degree was from Goucher College and her master's from the University of Pennsylvania, where she held a university scholarship. She earned the doctorate from The University of North Carolina in 1929 and received honorary doctorates from Goucher; Western College for Women, Oxford, Ohio; and The University of North Carolina.

Following service as a social worker in Philadelphia and Baltimore and as an instructor at Sweet Briar College, she became a research assistant at the Institute for Research in Social Science at The University of North Carolina in 1924 and assistant director of the institute in 1927. In 1924 she also was made an instructor in sociology and public welfare and later rose to the rank of professor, the first woman on the faculty to rise through all of the ranks to that position. In 1931 she became managing editor of the journal *Social Forces* and from 1951 to 1962 was its editor.

Professor Jocher held a special research assignment in 1930–31 on the President's Research Committee on Social Trends, and for several years beginning in 1947 she was a member of the Governor's Committee for Revision of Domestic Relations Laws in North Carolina, of the North Carolina Interracial Commission, and of the Committee on Services for Children and Youth in North Carolina. She was a member of and an officer in numerous professional organizations both at the state and the national level. With Howard W. Odum, she was the author of *An Introduction to Social Research* and *In Search of the Regional Balance of America*.

Miss Jocher died in Chapel Hill, survived by a niece.

SEE: Files of the Sociology Department and of the Office of the Secretary of the Faculty, University of North Carolina at Chapel Hill; *Who's Who in the South and Southwest* (1950).

WILLIAM S. POWELL

Joel, Lawrence (*22 Feb. 1928–4 Feb. 1984*), the first black man to receive the Medal of Honor for battlefield heroism, was born in the slums of Winston-Salem to Trenton and Mary Ellen Joel, but at age eight he was unofficially adopted by Mr. and Mrs. Clayton Samuel. During his teens he peddled firewood door-to-door, and at age seventeen he joined the merchant marines. In 1946 he enlisted in the army and, except for a four-year interval, served until 1973.

On 8 Nov. 1965 near Bien Hoa in South Vietnam, Company C of the 1st Battalion, 503rd Infantry, 173rd Airborne Brigade, was attacked by a Viet Cong force that killed or wounded nearly every man in the lead American squad. Joel, a medical aidman, bandaged his own wound, injected himself with morphine, and then attended his wounded comrades within sight of the enemy. When he received another bullet in the thigh, Joel continued to drag himself across the battlefield, treating thirteen more men before his medical supplies ran out. For his "courage, determination and professional skill," Joel was presented the Medal of Honor by President Lyndon B. Johnson at a White House ceremony on 9 Mar. 1967.

Joel's marriage to Dorothy Region produced two children—Tremaine and Deborah Louise—before it foundered. After his retirement from the army, Joel worked for the Veterans Administration in Hartford, Conn. However, suffering from diabetes and depression, he returned to Winston-Salem in 1982. Two years later he died there in a diabetic coma. He was buried in Arlington National Cemetery. In 1986 the Winston-Salem Board of Aldermen voted to name the city's new coliseum for Lawrence Joel.

SEE: Mel Allen, "The Battle Within," *Yankee*, March 1982; *Winston-Salem Journal*, 9 Mar., 9 Apr. 1967, 6, 8 Feb. 1984; *High Point Enterprise*, 21 Feb. 1986.

H. G. JONES

Johnson, Amos Neill (*5 June 1908–23 Apr. 1975*), physician, was born in Garland, Sampson County, the son of Jeff. Deems, Sr., and Mary Lily Wright Johnson. After attending the elementary school in Garland, he

became a student at the Blue Ridge School for Boys, Hendersonville, from which he was graduated in 1925. He received the bachelor of arts degree from Duke University in 1929. At Duke, the popular and scholarly Johnson was active in many campus organizations; in his senior year he was president of the student body. He also was a member of the football and baseball teams, and during the summers played baseball for the old Virginia, Piedmont, and Coastal Plain leagues.

In the fall of 1929 Johnson enrolled in the then two-year School of Medicine of The University of North Carolina, from which he received a certificate in medicine. Continuing his studies at the University of Pennsylvania School of Medicine at Philadelphia, he was graduated with the degree of doctor of medicine. Commenting on his desire to become a physician from an early age, Johnson joked that he was motivated by a determination to avoid farm work: "I had plenty of that as a boy."

After serving his internship at the Jackson Memorial Hospital in Miami, Fla., Johnson returned to Garland where he spent the rest of his life in general practice. Recognized throughout the area for his professional ability, he served on the staffs of the Sampson County Memorial Hospital and the Bladen County Memorial Hospital, Blandenboro. During the same period he was an instructor in general practice in the Duke University School of Medicine, Durham. For twelve years he participated in Duke's preceptorship program, which meant having a medical student constantly at his side for two-week intervals.

In addition to his busy practice, Johnson was active in local, state, and national medical associations as well as certain specialty organizations. For six years he was a member of the North Carolina Board of Medical Examiners (president, 1955). As president of the North Carolina Medical Society (1960–61), he sought to develop plans for prepaid medical care insurance in all brackets, especially for indigents. He was also president of the Sampson County Medical Society and of the Third District of the state medical society.

A charter member of the North Carolina chapter of the American Academy of Family Physicians, Johnson served as president and as chairman of its Committee on Education. In the national organization, he was for a time an official delegate from North Carolina and served successively as chairman of the Scientific Assembly and of the Commission on Education, chairman of the board of directors, president-elect, and president. From 1965 he represented the academy in the U.S. Congress, traveling regularly to Washington, D.C.—often one day a week—to appear before congressional committees, serve on panels, and consult with national leaders in both the executive and legislative branches of government. As a longtime member of the American Medical Association he was a perennial delegate from North Carolina, served as commissioner of the Joint Commission on Accreditation of Hospitals, and was a member of the ad hoc Committee to Study Training for Family Practice.

The American Board of Family Practice was a product of Johnson's interest and emphasis. He served as treasurer and president, and as its Washington consultant was the liaison officer between the medical profession and the government. Further, he was a member of the Executive Committee of the American Board of Medical Specialists and a director of the Universal Education Corporation.

During the same years he served, by gubernatorial appointment, on North Carolina's Commission on

Health Planning, the Commission to Study the Public School System, the Commission on Economic Development, the Committee for Court Reforms, and the Hospital Board of Controls. He was the medical adviser to the North Carolina Board of Health and for twelve years was a member of the Sampson County Board of Education. For many years he served on the Committee for Medical Affairs of The University of North Carolina, and was a member of the Board of Governors of the university system.

In the closing year of Dan K. Moore's administration, Johnson was cited by the governor as "Citizen of the Year." He was so honored again in 1975—one of the few to be given that award twice. In the latter year he was also named (posthumously) for the John G. Walsh Award, the highest honor accorded by the American Academy of Family Physicians; earlier he had received the academy's Certificate for Meritorious Service. The University of North Carolina Medical School gave him its Distinguished Alumnus Award in recognition of his leadership and contributions in the field of medicine, especially family practice.

His fellow practitioners remember Johnson for his pioneer plan called "the Physicians' Assistant Program." He had employed such a full-time assistant in his office for many years, and he later developed a physicians' assistant course, now available at the Duke University School of Medicine. On numerous occasions Johnson was called upon for professional testimony before state and national groups concerning ways and means of advancing health care for rural residents. He was a delegate to the White House Conference on the Aged and participated in subsequent conferences of a national scope, including the Surgeon General's Conference on the Prevention of Disability from Arthritis and the later White House Conference on Health. In addition, he was medical adviser to the Department of Health, Education, and Welfare (on cancer control), and to the U.S. Public Health Service (on the department's total health services and as a member of its Medical Assistance Committee).

Few North Carolina physicians in this century have received the professional and personal esteem granted Johnson. Immediately after his death, the *Tar Heel Practitioner*, the official publication of the North Carolina Academy of Family Physicians, devoted an entire issue in his memory. Political leaders, educators, and professional colleagues wrote of his tireless dedication to the major emphasis of his life: the vitalization and recognition of family practice as a basic component of medical care. The various sketches detail his multiple services in public offices, and especially recount his conspicuous leadership in national political affairs. It was reported that he wrote many memoranda, and perhaps some speeches, for congressional leaders—among them Senator Edward Kennedy, Congressman Paul Rodgers, and John Henley. Consulted by presidents and governors, he became known as an "astute medical politician." He was the author of the Family Practice Act of 1969, which passed the Congress with only one dissenting vote but later was vetoed by President Lyndon B. Johnson. When its advocates took the matter to court, the Federal Court of Appeals in Washington, D.C., ruled that the president was wrong in rejecting the bill. Amos Johnson guided the appeal, having been the first to question the propriety of the pocket veto.

On 16 Mar. 1934 Johnson married Mary Porter Allan, the daughter of Clifford Hollingsworth and Nan Martin Allan, of Fort Lauderdale, Fla. Of his wife, Johnson said: "She's worked as hard . . . as I have. She has al-

ways been my lab technician and secretary. She also handles all my financial affairs." The couple had two children: Mary Allan (Mrs. William R. Watts III) and Amos Neill, Jr. Johnson died in Bladen County. Funeral services were conducted at the Graves Memorial Presbyterian Church, Clinton, of which he was a member, and burial followed in the Clinton Cemetery.

SEE: *Bulletin*—Medical School of The University of North Carolina, Chapel Hill (March 1966); *Duke Alumni Register* (June 1975); William S. Powell, ed., *North Carolina Lives* (1962); Raleigh *News and Observer*, 25 Sept. 1960, 24 Apr. 1975; *Tar Heel Practitioner* 26 (May–June 1975); *Who's Who in America*, vol. 34 (1966).

C. SYLVESTER GREEN

Johnson, Andrew (29 Dec. 1808–31 July 1875), seventeenth president, was born in Raleigh, the son of Jacob Johnson and Mary McDonough, yeomen. His first decades remain obscure. James Russell Lowell wondered that "a great unknown" could father such an offspring; others speculated that he was "the living spit" of a Haywood. A Raleigh lady recalled that "my old Grandfather . . . sent his Coachman to whip him & his cousins . . . back to their cabin because they had a fancy to run naked on the road." That this tailor's apprentice decamped is of record. In his romantic past lie peregrinations in South Carolina and Tennessee before he settled at Greeneville, Tenn., in 1826. Johnson found the new environment congenial; within a decade he had married, prospered, and entered politics. His wife, Eliza McCardle (daughter of John and Sarah Phillips McCardle of Greeneville), bore ftve children, the last in 1852. Johnson the tailor was also a petty capitalist, exchanging goods and services; moreover, he acquired town property and made small loans. In a material sense, he exorcised "the grim and haggard monster" of poverty; in his mind, never.

Allegedly, when the mechanic-politician became alderman and mayor, "the tailor shop crowd" challenged the local aristocracy; yet Johnson was no pariah when elected representative to the state legislature in 1835. Hesitant amid uncertain party affiliations, he was before his service closed (house, 1835–37; senate, 1839–43) a staunch Jeffersonian—regular in voting, the foe of internal improvements, one of the obstructionist "Immortal Thirteen." He displayed radical democracy and sectionalism, advocating a "white basis" for congressional representation and sponsoring a "State of Franklin" to be created from East Tennessee and neighboring areas.

But overwhelming ambition could not rest; and Johnson, eyeing Congress, purportedly gerrymandered the First Tennessee District. For five terms (1843–53) he remained invincible, in great measure because of his political acumen. Possessing a genius for sensing the popular whim, this feared stump speaker stood forth as a doughty plebeian, champion of the common man, while casting opponents as nabobs, mouthpieces for the vested interests. In Congress he exhibited many lifelong characteristics. A loyal Democrat, he was not invariably a party man; sectionalist, but not necessarily *southern*; states' righter, but defender of the Union and the Constitution. Embracing such party shibboleths as low tariff, expansionism, and war with Mexico, he feuded with the leadership, notably with President James Knox Polk. Clashing with Jefferson Davis, he arraigned "an illegitimate, swaggering, bastard, scrub aristocracy." The tribune of the plebs labored for a homestead measure and popular election of the president and senators. The apostle of retrenchment opposed the Smithsonian Institution.

Virtually unknown nationally outside the House, Johnson was too well known in Tennessee, where Democrats wearied of his sinecure and Whigs "Henry-mandered" his district. He was on Golgotha. "My political garments have been divided and upon my vesture do they intend to cast lots"—a gloomy forecast for a decade which saw him in statehouse and Senate. Elected governor in 1853 and again in 1855, he vanquished such orators as the Whig Gustavus A. Henry and the "apostate" Meredith P. Gentry; in each close race he lost East Tennessee and won via the rural Middle Tennessee counties. The "radical" Johnson surfaced in a first inaugural which likened democracy unto a political ladder akin to Jacob's and envisioned "Democracy progressive" and the "Church Militant" converging towards theocracy.

Except for progress in public education, his governorship was undistinguished. Campaigns against internal improvements and the Bank of Tennessee failed; the assembly rejected his democratic constitutional "andy-johnsonisms." Not only had he assumed office inadequately prepared; not only did Governor Johnson, like President Johnson, lack effective liaison with the legislature; but the office was inherently weak, possessing neither patronage nor veto power. Yet, to the discomfiture of his opponents, he remained "the king of the Democracy." By 1856, the king dreamed of the vice-presidency or even the White House; but presently, Capitol Hill would suffice.

Chosen senator on the first ballot, Johnson returned to discord. When he had departed Washington in 1853, the sectional dilemma appeared solved; four years later, compromise had been aborted. The Tennessean did not immediately enter the vitrolic debate over slavery, considering it "in perfect harmony" with democracy and himself possessing several "household" Negroes. Instead, he concentrated on the homestead, presenting in May 1858 a rambling and discursive manifesto. By 1860 the measure, now espoused by Republicans and tolerated by proslavery men, passed only to be vetoed by James Buchanan. Meanwhile Johnson plunged into presidential politics, standing as a dark horse at Charleston; disappointed, and looking to 1864, he gave the Breckinridge ticket lukewarm support.

Swept up in the great denouement, the senator emerged as a national figure acclaimed by Unionists everywhere. In a ringing speech on 18–19 Dec. 1860, he denied the constitutionality of secession and urged defense of Southern rights within the Union; subsequently he denounced treason and conspiracy. In Tennessee, ironically, the "traitor" found himself divorced from democracy and consorting with Whiggery; his state seceded, the "martyr" stumped Kentucky and Ohio. He became an influential member of the Radical-dominated Joint Committee on the Conduct of the War. Johnson's unstinting patriotism brought appointment to the Tennessee governorship in February 1862. To an unprecedented Eng/Chang mission implicit in the Siamese "brigadier general and military governor" charged with restoring loyalty and civil government, he carried both assets and liabilities. It was an Augean task: refractory aristocrats and evasive "hermaphrodites," secesh parsons and pouting women, Graybacks and guerrillas, contentious generals and subalterns, matters great and small. Loyalty and restoration must await military supremacy. Called imaginatively "his finest hour," the governorship was more nearly a study in perseverance. And yet it enhanced his political fortunes. His steadfast

courage, his *brutum fulmen*—"*treason must be made odious and traitors impoverished*"—his "radical" espousal of abolition, his "availability" as War Democrat; these, with Lincoln's confidence and Republican approbation, propelled him into the vice-presidency. Assassination completed a progression.

What of the tailor become hierarch? For one past "the meridian of life," the president radiated vigor and purpose. Of medium height and sturdy frame, dark eyes and graying hair, he wore an expression that prompted a sobriquet "the Grim Presence." The frock coat and accoutrements, an estate that reached $110,000 in 1870, and a continuing self-education—though his speeches ne'er rang in runic rhyme—testified to his climb up Jacob's ladder. Fundamentally Johnson remained unchanged: a loner with few intimates, a champion of the underdog and an enemy of privilege, a shrewd, calculating politician, a man with a persecution complex, and a moralist whose mind contained "one compartment for right and one for wrong" but no middle chamber between. This Algerian figure now faced his sternest test.

Reconstruction theories ranged from "forgive and forget" to Carthaginian peace; to those of the latter persuasion, Johnson seemed an avenging angel. "By the gods, there will be no trouble now in running this government," proclaimed Benjamin Wade. In reality this Catonian image widely credited North and South was a distortion. Despite proscription of "high" and "property-tied" Confederates, his program, initiated between Congresses, was surprisingly lenient. Why the volte-face? Perhaps it reflected a stocktaking. Johnson discriminated between leaders and followers; intended that the South remain a white man's country; saw planter bloc replaced by Northern plutocracy; and, fatally stricken with the presidential virus, possibly contemplated a common man's democracy. Undoubtedly he had moderate counsel from the Sewards and the Blairs, and from Southerners.

Still, Reconstruction was not tunnel but labyrinth. Not all Northerners would forgive and forget; Congress, jealous of executive power, would reassert prerogative. Whether moderate, radical, or conservative, legislators generally believed they should preside over Reconstruction. And those Southerners—ex-Confederates in government, an apparently unreconstructed press, freedmen relegated to de facto slavery—*were* they loyal?

Another chapter in a historic tug-of-war had begun. Despite congressional exclusion of Southern representatives and creation of a Joint Committee on Reconstruction, the president remained optimistic. Early in 1866 he vetoed Freedmen's Bureau and Civil Rights bills; and, scenting victory, publicly identified Thaddeus Stevens and others as disunionists. Now sentiment swung against him, and in the ensuing year Congress passed over his veto such measures as the Fourteenth Amendment, the Tenure of Office Act, and the Military Reconstruction Act. His innovative midwestern "Swing around the Circle" during the congressional elections of 1866 was a disaster. Factors perhaps in toto irrepressible—among them his Tyler-like situation, his inflexibility and lack of congressional liaison, Southern mistakes, and Radical determination—defeated presidential Reconstruction.

Yet the drama had not ended; for Johnson, resisting the mandate by means open and sub rosa, added to the plot. Ouster had been bruited as early as 1866; and after his removal of Secretary of War Edwin McMasters Stanton challenged the Tenure of Office Act, enemies—

"Tray, Blanch, Sweetheart, little dogs and all," in Johnsonian parlance—procured in January 1868 impeachment for "high crimes and misdemeanors." The grand assize came in the spring, the Grim Presence comporting himself with dignity in absentia. In crucial roll calls which saw seven "recusant" Republicans side with the Democrats, conviction failed 35–19, one short of the necessary two-thirds. Interpretations of this crisis vary widely. Contemporaries often saw either Radical plot or just retribution. A legalistic approach stresses attack not only upon the man but also upon the presidency; a political persuasion contends that Johnson held a concept of office established only this century—thus, impeachment was a justifiable weapon against encroachment. These are converging polarities, each invoking checks and balances. Yen for power, high crimes, unindictable but impeachable—semantics and hypotheses redolent of Watergate—remind us that the historian is a creature of his or her times.

Scarcely Brownlow's "dead dog of the White House," Johnson was a lame duck not only for his term but also for another as well. Rejected by the democracy, his star descendant, he became per census "Ex Pres Retired"; yet, "Retired" to stage his own encore, this time for vindication. Again there was the strain of antimonopoly: let the public debt be repudiated! Again there was the Johnson mantra—no longer so binding. Losing Senate and House bids in 1869 and 1872, he was elected senator in January 1875. For one bittersweet month, a special session in March, he returned, the only former president to do so, and delivered a philippic against the incumbent Ulysses Grant. It was his envoi. Having survived facial tumor and cholera epidemic, he died of a stroke in Carter County, Tenn., and was interred in Greeneville.

In all likelihood the Johnson stereotype will persist: racist demagogue, vindictive and inflexible, power his compelling goal; man of the people, patriot and statesman "slandered and vilified by the press and the biased historians"—admixture of truth and falsehood. Ironically the realities, like the images, seem contradictory. Highly successful in many ways, Johnson always felt the sting of "huckletooth": of poverty, exclusion, obloquy, even of hatred. He suffered from a basic insecurity; hence his perennial war against "the interests," whether unskilled labor, slavocracy, or emerging financial-industrial combination. In this populist and free-soiler, radical and conservative commingle; in his career, one senses the clash of old and new. Was not the erstwhile tailor spokesman for a little America of limited government and equal opportunity, an America "of the people"? In the "implacable and unforgiving" Johnson, one detects a strong sense of lenience, a receptiveness to flattery, a vulnerability to the feminine sex. In his simplistic view of life but also in his complexities, the compleat Andrew Johnson symbolizes the nineteenth century.

SEE: Howard K. Beale, *The Critical Year* (1958); Michael Les Benedict, *The Impeachment and Trial of Andrew Johnson* (1973); Hubert Blair Bentley, "Andrew Johnson, Governor of Tennessee, 1853–57" (Ph.D. diss., University of Tennessee, 1972); David Bowen, "Andrew Johnson and the Negro" (Ph.D. diss., University of Tennessee, 1976); Albert Castel, "Andrew Johnson, His Historiographical Rise and Fall," *Mid-America* 45 (1963); *Congressional Globe*, 28th–32nd, 35th–40th Congresses; LeRoy P. Graf, "Andrew Johnson and Learning," *Phi Kappa Phi Journal* 42 (1962); LeRoy P. Graf and Ralph W. Haskins, eds., *The Papers of Andrew Johnson*, 5 vols.

(1967–); Ralph W. Haskins, "Andrew Johnson and the Preservation of the Union," East Tennessee Historical Society's *Publications*, no. 33 (1961), and "Internecine Strife in Tennessee: Andrew Johnson versus Parson Brownlow," *Tennessee Historical Quarterly* 24 (1965); Willard Hays, "Andrew Johnson's Changing Reputation," East Tennessee Historical Society's *Publications*, nos. 31, 32 (1959, 1960); Andrew Johnson Papers, Abraham Lincoln Papers (Library of Congress, Washington, D.C.); Johnson-Bartlett Collection (Greeneville, Tenn.); Eric McKitrick, *Andrew Johnson and Reconstruction* (1960), and ed., *Andrew Johnson: A Profile* (1969); Peter Maslowski, "Treason Must Be Made Odious" (Ph.D. diss., Ohio State University, 1972); James D. Richardson, *A Compilation of the Messages and Papers of the Presidents, 1789–1902* (1903); William T. M. Riches, "The Commoners: Abraham Lincoln and Andrew Johnson to 1861" (Ph.D. diss., University of Tennessee, 1976); Robert G. Russell, "Prelude to the Presidency: The Election of Andrew Johnson to the Senate," *Tennessee Historical Quarterly* 26 (1967); Oliver P. Temple, *Notable Men of Tennessee from 1833 to 1875* (1912); "This Clangor of Belated Mourning: James Russell Lowell on Andrew Johnson's Father," *South Atlantic Quarterly* 62 (1963); Hans Trefousse, *Impeachment of a President* (1975); Robert H. White, *Messages of the Governors of Tennessee*, 8 vols. (1952–72); Robert W. Winston, *Andrew Johnson: Plebeian and Patriot* (1928).

RALPH W. HASKINS

Johnson, Ann Swepson Boyd Hawkins Russell (6 *Jan. 1788–1861[?]*), proprietor-manager for seventeen years of the famous Warren County spa, Shocco Springs, was born in Mecklenburg County, Va. Her parents were Alexander Boyd, a well-known Scottish merchant and landowner of that county, and his wife, Ann Swepson, the daughter of Richard Swepson. The children of Alexander Boyd were William, Robert, Richard, Alexander, James, David, John, Jane Anderson, Ann Swepson, Mary Frances, and Susannah.

Ann Swepson Boyd's education was provided for until age sixteen by the terms of her father's will. Shortly before reaching that age she married, on 24 Dec. 1803, William Hawkins, a member of the illustrious Hawkins family of Granville-Warren-Vance counties, N.C., and later governor of North Carolina (1811–14). After Hawkins's untimely death in 1819, she married, on 8 Apr. 1824, Richard Russell, a wealthy planter of Warren County. Russell died in 1825, and on 9 June 1826 she married Robert R. Johnson, a socially prominent entrepreneur also of Warren County.

Johnson lived less than a year after their marriage. He had recently bought Shocco Springs, and within three months of his death his widow opened it for the season. Allotted the resort by her husband's administrators on condition that she relinquish all other claims to his estate, she finally purchased Shocco Springs at the auction of his land. In less than seven years Ann Johnson more than doubled the accommodations. Until 1844, when she sold the spa, she continued to develop the facility and to build its reputation for hospitality, excellent cuisine, and fashionable amusement. Season after season wealthy and prominent families returned for the frequent balls, supper parties, concerts, and social mingling as well as for the curative waters. In 1832, she also opened a girl's school there. Her achievements, known as far as New York, supplied the basis for later additional expansion of Shocco Springs.

Ann Johnson had nine children: Emily, Celestia,

Matilda, Lucy, William, Henrietta, and Mary Jane Hawkins; Louis (or Lewis) Henry Russell; and Roberta D. Johnson. She is said to have died in 1861 in Holly Springs, Miss.

SEE: Samuel A. Ashe, ed., *Biographical History of North Carolina*, vol. 5 (1906); George Anderson Foote, "Old Watering Places in Warren County," *Wake Forest Student* (19 Dec. 1899); William B. Hill, *The Boyds of Boydton* (1967); Mecklenburg County, Va., Wills (Boydton, Va.); Raleigh *Register*, 2 Jan. 1804, 1 Nov. 1822, 16 Apr. 1824, 3 Aug. 1841; *Roanoke Advocate*, 21 June 1832; Tarboro *Free Press*, 4 June 1830, 1 Aug. 1834; *Tarboro North Carolina Free Press*, 17 May 1831, 25 Dec. 1832; *Tarboro Press*, 5 Aug., 2 Sept. 1837; Warren County Deeds, Estate Records, Marriage Bonds (North Carolina State Archives, Raleigh); *Warrenton Reporter*, 16 Aug. 1825.

HELEN B. WATSON

Johnson, Archibald (29 Aug. 1859–27 Dec. 1934), editor, was born in what is now Spring Hill Township, Scotland County, the son of Duncan and Catherine Livingston Johnson, both of whom were of Highland Scots ancestry. He was six when the neighborhood fell directly in the path of one column of William T. Sherman's army, then driving Joseph E. Johnston north towards Durham Station for the surrender of the last Confederate army. Johnston, unable to halt Sherman, did what he could to delay him and so burnt all bridges behind him.

Duncan Johnson's house was within a mile of a bridge over the Lumber River, and it took Sherman's engineers three days to improvise a crossing; in the interim, the waiting army had time to apply Sherman's "scorched earth" policy to the neighborhood with the utmost rigor. Duncan Johnson had been a moderately affluent landowner and master of five or six "prime field hands" who, with their women and children, numbered from a dozen to a score of black people dependent on the farm. Within three days he was reduced from a man of substance, although less than wealth, to literal pauperism. Except for the house that sheltered the family, every structure on the place—barns, stables, corncrib, smokehouse, even wagon sheds—burned and all livestock and every wheeled vehicle were carried off; not even farm implements were left.

Thus early in life Archibald Johnson was acquainted with the harsh reality of the struggle for survival; if he remained relatively unscarred, it was because everyone he knew was very nearly in the same condition. Where everyone has to struggle for bare subsistence, the distinction between rich and poor vanishes; which is one, perhaps the main reason why the mature man, recognizing human excellence, never associated it with money.

Yet even in its evil days the community managed to maintain the Richmond Academy, one of those private schools that were predecessors of the modern high school system. Within its walls young Johnson acquired "little Latin and less Greek," but a respect for genuine learning that remained with him throughout life. Then, in the debates staged by the Richmond Temperance and Literary Society, he gained the knack of thinking on his feet and speaking clearly and persuasively.

But he was not cut out for a farmer. Soon after his marriage in 1885 to Flora Caroline McNeill, the youngest daughter of Hector McNeill, wartime high sheriff of Cumberland County, Johnson went into the mercantile business at Laurinburg. However, after a bout with typhoid fever kept him in bed for nine weeks, he turned to his true vocation as editor of the *Laurinburg Exchange* and later, for a year or two, of the *Red Springs Citizen*.

In 1895, John H. Mills, founder of the Thomasville Baptist Orphanage, retired and the trustees reorganized the institution. Mills, a devotee of vocational education before the term was invented, had set up a print shop, mainly to give some of the older boys an apprenticeship to the trade; from it he issued a weekly newspaper to plead the cause of the orphanage. He named the paper *Charity and Children*, edited it himself, and distributed it through some of the Baptist churches in the state. After his retirement, the trustees decided to divorce the paper from the routine management of the Thomasville Orphanage and to employ a professional newspaperman to edit it and also to act as field representative of the orphanage. For this they needed a person known to be able to write and speak.

After some search the trustees fixed upon Archibald Johnson, who held the job for thirty-nine years. Towards the end, failing health forced him to transfer the main burden of the work to the man who became his successor, the Reverend John Arch McMillan, but titular editor he remained until the day of his death. The reason for the trustees' generosity was that Johnson had converted a purely propaganda sheet with a circulation of 2,000 into a journal of opinion that eventually attained a weekly circulation of 30,000 copies. It became, in the opinion of Joseph P. Caldwell, then editor of the *Charlotte Observer*, "the most-quoted paper in the state."

In a way, Johnson's hand was forced. The orphanage was only one of many agencies of the Baptist State Convention, whose official organ was the *Biblical Recorder*, published in Raleigh and the recognized newspaper of record for the denomination's affairs. The function of *Charity and Children* was to speak for the orphanage alone, but to do that successfully it must be read, and to be widely read it must have something of interest other than institutional news. Church news, including matters of faith and dogma, were the preserve of the *Recorder*, and political partisanship of course was barred. But that left open the whole range of intellectual concerns, so Johnson restricted strictly orphanage news to one of his four pages and filled the rest with anything that happened to interest him. Because he was so completely Tar Heel born and Tar Heel bred, what interested him interested a great many other North Carolinians. The paper, from being a dead loss, became an important contributor to the revenues of the orphanage.

Naturally *Charity and Children* was controversial, but the editor was master of the art of speaking his mind good-humoredly; thus the dissent he aroused, though frequently vigorous, was also good-humored. Once he was censured by the state legislature because, after it passed a bill that he regarded as preposterous, he remarked that the general level of intelligence of that body approximated that of a gatepost. But the censure was exclusively official, for too many of the unofficial public heartily agreed with his observation.

Johnson's outstanding service to the state, however, came in the early twenties, when the Fundamentalist revolt against science was building up to enactment of the Tennessee "monkey law" that led to the Scopes trial in 1925. Certain Fundamentalist leaders, especially in Arkansas, Texas, and Kentucky, launched a concerted attack on North Carolina Baptists for retaining as president of Wake Forest College, a Baptist school, the biologist William Louis Poteat, who had done his graduate work at Woods Hole and the University of Berlin. At the time, the *Biblical Recorder* was edited by Livingston Johnson, Archibald's older brother. Although decidedly conservative in matters of dogma, the Johnson brothers knew Dr. Poteat and had the highest respect for his intellectual integrity; both were persuaded that he was a far more devout Christian than many of his detractors. So it happened that as the storm roared to its farcical climax at Dayton, Tenn., the two most influential Baptist newspapers in North Carolina sturdily resisted the attacks upon Poteat.

A few years later when The University of North Carolina, in its turn, was beleaguered and the legislature seemed about to enact a duplicate of the Tennessee law, seventeen of the twenty-one Wake Forest graduates sitting in the General Assembly voted with the university men, giving them a majority with eleven votes to spare.

It would be erroneous to attribute either the successful defense of Poteat or the successful resistance to the monkey law to the Johnson brothers. But they happened to be in conspicuous positions, not as commanders but rather as buglers of the victorious forces. Nevertheless, as the Scripture says, "if the trumpet give an uncertain sound, who shall prepare himself to the battle?" Their clarions were loud and clear, and that should be their memorial.

Survived by his wife, four daughters, and a son, Archibald Johnson was buried in the old Spring Hill churchyard near Wagram.

SEE: *Charlotte Observer*, 28 Dec. 1934; *Greensboro Daily News*, 23 June 1935; North Carolina Baptist State Convention, *Minutes*, 1935; *North Carolina Biography*, vol. 4 (1929, 1956); Raleigh, *Biblical Recorder*, 9 Jan. 1935.

GERALD W. JOHNSON

Johnson, Charles (d. 23 July 1802), state senator and congressman, was born in Scotland. According to family tradition, he was a member of the great Johnston family in southern Scotland. As a youth he took part in the unsuccessful rising of Prince Charles Edward in 1745. After the Battle of Culloden, he escaped to the Continent and dropped the "t" from his name. After a time he returned to Scotland and later went to London where he worked for the East India Company for several years.

After his arrival in North Carolina, Johnson located in the Albemarle region and married Ann Earl, the daughter of the Reverend Daniel Earl, rector of St. Paul's Church, Edenton, and owner of nearby Bandon plantation. After his marriage he pursued extensive agricultural interests.

Johnson rose to prominence in the region and became active in politics. An ardent Federalist, he aligned himself with Samuel Johnston, James Iredell, and Allen Jones. Johnson was elected to represent Chowan County in the state senate from 1781 to 1784 and from 1788 to 1792. During his second term, he was speaker of the senate (1789) while Samuel Johnston presided over the constitutional convention. Johnson vigorously supported ratification of the Constitution. He was elected to the Seventh Congress and served from 4 Mar. 1801 until his death at Bandon more than a year later. He was buried in Edenton. By his marriage to Ann Earl he left one son, Charles Earl.

SEE: Samuel A. Ashe, ed., *Biographical History of North Carolina*, vol. 2 (1905); *Biog. Dir. Am. Cong.* (1961).

JAMES ELLIOTT MOORE

Johnson, Charles Earl (13 Aug. 1851–9 Sept. 1923), businessman, was born in Raleigh, the son of Charles Earl and Frances Iredell Johnson. His mother was the daughter of James Iredell, governor of North Carolina in 1827–28. Young Johnson attended Lovejoy's Academy in Raleigh and also received instruction from the Reverend Dr. R. S. Mason. At age fourteen, he enrolled as a private in the Confederate Army shortly before the war ended. At seventeen he worked as a clerk at W. H. & R. S. Tucker, a Raleigh dry goods store, and in 1874–75 he was assistant secretary of the North Carolina Senate.

Johnson wished to study law, but the decimation of the family fortune during the Civil War and the death of his father in 1876 prevented him from doing so. Instead, he joined a large cotton firm, cotton at that time being the most important staple article in the trade of Raleigh. Within a year, he became manager of the firm of Lee, Whitaker and Johnson. In September 1877 he established his own cotton business, C. E. Johnson and Co., the first to build a cotton press in Raleigh. Johnson was also one of the first to recognize the advantage of exporting cotton directly from points of origin to the interior of the state, and direct exports by his company soon amounted to 150,000 bales annually. Later, as the consumption of cotton increased locally, Johnson's firm decreased exports. His new method of exports reduced the cost of handling cotton between producer and consumer. The company operated a large plant in Hamlet as well as in Raleigh.

In addition to his cotton business, Johnson was a longtime director of the Seaboard Air Line Railway and president of Carolina Ice Co. and Hamlet Ice Co. At the time of his death he was president of the Carolina Power & Light Co. Active in banking, he was the first president of the Mechanics Bank of Raleigh, vice-president of the National Bank of Raleigh, and president of Raleigh Banking and Trust. He also served as president of the Chesterfield Land and Lumber Co.

Although Johnson described himself as a "zealous supporter of the Democratic party," he never actively sought political office. Nevertheless, in 1905 Governor R. B. Glenn appointed him a member of his staff with the rank of colonel. Johnson also served as a member of the Raleigh city council. An Episcopalian, he was vestryman of Christ Church parish and for thirty years treasurer of the Diocese of North Carolina. He was an avid fisherman, and his tackle box was said to have been one of his most valued possessions.

On 7 Dec. 1876 Johnson married Mary Ellis Wilson of Charlotte, and they were the parents of three children: Mary Wilson (Mrs. Frank Kimbark), Charles Earl, Jr., and Fanny Hines (Mrs. Morris Harris). Johnson died of a heart attack and was buried in Oakwood Cemetery, Raleigh.

SEE: Samuel A. Ashe, ed., *Biographical History of North Carolina*, vol. 2 (1905); *North Carolina Biography*, vol. 4 (1919); Raleigh *News and Observer*, 10 Sept. 1923.

DAVID C. WRIGHT

Johnson, Charles Marion (9 Apr. 1891–2 June 1964), public official, was born at Burgaw, the son of M. H. and Minnie Norris Johnson. He attended school in his hometown, then Buies Creek Academy and the Bingham School at Mebane. After leaving school, he was employed for a year as assistant cashier in the Wilmington office of the Atlantic Coast Line Railway and then became traveling auditor for the Hilton Dodge Lumber Company at Savannah, Ga. Returning home, he was deputy clerk of court of Pender County for seven years followed by eighteen months as district tax supervisor under the Revaluation Act. Moving to state government, Johnson spent more than five years in various positions in the State Auditor's Office, serving first as a traveling auditor, one year as auditor of disbursements, and finally as deputy auditor.

After this apprenticeship in state finance, Johnson was appointed secretary to the County Government Advisory Commission by Governor Angus W. McLean. Through service in this position, he became familiar with the concerns of local government. He also became well known to the state's county commissioners, who appreciated his ability to deal with them in a frank, commonsense way. Johnson's manner was crisp but good-humored. His success in dealing with problems at the local level attracted the attention of Governor O. Max Gardner, who appointed him the first director of the Local Government Commission, which was created by the legislature in 1931.

Upon the resignation of the state treasurer, John Stedman, on 17 Nov. 1932, Governor Gardner named Johnson to be treasurer of North Carolina. This was shortly before the end of Gardner's administration, and his successor, J. C. B. Ehringhaus, recommended and secured from the legislature of 1933 a consolidation of the office of Director of Local Government and that of the state treasurer. Johnson thereby became the guardian of the credit not only of the state, but of its subdivisions as well. By his keen insight into, and his wise appraisal of, the financial problems of the state and its counties, cities, and towns, Johnson became a trusted adviser in matters of public finance and extremely popular with the people of North Carolina.

Johnson was elected to fill the unexpired term of Stedman, and then was regularly reelected for four-year terms until 1948 when he became a candidate for governor. He led in his party's primary by a small margin, but in a runoff W. Kerr Scott won and was elected governor. Johnson did not allow defeat to slow his pace, nor did he harbor any bitterness. Remaining active in both private and public life, he joined the First Securities Corporation in Durham and later became executive vice-president of the Bank of Charlotte. President Harry S Truman later appointed him collector of customs at Wilmington. In 1956 Johnson withdrew from public service and devoted himself to his varied business interests in Raleigh, except that he served two terms on the State Banking Commission by appointment of Governor Terry Sanford.

Johnson's tenure as state treasurer coincided with one of the most depressed and tragic periods in the history of North Carolina. Many local governments were in default, and the state had outstanding short-term borrowings in New York that were to have been paid out of current collections. The continued decline in the state's economy, however, made this impossible. It was up to Johnson, as treasurer, to be the right arm of governors Gardner and Ehringhaus in securing the renewal of the notes in New York (and the ultimate funding of them as a casual deficit under the provisions of the state constitution), and later to negotiate with the creditors of local governments for the purpose of getting them on a sound financial basis.

Johnson died of a heart attack at Rex Hospital, Raleigh, at age seventy-three. His wife, whom he married in 1920, was Ruth Moore of Burgaw; they were the parents of one son, Charles M., Jr., born in 1924.

SEE: Mattie Bloodworth, *History of Pender County, North Carolina* (1947); *North Carolina Biography*, vols. 3, 4 (1929, 1941); *North Carolina Manual* (1939–47); Raleigh *News and Observer*, 3 June 1964.

                                                              EDWIN GILL

Johnson, Edward Austin (23 Nov. 1860–24 July 1944), educator, historian, attorney, and politician, was one of eleven children of Columbus and Eliza Johnson, slaves belonging to a large slaveholder in Wake County. Johnson acquired his earliest education from a free black, Nancy Walton, and after emancipation attended a school in Raleigh directed by two white teachers from New England. These "Yankee" teachers introduced him to the Congregational church, in which he was active for the rest of his life.

In 1879 Johnson entered Atlanta University and upon graduation four years later became principal of the Mitchell Street School in Atlanta. In 1885 he returned to Raleigh to head Washington School, a position he held until 1891. As a principal and teacher, he came to recognize the critical need for works that would provide black children with information about "the many brave deeds and noble characters of their own race." To fill the void, Johnson wrote *A School History of the Negro Race in America* which was published in 1891 and later appeared in several revised editions. This textbook was the first by a black author to be approved by the North Carolina State Board of Education for use in the public schools, and it established his reputation as a scholar and historian. Johnson was the author of several other books, including *History of the Negro Soldiers in the Spanish-American War, Light Ahead for the Negro*, and *Negro Almanac and Statistics*, as well as numerous articles and pamphlets.

While a principal in Raleigh, Johnson enrolled in the law school at Shaw University and received a bachelor of law degree in 1891. Two years later he joined the law faculty at Shaw where he remained until 1907, serving first as professor and later as dean. Johnson acquired an enviable reputation as a trial lawyer and won all of the numerous cases that he argued before the North Carolina Supreme Court. Referring to his success as an attorney, a contemporary observed that "no man stands higher in the esteem of the substantial people of the Old North State than Mr. Johnson." In 1903 he helped to organize the National Bar Association.

Johnson also was associated with various business ventures. In 1897 he joined Warren C. Coleman and other black businessmen in North Carolina to establish a cotton mill in Concord. Johnson served first as vice-president and later as president of the Coleman Manufacturing Company, which was intended to become a model of Negro initiative and business acumen. The company did not fulfill the expectations of its incorporators and in fact ultimately went bankrupt. In 1898 Johnson and six other black men organized the North Carolina Mutual and Provident Association in Durham which in time became the largest Negro insurance company in the world. By the turn of the century, he had accumulated considerable real estate in Raleigh and in 1902 was one of only two black residents of the city whose income was sufficient to warrant payment of the state's income tax.

Throughout his career Johnson was active in the Republican party. He figured prominently in the party's local and state organizations and was a delegate to the Republican National Convention in 1892 and 1896. He was a member of Raleigh's Board of Aldermen for a term, and he served from 1899 to 1907 as assistant to the federal attorney for the district of eastern North Carolina. Unwilling to accept Booker T. Washington's advice that Negroes should eschew politics, Johnson deeply resented the disfranchisement of black citizens in the state that occurred in the wake of the "white supremacy" campaign of 1898. Rather than accept such legal proscriptions, he left the South for New York City.

Opening a law office in Harlem in 1907, Johnson quickly established a lucrative practice and became prominent in the economic, social, and political life of the black community. An active member of the Harlem Board of Trade and Commerce and the Upper Harlem Taxpayers Association, he also contributed generously of his time and money to the expansion of recreational facilities for Negro youth. Programs sponsored by churches and by the YMCA were of special concern to him.

As soon as Johnson arrived in Harlem, he began to insist that Negroes be nominated for office in areas where they constituted a majority of the voters. His own rise to political power in New York "symbolized a major transition in American Negro and urban history"—a black southerner who escaped the strictures on his civil and political rights by migrating to a northern city. He served as Republican committeeman from Harlem's Nineteenth Assembly District and in 1917 was elected to the state assembly in Albany, becoming the first Negro member of the New York legislature. As a legislator, according to a report by the Citizens Union, he "promoted measures of importance to his constituency." Of the four bills he piloted through the legislature, Johnson considered two of far-reaching significance: a civil rights act and a law establishing a state employment bureau. Defeated for reelection largely as the result of a redistricting of the city, Johnson remained active in local Republican circles. His final attempt to gain elective office took place in 1928, when he waged a vigorous, though unsuccessful campaign as a Republican candidate for Congress.

During the last decade of his life Johnson was almost blind. He died at age eighty-three following surgery and was survived by his only child, a daughter.

SEE: *Colored American*, 30 Apr. 1898; "Edward Austin Johnson," *Journal of Negro History* 24 (October 1944); Indianapolis *Freeman*, 6 July 1907; "The Life and Work of Edward Austin Johnson," *The Crisis* 40 (April 1933); *New York Times*, 24 July 1944; *Who's Who in Colored America, 1938–1940* (1940).

WILLARD B. GATEWOOD, JR.

Johnson, Gerald White (6 Aug. 1890–22 Mar. 1980), writer and newspaperman, was born in the community of Riverton in Scotland County, the son of Archibald and Flora Caroline McNeill Johnson. He received the A.B. degree from Wake Forest College and later studied at the University of Toulouse, France. A veteran of World War I, Johnson served with the 321st Infantry, 81st Division, U.S. Army (1917–19) and with the American Expeditionary Force, France, for one year.

His career in journalism began when, at age twenty, Johnson, with others, established the Thomasville *Davidsonian*; he soon moved to a position on the Lex-

ington *Dispatch*, where he worked from 1911 to 1913. Joining the staff of the *Greensboro Daily News*, he wrote editorials and music criticism until 1924, when he became a professor of journalism at The University of North Carolina. During his tenure on the university faculty, he helped President Harry Woodburn Chase in a successful campaign to fight antievolution bills in the General Assembly.

Johnson's journalistic career was climaxed by his affiliation with the *Baltimore Evening Sun* from 1926 to 1939, and *Baltimore Sun* from 1939 to 1943. As an editorial writer and columnist for the "Sunpapers," he was often called "Baltimore's second sage," a reference linking him with H. L. Mencken who was known as the sage of Baltimore. The two men remained friends through the years although their philosophies differed. In an obituary of Johnson, published in the *New York Times* on 24 Mar. 1980, Mencken was described as "cynical, pessimistic, racist and contemptuous of the 'booboisie,' " whereas Johnson was "patriotic, optimistic, a humanist and a liberal." Johnson's knowledge of the Bible and mythology, as well as his phenomenal memory, were legendary.

Because of his liberal philosophy, the editorialist left the Sunpapers in 1943. In a sketch published in *North Carolina Authors: A Selective Handbook*, he was quoted as saying that he found himself "completely out of line with the political policy of the *Baltimore Sun*, that I had served for 17 years, and although I was treated with the friendliest consideration it seemed only fair, both to the paper and to myself, to get out." From then on Johnson devoted his energies and talents to free-lance writing, though he held other positions for short periods of time. He substituted for Lewis Gannett on the New York *Herald Tribune* while Gannett was a war correspondent in Europe, was the American commentator for the *London Sunday Express* in 1947, and from 1952 to 1954 served as Sunday evening commentator for a Baltimore television station.

Between 1925 and 1976 Johnson published books on a regular basis. Biographies, essays, histories, commentaries on the American scene, novels—thought provoking all—were written by a man described in an editorial in the *Greensboro Daily News* of 25 Mar. 1980 as "a stirrer-upper, a writer who looked beyond his own time, a progressive voice in an often conservative wilderness."

Gerald Johnson did not regard himself as a historian. In a letter written in 1948, he said: "My books are pure journalism, not historiography. The historian writes authoritatively, for posterity; the journalist writes speculatively, for today. You will find in any of my books that the net result is not an affirmation, but a question, to wit, what significance has this man for us today? I try to give my answer, but it is speculative, not authoritative. It is merely the best guess I can make on the basis of the generally accepted facts.

"Mind you, I am not apologetic. My work has its own values but they are not the values that attach to history. To show the average man, the member of the reading public, how his acts and to a large extent his opinions are modified and controlled by what happened in the past is important—only less important than to discover and record the truth. The historian is the priest; the journalist is his acolyte; but they are, or should be, both servants of the truth."

Johnson's first book, written with William R. Hayward, was *The Story of Man's Work* (1925). This was followed by *What Is News? A Tentative Outline* and *Randolph of Roanoke: A Political Fantastic* (1926); *The Undefeated* and *Andrew Jackson: An Epic in Homespun* (1927); *The Secession* of the Southern States (1933); The Sunpapers of Baltimore (with Frank R. Kent, H. L. Mencken, and Hamilton Owens), A Little Night Music: Discoveries in the Exploitation of an Art, and The Wasted Land (1937); America's Silver Age: The Statecraft of Clay-Webster-Calhoun (1939); Roosevelt: Dictator or Democrat? (1941); American Heroes and Hero-Worship (1943); Woodrow Wilson: The Unforgettable Figure Who Has Returned to Haunt Us (1944); An Honorable Titan: A Biographical Study of Adolph S. Ochs (1946); The First Captain: The Story of John Paul Jones (1947); Liberal's Progress (1948); Our English Heritage (1949); Incredible Tale: The Odyssey of the Average American in the Last Half Century (1950); This American People (1951); Pattern for Liberty: The Story of Old Philadelphia and The Making of a Southern Industrialist: A Biographical Study of Simpson Bobo Tanner (1952); Mount Vernon: The Story of a Shrine . . . (1953); Lunatic Fringe (1957); Peril and Promise: An Inquiry into Freedom of the Press and The Lines Are Drawn: American Life since the First World War as Reflected in the Pulitzer Prize Cartoons (1958); Hod-Carrier: Notes of a Laborer on an Unfinished Cathedral and Communism: An American's View (1964); Franklin D. Roosevelt: Portrait of a Great Man (1967); The Imperial Republic: Speculation on the Future, If Any, of the Third U.S.A. (1972); and America-Watching (1976).

In 1959 Johnson published the first volume of a trilogy entitled America: A History for Peter, written to tell the story of America to his twelve-year-old grandson. The three books, America Is Born, America Grows Up, and America Moves Forward, were followed by four other books for young people: The Presidency and The Supreme Court (1962), The Congress (1963), and The Cabinet (1966). A History for Peter was the most successful, in terms of sales, of all his output.

In addition, Johnson wrote two novels: By Reason of Strength (1930), based on his family's migration from Scotland to America; and Number Thirty Six (1933), set in the South during his boyhood. Two mysteries were written under the pseudonym Charles North, a transliteration of North Carolina. Articles by him appeared in leading periodicals, and in 1954 Johnson became a contributing editor and weekly columnist for the New Republic. He also served as a speech writer during the presidential campaigns of Adlai E. Stevenson.

A member of Phi Beta Kappa, Johnson was awarded honorary degrees by Wake Forest University, the College of Charleston, the University of North Carolina at Chapel Hill, the University of the South, the University of North Carolina at Greensboro, Goucher College, and the Johns Hopkins University. He received the DuPont Commentator's Award; the Sidney Hillman Foundation Award; the George Foster Peabody Award; the North Carolina Award (the state's most prestigious medal); the Andrew White Medal from Loyola College, Baltimore; and the Maryland Civil Liberties Award.

A Democrat, Johnson was born into a family with strong Baptist connections but he himself was not active in any church. His father, Archibald Johnson, was editor of Charity and Children, a Baptist periodical published at the orphanage in Thomasville; and an uncle, Livingston Johnston, was editor of the Biblical Recorder, official organ of the Baptist State Convention. He was a cousin of North Carolina poet John Charles McNeill.

Johnson was described in his obituary in the Baltimore Sun of 23 Mar. 1980 as "a man who never seemed flustered or hurried. He was almost always seen with his cigar or pipe. As he aged and grew increasingly deaf, a hearing aid became indispensable. White-haired and with a white mustache, the writer, who was not a large man, looked frail in his later years, but his ideas

remained as robust as ever." Because of deafness, he had to give up flute playing, a hobby he had enjoyed. A dislocated hipbone required the use of a cane for several years before his death.

On 22 Apr. 1922, Johnson married Kathryn Hayward; they had two daughters, Kathryn (Mrs. Frederick Allen Sliger) and Dorothy (Mrs. Leonard van den Honert). His death was preceded by failing health during the last months of his life, and he died at the Edgewood Nursing Home. Following cremation at Greenmount Cemetery, Baltimore, Johnson's ashes were placed in a niche there.

SEE: Russell Brantley, "Celebrate the Life and Work of Gerald Johnson," Winston-Salem Sentinel, 2 Apr. 1980; Lloyd B. Dennis, "Native Tar Heel Gerald Johnson Still Prolific Writer in Baltimore," Raleigh News and Observer, 1 Mar. 1964; "G. W. Johnson Dies at 89; Was Writer," Baltimore Sun, 23 Mar. 1980; "Gerald W. Johnson," Greensboro Daily News, 25 Mar. 1980; "Gerald W. Johnson, Reporter-Historian," New York Times, 24 Mar. 1980; "Hopkins Honors State with Johnson," Raleigh News and Observer, 14 May 1977; Gerald W. Johnson to "Fannie Memory" [Memory F. Mitchell], 18 Feb. 1948 (North Carolina Collection, University of North Carolina Library, Chapel Hill); Lois Johnson, personal contact (Oxford); North Carolina Authors: A Selective Handbook (1952); "North Carolina-Born Author Dies at Age of 89," Raleigh News and Observer, 23 Mar. 1980; "Noted Author and Historian Johnson Dies," Greensboro Daily News, 23 Mar. 1980; Who's Who in America (1978–79).

MEMORY F. MITCHELL

Johnson, Herschel Vespasian (3 May 1894–16 Apr. 1966), foreign service officer, was born in Atlanta, Ga., the son of Arabelle Kenan Horne and William White Johnson. Arabelle Horne was a granddaughter of Governor Herschel V. Johnson of Georgia. Not related to his wife's family, William White Johnson also grew up in Georgia, reared by a strict Presbyterian grandmother. A well-read man with broad interests, he was in the insurance business and settled in Charlotte in 1900. Herschel attended the Charlotte public schools, and from the beginning was an able student and an omnivorous reader, never athletic, and as a child not especially sociable.

At The University of North Carolina, where he was graduated in 1916, Johnson majored in history and also concentrated on languages and literature. He was conspicuous as the energetic "inventor" of a student playreading club and dramatic workshop, and as the student who hung reproductions of Italian and other old masterpieces on the walls of his dormitory room. His classmates noted in the university annual his "cosmopolitan turn of mind . . . extensive reading in many fields of literature . . . keen perception and accurate judgment of men." He helped meet his college expenses with summer jobs in Charlotte and part-time jobs in Chapel Hill. He returned to the university in 1947 for an honorary LL.D. degree.

After graduation he taught French at Dr. Churchill Gibson Chamberlayne's school (later St. Christopher's) in Richmond, Va., and in 1917 enlisted in the army. He served overseas as first lieutenant, later captain, in the Fifty-fourth Infantry, with the Sixth Division in the Vosges Mountains and in the Meuse-Argonne offensive. Between the armistice and his return home, he spent five months in Burgundy, went twice to Italy, and was briefly in England, Scotland, and Paris. He attended Harvard Law School in 1919–20 and took the entrance examinations in Washington, D.C., for the Diplomatic Service. His appointment came on 15 Nov. 1920.

Johnson's first assignment abroad took him to Switzerland as third secretary to the legation at Berne (January–December 1921). From there he went to the legation in Sophia, Bulgaria, as second secretary for the next nineteen months. Bulgaria was unsettled by internal political strife and postwar economic adjustments, and twenty-nine-year-old Johnson was serving as chargé d'affaires when a coup d'état occurred in June 1923, with bloodshed in the streets. In July, he was assigned to the State Department's Division of Near Eastern Affairs in Washington for the next three years. Subsequently, for seven years (October 1926–February 1934), his province was Latin America.

He was second secretary at the legation in Tegucigalpa, Honduras (1926–28), where he also served as chargé d'affaires. His memories of 1928 included newsmaking visits by President-elect Hoover and by Charles A. Lindbergh. Johnson's next assignment was as first secretary in the Mexican Embassy under Ambassador Dwight W. Morrow. Morrow's tenure saw the establishment of more cordial U.S.-Mexican relations for the first time in nearly two decades, and ongoing negotiations concerning American oil investments and war-related claims in Mexico. Johnson was in charge during Morrow's absence from August 1929 until the following spring, when he was transferred to Washington. There he occupied the desk of the chief of the Division of Mexican Affairs for nearly four years.

From February 1934 to November 1941 he was at the embassy in London, as first secretary for three years and then counselor (second in command) for four years, with the rank of minister dating from February 1941. The London years were marked by critical international trade agreements, gathering war clouds, and the Nazi blitzkreig. Johnson represented his country at meetings of the Governing Body for Assistance to Refugees Arriving from Germany (1934), the International Sugar Council (1937–41), and the International Conference on Whaling (1937–39). He was responsible for aiding refugees and later for evacuating U.S. citizens in the war zone. At various times for a total of two years he was acting ambassador, including the interims following the death of Robert W. Bingham and the departure of Joseph P. Kennedy. It was Johnson who conveyed President Roosevelt's mediation proposal of 15 Apr. 1939 to the governments of Hitler and Mussolini. During the height of the blitz, Johnson lived at Claridge's Hotel and reported to his family in North Carolina that he was able to do a great deal of reading in the long hours in the bomb shelter.

Three days before the Japanese attack on Pearl Harbor, Johnson arrived in Stockholm to undertake the diplomatically ticklish role of U.S. minister in neutral Sweden, which was at that time surrounded by German-occupied territory. His work in assisting refugees continued. One of his duties was to discourage, as far as possible, Swedish exportation of strategic industrial materials to Germany. After the war, the Swedish press praised his intelligent understanding of Sweden's difficult position while he was handling negotiations between that nation and the United States. During the war years the legation grew from 40 to about 300, all of whom had to be airlifted in and out. The burgeoning staff had work to do in the country that served as "listening post" and "hotbed for intrigues of all the belligerants." When Johnson departed London in 1941, the

Times had called him a "skillful and tactful" administrator, liked for his "quiet and friendly way"; in Sweden he proved to be efficient under pressure and hard-driving, attending to his job seven days a week. He demanded—and got—"something close to perfection" from his junior staff. In April 1945 it was Johnson who handled the delicate communications in connection with Heinrich Himmler's unacceptable separate peace proposal, which had come via Count Folke Bernadotte of the Swedish Red Cross.

In May 1946 Johnson entered a new arena as deputy U.S. representative to the United Nations Security Council, serving under Edward R. Stettinius and replacing him in June as acting representative for six months. (Warren R. Austin, though on the scene, was not technically eligible to hold the post until after 1 Jan. 1947.) Johnson held the rank of ambassador from 9 July 1946. Under the rotation system he was president of the Security Council from 17 November to 17 December. In 1947 he served in the spring as alternate representative to the special session of the United Nations General Assembly on the Palestine question, and, in the fall, as representative to the second session of the General Assembly. He was deputy chief of the U.S. Mission to the United Nations from July 1947 to May 1948.

The main actions in which he participated during his two years at the United Nations were related to the Greek and Balkan crises, the Palestine question, and attempts to break the deadlock on negotiation procedures for both conventional disarmament and atomic control. He sparred with Russia's Gromyko and returned the fire of the Soviet delegate. Journalist Evelyn G. Kessel observed that Johnson "delivered his remarks courteously yet with provocative firmness—occasionally with a touch of sarcasm. Set jaw and narrow eyes gave a measure of his determination." Throughout these months his public addresses emphasized the urgency of atomic control, the importance of popular support for the United Nations as a place to thrash out disagreements, and his conviction that "we invite aggression . . . if we do not hold ourselves in readiness to take our full share of military responsibility for world security." In his home state he was chosen to receive the *Carolina Israelite*'s award for "Outstanding Brotherhood during 1947."

Johnson was temporarily felled by a heart attack in December 1947, recuperated in Puerto Rico and in Charlotte, and was in Washington five months later to take his oath of office as ambassador to Brazil.

From the time of his arrival in Rio de Janeiro in June 1948, Johnson was involved in negotiations concerning U.S. programs for Brazil's economic development; in the readjustment of outdated commercial relationships; and in attempts to gain Brazilian understanding of U.S. foreign aid programs that were weighted in favor of other areas of the world. *Time* magazine tagged him as his country's "New Explainer." There were misunderstandings to be resolved that arose from the overlapping functions of international agencies for planning, loans, and technical aid. Among the agreements signed during Johnson's ambassadorship were those providing for the Joint Commission for Economic Development and other broader technical cooperation agreements; programs in health and sanitation and vocational industrial education; an oil shale study in Brazil; and a Joint U.S.-Brazil Military Assistance Pact, in conformity with the United Nations charter and the U.S. Mutual Security Act of 1951. The military assistance pact, which included provisions for cooperative economic defense and commercial controls, was not immediately embraced by all parties in Brazil.

When President Dutra visited the United States in 1949, Johnson came home to serve as official host. On his return to Rio, he was accompanied by his mother; thereafter she made her home with him, graciously sharing his social and ceremonial duties. A new twelve-story American embassy was dedicated just before Johnson's departure in June 1953. At the end of his term, influential Rio newspapers were laudatory, and the Brazilian government soon afterwards awarded him the Order of the Southern Cross in the rank of grand cross.

On his retirement Johnson established a home in Charlotte where he led a relatively quiet life, especially in the years after his mother suffered a stroke. For several years he accepted invitations to speak, without remuneration, in and around Charlotte, and often he took these occasions to stress the importance of South America to the welfare and destiny of the United States. He served in 1958 on the fifteen-man North Carolina Constitutional Commission. His kin, his discussions with a circle of old friends—"The Philosophers Club," and, as always, his reading, were the happy stimulants of these later days. He was a member of St. Peter's Episcopal Church, the English-Speaking Union, and the Rotary Club in Charlotte; the Masonic order; Sigma Chi; the American Foreign Service Association; and the Metropolitan Club of Washington, D.C. Politically he was a Democrat.

In interviews with journalists, Johnson had testified to the lack of "Hollywoodish glamor" in the hard day-to-day work of a foreign service officer, but he relished that hard work for thirty-three years and liked every country he lived in. All his life he was intensely interested in the variety of events, people, places, art, and ideas that were his milieu. He was, as he said of himself, "a student by nature." He never married.

Johnson was buried in Elmwood Cemetery, Charlotte. An oil portrait, painted while he was in Brazil, is owned by the University of North Carolina at Charlotte. He gave a large part of his library to that institution in 1963. Some pieces from his fine collection of antique Chinese ceramics are now owned by the Mint Museum in Charlotte. His papers are preserved at the Truman Presidential Library in Missouri and at the University of North Carolina Library in Chapel Hill.

SEE: *Biographic Register of the United States Department of State,* 1 Apr. 1951; *Current Biography* (July 1946); Robert Burton House, *The Light that Shines, Chapel Hill, 1912–1916* (1964); Arabelle Horne Johnson family scrapbooks, 1928–54, 11 vols. (in possession of Mrs. Edgar A. Terrell, Charlotte); Herschel V. Johnson Papers (Southern Historical Collection, University of North Carolina Library, Chapel Hill); *Nat. Cyc. Am. Biog.,* vol. 54 (1973 [portrait]); *Who Was Who in America,* vol. 4 (1968).

ANNA BROOKE ALLAN

Johnson, James *(12 Feb. 1811–30 Nov. 1891),* Georgia lawyer, congressman, provisional governor, customs collector, and Superior Court judge, was born in Robeson County, N.C., the son of Peter and Nancy McNeill Johnson, whose parents had come from Scotland. Young James was among the Johnsons who moved into Henry County, Ga., newly created by the Georgia legislature's Land Lottery Act of 1821 from previously Indian-held territory between the Ocmulgee and Flint rivers. There is some reason to believe that his prepara-

tory schooling was completed under the Reverend James Gamble, the Presbyterian who opened Henry County Academy at McDonough, Ga., in 1827.

Aided by Presbyterian educational funds, Johnson attended Franklin College (now the University of Georgia) at Athens, where he and eleven classmates, including Alexander H. Stephens and William H. Crawford, Jr., received A.B. degrees in the summer of 1832. In February of his senior year, James represented the Phi Kappa Literary Society when the Georgia Guards celebrated the centennial of George Washington's birth. His toast on that occasion revealed admiration for Edward Livingston—"An able Secretary of State, a wise constructionist, distinguished alike for his political principles, and for his social virtues."

The graduate turned to teaching school and studying law. Beginning domestic life early, he married Ann Harris of Jones County, Ga., on 12 June 1834. They and their growing family became identified with rising Columbus, the seat of Muscogee County in western Georgia. In 1842 he and Wiley Williams advertised that they would "practice law in copartnership in the Chattahoochee Circuit, and in the adjoining counties of Alabama." In 1845 Johnson and a fellow member of the Columbus bar, Henry L. Benning, for whom the modern infantry center is named, helped inspire the community to nonpartisan commemoration of the death of General Andrew Jackson. In an election for clerk of the Inferior Court, Johnson lost to a Democrat, but in practice before the Superior Court around the Chattahoochee Circuit he gained increasing notice.

Following the impact of the Compromise of 1850, Johnson ran for Congress as an antitariff Unionist and defeated the states' rights candidate, none other than Benning. Though losing the next election to states' righter Alfred H. Colquitt, Congressman Johnson did sit honorably for one term (1851–53) in the U.S. House of Representatives with such conspicuous members of the Thirty-second Congress as Georgia's Alexander H. Stephens and Tennessee's Andrew Johnson.

Sometimes called a Whig, James Johnson in the later 1850s was attracted to the American, or Know-Nothing, party. The census of 1860 credited him with real and personal property worth $27,420, including thirty-one slaves in Muscogee County over age fifteen. Curiously, ten of them were listed as fugitives from the state. It is generally conceded that the Columbus attorney preserved a low profile during the Civil War, a conflict he called a tremendous mistake. His oldest son died in 1864. Union troops did not fight their way into Columbus until 16 Apr. 1865, a week after the surrender at Appomattox.

In picking an appropriate Georgian to begin reconstruction of the civil government of the exhausted state, President Andrew Johnson on 17 June appointed this conservative Columbus resident as provisional governor. A contemporary described the appointee as "a plain and unassuming gentleman of forty-five to fifty years of age, of medium size and height, who dresses throughout in black, has a regular and pleasantly inexpressive face, wears short chin and throat whiskers, and is slightly bald." Johnson's interim charge at Milledgeville, then the capital of Georgia, pleased at least the president and lasted for the six months ending 19 Dec. 1865, by which time Charles J. Jenkins had been elected governor and recognized in Washington, D.C.. James Johnson, at the president's suggestion, and Joshua Hill thereupon sought to become Georgia's first postwar U.S. senators, but on 30 Jan. 1866 the legislature preferred Alexander H. Stephens and Herschel V. Johnson.

The president tendered to James Johnson the collectorship of customs for the Port of Savannah, and the Columbus attorney endured this responsibility and routine from 1 Oct. 1866 to 31 May 1869. Meanwhile he did not hesitate to write to Washington, "I could devote myself to my profession with more pleasure and profit." When eventually he did get back to the familiar courthouses of the Chattahoochee Circuit, it was to preside as judge of the Superior Court from 1 July 1869 to 1 Oct. 1875, when he is said to have resigned. By 1880, though still engaging in light legal work, he with his wife and youngest son had withdrawn to a farm on the edge of Chattahoochee County, near Upatoi, ten miles east of Columbus. His health deteriorated, ending in paralysis, yet the octogenarian outlived his wife Ann and at least half of their ten children. Information about the children, based mainly on what N. K. Rogers reported in 1933 in his *History of Chattahoochee County, Georgia*, would include mention of these Johnsons: Richard Harris, Adelaide Victoria, George F., Lucius Q., Albert Lewis, James Edward, Walter Henry, Cornelia Ann, Charles Augustus, and Mary.

The Presbyterian Church in Columbus had been so recently destroyed by fire that the pastor had to conduct Johnson's large funeral from St. Paul's Methodist Episcopal Church. A long but garbled obituary was printed on the front page of the Columbus *Enquirer-Sun* for 1 Dec. 1891, and an editorial inside praised the late judge as a man of remarkable character who "although differing on the vital issues of the day with the vast majority of his people, always had their respect and esteem." The next day the paper mentioned that a committee of the Columbus bar had been appointed to prepare resolutions to be entered in the Muscogee Superior Court docket. It also noted that Johnson's body was carried to the city cemetery for interment.

SEE: Athens and Columbus entries, Georgia Newspaper Collection of microfilm (University of Georgia Library, Athens); *Biog. Dir. Am. Cong.* (1961); Census, congressional, and customs records (National Archives, Washington, D.C.); Andrew Johnson Papers (Library of Congress, Washington, D.C.); James Johnson folder and questionnaire (Special Collections, University of Georgia Library, Athens); Olive Hall Shadgett, "James Johnson, Provisional Governor of Georgia," *Georgia Historical Quarterly* 36 (1952).

H. B. FANT

Johnson, Jane Claudia Saunders (8 Mar. 1832–31 Dec. 1899), Confederate heroine, was born while her parents, Romulus M. Saunders and Anna Hayes Johnson, were living at Elmwood on Hillsborough Street in Raleigh. Her father, a native of Caswell County, was the state attorney general; her mother was a daughter of William Johnson, of South Carolina, a justice of the United States Supreme Court. Because she lived just two blocks from St. Mary's School (which her sister attended), she probably was educated there, but school records for those years do not exist. From 1846 to 1849 she lived abroad and spent the winters in Paris while her father was minister plenipotentiary to Spain, where he was secretly authorized by President James K. Polk to negotiate with Spain for the purchase of Cuba by the United States. Presented at the Spanish court, Jane became a friend of Eugnie de Montijo, Countess of Teba, and of her future husband, Charles Louis Napoleon Bonaparte, Napoleon III.

Saunders's appointment was terminated near the end of September 1849 and his family returned to Raleigh.

At Christ Episcopal Church on the evening of 25 June 1851 Jane Saunders married Bradley Tyler Johnson, twenty-two, of Frederick, Md., a graduate of Princeton and recently admitted to the bar. He became active in Maryland politics and in April and May 1861 recruited troops for the First Maryland Regiment for Confederate service. He and his colleagues hoped to steer the whole state in that direction and even had plans to kidnap the governor, who held Unionist sentiments. Their plans were thwarted, but they easily raised a battalion, largely in Baltimore. When their hopes for Maryland's entry into the Confederacy failed, the men went to Virginia to await formal organization and in hopes of securing equipment. They were soon joined by the militia from several Maryland counties as well as assorted local military units from the state. Bradley T. Johnson was captain of Company A, and his wife and their five-year-old son, Bradley Saunders Johnson, joined him.

Anxious to serve the South and to ensure that Maryland would be represented by its own sons in their own unit rather than have them absorbed into other units, the leaders faced a serious crisis. The men lacked uniforms, arms, and ammunition. Jane Saunders Johnson suggested that she be permitted to go to Raleigh to seek assistance. Her father's influence and her own acquaintance with leaders of the state might be effective, it was felt. Colonel Thomas J. Jackson, commanding officer, approved the plan, provided transportation, and assigned a captain and a lieutenant to escort her along a route that led to Winchester, Strasburg, Manassas Junction, and Richmond, and from Richmond to Raleigh. Leaving camp on 24 May 1861, they found the way blocked by Federal troops at Alexandria and had to change their route. Nevertheless, they reached Raleigh on the night of the twenty-seventh. The next morning, accompanied by her father, she called on Governor John W. Ellis to explain her purpose.

At the same time the Secession Convention was still in session, and delegates were inspired by word of the patriotism of so many Maryland men. It was also said that they greeted the news of Jane Saunders Johnson's mission with enthusiasm. Addressing the convention, former Congressman Kenneth Rayner said: "If great events produce great men—so in the scene before us we have proof that great events produce great women. . . . One of our own daughters, raised in the lap of luxury, blessed with the enjoyment of all the elements of elegance and ease, ha[s] quit her peaceful home, followed her husband to the camp, and leaving him in that camp, has come to the home of her childhood to seek aid for him and his comrades, not because he is her husband, but because he is fighting the battles of his country, against a tyrant."

Governor Ellis instructed one of his aides, Lieutenant Alexander W. Lawrence, an ordnance officer from Raleigh and undoubtedly known to Mrs. Johnson as they were the same age, to provide her with 500 rifles, 10,000 cartridges, 3,500 caps, and other "necessary equipments." Not lingering to enjoy a visit, Mrs. Johnson saw the equipment loaded in a boxcar and on the twenty-ninth boarded the car, took a seat atop the wooden box containing the rifles, and began the return trip. Word of her deed spread, and she was greeted by an "ovation" at every stop. The governor of Virginia gave her a quantity of camp kettles, hatchets, axes, and other equipment, and with money handed to her along the way she was able to order 41 tents in Richmond. Arriving in camp on 3 June, the equipment was promptly put to use by the troops.

Bradley Johnson saw service in numerous engagements in Virginia, was promoted to brigadier general, and late in 1864 and the early months of 1865 was commander of the Confederate prison at Salisbury, N.C., where he arranged for Federal officials to deliver some clothes and blankets to the prisoners held there. Mrs. Johnson was with her husband throughout much of the war, but the full extent of her travels is not clear from the records.

After the war Johnson practiced law in Richmond and served in the state senate (1875–79); he then practiced in Baltimore (1879–80) before moving to The Woodlands, the family home near Amelia Courthouse, Va. Mrs. Johnson died at The Woodlands and was buried in Baltimore. Veterans from among the troops that she helped to equip erected a large monument over her grave with the inscription ". . . in loving memory of a Noble Woman." In her will she directed that specific pieces of jewelry go to her daughter-in-law, Ann Rutherford Johnson; to a niece, Jeannie C. Saunders; to a cousin, Annie I. Poe; and to her sister-in-law, Mrs. Charles Schley of Milwaukee. Other gifts were left to her son, Bradley, Jr., and silver and china to her grandson, Bradley Tyler Johnson, Jr. She also left her grandson the regimental flag given to her by the men of her husband's unit during the Civil War.

SEE: *Confederate Veteran* 9 (July 1901); Bradley T. Johnson, *Maryland*, vol. 2, in Clement A. Evans, ed., *Confederate Military History* (1899); "Memoir of Jane Claudia Johnson," *Southern Historical Society Papers* 29 (1901); Raleigh *News and Observer*, 3 Jan. 1900; Raleigh *Register*, 28 June 1851; *Richmond Dispatch*, 2 Jan. 1900; Richmond *Times*, 2 Jan. 1900; J. Thomas Scharf, *History of Maryland*, vol. 3 (1879); Wake County Wills (North Carolina State Archives, Raleigh).

WILLIAM S. POWELL

Johnson, Jeff. Deems (6 June 1900–19 June 1960), attorney and North Carolina Supreme Court justice, was born in Garland, Sampson County, the son of Jeff. Deems and Mary Lily Wright Johnson. He was the third of five children. After completing his elementary and secondary education in Garland, he attended Trinity Park preparatory school in Durham in 1917–18. In the fall he enrolled in Trinity College and, having registered for military service on 12 Sept. 1918, joined the Student Army Training Corps in which he served as a private until discharged on 11 Dec. 1918, a month after the Armistice. He was graduated with the bachelor of arts degree in 1923. At Trinity he was active in many campus organizations, including several where membership was based on scholarship and leadership. Baseball was his favorite sport, and he gained wide note as a collegiate player, starring on championship teams during his four years there. During the summer he played for or managed baseball teams successively in Clinton, Mount Olive, Maxton, and Roanoke Rapids as well as in Meridian and Artesia, Miss. In his senior year he declined an offer from the Pittsburgh Pirates to play professional baseball.

After graduation Johnson taught history and government at Reynolds High School in Winston-Salem. In September 1924 he returned to Trinity College and entered the law school then headed by the inimitable dean, Samuel F. Mordecai. In 1926 he was graduated with a certificate in law (law degrees were not conferred then) from Duke University, the change in names having occurred in his first year of law study. He had the distinction of leading his class scholastically, and he passed the state bar examination in August.

Returning to Sampson County, Johnson opened an office in Clinton and made his home there for the rest of his life. He was an attorney for the town of Clinton from 1928 to 1941. He also served in the state senate for the two special sessions of 1936 and 1938 and the regular sessions of 1937 and 1941. His election was hailed as unusual because he won as a Democrat in a "rock-ribbed" Republican county. During the 1941 session, he was a member of the prestigious senate committee for the codification of the state laws. He was a member of the North Carolina Bar Association, of the county and national bar associations, and in 1939 of the executive committee of the Sixth Judicial District Bar.

On 1 July 1941 Governor J. Melville Broughton named Johnson a special judge of the Superior Court, Eastern Division, in which he rendered notable service for two terms (1941–45). Resuming the practice of law, he was a member of the North Carolina State Board of Law Examiners during the years 1948–50, and continued to be active in political and community affairs, serving as chairman of the Sampson County Democratic Executive Committee and one term as commander of the local post of the American Legion, which he joined in 1926.

Johnson was manager of the successful senatorial campaign of former Governor Broughton in 1948 and of the unsuccessful campaign of Senator Frank P. Graham in 1950 when he sought election to a full term following the interim appointment of Governor W. Kerr Scott.

After the death of Supreme Court Associate Justice A. A. F. Seawell on 14 Oct. 1950, Johnson's name was among the large number recommended to Governor Scott for the interim appointment, which the courts ruled would hold only until the general election in November. Johnson was not named to the vacancy, but instead was his party's nominee; winning the election, he took the oath on 29 Nov. 1950. Two years later he was reelected. In February 1955 Johnson was elected a trustee of Duke University, one of the few extra responsibilities he accepted while a member of the North Carolina Supreme Court. At its 1956 commencement The University of North Carolina conferred on him the honorary degree of doctor of laws.

At one time Johnson was chairman of the Methodist church's Board of Stewards in Clinton, and he served on the board of trustees of the church. He was also a longtime member of the local lodge of Ancient, Free, and Accepted Masons. On 17 Aug. 1935 he married Virginia Frances Faison, the daughter of Isham Francis and Isabel Pigford Faison of Faison. They had three children: Frances Faison, Mary Lily (Mrs. James Garland Nuckolls), and Jeff. Deems III.

Johnson died in Duke Hospital, Durham, and was buried in the Clinton city cemetery. A portrait, painted by Irene Price of Blowing Rock, is in the possession of the family.

SEE: Biographical data compiled by Jeff. Deems Johnson III; *North Carolina Biography*, vol. 3 (1956); *North Carolina Manual* (1937); Raleigh *News and Observer*, 19 Nov. 1950, 20 June 1960.

C. SYLVESTER GREEN

Johnson, John Lewis (13 Feb. 1818–3 Nov. 1900), physician, druggist, and dental surgeon, was a founder and leader of the Unionist secret society known as the Heroes of America, or "Red Strings," during the Civil War and Reconstruction. Born in Philadelphia, he was the son of Dr. Henry M. Johnson of Lynchburg, Va., and Hannah Lewis Johnson of New York.

Some time in his youth Johnson moved to Virginia,

and from there to Lexington, N.C., in 1841. In 1843 he began to study medicine with Dr. William Dillon Lindsay of Lexington, and in 1845 he returned to Philadelphia to attend Wilson's Medical School. After practicing medicine and selling patent medicines in Virginia, he moved back to Lexington in 1855 and went into the drug business with Dr. Samuel Pendleton. Johnson may have experienced hard times, for the 1860 census describes him as a brickmaker. In 1860 he moved to Forsyth County and established a practice in Winston, living in the village that is now called Union Cross.

The Civil War interrupted Johnson's fledgling practice in Winston, and in 1862 he served with the Confederate Army as an assistant surgeon under his old teacher, Dr. Lindsay. The circumstances of his enlistment are obscure, but he may have been conscripted or enlisted to avoid conscription, as his strong Unionist sympathies suggest that he would not have joined voluntarily. He served with the Army of Northern Virginia until after Fredericksburg, when he and Dr. Lindsay were captured. Johnson may have contrived to be captured because he was quickly exchanged.

Early in 1863 he began his career as a leading organizer of the Heroes of America, a secret society dedicated to the Union cause that arose in 1861 in the "Quaker" counties of Randolph, Davidson, Forsyth, and Guilford, close to Johnson's home. Johnson may have been a member of the organization from its creation; certainly from 1863 to 1869 he was one of its most active agents. In 1863, under cover of a job as a druggist in the Confederate hospital in Raleigh, Johnson took the lead in spreading the Heroes of America to many counties in central and eastern North Carolina, and also probably crossed into the Union lines at New Bern and Beaufort to establish contact between the society and the Union's occupying forces. He strongly supported the peace movement led by William W. Holden, editor of the Raleigh *North Carolina Standard*, and participated in a peace meeting in southern Wake County on 23 July 1863.

When the Heroes of America was exposed by the Confederates in June and July 1864, Johnson was forced to flee North Carolina. On his way north he decamped a company of Confederate soldiers to the Union lines, an event that was remembered locally as "Johnson's Raid." On arriving in Washington, D.C., he met with Benjamin Sherwood Hedrick, and initiated Hedrick and Daniel Reaves Goodloe—and probably President Lincoln, General Ulysses S. Grant, and Commissioner of Pensions Joseph Barrett as well—into the Heroes of America. Most likely Johnson and Hedrick set up a national Grand Council of the Heroes of America to cover the order's activities throughout the border states. Johnson then went to Cincinnati, where he attended a course of medical lectures, and in January 1865 he may have returned to North Carolina via Kentucky.

Johnson's family suffered greatly for his Unionist activities. He and his wife, Eliza Gafford, whom he had married at Danville, Va., on 3 Sept. 1839, had thirteen children between 1840 and 1867. Two of his sons died in a Confederate prison in Richmond, and a third was captured in West Virginia while trying to reach the North but survived imprisonment. One of his sons who died was scarcely a year old, which strongly suggests that his wife was arrested and incarcerated when Johnson's activities were exposed in 1864.

After the war, Johnson learned dentistry in Philadelphia and established a practice in Forsyth County. He became a Republican and remained active on the Grand Council of the Heroes of America (he was elected Grand Lecturer in 1867) until the order broke up about

1870 under pressure from the Ku Klux Klan. After its collapse Johnson presumably withdrew from politics, for little more is known of him until his death in Winston-Salem. He was buried at the Moravian Church in Union Cross, and his tombstone bears the Masonic emblem.

SEE: William T. Auman and David D. Scarboro, "The Heroes of America in Civil War North Carolina," *North Carolina Historical Review* 58 (October 1981); Documents in possession of Ben Johnson, Winston-Salem; J. G. de R. Hamilton, *Reconstruction in North Carolina* (1906); Letters of J. L. Johnson and letter of Jesse Wheeler to B. S. Hedrick, 27 Nov. 1864 (Benjamin Sherwood Hedrick Papers, Manuscript Collection, Duke University Library, Durham); Georgia Lee Tatum, *Disloyalty in the Confederacy* (1934); United States Congress, Senate, Testimony of Daniel Reaves Goodloe in *Select Committee to Investigate Alleged Denial of Elective Franchise and Other Outrages in Southern States, Testimony on North Carolina, with Minority Report*, S. Rept. 1, 42nd Cong., 1st sess., 1871.

WILLIAM T. AUMAN
DAVID D. SCARBORO

Johnson, Kate Ancrum Burr (14 Feb. 1881–22 Aug. 1968), public welfare administrator and civic leader, was born in Morganton. Her father was Frederick Hill Burr, whose American ancestry traced back to 1630 in Massachusetts and whose North Carolina ancestry went back to the early nineteenth century and to Wilmington. Her paternal grandfather, Colonel James Green Burr, served on the staff of Governor Zebulon B. Vance. Her mother was Lillian Walton whose Walton ancestors settled in Virginia before moving to Burke County, N.C., where descendants built Creekside and Brookwood, two beautiful antebellum homes.

Kate Ancrum Burr received preparatory education in Morganton and at Queens College, Charlotte. On 14 Apr. 1903 she married Clarence A. Johnson (d. 9 Sept. 1922), and they became the parents of two sons, Clarence A. and Frederick Burr. Although devoting most of her time to her family, she undertook civic activities in Raleigh, where the couple had settled following their marriage. By 1915 her public service had gained her the vice-presidency of the North Carolina Conference for Social Service (1915–16), but that proved to be only the early phase of a lifelong commitment to human rights and public welfare.

Although most of her career from 1915 fell in the area of public welfare, she early demonstrated her concern for women's rights and connected this dedication with her interest in penal reform, child welfare, and social justice. From involvement in the Episcopal church and its auxiliary activities she moved into the women's club movement, serving in various official capacities including president of the Raleigh Woman's Club, of which she was a charter member, and promoting woman suffrage and child welfare in the state. As president of the North Carolina Federation of Women's Clubs (1917–19), Mrs. Johnson worked effectively to interest women in social reform. She won respect for her capable leadership and was further recognized by her outstanding service (1917–18) to the state Liberty Bond commission.

In 1919, after a brief association with the North Carolina Department of Insurance, Kate Burr Johnson joined the staff of the Board of Charities and Public Welfare. Established by the state constitution of 1868, the board supervised and inspected all charitable and penal institutions. In 1917 the board's activities were expanded, a system of county superintendents was added, and the phrase "and Public Welfare" was appended to its title. Under this newly expanded board Mrs. Johnson served as director of child welfare from 1919 to 1921. During this time she received additional training through summer courses at the New York School of Social Work and The University of North Carolina. When the commissioner resigned in 1921, the board, various women's clubs, and even the governor endorsed her appointment as replacement. In July of that year she became the first woman in the nation to serve as a state commissioner of public welfare and the first North Carolina woman to head a major state department.

Commissioner Johnson served the state admirably from 1921 to 1930. Her tenure was marked by expansion of the board's work and staff, its reorganization into specialized bureaus, establishment of new institutions and more effective supervision of existing institutions, increased public and financial support of the board's activities, and changes in existing laws. Although a Democrat, the commissioner was first a devoted humanitarian and public servant; and, despite her limited training, she was in the forefront of professionalism in a neglected but rapidly emerging field in North Carolina. Under her supervision, studies were made of the problems and deficiencies in the penal system. Effective public relations work aided in gaining support for the board's programs, to which various women's organizations gave valuable assistance.

Kate Burr Johnson advocated separating inmates in all North Carolina institutions for criminals, delinquents, mental patients, and public wards into treatable groups by age, sex, and category. She promoted better understanding of the penal system, children's and women's conditions in industry, mental health and hygiene, and public welfare programs. Among the achievements either promoted by the board or introduced in North Carolina during her administration were a Mother's Aid program, institutions for juvenile offenders, a farm colony for women offenders, appropriations—though meager—for the institution for delinquent black girls established by the North Carolina Federation of Colored Women's Clubs, minor amendments to the child labor law, growth and development of public welfare programs, and improvements in conditions in prisons and on work gangs.

The Board of Charities and Public Welfare under Kate Burr Johnson persistently made proposals and budget requests to every session of the General Assembly. Frequently aiding her efforts was the Legislative Council of North Carolina Women, a clearinghouse for the legislative activities of seven major women's organizations in the state. A crusader, Mrs. Johnson utilized the Legislative Council, with which she had been affiliated almost from the moment of its inception in 1921, and other kindred groups to marshal pressure on governors and legislators. Although the commissioner herself remained aloof from direct political involvement, the Legislative Council and other organizations with which she was associated were politically active in promoting social justice.

In 1930 she accepted the post of superintendent of the New Jersey State Home for Girls in Trenton. There she continued her work in experimenting with new ideas and approaches. Among her achievements was the creation of a program of work classification for female offenders in New Jersey. She worked with authorities to develop local programs and agencies to deal with a variety of social problems, especially those related to child health and protection. In 1948, at age sixty-seven, she retired and returned to her home in Raleigh, where her career had begun decades before.

Over the years Kate Burr Johnson won national attention. She was either a member of or appointed to the American Association of Social Workers, National Probation Association, National Conference of Juvenile Agencies, New Jersey Conference of Social Work, American Prison Association, Executive Committee of the Child Welfare League of America, Business and Professional Women's Club, and American Academy of Social Sciences. From 1948 to 1953 she served on the North Carolina Prison Advisory Commission. In 1951 she was awarded the doctor of humane letters by the Woman's College of the University of North Carolina; and in 1954, the North Carolina Distinguished Service Award for Women by the Epsilon Beta chapter of Chi Omega fraternity.

Mrs. Johnson died at the Mayview Convalescent Home in Raleigh and was interred at the city's Oakwood Cemetery.

SEE: Kate Ancrum Burr Johnson Papers (Manuscript Collection, East Carolina University Library, Greenville); Raleigh *News and Observer*, 23 Aug. 1968; Gary Trawick and Paul Wyche, *100 Years, 100 Men, 1871–1971* (1971); Charles L. Van Noppen Papers (Manuscript Collection, Duke University Library, Durham [portrait]); *Who's Who in America*, vols. 13–25 (1924–49).

MOLLIE C. DAVIS

Johnson, Livingston (7 Nov. 1857–8 Feb. 1931), Baptist clergyman, administrator, and editor, was born in Richmond (now Scotland) County, the son of Duncan and Catharine Livingston Johnson. As a boy he worked on his father's farm in the summer and attended Spring Hill Academy in the winter. A valuable supplement to this schooling was his participation in debates and declamations of the Saturday afternoon programs of the Richmond Temperance and Literary Society, which his mother had helped to organize. After a year's study at Wake Forest College (1877–78), the young man returned to farming. Always an active church worker, he yielded to a strong conviction that he should preach and so attended the Southern Baptist Theological Seminary in Louisville for a year (1888–89). On 18 Apr. 1889 he was ordained to the Christian ministry in the Spring Hill Baptist Church, which his maternal great-grandfather, a native of Argyllshire, Scotland, had organized in 1813.

Soon after his ordination Johnson began a six-year ministry as pastor of five churches—Rockingham, Lilesville, Pleasant Grove, Cartledge's Creek, and Roberdel. Later he was pastor of the Lumberton Baptist Church (January–October 1895), First Baptist Church of Greensboro (1895–1900), and First Baptist Church of Rocky Mount (1916–17). This experience in country, town, and city churches—in all of which, Senator Josiah William Bailey said, he was "singularly beloved"—prepared him well for the two positions of leadership he held in the denomination. From 1901 to 1916 he was corresponding secretary (now called executive secretary) of the North Carolina Baptist State Convention, and from 1917 to 1930 he edited the *Biblical Recorder*, the Baptist state paper. While he was secretary, the denomination made marked progress in all phases of its work. Numerically North Carolina Baptists increased 61 percent; even more significant was the 321 percent increase in contributions to missions.

During his editorship of the *Biblical Recorder*, two highly controversial issues seriously threatened the unity of North Carolina Baptists. The first involved the widespread objection of religious fundamentalists to the teaching of evolution, which led in 1925 to the

Scopes trial in Dayton, Tenn. Several years earlier in North Carolina, such teaching had prompted harsh criticism of William Louis Poteat, a professor of biology who was then president of Wake Forest College. Extreme fundamentalists branded Poteat as unfit for the presidency of the college, accusing him of undermining the Christian faith of the students. Johnson, though his views differed from Poteat's, staunchly defended him as a devout Christian who, no matter what his convictions concerning the process by which God created man, held fast to the fundamental beliefs of the Christian faith.

The second controversy occurred during the 1928 presidential campaign of Republican Herbert Hoover versus Democrat Alfred E. Smith, one of the bitterest in the country's political history. A firm believer in the separation of church and state, Johnson held that a denominational paper should take no part in politics *unless* a moral issue was involved. Because of Smith's emphatic advocacy of repealing the Volstead Act, which made illegal the sale of alcoholic beverages in the United States, Johnson believed that the contest presented a clear-cut moral issue. Therefore, though he was a lifelong Democrat, as were most North Carolina Baptists, in his editorials he vigorously opposed Smith. Wishing to be fair, he opened the *Recorder* to letters from supporters of both candidates and repeatedly asserted that he was speaking only for himself, not for North Carolina Baptists.

Though the *Recorder* was, of course, primarily concerned with Baptist affairs, the paper during his editorship reflected the breadth of his interests and his warm sympathy. He made pleas for equality for blacks before the law and in employment, for increased support of the public schools, for federal aid to the unemployed during the depression, for prison reform, and for legislation that would reduce fraud and dishonesty in elections.

As secretary of the Baptist State Convention for fifteen years and as editor of the *Biblical Recorder* for thirteen, Johnson was called by Tom Bost of the *Greensboro Daily News* "the most influential and best beloved Baptist in North Carolina." In the centennial issue of the *Recorder*, 2 Jan. 1935, J. W. Bailey said he was "the foremost Baptist of his generation." According to Bailey, "Such was the kindliness of his heart and the brightness of his faith that few paused to consider his remarkable intellectual capacity or his indefatigable industry."

Johnson was for many years a trustee of Wake Forest College, of Meredith College, and of the Southern Baptist Theological Seminary, serving on the executive committee of the first two institutions. He was also a member of the executive committee of the Southern Baptist Convention and of the Baptist World Alliance. He was the author of two books: *History of North Carolina Baptists* (1908) and *Christian Statesmanship* (1913). Wake Forest awarded him the D.D. degree, and the administration building of Meredith College was named for him.

In 1882 Johnson married Mary Frances Memory of Whiteville, and they became the parents of five children: Wingate Memory, Foy Elisabeth, Duncan Munroe, Frances Livingston, and Mary Lynch. His funeral was held in the First Baptist Church of Raleigh, followed by burial in Oakwood Cemetery. There is a portrait of him in the classroom of the Livingston Johnson Bible Class of the First Baptist Church of Raleigh.

SEE: *Annual of North Carolina Baptist State Convention* (1900–1931); *Biblical Recorder* (1900–1931); Correspondence of Livingston Johnson (Baptist Collection, Wake Forest University, Winston-Salem); *Encyclopedia of Southern Baptists* (1958); Robert Melvin, "Livingston Johnson: A Study of a Baptist Editor's Role in Controversial Issues" (Thesis, Southeastern Seminary, 1952); *Who Was Who in America, 1897–1942*.

MARY LYNCH JOHNSON

Johnson, Norman Huff (24 Sept. 1880–5 June 1943), lawyer and economist, was born in Warrenton, the son of Edward Alston and Geneva Huff Johnson. He attended public schools and the Warrenton Academy before reading law under Judge Charles A. Cook and Benjamin G. Green. Johnson was a student at Wake Forest College from 1899 to 1900, when he received his license to practice law.

In 1901 Johnson was elected city attorney of Burlington, and in the course of his duties led the organization of the first retail merchants association to exchange credit information in the state in 1902. His similar efforts in several other cities resulted in 1903 in the formation of the North Carolina Retail Merchants Association, of which Johnson was elected attorney general. In 1904 he moved to Raleigh and established the *Merchants Journal*, a mercantile trade paper that was later merged with several others to form the *Merchants Journal and Commerce*, which had a wide circulation in the South. Johnson was a lobbyist for trade interests in the state legislature, successfully working for the repeal of unjust mercantile taxes and railroad freight regulations and for the passage of the bulk sales laws and the Pure Food law. In 1908 he was elected general counsel for the National Retail Merchants Association but declined the position to devote himself to his trade paper.

In 1913 Johnson moved the paper to Richmond, Va., and the next year he was elected general counsel and secretary of the Southern Wholesale Dry Goods Association, serving until its dissolution in 1928. Considered an expert on southern merchandising, he was under contract to the Thomas Brady Speakers' Bureau of New York City as the highest paid speaker on topics such as business, salesmanship, and advertising in the United States. During World War I he was also a noted speaker on government war projects.

In April 1941, Johnson was convicted of voluntary manslaughter in the gun slaying of his black hired hand and of possessing an illegal distillery. As the shooting was evidently in self-defense, he received only a two-year sentence which was suspended after the judge received a petition calling for suspension signed by sixty-nine of Johnson's neighbors.

Johnson married Alice Bouchillon Baird of Charlotte in 1906 and had two children: Norman Huff, Jr., and Martha Bouchillon. He was an Episcopalian and a Mason. He died in Richmond where he was buried in Oakdale Cemetery.

SEE: Correspondence of John T. Church, November 1977, and Mrs. John Kerr, Jr., September 1977 (in the author's possession); Richmond *Times-Dispatch*, 9 Apr., 4 Sept. 1941, 5 June 1943; Charles L. Van Noppen Papers (Manuscript Department, Duke University Library, Durham).

J. MARSHALL BULLOCK

Johnson, Robert Grady (5 May 1895–22 June 1951), lawyer, legislator, and politician, was born in Burgaw, the son of Joab F. and Myrtie Grady Johnson. He was graduated from Burgaw High School in 1913 and studied law at The University of North Carolina in 1914–15. From 1919 to 1925 he was assistant cashier of the Bank of Pender. In 1926, he studied law at Wake Forest College and was admitted to the bar.

Elected state senator from the Ninth District in 1929, Johnson represented Pender County in the General Assembly of 1931, 1933, and 1935, and was elected speaker of the state house of representatives in 1935. He served as secretary of the North Carolina Petroleum Industries Committee from January 1936 to September 1937. In May 1937 he was appointed a member of the state Highway and Public Works Commission, which elected him director of the state prisons. Serving in the latter post until 1941, Johnson introduced a system placing more emphasis on pleasant physical surroundings for prisoners, recreation, and prison industries. In 1941 he was chairman of the Alcoholic Beverage Control Board, and from 1942 to 1950 he was a member of the Utilities Commission. At various times Johnson also served on the board of trustees of The University of North Carolina, as register of deeds of Pender County, and as a member of the Pender County and state Democratic executive committees.

During World War I Johnson enlisted in the army as a private and served as a medical records clerk. He was a member of the American Legion and an active Mason. Johnson married Mrs. Louise White Freeman of Elizabeth City and they were the parents of three children: Louise Grady, Robert White, and Marion Lee. He was buried in Burgaw.

SEE: Mattie Bloodworth, *History of Pender County* (1947); *North Carolina Biography*, vols. 3, 4 (1941, 1956); *North Carolina Manual* (1949).

MARION L. JOHNSON

Johnson, Thor Martin (10 June 1913–16 Jan. 1975), musician and educator, was born in Wisconsin Rapids, Wis., the son of the Reverend Herbert B. and Anna Reusswig Johnson. In 1925 his father entered pastoral service in the Southern Province of the Moravian church, and the family moved to North Carolina, living for periods in Winston-Salem, Kernersville, and Mount Airy. Here, in the heartland of Moravian music, young Thor began his musical training. At age thirteen he organized and conducted a seventeen-member orchestra in Winston-Salem, demonstrating early the dedication and initiative of the distinguished musician and originator he became.

Johnson continued his musical training with formal studies at The University of North Carolina and conducted the North Carolina Little Symphony from 1932 until he received the A.B. degree in 1934. The next year he earned the Mus.M degree at the University of Michigan and conducted the university's Little Symphony until 1936. A scholarship awarded by the Beebe Foundation in 1935 enabled him to spend the following year in Europe. At the Salzburg Mozarteum he studied conducting under Felix Weingartner, Bruno Walter, and Nicolai Malko, and at the Conservatory of Leipzig under Hermann Abendroth. He later studied under Serge Koussevitsky in the United States.

When he returned from Europe, Johnson was appointed assistant professor of music at the University of Michigan, a post he held from 1937 to 1942. In 1938 he again became conductor of the University of Michigan Little Symphony, and in 1940 he began conducting the Grand Rapids Symphony Orchestra. During this period he also founded the Asheville (North Carolina) Mozart Festival, serving as its conductor from 1937 to 1941.

In 1942 Johnson left his posts in Michigan to enlist in the U.S. Army. While in the Army Air Corps he founded the U.S. Air Force Symphony Orchestra, the original soldier symphony in the U.S. armed forces.

After the war he spent a year as orchestral conductor at the Juilliard School of Music before becoming the permanent conductor of the Cincinnati Symphony Orchestra. The first American-born and American-trained conductor of a major American orchestra, Johnson held this position from 1947 to 1958. By 1951 he had earned a doctorate in music from The University of North Carolina; in the same year, he won the National Man of Music Award.

Devoted to the concept of the music festival and to the Moravian church, of which he was a member, Johnson began a revival of early American Moravian music in the 1950s. He was the musical director of eleven Moravian music festivals and was instrumental in establishing the Moravian Music Foundation (Winston-Salem), which he served as trustee for nineteen years.

In 1958 Johnson joined the music faculty at Northwestern University, teaching there with the rank of professor until 1964. From 1964 to 1967 he was director of the Interlochen Arts Academy, where he did much to develop the talents of youthful musicians, encouraging them to meet his demands for excellence in music while inspiring them with his personal warmth. In 1967 he became the music director of the Nashville Symphony Orchestra, a post he held until his death.

A musician of considerable reputation, Johnson appeared as guest conductor with most major American orchestras, including the Boston Symphony, Chicago Symphony, Philadelphia Orchestra, and New York Philharmonic. He received honorary doctorates from a number of colleges and universities and was the recipient of several prizes, including the Alice B. Ditson Prize in 1949 and the Sachs Award in 1950.

Johnson never married. He died in Nashville, Tenn., and was buried in God's Acre, the cemetery of the Home Moravian Church, Winston-Salem.

SEE: Miscellaneous Records (The Moravian Archive and the Moravian Music Foundation, Winston-Salem); *Who's Who in America* (1974–75).

CELIA C. SPARGER

Johnson, William Ransom (1782–18 Feb. 1849), legislator and horseman, was born in Warren County, the son of Marmaduke and Elizabeth Ransom Johnson. He probably attended Warrenton Academy, of which his father was a trustee. Johnson represented Warren County in the General Assembly from 1807 to 1814. Between 1803 and 1813 he raced the noted horses, Sir Archie and Pacolet, winning $30,000. Soon afterwards he moved to Virginia and began raising racehorses at Oakland. He was a member of the Virginia House of Delegates for Petersburg from 1818 to 1820 and from Chesterfield County in 1821–22. He was reelected to the house but resigned to serve in the senate from 1823 to 1826. He again held a seat in the house during the periods 1826–30 and 1833–37. By common consent he was the manager for the South in the South-North Races held in Washington, D.C., in 1823. From then until 1834 he managed nearly thirty other races of which the South won seventeen. For a generation Johnson was regarded as the leading American turfman, and he came to be known as "Napoleon of the Turf."

Johnson's wife, whom he married in 1803, was Mary Evans. He died in Mobile, Ala., and was buried at his Oakland plantation.

SEE: John L. Cheney, Jr., ed., *North Carolina Government, 1585–1979* (1981); Charles L. Coon, *North Carolina Schools and Academies, 1790–1840* (1915); Henry T. Shanks, ed., *The Papers of Willie Person Mangum*, vol. 3 (1953); *Who Was Who in America*, Historical Volume (1967).

WILLIAM S. POWELL

Johnson, Wingate Memory *(12 Aug. 1885–11 Sept. 1963)*, physician, writer, medical educator, and editor, was born in Riverton, a Scotland County community that was settled by his Scottish forebears. His father, Livingston Johnson, was a Baptist minister who served for fifteen years as corresponding secretary of the Baptist State Convention and later as editor of its weekly paper, the *Biblical Recorder*; his mother was Mary Frances Memory Johnson of Whiteville. Young Johnson received his early education in the public schools of North Carolina. From Wake Forest College he received the A.B. (1905), M.A. (1906), and Sc.D. (1940) degrees; from the Jefferson Medical School in Philadelphia he was awarded the M.D. (1908) and LL.D. (1952) degrees.

After a one-year internship at the Philadelphia Polyclinic, Johnson entered the general practice of medicine in Winston-Salem in 1910. Gradually confining his practice to internal medicine, he was one of the original diplomates of the American Board of Internal Medicine as well as a fellow of the American College of Physicians. In 1940, when Wake Forest's two-year medical school was moved to Winston-Salem and became the four-year Bowman Gray School of Medicine, Johnson was appointed professor of clinical medicine and was asked to organize the school's Private Diagnostic Clinic. Although he became an emeritus professor in 1958, he remained as chief of the clinic until his death. In 1953–54, he served as acting dean of the school for one year while Dean Carpenter was on leave of absence. His portrait hangs in the medical school.

Johnson's interest in writing became apparent during his college days, when he was editor of the *Wake Forest Student*. In 1928 *Harper's Magazine* published his first article, "A Family Doctor Speaks His Mind." He also wrote for the *Atlantic Monthly*, *American Mercury*, *Forum*, *Hygeia*, and numerous medical journals. His most widely read medical article was "Clinical Research in Private Practice," published in the *Journal of the American Medical Association* in 1938.

In 1936 Macmillan published the first of Johnson's books, *The True Physician: The Modern Doctor of the Old School*, giving advice to young physicians. His second work, *The Years after Fifty*, written for laymen, was published by Whittlesey House in 1947. In 1960 Paul B. Hoeber published *The Older Patient*, a book on geriatrics written by and for physicians and edited by Johnson.

Johnson's books and articles reflected his wide-ranging interests in education, family practice, medical economics, clinical research, pancreatitis, geriatrics, and mental hygiene. He was a member of the State Hospitals Board of Controls during the Broughton administration, and of the Governor's Coordinating Committee on Aging under Hodges and Sanford.

Registered as an "independent Democrat," Johnson was a Baptist and for twenty years (1920–40) served as a trustee of Wake Forest College. He was a member of Phi Beta Kappa and Alpha Omega Alpha honorary fraternities, of the American Association for the Advancement of Science, and of numerous medical organizations. He served one-year terms as president of the American Geriatric Society, his county and state medical societies, and the local Civitan and Torch clubs. At one time he was a vice-president of Civitan International, and in 1947–48 he served a one-year term as trustee of the American Medical Association. As president of the Medical Society of the State of North Carolina in 1938–39, he recommended the establishment of a state medical journal. When this recommendation was adopted in 1939, he was named the first editor of the *North Carolina Medical Journal*—a position he held until his death.

In 1914 Johnson married Undine Futrell of Scotland Neck. Their first child, Wingate, Jr., died at age two. Their two surviving children were Catherine (Mrs. E. W. Jackson), a medical editor of Durham, and Livingston, a cardiologist practicing in Shelby. After Johnson's death at the Baptist Hospital in Winston-Salem, his body was cremated and his ashes were sprinkled on the Lumber River near his birthplace in Scotland County.

SEE: *North Carolina Medical Journal* 2 (March 1941), 24 (December 1963); William S. Powell, ed., *North Carolina Lives* (1962); John S. Raymond, *Among Southern Baptists* (1936); *Who Was Who in America*, vol. 4 (1968).

CATHERINE JOHNSON JACKSON

Johnston, Elizabeth Johnston Evans *(3 May 1851–30 Dec. 1934)*, philanthropist, was born at Blandwood in Greensboro, the daughter of Peter G. Evans and his wife Eliza, who was the daughter of Governor John M. Morehead. Known throughout life as "Johnsie," the name given her by her father, she spent her early years at Beechwood, the Evans plantation near New Bern. During the Civil War Peter Evans, as colonel of the Sixty-third North Carolina Regiment (Cavalry), was gravely wounded in a charge at the Battle of Upperville, Va., on 21 June 1863 and died shortly afterwards in a prison hospital in Washington, D.C. When Colonel Evans had gone off to war, his young daughter had given him a silver cup bearing her name. Fifty years later, this relic was returned to her by E. P. Worcester, an old soldier in Los Angeles, who, as a private in the First Maine Cavalry, had found the cup on the battlefield.

After the death of her father, Elizabeth lived at her grandfather's home in Greensboro and was educated by tutors. On 1 Nov. 1871, at age twenty, she married General Robert Daniel Johnston, a Confederate hero and fourteen years her senior. The couple settled in Charlotte, where he practiced law and she was instrumental in the establishment of a hospital for blacks. In 1887, R. D. Johnston accepted the presidency of the Birmingham National Bank and the family moved to Alabama.

Soon after settling into their new home, the Johnstons engaged a tutor to prepare their oldest son, Gordon, for Princeton. The tutor conducted a Sunday school at the Pratt mines, operated by convicts, and began to take his charge with him. They were eventually joined by Mrs. Johnston, who became interested in the religious instruction of the prisoners. The plight of the younger convicts engaged her particular attention, and she conceived the idea of establishing a boys' training school for youthful offenders. Through her untiring efforts, a bill was passed by the Alabama legislature and the Alabama Boy's Industrial School was opened on 21 June 1900. It was said to be the first altruistic state institution of its kind and was unusual in that the board of managers was to be composed entirely of women. Under Mrs. Johnson's interest and guidance the school prospered, and for the rest of her life she was chairman of the board of managers. Her success with the training school was noted in her native state of North Carolina, which invited her to address the legislature on how it might establish a similar institution. In 1922 she was awarded a silver loving cup by the *Birmingham News* for her philanthropy.

With her appointment in 1901 as vice-regent of Alabama for the Mount Vernon Ladies' Association, Mrs. Johnston devoted the same energy to the preservation of the home of George Washington as she did to her school. She is said to have had an unusual ability to find Washington relics and was responsible for fourteen of these being placed in the mansion, including Washington's camp bed and the sash worn by General Edward Braddock in his last battle and given to his aide, Washington.

In her later years Mrs. Johnston lived in a house the Highland Book Club had built for her on the grounds of the Alabama Boy's Industrial School. She named it "Little Mount Vernon" and filled it with mementos of her career as vice-regent. After her death, the building became the school's library. Just before her eightieth birthday, the Alabama legislature passed a resolution to express the state's gratitude for her work in establishing the training school. Her success in public endeavors was said to have been due to her speaking ability and her great personal charm.

R. D. Johnston died many years before his wife. They had three sons—Gordon, Robert, and Evans—and four daughters—Elizabeth Evans (m. Maxwell Berry of Atlanta), Nancy Forney (m. Harvey Skey of Canada), Eugenia (m. William Eager of Birmingham), and Letitia (m. L. G. Firth of Pittsburgh). Mrs. Johnston died shortly after the death of her oldest son.

SEE: Mary Johnston Avery, *She Heard with Her Heart: The Life of Mrs. R. D. Johnston* (1944 [portrait]); "Evans Family," *Historical Southern Families*, vol. 3 (1955).

CLAIBORNE T. SMITH, JR.

Johnston, Gabriel (*ca.* 1698–17 July 1752), second royal governor of North Carolina, was born in Southdean, Borders Region, Scotland, where he was baptized on 28 Feb. 1698, the son of the Reverend Samuel and Isobel Hall Johnston. His father, minister of the Church of Scotland parishes of Southdean and, later, Dundee, was probably a descendant of the Elsieshields branch of the Johnstons of Annandale.

Young Johnston studied Greek and philosophy at the University of Edinburgh for four years from 1711, and in 1717 entered the University of St. Andrews as a divinity student, holding the Patrick Yeaman Bursary. He was graduated with a master of arts degree *per supplicationem* in 1720. The following year he studied medicine at the University of Leiden, but his interest seems not to have been serious, for within a month of his arrival in Holland he applied for a patent to teach Hebrew at St. Andrews. He received the royal appointment and in November 1722 was again at his alma mater, occupying the chair of Hebrew. In 1724 he was made Burgess and Guild Brother (gratis) of the city of Glasgow. Three years later he deserted his university post and went to London where, according to his own account, he lived in the household of Spencer Compton, Lord Wilmington, for seven years. During this time Johnston wrote political articles for the *Craftsman*, an anti-Walpole publication to which Bolingbroke, Pulteney, and Harley also contributed.

On 27 Mar. 1733 Johnston was appointed governor of North Carolina, taking his oaths of office in London that August. But he did not arrive in Brunswick Town,

at the mouth of the Cape Fear River, until 27 Oct. 1734 to assume his duties on 2 November.

Following the unpopular George Burrington, Johnston was hailed with almost unanimous delight by the Carolinians. Soon, however, the inevitable frictions arose between a chief executive sworn to promote the interests of the Crown and an assertively independent citizenry, equally determined to maintain the rights granted them by the Lords Proprietors. Johnston's most troublesome problems during his eighteen-year tenure, the longest of any North Carolina governor, were the conflict between the northern and southern sections of the colony, the misuse of blank patents, and the quit-rent controversy. Because his own salary and those of the other Crown officials were paid from the quitrents, this, of the three, most nearly touched his own well-being. At his death, his salary of £1,000 per year was found to be in arrears to the amount of £13,462 19d. The last of the debt was not collected by his heirs until forty-six years later.

Johnston antagonized the colonists by his stand on the collection of the quitrents, now double the amount paid by the settlers under the Lords Proprietors, and now to be collected in specie in designated places, instead of in produce at the farms, as formerly. His arbitrary removal of the government offices to New Town (later Wilmington) caused the eventual decay of Brunswick, making implacable enemies of the powerful Moore family and their adherents on the Cape Fear. Members of "The Family," as they were called, were also among the landholders who were enabled by the blank patents to appropriate Crown-held lands. Johnston's spirited opposition to this misuse of the patents further antagonized this element.

Despite almost constant opposition in North Carolina and lack of support from London, Johnston accomplished many reforms. During his term of office, the first printer was brought to the colony and the first newspaper was published. The laws of the colony were collected and printed. Forts were built along the coast for protection from Spanish depredation. A rent roll was drawn up. New counties were formed as the colony expanded towards the west. The governor introduced new agricultural methods at his plantation, Brompton, in Bladen County. Above all, he encouraged immigration, notably of his fellow Scots, so that the population of the province increased threefold during his tenure. His earnest attempts to establish free schools and to encourage the work of the Church of England in the colony met with apparent failure during his life but laid the groundwork for future success.

Arriving in North Carolina penniless and deeply in debt to his patrons, he soon made a most propitious marriage (ca. 1740) to Penelope Golland, stepdaughter of Governor Charles Eden, one of the wealthiest women in the province; she had been successively the widow of William Maule, John Lovick, and George Phenney. Their only child, Penelope, married John Dawson, of Williamsburg, son of the president of William and Mary College. Johnston's will mentions his son, Henry, and daughter, Carolina; these are thought to be two natural children; a third, "Polly," predeceased her father. After his first wife's death in 1741, he married Mrs. Frances Button. Governor Johnston died and was buried at Eden House, his plantation in Bertie County near Edenton.

He was bitterly criticized by his political opponents for what he himself called "management." They had stronger words for it: sharp practices, trickery, and fraud. In contrast to his predecessor's violent and profane behavior, Johnston's demeanor seems to have been consistently marked by self-control. He stated that he had known confusion and disorder, but had not made a single personal enemy in North Carolina.

Something of his personal standards may be learned from his instructions in his will concerning his "dear little girl," Penelope: that she should be brought up "in the Fear of God and under a deep Sense of being always in His Presence, confining her desires to things Plain, Neat and Elegant . . . not aspiring after the Gayety, Splendour and Extravagance and Especially to take care to keep within the Bounds of her Income and by no Means to Run in Debt."

No known portrait of him remains, although a miniature existed in 1893. Johnston County and Fort Johnston, at the mouth of the Cape Fear River, perpetuate his name in North Carolina.

SEE: C. M. Andrews and E. Andrews, eds., *Journal of a Lady of Quality* (1921); Bernard Burke, *The Dormant, Abeyant, Forfeited and Extinct Peerages* (1883); Walter Clark, ed., *State Records of North Carolina*, vol. 23 (1904); *DAB*, vol. 5 (1932); Granville Papers (Earl of Bath Collection, Longleat, Wiltshire, England); J. Bryan Grimes, *Abstracts of North Carolina Wills* (1956); Hayes Papers (Southern Historical Collection, University of North Carolina Library, Chapel Hill); C. L. Johnstone, *History of the Johnstones, 1191–1901* (1909); Charles Johnston Collection, Will of Gabriel Johnston (North Carolina State Archives, Raleigh); Hugh T. Lefler and Albert R. Newsome, *North Carolina* (1963); Newscastle and Townshend Papers (Additional Manuscripts, British Library, London); C. L. Raper, *North Carolina: A Study in English Colonial Government* (1904); William L. Saunders, ed., *Colonial Records of North Carolina*, vols. 4, 5 (1886–87); Hew Scott, *Fasti Ecclesiae Scoticanae* (1925); *Scottish Record Society* 56 (1925); J. L. Sprunt, *Chronicles of the Cape Fear* (1914); Nina M. Tiffany, ed., *Letters of James Murray, Loyalist* (1901); University of Edinburgh and University of St. Andrews Muniments.

JAQUELIN DRANE NASH

Johnston, George Doherty (*30 May 1832–8 Dec. 1910*), lawyer, mayor, legislator, Confederate officer, and educator, was born in Hillsborough, presumably at Heartsease, on East Queen Street. His father was George Mulhollan Johnston, a planter and surveyor, and the son of George and Martha Mulhollan Johnston. His mother was Eliza Mary Bond, the daughter of William H. and Frances Wilson Doherty Bond, and the granddaughter of Major George Doherty, a colonial officer. Her grandmother was Mary ("Polly") Freeman Burke, the widow of Governor Thomas Burke by her first marriage.

In August 1834 the family, accompanied by Miss Mary Williams Burke, a colorful great-aunt who was self-educated and took it upon herself to teach the local children, moved to Greensboro, Ala., where after only two weeks George's father died unexpectedly. The Court of Perry County awarded Miss Burke the guardianship of young George, whom she raised and taught while also looking after her beloved niece, George's mother. The family then settled in Marion, Ala., and George went on to attend Howard College. He was graduated in law at Cumberland University, Lebanon, Tenn., thereafter establishing a practice in Marion in 1855. Interested in local politics, he became mayor of Marion in 1856 and represented Perry County in the state legislature in 1857–58.

With the approach of the Civil War Johnston became a second lieutenant in Company G, Fourth Alabama

Regiment, which saw action at the Battle of First Manassas in Virginia. In January 1862 he was commissioned major in the newly organized Twenty-fifth Alabama Regiment, stationed at Mobile, in the army of General J. M. Withers. In the early spring this force joined General Albert S. Johnston's Army of the Mississippi and took part in the Battle of Shiloh, 6–7 Apr. 1862. During the battle the Twenty-fifth Alabama's commander, Colonel J. Q. Loomis, was wounded, and Major Johnston assumed command of the regiment, afterwards winning promotion to lieutenant colonel. Johnston led the regiment in some minor engagements and in the autumn of 1862 accompanied General Braxton Bragg's army on the Kentucky campaign, although it did not participate in any of the fighting. In the Battle of Murfreesboro during 31 Dec. 1862–2 Jan. 1863, Johnston led the regiment as a part of the First Brigade of General Withers's division; there he lost 105 men, a considerable portion of the regiment's original strength.

In September 1863 Johnston received a richly deserved promotion to the rank of colonel. On the nineteenth and twentieth of that month he led the regiment in the bloody Battle of Chickamauga as a part of General Z. C. Deas's brigade, Hindman's division. Here the regiment lost 110 out of 330 men sent into battle. In the Battle of Chattanooga Johnston fought on Missionary Ridge, 23–25 Nov. 1863, and then commanded the regiment during the grueling Atlanta campaign with such distinction that his superiors, generals Johnston, Hood, and Hindman, urged his promotion to brigadier general and brigade commander. In the brutal Battle of Atlanta on 22 July 1864, the gallant charge of his regiment broke through the Union lines and resulted in the capture of two flags, a 350-stand of small arms, and more prisoners than he had men in his regiment. For this his promotion was again urged by generals Bragg, Hood, Cheatham, and Brown. At last on 26 July 1864 he received the rank of brigadier general under a Confederate law providing for general officers of temporary rank, to rank from the same date (confirmed 21 Feb. 1865).

When he received notice of the promotion Johnston was leading Deas's old brigade—consisting of the Nineteenth, Twenty-second, Twenty-fifth, Thirty-ninth, and Fiftieth Alabama regiments and the Seventeenth Alabama Battalion Sharpshooters—in the Battle of Ezra Church, 28 July 1864. About three hours later he was seriously wounded by a bullet through his leg, but, supporting the wounded limb in his bridle rein, he continued to command the brigade until exhausted. He later accompanied Hood's army into Tennessee, although on crutches most of the time. After General William A. Quarles was wounded in the Battle of Franklin on 30 Nov. 1864, Johnston was assigned to command his brigade, consisting of the First Alabama, the Forty-eighth Tennessee, and consolidated Tennessee regiments. Johnston led this brigade in the Battle of Nashville, 15–16 December, and served in the rear guard during the retreat.

During the campaign through the Carolinas, Johnston continued to lead Quarles's brigade and fought in the Battle of Bentonville during 19–21 Mar. 1865. Here, and for a time afterwards, he led the division of General E. C. Walthall until the reorganization at Goldsboro. Just before the surrender of the Confederate Army commander, General Joseph E. Johnston, to Sherman, he refused to capitulate and made his way west to join the forces of Lieutenant General Richard Taylor in Alabama. No parole record for him has ever been found.

After the war Johnston returned to Marion, Ala., and

resumed his law practice in partnership with John F. Vary. He remained in Marion until 1868 when, after living in Dallas County for a time, he moved to Tuscaloosa. There he was commandant of cadets at the University of Alabama and later superintendent of the South Carolina Military Academy. He also served as U.S. Civil Service commissioner during the second term of President Grover Cleveland. Johnston engaged in expanding the subscription list to the series known as the Southern Historical Society Papers and was listed as its "General Agent." He returned to Tuscaloosa and was elected to the state senate.

Johnston died and was buried in Tuscaloosa. His first wife was Euphradia Poellnitz, and after her death he married Stella Searcy, who survived him.

SEE: C. A. Evans, *Confederate Military History*, vol. 7 (1899); *The News of Orange County*, 19 June, 24 July 1975; Ezra Warner, *Generals in Gray* (1959); Marcus J. Wright, *General Officers of the Confederate Army* (1911).

PAUL BRANCH

Johnston, Gordon (25 May 1874–8 Mar. 1934), military hero, was born in Charlotte, the son of Robert D. and Eliza Evans Johnston. The family had strong military traditions. His father was the youngest brigadier general in the Confederate Army, and his mother was the daughter of Colonel Peter Evans, who died of wounds received in a cavalry charge in the Battle of Upperville (1863). Mrs. Johnston, a great admirer of the noted contemporary British soldier, Charles George ("Chinese") Gordon, named her oldest son for him.

Johnston attended public school in Charlotte and the Pantops Academy in Virginia; he was graduated from Princeton with the B.A. degree in 1896. When the Spanish-American War broke out two years later, he enlisted as a sergeant in the Second Mississippi Infantry and soon afterwards became a private in the First U.S. Cavalry, the famous "Rough Riders." For a time he served as a mounted orderly to Colonel Theodore Roosevelt, forming a friendship that lasted until the latter's death in 1919. When the regiment went to Cuba, Johnston was left behind in Tampa to take charge of the horses and so missed action in the war. After the war he reenlisted, was assigned to the Forty-third U.S. Infantry, and in that command was promoted in 1899 to the rank of second lieutenant. Within a short time the division was sent to quell an insurrection in the Philippines. While commanding a small detachment of scouts, Johnston won his first distinction for gallantry in action after charging a superior force of insurgents to capture the town of Palo on 1 Feb. 1900.

Remaining in the army, he was detailed to the Signal Corps in 1904 and again assigned to the Philippines. In the spring of 1906, with an outbreak in the Maro country, Johnston volunteered for service with the troops sent there. At the engagement at Lake Lanao he led his men up the supposedly impregnable side of a crater, an action that figured largely in the resulting American victory. In the heat of battle Johnston was seriously wounded by a bullet through the shoulder and returned to the United States to recuperate. When the Mexican border situation led to mobilization of the National Guard units in 1916, Johnston was assigned to command the Twelfth New York Infantry. He attracted nationwide attention at the time by resigning his commission because he felt the mayor of New York had insulted his regiment by asking it to pass in review a second time. The affair was smoothed over and Johnston was restored to his command.

During World War I, he served as chief of staff of the Eighty-second Division in France and held other important commands. In his most noted exploit of the conflict, Johnston was credited with rescuing Major Whittlesey's "lost Battalion." After the war he returned to the scene of his former service and went to the Philippines with the Wood-Forbes Commission. As assistant to Leonard Wood, governor general of the Philippines, from 1921 to 1924, Johnston was delegated to organize a Guardian Society to care for Philippine orphans fathered by American servicemen. His success in this humanitarian cause won him high praise in Dr. Heiser's book, *An American Doctor's Odyssey*. In later years Johnston served in various commands in the United States. In 1928 he assisted General Frank R. McCoy in the elections in Nicaragua, and from 1929—when he was promoted to colonel—to 1931 he was military attaché to the American Embassy in Mexico. At the time of his death he was chief of staff of the Second Division at Fort Sam Houston, Tex.

Johnston was often referred to as the most decorated man in the U.S. Army, winning all the medals that the nation was authorized to confer and many awards from foreign governments. France made him a member of the Legion of Honor, and Japan awarded him the Third Class of the Imperial Order of Meiji. An outstanding horseman, he was an honor graduate of the infantry and cavalry schools in 1903 and attended the Royal Military Riding Academy in Hanover, Germany, in 1907. He was a member of the U.S. Army Officers Team in the International Horse Show in London in 1911. Johnston died of injuries suffered when he was thrown from his mount during a polo game at Fort Sam Houston. He was buried in Arlington National Cemetery.

Charles Kinsolving, president of the American Veterans Association which Johnston helped found, said of him: "He was one of the outstanding officers of American military life. He epitomized to me all that the American soldier should be. His sense of honor and justice and his devotion to his country was of the highest quality." Johnston was honored posthumously in 1943 when the name of Camp Carrabelle, Fla., was changed to Gordon Johnston. The camp was an important training center for invasion and commando tactics during World War II.

In 1904 Johnston married Anna Julia Johnson, the daughter of Dr. Robert Johnson of Baltimore. They had no children. In 1945 Mrs. Johnston endowed a carrel in his memory for the new library being planned at his alma mater, Princeton University, and donated his medals to be displayed in the library.

SEE: Alumni Records (Princeton University, Princeton, N.J.); Mary Johnston Avery, *She Heard with Heart: The Life of Mrs. R. D. Johnston* (1944); *New York Times*, 9 Mar. 1934.

CLAIBORNE T. SMITH, JR.

Johnston, James Cathcart (25 June 1782–9 May 1865), planter, was born in Edenton, the sixth child and fourth son of Samuel (1733–1816) and Frances Cathcart (1751–1801) Johnston. His father, a lawyer, was governor of North Carolina from 1787 to 1789 and a U.S. senator from 1790 to 1793. His great-uncle, Gabriel Johnston (ca. 1698–1752), was North Carolina's royal governor from 1734 to 1752. James Iredell (1751–99), a lawyer, judge, and United States Supreme Court justice, was his uncle.

Johnston spent much of his childhood and youth away from home at various schools. At age eight, he was sent to school on Long Island, N.Y., while his family lived in New York City and his father served in Congress. From 1792 to 1796 he attended Woodbury School located in New Jersey near Philadelphia and studied under the Reverend Andrew Hunter. He then entered the College of New Jersey (later Princeton University) where he was a member of the American Whig Society. Johnston was graduated in 1799 and returned to North Carolina to live at Hermitage Plantation near Williamston with his parents, his sisters Penelope, Helen, and Frances, and his brother Gabriel. Accustomed to a busy schedule of classes and studies and to the camaraderie of schoolmates, he found life at the secluded plantation very quiet. To while away idle hours, he read books and became especially absorbed in metaphysics and history. He studied French at The University of North Carolina from July to November 1800 and on his return home began to read law under his father. Johnston immediately became apprehensive about a legal career and lamented to friends that his studies were "rather dry and intricate." Nevertheless, he persevered and received a license to practice on 11 Apr. 1804. But while he had been completing his legal training, his attention had turned to agriculture. He began to manage his father's plantation in Pasquotank County and slowly drifted away from the law. Hard work and personal management of his plantations over the next sixty years made Johnston one of the state's most innovative and prosperous planters.

He lived at Hayes Plantation in Chowan County, located east of Edenton and bordered by Queen Anne's Creek and Edenton Bay. The farm had been purchased by Samuel Johnston in 1765 from David Rieusett, whose brother John had bought it from William and Harding Jones. Samuel gave the 665-acre plantation to his son in 1814 and instructed him to build a house on it, as the one there was uninhabitable. Johnston commissioned William Nichols, an English architect living in Edenton, to design the plantation house. Construction began in the fall of 1815, and Johnston and his sisters moved into it two years later. Nichols's plan featured a central section with two floors that was flanked by two single-story, curved wings with colonnades. The octagonal "Gothick" library at the end of one of the wings held Johnston's extensive collection of eighteenth- and nineteenth-century legal, political, and historical literature. The distinctive home was the focal point of the plantation that became famous throughout North Carolina. Over the years Johnston added to his Hayes property and by 1860 owned 1,374 acres of land.

The planter had extensive landholdings elsewhere in North Carolina. In Pasquotank County he owned several farms consisting of 2,740 acres. Poplar Plains, inherited from his father, was located along the Pasquotank River four miles below Elizabeth City. It adjoined his "Body" land and a plantation called Salem, which he purchased from Joseph Blount in 1819. Johnston's largest farm was Caledonia, located in Halifax County along the Roanoke River. Caledonia was also a bequest from his father, who had received it from his father-in-law, William Cathcart. Johnston bought more land and increased the plantation's size from 2,375 to 7,834 acres. He also owned some land in Northampton County.

Johnston spent much of his time traveling from plantation to plantation to personally oversee their operations. His largest crop was corn; in addition, he grew wheat, oats, cotton, flax, potatoes, peas, and beans. He raised cattle, hogs, and sheep. The plantation products to be sold at markets were floated down river on Johnston's boats to storage firms at Plymouth, Elizabeth City, or Edenton; then they were shipped, often by his

schooners and canal boats, to Savannah, Charleston, Norfolk, Baltimore, and New York. Commission merchants in these cities handled Johnston's profits, buying supplies for the plantations or investing the money in bank stocks and treasury notes for him.

Keenly interested in modern developments in agriculture, Johnston continually experimented with new farming techniques to improve his plantations. He cleared unused land, dug irrigation canals, and enriched his soil with fertilizers. He also invested in new agricultural machinery. Early in his career he built a windmill at Hayes but later dismantled it. He then constructed steam-powered saw, grist, and flour mills, which produced lumber, flour, and cornmeal for both plantation and market. In addition, he bought cotton gins and threshing machines. Johnston's innovations enabled him gradually to increase his agricultural production as well as the value and quality of his properties. Whereas in 1829 he described his plantations as "large and extensive but ragged and tattered in some places bare to the skin and almost to the bone," he proudly wrote in 1846 that they were "in better order" than he had ever had them.

Johnston displayed a moderate attitude towards slavery. He treated his slaves respectably and expected the same in return so that his plantations would operate smoothly. In 1860 he owned a total of 555 slaves—103 at Hayes, 181 at his Pasquotank County farms, and 271 at Caledonia. He was attentive to his slaves' needs and capabilities. They made their own clothes, and he regularly provided them with shoes, hats, blankets, medical care, and food. They were allowed to raise and to sell crops from their gardens. He trained several as overseers and frequently left the slaves at his Pasquotank plantations alone with little or no white supervision. He punished them when he considered such action necessary, yet expressed compassion for them in the problem of slave revolts. Johnston felt that insurrections were most dangerous for blacks, viewed with suspicion by nervous whites, and thought that during periods of unrest it was best "to be at home to protect the poor creatures who have no law to protect them and have nothing to work up to but the presence and protection of their master." Freedom for slaves was not beyond his consideration. Several facts point to this interpretation: in 1841 he anonymously donated $250 to the American Colonization Society; in the 1850s he loaned $1,000 to a freed and widowed black and her five children for their resettlement in Ohio; and during the Civil War, he wrote that he preferred to give a pass to his slaves who wanted to go to freedom behind the Federal lines rather than to have them run away and make him appear to be a hard master, and themselves to be rascals.

During his leisure hours Johnston traveled a great deal, claiming that it served as a "substitute for the pleasure of domestic life." He seems to have fallen in love only once with a Miss Jones, whom he met on a trip to Sweet Springs, Va., in the summer of 1821. She, however, flatly refused his proposal of marriage the following year. Johnston also enjoyed the change of scenery and company that travel afforded, and he frequently journed northward to New York City and Saratoga Springs to visit friends. In 1845 he leased a cabin at White Sulphur Springs in Greenbriar, Va., thereafter becoming a regular summer and fall visitor to this and other fashionable mountain resorts in Virginia. In 1859 he bought a farm at Cedar Creek in Bath County, Va., built a house and log cabins, and began planting crops. The Civil War, however, ended this plan for a private mountain retreat.

Johnston preferred a private life, shunning public duties—he wrote that he disliked "public applause." He held few public offices, serving only on the North Carolina Board of Internal Improvements (1820–21) and on the board of trustees of The University of North Carolina (1818–63). He was very interested in public events, especially politics. He greatly respected many Federalists, including Washington, Marshall, Jay, and Hamilton. He supported the Whig party and particularly admired Daniel Webster and Henry Clay, although he eventually became disillusioned with the Whigs. Johnston was deeply disturbed as the Union was propelled towards civil war in 1860–61. He thought that the United States Constitution was of superior quality but that it had been improperly administered under President Buchanan. The South, in his opinion, had degenerated into a state of anarchy. He also believed that the doctrine of the "wicked" Secessionists would set a harmful precedent: "when a state government brakes [*sic*] a most solemn contract with so little ceremony individuals will think it no sin to absolve themselves from any contract they may make and we may expect soon a general repudiation both of individuals as well as governments."

At his death Johnston willed his real and personal property to three friends and made them co-executors of his estate. Edward Wood, an Edenton businessman, received his Chowan County property, including Hayes Plantation. Christopher W. Hollowell, a resident of Pasquotank County who had helped manage Johnston's farms in that county, was given Poplar Plains and the other Pasquotank properties. Caledonia's manager, Henry J. Futrell, inherited the property in Halifax and Northampton counties. Johnston's closest living relatives were cousins, and he did not leave them any of his land for several reasons. He had frequently given them money during his lifetime, and he thought that they had been inconsiderate of him by leaving him alone and unprotected at Hayes during the Civil War. He also considered them incapable of maintaining his properties. After spending his entire life building and improving his plantations, he did not wish them to be destroyed by poor management or divided up among his numerous relatives. He believed his three heirs to be honest, industrious men. Furthermore, Hollowell and Futrell had been faithful to him and protected his property, and Wood was a capable businessman who would keep his beloved Hayes intact and operate it as a productive farm. Johnston's cousins challenged the legitimacy of his will and its accompanying letters of instruction to the executors by which some of them were to receive monetary gifts; they claimed that Johnston had been mentally unstable when he had written the will and the letters. The will was finally established as legal in 1867, but, because additional suits were brought against its executors, Johnston's estate was not settled until 1871.

Johnston was an Episcopalian. He was buried at Hayes Plantation.

SEE: Hayes Collection, Pettigrew Papers (Southern Historical Collection, University of North Carolina Library, Chapel Hill); Calder Loth and Julius Trousdale Sadler, Jr., *The Only Proper Style: Gothic Architecture in America* (1975); C. Ford Peatross and Robert O. Mellown, *William Nichols, Architect* (1979); Clyde Norman Wilson, Jr., "Carolina Cavalier: The Life of James Johnston Pettigrew" (Ph.D. diss., University of North Carolina, Chapel Hill, 1971).

MARTHA M. SMITH

Johnston, Jonas *(1740–29 July 1779)*, Revolutionary War officer, Edgecombe County official, and state legislator, was born near Courtland in present Southampton County, Va., the son of Jacob Johnston, Sr., and Mary Waller Johnston. In 1757 his parents settled on Town Creek in Edgecombe County, N.C. Although his formal education was limited, young Johnston had a natural gift for oratory accompanied by a keen, practical intelligence that soon elevated him to a position of leadership in the plantation society of which he was from early adulthood a respected and substantial member.

On 31 May 1771, the Edgecombe County Court appointed Johnston to the public office of magistrate to take the taxes and taxables. His potential capacity as a military leader was first recognized at the Battle of Moore's Creek Bridge on 27 Feb. 1776, when he served as captain of an Edgecombe County company in suppressing the Tory and Loyalist menace to the Patriot cause in North Carolina. About that time he was described as "robust in person, active, and capable of bearing much fatigue, vigilant and brave as an officer, and high-spirited and honorable as a man; which, joined to a mind distinguished for its strength and fortitude, rendered him an invaluable auxiliary in defense of the liberty of his country."

On 19 Apr. 1776, Johnston was appointed by the North Carolina Provincial Congress at Halifax "to receive, procure and purchase fire arms for the use of the troops," and three days later he became first major of the field officers of the Edgecombe Militia Regiment. On 12 November he was one of the three representatives from his county who took their seats in the Provincial Congress meeting at Halifax, which on 23 December ratified his appointment as a justice of the peace. He was still a member of the General Assembly in 1777 and on 2 September was named recruiting officer for his county in the Halifax Military District.

The records of the General Assembly contain numerous references to the important committees on which Major Johnston served constructively in 1777 and 1778, and a number of his surviving letters to Governor Richard Caswell reveal both his intelligence and his dedication to duty. Because of his election as entry taker in Edgecombe County, Johnston was forced to relinquish his place in the General Assembly on 28 Apr. 1778, but on 8 August he was properly seated again in the session at Hillsborough and ready to take part in the work of several committees.

At home between sessions, Johnston was occupied with a great variety of civic, domestic, and military duties. By 24 Nov. 1778 he held the rank of lieutenant colonel in the Edgecombe County Regiment, and on the following 19 January he was again seated in the General Assembly at Halifax. With the deteriorating military situation in South Carolina, Colonel Johnston rejoined the Edgecombe County Regiment and proceeded in early April to the vicinity of Camden and later of Charleston where, in the Battle of Stono Ferry on 20 June 1779, he "greatly distinguished himself for his personal courage and the skill with which he handled his men."

Subsequently Johnston was ordered to march his regiment against the Tories, who had become very troublesome in the Upper Pee Dee area. By the time his force reached Drowning Creek (now Lumber River), the colonel became so violently ill that he could proceed no farther and was taken to the home of his friend, Thomas Amis. There, the best of care could not save him. His wife, who had been sent for, arrived in a borrowed gig several days before his death. Because it was impossible for her to transport his body 140 miles through the summer heat, Johnston was buried in a small neighboring graveyard. Many years later, when his descendants wished to return his remains to the family cemetery in Edgecombe County, this graveyard could not be located.

On 17 Nov. 1768 Johnston married Esther Maund (15 Feb. 1751/52–19 Dec. 1840), the daughter of Lott and Prudence Hughlett Maund of Norfolk County, Va. She was described as "a woman who, in good sense, in resourcefulness, and in strength of character, seems to have been quite his equal." Esther Johnston never remarried, but completed the unfinished interior of their new home, carried on the plantation business, reared five children, and bravely endured the effects of paralysis during her last fifteen years of life. She was awarded a Revolutionary War Widow's Pension only a few years before her death. Her informative tombstone less than two miles east of Pinetops is still legible. A handsome bronze memorial to her husband is located in the lobby of the Edgecombe County Courthouse.

The Johnstons were the parents of Celia (25 May 1770–12 June 1840), Elizabeth Maund (9 Feb. 1772–October 1820), Prudence (15 Mar. 1775–12 Mar. 1855), Mary Ann (30 Dec. 1776–12 Feb. 1857), and William (14 Feb. 1779–7 Nov. 1793). Celia, who married Jesse Hines in 1791 and Elias Carr in 1797, was the mother of Richard Hines of Raleigh and the grandmother of Governor Elias Carr. Elizabeth married John Bell in 1789 and John Andrews in 1795. Prudence was the wife of Peter Hines and had three children; a son, the Reverend Peter Edmund Hines, was mayor of Wilson. Mary Ann married, on 18 Sept. 1794, Samuel Ruffin (4 Dec. 1773–17 May 1826), by whom she had ten children and many prominent descendants.

SEE: Coy K. Johnston and Hugh B. Johnston, *William Johnston of Isle of Wight County, Virginia, and His Descendants, 1648–1964* (1965).

HUGH BUCKNER JOHNSTON

Johnston, Joseph Forney (23 Mar. 1843–8 Aug. 1913), lawyer, governor of Alabama, and U.S. senator, was born at Mount Welcome, Lincoln County, the son of William and Nancy Forney Johnston. He attended the schools of North Carolina until age seventeen, when he moved to Alabama and entered high school in Talladega.

At the outbreak of the Civil War, Johnston enlisted in the Eleventh Alabama Regiment of the Confederate Army; by the end of the conflict he had attained the rank of captain in the Twelfth North Carolina Regiment. He was wounded in battles at Chickamauga, Spottsylvania Court House, New Market, and Petersburg. After the war he studied law in Jacksonville, Ala., under William H. Forney. He was admitted to the bar in 1866 and practiced in Selma until 1884, when he moved to Birmingham.

In Birmingham, a young but growing town, Johnston wasted no time in getting involved in various aspects of its expansion and economic development. He served as president of the Alabama State Bank from 1884 to 1894 and as president of the Sloss Iron and Steel Company from 1896 to 1900.

In 1896 Johnston ran as the Democratic nominee for governor, defeating Populist Albert T. Goodwyn by a vote of 128,549 to 89,290. His administration created several new state offices including those of the State Tax Commissioner, State Department of Insurance, and Chief Mine Inspector. Under his leadership, Alabama experienced renewed industrial growth, outside investments, greater funding for public education, and the development of hydroelectric power on the Tallapoosa River.

In his bid for a second term in 1898, Johnston defeated Gilbert B. Dean, another Populist, 110,551 to 50,052. This administration was marked by a loss of prestige and power because of some of the unpopular positions taken by the governor. In 1899, he became involved in a bitter dispute over the sale of coal lands owned by the University of Alabama to Sloss Sheffield Company. Johnston, who supported the sale, was the target of much criticism from people who claimed he had a conflict of interest in the deal. As a result of the controversy, the university kept the land and the governor's popularity floundered.

At the death of U.S. Senator Edmund W. Pettus in 1907, Johnston was appointed to serve the remainder of his term. Afterwards he was elected for a full term as senator and died in office.

On 12 Aug. 1869 Johnston married Theresa Virginia Hooper, and they became the parents of three sons, among whom were Edward Douglas and Forney. He was buried in Elmwood Cemetery, Birmingham.

SEE: *Biog. Dir. Am. Cong.* (1961); *DAB*, vol. 5 (1932); Thomas McAdory Owen, *History of Alabama and Dictionary of Alabama Biography*, vol. 3 (1921); Robert Sobel and John Raimo, eds., *Biographical Dictionary of the Governors of the United States, 1789–1978*, vol. 1 (1978); *Who Was Who in America*, vol. 1 (1897–1942).

SUZY CONNER

Johnston, Lancelot (1748–19 Sept. 1832), physician, Revolutionary War surgeon, and planter, was born in Ardess, County Fermanagh, Ireland, of Scottish ancestry. He received his medical education at the Medical College of the University of Dublin and emigrated to America before 1769, settling in that part of Orange County that soon became Caswell County. In 1771 he served for two months in the militia, and on 10 May 1777 he was commissioned by the Continental Congress as surgeon of the Ninth Battalion, Continental Army, "raised for the defending of American liberty and for repelling every hostile invasion thereof." On 26 Nov. 1778, he was appointed regimental surgeon of the Continental troops to be raised in the Hillsborough and Salisbury districts to assist in South Carolina, and was advanced £150 for the purchase of medicine and supplies. After the Battle of Camden he was sent there to help care for the wounded. His arrival was welcomed by the overworked Dr. Hugh Williamson, of Edenton, who wrote to the speaker of the North Carolina House of Commons: "We were happily reinforced by Dr. Johnston, a Senior Surgeon of great skill and Humanity in the Continental Service."

After the war, Johnston continued to serve as a physician to the residents of Caswell County and environs; he also was a planter of the farms he owned in the area. He died at his home in St. David's District (now Locust Hill township) and was buried in the family cemetery nearby.

In 1774 Johnston married Zerurah Rice, the daughter of Thomas Rice of Caswell County. They were the parents of six children: William, Lancelot, Elizabeth (m. Dr. E. E. Jones), and Polly (m. a Mr. Slade), all of whom moved to Madison, Ga.; and Thomas (m. Jane Bethell) and Zilphar (m. James Yancey), both of whom remained in North Carolina. Portraits of Dr. and Mrs. Johnston, said to have been painted by Thomas Sully, were sold by the family in the 1930s, but photographs of the portraits are owned by several descendants including Mrs. F. F. Bahnson, Jr., of Winston-Salem and Mrs. Clifford Bair of Chapel Hill.

SEE: Walter Clark, ed., *State Records of North Carolina*, vol. 12 (1895); Johnston Family Papers (Southern Historical Collection, University of North Carolina Library, Chapel Hill); William S. Powell, *When the Past Refused to Die: A History of Caswell County* (1977); William L. Saunders, ed., *Colonial Records of North Carolina*, vol. 10 (1890).

ANNA WITHERS BAIR
KATHARINE K. KENDALL

Johnston, Robert Daniel (*19 Mar. 1837–1 Feb. 1919*), Confederate officer, lawyer, and banker, was born of Scotch-Irish descent at Mount Welcome, Lincoln County. He was a member of a large family reared by Dr. William Johnston, a physician and successful iron manufacturer, who served at one time in the state legislature, and his wife Nancy Forney. Both of Johnston's grandfathers were officers in the American Revolution. As a child he benefited from the advantages available to a well-to-do family. Upon graduation from The University of North Carolina in 1858, Johnston studied law at the University of Virginia. Admitted to the bar of his native state, he practiced law until the outbreak of the Civil War.

When North Carolina seceded, Johnston was an officer in the Beattie's Ford Rifles, a Lincoln County militia company. He entered the Confederate Army as a captain of Company K, Twenty-third North Carolina Infantry. Four of his brothers also enlisted. Commissioned lieutenant colonel on 10 May 1862, Johnston participated in the Peninsular campaign, when he was wounded in the arm, face, and neck at Seven Pines. Cited for bravery at South Mountain and Sharpsburg, he continued to distinguish himself at Chancellorsville and Gettysburg. On 1 Sept. 1863 he was promoted to brigadier general to command five North Carolina regiments. In the battles of May 1864, he suffered a severe wound at Spotsylvania, only to return to lead his brigade in the Shenandoah Valley campaign of 1864. His performance in the Battle of Winchester on 19 September was particularly notable. Returning with his men to Petersburg, he endured the trench fighting until March 1865 when ordered to guard the Roanoke River area and to collect deserters. He was paroled at Charlotte in May 1865.

For the next twenty years Johnston practiced law in Charlotte as a partner of Colonel Hamilton C. Jones. In 1887 he moved to Birmingham, Ala., to assume the presidency of the Birmingham National Bank. The practice of law, numerous business investments, and mining promotions also contributed to make Johnston a leading citizen of the city. For a number of years he was registrar of the Federal Land Bank Office. Johnston and his wife were instrumental in the establishment of a state industrial school for boys near Birmingham.

In 1871 Johnston married Elizabeth Johnston Evans, and they were the parents of three sons and four daughters. He died in the home of a son in Winchester, Va., where he was buried.

SEE: Walter Clark, ed., *Histories of the Several Regiments and Battalions from North Carolina in the Great War, 1861–*

1865, vol. 2 (1901); *Confederate Veteran* 28 (1920); Clement A. Evans, ed., *Confederate Military History*, vol. 4 (1899); Douglas S. Freeman, *Lee's Lieutenants: A Study in Command*, vol. 3 (1944); William L. Sherrill, *Annals of Lincoln County, North Carolina* (1937); Ezra J. Warner, *Generals in Gray: Lives of the Confederate Commanders* (1959).

J. D. WERT

Johnston, Rufus Zenas (*7 June 1874–4 July 1959*), naval officer, was born in Lincolnton, the son of Robert Zenas, a Presbyterian minister, and Catherine Caldwell Johnston. He was educated in the Lincolnton public schools and was graduated from the U.S. Military Academy in 1895. Three years later Johnston served on the battleship *Oregon* during the Spanish-American War. Afterwards he saw service in the Philippine insurrection and the Boxer Rebellion in China. For distinguished conduct in 1914 at Vera Cruz, Mexico, he was awarded the Congressional Medal of Honor (the Vera Cruz engagement was the result of strained relations between a revolutionary Mexican government and the United States).

Johnston commanded the Newport Naval Training Station from 1915 until the country entered World War I. During the war he served as commander of the USS *Minneapolis* and received the Navy Cross for escorting 107 merchant supply vessels to France.

In 1925, Johnston was graduated from the Naval War College and made chief of staff at that institution. He was chief of staff of the First Naval District in Boston from 1928 until his retirement in 1930. Although Johnston retired as a captain, he was promoted to the rank of rear admiral, retired, in 1948. This was made possible by a law that allowed men on the retired list to be promoted provided they had been decorated for bravery.

After his retirement, Johnston resided in Newport, R.I. Becoming active in civic affairs, he served as chairman of the park commission and as a member of the board of managers of the Armed Services YMCA. He was a member of the U.S. Naval Institute and of the Army and Navy Club of Washington, D.C.

In 1903 Johnston married Emma Pegram of Richmond, Va. They had three children: Rufus Zenas, Jr., Elizabeth, and Catherine. Johnston died in Newport at age eighty-five.

SEE: *Nat. Cyc. Am. Biog.*, vol. 48 (1965 [portrait]); *New York Times*, 5 July 1959.

WARREN L. BINGHAM

Johnston, Samuel (*15 Dec. 1733–17 Aug. 1816*), Revolutionary War leader, governor, U.S. senator, judge, attorney, and planter, was born in Dundee, Scotland, the son of Samuel and Helen Scrymsoure Johnston. His uncle, Gabriel Johnston, who came to North Carolina in 1734 as royal governor, brought the elder Samuel and family to the colony sometime after March 1735. They resided at Poplar Spring Plantation on the main road between New Bern and Wilmington, in Onslow County, until the death of Samuel's father in October 1757. Young Johnston received his formal education at Yale but did not stay long enough to graduate; instead, he moved to Edenton in the fall of 1753 to read law under Thomas Barker.

In May 1755 Johnston was appointed clerk of the Court of Oyer and Terminer and General Gaol Delivery for the Edenton district, and in November 1756 he was licensed as an attorney. In 1759 he was elected to the Assembly, where he served without interruption until 1775, thus commencing almost fifty years of public service to his state and to the nation. In the spring of 1765 he bought Hayes Plantation, Edenton, where he and his family lived for about thirty years.

In 1770 Johnston purchased the post of deputy naval officer of the colony and served until November 1775. In the December 1770 session of the Assembly he sponsored a bill for punishing the Regulators who, he felt, were disturbing the peace by rioting against the legal authority of the colony's government. If the rioters did not turn themselves in, they were to be declared outlaws and liable to be shot on sight. This extremely harsh bill, which applied only to the Regulators and only for a limited time, became known to posterity as the "Johnston Act." Within five years, the man who introduced this legislation was a leader of North Carolina's revolt against royal authority.

Besides his usual committee assignments during each session of the Assembly, in December 1773 Johnston was named to the new Standing Committee of Correspondence and Enquiry. Its twofold purpose was to keep abreast of all Parliamentary proceedings affecting the American colonies and to correspond with the colonies regarding these proceedings.

A member of the First and Second Provincial Congresses, Johnston was named by both to take over and set the time of the next meeting in case Moderator John Harvey became incapacitated between assemblies. After Harvey died in May 1775, Johnston convened the Third Provincial Congress in August, at which time he was elected president of the Congress as well as treasurer of the Northern (Granville) District. On 9 September he was elected member-at-large of the Provincial Council, which was to govern the colony between congresses. From the end of May, when royal governor Josiah Martin fled from the palace in New Bern, until the middle of October, when Cornelius Harnett became chairman of the Provincial Council, Johnston was head of all government in North Carolina, the first nonroyal governor in function, if not in title. On 20 October the Council appointed him paymaster of troops for the Edenton district. When the Fourth Provincial Congress met on 4 Apr. 1776, Johnston was again chosen president.

In October 1776 Johnston received his first and only defeat at the polls when he sought election to the Provincial Congress, but he was not allowed to retire from public service. He was present at the Fifth Provincial Congress in December in his capacity as treasurer of the Northern District, and was kept informed and was consulted by the committee drawing up the state constitution. He was named by this congress to a legal commission to review the royal statutes worthy of being retained. In May 1777 the new congress reappointed him treasurer of the Northern District, but he declined the office. In 1779 he was returned to the legislature as state senator from Chowan County.

On 30 Apr. 1780 Johnston was chosen as one of North Carolina's delegates to the Continental Congress, but because of illness he did not arrive in Philadelphia until December. His attendance was faithful thereafter, and he was reelected for another term in July 1781 although he frequently asked to be relieved so he could return home to take care of his family and business. On 9 July 1781, according to the Journal of the Continental Congress, Johnston was elected president of that body. The entry for the next day states that he declined to accept the honor. He left Philadelphia on 12 July, and fellow delegate William Sharpe lamented the departure of "so able a representative and of so judicious and very agreeable [a] colleague."

In 1783 and 1784 Johnston served again as state senator from Chowan County. In June 1785 he was asked by the commissioners of New York and Massachusetts to serve as one of the judges in their boundary dispute. He accepted and thus helped to determine the present line between those two states.

Since his purchase of Hayes Plantation in 1765, Johnston divided his time between overseeing farming operations on his, and later his wife's, several plantations, and practicing law whenever he was not away on official public duties. He and his brother-in-law James Iredell frequently traveled the court circuits together on horseback. After the peace treaty was signed, Johnston was asked many times to recover Loyalist property that had been confiscated and sold by the state. One such case was *Bayard v. Singleton*, for which Johnston, Iredell, and William R. Davie were attorneys for the plaintiff. Although they lost (November 1787), the trial established the right of judicial review sixteen years before John Marshall's decision in *Marbury v. Madison* (1803). Because of this and similar cases, Johnston considered himself one of the most unpopular men in the North Carolina at that time and refused to run in the 1787 elections.

In Tarboro, where the Assembly was sitting, the state's Masons were also meeting for the purpose of reviving the Grand Lodge, which had been defunct since the break with England. On 11 Dec. 1787, Johnston was elected North Carolina's first Grand Master—there had only been Deputy Grand Masters until the American Revolution. Two days later the legislature unanimously elected Johnston governor on the first ballot, though he was not even a member of the legislature that year.

On 21 July 1788, the first convention was held at Hillsborough to consider ratification of the new federal Constitution. Johnston, leader of North Carolina's Federalists, was elected president unanimously although the Anti-Federalists controlled the convention. The delegates decided not to ratify at that time, and Johnston became a leader in the fight to have a second convention called for by the people. On 11 November of the same year he was reelected governor.

The second ratification convention was planned to meet simultaneously with the November 1789 legislature at Fayetteville. On the fourteenth Johnston was elected governor for the third time, and two days later he was unanimously elected president of the second ratification convention. On 21 November the delegates moved that North Carolina ratify the Constitution, the convention was disbanded, and the legislature resumed its business.

On the first ballot on 27 Nov. 1789, Samuel Johnston was elected North Carolina's first U.S. senator. He drew the short term and resigned his office of governor, arriving in New York early in the new year to assume his senatorial duties. When his term was completed, he returned home and moved his family from Edenton to the relatively higher and healthier area of Williamston, Martin County, where he had a farm and home he named the Hermitage. Johnston accepted an appointment as Superior Court judge and served from 1800 to 1813. Now seventy years old, he refused any more public offices.

On 29 May 1770 Johnston married Frances Cathcart, the daughter of his friend Dr. William Cathcart. She died at the Hermitage on 23 Jan. 1801. They had nine children, four of whom died before their second birthdays and one before he was six. The four who reached maturity were Penelope (m. John Swann), James Cathcart, Frances, and Helen. Johnston's only grandchild, Samuel Johnston Swann, died in childhood.

Johnston was a member of St. Paul's Church (Anglican), Edenton, where he served on the vestry (27 Apr. 1767–April 1776) and as church warden (30 Apr. 1768–16 Apr. 1770). Active in the founding of The University of North Carolina, he was the first trustee to be elected (1789). He often visited the school and was especially proud of the students in their public examinations at graduation. Johnston was buried in the family graveyard at Hayes Plantation, Edenton.

Of dignified mien and unquestionable integrity, Johnston was trusted by the electorate which turned to him again and again for leadership—first under royal rule, then in time of crisis during the Revolution, under the Articles of Confederation, and under the new federal government. The people felt that he was above political faction. Many of the state's political leaders esteemed him as their personal friend.

The only documented likeness of Samuel Johnston is an ivory miniature painted by Charles Wilson Peale, which is in the possession of the Reverend Charles E. Johnson. The portrait in the capitol in Raleigh, about which nothing is known, appears to have been copied from this miniature because of the similarity of the two paintings.

SEE: Anna W. Bair, "Samuel Johnston and the Ratification of the Federal Constitution in North Carolina" (M.A. thesis, DePaul University, 1969); Walter Clark, ed., *State Records of North Carolina*, vols. 20, 21 (1902, 1903); Hayes Papers (Southern Historical Collection, University of North Carolina Library, Chapel Hill); James Iredell Collection (Duke University Library, Durham); Charles E. Johnson Collection (North Carolina State Archives, Raleigh); William L. Saunders, ed., *Colonial Records of North Carolina*, vols. 6, 9 (1888, 1890).

ANNA WITHERS BAIR

Johnston, Samuel Iredell (28 Dec. 1806–12 Aug. 1865), Episcopal clergyman, was born in Windsor, the son of Colonel John Seymour and Elizabeth Cotten Johnston. His father was a brother of Governor Samuel Johnston of Hayes Plantation near Edenton and represented Bertie County in the state senate in 1795 and 1800. Shortly after his birth, the family moved to neighboring Hertford County to live with his maternal grandfather, Godwin Cotten. When John Johnston died in 1807, Cotten took charge of young Samuel and his sister Sallie Ann and raised them at his plantation, Mulberry Grove. In 1826 Johnston received the A.B. degree from The University of North Carolina, which later awarded him the A.M. degree in 1844. After reading law, he practiced briefly in Jackson.

Although his Cotten grandparents were devout Baptists, Johnston was exposed to the Episcopal church through visits with his father's family in Edenton. As his interest in the denomination grew, he determined to enter the ministry. After meeting with the Right Reverend Levi S. Ives, Bishop of North Carolina, he was admitted as a candidate for Holy Orders in 1832. He studied privately under another clergyman and was ordained to the diaconate by Bishop Ives at St. Matthew's, Hillsborough, on 20 July 1834. Johnston was soon sent to take charge of Calvary Church, Wadesboro, where he served for three years. In 1835 he was ordained to the priesthood by the Right Reverend Richard Channing Moore of Virginia. During his tenure at Wadesboro, Johnston established a parish library, worked among the local blacks, and held services at Morven.

In 1837 Johnston was named rector of St. Paul's Church, Edenton, and embarked on a ministry that would take him throughout the Albemarle section for the next twenty-eight years. At the beginning of his rectorship, he often held services at Windsor, Gatesville, and Hertford until churches could be erected at those places. Later, he worked with slaves on the plantations and was instrumental in persuading the Burgwyn, Pettigrew, and Skinner families to build chapels on their estates. Johnston also organized a parochial girls' school in Edenton, and he trained a number of young men while they were reading for deacon's or priest's orders.

Widely respected throughout the diocese, Johnston was frequently asked to preach to the diocesan convention and often represented North Carolina in the General Convention of the Episcopal church. In addition, he served on the important Standing Committee and on boards responsible for establishing a diocesan library and revising the canon law. Johnston was one of four clerical representatives selected in 1850 to investigate Bishop Ives and to examine his views on private confession and absolution, transubstantiation, prayers to the Virgin Mary, and veneration of the saints. In 1858 he was awarded the honorary doctor of divinity degree (institution unknown).

The Civil War marked the end of Johnston's highly successful ministry. In February 1862 he and his family fled from Edenton to Chapel Hill where his son-in-law, the Reverend Francis Hilliard, was rector. Poor health prevented his returning immediately to his parish at the end of the war. He died soon afterwards and was buried in Edenton.

On 25 Sept. 1829 Johnston married Margaret Ann Burgwin, the daughter of George William Bush Burgwin of the Hermitage near Wilmington. They were the parents of thirteen children: Samuel John (died young), James Cathcart, Maria Nash, Foster, Elizabeth Cotten, Gabriel, George Burgwin, infant twins, Iredell, Helen S., John, and Frances Ann.

SEE: *Diocesan Journals of the Episcopal Church in North Carolina*; Walter Burgwyn Jones, *The Jones-Burgwin Family History* (1913).

JAMES ELLIOTT MOORE

Johnston, Thomas Dillard (1 Apr. 1840–23 June 1902), lawyer, legislator, and congressman, was born at Waynesville in Haywood County, the son of William Johnston, a native of County Down, Ireland, and Lucinda Gudger Johnston, of the prominent Gudger family of Asheville. He was the first cousin of James Madison Gudger, Jr. His early education took place in the common schools of Haywood County, primarily the log school of James N. Terrell. For four years he attended the preparatory school of Colonel Stephen D. Lee near Asheville before entering The University of North Carolina as a sophomore in 1858. In less than a year, however, ill health caused his departure from Chapel Hill.

As the Civil War approached, Johnston was an opponent of secession; but when the conflict became imminent, he enlisted in the Rough and Ready Guards, a company formed at Asheville under Zebulon Vance. This group was soon incorporated into the Fourteenth

North Carolina Regiment, and young Johnston was elected a lieutenant of his company. Upon a later reorganization of the regiment, he was appointed adjutant. At the Battle of Malvern Hill he received three severe wounds, from which he nearly died. When he finally recovered he was appointed quartermaster of Colonel W. C. Walker's battalion and was promoted to the rank of captain, but his health soon failed once again and he resigned from the military.

After an extended period of recovery, he attended the law school of Judge James H. Bailey and his son W. H. Bailey at Black Mountain. On completing the course of study there in 1867, he was admitted to the bar.

Johnston's political career was launched in 1868 when he received the Democratic nomination for district solicitor, but his candidacy was voided by the military reconstruction government. Continuing to be a leader in the resurgence of the Democratic party, he was the first of that group since the war to be elected mayor of Asheville, in 1869, and then representative to the General Assembly from Buncombe County the following year, defeating the incumbent Republican. In the Assembly Johnston served on the judiciary and finance committees, and was named chairman of the House Committee on Constitutional Reform and one of the managers in the house of the impeachment of Governor William W. Holden. In the finance committee he drew up the bill that finally settled the state debt, although the bill was not passed by the senate for a few sessions. In 1872, he was reelected and was named to the Electoral College as a Greeley delegate. Two years later he did not seek reelection, but in 1876 he won a seat in the state senate from Buncombe and Madison counties, having run on a platform calling for the swift completion of the Western North Carolina Railroad. After only one term in the senate he returned to his private law practice.

In 1884 Johnston received the nomination for the Ninth District congressional seat being vacated by R. B. Vance, and was elected over Hamilton G. Ewart of Hendersonville. He was reelected two years later, but was defeated by Ewart in 1888. In Congress, his major accomplishment was to get a federal appropriation for the building of the federal courthouse in Asheville.

After his defeat, Johnston practiced law and stayed out of politics. On only one occasion did he speak out on a political matter and that was to denounce the government's proposal to repudiate the bonds that supported the building of the Spartanburg-Asheville Railroad.

On 10 July 1879 Johnston married Leila Bobo of Spartanburg, S.C., and they had two daughters: Leila Maie and Sarah Eugenia. He spent his last years in faltering health, which rapidly declined after the death of his wife in March 1902. He died three months later and was buried at Riverside Cemetery, Asheville.

SEE: John P. Arthur, *Western North Carolina: A History* (1914); Samuel A. Ashe, ed., *Biographical History of North Carolina*, vol. 7 (1907); *Asheville Citizen*, 30 Nov. 1886; *Asheville Daily Gazette*, 24 June 1902; *Biog. Dir. Am. Cong.* (1961); Jerome Dowd, *Sketches of Prominent Living North Carolinians* (1888); A. D. Smith, *Western North Carolina, Historical and Biographical* (1890).

MARTIN REIDINGER

Johnston, Thomas Pinkney (31 Oct. 1808–28 May 1883), pioneer Presbyterian missionary, was born in Rowan County, the son of William Smiley and Mary

Hall Johnston. He entered The University of North Carolina from Iredell County and was graduated in 1828. After studying at the Union Theological Seminary in Virginia from 1829 to 1832, he was licensed by the Presbyterian church in October 1832.

The first foreign missionary from the Synod of North Carolina, Johnston served in Trebizond, Turkey, for twenty years (1833–53). He was a home missionary of the Concord Presbytery and agent of the American Bible Society in Mississippi during the period 1854–59, and home missionary and colporteur in North Carolina from 1860 until 1882. His wife was Mary Ann Howe of Ohio. He died at the home of the Reverend J. H. Thornwell in Fort Mills, S.C., in the presence of his son, the Reverend F. H. Johnston.

SEE: Daniel L. Grant, *Alumni History of the University of North Carolina, 1795–1924* (1924); *Minutes of the Sixty-ninth Session of the Synod of North Carolina* (1883); L. L. Polk, *Handbook of North Carolina* (1879); E. C. Scott, *Ministerial Directory of the Presbyterian Church, U.S., 1861–1941* (1942).

WILLIAM S. POWELL

Johnston, William (1737–1785), merchant, land speculator, and Revolutionary patriot, was born in Harthwood, parish of Lochmaben, Shire of Annandale, in the south of Scotland, the son of Robert and Isabell Johnston. He was the great-nephew of North Carolina's royal governor, Gabriel Johnston, and the nephew of Samuel Johnston of Edenton, revolutionary and early state leader. By 1756 William Johnston was in North Carolina where he acquired 150 acres in Orange County. Soon afterwards he apparently was sheriff of Granville County and was a member of a commission named to divide St. John's Parish in that county and, with others, to erect public buildings in Bute County, which was formed from Granville. By 1767 he was living in Hillsborough where he served on the earliest board of commissioners. Johnston also acquired a plantation, Snow Hill, about fifteen miles northeast of the town, where he established a general store. After making Richard Bennehan a partner, his Little River Store served a large area of that part of the colony. In partnership with James Thackston, Johnston also opened a store in Hillsborough. In addition to these stores and his extensive farming interests, Johnston engaged in trade as far away as Wilmington and Cross Creek and operated gristmills on some of the swift creeks in the region.

During the Regulator uprising in Orange County, Johnston informed Governor William Tryon of conditions there, and he was referred to as a colonel. Although Johnston was given funds to be used in raising troops, there is nothing to suggest that he participated in military activity. Beginning about 1774 Johnston and other men, including Richard Henderson, became involved in land speculation when they acquired land across the mountains in the Tennessee and Kentucky area in violation of royal directives. They lost much of this land but received other land as compensation.

Johnston served as a member of the Hillsborough district committee of safety during the revolution and represented Hillsborough in the Provincial Congresses in the spring and winter of 1776. These two sessions drew up the Halifax Resolves calling for independence and prepared the state's first constitution. Johnston also was a member of a commission named to establish a gun factory in Hillsborough, and at Snow Hill he apparently produced gunpowder, lead, and rifle flints.

After the war Johnston acted privately as agent for Edmund Fanning of New York, formerly an unpopular colonial official in Orange County, but a man whom Johnston regarded as his friend. Johnston purchased Fanning's property scheduled for confiscation by the state and, in effect, saved it for Fanning.

Johnston's wife, Anne, ten years older than he, died at the age of 42 in February 1769, leaving a daughter. Johnston never remarried. The daughter, Amelia, later married Walter Alves and in about 1800 moved to Kentucky where she owned property inherited from her father. Johnston by his will granted freedom to his black servant woman, Esther, and made generous bequests to his widowed mother in Scotland and to other relatives living in England, Scotland, New York, and Virginia, as well as to his business partners.

SEE: Elizabeth Cometti, "Some Early Best Sellers in Piedmont North Carolina," *Journal of Southern History* 16 (Aug. 1950); William S. Powell, "William Johnston: Eighteenth-Century Entrepreneur," *The Durham Record* 1 (Fall 1983).

WILLIAM S. POWELL

Johnston, William (5 Mar. 1817–20 May 1896), attorney, was best known as a railroad builder and businessman of great frugality and sagacity; but, like many other public-spirited men of his day, he also was active intermittently in politics. Born on a farm in the lower Catawba valley near Cowans Ford in Lincoln (now Gaston) County, he was the son of Robert and Mary Reid Johnston whose union produced seven sons and five daughters. Both sides of the family were of Scottish descent; Johnston's paternal and maternal grandfathers, Colonel James Johnston and Captain John Reid, both had fought King George III and had served in the North Carolina Senate. Hard work and frugality were family characteristics. In later life William Johnston remembered fondly that when John Reid agreed to his parents' marriage he admonished Robert Johnston, the young suitor: "You make the money and Mary will take care of it." Apparently both parties to this union fulfilled their "duty" and inculcated the same spirit in their offspring.

After a bucolic boyhood Johnston received his first formal education from Robert G. Allison, who headed a nearby academy. Subsequently he attended The University of North Carolina, graduating in 1840, and was a member of the first law class conducted by Richmond M. Pearson at Richmond Hill—a school destined for fame. Admitted to the bar in 1842, he established a highly successful practice in Charlotte.

Although a competent and respected lawyer, Johnston was soon involved in building transportation systems. In the 1840s he headed the Charlotte and Taylorsville Plank Road Corporation. Under his direction some twenty-five miles of the road were built; but plank roads were beginning to be supplanted by railroads as a principal means of travel and transportation. In 1856 he abandoned his legal practice to become president of the Charlotte and South Carolina Railroad Company. He quickly demonstrated good management and fiscal acumen. The company's stock rose from $0.45 to par, thereby adding about $500,000 to the worth of the corporation. In 1859 Johnston also became president of the Atlantic, Tennessee, and Ohio Railroad Company, which was the culmination of an old idea to build a railroad from the Atlantic Ocean to the Ohio River. Construction of this privately financed venture began in

January 1861, and by March 1863 the link from Charlotte to Statesville had been completed. Meanwhile, however, Johnston's attention and energy had been diverted as the South turned to secession and war.

Johnston had been only incidentally interested in politics prior to 1861. By conviction and practice a Union Whig—but always an ardent supporter of Southern rights, the events of the late 1850s and the election of Abraham Lincoln caused him to embrace secessionism. He received the unanimous vote of the Mecklenburg County electorate as a delegate to the Secession Convention. After his vigorous support of the secession ordinance, hoping that withdrawal could be accomplished peacefully, Johnston's most notable action in the convention was successful sponsorship of a measure to relieve Hebrews of political disabilities under the constitution of 1835. When he learned that Jews were volunteering in Mecklenburg military units, his sense of justice required that he promote citizenship for this patriotic minority.

At the insistence of Governor John W. Ellis, Johnston, after resigning from the convention, reluctantly became commissary general of North Carolina with the rank of colonel. He served with distinction as the state prepared for war but resigned in the fall of 1861, believing that his direct management of his railroads would result in a more significant contribution to the Confederate cause. Upon the death of Ellis in 1862, Johnston—the candidate of the original Secessionists who had become hard-core Davis supporters—contested the governorship with Zebulon B. Vance, popular former Whig congressman and Unionist. Neither man canvassed the state, but the election elicited a vigorous newspaper response. Eleven journals supported Johnston and ten, Vance. The Johnston press denounced the youthful Vance as "anti-administration" and as the "Yankee" candidate; the Raleigh *Register*, a Confederate party organ, warned that his election would be construed "as an indispensable sign that the Union sentiment is in the ascendancy in the heart of the Southern Confederacy." Vance replied that he favored prosecution of the war "at all hazards and to the utmost extremity so long as the foot of an invader pressed the Southern soil." Colonel Vance, still commanding the Twenty-sixth North Carolina Regiment in Virginia, won an overwhelming victory. He carried 68 of the 80 counties and was elected by a vote of 54,423 to 20,448. The outcome of the election was not an accurate measure of Johnston's public repute, but rather reflected the unpopularity of the Confederate party and the public confidence and approbation enjoyed by Vance.

Despite his humiliating defeat, Johnston responded with characteristic efficiency and devotion to duty. He worked diligently to keep the Charlotte and South Carolina Railroad open as a means of transporting men and supplies vital to the Confederacy. By 1863 he had completed the forty-six mile link from Charlotte to Statesville in the ambitious plans of the Atlantic, Tennessee, and Ohio; but, as the plight of the Confederacy became desperate, he permitted that road to be cannibalized so that other routes could be kept operable. (He considered his work so important that in 1864 he declined President Davis's request that he become commissary general of Confederate armies.) When Wilmington, the last port on the East Coast open to blockade-runners, fell early in 1865, Johnston proposed to build a railroad from Augusta to Columbia in order to improve and shorten interior lines between the beleaguered armies of Robert E. Lee and Joseph E. Johnston. Although he raised one million dollars in Confederate script for the project, it was too late—the days of the Confederate States of America were numbered. In February 1865, William T. Sherman's advancing armies destroyed 60 of the 110 miles of track belonging to the Columbia and South Carolina. Bridges, depots, shops, and rolling stock as well as about one thousand bales of company cotton were burned or confiscated. Johnston succeeded in saving an additional one thousand bales of cotton, which was the company's only tangible asset.

Whereas historians have generally assumed that the federal government rebuilt many miles of devastated southern railroads during Reconstruction, the expenditures on behalf of the Charlotte and South Carolina were negligible. Undeterred, the energetic Johnston undertook what seemed an impossible task. With approximately $170,000 from the sale of cotton as company capital, he sought private subscriptions to rebuild a railroad through a devastated, pauperized countryside. In part, confidence in Johnston himself caused a favorable public response. In 1866, the road from Charlotte to Columbia reopened; and, despite the determined opposition of the monopolistic South Carolina Railroad Company, he also built the eighty-five mile Columbia to Augusta line at a cost of two million dollars in greenbacks, all secured by public subscription. The two lines merged to form the Charlotte, Columbia, and Augusta Railroad. In June 1871 the rebuilt railroad from Charlotte to Statesville reopened, again largely due to Johnston's efforts. No other man in the South had built or rebuilt more railroad mileage with private financing.

In 1873, Johnston retired from railroad management and turned his attention to his extensive personal and business interests in and near Charlotte. A charter member of the Commercial National Bank of Charlotte, he was frequently an adviser or director of other important financial and industrial enterprises. He served four terms as mayor of Charlotte (1875, 1876, 1877, and 1885) and, untrammeled by partisan considerations, promoted community advancement without regard to party. He was an unsuccessful congressional candidate in several elections, probably because his aggressive manner and reserved demeanor generated some enemies and more respect than popularity among his advocates.

In 1846 Johnston married Ann Eliza Graham (1826–81), the only child of Dr. George Franklin and Martha Ann Harris Graham. Dr. Graham (1794–1827) was a son of Joseph Graham; he abandoned Lincoln County for Memphis, Tenn., where he practiced medicine. The Johnstons had four children: Julia Martin (1846–1915), Frank Graham (1848–1916), Mary Cora (1852–1901), and William R. (1854–1922).

SEE: Samuel A. Ashe, ed., *Biographical History of North Carolina*, vol. 1 (1905), and *Cyclopedia of Eminent and Representative Men of the Carolinas of the Nineteenth Century*, vol. 2 (1892); W. A. Graham Clark, *Descendants of James Graham (1714–1763) of Ireland and Pennsylvania* (12 Oct. 1940); Charles L. Price, "Railroads and Reconstruction in North Carolina, 1865–1871" (Ph.D. diss., University of North Carolina, Chapel Hill, 1959); Raleigh *News and Observer*, 21 May 1896; William L. Sherrill, *Annals of Lincoln County, North Carolina* (1937).

MAX R. WILLIAMS

Jonas, Charles Andrew (14 Aug. 1876–25 May 1955), attorney, state senator and representative, congressman, and Republican party official, was born near Lin-

colnton, the son of Cephas and Martha Scronce Jonas who were transient tenant farmers. He attended public schools in Lincoln and Cleveland counties; and, after completing high school, he taught in the Lincoln County public schools for six years.

In debt throughout his school career, Jonas worked at small jobs to pay his way through The University of North Carolina. During his freshman year he won the Dialectic Society debaters' medal and as a junior was awarded the Intersociety medal for best debater. Finishing a four-year curriculum in three years, Jonas was graduated with honors in 1902 and several months later married Rosa Petrie, also from Lincoln County. He became a member of the board of trustees of The University of North Carolina in 1917.

After graduation, Jonas taught in the Winston public schools for one year. Between 1903 and 1906 he was the first superintendent of graded schools in Mount Holly and then headed a boarding school in Dallas. During these four years, he completed work at The University of North Carolina Law School, was admitted to the bar, and began a practice in Lincolnton in 1906.

Jonas was instrumental in founding the *Lincoln Times*, a newspaper first published in 1903, and later became its editor. He was postmaster of Lincolnton from 1907 to 1910 and then briefly city attorney. He first ran for elective office in 1912 as the Republican candidate for state senator in Lincoln and Catawba counties, but lost the race by a large number of votes.

On his second try for the state senate in 1914, Jonas was successful and was reelected in 1916. In 1918, 1926, and 1934 he was elected to separate terms in the state house of representatives. From 1921 to 1925 he was assistant district attorney for the Western District of North Carolina. Beginning in 1927 he served for fifteen years as Republican national committeeman, and he was a delegate from North Carolina to four Republican National conventions (1916, 1928–36). In 1928 Jonas was elected to a single term in Congress, serving from 1929 to 1931. He was defeated in the 1930, 1932, and 1942 congressional elections.

Following his defeat in 1930, Jonas was named U.S. district attorney for Western North Carolina and held the post for one year under recess appointment. Just before his appointment, Jonas had alleged that proper investigations had not been made into possibly fraudulent North Carolina elections. As a result, Senator Cameron A. Morrison, a North Carolina Democrat, objected to the nomination and Jonas's appointment was rejected.

Jonas was an outstanding Republican from a Democratic state. While in the North Carolina Senate, he introduced a woman suffrage bill applying only to school elections. In the senate in 1917 and again in the house in 1935, he introduced bills for better enforcement of prohibition laws in North Carolina. Jonas was active in securing passage of the congressional bill to establish the Kings Mountain Military Park. He also helped consolidate the North Carolina and South Carolina postal accounting offices, establishing the new location in his own district. In addition, he helped obtain appropriations of approximately $500,000 for a postal annex in Charlotte. He was a vocal advocate of tariff protection.

After several years of failing health, Jonas died in Charlotte. His wife died in 1962. Jonas was survived by three children: Celeste Gibson; Charles R., a congressman; and Donald. He was buried in Hollybrook Cemetery at the First Methodist Church, Lincolnton.

SEE: M. S. Beam, "A Biographical Sketch," *Charlotte News*, 31 Oct. 1918; *Biog. Dir. Am. Cong.* (1971); *Charlotte Observer*, 27 May 1955; Daniel L. Grant, *Alumni History of the University of North Carolina, 1795–1924* (1924); *Greensboro Daily News*, 26 May 1955; E. F. Mullen, "He's Bob's Opponent," *The State* 6 (16 July 1938 [portrait]); Raleigh *News and Observer*, 20 Feb. 1932, 18 Mar. 1944, 26 May 1955.

MARY A. BAKER

Jones, Alexander (14 Oct. 1802–22 Aug. 1863), physician, author, and journalist, was born in Rowan County, the son of Samuel Jones, a planter and schoolteacher who guided his son's early education. In 1818 young Jones went to live with his brother, Dabney, in Washington, Ga., where he was employed as a store clerk. Deciding that he wanted to become a physician, Jones began studying under a Dr. Dunn in Lexington, Ga. In the fall of 1820 he entered the medical school of the University of Pennsylvania. Soon after he was graduated in 1822, his father died and his estate was to be equally divided among seven children. Alexander, thinking that the shares allotted to his two sisters were insufficient to ensure their proper support and education, relinquished his portion to them.

Immediately after the settling of his father's estate, Jones and a fellow student sailed from New York City for Savannah, Ga., where Jones practiced medicine until 1837. In 1823 he was made an honorary member of the Georgia Medical Society, and two years later he was named dean of the Board of Medical Examiners of Georgia. In 1826–27 he served as secretary of the Central Medical Society of Georgia. In 1831 Jones asked the Georgia legislature for funds to enable him to complete a history of Georgia that had been begun by Joseph V. Beven in 1824. The appropriation was not passed and the project died.

During his residence in Georgia, Jones became interested in cotton culture and subsequently made several improvements in the cotton gin which were successfully adopted in the South. In 1840 the British East India Company sought to employ him and several other Americans to help establish a profitable cotton culture in India. These men went first to England, but, shortly before arrangements for sailing to India were completed, Jones decided that it would not be patriotic to contribute to the expansion of a crop that would compete with an important southern staple. He refused the $6,000 annual salary, plus expenses, offered by the British government, but not before providing a Parliamentary committee with information concerning American cotton culture. At least some of the other men went to India; it was reported, however, that the project failed because the "Hindoos" did not work well and they observed too many religious holidays to permit proper attention to the cotton fields.

Soon after returning from England, Jones settled in New York because the southern climate adversely affected his health. Under the pseudonym "Sandy Hook," he served as a correspondent for the New York *Journal of Commerce* as well as for several British newspapers. In 1846 Jones wrote the first news story to be transmitted by telegraph from New York to Washington, D.C.; it dealt with the launching of the *Albany*, a U.S. sloop of war, at the Brooklyn Navy Yard. He quickly grasped the importance of the telegraph in transmitting news reports. By 1847 a cipher code that he developed was used effectively to reduce the cost of transmitting news by telegraph. In an attempt to prevent telegraph operators from monopolizing the distribution of news by providing their services only to the highest bidder, six New York newspapers formed a cooperative news service. Jones became the first general agent for this organization, which later developed into the New York Associated Press. At his small office at 10 Wall Street, Jones received dispatches from the telegraph terminal in Jersey City and forwarded them to member newspapers. After three years in this position, he resigned in May 1851.

Also in 1851 Jones published two books: *Historical Sketch of the Electric Telegraph*, a detailed account of the history of the telegraph from the discovery of electricity to the organization of the New York Associated Press; and *Cuba in 1851*, an exposition of the trade advantages to be gained by the annexation of Cuba. From 1851 until his death twelve years later, Jones was a commercial reporter for the New York *Herald*.

Concurrent with his journalistic career, Jones continued to practice medicine. As an outstanding member of St. David's Society in New York, he pursued his interest in the history and welfare of the Welsh people. He was the author of *The Cymry of '76: Or Welshmen and Their Descendants of the American Revolution*, published in 1855. Jones died in New York after a year's illness. Following funeral services in St. Alban's Episcopal Church, he was buried in Greenwood Cemetery, Brooklyn. A lengthy, front-page obituary in the New York *Herald* made no mention of a wife, children, or other family.

SEE: Victor H. Bassett, "Two Physicians and Two Periods in the Medical History of Georgia," *Journal of the Medical Association of Georgia* 29 (1940); *DAB*, vol. 10; F. B. Marbut, *News from the Capital: The Story of Washington Reporting* (1971); New York *Herald*, 26 Aug. 1863; Victor Rosewater, *History of Cooperative News Gathering in the United States* (1930); Preston Wheeler, *American Biographies* (1940); *Who Was Who in America*, Historical Volume (1967).

JOAN J. HALL

Jones, Alexander Hamilton (21 July 1822–29 Jan. 1901), newspaper editor and Republican congressman, was born in Buncombe County near Asheville where he received his early education. He explained that during his youth he taught himself "to love the Union next to my God" by reading the lives of George Washington and other national heroes as well as the history of the United States. After his early schooling, he attended Emory and Henry College.

In 1843 Jones married Sarah D. Brittain (by whom he had five children—Charlotte, Julia, Hester, Thadeus, and Otto) and settled on a farm. After service in the War with Mexico, he developed rheumatism and his doctor advised him to give up farming. Therefore, in 1851 he moved with his family to Hendersonville and became a merchant. From this career Jones earned a modest living, owning $700 in real property and $9,000 in personal property in 1860. In that year, business circumstances led him into politics. While administrator of the Hendersonville *Times*, he was asked to fill the unexpired term of the editor. In this capacity he expressed his Whig philosophy, extolling the virtues of the Union and condemning secessionist efforts.

In 1861 Jones assumed a role in the campaign against calling a convention to vote on secession. He was a candidate for a seat in the convention but was not chosen.

During the Civil War he helped form a secret Union League, whose members pledged never to fight against the Union. He also wrote many articles under fictitious names, charging that the Confederates were traitors, that secession was achieved by undemocratic methods, and that the war was a rich man's cause and a poor man's fight. In 1862 he was an unsuccessful candidate for the state legislature as a Union man.

By 1863 Unionists in western North Carolina, including Jones, were forming companies to protect themselves against Confederate conscription officers. But Jones felt more had to be done, and on 31 Aug. 1863 he left for eastern Tennessee to join the Union Army. Arriving in Knoxville in early September, he reported to generals Samuel Carter and A. E. Burnside. From them, he received authorization to raise a regiment of North Carolina volunteers. However, just as he was starting his recruiting efforts, Jones was captured by the Confederates and spent many months imprisoned in Asheville, at Camp Vance, at Camp Holmes, and then at Libby Prison in Richmond. Finally, to win his release, he volunteered to serve in the Confederate Army. But in November 1864 he escaped from prison without fighting for the Confederacy. Jones made his way to Maryland and reported to the Federal officer in charge of the army stationed there. After being transported around by the army, he arrived back in Knoxville on 1 Mar. 1865. A month later the war ended without Jones having served officially in either army. (His name does not appear in either the Confederate or Union service records.)

On returning home to Hendersonville, Jones became active in Reconstruction politics, calling for the return of peace and harmony as well as for legal equality for blacks. He served in North Carolina's 1865 constitutional convention which abolished slavery, declared the ordinance of secession null and void, and repudiated the state's Confederate debt. In the same year he was elected to Congress from the Seventh Congressional District. Jones was the only congressman from North Carolina elected in 1865 who could take the then required test oath. However, along with the other Southern congressmen-elect, he was not permitted to take his seat.

In 1866 Jones established the *Henderson Pioneer*. As the paper's editor, he spoke for the Union and against Governor Jonathan Worth, for the common man and against the old slaveholding class. He also advocated internal improvements, including the construction of railroads, the encouragement of home manufacturing, and the development of mineral and other resources. He supported ratification of the Fourteenth Amendment and legal and political equality for blacks. In 1866 Jones served as a delegate to the Loyalist Convention, which met in Philadelphia. By 1867, he and his paper sided completely with the congressional Republicans' reconstruction policies. Jones became a charter member of North Carolina's Union League and an active politician in the Republican party. In July 1867 he moved his newspaper to Asheville, where it continued as a Republican paper under Jones's editorship until he turned to a new career the following year.

In July 1868, Jones was elected to Congress. After serving two terms (6 July 1868–3 Mar. 1871) in the Fortieth and Forty-first Congresses, he was defeated for reelection in 1870 when the Democrats swept the state. Jones remained in Washington until 1876; he then resided in Maryland until 1884, in Asheville until 1890, and in Oklahoma until 1897. In the latter year he moved to Long Beach, Calif., where he died and was buried in Signal Hill Cemetery.

SEE: *Appleton's Cyclopedia of American Biography*, vol. 3 (1888); J. P. Arthur, *Western North Carolina History* (1914); *Asheville Pioneer*, 1867–88; *Biog. Dir. Am. Cong.* (1950); B. S. Hedrick Papers (Duke University Library, Durham); *Henderson Pioneer*, 1866–67; A. H. Jones, *Knocking at the Door* (1866; pamphlet in the North Carolina Collection, University of North Carolina Library, Chapel Hill); James L. Lancaster, *The Scalawags of North Carolina, 1850–1868* (1976).

ROBERTA SUE ALEXANDER

Jones, Allen (24 Dec. 1739–10 Nov. 1798), colonial and state official and Revolutionary War officer, was born in Edgecombe (now Halifax County), the son of Robert ("Robin") Jones, colonial attorney general, and his wife, Sarah Cobb. Like his father, Allen was educated at Eton College in England. He was clerk of Superior Court for the Halifax district and from 1773 to 1775 represented Northampton County in the Assembly. By 1775 he actively opposed royal power in the colonies as a member of the Committee of Safety for Halifax. The following year Jones served as vice-president of the Provincial Congress that met at Halifax on 4 Apr. 1776. In that body he presided over or participated on the committee to empower North Carolina delegates in the Continental Congress to concur with those of other colonies in declaring independence, the committee to provide for the national defense, and the committee to establish a temporary form of government.

In 1778 Jones presided over the North Carolina Senate as speaker. He was a delegate to the Continental Congress meeting at Philadelphia in 1779–80. In 1782 he served as a member of the North Carolina Council of State, and in the years 1783, 1784, and 1787 he again represented Northampton County in the state senate.

As a man of military acumen, Jones professed to know little about the role he played. In a letter to Governor Richard Caswell on 8 Sept. 1777, he wrote: "I do not know whether my return is proper, for I confess my ignorance in military affairs." Nevertheless, the Halifax Congress had seen fit to name him a brigadier general on 22 Apr. 1776. He did have some military experience, however, for in 1771 he had assisted in the suppression of the Regulators at the Battle of Alamance. During the American Revolution he saw action in the fall of 1780, when for a time his forces were combined with those of General Horatio Gates.

Allen Jones had an equally prominent brother, Willie, who also took part in the Revolution. Surprisingly, the political views of the two men diverged after the war. Allen became a staunch Federalist, whereas Willie advocated states' rights.

Jones was married first, on 21 June 1762, to Mary Haynes; his second wife, whom he married on 3 Sept. 1768, was Rebecca Edwards, the sister of Isaac Edwards, formerly secretary to Governor William Tryon; and his third wife was a Miss Eaton. His son, Robin, died suddenly at age eight; his daughter, Sarah, married William R. Davie. Jones died and was buried at Mount Gallant, his plantation in Northampton County.

SEE: Samuel A. Ashe, ed., *Biographical History of North Carolina*, vol. 4 (1906); *Biog. Dir. Am. Cong.* (1961); Fairfax Braxton, "Patriots of North Carolina," *National Republic* (17 Apr. 1930); John L. Cheney, Jr., ed., *North*

Carolina Government, 1585–1974 (1975); John H. Wheeler, *Historical Sketches of North Carolina from 1584 to 1851* (1851) and ed., *Reminiscences and Memoirs of North Carolina and Eminent North Carolinians* (1884); *Who Was Who in America*, vol. 1 (1963).

TIMOTHY L. HOWERTON

Jones, Andrew Jackson *(1826–ca. 1 Apr. 1873)*, legislator, financier, and railroad president, was probably the son of William Jones of Bladen County. In the 1850 census he was recorded as a twenty-four-year-old farmer in that county. Little is known of his early life, but he later lived in Whiteville. Jones was active in state politics, representing Columbus County in the House of Commons in 1854–55 and in the North Carolina Senate for the sessions of 1865–66, 1868–69, and 1869–70. During most of the Civil War he acted as a purchasing agent for the Confederate government, procuring horses and mules for use by the army, yet he claimed after the war never to have lifted a hand against the Federal government. In January 1866 he declined appointment as U.S. treasury assessor for the Fayetteville District, but as a member of the General Assembly in 1869 his chief concerns were railroads, banking, and other corporate legislation, as well as a relentless pursuit of his own personal interests.

Jones came to be best known for his involvement in several sensational scandals between 1865 and 1871. In the former year he and State Treasurer William Sloan defrauded the state by selling state-owned cotton for their own benefit. Jones was later forced to return his share of the proceeds. He was also closely associated with George W. Swepson and the state's railroad "ring."

Despite his reputation for dishonesty, Jones was elected president of the Western Railroad in April 1869. During his two years in that position he squandered the greater part of $1,320,000 in special tax bonds, appropriated by the legislature for improving the Western Railroad. Some of this he lost in a notorious gambling binge in New York during the summer of 1869, but most was lost by his improvident speculation that fall. Jones, Swepson, and others pooled their respective companies' resources to control and drive up the value of their railroad bonds for personal gain. They were holding large amounts of these bonds when the market collapsed in the panic of September 1869.

Reports of this activity soon reached the legislature, and the Bragg Committee, in 1870, and the Shipp Commission, in 1871, were established to investigate. Jones was completely discredited in these proceedings, and he was replaced as president of the railroad. By November 1871, he was under criminal indictment in Cumberland and Moore counties for fraud and for failure to account to his successor for his railroad's tax bonds. In 1872 he was convicted in both cases and sentenced to prison. Both verdicts were appealed to the North Carolina Supreme Court; one was reversed on a technicality. Jones died in the spring of 1873 before the second case was heard. He apparently was survived by at least one son, Andrew J., Jr.

SEE: Wanda S. Campbell, *Abstracts of Wills of Bladen County, 1734–1900* (1962); Jonathan Daniels, *Prince of Carpetbaggers* (1958); Fayetteville *Eagle*, 8 Apr., 19 Aug. 1869; J. G. de R. Hamilton, *Reconstruction in North Carolina* (1941) and ed., *The Correspondence of Jonathan Worth*, 2 vols. (1909); *New York Times*, 5 Mar. 1872, 24 May 1873; *North Carolina Biography*, vol. 5 (1941); *North Carolina Legislative Documents, 1865–66* (Document 13);

Charles L. Price, "Railroads and Reconstruction in North Carolina, 1865–1871" (Ph.D. diss., University of North Carolina, 1959); Raleigh *Sentinel*, 26 Feb., 3 Mar. 1869, 6, 12 Mar. 1872, 26 Jan. 1873; *Report of the Commission to Investigate Fraud and Corruption under Act of Assembly: Session 1871–72* (1872); *Report of the Railroad Investigation Commission* (1871); Salisbury *Carolina Watchman*, 5 Apr. 1873; George W. Swepson Papers (North Carolina State Archives, Raleigh).

WILLIAM D. TITCHENER

Jones, Aquilla *(8 July 1811–12 July 1891)*, businessman and public official, was born near Salem in Stokes (now Forsyth) County, the son of Benjamin and Mary Jones of Welsh descent. In 1831 the family moved to Columbus, Ind., where another son, Elisha P., had been established for several years as a merchant. Aquilla became a clerk in the store and remained until August 1836, when he moved to Missouri for a year. Returning to Columbus, Aquilla operated a hotel briefly when, at the death of his brother, he acquired the store which he continued until 1856. He also succeeded his brother as postmaster and soon became a member of the first Columbus school board. As a large stockholder in 1849, he became president of the Columbus Bridge Co. and superintended the construction of a bridge across the White River.

Jones's political service included census taker and legislator (1842–43); he declined a presidential appointment as Indian agent for the Washington Territory as well as for New Mexico. In 1844 he was a delegate to the Democratic National Convention, and during the period 1850–52 he published the *Columbus Democrat*. He was elected state treasurer in 1856 but chose not to stand for reelection because he disagreed with the Democratic party's stand on slavery. On election to state office, he moved to Indianapolis and there became treasurer and afterwards president of the Indianapolis Rolling-Mill; he also served as treasurer of the Gatling Gun Co., president of the municipal waterworks, and postmaster.

As a young man Jones rose to the rank of major in the Indiana militia and during the Civil War served for less than two weeks with the 107th Regiment, Indiana Volunteers, in 1863.

In 1836 Jones married Sarah Ann Arnold, who died a year later. He married Harriet Cox in 1840, and they were the parents of ten children: Elisha P., John W., Emma, Benjamin F., Charles, Aquilla Q., Edwin S., William M. Frederick, Harriet, and Mary. A member of St. Paul's Episcopal Church, Jones died at his home in Indianapolis.

SEE: *Biographical Directory of the Indiana General Assembly* (1980); *A Biographical History of Eminent & Self-Made Men of the State of Indiana* (1880); Columbus (Ind.) *Evening Republican*, 13 July 1891; B. R. Sulgrove, *History of Indianapolis and Marion County* (1884 [engraving]); Stephen B. Weeks Scrapbook, vol. 6 (North Carolina Collection, University of North Carolina Library, Chapel Hill).

WILLIAM S. POWELL

Jones, Armistead *(23 Sept. 1846–24 Sept. 1925)*, lawyer, was born in Vance County, the son of Protheus Epps Armistead and Mary Francis Hawkins Jones. Through his father he was descended from Matthew Jones who lived in Warwick County, Va., during the middle 1600s, and from the Armistead, Tabb, and West-ward families of Virginia. His mother was a daughter of John Davis and Jane Boyd Hawkins of Vance County.

Jones attended Horner School at Oxford, but early in the Civil War—at age sixteen—he enlisted in the Con-federate Army as a member of Moseley's Battery and served with that command until the fall of Fort Fisher in 1865. After the war he moved to Raleigh and, while supporting himself as a telegraph operator, studied law under Judge William H. Battle; he was licensed in 1870.

Settling in Raleigh, Jones practiced law first in part-nership with his brother, William Westwood, and later with his son, William Branch. For several years Armi-stead was attorney for Wake County, and in 1900 he was appointed solicitor for the Judicial District which then comprised Chatham, Johnston, Wayne, and Wake counties. He was elected to the latter office on two oc-casions and served for eleven years. Jones declined an appointment by Governor David Fowle to the Superior Court, preferring advocacy in the courtroom. He served as chairman of the Wake County Democratic Commit-tee for twenty years and was an outstanding figure in the political life of the state.

On 3 Jan. 1872 Jones married Nancy Haywood Branch, the daughter of Confederate General Lawrence O'Bryan Branch and his wife Nancy Haywood Blount. They had three children: Nancy Branch (m. Thomas Martin Ashe), Mary Armistead (m. Alfred McGhee Maupin), and William Branch (m. Mary Seaton Hay). Jones was an Episcopalian and a member of Christ Episcopal Church, Raleigh. He died in Raleigh where he was buried in Oakwood Cemetery.

SEE: Grady Lee Ernest Carroll, *The City of Raleigh, North Carolina, and the Civil War Experience* (1979); *Confederate Military History*, vol. 4 (1899); Ernest Haywood, *Some Notes in Regard to the Eminent Lawyers Whose Portraits Adorn the Walls of the Superior Court Room at Raleigh, North Carolina* (1936); North Carolina Bar Association, *Proceedings* (1899–1948); Beauregard C. Poland, *North Carolina's Glorious Victory, 1898* (1898).

ARMISTEAD JONES MAUPIN

Jones, Cadwallader (*17 Aug. 1813–1 Dec. 1899*), law-yer, legislator, planter, and Confederate officer, was born at Mount Gallant, the Northampton County home of his paternal grandfather, General Allen Jones. The son of Cadwallader and Rebecca Edwards Long Jones of West Hill near Hillsborough, he was graduated in 1832 from The University of North Carolina, of which he be-came a trustee (1840–57). Jones began his legal career in Hillsborough in 1836, and was elected to the North Carolina House of Commons as a Democrat for the 1840 and 1842 sessions. He resigned on 20 Apr. 1843 to become solicitor of the Fourth Judicial District but was returned to the General Assembly for the 1848 and 1850 sessions. For a time he also served as a U.S. magistrate.

In 1857 Jones moved his young family to a cotton plantation overlooking the Catawba Valley near Rock Hill, S.C. His father had bought the 5,000-acre estate, also named Mount Gallant, in 1810, but it had re-mained unoccupied by the family during subsequent years. Jones represented South Carolina at the Rich-mond Democratic Convention of 1860 which nominated John C. Breckinridge for president.

On 13 Aug. 1861 Jones accepted a commission as cap-tain in the Confederate Army so that a local volunteer company could be raised. His first engagement was at Hilton Head in 1861, and he continued to fight in many of the well-known battles of the early years of the war: Mechanicsville, Malvern Hill, Second Manassas, and the Seven Days Campaign before Richmond. After the Battle of Sharpsburg in 1862, he was promoted to colo-nel in the Twelfth South Carolina Volunteers. Poor health forced him to resign from Gregg's Brigade before the end of the war, but he left four sons in the army: First Lieutenant Iredell Jones, who was stationed at Fort Sumter; Captain Cadwallader Jones, Jr., and Private Al-len Jones, who served in the same company as their fa-ther; and Johnstone Jones, who had been a cadet at the Citadel and enlisted in the Confederate Army at age fif-teen with the Arsenal Cadets of Columbia.

Soon after Jones's return home from the war, he was elected York District's representative to the South Caro-lina Senate. In 1865 he was a delegate to the state con-stitutional convention called to repeal the secession or-dinance, free the slaves, repudiate the war debt, and draw up a new constitution. Like other slaveholders, Jones was financially ruined by the war. He continued to plant cotton but lost money every year and was forced to sell off his land piece by piece until nothing was left of Mount Gallant.

On 5 Jan. 1836 Jones married Annie Isabella Iredell, the daughter of Governor James Iredell. They had ten children, nine of whom lived to maturity. In addition to the four sons who served in the war, there were two younger sons, Halcott Pride and Wilie (or Willie), who was later a brigadier general in the South Carolina state militia. The four daughters were Frances Iredell (Er-win); Rebecca Cadwallader, who died in her youth; An-nie Isabella (Robertson); and Helen Iredell (Coles). De-spite his poor health in middle age, Jones lived to the age of eighty-six and was the author, in the year of his death, of *A Genealogical History*. An Episcopalian, he died of natural causes in Columbia, S.C., at the home of his daughter Annie Robertson.

SEE: Battle Family Papers (Southern Historical Collec-tion, University of North Carolina Library, Chapel Hill); Douglas S. Brown, *A City without Cobwebs—Rock Hill, S.C.* (1953); John L. Cheney, Jr., ed., *North Carolina Gov-ernment, 1585–1974* (1975); Augusta B. Fothergill, *Peter Jones and Richard Jones Genealogies* (1924); Daniel L. Grant, *Alumni History of the University of North Carolina, 1795–1924* (1924); Cadwallader Jones, *A Genealogical History* (1899); Cadwallader Jones, Jr., Papers (South-ern Historical Collection, University of North Carolina Library, Chapel Hill); *Rock Hill* (S.C.) *Herald*, 2 Dec. 1899; *The State* (Columbia, S.C.), 2 Dec. 1899; John H. Wheeler, ed., *Reminiscences and Memoirs of North Carolina and Eminent North Carolinians* (1884).

BRENDA MARKS EAGLES

Jones, Calvin (*2 Apr. 1775–20 Sept. 1846*), physician, politician, and newspaper publisher, was born near Sheffield, Mass. His father, Ebenezer Jones, was of Welsh ancestry, a descendant of Thomas Ap Jones, who arrived in Massachusetts in 1651. His mother was a de-scendant of William Blackmore, who came from En-gland in 1665. Both parents were interested in their children's education, and Calvin apparently studied in the local schools and certainly read widely, but there is no evidence that he attended a college or university. It is likely that he apprenticed himself at about age four-teen to a local physician practicing in the Berkshires, and it is certain that in 1792, when he was seventeen, he received a certificate from the United Medical Society (now the Litchfield County Medical Association of Connecticut) which entitled him to practice medicine.

For some time Jones practiced in Freehold, N.Y., and there published *A Treatise on the Scarlet Fever, or Canker-Rash*; its preface was dated 10 Dec. 1793. In 1795 he moved to Smithfield, N.C., where he practiced for about eight years. In 1799 he was one of the small group of physicians who organized the first North Carolina Medical Society, serving as corresponding secretary during its five years of existence. Jones was also influential in the introduction of vaccination for smallpox in the state. The Raleigh *Register* for 11 Mar. 1800 contained a notice that he would inoculate against smallpox in April, but this was postponed to the following year. In 1801 he published in the *Register* a long letter on Jenner's vaccination for smallpox, which he urged physicians and the public to accept instead of the inoculation procedure. In 1799 and 1802, he was a member of the North Carolina House of Commons from Johnston County.

About 1803 Jones moved to Raleigh and became involved in various activities in addition to medicine. In 1807 he was elected to the House of Commons from Wake County. In association with Thomas Henderson he edited and published the Raleigh *Star* for several years, served as mayor (then called intendent of police) of Raleigh, and was active in the Masonic Order. In 1817 and 1819 he was Grand Master of Masons in North Carolina. Jones also served as adjutant general of the state militia for five years, including the period of the War of 1812. He invested in land, both in North Carolina and in Tennessee.

Jones continued his medical practice, read widely in scientific journals, published several articles between 1808 and 1819, and, while living in Wake Forest, taught several medical students. He was particularly interested in ophthalmology and became well known for his skill in removing cataracts. In addition to his interest in medical education, Jones served as a trustee of the Raleigh Academy and from 1802 to 1832 as a trustee of The University of North Carolina, to which he donated books for its library and his collection of "artificial and natural curiosities." In 1832 he sold Wake Forest, his 615-acre plantation near Raleigh, to the Baptist State Convention, and it became the site of Wake Forest College. At this time he moved to Bolivar, in West Tennessee, where he owned much land, and built a home, Pontine. The state of Tennessee bought his estate, where it built the Western Hospital for the Insane.

While living in Raleigh, Jones had been engaged to Ruina J. Williams, who died of tuberculosis in 1809. In 1819 he married her sister, Temperance Boddie Williams Jones, the widow of Dr. Thomas C. Jones. Their children were Montezuma (1822–1914); Octavia Rowena (1826–1917), who married Edward Polk of Bolivar; and Paul Tudor (1828–1904).

At one time there were three copies of Jones's portrait, the original of which hung in his home at Bolivar and later was taken by one of his descendants to Dallas, Tex. The copies were located at Wake Forest and in the Adjutant General's Office and the Grand Lodge Hall (Masonic) in Raleigh. The one at Wake Forest was later destroyed by fire.

SEE: S. R. Bruesch, "Calvin Jones, 1775–1846," *Bulletin of the History of Medicine*, vol. 31 (1957); M. D. Haywood, *Calvin Jones: Physician, Soldier, and Freemason, 1775–1846* (1919); Calvin Jones Papers (Southern Historical Collection, University of North Carolina Library,

Chapel Hill); D. Long, "Notes on the History of the Medical Society," *North Carolina Medical Journal* 15 (1954).

DOROTHY LONG

Jones, Edmund (15 Apr. 1848–25 Feb. 1920), soldier, attorney, and public servant, was born into a life of ease on his father's plantation, Clover Hill, situated about six miles north of Lenoir in Caldwell County. The family name has long been associated with the settlement of the upper Yadkin Valley and the development of a stable government there. He was the son of Sophia C. Davenport and Edmund Walter Jones, who spent his entire life at Clover Hill. Both his grandfathers, General Edmund Jones and Colonel William Davenport, were military heroes and men of distinction and honor in the area.

Jones's early background of luxury and refinement provided him with many advantages, including the best of scholastic training. After attending Bingham Military School, he entered The University of North Carolina but left in 1864, at age sixteen, to enlist as a private in Company F, Forty-first North Carolina Infantry, of the Confederate Army. Before he was seventeen Jones took part in the siege of Petersburg. Later he participated in General Wade Hampton's Raid, in which 2,500 cattle were captured from Ulysses Grant and brought behind Confederate lines. He remained with his brigade during the final stages of the Civil War, never missing a day of duty. Late in the conflict, Jones was engaged in the fighting on the road to Appomattox. He was a member of the force of thirty to forty men who made their way through the Northern lines to carry to President Jefferson Davis the first official notice that General Robert E. Lee was going to surrender. Jones then reported to General P. G. T. Beauregard, and was told to go home and await further orders. His three brothers also served the Confederate cause: Colonel John T. Jones was killed at the Battle of the Wilderness on 6 May 1864, Captain Walter T. Jones was mortally wounded at Gettysburg, and Captain William Davenport Jones, a member of General Collet Leventhorpe's staff, was also wounded.

After the war Edmund Jones reentered The University of North Carolina; he was enrolled from 1865 to 1868 but did not graduate. (The university subsequently awarded him the A.B. degree in 1911.) In 1868 he entered the law department of the University of Virginia, where he studied under John B. Minor. He then returned to Clover Hill in Caldwell County to farm and to start a political career.

In 1870, at age twenty-two, Jones was elected to the General Assembly. Serving from 1870 to 1872, he was a member of the legislature during the impeachment of Governor William W. Holden. In 1879 he served another term in the house. In 1881, Jones read law under Colonel George W. Folk, took the required examination, and was licensed to practice. He opened a law office at Lenoir and quickly rose to prominence in his profession, assuming a leadership role in the bar of western North Carolina. In 1885 Jones was appointed by President Grover Cleveland to the post of chief of the Customs Division of the Treasury Department, where he served until 1889. When offered the position again in 1893, he declined it, as acceptance would have meant giving up his legal career. In the same year, he served a third term in the North Carolina House of Representatives.

In April 1898, at the outbreak of the Spanish-American War, Jones mustered Company C of the Second North Carolina Volunteer Infantry, U.S. Army. He was captain of the company until it was dissolved at the end of the war. During the conflict he was in command of Fort Marion in St. Augustine, Fla. There he organized a military prison, which was continued after the war.

In 1916 Jones was a candidate in the Democratic primary for the office of attorney general. He finished second but did not demand a second run-off to which he was entitled.

On 29 Oct. 1872 Jones married Eugenia Lewis in Raleigh, her hometown. The daughter of Major A. M. Lewis, she died leaving four children: Augustus, Edmund, Eugene Patterson, and Sarah D. Jones later married Martha Snell Scott, a native of Caldwell County. He was a lifelong Episcopalian.

SEE: E. Carl Anderson, *The Heritage of Caldwell County*, vol. 1 (1983); Kemp P. Battle, *History of the University of North Carolina*, vol. 1 (1907); *Confederate Military History*, vol. 4 (1899); Daniel L. Grant, *Alumni History of the University of North Carolina, 1795–1924* (1924); North Carolina Bar Association, *Proceedings*, vol. 22 (1920); *North Carolina Biography*, vol. 4 (1919); W. W. Scott, *Annals of Caldwell County* (1930).

JOE O'NEAL LONG

Jones, Edward (10 Mar. 1762–8 Aug. 1841), legislator and lawyer, was born in Lisburn, Ireland. He was the second son of Dr. Conway and Mary Wray Todd Jones and the brother of William Todd Jones, the Irish patriot. On his mother's side he was descended from Bishop Jeremy Taylor.

Although he received little formal schooling, Jones was brought up in an educated family. In early life he was apprenticed to a linen merchant with the expectation that he would enter that business. On completing his apprenticeship he left Ireland for America in 1783 and settled in Philadelphia, where for a few years he was engaged in the mercantile business. When the enterprise failed, Jones moved to Wilmington, N.C., in 1786; he again tried the mercantile business and again failed.

Shortly after arriving in Wilmington Jones attracted the attention of Archibald Maclaine, one of the leading jurists of the state, who encouraged him to study law and assisted him in doing so. By 1788 Jones had received his license to practice. He found the legal profession much more to his liking and made a successful career for himself in the field. After only two years' residence in Wilmington, he was elected the borough's representative in the North Carolina House of Commons. His rapid rise to popularity was due to his attractive personality and to the influence of Archibald Maclaine. Jones was reelected to the house for three additional terms (1789–91).

In 1790 the General Assembly created the office of solicitor general to assist the attorney general in prosecuting cases on the overcrowded dockets of the superior courts. The legislature elected John Haywood the first solicitor general, but he held the office for only a few months. On his resignation in 1791, Edward Jones was elected to succeed him. Jones remained in the position until 1827. In estimating his ability as a solicitor general, Chief Justice Frederick Nash, a contemporary, said that he was "a thorough criminal lawyer, and administered that branch of the law with an energy and independence which was felt and acknowledged by the whole community. Very few of his bills of indictment were ever complained of, and still fewer quashed." Governor Charles Manly observed that Jones "discriminated with remarkable success the just rights of the State and those belonging to the prisoner, never urging a conviction with intemperate zeal for the gratification of a petty triumph."

About 1801 Jones moved from Wilmington to Chatham County, where he lived for the remainder of his life. He built a home about eight miles west of Pittsboro which he named Rock Rest. From 1804 to 1841 he was a member of the board of trustees of The University of North Carolina. Jones was one of those who in 1793 had donated funds to the university. He also gave books to the institution's library.

In 1790 Jones married in Wilmington Mary Elizabeth Mallett (1773–1837), the daughter of Peter and Eunice Curtis Mallett. They had ten children, four of whom died in infancy. The others were Du Ponceau, named for a friend in Philadelphia, Peter S. Du Ponceau; Johnston Blakeley, named for Jones's protégé, Captain Johnston Blakeley; Charlotte (m. William H. Hardin); Frances (m. the Reverend William Hooper); Louise (m. Abraham Rencher); and Elizabeth (m. John Eccles).

A member of the Episcopal church, Jones was buried in the churchyard of St. Bartholomew's Church, Pittsboro.

SEE: Kemp P. Battle, *History of the University of North Carolina*, vol. 1 (1907); Joseph B. Cheshire, "The Office of Solicitor General of North Carolina," *North Carolina University Magazine* 13 (1894); William Hooper, "Biographical Sketch of Edward Jones Esq.," *North Carolina University Magazine* 5 (1856); Raleigh *North Carolina Standard*, 19 Aug. 1841; Royal G. Shannonhouse, ed., *History of St. Bartholomew's Parish, Pittsboro, N.C.* (1933); Tombstone, St. Bartholomew's churchyard (Pittsboro); John H. Wheeler, ed., *Reminiscences and Memoirs of North Carolina and Eminent North Carolinians* (1884).

LAWRENCE F. LONDON

Jones, Frederick (1680[?]–June[?] 1722), merchant, lawyer, and planter, was a member of that class of Virginians called by Carl Bridenbaugh "First Families of the Chesapeake," families often founded by sea captains such as Jones's father. Roger Jones (1625[?]–1701) of Nottinghamshire served as a captain in the British Navy in Ireland and the West Indies during and after the Interregnum, and became involved in mercantile activities and land acquisition which made him wealthy. He and his first wife, Dorothy Walker, daughter of Sir John Walker of Mansfield, Nottinghamshire, accompanied Lord Thomas Culpepper, with whom Captain Jones was associated, to Virginia. They resided at Green Springs (1680–85) with the governor while Jones built landholdings, made commercial contacts, and coasted for pirates under Culpepper's commission.

Frederick was born in England, whereas his younger brother, Thomas (169?–1758), may have been born in Virginia. Merchant activities typically based on consanguinity drew young Frederick into the affairs of the firm of his father and Julius Deeds, "Merchants of London," and made him a part of that circulating elite that moved easily between North Carolina and Virginia during the Proprietary period. Jones's first wife, Jane Harding, died in 1719, and he married Sarah, daughter of Major Samuel Swann, Sr., and granddaughter of Alexander Lillington, both Carolinians of note. Responsible for extending the family mercantile activities into North Carolina after his parents' return to England, Jones spent a good part of his efforts from 1700 to 1710 in prosecuting the interests of family and friends in the colony's courts. His litigation with Thomas Cary made him a natural member of the anti-Cary faction led by Thomas Pollock, with whom he became allied during the latter's self-imposed political exile in Virginia.

Jones, a vestryman of Bruton Parish and "Director of Building" in Williamsburg, added thousands of acres to the family holdings in Virginia. Nevertheless, by 1710 when he settled in Chowan Precinct he had already supplied the glebe lands for the precinct's parish, St. Paul's, and patented 27,500 acres in Carolina. His estates continued to grow until his death, by which time he had patented 35,150 acres including a 17,000-acre estate in Chowan in 1721. To his career as merchant-lawyer, he added those of planter and politician.

As a member of the faction headed by Thomas Pollock and William Glover, Jones was involved in the struggle with the opposing party of Thomas Cary and John Porter that resulted in the unsuccessful Cary's Rebellion against the newly formed Hyde government (1710). The continuation of this conflict can be seen in the opposition of Edward Moseley, Cary's nominal ally, and the Vail, Moore, and Lillington family connections to Governor Charles Eden and his Council, of which Jones was a member. It is further reflected in the opposition of the Assembly led by Moseley to Governor Burrington.

The ascendancy of the Hyde government backed by Pollock coincided with Jones's permanent residence in the colony. In 1711 he served in the Assembly, but after his plantation was devastated in the Tuscarora War (1711–13) he returned to Virginia, serving as a justice of the peace in James City County in 1714. The year 1715 marks the beginning of his rapid political preferment. Returning to North Carolina, he was appointed vestryman of the Eastern parish of Chowan, became a commissioner of the library of St. Thomas Parish, Pamtecough Precinct (Beaufort County), and sat in the Assembly in 1715. He also became the deputy of Lord Proprietor Joseph Blake in 1716, taking his seat in the Council and serving until 1729, during which time the Council tried the case against Tobias Knight and the crew of pirate Teach (1718). In addition, Jones was chief justice of the General Court (1718–21), in which capacity he presided at the trial and conviction of Moseley on charges of "high crimes and misdemeanors" for seizing the records of the secretary of the colony. Ironically, Jones and Moseley remained friends until the former's death. Jones also served the colony in special capacities—as inspector of the boundaries of the Chowan Indian lands, boundary commissioner in the dispute with Virginia, and inspector in the controversy over illegal lapsing of patents, all in 1718; and as inspector of the boundaries of the Tuscarora settlement on the Moratuck (Roanoke) River in 1721.

At his death Jones's will divided his land among his three minor sons, William Harding, Frederick, and Thomas, who were then attending William and Mary Grammar School and in the care of their uncle, the chief executor of the estate. The entail on these properties was broken in 1759 by Jones's grandsons, Frederick and Harding. The remainder of the estate—personal property and slaves—fell to all six heirs including his daughters Jane (married to John Cotten), Martha, and Rebecca. The Virginia-Kentucky line of the family is descended from Jones's brother, Thomas, who in 1722 married the widow Elizabeth Pratt, daughter of William Cocke, secretary of state of Virginia.

SEE: Walter Clark, ed., *State Records of North Carolina*, vol. 23 (1904); J. Bryan Grimes, ed., *North Carolina Wills and Inventories* (1914); Hayes Papers (Southern Historical Collection, University of North Carolina Library, Chapel Hill); Ivor Noël Hume, "Archaeology: Handmaiden to History," *North Carolina Historical Review* 41 (1964); L. H. Jones, *Captain Roger Jones of London and Virginia* (1891); William P. Palmer, ed., *Calendar of Virginia State Papers and Other Manuscripts, 1652–1781*, vol. 1 (1875); William L. Saunders, ed., *Colonial Records of North Carolina*, vols. 1, 2, 5 (1886, 1887); Ellen G. Winslow, *History of Perquimans County* (1931).

CHARLES B. LOWRY

Jones, Hamilton Chamberlain (23 Aug. 1798–10 Sept. 1868), humorist, journalist, and lawyer, was born in Greenville, Va., the son of William Jones, who moved to Stokes County where he died in 1800. His widow married Colonel James Martin of Revolutionary fame. Young Jones was graduated in 1818 from The University of North Carolina; an exemplary student, he held the "fourth honor" in a class of fourteen, including future president James K. Polk. For several months he remained in Chapel Hill as a tutor in Greek, then went to New Bern early in 1819 to study law with William Gaston, joining about ten other students. He paid expenses there by tutoring the sons of a nearby farmer. After obtaining a law license, Jones settled in Salisbury to practice. On 11 July 1820 he married Ann Eliza Henderson, the daughter of Pleasant and Sarah Martin Henderson of Chapel Hill. He represented Rowan County in the North Carolina House of Commons in 1827, 1829, 1838, and 1840; in January 1849 he replaced John W. Ellis, who had resigned.

As a young man Jones became a popular raconteur; "often at social gatherings . . . the dancing room would be deserted, while all the company would form a circle around Ham Jones, as he recited with inimitable humor 'Cousin Sally Dilliard' and other stories." Without doubt, Jones's most famous story was "Cousin Sally Dilliard," about an intractable witness in a law case; after the first printing of the sketch in *Atkinson's Saturday Evening Post* of Philadelphia on 6 Aug. 1831, it was copied far and wide throughout the United States. It was a favorite of President Abraham Lincoln. On 28 July 1832, Jones published the first issue of the *Carolina Watchman*, an anti-Jackson weekly to oppose the other Salisbury newspaper, the pro-Jackson *Western Carolinian*. The scattered extant copies of the *Watchman* contain frequent bits and pieces of humor, including two more sketches by editor Jones, "The Lost Breeches" and "A Buncombe Story."

The *Watchman* was sold on 2 Aug. 1839, but Jones continued to write. *The Spirit of the Times*, edited by William T. Porter, solicited additional sketches from Jones. Among the six printed in this popular New York sporting weekly, "McAlpine's Trip to Charleston" and "Going to Muster in North Carolina" were second in popularity only to "Cousin Sally Dilliard." All were signed "By the author of Cousin Sally Dilliard," a byline considered sufficient to whet the funny bone of Porter's subscribers. Jones's nine extant sketches are outrageous, low-keyed farces, many of them lawyers' jests, geared to the humorous taste of the period. In 1845, when Porter included "Cousin Sally Dilliard" in his collection of comic sketches *The Big Bear of Arkansas and Other Tales*, Jones's reputation became nationwide.

For six years (1842–48) he served as solicitor for the Sixth North Carolina Judicial District, and was Supreme

Court reporter in Raleigh from 1853 until his resignation in 1863. Jones was responsible for volumes 46 through 60 of the *North Carolina Reports*, though the last was completed by P. H. Winston. He was a delegate to the Convention of 1861 and signed the North Carolina Ordinance of Secession.

Despite his peripatetic life, Jones was frequently to be found at Como, his country home near Salisbury. Of his ten children, four died in infancy; the others were Martha Martin (Mrs. Samuel Tate), Julia Hamilton, Alice Johnson (Mrs. Edward T. Broadnax), James Martin, Edmund Loftin, and Hamilton Chamberlain, Jr. He died at the home of his son-in-law, Dr. Tate, in Morganton.

SEE: Samuel A. Ashe, ed., *Biographical History of North Carolina*, vol. 7 (1908); Kemp P. Battle, "Ham C. Jones, the Elder," *Charlotte Observer* (undated clipping in the vertical file, North Carolina Collection, University of North Carolina Library, Chapel Hill), and *History of the University of North Carolina*, vol. 1 (1907); Archibald Henderson, *North Carolina: The Old North State and the New*, vol. 2 (1941 [portrait]); *Journal of the House of Commons* (1827–49); Raleigh *Daily Sentinel*, 16 Sept. 1868; Raleigh *Register*, 25 May 1861; Richard Walser, "Ham Jones: Southern Folk Humorist," *Journal of American Folklore* 78 (October–December 1965).

RICHARD WALSER

Jones, Hamilton Chamberlain, Jr. *(3 Nov. 1837–23 Aug. 1904)*, lawyer, Confederate officer, and state senator, was born at Como, his family's home near Salisbury, the son of Hamilton Chamberlain and Ann Eliza Henderson Jones. His father, whose parents had immigrated from Wales, was a lawyer, North Carolina Supreme Court reporter, and quoted wit and author. His mother was the daughter of Revolutionary War major Pleasant Henderson and the great-niece of Governor Alexander Martin.

Jones was educated at the Ben Sumner School near Salisbury and at The University of North Carolina, where he studied law under Judge W. H. Battle and was graduated in the top rank of his class in 1858. He then returned to Salisbury to continue the study of law in his father's office. In 1859 he was licensed in the county courts and a year later was admitted to the bar, remaining in the elder Jones's office to practice.

A determined Whig like his father, Jones ran unsuccessfully for the North Carolina Senate in 1860. The same year he stumped the state for John Bell, the Whig party's presidential candidate in what was to be the last race for the Whigs. Also like his father, he believed in the Southern states' right to secede but thought that it was unnecessary, and that the problems could be solved within the Union. When it became evident that North Carolina would secede, however, he supported the decision.

Jones was appointed a lieutenant of the Rowan Rifle Guard and was with the guard at the taking of Fort Johnston even before the state's formal secession ordinance and organization of troops for the war. After the state troops were organized, Governor John W. Ellis appointed him a captain of Company K, Fifth North Carolina Regiment, with which he fought in Virginia. While recovering from wounds received at the Battle of Williamsburg, Jones was promoted to lieutenant colonel of the Fifty-seventh North Carolina Regiment and later participated in the campaigns of Fredericksburg, Chancellorsville, and Gettysburg. He was captured at the

Rappahannock railroad bridge on 7 Nov. 1863 and taken to Washington, D.C., and later to the prison at Johnson Island on Lake Erie where he participated in a mammoth but unsuccessful attempt to escape. Following his return south in a special prisoner exchange, he was promoted to colonel of the Fifty-seventh Regiment and assumed command on the promotion of former commander Archibald C. Goodwin to brigadier general. Jones was again wounded—this time severely—while leading a charge on Grant's lines at Hare's Hill on 25 Mar. 1865. From these wounds he did not recover until after Lee's surrender. Jones briefly considered joining the continuing struggle west of the Mississippi but, on the advice of friends, decided to renew his allegiance to the Union.

He resumed his law practice in Salisbury until moving to Charlotte, where he established a partnership with General Robert D. Johnson in 1867. For a short time he and General Johnson edited the *Charlotte News*, a daily in which they assailed the abuses being inflicted on a South struggling to reconstruct. In 1869 he was appointed to fill an unexpired term in the state senate and was twice reelected. In the senate, he took an active role in the impeachment proceedings that resulted in the conviction and removal of Governor William W. Holden. In 1885 he was appointed U.S. district attorney for the western district of North Carolina by President Grover Cleveland, a position he held for one four-year term. After Jones's appointment, General Johnson dissolved their law partnership by moving to Birmington, Ala. On retiring from his post as district attorney, Jones formed a new partnership with Charles W. Tillet which lasted until his death. While practicing in Charlotte, he participated in nearly every prominent case that was tried in the area.

A Democrat following the demise of the Whig party, Jones served for several years as chairman of the Mecklenburg County Democratic Executive Committee; he has been credited with helping to make the county a Democratic stronghold.

In 1837 Jones married Sophia Convere Myers, the daughter of Colonel William R. Myers, who bore him six children. Known for his tireless service to his church, he was an officer of St. Peter's Episcopal Church in Charlotte for twenty-five years. The avid fisherman and hunter's legal prowess and character were revered by his colleagues and the various underprivileged citizens he defended and supported, as evidenced by the many glowing eulogies and memorials that followed his death.

SEE: Samuel A. Ashe, ed., *Cyclopedia of Eminent and Representative Men of the Carolinas of the Nineteenth Century*, vol. 2 (1892); *Charlotte Observer*, 26 Aug. 1904, 4 July 1905, 21 Jan. 1934; North Carolina Bar Association, *Proceedings* (1899–1948).

WILLIAM R. PITTMAN

Jones, James Addison *(20 Aug. 1869–25 May 1950)*, construction contractor, civic leader, and philanthropist, was born near Lexington in Davidson County, the son of Robert J. and Elizabeth Horney Jones. His parents were impoverished by the Civil War, and as a youth he was accustomed to hard work and frugal living on a farm. His limited education was gained in a few short terms in a country school. In later years his detailed estimates of involved construction projects were models of accuracy, completeness, and brevity, evidence of a high degree of self-education.

Jones's career in construction began in 1887 when he went to Charlotte before age eighteen to help build the city's first cotton mill. The contractor, a man named Cecil of Lexington, recruited several farm boys to work with him. Jones's first job was to help make bricks. For this he was paid twenty-five cents a day plus room and board in the crude construction camp. He next became a mason's tender and was soon on the scaffold as an apprentice mason. Within two years, he was said to have been the best and fastest mason on the job. Jones had great energy and a will to excel in all that he did. These traits, combined with integrity, good business sense, friendliness, loyalty to ideals, and a concern for the welfare of others characterized his career. In working with others he inspired them to do their best as he led the way.

Sometime between 1890 and 1894 Jones established himself as a general contractor, and within ten years he was building most of the large structures in and around Charlotte. Among these were the Cole Manufacturing plant, the first in the area to be constructed with reinforced concrete. The twelve-story Independence Building, completed in 1909, was the area's first skyscraper. In 1913 his son, Edwin L., became an employee in the business. His next son, Raymond A., who had completed studies at Georgia Tech, went on the payroll in 1916.

The company had a number of contracts when World War I began. Despite rising prices, all of these projects were completed, a fact that further enhanced Jones's reputation as a reliable contractor. In 1920 the business was incorporated as the J. A. Jones Construction Company, with Jones as president and principal stockholder and his sons Raymond and Edwin vice-president and secretary-treasurer, respectively. Jones continued as president until 1943, when he became chairman of the board but still remained vitally involved in all the company's affairs.

Under his leadership, the firm weathered the depression of the 1930s and came out of it with solid growth. A big help was the acquisition of a large contract to build a new military air base, Albrook Field, in the Canal Zone just as the depression began. During World War II the company made a notable record in shipbuilding and military construction in the United States and Central America. One of these was the Gaseous Diffusion Plant at Oak Ridge, Tenn., the largest construction project in the world up to that time.

Early in his career Jones accepted civic responsibilities in Charlotte, serving as alderman, a member of the executive committee of the board, and later as a member of the first city council. In 1917, when the Charlotte area suffered a severe drought, he—as a member of the executive board—led the city in moving from dependence on wells to drawing on the Catawba River for an adequate water supply.

In other business interests he was president of the Addison Realty Company, the Skyland Hotel Company, and the Highland Hotel Company; and a director of the Bank of Commerce, the Interstate Milling Company, and the Citizens Hotel Company. He served on the board of trustees of the Charlotte Memorial Hospital, the North Carolina Orthopedic Hospital of Gastonia, and the Hugh Chatham Memorial Hospital of Elkin.

An active churchman, Jones was a charter member of the Trinity Methodist Episcopal Church, South. When this church and Tryon Street Church merged in the mid-1920s to become First Methodist Church, he moved his membership to Dilworth Methodist Church where for many years he was chairman of the Board of Stewards. He had helped found the mission that became the Dilworth church, where the education building, completed in 1941, was named for him. Jones was elected a delegate from the Western North Carolina Conference to five Methodist General Conferences, the Uniting Conference, and three Jurisdictional Conferences from 1930 to 1948. For several years he was president of the Western North Carolina Conference Board of Church Extension. One of the founders and a trustee of the Charlotte Methodist Mission Society, he helped establish a number of Methodist churches in the city beginning in 1942.

His philanthropies were numerous and substantial. Greensboro College and Brevard College were given library buildings that bear his name. He contributed liberally to the Hugh Chatham Memorial Hospital in Elkin and to the Methodist Home for the Aged in Charlotte.

Jones was married four times. His first wife, whom he married in 1890, was Mary Jane Hooper of Charlotte, and they were the parents of twelve children: Edwin Lee, Bobbie, Raymond Allen, Hannibal Berryman, Frances Elizabeth, James Addison, Jr., Johnnie Hooper, Minnie Beatrice, William Franklin, Dorothy May, Paul Stewart, and Helen Estelle. Mrs. Jones died in February 1914, and in September 1915 Jones married Emma Lockhart Renn of Greensboro by whom he had two children, Emma Renn and Robert Joseph. Following the death of his wife in March 1919, he married Maude Boren of Pomona in September 1920, and they were the parents of a son, Charles Boren. She died in April 1941, and in January 1942 Jones married Rose Walsh, of Charlotte, who survived him.

He died at his home in Charlotte and was buried in the city's Elmwood Cemetery.

SEE: *Charlotte News*, 26 May 1950; *Charlotte Observer*, 26 May 1950; [Edwin L. Jones], *J. A. Construction Company* (1965).

GARLAND R. STAFFORD

Jones, James H. (*1831–8 Apr. 1921*), coachman and confidential courier for Confederate President Jefferson Davis and later a highly respected black public official in Wake County, was the free-born son of James H. and Nancy Jones of Wake County. There was some speculation that he was part Indian. The elder Jones died during his son's infancy, and young James learned the trade of brick mason and plasterer. His general education was derived from his life's experiences. During the winter months of the 1850s, he hired himself out as a gentleman's servant and waiter.

In the early summer of 1862, when the Peninsular campaign threatened Richmond for a brief time, Mrs. Varina Howell Davis and her children resided on the campus of Saint Mary's School in Raleigh. Jones was probably recommended to them as a servant and coachman by his former winter employer, Watt Otey, a brother of the Episcopal Bishop of Virginia. Jones was hired and accompanied the Davis family to the Confederate "White House" in Richmond in the fall of 1862.

For the rest of the war, Jones was the body servant, coachman, and confidential courier for President Davis. In April 1865 he drove the Davis family south from Richmond, through the Carolinas, and witnessed his employer's arrest near Irwinsville, Ga. Thereafter Jones passionately refuted the Northern allegation that President Davis was "dressed in female attire" when captured. He accompanied Davis to Fortress Monroe, Va., and in mid-1865 returned to his former home in Raleigh.

During the fall of 1865, Jones began a distinguished

career of public service when elected a delegate to the first freedmen's convention (State Convention of Colored Men), in Raleigh, which organized the Frederick Douglass Equal Rights League (later renamed the North Carolina State Equal Rights League). He was reelected a delegate to the second freedmen's convention (Colored State Educational Convention) in 1866. After this convention, Jones was appointed Grand Deputy of the state chapter of the Union League of America and served as a Union League organizer in North Carolina.

During the North Carolina Constitutional Convention of 1868, Jones was elected head doorkeeper and also canvassed for the document's adoption. Late that year he was named deputy sheriff of Wake County, a post he held until 1876 or 1877. In 1869 he assisted in the organization of Raleigh's Victor Hose Company, the city's first fire-fighting organization. The hose company was chartered by the state legislature in 1872, and Jones was elected its first foreman, serving until 1882. He also was elected president of the Colored Firemen of Raleigh.

In the 1870s, Jones was twice nominated by Wake County Republicans for a seat in the General Assembly but declined to run on both occasions. Elected city alderman for the Western Ward of Raleigh in 1873, he served for eighteen years with one or two intermissions. In 1876, he was instrumental in organizing the first black military company in North Carolina.

During the 1880s, he was engaged as a contractor for waterworks, street railways, and street grading in several southern towns. His last contract was with the Rock Bridge Company of Glasgow, Va., of which former Virginia Governor Fitzhugh Lee was president. Jones also served as a deacon of Raleigh's Congregational Church.

In 1893, while living in Alabama, Jones learned that the remains of Jefferson Davis were being moved to Hollywood Cemetery in Richmond, Va. Having maintained contact with the Davis family after the war, he was asked to drive the elaborate funeral car during a memorial service held at the Capitol in Raleigh on 30 May 1893.

Jones was a supporter of Republican leader General William Ruffin Cox, who became secretary of the U.S. Senate. Cox hired Jones for a post in the Senate Stationery Room, where Jones served until his death.

In 1906, Jones attended a ceremony in Richmond to lay the cornerstone for the Davis Monument and met with Mrs. Davis for the last time. Shortly before her death she sent him her husband's favorite buck horn handled walking cane. Jones later donated the cane and other Davis artifacts to the North Carolina Museum of History.

Jones died in Washington, D.C., and was buried in Mount Hope Cemetery, Raleigh. He was survived by a son who was a physician in Washington, D.C.

SEE: R. D. W. Connor, ed., *A Manual of North Carolina* (1913); Jefferson Davis Papers (North Carolina State Archives, Raleigh); "Jefferson Davis," Raleigh *News and Observer*, 20 May 1895; Charles N. Hunter Papers (Duke University Library, Durham); Interview with James Jones, *Washington Post*, January 1901; Elizabeth Reid Murray, *Wake: Capital County of North Carolina* (1984); "Negro Dies after Eventful Life," Raleigh *News and Observer*, 9 Apr. 1921; Photograph of James Jones (North Carolina State Archives, Iconographic Collection, Raleigh); Benjamin Quarles, *The Negro in the Civil War* (1953).

RAYMOND L. BECK

Jones, Jesse Weimar (*6 Nov. 1895–9 Mar. 1968*), newspaper editor, was born in Franklin, one of ten children of George Andrew and Harriette Sloan Jones. He entered The University of North Carolina in 1913 but was not in school in 1915–16; he returned in 1916–17 but was not graduated. In April 1918 he enlisted in the army and served for fifteen months during World War I, attaining the rank of sergeant first class in the medical corps. After the war he worked on newspapers in Greensboro, Andrews, Charlotte, and Asheville. For a time in World War II he was director of the Office of War Information in Raleigh.

In 1945 Jones acquired the *Franklin Press*, the weekly newspaper in his native town. His book, *My Affair with a Weekly*, published in 1960, relates his experiences as editor of the highly regarded small town paper. During his professional career he was president of the North Carolina Press Association, president of the International Editorial Writers Conference, and a visiting lecturer in the School of Journalism at The University of North Carolina. While in Chapel Hill he was tapped as an honorary member of the Order of the Golden Fleece, an honorary society.

Jones was nearly blind for most of his adult life. In 1920 he married Nell Thompson, and they became the parents of William and Elizabeth.

SEE: Alumni records, University of North Carolina, Chapel Hill; *Asheville Citizen*, 10 Mar. 1968; Weimar Jones, *My Affair with a Weekly* (1960); Raleigh *News and Observer*, 9 May 1954.

ROBERT O. CONWAY

Jones, John (*3 Nov. 1817–21 May 1879*), businessman and leader for blacks' rights, was born in Greene County, the son of a German named Bromfield and a free mulatto mother. Afraid that his father would take away her son, John's mother apprenticed him to a man named Shepherd on condition that he be taught a trade. Shepherd then bound the youth to a man named Claire who moved to Summerville in northwestern Georgia. There he was taught tailoring and remained until he was nearly twenty-one; by working longer hours than required, he was able to save a little money. He found further apprenticeship employment in Memphis, Tenn., where he made friends with a free black named Richardson, a blacksmith, and "formed a strong attachment for his daughter Mary." Richardson and his family moved to Alton, Ill., and as soon as he finished his apprenticeship, Jones made plans to follow. Some heirs of Claire, however, tried to sell him to planters moving to Texas. Jones appealed to his late master for aid; he obtained a horse which he rode day and night on his return to Greene County to collect evidence that he was free.

With about $100 Jones settled in Alton in 1844 and soon married Mary Richardson. In March of the following year they moved to Chicago. Jones rented a cottage and a small shop where he established himself as a tailor. He taught himself to read and write and soon built up a large trade among the gentry of the city. By 1871, shortly after his retirement, he was regarded as the wealthiest black in America with a fortune of around $100,000.

Before the Civil War, Jones's home was a station on the Underground Railroad through which he helped fugitive slaves escape to Canada; he also contributed generously to the welfare of needy blacks. In 1865 he was largely responsible for securing the repeal of the "Black Laws" of Illinois. The previous year he had written a pamphlet, *The Black Laws of Illinois, and a Few Reasons Why They Should Be Repealed*, as part of a campaign for that purpose. Jones was elected a Cook County commissioner in 1871 and was reelected to a second term. He led the fight to desegregate the schools of Chicago and was victorious in 1874. The first black to serve on the Chicago Board of Education, he donated land for a school that became the Jones Commercial School.

At his death Jones was survived by his wife and a daughter. He left bequests to relatives and friends, and an endowment to the Chicago Public Library and for educational purposes. He was buried in Graceland Cemetery. An early portrait of him is owned by the Chicago Historical Society.

SEE: Paul M. Angle, "John Jones and His Portrait," *Chicago History* 3 (Winter 1951–52 [portrait]); *Chicago Defender*, 21 July 1951; *Chicago Tribune*, 24 July 1955; Eugene P. Romayn Feldman, ed., *Figures in Negro History* (1964); Langston Hughes and others, *A Pictorial History of Blackamericans* (1983 [portrait]); Unidentified newspaper clipping, 21 May 1879, from the biographic files of the Chicago Historical Society.

WILLIAM S. POWELL

Jones, Johnston Blakeley (*12 Sept. 1814–1 Mar. 1889*), physician, was born at Rock Rest, the plantation of his father Edward Jones in Chatham County. Mary, his mother, was the daughter of Peter Mallett of Fayetteville. Young Jones was named for Johnston Blakeley, a naval hero in the War of 1812 and his father's protégé. He attended the Episcopal School for Boys in Raleigh and The University of North Carolina (1831–35), then entered the Medical School of South Carolina at Charleston. For health reasons he went to France for two years, continuing his studies in the prominent hospitals of Paris. After returning to America, he obtained a medical degree at Charleston. Jones was a man of striking appearance and in his student days in Paris was known as "the handsome American."

In 1841 Jones settled in Chapel Hill to practice. On 13 May 1842 he was a member of the group of churchmen who organized the Church of the Atonement, later named the Chapel of the Cross. Kemp P. Battle, who knew him well during his residence in Chapel Hill, wrote of him: "Jones was a man of genius and an acknowledged authority in his profession. He was, however, except when aroused by a dangerous case, fond of his ease and without ambition. I have known him to come to my father's home by a circuitous route in order to avoid a call for his services and spend hours in talking and reading Don Quixote." Battle also mentioned that Jones experimented in synesthesia, particularly the correlation between the senses of taste and smell. When The University of North Carolina closed following the Civil War, Jones moved to Charlotte where he eventually built up a large practice. He was one of the prime movers in the reorganization of the North Carolina Medical Society.

On 21 Oct. 1841 Jones married Mary Ann Stewart, the daughter of Gabriel Long Stewart, at times a legislator from Martin County, and his wife Ann, the daughter of Dr. Simmons Baker. Jones and his wife had five children. The oldest, Edward, died in the Civil War. Two surviving sons, J. B. and Dr. Simmons B., lived in Charlotte. The two daughters were Caroline B. and Mrs. Lucien H. Walker.

SEE: Samuel A. Ashe, ed., *Cyclopedia of Eminent and Representative Men of the Carolinas of the Nineteenth Century*, vol. 2 (1892); Howard A. Kelly and Walter L. Burrage, *American Medical Biographies* (1920).

CLAIBORNE T. SMITH, JR.

Jones, Joseph Seawell (*ca. 1806–20 Feb. 1855*), historian and humbug, was born in Warren County, the son of Edward J. and Elizabeth Seawell Jones. His father, a planter, owned a 2,000-acre tract near Shocco Springs; his mother was a sister of Judge Henry Seawell of the North Carolina Supreme Court and a niece of Nathaniel Macon. After attending various academies in Warren and Franklin counties, Jones entered The University of North Carolina in 1824. It was probably during his college days that he became known as "Shocco" Jones—to distinguish him from other students who had the same familiar surname.

At Chapel Hill Jones exhibited an inclination towards unconventional behavior that would characterize the remainder of his life. His refusal to apply himself to studies he disliked and his frequent absences from classes and chapel led to his dismissal in 1826. From 1829 to 1832 he intermittently attended the Harvard Law School, which awarded him the LL.B. degree in 1833. Although he had previously obtained a license to practice in the county courts of North Carolina, he apparently never made a serious effort to engage in the legal profession.

Instead, Jones devoted his attention for the next several years to two fields of endeavor: the writing of North Carolina history and "enjoying the fun of hoaxing people." His first book, *A Defence of the Revolutionary History of the State of North Carolina from the Aspersions of Mr. Jefferson* (1834), gave special prominence to a sympathetic treatment of the Regulator movement, a defense of the "Mecklenburg Declaration of Independence," and a vindication of the character of William Hooper. Although for the most part Jones's book measured up to the established standards of the day, it also revealed that facet of his personality for which he became famous—his "propensity to hoax and play upon the credulity of the public." Into his narrative he casually introduced "Miss Esther Wake," the supposed sister-in-law of Governor William Tryon, in whose honor he maintained Wake County was named. She was one of the earliest hoaxes that Jones imposed upon his fellowman. He apparently also originated the phrase, "Old North State."

In January 1834, the first of two celebrated "duels" involving Jones attracted the public eye. He allegedly participated in an affair of honor at Pawtucket, R.I., with a certain "Mr. Hooper," who had questioned the "delicate reputation of a Lady." Jones responded to a proclamation for his arrest issued by the governor of Rhode Island with a counterproclamation—to which he affixed the "Great Seal of Shocco"—offering a reward of tar and feathers for the governor's apprehension. He also avowed that the next duel he fought would be across the borders of Rhode Island, "which is not more than the usual distance between the parties in such cases convened." If a duel with "Mr. Hooper" took place, it was doubtless staged to publicize Jones's book.

He apparently planned a second and more ambitious historical work entitled "A Picturesque History of North Carolina," to be embellished with expensive engravings, but abandoned the enterprise because of its excessive cost. In January 1836, a correspondent of the *Richmond Enquirer* wrote that he had seen such a work but questioned that it was published in Raleigh as claimed. Jones undoubtedly was the author of this letter as well as a rejoining one testifying to the domestic production of such a handsome volume. No such book was in fact published. In the meantime he wrote a series of articles on North Carolina history which appeared in the *New-York Mirror*, the Raleigh *Register*, and other journals. These essays—perhaps originally intended for "A Picturesque History"—were collected in a small volume, *Memorials of North Carolina*, published in 1838.

Jones engineered his two most widely publicized hoaxes in 1839. In April, according to accounts in the Norfolk press, he killed a "Mr. H. Wright Wilson of New York" in an affair that took place near the Dismal Swamp Canal. Although his well-known "love of fun, frolick and hoax" raised doubts about the authenticity of this reported duel, the evidence produced that such an event had taken place appeared incontrovertible. It was not until five months later that a man whom Jones had duped into corroborating his account of the duel reluctantly concluded that "evidence" had been skillfully fabricated to make it appear that a fatal meeting had taken place.

Meanwhile, Jones had embarked on the most spectacular adventure of his career. A few weeks before his Dismal Swamp caper, he journeyed to Mississippi, a state hard hit by the economic recession of the late 1830s. Carrying impressive parcels labeled "Cape Fear Money" and "Public Documents," he let it be known that he had come to the state in a dual capacity: as an agent of the Bank of Cape Fear of Wilmington, he was seeking investment opportunities; and as an agent of the U.S. Treasury Department, he intended to compel Mississippi's two "pet banks" to repay the government deposits entrusted to them prior to the panic of 1837. He immediately became the most respected and feared man in the state. Wined and dined by applicants for loans, he was able to persuade the directors of one hard-pressed Columbus bank to name his stepfather, James Gordon, their new president. Many prominent Mississippians, including former Governor Hiram Runnels and Seargent S. Prentiss, then a candidate for the U.S. Senate, fell for his ruse. Not until October was it discovered that his parcel of "Cape Fear Money" contained nothing but blank pieces of paper and his "Public Documents" were actually old newspapers.

Though publication in 1840 of a widely reprinted newspaper account of "The Mammoth Humbug, or the Adventures of Shocco Jones in Mississippi, in the Summer of 1839" by Francis Leech brought Jones a measure of nationwide fame, he spent his remaining life in virtual obscurity. After leaving Mississippi for a while, he returned to the state to reside in Columbus with his mother and stepfather. After her death he lived a hermitlike existence in a cabin near the town, still fascinating occasional visitors to his retreat with his marvelous powers of conversation.

His contemporaries all agreed that Jones could have achieved a notable professional reputation if he had seriously utilized his obvious talents, but an irresistible compulsion to hoodwink his fellowman led him to seek distinction in a highly unorthodox manner. His death, before age fifty, served to remind the nation of the zany exploits of a remarkable individual who, according to the Raleigh *Register*, was "as famous in his day as 'Shocco Jones,' as ever was Mr. Randolph as 'John Randolph of Roanoke.' "

SEE: Edwin A. Miles, "Joseph Seawell Jones of Shocco—Historian and Humbug," *North Carolina Historical Re-*view 34 (October 1957), and ed., "Francis Leech's 'The Mammoth Humbug, or the Adventures of Shocco Jones in Mississippi, in the Summer of 1839,' " *Journal of Mississippi History* 21 (January 1959).

EDWIN A. MILES

Jones, Marmaduke (*ca. 1724–1787*), colonial official, was the nephew of Sir Marmaduke Wyvell, high sheriff of Yorkshire. Educated in England, he was in Wilmington by 1753, perhaps arriving from Jamaica. He served as assistant judge of the General Court (1760), Wilmington borough recorder (1760–66), attorney general of the colony (1766–67) by appointment of Governor William Tryon, and member of the governor's Council (1771–73) by appointment of King George III. On one occasion Jones described himself as a "merchant and Eminent Lawyer" and apparently he was, indeed, considered to be an exceptional lawyer. Governor Tryon in 1768 described him as "a gentleman not inferior to any of his profession in this country." In 1770 Tryon wrote that Jones was "a gentleman of the first eminence at the bar here. . . . He possesses a genteel and easy fortune, and his abilities I am persuaded will be serviceable in Council." During 1771 Jones was requested to assist in the prosecution of insurgents at Hillsborough after the Battle of Alamance, and in the same year he was appointed to a committee to correspond with and advise North Carolina's agent in England.

In 1772 Jones returned to England where he remained for two years, undoubtedly in connection with the illness and death in 1774 of his childless uncle, Sir Marmaduke, whose rank and property he expected to inherit. Due to this long absence, he resigned from the Council in 1773.

From London Alexander Elmsley wrote to a friend in North Carolina: "'Tis but too true that M^ke Jones is obliged to resume the practice of Law, his relations here treated him with a strange indifference and blasted all his hope of succeeding to the Wyvel Estate by suffering a recovery and conveying to a stranger." The baronetcy became dormant because Jones, the oldest surviving male heir, was "domiciled" in America, and the estate was awarded to Sir Marmaduke's half-sister. At her death in 1783 it passed to her husband. Jones returned to North Carolina, but had to reside in the colony a year before he could again be licensed to practice.

Although once more practicing law in Wilmington in 1774, he sold his real estate and personal property the following year. His movements during the American Revolution are vague. Aside from an appearance in 1779 as an attorney in the New Hanover County Court, he disappears from the record until 1783, when he was reported in London, preparing to return to Wilmington. He probably was again in England trying to reclaim his uncle's estate following the death of its most recent owner. In 1784 William Hooper wrote: "I have seen Marmaduke Jones: He is the greatest coxcomb alive."

Between 1784 and 1787, when he died, Jones pursued an active career as a Wilmington attorney. His will, dated 29 Aug. 1787, was proved in October. He was survived by one daughter, Elizabeth, who married Francis Brice. Apparently his wife was Judith Simmonds, sister of Peter Simmonds of Bladen County. She died in 1772, and afterwards he evidently married a widow Ivy, who had two daughters by her previous marriage (Ann Ivy Moore, wife of James Moore, and Mary Ivy De Rosset Boyd, wife of Dr. Moses John De Rosset and then of Adam Boyd).

SEE: John L. Cheney, Jr., ed., *North Carolina Government, 1585–1979* (1981); Walter Clark, ed., *State Records of North Carolina*, vols. 11 (1895), 22 (1907), 23 (1904), 25 (1906); G. E. Cokayne, *Complete Baronetage*, vol. 1 (1900); J. R. B. Hathaway, ed., *North Carolina Historical and Genealogical Register*, vol. 2 (1901); Don Higginbotham, ed., *The Papers of James Iredell, 1767–1783*, 2 vols. (1976); Donald R. Lennon and Ida Brooks Kellam, eds., *The Wilmington Town Book, 1743–1778* (1973); Catherine Douglass De Rosset Meares, *Annals of the De Rosset Family* (1906); New Hanover County deed books (North Carolina State Archives, Raleigh); William S. Powell, ed., *The Correspondence of William Tryon, 1758–1818*, 2 vols. (1980–81); William L. Saunders, ed., *Colonial Records of North Carolina*, vols. 5–9 (1887–90); Alexander McDonald Walker, ed., *New Hanover County Court Minutes, 1738–1800*, 4 vols. (1958–62).

DONALD R. LENNON

Jones, Nellie Rowe (Mrs. William Cecil) *(15 June 1887–28 June 1960)*, librarian and author, was born in Greensboro, one of two children of Dr. Walter Wheat and Mary Dyson Rowe, both originally from Philadelphia. Dr. Rowe, who moved to Greensboro in 1883, was one of the first resident dentists in the town and a prominent Baptist layman. Their son, Joseph Walter, died at a Navy training base during World War I.

Nellie Rowe was graduated from Greensboro High School and attended Greensboro College. In 1905, at age eighteen, she began to work in the Greensboro Public Library; she remained there until her retirement in 1949 after forty-two years of service, twenty-nine of them as head librarian. In 1915–16 she took a leave of absence to study at the Carnegie Library School in Atlanta, Ga. (now the School of Library Science at Emory University). On 23 Feb. 1938 she married William Cecil Jones, a retired Methodist minister who had served in both the North Carolina and the Western North Carolina Conferences of the Methodist church. At one time he had also been editor and publisher of the *Caswell Messenger*. Their mutual interest in writing and local history led to collaboration in writing numerous newspaper articles on Greensboro history.

Mrs. Jones's long association with the Greensboro Public Library was marked by significant growth and expansion of library services to Greensboro and Guilford County. During this period the library was moved twice into locations with expanded physical facilities. In 1906 it was moved from third-floor quarters in the old city hall to a home of its own made possible by the philanthropist and library benefactor, Andrew Carnegie. In 1939 it was relocated in the old First Presbyterian Church building. The church, erected during the pastorate of Dr. Jacob Henry Smith with an educational building added later in his memory, was of great sentimental value to Greensboro citizens. After a new Presbyterian church was built, the daughter and granddaughters of Dr. Smith purchased the old church property, remodeled it to become the Richardson Civic Center, and gave it to the city of Greensboro to house the library, the historical museum, and other community agencies.

Greensboro was a pioneer in county library service. On 15 Apr. 1915 it became the first library in North Carolina to open its doors to rural residents. Shortly after this a chain of book stations in community centers in the county was established to bring books directly to rural residents. In 1926, it became the second library in the state to provide bookmobile service to rural residents.

Mrs. Jones emphasized the importance of acquiring a well-rounded collection of books and materials to serve the varied needs of the community, stimulate interest in educational and cultural activities, and preserve the past for future generations. Her particular interest in local and state history led to the building of an outstanding collection of books, pamphlets, and clippings on these subjects. The clippings from newspapers and magazines, which were carefully classified and filed by subject in vertical files, are a significant part of the collection. Another special collection consists of materials on William Sydney Porter, a Guilford County native, who wrote as O. Henry. Both the history and the O. Henry collections are widely acclaimed by scholars and are used extensively by writers in these fields. These collections, together with a few others, are now housed in a special room in the fourth home of the library, a new building opened to the public in July 1964. This room was named the Caldwell-Jones Room in honor of Miss Bettie D. Caldwell, the first librarian, and Mrs. Jones for their interest and work in building these outstanding collections.

During Mrs. Jones's association with the library, the citizens of Greensboro and Guilford County took part in two world wars. Significant among the records of these years are her compilations of the war records of the service men and women: *Honor Roll for Guilford County, World War II*, published in five volumes; and *Soldiers, Nurses, Sailors of Guilford County in the World War*.

Mrs. Jones was active in the movement to establish a historical museum for the collection and preservation of relics and materials connected with the history of Greensboro and Guilford County. The museum, organized in 1924, was first housed in the basement of the public library. After its removal to several other temporary homes, it was permanently located in the Richardson Civic Center. In later years, when the library and other community agencies acquired other locations, the museum was expanded and given the whole building.

She was also active in the growth and expansion of library services statewide, lending her support to the Citizens Library Movement, professional organizations, and the campaign to secure state aid for public libraries. With Guilford a pioneer in county library work she was interested in providing library services to all citizens of North Carolina, both urban and rural. From 1925 to 1927 she was president of the North Carolina Library Association; and on her retirement in 1949, she was made an honorary member of the association for her contributions to library service at the local and state levels. Mrs. Jones was also a member of the Daughters of the American Revolution and of the Woman's Club, and an honorary member of the Altrusa Club and the Reviewers Book Club.

Her interest in children and in state history prompted her to write several books for children: *My Magic Storyland* (1929), *Discovering North Carolina* (1933), and *Crystal Locket* (1935).

Mrs. Jones died and was buried in Greensboro.

SEE: *Greensboro Daily News*, 30 June, 6 July 1960; "Mrs. Nellie Jones, Librarian, Is Dead," *Greensboro Daily News*, 30 June 1960; *Who's Who in the South and Southwest* (1947).

IRENE HESTER

Jones, Pembroke *(15 Dec. 1858–24 Jan. 1919)*, financier and social leader, was born in Wilmington, the son of John Pembroke and Jane London Jones. His father, a native of Virginia, was graduated from the U.S. Naval Academy in 1852 and during the Civil War was an officer in the Confederate Navy, serving for a time on the *Merrimac*. His mother died when he was young, and he was reared by a maternal aunt in Wilmington, Mrs. Platt K. Dickinson. She and her husband were childless, and on their deaths bequeathed to Jones what amounted for the times to a modest fortune. This enabled Jones to enter the rice milling business in Wilmington; he later expanded to New Orleans as well.

On his marriage to Sarah Wharton Green, the daughter of Colonel Wharton Green, in 1884, Jones and his wife became leaders in the civic and social life of Wilmington. During this period, Henry Walters, the railroad magnate, became ill of typhoid while in Wilmington on business. Mr. and Mrs. Jones took him into their home and nursed him back to health. A lifelong friendship followed; many years later Henry Walters married Mrs. Jones after the death of her husband. Moreover, Walters gave Jones financial advice which enabled him to accumulate a large fortune in railroad securities.

With their increased affluence, the Joneses moved to New York City and set as their goal acceptance into the "400," the innermost circle of New York and Newport society, then at its most flamboyant. (This era has been referred to by social historians as the Gilded Age.) They consulted Harry Lehr, the successor to Ward McAllister as social arbiter of New York, who agreed to sponsor them. Lehr advised Jones and his wife to feed New Yorkers well, and they would be eating out of their hands. Mr. and Mrs. Jones accordingly hired both a Russian chef and a black cook from the South, and they soon became noted for lavish entertaining. Given the hostility towards the South following the Civil War, it was no mean accomplishment for a young Southern couple to be accepted into this essentially alien world. After becoming established in New York and Newport, Jones purchased in 1908 the Theodore Havemeyer residence in Newport as a summer home. Naming the place Sherwood in honor of one of his ancestors, he almost completely rebuilt the house. The mansion, later converted into an apartment house, still stands on Bellevue Avenue.

After moving to New York, Jones maintained his interest in his native city and encouraged the development of Wilmington as a seaport. He and his wife continued to spend part of the year at their estate, Airlie, where Mrs. Jones developed a noted azalea garden. For many years they gave a Christmas tree party at Airlie and invited scores of children from prominent Wilmington families. Airlie, too, was the scene of numerous house parties at which Jones entertained business and social leaders of international prominence.

Caught up in the enthusiasm with which New York society supported the allied war effort, Jones—on 17 June 1917—placed his town house at 5 East 61st Street in New York City at the disposal of the Italian Royal War Mission. In 1918 he was a member of the War Trade Board in Washington, D.C. At the time of his death early in 1919, Jones was vice-president of the Carolina Shipbuilding Corporation, which then had several ships under construction in Wilmington.

Jones died in New York following an operation and was buried in Oakdale Cemetery, Wilmington. He and his wife were the parents of a son, Pembroke, and a daughter, Sarah, who married John Russell Pope, the architect. Mrs. Jones survived her husband and later married Henry Walters. Jones left $50,000 to city officials in Wilmington to purchase and maintain a park there to be named Pembroke Jones Park. The city bought the land for the park for considerably less than

that amount, and for many years the residual funds were used for maintenance. The main entrance of the park is on the corner of 14th and Market streets.

SEE: Mrs. Peter Bolhouse (Curator of Manuscripts, Newport Historical Society), personal contact; Elizabeth Drexel Lehr, *King Lehr and the Gilded Age* (1935); Lawrence F. London (Chapel Hill), personal contact; Marriage license of Pembroke Jones (Cumberland County Registry, Fayetteville); *New York Times*, 25 Jan. 1919; Wilmington *Morning Star*, 25 Jan. 1919; Cicero P. Yow to Claiborne T. Smith, Jr., 30 July 1980.

CLAIBORNE T. SMITH, JR.

Jones, Richard (1784–1860), farmer, miller, and legislator, was born in Virginia but moved to Caswell County, N.C., where he married Mary Ann ("Polley") Foster in 1811. Beginning with his wife's inherited farm on Moon Creek in present-day Locust Hill Township, Jones gradually enlarged his landholdings until he had accumulated 1,350 acres. His slaveholdings, however, apparently never exceeded ten. In addition to farming, he built and operated a water-powered gristmill, later known as "Page's Mill." Though addressed as "Captain," his title was probably honorary.

A Democrat, Jones was elected to the North Carolina House of Commons from Caswell County in 1846 and 1848. His votes generally reflected his partisanship on the issues dividing Democrats and Whigs, and his influence appears not to have been great. He usually voted against internal improvements legislation, but he supported the construction of a school for the deaf and blind.

Jones became vocal in connection with a resolution introduced early in 1847 regarding the War with Mexico. The resolution provided for an appropriation to equip and pay the expenses of a regiment of North Carolina volunteers, but its preamble reflected the Whig view that "by the action of the Executive and the subsequent sanction of Congress, this Republic is involved in a Foreign War." The Democrats attempted to remove this offending clause but were defeated by a party-line vote. They then sought to vote separately on the preamble and the resolution, but the chair ruled the question indivisible. When the resolution and its preamble came up for a decision, Jones and eighteen others voted in the negative on the second reading. The next day Jones, Wiatt Moye, and Elias Barnes submitted a resolution calling for the journal to be amended to show that, though they were recorded as voting against the measure, they were in fact in favor of the resolution but opposed the "untrue" preamble. They lost 60 to 51, but the introduction of their resolution assured its inclusion in the journal.

On the question of slavery, Jones strongly supported the traditional Southern stand. When, early in 1849, a series of resolutions was introduced denying the right of Congress to legislate on the subject of slavery in the territories, Jones supported six of the seven. He opposed the seventh resolution (substituted on motion of Edward Stanly) condemning all policies that threatened to weaken the Union. Interestingly, Jones voted against postponing indefinitely a bill that would have allowed a free man of color, Hillory Coor, to emancipate his wife, son, and two daughters.

An active member of Lick Fork Primitive Baptist Church, Jones was often sent by the church as a messenger to various Baptist associations. After the death of his first wife in 1852, he married two years later Elizabeth S. L. Johnson, an Edgecombe County widow.

His ten children, all by Mary Ann Jones, were Eliza Ann, John Edward, James Washington, Henry M., David A., Martha Jane, Thomas Jefferson, Mary, Fannie A., and Richard, Jr. Jones was buried next to his wife on his home tract near Watlington's store.

SEE: "Captain Richard Jones," *The Heritage of Caswell County* (1985); *Journal of the House of Commons* (1846–47, 1848–49).

H. G. JONES

Jones, Robert ("Robin"), Jr. (1718–2 Oct. 1766), attorney general of North Carolina, legislator, and agent of Earl Granville, was born in Surry County, Va., the son of Robert Jones, who practiced law in Surry County and served in the House of Burgesses. Educated at Eton, Robin Jones returned to Virginia where he also practiced law in Surry County. A resident of Albemarle Parish, he was a close friend of William Willie (pronounced Wiley). Sometime between 1750 and 1753 Jones moved to Northampton County, N.C., where he built a large residence, The Castle, the exact location of which is unknown. A member of the Assembly from Northampton County from 1754 to 1761, Jones was a man of wide learning and culture who took an interest in the evolving court system of the province. As collector of quitrents in the Granville District for Earl Granville, he acquired vast tracts of land and was soon one of the largest landowners on the Roanoke River.

In 1756, on the recommendation of Governor Arthur Dobbs, Jones was appointed attorney general of the province. Soon after taking office, he became embroiled in the controversy surrounding the administration of the Granville District. In November 1758 several residents of the district, dissatisfied with the high fees and poor administration of its land office, appealed to Jones to petition the Assembly on their behalf for redress. The Assembly ordered an investigation, and a committee concluded that both Francis Corbin and Joshua Bodley had generally followed Granville's instructions in the management of the land office. Corbin, it was determined, had been engaged in questionable practices, but the Assembly was satisfied with Bodley's conduct. The only immediate result of the investigation was the publication of the schedule of fees charged by Granville's agents.

The petitioners were not mollified, however, and, soon after the new year, the smoldering anger of the farmers in the district erupted in violence. On 24 Jan. 1759 a posse of embattled and intoxicated farmers led by Colonel Alexander McCulloch kidnapped Francis Corbin in Edenton and took him to Enfield, where he and Joshua Bodley were held captive and forced to give bond for the reformation of the Proprietary land office.

Many of the disaffected yeomen were especially hostile towards the eloquent and elegant Robin Jones. Following his 1756 appointment as attorney general, Jones earned the enmity of the Granville "courthouse ring" because of his identification with Governor Dobbs's removal from office of Robert Harris, a Granville justice who had openly expressed contempt for the governor. In retaliation, the Granville justices often refused to hold court. Pursuant to his duties as attorney general, Jones reported these actions to Dobbs who followed Jones's recommendations in making his next appointments of Granville justices, much to the displeasure of those already sitting.

On 23 Mar. 1759, "The Petition of Reuben Searcy and Others" was presented to the county court of Granville

and read in the presence of the justices. In this document, representing the views of "Sundry of the Inhabitants" of the county, "that Eloquent Gentleman" Robin Jones was accused of taking exorbitant legal fees, of preventing the appointment of justices of the peace favored by the petitioners, and "through his wiles and false insinuations to which art and chicanerie he owes his great success and high preferment in this Province" of imposing on "the inferior class of mankind" and on Governor Dobbs. The petitioners asked that Jones be prohibited from pleading at the Granville bar. Nothing directly resulted from the petition, but on 14 May Jones testified under oath before the governor and Council that "he had heared that it was intended by a great number of rioters to petition the court at Granville to silence him . . . and that if no such order was made, to pull him by the nose and also to abuse the court." Following a formal address to the governor by the Assembly on 15 May, a proclamation was issued and several rioters were jailed. During disorders in Enfield, farmers from surrounding counties broke into the jail and the prisoners escaped.

Meanwhile, after the disturbances, Francis Corbin had failed to bring the ringleaders to justice, and in England, as a result of the disorders and mismanagement of the land office, Thomas Child had persuaded Earl Granville to remove Corbin and Bodley from office. In September Child returned to North Carolina as the new attorney general, replacing Jones who then became Proprietary collector of quitrents for the district during the next year, when Child reformed many of the practices of the land office.

In the Assembly during 1760 and 1761 Jones was allied with Thomas Child, Thomas Barker from Edenton, and Francis Corbin, newly elected from Chowan County, in supporting the political and economic interests of the northern counties and in opposing the administration of Arthur Dobbs. Governor Dobbs denounced the group as "the northern Junto," in part reflecting his particular dislike of Child. Nevertheless, in July 1761 Jones once more received a commission from the governor as attorney general. Child, who was moving to Suffolk, Va., had recommended Jones as his successor, and in August 1761 he left active management of Proprietary affairs in Jones's hands. Jones also continued to serve as collector of Proprietary quitrents until the land office was closed in 1765.

During the next several years disorders continued sporadically in Granville and elsewhere, leading eventually to the August 1766 mass meeting at Sandy Creek, Orange County, where Regulator Advertisement Number 1 appeared. Jones may well have learned of the meeting, but in the summer of 1766 he was confined to his bed. On 20 August Samuel Johnston wrote to Thomas Barker in London, "your old friend R. J. is I am told on his last leggs." Johnston promised to visit Jones and to provide Barker with an account of his business affairs and Jones's health. When Johnston arrived in Halifax to settle with Jones for some monies received for land, he found Jones "so low as to be quite incapable of transacting that or any other business." According to Johnston, Jones "continued in that condition till about the middle of Sept. when a mortification was begun in his ankle and his surgeons at his request thought it proper to take off the limb above his knee. He underwent the operation with great firmness but survived it only a few days." Thus Jones did not serve in the 1766 Assembly to which he had been elected.

As late as 1773, Jones's role in the Granville disorders was criticized in the *Virginia Gazette* in Williamsburg.

Willie Jones was loyal to his father's memory, and his published reply was characteristically blunt: "You, sir, are a liar."

Unlike the will of his freethinking son, Willie, which reflected an acerbic disbelief, Robin Jones's will, dated 4 Apr. 1764, in which he left his considerable property to his wife and children, exhibited the pious standard form language of the time. Father and son did, however, share an aversion to mournful funerals. Robin Jones directed that no one go into mourning on his death, and that his funeral be "decent without any pomp according to . . . the Church of England & that on the occasion a few friends only . . . be assembled to attend my obsequies." In leaving Mary Eaton Jones a life estate in his Occoneechee Neck plantation, Jones berated his second wife, stating that "her conduct has been so void of the duties enjoined by the conjugal estate & the injuries she has done me so many & so great that I am conscious this provision far exceeds her merit."

In 1737 or 1738 Jones married Sarah Cobb of York County, Va., the daughter of Robert and Elizabeth Allen Cobb. They became the parents of five children: Allen (b. 24 Dec. 1739), Willie (b. 25 May 1741), Martha (b. 22 Aug. 1743), Charlotte (b. 7 Sept. 1746), and Robert (b. 2 Feb. 1749). After the death of his first wife, Jones married Mary ("Molly") Eaton, by whom he had one daughter, Elizabeth (b. 13 June 1766).

Robin Jones was connected by descent and marriage to some of the most influential members of the colonial Halifax circle. His oldest son was the Federalist general Allen Jones of Mount Gallant, whose daughter Sarah married Governor William R. Davie. A younger son, Willie Jones of The Grove, was an enigmatic Jeffersonian, whose daughters included Sally, who married Governor Hutchins G. Burton, and Martha Burke ("Patsy"), who married John Wayles Eppes of Buckingham County, Va., whose first wife had been Maria Jefferson. Robin Jones's daughter, Martha, married Dr. Thomas Gilchrist and their daughter married Colonel William Polk. Jones's youngest child, Elizabeth, married Jeffersonian Benjamin Williams, twice governor of North Carolina, who in 1799 ironically succeeded in office his wife's niece's Federalist husband, William R. Davie.

SEE: Archibald Henderson, "Robert Jones, III, Attorney General, One of Carolina's Neglected," Raleigh *News and Observer*, 2 Feb. 1941; Samuel Johnston to Thomas Barker, 20 Aug. 1766, 26 Oct. 1766, Hayes Collection (Southern Historical Collection, University of North Carolina Library, Chapel Hill); William Lunsford Long, "Willie Jones: A Brief Sketch of His Life and Political Influence in North Carolina," *University of North Carolina Magazine*, May 1909; William S. Powell, ed., *The Correspondence of William Tryon and Other Selected Papers*, vol. 1 (1980); Gertrude Richards, *Register of Albemarle Parish, Surry and Sussex Counties, Virginia* (1958); Blackwell P. Robinson, *William R. Davie* (1957) and "Willie Jones of Halifax," *North Carolina Historical Review* 18 (1941); William L. Saunders, ed., *Colonial Records of North Carolina*, vols. 5–7, 9 (1887–90).

JAMES P. BECKWITH, JR.

Jones, Robert Elijah (19 Feb. 1872–18 May 1960), Methodist clergyman and editor, was born in Greensboro and earned degrees at Bennett College, Greensboro, and Gammon Theological Seminary, Atlanta, Ga. He was ordained deacon by Bishop Hurst and elder by Bishop Mallalieu. Jones served pastorates in Leaksville, Lexington, and Thomasville, and in 1897 he became assistant manager of the *Southeastern Christian Advocate*. In 1901 he was field secretary of the Board of Sunday Schools, and in 1904 returned to the *Advocate* as editor.

In 1920 Jones was elected to the episcopacy and served in that capacity at the Central Jurisdictional Conference (black) until his retirement in 1944. Bishop Jones was a member of five General Conferences and a trustee of three institutions of learning. He founded the Gulfside Assembly at Waveland, Miss., and served as its president and in other high offices. In 1927, when awarded a bronze medal by the Harmon Foundation, he was recognized as one of the outstanding preachers and orators in black Methodism; two years later the foundation awarded him a gold medal for distinguished religious service. He was the recipient of honorary degrees from seven institutions. After retiring, he lived at the Gulfside Assembly. He was survived by a son, Robert E., Jr.

SEE: Lindo D. Addo and James H. McCallum, *To Be Faithful to Our Heritage: A History of Black Methodism in North Carolina* (1980).

GRADY L. E. CARROLL

Jones, Roland (18 Nov. 1813–5 Feb. 1869), attorney, congressman, and judge, was born in Salisbury, the son of Drucilla Brown and Samuel Jones. Samuel Jones was a man of some prominence in Rowan County. Besides having considerable landholdings, he operated an inn in Salisbury known as the Farmer's Hotel and served in the General Assembly (1819–20) and as county sheriff (1823).

Young Jones attended private schools in Rowan County and taught at the Wilkesboro Academy (1830–35). After graduation from the Cambridge (Mass.) Law School in 1838, he was admitted to the bar and began a practice in Brandon, Miss.; he also was editor of the *Brandon Republican* (1838–40). In 1840 Jones moved to Shreveport, La., where he continued to practice law. He served in the Louisiana House of Representatives (1844–48) and as district judge of Caddo Parish (1851–52). From March 1853 to March 1855 he served as a Democrat in the Thirty-third Congress but declined renomination in 1854 in order to resume his law practice. In 1860 he was again elected district judge, a position he held until 1868.

In 1844 Jones married Ann Neville Stokes, the daughter of North Carolina Governor Montfort Stokes, and the couple had six children: Montfort Stokes (m. Florence Burkett), Katherine Boylan (m. James B. Pickett), Mary Alice, Anne (m. Charles J. Randall), Roland, and Esmeralda Mathews. Jones died in Shreveport and was buried in Oakland Cemetery.

SEE: *Biog. Dir. Am. Cong.* (1971); James S. Brawley, *The Rowan Story* (1953) and materials provided by Brawley; James K. Greer, *Louisiana Politics, 1845–1861* (1930); "Jones File" (McCubbins Collection, Rowan Public Library, Salisbury); Lilla McLure and J. Ed Howe, *History of Shreveport and Shreveport Builders* (1937); Dunbar Rowland, ed., *Encyclopedia of Mississippi History*, vol. 2 (1907); Jethro Rumple, *History of Rowan County* (1881); Wilkes County Marriage Bonds (North Carolina State Archives, Raleigh).

LINDA ANGLE MILLER

Jones, Thomas (d. Sept.[?] 1797), lawyer and colonial and state official, a native of Gloucestershire, England, was clerk of court in Chowan County in 1758. Because there were numerous men of the same name in the colony, it is unlikely that his origins and the date of his arrival can ever be determined with certainty, although many families from Bristol, Gloucestershire, moved to North Carolina in the eighteenth century. It is clear, however, that Jones represented Chowan County in the colonial Assembly for three terms between 1773 and 1775 and in all five sessions of the Provincial Congress between 1774 and 1776. He also served on the Provincial Council in 1775–76 and on the Council of Safety in 1776. His letters, which are well written and grammatically correct, contain evidence of a classical education.

Jones was already established in Edenton when James Iredell, later noted as a jurist, arrived. The two men became close friends as well as neighbors. Iredell often visited Jones and his wife, and he copied some records for Jones as well as prepared a catalogue of Jones's extensive library. (One of Jones's books is preserved in the North Carolina Collection in Chapel Hill.) Jones participated in services at St. Paul's Anglican Church in Edenton, purchased a "gilt" copy of the *Book of Common Prayer* from a local merchant in 1772, and sang the psalms on one occasion in 1773, much to the delight of some of the ladies present.

As a member of the Provincial Council and the Provincial Congress, Jones played a significant role in the colony. The Council, composed of just thirteen men, was the most important agency of government at a critical time, and under its direction North Carolina was prepared for the coming revolution. The Council was responsible for the steps that led to victory at the Battle of Moore's Creek Bridge; it also laid the plans for and ordered the execution of General Griffith Rutherford's campaign against the Cherokee Indians. In the Provincial Congress Jones served on a select committee to provide for the defense of the province, and he also was on the Committee of Secrecy, Intelligence, and Observation. The latter committee reported the document that has come to be known as the Halifax Resolves—the first state action calling for independence from Great Britain. On 9 May 1776 Allen Jones and Thomas Jones, presumably unrelated, were appointed by the Provincial Congress to attend the Virginia Provincial Congress to recommend that both states fit out armed vessels to protect trade.

In the Provincial Congress Jones also served on the small committee that devised a temporary form of government to serve before a constitution was drawn up and a state government inaugurated. Finally, in December 1776, when the Provincial Congress was charged with writing a Declaration of Rights and a constitution, Jones was an important committee member. The constitution, in fact, was spoken of as "Jones's constitution." He was familiar with the constitutions of South Carolina and Connecticut, and pointed out some of their features for the committee's consideration. Jones was said to have been "a cunning and ingenious politician, [who] interceded and appeased the rage of the contending factions." With the adoption of the constitution, he was named first among eleven men charged with reviewing all past statutes and acts of assembly to determine which should remain in force.

Also in December 1776 the Congress passed a number of ordinances, and Jones is credited with having been responsible for the third of these. It secured all church property to whatever "religious Society, Church, Sect, [or] Denomination" it had belonged previously.

This clearly was an attempt to protect Anglican church property for the future.

Once the state was launched on the road to independence, Jones seems to have withdrawn from public life. His wife, the daughter of the late Reverend Clement Hall, apparently was dead by July 1776, as his children were with Mrs. Arthur Howe while he was attending the Provincial Congress. Jones's will, dated 26 June 1797, was probated in September. He left property to daughters Mary Brinn and Elizabeth Beasly; to sons Zachariah, Levi, and Thomas; and to grandchildren Elizabeth and Isaiah Sweeney. Sons James and Joshua in 1772 made purchases at the Johnston store, but they apparently died before their father.

SEE: Samuel A. Ashe, ed., *Biographical History of North Carolina*, vol. 4 (1906); John L. Cheney, Jr., ed., *North Carolina Government, 1585–1979* (1981); Chowan County Wills (North Carolina State Archives, Raleigh); Walter Clark, ed., *State Records of North Carolina*, vol. 23 (1904); Hayes Papers (Southern Historical Collection, University of North Carolina Library, Chapel Hill); Don Higginbotham, ed., *The Papers of James Iredell*, 2 vols. (1976); Jo. Seawell Jones, *Defence of the Revolutionary History of the State of North Carolina* (1834); William L. Saunders, ed., *Colonial Records of North Carolina*, vols. 9, 10 (1890).

WILLIAM S. POWELL

Jones, Thomas Laurens (21 Jan. 1819–20 July 1887), lawyer, legislator, and congressman, was born on his father's estate, White Oak, in Rutherford County. He was the son of George Jones, a planter of Welsh-English descent and a native of Orange County, Va. His mother, Elizabeth Mills Jones, also of English ancestry, was the daughter of Colonel William Mills. Jones received his preparatory education in Spartanburg, S.C., and attended Columbia College in Columbia, entering as a sophomore on 19 Dec. 1838. Subsequently, he was graduated in the class of 1840 at Princeton College, which awarded him an honorary degree in 1848. He received an LL.B. degree from the Harvard University Law School in 1847.

After leaving Harvard, Jones journeyed cross-country to New Orleans, visiting along the way with General Andrew Jackson and Henry Clay of Kentucky. Continuing his travels in Europe, he was for a time the guest of Washington Irving, then U.S. minister to Spain. Jones read law with James L. Pettigrue of Charleston, S.C., and was admitted to the bar in Columbia in 1846. The following year he moved to New York City where he practiced law until 1848. On 12 Sept. 1848 he married Mary K. Taylor, the daughter of Colonel James Taylor of Newport, Ky. Their children were James Taylor, Thomas, Laurens, and Elizabeth Mills (Mrs. Brent Arnold) of Cincinnati, Ohio.

In addition to his legal career, Jones became active in politics, serving from 1853 to 1855 in the Kentucky House of Representatives as a Democrat from Campbell County. He was elected to the U.S. House of Representatives for the Fortieth and Forty-first Congresses (4 Mar. 1867–3 Mar. 1871). Although not a candidate in 1870, he was again elected to the House for the Forty-fourth Congress (4 Mar. 1875–3 Mar. 1877).

Before the Civil War, Jones opposed secession; however, he is said to have opposed coercion as well. He was arrested in the summer of 1862 for "disloyalty" and sent to Camp Chase in Columbus, Ohio, as a political prisoner. After refusing to take the oath of allegiance to secure his release, he was paroled to Newport with the recommendation that the parole not be renewed.

Jones is credited with being the first member of Congress to favor a general amnesty in the postwar period. After his final term, he practiced law in Newport, Ky., until his death. A member of the Episcopal church, he was buried in Evergreen Cemetery, Newport.

SEE: *Biog. Dir. Am. Cong.* (1961); *Biographical Encyclopedia of Kentucky* (1878); Leonidas Polk, *Handbook of North Carolina . . .* (1879); *The War of the Rebellion*, ser. 2, vols. 4, 5 (1899); *Who Was Who in America*, Historical Volume, (1967).

DAVID ALLEN BENNINGTON

Jones, Thomas McKissick (16 Dec. 1816–13 Mar. 1892), lawyer, judge, legislator, and Confederate congressman, was born in Person County, the son of Wilson and Rebecca McKissick Jones. When Thomas was an infant, the family moved to Pulaski, Tenn., where he attended local schools and Wittenburg Academy. In 1831 he entered the University of Alabama, remaining until 1833 when he transferred to the University of Virginia. Returning to Pulaski in 1835, he read law for a year and on 14 June 1836 enlisted in the First Tennessee Mounted Volunteers. He also began to practice law and became interested in several business ventures. From 1842 to 1855 he was a director of a regional turnpike company; in 1855, a director and eventually president of the Nashville and Decatur Railroad; and a director of two local banks. By 1860 he owned fifty-four slaves and property valued at $91,500.

Jones was often mayor of Pulaski and on occasion was a member of the General Assembly; in 1847 he was a member of the Tennessee Senate. He was also a delegate to the Democratic National Conventions of 1856, 1860 (Charleston), and 1880. In 1861 Jones was a representative from Tennessee to the Provisional Congress of the Confederate States where he served on the committees for Flag and Seal and Naval Affairs. In the congress he spoke in opposition to martial law and demonstrated an interest in the welfare of soldiers. He was not a candidate for reelection. When Federal troops captured Pulaski in 1863, Jones was taken prisoner and sent to Nashville. Governor Andrew Johnson paroled him, however, on condition that he not communicate with members of the Confederate Congress or Confederate military commanders. After the war he resumed his law practice. In 1866 his son, Calvin, was one of six men who met in Jones's law office to organize the Ku Klux Klan.

In 1870 Jones was a delegate to the Tennessee Constitutional Convention. Interested in judicial questions, he urged that judges and chancellors be appointed by the governor so as to remove the judiciary from politics. In 1872 Jones was appointed for ten months as a judge of the Court of Arbitration for Middle Tennessee. At various times he also served as a special judge on the Tennessee Supreme Court.

On 25 Dec. 1838 Jones married Marietta Perkins and they became the the the parents of nine children: Calvin, Charles P., Thomas Wilson, Hume Field, Harriet, Edmund S., Lucy Anne, Lee Walthal, and Nicholas Tate. His second wife was Anne Perkins Wood, but they had no children. For twenty years Jones was a vestryman in the Episcopal church. In 1843 he joined the Masons and became Master Mason, Royal Arch Mason, and Knight Templar. He was buried in Maplewood Cemetery, Pulaski.

SEE: Thomas B. Alexander and Richard E. Beringer, *The Anatomy of the Confederate Congress* (1972); *Biographical Directory of the Tennessee General Assembly, 1796–1967* (1968); J. W. Caldwell, *Sketches of the Bench and Bar of Tennessee* (1896); *Journal of the Congress of the Confederate States*, vol. 1 (1904); Ezra J. Warner and W. Buck Yearns, *Biographical Register of the Confederate Congress* (1975).

RICHARD W. PARRIS

Jones, William Branch (22 June 1890–21 Sept. 1943), lawyer, was born in Raleigh, the son of Armistead and Nancy Haywood Branch Jones. Descended from the Armistead, Blount, Boyd, Branch, Haywood, and Hawkins families of North Carolina and Virginia, he was educated at the Raleigh Male Academy, North Carolina State College, and The University of North Carolina. He was admitted to the bar in 1901. Jones immediately began the practice of law with his father in Raleigh and followed his profession until the year of his death. After his father's death, he practiced alone until 1931 when he formed a partnership with Leon S. Brassfield. His nephew, Armistead Jones Maupin, became associated with the firm in 1939.

William Branch Jones (or "Buck," as he was widely known) became a trial lawyer of note and appeared in many important cases. A conservative Democrat, he was deeply interested in politics. He was president of various bar associations, and for a while he was president of the North Carolina Railroad. Jones was a lifelong member of Christ Episcopal Church.

On 22 Apr. 1903 he married Mary Seaton Hay, the daughter of Thomas T. Hay of Raleigh. They had one child, Isabelle Hay, who married William Carl Ethridge. Jones died in Duke Hospital, Durham, and was buried in Oakwood Cemetery, Raleigh.

SEE: Daniel L. Grant, *Alumni History of the University of North Carolina, 1795–1924* (1924); North Carolina Bar Association, *Proceedings* (1899–1948); *North Carolina Biography*, vols. 3, 4 (1929, 1941).

ARMISTEAD JONES MAUPIN

Jones, William Henry (23 Sept. 1883–4 Jan. 1963), educator, was born in Caswell County, the son of Thaddeus Cornelius and Rebecca Jane Roberts Jones. He attended rural schools in Caswell and Rockingham counties and was graduated in 1911 from The University of North Carolina, where in his senior year he was editor of *The Daily Tar Heel*, a member of the Golden Fleece, and a student assistant to Librarian Louis Round Wilson. Jones taught school in Caswell, Sampson, Buncombe, Durham, Washington, Robeson, and Pitt counties, and was principal of high schools in South Hill and Charlotte Courthouse, Va. In 1922 he became principal of Biltmore School near Asheville. Five years later he and Buncombe County Schools Superintendent A. C. Reynolds established a tuition-free county junior college at Biltmore, and Jones was promoted to superintendent of Biltmore Schools, encompassing the junior college, high school, and elementary school.

Biltmore Junior College's enrollment reached about three hundred students before the depression forced the charging of tuition. After Reynolds's retirement as county superintendent, Jones relinquished supervision of the junior college and Reynolds became its president. Later Biltmore was merged with Asheville College to form Asheville-Biltmore College, the predecessor of the University of North Carolina at Asheville.

In 1934 Jones became district supervisor of the Adult Education Program of the Emergency Relief Administration (later Works Progress Administration) with the office in Chapel Hill, and the following year he was appointed assistant state director of the program in Raleigh. For nine months preceding the termination of the program in 1943, Jones was state supervisor of the Adult Education Program. From 1945 until his retirement in 1960, he was employed by the Hospital Savings Association in Chapel Hill.

Jones was an avid gardener and an active Methodist layman. In 1916 he married Edna Lynch of Fairview, and they had three children: George Thaddeus (m. Mary Peres), Myra (m. Russell B. Davis and, after his death, Stewart Rogers), and Louise (m. Allen McCain Garrett). Jones died in Riverdale, Md., and his ashes were returned to North Carolina for burial in the old Chapel Hill Cemetery. His widow died in a fire at the Methodist Home, Durham, in 1976.

SEE: *Asheville Citizen-Times,* 16 Dec. 1962; *Chapel Hill Weekly,* 9 Jan. 1963; "William Henry Jones," *The Heritage of Caswell County* (1985); William Henry Jones Papers (North Carolina State Archives, Raleigh); *Statesville Record & Landmark,* 23 Dec. 1983.

H. G. JONES

Jones, Willie (*25 May 1741–18 June 1801*), Revolutionary patriot, consummate politician, Jeffersonian Democrat, and ardent states' righter, was born in Surry County, Va., of Welsh and English parentage. His father, Robin Jones, was sent to Eton where he is said to have attracted the attention of Earl Granville, who later appointed him as his agent for the province of North Carolina. Robin married Sarah Cobb of York County, Va., in 1737 or 1738. They were the parents of five children, including Willie's prominent, conservative brother, Allen, whose daughter, Sarah, married William Richardson Davie. In the early 1750s Robin Jones and his family moved to present Northampton County, N.C., about six miles from the then thriving and important borough town, Halifax. As Granville's land agent and as attorney general of North Carolina, he was probably the largest landed proprietor on the Roanoke River.

Willie (pronounced Wiley) was named for one of his godfathers, the Reverend William Willie of Albemarle Parish, Va. He and his brother Allen both attended their father's alma mater, Eton, which Willie left in 1758 to make the continental "grand tour." On his return to North Carolina, he found that Allen had built his home, Mount Gallant, on the Northampton side of the Roanoke and that his father had left him his large colonial home, The Castle, three miles south of present Jackson. Preferring to live in Halifax, he is said to have torn down his paternal home and built from these timbers, many of which may have come from England, a new home in the southern end of the town—The Groves, behind which was one of the finest race tracks in the colony. This home (which collapsed in the early 1900s) soon became the council hall of many stirring political meetings and the focal point for the belles and blades of the section—both groups of which sought Halifax as the political and social mecca of northeastern North Carolina.

Despite the imminence of war, Jones married Mary Montfort, the daughter of Colonel Joseph Montfort, appointed by the Duke of Beaufort as the first and only "Grand Master of Masons of and for America." Willie

and his wife had thirteen children, only five of whom lived to maturity. Of those who survived, two were sons who died unmarried. Thus there was not one to carry on the name of Jones. The three daughters who lived to maturity all married. Anna Maria married Joseph B. Littlejohn, who served as secretary to William R. Davie on the French mission of 1800. Martha (or Patsy) married U.S. Senator John Wayles Eppes of Buckingham County, Va., whose first wife was Maria, daughter of Thomas Jefferson. The third daughter, Sally Welch, married, first, Hutchins G. Burton, later governor, and second, Andrew Joyner of Poplar Grove near Weldon, N.C.

Willie Jones lived the life of a typical aristocratic planter of the times. According to the records of 1790, he owned, in District 9 of Halifax County alone, 9,942½ acres and 120 slaves, being one of the largest slaveholders in the state; his brother Allen owned 170 slaves. His first political venture was at age twenty-six when he represented Halifax County in the House of Commons in 1767, followed by another session in 1771. As might be expected from his heritage, he was identified during these early years with the royal governors, William Tryon and Josiah Martin, and their clique. He marched with Tryon's colonial militia to Orange County and was appointed Tryon's aide-de-camp on 15 May 1771, the day before Tryon's victory over the Regulators at the Battle of Alamance. Several days later Captain Jones was sent to raid the plantation of Herman Husband, a leading Regulator. When Tryon left North Carolina to become governor of New York, Jones "publicly lamented his removal . . . as a calamity to the province." As a further indication of his allegiance to the royal clique, he was appointed, on Governor Martin's recommendation, to His Majesty's Council of the Province of North Carolina on 9 Mar. 1774.

Jones's apostasy to the Whig cause in the approaching American Revolution was swift. He promptly refused the Council appointment and took his place among the leading radical elements of the Whig faction, which opposed the more conservative elements led by Samuel Johnston, William Hooper, Archibald Maclaine, and Jones's brother, Allen. He was elected to each of the five Provincial Congresses, but could not attend the fourth because he had been appointed superintendent of Indian Affairs for the Southern Colonies. At the Fifth Provincial Congress, he served on the committee to draft the state constitution and has been credited by many as its chief author.

Jones rapidly emerged as the acknowledged leader of the radical, democratic element in the state. He represented the borough of Halifax in the House of Commons in 1777 and 1778 and the county of Halifax in 1779 and 1780. He was senator in 1782, 1784, and 1788. He also served for a year in the Continental Congress (1780).

States' righter that he was, Jones refused appointment as a delegate to the Federal convention in 1787. His excuse to Governor Caswell was that he did not "think it will be in my power to attend there at the Time appointed." When the Constitution was submitted to the Hillsborough convention in 1788, he led the Anti-Federalist forces against its adoption. On the first day he proposed a vote without debate, declaring that "all the delegates knew how they were going to vote and he did not want to be guilty of lavishing public money." Defeated on this issue, he yielded to a full-scale, eleven-day debate in which he seldom participated, but exerted his influence against adoption behind the scenes. Particularly deploring the absence of a bill of rights, he cited a letter from Thomas Jefferson in Paris to James Madison at the Virginia convention, in which Jefferson wrote that he wished nine states would adopt it, not because it deserved ratification but in order to preserve the Union. Jefferson hoped, though, that the other four states would reject it—to ensure the adoption of amendments. Jones, in agreement, concluded: "For my part, I would rather be eighteen years out of the Union than adopt it in its present defective form."

When the final ballot was taken, the Anti-Federalists, by a vote of 184 to 84, carried a resolution neither rejecting nor ratifying the Constitution, but proposed a bill of rights of twenty parts as well as twenty-six amendments. Perhaps realizing that the efforts of such leading Federalists as William R. Davie and James Iredell had turned the tide, Jones did not run as a delegate to the Fayetteville convention of 1789, which ratified the Constitution by a vote of 195 to 77.

North Carolina's entrance into the Union marked Jones's retirement from the political arena, except that in 1796 he ran, and was defeated, for the post of presidential elector. The Jones tradition, however, was carried on by Nathaniel Macon, like Jones a man of aristocratic background imbued with a democratic attitude, who assumed leadership of the Jeffersonian party in the 1790s and held it for over three decades.

Jones's political retirement did not mean that he had forsaken other areas of public service. Not the least of these was his role as "the real founder of Raleigh." He served on the committee, appointed by the legislature in 1791, to locate the capital within ten miles of Isaac Hunter's plantation in Wake County. The committee purchased 1,000 acres of land from Joel Lane and laid off a city containing 400 acres. (It has been suggested that a statue be raised in Raleigh in honor of Jones, who actually parceled out the land. His name and those of other commissioners have been perpetuated in the names of the city's streets.) Soon afterwards he bought sixteen one-acre lots and later built a summer residence, Welcome, where he reportedly spent much of his time.

Still following the Jeffersonian tradition, Jones worked to carry out the constitutional mandate for a state university and served on the original board of trustees. Representing the Halifax judicial district, he also sat on the committees to select the location of the university and to choose its president. After donating $100 to support The University of North Carolina, he and his erstwhile political opponent, William R. Davie, issued a joint appeal in the *North Carolina Journal* for donations to the institution.

Because of his sympathy for the transmontane frontiersmen, the town of Jonesborough, "the oldest formally established town in Tennessee (1779)," was named for this "warm friend of over-mountain people." It was the first capital of the state of Franklin and is still the seat of Washington County. Also, Jones County in North Carolina was named for him.

The sudden decline in Jones's health was first revealed in a letter of 24 May 1801 from Nathaniel Macon to Thomas Jefferson, in which he wrote: "Your acquaintance, Mr. Willie Jones, is, I fear not long for this world. He is unable to walk, and there is no probability that he ever will again." Within a month Jones died at his seat in Raleigh. The Raleigh *Register* concluded his obituary with the statement that "it may with the greatest truth be said that Carolina has not produced a son of greater mental endowment than Mr. Jones, no one who lived more universally and deservedly respected or died more affectionately and sincerely regretted." He was buried on land now occupied by St. Augustine's College, but there is no trace of his grave. A search for it made in 1860 by Thomas Sherwood Haywood and others was unsuccessful.

Jones's will is a remarkable document. He directed that, if he died in Halifax, he should be buried beside his little daughter; or, if he died in Raleigh, he should be buried beside another small daughter. Reflecting his deistic philosophy, no monument or tombstone was to be placed over his grave. The will further stated: "No priest or other person is to insult my corpse by uttering any impious observations over my body. Let it be covered sunny and warm and there is an end. My family and my friends are not to mourn my death, even with a black rag—on the contrary, I give my wife and three daughters, Anna Maria, Sally and Patsy, each a Quaker-colored silk, to make their habits on the occasion."

Perhaps no man in North Carolina more aptly exemplified the eighteenth-century concept of noblesse oblige than did Willie Jones. An aristocrat and a man of great wealth, he was no demagogue or office seeker, but was instead a statesman whose guiding principles were the independence of sovereign people and the social and economic well-being of the masses, who looked to him as a father. Ingrained with this concept of service to the state and to the people, he devoted thirty years of his life to the application of this philosophy. A liberal in politics, education, and religion, he was indeed an "aristocratic democratic," cut from the same pattern as Thomas Jefferson.

SEE: Walter Clark, ed., *State Records of North Carolina*, vols. 12, 17, 19, 25 (1895–1906); Halifax *North Carolina Journal*, 1 Aug. 1792–13 May 1799; James Iredell Papers (Duke University Library, Durham); G. J. McRee, *Life and Correspondence of James Iredell*, 2 vols. (1857–58); Blackwell P. Robinson, "Willie Jones of Halifax," *North Carolina Historical Review* 28 (January, April 1941), and "Willie Jones of Halifax, North Carolina" (M.A. thesis, Duke University, 1939); William L. Saunders, ed., *Colonial Records of North Carolina*, vols. 9, 10 (1890); John H. Wheeler, *Historical Sketches of North Carolina from 1584 to 1851* (1851).

BLACKWELL P. ROBINSON

Jordan, Benjamin Everett (*8 Sept. 1896–15 Mar. 1974*), textile executive and U.S. senator, was born in Ramseur, the son of Ann Elizabeth Sellers and Henry Harrison Jordan, a Methodist minister. He attended Rutherford College Preparatory School and, in 1914–15, Trinity College (now Duke University). From 1915 to 1918 he worked in an uncle's jewelry store in Wellington, Kans. Jordan served in the U.S. Army Tank Corps in France in 1918 and with the occupation forces in Germany in 1919.

In 1920 he took a job with a textile mill in Gastonia, where he was plant superintendent of Myrtle Mill from 1923 to 1926 and of the Gray Mills from 1926 to 1927. In the latter year he was elected secretary-treasurer and general manager of the newly formed Sellers Manufacturing Company, organized by Jordan, his uncle Charles V. Sellers, a Burlington merchant, and other members of the Sellers family. The company purchased a textile mill on the Haw River at Saxapahaw which had been in receivership and standing idle for over three years. The plant was converted to the production of fine-combed cotton yarns intended to supply the local hosiery industry. By 1932 the corporation had purchased equipment for the production of mercerized combed yarns and silk yarn. As a result of plant improvements and the construction of a concrete dam in 1938, Sellers Manufacturing continued to grow. In the late thirties and forties the Sellers group purchased spinning mills in Cedar Falls, Burlington, and Wake Forest which were placed under Jordan's management. In the fifties the company added a dyeing process and equipment for the spinning and blending of synthetic fibers.

Jordan became active in the North Carolina Democratic party in the 1930s. In 1948 he and his brother, Henry, actively supported Kerr Scott's nomination for governor. After his election, Scott appointed Henry chairman of the North Carolina Highway Commission and Everett became chairman of the state Democratic party.

At the 1952 state Democratic convention, Jordan broke with Scott over the presidential nomination; Jordan supported Senator Richard Russell of Georgia, whereas Scott backed Adlai Stevenson. Scott resented Jordan's business alliance with Scott's political enemy, Senator Willis Smith, and Jordan's support of William B. Umstead's gubernatorial candidacy. Jordan continued as party chairman under Governor Umstead until his election as Democratic national committeeman in 1954—a post he held until his appointment to the Senate.

In April 1958 Governor Luther Hodges appointed Jordan to the U.S. Senate to fill the vacancy caused by the death of Kerr Scott, and in November Jordan was elected to fill the remainder of the term ending in January 1961. Several state newspapers suggested that Jordan was appointed as a "seat warmer" until Hodges could run for the Senate in 1960—although both Hodges and Jordan denied making a deal for Jordan not to seek reelection.

Jordan was elected to two full terms in the Senate in 1960 and 1966. His age and health were important issues in the 1972 Democratic primary in which he was defeated by Nick Galifianakis, who in turn lost the general election to Republican Jesse Helms.

By 1972 Jordan was fourth ranking Democrat on the Agriculture and Forestry Committee, third ranking Democrat on the Public Works Committee, and chairman of the Senate Rules Committee. He served alternately as chairman and vice-chairman of both the Joint Committee on the Library of Congress and the Joint Committee on Printing. Jordan was chairman of the Joint Committee on Inaugural Ceremonies in 1964–65 and 1968–69.

As a leader of the conservative wing of the state Democratic party, Jordan faithfully represented the state's tobacco and textile interests. He introduced the "acreage-poundage" legislation that brought sweeping changes in the tobacco marketing system and was instrumental in maintaining tobacco price supports. He also obtained federal appropriations for development of the state's water resources, harbor improvements, and an environmental health center in the Research Triangle Park. In 1964, he entered the national spotlight as chairman of the Rules Committee which investigated the activities of former Senate Democratic secretary Bobby Baker. Jordan's voting record was increasingly liberal during his tenure in the Senate. He generally supported the social welfare, educational, agricultural, and taxation programs of the Kennedy and Johnson administrations while opposing civil rights measures. He was regarded as a dove on the issue of the Vietnam War. In 1970 he broke ranks with other southern Democrats to vote in favor of the Cooper-Church amendment to the defense appropriations bill. The amendment passed,

limiting the president's power to extend U.S. participation in the war. In 1971 he supported the McGovern-Hatfield end-the-war amendment.

Jordan's civic activities included service as a member of the North Carolina Peace Officers Benefit and Retirement Commission (1943–48) and of the North Carolina Medical Care Commission (1945–51). He was a member of the board of trustees of American University, Duke University, and Elon College; chairman of the board of trustees of Alamance County General Hospital; a director of the Alamance County chapter of the American Red Cross; an active supporter of the Cherokee Council of the Boy Scouts of America; and president and a director of the Alamance County Tuberculosis Association.

In 1924 Jordan married Katherine McLean, daughter of Robert Clyde McLean, a Gastonia cotton merchant and realtor. They had three children: Benjamin Everett, Rose Ann (m. Roger Gant, Jr.), and John McLean. Jordan died of cancer at his home in Saxapahaw, thirty-seven months after an operation for cancer of the colon. He was buried in Pine Hill Cemetery, Burlington.

SEE: *Biog. Dir. Am. Cong.* (1970–71); Clippings file (North Carolina Collection, University of North Carolina Library, Chapel Hill); *Nat. Cyc. Am. Biog.* (1961–63); William S. Powell, ed., *North Carolina Lives* (1962); *Who's Who in America* (1970–71); *Who's Who in American Politics* (1969–70); *Who's Who in the South and Southwest* (1967–68); James Richard Young, *Textile Leaders of the South* (1963).

GEORGE W. TROXLER

Jordan, Charles Edward (*13 Apr. 1901–4 Feb. 1974*), university administrator, was born at Henrietta, the son of the Reverend H. H. and Annie Sellers Jordan. His father, a longtime and distinguished member of the Methodist Episcopal Church, South, was a native of Iredell County; his mother was a native of Randolph County. One of five children, Jordan had one sister, Mrs. Henry C. Sprinkle of Mocksville, and three brothers, all of whom were prominent in the state: B. Everett, of Saxapahaw, was a textile manufacturer and served for many years in the U.S. Senate; Henry was appointed chairman of the North Carolina Highway Commission by Governor W. Kerr Scott; and Frank was a clergyman in the Methodist church.

Charles E. Jordan entered Trinity College (now Duke University) in the fall of 1919 and was graduated with a bachelor of arts degree in 1923. He spent the next two years in Trinity's law school where he received a bachelor of laws degree in 1925. Although he passed the state bar examination and was licensed (1926) to practice in North Carolina, he undertook a career in educational administration. Jordan became assistant secretary of Duke University in 1925 and was promoted to secretary in 1941, serving in that capacity through 1957. He was vice-president in the Division of Public Relations (1946–66) and chairman of the university's Athletic Council (1949–63). Elon College awarded him the honorary doctor of laws degree at its commencement in June 1945.

For forty-seven years—from his student days until his retirement in 1966 because of deteriorating health—Jordan had a single objective to serve Duke University. He was a vital part of its stabilization and growth, projecting an image of scholarship and service to thousands of students who attended Duke during his tenure.

In a variety of affiliations, Jordan also served his community and state. While he was a member and chairman (1949–57) of the Durham County Board of Education, three bond issues for support of the schools were authorized by a popular vote and all county schools received full accreditation by the Southern Association of Colleges and Secondary Schools. He resigned the chairmanship in 1957 to accept appointment to the state Board of Education. Jordan was also president of the North Carolina State School Boards Association from 1953 to 1956. The new junior-senior high school built in southern Durham County was named for him in 1963.

From 1947 to 1949 Jordan was chairman of the Institutional Advisory Committee of the Veterans Administration Agency of the federal government. In addition, he was president of the North Carolina Symphony Society (1949–52), a member of the North Carolina Library Association (1955–57), and president of the Atlantic Coast Conference for intercollegiate athletics (1955–56). He was a member of the Rotary Club of Durham (president, 1940–41), Durham Chamber of Commerce (director, 1947–48), and Durham YMCA (director for more than a decade). His business connections included membership on the board of directors of the Home Savings and Loan Association (from 1936); Wachovia Bank, Durham (from 1949); and Occidental Life Insurance Company (from 1949).

An active member of the Duke Memorial United Methodist Church, Jordan was chairman of the Board of Stewards from 1936 to 1941. He also was a member of the board of trustees, North Carolina Conference of the Methodist church (treasurer, 1947–56; chairman, from 1956); Commission on Church Union, General Conference of the Methodist church (1952–56); and General Board of Education of the Methodist church (from 1956). From 1958 he was president of the North Carolina Methodist Board of Publications.

On 12 Dec. 1932 Jordan married Elizabeth Tyree of Durham, and they had two children: Charles Edward, Jr., and Elizabeth (Mrs. William B. Mewborne, Jr.). He died at his home in Durham at age seventy-two and was buried in Maplewood Cemetery.

SEE: Archives (Duke University Library, Durham); *Durham Morning Herald*, 6 Feb. 1974; *Durham Sun*, 5 Feb. 1974; Info Sheet (Office of Information Services, Duke University, Durham).

C. SYLVESTER GREEN

Jordan, Daniel William (20 June 1810–26 Jan. 1883), planter, collateral relative of John Jordan Crittenden of Kentucky, was born at Jordan Plains, Pitt County, of English ancestry. One Thomas Jordan migrated from England to Manhattan Island in the early seventeenth century and later settled in Maryland. Descendants migrated to Virginia and Hyde County, N.C. Daniel's grandfather, John Jordan III, was a delegate to the Provincial Congresses at Hillsborough and Halifax and was active in the American Revolution, served in the lower house of the General Assembly after the Revolution, and established the plantation known as Jordan Plains. Daniel's father, Valentine Smith Jordan, was a farmer; his mother, Sarah Jones Jordan, was a woman of some intellectual refinement and ambition.

Jordan attended Yankee Hall, a well-known school run by northern teachers in Pitt County, and later a school in New York, receiving a diploma in double entry bookkeeping in 1827. Returning home, he clerked in a store but found the work dull. Possessing an adventurous spirit, he rode a horse to Mississippi in 1833 to "scout" the region for possible settlement. Unable to

persuade his father to move, he migrated alone to Mississippi and entered cotton planting in 1834. In the panic of 1837, Jordan went bankrupt and fled his creditors; he returned to North Carolina about 1839–40.

In 1838 he married Emily Tuttle of Mississippi, and with her inheritance managed to recoup his fortunes by engaging in the naval stores industry, then expanding in North Carolina. In 1844 he purchased 800 acres of land in Brunswick County and entered the turpentine business with his brother-in-law, William Brinkley. Three years later he sold his interest and moved to a new plantation on Little River in All Saints Parish, Horry District, S.C., where he was said to have become the first large turpentine producer in South Carolina, turning out crude turpentine and conducting distilling and shipping operations. He was one of the few planters to attempt to solve marketing problems by constructing his own schooner and making direct shipments from his plantation to New York.

In 1860 Jordan sold his Little River plantation to N. F. Nixon and purchased Laurel Hill from Plowden C. J. Weston for $85,000. This well-known country seat was situated on a high bluff overlooking the Waccamaw River. The house was centered as the hub of a wheel with avenues of live oak trees leading from it. In 1860 it was estimated that Jordan owned over 10,000 acres of cotton, turpentine, and rice land and had over 250 slaves. During the Civil War he sold large amounts of rice to the Confederate government and engaged in salt manufacturing, with works capable of producing 50 bushels per day.

When Federal troops encroached on the South Carolina low country in 1864, Jordan, as other planters, took refuge with his family inland. He settled in Camden and engaged in cotton planting, making no effort in the postwar years to regain his coastal plantation. In 1879 he began a successful merchandise business with his son-in-law, Henry G. Carrison, by obtaining credit through Lyon Brothers, commission merchants in Baltimore, and repaying them with cotton in the fall.

Always an ardent states' rights Democrat, Jordan represented All Saints Parish in the South Carolina legislature for one term (1850–52) and held various local positions, such as commissioner of public buildings, free schools, and roads. He was a man of vaulting ambition and restless energy but at times failed to execute plans in detail. He sought always to live in the grand manner, and as he acquired wealth took his wife and daughter on a tour of northern resorts in 1853, indulged in expensive equipage, and ultimately became a member of the exclusive All Saints "Hot and Hot Fish Club." After his return from Mississippi he was usually addressed as "Colonel" but the source of the designation is unknown.

Jordan had five children: Sarah Malvina died in infancy; Sarah Victoria was drowned with her husband on their honeymoon in a Mississippi steamboat disaster in 1861; and a son, Valentine Smith, and daughters Cora Rebecca and Margaret Elizabeth survived him. Although of Episcopal heritage, he was buried in the Quaker cemetery in Camden.

SEE: D. W. Jordan Manuscripts (Duke University Library, Durham); *The Kershaw Gazette* (Camden, S.C.), 26 Jan. 1883; J. H. Rice, *The Aftermath of Glory* (1934); George C. Rogers, *History of Georgetown County, South Carolina* (1970); Albert Sidney Thomas, Genealogical table (in the author's possession).

PERCIVAL PERRY

Jordan, Gerald Ray *(11 Nov. 1896–15 Nov. 1964),* Methodist clergyman, professor, and author, was born in Kinston. He was graduated from Trinity College (now Duke University) with highest honors and received the B.D. degree from Emory University and the M.A. degree from Yale University. From 1921 to 1945 he served churches in Black Mountain, Asheville, Greensboro, Charlotte, High Point, and Winston-Salem. In 1945 Jordan became professor of homiletics and chapel preacher at the Candler School of Theology in Emory University, Atlanta, Ga. His teaching and his publications were recognized in 1960 when he was named Charles Howard Candler Professor in the School of Theology.

Jordan was an inveterate traveler, revival preacher, lecturer on college campuses, preacher to university groups, and prolific author. Among his books were *We Face Calvary and Life, Beyond Despair, Prayer That Prevails, Religion That Is Eternal, You Can Preach, Preaching during a Revolution,* and *Life-Giving Words.* His works were essentially devotional and inspirational in character, often reflecting a sensitivity to the relevance of the gospel to contemporary social issues.

In May 1939 he was a delegate to the Uniting Conference of the Methodist church in Kansas City, Mo. He was a delegate to the General Conference of 1938, 1940, 1944, 1948, and 1952, and a delegate to the Southeastern Jurisdictional Conference in 1940, 1944, 1948, 1952, and 1960. Jordan served on the board of trustees of High Point College and as a trustee of Scarritt College in Nashville, Tenn. For ten years he was a member of the General Board of Education and served on the Peace Commission. He was a keen student of Christian missions, an advocate of evangelism, and a pioneer in the use of television in the teaching of preaching. He received the honorary degrees of doctor of divinity from Duke University and Litt.D. from Lincoln Memorial University.

On 7 Mar. 1922 Jordan married Caroline Moody, and they became the parents of Gerald Ray, Jr., and Terrell Franklin. He died within a few months of retirement and was buried at the city cemetery of Decatur, Ga.

SEE: Boone M. Bowen, *The Candler School of Theology: Sixty Years of Service* (1974); Elmer T. Clark, *Methodism in Western North Carolina* (1966); Albea Godbold, ed., *Methodist History* (October 1968); Umphrey Lee and William Warren Sweet, *A Short History of American Methodism* (1956); Mildred Morse McEwen, *First United Methodist Church: Charlotte, North Carolina* (1983); *Minutes of the Annual Session of the Western North Carolina Conference* (1965).

GRADY L. E. CARROLL

Jordan, Pleasant *(17 Aug. 1812–27 May 1863),* lawyer and Arkansas attorney general, was born in Henderson County, the son of a Baptist minister who owned land along the French Broad River. Young Pleasant received an indifferent common school education before enrolling at a classical academy at Greenville, S.C., which was run on the manual labor plan. Lawrence Orr, congressman and ambassador to Russia, was a classmate. On graduation Jordan taught a term in a rural school. One of his pupils was Joseph E. Brown, a poor backwoods boy and hardworking student who sold two steers to pay for his schooling; he later became governor of Georgia.

Jordan had saved enough in teaching one term to enter the law office of Simpson Bobo at Spartanburg, S.C.

On completing his legal education, he moved with his brother, Fleming, to Arkansas, arriving in Little Rock in January 1843. Pleasant entered the office of Absalom Fowler, a prominent attorney, but later practiced with his brother. In 1849, he ran for the office of prosecuting attorney of the Fifth Judicial Circuit; at the time, he was described as a young man of "enterprise, energy, and high aspirations for eminence at the bar" but he was defeated at the polls. In 1861, however, Jordan won election as prosecuting attorney, a position that made him ex officio attorney general of Arkansas. He held the office until his death.

Jordan's goal was to be a cultured gentleman. During his short life he succeeded in building up a large legal library (inventoried in the probating of his estate), a sizable fortune, and a good reputation at the bar. He was a Whig in politics. In personal appearance he was five feet ten inches tall with black eyes, hair, and whiskers. Although raised a Baptist, Jordan joined the Campbellite denomination in Little Rock.

In 1851 he married Sallie E. Howell, the daughter of Seth Howell of Johnson County. The father of three girls and two boys, Jordan was buried at Mount Holly Cemetery in Little Rock.

SEE: John Hallum, *Biographical and Pictorial History of Arkansas* (1887); Little Rock *Arkansas Gazette,* 11 Jan. 1849, 6 June 1880.

MICHAEL B. DOUGAN

Jordan, Stroud *(11 Nov. 1885–28 Dec. 1947),* industrial chemist, was born at Caldwell Institute, Orange County, the son of Dr. Archibald Currie and Octavia Stroud Jordan. In 1905 he was graduated from The University of North Carolina, where he earned the master of science degree in 1907 and in 1909 received the first Ph.D. in chemistry awarded by the university.

Jordan held a Carnegie grant for research in New York City in 1905 before his appointment as professor at Gordon College in Massachusetts (1905–6) and instructor at the Massachusetts Institute of Technology (1909–11). From 1911 to 1920 he was chief chemist for the American Tobacco Company and originated the "toasting process," which became the basis for Lucky Strike cigarettes. In 1918 he volunteered for service in World War I and became a captain at Sixth Corps Headquarters with the Chemical Warfare Service of the Eighty-eighth Division; he served for a year in France. Afterwards Jordan was chief chemist for a large manufacturer of candy, became managing director of the Applied Sugar Laboratories, and in 1934 established the Stroud Jordan Laboratories in New York City. He served from 1934 to 1938 as chief of the Bureau of Standardization of the Department of Purchase for the city of New York, and from 1938 until his death he was director of research of the American Sugar Refining Laboratory. During World War II, as a dollar-a-year-man, he worked for a brief time in Washington, D.C.

Active in a number of professional organizations, Jordan was recognized as a brilliant chemist and an interpreter of highly technical information in lay terms. He was the author of four books on chemistry in confectionery manufacturing.

In 1912 he married Virginia Marshburn of Barnesville, Ga., and they were the parents of two daughters, Virginia and Dorothy Louise. He died of a heart attack at his winter home in Miami, Fla.

SEE: Alumni records (University of North Carolina, Chapel Hill); Maurice M. Bursey, *Carolina Chemists* (1982); Daniel L. Grant, *Alumni History of the University of North Carolina, 1795–1924* (1924); *New York Times*, 30 Dec. 1947.

WILLIAM S. POWELL

Joyner, Andrew (5 Nov. 1786–20 Sept. 1856), legislator and army officer, was born in Halifax County, the son of Henry (d. 1803) and Menie Troughton Joyner. An able legislator and promoter of internal affairs in state government, Andrew Joyner represented Martin County in the House of Commons from 1811 to 1813. During the War of 1812, he served for two years as a second major in the Third North Carolina Regiment of volunteers; in 1814 he was transferred to a new division and there made lieutenant colonel of the First Regiment. After the war he returned to his native county.

In 1826 Joyner and Cadwallader Jones formed the Roanoke Steamboat Company, which saw the first steamboat travel up the Roanoke River to Halifax on 15 Apr. 1829. In 1835 Joyner's Roanoke Navigation Company built the canal from Danville, Va., to Weldon—Weldon Orchard being an important railroad junction for the canal. Joyner was also president of the Seaboard and Roanoke and the Weldon and Portsmouth railroads.

From 1835 to 1852 he served in the North Carolina Senate, of which he was speaker three times (1838, 1840, 1846). As a Whig, Joyner promoted internal improvements in the legislature. In the 1836–37 session, he served on the Joint Committee of Twenty-Six (15 Whigs and 11 Democrats) to advise on the use of surplus revenues. Influenced by Dorothea Dix, he also supported a bill to establish a state school for the deaf, dumb, and blind in Raleigh.

Joyner was a trustee of The University of North Carolina for nineteen years (1836–56). In January 1839, he, David L. Swain, and William A. Graham formed a committee that reported in favor of providing new halls for the Dialectic and Philanthropic literary societies, especially for housing their growing libraries. Admired for his fairness and integrity, Joyner also served as a justice of the peace and an arbitrator in local disputes. His judicial endeavors earned his residence the name of "Colonel Joyner's Court of Equity."

By his first wife, Temperance Williams, the daughter of Colonel William Williams of Martin County, Joyner had five children: Elizabeth (m. the Reverend Robert Oswald Burton); Henry, a physician (m. Ann Elizabeth Pope); Martha Williams (m. Colonel Archibald Alexander Austin and later, in 1856 in Halifax County, Francis P. Haywood); Temperance (m. Dr. Willie Jones Eppes of Virginia); and Mary Camilla (m. William A. Daniel in 1850 in Warren County). In the fall of 1839, he married Sarah Wales Burton, the widow of Governor Hutchins G. Burton and the daughter of Willie and Mary Montford Jones of Halifax.

Joyner was baptized and confirmed in 1852 at St. Mark's Episcopal Church in Halifax. He was buried in the family cemetery at his plantation, Poplar Grove, four miles west of Weldon.

SEE: W. C. Allen, *History of Halifax County* (1918); Susie B. Anderson, *Abstract of Wills: Halifax County, North Carolina, 1760–1830* (1947); Samuel A. Ashe, ed., *Biographical History of North Carolina*, vol. 3 (1905); Kemp P. Battle, *History of the University of North Carolina*, vol. 1 (1907); Walter Clark, *History of the Raleigh and Gaston Railroad Company* (1877); J. G. de R. Hamilton, ed., *The Papers of Thomas Ruffin*, vol. 1 (1918); Legislature of North Carolina, *Report on the Progress and Present Condition of the Affairs of the Roanoke Navigation Company* (1831); Willie Jones Long Collection (Southern Historical Collection, University of North Carolina Library, Chapel Hill); North Carolina General Assembly, Committee on Internal Improvements, *Resolution to Investigate the Roanoke Navigation Company* (1852); H. D. Pegg, *The Whig Party in North Carolina* (1968); Dorothy Williams Potter, ed., *1820 Federal Census of North Carolina, Halifax County* (1972); Henry Thomas Shanks, ed., *The Papers of Willie Person Mangum*, vol. 3 (1953); Stuart Hall Smith and Claiborne T. Smith, Jr., *The History of Trinity Parish, Scotland Neck, Edgecombe Parish, Halifax County* (1955); John H. Wheeler, *Historical Sketches of North Carolina from 1584 to 1851* (1851).

EVA MURPHY

Joyner, Edmund Noah (26 July 1847–10 Oct. 1939), Episcopal priest, missionary, soldier, poet, and newspaper editor, was born in the Marlboro community near Farmville in Pitt County, the son of Dr. Noah and Emily Adelaide Williams Joyner. His father was an 1838 graduate of Jefferson Medical College, Philadelphia, and operated an extensive plantation in Pitt County. Edmund was one of eleven children. Three of his brothers, John Richard, Francis, and James, were also Episcopal priests; another, Robert Williams, was a physician; and a fifth brother, Andrew, was an attorney. His sisters were Clara Elizabeth (m. the Reverend Charles Daniel Malone), Sarah Lucy, and Harriette (m. the Reverend Hardy H. Phelps).

Probably the most unusual aspect of Joyner's career was his work as teacher, missionary, and advocate among the former slaves in the Carolinas during the decades immediately following the Civil War. Years before, on his parents' plantation, his mother had conducted Sunday school every Sunday afternoon for the slaves, whose infants were baptized and whose marriages and burial services were performed according to the *Book of Common Prayer*. Some slaves later related that "Marse Eddie" taught them to read, although such activity was illegal. From 1879 to 1884, while rector at Pittsboro, Joyner worked in the black community; in 1889 he was assigned by the Bishop of South Carolina to do missionary work among blacks in the vicinity of Columbia; and in 1892 he became archdeacon for all missionary activity among blacks throughout the state. During this period Joyner made what he called "raids" into northern states such as Michigan, New York, and Pennsylvania to raise money and preach in their Episcopal churches.

As a child Joyner was severely burned when he fell into a large cauldron of boiling cotton dye. At first it was thought he would not live. Virtually helpless for three years, he suffered a drawn ligament which greatly impaired walking. He used crutches but was eventually able to get around by himself.

Joyner was fourteen when the Civil War began. His two older brothers, Robert and John, left their studies at The University of North Carolina to volunteer for Confederate military service. Because the Joyner home in Pitt County was just inside the Confederate lines for most of the war, there was a constant flow of refugees and military wounded in residence. On 18 Oct. 1864, at age seventeen, Joyner enlisted in Company D, Thirteenth Battalion, North Carolina Light Artillery, in New Hanover County; the company was made up mostly of men from Pitt and Beaufort counties. He participated in both battles at Fort Fisher, where on 15 Jan. 1865 a minié ball took away a side of his skull and he was taken prisoner. When a local newspaper reported his head wound and capture, his parents thought that he was dead. He remained a prisoner at Point Lookout until 25 July, when he took the Oath of Allegiance. He returned home on Sunday, 30 July, astride a borrowed mule.

Still only eighteen, Joyner was sent by his father to the Davis School in Louisburg and the Horner School at Oxford. He briefly attended Trinity College at Hartford, Conn., but his eyes failed because of the wound in his temple and he was forced to withdraw. On 3 Jan. 1871 he married Mary Elizabeth Winfield of Chocowinity, and they had two children: Edmund Noah, Jr., and Mary Winfield.

Joyner got his first taste of journalism in 1872 when he purchased and for a short time operated a newspaper in Wilson. In 1873 he moved to Hickory Tavern (later Hickory) and opened a school, where his brother Andrew joined him as a teacher. In September of that year Joyner was ordained into the Episcopal ministry at Grace Church, Morganton, by Bishop Thomas Atkinson, whose conciliatory and nurturing attitudes towards the freed slaves he shared. He became the first rector of the Church of the Ascension, Hickory, which had been organized in May, and in the summer of 1873 he performed the first wedding ever held in a church in Hickory. In 1874 Joyner's mother died, and his father and two other brothers moved to Hickory to open a drugstore and medical practice. In the same year congregations at Statesville and Newton were added to his charge.

In 1879 Joyner moved to Pittsboro to become rector of St. Bartholomew's Church, and in 1881–82 he also served the Chapel of the Cross, Chapel Hill, which had no rector. On 24 July 1881 he assisted his lifelong friend, the Reverend Joseph Blount Cheshire, Jr., and Bishop Theodore B. Lyman in the consecration of St. Philip's, the first Episcopal church in Durham. Joyner was offered the full-time rectorship of the Chapel of the Cross but declined it, as Pittsboro at that time was a larger parish than Chapel Hill or Durham.

The Church Messenger, official newspaper of the Diocese of North Carolina, was then being published in Durham by the Reverend Charles J. Curtis. Because he had difficulty in getting it printed, Curtis decided to sell out. Joyner bought the paper and operated it as editor from 2 Feb. 1883 to 14 July 1887. He continued to live in Pittsboro and hired as associate editor C. B. Denson, principal of Pittsboro Academy. On 29 Feb. 1884, Joyner announced the move of the paper to Charlotte, where he expected it to merge with the *Church Herald* of South Carolina under a new name, *The Southern Guardian*. Joyner himself moved to nearby Rock Hill, S.C., taking charge of the church there and one at Yorkville. The newspaper merger fell through, so the *Messenger* retained its name. With the 29 Jan. 1885 issue, the Reverend Joseph Blount Cheshire, Jr., became co-editor and proprietor with Joyner; in September 1885 the Reverend R. W. Barnwell became associate editor. On 7 Jan. 1886, John Hirst, a Charlotte printer, became publisher, with Joyner as editor and Cheshire and Barnwell as associate editors. Barnwell left the paper on 4 Nov. 1886 "due to his distance from the base of operations." The 7 Feb. 1887 issue noted the departure of Cheshire due to heavy parish duties. By 16 June 1887, Joyner wrote that he "must retire" because of the growing demands of his work as pastor and missionary. In the last issue of the

paper on 14 July, he eloquently defended his own work in South Carolina among blacks.

Joyner also served as chaplain of a large association of labor unions centered in Columbia for twelve years, and twice as chaplain to the North Carolina Division of the United Confederate Veterans, a position he held at the time of his death. In 1905 he became General Missionary of the Missionary District of Asheville (later the Diocese of Western North Carolina), with residence and pastoral duties at Tryon. He took charge of St. James Church, Lenoir, about 1912.

His first wife having died, he married Elizabeth Andrews of Willington, S.C., in 1912. Their son, Archibald Andrews, was born in Lenoir, from which, after a pastorate of nine years, Joyner and his family retired to a remote settlement in Avery County, N.C., with no church, where they conducted "welfare work." After a few years he returned to South Carolina and remained in church work until 1928, when he "retired" once again to Hickory.

In addition to his writing as a newspaper editor, Joyner often wrote letters to church and secular journals in support of education and missionary work. In 1886 after a federal decree banned the placing of flowers on the graves of Confederate soldiers in Arlington Cemetery, a southern woman ignorant of the law was dragged away from the grave of her son and refused permission to leave flowers there. Outraged by this report, Joyner wrote a ten-stanza poem, "O Shame to the Foes of the Dead," which was printed in the Tarboro newspaper after Decoration Day.

His last act as a minister was to baptize his grandson, Edmund Lee Joyner, the son of his youngest child. Edmund Noah Joyner was buried in the churchyard at Calvary Church near Fletcher.

SEE: *The Church Messenger*, 1881–87; Norvin C. Duncan, *A Biographical Sketch of Rev. Edmund Noah Joyner* (1940); Thomas Felix Hickerson, *Happy Valley: History and Genealogy* (1940); Hickory *Piedmont Press*, 1873–79; Louis Manarin, comp., *North Carolina Troops, 1861–1865: A Roster*, vol. 1 (1966); Pittsboro *Chatham Record*, 1879–84; Charles J. Preslar, Jr., *A History of Catawba County* (1954); Laura Foster Renard, *The May, Lang, Joyner, Williams Family of North Carolina* (1974).

E. T. MALONE, JR.

Joyner, James Yadkin (7 Aug. 1862–24 Jan. 1954), educator, farmer, and North Carolina superintendent of public instruction, was a member of the generation of gifted educational statesmen who led North Carolina in an educational revival during the early twentieth century. He was born at Yadkin College in Davidson County, the youngest of seven children of John and Sarah ("Sallie") A. Wooten Joyner. His parents had recently moved to the western part of the state from their Lenoir County farm to escape the effects of the Civil War. Orphaned by age two, Joyner was reared on a farm in Lenoir County, first by his maternal grandfather Council Wooten, and, from age ten, by his uncle Shadrack I. Wooten. In later years, Joyner recalled the great influence on the development of his character exerted by his grandfather Wooten, a prominent planter near LaGrange and an influential Democrat. Wooten had served in the state house of representatives, at the Constitutional Convention of 1835, and on the Governor's Council (1860–62).

After studying under his grandfather and attending LaGrange Academy, Joyner entered The University of

North Carolina at age sixteen and three years later (1881) was graduated with the bachelor of philosophy degree. He became a friend of classmates Charles B. Aycock, Edwin A. Alderman, and Charles D. McIver. In later years, the university awarded Joyner the honorary LL.D.

In the fall of 1881, he returned to LaGrange Academy to teach Latin and other subjects. From 1882 to 1884, he served simultaneously as principal of the small private school and as public school superintendent of Lenoir County. In 1884 he moved to Winston to teach at the newly organized graded school, where Charles D. McIver was principal.

After one year at the progressive Winston school, Joyner entered the Greensboro law school of Robert P. Dick and John H. Dillard. Admitted to the bar in 1886, he moved to Goldsboro to practice but after three years his interest in education prevailed. From 1887 to 1889 he served as chairman of the Wayne County Board of Education, and in the summer of 1889 he joined the band of educators led by McIver and Alderman who traveled across the state conducting teacher institutes and providing most teachers their first professional training.

While living in Goldsboro, Joyner married Effie E. Rouse, of LaGrange, whom he had known since childhood. She attended LaGrange Academy, was graduated from Peace Institute, and taught for a year before her marriage. The Joyners became the parents of two sons, James Noah and William Thomas.

In 1889 Joyner succeeded Edwin A. Alderman as superintendent of the Goldsboro Graded Schools. The chairman of the board of trustees was his old friend, Charles B. Aycock. As city superintendent for four years, Joyner gained valuable experience and a growing reputation as the leader of an advanced school system.

The next nine years (1893–1902) found Joyner in Greensboro as a professor of English and dean of the new State Normal and Industrial College (now the University of North Carolina at Greensboro). He also was employed by president Charles D. McIver to assist in training women to become teachers. Joyner was able to combine his love of reading and poetry with his interest in teaching methods and became increasingly knowledgeable in education and administration. He continued to take part in summer teacher institutes and, in 1896, served as president of the state Teachers' Assembly. Joyner spoke out on educational issues, defended the principle of state support of higher education, and became a frequent contributor to the *North Carolina Journal of Education*. In 1901 he lobbied successfully for revision of the school law, and that spring he served on the newly authorized textbook commission.

During his stay in Greensboro, Joyner was active in civic affairs and a variety of organizations. He was an alderman and mayor pro tem, a trustee of the Agricultural and Technical College, and a member of the Democratic party and the Junior Order of United American Mechanics.

In February 1902 Governor Aycock appointed him superintendent of public instruction. Joyner entered the job at age thirty-nine with a total of seventeen years of teaching and administrative experience. The selection of Joyner to fill the unexpired term of deceased Thomas F. Toon met with strong endorsement from his fellow educators, and he received a vote of approval from the people in five subsequent elections.

The most dramatic period of Joyner's administration came in his first two years (1902–4), during the fight for increased school support led by Aycock, McIver, and Joyner. The three men spoke at educational rallies throughout the state to encourage the consolidation of school districts, the adoption of local state taxes, the construction of better buildings, and the lengthening of school terms. By 1904 there had been marked improvements in the areas of special taxes, new buildings, rural school libraries, and school enrollment. In Joyner's opinion, an educational "revolution" had occurred with the awakening of public support for universal public education.

During his seventeen years as state superintendent, two goals held special importance for Joyner—better training for teachers and the availability of public secondary education. For the teachers, he urged the establishment of teachers' colleges, better organization of institute work, a uniform state system of certification, and increased funds for black normal schools. Joyner called for the development of public high schools that would provide education not only for college-bound students, but also for the majority who were preparing for everyday life and citizenship. In order to adapt the work of rural schools to the local environment, he emphasized the need for the teaching of agriculture. He sought special facilities at rural high schools for the training of farmers and homemakers. Through these farm life schools, as they became known, Joyner hoped to fulfill his goal of preserving and improving the quality of rural life.

Although there continued to be deficiencies in some areas, there was notable progress in public education from 1902 to 1919, as Joyner's *Biennial Reports* recorded. At his urging, legislation was passed to establish teacher-training schools at Boone and Greenville (now Appalachian State and East Carolina universities), to consolidate the black normals into a more effective system, to provide the basis for a state system of teacher certification, to encourage the establishment of high schools, to promote the teaching of agriculture, and to establish mild regulations for compulsory attendance. In addition, Joyner strengthened and raised the prestige of his office, which provided increased services and numerous publications to aid school administrators and teachers.

A fundamental change in public attitudes had taken place during Joyner's tenure. Increased public support for a statewide system of public schools was reflected most notably in the increase of revenue for schools from local taxes. The state also broadened its financial responsibility. For the first time, the state appropriated money for the support of secondary education, and (in the farm life schools experiment) for vocational education. At Joyner's insistence, the legislature confirmed and extended state responsibility for teacher training. In the area of black education, he defeated efforts to require the division of school funds by race. Towards the end of his final term, an educational study commission was created to study the existing system of schools and to help plot the course for future development.

The last year of Joyner's service as state superintendent witnessed what has been termed his "crowning achievement." In November 1918 the voters approved a constitutional amendment that raised the required minimum school term from four to six months. In December 1918, at age fifty-six, Joyner made public his decision to retire, and in January 1919 he bequeathed to his successor, Eugene Clyde Brooks, plans for implementing the new six months requirement.

The progress achieved from 1902 to 1919 was due in part to the confidence inspired by Joyner's leadership, to his optimistic but moderate approach to change, to his efficient and honest performance of duty, and to his endorsement of financial aid from outside sources such as the Southern Education Board. In the opinion of contemporary Nathan W. Walker, Joyner was motivated in his fight for educational progress by an "intense desire to serve his people."

While state superintendent, Joyner was active in the Conference for Education in the South, the Association of Southern State Superintendents, and the National Education Association. He served terms as president of each of the organizations and made numerous addresses at annual meetings.

Joyner's retirement from school work in 1919 and his temporary return to his LaGrange farm drew him into a new career as farm leader and organizer. He became involved in the promotion of southern tobacco and cotton cooperatives, returning to Raleigh in 1922 as president of the North Carolina Tobacco Growers Association. From 1926 to 1932 he was a successful sales agent for the Prudential Life Insurance Company. Shortly after the death of his wife, Joyner returned to Lenoir County to personally manage his farms.

During the 1920s and 1930s Joyner remained highly interested in educational and farm problems, serving on state commissions concerned with adult education and with agricultural credit corporations. In the 1940s and 1950s, he was acclaimed the "grand old man of North Carolina education." He received tributes from the U.S. Commissioner of Education, the state Board of Education, and the state Grange. His hometown celebrated "Dr. J. Y. Joyner Day," and the Raleigh *News and Observer* honored him as "Tar Heel of the Week."

Joyner died at age ninety-one and was buried beside his wife in Oakwood Cemetery, Raleigh. Three years later, a portrait was presented by his family to Meredith College, which he had served as trustee for fifty-four years.

SEE: Samuel A. Ashe, ed., *Biographical History of North Carolina*, vol. 6 (1907); Willard B. Gatewood, Jr., *Eugene Clyde Brooks: Educator and Public Servant* (1960); Elmer D. Johnson, "James Yadkin Joyner, Educational Statesman," *North Carolina Historical Review* 33 (July 1956); Talmage C. Johnson and Charles R. Holloman, *The Story of Kinston and Lenoir County* (1954); James Yadkin Joyner Papers, Superintendent of Public Instruction Papers (North Carolina State Archives, Raleigh); Robert C. Lawrence, "Dr. J. Y. Joyner," *The State* 7 (22 July 1939); Oliver H. Orr, Jr., *Charles Brantley Aycock* (1961); Raleigh *News and Observer*, 23 July 1950; Gilbert Allen Tripp, "James Yadkin Joyner's Contributions to Education in North Carolina as State Superintendent" (M.A. thesis, University of North Carolina, Chapel Hill, 1939); *Who's Who in America* (1922–23).

GEORGE-ANNE WILLARD

Junaluska (*1779[?]–20 Nov. 1858*), Cherokee warrior and hero of Andrew Jackson's victory over the Creeks at Horseshoe Bend in 1814, was born near the head of the Little Tennessee River in either Macon County, N.C., or Rabun County, Ga. Although the date of his birth is uncertain, he signed four federal affidavits in 1849 indicating his age as "about seventy" and he was listed as seventy-two in the 1851 Cherokee census. The names of his parents are not known.

"Junaluska" is a corruption of the warrior's second Cherokee name. According to folk tradition, when he was born, his parents had great difficulty in finding an appropriate name for him. One day when his carry-

ing frame was placed against a tree while his parents worked, the frame fell over. He was then named Gul-ka-la-ski or "one falling from a leaning position." He was so-called until 1814. In that year he vowed to exterminate every Creek in battle, but, despite an overwhelming victory, did not achieve his goal. As a result, he called himself Tsu-na-la-hun-ski or "one who tries, but fails." Over the last four decades of his life, the name was gradually Anglicized into its present form.

Virtually nothing is known of Junaluska's life until 1811. During that year, the Shawnee chief Tecumseh visited the Cherokees at Soco Gap and urged them to join his war against the advancing American settlers. Junaluska spoke for the Cherokees—despite this instance of leadership, he never held the title of chief—and rejected Tecumseh's overtures. Junaluska also spoke for the tribal leadership when he extolled the advantages of the settled agricultural life-style adopted by the Cherokees.

In November 1813, he recruited one hundred Cherokees in western North Carolina who joined an army of five hundred braves already enrolled in Georgia, Tennessee, and Alabama to fight with Andrew Jackson against the Creeks. During his four months of service with this force, Junaluska performed feats that would make him a legendary figure in his lifetime. One account credits him with stopping a Creek prisoner from killing Jackson, although there is no documentation to support this story. There is much better evidence that Junaluska may have played a significant role in the battle between Jackson's force and the Creeks at Horseshoe Bend, Ala. When white militia stormed the fortified Creek position on 27 Mar. 1814, Junaluska and other Cherokees swam across the Tennessee River and secured the Creek canoes. Then they ferried the Cherokee force across the river and into a position at the rear of the Creeks. The outflanked Creeks continued to fight fiercely but were eventually overwhelmed by Jackson's army. Junaluska was recognized for his bravery—he was wounded in the shoulder—and his daring. The Cherokees, in particular, believed that his actions were responsible for the victory.

Junaluska returned to North Carolina and continued as a farmer. Little is known of this period in his life except that he appears to have been moderately successful. Under the provisions of the Treaty of 1819, he claimed 640 acres of land in Deep Gap. Later claims in 1843 asked for compensation for two farms of more than 300 acres each at Yularka and Cheoah. In 1838 Junaluska was forced by Federal troops to leave North Carolina and join most of the other Cherokees in the removal to Oklahoma. Traditional accounts maintain that during the forced move Junaluska's wife and children died due to the difficulty of the trip. The same accounts assert that Junaluska expressed deep resentment about Andrew Jackson's support for the removal process.

Upset by the loss of his family and longing for his native homeland, Junaluska walked the entire distance from Oklahoma to North Carolina in 1843. Having no legal status in the state, he was forced to live a precarious existence for the next three years. In 1847, a special act of the North Carolina legislature accorded him citizenship and a grant of 337 acres in recognition of his actions in aiding Jackson's army at Horseshoe Bend. This land was located at Cheoah and was apparently part of his holdings before he was forced to leave the state. One provision of the grant would embroil Junaluska and his heirs in controversy for two decades. The legislature had required that Junaluska not sell the land, but in 1850 he sold the grant to George W. Hayes for $1,000. Junaluska later left the same property to be used to support his wife. The controversy was not settled until 1872, when George Smythe, a northern businessman, acquired the land. The present town of Robbinsville occupies part of the grant.

Junaluska died at age seventy-nine. According to traditional accounts, he collapsed while walking to the healing springs of Citico, Tenn. In 1910, the General Joseph Winston Chapter of the Daughters of the American Revolution in Graham County erected a monument over Junaluska's grave on a wooded hill in Robbinsville.

He was married at least three times. One wife died before 1829, and there are no records of any children. Another wife and at least two sons accompanied him on the journey to Oklahoma during the 1838 removal, and they apparently died during the ordeal. On his return to North Carolina in 1843, he married Nicie (or Nisuh) and they had three children: Jimmy, Nalih, and Secqueyuh.

SEE: Documents covering Junaluska's life (Graham County Courthouse; Federal Courthouse, Asheville); William Holland Thomas Papers and microfilm records of Cherokee materials (National Archives, Washington, D.C.; Museum of the Cherokee Historical Society, Cherokee, N.C.). The only reasonably accurate account of his life is found in H. C. Wilburn, *Junaluska: The Man—The Name—The Places* (1951). The one surviving photograph is published in Ora Blackmun, *Western North Carolina: Its Mountains and Its People to 1880* (1977).

GORDON B. MCKINNEY

Justice, Amos Isaac (8 Dec. 1851–21 Dec. 1945), Baptist clergyman, was born in the Edneyville section of rural Henderson County. No record has been found identifying his parents, although it is known that his family moved to Rutherford County in 1853 and subsequently to Madison County. His father, probably a tenant farmer, was known to be an ardent churchman who saw to it that his children were "at home in the church." Further, his parents must have been better schooled than many others during the postwar period, for it was reported that Justice, at age sixteen, "began preaching and teaching while continuing efforts to advance his own studies and teaching." His formal schooling was limited to short periods of study at Judson College in Hendersonville under Professor W. C. McCarthey and later at Weaver College in Weaverville.

In 1867 Justice was ordained to the Baptist ministry in his home church in Madison County, and for the next sixty years he served churches in Madison, Buncombe, Polk, and Henderson counties. His last pastorate was at Marshall, from which he retired in 1930. Nevertheless, he continued to teach and to serve as supply preacher and interim pastor of many churches in the area until the age of ninety-three, when his hearing and eyesight failed and he entered a nursing home in Asheville. At the time of his death, he had long been the oldest active Baptist minister in the state.

During his ministry, Justice was pastor of thirty Baptist churches and was the leader in organizing five additional churches. He preached with great fervor, buttressing his sermons with wide reading and thoughtful interpretation of the Scriptures. His zeal for education provided the leadership that resulted in the organization of two educational institutions: Fruitland Institute in Henderson County and Fairview Institute in Buncombe County. A highlight of his career was the estab-

lishment of Fruitland Institute, near Hendersonville. Impressed with the need for formal educational facilities in that part of the state (around 1885, there was no high school in the four contiguous counties of Henderson, Polk, Rutherford, and Transylvania), Justice founded the school, became its first principal, and was involved in its administration for many years at great personal, physical, and financial sacrifice. He also sought funds to maintain the institution, which provided academic and Christian training for literally hundreds of students from the area. Wake Forest College, for one, accepted many Fruitland graduates who went on to become teachers, preachers, lawyers, congressmen, and business leaders across the state.

In denominational leadership, Justice served for years as moderator of the Carolina Association. His influence as a conciliatory and considerable force in solidifying church groups and organizations was widely felt throughout the Baptist State Convention, especially during the last quarter of the nineteenth century. One of his most successful undertakings led to the merging of the Western North Carolina Baptist Convention in 1898 with the North Carolina Baptist State Convention, which had been organized in Greenville in 1830. In that effort Justice worked with Albert Erskine Brown, a dedicated Baptist minister in western North Carolina.

In 1870 Justice married Minerva Fisher of Madison County. They were the parents of one son, James Foy, and five daughters: Lillie, Juliana, Minnie, May, and Lola. Justice died at age ninety-four; after funeral services in the First Baptist Church, Hendersonville, where he was a member, he was buried in the Hendersonville Cemetery.

SEE: *Asheville Citizen*, 22 Dec. 1945; *Minutes of the Carolina Baptist Association* (1881); *Report of the North Carolina Baptist Historical Commission* (1923).

C. SYLVESTER GREEN

Justice, Edwin (or Edward) Judson (10 June 1867–15 July 1917), lawyer, Democratic party leader, legislator, and special prosecutor, was born in Rutherfordton, one of six children and the oldest son of Margaret L. Smith and Michael Hoke Justice, a state senator and Superior Court judge. His family members were strong Baptists—among them his grandparents, the Reverend T. B. and Harriet Bailey Justice. He was graduated from Wake Forest College in 1887, then studied law with his father and at Colonel George N. Folk's Law School in Caldwell County. Justice practiced first in Rutherfordton with his father and, beginning in 1893, with his cousin, James William Pless, in Marion where he served a term as mayor in 1902.

In 1898 Justice was elected to the North Carolina House of Representatives from the Marion District. As a member of the Judiciary Committee, he helped draft the constitutional amendment on suffrage that disfranchised illiterate blacks; he also was chairman of the Corporation Committee and a member of the committees on Courts and Judicial Districts, Banks and Currency, Education, and Corporation Claims. During this session Justice began to criticize the Railroad Commission, citing its failure to protect the state's farmers, wholesalers, retailers, and manufacturers. At the same time, he became aware of the shortcomings of commission personnel as well as the statutory limitations of the commission itself; he urged that its powers be strengthened or that it be eliminated entirely. In the same legislative session, the Railroad Commission was replaced by the

Corporation Commission, which was endowed with broader powers and jurisdiction.

A senator from McDowell County in 1902, Justice became a member of the committees on Corporations, Appropriations, Federal Relations, the Judiciary, and the Deaf, Dumb, and Blind Asylums. He was chairman of the Railroads Committee where he became "the acknowledged authority on railroad regulation," equitable taxation on railroad properties, and the rate-making practices in force in North Carolina and neighboring states. Justice believed that the grossly unfair freight rates were mitigating against growth and prosperity for the state. His views were supported and augmented by the work of interest groups for organized political action, especially in Winston-Salem.

After the close of the 1903 session, Justice moved to Greensboro to form a law partnership with Edgar D. Broadhurst II, and to be closer to the center of the newly industrialized Piedmont. Building up a large practice, he represented some of the textile and furniture corporate structures. Because of his experience as president of the Blue Ridge Furniture Manufacturing Company in Marion and his banking interests, he was familiar with the problems facing these and other businesses. He was also active in civic affairs, drafting the charter for the city of Greensboro which incorporated the commission form of government.

In Greensboro he championed liberal causes, including attempts to rectify the unequal competition of state insurers with out-of-state firms and the high freight costs imposed on business and agriculture. Realizing that the solution to these and other problems lay in action by the legislature, he ran for a seat in the house of representatives from Guilford County in 1906. After his election he was chosen speaker, from which vantage point he introduced much needed legislation, debated his bills on the floor, and often urged support in the senate. The house in 1907 has been described as the most progressive body in the state during the Progressive Era.

Perhaps his greatest triumph in the 1907 session of the legislature was as the seasoned and skillful chairman of the joint legislative committee hearings at which railroad presidents and executives were summoned to testify on rate legislation and other matters. "With threats of subpoenas when necessary," Justice demanded information on rate discrimination; on money paid to newspapers, lobbyists, and executives for influence; and on the detailed earnings of the railroads. His forceful leadership and the widespread newspaper coverage of his work resulted in support for his efforts and the "perception of his goals as right and just." His achievements also "marked an end to the power of the railroad lobby in the state." Federal court injunctions and decisions forced the state to compromise on rate schedules. The onerous task of defending the state's actions before the higher courts, as well as the Interstate Commerce Commission, fell on Justice, who did so with some success.

Many other programs authorized in the 1907 session were held up by conservative forces in the government and in the state. Progressive leadership did not gain strength until about five years later under the impetus of Woodrow Wilson's candidacy for the presidency on the New Freedom platform. Justice was an early supporter of Wilson, later becoming his state campaign manager and delegate-at-large to the nominating convention.

Justice was returned to the house for the 1913 term, when stronger antitrust and antilobby legislation was

enacted and further reductions in the freight rates were negotiated by his committee. But he failed in his efforts to pass needed child labor laws, electoral reforms, and the provision of initiative, referendum, and recall legislation.

Late in 1913 President Wilson appointed Justice special assistant to the U.S. attorney general for the investigation of oil and land leases in California, Oregon, and Wyoming. Some of the corruption uncovered is said to have been reflected in the Teapot Dome scandal of the 1920s. Justice represented the U.S. Department of Justice in seeking to set aside the leases, prosecuting the Southern Pacific Railroad and allied oil companies, and recovering huge settlements in what may have been one of the biggest lawsuits in history to recover government property. He won every case brought to trial, settling other cases without the expense of a trial when defending companies offered favorable compromises after they were overwhelmed by the mass of his incriminating evidence. If he had lived to finish the investigation, his successes would have continued according to his associates in the Justice Department. Newspaper reports described him as the most able lawyer in the department.

Justice and his family moved to California and established a home in San Francisco, but he retained his partnership with Edgar Broadhurst in Greensboro. Justice died unexpectedly at the height of his national career. His death left unfinished his work in the West and unfulfilled the extension of his earlier successes in his home state.

His first wife, Lila Cutler of Wilmington, died leaving five daughters; Justice then married her sister, Lula Louisa, by whom he had two children. He was survived by his second wife and seven children: Marianna, Lila, Pauline, Margaret, Martha, Louisa, and Edwin J., Jr. Justice was buried in Berkeley, Calif.

In many newspaper accounts, public documents, and scholarly analyses of his work, his first name is often given as Edward rather than Edwin due to some early confusion. His son was named Edwin, Jr., evidently his preference.

SEE: Samuel A. Ashe, ed., *Cyclopedia of Eminent and Representative Men of the Carolinas of the Nineteenth Century*, vol. 2 (1892); A. W. Cooke, "Edwin Judson Justice," *North Carolina Bar Association Proceedings Report*, vol. 20 (1918); Josephus Daniels, *Editor in Politics* (1941); *Prominent People of North Carolina* (1906); Joseph F. Steelman, "Edward J. Justice: Profile of a Progressive Legislator, 1899–1913," *North Carolina Historical Review* 48 (April 1971); *Who Was Who in America*, vol. 1 (1943).

CLARA HAMLETT ROBERTSON FLANNAGAN

Justice, Michael Hoke (13 Feb. 1844–12 Feb. 1919), Confederate ordnance officer, attorney, state senator, and Superior Court judge, was born in Rutherford County. He was the fourth of six children of the Reverend Thomas Butler Justice, a Baptist minister from Buncombe County, and his wife Harriet Bailey, formerly of Henderson County. Other Baptist ministers in the family included a great-uncle, Thomas Justice, and two brothers, Charles Baylum Justice and Thomas Butler Justice.

After attending school in Rutherford County, young Justice entered the Rutherfordton Academy at age ten. Five years later he transferred to Golden Grove Seminary near Spindale for several more years of study. On 14 July 1862, at age eighteen, he enlisted in Company F,

Sixty-second North Carolina Regiment, of the Confederate Army; later he was promoted to ordnance sergeant. At the end of the war he began studying law under Judge John B. Bailey in Asheville and was licensed in January 1868. Establishing an office in Rutherfordton, he practiced law until appointed judge.

After the war Justice was elected mayor of Rutherfordton. In 1876 he became the first Democrat since the end of the Civil War to serve as senator for the Thirty-ninth District, made up of Rutherford and Polk counties. In 1884 he became the Democratic presidential elector for his district. Later he was a state senator in the legislative sessions of 1897, 1899, and 1901, serving as chairman of the Judiciary Committee in 1899 and 1901. In a speech to the 1900 Democratic convention, Justice presented Charles B. Aycock as a gubernatorial candidate. In 1901 Governor Aycock appointed him a Superior Court judge for the Sixteenth Judicial District. While Governor Locke Craig was in office, Justice served as chairman of a commission to establish controversial regulations for railroad freight. During the state Democratic convention of 1904 held in Greensboro, he was nominated for the Supreme Court by W. T. Crawford but lost the election to Judge Hoke.

Justice was a member of the First Baptist Church in Rutherfordton and attained the highest rank in the Masonic Order. He was a member of the Rutherfordton Hotel and Improvement Company, and served on the board of directors and as counsel for the Citizens' Building and Loan Association. The charter for the Asheville and Thermal Belt Railroad Company was written by Justice. As a director he also supported the Rutherfordton Military Institute.

On 21 Mar. 1865 Justice married Margaret ("Maggie") L. Smith, the daughter of James M. and Martha Smith of Buncombe County; they had six children: Edwin J., Charles, Butler Alexander, Martha McCree, Gaston Bailey, and Michael Hoke, Jr. In 1895 he married Lula B. Tanner, the daughter of Andrew and Amy Carolina Tanner of Saluda, and they had a daughter, Louisa. Justice died on the day before his seventy-fifth birthday and was buried in the Rutherfordton Cemetery. Two oil portraits of him are in the possession of his descendants.

SEE: Samuel A. Ashe, ed., *Cyclopedia of Eminent and Representative Men of the Carolinas of the Nineteenth Century*, vol. 2 (1892); *Centennial of the Supreme Court of North Carolina, 1819–1919* (1919); Clarence W. Griffin, *History of Old Tryon and Rutherford Counties, North Carolina, 1730–1936* (1937); John R. Logan, *Sketches, Historical and Biographical, of the Broad River and King's Mountain Baptist Association, from 1800 to 1882* (1887); M. G. McGuinn to the author; *North Carolina Biography*, vol. 5 (1941); Charles L. Van Noppen Papers (Manuscript Department, Duke University Library, Durham).

B. W. C. ROBERTS

Kalberlahn, Hans Martin (*30 Mar. 1722–28 July 1759*), physician, was born in Drontheim, Norway. His parents were of the Lutheran faith, and he was sent to school regularly in the Lutheran fashion. After completing elementary school at age fifteen, he entered training as a surgeon. On completion of his studies in 1743, at age twenty-one, he set out on his "wander-Jahre," a practice to put the finishing touch on the education of European youth of that period. With his credentials, the young man traveled from city to city to get to know the world, practicing his profession to make his way. He visited Travemunde, Bergen, Hamburg, Lübeck, Copenhagen, and Slagelse. Returning to Copenhagen in 1745, Kalberlahn became associated with a surgeon and remained for two years. During this period he was frequently in the company of the Moravian Brethren. He became particularly interested in the missionary work of the Moravians and desired to become more involved with that religious group. In 1747 he traveled to the Moravian center of Herrnhaag near Frankfurt, Germany, where he worked with Dr. John Matthew Otto. When Otto emigrated to Pennsylvania in 1750, Kalberlahn replaced him as physician for the Single Brethren.

In 1753, the governing board of the Moravian church appointed Kalberlahn physician for the initial group of pioneers assigned to carry the gospel to the Indians in the vicinity of Wachovia, N.C. Kalberlahn left Herrnhaag on 2 May and arrived in Bethlehem, Pa., on 14 September. Twenty-four days later he set out with thirteen other single men on a long, hard journey to the primitive area of Rowan County, N.C., arriving at a place called Bethabara on 17 November.

The settlers in Bethabara had in Kalberlahn a beloved physician who served them faithfully, not only in medicine but also in many other ways. Moreover neighbors—who previously had not known where to turn when they were ill—began flocking to him from a one-hundred-mile radius. He set their broken bones, healed their wounds, did the necessary surgery, and sheltered the sick for considerable periods of time. He also visited the homes of those who were too ill to travel. At times he was away for as long as five days, visiting the sick in the Yadkin valley, the mountains of Virginia, and other distant areas.

Kalberlahn planted an extensive herb garden in 1756 and introduced several new botanicals to North Carolina. Most of his medications had to be manufactured from plants that were grown in the area. One popular medication at this time was tar water, reputed to be a preventative against smallpox. According to Moravian records, each year the men gathered pine boughs to make tar for the medicine that Kalberlahn needed.

In April 1758 he returned to Bethlehem, Pa., to work for a time with his former colleague, Dr. Otto. While in Pennsylvania he met and married Anna Catharina Antes, who accompanied him on his return to Bethabara in May 1759.

Kalberlahn found the place crowded with refugees from the French and Indian War. To compound the problem, there had been a famine in the area that spring and many of the refugees and inhabitants were underfed. The two forts at Bethabara were overflowing with hungry, frightened neighbors who had sought refuge from marauding Indian bands. In the latter part of June, a severe epidemic of fever—most likely typhus, promoted by malnourishment and crowded conditions—broke out and swept rapidly through Bethabara, lingering until cold weather appeared. Out of two hundred sheltered there, only fourteen were spared the disease. Its fourth victim was Kalberlahn, who died after a four-day illness, one day before the first anniversary of his marriage, at age thirty-seven. In the records, the tall, blue-eyed, blond physician is described as "an angel of mercy" and "the sainted Kalberlahn."

SEE: Adelaide L. Fries, ed., *Records of the Moravians in North Carolina*, vol. 1 (1922); Memoir of Hans Martin Kalberlahn and Christian G. Reuter, "Flora and Fauna in Wachovia" (Moravian Archives, Winston-Salem).

LAURA M. MOSLEY

Kapp, John Jacob (*30 Dec. 1729–6 Dec. 1807*), early Moravian miller, was born in Münchenstein, near Basel, Switzerland. His parents, Johannes and Judith Kapp, were members of the Reformed church. Fleeing religious persecution and economic hardship, they left Switzerland for Pennsylvania in 1740. Most of the family, including Kapp's mother, died at sea. His father remarried and settled in Lancaster County, Pa., where he carried on his trade as a cartwright. Perhaps not wholly at home with his father's second family, John Jacob Kapp was attracted to the teachings of the Moravian missionaries from Bethlehem, Pa. In 1748 he joined the Moravian church, accepting its idea of a Christian communal society.

Kapp was one of twenty-two Single Brethren selected to start a Moravian settlement at Christian's Spring, Pa., in 1749. Five years later, he was asked by the church to go with seven other men in the second band of settlers to the new Moravian town of Bethabara in western North Carolina. The settlement was less than a year old when they arrived on 26 Oct. 1754. Kapp's inclusion in the group was part of a carefully drawn plan typical of Moravian settlements. He was a skilled woodworker who had other mechanical abilities. One of his assignments was to work with two men sent to find a site for and build a mill. On 28 Nov. 1755, they put into operation the first gristmill in northwestern North Carolina. Besides the Moravian groups, it served on a custom-grinding basis settlers on the Yadkin, in the Quaker community of New Garden (now Guilford College), in the Irish settlement of modern Davidson County, and along Town Fork Creek (now Stokes and Rockingham counties). Kapp served as assistant to the first miller. He was also vestryman for Dobbs Parish, the Anglican designation for the area Moravians knew as Wachovia.

During the French and Indian War, Kapp was in charge of caring for the hundreds of refugees who sought safety from Cherokee attacks with the Moravians of Bethabara. He helped supervise the building of a stockade around the gristmill and ten log cabins to house the refugees. He worked, too, to feed a starving region. Only the Moravians had food during a time of war-ruined crops, and Kapp, through his post at the mill, helped distribute supplies. In 1759, he assisted with another project aimed at easing the refugee crunch—the founding of nearby Bethania, where Moravian Brethren and nonmembers could live outside the traditional communal society.

At war's end in 1763, Kapp returned to his routine as assistant miller, becoming chief on the retirement of the first miller nine years later. He held the position for thirty years. Because his work at the mill gave him an unusual amount of contact with outsiders, Moravian leaders and ministers found him a useful companion in their political and religious journeys outside Wachovia.

During the American Revolution, Kapp the miller ground grain for both sides between the battles of Kings Mountain and Guilford Court House, but Kapp the man upset the carefully neutral leadership of the church by early declaring his sympathy for the Patriot cause.

He spent the rest of his years quietly pursuing his trade, raising his family, and practicing his faith. Unlike many millers of his time, he amassed no great estate; in Moravian society, the profits from work were turned back to the church and all in the community were provided for according to their needs. Retiring from the mill in April 1802, Kapp moved into the village of Bethabara where he died five years later of influenza. He was buried in God's Acre, the graveyard at Bethabara.

His service during the French and Indian War was recognized in 1903, when a plaque was erected at Bethabara. However, his greatest legacy was the milling tradition carried through five generations. His son, Henry, ran the first mill in nearby Bethania and later established another near the northern boundary of Wachovia. Henry's son, Thomas, established another mill three miles northwest of Bethania. John M. Kapp, another grandson of the original miller, operated "Kapp's Mill" on the Mitchell River in the Mountain View community of Surry County. The last of the mills operated into the 1920s.

Kapp was married three times. His first wife, Margaretha Schor (or Shore), arrived in Bethabara as a refugee in the French and Indian War. They were married in 1764 and had four children, two of whom had their own families. The oldest son, John Frederick, moved with his family to Tennessee in 1794. The second son, Henry, remained in Wachovia; to his line belong the Kapps now living in and around Forsyth County. There is some indication that eastern North Carolina families with the name of Capp and Capps may be descended from John Jacob Kapp as well. His second marriage—to Elisabeth Everit in 1779—produced no surviving children. But he had two by Louisa Doll, whom he married in 1783. Their son is known to have left Bethabara in the early nineteenth century.

SEE: Adelaide L. Fries, ed., *Records of the Moravians in North Carolina*, vols. 1–6 (1922–43); Johannes Kapp Memoir (Moravian Archives, Bethlehem, Pa.); John Jacob Kapp Memoir (Moravian Archives, Winston-Salem); M. Keith Kapp with Hunter James, "And Well to Grind the Grain," *The Three Forks of Muddy Creek* 2 (1975); Emma L. Lehman, "Family Register of Mary Amanda Kapp" (1895 manuscript in the possession of Mrs. Herbert Weber, Charlotte); Stokes County Wills (Danbury).

M. KEITH KAPP

Keen, Thomas William (*8 Sept. 1823–16 Jan. 1886*), physician, tobacco dealer, and legislator, was born in Pittsylvania County, Va., the son of Ashford T. Keen (1796–1876) and his first wife, Elizabeth Edwards Keen. He was educated in a private school in Franklin County, Va., after which he attended the Medical University of Maryland, graduating in 1843. The following year he settled in Rockingham, N.C., and began a medical practice. After 26 Feb. 1846, he married Aramenta D. Adams (1827–1914). They had two daughters, one who died in infancy and Mary E. (1849–76), who married P. B. Kennedy of Salisbury.

Keen was active in the Democratic party of Rockingham County, serving on the county committee and a term in the North Carolina House of Commons (1848–49). In 1849 he ran for the U.S. House of Representatives, but was defeated. Later he declined appointment by President James Buchanan as U.S. consul to Dundee, Scotland. In the presidential campaign of 1869, Keen served as an elector on the Douglas ticket. During the Civil War, he was appointed surgeon with the Eleventh North Carolina Volunteers (Twenty-first North Carolina Regiment) and, while his unit was stationed at Pageland, Va., participated in the Battle of the Potomac. In September 1861 he resigned, probably because of poor health, but in 1864 he was serving at Kinston as a member of the Sixth Regiment of North Carolina Home Guards and as a surgeon of the Third Military District.

After the war, Keen took up residence in Salisbury where he went into tobacco manufacturing and sales in the firm of Keen and Kennedy, which he established with his son-in-law, P. B. Kennedy. He was elected mayor of Salisbury three times and served as president of the agricultural fair in 1873–75. In 1877 after some difficulties with his tobacco business, Keen moved to Reidsville and the next year to Danville, Va., where he engaged in medical practice, the tobacco business, and politics. In 1883 and 1885 he was elected to the Virginia House of Delegates. At the beginning of 1886, after a speech pleading for state-supplied books for school children, Keen collapsed on the floor of the legislative chambers and died of apoplexy. He was buried on 19 January in the Lutheran Cemetery, Salisbury, after funeral services at the First Presbyterian Church.

SEE: John L. Cheney, Jr., ed., *North Carolina Government, 1585–1974* (1975); *House Journal, General Assembly of Virginia, 1885–1886*; Weymouth Jordan, ed., *North Carolina Troops, 1861–1865*, vol. 4 (1973); *Norfolk Virginian*, 17 Jan. 1886; David S. Reid Papers (North Carolina State Archives, Raleigh); *Richmond Dispatch*, 19 Jan. 1886; Rockingham County Marriage License Index (North Carolina State Archives, Raleigh); *Salisbury Herald*, 21 Jan. 1886; William H. Thomas Papers (Duke University Archives, Durham); U.S. Census, Rockingham County, N.C. (1860), Pittsylvania County, Va. (1880).

LINDLEY S. BUTLER
GEORGE K. SCHWEITZER

Keener, Walter Ney (2 Aug. 1880–25 Nov. 1931), newspaper editor, was born in rural Lincoln County, the son of Elijah Washington and Rhoda Caroline Loftin Keener. After attending local schools, he entered Wake Forest College from which he was graduated with a bachelor of arts degree in 1902. Returning to Wake Forest for another year, he received the bachelor of laws degree in 1903 and passed the state bar examination in the late summer. In his home county he opened an office in Lincolnton, and in the fall purchased the *Lincoln County News* in partnership with A. L. Quickel; he edited the paper while establishing his law practice. In 1906 he bought his partner's interest but sold the paper in 1907 when he formed a law partnership with Walter Feimster. In the legislative session of 1907–8, Keener represented Lincoln County in the North Carolina House of Representatives.

In 1909 he abandoned the law in favor of journalism and was in succession city editor of the *Raleigh Times* (1909–11), managing and city editor of the *Durham Sun* (1912–13), city editor of the *Charlotte Chronicle* (1913–14), editor of the *High Point Enterprise* (1914–16), and editor of the *Wilmington Dispatch* (1917–18). In 1918 he returned to Durham to become editor of the *Durham Morning Herald*; when the Durham Herald Company acquired the afternoon newspaper, the *Durham Sun*, he became editor of both papers, a post he held with distinction until his death.

Keener was noted for his pertinent and incisive editorials, and for the comprehensive coverage the papers gave all areas of news. An editorial comment in the Raleigh *News and Observer* described him as "a man of inquiring mind, ready decisions, strong opinions, and as an editorial writer [he] expressed himself forcefully and effectively—Walter Keener was frank, independent, and courageous, with a deep aversion to sham and pretense wherever it appeared."

He was a member of the First Presbyterian Church, Durham, and participated in many of its lay programs; a Mason; and a charter member of the Kiwanis Club of Durham, of which he was secretary for six years. For a number of years he served on the executive committee

of the North Carolina School for the Blind and Deaf. Although an active Democrat, he never ran for political office after beginning his newspaper career.

On 2 Feb. 1904 Keener married Mamie E. Dunn of Wake Forest, and they were the parents of two sons, Walter Ney, Jr., and John Washington. She died in 1918. Four years later he married Ruth Duhling of Durham and they had one son, Edward Bruce.

Keener died in Durham at age fifty-two and was buried in the cemetery at Wake Forest.

SEE: *North Carolina Biography*, vol. 3 (1929); E. I. Olive, *Wake Forest Alumni Directory* (1961); Raleigh *News and Observer*, 26 Nov. 1932; *Who Was Who in America*, vol. 1 (1943).

C. SYLVESTER GREEN

Keith, Robert (fl. 1782–85), printer and journalist, originally from Philadelphia, went to Charleston, S.C., in 1782 and became a partner of John McIver, Jr. He settled in New Bern in 1783. From James Davis, the state's first printer and first journalist, he borrowed both equipment and newspaper title; the first issue of Keith's *North Carolina Gazette, or Impartial Intelligencer and Weekly General Advertiser* appeared on 28 Aug. 1783. In the first issue, he remarked that the state had been without a newspaper for several years—James Davis had ceased publication of his *North Carolina Gazette* in November 1778—and he felt the citizens were eager to have one again. He gave his address as "near the Church," the same address used by Davis and his son Thomas. In addition to his newspaper, Keith also had a bookstore and trained printers' apprentices. One of them apparently was Francis Xavier Martin, who later published his own version of the *North Carolina Gazette* before becoming a well-known author and jurist in the Louisiana Territory.

The last known issues of the *Gazette* bearing Keith's imprint are dated early September 1784, and he evidently ceased publication soon afterwards. It is not known whether he continued in the printing trade, but James Davis's will of 1785 bequeathed his printing equipment to his son Thomas and mentioned that some was in the hands of Robert Keith.

SEE: C. S. Brigham, *History and Bibliography of American Newspapers, 1690–1820*, vol. 2 (1947); C. C. Crittenden, *North Carolina Newspapers before 1790* (1928); D. C. McMurtrie, *A History of Printing in the United States* (1936); Stephen B. Weeks, *The Press of North Carolina in the 18th Century* (1981).

THOMAS A. BOWERS

Kemp, James Hal (27 Mar. 1904–21 Dec. 1940), orchestra and band leader, was born in Marion, Ala., the son of T. D. and Leila Rush Kemp. His mother was a poet. Hal Kemp began his musical training while working at Marion's Bonita Theater, playing piano. After his family moved to Charlotte, he attended and was graduated from Charlotte Central High School. While in high school he organized his first dance band, a five-piece combo called "The Merrymakers."

In 1922 Kemp entered The University of North Carolina, where he organized a campus band known as the "Carolina Club Orchestra." During the summer vacations, the band performed in Europe. Active on campus, Kemp was a member of the Musical Club, band, orchestra, glee club, and Delta Sigma Phi and Lambda Phi Epsilon fraternities. He was also president of the

Wigue and Masque, the dramatic arts association. During his senior year he formed a seven-piece combo, the forerunner of his nationally known orchestra, which included future musicians Skinnay Ennis, John Scott Trotter, and Saxie Dowell. On the advice and encouragement of bandleader Fred Waring, the orchestra went professional after Kemp's graduation in 1926.

Later that year Kemp's orchestra appeared in Buffalo, N.Y., and started playing in theaters and hotels throughout Europe and the United States. Kemp developed a national reputation following a long stint at the Blackhawk in Chicago in 1932. In the same year he married Betsy Slaughter, a Dallas, Tex., debutante, and moved to a permanent residence in Shongum Lake, N.J. They had two children, Hal, Jr. ("Tippy"), and Sally Rush.

Kemp was proficient in playing trumpet, clarinet, and saxophone. He was recognized for the clean, smooth style in the saxophone and brass sections of his orchestra, as well as the unusual choral arrangements. The band's theme song, which Kemp arranged, was "I'll Be with You When the Summer Is Gone." The band recorded a number of other popular tunes during the late 1930s, including "Got a Date with an Angel," "Lamplight," "Remember Me," "The Loveliness of You," "The Breeze and I," and "Way Back in 1939 A.D." It also played for a number of radio shows, including "Penzoil Parade," "CBS-Time to Shine," "Penthouse Party," and "Chesterfield Program."

Bandleader Kay Kyser credited Kemp with encouraging him to enter the field. Several vocalists achieved fame with Kemp's band—among them Maxine Gray and Bob Allen.

Kemp's band was the first to be featured in a motion picture, *Radio City Revels of 1938*. Receiving wide acclaim, it was named by *Variety* magazine as the favorite "sweet-swing" band of 1938 and received the Associated Collegiate Press All-American Musical Award for 1938.

In 1938 Kemp was divorced, and on 13 Jan. 1939 he married Martha Stephenson, of New York but originally from Alabama. In the latter year he served as a guest conductor of the Chicago Symphony, partially fulfilling his secret ambition to be a symphony conductor. His dreams were cut short, however, on 19 Dec. 1940 when he was severely injured in a head-on automobile collision near Madera, Calif., while traveling from Los Angeles to San Francisco to play an engagement. From a punctured lung he developed pneumonia and died two days later. His death came less than two months before he was scheduled to play his most prestigious engagement, a three-month stand at the New York Waldorf-Astoria.

SEE: *Charlotte Observer*, 21–22 Dec. 1940; University of North Carolina, *Alumni Directory* (1954), Alumni Records (Alumni House, Chapel Hill), and *Yackety-Yack* (1926).

WILLIAM B. ALLEN

Kenan, Daniel Love (18 Dec. 1780–14 Oct. 1840), local official and legislator, was born in Duplin County, the son of Colonel James and Sarah Love Kenan. Of Scotch-Irish descent, his grandparents immigrated from Ireland to Wilmington in the 1730s. Young Kenan was educated at Grove Academy. In 1807 he was acting deputy coroner, and in 1809 he was elected sheriff of the county. The 1810 census of Duplin County is signed by him as assistant marshall; he was one of the justices

in 1812 and 1815, and in the period 1813–17 he also served as postmaster of the county seat. He was elected to the House of Commons for the 1820 session and to the North Carolina Senate for the 1821–22 session. Kenan's interest in education was demonstrated when he served as Duplin's representative on the board of trustees of the Smithville Academy in Brunswick County and as an original trustee of the Line Academy, established in 1825 on the line between Duplin and Sampson counties. An active Mason, he was secretary of Pine Lodge No. 89.

Kenan, a man of vision, moved to Florida in 1831 as that state began to develop. Although Kenansville, Fla., was named for him, he settled in Quincy. There he joined the local Masonic lodge and was elected Master the following year. In 1836 he represented Gadsden County, Fla., in the Legislative Council, and again served in 1837 and 1838. In the latter year he was one of the charter members and ruling elders in organizing Old Philadelphia Presbyterian Church in Quincy. His name appears among the thirty largest planters of tobacco and cotton and as owner of thirty slaves.

Kenan's first wife was Mary James, whom he married in Duplin County in 1809; she died in 1811. Secondly, in 1812 he married her sister, Elizabeth, who lived until sometime between 1825 and 1830. His third wife, to whom he was married between 1836 and 1840, was Mrs. Ann Wilkinson, who survived him. Kenan's children by his first wife were Thomas James and Sarah Elizabeth. By his second wife he had William Owen, Mary James, Temperance Jane, Michael Molten, Susan Catharine, and Daniel Lafayette. He died in Quincy, Fla.

SEE: *Cape Fear Recorder*, 28 Oct. 1829; Correspondence between Elizabeth Johnston Blanks and her sister, Catharine Kenan Price, 1833–88 (Manuscript Department, Duke University Library, Durham); A. T. Outlaw, *The Historical Background of Duplin County, North Carolina* (1949) and *Official Directory of Duplin County, North Carolina, 1740–1935* (1935); Probate Records (Gadsen County, Fla.); *Quincy Sentinel*, 15 Nov. 1838; Records of the Post Office Department (National Archives, Washington, D.C.); Alvaretta Kenan Register, ed., *The Kenan Family* (1967); U.S. Census of 1810.

ALVARETTA KENAN REGISTER

Kenan, Felix (d. 1785), sheriff of Duplin County and active Tory in the American Revolution, is said by family tradition to have settled in the 1730s with his two brothers, Thomas and William, in the upper part of New Hanover County that later became Duplin. In 1754 Felix was a member of the company of militia commanded by a Captain Gregg, and in June 1758 he was appointed a justice of the peace for Duplin County which had been created in 1750. He remained a justice until 1770. From 1762 to 1768 he served as a member of the colonial Assembly, where his committee assignments dealt mainly with fiscal matters; he also was a member of the committee that determined the location of Fort Johnston.

Kenan was involved in area land matters, serving on the Claims Commission for the county from 1764 to 1769, and as a member of the 1766 commission that determined the boundary between New Hanover and Duplin counties. During much of this time he was also land agent and attorney for Henry McCulloch, who owned large tracts of land in the area. Kenan was sheriff on two occasions—in 1760–61 and again from 1769 to

1776. In May 1776 he was removed from the office because of his involvement in Tory activities, particularly at the Battle of Moore's Creek Bridge in February when he bore arms with the Loyalist forces under General Donald MacDonald. He was captured by the Patriots and returned to Duplin County. On 11 May 1776 the Assembly passed a resolution removing him from the office of sheriff, noting that he had been "inimical to the Liberties of America" and was "truly unworthy to execute any longer the trust and confidence reposed in him by his appointment as Sheriff." In March 1777 he was rumored to be at the head of a Tory insurrection in the state, and in July his arrest was ordered for his alleged involvement in a conspiracy against Governor Richard Caswell. Surviving records, however, do not reveal whether he actually was detained. One report said that Kenan "had not the independence to be a Tory, or the honesty to be a Whig."

In 1754 Kenan married Catharine Norris Love, the daughter of George and Sarah Norris and widow of Daniel Love. Their children were William and Rose, both sons, and Nancy and Jane. He died in Duplin County sometime between 9 Apr. and 18 July 1785 and was buried near the Duplin-Sampson county line.

SEE: Walter Clark, ed., *State Records of North Carolina*, vols. 11, 22, 23 (1895, 1907, 1904); William S. Powell, ed., *The Correspondence of William Tryon*, 2 vols. (1980–81); Alvaretta Kenan Register, ed., *The Kenan Family* (1967); Lorenzo Sabine, *Biographical Sketches of Loyalists in the American Revolution*, vol. 1 (1864); William L. Saunders, ed., *Colonial Records of North Carolina*, vols. 9, 10 (1890).

NEIL C. PENNYWITT

Kenan, James (23 Sept. 1740–23 May 1810), colonial and state official and Revolutionary officer, was born at his father's plantation, The Lilacs, in Turkey, N.C., the oldest son of Thomas and Elizabeth Johnston Kenan. Elected sheriff of Duplin County, he served from 1762 to 1766 and again from 1785 to 1786. Kenan led a company of volunteers to Wilmington in 1765 to oppose enforcement of the Stamp Act, and he was a member of the Assembly in 1773 and 1774 and of the Provincial Congress in August 1774, August 1775, and November 1776. He was chairman of the Duplin Safety Committee and a member of the Wilmington Committee.

As colonel of the Duplin militia, Kenan participated in military operations during the American Revolution. Immediately after the war he was chosen brigadier general for the Wilmington District. He served ten terms in the North Carolina Senate between 1777 and 1793, was a member of the state constitutional convention in 1788–89, and became councilor of state. He also was a trustee of The University of North Carolina.

Kenan married Sarah Love in 1770, and they had eight children: Thomas, Catherine, Elizabeth, Owen, Susannah, Daniel Love, Sarah, and Jane. A member of the Presbyterian church, he died at his plantation in Turkey. His grave has since been moved to the Liberty Hall Restoration in Kenansville.

SEE: Walter Clark, ed., *State Records of North Carolina*, vols. 12, 19–21 (1895–1903); W. R. Kenan, Jr., ed., *Incidents by the Way* (1946); Faison W. McGowen, ed., *Duplin History and Government* (1971); Alvaretta Kenan Register, ed., *The Kenan Family* (1967).

THOMAS S. KENAN III

Kenan, Owen Hill (23 May 1872–2 July 1963), physician, was born in Kenansville, the oldest child of James Graham and Anne Elizabeth Hill Kenan. After graduation from The University of North Carolina in 1894, he received a medical degree from the University of Pennsylvania. He practiced medicine first in Kenansville and later in New York City and Palm Beach, Fla.

A world traveler, Kenan was one of the few survivors of the *Lusitania* disaster when the vessel was torpedoed by a German submarine off the Irish coast in 1915. He joined the French Army and was awarded the French Medal of Honor. When the United States entered World War I, he joined an American unit and attained the rank of colonel. In later years he lived and maintained homes in Paris, France; Palm Beach, Fla.; and Wilmington, N.C. He was an art collector and an authority on eighteenth-century French art.

Kenan was a member of St. James Episcopal Church, Wilmington, and of Bethesda By the Sea Episcopal Church, Palm Beach; he was buried in Arlington National Cemetery. He never married.

SEE: Kenan family records in the author's possession; Alvaretta Kenan Register, ed., *The Kenan Family* (1967).

THOMAS S. KENAN III

Kenan, Owen Rand (4 Mar. 1804–3 Mar. 1887), planter, legislator, and Confederate congressman, was born in Kenansville on land that his Scotch-Irish grandfather, Thomas Kenan, had acquired about 1735. His parents were Thomas and Mary Rand Kenan. He studied medicine briefly, then decided to read law. Kenan first practiced in Kenansville, but when the rest of the family moved to Alabama in 1833 he took over the Duplin County property as the oldest son. Soon cotton and tobacco planting became his chief interest. He rebuilt Liberty Hall, which had been destroyed by fire, and in 1836 he married Sarah Rebecca Graham, a local lady of Scottish descent. They had one daughter, Annie Dickson, and three sons: Thomas Stephen, James Graham, and William Rand. All the sons later served as officers in the Forty-third North Carolina Regiment, Confederate Army.

Kenan was elected to the North Carolina House of Commons as a Democrat in 1834, 1835, and 1836, serving successively on the committees of Privileges and Elections, Education, and Propositions and Grievances. For the next few years, he abstained from active politics and Liberty Hall became one of the main centers of Duplin County social affairs. After Lincoln's election to the presidency in 1860, Kenan became a strong Secessionist. In the fall of 1861 he campaigned for a seat in the Confederate House of Representatives on the promise to cooperate fully with the Confederacy. He won easily over two more conservative opponents.

In Richmond, where he served on the Committee on Accounts, Kenan was one of North Carolina's few strong supporters of vigorous wartime legislation. It was only in his opposition to the tax in kind on agricultural production and to arbitrary curbs on inflation, both of which he felt would overburden his productive agricultural district, that Kenan placed local over national considerations. At the end of his two-year term Kenan stated that in North Carolina there was not enough discontent with the Confederacy to merit concern, but he did not seek reelection. After the Civil War, he devoted himself entirely to his law practice and to planting.

Kenan's contemporaries described him as quiet,

though affable and hospitable. He died at home and was buried in the Graham family cemetery near Kenansville.

SEE: Samuel A. Ashe, ed., *Biographical History of North Carolina*, vol. 3 (1906); *Journal of the Confederate Congress*, vols. 5–6 (1905); *Journal of the House of Commons of North Carolina* (1834–36); Faison W. McGowen and Pearl C. McGowen, eds., *Flashes of Duplin History and Government* (1971); Raleigh *News and Observer*, 4 Mar. 1887; Alvaretta Kenan Register, ed., *The Kenan Family* (1967); Wilmington *Daily Journal*, 1861–63.

BUCK YEARNS

Kenan, Sarah Graham (17 Feb. 1876–16 Mar. 1968), philanthropist, was born in Wilmington of which she remained a lifelong resident. The daughter of Mary Hargrave and William Rand Kenan, a native of Kenansville, she attended school in Wilmington and New York City; she was graduated from St. Mary's Junior College in Raleigh. On 19 Dec. 1912 she married her cousin Graham Kenan, a lawyer in Wilmington; he died on 5 Feb. 1920 in New York City, where he had recently opened a law office. The couple had no children. After the death of her husband, Mrs. Kenan purchased a house on Market Street in Wilmington in order to live near her sister Jessie; the brick colonial residence was altered and modernized by Tom Hastings, architect of Carrere and Hastings of New York City. Mrs. Kenan traveled extensively, spending time in Palm Beach and St. Augustine, Fla., as well as in Wilmington in winter and Lake Placid, N.Y., in summer. She also traveled abroad and was an avid art collector most of her life.

Mrs. Kenan was the sister-in-law of Henry Morrison Flagler, who with John D. Rockefeller founded the Standard Oil Company. The Flagler fortune was left to Mrs. Kenan's sister, Mary Lily Flagler Bingham. At her death in 1917 it was divided equally between Mrs. Kenan, her brother William Rand Kenan, Jr., of New York, and her sister Jessie Kenan Wise of Wilmington. Because Mrs. Kenan lived a quiet life and shunned publicity, most of her philanthropic activity went unnoticed. Nonetheless, during her lifetime gifts to charitable foundations and educational institutions exceeded $12 million. The present report of philanthropic donations of the Sarah Graham Kenan Foundation lists substantial gifts received by the Catherine Kennedy Home in Wilmington, the Duplin County Board of Education, New Hanover County private schools, the Diocese of East Carolina and St. James Episcopal Church in Wilmington, the Duke University Medical School, the North Carolina Museum of Life and Science, St. Mary's College, the Thalian Hall Commission in Wilmington, Durham Academy, the Kenansville Board of Education, the University of North Carolina at Wilmington, and others. On 18 Nov. 1968 James Graham Kenan gave a gift deed of Mrs. Kenan's home on Market Street to the state of North Carolina for the board of trustees of Wilmington College (now the University of North Carolina at Wilmington). This gift from her nephew included some of the fine furnishings and art treasures collected by Mrs. Kenan. The home is now the residence of the chancellor of the University of North Carolina at Wilmington. Mrs. Kenan's portrait hangs in the lobby of the Sarah Graham Kenan Auditorium on the Wilmington campus.

On 20 Mar. 1968 the funeral service for Mrs. Kenan was held at St. James Episcopal Church, Wilmington. She was interred in Oakdale Cemetery, where her parents were also buried.

SEE: Daniel L. Grant, *Alumni History of the University of North Carolina, 1795–1924* (1924); Information Service, University of North Carolina at Wilmington; New Hanover County Deed Books (North Carolina State Archives, Raleigh); Raleigh *News and Observer*, 17 Mar. 1968; Wilmington *Morning Star*, 20 Mar. 1968; Wilmington *Sunday Star-News*, 17 Mar. 1968.

IDA BROOKS KELLAM

Kenan, Thomas (26 Feb. 1771–22 Oct. 1843), legislator and congressman, was born in Duplin County, the son of James and Sarah Love Kenan. He represented Duplin County in the House of Commons in 1798–99 and in the Senate in 1804. Kenan served in the Ninth, Tenth, and Eleventh Congresses from 4 Mar. 1805 to 3 Mar. 1811. He owned and operated Laughlin Plantation on the Northeast Cape Fear River, which consisted of over 5,000 acres.

In 1833 Kenan moved his family to Selma, Ala., where he purchased a large plantation and built a handsome home, which still stands. For several years he served in the Alabama House of Representatives.

Kenan married Mary Rand of Raleigh in 1800, and they had ten children: Catherine Elizabeth, Sarah, Owen Rand, Julia Susannah, James, Thomas Daniel, John Rand, Daniel Love, William Kimbro, and Mary Rand. A member of the Presbyterian church, Kenan died at his plantation and was buried at Valley Creek Cemetery near Selma.

SEE: Kenan family records in the author's possession; Faison W. McGowen and Pearl C. McGowen, eds., *Flashes of Duplin History and Government* (1971); Alvaretta Kenan Register, ed., *The Kenan Family* (1967).

THOMAS S. KENAN III

Kenan, Thomas Stephen (12 Feb. 1838–23 Dec. 1911), lawyer, Confederate colonel, attorney general, and clerk of the North Carolina Supreme Court, was born in Kenansville, the son of Owen Rand and Sarah Rebecca Graham Kenan. He attended Grove Academy and the Central Military Institute at Selma, Ala., before spending a year at Wake Forest College. Afterwards he enrolled in The University of North Carolina as a sophomore and was graduated in 1857. There followed two more years of study at Judge Richmond Pearson's private law school in Yadkin County. In 1860, Kenan opened an office for the practice of law in Kenansville. In 1859 Thomas and his brother, James, organized a local militia company which they called the Duplin Rifles.

Three days after the attack on Fort Sumter, which marked the beginning of hostilities in the Civil War, the entire personnel of the Duplin Rifles volunteered for active service for the customary six-month period. The unit was designated Company C, Twelfth North Carolina Regiment, with Thomas Kenan as captain. Sent to the Norfolk, Va., area, the company saw little action as it was not equipped to respond to the long-range shelling inflicted in the region by Federal forces.

At the end of the six-month enlistment period, Company C was mustered out and the men returned home. Just before Christmas, 1861, the company was reorganized, but some of the men dropped out to assist in forming additional units. The Kenan brothers, however, remained with the company which was then designated as Company A, Forty-third Regiment, and so continued throughout the war. In May 1862 the regiment reported to Camp Mangum near Raleigh for additional training, but while there Thomas Kenan received word that he had been made colonel of the Thirty-eighth Regiment then being formed at Goldsboro. He declined the promotion, but soon was made colonel of his own regiment, the Forty-third. James became captain of the company in one of the rare instances in which two brothers served together as commissioned officers, one under the other.

For a time the regiment was stationed around Wilmington but was sent back to the Richmond, Va., area for service during a proposed advance by General Robert E. Lee into Maryland in September 1862. Some of Kenan's men were employed around Suffolk to prevent Federal movements in the rear of Lee's force. The enemy had occupied much of coastal North Carolina early in the war and moved up the rivers to Washington and Plymouth. In December, New Bern was threatened. The Forty-third was ordered to the Goldsboro area in a futile attempt to save a vital railroad bridge between there and New Bern. Although the bridge was destroyed, it was quickly rebuilt after Federal forces withdrew. Kenan and his men remained in the vicinity of Kinston to prevent further inland movements.

Kenan's regiment and the others in its brigade soon began the movement that was to be the most dramatic and tragic of the war, the taking of the Army of Northern Virginia into enemy territory in Pennsylvania in June 1863. His men were now seasoned soldiers, trained and equipped at the height of their military attainments, confident that war should be carried into the enemy's territory. At Brandy Station, a fierce engagement between opposing cavalry forces resulted in a Confederate victory. Kenan's regiment shared the spoils of at least one Federal cavalry storage area for some much needed supplies.

Movements were by now reasonably clear to everyone: General Lee was on his way to Gettysburg and the supplies that might well be obtained by a successful operation there. By way of Hagerstown and Chambersburg, Kenan's regiment reached the Carlisle Barracks, which it and the others occupied while making final preparations for the Gettysburg campaign, which began on 1 July 1863.

In the afternoon the Forty-third Regiment was a part of the force that carried the lines to Seminary Ridge and occupied that position, the Federals having retreated before the Confederate onslaught. Both sides suffered heavy losses, however. During 2 July infantry action under Kenan's command was minor, while the opposing artillery waged a heavy bombardment that became the talk of veterans for many years to come. General Lee's actual presence in full view of the fighting men was an encouraging bit of strategy.

At daybreak on Friday, 3 July, Kenan's regiment was chosen to lead the attack on Culp's Hill, passage to which was cluttered by fallen trees, boulders, and difficult terrain. The charge failed, and Colonel Kenan, wounded severely by a bullet in the leg, was sent to the rear for transfer to the hospital wagon train. He was among the many who were captured by the Federal forces crowding around the retreating Confederates, and on 6 July he was admitted to the army hospital at Frederick, Md. A month later he was transferred to the larger hospital at Baltimore where two more weeks of recuperation enabled him to move on crutches. He was then sent to Sandusky, Ohio, for commitment to the great Federal prison on Johnson's Island.

While these events were ending the war for Kenan, the South's great stronghold at Vicksburg, Miss., fell, in what many Southerners considered the turning point of the war, rather than the events at Gettysburg. But of more personal concern to Kenan was the raid carried

out by the enemy from New Bern in which his family's sword factory at Kenansville was destroyed. When and how much he knew of this, of course, is unknown, but he was wounded at nearly the same time as the raid on Kenansville.

Both Thomas and James were at Johnson's Island enduring the boredom of inactivity and suffering through the cold of two winters. They joined other Confederate prisoners in attempting to tunnel a passage under the walls; however, after many weeks of labor and concealment of the rubble, their scheme was discovered and frustrated. The colonel somehow managed to secure a copy of Blackstone's *Commentaries* and was able to spend some of his time profitably in review and study.

In February 1865 Kenan was a member of a committee of prisoners who sought permission to establish a form of self-government within the prison. Their suggestion was favorably received, but the approaching end of the war prevented its implementation. Late in March the Kenan brothers were among about three hundred prisoners paroled and sent to the vicinity of Richmond although not permitted to rejoin their former commands. They briefly toyed with the idea of participating in the Trans-Mississippi movement for a sort of Confederate government-in-exile, but the surrender of Lee at Appomattox and General Joseph E. Johnston at Durham nullified their plans.

From Virginia Kenan made his way to Greensboro. On his arrival, the railroad to Salisbury was so badly damaged that trains were not running. He walked to Salisbury and took a train to Charlotte, where he found a kindly hotel keeper who provided accommodations. On 12 May he was officially paroled, and five days later he was back in Kenansville ready to resume a position of leadership in the community. Without loss of time he became a candidate for the General Assembly, was elected, and served in the sessions of 1865–66 and 1866–67. He then was a candidate for Congress in 1868, but by that time the political leadership of the state had changed and he was defeated.

In 1868 Kenan married Sallie Dortch, daughter of Dr. Lewis Dortch of Edgecombe County, and the following year they moved to Wilson. His law practice there flourished and in 1872 he was elected mayor and inaugurated a progressive administration. In 1876 he supported the gubernatorial candidacy of Zebulon B. Vance in a campaign that returned the Democratic party to power and elevated Kenan to the office of attorney general. He was reelected for a second four-year term. During this time he also served as reporter for the North Carolina Supreme Court.

Kenan rendered further service as a member of the board of trustees of The University of North Carolina, as president of the university's alumni association, and as a member of the executive committee of the Confederate Memorial Association. He also supported a movement that resulted in a Soldiers' Home in Raleigh. As the century drew to a close, plans were under way for a five-volume history of the military units furnished by North Carolina to the Civil War. To this work Kenan contributed a history of his regiment, of his brother's company, and of his experiences as a prisoner on Johnson's Island. The College of Medicine of the University of Virginia adopted a plan to have on its board of trustees members from the surrounding states, and for this Kenan was chosen from North Carolina. The North Carolina Bar Association also elected him its president for a term.

With no children of their own, the Kenans played host to many people and functions for eastern North Carolina. One of the most elegant such occasions was in connection with the marriage of Thomas's niece, Mary Lily Kenan, to railroad magnate, Henry M. Flagler, in 1901. Kenan's health gradually declined before he died at his home in Raleigh. He was buried in that city's Oakwood Cemetery.

SEE: Samuel A. Ashe, ed., *Biographical History of North Carolina*, vol. 3 (1906); Walter Clark, ed., *Histories of the Several Regiments and Battalions from North Carolina in the Great War, 1861–1865*, vol. 3 (1901); Confederate personnel records (National Archives, Washington, D.C.); "Descriptive Booklet of Johnson's Island and Confederate Cemetery," *Sandusky* (Ohio) *Register*, June 1945; Charles Frohman, "The Civil War Years," in *A History of Sandusky and Erie County* (n.d.); Thomas S. Kenan to James Dickson, 7 Feb. 1864 (letter exhibited at Liberty Hall, the Kenan home, in Kenansville); Alvaretta Kenan Register, ed., *The Kenan Family* (1967); Dudley A. White II, "A Report on Johnson's Island" (unpublished paper, Washington and Lee University, Lexington, Va., 1952).

A. M. FOUNTAIN

Kenan, William Rand *(4 Aug. 1885–14 Apr. 1903)*, merchant and port collector, was born in Kenansville, the son of Thomas and Mary Rand Kenan. After attending Grove Academy, he entered The University of North Carolina in 1860 at age fifteen. In 1863 he withdrew from the university to enlist as a private in the Duplin Rifles of the Forty-third North Carolina Regiment, rising to the rank of captain. He subsequently moved to Wilmington and became a life insurance agent and later a wholesale merchant. Kenan was collector of the port of Wilmington under President Grover Cleveland. He served as treasurer of the Presbyterian Church and was ordained first a deacon and then a ruling elder. In February 1903 he was appointed a trustee of The University of North Carolina, two months before his death in Wilmington where he was buried in Oakdale Cemetery.

Kenan married Mary Hargrave of Chapel Hill in 1864, and they had four children: Mary Lily, Jessie Hargrave, William Rand, Jr., and Sarah Graham. A portrait of William Rand Kenan is in the possession of his daughter Sarah's nephew, James Graham Kenan of Atlanta, Ga. In his memory, his children established the Kenan Professor Trust Fund at The University of North Carolina and donated the funds for Kenan Memorial Stadium, also in Chapel Hill.

SEE: Kenan family records in the author's possession; W. R. Kenan, Jr., ed., *Incidents by the Way* (1946); Alvaretta Kenan Register, ed., *The Kenan Family* (1967).

THOMAS S. KENAN III

Kenan, William Rand, Jr. *(30 Apr. 1872–28 July 1965)*, scientist, businessman, and philanthropist, was born in Wilmington. His father, William Rand Kenan, was born in Kenansville and became a wholesale merchant; his mother was Mary Hargrave, of Chapel Hill, whose family gave some of the land for The University of North Carolina when it was founded. Young Kenan attended Horner's Military School at Oxford before entering The University of North Carolina in 1890; he was graduated with the B.S. degree in 1894.

While in Chapel Hill, Kenan assisted in the discovery of calcium carbide, the major basis for the manufacture of acetylene; this led to the eventual formation of the Union Carbide Company. Before he was twenty-six, he

traveled around the world in the employment of Union Carbide. In 1900 he moved to Lockport, N.Y., and acquired an interest in the Traders Paper Company, becoming assistant manager. In 1899 he had met Henry Morrison Flagler, who was a partner of John D. Rockefeller in the formation of the Standard Oil Company. At that time Flagler was the major developer of the east coast of Florida and had begun construction of his Florida East Coast Railroad and a chain of resort hotels. Impressed with Kenan's mechanical ability, Flagler hired him as a consultant for all his Florida enterprises. Their relationship was strengthened when Flagler married Kenan's sister, Mary Lily, in 1901. Kenan built the first generator for Flagler's Miami Power and Water Company (later Florida Power and Light). At Flagler's death, Kenan became a trustee of the Flagler estate and later president of the Florida East Coast Railroad, Florida East Coast Hotel Company, Florida East Coast Car Ferry Company, Model Land Company, Miami Power and Water Company, West Palm Beach Water Company, and P. & O. Steamship Company.

Kenan also established Randleigh Farms in Lockport, N.Y., a scientific breeding and dairy farm. For his contributions to dairy science, he was awarded the Master Breeders Award.

As a philanthropist, Kenan gave generously to his church, the First Presbyterian Church of Lockport, and to the Memorial Hospital of Lockport. He also founded Camp Kenan for the Lockport YMCA and endowed its operations. Among his gifts to The University of North Carolina, he donated the funds to build Kenan Memorial Stadium in honor of his parents.

Kenan was buried in Lockport beside his wife, Alice Pomroy Kenan, whom he married in 1904; she died in 1948. They had no children. Kenan's will established the William R. Kenan, Jr., Charitable Trust, which has continued to make generous grants to The University of North Carolina. The first major gift from this trust was a $5 million endowment for the William R. Kenan, Jr., Professorships. There is a portrait of him at the university in Chapel Hill.

SEE: Kenan family records in the author's possession; W. R. Kenan, Jr., ed., *Incidents by the Way* (1946); *New York Times*, 29 July 1965; Alvaretta Kenan Register, ed., *The Kenan Family* (1967).

THOMAS S. KENAN III

Kendall, Henry Eli, Jr. *(24 Aug. 1905–4 Dec. 1981)*, engineer and state government official, was born in Shelby of English and Scottish ancestry, the son of Henry E., Sr., a pharmacist, and Mary Whitelaw Wiseman Kendall, of Danville, Va. He was a brother of Henry Wiseman Kendall, editor of the *Greensboro Daily News*. As a youth Kendall worked in his father's drugstore, and he was graduated from Shelby High School in 1922 as valedictorian. At North Carolina State College, from which he received the B.S. degree in 1926, he was president of the student body.

After employment by the Plumer Wiseman Engineering Co. of Danville, Va., Kendall went to Shanghai, China, in 1930, where for six years he was office manager of Dibrell Brothers Tobacco Co. Returning to North Carolina in 1936, he settled in Raleigh and became chief of plant operations of the State School Commission (which was given the duties of the State Board of Equalization on its creation in 1933).

Kendall entered the U.S. Army Corps of Engineers as a first lieutenant in 1942, serving in Europe, the Philippines, and Japan until his discharge in 1946 as a lieutenant colonel. In July 1946 Governor R. Gregg Cherry named him chairman of the Unemployment Compensation Commission, and the next year he supervised the return of the U.S. Employment Service to the state of North Carolina and the reorganization of his agency to the Employment Security Commission. Reappointed by the six succeeding governors, Kendall served as chairman for twenty-seven years until his retirement in 1973. His duties included collecting taxes and paying claims to the unemployed, as well as supervising sixty local offices in North Carolina. Working under a federal-state cooperative program, Kendall was noted for his conservative approach and for implementing the Work Incentive and Comprehensive Employment Training Acts in the state.

Serving twice as president of the national Interstate Conference of Employment Security Agencies, Kendall was on the executive committee of the President's Committee on Employment of the Handicapped, a member of the coordinating committees on Aging and the Status of Women, chairman of the Governor's Advisory Committee on Implementing the Manpower Development and Training Act, and on the board of directors of the Manpower Development Corporation for eight years. For ten years he also was a director of the State Employees Credit Union.

Kendall was a Mason and a member of the North Carolina Society of Engineers, of the Lions Club, and of the American Philatelic Society. He was also a member of the Veterans of Foreign Wars and of the administrative committee of the North Carolina Division of the American Legion. In 1950–51 he was president of the General Alumni Association of North Carolina State College, the only alumnus to serve in that position who had also been a student body president. In 1973 the North Carolina Citizens Association awarded him its citation for Distinguished Public Service. After his retirement, Kendall served as legislative chairman of the Retired State Governmental Employees Association and on the Foundations Board of North Carolina State University.

On 21 June 1947 he married Katharine Kerr of Yanceyville. A Presbyterian, he served as deacon, elder, and treasurer of White Memorial Church in Raleigh. Kendall was buried in the Presbyterian church cemetery, Yanceyville.

SEE: *North Carolina Manual* (1949–71); Raleigh *News and Observer*, 5 Dec. 1981; *Shelby Daily Star*, 4 Dec. 1981; Lee B. Weathers, *The Living Past of Cleveland County* (1956).

KATHARINE KERR KENDALL

Kendall, Henry Wiseman (*19 Mar. 1897–1 Jan. 1968*), newspaper editor, was born in Shelby, the son of Henry E., Sr., and Mary Whitelaw Wiseman Kendall. He attended local public schools, and was graduated from high school in 1914 and from Trinity College (now Duke University) in 1918. Kendall worked briefly for the *Morning New Bernian*, edited business market reports for the U.S. Department of Agriculture, Washington, D.C., in 1919–20, and became editor of the Rocky Mount *Evening Telegram* in 1920. In 1930 he joined the *Greensboro Daily News* as associate editor; he was advanced to editor in 1942 and served until 1965.

In his writings Kendall was persistent in championing those who most needed help. He favored institutions for treatment for the mentally ill, and he spoke

out on issues such as poorly supervised jails, public education, and highway safety. In 1947 he received the North Carolina Press Association's award for the best editorial. Kendall served on the North Carolina Education Study Commission during the period 1947–49 and was a member of the Hospital Board of Control (later the Department of Mental Health) from 1953 to 1965. He was also active in the Association for Retarded Children, and the Guilford County Center is named in his honor.

Kendall was the recipient of an honorary doctor of literature degree from Duke University (1960), the outstanding citizen of the year award from Greensboro (1958), and, posthumously, the Edward R. Murrow award for reporting. A Rotarian, a Presbyterian, and a Democrat, he was a member of the American Society of Newspaper Editors and chairman of the Board of Visitors of Peace College, Raleigh.

Survived by his wife, the former Mary Leslie Moss, he was buried in Sunset Cemetery, Shelby.

SEE: *Greensboro Daily News*, 2 Jan. 1968; *Who Was Who in America*, vol. 4 (1968).

KATHARINE KERR KENDALL

Kendrick, Benjamin Burks (*16 Oct. 1884–27 Oct. 1946*), historian, was born at Woodland, Talbot County, Ga., the son of William Thomas and Levicie Maddox Kendrick. The Kendrick family was substantial and of English origins. After graduating from Mercer College in 1905, Kendrick taught for four years in the public high schools of Georgia. In 1909 he entered Columbia University, where he remained until 1923 as graduate student, instructor, assistant, and associate professor. Like many other southern students he took his doctorate with William A. Dunning (1914), but was perhaps equally influenced by another member of the Columbia faculty, Charles A. Beard.

In 1923 Kendrick went to Greensboro as professor of history at the Woman's College of the University of North Carolina. From 1930 until a stroke forced his retirement in 1943, he was chairman of the college's Department of History and Political Science. Kendrick was one of the signers of the original organizational notice of the Southern Historical Association, of which he was president in 1941. He also served on the executive council of the American Historical Association and was active in the Social Science Research Council, where he was chairman of the Southern Regional Committee (1930–35).

Kendrick's first published work was his dissertation, *The Journal of the Joint Committee of Fifteen on Reconstruction* (1914), in which he edited the record of proceedings of that important congressional committee (previously unavailable to the public) and wrote a history of the committee. *The Journal* included the first serious examination of the genesis of the Fourteenth Amendment and its controversial application to business corporations. He next published, with Louis M. Hacker, who had been his student at Columbia, a college textbook, *The U.S. Since 1865*, which appeared in three editions (1931, 1934, and 1938). Kendrick also wrote at least ten articles, chiefly contemporary social commentary. A progressive social scientist, he was dedicated to the social and economic uplifting of the South, but, unlike many others, he was a regional loyalist as well, ready to vindicate the past of the South which he believed had been more sinned against than sinner.

In *The South Looks at Its Past* (1935), a still interesting interpretation of southern history written by Kendrick and his colleague Alex M. Arnett, the authors sought to reconcile the progressive thrust of the 1930s with the best in the social and cultural heritage of the Old South, thus falling somewhere between the Chapel Hill and Nashville schools of southern thought.

Kendrick's stance as a historian is perhaps best illustrated by his presidential address to the Southern Historical Association, entitled "The Colonial Status of the South," delivered one month before Pearl Harbor. This paper clearly revealed him as a combination of southern loyalist and Beardian progressive. The main theme of three centuries of southern history, according to Kendrick, was the region's colonial exploitation by the business interests of the Northeast. History had offered only one opportunity to escape that status, which had been lost when the South joined the North in one government in 1787. "At present," Kendrick believed, "finance capitalism and imperialism," which might even then be maneuvering the United States into the war, "hold the region in so firm a grip that no escape from the colonial status appears possible" without some catastrophic upheaval.

In 1909 Kendrick married Elizabeth Shields at Hudson, N.Y. They had four children. Described as redhaired, stocky, friendly, forthright, and practical, Kendrick was a Presbyterian and was active as a bank director and real estate developer in Greensboro. At the time of the consolidation of The University of North Carolina, he was elected by the faculty of the Woman's College as its representative on the Consolidated University Advisory Council. In 1934 he was a major candidate for appointment as president of the University of Tennessee. He died at his retirement home in Cedar Grove, Maine, and was buried nearby at West Dresden.

SEE: *Greensboro Daily News*, 28, 29 Oct. 1946; Information and photograph on file at the Walter Clinton Jackson Library (University of North Carolina, Greensboro); *Journal of American History*, vol. 52 (1946–47); *Journal of Southern History*, vol. 13 (1947); *Who's Who in America* (1946–47).

CLYDE WILSON

Kennedy, David (20 Jan. 1768–2 May 1837), gunsmith and Revolutionary War soldier, was the son of John Alexander and Mary Tandy Thomas Kennedy. She was the widow of John Thomas of Maryland. The elder Kennedy was a noted gun maker in Philadelphia, where he furnished guns for the Continental Army until forced to flee to North Carolina after Philadelphia fell to the British in September 1777.

David Kennedy was the oldest son and widely known as an excellent fiddler. With a partner, William Williamson, David, having learned the trade from his father, began a gun factory in what is now the northeastern corner of Moore County, near present-day Robbins. He soon bought his partner's interest, and at least for a time his brother Alexander, and perhaps another brother John, worked with him. An old mill was purchased on Bear Creek, a dam constructed across the creek, and water-powered machinery installed. Using power drills, riflers, hammers, and polishing machinery, the brothers soon did a large business. The earliest name of the community was Mechanicks Hill and the factory was called Mechanicsville. In 1810 it was reported that David made a profit of about $15,000, while his brother Alexander earned $1,000. In that year the factory made 650 rifles valued at $9,500. During the War of 1812 it had a government contract to make "Yauger" rifles, which were tested on a range that fired across Bear Creek. At the time of its peak production the factory employed more than seventy-five workmen, but after the war only a few dozen were employed. Some of the rifles from the Kennedy shop still exist.

From 1787 to 1790 Kennedy served in the General Assembly, and by 1835 he was receiving a pension for Revolutionary War service. Towards the end of his life misfortune befell him after he became surety for his brother Alexander's investment in a store. Alexander was too generous in granting credit to his customers, and his financial condition became so bad that he had to sell the business. To meet the loss, David was also obliged to dispose of his gun factory, his 778 acres of land, and his large, beautiful home. Facing financial ruin, Kennedy packed his few belongings and moved to Alabama where he died after a few years. Some years later gold was discovered on the land formerly owned by Kennedy, and it produced many thousands of dollars worth.

David and Alexander Kennedy were trustees of Mount Parnassus Academy at Carthage, chartered in 1809. In the early 1820s David gave the land and paid for building the Mechanics Hill Baptist Church, reportedly the first place of worship in upper Moore County.

On 24 May 1788 Kennedy married Joanna Moore, the daughter of Edward Moore, and they became the parents of ten children: Edward, John, Hiram and Martha (twins), W. M., Elizabeth, Elias M., Aaron, Enoch S., and Lydia.

SEE: Walter Clark, ed., *State Records of North Carolina*, vols. 20, 22 (1902, 1907); Albert R. Newsome, ed., "Twelve North Carolina Counties in 1810–1811, Moore County," *North Carolina Historical Review* 6 (1929); Blackwell P. Robinson, *A History of Moore County, 1747–1847* (1956); Manly Wade Wellman, *The County of Moore, 1847–1947* (1962).

K. S. MELVIN

Kennedy, John Bryan ("Jack") (10 Apr. 1845–27 Sept. 1915), physician, Confederate soldier, planter, and educational leader, was born at The Meadows, four miles west of Goldsboro, the son of John Thomas and Elizabeth Anne Cox Kennedy. Young Kennedy, a birthright Quaker, received his earliest education at home from his mother; after 1853, he attended the Wayne Institute and Normal College in Goldsboro, established that year by his father and others.

On 15 Apr. 1861, when he was just sixteen, he joined his father and other Wayne County men in boarding a train to go to Fort Macon on the coast in hope of taking it from Federal control. In New Bern they learned that the fort had already been secured and so returned to Goldsboro where they organized the Goldsboro Rifles, soon to become Company A, Twenty-seventh North Carolina Infantry. Kennedy was a private in the company. In February 1862 he transferred to the Thirty-fifth Regiment as a sergeant and saw service in March at the Battle of New Bern and in June and July at the Seven Days' Battle around Richmond. In July he was discharged because he was under eighteen. As soon as he was old enough, however, he reenlisted, was trained as a telegraph operator, and was assigned to Fort Fisher below Wilmington. He was there when the fort fell to Union forces near the end of the war and escaped capture by swimming the Cape Fear River. Returning to Goldsboro, he joined Confederate forces in the vicinity.

Soon afterwards he joined President Jefferson Davis's party as it moved across North Carolina and served as a bodyguard and telegrapher until they reached Washington, Ga. There he was discharged but went to Texas to join the forces of General Kirby Smith in hope of continuing the war.

After returning home briefly, Kennedy left for Mississippi in the winter of 1866 to study at an academy in Mount Pleasant, Miss. There he married his cousin, Mrs. Sarah Eliza Cox Crutcher, a widow, and they soon returned to Wayne County, N.C., which was also her birthplace. Kennedy studied medicine with a local physician and in 1868 enrolled in Washington College, Baltimore, where he studied medicine for a year before transferring to medical school in Nashville, Tenn., from which he was graduated in 1870. He set up a practice in rural Wayne County; on a large farm, he also practiced progressive farming methods.

Kennedy was active in a local medical society, presenting papers recounting his research and experience in cases of tetanus and appendicitis, and he collaborated with Dr. Hubert Royster of Raleigh in a pioneer appendicitis operation.

To provide a means of education for local youth, he established Falling Creek Academy near his home and was a trustee for many years. He also presented a medal for scholastic excellence to the graduating senior each year. In addition, he was a strong supporter of improved public schools.

Although born a Quaker, after 1870 Kennedy was a member of the Methodist church in which he served as a steward. His first wife died in 1882, leaving four sons: William Alfonzo, John Richard, Henry Cox, and James Matthew. In 1892 he married Katherine Amelia Bridgers, and they were the parents of Henry Bridgers and Sarah Amelia. Kennedy also reared two wards, Zebulon and Nancy Snipes, whose parents, patients of Dr. Kennedy, had died. He was buried in the churchyard at Falling Creek Methodist Church.

SEE: Frank A. Daniels, *History of Wayne County* (1914); Jefferson Davis, *The Rise and Fall of the Confederate Government* (1881); A. J. Hanna, *Flight into Oblivion* (1959); Military Service Records (National Archives, Washington, D.C.); *Mount Olive Tribune*, Industrial Issue (1907); *Proceedings of the First Semi-Annual Meeting of the Eastern Medical Association* (1873); *Southern Historical Society Papers*, vol. 9 (December 1881), vol. 12 (1894).

JOHN BAXTON FLOWERS III

Kennedy, John Thomas (5 Mar. 1824–21 Jan. 1913), planter, Confederate officer, and public official, was born at his father's Oak Hill plantation in west-central Wayne County, the son of John and Sarah Everett Becton Kennedy, Quakers. His earliest education was at home under his mother; then, with his brother, Joseph Everett, he attended Waynesborough Academy at the county seat, Waynesborough. When he was about eighteen he began farming, and in 1843 he married Elizabeth Anne Cox. They settled on land given him by his father which they called The Meadows.

By the mid-1840s Kennedy was demonstrating an interest in politics and he became a justice of the peace for the county. At about the same time he and his brother, Joseph, and a half brother, John E. Becton, using their slaves, contracted to lay the roadbed for the North Carolina Railroad between Selma and Pine Level. As contractors they also built the office for the Bank of New Bern in Waynesboro, as the county seat was then

called. In 1850 they had the contract to construct the new brick courthouse there. Kennedy in 1853 joined other men to form a stock company which established the Wayne Institute and Normal College; four years later he and others founded the Wayne Female College in Goldsboro.

In mid-April 1861, before North Carolina had seceded, he and his sixteen-year-old son, John, were among members of two companies of militia setting out for New Bern en route to take Fort Macon from Federal control. In New Bern they learned that the fort had already been secured for the state, and they returned home. In October, after the state had left the Union, Kennedy enlisted in the Thirty-fifth North Carolina Regiment of infantry and became first lieutenant in one of the companies; his son was a private in the same regiment. During the following spring he raised two companies from Wayne, Johnston, and Wake counties and partially outfitted them. With two other companies from the state, they were assigned to a Georgia regiment in August 1862. Kennedy was promoted to major, and in 1863 he became a lieutenant colonel; he served with the Georgia regiment until the spring of 1864, frequently engaged in scouting duty and in skirmishes in eastern North Carolina.

In July 1864 Kennedy was promoted to colonel to take command of the newly formed Sixteenth Battalion, North Carolina Cavalry. He was in enemy hands at the time, however, having been hit in the back by Union sharpshooters at Spring Hill, Va., at the end of May 1864 and captured. Exchanged in August, he was with his new command by the end of November. The war ended in the spring of 1865, and he was paroled at Goldsboro on 15 May.

As a Democrat Kennedy was elected a delegate from Wayne County to the constitutional convention in Raleigh in 1865, but he was in a minority and, discontented with the convention's actions, resigned his seat. In February 1866 he was elected sheriff and remained in office until 1874. During this time the whipping post was abolished as a means of punishment in the county. Also during this period Kennedy joined some neighbors, as well as some men from adjoining Johnston County, in an effort to encourage European immigrants to move to that region as farm laborers, but they met with only limited success. In 1877 he became steward of the new State Hospital for the Colored Insane near Goldsboro, where he superintended the production of farm crops for the staff and patients.

In the elections of November 1884, Kennedy narrowly won a seat in the state senate. His committee assignments included those on Institutions for the Deaf, Dumb, and Blind; Education; Agriculture; and Military Affairs. He introduced a bill to prohibit the sale of "spirituous liquors, or other intoxicating drinks" in state institutions. Kennedy did not seek reelection and retired to his farm. Because of poor health, he fell into debt and asked friends in state government for employment. Between 1889 and 1900, at age seventy-four, he became a janitor in the museum section of the Department of Agriculture. His wife died in 1901, and he returned briefly to Goldsboro. In 1904, however, he became assistant curator at the state museum and helped prepare the state's exhibition for the St. Louis World's Fair. Further illness resulted in his moving to the Confederate Soldiers' Home in Raleigh where he remained until his death.

Kennedy and his wife were the parents of eleven children: John Bryan, Sarah Eliza, Micajah Thomas, William Frederick, Silas Cox, Mary Elizabeth, Matthew

Everett, Thomas Simpson, Richard Lee, Robert Dearing, and Sidney Davis.

SEE: *Branson's North Carolina Agricultural Almanac* (1881–93); *Branson's North Carolina Business Directory* (1867–68); Frank Daniels, *History of Wayne County* (1916); Department of Agriculture, *Report* (1899–1900, 1905, 1907, 1909); *Goldsboro Argus*, 24 Mar. 1900; *Goldsboro News Argus*, Centennial Edition (October 1947); *Journal of the General Assembly*, 1885 session; Louis A. Manarin, ed., *North Carolina Troops, 1861–1965*, vol. 2 (1968); *Proceedings of the Constitutional Convention* (1865); Wayne County Records (North Carolina State Archives, Raleigh).

JOHN BAXTON FLOWERS III

Kennedy, William (31 July 1768–11 Oct. 1834), lawyer and congressman, was the son of John and Sarah Kennedy of Beaufort County. Nothing is known of his early life and education. As a young man he was admitted to the bar and began the practice of law in Pitt County but later lived in Beaufort County, where he owned several large tracts of land. Generally allied with the Federalist party, he at times associated himself with the Jeffersonian Republicans.

On 4 Mar. 1803, Kennedy entered Congress and served until 3 Mar. 1805. Reelected, he served in the session of 1809–11 but was defeated in his campaign for still another term. Thomas Blount, who won the election, died in office, and at the next election Kennedy was again elected, serving during the years 1813–15. As a member of Congress during the War of 1812, he supported the war measures of the administration, although he was one of the North Carolina congressmen who voted in 1814 to lift the embargo. Defeated in his bid for reelection, he retired to Beaufort County and made his principal seat on a plantation above the town of Washington.

Kennedy's wife, Elizabeth, died in 1818. An infant daughter had died the year before. Kennedy's will, dated 20 Sept. 1833, left a large amount of land, personal property, and more than thirty slaves to his three children: Frances, Sophrorisba, and William L. He was buried in the family cemetery near Washington.

SEE: *Biog. Dir. Am. Cong.* (1961), which confuses Kennedy with another man of the same name; W. Frank Craven, "William Kennedy" (unpublished sketch in the author's possession); Sarah M. Lemmon, *Frustrated Patriots: North Carolina in the War of 1812* (1973); William H. Masterson, ed., *The John Gray Blount Papers*, vol. 3 (1965); *New Jersey Gazette*, 13 Oct. 1779; Will and Estate Papers, Beaufort County (North Carolina State Archives, Raleigh).

JOHN BAXTON FLOWERS III

Kephart, Horace Sowers (8 Sept. 1862–2 Apr. 1931), writer, outdoorsman, and librarian, was born in East Salem, Pa., the son of Isaiah L., a teacher, editor, and clergyman, and Mary Elizabeth Sowers Kephart. His ancestors had been among the first settlers of the mountain wilderness west of the Susquehanna. In 1867 the family moved to Jefferson, Iowa, and in 1871 to Western, Iowa, where Kephart attended Western College for a year. In 1876 his family returned to Pennsylvania, and he entered Lebanon Valley College in Annville, graduating with the A.B. degree in the spring of 1879. That fall he enrolled in the College of Liberal Arts

of Boston University. In addition to studying under Alphaeus Hyatt—the distinguished zoologist—he enjoyed "the blessed privilege of studying whatever I pleased in the Boston Public Library." Thus evolved his career for the next twenty years.

In 1880 Kephart went to Cornell University, in Ithaca, N.Y., where he assumed supervision of cataloguing the library's holdings and took courses in history and political science. At the library he worked for Cornell's first librarian, Willard Fiske, who became a personal friend and benefactor. Independently wealthy, Fiske moved to Italy in 1883 and established his residence at the Villa Forini in the eastern quarter of Florence, where he began to assemble some of the world's finest collections of Dante and Petrarch, Icelandic history and literature, and the Rhaeto-Romanic language. In 1885 he brought Kephart to the Villa Forini to assist in cataloguing and purchasing these materials. In this capacity, Kephart worked in the major libraries of Italy and the Royal Library in Munich. In addition, he took lectures at the Institute di Studii Superiori under Paolo Mantegazza—an eminent physiologist and anthropologist—and made walking trips in the Apennines and Alps.

In 1886 Kephart returned to the United States and accepted a position as assistant librarian at Yale College in New Haven, Conn. The following year he married Laura Mack of Ithaca. While in New Haven, Kephart began his career as a writer. Most of his early writings are related to library matters, but he was also developing an interest in American frontier history. Largely as a result of this interest, he accepted in 1890 the directorship of the St. Louis Mercantile Library Association, "the oldest library west of the Mississippi." Here Kephart built one of the finest collections of Western Americana then in existence. He became an authority in the field, consulted by historians and writers such as Hiram Chittenden and Emerson Hough.

As an exceptionally competent librarian, Kephart resided with his wife and six children in St. Louis for over a decade. After the turn of the century, however, his outlook on life underwent fundamental changes. His interests and writings shifted from librarianship to outdoor life, firearms, and frontier history. He became disenchanted with the basic context of his home life, and he developed a serious drinking problem. As time passed, his main pleasure came from solitary excursions into the Ozark Mountains and the Arkansas swamps. "I love the wilderness because there are no shams in it," he wrote in a notebook. The extended wilderness trips alienated the library's directors, and late in 1903 he was forced to resign from the Mercantile Library. In April 1904 he suffered a nervous collapse and was taken to his parents' home in Dayton, Ohio. His wife returned with their children to Ithaca.

In Dayton, Kephart was preoccupied with the desire to forge for himself a literary career, while at the same time living a wilderness-frontier existence "so that I might realize the past in the present." He was seeking a "Back of Beyond" in which he could find "a . . . place to begin again." After much study he chose the mountains of western North Carolina. In the summer of 1904 he journeyed south by train and set up camp on Dick's Creek, several miles west of Dillsboro in Jackson County. Then, in October, he obtained permission to use an abandoned two-room cabin on the Little Fork of the Sugar Fork of Hazel Creek on the western slope of the Great Smokies in Swain County. From this vantage point he studied the land and the people, supporting his few needs by writing for the popular outdoor and sporting journals of the day. By 1906 he had compiled enough material on how to live in the wilderness to publish *Camping and Woodcraft*, a storehouse of practical advice, lore, anecdote, and adventure, which became in time the standard work in its field.

Kephart left the Hazel Creek watershed in 1907 and traveled in other parts of the Southern Appalachians. In 1910 he returned to Swain County, where he lived in a boardinghouse in Bryson City most of the year, but during the summers he camped, mostly alone, at favorite sites in the backcountry. Two books on subjects on which he was an authority, *Camp Cookery* and *Sporting Firearms*, appeared in 1910 and 1912. The first edition of his major work, *Our Southern Highlanders*, was published in 1913 (revised and expanded in 1922). Drawing on materials that he collected firsthand (primarily on Hazel Creek and in the Bryson City area) or that he carefully researched, Kephart produced a literary work that is at once historical, sociological, and autobiographical. No book devoted to the Southern Appalachians has been more widely known, read, and respected. It is the classic study of the region.

After 1913 Kephart published *Camping* (1916) and *The Camper's Manual* (1923), edited a series of eleven volumes of adventure and exploration ("Outdoor Adventure Library," 1915–17), and labored on a novel entitled "Smoky Mountain Magic" that never got out of typescript. He was active in the establishment of the Appalachian Trail, particularly in plotting the route the trail was to follow through the Smokies and on into northern Georgia. But his most important writing and the major portion of his energies during the 1920s and early 1930s were devoted to the movement that culminated in the establishment of the Great Smoky Mountains National Park. His role in the movement was considerable. He was killed in an automobile accident near Bryson City (where he was buried) before the park became an actuality, but he died knowing it was assured. Two months before his death the U.S. Geographic Board designated that a peak on the high divide of the Smokies, about eight miles northeast of Clingman's Dome, be named Mount Kephart. He was the first living American so honored.

SEE: Jim Casada, "Writers of the Purple Prose," *Wildlife in North Carolina* 52 (January 1988); George Ellison, Introduction to *Our Southern Highlanders*, by Horace Kephart (1976); Horace Kephart, "Horace Kephart By Himself," *North Carolina Library Bulletin* 5 (June 1922); Clarence Miller, "Horace Kephart, A Personal Glimpse," *Missouri Historical Society Bulletin* 16 (July 1959).

GEORGE ELLISON

Ker, David (*February 1758–21 Jan. 1805*), minister, educator, lawyer, and judge, was born in Down Patrick, Ireland, of Scottish ancestry. He was graduated from Trinity College, Dublin, and was connected with Temple Patrick Presbytery. There is no record as to when he and his family reached North Carolina, but his name first appeared on the rolls of Orange Presbytery in 1789. Two years later he moved to Fayetteville, began regular Sabbath services at the courthouse, and taught school during the week. His school salary was about $400, and his congregation paid him a similar amount. The Reverend William Henry Foote recorded that Ker did not administer the ordinance of Holy Communion during his three years in Fayetteville and that no one knew whether there was a baptism.

In 1794 Ker left Fayetteville for Chapel Hill, where he became the first professor and first presiding professor of The University of North Carolina when it opened in 1795. The man who had been described earlier as "a man of piety and learning" became an "outspoken infidel." When attempts were made to change the organization at the school and install a president with Ker as professor of languages, he objected. He lived in what would be the residence of the president and demanded that, if he were forced to leave it, his salary be increased annually to include the value of the house. The trustees would not agree to his demands, and Ker remained in his position until July 1796. Because of the disorders in the student body during the previous session, Ker resigned against his will and the trustees accepted his resignation. Part of the dissatisfaction with Ker was based on his being "a furious Republican" as well as an "infidel," and the unrest and unruliness among the students probably stemmed somewhat from the discussion of his philosophy.

Leaving the university in a disgruntled frame of mind, Ker moved to Lumberton. In 1793 General John Willis, the Revolutionary War hero on whose plantation the town of Lumberton was built, was the prime mover in getting the legislature to authorize the establishment of an academy in Lumberton. In 1796, the General Assembly passed another law authorizing the trustees of the school "to lay off and sell a part of the town Commons, to raise a fund for the purpose of building said academy." The academy was ready for David Ker, who became its first principal while studying law and engaging in a small mercantile business. He subsequently was admitted to the bar.

In 1800, when General Willis emigrated to Mississippi, Ker, who also moved there at the same time, probably went as tutor to the Willis children. Ker settled in the Natchez neighborhood and, in 1801, opened in that town the first public school for females in the Mississippi Territory; he was assisted in the undertaking by his wife and daughters, who were "highly finished scholars and very elegant ladies." During the same year he was appointed sheriff and became clerk of court, both of Adams County. In the summer of 1802, President Thomas Jefferson appointed him to a judgeship, which gave "much satisfaction" to the citizens of the Mississippi Territory.

Early in 1805 Ker held court in an open, unheated house in severe weather and contracted an illness that ended his life. His widow taught school to support the family and outlived him by more than four decades. A devoted Christian, she burned all of Ker's papers after his death, fearing that his writings might wrongly influence others. He was described variously as "able and impartial," as having versatility in his genius, as being the "ablest and best judge on the bench," and as a "man of fine education, a classical scholar, well read in the principles of moral and natural philosophy, of law and religion."

Ker and his wife Mary had five children: David died unmarried at age twenty-three, John became a successful physician, Sarah married a Cowden, Eliza married Rush Nutt, and Martha (or Patsey) married William Terry. There are many of Ker's descendants throughout the United States, especially in Mississippi and Louisiana. Portraits of Ker and his wife are in the Southern Historical Collection at the University of North Carolina at Chapel Hill.

SEE: Kemp P. Battle, *History of the University of North Carolina*, vol. 1 (1907); Kate Britt Biggs, "Robeson County History," *Robeson County* (Lumberton) *Enter-*

prise, 18 July 1965; *Biographical and Historical Memoirs of Mississippi* (1891); William Henry Foote, *Sketches of North Carolina, Historical and Biographical, Illustrative of the Principles of a Portion of Her Early Settlers* (1846); Robert C. Lawrence, *The State of Robeson* (1939); *Laws of North Carolina* (1793, 1796); "Lumberton Education History Dates Back to 1791," *The Robesonian* (26 Feb. 1951); Edward Mayes, *History of Education in Mississippi* (1899); Dunbar Rowland, *Courts, Judges and Lawyers of Mississippi, 1798–1935* (1935); Jethro Rumple, *The History of Presbyterianism in North Carolina* (1966); John H. Wheeler, *Historical Sketches of North Carolina from 1584 to 1851* (1851).

MAUD THOMAS SMITH

Kern, Paul Bentley (*16 June 1882–16 Dec. 1953*), Methodist bishop and educator, was born at Alexandria, Va., the son of Dr. John A. and Margaret Virginia Eskridge Kern. His father was a longtime professor of English Bible at Randolph-Macon College, briefly president of that institution, and later professor at Vanderbilt University.

Kern was a student at Randolph-Macon during the years 1897–99 and was graduated from Vanderbilt in 1905. Ordained deacon and elder by Bishop Elijah E. Hoss, he became assistant director of the correspondence school of the Vanderbilt University School of Religion for training ministers. From 1910 to 1915 he was successively pastor of churches in Nashville, Bellbuckle, and Murfreesboro, Tenn. For the next five years he was professor of ministerial efficiency at Southern Methodist University, where from 1920 to 1926 he was dean of the School of Theology. In 1926 Kern became pastor of a church in San Antonio, Tex., and remained in the post until elected bishop in 1930. Assigned to the Orient for four years, he next became presiding bishop of the four conferences in the Carolinas from 1934 to 1938. Other assignments took him to Cuba, Florida, and Tennessee until he retired in 1952. He was a frequent lecturer at Southern Methodist University, Vanderbilt University, Emory University, and elsewhere from 1930 until his retirement.

Bishop Kern was the author of *A Methodist Church and Its Works* (with Worth M. Tippy), *The Miracle of the Galilean: Methodism Has a Message*, and *The Basic Beliefs of Jesus: A Story of the Assumptions Behind Life*. In 1948 he was a delegate from the Methodist church to the World Council of Churches at Amsterdam, and in 1952 at the General Conference in San Francisco he presented the Episcopal Address which attracted nationwide attention for its incisiveness and comprehensive pronouncements on many subjects. The recipient of honorary degrees from seven colleges and universities, he was called a "vigorous, progressive, dynamic leader."

In 1952 a campaign was conducted and funds were raised for the construction of a youth center at the Lake Junaluska Assembly Grounds and named in his memory. He was a longtime trustee of the Assembly and made his home at Lake Junaluska. There he and E. O. Harbin were instrumental in founding the Youth Caravan Movement of the Methodist church.

Kern married Lucy Campbell, and they were the parents of John Campbell, Virginia, and Katherine. There is a portrait and a manuscript biography of him at Southern Methodist University. He was buried in Nashville, Tenn.

SEE: Elmer T. Clark, *Methodism in Western North Carolina* (1966); *Discipline of the Methodist Church* (1939); *Methodist History* (October 1968); *Michigan Christian Advocate* (December 1953); Walter N. Vernon, *Methodism Moves Across North Texas* (1967); *Who's Who in America* (1952).

GRADY L. E. CARROLL

Kerr, Daniel Wilson (*10 July 1796–15 May 1850*), clergyman, educator, and publisher, born in Cumberland County, Va., was a descendant of early colonists who first settled in Virginia's Norfolk County. The literary ability that was evident in Kerr's professional accomplishments indicates that he received a classical education in his youth. However, except that he married Rebecca Barham Davis, a cultured and refined lady, nothing has been found about his life until 1818, when he joined the Christian church founded by James O'Kelly. The following year he became a minister.

By 1826 Kerr was in North Carolina, for in that year he became principal of a school incorporated as the Wake Forest Pleasant Grove Academy, which was located twelve miles north of Raleigh on the road to Oxford. In 1836 he moved to Orange County and opened Mt. Pleasant Academy on 15 January. Located twelve miles northeast of Hillsborough and within a short distance of Mt. Zion Christian Church, the academy accepted only male boarding students and advertised that its courses would sufficiently prepare them for entrance into the state university. Within a few months, Principal Kerr changed the name of the school to Junto Academy and conducted it as such until 1849, when he moved it to Pittsboro.

Kerr was a member of the North Carolina and Virginia Christian Conference, one of several independent units composing the southern Christian church in the first half of the nineteenth century. Beginning in 1830 and for two decades thereafter, he served with distinction on numerous conference committees. His most outstanding contribution to the organization was his persistent efforts to found a church publication, through which he hoped to promote a union of the various conferences into one central governmental body. In 1833 he served on a conference committee that made a vain attempt to launch the *Christian Intelligencer*, and in 1840 he was a member of a similar committee that tried unsuccessfully to publish the *Christian Protestant and Advocate of Union*. After these failures, the Christians officially decided to endorse the *Christian Palladium*, published in Bloomfield, N.Y., by the northern Christian church. Kerr was delegated by the conference to serve as one of its official correspondents to the paper, and prospects appeared favorable for an eventual merger of the two Christian churches into one. However, the *Palladium* somewhat enthusiastically espoused the arguments of the Abolitionists, which alienated the southerners, and the merger was not consummated until 1922.

The thwarted conference, prodded by Kerr and others, decided to make a third attempt to found a periodical and, in a meeting at Union Chapel in Orange (now Alamance) County on 14 May 1842, voted to establish the *Christian Sun* with Kerr as editor. This time their plan succeeded and the first issue, printed by Dennis Heartt in Hillsborough, was dated 1 Jan. 1844, although not actually issued until February. The front page carried the caption "The Lord is a Sun and Shield" and an appealing editorial from the pen of the editor.

As a result of Kerr's promotional efforts, the Southern Christian Association was organized, composed of members from the various Christian conferences to supervise the management and promote the circulation of the paper. Largely due to Kerr's efficiency, the *Sun* survived and its influence increased; except for its suspension during the Civil War, it appeared regularly over a wide southern area until discontinued by the church in 1965. The promotional campaign carried on through the columns of the paper was the primary cause of a meeting in 1856 of the various Christian conferences, significantly at Union Chapel, on which occasion the organization of the Southern Christian Convention was accomplished. Kerr's dream of union was thus realized, but he did not live to witness its fulfilment for he was stricken with paralysis and died at age fifty-four. W. S. Gunter, one of his students, who was also clerk of the Superior Court of Chatham County, assisted Mrs. Kerr in publishing the *Sun* until the church could make new arrangements.

The Kerrs had no children and, after her husband's death, Mrs. Kerr taught in a school for young ladies in Alamance County. The editor was buried at Pittsboro and reinterred in 1857 at Union Chapel. On 14 Nov. 1944, the North Carolina and Virginia Conference of the Congregational Christian church (now the United Church of Christ) met at the site of Junto Academy and unveiled a suitable marker of native field stone to commemorate Kerr's career and the founding of the *Christian Sun*.

SEE: *Burlington Daily Times-News*, 15 Nov. 1944; Chatham County Deeds (Chatham County Courthouse, Pittsboro); *Hillsborough Recorder*, 5 Feb. 1836, 1 Aug. 1838; Peter J. Kernodle, *Lives of Christian Ministers* (1909); *Minutes of the Conferences of the Christian Church, South*, Files of *Christian Sun*, and Files of *Christian Palladium* (Church History Room, Elon College); Orange County Deeds (Orange County Courthouse, Hillsborough).

DURWARD T. STOKES

Kerr, John (*4 Aug. 1782–29 Sept. 1842*), Baptist minister and congressman, was born in Gloucester District, southern Caswell County, of Scottish and English ancestry. He was the son of Mary Graves and John Kerr, a planter. Young Kerr was first employed as a teacher in the common English school begun by his uncle, General Azariah Graves, in Caswell County. In 1801, after attending a revival at Crossroads Presbyterian Church, he was converted, baptized, and began to preach. His first pastorate was in 1805 near Halifax, Va., at Arbor and Mary Creek churches. Elected to Congress as a Democrat from Virginia, he served from 1813 to 1815; although an unsuccessful candidate in the next election, he was subsequently elected to fill a vacancy and served again from 1815 to 1817. He was not a candidate for reelection.

Kerr seriously considered leaving the ministry for a legal and political career. While on a preaching mission, however, he was thrown from his gig and almost died from his injuries. Believing that his complete recovery was due to divine intervention, he cast aside his political ambitions.

Early in 1825 he was invited to preach for two weeks at the First Baptist Church in Richmond, Va. That February the church offered him the position of pastor at an annual salary of $1,000, which he accepted. His preaching drew great crowds, and it is said that he "took Richmond by storm." A deliberate, forceful, and emotional speaker, his sermons often lasted for two hours. During his tenure, he served as first agent of the Roanoke Baptist Association, first president of the Virginia Baptist Education Society, and president of the

Baptist General Association of Virginia. In 1830 he presided over the meeting of the Education Society out of which the University of Richmond was born.

Kerr's desire to engage in evangelistic preaching caused him to resign the Richmond pastorate in 1832 and settle on a farm near Danville. From then until his death, Elder Kerr, as he was called in Baptist churches, was a leader in the establishment of missionary Baptist churches, preaching at camp meetings in Virginia and North Carolina. At one camp meeting in Northumberland County, Va., it was reported that 150 people joined the church. His crusades in Caswell County led to the founding of the First Baptist Church in Yanceyville and the Sycamore Church in southern Stony Creek township. In 1845, the latter church was renamed Kerr's Chapel in his honor.

In 1805 Kerr married Mrs. Elizabeth Williams of Halifax, Va., and they became the parents of six children: John, Jr., Nathaniel W. Williams, Sarah Lanier, Mary Graves, Martha (m. Dr. James Martin of Mocksville), and Frances (m. Thomas Dickson Connally of Milton). He died at his home near Danville and was buried in the Baptist church cemetery, Yanceyville. The Reverend J. B. Jeter, who succeeded him as pastor in Richmond, preached the funeral service on 25 June 1843, nine months after his death. Kerr's portrait was owned by a great-grandson, John Motley Morehead of New York City.

SEE: *Biog. Dir. Am. Cong.* (1961); John Motley Morehead, comp., *The Morehead Family of North Carolina* (1921); *Virginia Baptist Preacher*, September 1843; Blanche White, *First Baptist Church, Richmond, 1780–1955* (1955).

KATHARINE K. KENDALL

Kerr, John, Jr. (*10 Feb. 1811–5 Sept. 1879*), congressman, judge, and legislator, was born in Halifax County, Va., of Scottish and English ancestry, the son of Elizabeth Williams and John Kerr, a Baptist minister and congressman. He attended school and studied law in Richmond, where his father was pastor of the First Baptist Church. In 1832 he settled in Yanceyville, Caswell County, N.C., the home county of his father and grandparents, and in April took an oath to practice as an attorney before the county court. The frequency of his name on deeds, wills, and court cases in Caswell records indicates that his legal practice was large.

Active in politics and a forceful orator in judicial circles, Kerr was an unsuccessful candidate for governor in 1852 on the Whig ticket. He may have lost the election because of his campaign to allow the people to vote on a state constitutional amendment rather than to have the legislature adopt it. Soon afterwards, however, he was elected as a Whig to the Congress of 1853–55. Kerr was a staunch believer in slavery, and in October 1854 the citizens of Yanceyville honored him with a public dinner for his efforts to promote passage of the Kansas-Nebraska Act. In the same year he was speaker for the first Agricultural Fair in Yanceyville. In 1858–60 he served in the General Assembly, and in 1862–63 he was a judge of the Superior Court. With the fall of the Whig party, he became a Democrat.

After the Civil War, Kerr suffered much humiliation from Reconstruction forces and during the Kirk-Holden war was arrested by George Kirk—along with other residents of Caswell County—and imprisoned in Raleigh. His denial of a writ of habeas corpus before the Supreme Court on 2 Aug. 1870 shocked the country and aroused sympathy from his state. In 1874 he was again named a Superior Court judge and served until his death. During his last tenure, he moved to Reidsville to take advantage of rail transportation to meet court schedules.

Active in educational affairs, Kerr was an organizer and trustee of the Yanceyville Female Academy in 1836; solicited funds for the establishment of Wake Forest College, of which he served as a trustee from 1844 to 1856; and was a trustee of The University of North Carolina from 1846 to 1868, as well as escheats officer for Caswell County. In 1879 The University of North Carolina awarded him the honorary doctor of laws degree. At the time of his death, Kerr was president of the Historical Society of North Carolina. An ardent and uncompromising Baptist, he served as president of the Beulah Baptist Association and as president of the Baptist State Convention during the periods 1875–76 and 1877–78.

Kerr died in Reidsville and was buried in the Yanceyville Baptist cemetery. He was married twice, first in 1835 to Evelina B. Campbell, of Orange County, by whom he had seven children: John Marshall, Mary, William Alexander, Nathaniel, Elizabeth Williams, Fannie, and E. C. His second wife was Anne Eliza Royall, of Chesterfield County, Va., who went to Yanceyville to teach music. They had five children: Junius Royall, Sallie, Grace, Annot Lyle, and Laura.

SEE: Biblical Recorder, September 1879; Biog. Dir. Am. Cong. (1971); Greensboro Patriot, 6 Sept. 1879; Minutes of the Baptist State Convention, 1875–1878; John Motley Morehead, comp., The Morehead Family of North Carolina (1921); North Carolina Manual (1913); G. W. Paschal, History of Wake Forest College, 3 vols. (1935–43); Herbert D. Pegg, The Whig Party in North Carolina, 1834–1861 (1968[?]); U.S. Census, 1850, 1860, 1870; John H. Wheeler, ed., Reminiscences and Memoirs of North Carolina and Eminent North Carolinians (1884).

KATHARINE K. KENDALL

Kerr, John Hosea (30 Dec. 1873–21 June 1958), lawyer, Superior Court solicitor and judge, and congressman, was born at Yanceyville, the son of John Hosea McNeill and Eliza Catherine Yancey Kerr, great niece of Bartlett Yancey and granddaughter of James Yancey. His father was an officer in the Confederate Army and served for a number of years as clerk of court in Caswell County. Young Kerr was educated in the Yanceyville schools and Bingham School at Mebane; he received the bachelor of arts degree from Wake Forest College in 1895. One of the early students of law at Wake Forest, he was awarded the honorary doctor of law degree from the college on 4 June 1945.

In the fall of 1895, Kerr received his license and began to practice law in Warrenton. He served as town attorney and for two terms as mayor (1897–98). In these positions he was instrumental in having the Warrenton charter amended to permit the municipality to own and operate businesses, including a dispensary for the sale of spirits, wine, and beer; a telephone company; a hotel; and a railroad. This policy brought Warrenton to the attention of local governments nationwide. In 1905 Kerr was elected solicitor of the Third Judicial District, a post he held for ten years. In November 1916 he was elected judge of the Superior Court and served until 1923. On the death of Claude Kitchin in 1923, Kerr was elected as a Democrat to Congress where he served fifteen consecutive terms until 1952. He was the third generation

of his family bearing the name John Kerr to be elected to Congress.

While in Congress, he took a deep interest in the agricultural life of his district; he was particularly active in legislation affecting the cotton, peanut, and tobacco crops. Among his committee assignments, he was a member of the Public Buildings Committee, which was instrumental in the erection of many government buildings in the 1930s and 1940s—including the United States Supreme Court Building. On the Appropriations Committee, he served as vice-chairman of the subcommittee that handled military appropriations during World War II, and he was chairman of the Subcommittee on Subversive Organizations. Kerr was coauthor of the Kerr-Coolidge Immigration bill and the Kerr-Smith Tobacco Act of 1934. The latter legislation evolved into a governmental program of price supports and allotments for tobacco farmers, which proved to be of tremendous economic benefit to North Carolina and other tobacco-producing regions.

During the administration of President Franklin D. Roosevelt, Kerr was a close personal friend of Secretary of State Cordell Hull and was sent on diplomatic missions to Hawaii, Central America, and Europe. He served as chairman of the U.S. delegation to the Inter-America Travel Congress at Mexico City in 1941.

The Second Congressional District, which Kerr served for twenty-nine years, was traversed by the Roanoke River. The Roanoke had a history of severe flooding, and in 1940 the waters produced by a devastating flood crested at Weldon at fifty-eight feet, six inches. In this thirtieth major flood along the Roanoke River basin since the Civil War, the entire crop in the Roanoke Valley was destroyed. The frequency of damaging floods caused Kerr to begin action for the location of a flood control project on the Roanoke River. Against the resistance of many, he secured passage of a congressional appropriation authorizing the investigation of such a project and a survey. Kerr secured the assistance of several colleagues from Virginia and North Carolina, and a flood control and hydroelectric source dam was erected at Buggs Island, Va., at a cost of $100 million. Members of Congress paid tribute to his efforts by naming the facility, which was dedicated on 3 Oct. 1952, the John H. Kerr Dam and Reservoir. This project led to construction of Gaston Dam near Roanoke Rapids by the Virginia Electric and Power Company. The recreational features alone of the two projects (Kerr Lake having 880 miles of shoreline) has produced an economic revolution in the Roanoke Valley, which runs through northeastern North Carolina and southside Virginia.

On 15 Feb. 1899 Kerr married Ella Lillian Foote, the daughter of Henry Alexander and Minnie Young Foote of Warrenton; her father was an attorney and the owner and publisher of the Warrenton Gazette. They were the parents of two sons: John H., Jr., an attorney and a member of the North Carolina House of Representatives and Senate for twelve terms (speaker of the house, 1943); and James Yancey, an attorney and tobacconist. Kerr was a Mason, a member of the Warrenton Baptist Church, a trustee of The University of North Carolina, and a member of the Board of Visitors of the U.S. Military Academy at West Point. He died in Warrenton, where he was buried in Fairview Cemetery.

SEE: Biog. Dir. Am. Cong. (1950); John L. Cheney, Jr., ed., North Carolina Government, 1585–1974 (1975); Congressional Record, 5 July 1952; History of North Carolina, vol. 5 (1919); Robert C. Lawrence, Here in Carolina (1939); Elizabeth Wilson Montgomery, Sketches of Old

Warrenton (1924); William S. Powell, *When the Past Refused to Die: A History of Caswell County, North Carolina, 1777–1977* (1977); Parke Rouse, Jr., *Below the James Lies Dixie* (1968); W. O. Saunders, "The Town That Had Faith in Itself," *Colliers*, 17 Mar. 1923; Warrenton, *The Warren Record*, 27 June 1958; Manly Wade Wellman, *The County of Warren, North Carolina* (1959); *Who Was Who in America, 1951–1960*, vol. 3 (1963).

JOHN H. KERR III

Kerr, John Hosea, Jr. *(19 May 1900–28 May 1968)*, attorney and legislator, was born in Warrenton, the son of John Hosea and Ella Foote Kerr. He received his early education in the schools of Warrenton where he was an honor graduate and valedictorian of the Graham Academy in 1917. During the latter year he entered The University of North Carolina, from which he received the A.B. degree in 1921. In Chapel Hill, Kerr distinguished himself as a debater in the Philanthropic Literary Society and served as business manager of the *Tar Heel* while Thomas Wolfe was editor.

Kerr studied law at Wake Forest College (1922–23) and was admitted to the bar in 1923. After an additional year of legal study at George Washington University, he began a practice in Rocky Mount. In 1928, he was elected to his first term in the General Assembly as a member of the house for Edgecombe County. He returned to Warrenton in 1931 and established a permanent practice. In 1938 Kerr was again elected to the house, now representing Warren County, and was continuously reelected until 1949; for the 1943 session he served as speaker. After a single term in the state senate (1955–57), he served three more terms in the house (1957–63) before declining to seek reelection.

The legislator from Warrenton was the most noted orator and one of the most influential members in the General Assembly of his day. His speeches were presented ex tempore and none of the major addresses survive in recorded form. The most famous was delivered during the 1947 session in support of the Humber bill to establish the North Carolina Museum of Art. This bill, which sought an appropriation of one million dollars, had not previously attracted significant legislative support. Kerr's speech began: "I know that I am facing a hostile audience, but man cannot live by bread alone." The address was commonly credited with securing passage of the bill; among significant speeches in the state's legislative history, it was perhaps equaled only by the James C. Dobbin speech in support of the state mental hospital.

Despite extreme conservatism in fiscal and social matters, Kerr achieved a considerable record in support of innovative state programs. It is said that he obtained the initial state appropriation for the North Carolina Institute of Government, and he was an influential supporter of the North Carolina School of the Arts.

In addition to his legislative service, Kerr was an official of the state Democratic party, a trustee of The University of North Carolina, and a promoter of local improvements in Warrenton.

On 12 Nov. 1932 he married Mary Hinton Duke of Richmond, Va., and they had one child, John H. Kerr III. He died at age sixty-eight and was buried in Fairview Cemetery, Warrenton.

SEE: *Durham Morning Herald*, 16 Jan. 1959, 29 Jan. 1961; Daniel L. Grant, *Alumni History of the University of North Carolina, 1795–1924* (1924); Archibald Henderson, *The Campus of the First State University* (1949); *North Carolina Architect*, May–June 1967; Raleigh *News and Observer*, 30 May 1968.

GEORGE T. BLACKBURN II

Kerr, Washington Caruthers *(24 May 1827–9 Aug. 1885)*, geologist, was born in eastern Guilford County in the Alamance Creek–Alamance Church region. His Scotch-Irish parents were William M. Kerr, a small farmer, and Euphence B. Doak, who reportedly possessed unusual mechanical talent. When "W. C." was a small child, the family moved to the Haw River area in western Orange County, which in 1849 became the eastern section of the new county of Alamance. His father died about 1835 and his mother in 1840, leaving four sons and two daughters. W. C., quick and bright, was the namesake of the family's pastor, the Reverend Eli Washington Caruthers. Indeed, Caruthers was then the state's outstanding Presbyterian as well as principal of a good preparatory school in Guilford County. Cared for and guided by his mentor, young Kerr entered the sophomore class at The University of North Carolina and was graduated in 1850 with highest honors. He taught for one year at Williamston in Martin County, and for another year at Marshall University in northeastern Texas.

In 1852 Kerr was appointed as a computer in the office of the *Nautical Almanac* at Cambridge, Mass., and held the post for almost five years. He also studied at the Lawrence Scientific School and came in contact at Harvard University with such luminaries as Louis Agassiz, naturalist, and Asa Gray, botanist. Between 1857 and 1862 he served as professor of chemistry, mineralogy, and geology at Davidson College, teaching upper-level courses. One of his students recalled in later years: "We used to call him 'Steam Engine,' instead of Kerr, such was his promptness to time and rapid motion." Another remembered: "He was a man of small physical stature,—with massive forehead whose amplitude was increased by baldness and his way of wearing his hair. His face was thin and intellectual—his eyes blue and piercing . . . his voice . . . clear and penetrating. He . . . could not brook shamming or laziness. His rebukes were often cutting—always deserved." Kerr's contribution to the Confederacy (1862–64) was as chemist and superintendent of the Mecklenburg Salt Company at Mount Pleasant, S.C., near Charleston; he improved the manufacturing process and cut the cost of firewood by half.

Governor Zebulon B. Vance appointed Kerr state geologist in 1864, but conditions in North Carolina during the final year of the Civil War precluded either systematic work or a salary. In 1866 he was reappointed by Governor Jonathan Worth. Kerr evaluated in Raleigh the "geological reconnaissance" performed by Chapel Hill professors Denison Olmsted and Elisha Mitchell in the 1820s (the first state survey in the nation), and the more detailed survey of state geologist Ebenezer Emmons during the 1850s. Neither, however, covered adequately the western quarter of the state, where most of the mineral resources were located. With an eye on economic development, Kerr concluded that the region beyond the Catawba River merited particular attention, and that an accurate geographic and topographical map of North Carolina should be produced.

Although not a trained specialist, Kerr was a keen observer and hard worker. His first official report stated that he had traveled, "mainly in the saddle," 1,700 miles in less than four months; his second, 4,000 miles in eleven months. The legislature appropriated only

$5,000 annually for all geologic operations, which meant that Kerr could have no permanent assistants. Nevertheless, by 1870 his own statewide survey was ready for publication. The lawmakers, however, placed so low a priority on the work that it did not appear until 1875—a major frustration. Kerr's 325-page *Report of the Geological Survey of North Carolina* concentrated on topography, climate, geology, soils, fertilizers, and ores. His large fold-out geologic map was tinted in five colors by Mrs. Cornelia Phillips Spencer of Chapel Hill. The base for this map was that of the federal Coast Survey. After fifteen years of intermittent labor, Kerr in 1882 had calculated his own base, thus providing by far the most accurate map of North Carolina up to that time.

As state geologist he touched every county and, when not in the saddle, employed buggy, spring wagon, boat, handcar, or train. Always he collected specimens for the state museum in Raleigh. His correspondence was voluminous, his conferences frequent, his popular talks and articles many. He was a leading member of the state Board of Agriculture, lectured regularly on geology and related sciences at The University of North Carolina, and prepared displays of the state's resources for expositions both at home and abroad. A respectable number of his professional papers were read before, and published by, several scientific societies.

Kerr made two important theoretical contributions to geologic science. He was first in the United States to explain a phenomenon that many North Carolinians and South Carolinians had often noticed: along rivers flowing from west to east, their south banks presented bluffs and high ground, their north banks low plains and swamps. Citing Ferrel's "law of motion" (1859), Kerr deduced that this condition resulted from the coordinate action of stream flow and rotation of the earth. He was also first to describe the alternate freezing and thawing that produced "deep movement and bedded arrangement of loose materials on slopes," even very slight slopes—a "frost drift" analogous to "glacial drift." But his belief that glaciation occurred as far south as North Carolina was not accepted.

The satisfactions of his work were countered by certain vexations. Chief among them was the periodic meeting of the legislature and the inevitable confrontation between the state geologist, who favored plans for long-range economic development, and legislators, who expected immediate results for funds appropriated. To Kerr it was "real torture." Never robust, his health gradually deteriorated (from catarrah of the digestive organs) after age forty. Yet this period witnessed his greatest productivity. An associate declared that Kerr was "often impatient, often despondent" but "clung to his work, impelled and sustained by nervous energy alone."

In August 1882 he resigned his position to join the U.S. Geological Survey; some of his duties were in Appalachia, some in Washington. While in Washington, he prepared a report on the cotton production and general agriculture of North Carolina and Virginia for the Tenth Census, and wrote the article "North Carolina" for the ninth edition (1884) of the *Encyclopaedia Britannica*. Finally his failing health persuaded him to give up regular work, resign from the Geological Survey, and spend summers in Asheville and winters in Tampa, Fla. The Elisha Mitchell Scientific Society at Chapel Hill elected him president in 1884, and the university honored him with the Ph.D. in 1879 and the LL.D. in 1885. During his lifetime Kerr was almost the only North Carolina-born scientist active in the state. His great service was to open the eyes of the people to their own natural resources, especially minerals. He died, of consumption, at Asheville and was buried in Oakwood Cemetery, Raleigh.

Kerr married Emma Hall of Iredell County in 1853. Their three children were William Hall, automatic-bagging inventor and manufacturer; Alice Spencer, a teacher who died of consumption at twenty-one; and Lizzie, who married Professor George F. Atkinson of Chapel Hill. In a letter to Lizzie from Burnsville dated 17 Nov. 1882, Professor Kerr, as most people called him, unconsciously left a portrait of himself: "I came in here Monday morning from Grandfather [Mountain], Tuesday went to Tom Wilsons, Wednesday to top of [Mount] Mitchell. Ground frozen hard & ice in path to top, & little lines of snow in the furrows of the rocks & whitening the top branches of the balsam trees. Day pleasant . . . I have taken board for party at Ray's, 4 men & 4 horses."

SEE: *At Home and Abroad* (Charlotte), February 1883; Davidson College *Monthly*, February 1891; J. A. Holmes, Elisha Mitchell Scientific Society *Journal* (1887 [portrait]); A. S. Kerr Papers (Southern Historical Collection, University of North Carolina Library, Chapel Hill); *South-Atlantic*, August 1878; C. P. Spencer Papers, Orange County Wills and Estates (North Carolina State Archives, Raleigh); George Troxler, *Journal of Presbyterian History*, June 1967.

STUART NOBLIN

Kester, Howard Anderson ("Buck") *(21 July 1904– 12 July 1977)*, clergyman, educator, and social reformer, was born near Martinsville in Henry County, Va. He was the youngest of three children of Nannie Holt, of Lynchburg, Va., and William Hamilton Kester, originally of Washingtonville, Pa. Kester's later radicalism stemmed neither from the economic deprivations nor the abundance of his childhood, for his family though not affluent enjoyed a measure of middle-class respectability. His father was a tailor, Presbyterian elder, and respected member of his community; however, economic difficulties in 1916 did prompt William Kester to move his family to Beckley, W.Va.

Howard Kester returned to Virginia in 1921, enrolling in Lynchburg College in preparation for the ministerial career to which his parents had dedicated him at his baptism. But already he experienced doubts about the relevance of the church to social problems of his day. Over the next six years his experiences helped transform these doubts into a positive conviction that the church had fallen short of its prophetic mission.

While at Lynchburg Kester served briefly as a student pastor in the coal fields of West Virginia, where his open support for striking miners among his parishioners roused the ire of Presbytery authorities. During these years he became deeply involved in YMCA work in the South, striving to integrate the student Christian movement in the region and coordinating the YMCA's efforts to raise money for the relief of European students suffering in the aftermath of World War I. These activities intensified his commitment to the promotion of economic and racial justice and, for a time at least, to the cause of pacifism.

In the fall of 1925 Kester enrolled in Princeton Theological Seminary, but left within a year because of his conviction that the seminary overemphasized dogma at the expense of Christianity's social dimension. Seeking a more satisfying theological education, he entered

Vanderbilt University in the fall of 1926. His attempts to sponsor interracial fellowship meetings among students in the Nashville area and his unpopular political views cost the young radical his job as assistant director of the Vanderbilt YMCA in March 1927. This loss of his only means of financial support occurred just three weeks after his marriage on 18 February to Alice Harris of Decatur, Ga. His dismissal was the first of many turbulent episodes the couple would share as a result of their commitment to social change.

In the spring of 1927 Kester became youth secretary of the Fellowship of the Reconciliation and moved to New York City. Two years later he resumed his theological training in Nashville, receiving the B.D. degree from Vanderbilt in 1931. His unorthodox religious and social views made conventional church authorities wary of him and he was not ordained until 1936 when, after twice having been rejected by the Presbyterians, he was accepted for ordination by the Congregational church.

After his graduation from Vanderbilt Kester joined the Socialist party and became active in organizational work in central Tennessee. In 1932 he ran for Congress on the Socialist ticket. Although soundly defeated, he continued to work for the party until the late 1930s, serving as national executive committeeman in 1937.

Meanwhile the young activist worked for social justice throughout the South. He later said of these years, "Wherever trouble brewed we tried to go." He served as southern secretary of the Fellowship of Reconciliation until 1934, when a dispute over the role of violence in the class struggle caused him and other leading members to resign. Several of those who withdrew from the fellowship, among them Reinhold Niebuhr, organized the Committee for Economic and Racial Justice and financed Kester's work in the South. Under the sponsorship of Niebuhr's committee, Kester investigated lynchings for the NAACP and the American Civil Liberties Union, helped organize the Fellowship of Southern Churchmen, assisted in the organization of the Southern Tenant Farmers' Union, publicized the plight of many of the South's rural poor with his book *Revolt Among the Sharecroppers* (1936), lectured for the League for Industrial Democracy, and began publishing *Prophetic Religion*, the journal of the Fellowship of Southern Churchmen.

In 1939 the Kesters and their daughter Nancy Alice (b. 27 Apr. 1934) moved from Nashville to High Top Colony near Black Mountain, N.C. The Fellowship of Southern Churchmen, to which Kester now devoted most of his time, assumed responsibility for his work in the fall of 1941, but financial difficulties—stemming from a lack of interested sponsors for the group during World War II—soon resulted in the fellowship's inability to meet its commitment to the Kesters.

In December 1943 Howard and Alice Kester accepted positions with the Penn Normal, Agricultural, and Industrial School on St. Helena Island off the coast of South Carolina. He became the institution's principal and she its director of instruction. In December 1948 the Kesters resigned after the school had become a facility for adult education and a community service center. For a brief time in 1949–50 they lived in New York City, where they directed the Congregational Christian Service Committee's program for the relocation of persons displaced by World War II. In the late spring of 1950 Kester became the director of the Campbell Folk School at Brasstown, N.C., and remained for eight months. From early 1952 to 1957 he was executive secretary of the Fellowship of Southern Churchmen, and in the fall of 1957 he joined the staff of Eureka College

in Eureka, Ill., as director of student life, professor of history, and dean of students.

In 1960 the Kesters returned to North Carolina where Howard managed Christmont Assembly, a project of the Christian Churches (Disciples of Christ) near Black Mountain. From 1965 to 1971 he served on the faculty of Montreat-Anderson College as an instructor in the department of social studies and as dean of students. His wife's death on 6 Apr. 1970 and a heart attack he suffered eleven months later prompted Kester to retire to his home at High Top Colony. In January 1977 he married Elizabeth Moore Harris, Alice Kester's sister-in-law and the couple's friend for nearly a half century. Kester died the following July and was buried at Mountain View Memorial Park in Swannanoa.

In 1926 the president of Princeton Theological Seminary had accused Howard Kester of having rejected eighteen centuries of Christian tradition, a judgment in which this pioneer of southern social activism later concurred. But Kester never rejected the teachings of Christ; rather, he desired a return to what he understood to be the basic teachings of New Testament Christianity, and therein lay his radicalism.

SEE: *Asheville Citizen*, 15 July 1977; *Charlotte Observer*, 15 July 1977; John Egerton, *A Mind to Stay Here: Profiles from the South* (1970); Fellowship of Southern Churchmen Papers, Howard Anderson Kester Papers, Southern Oral History Program Collection, Series B (Southern Historical Collection, University of North Carolina Library, Chapel Hill); Donald B. Meyer, *The Protestant Search for Political Realism, 1919–1941* (1960).

ROBERT F. MARTIN

Kilgo, John Carlisle (22 July 1861–11 Aug. 1922), college president, Methodist bishop, and moral and religious leader, was born in a small brick parsonage in Laurens, S.C., the son of James Tillman and Catherine Mason Kilgo. His father, whose Scotch-Irish ancestors were from Wake County, was a Methodist minister for thirty years; his mother was a native of Fairfield County, S.C.

Young Kilgo received his early education in the sections of South Carolina where his father preached. At McArthur Academy, which was organized along the lines of English schools with strict rules and discipline, he established his own lifelong code. Afterwards he attended Gaffney Seminary and in 1880 enrolled at Wofford College, which he was forced to leave at the end of his sophomore year because of poor eyesight. He then became a public schoolteacher for a year at Clio, S.C. In May 1882, he was licensed to preach and joined the South Carolina Conference of the Methodist Episcopal Church, South. His first charge was as a junior preacher on the Bennettsville Circuit. From 1882 to 1888 he served as a preacher in the South Carolina Conference. His appointments also included Timmonsville Circuit, Rock Hill Circuit, and Little Rock Circuit. He established a unique record as a public orator and became known as one of the outstanding preachers in the state.

In 1888 Kilgo was made financial agent of Wofford College, which was owned by the South Carolina Conference of the Methodist church. His duties were to increase the endowment of the college and to awaken greater interest in the school. In this capacity, he was able to continue his formal education, receiving the M.A. degree from Wofford in 1892. He was also appointed to the chair of philosophy and political economy. Later he received honorary degrees from Randolph-Macon and Wofford (doctor of divinity, 1895), Tulane University (doctor of laws, 1910), and Trinity College (doctor of laws, 1916).

His basic educational concept asserted that true higher education could be obtained only in institutions conducted under Christian auspices. Although an advocate of a strong public school system, he believed that higher education was the domain of private colleges rather than the state. Also at Wofford Kilgo developed his views regarding the education of women. In his opinion, women should receive the same educational opportunities as men; moreover, coeducation was the only answer because female colleges were inferior.

On 31 July 1894 Kilgo was nominated for president of Trinity College (now Duke University) and unanimously elected. He arrived in Durham and assumed the office on 16 August. On his first Sunday, he preached at both Methodist churches and captured the attention of the congregations. He immediately impressed the people of Durham with his ability as a preacher and an educational leader, demonstrating that he had a strong hold on Methodism in the state. There was a general rally behind him as he proceeded to rebuild the college.

Kilgo spent a large part of his first year at Trinity defending the cause of Christian education. In 1896, while still in his thirties, he joined Josiah W. Bailey, editor of the *Biblical Recorder*, in leading a statewide fight against taxes to support secular schools. To pursue his argument, he founded a monthly newspaper, the *Christian Educator*, which was published until 1898.

A personal and much publicized battle with one of his trustees began in June 1897 over a disagreement on faculty tenure. His opponent was Judge Walter Clark, a leading Methodist layman who, like Kilgo, was an able leader and a hard-hitting fighter. The two men exchanged a series of vituperative letters, which grew longer and more heated as time went on. In the dispute, the Trinity Board of Trustees supported Kilgo and asked Clark to resign. When the controversy was leaked to the press, Clark made further accusations and Kilgo called for an investigation to clear his name. Some of the statements made by the antagonists took them into the courts, and over the next several years there were three trials for slander and three appeals to the state Supreme Court. Finally, the case was dismissed and the dismissal upheld in November 1905. The Clark-Kilgo controversy was said to have mixed elements of "comic opera and war to the knife." The struggle was essentially a personal conflict between two strong-willed men who were accustomed to being "right."

Meanwhile, the resources of Trinity College grew in money, faculty, and equipment. In 1897 women began to arrive in modest numbers, and by the turn of the century the atmosphere of the college was attuned to the ambitions and attitudes of modern scholarship. In Kilgo, students and faculty had a champion who was increasingly disturbed about any restriction on their right to speak out. During his administration the college achieved a national reputation as a southern institution that permitted true academic freedom. This reputation was the result of his unshakeable convictions about, and constant fight for, the right of academic persons to enjoy free inquiry and free speech— rights that were widely denied and violated throughout the nation at the time.

The policy of academic freedom was tested in 1903 when Professor John Spencer Bassett published an article entitled "Stirring Up the Fires of Race Antipathy" in the *South Atlantic Quarterly*, a magazine he had launched. In his essay, Bassett suggested that politicians and political newspapers were exploiting the race issue for partisan ends. He predicted that blacks would win equality and called Booker T. Washington one of the greatest men born in the South, next to Robert E. Lee.

Led by Josephus Daniels, most of the Democratic press in North Carolina leveled a storm of abuse against Bassett and, in many cases, against Kilgo and the institution that harbored them. This occurred at a time when colleges had to worry about recruiting. In view of the uproar, Bassett offered to resign. The critical question became whether the trustees of Trinity, meeting in a special session on 1 Dec. 1903, would sacrifice the professor in order, presumably, to buy peace and public approval.

Though the students, faculty, and president of Trinity rallied wholeheartedly in defense of Bassett's right to free speech, the final power of decision lay with the trustees. After a long, dramatic meeting at which Kilgo made an impassioned plea for academic free speech, the trustees voted to refuse Bassett's resignation. In addition, they issued a ringing statement that has become one of the classic documents in the history of academic freedom in the United States.

By no means timid and indeed almost welcoming a fight, President Kilgo injected much of his own philosophy and personality into his statement of the spirit and purpose of the college. He made many contributions to the cause of higher education in the South, but his championship of academic freedom at Trinity has been considered by many as his most important educational work.

Kilgo is also credited for his part in stimulating the interest of the Duke family in the college—both through his close friendship with the family and by bringing outstanding teachers to the institution. It has been said that had it not been for Kilgo, there never would have been a Duke University.

During his sixteen-year tenure, Kilgo rebuilt Trinity from a small, poor college to one of the best known and most richly endowed institutions in the South while continuing the noble traditions already begun. In addition to raising scholastic standards, he remained true to his conviction that a school of higher education should make public opinion rather than be subservient to it. He maintained that Trinity should not avoid taking a stand on controversial issues for fear of adverse criticism. Under Kilgo's leadership, the search for truth became the primary concern of the school. Further, he upheld the religious and moral factors in higher education. He had a profound respect for the power of ideas, believing that "every thought left its mark somewhere." He never allowed the constituency of Trinity College or the citizens of North Carolina to forget that the forces of religion and education should unite in the common task of producing a nobler civilization.

Kilgo's moral and religious leadership extended beyond the campus. In constant demand as a preacher and lecturer, he was said to be the greatest preacher of his day in North Carolina. On many occasions Kilgo was asked to present the cause of Christian education in various sections of Southern Methodism. As a member of the General Conference from 1894 to 1910, he played an important role in the affairs of the denomination. In four consecutive General Conferences he was a member of the committee on episcopacy. In 1901 he was an official delegate from the Methodist Episcopal

Church, South, to the Ecumenical Methodist Conference in London.

His educational and religious leadership led to Kilgo's election as bishop of the Methodist Episcopal Church, South—on the first ballot—at the General Conference in 1910. He was consecrated on 19 May. Because his episcopal duties made it impossible for him to continue as president of Trinity College, he tendered his resignation to the board of trustees on 3 June 1910 and retired from the post on 1 July.

In view of his many years of service to the college, and the value that might come from his continued presence, a home was erected for him at the northeastern corner of the campus. In 1912 the first number of the college annual was dedicated to Bishop Kilgo. He served on the board of trustees from 1910 to 1917 and in the latter year as chairman. In June 1915 the board elected him president emeritus, a salaried position with the duties of advising and assisting the executive committee and his successor, President William P. Few. During this time his ties with the Duke family and the Methodist church also continued to benefit the college.

By 1914 Kilgo's residence in Durham was proving too taxing. Because his episcopal duties required constant travel, mostly to the west, he decided to move to Charlotte. Shortly before his departure, he became involved in one more controversy which led to a sad break with the college. On Thanksgiving two students hoisted a sophomore class pennant, bearing the numerals "17," to the top of the campus flagpole. Kilgo, who had made much of the flagpole, considered the "treasonable" act to be a desecration of Old Glory. Becoming angry, he inquired whether the guilty parties were "sons of buffaloes," denounced them publicly, and demanded that they be found. The incident was blown out of proportion and Kilgo left, disappointed that the board took no action.

More than that, he was unwilling to forgive and forget. He believed the offending students should not receive their degrees. At the board meeting in June 1917, Kilgo was elected chairman to replace the former chairman, who had just died. When the names of the graduates were presented for approval, he refused to vote for them and sign their diplomas. The board overruled him and the diplomas were signed by the vice-chairman. On 21 November, the board accepted his resignation as trustee and president emeritus. At the time he was described as "the real builder of the new Trinity," and his moral leadership was singled out as his most significant contribution.

As bishop, Kilgo impressed those who heard him with his deep spirituality and evangelistic consecration. He electrified audiences throughout the state and the South. "With an eye that shone like an eagle, a high forehead, projecting chin and stentorian voice, he could thrill multitudes as few men ever could." Soon after taking office, the bishop was involved in the church battle on unification, which he strongly opposed.

Kilgo was a member of the Education Commission of the Methodist Episcopal Church, South, which founded and incorporated Emory University. He was a trustee from 1915 and vice-president of the board from 1917 until his death. In 1916 and 1917 he was a special lecturer on homiletics at Emory. After 1918 his health gradually failed, and by 1920 he was relieved of his episcopal duties. In 1922, while returning from the General Conference at Hot Springs, Ark., Kilgo became seriously ill. He died of a bone malignancy in Charlotte, where he was buried.

On 20 Dec. 1882, Kilgo married Fannie Nott Turner of Gaffney, S.C. They had five children: Edna Clyde, James Luther, Walter Bissell (who died at age six), Fannie, and John Carlisle, Jr.

Many of Kilgo's sermons were published. His writings, articles, and personal papers are in the Manuscript Department of the Perkins Library of Duke University, which also maintains several portraits.

SEE: Samuel A. Ashe, ed., *Biographical History of North Carolina*, vol. 3 (1917); Aubrey Lee Brooks, *Walter Clark, Fighting Judge* (1944); Josephus Daniels, *Editor in Politics* (1941); Wyatt J. Dixon, *Ninety Years of Duke Memorial Church, 1886–1976* (1977 [portrait]); Robert F. Durden, "Bassett's Affair with Destiny," *Duke Alumni Register* 65 (1978 [portrait]), and *The Dukes of Durham, 1865–1922* (1975); Emory University catalogues, 1915–22; Paul Neff Garber, *John Carlisle Kilgo, President of Trinity College, 1894–1910* (1937 [portrait]); Fannie Kilgo Groome to the author, 20 Jan. 1979; Louise Kilgo Hudson to the author, 15 Jan. 1979; Stevie Johnston, "Laryngitis Hits Marse Jack," *Duke Chronicle*, 13 Apr. 1966; John Carlisle Kilgo Papers (Manuscript Department, Duke University Library, Durham); D. W. Newsom, ed., *Chapel Talks by John Carlisle Kilgo* (1922); Hersey Everett Spence, "I Remember," *Recollections and Reminiscences of Alma Mater* (1954); *Trinity Alumni Register*, 1922–23.

ELIZABETH H. COPELAND

Kimberly, John (1 Sept. 1817–6 Mar. 1882), chemist and educator, was born in Brooklyn, N.Y., the son of David and Elizabeth Ferris Kimberly. After receiving the B.A. from Yale and the M.A. from the Harvard Science School, he moved to North Carolina to teach at the Buckhorn Academy in Murfreesboro. He was awarded an honorary master of arts degree by The University of North Carolina in 1846.

In January 1857 Kimberly was elected to the chair of agricultural chemistry at The University of North Carolina vacated by Benjamin Hedrick. This position included laboratory instruction as well as teaching. Two years later, he persuaded the university that his usefulness as a teacher of chemistry would be greatly increased if he could study the newest discoveries in European chemistry. Kimberly and his wife spent the year 1859 abroad, mostly at Heidelberg, where he studied under Robert Bunsen. Returning to Chapel Hill, he significantly upgraded the laboratory offerings, incidentally instituting the first laboratory fee for supplies; students were also expected to provide their own glassware, dishes, crucibles, and expensive reagents.

Professor Kimberly was much admired for the strength of the agricultural chemistry program, one of the first in the country to offer practical laboratory instruction. (At the time, the idea of teaching students to work with their hands was revolutionary to the concept of a university.) He had little time, however, to build his program on the new ideas from Europe, for the Civil War set plans askew. Kimberly remained at the university when many students and faculty members went off to war. His responsibilities for courses in applied chemistry were increased by the assumption of the theoretical chemistry offerings when Professor William Martin left in 1861, and by November of that year he was directing all offerings in four departments—at a reduced salary.

Kimberly's contribution to the war effort was singular in North Carolina. In addition to teaching the dwindling classes at the university, he formed a company to make sulfuric acid and nitric acid for the Confederate

Army and for North Carolina manufacturers; the nitric acid was then used to make gunpowder. He also performed analyses for the North State Iron and Brass Works. His advice on identifying sources of raw materials, the practical chemistry of chemical and steel manufacturing, and business aspects of chemical manufacturing was sought across the Confederacy. Much of his surviving correspondence with the Confederate States Nitre and Mining Bureau deals with improvements in procedures for the development of these products vital to the war effort.

In 1863 Governor Zebulon B. Vance assigned him responsibility for forming and directing a company of students to defend the university from attack by Union forces. Losses in the family of Mrs. Kimberly prompted him to obtain passports for his wife and children to move through the lines at Elizabeth City, thence to his father's home in Brooklyn, and finally to her family in Nashville.

Although the papers and money he buried before the arrival of the occupying Union forces were later lost through discovery, Kimberly was still able in the summer of 1865 to use some of the profits from his wartime businesses to purchase property in the western part of the state. Early in 1866, he went to Asheville at the urging of Governor David L. Swain and bought a 600-acre farm near Asheville, to which he retired during the summer, foreseeing the collapse of the university.

When it reopened in 1875, Kimberly was again offered his former chair. After a year as professor of agriculture, he resigned and returned to the farm. There his health declined for several years before his death. The homestead was on present Kimberly Avenue, and the farm covered what is now north Asheville.

In 1840 Kimberly married Caroline A. Capehart, and they had four children, two of whom survived to adulthood: Elizabeth Ferris and Emily Southall. Caroline died in 1848. On 8 Dec. 1858, he married Elizabeth ("Bettie") Meredith Maney, then of Nashville, Tenn. Their eight children were Annie Rebecca (b. 10 Oct. 1859), Thomas Maney (b. 31 Mar. 1861), John (b. 26 Aug. 1862), Mary (b. 18 June 1864), David (b. 16 Mar. 1867), William (died in infancy), George Maney (b. 1 Aug. 1870), and Frances ("Fannie") Maney (b. 22 May 1872). Kimberly and his second wife, who died on 24 Mar. 1876, were buried in Trinity Episcopal churchyard and later reinterred in Riverside Cemetery, Asheville.

SEE: M. M. Bursey, *Carolina Chemists* (1982); John Kimberly Papers (Southern Historical Collection, University of North Carolina Library, Chapel Hill); D. C. Ward, ed., *The Heritage of Old Buncombe County*, vol. 1 (1981 [portrait]).

MAURICE M. BURSEY
SALLIE CARTER THOMASON

Kinchen, John (*ca. 1745–94*), lawyer, Revolutionary patriot, and legislator, was born at the home of his father, William Kinchen, Jr., a well-to-do merchant-planter who settled on the south side of the Roanoke River a few miles below Halifax; at the time of his early death in 1758, William represented Edgecombe County in the Assembly. John's mother, Mary, was the daughter of John Dawson of Northampton, a member of the Council. His Kinchen grandfather was the subject of one of William Byrd's rare compliments: "[A] man of Figure and Authority in N Carolina," wrote Byrd. "By the Benefit of a little pains, and good Management, this worthy Magistrate lives in much Affluence."

The well-known lawyer, Blake Baker, a neighbor and relation, was chosen guardian for William Kinchen's children, and it is virtually certain that John Kinchen read law under his guidance. By 1767 the young man had entered practice in Halifax and had begun amassing an interesting library. The earlier volumes that he owned included the works of Francis Bacon, Algernon Sidney, John Locke, Voltaire's *Lettres Philosophiques*, and Montesquieu's *De l'Esprit des Lois*. He bought Laurence Sterne's sermons as well as his *Sentimental Journey*, and he acquired Smollett's *Roderick Random*.

By 1770 Kinchen had decided to pursue his legal career in the rapidly developing area of Orange County. He sold the 1,300 acres in Occoneechee Neck, Northampton County, that he had inherited from his father and moved to Hillsborough. In 1774 he sold his house and lots in Halifax to John Webb of Chowan, the man who probably took over Kinchen's Halifax practice. In Orange Kinchen soon attracted as a client "one of the most cautious and successful business men" of the colony, the Scottish merchant, William Johnston. Within a few years he was recognized "as a wise counsellor, good business man, and an excellent lawyer." In the St. Mary's community, a few miles northeast of the county seat, Kinchen purchased a plantation residence that he called Tar Hill, but his law office seems to have been located in Hillsborough. He continued to add books to his shelves—among them, the complete works of Alexander Pope and James Thomson's *The Seasons*, Hume's *Essays*, and the writings of the Edinburgh "common sense" philosophers, Thomas Reid and Dugald Stewart. Nor was he slow to acquire the Parliamentary speeches of Edmund Burke when they appeared in 1774 and 1775.

In the right place at the right time, Kinchen gained the confidence of his fellow citizens. This trust was first demonstrated when he—together with Thomas Hart, Thomas Burke, and Francis Nash—was chosen to represent Orange County in the Provincial Congress that met in New Bern in April 1775. The county again appointed him as a delegate to the Third Provincial Congress that met in Hillsborough in August. During that session, Kinchen and Thomas Person of Granville were named to represent the newly created Hillsborough District in the Provincial Council, as near an executive head as the province boasted. He served on the Council in 1775 and 1776. In March of the latter year, carrying out a recommendation of the Continental Congress, the Council chose Kinchen and Abner Nash as North Carolina's committee to confer in Charleston with similar representatives from South Carolina and Georgia "upon weighty and important matters relative to the defence and security of these colonies."

In the Fourth Provincial Congress meeting in Halifax in April 1776, Kinchen headed the delegation which included General John Butler, Nathaniel Rochester, Thomas Burke, and James Saunders. It was in this body that Kinchen's Whig reliability was most strongly manifested: he was made a member of the committee responsible for setting the agenda of the Congress, the committee on ways and means, the committee to issue paper money, and the committee to procure guns and bayonets. Most significantly, he was appointed to a special committee to consider "the usurpations and violences attempted and committed by the King and Parliament of Britain against America, and the further measures to be taken for frustrating them, and for the better defence of the province." The other members of this committee were Cornelius Harnett, Allen Jones, Thomas Burke, Abner Nash, Thomas Person, and Thomas Jones. In reporting this action of the Congress a century later, William L. Saunders wrote: "The committee was an exceptionally strong one, every member of it having a notable record, unless it be Mr. Kinchen, of Orange, about whom not much is now known, save that he was a lawyer and lived in Hillsborough. The fact, however, that he was put upon that committee is strong proof that he was a strong man, for it was a committee upon which there was no room for mere figure heads." Four days after their appointment, these seven men presented for adoption the resolution that empowered North Carolina's delegation in the Continental Congress "to concur with the delegates of the other colonies in declaring Independency," a resolution that was adopted unanimously. Echoing Saunders, Stephen B. Weeks wrote that "the very fact that the officers of that Congress thought enough of Kinchen to put him into such good company is perhaps the very best possible proof of his ability and sufficiency."

The election to choose delegates from Orange for the Fourth Provincial Congress scheduled for 1777 was a spirited one; its results demonstrated that John Kinchen, who was not selected, held less radical views than the successful candidates. Early in 1777, however, in an attempt to alleviate problems that had arisen from the breakdown in the court system, Governor Richard Caswell directed Kinchen and John Penn of Granville to sit as judges of the special Court of Oyer and Terminer called for the Hillsborough District. When he received the commission, Kinchen wrote Penn that he "could not by any means reconcile [himself], acting in so important a department without a co-adjutor . . . especially as the criminal laws of this State are now rendered extremely vague & uncertain." This was a conservative and lawyerly position; hence it is surprising that Penn responded with "a very faint" excuse, yet giving Kinchen "to understand that he would sit in conjunction with [him]." When Penn failed to appear at the time set for the court to open, Kinchen declined to sit alone. Fearing that this action might be misrepresented, he wrote to Governor Caswell: "[I]t is with real concern, I inform your Excellency, that together with Mr. Penn's inflexible obstinacy, & my diffidence from consciousness of my inexperience & want of abilities to discharge the very important & arduous duty of a Judge, there was no Court." The Hillsborough lawyer, Francis Nash, considered Kinchen to be Penn's superior as an attorney, but he interpreted this incident as evidence that Kinchen was "very modest and self-distrustful in public affairs."

Modest he may have been, but this characteristic did not deter the citizens of Orange from electing Kinchen to represent them in the state senate of 1779. In that post he played a conservative role, introducing a bill to set up an academy in Hillsborough and two bills dealing with problems posed by the institution of slavery, one designed to prevent the theft of slaves and another to provide for the sale of slaves who had been freed illegally.

In October 1779, when the General Assembly was called on to choose two persons to fill positions in North Carolina's delegation to the Continental Congress, John Kinchen was one of the six nominees. His failure to be elected on that occasion was the first in a series of similar defeats extending over the next few years. Notwithstanding, he was named to the important Board of Auditors created to try to bring order out of the financial chaos in which the new state found itself. In recognition of his efforts to obtain an academy for his constituents, Kinchen was named a trustee of Science Hall, the resulting institution. In 1781, for reasons not disclosed in the records, he resigned from the Board of Auditors, only to be nominated almost imme-

diately for the Council of State, a post to which he was not elected.

One of the most publicized trials of North Carolina's Revolutionary period occurred in March 1782. Three prominent Tories—Colonel Samuel Bryan, Lieutenant Colonel John Hampton, and Captain Nicholas White—had been arrested and were tried in Salisbury. The able Alfred Moore was the prosecutor; the defendants were represented by an equally eminent team of lawyers: William R. Davie, Richard Henderson, John Penn, and John Kinchen. Theirs was an unpopular assignment, for public sentiment ran strongly for conviction. Despite their efforts, their clients were convicted and sentenced to die. Davie, Henderson, and Kinchen sent Governor Thomas Burke the record of the trial and petitioned for clemency, stating that they felt that executing these soldiers would be a reflection on the state. Burke concurred, pardoned the men, and exchanged them for American officers in British hands. It was now apparent that John Kinchen, although clearly a patriot, had aligned himself with the conservative camp.

After ten years in Orange County, Kinchen decided to return to his native Halifax. Although the precise date of his (probable) marriage to Mary Martin, the daughter of James Martin of that county, is unknown, the age of their son, Henry Martin, suggests that it took place in the mid-1770s. Census records indicate that Mary Martin Kinchen died not many years after the birth of their son. This change in Kinchen's domestic life may have accounted for his leaving Hillsborough; but another possibility is that his growing conservatism undermined his political popularity in Orange. Whatever the reason, in 1780 Kinchen reopened his law practice in Halifax; he seems also to have begun to develop mercantile interests in the Roanoke valley. In October of that year he stood as godfather at Elk Marsh, the Benjamin McCulloch plantation near Halifax, for twin children of the owner. Not long afterwards Kinchen was married a second time to a person whose name is unknown, who by 1790 had become the mother of two sons, both of whom died shortly after the census of 1790 was taken. Soon their daughter, Peggy, was born.

Having left the scene of his initial prominence, Kinchen seems to have been lost track of by North Carolina historians, yet his change of address had little effect on the confidence in which he was held by the General Assembly. In 1782 he was nominated by the lower house, along with Alfred Moore, his opponent in the Tory trial, for the post of attorney general of the state. In light of the popularity of the cause Moore advocated in Salisbury, it is not surprising that he, not Kinchen, was elected. Two years later, when nominated a third time for delegate to the Continental Congress, Kinchen was again defeated. Precisely the same action recurred in 1785. His conservatism did not make him a popular candidate. It was not until 1787 that he was again chosen for a governmental post; together with Whitmel Hill, Charles Johnston, and the radical Willie Jones, Kinchen was elected to the Council of State. In 1788 he was reelected for a term to begin in 1789, but on 8 April of that year he wrote from Halifax to Governor Samuel Johnston: "My ill state of health continuing without the least abatement, I am reduced to the necessity of trying a Change of Climate, in the course of the Spring or early in the Summer, and of course cannot have it in my power to attend to the duties of a Member of the Council."

The wasting illness from which Kinchen suffered—probably tuberculosis—did not prevent him from riding the court circuit from Halifax to Edenton to Hillsborough and Salisbury, possibly as far west as Morganton. He continued his interest in public affairs, acquired a copy of the North Carolina constitutional debates when they were published in 1788, and bought his friend James Iredell's revision of the statutes applicable in North Carolina when it appeared in 1791—an indication of his intention to maintain an active practice.

In 1791, two years after resigning from the Council of State, Kinchen moved his residence from Halifax to a plantation on the northern side of the Tar River several miles northwest of Louisburg in the new county of Franklin. (It was ironic that the land Kinchen bought had not long before belonged to John Penn.) The "Change of Climate" he hoped to find in the higher ground near the Granville-Franklin border did not stem the course of Kinchen's illness, and he died in the early months of 1794.

The will that Kinchen drew for himself and signed on 23 Apr. 1793 merits study. It shows that he left a pregnant wife and two minor children, Henry Martin by his first wife and Peggy by his second. After naming James Lyne of Granville, a connection of the first Mrs. Kinchen, as guardian for his son, Kinchen urged that the boy "be educated in the best manner his Circumstances will admit and above all things brought up most rigidly to whatever business or profession his Capabilities or inclination may lead to or point out." Like the books listed in Kinchen's inventory, this testamentary injunction is valuable evidence of the man's philosophy and personality. In choosing executors to serve with his wife, Kinchen drew on his friends at the bar—William R. Davie and Blake Baker, Jr. (soon to become attorney general)—as well as new friends in Franklin, Dr. Richard Fenner, John Thomas, and Francis Taylor.

Henry Martin Kinchen was enrolled in the first class of the new University of North Carolina, and on 3 June 1795 he became a member of the debating group from which sprang the well-known Dialectic and Philanthropic societies. By early 1808 the second Mrs. John Kinchen and her daughter Peggy had died, nor had the child unborn in 1793 survived. Thus, Henry Martin Kinchen was his father's sole heir, but the young man's career was cut short by illness. Now of age, he sold all of his father's Franklin lands and died soon thereafter, unmarried, in the summer of 1808. The fact that John Kinchen had no descendants to keep his name alive no doubt contributed to the general lack of information about him that has plagued historians.

SEE: John L. Cheney, Jr., ed., *North Carolina Government, 1585–1979* (1981); Walter Clark, ed., *State Records of North Carolina*, 16 vols. (1895–1906); Don Higginbotham, ed., *The Papers of James Iredell*, 2 vols. (1976); William L. Saunders, ed., *Colonial Records of North Carolina*, 10 vols. (1886–90); Stephen B. Weeks, "John Kinchen" (typescript in Charles L. Van Noppen Papers, Manuscript Department, Duke University Library, Durham); Wills and Deeds of Franklin, Halifax, Northampton, and Orange Counties (North Carolina State Archives, Raleigh).

HENRY W. LEWIS

King, Carl Howie *(25 Jan. 1898–27 June 1967)*, Methodist clergyman and Christian educator, was born in Mecklenburg County, the second of six children of Elam Newton and Roxie Taylor King. His education began at Nutwood Academy, a local subscription school; he later attended Rutherford College, Trinity College (now Duke University; B.A., 1924), Yale University Divinity School (B.D., 1927), and the Yale Graduate School of Education. In 1955 High Point College awarded him the honorary D.D. degree. While in New England, Howie served as executive secretary of the New Haven, Conn., Council of Churches as well as director for two years of a summer camp, Camp Tekoa, near Westfield, Mass. In 1929 he was appointed director of Christian Education in the Virginia Conference of the Methodist church by one of its leading churches, Court Street in Lynchburg. Despite a successful ministry, program support was curtailed because of the economic depression and the position was terminated in 1932. King returned to his native county and the Western North Carolina Conference to serve the three Methodist churches near Charlotte.

The period of the Great Depression was no less tumultuous for the Methodist Episcopal Church, South, with external debate over the prospect of merger with the Methodist Episcopal church and the Methodist Protestant church, and internal debate over—among other issues—the structure of its demonstrated commitment to Christian education. When the General Conference met in Dallas, Tex., in 1930, its Sunday School Board, Epworth League Committee, and Board of Higher Education had amassed such power and influence that they were often more competitive than cooperative. That historic conference reorganized the educational program under the direction of a single Board of Education with the philosophy that from "the 'cradle roll' through church school, college, and university, and through life, Christian education should be one ongoing process." With the commitment to Christian education reaffirmed and the means to implement it reorganized from the local church through the General Conference, Bishop Paul B. Kern of the Western North Carolina Conference, who before his election as bishop had led the successful movement to consolidate the educational boards, began to establish the program in his area. Due to the depression, however, the Conference was unable to adequately support the venture financially, resulting in the shifting of key personnel. In 1934, after there had been two Conference leaders in three years, Bishop Kern appointed Carl H. King executive secretary of the Conference Board of Education, a position he held for the next thirty-three years. At the time of his retirement in 1967, his tenure represented the longest appointment in that capacity in the United Methodist church.

With quiet persistence King assembled an exemplary staff to implement the new educational program, successfully integrated the competing programs after the unification of the Methodist church in 1939, and survived the vicissitudes of World War II and the postwar era; his became one of the strongest Conference educational programs in the Methodist church. From among the varied programs, the executive secretary was perhaps most proud of the precedent-setting program for junior high camping, the annual series of Christian Workers Schools, the Scandinavian Youth Caravan, and the innovative program of financial assistance for the Methodist colleges in the Conference, the sustaining fund.

Begun in 1936, the camping program grew from a two-week venture of 80 participants in rented facilities with separate camps for boys and girls, to a full summer program in 1965 that served an average of 1,200 participants at a fully integrated conference-owned facility, Camp Tekoa, near Hendersonville. By the 1960s the Christian Workers Schools, which grew out of the merger of the traditional Cokesbury Leadership Schools and the Standard Training Schools, involved approximately 12,000 participants annually in about three dozen local churches. With teachers recruited from church colleges, divinity school facilities, directors of Christian education, ministers, and lay personnel nationwide, these training schools of from three to five days' duration offered programs where many church lay people received their first courses in the interpretation of the Bible, teaching methods and materials, the development of a personal faith, child psychology, and church organization and administration. In 1950–51 Dean Luther A. Weigle, King's former professor at Yale and chairman of the committee that translated the Revised Standard Version of the Bible, introduced the new translation to Methodists in the Conference through the Christian Workers Schools, thus undoubtedly helping to spare the area of much of the controversy that often accompanied the introduction of that major translation of the Bible. The sustaining fund, begun in the inflationary time of 1949, provided Conference support for faculty salaries, and later endowment development, at its Methodist colleges and the Duke Divinity School. The fund's annual contribution grew from around $75,000 in 1949 to over $500,000 in 1967. The Scandinavian Youth Caravan, begun in 1955, had the distinctive feature of alternate annual visitations of college students and young adults from western North Carolina and Scandinavia to observe and work in their respective local church and Conference youth programs.

Throughout King's tenure as executive secretary, thousands of lay and clerical persons traveled to the camps and assemblies he supervised during the summer in the mountains of North Carolina; during the rest of the year, he traveled to many local churches from the centrally located offices in Salisbury and after 1960, Statesville. His style was to plan carefully, work behind the scenes with proven local and Conference leadership, and let what accolades there might be fall to others. Yet by recognition and reputation he was probably known by more Methodists than any other Conference leader. At a testimonial dinner in 1967 Professor W. Arthur Kale, King's predecessor as executive secretary, praised King's educational ministry.

King was ordained deacon in 1933 and elder in 1936. He served as a member of the General Board of Education of the Methodist church; as a delegate to the General Conference in 1952, 1964, and 1966 (special), and to the Southeastern Jurisdictional Conference in 1948, 1952, 1956, 1960, and 1964; and as a delegate to the Golden Anniversary, White House Conference on Children and Youth, in 1960. He also was a trustee of Bennett College, Pfeiffer College, and Lake Junaluska Assembly.

In 1927 he married Mary Elizabeth Eskridge who was also a trained, experienced Christian educator and a leader in the women's work of the United Methodist church. With complimentary talents, they worked effectively as a team officially and unofficially. They had two children, Carl Howie, Jr., and William Eskridge. King was buried at Hickory Grove United Methodist Church, Charlotte, the church of his youth in his home community.

SEE: *Journal of the 1968 Session of the Western North Carolina Annual Conference of the United Methodist Church* (photograph); Carl H. King, *Historical Highlights of the Educational Ministry: Western North Carolina Conference Seventy-five Years, 1890–1965* (1965); Carl Howie and Mary Eskridge King Papers (Manuscript Department, Duke University Library, Durham).

WILLIAM E. KING

King, Mary Elizabeth Eskridge (17 Sept. 1901–28 June 1973), Christian educator, was born in Arbovale, Pocahontas County, W.Va., the oldest of six children of William Augustus and Mary Riley Eskridge. She was graduated from Blackstone Junior College in Virginia in 1921 and taught in the public schools in her hometown of Marlinton, W.Va., before entering Trinity College at Durham in the fall of 1923. In June 1925, she received the B.A. degree from Duke University as a member of the first graduating class of the recently renamed Trinity College. Active in various student organizations, she was named a charter member of the university's senior honor society for women.

After again teaching in her hometown for two years, she married the Reverend Carl Howie King, a college classmate then at the Yale University Graduate School, on 22 June 1927. They had two children, Carl Howie, Jr., and William Eskridge. A longtime coworker in Christian education with her husband, who was executive secretary of the Board of Education of the Western North Carolina Conference of the Methodist church from 1934 to 1967, she assisted him as program director of the Conference's junior high summer camps; as teacher, director, counselor, and dean of Conference summer youth assemblies at Lake Junaluska; as certified teacher in Christian workers', training, and leadership schools; and as co-counselor of the initial Conference Scandinavian Youth Caravan in 1955.

Apart from the responsibilities she shared in her husband's work, Mary King became a leader in the Methodist church in her own right. Short of stature and gentle in manner but ever intellectually alert and physically active, she respected people as individuals regardless of age; this trait enabled her to be a successful teacher and to be especially effective with youth. Her special interests were in the areas of social concerns, mission, and youth work. In the Women's Society of Christian Service (later the United Methodist Women), she served successively as president of her local church group in Salisbury, as district secretary of Christian social relations, as Conference secretary of student work, as Southeastern Jurisdictional secretary of youth work, and as Conference president. As Conference president of the Women's Society she played a major role in preparing not only the women but also the entire Conference for the merger of the white Conference with the black North Carolina-Virginia Conference in 1968.

In the Western North Carolina Conference of the Methodist church, Mary King was at various times a member of the Board of Christian Social Concerns, Board of Missions, Deaconess Board, Town and Country Commission, Conference Committee on Extremism, and Special Committee on Priorities. At the time, the percentage of women leaders recognized by men was far from commensurate with their membership in the church. Thus a special honor and responsibility was her election as a Conference delegate to the Southeastern Jurisdictional Conference in 1964 and 1972, and as a delegate to the General Conference (the governing body of the United Methodist church) in 1964, 1966, and 1972. In 1972 she was the first woman in the history of the Western North Carolina Conference to head the lay delegation to the General Conference, as well as the first woman lay leader of her local congregation, the First Methodist Church in Charlotte. From 1968 to 1973 she was a member of the World Division of the Global Board of Ministries (formerly the Board of Missions) of the United Methodist church.

In addition to church activities, Mary King was a member of the Salisbury Interracial Council and the American Association of University Women, and president of the Salisbury Parent-Teacher Association and the Duke University Alumnae Association. She was also a trustee of Pfeiffer College and Bennett College. On her death at age seventy-two, she was buried at Hickory Grove United Methodist Church, Charlotte, the community church of her husband.

SEE: *Charlotte News*, 29 Aug. 1968; *Charlotte Observer*, 17 Apr. 1972 (photograph), 29, 30 June, 4 July 1973; *Duke Alumni Register*, June 1947 (photograph); Carl Howie and Mary Eskridge King Papers (Manuscript Department, Duke University Library, Durham).

WILLIAM E. KING

King, Pendleton (*2 Apr. 1844–31 July 1913*), educator, scholar, and diplomat, was born at Kings Crossroads near Stokesdale in Guilford County. His parents, John and Lydia Ann Bowman King, had nine sons. Young King attended Oak Ridge Academy and New Garden Boarding School (now Guilford College) before entering Haverford College, from which he was graduated in 1869. He taught at both Oak Ridge and New Garden, serving as principal teacher in the Boys School of the latter institution in 1870–71. King returned to Haverford for the A.M. degree in 1872 and then joined the faculty of Louisiana University, at Baton Rouge, where he taught English and natural history for three years.

After a year in Philadelphia, he spent three years in Europe, traveling and studying at the University of Berlin and in Paris. While abroad he married Helen Ninde of Fort Wayne, Ind., and had two children, Helen and Rush Ninde.

On returning to the United States, King was active in the Democratic party. In 1884, G. P. Putnam and Sons published his *Life and Public Service of Grover Cleveland*, a campaign biography that so impressed the subject that King was appointed first secretary in the American Legation at Constantinople. He served in Turkey from 9 Mar. 1886 to 5 June 1890, frequently as chargé d'affaires ad interim in the absence of ministers Sunset Cox and Oscar Strauss. On several occasions he was active in protecting the rights of American Jews in Palestine.

On 1 June 1894 King was appointed chief of the Bureau of Indexes and Archives of the Department of State, a post he held until 12 Dec. 1905 when commissioned as consul at Aix la Chapelle, Germany. He served in that position until his death at Giessen, Germany, of heart failure following surgery for gallstones. He was buried at Fort Wayne, Ind.

King's career was unusual in that he served in all three of the then relatively separate branches of diplomacy—the diplomatic service, the consular corps, and the Department of State. He was a bibliophile and his collection of 7,000 books, which he willed to the Greensboro Carnegie Library, was acquired by the university library in Chapel Hill in 1921–22.

SEE: Dorothy Gilbert, *Guilford, a Quaker College* (1937); Pendleton King Papers (Southern Historical Collection, University of North Carolina Library, Chapel Hill); Record Group 59 (National Archives, Washington, D.C., under King's file number 123.K 581); U.S. Department of State, *Foreign Relations of the United States* (1886–90).

WILLIAM F. SHEPPARD

King, Rufus P. (*15 Apr. 1843–24 Feb. 1923*), Quaker minister, was born in Orange County, the son of Emily

King; the name of his father is unknown. Emily was also the mother of Missouri (b. 1844), Dolphin (b. 1845), Frank (b. 1847), and Giraldo (b. 1848). In 1855 Rufus, Missouri, and Giraldo were apprenticed to Walter A. Thompson to learn the "art and mystery of Farming." Rufus had no formal schooling. Enlisting in the Confederate Army on 26 Feb. 1862, he served in Company G, Eleventh Regiment, until captured at Falling Waters, Md., on 14 July 1863. He was confined at Old Capitol Prison, Washington, D.C., until he was transferred first to Point Lookout, Md., and afterwards to Savannah, Ga., where he was exchanged late in 1864. King had returned to duty by February 1865 but deserted to the enemy on or about 20 March. He was released about five days later after taking the oath of allegiance and soon joined a group of refugees going to the West.

His first knowledge of Quakers came from an Indiana family that took him in, cared for him, and taught him their values. In Indiana, he attended Spiceland Academy and was recorded as minister in 1869 at age twenty-six. Returning to North Carolina in 1878, he attended New Garden Boarding School for a year. In 1880 he married Alice R. Carr, and they established their home near Springfield Monthly Meeting south of High Point. The couple became the parents of three children: Emma, Edward, and Annabella.

While still in Indiana King began his ministry of visiting meetings and families, preaching at every opportunity, and made his first long journey—to England, Ireland, Norway, and Denmark. It was from Springfield, however, that he pursued his most extensive, worldwide ministry from 1881 to 1911, telling how God had wondrously preserved him through his Civil War experiences. His travels "in the love of the Gospel" were remarkable. He went to New England, the Midwest, Australia, New Zealand, Tasmania, France, England, and Jamaica. Between 1890 and 1904 he visited more than fifty yearly, monthly, and other meetings.

King probably was in close touch with more prominent Friends the world over than any other Quaker. The illiterate boy had become one of the most widely known and beloved ministers among the Quakers of his day, yet he cherished the simple, poor, and unloved of the world. He was buried at Springfield Friends cemetery.

SEE: B. Russell Branson, "Rufus P. King, Man of God" (1972 manuscript in the Quaker Collection, Guilford College Library, Greensboro); Fernando Cartland, *Southern Heroes, or the Friends in War Times* (1895); Emma King, "Rufus P. King," *Quaker Biographies*, ser. 2, vol. 2 (n.d.); Orange County Apprenticeship records and Bastardy Bonds (North Carolina State Archives, Raleigh).

B. RUSSELL BRANSON

King, William Rufus Devane (*7 Apr. 1786–18 Apr. 1853*), congressman, diplomat, U.S. senator, and vice-president of the United States, was born in Sampson County, the second son of William and Margaret Devane King. His father was a Revolutionary patriot, planter, justice of the peace, delegate to the North Carolina ratification convention in 1789, and member of the North Carolina House of Commons. His mother was a descendant of a prominent Huguenot family.

Brought up in relative affluence, King attended Grove Academy near Kenansville, Fayetteville Academy, and the Preparatory School at The University of North Carolina. He was a student at the university from 1801 until 1804, when he left at the end of his ju-

nior year to study law under William Duffy at Fayetteville. In late 1805 he obtained a license to practice and
set up an office in Clinton.

King sought a seat in the North Carolina House of
Commons in 1808 and was elected as a Republican. In
the ensuing session, he defended resolutions to support measures taken by the Jefferson administration
against the aggressive actions of France and Great Britain. A productive member of the house, he was reelected in 1809 but resigned before the end of the session to become solicitor of the First Circuit of the state
court.

In 1810, he was elected to represent the Wilmington
District in the United States Congress. Only twenty-five
when the Twelfth Congress met in November 1811,
King joined an able group of young men with whom he
was destined to be associated for most of his life, including John C. Calhoun and Henry Clay. A member of
the youthful War Hawk faction, King supported measures to strengthen the military power of the United
States and generally approved the conduct of the War
of 1812. Though neither an ardent expansionist nor a
staunch defender of the carrying trade, he maintained
that American rights should be asserted.

Reelected without opposition in 1813 and 1815, King
joined other young political figures in supporting early
phases of the nationalistic program proposed by President James Madison after the War of 1812. Before his
full influence on the program could be exerted, however, he resigned his seat in the House of Representatives in April 1816 to become secretary of the legation to
the Court of Naples and the Two Sicilies and to the
Court of Russia. His objective was to acquire knowledge about Europe through travel and observation.
Joining William Pinkney, who had been named minister
to the two courts, King went first to Naples and later to
Russia. In the summer of 1817, he resigned his post and
returned to the United States.

In 1818 King moved to Alabama to take advantage of
the unprecedented economic opportunity there and to
enhance his political career. He acquired large landholdings in Dallas County and played a major part in
the founding of Selma. Elected to represent Dallas
County in the Alabama Constitutional Convention of
1819, he was appointed to the Committee of Fifteen established to draw up a proposed draft of the constitution. In convention debates, King supported a more
conservative constitution as opposed to one characterized by "extreme" democracy.

In 1819, he was elected by the new state legislature to
represent southern Alabama in the U.S. Senate. On
Capitol Hill he supported the Missouri Compromise
and became a leader in the fight for generous land legislation and an opponent of protective tariffs. He exerted a powerful influence in support of the Land Act
of 1820 and relinquishment laws for the benefit of western farmers who had overbought government land.

King was reelected to the Senate in 1822 by a narrow
margin and in 1828 without opposition. Although he
supported John Quincy Adams for president in 1824,
he soon became disillusioned with his policies and
joined many other Alabamians in endorsing Andrew
Jackson. He opposed the tariff acts of 1824 and 1828
and took a special interest in Indian removal and in
public land measures. After Jackson's election, King became one of the major administration leaders in the
Senate.

A supporter of a low tariff but a foe of the principle
of nullification, King feared the consequences in the
South of the continuation of the protective tariff. Dur-

ing debates that preceded adoption of the Tariff of 1832,
he spoke against its protective features, called on his
protectionist colleagues for conciliatory steps, and eventually voted for an amended bill that offered some miti-
gation of the protective system. When South Carolina
attempted to nullify tariff laws in 1832, King opposed
both nullification and the Force bill which was designed
to punish South Carolina. He took a lead in seeking
adoption of the Tariff of 1833, which led to a peaceful
settlement of the issue.

While King was chairman of the Public Lands Committee during the Twenty-second Congress, the committee issued a report opposing a distribution scheme
favored by a group led by Henry Clay and advocating
instead a reduction in the price of public land. The report constituted a source document for later advocates
of cheap public land and opponents of the distribution
of government revenues. Throughout his tenure in the
Senate, King continued to support land policies that
were beneficial to settlers and to oppose distribution. In
1832, he opposed the bill proposing recharter of the
Bank of the United States because it had been presented for partisan reasons and because no modifica-
tions had been proposed to correct abuses. Subsequently, he vigorously opposed the bank's efforts to
force reconsideration of the bank measure.

As a delegate to the Democratic convention in Baltimore in 1832, King was appointed to the Committee on
Rules and reported for the committee a rule requiring a
two-thirds vote for the selection of a nominee, a rule
continued by the Democratic party until 1936. Although
he opposed the nomination of Martin Van Buren for the
vice-presidency, the Alabama senator supported the
party ticket.

Despite severe criticism by the advocates of nullification because of his stand at the time of the crisis, King
was reelected to the Senate in 1834 with only slight opposition. While maintaining his reservations about Martin Van Buren, he supported him for the presidency in
1836. Deeply concerned about the panic of 1837 because
it brought personal suffering and threatened to split the
Democratic party, he supported repeal of the Distribution Act and creation of the Independent Treasury System as a means to help alleviate existing problems.

When trouble arose in the 1830s over the distribution
of Abolitionist literature in the South and the reception
of Abolitionist petitions by the Senate, King took a
moderate position. He supported the view that the distribution of literature should be limited at the source
and that petitions should be received by the Senate and
rejected.

At the close of the Twenty-fourth Congress, he was
elected president pro tempore of the Senate and served
until 1841. Previously, he had presided over the Senate
many times and was regarded as the foremost ex-
pounder of Senate rules.

As early as 1838, King began to think of securing the
Democratic vice-presidential nomination in 1840. But
despite strong support for him in Alabama and Pennsylvania, the Democratic National Convention failed to
agree on a single vice-presidential candidate. Rather
than divide the party, King withdrew in favor of Richard M. Johnson. Late in 1840, he was reelected to the
Senate for a fifth term but with strong opposition from
his Whig opponent, John Gayle.

After 1841, King was one of the leaders of the opposition in the Whig-controlled Senate. As such, he opposed attempts to repeal the Independent Treasury Act,
to revive the Second Bank of the United States in new
forms, to provide for distribution of governmental rev-

enues to the states, to impose a higher tariff, and to restrict the Senate's right to full debate on all issues. Though only partially successful in his resistance to the Whig program on banking and manufacturing, King won the fight to protect the Senate's right to full debate. In taking such positions, he was thrown in support of John Tyler, the states' rights Whig who succeeded to the presidency after the death of William Henry Harrison. He also supported Tyler in his quest for the annexation of Texas.

As the election of 1844 neared, strong support again developed for King for the vice-presidency. However, when Van Buren lost the presidential nomination to James Knox Polk, a southerner, his hopes were shattered.

In April 1844 King resigned from the Senate to become minister to France, serving until September 1846. In that position, he contributed greatly to the success of three measures important to the United States: the annexation of Texas, the settlement of the Oregon boundary, and the Mexican War. King convinced the French government that it would be unwise to join England in its proposed plan of intervention in Texas, thus permitting the United States to annex Texas without fear of foreign interference. He also obtained assurances that France would not intervene against the United States in England's behalf during the Oregon controversy and that it would not act in a manner unfriendly to the United States during the Mexican War.

Returning to Alabama in November 1836, King declined to become a candidate for governor in 1847 and instead began a campaign to unseat Dixon Hall Lewis, who had been elected to his old seat in the Senate. Opposed by both the Whigs and the Lewis element of the Democratic party in the 1847 contest, however, he was unable to secure a majority in the legislature and suffered his only defeat at the state level. Shortly afterwards, he was nominated for the vice-presidency by the Alabama Democratic party but received only scattered support at the National Convention. When Arthur P. Bagby resigned from the Senate in June 1848, King was appointed to replace him; he was elected to the seat in 1849 after making concessions to the states' rights wing of the Democratic party.

King performed his last great service as senator during the crisis of 1850. One of the leading advocates of compromise in the Senate, he took a moderate position himself and called on both northerners and southerners to make concessions in order to save the Union. Chosen presiding officer of the Senate after the death of President Zachary Taylor, King sought to influence his colleagues to take a less emotional approach to the problems before them. As chairman of the Committee on Foreign Relations, he was instrumental in securing adoption of the Clayton-Bulwer Treaty.

Although responsible for ensuring passage of the compromise measures of 1850, King deserves even more credit for bringing about the acceptance of these measures by the South. Conceding that southerners had just cause to complain about this legislation, he nevertheless advised acquiescence and spoke against taking steps that might threaten the Union. He also took a lead in reorganizing the Democratic party in Alabama and in settling North-South differences within the national party.

Partly in recognition of his distinguished record and partly to conciliate the supporters of James Buchanan, King was chosen as the vice-presidential nominee of his party in 1852. But by the time of his landslide victory, he was extremely ill with tuberculosis. In December 1852 he resigned from the Senate and went to Cuba to recover his health. By authorization of a special act of Congress, he was sworn in as vice-president in Cuba on 24 Mar. 1853. He returned to the United States in April and died the same month.

Although King attracted less attention and received less recognition than some of his more colorful contemporaries, he made significant contributions to his state and country. Probably no other elected representative in American history has equaled his ability as presiding officer of the Senate. Acknowledged as the outstanding authority on Senate rules, he was elected president pro tempore on many occasions; moreover, other presiding officers often called on him to preside during their absence. From the floor, King was vigilant to see that presiding officers followed established rules and that decorum was maintained. His moderation and firmness contributed to the reduction of sectional antagonism growing out of the slavery question. Throughout his political career, he maintained an allegiance to the party of Jefferson. He was a staunch supporter of states' rights and a strong opponent of a broad construction of the Constitution.

King, who never married, was a member of the Episcopal church. In appearance, he was tall and slender. He was praised for his courtly manners, courtesy, hospitality, and scrupulous attention to monetary obligations. Portraits of him appear in the State Archives Building in Montgomery, Ala., and at The University of North Carolina. After his death at his home in Dallas County, his body was interred in a vault on the plantation but was later moved to the City Cemetery in Selma.

SEE: Samuel F. Bemis, ed., *The American Secretaries of State and Their Diplomacy*, vol. 5 (1927–29); *Biog. Dir. Am. Cong.* (1928); Lewy Dorman, *Party Politics in Alabama from 1850 through 1860* (1935); Walter Jackson, *Alabama's First United States Vice President, William Rufus King* (1952); John M. Martin, "William R. King and the Compromise of 1850," *North Carolina Historical Review* (Autumn 1962), "William R. King: Jacksonian Senator," *Alabama Review* (October 1965), and "William R. King and the Vice Presidency," *Alabama Review* (January 1963); *Obituary Addresses on the Occasion of the Death of the Hon. William R. King* (1854); Albert J. Pickett, *History of Alabama* (1851).

JOHN M. MARTIN

Kingsbury, Theodore Bryant (*28 Aug. 1828–4 June 1913*), clergyman, author, literary critic, and journalist, was born in the Guion Hotel at Raleigh, the son of Russell and Mary Sumner Bryant Kingsbury. His father, a native of Connecticut, was a lineal descendant of Henry Kingsbury who emigrated from England to Massachusetts with John Winthrop in 1630, and with his wife was among the original twenty-six members of the First Church, Boston. Russell Kingsbury arrived in North Carolina between 1812 and 1815 and settled in Granville County, where he became a farmer and merchant. A lover of books, he owned and read works by some of the best authors. He served as a town commissioner of Oxford and as a trustee of the Oxford Male and Female academies. Theodore Bryant Kingsbury's mother, a native of Scotland Neck and a member of a prominent North Carolina family, died in 1836 when he was eight.

Kingsbury's delicate health during childhood, plus his father's example, caused him to form an early taste for books rather than the active sports that fascinated his young friends. According to memoranda of his readings that he kept as a youth, he was a habitual reader from age nine, perusing the writings of Plutarch, Hume, Smollett, Miller, Josephus, and Shakespeare as well as Rollin's *Ancient History*, certain volumes of Jared Sparks's *Library of American Biography*, and other solid works. He studied at the Oxford Male Academy and later at the Lovejoy Academy, Raleigh, where he was captain of the student cadet corps. In 1847–48 he attended The University of North Carolina, where he gained recognition as a skillful writer, but left without graduating. His father wished him to study law and offered to finance his way through the Harvard Law School, but the young man chose instead to enter the mercantile business, which he followed for seven years.

Early in 1858 Kingsbury became editor of the *Leisure Hour: A Literary and Family Journal*, a weekly newspaper owned and published by F. K. Strother at Oxford. Kingsbury filled the paper's columns with scholarly essays on literature, history, and biography, attracting favorable attention outside the state and drawing high praise from—among others—John R. Thompson, editor of the *Southern Literary Messenger* of Richmond, Va., and Paul H. Hayne, the noted poet, then editor of *Russell's Magazine* published in Charleston, S.C. At home the *Leisure Hour* was less well received. When Kingsbury relinquished his editorship on 27 Jan. 1859, Strother pledged to continue the paper, promising to make it "a news weekly of the family and literary type"; he hoped to dispel the reputation it had acquired under Kingsbury that it took two people to read it—one to hold the paper and the other to look up words in the dictionary.

In June 1859 Kingsbury declined a professorship of literature at Trinity College in order to prepare himself for the Methodist ministry, which he soon entered. On three separate occasions he declined the editorship of the *North Carolina Christian Advocate*, the official organ of North Carolina Methodists. About 1866 he left the Methodist Episcopal Church, South, and became a Baptist as a consequence of his changed views on baptism, which he set forth in a book of 275 pages, *What Is Baptism?* (1867). From 1866 to 1869, he served as pastor of the First Baptist Church, Warrenton, while editing— from 9 Jan. 1867—a new weekly and semiweekly newspaper, the Warrenton *Indicator*. He also briefly held a post with the Southern Baptist Convention. In 1868 Wake Forest College awarded him the honorary degree of doctor of divinity in recognition of his services to the Baptist denomination.

In March 1869 Kingsbury left the ministry to become associate editor of the Raleigh *Sentinel*, of which Josiah Turner was editor and which was published during this period as a weekly, semiweekly, and daily. In 1874 and 1875 Kingsbury edited S. D. Poole's *Educational Journal*. In September 1874, when the periodical was moved from New Bern to Raleigh, he became associate editor of Poole's literary and historical magazine, *Our Living and Our Dead*, which after October 1873 served as the official journal of the North Carolina branch of the Southern Historical Society. Kingsbury wrote numerous historical and biographical sketches for the magazine as well as many essays on such subjects as education, southern textbooks, plagiarism, and poetry. Though he was one of the better informed southern literary critics of the period, he reviewed few books in detail, having little time to read.

In 1876 he accepted a position on the editorial staff of the Wilmington *Morning Star*, where he remained until becoming editor of the Wilmington *Messenger* in 1888. From May 1902, when he retired from the *Messenger*,

until 3 Sept. 1911, he contributed weekly articles on a variety of subjects to the Sunday edition of the Raleigh *News and Observer*. By his own generation Kingsbury was highly regarded as both an editor and a literary critic, and in 1888 he received an honorary doctor of letters degree from The University of North Carolina. The total volume of his writings was enormous and included a great deal of historical and biographical material. In addition to his contributions to the magazines and newspapers he served in an editorial capacity, he wrote a number of books—among them a guide to the Philadelphia Centennial Exposition—and was the author of some twelve sketches in *Biographical Contributions of Harvard University*, edited by Justin Winsor.

On 1 May 1851 Kingsbury married Sallie Jones Atkinson, the daughter of General Roger P. Atkinson of Virginia, a relative of descendants of Thomas Jefferson, the Randolphs, Lees, and Pryors, and his wife, Margaret M. Littlejohn Atkinson, formerly of Oxford. The couple had nine children. Kingsbury died at his home in Wilmington, survived by his widow, two daughters, and a son, Dr. Walter Russell Kingsbury. Funeral services were conducted from the residence, with burial the following day at Oxford.

Before the Civil War Kingsbury was a Henry Clay Whig; after the war he was a Democrat. In later life he reaffiliated with the Methodist church.

SEE: Samuel A. Ashe, ed., *Biographical History of North Carolina*, vol. 1 (1905); Ray M. Atchison, "Our Living and Our Dead: A Post-Bellum North Carolina Magazine of Literature and History," *North Carolina Historical Review* 40 (Autumn 1963), and "Southern Literary Magazines, 1865–1887" (Ph.D. diss., Duke University, 1956); "Death of Dr. T. B. Kingsbury," Wilmington *Morning Star*, 5 June 1913; Francis B. Dedmond, ed., "Editor Haynes to Editor Kingsbury: Three Significant Unpublished Letters," *North Carolina Historical Review* 31 (January 1955); Guion Griffis Johnston, *Ante-Bellum North Carolina: A Social History* (1937); Theodore Bryant Kingsbury Papers (Southern Historical Collection, University of North Carolina Library, Chapel Hill); Elizabeth W. Montgomery, *Sketches of Old Warrenton, North Carolina* (1924); Calvin Henderson Wiley Papers (North Carolina State Archives, Raleigh).

W. CONARD GASS

Kirk, George W. *(25 June 1837–17 Feb. 1905)*, Union army officer in the mountains and leader of the state militia against the Ku Klux Klan, was born and raised in Greene County, Tenn. He received a liberal education, and in 1860 married Marie L. Jones.

Early in the Civil War, Kirk may have joined or been conscripted into the Confederate Army. His sentiments were outspokenly Unionist, however, and by 1862 he left the state to join the Federal army. He received several promotions, emerging from the war as a colonel. In 1864 and 1865, after raising a cavalry regiment among the mountain Unionists of North Carolina and Tennessee, he developed a reputation as leader of a series of daring and destructive raids into western North Carolina. In June and July 1864 he took 130 men from Morristown, Tenn., to Camp Vance, near Morganton, captured its garrison, and destroyed considerable military and railroad equipment before slipping back through the mountains. He led later forays into Caldwell, McDowell, Haywood, Watauga, and Macon counties before hostilities ended in May 1865. In many of these operations Kirk and his men lived off the land, seizing and destroying the property of Confederate supporters and thereby winning their undying enmity.

After the war, in 1866, Kirk settled briefly in Asheville and in Rutherfordton, where he opened a small store. But he soon returned to Tennessee and engaged principally in farming in Washington County. In 1867 he was commissioned in the Tennessee militia, and two years later commanded a regiment that occupied Jackson and Overton counties and arrested several Ku Klux Klansmen.

In June 1870, while visiting Washington, D.C., as a war claims agent, he was commissioned by Governor W. W. Holden to raise a regiment of North Carolina militia in the mountains for the purpose of quelling Ku Klux terrorism in Alamance and Caswell counties. He enlisted over 600 men, some of them wartime comrades-in-arms and perhaps a third of them fellow Tennesseans. In July he took 200 of the recruits to Alamance and Caswell, where they proceeded to arrest about 100 men charged with murder and other serious crimes. Opponents charged the militia with atrocities, but with a few exceptions not under his immediate surveillance, Kirk's prisoners testified to fair treatment. Although the so-called Kirk-Holden war succeeded in breaking up Klan organization and activity in the two counties, the prisoners were never punished owing to the collusion of local officials and the governor's inability to try them by special tribunal. Moreover the campaign triggered an adverse political reaction, helping Democrats to win the August legislative elections and providing grounds for their later impeachment of Governor Holden.

Kirk was immediately subjected to legal retaliation by his recent prisoners. When the militiamen were disbursed in September, he went to Raleigh under an arranged Federal arrest in order to evade sheriffs and process servers. In December, cleared of Federal charges and threatened with mob violence, he returned secretly and by a circuitous route to his home in Tennessee.

Not long afterwards Kirk moved to Washington, D.C., and served as an officer of the police force guarding the government buildings. For several years he was employed in the Patent Office. He then returned to the mountains, took up mining, and reportedly made and lost several fortunes. In 1898, suffering from heart and kidney ailments, he went to California where he moved about, chiefly in the mining districts. By 1900 he was living in Oakland. He died at Gilroy, Calif., survived by his wife and two sons, John A., an architect and highway construction official at Gilroy, and W. T. S., a mining engineer in Alameda.

SEE: John G. Barrett, *The Civil War in North Carolina* (1963); *Gilroy* (Calif.) *Advocate*, 18 Feb. 1905; J. G. de R. Hamilton, *Reconstruction in North Carolina* (1914); *San Francisco Call*, 9 June 1900, 25 Apr. 1901 (portraits); Allen W. Trelease, *White Terror: The Ku Klux Klan Conspiracy and Southern Reconstruction* (1971); Ina W. Van Noppen, "The Significance of Stoneman's Last Raid," *North Carolina Historical Review* 38 (1961).

ALLEN W. TRELEASE

Kirkland, William Alexander (3 July 1836–12 Aug. 1898), naval officer, was born in Hillsborough, the son of Anna McKenzie Cameron and Alexander McKenzie Kirkland, a merchant. In 1850, at age fourteen, he entered the Naval Academy at Annapolis. He was attached to the *Portsmouth* in 1851 and then to the *St. Lawrence* before returning to the Naval Academy in 1856, where he was promoted to passed midshipman.

Between 1856 and 1863 Kirkland served in various ships attached to the Brazil Squadron. He was promoted to lieutenant in 1858 and to lieutenant commander in 1862. In 1863, he received orders to the *Jamestown* and from there to the *Wyoming* in the East India Squadron. He was on the *Wyoming* when she attacked the forts on the Shimonoseki Straits in Japanese waters.

In 1864 he returned to the United States and received his first command, the gunboat *Owasco*, which was attached to Rear Admiral David G. Farragut's Western Gulf Blockading Squadron. He then commanded until the end of the Civil War the river monitor *Winnebago*, which was involved—in the last months of the conflict—in the fighting in and around Mobile Bay. The *Winnebago* blockaded the surviving vessels of the Confederate naval forces at Mobile in the Tombigbee River and was present at their surrender.

Kirkland went back to South America in 1866, this time in command of the *Wasp*. Two years later Rear Admiral Charles H. Davis, who commanded the South Atlantic Squadron, ordered him to ascend the Paraguay River and rescue Charles A. Washburn, the American minister in Asunción. Paraguay was involved in the War of the Triple Alliance, and Washburn was in danger because of his alleged involvement in a plot to assassinate Francisco Solano López, dictator of Paraguay. Kirkland, who spoke Spanish fluently, in an interview with López threatened war if the minister was not allowed to depart. Although Kirkland acted on his own authority, López bowed to gunboat diplomacy and permitted Washburn to leave on the *Wasp*. In South America Kirkland acquired the name "El Rubio" because of the publicity given the incident. More than likely his conduct in this affair was at least partly responsible for his promotion to commander in 1869.

In the decade that followed he spent two years ashore (1874–75) on ordnance duty, and the remainder afloat in various commands. He was promoted to captain in 1880, while commanding the *Shenandoah* on the South American station. From 1883 to 1893 he remained ashore, commanding in succession the Norfolk Navy Yard, receiving ship *Colorado*, New York Navy Yard, receiving ship *Vermont*, Harbor of New York, League Island Navy Yard, and, as governor, the Naval Home in Philadelphia. He was promoted to commodore while governor, and shortly afterwards to rear admiral.

In 1894 Kirkland was given command of the South Atlantic Squadron, but within a few months, at his own request, was assigned the European Squadron. Command of a squadron was usually for two years, and Kirkland expected to be promoted to vice admiral when he returned to the United States. In the summer of 1895, his squadron attended the naval review at Kiel, Germany, during the ceremonies for the opening of the Kaiser Wilhelm Canal. Unfortunately, the remainder of his tour was marred by controversy which ultimately led to his removal from the European Squadron command. First he was reprimanded by the secretary of the navy for writing a letter of congratulation (published in the newspapers) to the recently elected president of France, then relieved of his command by President Grover Cleveland for alleged public statements critical of American missionaries in Turkey. The European Squadron had been ordered to the eastern Mediterranean to protect the missionaries during the Armenian massacres. Cleveland ordered Kirkland to be replaced in October 1895, after the rear admiral made antimissionary remarks widely publicized in the press. Religious and missionary organizations also desired him removed because of his refusal to keep the squadron in Turkish waters, although Kirkland had reported that the missionaries were in no immediate danger.

Kirkland was not promoted to vice admiral, despite Assistant Secretary of the Navy Theodore Roosevelt's recommendation. From 1896 until his death, he commanded the Mare Island Navy Yard. At the time of his death he was first on the list of rear admirals, having had forty-eight years of service. He was buried in the Naval Academy Cemetery at Annapolis, Md.

Kirkland was a respected and colorful officer in the old navy, where he was known throughout the fleet as "Red Bill" because of his sandy hair, florid complexion, and fiery nature. In 1860 he married Consolación Victoria Gowland of Montevideo, Uruguay; she died in February 1909. They had five children (Anna Rebecca, Maria Isabel, Florencia Maria, Roberto Lathrop Gowland, and William Alexander), all born in Montevideo.

SEE: William A. Kirkland Papers (Manuscript Collection, East Carolina University, Greenville); *New York Times*, 18 Aug. 1898; Paraguayan Investigation (H.R., 41st Cong., 2d sess., Report No. 65, vol. 2, Washington, D.C., 1870); Charles A. Washburn, *The History of Paraguay* (1871).

WILLIAM N. STILL

Kirkland, William Wheedbee (13 Feb. 1833–12 May 1915), Confederate officer, businessman, and postal official, was born at Ayr Mount, the home of the Kirkland family east of Hillsborough. His father was John Umstead Kirkland, the son of Scottish merchant William Kirkland who came to the United States from Ayr, Scotland, and built Ayr Mount. His mother was Elizabeth A. Simpson Kirkland, the daughter of Samuel Simpson, a prominent merchant of New Bern. Young Kirkland was appointed to the U.S. Military Academy at West Point but did not graduate. In 1855 he was commissioned a second lieutenant in the U.S. Marine Corps, from which he resigned in August 1860.

When the Civil War broke out, Kirkland's name was sent to the Confederate Congress for appointment to the rank of captain in the Regular Confederate Army on 16 Mar. 1861. When the Twenty-first North Carolina Regiment was formed in June, he was elected its colonel. Kirkland established a vigorous regimen of discipline and drill. Soon the Twenty-first was sent to Virginia to join Beauregard's army along Bull Run, arriving on 18 July in time to participate in the engagement at Mitchell's Ford. During the first Battle of Bull Run, three days later, Kirkland was field officer of the day for General M. L. Bonham's brigade, to which his own regiment had been attached. His force helped guard the Confederate right flank and was not engaged in the more serious fighting on the left.

In October 1861 Kirkland's regiment became part of Brigadier General Isaac Trimble's brigade, of Ewell's division, and in early 1862 participated in General "Stonewall" Jackson's famous Valley campaign. On 25 May, when Trimble's brigade led the Confederate attack in the first Battle of Winchester, the Twenty-first North Carolina advanced through intense fire to drive the Union forces from behind a stone wall. In this charge Kirkland was seriously wounded in the thigh but refused to leave the field, waving his sword and cheering his men on. The injury kept him out of service for about a year, during which time he was able to perform minor duties as a temporary staff officer to General Patrick Cleburne in Tennessee.

Rejoining his regiment, he participated in the Gettysburg campaign. During the fighting at Gettysburg,

Kirkland's regiment took part in the ill-fated charge on Cemetery Ridge on the evening of 2 July 1863. On 31 August Kirkland was promoted to brigadier general, to rank from 29 August (confirmed 16 Feb. 1864), and on 7 September was given command of Pettigrew's North Carolina brigade, which consisted of the Eleventh, Twenty-sixth, Forty-fourth, Forty-seventh, and Fifty-second regiments. On 14 October, in the unfortunate Battle of Bristoe Station, Kirkland's brigade—in conjunction with the North Carolina brigade of Brigadier General John R. Cooke—stumbled into a trap and was decimated. In a very short time the brigade lost 602 men and Kirkland was again seriously wounded. His actions in this battle were commended in the reports of generals Heth and A. P. Hill, division and corps commanders respectively.

After having been incapacitated for a number of months, Kirkland once again returned to duty and participated in the Battle of the Wilderness, on 5–6 May 1864, in which his brigade suffered severe losses. His command also fought in the Battle of Spotsylvania Court House on 8–21 May and in the actions along North Anna River and Totopotomoy Creek. On 2 June, during the Battle of Cold Harbor, he was again wounded by a sharpshooter. During his absence, his brigade passed to Brigadier General William MacRae. When Kirkland returned to the field in August, he was assigned to Martin's brigade of Hoke's division, consisting of the Seventeenth, Forty-second, and Sixty-sixth North Carolina regiments. Stationed north of the James River in the Richmond Defenses during the siege of Petersburg, the brigade took part in the battles around Fort Harrison. In the fall and winter of 1864, Kirkland's brigade remained on this front where it had the reputation for being one of the most disciplined brigades in the army. General Robert E. Lee ordered the defense lines strengthened and the camps policed during the winter and, on inspecting the lines, found that Kirkland's camp and defenses had the best appearance. Lee complimented him for this and summoned the other officers in the corps to observe Kirkland's camp and model their own after his.

In December 1864, Hoke's division was sent to Wilmington to aid in the defense of the Cape Fear River and Kirkland's brigade accompanied it back to its native state. Although Union naval and land forces under General Benjamin Butler were preparing to attack Fort Fisher, Kirkland was hurried forward to Sugar Loaf with the first two of his regiments to arrive from Virginia. When the Union forces landed on the beach on Christmas Day, Kirkland deployed his regiments as skirmishers covering the entire island and checked the Union advance, though outnumbered six times over. Butler abandoned his attack, but in January 1865 the Union forces tried again to capture the fort; this time they were able to land and establish a defense line before Hoke's division could stop them. Kirkland's skirmishers attacked and drove in Union skirmishers but then were ordered back. After the fall of Fort Fisher, Hoke's division retreated back to Wilmington and Kirkland's brigade formed the rear guard.

When Wilmington was abandoned, Kirkland's command held the bridge over the Northeast Branch of the Cape Fear while the rest of the division retreated across it. Moving then to Kinston, the brigade participated in Hoke's charge against Union forces left in the Battle of Wise's Forks on 8 Mar. 1865, which resulted in the capture of hundreds of Union prisoners. Two days later Kirkland's brigade was sent out on reconnaissance to determine the enemy's position, but somehow the order was interpreted as an attack. The brigade hurled itself against the Union entrenchments in a futile and costly assault. On 19–21 March Kirkland's forces took a conspicuous part in the Battle of Bentonville. It is said that during the fighting General Joseph Johnston, the Confederate Army commander, inquired as to who was responsible for the heavy firing at the front. When told the enemy was attacking, Johnston said, "I am glad of it. I would rather they would attack Kirkland than any one else."

At the end of the war, Kirkland was paroled at Greensboro on 1 May 1865. Afterwards he settled in Savannah, Ga., where for some years he engaged in the commission business. Later he moved to New York City and took a position in the post office. Invalided near the turn of the century, he spent his last years in a soldiers' home in Washington, D.C. He was buried in an unmarked grave on the outskirts of Shepherdstown, W.Va.

Kirkland's wife was Susan A. Hardee, the niece of Lieutenant General William J. Hardee, of Georgia, eminent author of military tactics and prominent Confederate officer who led a corps in most of the engagements of the Army of Tennessee. Their marriage license is dated 16 Feb. 1859. Kirkland's daughter, Bess, became famous on the Broadway stage under the name Odette Tyler.

SEE: Walter Clark, ed., *Histories of the Several Regiments and Battalions from North Carolina in the Great War, 1861–1865*, vols. 2, 4 (1901); C. A. Evans, *Confederate Military History*, vol. 4 (1899); Ezra Warner, *Generals in Gray* (1959); M. J. Wright, *General Officers of the Confederate Army* (1911).

PAUL BRANCH

Kirkland, Winifred Margaretta (25 Nov. 1872–14 May 1943), writer, was born in Columbia, Pa., the oldest child of George Henry and Emma Matilda Reagan Kirkland. After attending Packer Institute in Brooklyn, she received the A.B. degree from Vassar College in 1897, then spent two years at Bryn Mawr College as a graduate student. For many years she taught English in private schools in Bryn Mawr and Baltimore.

In 1903 the *Youth's Companion* published her story "The Mistress of Corridor B," which was followed by other periodical acceptances. The first of her thirty-four books was *Polly Pat's Parish* (1907), a juvenile. In 1908 Miss Kirkland gave up teaching to devote full time to writing. Until 1924 she lived at 46 Panola Place in Asheville, to which her father, an Episcopal clergyman, had retired. The Patterson Memorial Cup was presented to her in 1920 for *The View Vertical and Other Essays* as the work displaying "the greatest excellence and the highest literary skill and genius" by a resident North Carolinian. Her last years were spent in New York City and Sewanee, Tenn., where she died. She was survived by a brother and a sister, Frances.

Among the informal essays in *The View Vertical* are friendly excursions into "Drudgery as a Fine Art," "Courtesies and Calories," "Robinson Crusoe Re-read," and "The Pleasures of the Preposition." The Littleville of *My Little Town* (1917) is presumably Asheville, and in the book the author tells about the Christmas season at "our little Rectory." *The Joys of Being a Woman, and Other Papers* (1918) is a volume of early feminist essays by "a ministerial child." *Chaos and a Creed* (1925), first published under the pseudonym of James Priceman, was reissued five years later as "by Winifred Kirkland." With her sister Frances, she collaborated on five books (1930–

34) about the girlhoods of famous women. *The Easter People: A Pen-Picture of the Moravian Celebration of Resurrection* appeared in 1923. Among her twenty-one titles on religious subjects, thirteen are brief gift books, a few of which were previously published in the *Atlantic Monthly*. She wrote four juvenile novels.

SEE: Files in the Pack Memorial Library, Asheville, and in the alumnae offices at Vassar College and Bryn Mawr College; *New York Times*, 15 May 1943; *North Carolina Authors* (1952); *Who Was Who in America*, vol. 2 (1950). At the Vassar College Library there is a collection, though incomplete, of Miss Kirkland's magazine articles and books.

RICHARD WALSER

Kitchin, Alvin Paul (13 Sept. 1908–22 Oct. 1983), attorney and congressman, was born in Scotland Neck, the son of Alvin Paul, Sr., and Carrie Virginia Lawrence Kitchin. His family included Governor W. W. Kitchin, Congressman Claude Kitchin, and President Thurman D. Kitchin of Wake Forest College. Alvin Paul Kitchin, Sr., served in the state house of representatives in 1907 and 1909, and in the senate in 1911.

Young Kitchin attended local public schools and was graduated from Oak Ridge Military Academy in 1925. He took undergraduate courses at Wake Forest College for two years and was enrolled at the law school for an additional two years but received no degrees. In January 1930 he passed the state bar examination and began a practice in his native town. He served as chairman of the Halifax County Board of Elections in 1932, and in the fall began a brief period of employment with an engineering and construction firm in Richmond, Va. In January 1933 Kitchin joined the Division of Investigation, U.S. Department of Justice (now the Federal Bureau of Investigation), where he became responsible for several branch offices. Resigning in August 1945, he moved to Wadesboro and joined the law firm of Taylor, Kitchin, and Taylor.

In his new home, Kitchin was a member of the Anson County Board of Elections for six years. In November 1956 he was elected to Congress, where he served a total of three terms and was a member of the Armed Services Committee. The 1960 census necessitated redistricting, and Kitchin's opponent in the November 1962 election was five-term Congressman Charles Raper Jonas, a Republican, who defeated him. In January 1963, Senator Sam J. Ervin named Kitchin chief counsel and staff director of the Senate Judiciary Subcommittee on Codification and Revision. After three years Kitchin returned to his law practice in Wadesboro, where he spent the remainder of his life. He was buried in the town's East View Cemetery.

Kitchin married Dora Bennett Little of Wadesboro on 13 Oct. 1934, and they were the parents of Alvin Paul, Jr., and Henry Little.

SEE: *Greensboro Daily News*, 22 May 1966; *North Carolina Manual* (1961); William S. Powell, ed., *North Carolina Lives* (1962); Raleigh *News and Observer*, 10 June 1956, 13 Jan. 1957, 17 Aug. 1962, 11 Jan. 1963, 23 Oct. 1983.

LEE BOUGHMAN

Kitchin, Claude (24 Mar. 1869–31 May 1923), attorney and congressman, was born in Halifax County near Scotland Neck, the third of eleven children of William Hodge and Maria Arrington Kitchin. His father, a Civil

War veteran, practiced law in Scotland Neck while maintaining the family tradition as a cotton planter. Young Kitchin attended Vine Hill Academy in Halifax County and then, no doubt because of his Baptist heritage, enrolled at Wake Forest College; seven of his brothers also attended that institution, and one of them, Dr. Thurman Delna Kitchin, became its president. Claude, an excellent student, read law after his graduation in 1888 while serving as assistant registrar of deeds in the county. He was admitted to the bar in September 1890 and developed a successful practice. In the latter year he married Kate Mills, the daughter of Luther Rice Mills, a senior member of the Wake Forest faculty. The Kitchins had nine children.

In the years between Reconstruction and the end of the century, times were hard for farmers in the Tidewater and Piedmont. The Farmers' Alliance was strong in that area, and the elder Kitchin was one of its leaders. In the 1890s, when Republicans and Populists were considering fusion, black people voted in considerable numbers in eastern North Carolina; indeed, George White, a black Republican, was elected to the U.S. House of Representatives from the Second District where the Kitchins lived. During this period Claude Kitchin, though interested in politics, played no leading role. But he had become so well known that he was appointed to the North Carolina Democratic Executive Committee for the state election of 1898, and helped Furnifold M. Simmons, chairman of the executive committee, organize the "White Supremacy" campaign which restored the legislature to Democratic control. This campaign was characterized by intimidation and corruption at the polls, practices that its leaders believed were justified in order to eliminate the influence of an allegedly inferior race from the political scene.

In the Second District, Claude Kitchin helped mobilize the Red Shirts, bands of armed men who rode through rural communities warning blacks not to vote. Apparently he was also aware that trick ballot boxes made it possible to count only certain votes. His effectiveness in this campaign led to his nomination and election as congressman by his district. From then until his death, in eleven more consecutive elections, Kitchin met no significant opposition for the congressional post.

His early years in Congress were ones of preparation. He retained close ties with his constituents and supported efforts to create a Bryan-oriented Democratic party in his state, and to help his brother William undermine the organization that had elected Simmons senator in 1900. The Kitchins were only partially successful in this attempt. William Kitchin defeated Simmons's candidate, Locke Craig, for governor in 1908, but Simmons came back to defeat William Kitchin in the Senate race of 1912.

In the meantime, Claude Kitchin was slowly building up a reputation in the House. He was first assigned to the Committee on Claims, where he worked conscientiously although he rarely spoke on the floor. He gave the House at least one demonstration of his legal skills by an analysis of the French spoliation claims, which, according to one fellow congressman, settled that ancient issue once and for all. Then in 1904, he exhibited the sarcasm and wit—for which he was to be noted in debate—by a frontal attack on Theodore Roosevelt.

Kitchin made no significant contribution to the *Congressional Record* again until 1909, when he entered the debate over the Payne-Aldrich tariff (which he designated the "Pain-All-Rich Tariff"). His brilliant arguments startled veteran Republicans and were ap-

plauded by his Democratic colleagues. Indeed, he so impressed the hierarchy of his party that when committee appointments were next made, he was named to the prestigious Ways and Means Committee, of which Oscar Underwood was chairman. For the Democratic party, chairmanship of Ways and Means automatically made its occupant majority leader of the House. In 1915, the year after Underwood was elected senator, the fortunes of seniority elevated Kitchin to the dual post.

Kitchin's relations with Woodrow Wilson were a complex of enthusiasm and strain. He had supported Wilson for the presidency in 1912 and had been an architect of one of his administration's principal legislative victories, the Underwood-Simmons tariff and the income tax, but he had opposed Wilson's proposal to charge American coastal shipping for using the Panama Canal. As World War I shifted the government's attention to foreign policy, Kitchin became increasingly alarmed by the possibility of U.S. intervention. In general, he favored rigid impartiality towards belligerents and the avoidance of war at all costs. Moreover, he was against unusual expenditures for defense and thus opposed Wilson's conversion to preparedness in 1915. He was selective in establishing his position on the issue, for although he voted for the National Defense Act of 1916 (to strengthen the army and make important organizational changes), he opposed Secretary of War Garrison's Continental Army and voted against the administration's program for expansion of the navy. On other domestic matters, he usually supported the president's position but did not hesitate to declare his independence. For example, like most of his southern colleagues, he opposed the federal Child Labor Law of 1916 and voted to override Wilson's veto of the Immigration Act of 1917. Yet, as in 1912, there was no question that he would go down the line for the Democratic candidate in 1916 because, as he said in Durham on 7 October, "Woodrow Wilson is the only star in this firmament of nations with peace and good will to men."

Kitchin's finest hour came in response to Wilson's appeal to Congress to declare war on Germany. In a dramatic midnight speech, on 5 Apr. 1917, Kitchin emotionally told a packed House that he was "unwilling for my country by statutory command, to pull up the last anchor of peace in the world and extinguish during the long night of a world-wide war the only remaining star of hope for Christendom." Knowing that by voting against a declaration of war he was choosing an unpopular path, he offered to walk it "barefoot and alone." Fifty congressmen voted with him—five from the South, including E. Yates Webb of North Carolina.

Kitchin was both denounced and praised for his stand. Some critics argued that he should give up his majority leadership, but he refused to do so voluntarily and asserted that, because the Congress had spoken, he would loyally support the war effort. As chairman of Ways and Means, he was responsible for seeing that unprecedented revenue legislation was carried through Congress. The first war loan of $7 billion, as he told the House, was the "most momentous project ever taken by the United States," providing for more funds than had ever been authorized by "any legislative body in the history of the entire world." The same superlatives were applied to the tax bill, passed with more opposition in October 1917. Kitchin consistently fought to increase the proportion of expenditures to be borne by taxes as opposed to loans so that the cost of the war would fall less heavily on future generations, and to impose the heaviest burden on excess profits. In defending these principles he occasionally found himself at odds with the Senate Finance Committee, led by fellow North Carolinian F. M. Simmons. Both were forced to compromise. Kitchin and Simmons were jointly responsible for three war loans (liberty bonds) and a victory loan, all passed without dissent, the War Finance Corporation (5 Apr. 1918), and two tax bills; the second, designed to help pay for the skyrocketing expenses of the second year of the war, aimed at raising about $8 billions—more than four times the estimated returns from the first. But so great was the difficulty in getting agreement on this measure that it was not passed until three months after the armistice.

In the elections of 1918, the Republicans carried the House of Representatives. When the Sixty-sixth Congress met in May 1919, Champ Clark, who had been speaker of the House, became minority leader and Kitchin became ranking Democrat on the Ways and Means Committee. On 9 Apr. 1920, Kitchin made one of his infrequent speeches in Congress on a subject unrelated to finance. On this occasion he opposed, with characteristic wit and eloquence, a separate peace with Germany on the ground that it would place Germany on an equal footing with the United States in determining the terms of peace. At the end of the speech, he collapsed with a paralytic stroke. He was able to return to his seat briefly in December, but dizzy spells continued, and he went to Albany, N.Y., for brain surgery which appeared to be successful. When Congress met on 11 Apr. 1921, Champ Clark had died and Kitchin was elected minority leader. Although unable to be active in that position, he was reelected in 1923. During the winter of 1922–23 he contracted influenza and pneumonia, and, as a result of complications from these ailments, was taken to a hospital in Wilson, N.C., where he died. He was buried in the Baptist cemetery at Scotland Neck.

Kitchin had once been a man of magnificent physique and powerful voice, tall, erect, black haired, and black eyed. During the last three years of his life, he courageously fought his physical incapacity. When unable to go to the Capitol, he urged his Democratic colleagues by letter to retain the excess profits tax, to fight to the end against increasing tariff duties, and to refuse to compromise with the Republicans who advocated lowering rates on upper incomes.

Opinions varied as to Kitchin's abilities. Senator John Sharp Williams of Mississippi, shortly after Kitchin's antiwar vote in 1917, wrote privately that he "never was any account" and called him "a constitutional dashboard kicker." The New York Times, which seemed incapable of accepting anyone from Scotland Neck as majority leader of the House, became particularly critical when in the War Revenue bill he advocated increases in rates for second-class mail. After his death, the editor of the Greensboro News bewailed his having been majority leader during the war, calling him a "broken reed," unable "to make a new judgment based on the facts as they existed, and not on ancient shibboliths and venerable formulas."

Yet he had enthusiastic defenders. J. G. de Roulhac Hamilton, who disagreed with him on the war issue, praised him for his sincerity and courage. Few denied his ability as a debater. "I do not recall any instance where Mr. Kitchin has ever been embarrassed and in almost every instance his questioner was covered with confusion and laughter," said Representative John Small. "But there is no poison in his arrow, and he has numerous friends among Republicans." A veteran Republican congressman, James R. Mann, who had frequently debated with Kitchin, confirmed this judgment

and described Kitchin's words in debate as "like a brick in a towel." He treated his victims, according to Francis H. Gillette, Republican speaker of the House in 1923, "as if he loved them . . . and they generally reciprocated."

Kitchin devoted his energies to revenue legislation, and an ability to do mental arithmetic no doubt helped him in the mastery of taxes and tariffs. Although much more populistically inclined, he matched the ability of F. M. Simmons, a longtime member of the Finance Committee and Kitchin's longtime rival on the state and national levels, in dealing with financial legislation and with Treasury experts. Simmons's respect for Kitchin grew, as did that of his fellows in the House. Some even hazarded the opinion that, had his health been good, the independent Republicans in the House would have joined the Democrats to make him majority leader in the Sixty-eighth Congress despite the theoretical majority held by the Republicans. By that time, however, he was mortally ill, "as truly a casualty of the war," said Clarence Cannon of Missouri, "as if he had died leading the charge upon the crimson fields of France."

SEE: Alex Mathews Arnett, Claude Kitchin and the Wilson War Policies (1937); Congressional Record, scattered issues; DAB, vol. 5 (1932); Greensboro News, 1 June 1923; Claude Kitchin Papers, Edward Yates Webb Papers (Southern Historical Collection, University of North Carolina Library, Chapel Hill); Arthur Link, ed., Wilson: Campaigns for Progressivism and Peace (1965), Wilson: Confusion and Crisis (1964), Wilson: The New Freedom (1960), and Wilson: The Struggle for Neutrality (1956); William G. McAdoo Papers, Woodrow Wilson Papers (Library of Congress, Washington, D.C.); Raleigh News and Observer, 1 June 1923.

RICHARD L. WATSON, JR.

Kitchin, Thurman Delna (17 Oct. 1885–28 Aug. 1955), physician and educator, was born at Scotland Neck, the son of William Hodge and Maria Arrington Kitchin, as one of a family of eleven children. After attending the Vine Hill Male Academy at Scotland Neck, he entered Wake Forest College, from which he received the A.B. degree in 1905. Medical studies during his senior year and a year at The University of North Carolina in 1905–6 prepared him for the last two years in medicine at the Jefferson Medical College in Philadelphia, where he was awarded the M.D. degree in 1908.

In the same year Kitchin began a medical practice in Lumberton, where he remained until 1910; he then moved to Scotland Neck to practice. In 1917 he accepted an appointment as professor of physiology in the two-year Medical School at Wake Forest College, and in 1919 he became its dean. He was appointed president of Wake Forest in the summer of 1930, succeeding Francis Pendleton Gaines. Although not having reached a compulsory retirement age, Kitchin decided in 1950 to relinquish his position.

During his tenure as dean of the Medical School and also later as president of the college, Kitchin faced certain dissensions and disturbances. Despite these difficulties and the stringencies of the Great Depression followed by World War II, Wake Forest achieved substantial growth under his administrative direction. As dean he was obliged in 1926 to deal with a schism in the medical faculty, which culminated in the resignation of two of its members. It was partially because of this that some who later opposed his candidacy for president of the college called him "devisive," however unjust and unfounded his supporters considered the charge.

The circumstances surrounding his appointment as president of Wake Forest were particularly unfortunate and apparently not of his own making. In the spring of 1930, a group of faculty members circulated a petition among faculty and students calling for Kitchin as president. This immediately divided the faculty, even before the special committee of trustees had a sufficient opportunity to survey the field for possible candidates. The debate soon spread to alumni and members of the Baptist church. Opposition to Kitchin centered mainly on two points: that he was not a humanistic scholar and that he had not distinguished himself as a Baptist leader. Kitchin knew that he was neither. Believing, however, that he possessed equivalent talents, which experience proved to be the case, he accepted the appointment. Many of his opponents, recognizing the need to preserve unity at the college, agreed to work with him peaceably, so the controversy gradually subsided. To allay further doubt about his religious beliefs, he published statements in the summer of 1930 that seemed to satisfy North Carolina Baptists, at least for the time.

Apart from his medical ability, another quality helped Kitchin in the discharge of his presidential duties—his political talent and acumen. With a father who had been elected to Congress from the Second North Carolina District, a brother, William Walton, who had been governor, and another brother, Claude, who had been Democratic leader in the U.S. House of Representatives, it was natural that Thurman Kitchin should possess like capacities which he chose to apply to a private institution rather than in public office. He thus belonged among those college presidents who are skilled administrators rather than scholars, each perhaps, according to given situations, being equally effective. His political inclinations helped him to maintain good relations with alumni, to withstand Baptist attacks, and to promote the interests of the college.

Many beneficial changes were made at Wake Forest during the Kitchin administration. The need for funds prompted a vigorous campaign for new students; as a result, undergraduate enrollment increased from 617 in 1929–30 to 1,107 in 1940–41. In 1935, to meet the admission standards of the American Association of Law Schools, the Law School was reorganized, a new dean appointed, and the curriculum broadened. During World War II, when there were few male students, women were first admitted as undergraduates in 1942. The Medical School was defended against the attacks of the American Medical Association on two-year institutions until it was possible to expand to a four-year program in Winston-Salem in 1941. That year a chapter of Phi Beta Kappa was also established.

Under President Kitchin, the college's physical plant was refurbished and expanded. Two campus buildings that had been destroyed by an incendiary in 1933 and 1934 were replaced, funds were donated for a new building for the Medical School, a new dormitory and a new gymnasium were erected, and the North Carolina State Convention provided a new and much larger chapel. Although Kitchin did not take a very active part in these proceedings, it was late in his administration, during spring 1946, that the Z. Smith Reynolds Foundation made the offer that led to the college's relocation in Winston-Salem in 1956.

Especially while he was dean of the Medical School, Kitchin served on various state committees and boards dealing with medical and medico-social affairs, such as the problems of the feebleminded, the direction of the North Carolina Sanitarium, unemployment compensation, and the concerns of the Employment Security Commission. He was president of the Southern Medical Association in 1928–29 and enjoyed the distinction of election as a Fellow of the American College of Physicians. Kitchin was awarded honorary degrees by Duke University (1931), The University of North Carolina (1933), and Davidson College (1947). He was the author of *Lectures on Pharmacology* (1929), *The Doctor and Citizenship* (1934), and *Doctors in Other Fields* (1938).

On 3 Nov. 1908 he married Reba Calvert Clark of Scotland Neck. They were the parents of Thurman Delna, Jr., Irwin Clark, and William Walton. Kitchin died at Wake Forest after suffering for some time from a heart ailment common in his family; he was buried at Scotland Neck the following day, survived by his widow and three sons.

SEE: *Biblical Recorder*, scattered issues; *Journal of the American Medical Association*, vol. 159 (22 Oct. 1955); Kitchin Papers (Manuscript Department, Wake Forest University, Winston-Salem); Minutes of the Faculty and Trustees of Wake Forest College (Wake Forest Archives, Winston-Salem); *Nat. Cyc. Am. Biog.*, vol. 42 (1958 [portrait]); *New York Times*, 29 Aug. 1955; *Old Gold and Black* (Wake Forest), scattered issues; G. W. Paschal, *History of Wake Forest College*, 3 vols. (1935–43); *Who Was Who in America*, vol. 3 (1960).

C. P. WEST

Kitchin, William Hodge (22 Dec. 1837–2 Feb. 1901), orator and politician, was born in Lauderdale County, Ala., the son of Boas and Arabella Smith Kitchin. When he was four, his parents returned to their native North Carolina and settled in Halifax County, where he resided for the rest of his life. Kitchin attended Emory and Henry College in Virginia but left when the Civil War broke out, enlisting as a private in the Second North Carolina Volunteer Regiment. Eventually promoted to captain, he fought with the Army of Northern Virginia until wounded and captured in 1864.

After the war, the young veteran (now nicknamed "Captain Buck") attended to his farm and business activities in Scotland Neck. He became interested in politics and studied law, earning his license in 1869. The Democrats of the Second Congressional District selected him as their "forlorn hope" in 1872, and though he had no chance of winning a seat in Congress from the "black second," he made blistering stump speeches designed to build party morale. On election day he was overwhelmed, carrying only one of the ten counties in his district.

Six years later, in 1878, Kitchin won the nomination for Congress a second time. His chances for victory were better in this election because the majority party was deeply divided, with black politicians James E. O'Hara and James H. Harris each claiming to be the regular Republican candidate. Kitchin won the election but only after county canvassing boards in Halifax and two other black counties rejected hundreds of O'Hara ballots on flimsy technicalities. O'Hara contested the election in the state courts and in the House, but to no avail.

As a member of Congress, Kitchin showed himself to be an intensely partisan, old-fashioned Democrat. He condemned not only Republican "bayonet rule" and corrupt practices, but also "undemocratic" internal improvements from which the South might benefit. In his bid for reelection in 1880 he was defeated by Orlando Hubbs, a northern-born white Republican. With the Republicans united it was virtually impossible for a Democrat to win. The voting in Halifax was once again tainted by charges of fraud, and a federal grand jury later indicted seven election officials, two of whom were convicted.

Although Kitchin held no significant office in the 1880s, he gained a reputation as a powerful orator, and his services were often in demand during political campaigns. A tall man with a full black beard, he "stirred party passion as no other man of his day," remembered Josephus Daniels. As Democratic elector-at-large in 1884, he sparked controversy when he publicly declined to make further appeals for the black vote. In 1888, he commented: "You may talk tariff, revenue, corruption, fraud, pensions and every other evil . . . till doomsday and not one man in ten will remember what you said three minutes after you stop. . . . But when you talk negro equality, negro supremacy, negro domination to our people, every man's blood rises to boiling heat at once."

For four years Kitchin was a journalist—as well as lawyer, farmer, businessman, and politician. From 1883 to 1887 he edited the Scotland Neck *Democrat*, dispensing commentary on a wide range of subjects with his usual vigor. He quickly became disgusted with Democratic President Grover Cleveland, partly because of Cleveland's stand on racial issues. "I would prefer the Devil himself for President to Cleveland, provided he was not a Republican," he wrote to Senator Zebulon Vance in 1887, and he strongly opposed Cleveland's nomination in 1888 and 1892.

Kitchin was a leading contender for the Second District's congressional nomination in 1892, though in the end he lost to Frederick A. Woodard of Wilson. Halifax County Democrats nominated him for the General Assembly, and, in a year of confusing political realignment—as the new Populist party struggled with the two old parties—Kitchin was victorious.

Despite his years of fervent loyalty to the Democratic party, Kitchin was so distressed by the Cleveland administration that he joined the Populists in the spring of 1894. A strong supporter of free silver, but not other Populist ideas such as government ownership of the railroads, Kitchin lent his influence to the Populist-Republican fusion which swept to power in the 1894 elections. By the next campaign, however, he was working with the Democrats again, praising the free-silver candidate, William Jennings Bryan, and warning the voters of the threat to white supremacy posed by the Fusionists. Kitchin formally returned to the Democratic party at the end of 1897, though he had been a Democrat in all but name for over a year. In the dramatic elections of 1898 and 1900, he and his sons William and Claude denounced the dangers of "Negro domination." Kitchin died in 1901 shortly before Claude took his seat as a representative of the Second District in the Fifty-seventh Congress. William represented North Carolina's Fifth District for six terms and was elected governor of the state in 1908.

Kitchin married Maria F. Arrington of Halifax, and they had eleven children. In religion, he was, as he once described himself, a "militant Baptist."

SEE: Eric D. Anderson, *Race and Politics in North Carolina, 1872–1901* (1981); Biog. Dir. Am. Cong. (1961); H. L. Ingle, "A Southern Democrat at Large: William Hodge Kitchin and the Populist Party," *North Carolina Historical Review* 45 (1968); Raleigh *State Chronicle*, 4 May 1888; W.

F. Tomlinson, *Biography of the State Officers and Members of the General Assembly* (1893).

ERIC ANDERSON

Kitchin, William Walton (9 Oct. 1866–9 Nov. 1924), lawyer, congressman, and governor of North Carolina, was born in rural Halifax County near Scotland Neck, the son of William Hodge and Maria Figus Arrington Kitchin. His father was a captain in the Twelfth Regiment of the North Carolina Infantry in the Civil War. Young Kitchin received his early education in local schools, including the Vine Hill Academy in Halifax County, after which he entered Wake Forest College and was graduated in 1884, at age eighteen, with the B.A. degree.

After leaving Wake Forest he taught for a session at Vine Hill Academy, then spent one year (1885–86) as editor of the *Democrat* in Scotland Neck. In 1887 he studied law at The University of North Carolina under Professor John Manning, having already read law with his father for more than a year. He passed the North Carolina bar examination in the same year. Late in 1887 Kitchin went to Texas, but there is no record of his activity there; he returned to North Carolina and settled in Roxboro in 1888 to practice law. Two years later, as chairman of the Democratic executive committee of Person County, he began his political career.

Kitchin is credited with having led Person County back into "the Democratic fold" after years of Republican dominance. He was an unsuccessful candidate for the state senate in 1894, but in 1896 won his party's nomination for a seat in the U.S. House of Representatives from the Fifth Congressional District. Thomas Settle, a Republican, was the incumbent. Kitchin was the only Democrat elected from North Carolina that year. Reelected for six terms, he served from 1896 to 1908.

Those who have appraised Kitchin's performance on Capitol Hill find little to write about. He was a member of the Committee on Naval Affairs and of the Congressional Campaign Committee for the Democratic party. One of his best known speeches in Congress was in defense of the Suffrage Amendment at a time when white supremacy and suffrage were pertinent issues in his state.

In any case, Congressman Kitchin retained the respect of his party. When the Democratic convention met in Charlotte in 1908, he won the gubernatorial nomination—but only after sixty-one rounds of balloting. His opponents were Locke Craig, later elected governor, and Ashley Horne. All three candidates were popular political leaders in North Carolina. Kitchin won the election in November over the Republican nominee, J. Elwood Cox, and took office on 12 Jan. 1909.

If his years in Congress were lackluster, his tenure as governor was highly successful. It was a time of tremendous increases in expenditures for public education, public health service to the feebleminded, and expansion of swampland affected by significant drainage laws. In addition, those years saw great expansion of railroads and general improvement in the stability of the state's banking institutions.

During his last year as governor, Kitchin's was one of four names mentioned in the state's first regular popular election to the U.S. Senate: Charles Brantley Aycock (d. 1912), who was mentioned early; Chief Justice Walter Clark of the North Carolina Supreme Court, a jurist of great wisdom and poise; Furnifold M. Simmons, the incumbent U.S. senator who had in his term scored a distinctive record in Washington; and Kitchin, who had served a dozen years in Congress and over three years as a progressive governor. The North Carolina press reported it as a vigorous campaign. Although there was some doubt as to the ultimate winner, Senator Simmons emerged victor with a clear majority over Clark and Kitchin.

After completing his term Governor Kitchin practiced law in Raleigh, where he formed a partnership with James S. Manning that lasted for six years. In 1919 he suffered a stroke and retired to his home in Scotland Neck.

On 22 Dec. 1892 Kitchin married Musette Satterfield, of Roxboro, the daughter of William Clement Satterfield. They had five children: Sue Arrington, Anniemaria, Elizabeth Musette, Clement, and William Walton, Jr.

Kitchin was an active member of Baptist churches where he lived, as well as a member of three fraternal orders: Ancient, Free, and Accepted Masons; Improved Order of Odd Fellows; and Knights of Pythias. He died in Scotland Neck; after funeral services in the Baptist Church there, he was buried in the local cemetery. A portrait of him, presented by R. O. Everett of Durham, hangs in the Person County Courthouse, and there is another portrait in the capitol in Raleigh.

SEE: *Biog. Dir. Am. Cong.* (1928); *DAB*, vol. 5 (1932); *General Catalog of Wake Forest College* (n.d.); *New York Times*, 10 Nov. 1924; *North Carolina Biography*, vol. 3 (1941); *Proceedings of the North Carolina Bar Association* (1925); *Prominent People of North Carolina* (1906); Raleigh *News and Observer*, 10 Nov. 1924; *Wake Forest Student* (January 1909); *Who's Who in America* (1924–25).

C. SYLVESTER GREEN

Kittrell, Pleasant Williams (13 Apr. 1805–25 Sept. 1867), physician, politician, legislator, and planter, was born at his father's plantation near Chapel Hill, although some accounts based on family tradition show his birthplace as Kittrell Springs in Granville (now Vance) County. He was the son of Rowland Bryant and Mary A. Norman Kittrell. During his childhood and adolescent years he lived in a rural home adjacent to the campus of The University of North Carolina, from which he was graduated with honors in 1822, at age seventeen. Kittrell apprenticed in medicine with Dr. John King of Anson County and studied at the Medical College of the University of Pennsylvania during the 1824–25 academic year. Afterwards he practiced medicine, acquired land and slaves as an active planter, and was postmaster at Sneedsborough, on the Pee Dee River, in Anson County. In 1833 he was elected to the first of two terms in the North Carolina legislature, and the following year was appointed a member of the board of trustees of The University of North Carolina.

In 1837, after the death of his father, who had migrated to Alabama about 1830, Kittrell moved with his family and servants to Greene County, Ala., to claim a substantial inheritance of farmland and slaves. His application to practice medicine is supported by an affidavit, dated 1845, citing his study under Dr. John King in North Carolina. Kittrell again became involved in politics and was elected to two terms in the Alabama legislature, in 1844 and 1846. He was awarded an honorary master of arts degree by the University of Alabama in 1847.

Kittrell left Alabama in 1850 with other Greene County families (including the family of his father-in-law, Dr. Langston James Goree, of Perry County, Ala.),

moved to Texas, and settled at a new plantation, Prairie View, near Huntsville in Walker (now Madison) County. He conducted an active medical practice and extensive stock raising and farming activities in Walker, Madison, Trinity, and Polk (now San Jacinto) counties, which are described in detail in journals he maintained from 1854 to 1867. Kittrell also served two terms in the Texas legislature from 1855 to 1858. He was chairman of the House Committee on Education and led the fight for the University Act of 1858, which was passed and adopted, authorizing the establishment of a state university. In 1866 he was appointed to the first board of trustees of the University of Texas. The turmoil of Reconstruction delayed the opening of the university until 1886, but Kittrell shared with Dr. Oscar Cooper the traditional title, "Father of the University of Texas." In addition, he was a trustee of Austin College (now at Sherman, Tex.) and Andrew Female College at Huntsville.

In 1858 he moved from Prairie View, now in Madison County, which he helped create in 1856, to his plantation in eastern Walker County, Cedar Grove, fourteen miles from Huntsville. Cedar Grove was adjacent to Raven Hill, the plantation of his widowed sister, Sarah Williams Kittrell Goree, and formerly the home of his friend and political foe, General Sam Houston. Census and tax records for 1860 show that Kittrell was the wealthiest planter and slaveholder in Walker County; the strife and hardship of the Civil War years that followed are only suggested by his personal journals that tell of a loan made by a former slave and freedman, Jordan Goree, that enabled him to pay his taxes the year after the Civil War ended.

On 23 Mar. 1826 Kittrell married Mrs. Ann Pegues Evans, a widow of Chesterfield District, S.C., who died in Alabama in 1847. In 1848 he married Mary Frances Goree, of Marion, Perry County, Ala.; she died in 1907.

Kittrell was active and influential in the establishment and administration of institutions of higher education in three states, as well as an upright and vocal but contentious and controversial politician. A determined Secessionist, he strongly opposed Governor Sam Houston's efforts to keep Texas in the Union prior to the Civil War. Kittrell died in the same bedroom as had Sam Houston four years earlier, in the Steamboat House at Huntsville, a victim of yellow fever. He was buried at Oakwood Cemetery, Huntsville. His portrait hangs in the foyer of the president's office at the University of Texas, and he is memorialized at the Education Hall of Fame in Dallas.

SEE: Kemp P. Battle, *History of the University of North Carolina*, vol. 1 (1907); Edwin Sue Goree, *A Family Mosaic* (privately printed, 1961); Archibald Henderson, *Campus of the First State University* (1949); Norman Goree Kittrell, *Governors Who Have Been, and Other Public Men of Texas* (1921); Pleasant Williams Kittrell, personal journals, 1854–67 (Archives, The University of Texas); Mary L. Medley, *History of Anson County, North Carolina, 1750–1976* (1976); John Payne, "Diary of an East Texas Doctor" (1971 manuscript, Sam Houston State University).

LANGSTON JAMES GOREE V

Kluttz, Theodore Franklin (4 Oct. 1848–19 Nov. 1918), businessman, lawyer, and congressman, was born in Salisbury, the son of Elizabeth Moose and Caleb Kluttz, who at the time was sheriff of Rowan County. Orphaned at an early age, Kluttz lived a moderate existence and became self-supporting while he was still very young. At age sixteen he began work as a clerk in the local drugstore of Henderson and Enniss. Four or five years later, he bought Enniss's share of the business and became a partner. The drugstore's name was promptly changed to Theodore F. Kluttz and Co.

By 1880 his store was enjoying such prosperity that he felt comfortable in pursuing his dream of a career in law. At age thirty-two, he began his studies under James M. McCorkle. On admission to the bar, Kluttz joined McCorkle's practice and continued a partnership with him until McCorkle's death. Kluttz's success as a lawyer equaled (and even surpassed) his success as a businessman. He was recognized for his studious, energetic, and eloquent approach to the law; good judgment; and abilities as advocate, defender, and arbitrator.

His interest in business continued throughout most of his life, and he was associated with numerous efforts to promote growth and prosperity in his city and county. Kluttz served as vice-president of the Yadkin Railroad Company and president of the Salisbury Building and Loan Association, Davis and Wiley Bank, Salisbury Chamber of Commerce, Rowan Knitting Company, and Chestnut Hill Cemetery Association. He was also a director in various industries, including the North Carolina Railroad Company, Salisbury Water Works, North Carolina Steel and Iron Company, and Salisbury Cotton Mills.

Kluttz was active in politics as well. In 1880 he served as district presidential elector on the Hancock ticket, and in 1896 he was chairman of the North Carolina delegation to the Democratic National Convention. At the convention, he made an exhilarating speech seconding the nomination of William Jennings Bryan. Later that year, he served as a Democratic presidential elector on the Bryan ticket.

His own political career began in 1898, when he was elected to the Fifty-sixth Congress as a representative from the Seventh District. Kluttz served again during the Fifty-seventh and Fifty-eighth Congresses, but this time as a representative from the Eighth District due to reapportionment. He declined to be renominated in 1905 and returned to his law practice in Salisbury. In 1912, he started a two-year term as judge of the Rowan County Court.

In 1873 Kluttz married Sallie Caldwell, a sister of Joseph Caldwell, and they had six children. He was a member of the Presbyterian church and served as deacon.

Kluttz was buried in Chestnut Hill Cemetery, Salisbury.

SEE: Samuel A. Ashe, ed., *Cyclopedia of Eminent and Representative Men of the Carolinas of the Nineteenth Century*, vol. 2 (1892); North Carolina Bar Association, *Proceedings of the Twenty-first Annual Session (5–7 Aug. 1919)*; *Prominent People of North Carolina* (1906); A. Davis Smith, *Western North Carolina, Historical and Biographical* (1890).

SUZY CONNER

Knapp, Joseph Palmer (14 May 1864–30 Jan. 1951), publisher, financier, philanthropist, and conservationist, was born in Brooklyn, N.Y., the son of Phoebe Palmer and Joseph Fairchild Knapp, a founder of the Metropolitan Life Insurance Company. He was educated at the Polytechnical Institute in Brooklyn and Columbia University, from which he was graduated in 1884.

A substantial inheritance left by his father enabled Knapp to invest in a variety of business ventures, primarily associated with printing and publishing. In 1895 he founded the American Lithographic Company, and was instrumental in developing a multicolor process that carried a sheet of paper over a number of cylinders, from each of which an impression was made in a different color. With control of this process he began printing the *Associated Sunday Magazine* in 1903, thus providing newspapers with their first weekly magazine supplement. For many years, as a principal stockholder and chairman of the board of the Crowell-Collier Publishing Company, he was the publisher of several of the nation's largest circulation magazines including *Collier's*, *The American Magazine*, *The Women's Home Companion*, and *Country Home*. For most of his adult life he was a director of the Metropolitan Life Insurance Company, serving for many years as chairman of its finance committee.

Among the specialized printing jobs for which the multicolor presses of the American Lithographic Company were particularly well suited was the production of millions of small pictures of popular baseball players which were packaged with cigarettes. In this way he became associated with James B. Duke, founder of the American Tobacco Company, from whom Knapp gained considerable information about North Carolina. But duck hunting, not baseball, was the reason for his first trip to eastern North Carolina, and that initial visit to the Currituck area in 1916 marked the beginning of a long association between the New York financier and the sparsely populated coastal county of Currituck. Knapp soon purchased a hunting club and an island, Mackey Island, from author Thomas Dixon, and designed a spacious colonial home which was completed there in 1920. For many years he and his wife, the former Margaret Rutledge of Summit, Miss., spent part of each year in their River House apartment in the heart of New York City and the remainder on isolated Mackey Island in the middle of Currituck Sound.

Concerned about the lack of educational opportunities for the young people of the county, he offered to supplement whatever could be raised locally in order to bring about needed improvements. His first donation to the Currituck schools, in 1923, was for $50,000; until his death he continued to make annual contributions. With his assistance modern school buildings were constructed, together with comfortable houses for teachers as an inducement to attract capable instructors; school buses were purchased; teaching salaries were supplemented; and Currituck took the lead among North Carolina counties in providing textbooks and school lunches for all students, in employing school nurses and vocational teachers, and in extending the school term to nine months, setting an example for the state to follow later.

Knapp extended his largess to the people of Currituck County far beyond the public schools, employing agricultural experts to advise the farmers, furnishing credit for the operation of a Currituck Mutual Exchange through which farmers could finance their crops, and making substantial annual donations to the public welfare fund. In a published report in 1932, the clerk to the Currituck County Board of Commissioners said: "Mr. Knapp has given us more this year than we have paid in taxes."

In September 1947 Governor R. Gregg Cherry announced that Joseph Knapp, through his Knapp Foundation, Inc., had given a quarter of a million dollars to the state for a two-year survey of school needs and for fisheries research, projects the governor described as "a tribute to Joseph P. Knapp's lifelong interest in the betterment of mankind."

Ironically, Knapp's final, and possibly his most important, contribution to his adopted state did not reach fruition until after his death. This was the provision of funds, by the Knapp Foundation and at the insistence of his widow, for the construction of the Institute of Government building in Chapel Hill.

Knapp, the father of two children, Joseph Fairchild and Claire Knapp Dixon, was buried in Memorial Cemetery near Moyock in Currituck County.

SEE: Albert Coates, "Joseph Palmer Knapp in North Carolina," *Popular Government* 27 (March 1961); *Durham Morning Herald*, 30 Sept. 1947, 4 Nov. 1951; Raleigh *News and Observer*, 17 Feb. 1929.

DAVID STICK

Knight, Edgar Wallace (9 Apr. 1886–7 Aug. 1953), university professor and distinguished historian of American education, was born in Northampton County near the town of Woodland. His parents were John Washington and Margaret Davis Knight, small farmers whose chief crop was tobacco. Knight received his early education at the local schools and at Trinity Park, the preparatory school for Trinity College (now Duke University). He was graduated from Trinity College with a bachelor's degree and membership in Phi Beta Kappa in 1909, and with a master's degree in 1911. From Trinity he went directly to Teachers College, Columbia University, where he earned the Ph.D. degree in 1913.

Both at Trinity and Columbia, Knight studied under teachers who exerted a profound influence on his future. At Trinity professors Edwin Mims and John Spencer Bassett were his instructors and Dean Samuel Fox Mordecai of the law school was his warm friend. At Columbia, where he minored in history, he was a student of James Harvey Robinson and William A. Dunning, with the latter undoubtedly influencing his choice of dissertation topic; the study was completed under Professor Paul Monroe and published as a monograph entitled, *The Influence of Reconstruction on Education in the South*.

Knight's first experience in the classroom was at Trinity Park, where he taught English and history for two years while enrolled part-time as a graduate student at Trinity College. In the summer of 1910 he taught history at East Carolina Teachers Training School in Greenville. After graduation from Columbia, Knight returned to Trinity with an appointment as assistant professor of education; he was promoted to professor and remained in that position until 1917, when he became superintendent of Wake County Schools. In 1918, with the nation involved in World War I, he was appointed assistant educational director for the southeastern states of the Committee on Education and Special Training for the War Plans Division of the General Staff. In 1919 Knight joined the faculty of The University of North Carolina, and from that date Chapel Hill remained his home even though he held visiting professorships at a number of colleges and universities, including Darmouth, Columbia, Michigan, and Duke. In 1934 his reputation as a teacher and scholar was recognized by his appointment to one of the university's distinguished chairs, a Kenan professorship. Duke University, in 1952, conferred on him the degree, doctor of literature.

Knight was a magnificent teacher—unorthodox but inspiring, understanding and sympathetic, but de-

manding, and possessing little patience with careless or second-rate work from students or colleagues. In every respect he was a scholar; his enthusiasm for research in the history of American education seemed boundless, and to a remarkable degree he was able to transmit this to students, a fact that made his afternoon seminars particularly valuable. When a student's research efforts deserved recognition, Knight was quick to give praise and generous in giving credit when a reference was made to the student's work.

His research was directed chiefly towards the history of education in the antebellum South. He wrote extensively in that field, but in addition published numerous articles reflecting his awareness of the educational problems of the twentieth century. Throughout his career he was a critic of educational practices that he regarded as superficial, and in his writings treated them in a highly amusing fashion. Educational workshops, college and university administrators, enthusiasts for curriculum revision, and the proliferation of college degrees each were exposed to his sharp wit in books and articles such as "Consider the Deans, How They Toil," *What College Presidents Say*, "The Butter Curriculum," and "Getting Ahead by Degrees."

Friends and former students have fond memories of Knight's humor, for it was a quality very much a part of him. He was convinced that humor had a place in the classroom as well as in life, and he frequently used it to illustrate the weakness of an educational fad, to emphasize an important point, or to dispel Monday's gloom after the Saturday defeat of a Carolina football team. The humor was sudden and sometimes devastating, but never vengeful or designed to hurt. In the classroom there was almost an informal atmosphere, yet it was controlled informality that never degenerated into idle or pointless chatter as might have been the case under a less skillful person.

As a productive scholar Knight wrote more than 30 books and 150 articles, while also giving freely of himself to the university, to the community, and to the numerous agencies that called on him for advice. For twenty-eight years he was an active member of the Administrative Board of The University of North Carolina Graduate School, and served on numerous other university boards and committees. Within the state he was a member of the board of trustees of Louisburg College and of North Carolina College (now North Carolina Central University), a member of the state Library Commission and of the state Textbook Commission, assistant superintendent of Orange County Public Schools for several years (without pay), and for thirty years (1922–52) a member of the Chapel Hill School Board. The U.S. government on more than one occasion called on his services. At the beginning of World War II he was asked to become director of the qualifying tests for civilians in the Naval Training College Programs, and in the years immediately following he was active in the work of the Educational Policies Commission. During the years of military occupation in Germany and Japan, Knight resisted any invitations to participate in the educational programs. The lessons of Reconstruction were on his mind, and he quite frankly feared the errors that our government might again make.

In 1925, by virtue of a grant from the Social Science Research Council, Knight spent some time in Denmark observing the rural and folk schools. An account of this trip appeared in book form under the title, *Among the Danes*. During the academic year 1930–31 he was in China as a member of a special commission organized by the Institute of Social and Religious Research to study educational conditions in that country. In 1933, with his friends professors Paul Monroe and William C. Bagley of Teachers College, Columbia University, he went to Iraq, where the three worked as a commission to assist the government with its schools. And then Knight spent some time studying the educational systems of England and France. There was, indeed, nothing provincial about his scholarly interests.

Knight's monumental work was his *Documentary History of Education in the South Before 1860*, published in five volumes, the first of which appeared in 1949. Unfortunately, he did not live to see the final volume which was released from the press in December 1953, a few months after his death. The main body of his writings dealt with the history of education, and his most widely known work was the textbook, *Education in the United States*, which appeared first in 1929 and in revised editions in 1934, 1941, and 1951.

On 28 June 1916 Edgar Knight and Annie Mozelle Turner, a native of Orange County, were married in Durham Memorial Methodist Church. They were the parents of two daughters, Ann (Mrs. Strother Calloway Fleming, Jr.) and Jane (Mrs. James Minor Ludlow). Death came as the result of a heart attack, and he was buried in the Chapel Hill Cemetery.

Knight was intensely loyal to his state and to The University of North Carolina. As an individual, he was in every respect a gentleman; as a historian, he ranked with the best; and as a scholar, he retained a clear perspective. Knight was no reformer, but for forty years, in the midst of changing educational theories and philosophies, he spoke and wrote about the need for good teaching and sound learning. So far as he was concerned, there was no substitute; nor was there a substitute for excellence.

SEE: William E. Drake, "Edgar Wallace Knight as I Knew Him," *Educational Forum* 25 (November 1960); Clifton L. Hall, "Edgar W. Knight: Educational Historian, 1886–1953," *Teachers College Record* 55 (February 1954); Almonte C. Howell, ed., *The Kenan Professorships* (1956); Forrest L. Rollins, "The Educational Philosophy of Edgar Knight" (Ph.D. diss., George Peabody College for Teachers, 1968); *Who Was Who in America*, vol. 3 (1960).

J. ISAAC COPELAND

Knight, Tobias (d. 11 June 1719), government official, judge, and attorney, lived in Bath. The earliest record of Knight appears in the *Colonial Records of North Carolina*, dated 16 Apr. 1710, where he is recognized as a member of the governing council of the colony. In 1711, he was a member of the party that asked the queen for support against the Indians who were terrorizing the colony at that time. In the same year he was made "Commissioner and Trustee for the due Inspection and Preservation of the Library."

On 12 July 1712 Knight was appointed deputy proprietor to John Danson, and on 17 Dec. 1714 his power was extended as he became deputy proprietor to Lord Craven. Also in 1712, Knight became secretary of the government of North Carolina under Governor Charles Eden, as well as the collector of "her Matyes Customs in Currituck District." The records show that by 1712 Knight had married Catherine Glover, widow of former Governor William Glover. There was something of a scandal involved here, for Glover some years before had borrowed money from the church and had died before paying it back. Knight let it be known that he would not repay the money even though he had married Glover's widow. Some members of the community thought that Knight was "robbing the Church."

Three years later, the colonial government authorized him to receive prisoners from Virginia, and to present them to the magistrate. For this service he was paid 20c [sic] for each prisoner. Also in 1715, he was made vestryman in the West Parish of the Pasquotank Precinct of the Anglican church.

On 1 Aug. 1717 Knight was chosen by the "Governor and advice and consent of the Council . . . Chief Justice of the Province," and served in this capacity until shortly before his death. The following year, on 5 June 1718, he purchased a tract of land near Bath known as Archbell Point. This property had belonged to Landgrave Robert Daniel (one of the first to live in or near Bath) and Knight bought it from Daniel's widow. As a result of the transaction, Knight became a neighbor of Governor Charles Eden.

On 22 Nov. 1718 Edward Teach, more commonly known as Blackbeard, the notorious pirate, was killed by an expedition sent by Governor Alexander Spotswood of Virginia. Some of Teach's slaves survived the engagement and were taken to Williamsburg, where they were tried in a Court of Admiralty for piracy. On 12 Mar. 1719, they gave testimony that was damaging to Knight. The evidence was of sufficient strength that Governor Spotswood sent depositions to North Carolina for consideration. Knight was accused of accessory to piracy and his trial began on 27 May 1719 at the home of Fredrick Jones. Governor Eden, sitting with the governing council, heard the testimony. Knight spoke for himself; and his defense "leaves no doubt that he was an attorney of not inconsiderable ability," for the governor and council "investigated the charges and . . . gravely pronounced him intirely innocent."

Nevertheless, Knight resigned the office of chief justice of the colony. Shortly afterwards, Captain Ellis Brand wrote to the Lords Commissioners of Admiralty complaining that Knight and others were assisting pirates. Knight, however, died before an investigation could be launched. The question of his involvement (as well as that of Governor Eden) with Blackbeard has excited historians for centuries. Governor Eden has been criticized for finding Knight innocent given the amount of evidence that was brought against him, although the trial followed legal procedure in regard to the submission of evidence. Much of the evidence against Knight could not have been used in a court of law. However, "convincing" evidence cannot be found for either side.

Knight died after a long illness, and his estate was left to his wife Catherine, the executrix, and his stepdaughter, Elizabeth Glover.

SEE: Walter Clark, ed., *State Records of North Carolina*, vols. 23, 25 (1904, 1906); J. Bryan Grimes, *Abstracts of North Carolina Wills* (1910); Francis L. Hawks, *History of North Carolina*, vol. 2 (1858); Robert E. Lee, *Blackbeard the Pirate* (1974); Ursula F. Loy and Pauline M. Worthy, *Washington and the Pamlico* (1976); William L. Saunders, ed., *Colonial Records of North Carolina*, vols. 1, 2, 4 (1886).

JAMES D. GILLESPIE

Knox, Andrew (ca. 1733–76), merchant and public official, was a resident of Perquimans County where he had acquired land on both sides of the Yeopim Road between the Yeopim and Perquimans rivers. He owned the sloop *Franklin* with which he engaged in coastal shipping to supply his own store and others. About 1754 he married Christian Halsey, the daughter of William and Martha Halsey. Their first child, Ann, was born on 16 July 1755.

From 1761 to 1769 Knox was sheriff of Perquimans County, and from 1764 to 1775 he served in the Assembly. He was a member and clerk of the Provincial Congress in 1774 and 1775. Among his legislative assignments were the Committee to Regulate the Several Public Offices in the Province (1766) and the Committee to Issue Paper Currency (1775). In 1771, as a member of the legislature, he went to Rowan County in an attempt to pacify the Regulators there. In 1773 he was commissioner for the town of Hertford, and in 1775 he was a lieutenant colonel in the militia of the Edenton District, where he also served as commissary for the militia.

Knox had five children: Ann, Sarah, Christian, Andrew, and Hugh. He died shortly before 20 Jan. 1776, the date on which his will was probated.

SEE: Walter Clark, ed., *State Records of North Carolina*, vols. 22, 23 (1904–7); William L. Saunders, ed., *Colonial Records of North Carolina*, vols. 7–9 (1890); Mrs. Watson Winslow, *History of Perquimans County* (1931).

ELMER D. JOHNSON

Koch, Frederick Henry (12 Sept. 1877–16 Aug. 1944), university professor of dramatic art and promoter of the American folk play, was born in Covington, Ky., in a family of nine boys and one girl. His father, August William Koch, was of German ancestry; his mother, Rebecca Cornelia Julian Koch, came from French stock. August, an accountant and cashier in the Etna Life Insurance Company, was a freehand artist and inventor. His imaginative bent showed up in his children: three of his sons became architects, the daughter a singer. From his father Frederick obtained creative talents, from his mother a playful disposition.

Koch grew up in Illinois. He attended Peoria High School and Caterals Methodist College, then Ohio Wesleyan, from which he was graduated with the A.B. degree in 1900. Wishing passionately to become an actor, he spent some time at the Emerson School of Oratory in Boston, but when his family frowned on his histrionic ambition, Koch enrolled at Harvard to study English literature. Unable to stifle completely his thespian urge, however, he traveled around the countryside giving readings of Shakespeare. He was awarded the M.A. degree in 1909.

At Harvard Koch fell under the dramatic influence of George Pierce Baker who was, at the time, stirring a group of young men and women to write plays on native American subjects. After graduation, Koch took an extended trip to Greece, North Africa, Syria, Egypt, and Palestine. At Athens he met an Irish-American girl, Loretta Jean Hanigan, whom he married in 1910. They had four sons: Frederick, George, Robert, and William. From 1905 to 1918 Koch taught English at the University of North Dakota where, besides conducting courses in literature, he founded the Dakota Playmakers. The Playmakers produced one-act plays on the life of the state, written by students. The plays were trouped around North Dakota and presented to schools and communities, some of which had never before seen a dramatic performance.

Informed of the singularly productive work being done by Professor Koch in the Midwest, President Edward Kidder Graham of The University of North Carolina wished to develop similar creative activity at his institution. In 1918 he wrote to Koch and persuaded him to come to the Southeast. In Chapel Hill, Koch taught dramatic literature and playwriting for twenty-six years. Young men and women from every section of the state came to work with him, and they were soon joined by students from other states, then from abroad: Canada, England, Germany, Egypt, Korea, Japan, the Philippines, Mexico, Chile, and elsewhere. Among the dramatists, novelists, and short-story writers (authors who were inspired and guided in one way or another by the lively theater man from the Midwest) were Thomas Wolfe, Paul Green, Betty Smith, Jonathan Daniels, Noel Houston, Joseph Mitchell, Frances Gray Patton, Bernice Kelly Harris, Le Gette Blythe, Howard Richardson, and Josefina Niggli.

To provide a means for his authors to see their work in performances, Koch organized a producing group, the Carolina Playmakers, modeled on the Playmakers of North Dakota. Many of the actors, directors, dancers, and designers who received instruction at The University of North Carolina later entered the professional world of the stage, motion pictures, and television. The university group—again following the example of the Dakota students—trouped their plays all over North Carolina, and extended their tours to such far-off places as New York, Boston, Dallas, and St. Louis.

With the help of the University Extension Department and its associates, Koch established a Bureau of Community Drama, with a field secretary, which developed dramatic centers in other parts of the state. The productions of high school, college, and community groups were brought yearly to the university in Chapel Hill where they were staged in a spring Festival. Thirty years after Koch's death, the yearly Festival was still being held.

Selected student-written plays were published by Koch in five volumes: *Carolina Folk Plays* (in four series) and *American Folk Plays*. He sponsored single authors' works in *Alabama Folk Plays*, by Kate Porter Lewis; *Folk Plays of Eastern Carolina*, by Bernice Kelly Harris; and *Mexican Folk Plays*, by Josefina Niggli. Some of Miss Niggli's short stories were combined and issued in a motion picture, *Sombrero*. Outdoor historical plays, inspired by Koch and written by Paul Green and Kermit Hunter, were produced and published.

Koch used the term "folk play" in the sense of the German *volk* (common people), thus describing his employment of the word: "The term 'folk,' as we use it, has nothing to do with the folk play of medieval times. But rather is it concerned with folk subject matter: with the legends, superstitions, customs, environmental differences, and the vernacular of the common people. For the most part they are realistic and human; sometimes they are imaginative and poetic." The early plays of Eugene O'Neill and Paul Green, Koch regarded as folk plays; the dramas of such writers as Bernard Shaw and John Von Druten were not.

A man of remarkable energy and enthusiasm, Koch remained active until the time of his death. He was buried in the old Chapel Hill Cemetery.

SEE: Frederick Henry Koch, ed., *American Folk Plays* (1939), *Carolina Folk Plays* (1941), and *The Carolina Play-Book* (1928–44); Kenneth Macgowan, *Footlights Across America* (1929); Arthur Hobson Quinn, *A History of the American Drama* (1951); Samuel Selden, *Frederick Henry Koch: Pioneer Playmaker* (1954 [portrait]).

SAMUEL SELDEN

Koopman, Augustus (2 Jan. 1869–31 Jan. 1941), painter and etcher, was born in Charlotte, the son of Bernard and Johanna Koopman. After attending Central High School in Philadelphia, he began art studies at the Pennsylvania Academy of Fine Arts. Later he went to Paris, where he entered the École des Beaux Arts and studied under Bouguereau and Robert Fleury. On 6 May 1897 he married Louise Lovett Osgood of Cohasset, Mass. Koopman made France his home, wintering in Paris and spending the spring and summer in Étaples and in the nearby village of Équihen. He taught painting in Paris from 1896 to 1899 and specialized in portraits while in London from 1902 to 1906.

Koopman has often been called a painter of emotionalism. He found inspiration in the ocean and its storms, disasters, and boats. His *Horses Running to Meet a Boat*, owned by the St. Paul Art Institute, is a notable representation of his subject. *The Wind Storm* and *A Windy Day* are also full of movement and typify Koopman's intense attraction to the sea. In contrast to these is *Return of the Shrimpers*, which depicts a quiet group making their way home from their boats. For this painting he received a medal in 1904 at the St. Louis Exposition and was invited to exhibit it at the Venice International Art Exposition in 1910. He was an exhibitor at Paris, Munich, London, Venice, and American exhibitions. His early work had many of the qualities characteristic of the modern Dutch artists, especially the marine painters Mesdag and Blommers. Later he became influenced by the impressionists and postimpressionists, and many of his pictures of this later period gained a unique popularity because of their individuality.

Koopman's works covered many themes. He was not essentially a marine painter; he was also a figure painter, using his own children as models. He painted a notable decoration, *Industrial Arts*, for the U.S. government pavillion at the Paris Exposition in 1900. His figure pictures, *The Crystal Gazers* and *Old Troubadour*, are painted with great charm of pose and color. His drypoints and etchings were usually fishermen, scenes in cafés, and figures, all done in careful line.

In 1912 Koopman was elected an associé of the Société Nationale des Beaux Arts, a great honor in the artist's world, and he received many awards, medals, and prizes. Among these were the special silver medal for his decoration at the Paris Exposition, the bronze medals at the Pan-American Exposition at Buffalo (1901) and at the St. Louis Exposition, and a silver medal at the Appalachian Exposition at Knoxville (1911). His portraits and decorations are represented in French and American collections in St. Louis, St. Paul, and Detroit museums; the Philadelphia Art Club; and the Brooklyn Institute of Arts and Sciences. His etchings are represented in the Congressional Library in Washington, D.C., and there is a collection in the New York Public Library. He died of paraylsis in Étaples.

SEE: *DAB*, vol. 5 (1932); *New York Times*, 3 Feb. 1914; E. A. Taylor, "The Paintings of Augustus Koopman," *International Studio*, May 1914; *Who Was Who in America*, vol. 1 (1942).

AMANDA B. BURTON

Kornegay, Wade Hampton (17 Apr. 1865–19 Nov. 1939), lawyer and judge, was born near Outlaw's Bridge in Duplin County while his father was serving in the Confederate Army. He was the son of Henry Robert Kornegay, a Baptist minister, lawyer, and clerk of Superior Court, and his wife Jeanette Williams, a native of Wayne County. Shortly after the Civil War, the family moved to Kenansville where Kornegay attended the Grove Academy and the Millard Seminary. At age fifteen he enrolled at Wake Forest College; he received the Silcox Greek medal in 1883 and was valedictorian when he was graduated in 1884 with the master of arts degree.

After teaching school for four years in Richmond, Kornegay attended law school at the University of Virginia during the summer of 1889 and then studied law at Vanderbilt University. He completed a two-year course in one year and received an LL.B. from Vanderbilt in 1890.

In 1891 Kornegay opened a law office in Vanita, Indian Territory (now Oklahoma), where he practiced law for forty-eight years until his death. He issued the call to Democrats in the Indian Territory to meet and choose delegates to the national convention in 1892. A leading citizen of the territory, Kornegay later helped lead the movement to form the new state of Oklahoma and served as a member of the constitutional convention of 1907, which drafted the state's constitution. He was a supporter and friend of William H. ("Alfalfa Bill") Murray. In 1931 Governor Murray appointed him to an unexpired term on the Oklahoma Supreme Court. Kornegay served for less than two years and did not seek reelection.

In November 1892 he married Nannie Louise Stafford of the Indian Territory. They had four children: Jeanette, Clarence Stafford, Wade Hampton, Jr., and Fay Louise. Kornegay, a member of the Presbyterian church, died of a heart attack and was buried in the Fairview Cemetery at Vanita. His pallbearers included former Governor Murray and Governor Leon C. Phillips.

SEE: *Chronicles of Oklahoma*, vol. 18 (1940); Raleigh *News and Observer*, 6 Feb. 1949; *Who Was Who in America*, vol. 1 (1981).

CHARLES W. EAGLES

Kramsch, Samuel Gottlieb (7 Sept. 1756–2 Feb. 1824), minister, educator, and botanist, was born in Rudelstadt, Silesia, the son of Lutheran pastor Johann Gottlob and Ursula Regina Kahl Kramsch. He was educated at the Moravian school at Gnadenberg. After working briefly in an apothecary shop, he accepted a temporary teaching position which he discovered to be to his liking. Already proficient in Latin, Greek, and French, he thought briefly of studying medicine, chemistry, or natural philosophy. Teaching, however, appealed to Kramsch, and in 1783 he was called to head a boys' school at Bethlehem, Pa. En route to America in the summer of that year, he saw the last English fleet returning to England after the American Revolution. Reaching Bethlehem on 6 November, he soon was ordained a deacon of the Moravian church and in addition to teaching was the spiritual leader of the single brothers in the town.

In 1788 Kramsch was called to Salem, N.C., as a teacher and as spiritual leader of the single brothers there. He soon established a practice which he followed for sixteen years: preaching regularly in a thirty-mile-area around Salem, often to Lutheran and Methodist congregations as well as to Moravians. On at least one occasion he was invited to preach to a Baptist congregation. He sometimes baptized, married, and buried people without regard to their denomination when no other clergyman was available. At a funeral in 1800, before the Episcopal church was established in the state, he used the "English Church burial liturgy" in compliance with the dying request of a man over ninety.

In addition, Kramsch taught in the boys' school and in February 1789 began English reading classes for men; in December he also began an evening school for older boys. Between 1790 and 1792 he was head of the boys' school, and in the spring of 1791 was one of those who dined with George Washington when he was in Salem. Kramsch conducted the president on a visit to the school, and Washington also observed one of Kramsch's reading classes. In 1792, he was called to take charge of an English-speaking congregation at Hope some distance from Salem. Because he was still single and Moravians expected their clergymen to be married, he went to Pennsylvania in August and was back by early December with his bride, the former Susanna Elisabeth Langaard, daughter of a professor at the Bethlehem Female Seminary and herself a gifted teacher and musician. They served the Hope congregation well until mid-January 1803, when the family, now including daughters Louise Charlotte and Christiana Susanna, settled in Salem.

Kramsch in Salem became associate pastor and established a girls' boarding school. Under his direction plans were made, the cornerstone was laid on 6 Oct. 1803, and a teaching staff was engaged; on 15 May 1804 the first students arrived to enter what would become Salem College. Other students arrived from various parts of the state and from as far away as Georgia to study under several good teachers, including the Reverend and Mrs. Kramsch. In mid-November 1805, however, it was discovered that "Br. Kramsch in his associations with the sisters and children of the Girls Boarding School has behaved in a most improper and objectionable manner." Exactly what he did is not recorded, but he was removed from his position at the school, excluded from the Communion, and removed from the Board of Elders.

For a time Kramsch became a shopkeeper, while his wife was named to look after the women visitors to Salem. In 1813 he was recalled to Hope where he served faithfully and well until 1819, when failing eyesight forced his retirement. He underwent operations on his eyes—in Raleigh, by Dr. Calvin Jones, in 1814 and in Salisbury in May 1823—with moderate success. His last years were spent in Salem where an apartment at the school was made available to the family, and he was buried in Salem.

Outside North Carolina Kramsch was known as a botanist. He studied, identified, recorded, and reported plants in both Pennsylvania and North Carolina and corresponded widely with other botanists. He also took his pupils on field trips. In North Carolina he was visited by such noted botanists as Henry Izard, August Gotthold Vemler, Ludwig David von Schweinitz, and John E. LeConte, and he sent plants and seeds to still others.

SEE: William Darlington, *Memoirs of John Bartram and Humphry Marshall with Notices of Their Botanical Contemporaries* (1849); Adelaide L. Fries, ed., *Records of the Moravians in North Carolina*, vols. 5–8 (1941–54); Frances Griffin, *Less Time for Meddling: A History of Salem Academy and College, 1772–1866* (1979); "Memoir of Samuel Gottlieb Kramsch" (Moravian Archives, Winston-Salem).

WILLIAM S. POWELL

Krider, Jacob (*17 Aug. 1788–17 Oct. 1874*), printer, publisher, and planter, was born in Pennsylvania, the son of Barnabus and Peggy Krider. Barnabus Krider moved with his family to Salisbury, N.C., sometime after 1800 and remained there until his death in 1823. Jacob's education and early years in Salisbury are not known; however, it can be assumed that he was involved to some extent with his father's print shop as he became affiliated with the printer Francis Coupee as early as 1811. Under the name of Coupee and Krider they printed a number of religious tracts and other materials. In 1813 Coupee and Krider founded the *North Carolina Magazine, Political, Historical, and Miscellaneous*, one of the first periodicals in western North Carolina. The first issue appeared in August 1813, with monthly issues through December 1813, when the magazine folded—perhaps in part because of Krider's involvement in the mustering of militia to fight the Creek Indians during the War of 1812. Krider became captain of the First Company, Seventh Regiment, commanded by Colonel Jesse A. Pearson. The company rendezvoused in Salisbury on 1 February, marched on 1 March, and returned to Salisbury about 1 August.

On 29 June 1815 Krider married Sarah Wood (1792–1880), and in 1817 was among a group of businessmen who subscribed the support for the first fire company in Salisbury. He was then operating a tavern with his brother-in-law, Thomas Holmes, and a store with David Wood. Krider also returned to the printing trade and in 1819 issued James H. Conway's *The North Carolina Calculator*. In June 1820 he founded *The Western Carolinian* in partnership with Lemuel Bingham, but in 1821 he sold his interest to Philo White. *The Western Carolinian* supported many of the political ambitions of Charles Fisher and was a strong voice for western interests in the state until it ceased publication in 1842.

About 1822 Krider moved with his family onto a tract of land in Scotch-Irish Township that he purchased in the same year from Robert Bunton. The plantation he established there, Mt. Vernon, was adjacent to the grist and sawmills operated by his father-in-law, Daniel Wood. Krider's wife inherited the mills and property on which they sat at her father's death in 1829. Krider continued to operate the mills, and for the remainder of his life he was a miller, merchant, and planter in the Third Creek community.

With his removal from Salisbury to the country, Krider moved his membership from the Presbyterian Church in Salisbury to the Third Creek Church. In 1833, he served as chairman of the building committee that raised funds for and oversaw the construction of a brick structure, which has been occupied by the church since its completion in 1835. He and his brother-in-law, William Burton Wood, were two of the three church members who subscribed as much as $100 to the building fund. On 22 May 1842, Krider was ordained an elder at Third Creek Church and held that position until his death.

The Kriders had three daughters and five sons. Mary Letitia (1816–51) married the Reverend James Elijah Morrison, Margaret C. (1823–79) married John Giles Fleming, and Julia (1833–1912) married first Richard Wainwright Griffith and second John Graham. Krider's oldest child, William H. (1819–61), never married. The second and third sons, Thomas Albert (b. 1821) who married the widow Jane Wood, and Daniel Wood (1825–82) who married Margaret A. Lowe, became doctors. The fourth son, Charles C. Krider (1827–91) who married Margaret A. McKinnon, was sheriff of Rowan County for ten years (1880–90). The fifth son, Barnabus

Scott Krider (1829–65), attended Davidson College and the Columbia and Princeton theological seminaries; he married Maria Catherine Cowan.

Krider, his wife, and five of their children were buried at Third Creek Church. His house, Mt. Vernon, which passed out of the family in 1892, still stands in Rowan County.

SEE: James S. Brawley, *The Rowan Story* (1953); Deeds and Wills of Rowan County (North Carolina State Archives, Raleigh); John Kerr Fleming, *The Cowans from County Down* (1971) and *History of the Third Creek Presbyterian Church* (1967); Walter Lingle, *Thyatira Presbyterian Church* (n.d.); Daniel Miles McFarland, "North Carolina Newspapers, Editors, and Journalistic Politics," *North Carolina Historical Review* (July 1953); North Carolina Imprint File (North Carolina Collection, University of North Carolina Library, Chapel Hill); Jethro Rumple, *A History of Rowan County, North Carolina* (1881); Salisbury *Carolina Watchman*, 22 Oct. 1874; Salisbury *Western Carolinian*, scattered issues; Maurice Toler, *Muster Rolls of the Soldiers of the War of 1812 Detached from the Militia of North Carolina in 1812 and 1814* (1976).

DAVYD FOARD HOOD

Kyser, James Kern ("Kay") (*18 June 1906–23 July 1985*), orchestra leader, actor, and Christian Science lecturer, was born in Rocky Mount, the son of Paul B. and Emily Royster Howell Kyser. As a student at The University of North Carolina in 1926, he organized his first band and played for college dances. At Chapel Hill he was also a cheerleader and later wrote the fight song, "Tar Heels on Hand." Following his graduation in 1928 he took his band on tour, playing for theaters, hotels, nightclubs, and radio around the nation. In 1934, over the National Broadcasting Company, he began a weekly program, "College of Musical Knowledge," which quickly became one of the most popular programs on the air. He introduced and featured many singers and instrumentalists who worked with his orchestra as well as with others.

With a good ear for music and a keen sense of humor, his career flourished and he acted in a number of motion pictures and recorded for Columbia Recording Corp. During World War II he frequently entertained troops overseas. It was while thus engaged that Kyser became impressed by the sacrifice many servicemen were making and resolved to end his career in which he played and entertained for money. He was unable to free himself from professional commitments, particularly television, until 1950, but from that time he devoted himself to other matters. In 1951 he moved to Chapel Hill and spent three years helping to plan and raise funds for public television and enlarging the health affairs program at The University of North Carolina.

As a youth Kyser had been impressed by his mother's recovery from pneumonia through Christian Science when physicians had given up hope for her. Although raised as a member of the Baptist church, he was long interested in Christian Science and in 1967 became head of the film and broadcasting division of the Christian Science church, spending much time in the church's headquarters in Boston. He also was a lecturer for the church and traveled widely.

Kyser married Georgia Carroll, a soloist with his orchestra, and they became the parents of three daughters: Amanda, Carroll, and Kimberly. He was buried in the old Chapel Hill Cemetery.

SEE: *Chapel Hill Newspaper*, 24, 28 July 1985; Raleigh *News and Observer*, 24 July 1985; *Who's Who in America* (1942, 1948, 1953).

WILLIAM S. POWELL